A PEOPLE AND A NATION

A PEOPLE

A

AND A NATION
History of the United States

Second Edition

MARY BETH NORTON
Cornell University

DAVID M. KATZMAN
University of Kansas

PAUL D. ESCOTT
University of North Carolina, Charlotte

HOWARD P. CHUDACOFF
Brown University

THOMAS G. PATERSON
University of Connecticut

WILLIAM M. TUTTLE, JR.
University of Kansas

HOUGHTON MIFFLIN COMPANY   BOSTON
Dallas   Geneva, Illinois   Lawrenceville, New Jersey   Palo Alto

Mary Beth Norton

Now a professor of history at Cornell University, Mary Beth Norton was born in Ann Arbor, Michigan, and received her B.A. from the University of Michigan (1964). Harvard University awarded her the Ph.D. in 1969, the year her dissertation won the Allan Nevins Prize. Her writing includes *The British-Americans: The Loyalist Exiles in England, 1774–1789* (1972) and *Liberty's Daughters: The Revolutionary Experience of American Women, 1750–1800* (1980). With Carol Berkin she has edited a book of original essays, *Women of America: A History* (1979). Her many articles have appeared in such journals as the *William and Mary Quarterly, Signs,* and the *American Historical Review.* Mary Beth has served on the National Council on the Humanities. From 1983 to 1985 she was president of the Berkshire Conference of Women Historians, and in 1984 she was elected vice president for research of the American Historical Association. Besides holding honorary degrees from Siena College and Marymount Manhattan College, she has received research assistance from the Shelby Cullom Davis Center, Charles Warren Center, National Endowment for the Humanities, and the American Antiquarian Society.

David M. Katzman

A graduate of Queens College (B.A., 1963) and the University of Michigan (Ph.D., 1969), David M. Katzman is now a professor of history at the University of Kansas. Born in New York City, David is known for his work in labor, social and black history. His book *Seven Days a Week: Women and Domestic Service in Industrializing America* (1978) won the Philip Taft Labor History Prize. He has also written *Before the Ghetto: Black Detroit in the Nineteenth Century* (1973) and contributed to *Three Generations in Twentieth-Century America: Family, Community and the Nation* (Second Edition, 1981). With William M. Tuttle, Jr., David has edited *Plain Folk: The Life Stories of Undistinguished Americans* (1981). The Guggenheim Foundation, National Endowment for the Humanities, and Ford Foundation have awarded him research assistance. He has written articles for the *Dictionary of American Biography* and has served as the associate editor of the journal *American Studies.* For 1984–1985 he was Visiting Professor of Economic and Social History, University of Birmingham, England.

Paul D. Escott

Born and reared in the Midwest (St. Louis, Missouri), Paul D. Escott studied in New England and the South. His interest in southern history and the Civil War era probably began with southern parents, but it became conscious at Harvard College (B.A., 1969) and matured at Duke University (Ph.D., 1974). Now a professor of history at the University of North Carolina, Charlotte, Paul has written *After Secession: Jefferson Davis and the Failure of Confederate Nationalism* (1978), *Slavery Remembered: A Record of Twentieth-Century Slave Narratives* (1979), and *Many Excellent People: Power and Privilege in North Carolina, 1850–1900* (1985). Paul's articles have appeared in such journals as *Civil War History, Georgia Historical Quarterly,* and *Journal of Southern History.* Active in the profession, he has served on committees of the Southern Historical Association. Fellowships from the Whitney M. Young, Jr., Memorial Foundation, the American Philosophical Society, and the Rockefeller Foundation have aided his research.

Howard P. Chudacoff

A professor of history at Brown University, Howard P. Chudacoff was born in Omaha, Nebraska, and received his degrees from the University of Chicago (A.B., 1965; Ph.D., 1969). At Brown he has co-chaired the American Civilization Program. His books include *Mobile Americans: Residential and Social Mobility in Omaha, 1880–1920* (1972) and the *Evolution of American Urban Society* (Third Edition, 1986). His many articles on topics in urban and social history have appeared in such journals as the *Journal of Family History, Reviews in American History,* and the *Journal of American History.* Howard has lectured and presented papers at many universities and historical meetings, and has received research awards from the Rockefeller Foundation, National Endowment for the Humanities, and the Population Studies and Research Center of Brown University.

Thomas G. Paterson

Thomas G. Paterson was born in Oregon City, Oregon. He graduated from the University of New Hampshire (B.A., 1963) before earning his doctorate from the University of California, Berkeley in 1968. He is now a professor of history at the University of Connecticut. His books include *Soviet-American Confrontation* (1973), *On Every Front* (1979), and *American Foreign Policy: A History* (Second Edition, 1983). Among his edited scholarship is *Major Problems in American Foreign Policy* (Second Edition, 1984). The author of over thirty articles, Tom's work has appeared in the *American Historical Review* and the *Journal of American History.* He has served on the editorial boards of the *Journal of American History* and *Diplomatic History,* on committees of the Organization of American Historians and Society for Historians of American Foreign Relations, and on the Board of Trustees of Stonehill College. Tom has also directed National Endowment for the Humanities Summer Seminars for College Teachers. His research has been assisted by the American Philosophical Society, Institute for the Study of World Politics, National Endowment for the Humanities, and others.

William M. Tuttle, Jr.

A native of Detroit, Michigan, who graduated from Denison University (1959) and the University of Wisconsin, Madison (Ph.D., 1967), William M. Tuttle, Jr. is now a professor of history at the University of Kansas. Bill has written the award-winning *Race Riot: Chicago in the Red Summer of 1919* (1970) and has edited *W. E. B. Du Bois* (1973) and, with David M. Katzman, *Plain Folk* (1982). As an historical consultant, he has helped prepare several public television documentaries and docudramas. Bill's numerous articles have appeared in the *Journal of Negro History, Labor History, Agricultural History, Technology and Culture,* and the *Journal of American History.* The Guggenheim Foundation, National Endowment for the Humanities, and American Council of Learned Societies have provided him with research assistance. He has also been awarded fellowships from the Institute of Southern History at Johns Hopkins University, Charles Warren Center at Harvard, and Stanford Humanities Center. He was elected to the Nominating Board of the Organization of American Historians.

ABOUT THE COVER

Delivery Man. This delivery man, carrying a splint basket and leather pack, was possibly a shop sign advertising a nineteenth-century grocery store. Dated about 1875, this 28½-inch figure has real buttons; the cap, boots, and arms were carved as separate pieces and then attached. It would have been placed on a pedestal located directly above the doorway of a grocery store to depict the trade of the shop. Subsequently, it came to the Henry Ford Museum in Dearborn, Michigan, to join the collections of American decorative, mechanical, and industrial arts established by Henry Ford. From the collections of Henry Ford Museum and Greenfield Village.

Printed in the U.S.A.
Library of Congress Catalog Card Number: 85-60316
ISBN: 0-395-35953-8
DEFGHIJ-D-898

CONTENTS

Chapter 12

REFORM, POLITICS, AND EXPANSION, 1824–1844

Chapter 13

TERRITORIAL EXPANSION AND SLAVERY: THE ROAD TO WAR, 1845–1861

Chapter 14

TRANSFORMING FIRE: THE CIVIL WAR, 1861–1865

Chapter 19

EVERYDAY LIFE AND CULTURE, 1877–1920

Chapter 20

GILDED AGE POLITICS, 1877–1900

Chapter 21

THE PROGRESSIVE ERA, 1895–1920

Chapter 29

THE COLD WAR AND AMERICAN POLITICS, 1945–1953

Chapter 30

AN AGE OF FRAGILE CONSENSUS, 1953–1961

Chapter 31

AMERICAN SOCIETY DURING THE POSTWAR BOOM, 1945–1960s

APPENDIX

MAPS/CHARTS

PREFACE

The generous reception given to the first edition of this volume by our colleagues in history, the encouragement and suggestions of the many instructors who used the book in their classrooms, and the appearance of new scholarship in the last few years have afforded us the opportunity to improve and update *A People and a Nation*. In this second edition we have retained and strengthened those characteristics of the first edition that students and faculty found attractive. As teachers and students we are always recreating our past, rediscovering the personalities and events that have shaped us, inspired us, and bedeviled us. This book is our rediscovery of America's past—its people and the nation they founded and sustained. Sometimes we find this history comforting, sometimes disturbing. As with our own personal experience, it is both triumphant and tragic, filled with injury as well as healing. As a mirror on our lives, it is always significant.

We draw on recent research as well as on seasoned, authoritative works to offer a comprehensive book that tells the whole story of American history. Presidential and party politics, congressional legislation, Supreme Court decisions, diplomacy and treaties, wars and foreign interventions, economic patterns, and state and local government have been the stuff of American history for generations. Into this traditional fabric we weave social history, broadly defined. We investigate the history of the majority of Americans—women—and of minorities. We study the history of social classes, and we illuminate the private, everyday life of the American people.

Characteristics of the Book

From the ordinary to the exceptional—the factory worker, the slave, the office secretary, the local merchant, the small farmer, the plantation owner, the ward politician, the president's wife, the film star, the scientist, the army general—Americans have had personal stories that have intersected with the public policies of their government. Whether victors or victims, all have been actors in their own right, with feelings, ideas, and aspirations that have fortified them in good times and bad. All are part of the American story; all speak here through excerpts from their letters, diaries, and other writings, and oral histories.

Several questions guided our telling of this narrative. On the official, or public, side of American history, we emphasize Americans' expectations of their governments and the everyday practice of those local, state, and federal institutions. We identify the mood and mentality of an era, in which Americans reveal what they think about themselves and their public officials. And in our discussion of foreign policy we particularly probe its domestic sources.

Major Themes

In the social and economic spheres, we emphasize patterns of change in the population, geographic mobility, and people's adaptation to new environments. We study the interactions of people of different races, ethnic backgrounds, religions, and genders, the social divisions that emerged, and the efforts made, often in reform movements, to heal them. As well, we focus on the effects of technological development on the economy, the worker and workplace, and lifestyles.

In the private, everyday life of the family and the home, we pay particular attention to sex roles, childbearing and childrearing, and diet and dress. We ask how Americans have chosen to entertain themselves, as participants or spectators, with sports, music, the graphic arts, reading, theater, film, and television. Throughout American history, of course, this private part of American life and public policy have interacted and influenced one another.

Students and instructors have liked our use of clear, concrete language, and have commented on how enjoyable the book is to read. They have also told us that we challenged them to think about the meaning of American history, not just to memorize it; to confront our own interpretations and at the same time to understand and respect the views of others; and to show how an historian's mind works to ask questions and to tease conclusions out of a mass of information.

For this revised edition, the authors met to discuss at length the themes and questions of the book. We reviewed numerous reports from instructors and worked to incorporate their suggestions. We also researched the most recent scholarship, alert to new evidence and new interpretations. As well, we examined every line of the text with an eye to conciseness, clarity, and readability. In the course of writing, the six of us read and reread one another's drafts and debated one another with a friendly spririt and mutual respect that strengthened us as scholars.

Several changes in this second edition stand out. First, that part of the book devoted to the post-1941 years has been substantially reorganized to match the way most instructors teach that **Changes in the** period. All of the material on the **Second Edition** Second World War—domestic and foreign—is now in Chapter 28. The Truman years are covered in Chapter 29 and the Eisenhower years in 30. They are followed by a chapter (31) on the social history of the postwar period. Chapter 32, a foreign policy segment, has been recast to emphasize the origins, experience, and aftermath of the Vietnam War. Chapter 33 then treats the domestic effects of the war and political and economic events for 1961–1973, whereas Chapter 34 does so for 1973–1981. Finally, an altogether new Chapter 35 studies the Reagan years and the interaction among social, political, economic, and diplomatic currents in the 1980s.

Second, Chapter 1 has been significantly reworked to provide the stories of the three divergent cultures—Native American, African, and European—that intersected in the New World to mold the early history of the United States. Third, we have expanded our coverage of Asians and Hispanics, constitutional history, and the nuclear arms race. Fourth, throughout the book we have explained the significance of gender in employment—the sexual division of labor. Fifth, we have set out more prominently the themes of each chapter, following the opening vignette. And, finally, A People and a Nation has a new look. Not only have new illustrations and maps been added—they have also been improved through the use of full color. Full color makes the maps (all ninety of them) easier to read and understand and the illustrations (all historically accurate because they are contemporaneous with a chapter's period) truer prints of their originals.

As in the first edition, each chapter opens with the story of an American, ordinary or exceptional, whose experience was representative of the times or whose commentary facilitates our understanding of the chapter themes, which immediately follow this vignette. To help students study and **Study Aids** review, we use bold-typed notes—like the one here—to highlight key personalities, events, concepts, and trends. Significant concepts and words are defined and italicized; important events are listed in a chart near the end of most chapters; and suggested readings for further study close each chapter. The Appendix, updated and expanded, is a unique compendium providing a historical overview of the American people and their nation.

To make the book as useful as possible for students and instructors, several learning and teaching ancillaries are available, including a *Study Guide* and *Computerized Study Guide*, an *In-* **Ancillaries** *structor's Manual*, a *Test Items* file, a *Computerized Test Items* file, and *Map Transparencies*. The *Study Guide*, which was prepared by George Warren and Cynthia Ricketson of Central Piedmont Community College, includes an introductory chapter on study techniques for history students, as well as learning objectives and a thematic guide for each chapter in the text and exercises on evaluating and using information and on finding the main idea in passages from the text, as well as test questions on the content of each chapter. The *Study Guide* is also available in a computerized version that provides the student with tutorial instruction. The *Instructor's Manual*, by Richard Rowe of Golden West College, contains chapter outlines, suggestions for lectures and discussion, and lists of audio-visual resources. The accompanying *Test Items* file, also by Professor Rowe, offers more than 1,500 multiple-choice and essay questions and more than 700 identification terms. The test items are available to adoptors on computer tape and disk. In addition, there is a set of forty full-color map transparencies available on adoption.

Though each of us feels answerable for the whole, we take primary responsibility for particular chapters: Mary Beth Norton, Chapters 1–7, David M. Katzman, Chapters 8–10, 12; Paul D. Escott, Chapters 11, 13–15; Howard P. Chudacoff, Chapters 16–21, 24; Thomas G. Paterson, Chapters 22–23, 25, 27, 30, 32, and part of 35; William M. Tuttle, Jr., Chapters 26, 28–29, 31, 33–34, and part of 35. Thomas G. Paterson also served as the coordinating author and prepared the Appendix.

Acknowledgments

Many instructors have read and criticized the successive drafts of our manuscript. Their constructive suggestions have informed and improved this second edition. We heartily thank:

John K. Alexander, *University of Cincinnati*
Roberta Alexander, *University of Dayton*
John Borden Armstrong, *Boston University*
James Barrett, *University of Illinois*
John Britton, *Francis Marion College*
Richard Burns, *California State University, Los Angeles*
Ballard Campbell, *Northeastern University*
Ron Carden, *South Plains College*
Patricia Cohen, *University of California, Santa Barbara*
Frank Costigliola, *University of Rhode Island*
Jay Coughtry, *University of Nevada, Las Vegas*
William Fleming, *Pan American University*
James Gormly, *Pan American University*
Maurine Greenwald, *University of Pittsburgh*
Linda Guerrero, *Palomar College*
James Hijiya, *Southeastern Massachusetts University*
Richard J. Hopkins, *Ohio State University*

George Juergens, *Indiana University*
Harry Lupold, *Lakeland Community College*
Bart McCash, *Middle Tennessee State University*
John Muldowny, *University of Tennessee*
Leonard Murphy, *San Antonio College*
Paul L. Murphy, *University of Minnesota*
Philip Nicholson, *Nassau Community College*
Lawrence Powell, *Tulane University*
Howard Rabinowitz, *University of New Mexico*
Roy Rosenzweig, *George Mason University*
James H. Sasser, *Central Piedmont Community College*
Constance Schulz, *University of South Carolina*
Peter Shattuck, *California State University, Sacramento*
Rebecca Shoemaker, *Indiana State University*
Harvard Sitkoff, *University of New Hampshire*
William R. Swagerty, *University of Idaho*
Emory Thomas, *University of Georgia*
James Walter, *Sinclair Community College*
Nelson Woodard, *California State University, Fullerton*

We acknowledge with thanks as well the contributions of Ruth Alexander, Nancy Fisher Chudacoff, J. Garry Clifford, Christopher Collier, Mary Ellen Erickson, Elizabeth French, William Gienapp, James L. Gormly, Frederick Hoxie, Nathan Huggins, Jacqueline Jones, Sharyn A. Katzman, Freeman Meyer, William H. Moore, Holly Izard Paterson, Shirley Rice, Barney J. Rickman, III, Janice Riley, Daniel Usner, Deborah White, David Wyllie, and Thomas Zoumaras. We also appreciate the continued guidance and generous assistance of the staff of the Houghton Mifflin Company.

T.G.P.

A PEOPLE AND A NATION

THE MEETING OF
OLD WORLD AND NEW
1492–1650

CHAPTER 1

"*It spread over* the people as great destruction," the old man told the priest. "Some it quite covered [with pustules] on all parts—their faces, their heads, their breasts. . . . There was great havoc. Very many died of it. They could not stir; they could not change position, nor lie on one side, nor face down, nor on their backs. And if they stirred, much did they cry out. Great was its destruction. Covered, mantled with pustules, very many people died of them. And very many starved; there was death from hunger, [for] none could take care of [the sick]; nothing could be done for them."

It was, by European reckoning, September 1520. Spanish troops led by Hernando Cortés had abandoned the Aztec capital of Tenochtitlan after failing in their first attempt to gain control of the city. But they had unknowingly left behind the smallpox germs that would ensure their eventual triumph. By the time the Spaniards returned three months later, the great epidemic described above had fatally weakened Tenochtitlan's inhabitants. Even so, the city held out for months against the Spanish siege. But in the Aztec year Three House, on the day One Serpent (August 1521), Tenochtitlan finally surrendered. The Spaniards had conquered Mexico, and on the site of the Aztec capital they built what is now Mexico City.

After many millennia of separation, inhabitants of the Eastern Hemisphere—the so-called Old World—had encountered the residents of the Americas, with catastrophic results for the latter and untold benefits for the former. By the time Spanish troops occupied Tenochtitlan, the age of European expansion and colonization was already well under way. Over the next three hundred and fifty years, Europeans would spread their civilization across the globe. They would come to dominate native peoples in Asia and Africa as well as in the New World of the Western Hemisphere. The history of the thirteen tiny English colonies in North America that eventually became the United States must be seen in this broader context of worldwide exploration and exploitation.

That context is complex. After 1400, European nations sought to improve their positions relative to neighboring countries not only by fighting wars on their own continent but also by acquiring valuable colonies elsewhere in the world. Simultaneously, the warring tribes and nations of Asia, Africa, and the Americas attempted to use the alien intruders to their own advantage or, failing that, to adapt successfully to the Europeans' presence in their midst. All the participants in the resulting interaction of divergent cultures were indelibly affected by the process. The contest among Europeans for control of the Americas and Africa changed the course of history in all four continents. Strategies selected by American and African tribes influenced the outcome of the Europeans' contest as well as determining the fate of their own societies. Although Europeans emerged politically dominant at the end of the long process of interaction among divergent cultures, they by no means controlled every aspect of it.

Nowhere is that lack of European control shown more clearly than in the early history of the English settlements in North America. England's first attempts to establish colonies on the mainland failed completely. Its second tries—in the early seventeenth century—succeeded only because neighboring Indians assisted the newcomers. The English colonists prospered by learning to grow such unfamiliar American crops as corn and tobacco and by developing extensive trading relationships with Native Americans. Eventually, as shall be seen in Chapter 2, they discovered a third source of prosperity—importing enslaved African laborers to work in their fields.

Only in this last case were the English able to exert more than partial control over the success of their efforts. To achieve the first goal of providing food, they had to adopt agricultural techniques suited both to the new crops and to an alien environment. As for the second goal, maintaining the trade networks essential to their survival required them to deal regularly on a more or less equal basis with people who seemed very different from themselves and who were far more familiar with America than they were. The early history of the United States, in short, can best be understood as a series of complex interactions among different peoples and environments rather than as the simple story of a triumph by only one of those groups—the English colonists.

SOCIETIES OF THE AMERICAS AND AFRICA

In the Christian world, it was the year 1400; by the Muslim calendar, 802; by Chinese count, 2896, the year of the hare; and to the Maya, who had the most accurate calendar of all, the era started with the date 1 Ahau 18 Ceh. Regardless of the name or the reckoning system, the two-hundred-year period that followed changed the course of world history. For thousands of years, human societies had developed largely in isolation from each other. The era that began in the Christian fifteenth century brought that long-standing isolation to an end. As European explorers and colonizers sought to exploit the resources of the rest of the globe, peoples from different races and cultural traditions came into regular contact for the first time.

The civilizations that had developed separately had several basic characteristics in common. All had political structures governing their secular affairs, kinship systems regulating their social life, and one or more sets of indigenous religious beliefs. In addition, they all organized their work assignments on the basis of the sexual division of labor. Throughout the world, men and women performed different tasks, although the specific definitions of those tasks varied. Many, but not all, of the societies shared yet another characteristic: they relied on agriculture for their essential food supply. (Some of the world's societies were nomadic, surviving by moving continually in search of wild animals and edible plants.) Agricultural civilizations, assured of steady supplies of meat, grains, and vegetables, did not have to devote all their energies to mere subsistence. They accumulated wealth, produced ornamental objects, and created elaborate rituals and ceremonies. In brief, they developed distinctive cultural traditions.

These cultural distinctions became the focal point for the interactions that occurred in the fifteenth century and thereafter among the various human societies. The basic similarities were obscured by the shock of discovering that not all people were the same color as oneself, that other folk worshipped other gods, or that some people defined the separate roles of men and women differently from the way one's own society did. Because three major human groups—Native Americans, Africans, and Europeans—met and mingled on the soil of the Western Hemisphere during the age of European colonization, their relationships can be examined in that context.

Since the earliest known humanlike remains, about 3 million years old, have been found in what is now Ethiopia, it is likely that human beings originated on the continent of Africa. During many millennia, the growing human population slowly dispersed to the other continents. Some of the peoples participating in this vast migration crossed a now-submerged stretch of land that joined the Asian and North American continents at the site of the Bering Strait. These forerunners of the Native American population, known as Paleo-Indians, probably **Paleo-Indians** arrived in the Americas more than thirty thousand years ago—about the same time that parts of present-day China and the Soviet Union were also being settled. The Paleo-Indians were nomadic hunters of game and gatherers of wild plants. Over many centuries, they spread through North and South America, probably moving as extended families, or "bands." ("Tribes" were composed of groups of allied bands.)

By approximately 5,500 years ago (or B.P., the archeologists' term for *before the present*), Indians living in central Mexico had begun to cultivate food crops. Their most important products were maize (corn), squash, beans, gourds, and chili peppers. As knowledge of agricultural techniques spread, most Indian groups started to live a more stationary existence. Some established permanent settlements; others moved two or three times a year among fixed sites. Over the centuries, groups of North American Indians adapted their once-similar ways of life to specific and very different geographical settings, thus creating the diversity of cultures that Europeans encountered when they first arrived (see map, page 6).

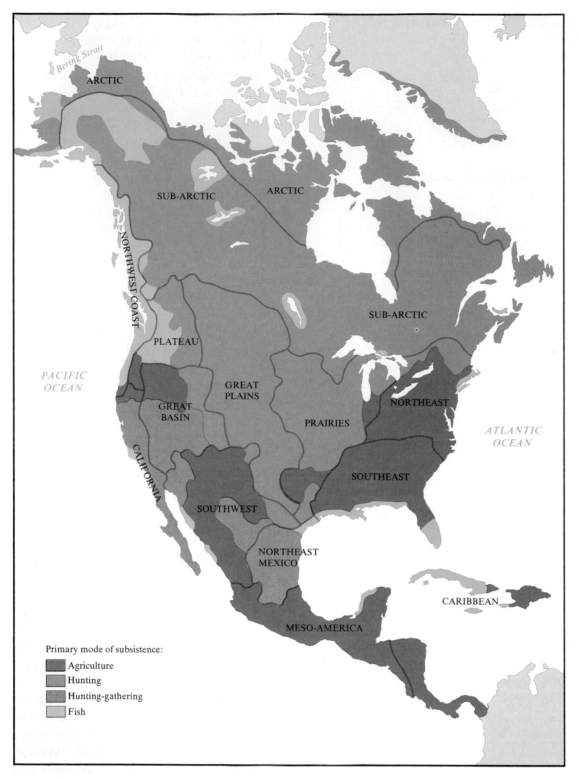

Indian Cultures of North America

       Chapter 1: THE MEETING OF OLD WORLD AND NEW, 1492–1650

The French artist Jacques Le Moyne, who visited northern Florida in 1564–1565, showed one aspect of the sexual division of labor as practiced by the Indians of the region. At planting time, the men break up the ground with hoes made from fish bones while the women dig holes into which they drop the seeds.   Library of Congress.

Those Indian bands that lived in environments not well suited to agriculture—because of a lack of adequate rainfall, for example—continued the nomadic lifestyle of their ancestors. Within the area of the present-day United States, these tribes included the Paiute and Shoshoni, who inhabited the Great Basin (now Nevada and Utah). Bands of such hunter-gatherers were small, because of the difficulties of finding sufficient food for more than a few people. They were usually composed of one or more related families, with men hunting small animals and women gathering seeds and berries. Where large game was more plentiful and food supplies therefore more certain, as in present-day Canada or the Great Plains, bands of hunters could be somewhat larger.

In more favorable environments, Indians combined agriculture in varying degrees with gathering, hunting,

and fishing. The more heavily a tribe relied on agriculture, the less likely it was to be highly mobile, since fields required attention. The cultivation of crops also tended to increase the size of Indian communities, because of the greater availability of food. Those tribes that lived near the sea coasts, like the Chinook of present-day Washington and Oregon, consumed large quantities of fish and shellfish, in addition to growing crops and gathering seeds and berries. Tribes of the interior (for example, the Arikara of the Missouri River valley) hunted large game animals while also cultivating fields of corn, squash, and beans. That was true, too, of the Algonkian tribes that inhabited much of what is now eastern Canada and the northeastern United States. (Indians are often described by linguistic groups, since large numbers of tribes spoke related languages and shared similar cultures. For example, the most important linguistic groups east of the Mississippi River were the Algonkians and the Iroquoians, found primarily in the north, and the Muskogeans of the south.)

Agricultural Indians differed in how they assigned the task of cultivating crops to the sexes. In the Southwest, the Pueblo peoples, who began raising squash and beans by 3000 B.P., defined agricultural labor as "men's work." In the East, by contrast, Algonkian, Iroquoian, and Muskogean peoples allocated agricultural chores to women. Among these eastern tribes, men's major assignments were hunting large animals and clearing the land. In all the cultures, women gathered wild foods, prepared the food for consumption or storage, and cared for the children.

Sexual Division of Labor in America

The southwestern and eastern agricultural Indians had similar social organizations. They lived in villages, sometimes sizable ones with a thousand or more inhabitants. Pueblo villages were large multistoried buildings, constructed on terraces along the sides of cliffs or other easily defended sites. Northern Iroquois villages were composed of large, rectangular, bark-covered structures (long houses), and Muskogeans and southern Algonkians lived in similarly large houses made of thatch. Most of the eastern villages were also laid out defensively, often being surrounded by wood palisades and ditches. In these cultures, each dwelling housed an extended family defined *matrilineally* (that is, through the female line). The families in such dwellings were linked together into clans, again defined by matrilineal kinship ties.

In both southwestern and eastern cultures, the most important political structures were those of the village. Indeed, among Pueblo and Muskogean peoples the village council, composed of ten to thirty men, was the highest political authority; there was no government at the tribal level. The Iroquois, by contrast, had an elaborate political hierarchy linking villages into tribes, and tribes into a widespread confederation. (The Iroquois Confederacy will be discussed in detail in Chapter 2.) In all the cultures, political power was divided between civil and war chiefs, who had authority only so long as they retained the confidence of the people.

Indian Politics and Religion

The political position of women varied from tribe to tribe. Women were more likely to assume leadership roles among the agricultural peoples (especially where females were the chief cultivators) than among nomadic hunters. For example, women could become chiefs of certain Algonkian bands, but they never held that position in the hunting tribes of the Great Plains. Iroquois women did not become chiefs, yet tribal matrons nevertheless exercised political power, as will be seen in Chapter 2. Probably the most powerful female chiefs were found in what is now the southeastern United States. In the mid-sixteenth century a female ruler known as the Lady of Cofitachique governed a large group of villages in present-day western South Carolina.

Indian religious beliefs varied even more than did their political systems. One common thread was that they were all *polytheistic*; that is, they all involved a multitude of gods. Another was the relationship of the most important rituals to the tribe's chief means of subsistence. That is, the major deities of agricultural Indians like Pueblos and Muskogeans were associated with cultivation, and their chief festivals centered on planting and harvest. The most important gods of hunting tribes (like the Siouan-speakers of the Great Plains), by contrast, were associated with animals, and their major festivals were related to hunting. The tribe's main source of food and women's role (or lack of role) in its production helped to determine women's potential as religious leaders. Women held the most prominent positions in those agricultural societies (like the Iroquois) in which they were also the chief food producers.

The most advanced Indian civilizations on the North American continent were located in present-day Mexico and Guatemala (Mesoamerica). The major Indian societies encountered by the Spanish in the sixteenth century— the Aztec and the Maya—were the heirs of earlier civilizations (such as the Olmec), which had also built great empires. Characteristic of these Mesoamerican cultures were large cities, ceremonial sites featuring massive pyramid-shaped temples, rule by an hereditary elite of warrior-priests, primary dependence on agriculture for food, and religious practices that included human sacrifice. The Aztec, who entered central Mexico in the fourteenth century, were a warlike people who had consolidated their control over the entire region by the

Aztec and Maya

John White, an artist who accompanied the exploratory mission Raleigh sent to America in 1585, sketched Pomeioc, a typical Algonkian village composed of houses made from woven mats stretched over poles, and surrounded by a defensive wooden palisade.   Library of Congress.

time of Cortés's arrival. The Maya, whose civilization was already in decline when the Spaniards came, were the intellectual leaders of Mesoamerica. They invented systems of writing and mathematics, and their calendar was the most accurate then known.

In the fifteenth century, then, a wide variety of Indian cultures, comprising perhaps 4 to 6 million people, inhabited North America. In modern Mexico, hereditary rulers presided over vast agricultural empires. Along the Atlantic coast of the present-day United States, Indians likewise cultivated crops, but their political systems differed greatly from those of Mesoamerica. To the north and west, in what is now Canada and the Great Plains, lived nomadic and seminomadic societies primarily dependent on hunting large animals. Still farther west were the hunter-gatherer bands of the Great Basin and the agricultural Indians of the Southwest. Finally, on the Pacific coast lived tribes that based their subsistence chiefly on fish. All told, these diverse groups spoke well over one thousand different languages. For obvious reasons, they did not consider themselves as one people, nor did they—for the most part—think of uniting to repel the European invaders. Instead, each tribe or band continued to pursue the same goal it always had: bettering its own circumstances relative to its neighbors, regardless of who those neighbors were.

Fifteenth-century Africa, like fifteenth-century America, housed a variety of cultures adapted to different geographical settings (see map, page 10).

Africa: Its Peoples

Many of these cultures were of great antiquity. In the north, along the Mediterranean Sea, lived the Berbers, a Muslim people of Middle Eastern origin. (Muslims are adherents of the Islamic religion founded by the prophet Mohammed in the seventh century.) On the east coast of Africa, city-states dominated by Muslim merchants engaged in extensive trade with India, the Moluccas (part of

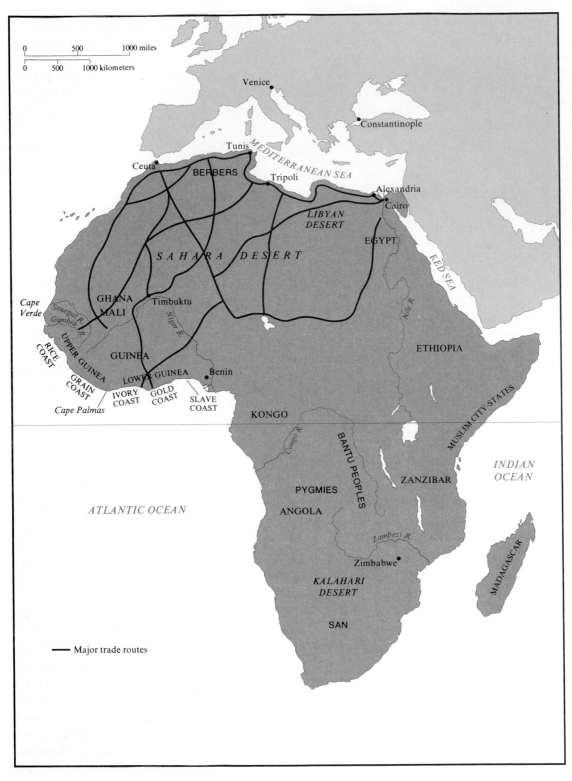

Africa and Its Peoples, ca. 1400

Scale:
0 — 500 — 1000 miles
0 — 500 — 1000 kilometers

Venice

Constantinople

MEDITERRANEAN SEA

Tunis

Ceuta

BERBERS

Tripoli

Alexandria

Cairo

LIBYAN DESERT

EGYPT

RED SEA

SAHARA DESERT

Cape Verde

Senegal R.

Gambia R.

GHANA

MALI

Timbuktu

Niger R.

Nile R.

ETHIOPIA

RICE COAST

UPPER GUINEA

GRAIN COAST

GUINEA

LOWER GUINEA

IVORY COAST

GOLD COAST

SLAVE COAST

Benin

Cape Palmas

KONGO

MUSLIM CITY STATES

Congo R.

BANTU PEOPLES

ZANZIBAR

INDIAN OCEAN

PYGMIES

ANGOLA

ATLANTIC OCEAN

Zambezi R.

Zimbabwe

MADAGASCAR

KALAHARI DESERT

SAN

—— Major trade routes

modern Indonesia), and China. Through these ports passed a considerable share of the trade between the eastern Mediterranean and Far East; the rest followed the long land route across Central Asia known as the Silk Road.

In the African interior, south of the Mediterranean coast, lie the great Sahara and Libyan deserts, huge expanses of nearly waterless terrain that pose a formidable barrier to travel. Below the deserts, much of the continent is divided between tropical rain forests and grassy plains. Over the centuries, this fertile landscape came to be dominated by Bantu peoples, who left their homeland in modern Nigeria about two thousand years ago and slowly migrated southward across the continent, assimilating and conquering other ethnic groups (like the Pygmies and the San) as they went. The capital of their empire was the great city whose ruins are now known as Zimbabwe, the "stone houses."

Most of the unwilling black migrants to the Americas came from West Africa, or Guinea, a land of tropical forests and small-scale agriculture that had

West Africa (Guinea) been inhabited for at least ten thousand years before Europeans set foot there in the fifteenth century.

The northern region, or Upper Guinea, was heavily influenced by Islamic culture. As early as the eleventh century, many of its inhabitants had become Muslims; more important, the trans-Saharan trade between Upper Guinea and the Muslim Mediterranean was black Africa's major connection to Europe and the Middle East. In return for salt, dates, and such manufactured goods as silk and cotton cloth, Africans exchanged ivory, gold, and slaves with the northern merchants. (Slaves, who were mostly captives of war, were in great demand as household servants in the homes of the Muslim Mediterranean elite.) This commerce was controlled first by the great kingdom of Ghana (ca. 900–1100), then by its successor, the empire of Mali, which flourished in the fourteenth and fifteenth centuries. Black Africa and Islam intersected at the city that was the intellectual and commercial heart of the trade, the near-legendary Timbuktu. A cosmopolitan center, Timbuktu attracted merchants and scholars from all parts of North Africa and the Mediterranean.

Along the coast of West Africa and in the south, or Lower Guinea, Islam had less influence. There,

most Africans continued to practice their indigenous religions, which—like those of the agricultural Indians of the Americas—revolved around rituals designed to ensure good harvests. The vast interior kingdoms of Mali and Ghana had no counterparts on the coast. Throughout Lower Guinea, individual villages composed of groups of kin were linked into small, often rigidly hierarchical kingdoms. At the time of initial contact with Europeans, the region was characterized by fragmented political and social authority.

Just as the political structures varied, so too did the means of subsistence pursued by the different peoples of Guinea. Upper Guinea runs roughly north-south from Cape Verde to Cape Palmas. Its northernmost region was the so-called Rice Coast, lying just south of the Gambia River (present-day Gambia, Senegal, and Guinea). The people who lived there fished and cultivated rice in coastal swamplands. The Grain Coast, the next region to the south, was thinly populated and not readily accessible from the sea because it had only one good harbor (modern Freetown, Sierra Leone). Its people concentrated on farming and animal husbandry.

South of the Grain Coast, at Cape Palmas, the coastline turns east, and Lower Guinea begins. The Ivory Coast and the Gold Coast were each named by Europeans for the major trade goods they obtained there. The Gold Coast, comprising thirty little kingdoms known as the Akan States, later formed the basis of the great Asante kingdom. Initially many of the slaves destined for sale in the Americas came from the Akan States. By the eighteenth century, though, it was the next section of Lower Guinea, the modern nations of Togo and Benin, that supplied most of the slaves sold in the English colonies. The Adja kings of the region, which became known as the Slave Coast, encouraged the founding of slave trading posts and served as middlemen in the trade.

The ancient kingdom of Benin (modern Nigeria), which lay east of the Slave Coast and west of the Niger River, was the strongest and most centralized coastal state in Guinea. Long before Europeans arrived it was, like Mali, a center of trade for West and North Africa. Like the peoples of the Rice Coast, those who lived in Benin along the delta of the Niger made much of their living from the water. They fished, made salt, and used skillfully constructed dugout canoes to carry on a wide-ranging commerce.

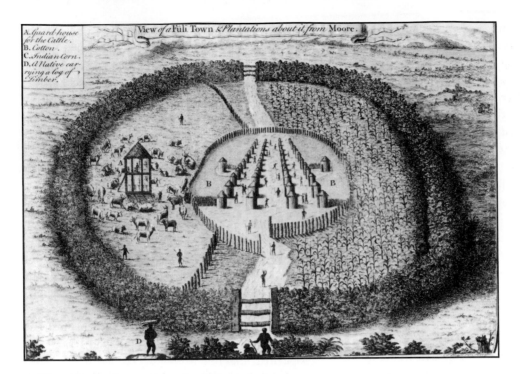

A West African village as drawn by a European observer. A wooden defensive palisade surrounds the circular houses made of woven plant materials. In this the African village resembles Pomeioc, the Indian village pictured on page 9. But note a major difference—a herd of livestock enclosed in a larger fence. Note also that the Africans are growing Indian corn, thus illustrating the exchange of plants between America and Africa (see page 19). Library of Congress.

The societies of West Africa, like those of the Americas, assigned different tasks to men and women. In general, the sexes shared agricultural duties, but in some Guinean cultures women bore the primary responsibility for growing crops, whereas in others men assumed that chore. In addition, men hunted, managed livestock, and did most of the fishing. Women were responsible for childcare, food preparation, and cloth manufacture. Everywhere in West Africa women were the primary local traders. They had charge of the extensive local and regional networks through which goods were exchanged among the various families, villages, and small kingdoms.

Sexual Division of Labor in West Africa

Despite their different modes of subsistence and deep political divisions, the peoples of West Africa had largely similar social systems organized on the basis of what anthropologists have called the dual-sex principle. In the societies of West Africa, each sex handled its own affairs: just as male political and religious leaders governed the men, so females ruled the women. In the Dahomean kingdom, every male official had his female counterpart; in the Akan States, chiefs inherited their status through the female line and each chief had a female assistant who supervised women's affairs.

Indigenous religious beliefs likewise stressed the complementary nature of male and female roles. Both women and men served as heads of the cults and secret societies that directed the spiritual life of the villages. Although African women rarely held formal power over men (unlike some of their Native American contemporaries), they did govern other females.

The West Africans brought to the Americas, then, were agricultural peoples, skilled at tending livestock, hunting, fishing, and manufacturing cloth from plant fibers and animal skins. Both men and women were accustomed to working communally, alongside other members of their own sex. They were also accustomed to a relatively egalitarian relationship between the sexes. In the New World, they entered societies that used their labor but had little respect for their cultural traditions. Of the three peoples whose experience intersected in the Americas, their lives were the most disrupted.

EUROPE AND
ITS EXPLORATIONS

After 1400, Europe had begun to recover from centuries of decline. Northern Europe—England and France in particular—had long been an intellectual and economic backwater, far outstripped in importance by the states of the Mediterranean, especially the great Italian city-states like Venice and Florence. The cultural flowering known as the Renaissance began in those city-states in the fourteenth century and spread northward, awakening Europeans' intellectual curiosity. At the same time, the pace of economic activity quickened. Near-constant warfare (for example, the Hundred Years' War between England and France, which ended in a French victory in 1453), promoted feelings of nationalism within the combatant countries. All these developments helped to set the stage for extraordinary political and technological change after the middle of the fifteenth century.

Yet in the midst of that change the life of Europe's common people remained basically untouched for at least another century. European societies were hierarchical, with a few wealthy aristocratic families wielding arbitrary power over the majority of the people. Europe's kingdoms accordingly resembled those of Africa or Mesoamerica, but differed greatly from the more egalitarian, consensus-based societies found in America north of Mexico. Most Europeans, like most Africans or Native Americans, lived in small agricultural villages. But because the Roman Catholic church—to which almost all Europeans belonged—insisted on *exogamy* (marriage to nonrelatives), villages were not based solely, or even primarily, on kinship groups, as they were in Africa or the Americas. On those continents, the kin groups that constituted a village together controlled the surrounding land. Europe had no comparable coresident extended families; perhaps that was why European land tended to be held by individual farmers rather than by villages as a whole.

Even though European farmers, or peasants, had separate landholdings, they nevertheless worked their fields communally, like most Africans and Native Americans. That was because fields had to lie fallow every second or third year to regain their fertility after having been planted with wheat or rye, the most common European food grains. A family could not have ensured its own food supply in alternate years had not the work and the crop been shared annually by all the villagers.

In European cultures, men did most of the field work, with women helping out chiefly at planting and harvest. At other times, women's duties consisted primarily of childcare and household tasks (including food preservation, milking cows, and caring for poultry). If a woman's husband was an artisan or storekeeper, she might assist him in business. Since Europeans usually kept domesticated animals (especially pigs, sheep, and cattle) to use for meat, hunting had little economic importance in their cultures. Rather, hunting was viewed mainly as a sport for male aristocrats.

Sexual Division of Labor in Europe

Whereas in African or Native American societies women often played major roles in politics and religion, in Europe men were dominant in all areas of life. A few women from noble families—for example, Queen Elizabeth I of England—achieved status or power, but the vast majority of European women were excluded from positions of political authority. In the Catholic church, leadership roles were reserved for men, who alone could become priests and bishops. At the familial level, husbands and fathers expected to control the lives of their wives, children, and servants (a *patriarchal* system of family governance). In short, European women held inferior positions in both public and private realms.

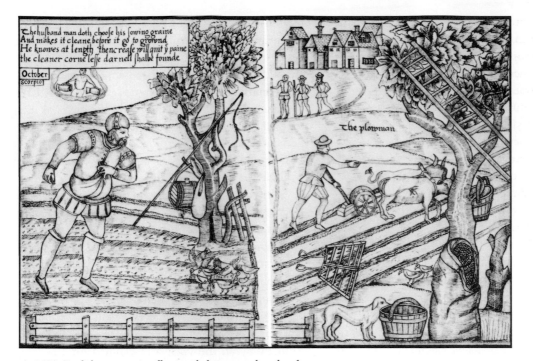

A 1622 English manuscript illustrated the seasonal cycle of work for ordinary farmers. In October, the month shown here, the wise husbandman (farmer) plowed his fields and sowed a crop of winter wheat (which the English called corn). Note that these scenes contain only men, showing that the sexual division of labor in European agriculture was quite different from that of the Indians illustrated on page 7. *Folger Shakespeare Library.*

The traditional hierarchical social structure of Europe changed little in the fifteenth century, but the opposite was true of politics. The century witnessed rapid and dynamic political change,

Political and Technological Change

as ruthless monarchs expanded their territories through conquest and marriage and centralized previously diffuse political power in their own hands. In England, Henry VII in 1485 founded the Tudor dynasty and began uniting a previously divided land. In France, the successors of Charles VII unified the kingdom and established new, more secure sources of revenue. Most successful of all, at least in the short run, were Ferdinand of Aragon and Isabella of Castile. In 1469 they married and combined their kingdoms, thus creating the foundation of a strongly Catholic Spain. In 1492, they defeated the Muslims (who had lived on the Iberian peninsula for centuries) and expelled all Jews from their domain.

The fifteenth century also brought significant technological change to Europe. Movable type and the printing press, invented in Germany in the 1450s, made information more widely and more readily accessible than ever before. Other discoveries led to the development of navigational instruments like the astrolabe, which allowed oceanic sailors to estimate their position by measuring the relationship of sun, moon, or stars to the horizon. Such inventions simultaneously stimulated Europeans' curiosity about fabled lands across the seas and enabled them to think about reaching exotic places by ship. For example, Marco Polo's *Travels*, which described a Venetian merchant's adventures in thirteenth-century China and reported that that nation was bordered on the east by an ocean, circulated widely among Europe's educated elites after it was printed in 1477. This book led many Europeans to believe that they could trade directly with China via ocean-going vessels, instead of relying on the Silk Road or the trade route through East Africa. That would also allow them to circumvent the Muslim merchants who had hitherto controlled their access to Asian goods.

Thus the European explorations of the fifteenth and sixteenth centuries were made possible by technological advances and by the financial might of newly powerful national rulers. But the primary motivation for the exploratory voyages was a desire for direct access to the wealth of the East. That motive was supported by a secondary concern to spread Christianity around the world. The linking of materialist and spiritual goals might seem contradictory today, but fifteenth-century Europeans saw no necessary conflict between the two. Explorers and colonizers could honestly wish to convert heathen peoples to Christianity. At the same time they could also hope to increase their nation's wealth by establishing direct trade with China, India, and the Moluccas, the sources of spices like pepper, cloves, cinnamon, and nutmeg (needed to season the bland European diet), silk, dyes, perfumes, jewels, and gold.

Motives for Exploration

The seafaring Portuguese people, whose land was located on the southwestern corner of the continent of Europe, began the age of European expansion in 1415 when they seized control of Ceuta, a Muslim city in North Africa (see map, page 10). Prince Henry the Navigator, son of King John I, realized that vast wealth awaited the first European nation to tap the riches of Africa and Asia directly. Each year he dispatched ships southward along the coast of Africa, attempting to discover a passage to the East. Not until after Prince Henry's death did Bartholomew Dias round the southern tip of Africa (1488) and Vasco da Gama finally reach India (1498). Long before that, the Portuguese had established trading posts in Guinea, so that they no longer needed to use the long trans-Saharan trade route through Timbuktu. They earned immense profits by transporting African goods swiftly to Europe. Among their most valuable cargoes were slaves; when they carried African Muslim prisoners of war back to the Iberian peninsula, the Portuguese introduced the custom of black slavery into Europe.

Spain, with its reinvigorated monarchy, was the next country to sponsor exploratory voyages, chiefly those of Christopher Columbus, a Genoese sea captain.

Christopher Columbus

Like other experienced sailors, Columbus believed the world to be round. (Only ignorant folk still thought it was flat.) Where he differed from his contemporaries was in his estimate of its size. He believed that Japan lay only 3,000 miles from the southern European coast—the distance is actually 12,000 miles—and therefore that it would be easier to reach the East by sailing west than by making the difficult voyage around the southern tip of Africa.

After being rejected as a crackpot by the monarchs of France, Portugal, and England, Columbus sought and received financial backing from Queen Isabella. Envious of Portuguese successes, she hoped to gain a foothold in Asia for her nation. On August 3, 1492, with three ships under his command—the *Pinta*, the *Niña*, and the *Santa Maria*—Columbus sailed west from the port of Palos in Spain. On October 12, he landed on an island in the Bahamas, which he named San Salvador and claimed for the king and queen of Spain. Because he thought he had reached the Indies, he called the inhabitants of the region Indians.

Columbus made three more voyages to the west, during which he explored most of the major Caribbean islands and sailed along the coasts of Central and South America. Until the day he died in 1506, Columbus continued to believe that he had reached Asia. Even before his death, others knew better. Because the Florentine Amerigo Vespucci (who explored the South American coast in 1499) was the first to publish the idea that a new continent had been discovered, a mapmaker in 1507 labeled the land *America*.

More than five hundred years earlier, Norse explorers had briefly colonized present-day Newfoundland, but it was the voyages of Columbus and his successors that finally brought the Old and New Worlds together. John Cabot (1497), Giovanni da Verrazano (1524), Jacques Cartier (1534), and Henry Hudson (1609 and 1610) all explored the North American coast (see map, page 17). They were primarily searching for the legendary, nonexistent "Northwest Passage" through the Americas, hoping to find an easy route to the riches of the East. Although they did not attempt to plant colonies in the Western Hemisphere, their discoveries interested European nations in the New World for its own sake.

Only Spain immediately moved to take advantage of the discoveries. On his first voyage, Columbus had established a base on the island of Hispaniola. From there, Spanish explorers fanned out around the Caribbean basin: in 1513, Juan Ponce de León reached Florida and Vasco Nuñez de Balboa crossed the Isthmus of Panama and found the Pacific Ocean. Less than ten years later, the Spaniards' dreams of wealth were realized when Cortés conquered the Aztec empire, killing its ruler, Moctezuma, and seizing a fabulous treasure of gold and silver. Venturing northward, conquistadores like Juan Rodriguez Cabrillo (who sailed along the California coast), Hernando de Soto (who discovered the Mississippi River), and Francisco Vásquez de Coronado (who explored the southwestern portion of what is now the United States) found little of value. By contrast, Francisco Pizarro, who explored the western coast of South America, conquered and enslaved the Inca in 1535, thus acquiring the richest silver mines in the world. Just half a century after Columbus's first voyage, the Spanish monarchs—who treated the American territories as their personal possessions—controlled the richest, most extensive empire Europe had known since ancient Rome.

Conquistadores

Spain established the model of colonization that other countries later attempted to imitate, a model with three major elements. First, the crown maintained tight control over the colonies, establishing a rigidly hierarchical government that allowed little autonomy to New World jurisdictions. (That control included, for example, allowing only selected persons to migrate to America and insisting that the colonies import all their manufactured goods from Spain.) Second, the colonies' wealth was based on the exploitation of both the native population and slaves imported from Africa. A Spanish law adopted in 1542 forbade the enslavement of Indians, but the conquerors, accustomed to African slavery in their homeland, had no similar scruples about blacks. And many Indians, though technically not enslaved, labored in mines and fields in a status resembling peonage (perpetual service for debt). Third, the colonists sent from Spain were almost wholly male. They married Indian—and later black—women, thereby creating the racially mixed population that characterizes Latin America to the present day.

The New World's gold and silver, though a boon at first, ultimately brought about the decline of Spain as a major power. The influx of hitherto undreamed-of wealth led to rapid inflation, which (among other adverse effects) caused Spanish products to be overpriced in international markets and imported goods to become cheaper in Spain. The once-profitable Spanish textile manufacturing industry collapsed, as did scores of other businesses. The seemingly endless income from New World colonies also emboldened successive Spanish monarchs to spend lavishly on wars against the Dutch and the English. Several times in the late sixteenth and early seventeenth centuries the monarchs repudiated the state debt, thus wreaking havoc with the nation's finances. When the South American mines started to give out in the mid-seventeenth century, Spain's economy crumbled and the nation lost its political pre-eminence.

American civilizations suffered even more. The Spaniards deliberately leveled Indian cities, building cathedrals and monasteries on sites once occupied by Aztec, Incan, and Mayan temples. Despite the protests of some priests, they sought to erase all vestiges of the great Indian cultures by burning whatever written records they found. As a result, present-day knowledge of the Aztec, Maya, and Inca civilizations rests almost entirely on architectural remains, pottery artifacts, and a few records left by priests who sympathized with the Indians.

The native peoples to the north initially fared somewhat better because the English, French, and Dutch, unlike the Spanish, did not immediately start to colonize the coast their sailors had explored. Instead, they left the region to European mariners, who came to fish in the rich waters off Newfoundland. Eventually, these fishermen learned that they could supplement their profits by exchanging cloth and metal goods (like pots and knives) for the Indians' beaver pelts, which Europeans used to make fashionable felt hats. At first the Europeans conducted their trading from ships sailing along the coast, but later they established permanent outposts on the mainland to centralize and control the traffic in furs. Among the most successful of these were the French trading posts at Quebec (1608) and Montreal (1642), on the St. Lawrence River; the Swedish settlement at Fort Christina (1638) on the Delaware River; and

Northern Traders

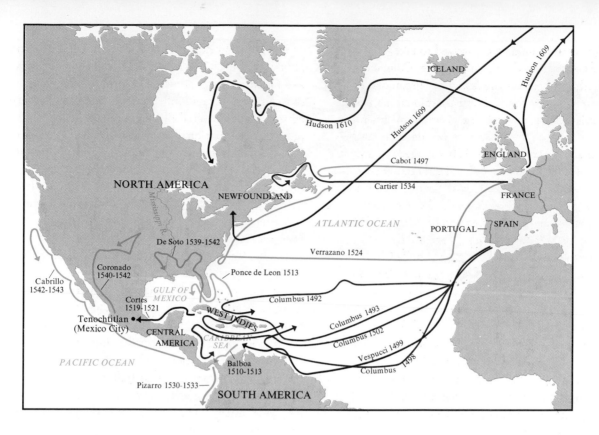

European Explorations in America

the Dutch forts of New Amsterdam and Fort Orange on the Hudson River, both founded in 1624. All were inhabited chiefly by male adventurers, whose sole aim was to send as many pelts as possible home to Europe.

Even though the northern Europeans did not conquer the Indians, as the Spanish had, their trading activities had a significant effect on the native societies. The Europeans' insatiable demand for furs, especially beaver, was matched by the Indians' desire for European goods that could make their lives easier and establish their superiority over neighboring tribes. Some tribes concentrated so completely on trapping for the European market that they abandoned their traditional modes of subsistence. The Abenaki of Maine, for example, became partially dependent on food supplied by their neighbors to the south, the Massachusett tribe, because they devoted most of their energies to catching beaver to sell to French traders. The Massachusett, in turn, intensified their production of foodstuffs, which they traded to the Abenaki in exchange for the European metal tools that they preferred to their own handmade stone implements. The northeastern tribes, in other words, began to change their traditional ways of life: some specialized in producing pelts for the market, others in supplying foodstuffs to the fur hunters, who became the agriculturalists' major source of European trade goods, rather than the Europeans themselves.

The Europeans' greatest impact on the Americas was, however, unintended. Diseases carried from the Old World to the New by the alien invaders killed hundreds of thousands, even millions, of Native Americans, who had no immunity to germs that had infested Europe, Asia, and Africa for centuries. The greatest killer was smallpox, which was spread by direct human contact. The epidemic that hit Tenochtitlan in 1520 had begun in Hispaniola two years earlier. Pizarro easily conquered the Inca partly because their society had been devastated by the epidemic shortly before his arrival. Smallpox was not the only villain; influenza, measles, and other diseases added to the destruction.

Killer Diseases

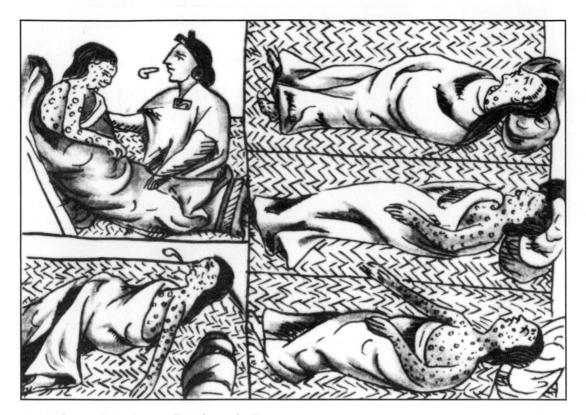

Aztec Indians suffering from smallpox during the Cortes invasion. From Fray Bernardo de Sahagun's General History of the Things of New Spain (Historia de las Cosas de Nueva Espana), *published in the sixteenth century.* Library of Congress.

The statistics are staggering. When Columbus landed on Hispaniola in 1492, more than 3 million Indians resided there. Fifty years later, only five hundred were still alive.

Even in the north, where smaller Indian populations encountered only a few European explorers, traders, and fishermen, disease ravaged the countryside. A great epidemic, most likely chicken pox, swept through the Indian villages along the coast north of Cape Cod in 1616–1618. The mortality rate may have been as high as 90 percent. An English traveler several years later commented that the Indians had "died on heapes, as they lay in their houses," and that bones and skulls covered the remains of their villages. Because of this dramatic depopulation of the area, just a few years later English colonists were able to establish settlements virtually unopposed by native peoples. As one historian has observed, America was more a widowed land than a virgin one when the English arrived there.

The Americans, though, took a revenge of sorts. They gave the Europeans a virulent form of syphilis. The first recorded case of the new disease in Europe occurred in Barcelona, Spain, in 1493, shortly after Columbus's return from the Caribbean. Although less deadly than smallpox, syphilis was extremely dangerous and debilitating. It spread quickly through Europe and Asia, carried by soldiers, sailors, and prostitutes, even reaching China by 1505.

The exchange of diseases was only part of a broader mutual transfer of plants and animals that resulted directly from Columbus's voyages. The two hemispheres had evolved separately over millions of years, developing widely different forms of life. Many large

Exchange of Plants and Animals

mammals were native to the connected continents of Europe, Asia, and Africa, but the Americas contained no domesticated beasts larger than dogs and llamas. On the other hand, the vegetable crops of the New World—particularly corn, beans, squash, manioc, and potatoes—were more nutritious and produced higher yields than those of the Old, like wheat and rye. In time Indians learned to raise and consume European domestic animals, and Europeans and Africans became accustomed to planting and eating American crops. As a result, the diets of all three peoples were vastly enriched. One consequence was the doubling of the world's population over the next three hundred years, after centuries of stability.

The exchange of two other commodities significantly influenced European and American civilizations. In America, Europeans discovered tobacco, which was at first believed to have beneficial medicinal effects. Smoking and chewing the "Indian weed" became a fad in the Old World. Tobacco cultivation was later to form the basis for the prosperity of the first successful English colonies in North America. Despite the efforts of such skeptics as King James I of England, who in 1604 pronounced smoking to be "loathsome to the eye, hatefull to the Nose, harmfull to the brain, [and] dangerous to the Lungs," tobacco's popularity has continued to the present day.

More important was the impact of the horse on some Indian cultures. Spaniards brought the first horses to America; inevitably, some fell into the hands of the Native Americans. They were traded northward among the tribes and eventually became essential to the life of the nomadic buffalo hunters of the Great Plains. The Apache, Comanche, and Blackfeet, among others, used horses for transportation and hunting, calculated their wealth in the number of horses owned, and waged wars primarily from horseback. Because their horses continually needed fresh pastures, they had to move their camps frequently. Some tribes that had previously cultivated crops abandoned agriculture altogether. As a result of the acquisition of horses, then, a mode of subsistence that had been based on hunting several different animals, combined with some gathering and agriculture, became one focused almost wholly on hunting buffalo.

ENGLAND COLONIZES THE NEW WORLD

When Englishmen began to think about planting colonies in the Western Hemisphere, they took Spain's possessions in the New World as both a model and a challenge. New Spain's existence posed a threat to England, Spain's greatest rival, not only because of the wealth Spain derived from the colonies, but also because of their strategic importance. Even remote outposts could be of use to warring countries. By establishing its own settlements, England could prevent Spain from dominating the Western Hemisphere and could also gain direct access to valuable American commodities.

England's first colonial planners thus hoped to reproduce Spanish successes by dispatching to America men who would exploit the native peoples for their own and their nation's benefit. In

Raleigh's Roanoke Colony

the 1580s, a group that included Sir Humphrey Gilbert and his younger half-brother Sir Walter Raleigh promoted a scheme to establish outposts that could trade with the Indians and provide bases for attacks on New Spain. Approving the idea, Queen Elizabeth I authorized Raleigh and Gilbert to colonize North America. Gilbert failed to plant a colony in Newfoundland, dying in the attempt, and Raleigh was only briefly more successful. In 1587 he sent 117 colonists to the territory he named Virginia (for Elizabeth, the "Virgin Queen"). They established a settlement on Roanoke Island, in what is now North Carolina, but in 1590 a supply ship could not find them. The colonists had vanished, leaving only the word "Croatoan" (the name of a nearby island) carved on a tree.

The failure of Raleigh's attempt to colonize Virginia ended English efforts at settlement in North America for nearly two decades. When, in 1606, Englishmen decided to try once more, they again planned colonies that imitated the Spanish model. Success came only when they abandoned that model and founded settlements very different from those of other European

TUDOR AND STUART MONARCHS OF ENGLAND
1509–1649

Monarch	Years of Reign	Relation to Predecessor
Henry VIII	1509–1547	son
Edward VI	1547–1553	son
Mary I	1553–1558	half-sister
Elizabeth I	1558–1603	half-sister
James I	1603–1625	cousin
Charles I	1625–1649	son

powers. Unlike Spain, France, or the Netherlands, England eventually sent large numbers of men *and women* to set up *agriculturally based* colonies in the New World. Before the history of those colonies is discussed, it is important to examine the two major developments that prompted approximately two hundred thousand ordinary English men and women to move to North America in the seventeenth century and that led their government to encourage them.

The first development was a significant change in English religious practice, a transformation that eventually led large numbers of English dissenters to

English Reformation

leave their homeland. In 1533, Henry VIII, wanting a male heir and infatuated with Anne Boleyn, sought to annul his marriage to his Spanish-born queen, Catherine of Aragon, despite nearly twenty years of marriage. When the pope refused to approve the annulment, Henry left the Roman Catholic church, founded the Church of England, and—with Parliament's concurrence—proclaimed himself its head. The English people welcomed the schism, because they had little respect for the English Catholic church, which was at the time filled with corrupt bishops and ignorant, drunken priests. At first the reformed Church of England differed little from Catholicism in its practices, but under Henry's daughter Elizabeth I (child of his marriage to Anne Boleyn), new currents of religious belief that had originated on the European continent early in the

sixteenth century dramatically affected the English church.

The leaders of the continental Protestant Reformation were Martin Luther, a German monk, and John Calvin, a French cleric and lawyer. Combating the Catholic doctrine that priests had to serve as intermediaries between lay people and God, they both insisted that each person could interpret the Bible for him or herself. (One result of that notion was the spread of literacy: to understand and interpret the Bible, people obviously had to learn how to read it for themselves.) Both Luther and Calvin rejected Catholic rituals and denied the need for an elaborate church hierarchy. They also asserted that salvation came through faith alone, rather than—as Catholic teaching had it—through a combination of faith and good works. Calvin, though, went further than Luther in stressing God's absolute omnipotence and emphasizing the need for people to submit totally to His will.

Elizabeth I tolerated religious diversity among her subjects as long as they generally acknowledged her authority as head of the Church of England. Ac-

Puritans

cordingly, during her long reign (1558–1603) Calvin's ideas gained influence within the English church. By the early seventeenth century, many English Calvinists believed that the Reformation had not gone far enough. Henry had simplified the church hierarchy; they wanted to abolish it altogether. Henry had subordinated the church to the interests of the state; they wanted a church free from political interference. And the Church of England, like the Catholic church, continued to define its membership as including everyone in the state. Some Calvinists preferred a more restricted definition; they wanted to confine church membership to persons believed to be "saved." Because these seventeenth-century English Calvinists said they wanted to *purify* the church, they became known as Puritans.

Elizabeth I's Stuart successors, her cousin James I (1603–1625) and his son Charles I (1625–1649) were less tolerant of Puritans than she. As Scots, they also had little respect for the traditions of representative government that had developed in England under the Tudors and their predecessors. The wealthy, taxpaying landowners who sat in Parliament had grown accustomed to having considerable influence on government policies, especially taxation. But James I, taking a position later endorsed by his son, publicly declared his adherence to the theory of the divine right of kings. The Stuarts insisted that a monarch's power came directly from God and that his subjects had no alternative but to obey him. A king's authority, they argued, was absolute, just like the authority of a father over his children. Both James I and Charles I believed that their authority included the power to enforce religious conformity among their subjects and so they authorized the persecution of Puritans, who were challenging many of the most important precepts of the English church. Consequently, in the 1620s and 1630s a number of English Puritans decided to move to America, where they hoped to put their religious beliefs into practice unmolested by the Stuarts or the church hierarchy.

The second major development that led English folk to move to North America was the onset of dramatic social and economic change caused by the doubling of the English population in the 150-year period after 1530. All those additional people needed food, clothing, and other goods. The competition for goods led to high inflation, coupled with a fall in real wages as the number of workers increased. In these new economic and demographic circumstances, some English people—especially those with sizable landholdings that could produce food and clothing fibers for the growing population—sub-

Social Change in England

Puritan doctrines aroused so much controversy in sixteenth- and seventeenth-century England that clergymen with Puritan beliefs were occasionally physically attacked while they were preaching. Such an incident is illustrated in this English cartoon of the period. Library of Congress.

stantially improved their lot. Others, particularly landless laborers or those with very small amounts of land, fell into unremitting poverty. When landowners raised rents or decided to enclose and combine small holdings into large units, they forced tenant farmers off the land. Consequently, geographical as well as social mobility increased, and the population of the cities (especially London) swelled.

Well-to-do English people reacted with alarm to what they saw as the disappearance of traditional ways of life. The streets and highways were filled with steady streams of the landless and the homeless. Officials became obsessed with the problem of maintaining order and came to believe that England was overcrowded. They concluded that colonies established in the New World could siphon off England's "surplus population," thus easing the social strains at home. For similar reasons, many English people decided that they could improve their circumstances by migrating from a small, land-scarce, apparently overpopulated island to a large, land-rich continent. Such economic considerations affected English people's decisions to migrate to the colonies as much as, if not more than, a desire for escape from religious persecution.

The initial impetus for the establishment of what was to become England's first permanent colony in

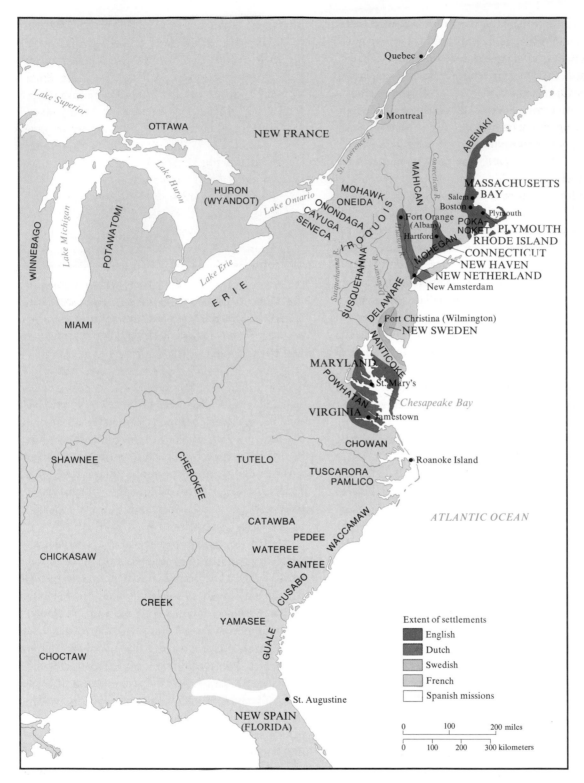

European Settlements and Indian Tribes in America,
1650

Chapter 1: THE MEETING OF OLD WORLD AND NEW, 1492–1650

the Western Hemisphere came from a group of merchants and wealthy gentry. In 1606, envisioning the possibility of earning great profits from a New World settlement, they set up a joint-stock company, the Virginia Company, to plant colonies in America.

Joint-stock companies had been developed in England during the sixteenth century as a mechanism for pooling the resources of a large number of small

Joint-Stock Companies

investors. These forerunners of modern corporations were funded through the sale of stock. Until the founding of the Virginia Company, they had been used primarily to finance trading voyages; for that purpose they worked well. No one person risked too much money, and investors usually received quick returns. But joint-stock companies turned out to be a poor way to finance colonies, because the early settlements required enormous amounts of capital and with rare exceptions failed to return much immediate profit. The colonies founded by joint-stock companies accordingly suffered from a chronic lack of capital—for investors did not want to send good money after bad—and from constant tension between stockholders and colonists (who claimed they were not being adequately supported).

The Virginia Company was no exception to this rule. Chartered by King James I in 1606, the company tried but failed to start a colony in Maine, and barely

Founding of Virginia

succeeded in planting one in Virginia. In 1607 it dispatched 144 men and boys to North America. Ominously, only 104 of them survived the voyage. In May of that year, they established the settlement called Jamestown on a swampy peninsula in a river they also named for their monarch. The colonists were ill equipped for survival in the unfamiliar environment, and the settlement was afflicted by dissension and disease.

By January 1608, only 38 of the original colonists were still alive. Many of the first migrants were gentlemen unaccustomed to working with their hands and artisans with irrelevant skills like glassmaking. Having come to Virginia expecting to make easy fortunes, most could not adjust to the conditions they encountered. They resisted living "like savages," retaining English dress and casual work habits despite their desperate circumstances. Such attitudes, combined with the effects of chronic malnutrition and

epidemic disease, took a terrible toll. Only when Captain John Smith, one of the colony's founders, imposed military discipline on the colonists in 1608 was Jamestown saved from collapse. Still, after Smith's departure, some colonists resorted to cannibalism during the notorious "starving time," the winter of 1609 to 1610. Although conditions later improved somewhat, as late as 1624 only 1,300 of approximately 8,000 English migrants to Virginia remained alive.

That the colony survived at all was a tribute not to the English but rather to the Indians within whose territories they settled (see map). The Powhatan

Powhatan Confederacy

Confederacy—a group of six Algonkian tribes—is known by the name of its leader. Powhatan, a powerful figure, was consolidating his authority over some twenty-five other small tribes in the area at the time the Europeans arrived. Fortunately for the Englishmen, Powhatan viewed them as potential allies instead of threats to his control of the region. And, indeed, Powhatan found the English colony a reliable source of such items as steel knives and guns, which gave him a technological advantage over his Indian neighbors. In return, Powhatan's tribes traded their excess corn and other foodstuffs to the starving colonists. In 1614, Powhatan signed a formal treaty with the settlers and sealed the deal in traditional fashion by marrying his daughter Pocahontas to John Rolfe, one of the English colony's most prominent residents.

Yet the relationship between the Jamestown colony and the coastal tribes was an uneasy one, like later relationships between other colonies and their neighboring tribes. English and Algonkian peoples had much in common (deep religious beliefs, a lifestyle oriented around agriculture, clear political and social hierarchies, and sharply defined sex roles). Yet the English and Indians themselves usually focused on their cultural differences, not their similarities. English men thought that Indian men were lazy because they hunted (a sport in English eyes) and did not work in the fields, whereas Indian men thought English men effeminate because they did "women's work" of cultivation. In the same vein, the whites believed that Indian women were oppressed since they did heavy field labor.

Other differences between the two cultures caused serious misunderstandings. Although both societies

Pocahontas (1595/96?–1617), here called Matoaka alias Rebecka, portrayed in Elizabethan dress. During her visit to England with her husband John Rolfe in 1616, the Indian princess became the toast of London society. She died the following year, just as she was leaving England to return to her homeland, and was buried in the parish church at Gravesend. National Portrait Gallery, Smithsonian Institution, Washington, D.C.

were hierarchical, the nature of the hierarchies differed considerably. Among the east-coast Algonkian tribes, people were not born to automatic positions of leadership, nor were political power and social status necessarily inherited through the male line. The English gentry did inherit their position from their fathers, and English political and military leaders tended to rule autocratically. By contrast, the authority of Indian leaders rested largely on the consent of their fellow tribesmen. Accustomed to the European concept of powerful kings, the English sought such figures within the tribes. Often (for example, when negotiating treaties) they willfully overestimated the ability of chiefs to make independent decisions for their people.

Algonkian and English Cultural Differences

Furthermore, the Indians and the English had very different notions of property ownership. In most eastern tribes, land was held communally by the entire group. It could not be bought or sold absolutely, although certain rights to use the land (for example, for hunting or fishing) could be transferred. The English, on the other hand, were accustomed to individual farms and to buying and selling land. In addition, the English refused to accept the validity of Indian claims to traditional hunting territories, insisting that only land intensively cultivated could be regarded as owned or occupied by a tribe.

An aspect of the cultural clash that needs particular emphasis is the English settlers' unwavering belief in the superiority of their civilization. Although in the early years of colonization they often harbored thoughts of living peacefully alongside the Indians, they always assumed that they themselves would dictate the terms of such coexistence. They expected the Indians to adopt English customs and to convert to Christianity. They showed little respect for traditional Indian ways of life, especially when they believed their own interests were at stake. That attitude was clearly revealed in the Virginia colony's treatment of the Powhatan Confederacy in the years following the treaty of 1614.

What upset the previous balance between the English and the Indians was the spread of tobacco cultivation. In tobacco the settlers and the Virginia Company found the salable commodity for which they had been searching. John Rolfe planted the first crop in 1611. In 1620 Virginians exported 40,000 pounds of cured leaves, and by the end of that decade shipments had jumped dramatically to 1.5 million pounds. The great tobacco boom had begun, fueled by high prices and substantial profits for planters. The price later fell almost as sharply as it had risen, and it fluctuated wildly from year to year in response to increasing supply and international competition. Nevertheless, tobacco became the foundation of Virginia's prosperity.

Tobacco: The Basis of Virginia's Success

Successful tobacco cultivation required abundant land, since the crop quickly drained soil of nutrients. Planters soon learned that a field could produce only about three satisfactory crops before it had to lie fallow for several years to regain its fertility. Thus the once small English settlements began to expand rapidly: eager planters applied to the Virginia Company for large land grants on both sides of the James River and its tributary streams. Lulled into a false sense of security by years of peace, the planters established farms at some distance from one another along the river banks—a settlement pattern convenient for tobacco cultivation but poorly designed for defense.

Opechancanough, Powhatan's brother and successor, watched the English colonists steadily encroaching on Indian lands and attempting to convert members of the tribes to Christianity. He recognized the danger his brother had overlooked. On March 22 (Good Friday), 1622, under his leadership, the confederacy launched coordinated attacks all along the river. By the end of the day 347 colonists (about one-quarter of the total) lay dead, and only a timely warning from two Christianized Indians saved Jamestown itself from destruction.

The Virginia colony reeled from the blow but did not collapse. Reinforced by new shipments of men and arms from England, the settlers launched a series of attacks on Opechancanough's villages. In April 1644 Opechancanough tried one last time to repel the invaders, but he failed, dying in the war that ensued. In 1646, survivors of the Powhatan Confederacy accepted a treaty formally subordinating them to English authority. Although they continued to live in the region, their alliance crumbled and their efforts to resist the spread of white settlement ended.

LIFE IN THE CHESAPEAKE: VIRGINIA AND MARYLAND

The 1622 Indian uprising that failed to destroy the Virginia colony did succeed in killing its parent company, which had never made any profits from the enterprise. (The heavy costs had offset all the company's earnings.) In 1624 James I revoked the charter and made Virginia a royal colony, ruled by the king through appointed officials. At the same time, though, he continued an important policy designed to attract settlers, which the company had first adopted in 1617. Under the "headright" system, every new arrival was promised a land grant of fifty acres; those who financed the passage of others received headrights for each. To ordinary English farmers, many of whom had owned little or no land, the headright system offered a real incentive to migrate to Virginia. To wealthy gentry, it promised even more: the possibility of establishing vast agricultural enterprises worked by large numbers of laborers.

In 1619, the company had introduced a second policy that James was more reluctant to retain: it had authorized the landowning men of the major Virginia settlements to elect representatives to a legislature called the House of Burgesses. Although England was a monarchy, English landholders had long been accustomed to electing members of Parliament and controlling their own local governments. In accordance with his belief in the absolute power of the monarchy and his distrust of legislative bodies, James at first abolished the Virginia assembly. But the settlers protested so vigorously that by 1629 the House of Burgesses was functioning once again. Only two decades after the first permanent English settlement was planted in the New World, the colonists were insisting on governing themselves at the local level. They thus ensured that the political structure of England's American possessions would differ from that of New Spain, which was ruled autocratically by the Spanish monarchs.

By the 1630s, tobacco was firmly established in Virginia as the staple crop and chief source of revenue. It quickly became just as important in the second English colony planted on Chesapeake Bay: the proprietorship of Maryland, chartered **Founding of** by the king in 1632. (Because **Maryland** Virginia and Maryland both bordered Chesapeake Bay—see map, page 22—they are often referred to collectively as "the Chesapeake.") The Calvert family, who founded Maryland, intended the colony to serve as a haven for their fellow Roman Catholics, who were being persecuted in England. Cecilius Calvert, second Lord Baltimore, became the first colonizer to offer prospective settlers freedom of religion, as long as they were practicing Christians. He did so because he realized that his Catholic coreligionists would likely compose a minority of the colony's population. Only in that respect did Maryland differ from Virginia, where the Church of England was the sole officially recognized religion.

In other ways the two Chesapeake colonies resembled each other. In Maryland as in Virginia, tobacco planters spread out along the river banks, establishing isolated farms instead of towns. The region's deep, wide rivers offered dependable water transportation in an age of few and inadequate roads. Each farm or group of farms had its own wharf, where oceangoing vessels could take on or discharge cargo. As a result, Virginia and Maryland had few towns, for these colonies did not need commercial centers in order to buy and sell goods.

The planting, cultivation, and harvesting of tobacco had to be done by hand; these tasks did not take much skill, but they were repetitive and time-consuming. When the headright system was adopted in Maryland in 1640, a prospective tobacco planter anywhere in the Chesapeake could simultaneously obtain both land and the labor to work it. Good management could make the process self-perpetuating: a planter could use his profits to pay for the passage of more workers, and thus gain title to more land.

There were two possible sources of laborers for the growing tobacco farms of the Chesapeake: Africa and England. In 1619, a Dutch privateer brought more than twenty blacks to Virginia; they were the first known black inhabitants of the English colonies in North America. Over the next few decades small numbers of blacks were carried to the Chesapeake, but even as late as 1670 the black population of Virginia was at most 2,000 and probably no more than 1,500, making up less than 5 percent of the inhabitants. Rather than relying on Africa or the West Indies, then, Chesapeake tobacco planters first looked to England to supply their labor needs. Because men did the agricultural work in European societies, planters and workers alike assumed that field laborers should be males, preferably young, strong ones. Such laborers migrated to America as indentured servants; that is, in return for their passage they contracted to work for planters for periods ranging from four to seven years.

Indentured servants accounted for 75 to 85 percent of the approximately 130,000 English migrants to Virginia and Maryland during the seventeenth century. Roughly three-quarters of them were **Migrants to** men between the ages of fifteen and **the Chesapeake** twenty-four. Most had been farmers and laborers; some had additional skills. They were what their contemporaries called the "common" or "middling" sort. Judging by their youth, though, most had probably not yet established themselves in England.

Many of the servants came from areas of England that were experiencing especially severe societal disruption during that era of economic change. Some had already moved several times within England before they decided to migrate to America. For such people the Chesapeake appeared to offer good prospects. Once they had fulfilled the terms of their indentures, servants were promised "freedom dues" consisting of clothes, tools, livestock, casks of corn and tobacco, and sometimes even land. From a distance at least, America seemed to hold out chances for advancement unavailable in England.

Still, their lives as servants were difficult. They typically worked six days a week, ten to fourteen hours a day, in a climate much warmer than they were accustomed to. Their masters **Conditions of** could discipline or sell them, and **Servitude** they faced severe penalties for running away. Even so, the laws did offer them some protection. For example, their masters had to supply them with sufficient food, clothing, and shelter, and they could not be beaten excessively.

On occasion, servants turned to the courts with complaints of mistreatment, although many incidents must have gone unreported. Judges clearly favored masters, yet tried to prevent the worst atrocities. In early Maryland, for example, the courts carefully investigated cases in which servants died under mysterious circumstances, in order to assure themselves that a master was not responsible for the death in question. A 1655 case illustrated the way the Maryland courts balanced the financial interests of masters against the physical well-being of servants. A runaway maidservant, who complained of "Extream Usage" and was known to have been beaten by her mistress for "two hours by the clock," was ordered freed from her indenture. Yet the court insisted that she compensate her master for the loss of her time. Sympathetic planters attending court that day contributed the amount she needed.

Servants and planters alike had to contend with epidemic disease; death rates in the Chesapeake were

The difficulties of the early settlers in Virginia prompted the printing of this broadside in 1622. It advised prospective emigrants to take adequate supplies of food, clothing, weapons, tools, and household goods with them to America, offering specific suggestions aimed at individuals and at families of six persons. Courtesy of the John Carter Brown Library at Brown University.

higher than in England. Migrants first had to survive the process the colonists called seasoning—a bout with disease (probably malaria) that usually occurred during their first summer in the Chesapeake. They then had to endure recurrences of malaria, along with dysentery, influenza, typhoid fever, and other diseases. As a result, approximately 40 percent of male servants did not survive long enough to become freedmen. Even young men of twenty-two who had successfully weathered their "seasoning" could expect to live only another twenty years at best.

For those who survived the term of their indentures, however, the opportunities for advancement were real. Until the last decades of the century, former servants were usually able to become independent planters ("freeholders") and to live a modest but comfortable existence. Some even assumed such positions of political prominence as justice of the peace or militia officer. But in the 1670s tobacco prices entered a fifty-year period of stagnation and decline. At the same time, good land grew increasingly scarce and expensive. In 1681 Maryland dropped its legal requirement that servants receive land as part of their freedom dues, forcing large numbers of freed servants to live as wage laborers or tenant farmers instead of acquiring freeholder status. By 1700 the Chesapeake was no longer the land of opportunity it had once been.

Life in the seventeenth-century Chesapeake was hard for everyone, regardless of sex or status. Farmers (and sometimes their wives) toiled in the fields alongside the servants, laboriously clearing

Family Life in the Chesapeake the land of trees, then planting and harvesting not only tobacco but also corn, wheat, and vegetables. Chesapeake households subsisted mainly on pork and corn, a filling but monotonous and not particularly nutritious diet. Thus the health problems caused by epidemic disease were magnified by diet deficiencies and the near-impossibility of preserving food for safe winter consumption. (Salting, drying, and smoking, the only methods the colonists knew, did not always prevent spoilage.) Few households had many material possessions other than farm implements, beds, and basic cooking and eating utensils. Even their houses were little more than shacks. Planters devoted their income to improving their farms, buying livestock, and purchasing more laborers rather than to improving their lifestyle. Instead of making such items as clothing and tools, planter families concentrated their energies solely on growing tobacco, importing necessary manufactured goods from England.

The predominance of males, the incidence of servitude, and the high mortality rates combined to produce unusual patterns of family life. Female servants normally were not allowed to marry during their terms of indenture, since masters did not want pregnancies to deprive them of workers. Many male ex-servants could not marry at all, because there were so few women. On the other hand, nearly every adult free woman in the Chesapeake married, and the many widows commonly remarried within a few months of a husband's death. Yet because their marriages were delayed by servitude or broken by death, Chesapeake women bore only one to three children, in contrast to English women, who normally had at least five.

Thus seventeenth-century Chesapeake families were relatively few, small, and short-lived. The migrants could not reproduce the English patriarchal system, even if they wanted to, for they came to America as individuals free of paternal control and they tended to die while their own children were still quite young. (In one Virginia county, for example, more than three-quarters of the children had lost at least one parent by the time they either married or reached twenty-one.)

As a result of the demographic patterns that led to a low rate of natural increase, migrants made up a majority of the Chesapeake population throughout the seventeenth century. That fact had important implications for politics in Maryland and Virginia. Since migrants dominated the population, they also composed the vast majority of the membership of both Virginia's House of Burgesses and Maryland's House of Delegates (established in 1635). So too they dominated the governors' councils in both colonies. (The council acted in three important capacities: as part of the legislature, as the colony's highest court, and as executive advisor to the governor.)

Chesapeake Politics

English-born colonists naturally tended to look to England for solutions to their problems, and migrants frequently relied on English allies to advance their cause. The seventeenth-century leaders of the Chesapeake colonies engaged in bitter and prolonged struggles for power and personal economic advantage; these struggles then crossed the Atlantic, and decisions made in America were laid open to reversal in London. The incessant quarreling and convoluted political tangles thwarted the Virginia and Maryland governments' ability to function effectively.

Representative institutions based on the consent of the governed, it is often argued, are a major source of political stability. In the seventeenth-century Chesapeake, most property-owning white males could vote, and such freeholders chose as their legislators the local elites who seemed to be the natural leaders of their respective areas. But because of the nature of the population, the existence of the assemblies did not lead to political stability. Indeed, the contrary may well have been true. Virginia and Maryland paid a high political price for their unusual demographic patterns.

THE FOUNDING OF NEW ENGLAND

The economic motives that prompted English people to move to the Chesapeake colonies also drew men and women to New England, as the area north and east of the Hudson River soon came to be called (see map). But because Puritans organized the New England colonies, and also because of environmental differences between the two regions, the northern settlements turned out very differently from those in the South. Except for the Catholics who moved to Maryland (where they made up a minority of the population), migrants to the Chesapeake seem to have been little affected by religious motives. Yet religion was a primary motivating factor in the minds of many, though certainly not all, of the people who colonized New England. The Puritan church quickly became one of the most important institutions in colonial New England; in the Chesapeake, neither the Church of England nor Roman Catholicism had much impact on the settlers. In addition, the northern landscape and climate were not suitable for staple-crop production, and so diversified small farms became the dominant economic units.

Religion was a constant presence in the lives of pious Puritans. As followers of John Calvin, they believed that an omnipotent God predestined souls to heaven or hell before birth, and that Christians could do nothing to change their ultimate fate. One of their primary duties as Christians, though, was to assess the state of their own souls. They thus devoted themselves to self-examination and Bible study, and families prayed together each day under the guidance of the husband and father. Yet even the most pious

Puritan Beliefs

could never be absolutely certain that they were numbered among the saved. Consequently, devout Puritans were filled with anxiety about their spiritual state. Many kept diaries in which they minutely examined their everyday feelings for signs of their status.

Some Puritans (called Congregationalists) wanted to reform the Church of England rather than abandon it. Another group, known as Separatists, believed that church to be so corrupt it could not be salvaged. The only way to purify it, they believed, was to start anew, establishing their own religious bodies, with membership restricted to the saved (as nearly as they could be identified).

Separatists were the first to move to New England. In 1609 a group of Separatists migrated to Holland, where they found the freedom of worship denied them in Stuart England. But they were nevertheless troubled by the Netherlands' too-tolerant atmosphere; the nation that tolerated them also tolerated other religions and behaviors they abhorred. Hoping to isolate themselves and their children from the corrupting influence of worldly temptations, they received permission from a branch of the Virginia Company to colonize the northern part of its territory.

In September 1620, more than one hundred people, only thirty of them Separatists, set sail from Plymouth, England, on the old and crowded *Mayflower*. Two months later they landed in America, but farther north than they had intended to be. Still, given the lateness of the season—winter was closing in—they decided to stay where they were. They established their colony on a fine harbor that had been occupied by an Indian village destroyed in the great epidemic of 1616–1618. Their settlement was named after the city from which they had sailed.

Founding of Plymouth

Even before they landed, the Pilgrims had to surmount their first challenge—from the "strangers," or non-Puritans, who had sailed with them to America. Because they landed outside the jurisdiction of the Virginia Company, some of the strangers questioned the authority of the colony's leaders. In response, the Mayflower Compact, signed in November 1620 while everyone was still on board the ship, established a "Civil Body Politic" and a rudimentary legal authority for the colony. The settlers elected a governor and

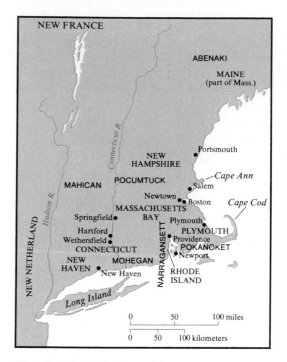

New England Colonies, 1650

at first made all decisions for the colony at town meetings. Later, after more towns had been founded and the population had increased, Plymouth, like Virginia and Maryland, created an assembly to which the landowning male settlers elected representatives.

A second challenge facing the Pilgrims in 1620 and 1621 was, quite simply, survival. Like the Jamestown settlers before them, they were poorly prepared to survive in the new environment. Their difficulties were compounded by the season of their arrival, for they barely had time to build shelters before winter descended on them. Only half of the *Mayflower's* passengers were still alive by spring. But, again like the Virginians, the Pilgrims benefited from the political circumstances of their Indian neighbors.

The Pokanoket (also known as the Wampanoag) controlled the area in which the Pilgrims had settled, yet their villages had suffered terrible losses in the epidemic of 1616–1618. In order to protect themselves from the powerful Narragansett Indians of the southern New England coast (who had been spared the ravages of the disease), the Pokanoket decided to ally themselves with the newcomers. In the spring of 1621,

Algonkian men of the northeastern tribes carved wooden utensils of great beauty. This bowl, dating from before 1630, was probably made by a young Pokanoket or Massachusett man for his bride. The heads of two mythic animals serve as handles. Private Collection, New York City. Photo: Robert and Aida Mates.

their leader, Massasoit, signed a treaty with the Pilgrims, and during the colony's first difficult years the Pokanoket supplied the English with essential foodstuffs. The settlers were also assisted by Squanto, an Indian whose village had been wiped out by the epidemic. Squanto spoke English—he had been captured by traders and held prisoner in England for several years—and so he served as the Pilgrims' interpreter, as well as their major source of information about the unfamiliar environment.

Before the 1620s had ended, another group of Puritans—this time Congregationalists, not Separatists—launched the colonial enterprise that would

Founding of Massachusetts Bay

come to dominate New England and would absorb Plymouth in 1691. When Charles I, who was more hostile to Puritan beliefs than his father James I, became king in 1625, some non-Separatists began to think about settling in America. A group of Congregationalist merchants sent out a body of settlers to Cape Ann, north of Cape Cod, in 1628. The following year the merchants obtained a royal charter, constituting themselves as the Massachusetts Bay Company.

The new company quickly attracted the attention of Puritans of the "middling sort" who were becoming increasingly convinced that they would no longer be able to practice their religion freely in England. They remained committed to the goal of reforming the Church of England, but came to believe they should pursue that aim in America rather than at home. In a dramatic move, the Congregationalist merchants boldly decided to transfer the headquarters of the Massachusetts Bay Company to New England. The settlers would then be answerable to no one in the mother country and would be able to handle their affairs, secular and religious, as they pleased.

The most important recruit to the new venture was John Winthrop, a pious but practical landed gentleman from Suffolk and a justice of the peace.

Governor John Winthrop

In October 1629, the members of the Massachusetts Bay Company elected the forty-one-year-old Winthrop as their governor. With the exception of isolated years in the mid-1630s and early 1640s, he served in that post until his death in 1649. It thus fell to Winthrop to organize the initial segment of the great Puritan migration to America. In 1630 more than one thousand English men and women came to Massachusetts—most of them to Boston, which soon became the largest town in North America. By 1643 nearly twenty thousand compatriots had followed them.

On board the *Arbella*, en route to New England in 1630, John Winthrop preached a sermon, "A Modell of Christian Charity," laying out his expectations for the new colony. Above all, he stressed the communal nature of the endeavor on which he and his fellow settlers had embarked. God, he explained, "hath so disposed of the condition of mankind as in all times some must be rich, some poor, some high and eminent in power and dignity, others mean and in subjection." But differences in status did not imply differences in worth. On the contrary: God had planned the world so that "every man might have need of other, and from hence they might be all knit more nearly together in the bond of brotherly affection." In America, Winthrop asserted, "we shall be as a city upon a hill, the eyes of all people are upon us." If the Puritans failed to carry out their "special commission" from God, "the Lord will surely break out in wrath against us."

Winthrop's was a transcendent vision. The society he foresaw in Puritan America was a true commonwealth, a community in which each person put the good of the whole ahead of his or her private concerns. It was, furthermore, to be a society whose members all lived according to the precepts of Christian charity, loving and aiding friends and enemies alike. Of course, such an ideal was beyond human reach. Early New England had its share of bitter quarrels and unchristian behavior. What is remarkable is how long the ideal prevailed as a goal to be sought, if seldom or never attained.

The Puritans' communal ideal was expressed chiefly in the doctrine of the covenant. They believed God had made a covenant—that is, an agreement or contract—with them when He chose them for the special mission to America. In turn they covenanted with each other, promising to work together toward their goals. The founders of churches and towns in the new land often drafted formal documents setting forth the principles on which such institutions would be based. The same was true of the colonial governments of New England. The Pilgrims' Mayflower Compact was a covenant; so too was the Fundamental Orders of Connecticut (1639), which laid down the basic law for the settlements established along the Connecticut River valley in 1636 and thereafter.

Ideal of the Covenant

The leaders of Massachusetts Bay likewise transformed their original joint-stock company charter into the basis for a covenanted community based on mutual consent. Under pressure from the settlers, they gradually changed the General Court, officially merely the company's governing body, into a colonial legislature and opened the status of freeman, or voting member of the company, to all adult male church members resident in Massachusetts. Less than two decades after the first large group of Puritans had arrived in Massachusetts Bay, the colony had a functioning system of self-government composed of a governor and a two-house legislature. The General Court also established a judicial system modeled on England's and in 1641 adopted a legal code, *The Laws and Liberties of Massachusetts*, spelling out crimes and their proper punishments.

The colony's method of distributing land helped to further the communal ideal. Unlike Virginia and Maryland, where individual applicants sought headrights for themselves and their servants, in Massachusetts groups of families—often from the same region of England—applied together to the General Court for grants of land on which to establish towns. The

men who received the original town grant had the sole authority to determine how the land would be distributed. Understandably, they copied the villages from which they came. First they laid out town lots for houses and a church. Then they gave each family parcels of land scattered around the town center: pasture here, a woodlot there, an arable field elsewhere. They also reserved the best and largest plots for the most distinguished among them (usually including the minister); people who had been low on the social scale in England were given much smaller and less desirable allotments. Even when migrants began to move beyond the territorial limits of the Bay Colony into Connecticut (1636), New Haven (1638), and New Hampshire (1638), the same pattern of town land grants was maintained.

New England Towns

Thus New England settlements initially tended to be more compact than those of the Chesapeake. Town centers grew up quickly, developing in three distinctly different ways. Some, chiefly isolated agricultural settlements in the interior, tried to sustain Winthrop's vision of harmonious community life based on diversified family farms. A second group, the coastal towns like Boston and Salem, became bustling seaports, serving as the places of entry for thousands of new migrants and as focal points for trade. The third category, commercialized agricultural towns, grew up in the Connecticut River valley. There the easy water transportation made it possible for farmers to sell surplus goods readily. In Springfield, Massachusetts, for example, the merchant-entrepreneur William Pynchon and his son John began as fur traders and ended as large landowners with thousands of acres on which tenant farmers produced grain for export. Even in Puritan New England, in other words, the acquisitive, individualistic spirit characteristic of the Chesapeake found some room for expression.

The migration to the Connecticut valley ended the Puritans' relative freedom from clashes with neighboring Indians. The first English settlers in the valley moved there from Newtown (Cambridge), under the direction of their minister, Thomas Hooker. Connecticut was fertile, though remote from the other English towns, and the wide river promised ready access to the ocean. The site had just one problem: it fell within the territory controlled by the Pequot Indians.

John Eliot, painted in 1659 by an unknown artist. Determined to convert the New England Indians to Christianity, Eliot translated the Bible into their language. His Up-Biblum was published in 1663, the first Bible printed in the English colonies. Huntington Library.

many of them women and children. The few surviving Pequots were captured and enslaved.

Just five years later the Narragansett leader Miantonomi realized that the Pequot had been correct in assessing the danger posed by the Puritan settlements. He in turn attempted to forge a pan-Indian alliance, telling other bands that "so are we all Indians as the English are . . . so must we be one as they are, otherwise we shall all be gone shortly." But his words fell on deaf ears, and he was killed in 1643 by other Indians acting at the English colonists' behest.

For the next thirty years, the New England Indians tried to accommodate themselves to the spread of white settlement. They traded with the whites and sometimes worked for them, but for the most part they resisted acculturation or incorporation into English society. Indeed, most whites showed little interest in the Indians except as laborers or producers of valuable trade goods. Only a few Puritan clerics (most notably John Eliot) seriously attempted to convert the Massachusetts Bay Indians to Christianity. Since most of them insisted that converts give up their traditional seminomadic lifestyle to reside in English-style houses and towns, they met with relatively little success. At the peak of Eliot's efforts, only 1,100 Indians lived in the fourteen "Praying Towns" he had established, and just 10 percent of those town residents had been formally baptized.

LIFE IN NEW ENGLAND

Two sets of comparisons will help to illuminate the lives of early New Englanders: first, with the Indians of the region, and second, with the Chesapeake colonists.

The major contrast between the lifestyles of Indian and white residents of New England was the mobility of the former and the stability of the latter. The **Indian and English Lifestyles Compared** agricultural Algonkians of New England commonly moved four or five times during the course of a year to take full advantage of their environment. In the spring, women

Pequot dominance was based on their role as primary middlemen in the trade between New England Indians and the Dutch in New Netherland. The arrival of English settlers signaled the end of **Pequot War** Pequot power over the regional trading networks, for their tributary bands could now trade directly with Europeans. Clashes between the Pequot and the English began even before the Connecticut valley settlements were established, but their founding tipped the balance toward war. After trying without success to enlist other Indians to resist English expansion into the interior, the Pequot (after an English raid on their villages) attacked the new town of Wethersfield in April 1637, killing nine and capturing two of the colonists. In retaliation, a Massachusetts Bay expedition the following month attacked and burned the main Pequot town on the Mystic River. The Englishmen and their Narragansett Indian allies slaughtered at least four hundred people,

Fairbanks House, Dedham, Massachusetts, built ca. 1637 (as photographed in 1880). Unlike their Indian neighbors or the English residents of the Chesapeake, the migrants to New England constructed dwellings designed to last for many years. Later additions (like those shown on the right of this picture) expanded the size of the original small and simple houses. Society for the Preservation of New England Antiquities.

would plant the fields, but once the crops were well established they would not need regular attention for several months. Accordingly, villages then broke into small mobile bands; women occupied themselves with gathering, men with hunting and fishing. The village would reassemble for harvest, then once again disperse for the fall hunting season. Finally, the people would spend the harsh winter months together, probably in some protected valley, before returning to their fields again in the spring. And every few years they would alter the site of those fields, thus avoiding any need to use fertilizer.

The English settlers, by contrast, lived year-round in the same location. Unlike the Indians or the Chesapeake colonists, New Englanders constructed sturdy, permanent dwellings intended to last for many years. (Indeed, some survive to this day.) They used the same fields again and again, believing it was less arduous to employ fertilizer than to clear new fields every few years. Although they hunted and fished, their chief source of meat was the livestock they bred on their farms. Hogs in particular reproduced so rapidly that they caused major problems for the settlers. Farmers had to fence their croplands to keep hogs, sheep, and cattle from eating the growing plants; many disputes between neighbors or even entire towns had their origins in one side's livestock having invaded the other side's fields. When New Englanders began to spread out over the countryside, the reason was not so much human crowding as it was animal crowding. All the livestock constantly needed more grazing land on which to survive.

In their heavy reliance on cattle and hogs, white New Englanders resembled their Chesapeake counterparts. But in other ways they differed sharply from them. The contrast between Chesapeake and New England settlement patterns has already been made clear; in addition, the regions varied in their family organization and behavior and with respect to the importance of religion in the settlers' daily lives.

Unlike migrants to the Chesapeake, Puritans commonly moved to America in family groups. Thus, the age range of New Englanders was wide and the sexes more balanced numerically, so that the population could immediately begin to reproduce itself. Moreover, New England's climate was much healthier than that of the Chesapeake. Once Puritan settlements had survived the difficult first two or three years and established self-sufficiency in foodstuffs, New England proved to be even healthier than the mother country. Though adult male migrants to the Chesapeake lost about ten years from their English life expectancy of fifty to fifty-five years, their Massachusetts counterparts gained about ten years.

Consequently, although Chesapeake population patterns made for families that were few in number, small in size, and transitory, the demographic characteristics of New England made families there numerous, large, and long-lived. In New England most men were able to marry; migrant women married young (at twenty, on the average); and marriages lasted longer and produced more children, who were more likely to live to maturity. If seventeenth-century Chesapeake women could expect to rear one to three healthy children, New England women could anticipate raising five to seven.

Family Life in New England

The nature of the population had other major implications for family life. New England in effect created grandparents, since in England people rarely lived long enough to know their children's children. And whereas seventeenth-century southern parents normally died before their children married, northern parents exercised a good deal of control over their adult children. Young men could not marry without acreage to cultivate, and because of the communal land-grant system they were dependent on their fathers to supply them with that land. Daughters, too, needed the dowry of household goods their parents would give them when they married. Yet parents needed their children's labor and were often reluctant to see them marry and start their own households. That at times led to considerable conflict between the generations. On the whole, though, children seem to have obeyed their parents' wishes, for they had few alternatives.

Another important difference lay in the influence of religion on New Englanders' lives. The governments of Massachusetts Bay, Plymouth, Connecticut, and the other early northern colonies were all controlled by Puritans. Congregationalism was the only officially recognized religion; members of other sects had no freedom of worship except in Rhode Island. Elsewhere, except in Connecticut, only male Puritans could vote in colony elections, although non-Puritans voted in town meetings. All households were taxed to build meetinghouses and pay ministers' salaries. Massachusetts' *Body of Laws and Liberties* incorporated regulations drawn from Old Testament scriptures into the legal code of the colony. Moreover, penalties were prescribed for expressing contempt for ministers or their preaching, and for failing to attend church services regularly.

In the New England colonies, church and state were intertwined. Puritans objected to secular interference in religious affairs, but at the same time expected the church to influence the conduct of politics. They also believed that the state had an obligation to support and protect the one true church—theirs. As a result, though they came to America seeking freedom to worship as they wished, they saw no contradiction in their refusal to grant that freedom to others. Indeed, the two most significant divisions in early Massachusetts were caused by religious disputes and by Massachusetts Bay's unwillingness to tolerate dissent.

Roger Williams, a Separatist, migrated to Massachusetts Bay in 1631 and became assistant pastor at Salem. Williams soon began to express the eccentric ideas that the king of England had no right to give away land belonging to the Indians, that church and state should be kept entirely separate, and that Puritans should not impose their religious beliefs on others. Banished from Massachusetts in 1635, Williams founded the town of Providence on Narragansett Bay. Because of his beliefs, Providence and other towns in what became the colony of Rhode Island adopted a policy of tolerating all religions, including Judaism.

Roger Williams

IMPORTANT EVENTS

1492	Christopher Columbus reaches Bahama Islands	1611	First Virginia tobacco crop
1513	Ponce de Leon reaches Florida	1619	First blacks arrive in Virginia
1518–30	Smallpox pandemic decimates Indian population of Central and South America	1620	Plymouth Colony founded
		1622	Powhatan Confederacy attacks Virginia colony
1521	Tenochtitlan surrenders to Cortés; Aztec empire falls to Spaniards	1624	Dutch settle on Manhattan Island
1533	Henry VIII divorces Catherine of Aragon; English reformation begins	1625	Charles I becomes king
		1630	Massachusetts Bay Colony founded
1539–42	Hernando de Soto explores southeastern United States	1634	Maryland founded
1540–42	Francisco Vásquez de Coronado explores southwestern United States	1635	Roger Williams expelled from Massachusetts Bay; founds Providence, Rhode Island
1558	Elizabeth I becomes queen	1636	Connecticut founded
1587–90	Sir Walter Raleigh's Roanoke colony fails	1637	Pequot War Anne Hutchinson expelled from Massachusetts Bay
1603	James I becomes king	1646	Treaty ends hostilities between Virginia and Powhatan Confederacy
1607	Jamestown founded		

The other dissenter, and an even greater challenge to Massachusetts Bay orthodoxy, was Anne Marbury Hutchinson. A skilled midwife popular with the women of Boston, she was a follower of John Cotton, a minister who stressed the covenant of grace, or God's free gift of salvation to unworthy, utterly helpless human beings. (By contrast, most Massachusetts clerics emphasized the need for Puritans to engage in good works, study, and reflection in preparation for receiving God's grace.) In 1636 Hutchinson began holding women's meetings in her home to discuss Cotton's sermons. Soon men also started to attend. Hutchinson emphasized the covenant of grace more than did Cotton himself and she even

Anne Hutchinson

adopted the belief that the elect could communicate directly with God and be assured of salvation. Such ideas had an immense appeal for Puritans. Anne Hutchinson offered them certainty of salvation instead of a state of constant tension. Her approach also made the institutional church less important.

Hutchinson's ideas were a dangerous threat to Puritan orthodoxy, so in November 1637 she was brought before the General Court of Massachusetts. She was charged with claiming that the colony's ministers preached salvation through works. For two days she defended herself cleverly against her accusers, matching scriptural references and wits with John Winthrop himself. Finally, in an unguarded moment late in the second day, Hutchinson declared that God had spoken to her "by an immediate revelation." That heretical assertion assured her banishment; she and her family, along with some faithful followers, were exiled to Rhode Island.

The authorities in Massachusetts Bay perceived Anne Hutchinson as doubly dangerous to the existing order: she threatened not only religious orthodoxy but also traditional gender roles. Puritans believed in the equality before God of all souls, including women, but they also considered women inferior to men, forever tainted by Eve's guilt. Christians had long followed St. Paul's dictum that women should keep silent in church and be submissive to their husbands. Anne Hutchinson did neither. The magistrates' comments during her trial reveal that they were almost as outraged by her "masculine" behavior as by her religious beliefs. Winthrop charged her with having set wife against husband, since so many of her followers were women. Another judge told her bluntly: "You have stept out of your place, you have rather bine a Husband than a Wife and a preacher than a Hearer; and a Magistrate than a Subject."

The New England authorities' reaction to Anne Hutchinson reveals the depth of their adherence to European gender-role concepts. To them, an orderly society required the submission of wives to husbands as well as the obedience of subjects to rulers. Indeed, one reason why they perceived Indian societies as disorderly was because Indian women seemed to be largely independent of male authority. English people intended to change many aspects of their lives by colonizing North America, but not the sexual division of labor or the assumption of male superiority.

In 1630 John Winthrop wrote to his wife Margaret, who was still in England, "my deare wife, we are heer in a paradise." He was, of course, exaggerating. Yet even though America was not a paradise, it was a place where English men and women could free themselves from Stuart persecution or attempt to better their economic circumstances. Many died, but those who lived laid the foundation for subsequent colonial prosperity. That they did so by dispossessing the Indians bothered few besides Roger Williams. By the middle of the seventeenth century, English people had unquestionably come to North America to stay.

The permanent presence of Europeans on the soil of the Americas signaled major changes for the peoples of both Old and New Worlds. European political rivalries, once confined to their own continent, now spread around the globe, as the competing nations of England, Spain, Portugal, France, and the Netherlands vied for control of the peoples and resources of Asia, Africa, and the Americas. Because of the varying nature of Indian societies, France and the Netherlands earned their profits from Indian trade rather than imitating the Spanish example and engaging in wars of conquest. Although they too at first relied on trade, the English colonies soon took another form altogether when so many English people of the "common sort" decided to migrate to North America. In the years to come, the European rivalries would grow even fiercer, and residents of the Americas—whites, Indians, and blacks alike—would inevitably be drawn into them. Not until after France and England in the mid-eighteenth century had fought the greatest war yet known, and until the thirteen American colonies had won their independence, would those rivalries cease to affect Americans of all races.

SUGGESTIONS FOR FURTHER READING

General

Charles M. Andrews, *The Colonial Period of American History: The Settlements*, 3 vols. (1934–1937); Gary B. Nash, *Red, White, and Black: The Peoples of Early America*, 2nd ed. (1982); John E. Pomfret, *Founding the American Colonies, 1583–1660* (1970); Robert V. Wells, *Revolutions in Americans' Lives: A Demographic Perspective on the History of Americans, Their Families, and Their Society* (1982).

Indians

Harold E. Driver, *Indians of North America*, 2nd ed. (1969); Alvin Josephy, Jr., *The Indian Heritage of America* (1968); Alice B. Kehoe, *North American Indians: A Comprehensive Account* (1981); Eleanor B. Leacock and Nancy O. Lurie, eds., *North American Indians in Historical Perspective* (1971); Smithsonian Institution, *Handbook of North American Indians*, 6: *Subarctic* (1981), 8: *California* (1978), 9, 10: *The Southwest* (1979, 1983), 15: *The Northeast* (1978); Robert F. Spencer, Jesse D. Jennings, *et al.*, *The Native Americans: Ethnology and Backgrounds of the North American Indians*, 2nd ed. (1977).

Africa

Robin Hallett, *Africa to 1875* (1970); George P. Murdock, *Africa: Its Peoples and Their Culture History* (1959); Richard Olaniyan, *African History and Culture* (1982); Roland Oliver, ed., *The Cambridge History of Africa*, vol. 3: *c. 1050–c. 1600* (1977); Roland Oliver and J. D. Fage, *A Short History of Africa* (1975).

England

Carl Bridenbaugh, *Vexed and Troubled Englishmen, 1590–1642*, rev. ed. (1976); Mildred Campbell, *The English Yeoman under Elizabeth and the Early Stuarts* (1942); Peter Laslett, *The World We Have Lost* (1965); Wallace Notestein, *The English People on the Eve of Colonization 1603–1630* (1954); Lawrence Stone, *The Crisis of the Aristocracy, 1558–1641* (1965); Michael Walzer, *The Revolution of the Saints* (1965); Keith Wrightson, *English Society 1580–1680* (1982).

Exploration and Discovery

Fredi Chiappelli, *et al.*, eds., *First Images of America: The Impact of the New World on the Old*, 2 vols. (1976); Alfred W. Crosby, Jr., *The Columbian Exchange: Biological and Cultural Consequences of 1492* (1972); J. H. Elliott, *The Old World and the New, 1492–1650* (1970); Charles Gibson, *Spain in America* (1966); Samuel Eliot Morison, *The European Discovery of America: The Northern Voyages, A.D. 1500–1600* (1971), *The Southern Voyages, A.D. 1492–1616* (1974); J. H. Parry, *The Age of Reconnaissance* (1963); David B. Quinn, *North America from Earliest Discovery to First Settlements* (1977).

Early Contact Between Whites and Indians

James Axtell, *The European and the Indian: Essays in the Ethnohistory of Colonial North America* (1981); William Cronon, *Changes in the Land: Indians, Colonists, and the Ecology of New England* (1983); Francis Jennings, *The Invasion of America: Indians, Colonialism, and the Cant of Conquest* (1975); Karen O. Kupperman, *Roanoke, The Abandoned Colony* (1984); Karen O. Kupperman, *Settling with the Indians: The Meeting of English and Indian Cultures in America, 1580–1640* (1980); Kenneth Morrison, *The Embattled Northeast: The Elusive Ideal of Alliance in Abenaki-Euroamerican Relations* (1984); Neal Salisbury, *Manitou and Providence: Indians, Europeans, and the Making of New England, 1500–1643* (1982); Bernard Sheehan, *Savagism and Civility: Indians and Englishmen in Colonial Virginia* (1980); Alden T. Vaughan, *American Genesis: Captain John Smith and the Founding of Virginia* (1975); Alden T. Vaughan, *The New England Frontier: Puritans and Indians 1620–1675*, rev. ed. (1979).

New England

David Grayson Allen, *In English Ways: The Movement of Societies and the Transferal of English Law and Custom to Massachusetts Bay in the Seventeenth Century* (1981); Ben Barker-Benfield, "Anne Hutchinson and the Puritan Attitude Toward Women," *Feminist Studies*, I (1972), 65–96; Charles E. Clark, *The Eastern Frontier: The Settlement of Northern New England, 1610–1763* (1970); John Demos, *A Little Commonwealth: Family Life in Plymouth Colony* (1970); Philip J. Greven, Jr., *Four Generations: Population, Land, and Family in Colonial Andover, Massachusetts* (1970); Stephen Innes, *Labor in a New Land: Economy and Society in Seventeenth-Century Springfield* (1983); Sydney V. James, *Colonial Rhode Island* (1975); Lyle Koehler, *A Search for Power: The 'Weaker Sex' in Seventeenth-Century New England* (1980); George Langdon, *Pilgrim Colony: A History of New Plymouth, 1620–1691* (1966); Kenneth A. Lockridge, *A New England Town: The First Hundred Years (Dedham, Massachusetts, 1636–1736)* (1970); Edmund S. Morgan, *The Puritan Dilemma: The Story of John Winthrop* (1958); Edmund S. Morgan, *The Puritan Family: Religion and Domestic Relations in Seventeeth-Century New England*, rev. ed. (1966); Sumner Chilton Powell, *Puritan Village: The Formation of a New England Town* (1963); Darrett Rutman, *Winthrop's Boston: A Portrait of a Puritan Town, 1630–1649* (1965); Darrett Rutman, *American Puritanism: Faith and Practice* (1970); Alan Simpson, *Puritanism in Old and New England* (1955).

Chesapeake

Lois Green Carr and Lorena Walsh, "The Planter's Wife: The Experience of White Women in Seventeenth-Century Maryland," *William and Mary Quarterly*, 3rd ser., 34 (1977), 542–571; Wesley Frank Craven, *The Southern Colonies in the Seventeenth Century, 1607–1689* (1949); Wesley Frank Craven, *White, Red, and Black: The Seventeenth Century Virginian* (1971); David Galenson, *White Servitude in Colonial America: An Economic Analysis* (1981); Ivor Noel Hume, *Martin's Hundred: The Discovery of a Lost Colonial Virginia Settlement* (1979); Karen O. Kupperman, "Apathy and Death in Early Jamestown," *Journal of American History*, 66 (1979), 24–40; Gloria L. Main, *Tobacco Colony: Life in Early Maryland, 1650–1720* (1983); Edmund S. Morgan, *American Slavery, American Freedom: The Ordeal of Colonial Virginia* (1975); Darrett Rutman and Anita Rutman, *A Place in Time: Middlesex County, Virginia, 1650–1750* (1984); Abbot E. Smith, *Colonists in Bondage: White Servitude and Convict Labor in America, 1607–1776* (1947); Thad W. Tate and David L. Ammerman, eds., *The Chesapeake in the Seventeenth Century: Essays on Anglo-American Society & Politics* (1979); *William and Mary Quarterly*, 3rd ser., 30, No. 1 (Jan. 1973): *Chesapeake Society*.

American Society Takes Shape

1650–1720

Chapter 2

Olaudah Equiano was eleven years old in 1756 when black raiders seeking slaves for white traders kidnapped him and his younger sister from their village in what is now Nigeria. Until then, he had lived peacefully with his father and mother, his father's other wives, and his seven siblings and half-siblings in a mud-walled compound resembling a small village. Equiano and other members of the Ibo tribe were, he later observed, "habituated to labour from our earliest years." Men, women, and children worked together to cultivate corn, yams, beans, cotton, tobacco, and plantains (a type of banana). Men also herded cattle and goats, and the women spun and wove cotton into clothing. Equiano's family, like others in the region, held prisoners of war as slaves. With what may have been idealizing hindsight, he later recalled that the slaves did "no more work than other members of the community, even their master; their food, clothing, and lodging were nearly the same."

Equiano's experiences as a captive differed sharply from the life he had led as a child in his father's house. For months he was passed from master to master, finally arriving at the coast, where an English slave ship lay at anchor. Terrified by the light complexions, long hair, and strange language of the sailors, he was afraid that "I had gotten into a world of bad spirits and that they were going to kill me." Equiano was placed below decks, where "with the loathsomeness of the stench and crying together, I became so sick and low that I was not able to eat, nor had I the least desire to taste anything." The whites flogged him to make him eat, and he thought about jumping overboard but he was too closely watched. At last some other Ibos told him that they were being taken to the whites' country to work. "I then was a little revived," Equiano remembered, "and thought if it were no worse than working, my situation was not so desperate."

After a long voyage during which many of the Africans died of disease caused by the cramped, unsanitary conditions and poor food, the ship arrived at Barbados, a British island in the West Indies. (In the 1620s and 1630s, English people settled on a number of Caribbean islands where they soon began to rely on slave labor to raise a lucrative crop—sugar cane.) Equiano and his shipmates feared that "these ugly men" were cannibals, but experienced slaves were brought on board to assure them that they would not be eaten and that many blacks like themselves lived on the islands. "This report eased us much," Equiano recalled, "and sure enough soon after we landed there came to us Africans of all languages." Everything in Barbados was new and surprising, but Equiano later remarked particularly on two-storied buildings and horses, neither of which he had ever seen.

Equiano was not purchased in the West Indies because planters there preferred older, stronger slaves. Instead, he was carried to Virginia along with the other less-valuable Africans. There, on the plantation of his new owner, he was separated from the other Africans and put to work weeding and clearing rocks from the fields. "I was now exceedingly miserable and thought myself worse off than any of the rest of my companions," Equiano reported, "for they could talk to each other, but I had no person to speak to that I could understand. In this state I was constantly grieving and pining and wishing for death rather than anything else."

But Equiano did not remain in Virginia for long. Bought by a sea captain, Olaudah Equiano eventually became an experienced sailor. He learned to read and write English, purchased his freedom at the age of twenty-one, and later actively supported the English antislavery movement. In 1789 Equiano published *The Interesting Narrative of the Life of Olaudah Equiano . . . Written by Himself*, from which this account of his captivity is drawn. Until he was purchased by the sailor, Equiano's experiences differed very little from those of other Africans who were forced into slavery in the English colonies of the New World. Like him, many were sold by black slavers and taken first to the West Indies, then to North America. His *Interesting Narrative*, one of a number of memoirs by former slaves, depicts the captives' terror powerfully and convincingly.

Charles II, who returned from exile to become king in 1660, consolidated England's hold over eastern North America by chartering six new colonies. Moreover, his commercial policies ensured that the economies of the American settlements would be closely linked to that of England. National Portrait Gallery, London.

Equiano's life story illustrates one of the major developments in colonial life during the century after 1650: the importation of more than two hundred thousand unwilling, captive Africans into North America. The introduction of the institution of slavery and the arrival of large numbers of West African peoples dramatically reshaped colonial society. Indeed, the geographic patterns of that migration continue to influence the United States to the present day.

The other important trends in colonial life between 1650 and 1720 were external rather than internal. That is, they pertained to the English colonists' relationships with others: first, with England itself, and second, with their neighbors in America. Although in the early years of settlement events in England had little direct impact on North America, that situation changed when civil war broke out in the

colonists' homeland in 1642. First the Puritan victory in the war, then the restoration of the Stuart monarchy, and finally the Glorious Revolution of 1688 and 1689 indelibly affected the residents of England's American possessions. By the end of the seventeenth century, the New World colonies were no longer isolated outposts but an integral part of a far-flung mercantile empire. As such, policies made in distant London became constant reminders that they were tied, willingly or not, to the world of Europe.

The English colonists likewise interacted regularly with their neighbors on the American continent— their Indian trading partners and other transplanted Europeans, with whom they increasingly competed for control of North America. As the English settlements expanded, they came into violent conflict not only with the powerful Indian tribes of the interior but also with the Dutch, the Spanish, and especially the French. By 1720, war—between Europeans and Indians, among Europeans, and among Indians allied with different colonial powers—had become an all-too-frequent feature of American life.

THE ENGLISH CIVIL WAR, THE STUART RESTORATION, AND THE AMERICAN COLONIES

By the time Charles I became king in 1625, members of the Puritan sect dominated Parliament. For eleven years (1629–1640) Charles, who wanted to suppress Puritanism, refused to call Parliament into session, ruling the nation arbitrarily. When Parliament finally met, it passed laws limiting the monarch's authority. In 1642 civil war broke out between supporters of the king and those who favored Parliament. Four years later, Parliament triumphed; Charles I was executed in 1649.

Oliver Cromwell, the leader of the parliamentary army, assumed control of the government, taking the title of Lord Protector in 1653. After Cromwell's death in 1658, Parliament decided to restore the

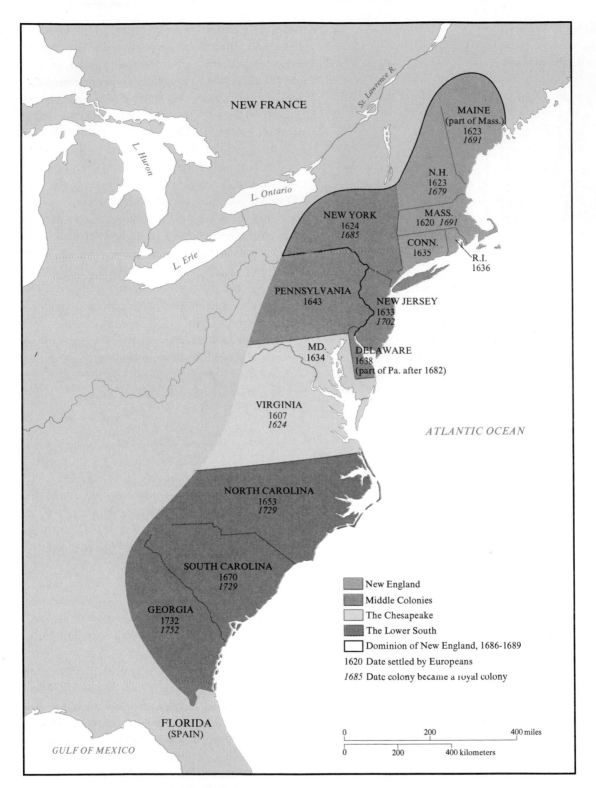

New France

St. Lawrence R.

L. Huron

L. Ontario

L. Erie

MAINE
(part of Mass.)
1623
1691

N.H.
1623
1679

NEW YORK
1624
1685

MASS.
1620 *1691*

CONN.
1635

R.I.
1636

PENNSYLVANIA
1643

NEW JERSEY
1633
1702

MD.
1634

DELAWARE
1638
(part of Pa. after 1682)

VIRGINIA
1607
1624

ATLANTIC OCEAN

NORTH CAROLINA
1653
1729

SOUTH CAROLINA
1670
1729

GEORGIA
1732
1752

	New England
	Middle Colonies
	The Chesapeake
	The Lower South
	Dominion of New England, 1686-1689

1620 Date settled by Europeans

1685 Date colony became a royal colony

FLORIDA
(SPAIN)

GULF OF MEXICO

0   200   400 miles

0   200   400 kilometers

*The American Colonies in the Early Eighteenth
Century*

monarchy if Charles I's son and heir would agree to certain restrictions on his authority. In 1660, Charles II assumed the throne, having promised to seek Parliament's consent for any new taxes and to support the Church of England. Thus ended the tumultuous chapter in English history known as the Interregnum (Latin for "between reigns").

The Civil War and Interregnum had both short-term and long-term consequences for England's American colonies. Political disruption in the mother country fostered similar disruption in America, especially in the Chesapeake. Both Virginia and Maryland were wracked by disputes over the structure of political and religious authority. In Maryland, for example, the provincial court could not meet from 1644 to 1647 because of a Protestant uprising. During those years, no debts could be collected, no crimes prosecuted, and no wills probated.

The effects on New England were long-term and quite different. Puritan New Englanders welcomed the victory of their compatriots across the Atlantic, and some of them even packed up and returned home to the mother country. More important, because the Puritan triumph in England removed dissenters' major incentive for moving to America, migration to Massachusetts Bay largely ceased after 1640. This had a profound impact on the colony's economy and on its subsequent development. The Stuart Restoration, which again placed Anglicans (members of the Church of England) in power, effectively isolated the New England Puritans within the empire. Stuart monarchs proved to be highly suspicious of New Englanders, whose coreligionists had executed Charles I, and the Puritans thereafter found it difficult to deal with English officials. By the last quarter of the century, friction between the northern colonies and the mother country had increased substantially. These developments will be considered in detail later in this chapter (see pages 57–62).

The reign of Charles II (1660–1685) had enormous significance for the future United States. Six of the thirteen colonies that eventually would form the nation were either founded or came under English rule during that period: New York, New Jersey, Pennsylvania (including Delaware), and North and South Carolina (see map). All were proprietorships; that is, like Maryland they were granted in their entirety to one man or a group of men, who both held title to the soil and controlled the government. Charles II gave these vast American holdings as rewards to the men who had supported him during his years of exile. Several of his favorites even shared in more than one grant.

One of the first to benefit was Charles's younger brother James, the Duke of York. In March 1664, acting as though the Dutch colony of New Netherland did not exist, Charles II gave James the region between the Connecticut and Delaware rivers, including the Hudson Valley and Long Island. James immediately organized an invasion fleet. In late August the vessels anchored off Manhattan Island and demanded New Netherland's surrender. The Dutch complied without firing a shot. Although the Netherlands briefly regained control of the colony in 1672 during one of the Anglo-Dutch wars, it permanently ceded the province in 1674.

Thus England acquired a tiny but heterogeneous possession. New Netherland had been founded in 1624, but had remained small in comparison to its

New Netherland Becomes New York

English neighbors. As a trading outpost of the Dutch West India Company, whose chief economic interests lay elsewhere (in Africa, Brazil, and modern-day Indonesia), New Netherland was neglected. And because the Dutch were not afflicted by the economic and religious pressures that caused English people to move to the New World, migration was sparse. Even a company policy of 1629 that offered a large land grant, or patroonship, to anyone who would bring fifty settlers to the province failed to attract takers. (Only one such tract—Rensselaerswyck, near modern Albany was ever fully developed.) In the mid-1660s, when the Duke of York assumed control, New Netherland had only about five thousand inhabitants.

Logically enough, the Dutch made up the largest proportion of the population. There was also an appreciable minority of English people in the colony, for Puritan New Englanders had begun to settle on Long Island as early as the 1640s. New York, as it was now called, also included sizable numbers of Germans, French-speaking Walloons, Scandinavians (New Netherland had swallowed up Swedish settlements on the Delaware River in 1655), and Africans, as well as an additional smattering of other European peoples. Because the Dutch West India Company

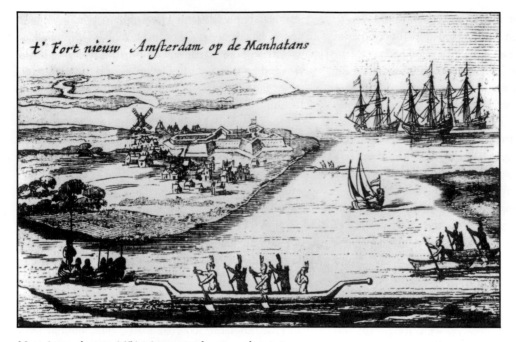

New Amsterdam in 1651. Appropriately, given their importance to the survival of the colony, fur-trading Indians and vessels of the Dutch West India Company figure prominently in the earliest known view of the Dutch outpost on Manhattan Island.   Library of Congress.

actively imported slaves into the colony after its efforts to attract white settlers had failed, almost one-fifth of New York City's approximately 1,500 inhabitants were black. Slaves thus constituted a higher proportion of New York's urban population than of the Chesapeake's at the same time. One observer commented that eighteen different languages could be heard in the colony.

Recognizing the diversity of the population, the Duke of York's representatives moved cautiously in their efforts to establish English authority. The Duke's Laws, a legal code proclaimed in March 1665, at first applied only to the Puritan settlements on Long Island; they were later extended to the rest of the colony. Dutch forms of local government were maintained and Dutch land titles confirmed. Religious toleration was guaranteed through a sort of multiple establishment: each town was permitted to decide which church to support with its tax revenues. Furthermore, the Dutch were allowed to maintain their customary legal practices. Until the 1690s, for example, many Dutch couples wrote joint wills, which were

enforced in New York courts even though under English law married women could not draft wills. Much to the chagrin of English residents of the colony, the Duke's Laws made no provision for a representative assembly. Like other Stuarts, James was suspicious of legislative bodies, and so not until 1683 did he agree to the colonists' requests for an elected legislature. Before then, New York was ruled by an autocratic governor, as it had been under the Dutch.

The English takeover thus had little immediate effect on the colony. Its population grew slowly, barely reaching eighteen thousand by the time of the first English census in 1698. Until the second decade of the eighteenth century, New York City remained a commercial backwater within the orbit of Boston.

One of the chief reasons why the English conquest brought so little change to New York was that the Duke of York quickly regranted the land between the Hudson and Delaware rivers—New Jersey—to his friends Sir George Carteret and **Founding of** John Lord Berkeley. That left his **New Jersey** own colony confined between Connecticut to the east and New Jersey to the west, depriving it of much fertile land and hindering its economic growth. He also failed to promote migration. Meanwhile the New Jersey proprietors acted rapidly to attract settlers, promising generous land grants, freedom of religion, and—without authorization from the crown—a representative assembly. In response, large numbers of Puritan New Englanders migrated southward to New Jersey, along with some Dutch New Yorkers and a contingent of families from Barbados.

Within twenty years, Berkeley and Carteret sold their interests in New Jersey to separate groups of investors. Because of the resulting large number of individual proprietary shares, and because the governor of New York had granted lands in New Jersey before learning that the duke had given it away, land titles in northern New Jersey were clouded for many years to come. Nevertheless, New Jersey grew quickly; at the time of its first census in 1726, it had 32,500 inhabitants, only 8,000 fewer than New York.

The purchasers of all of Carteret's share (West Jersey) and portions of Berkeley's East Jersey were Quakers seeking a refuge from persecution in England. The Quakers, formally known as the Society of Friends, denied the need for an intermediary between the individual and God. Anyone, they believed, could receive the "inner light" and be saved, and all were equal in God's sight. They had no formally trained clergy; any Quaker, male or female, who felt the call could become a "public Friend" and travel from meeting to meeting to discuss God's word. Moreover, any member of the Society could speak in meetings if he or she desired. In short, the Quakers were true religious radicals in the mold of Anne Hutchinson. (Indeed, Mary Dyer, who followed Hutchinson into exile, became a Quaker, returned to Boston as a missionary, and was hanged for preaching Quaker doctrines).

The Quakers obtained a colony of their own in 1681, when Charles II granted the region between Maryland and New York to William Penn, one of the sect's most prominent members.

Pennsylvania, a Quaker Haven The pious yet fun-loving Penn was then thirty-seven years old. Penn's father, Admiral William Penn, had originally served Oliver Cromwell, but later joined forces with Charles II and even loaned the monarch a substantial sum of money. The younger Penn became a Quaker in the mid-1660s, much to his father's dismay. But despite Penn's radical political and religious beliefs, he and Charles II were close personal friends. Were it not for their friendship (and the desire of Charles's advisors to rid England of religious dissenters), the despised Quakers would never have won a charter for an American settlement. As it was, the publicly stated reason for the grant—repayment of the loan from Penn's father—was just that, a public rationalization for a private act.

William Penn held the colony as a personal proprietorship, and the vast property holdings earned profits for his descendants until the American Revolution. Even so, Penn, like the Roman Catholic Calverts of Maryland before him, saw the province not merely as a source of revenue but also as a haven for his persecuted coreligionists. Penn offered land to all comers on liberal terms, promised toleration for all religions (though only Christians were given the right to vote), guaranteed such English liberties as the right to bail and trial by jury, and pledged to establish a representative assembly. He also publicized the ready availability of land in Pennsylvania through promotional tracts printed in German, French, and Dutch.

Penn's activities and the natural attraction of his lands for Quakers gave rise to a migration whose magnitude was equaled only by the Puritan exodus to New England in the 1630s. By mid-1683, over three thousand people—among them Welsh, Irish, Dutch, and Germans—had already moved to Pennsylvania, and within five years the population had reached twelve thousand. (By contrast, it took Virginia more than thirty years to achieve a comparable population.) Philadelphia, carefully planned to be the major city in the province, drew merchants and artisans from throughout the English-speaking world. From mainland and West Indian colonies alike came Quakers seeking religious freedom; they brought with them years of experience on American soil and well-established trading connections. Pennsylvania's lands were both plentiful and fertile, and the colony soon began exporting flour and other foodstuffs to the West Indies. Practically overnight Philadelphia acquired more than two thousand citizens and began to challenge Boston's commercial pre-eminence.

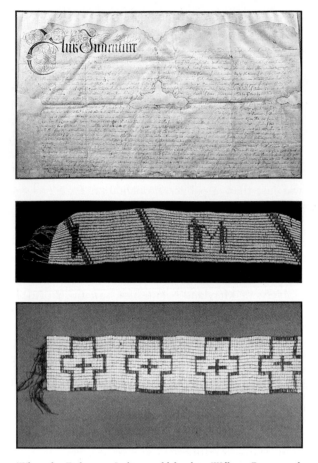

When the Delaware Indians sold land to William Penn, each side recorded the deed in its own way. The English drew up a written document, signed and sealed by all concerned; the Delawares prepared wampum belts portraying the four tribal groups participating in the sale and the peaceful agreement between Indians and whites (shown standing hand in hand). Deed and top belt: Historical Society of Pennsylvania; bottom belt: Courtesy Museum of the American Indian.

A pacifist with egalitarian principles, Penn was determined to treat the Indians of Pennsylvania fairly. He carefully purchased tracts of land from the Delaware (or Lenni Lenape), the dominant tribe in the region, before selling them to settlers. Penn also established strict regulations for the Indian trade and forbade the sale of alcohol to tribesmen. In 1682 he visited a number of Lenni Lenape villages, after taking pains to learn the language. "I must say," Penn commented, "that I know not a language spoken in Europe that hath words of more sweetness in Accent and Emphasis, than theirs."

Penn's Indian policy provides a sterling example of the complexity of the interaction among whites and Indians, because it prompted several tribes to move to Pennsylvania. Indians from western Maryland, Virginia, and North Carolina came northward near the end of the seventeenth century to escape repeated clashes with white settlers. The most important of these tribes was the Tuscarora, whose experiences will be described later in this chapter. Likewise, the Shawnee and Miami chose to move eastward from the Ohio valley. By a supreme irony, however, the same toleration that attracted Indians to Penn's domains also brought non-Quaker Europeans who showed little respect for Indian claims to the soil. In effect, Penn's policy was so successful that it caused its own downfall. The Scotch-Irish, Palatine Germans, and Swiss who settled in Pennsylvania in the first half of the eighteenth century clashed repeatedly over land with tribes that had also recently migrated to the colony.

The other proprietary colony, granted by Charles II in 1663, encompassed a huge tract of land stretching from the southern boundary of Virginia to Spanish Florida. The area had great strategic importance; a successful English settlement there would prevent the Spanish from pushing further north. The semitropical land was also extremely fertile, holding forth the promise of producing such exotic and valuable commodities as figs, olives, wines, and silk. The proprietors named their new province Carolina in Charles's honor (in Latin his name was Carolus). The "Fundamental Constitutions of Carolina," which they asked

Founding of Carolina

the political philosopher John Locke to draft for them, set forth an elaborate plan for a colony governed by a hierarchy of landholding aristocrats and characterized by a carefully structured distribution of political and economic power. But Carolina failed to follow the course the proprietors laid out. Instead it quickly developed two distinct population centers, which in 1729 permanently split into two separate colonies.

The Albemarle region that became North Carolina was settled by Virginians. They established a society much like their own, with an economy based on tobacco cultivation and the export of such forest products as pitch, tar, and timber. Because North Carolina lacked a satisfactory harbor, its planters continued to rely on Virginia's ports and merchants to conduct their trade, and the two colonies remained tightly linked.

South Carolina developed quite differently. Its first settlers, who founded Charleston in 1670, came from Barbados. That tiny island had been colonized by the English in 1627 and was already overcrowded less than fifty years later. When white planters from Barbados moved to the mainland of North America, they brought with them the slaves who had worked on their sugar plantations. By so doing they irrevocably shaped the future of South Carolina and the subsequent history of the United States.

THE FORCED MIGRATION OF AFRICANS

During the first six decades of English settlement in America few blacks were imported into the mainland colonies. After 1670 that pattern changed dramatically. Why did the change occur, in the Chesapeake as well as in South Carolina? And, more important, since England itself had no tradition of slavery, why did English settlers in the New World begin to enslave Africans at all? The answers to both questions lie in the combined effects of economics and racial attitudes.

The English were an ethnocentric people. As was seen in Chapter 1, they believed firmly in the superiority of their values and civilization, especially when compared with the native cultures of Africa and North America. Furthermore, they believed that fair-skinned peoples like themselves were superior to the darker-skinned races. Those beliefs alone did not cause them to enslave Indians and Africans, but the idea that other races were inferior to whites helped to justify slavery.

Although the English had not previously practiced slavery, other Europeans had. The Spanish and Portuguese, for example, had long enslaved African Muslims and other "heathen" peoples. Further, Christian doctrine could even be interpreted as allowing enslavement as a means of converting such people to the true faith. European colonizers needed a large labor force to exploit the riches of the New World, and few free people were willing to work as wage laborers in the difficult and dangerous conditions of South American mines or Caribbean sugar plantations. Needing bound laborers, then, Europeans sought them chiefly in the ranks of dark-skinned non-Christians.

The most obvious source of workers would have been the Indians native to the Americas. But, for a variety of reasons, although some Indians were indeed enslaved (see page 54), they could not supply all the Europeans' labor needs. As was noted in Chapter 1, alien diseases had taken a terrible toll of the Native Americans; in addition, in the Spanish colonies Indian slavery was not only illegal but also actively discouraged by the Catholic Church. No such religious motive worked against Indian slavery in the English settlements, but they also had good reason not to enslave too many Indians. For one thing, the native peoples' familiarity with the environment enabled them to escape easily from their white masters. For another, the presence of Indian slaves in a white settlement might provoke retaliatory raids from their fellow tribesmen. Colonial authorities also feared that if they enslaved Indian captives, the tribes might treat captured whites in a similar fashion.

Africans were a different story. Transported far from home and set down in alien surroundings, like Olaudah Equiano they were frequently unable to communicate with their fellow workers. They were also the darkest (and thus, to European eyes, the most inferior) of all peoples. Black Africans therefore seemed to be ideal candidates for perpetual servitude. By the time the English established settlements in the Caribbean and North America, Spanish colonists had already held Africans in slavery for over a century. The English newcomers to the New World, in other words, had a ready-made model to copy.

Nevertheless, a fully developed system of lifelong slavery did not emerge immediately in the English colonies. Lack of historical evidence makes it difficult to determine the legal status of blacks during the first two or three decades of English settlement, but many of them seem to have been indentured, like whites, which meant that they eventually became free. (Massachusetts, in 1641, was the first to mention slavery in its legal code.) After 1640,

Slavery Established

some blacks were being permanently enslaved in each of the English colonies. By the end of the century, the blacks' status was fixed. Barbados adopted a comprehensive slave code as early as 1661, and the mainland provinces soon did the same. In short, even before the expansion of slavery in North America, the English settlements there had established the legal basis for a slave system.

But why did Chesapeake tobacco planters, who had long relied on indentured English servants, begin to purchase blacks in ever-increasing numbers near the end of the seventeenth century? The answer was simple: After about 1675 they could no longer obtain an adequate supply of white workers. A falling birth rate and improved economic conditions in England decreased the number of possible migrants to the colonies. At the same time new English settlements in North America had started to compete with the Chesapeake for settlers, both indentured and free. As a result, the number of servant migrants to the Chesapeake leveled off after 1665 and fell in the 1680s. After 1674, when the shortage of servants became acute, imports of Africans increased dramatically. As early as 1690, the Chesapeake colonies contained more black slaves than white indentured servants, and by 1710 one-fifth of the region's population was black. Slaves usually cost about two-and-a-half times as much as servants, but they repaid the greater investment by their lifetime of service.

Yet not all white planters could afford to devote so much money to purchasing workers. Accordingly, the transition from indentured to enslaved labor increased the social and economic distance between richer and poorer planters. Whites with enough money could acquire slaves and accumulate greater wealth, while less affluent whites could not even buy indentured servants, whose price had been driven up by scarcity. In addition, the transition to slave labor ended what had become a common way for poorer white planters to earn essential income: renting parts of their property to newly freed servants. Deprived of that source of capital—since there were far fewer ex-servants—many marginal planters sank into landless status. As time passed, white Chesapeake society thus became more and more stratified; that is, the gap between rich and poor steadily widened. The introduction of large numbers of Africans into the Chesapeake, in other words, had a significant impact on white society, in addition to reshaping the population as a whole.

In South Carolina, as has been seen, the first slaves arrived with the first white settlers. Indeed, one-quarter to one-third of South Carolina's early population was black. The Barbados whites quickly discovered that Africans had a variety of skills well suited to the semitropical environment of South Carolina. African-style dugout canoes became the chief means of transportation in the colony, which was crisscrossed by rivers. Fishing nets copied from African models proved to be more efficient than those of English origin. The baskets slaves wove and the gourds they hollowed out came into general use as containers for food and drink. Africans' skill at killing crocodiles equipped them to handle alligators as well. And, finally, slaves adapted African techniques of cattleherding for use in the American context. Since meat and hides, not the exotic products originally envisioned, were the colony's chief exports in its earliest years, blacks obviously contributed significantly to South Carolina's prosperity.

Blacks in South Carolina

The similarity of South Carolina's environment to West Africa, coupled with the large number of blacks in the population, ensured that more aspects of West African culture survived in that colony than elsewhere on the mainland of North America. Only in South Carolina did black parents continue to give their children African names; only there did a dialect develop that combined English words with African terms. (Known as Gullah, it was used in certain areas until the twentieth century.) African skills remained useful, and so techniques that in other regions were lost when the migrant generation died were instead passed down to their children. And in South Carolina, as in West Africa, black women were the primary traders, dominating the markets of Charleston as they did those of Gambia or Benin. One white observer commented that "these women have such a connection with and influence on the country negroes who come to that market, that they generally find means to obtain whatever they choose, in preference to any white person; thus they forestall and engross many articles, which some hours afterwards you must buy back from them at 100 or 150 per cent advance."

Blacks' central position in the colony's economy was firmly established near the end of the seventeenth

Mulberry Plantation, South Carolina, in the late eighteenth century. The mansion house on this indigo and rice planta-tion (built 1708) is surrounded by slave quarters—African-style huts constructed by Africans and their Afro-American children. Some of the tiny houses survived into the twentieth century.   Painting by Thomas Coram. Carolina Art Asso-ciation/Gibbes Art Gallery.

century, when South Carolinians began to cultivate a new staple crop: rice. English people knew little about the techniques of growing and processing rice, and their first attempts to raise it were unsuccessful. But slaves from Africa's Rice Coast (see page 11) had spent their lives working with the crop. Signif-icantly, the importation of large numbers of Africans coincided with the successful introduction of rice as a staple crop in South Carolina. Although the evidence is circumstantial, it seems likely that the Africans' expertise enabled their English masters to cultivate the crop profitably. In the mid-eighteenth century a South Carolina merchant commented that "the Slaves from the River Gambia are preferr'd to all others with us save the Gold Coast." After rice had become South Carolina's major export, 43 percent of the Africans imported into the colony came from rice-producing regions.

South Carolina later developed a second staple crop, and it too made use of blacks' special skills. The crop was indigo, much prized in Europe as a blue dye for clothing. In the early 1740s, Eliza Lucas, a young white West Indian woman who was managing her father's South Carolina plantations, began to experiment with indigo cultivation. Drawing on the knowledge of white and black West Indians, she developed the planting and processing techniques later adopted throughout the colony. Indigo was grown on high ground, and rice was planted in low-lying swampy areas; rice and indigo also had opposite growing seasons. Thus the two crops complemented each other perfectly. Although South Carolina indigo never matched the quality of that raised in the West Indies, the indigo industry flourished because Parliament of-fered Carolinians a bounty on every pound they ex-ported to Great Britian.

After 1700 white southerners were irrevocably committed to black slavery as their chief source of

In the early eighteenth century, the king of Dahomey formed a women's brigade to help him conquer neighboring kingdoms. This contemporary print, which shows him leading his armed female troops to war, both illustrates the continuing importance in West Africa of dual-sex social organization and shows the significant political changes caused by the slave trade, as rulers sought to extend their power over wider areas. (The women's brigade was not disbanded until 1892.) The New York Public Library, Astor, Lenox, and Tilden Foundations.

labor. The same was not true of white northerners.

Slavery in the North

Only a small proportion of the slaves brought to the English colonies in America went to the northern mainland provinces, and most of those who did worked as domestic servants. Lacking large-scale agricultural enterprises, the rural North did not demand many enslaved laborers. In northern urban areas, though, white domestic servants were hard to find and harder to keep (because higher wages were paid for other jobs in the labor-scarce economy), and blacks there filled an identifiable need. In some northern colonial cities (notably Newport, Rhode Island, and New York City), black slaves accounted for more than 10 percent of the population.

The introduction of large-scale slavery in the South, coupled with its near-absence in the North, accentuated regional differences that had already begun to develop in England's American colonies. To the distinction between diversified agriculture and staple-crop production was now added a difference in the race and status of most laborers. That difference was one of degree, but it was nonetheless crucial. In the latter years of the seventeenth century, white southern planters chose a course of action that nearly two centuries later took the future United States into civil war.

Between 1492 and 1770 more Africans than Europeans came to the New World. But just 4.5 percent of them (345,000 persons by 1861, or 275,000 during the eighteenth century) were imported into the region that later became the United States. By contrast, 42 percent of the approximately 9.5 million enslaved blacks were carried to the Caribbean, and 49 percent went to South America, mainly to the Portuguese colony of Brazil. The magnitude of this trade in slaves raises three important and related questions. First, what was its impact on West Africa, the source of most of the slaves taken to North America? Second, how was the trade organized and conducted? Third, what was its effect on the blacks it carried?

The West African coast was one of the most fertile

Cape Coast Castle in 1692. Built by the Royal African Company, this fort on the Gold Coast was one of the most important English slave-trading posts in West Africa. After Greenhill.

and densely inhabited regions of the continent. Despite the extent of forced migration to the Western Hemisphere, the area was not noticeably depopulated by the trade in human beings. (Further south, though, Angola—which was the chief source of slaves carried by the Portuguese to Brazil—did suffer severe depopulation.) In Guinea, the primary consequences of the trade were political. The coastal kings who served as middlemen in the trade used it as a vehicle to consolidate their power and extend their rule over larger territories. They controlled European traders' access to slaves and at the same time controlled inland peoples' access to desirable European trade goods like cloth, beads, alcohol, tobacco, firearms, and iron bars that could be made into knives and other tools. The centralizing tendencies of the trade thus helped in the formation of such powerful eighteenth-century kingdoms as Dahomey and Asante (created from the Akan States; see page 11).

West Africa and the Slave Trade

These West African kings played a crucial role in the functioning of the slave trade. Europeans set up permanent slave-trading posts in Lower Guinea under the protection of local rulers, who then supplied the resident Europeans with slaves to fill the ships that stopped regularly at the coastal forts. In Upper Guinea, the lack of good harbors caused a somewhat different trading pattern: Europeans would sail along the coast, stopping to pick up cargoes when signaled from the shore. Most persons thereby sold into American slavery were wartime captives (including leaders of high status), criminals sentenced to enslavement, or persons seized for nonpayment of debts. A smaller proportion had been kidnapped, like Olaudah Equiano.

The Portuguese, who initially controlled most of the slave trade, were supplanted by the Dutch in the middle of the seventeenth century. The Dutch in turn lost out to the English, who came to dominate the trade through the efforts of the Royal African Company, a joint-stock company chartered by Charles II in 1672. Holding a monopoly on all English trade

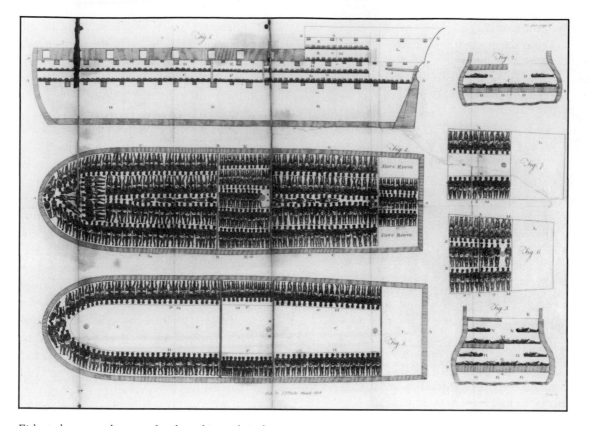

Eighteenth-century diagram of a slave ship, with its human cargo stowed according to British regulations. Many captains did not give slaves even this much room. On the assumption that a large number of Africans would die en route, shipmasters packed as many slaves as possible into the hold to increase their profit. Library of Congress.

with black Africa, the company built and maintained eight forts, dispatched to West Africa hundreds of ships carrying English manufactured goods, and transported more than 120,000 slaves to England's American colonies. Yet even before the company's monopoly expired in 1712 many individual English traders had illegally entered the market for slaves. By the early eighteenth century, such independent traders were carrying most of the Africans imported into the colonies, making slaves more readily available in Anglo-America than they had been previously.

At first, most of the slaves imported into the English colonies went to the Caribbean islands. As mainland planters began to purchase slaves in greater numbers, some blacks were re-exported from the West Indies to meet the demand. Even before the end of the seventeenth century, though, most blacks brought to the future United States came directly from Africa. And although Chesapeake and South Carolina planters initially bought approximately equal numbers of slaves, by the middle of the eighteenth century Carolinians were purchasing three times as many blacks each year as Virginians and Marylanders combined. One result was that blacks made up a majority of the population of South Carolina even before midcentury.

The experience of the Middle Passage (thus named because it was the middle section of the so-called triangular trade among England, Africa, and the Americas; see pages 58–59) was always traumatic and sometimes fatal for the Africans who made up the ship's cargo. An average of 10 to 20 percent of the slaves died en route, but on voyages that were particularly long or were hard hit by epi-

The Middle Passage

demic diseases, the mortality rates were much higher. In addition, some slaves usually died either before the ships left Africa or shortly after their arrival in the New World. Their white captors died at the same, if not higher, rates, chiefly through exposure to alien African germs. Just 10 percent of the men sent to run the Royal African Company's forts in Lower Guinea lived to return home to England, and one in every four or five white sailors died on the Middle Passage. Once again, the exchange of diseases that accompanied the interaction of alien peoples caused unanticipated death and destruction.

On shipboard, men were usually kept shackled in pairs, while women and children were released from any bonds once the ship was well out at sea. The slaves were fed a vegetable diet of beans, rice, yams, or corn, cooked together in various combinations to create a warm mush. In good weather, they were normally allowed on deck for fresh air, because only healthy slaves commanded high prices. Many ships also carried a doctor whose primary role was to treat the slaves' illnesses. The average size of a cargo was about 250 slaves, although since the size of ships varied greatly, so too did the number of slaves carried.

Records of slave traders reveal numerous instances of Africans' resistance to captivity. Recall that Olaudah Equiano contemplated suicide; many of his fellow captives took that means of avoiding servitude. Others participated in shipboard revolts; more than 150 occurred during the three-hundred-year history of the Middle Passage. Yet most of the Africans who embarked on the slave vessels arrived in the Americas alive and still in captivity; the whites saw to that, for only thus could they make a profit. The kind of life those Africans found in their new homes will be discussed in Chapter 3.

RELATIONS BETWEEN WHITES
AND INDIANS

Everywhere in North America, European colonizers depended heavily on the labor of native peoples. But their reliance on the Indians took varying forms in different parts of the continent. In the Northeast, France, England, and the Netherlands competed for the pelts supplied by Indian hunters. In the Southeast, England, Spain, and later France each tried to control a thriving trade with the tribes in deerskins and Indian slaves. Finally, in the Southwest, Spain attempted to exploit the agricultural and artisan skills of the Pueblo peoples (see page 8).

Spanish colonizers first settled in the present-day United States during the last half of the sixteenth century. In 1565, Pedro Menendez de Aviles, a Spanish noble, along with a group of soldiers, settlers, and priests, established the first permanent settlement in the United States: St. Augustine, Florida. Just over thirty years later (1598) a similar group led by Juan de Oñate, a Mexican-born adventurer, colonized New Mexico. The Spaniards had three goals: to gain wealth for themselves, preferably through finding precious metals; to claim new territories for their monarch; and to convert the Indians to Christianity. They located few precious metals, although some of the westerners did become wealthy by other means. They were more successful in achieving their other aims. In both Florida and the Southwest, Franciscans set up long chains of missions, and by the late eighteenth century Spain claimed a vast territory that stretched from California (initially colonized in 1769) through Texas (chiefly settled after 1700) to the Gulf Coast.

But Spain's ability to control such an immense area was questionable, to say the least. Nowhere was that more clear than in New Mexico, the heartland of northern New Spain. During the seventeenth century, Spanish settlers and missionaries based at Santa Fé (founded 1610) ruthlessly forced Indian laborers—slaves in all but name—to work their fields and care for their livestock. The Franciscans also adopted brutal and violent tactics as they tried to wipe out all vestiges of the native religion. Finally, in 1680 the Pueblos revolted under the leadership of Popé, a respected medicine man, and successfully drove the Spaniards out of New Mexico. Although Spanish authority was nominally restored in 1692, Spain had learned its lesson. From that time on Spanish governors stressed cooperation, rather than confrontation, with the Pueblos and no longer attempted to reduce them to bondage or to violate

Popé and the Pueblo Revolt

their cultural integrity. The Pueblo revolt was the most successful and longest sustained Indian resistance movement in colonial North America.

Along the eastern seaboard Europeans valued the Indians as hunters rather than as agricultural workers, but they were no less dependent on Indian labor than were the Spanish in the west. The Dutch and French settlements in North America were little more than trading posts. Although the English colonies eventually began to market their own products, in the earliest phase of each colony's history its primary exports were furs and skins obtained from neighboring Indians.

South Carolina provides a case in point. The Barbadians who colonized the region moved quickly to establish a vigorous trade in deerskins with nearby tribes. During the first decade of the eighteenth century, South Carolina exported to Europe an average of 54,000 skins annually, a number that later climbed to a peak of 160,000. The trade gave rise to other exchanges that reveal the complexity of the economic relationships among Indians and Europeans. For example, the horses white Carolinians needed to carry the deerskins came from the Creek Indians, who had in turn obtained them from the Spaniards through trade and capture.

Another important component of the Carolina trade was traffic in Indian slaves. The warring tribes of South Carolina (especially the Creek) profited **Indian Slave Trade** from selling their captive enemies to the whites, who then either kept them in the colony as slaves or exported them to the West Indies or other mainland settlements. There are no reliable statistics on the extent of the trade in Indian slaves, but in 1708 they made up 14 percent of the population of South Carolina. Many were Christians converted by the Spanish missions in northern Florida, then captured by Englishmen and their Indian allies.

A major conflict between white Carolinians and neighboring tribes also added to the supply of Indian slaves. In 1711, the Tuscarora, an Iroquoian people who had migrated southward many years earlier, attacked the Swiss-German settlement of New Bern, which had expropriated their lands without payment. The Tuscarora had been avid slavers and had sold many captives from weaker Algonkian tribes to the whites. Those tribes seized the opportunity to settle old scores, joining with the English colonists to defeat their enemy in a bloody two-year war. In the end, more than a thousand Tuscarora were themselves sold into slavery, and the remnants of the tribe drifted northward, returning to their ancient homeland in northern Pennsylvania and southern New York.

The abuses of the slave trade led to the most destructive Indian war in Carolina. White traders regularly engaged in corrupt, brutal, and fraudulent practices. They were notorious for cheating the Indians, physically abusing them (including raping the women), and selling friendly tribesmen into slavery when no enemy captives came readily to hand. In the spring of 1715 the Yamasee, aided by the Creek and a number of other tribes, retaliated by attacking the English colonists. As the raids continued through the summer, white refugees streamed into Charleston by the hundreds. At times the Creek-Yamasee offensive, often guided by information from Indian slaves held by the whites, came close to driving the intruders from the mainland altogether. But then colonial reinforcements arrived from the north, and the Cherokee joined the whites against their ancient enemies, the Creek. Their cause lost, the Yamasee moved south to seek Spanish protection, and the Creek retreated to their villages in the west. Still, it was years before South Carolina fully recovered from the effects of the Yamasee War.

That the Yamasee could escape by migrating southward exposed the one remaining gap in the line of English coastal settlements, the area between the **Founding of Georgia** southern border of South Carolina and Spanish Florida. The gap was plugged in 1732 with the chartering of Georgia, the last of the colonies that would become part of the United States. Intended as a haven for debtors by its founder James Oglethorpe, Georgia was specifically designed as a garrison province. Since all its landholders were expected to serve as militiamen to defend English settlements, the charter prohibited women from inheriting or purchasing land in the colony. The charter also prohibited the use of alcoholic beverages and forbade the introduction of slavery. Such provisions reveal the founders' intention that Georgia should be peopled by sturdy, sober yeoman farmers who could take up their weapons against the Indians or Spaniards at a moment's notice. None of the conditions could be enforced, however, and all had been abandoned by 1752, when Georgia became a royal colony.

In the Northeast, relationships were complicated by the number of European nations and Indian tribes involved in the fur trade. Before the large-scale migration of English people, the Dutch at Fort Orange (Albany) on the upper Hudson River competed for control of the fur trade with the French on the St. Lawrence. In the 1640s, the Iroquois, who traded chiefly with the Dutch, went to war against the Huron, who traded primarily with the French. The Iroquois' object was to become the major supplier of pelts to the Europeans, and they achieved that goal by practically exterminating the Huron tribe through the use of guns obtained from their Dutch allies. The Iroquois thus established themselves as a major force in the region, one that Europeans could ignore only at their peril.

The Iroquois nation was not one tribe, but five: the Mohawk, Oneida, Onondaga, Cayuga, and Seneca. (In 1722 the Tuscarora became the sixth.) Under

Iroquois Confederacy

the terms of a defensive alliance forged early in the sixteenth century, key decisions of war and peace for the entire Iroquois Confederacy were made by a council composed of tribal representatives. Each tribe retained some autonomy, and no tribe could be forced to comply with a council directive against its will. The Iroquois were unique among Indians not only because of the strength and persistence of their alliance but also because of the role played by their tribal matrons. The older women of each village chose its chief and could either start wars (by calling for the capture of prisoners to replace dead relatives) or stop them (by refusing to supply warriors with necessary foodstuffs).

Before the arrival of the Europeans, the Iroquois had waged wars primarily for the purpose of acquiring captives to replenish their population. Contact with white traders brought ravaging disease as early as 1633 and thus intensified the need for captives. At the same time the arrival of whites created an economic motive for warfare: the desire to control the fur trade and gain unimpeded access to European goods. The war with the Huron was but the first of a series of

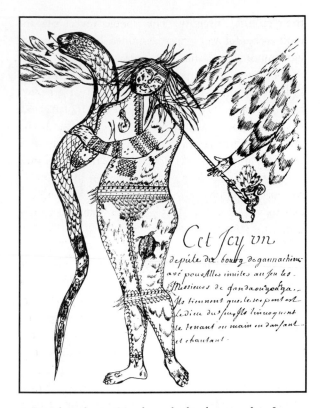

A French settler in Canada made this drawing of an Iroquois about 1700. The artist's fascination with his subject's mode of dress and patterned tattoos is evident. Such pictorial representations of "otherness" help to suggest the cultural gulf that divided the European and Indian residents of North America. Library of Congress.

conflicts with other tribes known as the Beaver Wars, in which the Iroquois fought desperately to maintain a pre-eminent position in the trade. In the mid-1670s, just when it appeared they would be successful, the French stepped in to prevent an Iroquois triumph (which would have destroyed France's plans to trade directly with the Indians of the Great Lakes and Mississippi Valley regions). Over the next twenty years the French launched repeated attacks on Iroquois villages. The English, who replaced the Dutch at Albany after 1664, offered little assistance other than weapons to their trading partners and nominal allies. Their people and resources depleted by constant warfare, the Iroquois in 1701 negotiated neutrality treaties with France, England, and their tribal neighbors. For the next half-century they maintained their power through diplomacy and trade.

The Beaver hunting spoken
of in y. 16 letter.
A. the Iroquese surprising their enemies at hunting.
B. the huntsmen coming in a body to meet 'em
C. a savage taken prisoner of war
D. a savage surpris'd and kill'd in the action
E. the Iroquese in Ambush firing upon y Canons
G. the Iroquese shooting upon y Canons that fly.
H savages flying to their Canons
I Canoes of bark
I savages put to flight
M women flying with their Children

A hut for 10 huntsmen

The precinct of a hut for ten huntsmen
plac'd in y middle

A pool or little lake in y midst of which y
beavers build their kennels

A European's diagram of one of the Iroquois Beaver Wars.
At the bottom of the picture, the main body of the Iroquois
attacks a group of beaver hunters (note that the Iroquois
have guns and their opponents only bows and arrows); in
the center are the beaver pools and hunting camps. At letter
M, women are fleeing from the fighting, carrying their
children to safety. At the top, groups of hunters paddle off
in their canoes.   Library of Congress.

In the Carolinas and the middle colonies, then, it was friction arising from trade relationships that produced the major conflicts between whites and Indians. But in Virginia, the cause of a renewed outbreak of violence was the white colonists' hunger for land on which to grow still more tobacco.

By the early 1670s, some Virginians were eagerly eyeing the rich lands north of the York River that had been reserved for Indians under earlier treaties. Using as a pretext the July 1675 killing of a white servant by some Doeg Indians, they attacked not only the Doeg but also the Susquehannock, a powerful tribe that had recently occupied the region. In retaliation, Susquehannock bands began to raid frontier plantations in the winter of 1676. The land-hungry whites rallied behind the leadership of Nathaniel Bacon, a planter who had arrived in the colony only two years before. Bacon and his followers wanted, in his words, "to ruine and extirpate all Indians in generall." Governor William Berkeley, however, hoped to avoid setting off a major war.

Berkeley and Bacon soon clashed. After Bacon

forced the House of Burgesses to authorize him to attack the Indians, Berkeley declared Bacon and his men to be in rebellion. As the chaotic summer of 1676 wore on, Bacon alternately pursued Indians and battled with the governor's supporters. In September he marched on Jamestown itself and burned the capital to the ground. But after Bacon died of dysentery the following month, the rebellion collapsed. A new Indian treaty signed in 1677 opened much of the disputed territory to whites.

Bacon's Rebellion

It was more than coincidence that New England, which had also been settled more than fifty years earlier, was wracked by conflict with Indians at precisely the same time. In both areas the whites' original accommodation with the tribes—reached after the defeat of the Pequot in the North and the Powhatan Confederacy in the South—no longer satisfied both parties. In New England, though, it was the Indians, rather than the whites, who felt aggrieved.

In the half-century since the founding of New England, white settlement had spread far into the interior of Massachusetts and Connecticut. In the process the whites had completely surrounded the ancestral lands of the Pokanoket (Wampanoag) on Narragansett Bay. Their chief, Metacomet (known to the whites as King Philip), was the son of Massassoit, who had signed the treaty with the Pilgrims in 1621. Troubled by white encroachments on Pokanoket lands and equally concerned about the impact European culture and Christianity were having on his people, Metacomet in late June 1675 led his warriors in attacks on nearby white communities.

King Philip's War

By the end of the year, two other local tribes, the Nipmuck and the Narragansett, had joined Metacomet's forces. In the fall, the three tribes jointly attacked settlements in the northern Connecticut River valley; in the winter and spring of 1676, they devastated well-established villages and even attacked Plymouth and Providence. Altogether, the alliance totally destroyed twelve of the ninety Puritan towns and attacked forty others. A tenth of the able-bodied adult males in Massachusetts were captured or killed; proportional to population, it was the most costly war in American history. New England's very survival seemed to be at stake.

But the tide turned in the summer of 1676. The Indian coalition ran short of food and ammunition, and whites began to use "praying Indians" as guides and scouts. After Metacomet was killed in an ambush in August, the alliance crumbled. Many surviving Pokanokets, Nipmucks, and Narragansetts, including Metacomet's wife and son, were captured and sold into slavery in the West Indies. The power of New England's coastal tribes was broken. Thereafter they lived in small clusters, subordinated to the whites and often working as servants or sailors. Only on the isolated island of Martha's Vineyard were some surviving Pokanokets able to preserve their tribal identity intact.

NEW ENGLAND AND THE WEB OF IMPERIAL TRADE

The New England settlements that Metacomet attacked had changed in three major ways since the early years of colonization. The population had grown dramatically; the nature of the residents' religious commitment had altered; and the economy had developed in unanticipated ways.

The expansion of the population was the result not of continued migration from England (for that had largely ceased after 1640), but rather of natural increase. The original settlers' many children also produced many children, and subsequent generations followed suit. By 1700, New England's population had quadrupled to reach approximately 100,000. That placed great pressure on the available land, and many members of the third and fourth generations of New Englanders had to migrate—north to New Hampshire or Maine, south to New York, west beyond the Connecticut River—to find sufficient farm land for themselves and their children. Others abandoned agriculture and learned skills like blacksmithing or carpentry so that they could support themselves in the growing number of towns that dotted the countryside in that area.

Population Pressures

In addition, American-born Puritans did not display

the same religious fervor that had prompted their ancestors to cross the Atlantic. Many of them had not experienced the gift of God's grace, or "saving faith," which was required for full membership in the Congregational church. Yet they had been baptized as children, attended church services regularly, and wanted their own infants to be baptized, even though that sacrament was supposed to be available only to the children of church members. A synod of Massachusetts ministers, convened in 1662 to consider the problem, responded by establishing a category of "halfway" membership in the church. In a statement that has become known as the Halfway Covenant, the clergymen declared that adults who had been baptized as children but were not full church members could have their children baptized. In return, such parents had to acknowledge the authority of the church and live according to moral precepts. They were not allowed to vote in church affairs or take communion.

Halfway Covenant

The Halfway Covenant attempted to deal with one problem of changing religious mores, but it did not touch another: a newly noticeable difference between the experiences of the two sexes. By the end of the seventeenth century, women were more likely than men to experience "saving faith" and so they made up a majority in many New England congregations. Searching for the cause of this phenomenon, Cotton Mather—the most prominent member of a family of distinguished ministers—speculated that the fear of dying in childbirth made women especially sensitive to their spiritual state. Modern historians have also argued that women were attracted to religion because the church offered them a spritual equality that offset their secular inferiority. Whatever the explanation, Mather's increasingly female audiences prompted him to deliver sermons outlining women's proper role in church and society—the first formal examination of that theme in American history. Mather was the first of many men to urge American women to be submissive to their husbands, watchful of their children, and attentive to religious duty.

The differential rate of church membership in late-seventeenth-century New England suggests a growing division between pious women and their more worldly husbands. That split reflected significant economic changes, which constitute the third major way in which the Puritan colonies were being transformed.

New England's first economic system had been based on two pillars: the fur trade and the constant flow of migrants. Together those had allowed New Englanders to acquire the manufactured goods they needed: the fur trade gave them valuable pelts to sell in England, and the migrants were always willing to exchange clothing and other items for the earlier settlers' surplus seed grains and livestock. But New England's supply of furs was limited, because the region lacked rivers giving ready access to the interior of the continent, and the migrants stopped coming with the outbreak of civil war in England. Thus in 1640 that first economic system collapsed.

The Puritans then began a search for new salable crops and markets. They found such crops in the waters off the coast—fish—and on their own land—grain and wood products. By 1643 they had also found the necessary markets: first the Wine Islands (the Azores and Canaries) in the Atlantic, and then the new English colonies in the Caribbean, which were beginning to cultivate sugar intensively and to invest heavily in slaves. The islands lacked precisely the goods New England could produce in abundance: cheap food (corn and salted fish) to feed the slaves, and wood for barrels to transport wine (from the Atlantic islands) and molasses (from the Caribbean colonies).

New England's Trading System

Thus developed the series of transactions that has become known, inaccurately, as the triangular trade. Since New England's products duplicated England's, the northern colonists sold their goods in the West Indies and elsewhere to earn the money with which to purchase English products. (Southerners did not have the same problem. Their crops—tobacco, rice, and indigo—could be sold directly to England.) There soon grew up in New England's ports a cadre of merchants who acquired—usually through barter—cargoes of timber and foodstuffs, which they then dispatched to the West Indies for sale. In the Caribbean the ships sailed from island to island, exchanging fish, barrel staves, and grains for molasses, fruit, spices, and slaves.

Once they had a full load, the ships returned to Boston, Newport, or New Haven to dispose of their

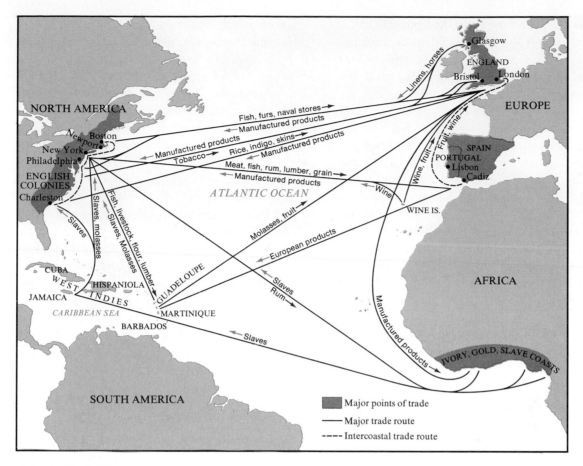

Atlantic Trade Routes

cargoes. New Englanders then traded those items they did not consume to other colonies or to England. Most important, they distilled West Indian molasses into the more valuable rum, a widely used alcoholic beverage. Rum was a key component of the only part of the trade that could be termed triangular: Rhode Islanders took rum to Africa and traded it for slaves, whom they carried to the West Indies to exchange for more molasses to produce still more rum. With that exception, the trading pattern was not a triangle but a shifting set of shuttle voyages (see map). Its sole constant was uncertainty, due to the weather, rapid changes of supply and demand in the small island markets, and the delicate system of credit on which the entire structure depended.

The network of seventeenth-century trade, which had achieved mature form by the 1660s, was fueled

not by cash (no one had much of that) but by credit in the form of bills of exchange. These were, in effect, promissory notes in which one merchant pledged to pay another a certain sum on demand. Bills of exchange passed from hand to hand, circulating much as currency does today. Ultimately, though, their value rested on trust and the credit standing of the first merchant in the chain. That was one of the major reasons why the seventeenth-century mercantile community was composed chiefly of men related to each other by blood or marriage. A Bostonian who needed a reliable representative in Barbados would send his brother-in-law, son, or cousin to handle his interests; a London merchant might dispatch a relative to Boston for the same reason.

The Puritan New Englanders who ventured into commerce were soon differentiated from their rural

Sea Captains Carousing in Surinam, *a scene that could have occurred in any tavern in any Caribbean port. Several recognizable Rhode Island merchants are included among the merrymakers. Painted by John Greenwood (1758), a Bostonian who lived in Surinam (Dutch Guiana), on the northern coast of South America.   The St. Louis Art Museum.*

Puritans and Anglicans

counterparts by their ties to a wider transatlantic world and by their preoccupation with material endeavors. Moreover, as time passed, increasing numbers of Puritans became involved in trade. Small investors who owned shares of voyages soon dominated the field numerically if not monetarily. The gulf between commercial and farming interests widened after 1660, when—with the end of the Interregnum and the restoration of the Stuarts to the English throne—Anglican merchants began to migrate to New England. Such men had little stake in the survival of Massachusetts Bay and Connecticut in their original form, and some were openly antagonistic to Puritan traditions. As non-Congregationalists they were denied the vote and they could not practice their religion freely. They resented their exclusion from the governing elite, believing that their wealth and social status entitled them to political power. Congregationalist clergymen returned their hostility in full measure and preached sermons called jeremiads lamenting New England's new commercial orientation. The Reverend Increase Mather (Cotton Mather's

father) reminded his congregation in 1676 that "*Religion and not the World* was that which our Fathers came hither for."

But Mather spoke for the past, not the future or even for his own contemporaries. By the 1670s, New England and the other American colonies were deeply enmeshed in an intricate international trading network. The seventeenth-century colonies should not be seen as primitive, isolated, self-sufficient communities. Indeed, the early colonies were, if anything, more dependent on overseas markets and imported goods than was eighteenth-century America. During the 1600s, the colonies lacked sufficient population to support an elaborate internal economy. (For example, all attempts to establish ironworks or glass factories in the first decades of settlement failed because there simply were not enough colonial customers for their products.) Furthermore, the colonies' economic fortunes largely depended on the sale of their exports in foreign markets: furs, deerskins, tobacco, rice, indigo, fish, and timber products together formed the basis for Anglo-America's prosperity.

At mid-century, this valuable American commerce

attracted the attention of English officials seeking a new source of revenue after the disruptions of the Civil War. They realized that the colonies could make important contributions to England's economic well-being. Tobacco from the Chesapeake and sugar from the West Indies had obvious value, but other colonial products also had profitable potential. The king needed tax revenues, and English merchants wanted to ensure that they—not their Dutch rivals—reaped the benefits of trading with the English colonies. Parliament and the restored Stuart monarchs accordingly began to design a system of laws that would, they hoped, confine the profits of colonial trade primarily to the mother country.

They based their commercial policy on a series of assumptions about the operations of the world's economic system. Collectively, these assumptions are usually called *mercantilism,* though neither the term itself nor a unified mercantilist theory was formulated until a century later. The economic world was seen as a collection of national states, each competing for shares of a finite amount of wealth. What one nation gained was automatically another nation's loss. Each nation's goal was to become as economically self-sufficient as possible while maintaining a favorable balance of trade with other countries (that is, exporting more than it imported). Colonies had an important role to play in such a scheme. They could supply the mother country with valuable raw materials to be consumed at home or sent abroad, and they could serve as a market for the mother country's manufactured goods.

Parliament applied that mercantilist theory to the American colonies in a series of laws known as the Navigation Acts. The major acts—passed in 1651,

Navigation Acts

1660, 1663, and 1673—established three main principles. First, only English or colonial merchants and ships could engage in trade in the colonies. Second, certain valuable American products could be sold only in the mother country. At first these "enumerated" goods were wool, sugar, tobacco, indigo, ginger, and dyes; later acts added rice, naval stores (masts, spars, pitch, tar, and turpentine), copper, and furs to the list. Third, all foreign goods destined for sale in the colonies had to be shipped via England and pay English import duties. Some years later, a new series of laws declared a fourth principle: the colonies could not make or export items that competed with English products (such as wool clothing, hats, and iron).

The intention of the Navigation Acts was clear: American trade was to center on England. The mother country was to benefit from both colonial imports and exports. England had first claim on the most valuable colonial exports, and all foreign imports into the colonies had to pass through England first, enriching its customs revenues in the process. Moreover, English and colonial shippers were given a monopoly of the American trade. However, the American provinces, especially those in the north, did produce many goods that were not enumerated—such as fish, flour, and barrel staves. These products could be traded directly to foreign purchasers as long as they were carried in English or American ships.

The English authorities soon learned that it was easier to write mercantilist legislation than to enforce it. The many harbors of the American coast provided ready havens for smugglers, and colonial officials often looked the other way when illegally imported goods were offered for sale. In ports such as Curaçao in the Dutch West Indies, American merchants could easily dispose of enumerated goods and purchase foreign items on which duty had not been paid. Consequently, Parliament in 1696 enacted another Navigation Act designed to strengthen enforcement of the first four. This law established in America a number of vice-admiralty courts, which operated without juries. In England such courts dealt only with cases involving piracy, vessels taken as wartime prizes, and the like. But since American juries had already demonstrated a tendency to favor local smugglers over customs officers (a colonial customs service was started in 1671), Parliament decided to remove Navigation Act cases from the regular colonial courts.

England took another major step in colonial administration in 1696 by creating the Board of Trade and Plantations to replace the loosely structured standing committee of the Privy

Board of Trade Council that had handled colonial affairs since 1675. The fifteen-member Board of Trade thereafter served as the chief organ of government concerned with the American colonies. It gathered information, reviewed Crown appointments in America, scrutinized legislation passed by colonial assemblies, supervised trade policies, and advised successive ministries on colonial issues. Still, the Board of Trade did not have any direct powers of enforcement. Furthermore, it shared jurisdiction over American affairs not only with the customs service and the navy but also with the secretary of state for the southern department (the member of the ministry responsible for the colonies). In short, although the Stuart monarchs' reforms considerably improved the quality of colonial administration, supervision of the American provinces remained decentralized and haphazard.

Even inefficient enforcement of the Navigation Acts was too much for many colonists, and they resisted the laws in various ways—not only by attempting to circumvent them but also by formally protesting to the government in London. Governor William Berkeley of Virginia was among the most vocal critics of the new laws. Tobacco prices declined significantly after 1660, causing serious economic problems in both Virginia and Maryland. Thus when English officials asked Berkeley about the state of trade in Virginia, he responded unhesitatingly that great hardship had resulted from "that severe act of Parliament which excludes us from having any commerce with any nation in Europe but our own," thereby preventing the development of new markets for tobacco. But such protests had little effect, chiefly because policymakers in England were more concerned about preserving the revenues obtained from colonial trade than about any adverse impact the acts might have on the colonies.

COLONIAL POLITICAL DEVELOPMENT AND IMPERIAL REORGANIZATION

English officials who dealt with colonial administration in the 1670s and 1680s were confronted not only by resistance to the Navigation Acts but also by a bewildering array of colonial governments. Massachusetts Bay still functioned under its original corporate charter, and its New England neighbors Connecticut and Rhode Island had been granted similar corporate status by Charles II in 1662 and 1663, respectively. Virginia was a royal colony, and New York became one when its proprietor ascended the throne in 1685 as James II, but all the other mainland settlements were proprietorships. Further, the latter had varying political structures, for the royal charters gave the proprietors a great deal of leeway in governing their possessions.

Still, the political structures of the colonies shared certain characteristics. Most were ruled by a governor and a two-house legislature. In New England, the

Colonial Political Structures

governors were elected by the people or the legislature; in the Chesapeake, they were appointed by the king or the proprietor. A council, elected in some colonies and appointed in others, advised the governor on matters of policy and sometimes served as the province's highest court. The council also had a legislative function: initially its members met jointly with representatives elected by their districts to debate and vote on laws affecting the colony. But as time passed, the fundamental differences between the two legislative groups' purposes and constituencies led them to separate into two distinct houses. In Virginia, that important event occurred in 1663; in Massachusetts Bay it had happened earlier, in 1644. Thus developed the two-house legislature still used in almost all of the United States.

While provincial governments were taking shape, so too were local political institutions. In New England, elected selectmen governed the towns at first, but by the end of the century the town meeting, held at least annually and attended by most adult white townsmen, handled most matters of local concern. In the Chesapeake the same function was performed by the judges of the county court and by the parish vestry, a group of laymen charged with overseeing church affairs, whose power also encompassed secular concerns.

By late in the seventeenth century, therefore, the American colonists were accustomed to exercising a considerable degree of local political autonomy. The tradition of consent was especially firmly established in New England. Massachusetts, Connecticut, and Rhode Island were, in effect, independent entities, subject neither to the direct authority of the king

STUART MONARCHS OF ENGLAND
1660–1714

Monarch	Reign	Relation to Predecessor
Charles II	1660–1685	son
James II	1685–1688	brother
Mary ⎫	1688–1694	daughter
William ⎭	1688–1702	son-in-law
Anne	1702–1714	sister, sister-in-law

nor to a proprietor. Everywhere in the English colonies, white males owning more property than a stated minimum (which varied from province to province) expected to have an influential voice in how they were governed, and especially how they were taxed.

After James II became king, these expectations clashed with those of their monarch. The new king and his successors sought to bring order to the apparently chaotic state of colonial administration by tightening the reins of government and reducing the colonies' political autonomy. (Simultaneously, of course, they used the Navigation Acts to reduce the colonies' economic autonomy.) They began to chip away at the privileges granted in colonial charters and to reclaim proprietorships for the Crown. New Hampshire (1679), its parent colony Massachusetts (1691), New Jersey (1702), and the Carolinas (1729) all became royal colonies. The charters of Rhode Island, Connecticut, Maryland, and Pennsylvania were temporarily suspended as well, but were ultimately restored to their original status.

The most drastic reordering of colonial administration was attempted in 1686 through 1689, and its chief target was Puritan New England. Reports from America had convinced English officials that New England was a hotbed of smuggling. Moreover, the Puritans refused to allow freedom of religion and insisted on maintaining laws that often ran counter to English practice. New England thus seemed an appropriate place to exert English

Dominion of New England

authority with greater vigor. The charters of all the colonies from New Jersey to Maine (then part of Massachusetts) were revoked and a Dominion of New England was established in 1686 (see map, page 42). Sir Edmund Andros, the governor, was given immense power: all the assemblies were dissolved, and he needed only the consent of an appointed council to make laws and levy taxes.

New Englanders endured Andros's autocratic rule for more than two years. Then came the dramatic news that James II had been overthrown in a bloodless rebellion (known as the Glorious Revolution) and had been replaced on the throne by his daughter Mary and her husband, the Dutch prince William of Orange. Seizing the opportunity to rid themselves of the hated Dominion, New Englanders jailed Andros and his associates, proclaimed their loyalty to William and Mary, and wrote to England for instructions as to the form of government they should adopt. Most of Massachusetts Bay's political leadership hoped that the new monarchs would renew their original charter, which had been revoked in 1684 prior to the establishment of the Dominion.

In other American colonies too, the Glorious Revolution proved to be a signal for revolt. In Maryland the Protestant Association overturned the government of the Catholic proprietor, and in New York Jacob Leisler, a militia officer of German origin, assumed control of the government. Like the New Englanders, the Maryland and New

Glorious Revolution in America

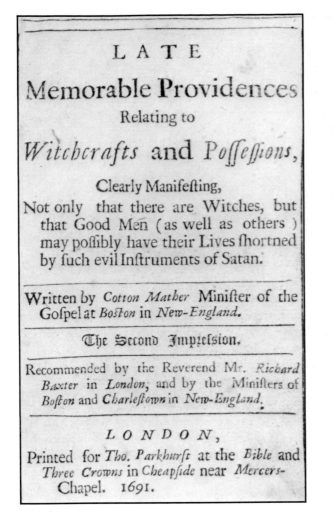

LATE
Memorable Providences
Relating to
Witchcrafts and *Poffeffions,*
Clearly Manifefting,
Not only that there are Witches, but
that Good Men (as well as others)
may poffibly have their Lives fhortned
by fuch evil Inftruments of Satan.

Written by *Cotton Mather* Minifter of the
Gofpel at *Bofton* in *New-England.*

The Second Impreffion.

Recommended by the Reverend Mr. *Richard
Baxter* in *London;* and by the Minifters of
Bofton and *Charleftown* in *New-England.*

LONDON,
Printed for *Tho. Parkhurft* at the *Bible* and
Three Crowns in *Cheapfide* near *Mercers-
Chapel.* 1691.

*Shortly before the hysteria at Salem Village, the prominent
New England minister Cotton Mather published this treatise
on witchcraft. The incidents in Salem Village were not isolated but rather reflected the New Englanders' everyday view
of the world. They often used witchcraft to explain otherwise
inexplicable events. Folger Shakespeare Library.*

York rebels allied themselves with the supporters of
William and Mary. They saw themselves as carrying
out the colonial phase of the English revolt against
Stuart absolutism. The problem was that the new
monarchs and their colonial administrators did not
view American events in the same light.

The Glorious Revolution occurred in the mother
country because members of Parliament feared that
once again, just as in Charles I's reign, a Stuart king
was attempting to seize absolute power. James II, like
his father, had levied taxes without parliamentary
approval. He had also announced his conversion to
Roman Catholicism. The Glorious Revolution affirmed
the supremacy of Parliament and of Protestantism
when Parliament offered the throne to the Protestants
William and Mary. But—and this was the difficulty
for the colonists—it did not directly affect English
policies toward America. William and Mary, like
James II, believed that the colonies were too independent and that England should exercise tighter
control over its unruly American possessions.

Consequently, the only American rebellion that
received royal sanction was that in Maryland, which
was approved primarily because of its anti-Catholic
thrust. In New York, Jacob Leisler was hanged for
treason, and Massachusetts, to the dismay of its Puritan
leaders, became a royal colony, complete with an
appointed governor. The province was allowed to
retain its town meeting system of local government
and to elect its council, but the new charter issued
in 1691 removed the traditional Puritan religious test
for voting. An Anglican parish was even established
in the heart of Boston. The "city upon a hill," at
least as envisioned by John Winthrop, was no more.

Compounding New England's difficulties in a time
of political uncertainty and economic change was a
war with the French and their Indian allies. King
Louis XIV of France allied himself with the deposed
James II, and England therefore declared war on
France in the summer of 1689. In Europe, the conflict,
which lasted until 1697, was known as the War of
the League of Augsburg, but the colonists called it
King William's War. The American phase of the war
was fought chiefly on the northern frontiers of New
England and New York; among the English settlements
devastated by enemy attacks in 1690 were Schenectady, New York, and Casco (Falmouth), Maine. Expeditions organized by the colonies against Montreal
and Quebec that same year both failed miserably,
and throughout the rest of the war New England
found itself on the defensive.

In this period of extreme stress there occurred the
famous outbreak of witchcraft accusations in Salem
Village (now Danvers), Massachusetts, a rural community adjoining the bustling port

**Witchcraft in
Salem Village**
of Salem Town. Like their contemporaries elsewhere, seventeenth-
century New Englanders believed
in the existence of witches, whose evil powers came
from the devil. If people could not find rational

Chapter 2: AMERICAN SOCIETY TAKES SHAPE, 1650–1720

explanations for their troubles, they tended to suspect they were bewitched. Before 1689, 103 New Englanders, most of them middle-aged women, had been accused of practicing witchcraft, chiefly by neighbors who had suffered misfortunes that they attributed to the suspected witch (with whom they usually had an ongoing dispute). Although most such accusations occurred singly, on occasion a witchcraft panic could result when one charge set off a chain reaction of similar charges (that happened in Hartford, Connecticut, in 1662 and 1663, for example). But nothing else in New England's history ever came close to matching the Salem Village cataclysm.

The crisis began in early 1692 when a group of adolescent girls accused some older women of having bewitched them. Before the hysteria spent itself ten months later, nineteen people (including several men, most of them related to accused female witches) had been hanged, another pressed to death by heavy stones, and more than one hundred persons jailed. Historians have proposed various explanations for

this puzzling episode, but to be understood it must be seen in its proper context—one of political and legal disorder, of Indian war, and of religious and economic change. It must have seemed to Puritan New Englanders as though their entire world was collapsing. At the very least they could have had no sense of security about their future.

Nowhere was that more true than in Salem Village, a farming town torn between old and new styles of life because of its position on the edge of a commercial center. And for no residents of the village was a feeling of insecurity sharper than it was for the girls who issued the initial accusations. Many of them had been orphaned in the recent Indian attacks on Maine; they were living in Salem Village as domestic servants. Their involvement with witchcraft began when they experimented with fortunetelling as a means of foreseeing their futures, in particular the identity of their eventual husbands. As the most powerless people in a town apparently powerless to affect its fate, they offered their fellow New Englanders a compelling explanation for the seemingly endless chain of troubles afflicting them: their province was under direct attack from the devil and his legion of witches. Interpreted thus, it is not the number of witchcraft accusations that seems surprising but rather their abrupt cessation in the fall of 1692.

There were two reasons for the rapid end to the crisis. First, the accusers had grown too bold. When they started to charge some of the colony's most distinguished and respected residents with being in league with the devil, members of the ruling elite began to doubt their veracity. Second, the new royal charter was fully implemented in late 1692, ending the worst period of political uncertainty and removing a major source of psychological stress. The war continued, and the Puritans were not entirely pleased with the charter, but at least order had formally been restored.

Over the course of the next three decades, Massachusetts and the rest of the English colonies in America accommodated themselves to the new imperial order. Most colonists did not like the class of alien officials who arrived in America determined to implement the policies of king and Parliament, but they adjusted to their demands and to the trade restrictions imposed by the Navigation Acts. They fought another imperial war—the War of the Spanish Succession, or Queen Anne's War—from 1702 to 1713, without enduring the psychological stress of the first, despite the heavy economic burdens the conflict imposed. Colonists who allied themselves with royal governors received patronage in the form of offices and land grants and composed "court parties" that supported English officials. Others, who were perhaps less fortunate in their friends, or more principled in defense of colonial autonomy (opinions differ), made up the opposition, or "country" interest. By the end of the first quarter of the eighteenth century, most men in both groups were native-born Americans, members of elite families whose wealth derived from staple-crop production in the south and commerce in the north.

During the seventy years from 1650 to 1720, then, the English colonies in America had changed dramatically. In 1650, there were just two isolated centers of population, New England and the Chesapeake; in 1720, nearly the entire eastern coast of mainland North America was in English hands. What had been

a migrant population was now mostly American-born; economies originally based on the fur trade had become far more complex and more closely linked with the mother country; and a wide variety of political structures had been reshaped into a more uniform pattern. Yet at the same time the introduction of large-scale slavery into the Chesapeake and the Carolinas had irrevocably differentiated their societies from those of the colonies to the north. Staple-crop production for the market was not the key distinguishing feature of the southern regional economies; rather, their uniqueness lay in their reliance on a racially based system of perpetual servitude.

By 1720, the essential elements of the imperial structure that would govern the colonies until 1775 were in place. And the regional economic systems originating in the late seventeenth and early eighteenth centuries continued to dominate American life for another century—until after independence had been won. This period, in other words, established the basic economic and political patterns that were to structure all subsequent changes in colonial American society.

SUGGESTIONS FOR FURTHER READING

General

Charles M. Andrews, *The Colonial Period of American History*, vol. 4 (1938); George Louis Beer, *The Old Colonial System, 1660–1754*, 2 vols. (1912); Carl Bridenbaugh, *Cities in the Wilderness: The First Century of Urban Life in America, 1625–1742* (1938); Wesley Frank Craven, *The Colonies in Transition, 1660–1713* (1968); Jack P. Greene and J. R. Pole, eds., *Colonial British America: Essays in the New History of the Early Modern Era* (1984); Gary Walton and James Shepherd, *The Economic Rise of Early America* (1979).

Africa and the Slave Trade

Jay Coughtry, *The Notorious Triangle: Rhode Island and the African Slave Trade 1700–1807* (1981); Philip D. Curtin, *The Atlantic Slave Trade: A Census* (1969); Basil Davidson, *Black Mother* (1969); David B. Davis, *The Problem of Slavery in Western Culture* (1966); Henry Gemery and Jan Hogendorn, eds., *The Uncommon Market: Essays in the Economic History of the Atlantic Slave Trade* (1979); Herbert Klein, *The Middle Passage* (1978); Daniel C. Littlefield, *Rice and Slaves: Ethnicity and the Slave Trade in Colonial South Carolina* (1981); James Rawley, *The Transatlantic Slave Trade: A History* (1981).

Blacks in Anglo-America

T. H. Breen and Stephen Innes, *"Myne Own Ground": Race and Freedom on Virginia's Eastern Shore, 1640–1676* (1980); Richard S. Dunn, *Sugar and Slaves: The Rise of the Planter Class in the English West Indies, 1624–1713* (1972); Lorenzo Johnson Green, *The Negro in Colonial New England* (1942); Edgar J. McManus, *Black Bondage in the North* (1973); Russell Menard, "From Servants to Slaves: The Transformation of the Chesapeake Labor System," *Southern Studies*, 16 (1977), 355–390; Edmund S. Morgan, *American Slavery, American Freedom: The Ordeal of Colonial Virginia* (1975); Peter H. Wood, *Black Majority: Negroes in Colonial South Carolina from 1670 Through the Stono Rebellion* (1974).

Indian-White Relations

Henry Bowden, *American Indians and Christian Missions: Studies in Cultural Conflict* (1981); Judith K. Brown, "Economic Organization and the Position of Women among the Iroquois," *Ethnohistory*, 17 (1970), 151–167; David H. Corkran, *The Creek Frontier, 1540–1783* (1967); Verner W. Crane, *The Southern Frontier, 1670–1732* (1929); Francis Jennings, *The Ambiguous Iroquois Empire* (1984); Elizabeth A. H. John, *Storms Brewed in Other Men's Worlds: The Confrontation of Indians, Spanish, and French in the Southwest, 1540–1795* (1975); Douglas Leach, *Flintlock and Tomahawk: New England in King Philip's War* (1958); Daniel K. Richter, "War and Culture: The Iroquois Experience," *William and Mary Quarterly*, 3rd ser., 40 (1983), 528–559; Allen W. Trelease, *Indian Affairs in Colonial New York: The Seventeenth Century* (1960); C. A. Weslager, *The Delaware Indians: A History* (1972); J. Leitch Wright, Jr., *The Only Land They Knew: The Tragic Story of the American Indians in the Old South* (1981).

New England

Bernard Bailyn, *The New England Merchants in the Seventeenth Century* (1955); Paul Boyer and Stephen Nissenbaum, *Salem Possessed: The Social Origins of Witchcraft* (1974); Richard Bushman, *From Puritan to Yankee: Character and the Social Order in Connecticut, 1690–1765* (1967); John Demos, *Entertaining Satan: Witchcraft and the Culture of Early New England* (1982); Mary Maples Dunn, "Saints and Sisters: Congregational and Quaker Women in the Early Colonial Period," *American Quarterly*, 30 (1978), 582–601; Perry Miller, *The New England Mind: From Colony to Province* (1953); Richard Pares, *Yankees and Creoles: The Trade Between North America and the West Indies Before the American Revolution* (1956); Robert G. Pope, *The Half-Way Covenant: Church Membership in Puritan New England* (1969); Laurel Thatcher Ulrich, *Good Wives: Image and Reality in the Lives of Women in Northern New England 1650–1750* (1982).

New Netherland and the Restoration Colonies

Edwin B. Bronner, *William Penn's "Holy Experiment": The Founding of Pennsylvania 1681–1701* (1962); Thomas J. Condon, *New York Beginnings: The Commercial Origins of New Netherland* (1968); Wesley Frank Craven, *New Jersey and the English Colonization of North America* (1964); Mary Maples Dunn, *William Penn: Politics and Conscience* (1967); Michael Kammen, *Colonial New York: A History* (1975); Robert C. Ritchie, *The Duke's Province: A Study of Politics and Society in Colonial New York, 1660–1691* (1977); Robert M. Weir, *Colonial South Carolina: A History* (1983).

Colonial Politics

Bernard Bailyn, "Politics and Social Structure in Virginia," in *Seventeenth-Century America: Essays in Colonial History*, ed. James M. Smith (1959), 90–115; Lois Green Carr and David W. Jordan, *Maryland's Revolution of Government 1689–1692* (1974); Richard R. Johnson, *Adjustment to Empire: The New England Colonies, 1675–1715* (1981); Kenneth A. Lockridge and Alan Kreider, "The Evolution of Massachusetts Town Government, 1640–1740," *William and Mary Quarterly*, 3rd ser., 23 (1966), 549–574; David S. Lovejoy, *The Glorious Revolution in America* (1972); Jack M. Sosin, *English America and the Restoration Monarchy of Charles II: Transatlantic Politics, Commerce, and Kinship* (1980).

Imperial Administration

Viola F. Barnes, *The Dominion of New England: A Study in British Colonial Policy* (1923); Thomas C. Barrow, *Trade and Empire: The British Customs Service in Colonial America 1660–1775* (1967); Lawrence A. Harper, *The English Navigation Laws: A Seventeenth-Century Experiment in Social Engineering* (1939); Michael Kammen, *Empire and Interest: The American Colonies and the Politics of Mercantilism* (1970); I. K. Steele, *Politics of Colonial Policy: The Board of Trade in Colonial Administration* (1968); Stephen Saunders Webb, *The Governors-General: The English Army and the Definition of the Empire, 1569–1681* (1979); Stephen Saunders Webb, *1676: The End of American Independence* (1984).

GROWTH AND DIVERSITY
1720–1770

CHAPTER 3

In June 1744, Dr. Alexander Hamilton, a thirty-four-year-old Scottish-born physician living in Annapolis, Maryland, paid his first visit to Philadelphia. There he encountered two quite different worlds. One consisted of men of his own status, the merchants and professionals he called "the better sort." Hamilton mingled with them at the Governor's Club, "a society of gentlemen that met at a taveren every night and converse on various subjects." The night Hamilton attended, the "entertaining" discussion focused on Cervantes and some English poets.

Hamilton reacted differently to the other world of Philadelphia, that composed of people he variously termed "rabble," "a strange medley," or "comicall, grotesque phizzes." Most spoke, he thought, "ignorantly," regardless of the subject. One evening he dined at a tavern with "a very mixed company" of twenty-five men. "There were Scots, English, Dutch, Germans, and Irish; there were Roman Catholicks, Church men, Presbyterians, Quakers, Newlightmen, Methodists, Seventh day men, Moravians, Anabaptists, and one Jew." Some discussed business, and a few argued about religion, but the "prevailing topick" was politics and the threat of war with France. Hamilton refused to be drawn into any of the conversations. As a gentleman, he consciously set himself apart from ordinary folk, commenting on their behavior but not participating in their exchanges.

And what of the women in Philadelphia? Hamilton met few of them, other than his landlady and one of her friends. "The ladies," he explained, "for the most part, keep att home and seldom appear in the streets, never in publick assemblies except att the churches or meetings." Hamilton was referring, of course, to women of "the better sort." He could hardly have walked the streets of the city without seeing many female domestic servants, market women, and wives of ordinary laborers going about their daily chores.

Despite his obvious biases, Dr. Hamilton was an astute observer of mid-eighteenth-century Philadelphia. The residents' chief employment, he wrote, "is traffick and mercantile business"; and the richest merchants of all were the Quakers. Members of that sect also controlled the government of Pennsylvania,

but, Hamilton noted, "the standing or falling of the Quakers in the House of Assembly depends upon their making sure the interest of the Palatines [Germans] in this province, who of late have turned so numerous that they can sway the votes which way they please." And Hamilton deplored the impact on the city of the Great Awakening, a religious revival that was then sweeping the colonies. "I never was in a place so populous where the gout [taste] for publick gay diversions prevailed so little," he remarked. "There is no such thing as assemblys of the gentry among them, either for dancing or musick; these they have an utter aversion to ever since Whitefield preached among them."

Hamilton's comments provide an excellent introduction to mid-eighteenth-century American life, for the patterns he observed in Philadelphia were not unique to that city. Although ethnic diversity was especially pronounced in urban areas, by midcentury non-English migrants were settling in many regions of the mainland colonies. Their arrival not only added noticeably to the total population, it also altered political balances worked out before 1720 and affected the religious climate by increasing the number of different sects. The diverse group of men Hamilton encountered in that tavern could have been duplicated in other cities and even in some rural areas.

Hamilton correctly recognized that the Quakers maintained control of Pennsylvania politics because they had managed to win the support of recent German immigrants. The ruling elites in other provinces handled immigrants in a way that eventually was to backfire on them: they ignored the newcomers, refusing to allow them adequate representation and government services. Through these tactics such elites, now primarily native-born, established stable political regimes in each of the colonies. They contended with English-born governors and councillors for control of their colonies' governmental machinery, and in some cases they won. These victories were to serve them well when they began battling for independence later in the century.

In addition, Hamilton accurately assessed the importance of commerce in Americans' lives. The web of imperial trade woven before 1720 became even more complex and all-encompassing during the next fifty years. Americans of all descriptions were tied to an international commercial system that fluctuated wildly for reasons having little to do with the colonies, but whose effects were nonetheless inescapable. As the colonies would learn when they attempted to break their trade ties with Great Britain at the time of the Revolution, they were heavily dependent on England for both imported manufactured goods and markets for their exports.

As a well-educated man, Dr. Hamilton was heavily influenced by the Enlightenment, the major European intellectual movement of the day. The Enlightenment stressed reason and empirical knowledge, deliberately discarding superstition and instinct as guides to human behavior. Hamilton, like other enlightened thinkers, believed above all in rationality. To him, God was a distant presence who had ordered the world, setting forth natural laws that humans could discover through careful investigation and logical thought. From this perspective came Hamilton's distaste for the Great Awakening, since that revival drew primarily on the Calvinistic concept of a God that people could never fully comprehend. Moreover, the hallmark of the Great Awakening was emotion, expressed in a single identifiable moment of conversion. To a believer in the primacy of reason, the passions of the newly converted were more than foolish—they were idiotic.

The Enlightenment affected Dr. Hamilton in another way as well, for it helped to create the elite world of which he was a part, a world that seemed so different from that of ordinary folk. Wealthy, well-read Americans participated in a transatlantic intellectual community, whereas most colonists of "the lesser sort" could neither read nor write. Hamilton and his peers lived in comfortable houses and entertained at lavish parties; most colonists struggled just to make ends meet. Hamilton could take a leisurely four-month journey for his health (for his visit to Philadelphia was but one stop on a long trip), but most Americans had to work daily from dawn to dark. The eighteenth century, then, brought an increasing gap between rich and poor. The colonies had always been composed of people of different ranks, but by the last half of the century the social and economic distance between those ranks had widened noticeably.

Above all, the eighteenth-century colonies present a picture of growth and diversity. Population increased dramatically, and the area settled by whites and blacks expanded until it filled almost all of the region between the Appalachian mountains and the Atlantic Ocean. At the same time, the colonies became more diverse; the two original regional economies (the Chesapeake and New England) became four (those two plus the middle colonies and the Lower South). By midcentury, many of the colonies, not just New York, were home to a variety of ethnic groups and religious sects. The urban population, though still tiny by today's standards, grew larger; and in the cities were found the greatest extremes of wealth and poverty. Such changes transformed the character of England's North American possessions. The colonies that revolted in unison against British rule after 1765 were very different from the colonies that revolted separately against Stuart absolutism in 1689.

POPULATION GROWTH AND ETHNIC DIVERSITY

One of the most striking characteristics of the mainland colonies in the eighteenth century was their rapid population growth. Only about 250,000 Euro- and Afro-Americans resided in the colonies in 1700; thirty years later that number had more than doubled, and by 1775 it had become 2.5 million. Although migration accounted for a considerable share of the growth, most of it resulted from natural increase. Once the difficult early decades had passed, the American population doubled approximately every twenty-five years. Such a rate of growth is essentially unparalleled in human history. It had a variety of causes, the chief one being the youthful marriage age of women (early twenties for whites, late teens for blacks); since married women became pregnant every two or three years, this meant that women normally bore five to eight children. Because the eighteenth-century colonies, especially those north of Virginia, were very healthful places to live, a large proportion of the children born reached maturity and

This portrait of an eighteenth-century family shows the typical colonial childbearing pattern in the large number of "stairstep" children, born at approximately two-year intervals. National Gallery of Art, Washington, D.C., Gift of Edgar William and Bernice Chrysler Garbisch.

began families of their own. As a result, in 1775 about half the American population, white and black, was under sixteen years of age. (In 1980, by contrast, only about one-third of the American population was under sixteen.)

Such a dramatic phenomenon did not escape the attention of contemporaries. As early as the 1720s, Americans began to point with pride to their fertility, citing population growth as evidence of the advantages of living in the colonies. In 1755 Benjamin Franklin published his *Observations Concerning the Increase of Mankind*, which predicted that in another century "the greatest Number of Englishmen will be on this Side the Water. What an Accession of Power to the British Empire by Sea as well as Land!" he rhapsodized. "What Increase of Trade and Navigation!"

Interestingly enough, Franklin's purpose in writing his *Observations* was to argue that Britain should

prevent Germans from migrating to Pennsylvania. Since the English population in America was increasing so rapidly, he asked, "why should the Palatine Boors be suffered to swarm into our Settlements? . . . Why should Pennsylvania, founded by the English, become a Colony of *Aliens*, who will shortly be so numerous as to Germanize us instead of our Anglifying them, and will never adopt our Language or Customs?"

Whether Franklin's fears were shared by a majority of his American-born contemporaries is not known. But the eighteenth-century migration to the English colonies was massive; it comprised approximately 375,000 whites and 275,000 blacks (see map). Because some of the whites (for example, convicts sentenced to exile by English courts) and all the blacks did not choose freely to come to the colonies, nearly half the eighteenth-century migrants moved to America against their will. That contrasts sharply with the nineteenth-century pattern of voluntary migration from Europe that is discussed in Chapter 10.

Africans made up the largest single racial or ethnic group that came to the colonies during the eighteenth century. More important than the number of black migrants, however, is the fact that in the first half of the century the black population of the mainland colonies began to grow faster through natural increase than through importation. In the slaveholding societies of South America and the Caribbean, a surplus of males over females and appallingly high mortality rates together produced very different slave population patterns. There, only massive and continuing importations from Africa were able to maintain the enslaved work force at adequate levels. South Carolina, where rice cultivation was difficult and unhealthy work (chiefly because malaria-carrying mosquitoes bred in the rice swamps) and where planters preferred to purchase males, bore some resemblance to such colonies in that it too required a constant influx of Africans. But in the Chesapeake the black population grew primarily through natural increase after 1740. As shall be seen later in this chapter, that increase had significant implications for the society and economy of the region.

The German migrants who so worried Franklin numbered about 100,000. Most of them emigrated from the Rhineland between 1730 and 1755, usually landing in Philadelphia. They became known locally as the Pennsylvania Dutch (a corruption of *Deutsch*); late in the century they and their descendants made up one-third of the colony's residents. But many other Germans moved west and then south along the eastern slope of the Appalachian mountains, eventually finding homes in western Maryland and Virginia. Others sailed first to Charleston or Savannah and settled in the interior of South Carolina or Georgia. A smaller number found land along the Mohawk River Valley in northern New York. The German immigrants belonged to a wide variety of Protestant sects—primarily Lutheran, German Reformed, and Moravian—and therefore added to the already substantial religious diversity of the middle colonies.

Many Germans arrived in America as redemptioners. Under that variant form of indentured servitude, migrants paid as much as possible of the cost of their

German Immigration

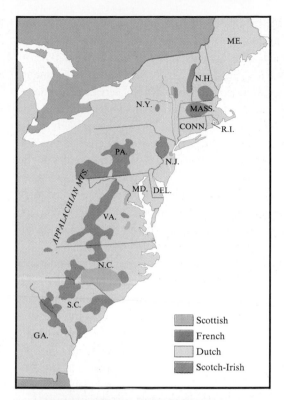

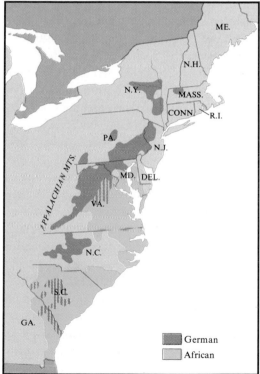

Non-English Ethnic Groups in the British Colonies, ca. 1775

passage before sailing from Europe. After they landed in the colonies, the rest of the fare had to be "redeemed." If poor folk had no friends or relatives in America willing to take on the burden of payment, they were indentured for a term of service proportional to the amount they still owed. That term could be as brief as a year or two, but was more likely to be four. In contrast to the unmarried English indentured servants who had migrated to the Chesapeake in the seventeenth century, German redemptioners often traveled in family groups. In America, the family was sometimes divided among different purchasers, or one member (often a son or daughter) was indentured to pay for the others' passages.

The largest group of white non-English immigrants to America was the Scotch-Irish, chiefly descended from Presbyterian Scots who had settled in Protestant portions of Ireland during the seventeenth century. Perhaps as many as 250,000 Scotch-Irish people moved to the colonies. Fleeing economic distress and religious discrimination at home—Irish law favored Anglicans over Presbyterians and other dissenters—they were lured as well by hopes of obtaining land in America. Like the Germans, the Scotch-Irish often landed in Philadelphia. They also moved west and south from that city, settling chiefly in the western portions of Pennsylvania, Maryland, Virginia, and the Carolinas. Frequently unable to afford to buy any acreage, they squatted on land belonging to Indian tribes, land speculators, or colonial governments.

Scotch-Irish and Scottish Immigration

The more than 25,000 Scots who came directly to America from Scotland should not be confused with the Scotch-Irish. Many Scottish immigrants were supporters of Stuart claimants to the throne of England, or Jacobites (so called because the Latin name for James was Jacobus). After the death of William and Mary's successor Queen Anne in 1714, the British throne passed to the German house of Hanover, in the person of King George I. In 1715 and again in 1745, Jacobite rebels attempted unsuccessfully to capture the crown for the Stuart pretender, and many were exiled to America as punishment for their treason. Most of the Jacobites settled in North Carolina. Ironically, they tended to become loyalists during the Revolutionary War because of their strong commitment to monarchy. Another wave of Scottish immigration began in the 1760s and flowed mainly into northern New York; most of these new arrivals settled as tenants on large tracts of land in the Mohawk River valley.

Because of these migration patterns and the concentration of slaveholding in the South, half the colonial population south of New England was of non-English origin by 1775. Whether the migrants assimilated readily into Anglo-American culture depended largely on the patterns of settlement, the size of the group, and the strength of the migrants' ties to their common culture. The Huguenots, for instance, were French Protestants who fled religious persecution in their homeland after 1685. They settled in tiny enclaves in American cities like Charleston and New York, but were unable to sustain either their language or their distinctive religious practices. Within two generations they had been almost wholly absorbed into the dominant culture. The equally small group of colonial Jews, by contrast, largely maintained a separate identity. The Jews in early America were Sephardic in origin, most of them descended from persons who had originally migrated first to the Netherlands to escape persecution in Spain and Portugal, and from there to the Dutch colonies in the New World. In a few cities—most notably New York and Newport, Rhode Island—they established synagogues and worked actively to preserve their culture (for example, by opposing intermarriage with Christians).

Members of the larger groups of migrants (the Germans, Scotch-Irish, and Scots) found it easier to sustain Old World ways if they wished. Countless local areas of the colonies were settled almost exclusively by one group or another. Near Frederick, Maryland, a visitor would have heard more German than English; in Anson and Cumberland Counties, North Carolina, that same visitor might have thought she was in Scotland. Where migrants from different countries settled in the same region, ethnic antagonisms often surfaced. One German clergyman, for example, explained his efforts to stop German young people from marrying persons of different ethnic origins by asserting that the Scotch-Irish were "lazy, dissipated and poor" and that "it is very seldom that German and English blood is happily united in wedlock."

Recognizing that it was to their benefit to keep other racial and ethnic groups divided, the dominant whites on occasion deliberately fostered such antagonisms. When the targets of their policies were Eu-

Spencer Hall shipyard, Gray's Inn Creek, Kent County, Maryland, about 1760. The earliest known view of a Chesapeake Bay shipyard, this oil painting on a wooden panel shows the wide variety of ships that sailed on the bay, as well as (in the background) lumbermen preparing a supply of timber.   Maryland Historical Society.

ropean migrants, the goal was the maintenance of political and economic power. When the targets were Indians and blacks, as they were in South Carolina, the stakes were considerably higher. In 1758 one official remarked, "it has been allways the policy of this government to create an aversion in them [Indians] to Negroes." The reason? South Carolina whites, who composed a minority of the population of the colony, wanted to prevent Indians and blacks from making common cause against them. So that slaves would not try to run away to join the Indians, whites hired Indians as slave catchers. So that Indians would not trust blacks, whites used blacks as soldiers in Indian wars.

Although the dominant elites probably would have preferred to ignore the colonies' growing racial and ethnic diversity, they could not do so for long and still maintain their power. When such men decided to lead a revolution in the 1770s, they recognized that they needed the support of non-English Americans. Not by chance, then, did they begin to speak of "the rights of man," rather than "English liberties," when they sought recruits for their cause.

ECONOMIC GROWTH AND DEVELOPMENT

The eighteenth-century American economy was characterized more by sharp fluctuations than by a consistent long-term trend. There were two primary causes of the fluctuations: the impact of European wars and variations in the overseas demand for American products. The dramatic increase in colonial population was the only source of stability in the shifting economic climate.

Each year the rising population generated ever-greater demands for goods and services, which led to the development of small-scale colonial manufacturing and to the creation of a complex network of internal trade. As the area of settlement expanded, new roads, bridges, mills, and stores were built to serve the new communities. A lively coastal trade developed; by the late 1760s more than half (54 percent) of the vessels leaving Boston harbor were sailing to other mainland colonies rather than to foreign ports. Such ships were not only collecting goods for export and distributing imports, but also selling items made in America. In the middle decades of the eighteenth century, the colonies finally began to move away from their earlier pattern of near-total dependence on Europe for manufactured goods. For the first time, the American population sustained sufficient demand to encourage home-grown manufacturing enterprises.

The major energizing—yet destabilizing—influence on the colonial economy was foreign trade. Colonial prosperity still depended heavily on overseas demand for American products like tobacco, rice, indigo, fish, and barrel staves, for it was through the sale of such items that the colonists earned the credit they needed to purchase English and European imports. If the demand for American exports slowed, the colonists' income dropped and so did their demand for imported goods. Accordingly, even small merchants could be affected by sudden economic downswings they had not anticipated. In 1754, a woman who ran a small dry-goods store in Boston reported to her brother (her chief financial backer) that another female merchant had been "obliged to sell all her goods this week," to pay her creditors. "Such things make me double my diligence," she commented, "and endeavor to keep my self as clear [from debt] as is possible."

Despite fluctuations, there was a slow growth in the economy over the course of the eighteenth century, which resulted in higher standards of living for all property-owning Americans. Estate

Rising Standard of Living

inventories show that in the first two decades of the century households began to acquire amenities like crude earthenware dishes (for eating, food storage, and dairying), chairs, and knives and forks. (Seventeenth-century colonists had used only spoons.) Diet also improved; inventories reveal larger quantities and wider varieties of stored foods. After 1750, luxury items like silver plate appeared in the homes of the wealthy, and the "middling sort" started to purchase imported English ceramics and teapots. Even the poorest property owners showed some improvement in the number and type of their household possessions. Probably this was caused by the falling price of British manufactures relative to the income Americans earned from their exports.

Yet the benefits of economic growth were not evenly distributed: wealthy Americans improved their position relative to other colonists. The native-born elite families who dominated American political, economic, and social life by 1750 were those who had begun the century with sufficient capital to take advantage of the changes caused by population growth. They were the urban merchants who exported raw materials and imported luxury goods, the large landowners who rented small farms to German or Scotch-Irish tenants, the slave traders who supplied white planters with their bondspeople, and the owners of rum distilleries. The rise of this group of monied families helped to make the social and economic structure of mid-eighteenth-century America more rigid than it had been previously. The new non-English immigrants did not have the opportunities for advancement that had greeted their English predecessors.

At the very bottom of the social scale, poverty increased in colonial cities, particularly Boston. Families of urban laborers lived on the edge of destitution.

Urban Poverty

In Philadelphia, for instance, a male laborer's average annual earnings fell short of the amount needed to supply his family with the bare necessities. Even in a good year, then, other members of the family (wife or children) had to do wage work; in a bad year, the family could be reduced to beggary. By the 1760s, urban poor-relief systems were overwhelmed with applicants for assistance, and some cities began to build workhouses or almshouses to shelter the growing number of poor people. How could that have happened at a time when the lot of the average American family was improving?

A possible answer is that, although the living standard of property owners was rising, some colonists were being deprived of any access to property. Such

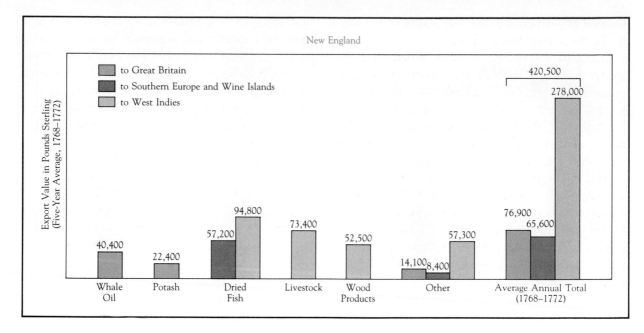

New England

Regional Trading Patterns: New England *Source: James F. Shepherd and Gary M. Walton, Shipping, Maritime Trade, and the Economic Development of Colonial America (1972), Tables 2–5, pp. 211–226.*

people clustered in the cities where they could more easily find work. Another explanation might be that poverty was a stage people passed through at particular points in their lives rather than a constant condition. That is, a laborer's family afflicted by disease, a youth not yet established in a trade, a recent immigrant, or an elderly or infirm person might be among the poor at one time but not at another. Again, such people were more likely to be found in a city than in the countryside. A third answer points to the preponderance of women, mostly widows, among the urban poor. Since women in the eighteenth century, like women today, were paid about half the wages men earned for the same or comparable work, it may well be that urban poverty was primarily a sex-typed phenomenon, with poor *men* being the aberration rather than the rule. In any event, it is not clear whether poverty was rising in rural areas, and that was where more than 90 percent of the American population lived.

Within this overall picture, it is important to distinguish among the various regions: New England, the middle colonies, the Chesapeake, and the Lower South (the Carolinas and Georgia). In New England, three elements combined to exert a major influence on economic development: the nature of the landscape, New England's leadership in colonial shipping, and the impact of the imperial wars. New England's soil was rocky and thin, and farmers did not normally produce large surpluses of grains or other crops to sell abroad. Farms were worked primarily by family members; the region had relatively few hired laborers. It also had the lowest average wealth per freeholder in the colonies. New England had its share of wealthy men, though; they were the merchants and professionals whose income was drawn from overseas trade, primarily with the West Indies.

Boston's central position in the New England economy and its role as a shipbuilding center ensured that it would be directly affected by any resumption of warfare. Thus when England declared war on Spain in 1739, setting off the conflict that was known in Europe as the War of the Austrian Succession and in America as King George's War, the first impact on Boston's economy

New England and King George's War

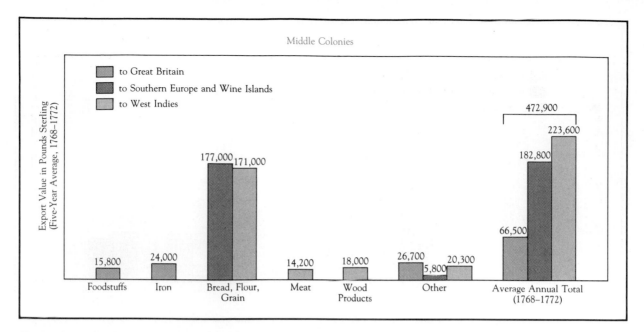

Regional Trading Patterns: Middle Colonies *Source: James F. Shepherd and Gary M. Walton, Shipping, Maritime Trade, and the Economic Development of Colonial America (1972), Tables 2–5, pp. 211–226.*

was positive. Ships—and sailors—were in great demand to serve as privateers (privately owned vessels authorized by the British to capture the enemy's commercial shipping). Wealthy merchants like Thomas Hancock became even wealthier by profiting from contracts to supply military expeditions.

But Boston suffered heavy losses of manpower both in several Caribbean battles and in forays against the French in Canada after 1744, when France became Spain's ally. The most successful expedition was also the most costly. In 1745 a Massachusetts force captured the French fortress of Louisbourg, which guarded the mouth of the St. Lawrence River, but the colony had to levy extremely heavy taxes on its residents to pay for the expensive effort. For decades Boston's economy felt the continuing effects of King George's War. The town was left with unprecedented numbers of widows and children on its relief rolls, the boom in shipbuilding ended when the war did, and taxes remained high. As a final blow, Britain gave Louisbourg back to France in the treaty of Aix-la-Chapelle (1748).

Because of one key difference between the northernmost and the middle colonies, the latter were more positively affected by King George's War and

its aftermath. That difference was the greater fertility of the soil in New York and Pennsylvania, where commercial farming was already the norm. (An average Pennsylvania farm family consumed only 40 percent of what it produced, selling the rest.) New York and New Jersey both had many tenant farmers, who rented acreage from large landowners and often paid their rental fees by sharing crops with their landlords. Prosperous middle-colony property holders were thus in an ideal position to profit from the wartime demand for foodstuffs, especially in the West Indies. After the war a series of poor grain harvests in Europe caused flour prices to rise even more rapidly. Philadelphia and New York, which could draw on large, fertile grain- and livestock-producing areas, took the lead in the foodstuffs trade while Boston, which had no such fertile hinterland, found its economy stagnating.

Prosperity of the Middle Colonies

The increased European demand for grain (and consequent higher prices) in the mid-eighteenth century also had a significant impact on the Chesapeake. After 1745, some Chesapeake planters began to convert tobacco fields to wheat and corn, because the

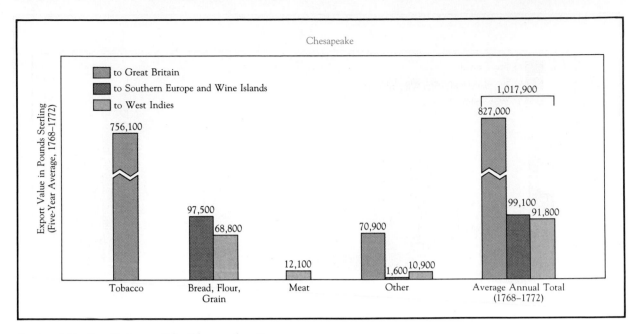

Chesapeake

Export Value in Pounds Sterling (Five-Year Average, 1768–1772)

- to Great Britain
- to Southern Europe and Wine Islands
- to West Indies

Tobacco: 756,100

Bread, Flour, Grain: 97,500 / 68,800

Meat: 12,100

Other: 70,900 / 1,600 / 10,900

Average Annual Total (1768–1772): 1,017,900 / 827,000 / 99,100 / 91,800

Regional Trading Patterns: The Chesapeake Source: James F. Shepherd and Gary M. Walton, Shipping, Maritime Trade, and the Economic Development of Colonial America *(1972), Tables 2–5, pp. 211–226.*

price of grain was rising faster than that of tobacco. They saw the benefit of diversifying their crops, so they would not be so dependent on one product for their income. But tobacco still ruled the region, and it was the largest single export from the mainland colonies as a whole. (The value of tobacco exports was nearly double that of grain products, the next contender.) Thus it is useful to focus briefly on tobacco's continuing impact on the Chesapeake.

Two major results of the region's concentration on tobacco growing can be discerned in the mid-eighteenth century. The first derived from the sub-stitution of enslaved for indentured labor. The offspring of slaves were also slaves, whereas the children of servants were free. The conse-quences of that fact were not clear until the black population of the Chesapeake began to grow through natural increase, which occurred between 1720 and 1740. It then became evident that a planter who began with only a few slave families could watch the size of his labor force increase steadily over the years without making additional major investments in workers. Not co-

Natural Increase of Black Population

incidentally, the first truly large Chesapeake plan-tations appeared in the 1740s. Some years later, the slaveholder Thomas Jefferson indicated that he fully understood the connections when he declared, "I consider a woman who brings a child every two years more profitable than the best man of the farm. What she produces is an addition to the capital, while his labors disappear in mere consumption."

The second effect of tobacco cultivation on the Chesapeake related to patterns of trade. In the first half of the eighteenth century, wealthy planters served as middlemen in the tobacco trade. They collected and shipped tobacco grown by their less prosperous neighbors, extended credit to them, and ordered the English imports they wanted. Indeed, they often prof-ited more from fulfilling these functions than from selling their own crops. In the process, though, they went heavily into debt to English merchants, because the entire system operated on credit.

Beginning in the 1740s, a major change in the system of marketing tobacco affected all Chesapeake planters, though in varying ways. That change was the entry into the tobacco trade of Scottish merchants, who organized

Scots Factors

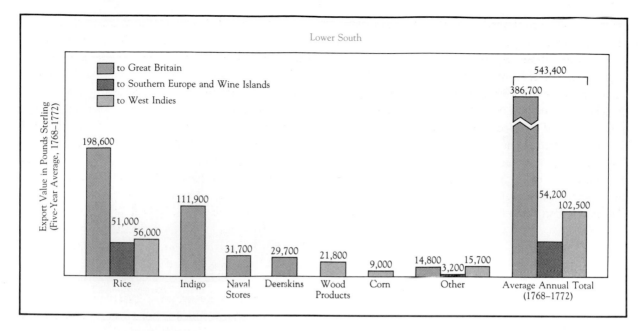

Lower South

Legend:
- to Great Britain
- to Southern Europe and Wine Islands
- to West Indies

Export Value in Pounds Sterling (Five-Year Average, 1768-1772)

Rice: 198,600 / 51,000 / 56,000
Indigo: 111,900
Naval Stores: 31,700
Deerskins: 29,700
Wood Products: 21,800
Corn: 9,000
Other: 14,800 / 3,200 / 15,700
Average Annual Total (1768-1772): 386,700 / 54,200 / 102,500 — 543,400

Regional Trading Patterns: The Lower South *Source: James F. Shepherd and Gary M. Walton,* Shipping, Maritime Trade, and the Economic Development of Colonial America *(1972), Tables 2–5, pp. 211–226.*

their efforts differently from their London-based competitors. They stationed representatives (called factors) in the Chesapeake to purchase tobacco, arrange for shipments, and sell imports. The arrival of the Scots factors created genuine competition for the first time and thus pushed up tobacco prices. The Scots provided planters with an alternative system for marketing their crops. Large planters could avoid going into debt, and smaller planters could decrease their economic dependence on their wealthier neighbors. When the Chesapeake finally began to develop port towns later in the century, they grew up in centers of Scots mercantile activity (like Norfolk, Virginia) or in regions that had largely converted to grain production (like Baltimore, Maryland).

Lower South Trade Patterns

The Lower South, like the Chesapeake, depended on staple crops and an enslaved labor force for its prosperity, but its pattern of economic growth was distinctive. In contrast to tobacco prices, which rose slowly through the middle decades of the century, rice prices climbed steeply, doubling by the late 1730s. The sharp rise was caused primarily by a heavy demand for rice in southern Europe.

Because Parliament removed rice from the list of enumerated products in 1730, South Carolinians were able to do what colonial tobacco planters never could: trade directly with continental Europe. But dependence on European sales had its drawbacks, as rice growers discovered at the outbreak of King George's War in 1739. Trade with the continent was completely disrupted, rice prices plummeted, and South Carolina entered a depression from which it did not emerge until the following decade. Still, by the 1760s prosperity had returned; indeed, in that period the Lower South experienced more rapid economic growth than the other regions of the colonies. Partly as a result, it had the highest average wealth per freeholder in Anglo-America by the time of the Revolution.

Each region of the colonies, then, had its own economic rhythm derived from the nature of its export trade. King George's War initially helped New England and hurt the Lower South, but in the long run those effects were reversed. In the Chesapeake and the middle colonies, the war initiated a long period of prosperity. The variety of these economic experiences points up a crucial fact about the eighteenth-century mainland colonies: they did not compose a unified

Chapter 3: GROWTH AND DIVERSITY, 1720–1770

whole. They were linked economically into regions, but they had few political or social ties beyond or even within those regions.

Despite the growing coastal trade, the individual colonies' economic fortunes depended not on their neighbors in America but rather on the shifting markets of Europe and the West Indies. Had it not been for an unprecedented crisis in the British imperial system (which will be discussed in Chapter 4), it is hard to see how they could have been persuaded to join in a common endeavor. Even with that impetus, as will become evident, they found unity difficult to maintain.

DAILY LIFE

The basic unit of colonial society was the household. Headed by a white male (or perhaps his widow), the household was the chief mechanism of production and consumption in the colonial economy. Its members—bound by ties of blood or servitude—worked together to produce goods for consumption or sale. The white male head of the household represented it to the outside world, serving in the militia or political posts, casting the household's sole vote in elections. He managed the finances and held legal authority over the rest of the family—his wife, his children, and his servants or slaves. (Eighteenth-century Americans used the word *family* for people who lived together in one house, whether or not they were blood kin.) Such households were considerably larger than American families today; in 1790, the average home contained 5.7 whites. And most of those large families were nuclear—that is, they did not include extended kin like aunts, uncles, or grandparents.

The vast majority of eighteenth-century American families—more than 90 percent of them—lived in rural areas. Therefore nearly all adult white men were farmers and all adult white women farm wives. Though men might work as millers, blacksmiths, or carpenters, and women might sell surplus farm produce to neighbors, they typically did so in addition to their

Sexual Division of Labor among White Americans

primary agricultural tasks. In colonial America, as in the societies discussed in Chapter 1, household tasks were allocated by gender. The master, his sons, and his male servants or slaves performed one set of chores; the mistress, her daughters, and her female servants or slaves, an entirely different set. So rigid were the gender classifications that when households for some reason lacked a master or mistress the appropriate jobs were often not done. For example, a foreign traveler visiting a Pennsylvania farm remarked that its owner, a bachelor, did not keep poultry or make cheese or clothing because "these domestic farm industries . . . can be carried on well only by women." Only in emergencies and for brief periods of time would women do "men's work" or men do women's.

The mistress of the rural household was responsible for what were termed indoor affairs. She and her female helpers prepared the food, kept the house clean and neat, did the laundry, and often made the clothing. In eighteenth-century America, these basic chores were enormously complex and time-consuming. Preparing food involved planting and cultivating a garden, harvesting and preserving vegetables, salting and smoking meat, drying apples and pressing cider, milking cows and making butter and cheese, not to mention cooking and baking. Making clothing (the chief job of daughters) meant processing raw wool and flax fibers, spinning thread, weaving cloth, dyeing and softening the cloth, and finally cutting out and sewing garments by hand. Nor was keeping one's clothes and home clean an easy job, since the soap had to be made in the household—from ashes, rendered fat, and lye—and water had to be carried by hand from a well or stream. No wonder one harried Long Island housewife filled her diary in 1768 and 1769 with such entries as these: "It has been a tiresome day it is now Bed time and I have not had won minutts rest"; "full of freting discontent dirty and miserabel both yesterday and today."

The head of the household and his male helpers, responsible for outdoor affairs, also had heavy work loads. They had to plant and cultivate fields, build fences, chop wood for the fireplaces, harvest and market crops, and butcher cattle and hogs to provide the household with meat. Only in the plantation South and in northern cities could even a few adult white males lead lives free from arduous physical

In 1775, a Connecticut woman, Prudence Punderson, created this needlework picture, which she entitled The First, Second, and Last Scene of Mortality. *At right she depicted a baby tended by a black servant; at center a mature woman doing needlework; and at left a coffin. Thus she summed up a woman's life from birth to the grave, with traditionally female work—like her picture itself—at its core.* Connecticut Historical Society, Hartford.

labor. Indeed, so extensive was the work involved in maintaining an eighteenth-century farm household that a married couple could not do it alone. They had to have help—if not children, then servants or slaves.

Farm households were governed by the seasons and by the hours of daylight. (Candles too had to be manufactured at home; they were too precious to be wasted, so most people rose and went to bed with the sun.) Men and boys had the most leisure in the winter, when there were no crops that needed care. Women and girls were freest in the summer, before embarking on autumn food preservation and winter spinning and weaving. Other activities, including education, had to be subordinated

Rhythms of Rural Life

to seasonal work. Thus farm boys attended school in the winter, and their sisters went to classes in the summer. The seasons also affected travel plans. Because the roads were muddy in spring and fall, most visiting took place in summer and, in the North, in winter, when sleighs could be used.

Because most farm families were relatively isolated from their neighbors and had these heavy seasonal work obligations, rural folk took advantage of every possible opportunity for socializing. Men taking grain to be milled would stop at a crossroads tavern for a drink and conversation with friends. Women gathering to assist at childbirth would drink tea and exchange news. Barbecues and week-long house parties were popular among southern planter families. The Reverend Charles Woodmason, an Anglican missionary, found to his consternation that residents of the Carolina backcountry regarded his church services as social events. "No making of them sit still during Service—but they will be in and out—forward and backward the whole Time (Women especially) as Bees to and fro to their Hives," he wrote of one congregation in 1768. And work itself provided opportunities for visiting. Harvest frolics, corn-husking bees, barn raisings, quilting parties, spinning bees, and other communal endeavors brought together neighbors from miles around, often for several days of work followed by feasting, dancing, and singing in the evenings.

The few eighteenth-century colonial cities were nothing but large towns by today's standards. (The largest, Boston and Philadelphia, had just seventeen thousand and thirteen thousand inhabitants, respectively.) Still, city life differed considerably from rural life. A young Massachusetts man who had moved to Providence described one difference to his farmer father: the city, he remarked, was filled with "Noise and Confusion and Disturbance. I must confess, the jolts of Waggons, the Ratlings of Coaches, the crying of Meat for the Market, the Hollowing of Negros and the ten thousand jinggles and Noises, that continually Surround us in every Part almost of the Town, Confuse my thinking." In the cities, lives were governed by clocks instead of the sun and by work schedules that did not depend so wholly on the seasons. True, a city wife might preserve a ham in the fall, and a merchant's business might vary according to the weather (which determined sailing schedules), but city dwellers were not inextricably tied to the seasons. Year-round, they could purchase foodstuffs and wood at city markets and cloth at dry-goods stores. They could see friends any time they wished. Wealthy urbanites had plenty of leisure time to read, take walks around town or rides in the countryside, play cards, or attend dances, plays, and concerts, for by midcentury most colonial cities had theaters and assembly halls.

Rhythms of Urban Life

City people also had much more contact with the world beyond their own homes than did their rural compatriots. By the middle of the century, every major city had at least one weekly newspaper, and most had two or three. Newspapers printed the latest "advices from London" (usually two to three months

In eighteenth-century colonial cities, where most of the buildings were constructed of wood, fire was an ever-present danger. Thus the young men of the towns formed volunteer fire companies, which not only served a useful purpose but also provided their members with convivial companionship. New York Public Library.

old) and news of events in other English colonies, as well as reports on matters of local interest. The local newspaper was available at taverns and inns, so people who could not afford to buy it could nevertheless read it. (Even illiterates could acquaint themselves with the latest news, since the paper was often read aloud by literate customers.) However, contact with the outside world also had drawbacks. Sailors sometimes brought exotic and deadly diseases into port with them. Cities like Boston, New York, and Philadelphia endured terrible epidemics of smallpox and yellow fever, which the countryside largely escaped.

Cities attracted many migrants from rural areas. Young men came to learn a skill through an apprenticeship, for cities housed the artisans who printed books and newspapers, crafted fine furniture, made shoes, or created expensive gold or silver items. Ordinary laborers too came seeking work, and widows came looking for a means of supporting their families. Without an adult man in the household, a woman had a difficult time running a farm. Consequently, widows tended to congregate in port cities, where they could sell their services as nurses, teachers, seamstresses, servants, or prostitutes, or (if they had some capital) open shops, inns, or boardinghouses. In rural areas, where the economy was based largely on subsistence agriculture and most families produced nearly all their own necessities, there was little demand for the services that landless women and men could perform. In the cities, though, someone always needed another servant, blacksmith, or laundress.

Only widows and the very few never-married women could legally run independent businesses. An unmarried colonial woman had the same legal rights as a man (with the exception of vot-

Status of Women

ing), but an Anglo-American wife was subordinate to her husband in law as well as custom. Under the common-law doctrine of coverture, a married woman became one person with her husband. She could not sue or be sued, make contracts, buy or sell property, or draft a will. Any property she owned prior to marriage became her husband's after the wedding; any wages she earned were legally his; and all children of the marriage fell under his absolute control. Moreover, since divorces were practically impossible to obtain, men and women had little chance to escape from a bad marriage.

Anglo-American men expected their wives to defer to their judgment. Most wives seem to have accepted secondary status without murmuring. When girls married, they were commonly advised to devote themselves to their husbands' interests. "Let your Dress your Conversation & the whole Business of your life be to please your Husband & to make him happy & you need not fail of being so your self," a New Yorker told his daughter in the 1730s. That women followed such advice is evident in their diaries. A Virginia woman remarked, for example, that "one of my first resolutions I made after marriage, was never to hold disputes with my husband." It was wives' responsibility, she declared, "to give up to their husbands" whenever differences of opinion arose between them. Not until very late in the eighteenth

century, during and after the American Revolution, would such women as Abigail Adams begin to question these traditional notions.

The man's legal and customary authority extended to his children as well. Indeed, childrearing was the one task regularly undertaken by both men and women in colonial America; all their other chores were divided by sex. Women cared for infants and toddlers, but thereafter both parents disciplined the children. The father set the general standards by which they were raised and usually had the final word on such matters as their education or vocational training. White parents normally insisted on unquestioning obedience from their offspring, and many freely used physical punishment to break a child's will. In the homes of America's elite families, though, more nurturant childrearing practices seem to have prevailed. In such households, the most burdensome chores were performed by white or black servants, freeing parents to spend more time with their offspring and reducing the need for strict disciplinary measures. The relaxed upbringing of these wealthy youngsters foreshadowed nineteenth-century white Americans' greater indulgence of their children.

Not all families in the English colonies, of course, were white. And more than 95 percent of black families were held in perpetual bondage. In South Carolina, a majority of the population was black; in Georgia, about half; and in the Chesapeake, 40 percent. Although the populations of some backcountry areas of Virginia, Maryland, and the Carolinas were less than one-fifth black, some parts of the Carolina lowcountry were nearly 90 percent black by 1790. A trend toward consolidation of landholding and slave ownership after 1740 had a profound effect on the lives of Afro-Americans. In areas with high proportions of blacks in the population, most slaves resided on plantations with at least nine other bondspeople. Although many southern blacks lived on farms with only one or two other slaves, the majority had the experience of living and working in a largely black setting.

The size of such plantation households allowed for the specialization of labor. Encouraged by planters whose goal was to create as self-sufficient a household as possible, Afro-American men and women became highly skilled at tasks whites believed appropriate to their sex. Each large plantation had its own male

Sexual Division of Labor among Black Americans

blacksmiths, carpenters, valets, shoemakers, and gardeners, and female dairymaids, seamstresses, cooks, and at least one midwife, who attended pregnant white and black women alike. These skilled slaves—between 10 and 20 percent of the black population—were as essential to the smooth functioning of the plantation as the ordinary field hands who labored "in the crop." But whites assigned most male and female slaves to work in the fields. Since West African women were accustomed to agricultural labor (see page 12), that task must have coincided with their own cultural expectations. But whites had a different concept of sexual division of labor. To them black women's work in the fields connoted inferior status.

The typical Chesapeake tobacco plantation was divided into small "quarters" located at some distance from one another. White overseers supervised work on the distant quarters, while the planter personally took charge of the "home" quarter (which included the planter's house). In the Carolina lowcountry, where planters usually spent months in Charleston in the hope of avoiding the malaria and yellow fever seasons, blacks often supervised their fellow slaves. Planters commonly assigned "outlandish" (African-born) slaves to do field labor in order to accustom them to plantation work routines and to enable them to learn some English. Artisans, on the other hand, were usually drawn from among the plantation's American-born blacks. In such families skills like carpentry and midwifery were passed down from father to son and from mother to daughter; such knowledge often constituted a slave family's most valuable possession.

Plantation Life

Eighteenth-century planters were considerably less worried that their slaves might run away than were their counterparts seventy-five years later, and with good reason. All the English colonies legally permitted slavery, so blacks had few places to go to escape bondage. Sometimes recently arrived Africans tried to steal boats to return home or ran off in groups to the frontier, where they attempted to establish traditional villages. Occasionally slaves from South Carolina tried to reach Spanish Florida. But Afro-Americans usually recognized that they had few long-term alternatives to remaining on their plantations.

About 1784, slave artisans on the plantation of Joel Lane, near Raleigh, North Carolina, fashioned this beautiful china cabinet. Every plantation had its share of skilled slaves. Planters reserved traditionally male jobs like cabinet-making for their male slaves, assigning skilled women to "feminine" tasks like spinning, dairying, and cooking. Index of American Design, National Gallery of Art, Washington, D.C.

This is not to say that Afro-American slaves never ran away. They did, in large numbers. But they did so to visit friends or relatives, or simply to escape their normal work routines for a few days or months; they could have had little hope of remaining permanently at large. In a society in which blackness automatically connoted perpetual servitude, no black person anywhere could claim free status without being challenged. And, from the blacks' perspective, violent resistance had even less to recommend it than running away. Whites may have been in the minority in some areas, but they controlled the guns and ammunition. Even if a revolt succeeded for a time, whites could easily muster the armed force necessary to put it down. Only in very unusual circumstances, therefore—as will be seen in the last section of this chapter—did colonial blacks attempt to rebel against their white oppressors.

An Overseer Doing His Duty, *by Benjamin H. Latrobe.*
Most slave women were field hands like these, sketched in
1798 near Fredericksburg, Virginia. White women were
believed to be unsuited for heavy outdoor labor. Maryland
Historical Society.

**Black
Families**

Afro-Americans did try to improve the conditions
of their bondage and gain some measure of control
over their lives. Their chief vehicle for doing so was
the family. Planters' records reveal
how members of extended kin groups
provided support, assistance, and
comfort to each other. They asked
to live on the same quarters, protested excessive
punishment administered to relatives, and often requested special treatment for children or siblings. On
one Virginia plantation, for instance, a mother arranged for her daughter to be treated by a particular
black doctor, and a father successfully convinced his
master that his daughter should be allowed to live
with her stepmother. The extended-kin ties that developed among Afro-American families who had lived
on the same plantation for several generations served
as insurance against the uncertainties of existence
under slavery. If a nuclear family was broken up by
sale, there were always relatives around to help with

childrearing and other tasks. Among colonial blacks,
in other words, the extended family probably served
a more important function than it did among whites.

Yet blacks were always subject to white intrusions
into their lives. Black house servants had to serve
the white family rather than their own, and even
field hands were constantly at the whites' beck and
call. Still, most black families managed to carve out
a small measure of autonomy. On many plantations,
slaves were allowed to plant their own gardens, hunt,
or fish in order to supplement the standard diet of
corn and salt pork. Some Chesapeake mistresses permitted their female slaves to raise chickens, which
they could then sell or exchange for such items as
extra clothing or blankets.

In South Carolina, slaves were often able to accumulate personal property, because most rice and
indigo plantations operated on a task system. Once
slaves had completed their assigned tasks for the day,
they were free to work for themselves. (Occasionally

Chapter 3: GROWTH AND DIVERSITY, 1720–1770

they could even cultivate rice or indigo crops of their own.) In Maryland and Virginia, where by the end of the century some whites had begun to hire out their slaves to others, blacks were sometimes allowed to keep a small part of the wages they earned. Such advances were slight, but against the bleak backdrop of slavery they deserve to be highlighted.

Relations between blacks and whites varied considerably from household to household. In some, masters and mistresses enforced their will chiefly

Black-White Relations through physical coercion. Thus one woman's diary noted matter-of-factly: "December 1: Lucy whippt for getting key of Celler door & stealing apples. December 2: Plato Anthoney & Abraham Pegg's housband whipt for Hog stealing." On other plantations, masters were more lenient and respectful of slaves' property and their desire to live with other members of their families. But even in households where whites and blacks displayed genuine affection for one another, there were inescapable tensions. Such tensions were caused not only by the whites' uneasiness about the slave system in general but also by the dynamics of day-to-day relationships when a small number of whites wielded absolute legal power over the lives of many blacks.

Thomas Jefferson was deeply concerned about that issue. In 1780 he observed, "The whole commerce between master and slave is a perpetual exercise of the most boisterous passions, the most unremitting despotism on the one part, and degrading submission on the other. Our children see this, and learn to imitate it. . . . The man must be a prodigy who can retain his manners and morals undepraved by such circumstances." Thus, what troubled him most was the impact of the system on whites, not on the people they held in bondage. Before the Revolution, only a tiny number of Quakers (most notably John Woolman in his *Some Considerations on the Keeping of Negroes*, published in 1754) took a different approach, criticizing slavery out of sympathy for blacks. The other white colonists who questioned slavery took Jefferson's approach, stressing the institution's adverse effect on whites, and they were extremely few in number. A labor system so essential to the functioning of the colonial economy met with little open challenge.

In the third quarter of the eighteenth century, the daily work routines of most Americans had changed little from those of their Old World ancestors. Ordinary white folk lived in farm households, their lives governed by the sexual division of labor. Most Afro-Americans were held in perpetual bondage, but their work was performed as it had been in West Africa, communally in the fields. Even in colonial cities life differed little from European cities in previous centuries. Yet if the routines of daily life seemed fixed and unchanging, the wider context in which those routines occurred did not. In both Europe and America the eighteenth century was a time of great cultural and intellectual ferment. The movement known as the Enlightenment at first primarily influenced the educated elites. Ordinary people seemed little touched by it. But since enlightened thinking played a major part in the ideology of the American Revolution, it was eventually to have an important impact on the lives of all Americans.

COLONIAL CULTURE

The older, traditional form of colonial culture was oral, communal, and—for at least the first half of the eighteenth century—intensely localized. The newer culture of the elite was print-oriented, more individualized, and self-consciously cosmopolitan. The two will be discussed separately but they also mingled in a variety of ways, since people of both descriptions lived side by side in small communities.

A majority of the residents of British America (almost all the blacks, half the white women, and at least one-fifth of the white men) could neither

Oral Culture read nor write. That had important consequences for the transmission and development of American culture. In the absence of literacy, the primary means of communication was face-to-face conversation. Information tended to travel slowly and within relatively confined regions. Different locales developed divergent cultural traditions, and those differences were heightened by racial or ethnic variations.

When Europeans or Africans migrated to the colonies, they left familiar environments behind but brought with them sets of cultural assumptions about how society should work and how their own lives fitted into the broader social context. In North America, those assumptions influenced the way they organized their lives. Yet Old World customs usually could not be recreated intact in the New World, because people from different origins now resided in the same communities. Accordingly, the colonists had to forge new cultural identities for themselves.

In New England, communal culture centered on the church and on religious observances in the civic sphere. Colonial governments proclaimed official days of thanksgiving (for good harvests, victories in war, and so forth) or days of fasting and prayer (when the colony was experiencing difficulties). Everyone in the community was expected to participate in the public rituals held on such occasions. Militia musters (known as training days), normally scheduled once a month, were similar moments that brought the community together, since all able-bodied men between the ages of sixteen and sixty were members of the militia.

Attendance at church was perhaps the most important public ritual in New England. Church services publicly affirmed one's standing in the community.

Religious Rituals In Congregational (Puritan) churches, seating was assigned by church leaders: each family had its own pew, whose location at the front, back, or sides of the church depended on the family's wealth and social prominence. A similar statement about the local status hierarchy was conveyed at Anglican parishes in Virginia. There too families purchased their own pews, and in some parishes the landed gentlemen customarily strode into church as a group just before the service was to begin, deliberately drawing attention to their exalted position. Quite a different message came from the entirely egalitarian, but sex-segregated, seating system used in Quaker meetinghouses. Where one sat in colonial churches, in other words, symbolized one's place in society and the values of the local community.

Other aspects of the service also reflected communal values. In most colonial churches, trained clergymen delivered formal sermons, but in Quaker services members of the meeting spoke informally to each other. Communal singing in Congregational churches added an egalitarian element to an otherwise status-conscious experience. Not by accident was the first

book printed in the colonies *The Bay Psalm Book* (1640), consisting of Old Testament psalms recast in short, rhyming, metrical lines so they could be easily learned, remembered, and sung even by people who could not read. Communal singing helped to reduce the ritual significance of hierarchical seating arrangements, bringing a kind of crude democracy into the church. Everyone participated in the singing on an equal basis and all had an equal voice in deciding which version of the psalms to use and whether instruments should accompany the singing.

In the Chesapeake, some of the most important cultural rituals were civic in nature, in particular court and election days. When the county court was in session, men would come from

Civic Rituals miles around to sue one another for debt, appear as witnesses, serve as jurors, or simply observe the goings-on. Attendance at court functioned as a method of civic education; from watching the proceedings men learned what behavior their neighbors expected of them. Elections served the same purpose, for freeholders voted in public. An election official, often flanked by the candidates for the office in question, would call each man forward in turn to declare his preference. The voter would then be thanked politely by the gentleman for whom he had cast his oral ballot. Traditionally, the candidates also treated their supporters to rum at nearby taverns. (Note, in this context, that public rituals in the Chesapeake region were more male-centered than those in New England, where rituals focused on religion, in which women participated fully, rather than politics.)

In such settings as church and courthouse, then, elite and ordinary folk alike participated in the oral, communal culture that served as the cement holding their communities together. But the genteel residents of the colonies also took part in a newer kind of culture, one organized through the world of print and the message conveyed by reading as well as by observing one's neighbors.

Literacy was certainly less essential in eighteenth-century America than it is today. People—especially women—could live their entire lives without ever being called upon to read a book

Attitudes Toward Education or write a letter. Thus education beyond the bare rudiments of reading, writing, and "figuring" was usually regarded as a frill for either sex. Men might have to know how to read a contract or keep rough accounts, and women might need or want to read the Bible, but beyond that little learning appeared to be necessary. Education accordingly was an accomplishment, a sign of status. Only parents who wanted their children to be distinguished from less fortunate peers (perhaps for reasons of piety, or a desire for upward mobility or maintenance of status) were willing to forgo their children's valuable labor to allow them to attend school. And when parents did so, the education they gave their sons differed from that given their daughters. Girls ordinarily received little intellectual training beyond the rudiments, though they might learn music, dancing, or fancy needlework (since those skills all connoted genteel status). Elite boys, on the other hand, studied with tutors or attended grammar schools that prepared them to enter college at age fourteen or fifteen.

Not surprisingly, therefore, the colonial system of higher education for males was more fully developed than was basic instruction for either sex. The first American colleges were chiefly designed to train young men for the ministry. Following the earlier examples of Harvard (1636), William and Mary (chartered 1693, but not a functioning entity until 1726), and Yale (1701), the colleges founded in the mid-eighteenth century—those now known as Princeton (1747), Columbia (1754), Brown (1765), and Rutgers (1766)—were intended to supply clergymen to fill the pulpits of Presbyterian, Anglican, Baptist, and Dutch Reformed churches, respectively. (Dartmouth College, founded 1769, though not explicitly aimed at educating clerics, also had a religious purpose, that of Christianizing the Indians.) But during the eighteenth century the curriculum and character of all these colleges changed considerably. Their students, the sons of the colonial elite, were now interested in careers in medicine, law, and business instead of the ministry. And the learned men who headed the colleges, though ministers themselves, were deeply affected by the Enlightenment.

In the seventeenth century, some European thinkers had begun to analyze nature in an effort to determine the laws that govern the universe. They and their successors in subsequent centuries

The Enlightenment employed experimentation and abstract reasoning to discover general

A colonial boy's education included not just reading and writing but instruction in the duties of the patriarchal role. The unpublished picture book, The Ages of Man, *prepared about 1760, taught its young male readers that a mature man should demonstrate "love and care" for his children. Free Library of Philadelphia, Rosenbach Collection.*

principles behind such everyday phenomena as the motions of the planets and stars, the behavior of falling objects, and the characteristics of light and sound. Above all, the Enlightenment philosophers emphasized acquiring knowledge through reason, rather than through intuition and revelation. They took a particular delight in challenging previously unquestioned assumptions; for example, John Locke's *Essay Concerning Human Understanding* (1690) disputed the notion that human beings were born already imprinted with innate ideas. All knowledge, Locke asserted, came rather from one's observations of the external world.

The Enlightenment had an enormous impact on well-to-do, educated people in Europe and America. It supplied them with a common vocabulary and a unified view of the world, one that insisted that the enlightened eighteenth century was better than all previous ages. It joined them in a common endeavor, the effort to make sense of God's orderly creation. Thus American naturalists like John and William Bartram supplied European scientists with information about New World plants and animals, so that they could be fitted into newly formulated universal classification systems. So too Americans interested in astronomy took part in 1769 in an international effort to learn about the workings of the solar system by studying a rare occurrence, the transit of Venus across the face of the sun.

These intellectual currents had a dramatic effect on the curriculum of the colonial colleges. Whereas in the seventeenth century Harvard courses focused on the study of the ancient languages and theology, after the 1720s colleges began to introduce courses in mathematics (including algebra, geometry, and calculus), the natural sciences, law, and medicine (including anatomy and physiology). The young men educated in such colleges—and their sisters at home, with whom they occasionally shared their books and ideas—developed a rational outlook on life that differentiated them from their fellow colonists. This was the world of Dr. Alexander Hamilton and his associates. When he left Annapolis in 1744, he carried letters of introduction to "the better sort" in all the places he intended to visit. Such people had learned the value of reading, of regular correspondence with like-minded friends, of convivial gatherings at which the conversation focused on the books most recently imported from Europe (especially the daring novels by Samuel Richardson).

Well-to-do graduates of American colleges, along with others who like Hamilton had obtained their education in Great Britain, formed the core of genteel culture in the colonies. Men and **Elite Culture** women from these families wanted to set themselves apart from ordinary folk. Beginning in the 1720s they constructed grandiose residences for themselves, substantial houses furnished with imported carpets, silver plate, and furniture. They entertained their friends at elaborate dinner parties and balls, at which all present dressed in the height of fashion. They cultivated polite manners and saw themselves as part of a transatlantic and intercolonial network.

In what ways, if at all, did this genteel, enlightened culture affect the lives of the majority of colonists? Certainly no resident of the colonies could have avoided some contact with members of the elite, even if it was only an occasional glimpse of them. Some groups were more directly affected; for example, the elite's demand for consumer goods of all kinds led to the growth of artisan industries (like silversmithing or fine furniture-making) in the colonies. But the Enlightenment's most immediate impact on all Americans was in the realm of medicine.

The key figure in the drama was the Reverend Cotton Mather, the Puritan clergyman, who was a member of England's Royal Society, an organization of the intellectual elite. In a Royal **Smallpox** Society publication Mather read **Inoculations** about the benefits of inoculation (deliberately infecting a person with a mild case of a disease) as a protection against the dreaded smallpox. In 1720 and 1721, when Boston suffered a major smallpox epidemic, Mather and a doctor ally urged people to be inoculated; there was fervent opposition, including that of Boston's leading physician. When the epidemic had ended, the statistics bore out Mather's opinion: of those inoculated, fewer than 3 percent died; of those who became ill without inoculation, nearly 15 percent perished. Though it was midcentury before inoculation was generally accepted as a preventive procedure, enlightened methods had provided colonial Americans with protection from the greatest killer disease of all.

If the lives of genteel and ordinary folk in the eighteenth-century colonies seemed to follow different patterns, there was one man who in his person appeared to combine their traits; ap- **Benjamin** propriately enough, he later became **Franklin,** for Europeans the symbolic Amer- **the Symbolic** ican. That man was Benjamin **American** Franklin. Born in Boston in 1706, he was the perfect example of a self-made, self-educated man. Apprenticed at an early age to his older brother James, a Boston printer and newspaper publisher, Franklin ran away to Philadelphia in 1723. There he worked as a printer and eventually started his own publishing business, printing the *Pennsylvania Gazette* and *Poor Richard's Almanack* among other books. The business was so successful that Franklin was able to retire from active control in 1748, at forty-two. He thereafter devoted himself to intellectual endeavors and public service (as deputy postmaster general for the colonies, as an agent representing colonial interests in London, and finally as a diplomat during the Revolution). Franklin's *Experiments and Observations on Electricity* (1751) was the most important scientific work by a colonial American; it established the terminology and basic theory of electricity still in use today.

In 1749 and 1751 Franklin published pamphlets proposing the establishment of a new educational institution in Pennsylvania. The purpose of Franklin's "English School" was not to produce clerics or scholars but to prepare young men "for learning any business, calling or profession, except such wherein languages are required." He wanted to enable them "to pass through and execute the several offices of civil life, with advantage and reputation to themselves and country." The College of Philadelphia, which he founded in 1755, was intended to graduate youths who would resemble Franklin himself—talented, practical men of affairs competent in a number of different fields.

Franklin and the student he envisioned thus fused the conflicting tendencies of colonial culture. Free of the Old World's traditions, the ideal American would achieve distinction through hard work and the application of common-sense principles. Like Franklin, he would rise from an ordinary family into the ranks of the genteel, thereby transcending the cultural boundaries that divided the colonists. He would be unpretentious but not unlearned, simple but not ignorant, virtuous but not priggish. The American would be a true child of the Enlightenment, knowledgeable about European culture yet not bound by its fetters, advancing through reason and talent alone. To him all things would be possible, all doors open.

The contrast with the original communal ideals of the early New England settlements could not have been sharper. Franklin's American was an individual, free to make choices about his future, able to contemplate a variety of possible careers. John Winthrop's American, outlined in his "Modell of Christian Charity" (see pages 30–31), had been a component of a greater whole that required his unhesitating, unquestioning submission. But the two visions had one point in common: both described only white males. Neither blacks nor females played any part in them.

Benjamin Franklin (1706–1789), painted by the itinerant artist Robert Feke in 1746, when Franklin was forty. The portrait shows Franklin at the height of his business career, a prosperous Philadelphian. Harvard University Portrait Collection, Bequest, Dr. John C. Warren in 1856.

Not until many years later would America formally recognize what had been true all along: that females and nonwhites had participated in the creation of the nation's cultural traditions.

POLITICS AND RELIGION: STABILITY AND CRISIS AT MIDCENTURY

In the first decades of the eighteenth century, colonial political life developed a new stability. Despite the large migration from overseas, a majority of the residents of the mainland colonies were now native-born. Men from genteel families dominated the political structures in each province, for voters (white men who met property-holding requirements) tended to defer to their well-educated "betters" on election days. (Whether that deference was voluntary or forced is disputed among historians, but the result was the same.) The most noticeable consequence of such deferential behavior was a declining rate of turnover among elected officials in most of the colonies.

Logically enough, colonial political leaders sought to increase the powers of the elected assemblies relative to those of the governors and other appointed officials.

Rise of the Assemblies Colonial assemblies began to claim privileges associated with the British House of Commons, such as the right to initiate all tax legislation and to control the militia. The assemblies also developed effective ways of influencing British appointees, especially by threatening to withhold their salaries. In some colonies (like Virginia and South Carolina), the elite members of the assemblies most often presented a united front to royal officials, but in others (like New York), they fought with each other long and bitterly. It was in the latter province that the first steps on the road to modern American democracy were taken. In their attempts to win hotly contested elections, New York's genteel leaders began to appeal to "the people," competing openly for the votes of ordinary freeholders.

Yet eighteenth-century assemblies bore little resemblance to twentieth-century state legislatures. In the first place, much of their business was what today would be termed administrative; only on rare occasions did they formulate new policies or pass laws of major importance. Second, members of the assemblies conceived of their role differently from modern legislators. Instead of believing that they should act *positively* to improve the lives of their constituents, eighteenth-century assemblymen saw themselves as acting *negatively* to prevent encroachments on the people's rights. That is, in their minds their primary function was to stop the governors or councils from enacting (for example) oppressive taxes; it was not to pass laws that would actively benefit their constituents.

By the middle of the century, politically aware colonists commonly drew analogies between their governments and the balance between king, lords, and commons found in Great Britain—a combination that was thought to produce a stable polity. Although

the analogy was not exact, the colonists equated their governors with the monarch, their councils with the aristocracy, and their assemblies with the House of Commons. All three were thought essential to good government, but Americans did not regard them with the same degrees of approval. They saw the governors and appointed councils as aliens who posed a potential threat to colonial freedoms and customary ways of life. As representatives of England rather than America, the governors and councils were to be feared rather than trusted. Colonists saw the assemblies, on the other hand, as the people's protectors. And for their part, the assemblies regarded themselves as representatives of the people.

But again, such beliefs should not be equated with modern practice. The assemblies, firmly controlled by dominant families whose members were re-elected year after year, rarely responded to the concerns of their poorer constituents. Although settlement continually spread westward, assemblies failed to reapportion themselves to provide adequate representation for newer communities—a lack of action that led to serious grievances among frontier dwellers, especially those from non-English ethnic groups. Moreover, the assemblies occasionally acted in a manner that appears oppressive to modern eyes. For example, in 1735 the New York assembly jailed the printer John Peter Zenger for publicly criticizing its actions in his newspaper. Thus it is important to distinguish between the colonial *ideal*, which placed the assembly to the forefront in the protection of people's liberties, and the *reality*, in which the people protected tended chiefly to be the wealthy and well-born and the assembly members themselves.

At midcentury, the political structures that had stabilized in a period of relative calm confronted a series of crises. None affected all the mainland provinces, but on the other hand no colony escaped wholly untouched by at least one. The crises were of various sorts—ethnic, racial, economic, religious—and they exposed the internal tensions building in the pluralistic American society. They foreshadowed the greater disorder of the revolutionary era. Most important, they demonstrated that the political accommodations arrived at in the aftermath of the Glorious Revolution were no longer adequate to govern Britain's American empire. Once again, changes appeared necessary.

In 1748, the colony of Massachusetts constructed its impressive State House in Boston. Here met the Assembly and the Council. The solidity and imposing nature of the building must have symbolized for its users the increasing consolidation of power in the hands of the Massachusetts legislature. Library of Congress.

One of the first—and greatest—of the crises occurred in South Carolina. Early one morning in September 1739, about twenty South Carolina slaves gathered

Stono Rebellion

near the Stono River south of Charleston. After seizing guns and ammunition from a store, they killed the storekeepers and some nearby planter families. Then, joined by other slaves from the area, they headed south toward Florida in hopes of finding refuge in that Spanish colony. By midday, however, the alarm had been sounded among whites in the district. In the late afternoon a troop of militia caught up with the fugitives, then numbering about a hundred, and attacked them, killing some and dispersing the rest. More than a week later, the whites finally captured most of the remaining con-

spirators. Those not killed on the spot were later executed, but for more than two years afterward renegades were rumored to be still at large.

The Stono Rebellion shocked white South Carolinians and residents of other colonies as well. Laws governing the behavior of blacks were stiffened throughout British America. But the most immediate response came in New York, which itself had suffered a slave revolt in 1712. There the news from the South, coupled with fears of Spain generated by the outbreak of King George's War, set off a reign of terror in the summer of 1741. Hysterical whites transformed a biracial gang of thieves and arsonists into malevolent conspirators who wanted to foment a slave uprising under the guidance of a supposed priest in the pay of Spain. By summer's end, thirty-one blacks and four whites had been executed for participating in the "plot." Not only did the Stono Rebellion and the New York Conspiracy expose and confirm whites' deepest fears about the dangers of slaveholding, they also revealed the assemblies' inability to prevent serious internal disorder. Events of the next two decades confirmed that pattern.

By midcentury, most of the fertile land east of the Appalachians had been purchased or occupied. As a result, conflicts over land titles and conditions of landholding grew in number and

Land Riots frequency as colonists competed for control of land good for farming. In 1746, for example, New Jersey farmers holding land under grants from the governor of New York (dating from the brief period when both provinces were owned by the Duke of York) clashed violently with agents of the East Jersey proprietors. The proprietors claimed the land as theirs and demanded annual payments, called quitrents, for the use of the property. Similar violence occurred in the 1760s in the region that later became Vermont. There, farmers (many of them migrants from eastern New England) holding land grants issued by New Hampshire battled with speculators claiming title to the area through grants from New York authorities.

The most serious land riots of the period took place along the Hudson River in 1765 and 1766. Late in the seventeenth century, Governor Benjamin Fletcher of New York had granted several huge tracts in the lower Hudson valley to prominent colonial families. The proprietors in turn divided these estates into small farms, which they rented chiefly to poor Dutch and German migrants, who evidently regarded tenancy as a step on the road to independent freeholder status. By the 1750s, some proprietors were earning as much as £1,000 to £2,000 annually from quitrents and other fees.

After 1740, though, increasing migration from New England brought conflict to the great New York estates. The mobile New Englanders, who had moved in search of land, did not want to become tenants. Many squatted on vacant portions of the manors and resisted all attempts to evict them. In the mid-1760s, the Philipse family brought suit against the New Englanders, some of whom had lived on Philipse land for twenty or thirty years. New York courts upheld the Philipse claim and ordered the squatters to make

way for tenants with valid leases. Instead of complying, the farmers organized a rebellion against the proprietors. For nearly a year the insurgent farmers controlled much of the Hudson valley. They terrorized proprietors and loyal tenants, freed their friends from jail, and on one occasion battled a county sheriff and his posse. The rebellion was put down only after British troops dispatched from New York City captured its most important leaders.

Violent conflicts of a different sort erupted just a few years later in the Carolinas. The "Regulator" movements of the late 1760s (South Carolina) and early 1770s (North Carolina) pitted

The Regulators backcountry farmers against the eastern planters who controlled their provinces' governments. The frontier dwellers, most of whom were Scotch-Irish, protested their lack of an adequate voice in colonial political affairs. The South Carolinians for months policed the countryside in vigilante bands, contending that law enforcement in the region was too lax. The North Carolinians, many of whose grievances had their origin in heavy taxation, fought a battle with eastern militiamen at Alamance in 1771. Regional, ethnic, and economic tensions thus combined to create these disturbances, which ultimately arose from frontiersmen's dissatisfaction with the Carolina governments.

The most widespread of all midcentury crises occurred not in politics but in religion. From the late 1730s through the 1760s, waves of religious revivalism—known collectively as the

First Great Great Awakening—swept over var-
Awakening ious parts of the colonies, primarily New England (1735–1745) and Virginia (1750s and 1760s). Eighteenth-century America was ripe for religious renewal, because orthodox Calvinists were troubled by the influence on religion of Enlightenment rationalism (which denied innate human depravity). The Great Awakening was also related to the colonies' new population patterns. Because many of the recent immigrants and residents of the backcountry had no religious affiliation, they offered evangelists a likely source of converts.

The first indications of what was to become the Great Awakening occurred in western Massachusetts, in the Northampton congregation of the Reverend Jonathan Edwards, a noted preacher and theologian. During 1734 and 1735, Edwards noticed a remarkable response in his flock (and especially its more youthful members) to a message based squarely on Calvinist principles. Individuals, Edwards argued, could attain salvation only through recognition of their own depraved natures and the need to surrender completely to God's will. Such surrender, when it came, brought release from worry and sin; it was an intensely emotional experience. Indeed, people in Edwards's congregation began to experience that surrender as a single identifiable moment of conversion.

The effects of such conversions remained isolated until 1739, when George Whitefield, an English adherent of the Methodist branch of Anglicanism, arrived in America. For fifteen months

George Whitefield

Whitefield toured the colonies, preaching to large audiences from Georgia to New England and concentrating his efforts in the major cities: Boston, New York, Philadelphia, and Charleston. An effective orator, Whitefield was the chief generating force behind the Great Awakening. Everywhere he traveled, his fame preceded him; thousands turned out to listen—and to experience conversion. At first, regular clerics welcomed Whitefield and the native itinerant evangelist preachers who sprang up to imitate him. Soon, however, many clergymen began to realize that "revived" religion, though it filled their churches, ran counter to a more rational approach to matters of faith. Furthermore, they disliked the emotional style of the revivalists, whose itinerancy also disrupted normal patterns of church attendance.

Opposition to the Awakening heightened rapidly, and large numbers of churches splintered in its wake. "Old Lights"—traditional clerics and their followers—engaged in bitter disputes with the "New Light" evangelicals. American religion, already characterized by numerous sects, became further divided as the major denominations split into Old Light and New Light factions, and as new evangelical sects—Methodists and Baptists—quickly gained adherents. Paradoxically, the angry fights and the rapid rise in the number of distinct denominations eventually led to an American willingness to tolerate religious diversity. No one sect could make an unequivocal claim to orthodoxy and so they all had to coexist if they were to exist at all.

The most important effect of the Awakening was its impact on American modes of thought. Common

George Whitefield (1714–1770), an English evangelist who made frequent tours of the American colonies. This portrait, painted in England, shows the effects his powerful preaching had on his listeners.   National Portrait Gallery, London.

folk had long been expected to accept unhesitatingly the authority of their "betters," whether wealthy gentry, government officials, or educated clergymen. The message of the Great Awakening directly challenged that tradition of deference. The revivalists, many of whom were not ordained clergymen, claimed they understood the word of God far better than orthodox clerics. The Awakening's emphasis on emotion rather than learning as the road to salvation further undermined the validity of received wisdom. Supported by the belief that God was with them, New Lights began to question not only religious but also social and political orthodoxy.

Nowhere was this trend more evident than in Virginia, where the plantation gentry and their ostentatious lifestyle dominated society. By the 1760s, Baptists had gained a major foothold in Virginia, and their beliefs and behavior were openly at odds with the way most gentry families lived. They rejected as sinful the horse racing, gambling, and dancing that occupied much of the gentry's leisure time. Like the Quakers before them, they dressed plainly and simply, in contrast to the fashionable opulence of the gentry. Most strikingly of all, they addressed each other as "brother" and "sister" and organized their congregations on the basis of equality. And at least some Baptist congregations included blacks as well as whites, which was truly revolutionary.

At midcentury the Great Awakening injected an egalitarian strain into American life. Although primarily a religious movement, the Awakening also had important social and political consequences, calling into question habitual modes of behavior in the secular as well as the religious realm. In combination with the other changes occurring in the colonies—the increasing ethnic and racial diversity, the expanding economy, the introduction of new lifestyles and forms of thought—the Great Awakening helped to break Americans' ties to their limited seventeenth-century origins. A century and a half

after English people had first settled in North America, the colonies were only nominally English. Rather, they mixed diverse European, American, and African traditions into a novel cultural blend. That culture owed much to the Old World, but just as much, if not more, to the New. In the 1760s Americans began to recognize that fact. They realized that their interests were not necessarily those of Great Britain, or of its rulers; for the first time they offered a frontal challenge to British authority.

SUGGESTIONS FOR FURTHER READING

General

Jack P. Greene and J. R. Pole, eds, *Colonial British America: Essays in the New History of the Early Modern Era* (1984); James A. Henretta, *The Evolution of American Society, 1700–1815* (1973); Richard Hofstadter, *America at 1750: A Social Portrait* (1971); Robert V. Wells, *The Population of the British Colonies in America before 1776: A Survey of Census Data* (1975).

Rural Society

Carl Bridenbaugh, *Myths and Realities: Societies of the Colonial South* (1963); Rhys Isaac, *The Transformation of Virginia 1740–1790* (1982); Christopher Jedrey, *The World of John Cleaveland: Family and Community in Eighteenth-Century New England* (1979); Sung Bok Kim, *Landlord and Tenant in Colonial New York: Manorial Society, 1664–1775* (1978); James T. Lemon, *The Best Poor Man's Country: A Geographical Study of Early Southeastern Pennsylvania* (1972); Michael Zuckerman, *Peaceable Kingdoms: New England Towns in the Eighteenth Century* (1970).

Urban Society

Carl Bridenbaugh, *Cities in Revolt: Urban Life in America, 1743–1776* (1955); Gary B. Nash, *The Urban Crucible: Social Change, Political Consciousness, and the Origins of the American Revolution* (1979); Frederick B. Tolles, *Meeting House and Counting House: The Quaker Merchants of Colonial Philadelphia 1682–1763* (1948); Stephanie Grauman Wolf, *Urban Village: Population, Community, and Family Structure in Germantown, Pennsylvania, 1683–1800* (1976).

Economic Development

Paul G. E. Clemens, *The Atlantic Economy and Colonial Maryland's Eastern Shore: From Tobacco to Grain* (1980); Marc Egnal, "The Economic Development of the Thirteen Continental Colonies, 1720–1775," *William and Mary Quarterly*, 3rd ser., 32 (1975), 191–222; Alice Hanson Jones, *Wealth of a Nation To Be: The American Colonies on the Eve of the Revolution* (1980); Edwin J. Perkins, *The Economy of Colonial America* (1980); Jacob M. Price, "Economic Function and the Growth of American Port Towns in the Eighteenth Century," *Perspectives in American History*, 8 (1974), 123–186; James F. Shepherd and Gary M. Walton, *Shipping, Maritime Trade and the Economic Development of Colonial North America* (1972); Gary M. Walton and James F. Shepherd, *The Economic Rise of Early America* (1979).

Politics

Bernard Bailyn, *The Origins of American Politics* (1968); Patricia U. Bonomi, *A Factious People: Politics and Society in Colonial New York* (1971); Edward M. Cook, Jr., *The Fathers of the Towns: Leadership and Community Structure in Eighteenth-Century New England* (1976); Jack P. Greene, *The Quest for Power: The Lower Houses of Assembly in the Southern Royal Colonies 1689–1776* (1963).

Immigration

Jon Butler, *The Huguenots in America: A Refugee People in New World Society* (1983); R. J. Dickson, *Ulster Immigration to Colonial America, 1718–1775* (1966); Albert B. Faust, *The German Element in the United States*, 2 vols. (1909); Ian C. C. Graham, *Colonists from Scotland: Emigration to North America 1707–1783* (1956); James G. Leyburn, *The Scotch-Irish: A Social History* (1962).

Blacks

Ira Berlin, "Time, Space, and the Evolution of Afro-American Society in British Mainland America," *American Historical Review*, 85 (1980), 44–78; Herbert Gutman, *The Black Family in Slavery and Freedom 1750–1925* (1976); Allan Kulikoff, "The Origins of Afro-American Society in Tidewater Maryland and Virginia, 1700 to 1790," *William and Mary Quarterly*, 3rd ser., 35 (1978), 228–259; Gerald W. Mullin, *Flight and Rebellion: Slave Resistance in Eighteenth-Century Virginia* (1972).

Women and Family

J. William Frost, *The Quaker Family in Colonial America* (1972); Philip J. Greven, *The Protestant Temperament: Patterns of Child-Rearing, Religious Experience, and the Self in Early America* (1977); Mary Beth Norton, *Liberty's Daughters: The Revolutionary Experience of American Women, 1750–1800* (1980); Daniel Blake Smith, *Inside the Great House: Planter Family Life in Eighteenth-Century Chesapeake Society* (1980); Daniel Scott Smith, "Parental Power and Marriage Patterns: An Analysis of Historical Trends in Hingham, Massachusetts," *Journal of Marriage and the Family*, 35 (1973), 419–428.

Colonial Culture and the Enlightenment

Daniel J. Boorstin, *The Americans: The Colonial Experience* (1958); Richard Beale Davis, *Intellectual Life in the Colonial South, 1585–1763*, 2 vols. (1978); Howard Mumford Jones, *O Strange New World. American Culture: The Formative Years* (1964); Henry F. May, *The Enlightenment in America* (1976); Louis B. Wright, *The Cultural Life of the American Colonies, 1607–1763* (1957).

Education

James Axtell, *The School upon a Hill: Education and Society in Colonial New England* (1974); Bernard Bailyn, *Education in the Forming of American Society* (1960); Patricia Cline Cohen, *A Calculating People: The Spread of Numeracy in Early America* (1982); Lawrence A. Cremin, *American Education: The Colonial Experience 1607–1783* (1970); Kenneth A. Lockridge, *Literacy in Colonial New England: An Inquiry into the Social Context of Literacy in the Early Modern West* (1974).

Science and Medicine

Jane Donegan, *Women and Men Midwives: Medicine, Morality, and Misogyny in Early America* (1978); John Duffy, *Epidemics in Colonial America* (1953); Brooke Hindle, *The Pursuit of Science in Revolutionary America* (1956); Raymond P. Stearns, *Science in the British Colonies of America* (1970).

Religion and the Great Awakening

Carl Bridenbaugh, *Mitre and Sceptre: Transatlantic Faiths, Ideas, Personalities, and Politics, 1689–1775* (1962); J. M. Bumsted and John E. Van de Wetering, *What Must I Do To Be Saved? The Great Awakening in Colonial America* (1976); Edwin S. Gaustad, *The Great Awakening in New England* (1957); Alan E. Heimert, *Religion and the American Mind: From the Great Awakening to the Revolution* (1966); William McLoughlin, *Isaac Backus and the American Pietistic Tradition* (1967); Patricia Tracy, *Jonathan Edwards, Pastor* (1980).

SEVERING THE BONDS
OF EMPIRE
1754–1774

CHAPTER 4

*I*n *late October* 1769, the young Boston shopkeeper Betsy Cuming was visiting a sick friend when outside the house she heard "a voilint Skreeming Kill him Kill him." Betsy ran to the window and saw John Mein, a bookseller and newspaper publisher, being chased by "a larg Croud of those who Call themselves Gentelman, but," she added, "in reality they ware no other then Murderers for there disigne was certinly on his life." Later that evening a crowd of at least a thousand men and boys passed the door, "& on a Kart a Man was Exibited as we thought in a Gore of Blod." Betsy concluded that the mob had caught Mein, but she was mistaken. She learned the next day that the victim was a customs informer seized by the crowd after Mein had taken shelter in a British army guardhouse. That same night, Mein fled to a vessel anchored in the harbor. He later sailed to England and never returned to the city.

What had John Mein done to arouse the antagonism of the "gentlemen" of Boston? He published a newspaper, the *Boston Chronicle*, which generally supported the British side in the current disputes with the colonies. The offense that led to the mobbing, though, was more specific: he had printed several lists of names of local merchants who had recently cleared imports through the Boston customs house. The Mein incident thus involved one of the first recorded examples in American history of a carefully orchestrated political "leak" from official sources. Some administrator had given the printer access to the supposedly private customs records. But why was the information Mein revealed so explosive? Because in the fall of 1769 many American merchants had signed an agreement not to import goods from Great Britain; Mein's lists indicated that some of the most vocal supporters of nonimportation (including the patriot leader John Hancock) had been violating the agreement. That was why the "gentlemen" of Boston had to silence the outspoken publisher.

John Mein was not the first, and he would be far from the last, resident of the colonies who found his life wholly disrupted by the growing political antagonism between England and her American possessions. Indeed, even Betsy Cuming herself was eventually forced into exile in Nova Scotia because she opposed the trend of American resistance to Great Britain. Long afterwards, John Adams identified the years between 1760 and 1775 as the period in which the true American Revolution had occurred. The Revolution, Adams declared, was completed before the fighting started, for it was "in the Minds of the people," involving not the actual winning of independence but rather a shift of allegiance from England to America. Today, not all historians would agree with Adams's assertion that that shift constituted the Revolution. But none would deny the importance of the events of those crucial years, which led to the division of the American population along political lines and started the colonies on the road to independence.

The story of the 1760s and early 1770s is one of an ever-widening split between England and America, and among their respective supporters in the colonies. In the long history of British settlement in the Western Hemisphere, there had at times been considerable tension in the relationship between individual provinces and mother country. Still, that tension had rarely been sustained for long, nor had it been widespread, except in 1688 and 1689. The primary divisions affecting the colonies had been internal rather than external. In the 1750s, however, a series of events began to change all that, shifting the colonists' attention from domestic matters to their relations with Great Britain. It all started with the French and Indian War (1754–1763).

Britain's overwhelming victory in that war forever altered the balance of power in North America. France was ousted from the continent, an event with major consequences for both the Indian tribes of the interior and the residents of the British colonies. Northern Indians could no longer play European powers off against one another, and so they lost one of their major diplomatic tools. Anglo-Americans, for their part, no longer had to fear a French threat on their borders. Some historians have argued that if the colonies had had to worry about the continuing presence of France on the North American mainland, the Revolution could never have occurred. The British

A LIST of the Names of *those*
who AUDACIOUSLY continue to counteract the UNIT-
ED SENTIMENTS of the BODY of Merchants thro'out
NORTH-AMERICA ; by importing British Goods
contrary to the Agreement.

John Bernard,
(In King-Street, almoft oppofite Vernon's Head.

James McMafters,
(On Treat's Wharf.

Patrick McMafters,
(Oppofite the Sign of the Lamb.

John Mein,
(Oppofite the White-Horfe, and in King-Street.

Nathaniel Rogers,
(Oppofite Mr. Henderfon Inches Store lower End
King-Street.

William Jackfon,
At the Brazen Head, Cornhill, near the Town-Houfe.

Theophilus Lillie,
(Near Mr. Pemberton's Meeting-Houfe, North-End.

John Taylor,
(Nearly oppofite the Heart and Crown in Cornhill.

Ame & Elizabeth Cummings,
(Oppofite the Old Brick Meeting Houfe, all of Bofton.

Ifrael Williams, Efq; *& Son,*
(Traders in the Town of Hatfield.

And, *Henry Barnes,*
(Trader in the Town of Marlboro'.

The following Names fhould have been inferted in
the Lift of Juftices.

County of Middlefex.	County of Lincoln.
Samuel Hendley	
John Borland	John Kingfbury
Henry Barnes	
Richard Cary	County of Berkfhire.
County of Briftol.	Mark Hopkins
George Brightman	Elijah Dwight
County of Worcefter.	Ifrael Stoddard
Daniel Blifs	

A blacklist printed in the North American Almanac for
1770 identified those Boston merchants who had ignored the
nonimportation agreement. Among their number were both
John Mein, the object of the mob's wrath the previous
October, and Betsy (Elizabeth) Cuming, the narrator of the
story, who—with her sister Anne—ran a small dry-goods
store. *Library of Congress.*

colonies would never have dared to break with their
mother country, it is said, if an enemy nation and
its Indian allies had controlled the interior of the
continent.

The British victory in 1763, then, constituted a
major turning point in American history because of
its direct effect on white and Indian residents of
North America. It also had a significant impact on
Great Britain, one that soon affected the colonies
as well. To win the war, Britain had gone heavily

into debt. To reduce the debt, Parliament for the
first time laid revenue-raising taxes on the colonies.
That decision exposed differences in the political
thinking of Americans and Britons—differences that
had until then been obscured by the use of a common
political vocabulary.

During the 1760s, a broad coalition of white
Americans, men and women alike, resisted new tax
levies and attempts by British officials to tighten
controls over the provincial governments. America's
elected leaders became ever more suspicious of Britain's
motives as the years passed. They laid aside traditional
intercolonial antagonisms to coordinate their response
to the new measures, and they slowly began to reorient
their political thinking. As late as the summer of
1774, though, most were still seeking a solution within
the framework of the empire; few harbored thoughts
of independence. When independence, as opposed
to loyal resistance, did become the issue, the coalition
of the 1760s broke down. That, however, did not
happen until after the battles of Lexington and Concord in April 1775. Before then, only a few Americans,
most of them closely connected to colonial administration or the Church of England, opposed the
trend of resistance.

RENEWED WARFARE AMONG
EUROPEANS AND INDIANS

While the English colonists had been consolidating control of the Atlantic seaboard, the
French and Spanish had been extending their influence
into the interior of North America around the edges
of English settlement. The Spanish outposts in Florida
and along the coast of the Gulf of Mexico posed
little threat to the English, for Spain's days as a major
power had passed. The French, though, were another
matter. In the late seventeenth and early eighteenth
centuries France had explored the Great Lakes and
Mississippi valley regions, establishing a long chain
of forts and settlements stretching from New Orleans
at the mouth of the Mississippi to Michilimackinac
at the junction of Lakes Huron and Michigan. From

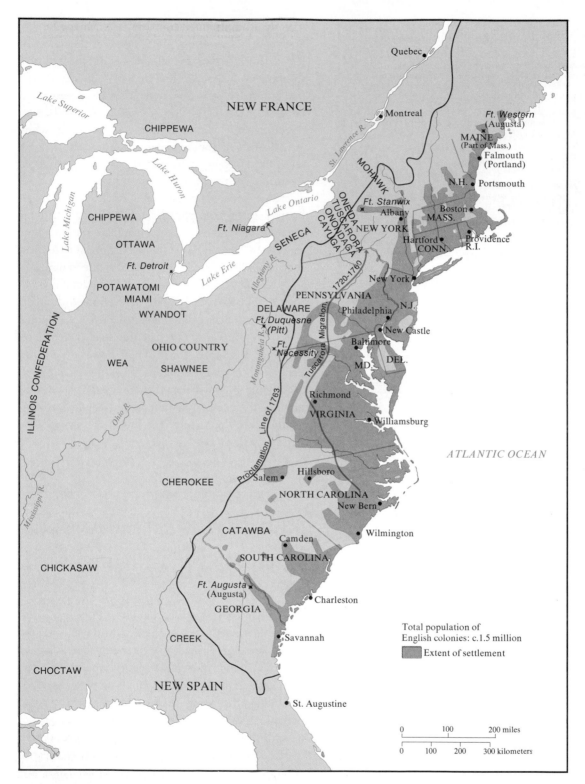

European Settlements and Indian Tribes, 1750

Chapter 4: SEVERING THE BONDS OF EMPIRE, 1754–1774

these posts they traded for furs with the tribes whose territories lay west of the Appalachian mountains. In none of the three wars fought between 1689 and 1748 was England able to shake France's domination of the North American interior, which rested on control of the inland system of rivers and lakes. Under the Peace of Utrecht, which ended Queen Anne's War in 1713, the English won control of such peripheral northern areas as Newfoundland, Hudson's Bay, and Nova Scotia (Acadia). But Britain made no additional territorial gains in King George's War (see map).

During both Queen Anne's War and King George's War, the Iroquois Confederacy adhered to the policy of neutrality it first developed in 1701 (see page 55).

Iroquois Neutrality While English and French forces fought for nominal control of the North American continent, the confederacy that actually dominated a large portion of that continent took no formal role. Instead, the Iroquois council skillfully played the Europeans off against one another, refusing to commit its warriors fully to either side despite being showered with presents by both. When the Iroquois went to war in those years, it was against a traditional southern enemy, the Catawba. Since the French repeatedly urged them to attack the Catawba (a tribe allied with the English), the Iroquois thereby achieved two desirable goals. They kept the French happy and simultaneously consolidated their control over the entire interior region north of Virginia. In addition, these southern wars (by identifying a common enemy) enabled the confederacy to cement its alliance with its weaker tributaries, the Shawnee and Delaware, and to ensure the continued subordination of those tribes.

But even the careful Iroquois diplomats could not prevent the region inhabited by the Shawnee and Delaware (now western Pennsylvania and eastern Ohio) from providing the spark that set off a major war. That conflict spread from America to Europe (a significant reversal of previous patterns) and proved decisive in the contest for North America. Trouble began in 1752 when English fur traders ventured into the area, known as the Ohio country. The French could not permit their English rivals to dominate the region, for it contained the source of the Ohio River, which offered direct access by water to their posts

In 1754 Benjamin Franklin produced his famous cartoon calling for unity among the English colonies in the face of the threat from the French and Indians. Later, during the Revolution, it was widely used as a symbol of the colonies' need to unite against Great Britain.   Library of Congress.

on the Mississippi. A permanent English presence in the Ohio country could challenge France's control of the western fur trade and even threaten its prominence in the Mississippi valley. Accordingly, in 1753 the French pushed southward from Lake Erie, building fortified outposts at strategic points along the rivers of the Ohio country.

In response to the threat posed by the French to their western frontiers, delegates from seven northern and middle colonies gathered in Albany, New York, in June 1754. With the backing of administrators in London, they sought two goals: to persuade the Iroquois to abandon their traditional neutrality, and to coordinate the defenses of the colonies. In neither aim were they successful. The Iroquois, while listening politely to the colonists' arguments, saw no reason to change a policy that had served them well for half a century. And although the Albany Congress delegates adopted a Plan of Union (which would have established an elected intercolonial legislature with the power to tax), the plan was uniformly rejected by their provincial governments—primarily because those governments feared a loss of autonomy.

The delegates to the Congress did not know that, while they deliberated, the war they sought to prepare for was already beginning. Governor Robert Dinwiddie

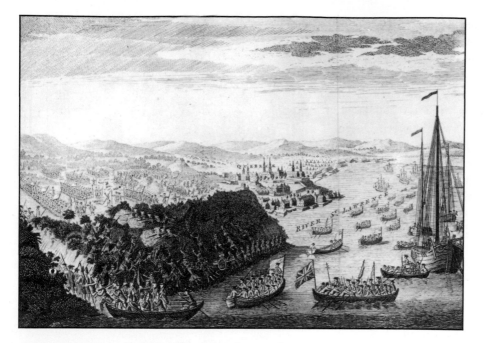

On the night of September 13, 1759, British forces under General James Wolfe scaled the heights of Quebec and defeated the French army led by General Louis Joseph Montcalm. Both generals died on the battlefield. Library of Congress.

of Virginia had sent a small militia force westward to counter the French moves. Virginia claimed ownership of the Ohio country, and Dinwiddie was eager to prevent the French from establishing a permanent post there. But the Virginia militiamen arrived too late. The French had already taken possession of the strategic point—now Pittsburgh—where the Allegheny and Monongahela rivers meet to form the Ohio, and they were busily engaged in constructing Fort Duquesne. The foolhardy and inexperienced young colonel who commanded the Virginians attacked a French detachment, then allowed himself to be trapped by the French in his crudely built Fort Necessity at Great Meadows, Pennsylvania. After a day-long battle (on July 3, 1754), during which more than one-third of his men were killed or wounded, the twenty-two-year-old George Washington surrendered. He signed a document of capitulation, and he and his men were allowed to return to Virginia.

Beginning of the French and Indian War

Washington had blundered grievously. He had started a war that would eventually encompass nearly the entire world. He had also ensured that the tribes of the Ohio valley, many of whom had moved west to escape Iroquois domination and to trade directly with the French, would for the most part support France in the coming conflict. The Indians took Washington's mistakes as an indication of Britain's inability to win the war, and nothing that occurred in the next four years made them change their minds. In July 1755 a combined force of French and Indians ambushed General Edward Braddock, two regiments of British regulars, and some colonial troops a few miles south of Fort Duquesne. Braddock was killed and his men demoralized by their complete defeat.

For three more years one disaster followed another for Great Britain. The war went so badly that Britain began to fear that France would attempt to retake Newfoundland and Nova Scotia. Trying to consolidate their control of the region, the British administrators of Nova Scotia forced its French residents to leave the homes they had occupied for generations. After years of wandering, many of these Acadian exiles made their way to Louisiana, where they became known as Cajuns.

At last, under the leadership of William Pitt, who was named secretary of state in 1757, the British mounted the effort that won them the war in North America. In July 1758 they recaptured the fortress at Louisbourg; in a surprise night attack in September 1759 they broke down the defenses of Quebec. Sensing a British victory, the Iroquois abandoned their policy of neutrality and allied themselves with the British, hoping to gain some diplomatic leverage by that decision. A year later the British took Montreal, the last French stronghold. The war in America thus ended in 1760, though fighting continued for three more years in the Caribbean, India, and Europe.

When the Treaty of Paris was signed in 1763, France ceded its major North American holdings to Britain. Spain, an ally of France toward the end of the war, gave Florida to the victorious English. And since Britain feared the presence of France in Louisiana, it forced the French to cede that region to Spain, a weaker power. No longer would the English seacoast colonies have to worry about the threat to their existence posed by France's extensive North American territories (see maps).

Pitt achieved this stunning victory by encouraging cooperation between the colonists and Great Britain. In the early years of the war—the years of England's many defeats—British army and navy officers had adopted coercive recruiting techniques. They arbitrarily commandeered supplies from American farmers and merchants and ordered the quartering of royal troops in private homes. All these actions aroused the colonists' ire. Pitt, by contrast, agreed to reimburse the colonies for their military expenditures and placed troop recruitment wholly in local hands. Consequently, Americans (especially New Englanders) began to support the war effort more fully. As many as one-third of all Massachusetts men between the ages of sixteen and twenty-nine served for a time in the provincial army.

Yet British commanders denigrated the American contributions to the winning campaigns. For one thing, most of the actual fighting was carried on by British regulars, with colonial troops being relegated

BEFORE 1754

▨ English	▨ New Spain
▨ New France	▨ Russian

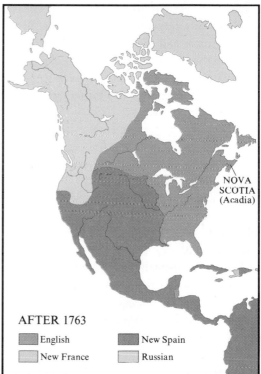

AFTER 1763

▨ English	▨ New Spain
▨ New France	▨ Russian

European Claims in North America

Anglo-American Tensions

to support roles (a practice the Americans resented). For another, the British army leaders alleged that American merchants were prolonging the conflict by continuing to trade with the French West Indies. (The Americans responded that their economies would collapse without the West Indian trade, and that in any event the French islands were contributing little to the mainland war.) And, finally, redcoat officers and enlisted men alike looked down on their American counterparts as undisciplined and ignorant of military procedures. As one arrogant colonel declared, "The Provincials [are] sufficient to work our Boats, drive our Waggons, and fell our Trees, and do the Work that in inhabited Countrys are performed by Peasants."

Over the decade and a half following the close of the American phase of the war in 1760, as the colonies and Great Britain moved slowly toward a confrontation, each drew on impressions of the other gained during the French and Indian War. The British dismissed any suggestion of American military prowess with a laugh. The Americans, meanwhile, remembered the threat of arbitrary military power, the British officers' arrogance, and their own wounded pride. In other words, the victorious alliance of colonies and mother country had done nothing to dispel—and possibly much to promote—the gathering clouds of disagreement.

1763: A TURNING POINT

The overwhelming British victory over France had an irreversible impact on North America. Its effects were felt first by the Indian tribes that had used the competition among European powers to maintain their autonomy. With France excluded from the continent altogether and Spanish territory now confined to the area west of the Mississippi, the diplomatic strategy that had served the tribes well for so long could no longer be employed. The consequences were immediate and devastating.

Even before the Treaty of Paris, southern Indians had to adjust to the new circumstances. After the British gained the upper hand in the American war in 1758, the Creek and Cherokee lost their ability to force concessions from the British by threatening to turn instead to the French or the Spanish. In desperation and in retaliation for British atrocities, the Cherokee attacked the Carolina and Virginia frontiers in 1760. Although initially victorious, the tribesmen were defeated the following year by a force of British regulars and colonial militia. Late in 1761 the two sides concluded a treaty under which the Cherokee allowed the construction of English forts in tribal territories and also opened a large tract of land to white settlement.

The fate of the Cherokee in the South was a portent of things to come in the Northwest. There, the western tribes—the Ottawa, Chippewa, and Potawatomi—became angry when Great Britain, no longer facing French competition, raised the price of trade goods and ended the practice of paying rent for forts. In addition, the British allowed settlers to move into the Monongahela and Susquehanna valleys, onto Delaware and Iroquois lands.

Pontiac, the war chief of an Ottawa village near Detroit, understood the implications of such British actions. Only unity among the western tribes, he realized, could possibly prevent total dependence on and subordination to the victorious British. Using his considerable powers of persuasion, in the spring of 1763 he forged an unprecedented alliance among the Huron, Chippewa, Potawatomi, Delaware, and Shawnee tribes, even gaining the participation of some Mingoes (Pennsylvania Iroquois). Pontiac then laid seige to the fort at Detroit while his war parties attacked the other British outposts in the Great Lakes region. Detroit withstood the siege, but by the end of June all the other forts west of Niagara and north of Fort Pitt (old Fort Duquesne) had fallen to the Indian alliance.

Pontiac's Uprising

That was the high point of the uprising. The tribes raided the Virginia and Pennsylvania frontiers at will throughout the summer, killing at least two thousand whites. But they could not take the strongholds of Niagara, Fort Pitt, or Detroit. In early August, a combined force of Delawares, Shawnees, Hurons, and Mingoes was soundly defeated at Bushy Run, Pennsylvania, by troops sent from the coast. Conflict ceased when Pontiac broke off the siege of Detroit

In 1764, Colonel Henry Bouquet, the victor the preceding year at the battle of Bushy Run, negotiated with representatives of the Seneca, Shawnee, and Delaware at a council held on the Muskingum River in the Ohio country. The agreement reached there opened part of the region to white settlement.   Library of Congress.

in late October, after most of his warriors had returned to their villages. A formal treaty ending the war was finally negotiated in 1766.

In the aftermath of the bloody summer of 1763, Scotch-Irish frontiersmen from Paxton Township, Pennsylvania, sought revenge on the only Indians within reach, a peaceful band of Christian converts living at Conestoga. In December the whites raided the Indian village twice, killing twenty people. Two months later hundreds of frontier dwellers known to history as the Paxton Boys marched on Philadelphia to demand military protection against future Indian attacks. City officials feared violence and mustered the militia to repel the westerners, but the protesters presented their request in an orderly fashion and returned home.

Pontiac's uprising and the march of the Paxton Boys showed that Great Britain would not find it easy to govern the huge territory it had just acquired from France. The central administration in London

Proclamation of 1763

had had no prior experience in managing such a vast tract of land, particularly one inhabited by two hostile peoples—the remaining French settlers along the St. Lawrence and the many Indian tribes. In October, in a futile attempt to assert control over the interior, the ministry issued the Proclamation of 1763, which declared the headwaters of rivers flowing into the Atlantic from the Appalachian Mountains to be the temporary western boundary for colonial settlement. The proclamation was intended to prevent future clashes between Indians and colonists by forbidding whites to move onto Indian lands until the tribes had given up their land by treaty. But many whites had already established farms west of the proclamation line, and the policy was doomed to failure from its outset.

The proclamation directly affected only frontier families; other decisions made in London in 1763 and thereafter had a much broader impact in British

King George III in his coronation robes, 1760, painted by Allan Ramsay. Colonial Williamsburg photograph.

North America. The victory in the French and Indian War both posed problems for and offered opportunities to the British government. The most pressing problem was Britain's immense war debt. The men who had to solve that problem were King George III and his new prime minister, George Grenville.

In 1760 George III, then twenty-two years old, succeeded his grandfather, George II, on the English throne. The young king, a man of mediocre intellect and even more mediocre education, **George III** was unfortunately a poor—or, more accurately, an erratic—judge of character. During the crucial years between 1763 and 1770, when the rift between England and the colonies was growing ever wider, he replaced ministries with bewildering rapidity. The king, though determined to assert the power of the monarchy, was immature and unsure of himself. He often substituted stubbornness for intelligence, and he regarded adherence to the status quo as the hallmark of true patriotism.

The man he selected as prime minister in 1763,

George Grenville, believed that the American colonies should be more tightly administered than in the past. Grenville confronted a financial crisis: England's burden of indebtedness had nearly doubled since 1754, from £73 million to £137 million. Annual expenditures before the war had amounted to no more than £8 million; now the yearly interest on the debt alone came to £5 million. Obviously, Grenville's ministry had to find new sources of funds, and the English people themselves were already heavily taxed. Since the colonists had been major beneficiaries of the wartime expenditures, Grenville concluded that the Americans should be asked to pay a greater share of the cost of running the empire.

It did not occur to Grenville to question Great Britain's right to levy taxes on the colonies. Like all his countrymen, he believed that the government's legitimacy derived ultimately from **Theories of** the consent of the people, but he **Representation** defined consent far more loosely than did the colonists. Americans had come to believe that they could be represented only by men for whom they or their property-holding neighbors had actually voted; otherwise they could not count on legislators to protect them from oppression. To Grenville and his English contemporaries, Parliament—king, lords, and commons acting together—by definition represented all English subjects, wherever they resided (even overseas) and whether or not they could vote. According to this theory of government, called *virtual representation,* the colonists were said to be virtually, if not actually, represented in Parliament. Thus their consent to acts of Parliament could be presumed.

In other words, the Americans and the English began at the same theoretical starting point but arrived at different conclusions in practice. In England, members of Parliament saw themselves as *collectively* representing the entire nation, composed of nobility and common folk. Only members of the House of Commons were elected, and the particular constituency that chose a member had no special claim on his vote. In the colonies, by contrast, members of the lower houses of the assemblies were viewed as *individually* representing the voters who had elected them. Before Grenville proposed to tax the colonists, the two notions existed side by side without apparent contradiction. But the events of the 1760s pointed up the difference between the English and colonial definitions of representation.

The same events threw into sharp relief Americans' attitudes toward political power. The colonists had become accustomed to a government that wielded only limited authority over them and affected their daily lives very little. In consequence, they believed that a good government was one that largely left them alone, a view in keeping with the theories of a group of British writers known as the Real Whigs. Drawing on a tradition of English dissenting thought that reached back to the days of the Civil War, the Real Whigs stressed the dangers inherent in a powerful government, particularly one headed by a monarch. They warned that the people had to guard constantly against the government's attempts to encroach on their liberties. Political power was always to be feared, wrote John Trenchard and Thomas Gordon in their essay series *Cato's Letters* (originally published in England in 1720–1723 and reprinted many times thereafter in the colonies). Rulers would try to corrupt and oppress the people. Only the perpetual vigilance of the people and their elected representatives could preserve their fragile yet precious freedoms.

Britain's attempts to tighten the reins of government and raise revenues from the colonies in the 1760s and early 1770s convinced many Americans that the Real Whigs' reasoning applied to their circumstances. They began to interpret British measures in light of the Real Whigs' warnings and to see evil designs behind the actions of Grenville and his successors. Historians disagree over the extent to which those perceptions were correct, but by 1775 a large number of colonists unquestionably believed they were. In the mid-1760s, colonial leaders did not, however, immediately accuse Grenville of an intent to oppress them. They at first simply questioned the wisdom of the laws Grenville proposed.

The first such measures, the Sugar and Currency Acts, were passed by Parliament in 1764. The Sugar Act revised the existing system of customs regulations; **Sugar and Currency Acts** laid new duties on certain foreign imports into the colonies; established a vice-admiralty court at Halifax, Nova Scotia; and included special provisions aimed at stopping the widespread smuggling of molasses, one of the chief commodities in American trade. Although the Sugar Act appeared to resemble the Navigation Acts (see page 64), it broke with tradition because it was explicitly designed to raise revenue, not to channel American trade through Britain. The Currency Act in effect outlawed colonial issues of paper money. (For years, the colonies had printed their own money to supplement the private bills of exchange that circulated chiefly among merchants.) Americans could accumulate little hard cash, since they imported more than they exported; thus the act seemed to the colonists to deprive them of a useful medium of exchange.

The Sugar and Currency Acts were visited upon an economy already in the midst of depression. A business boom had accompanied the French and Indian War, but the brief spell of prosperity ended abruptly in 1760, when the war shifted overseas. Urban merchants could not sell all their imported goods to colonial customers alone, and without the military's demand for foodstuffs, American farmers found fewer buyers for their products. The bottom dropped out of the European tobacco market, threatening the livelihood of Chesapeake planters. Sailors were thrown out of work, and artisans found few employers to hire them. In such circumstances, the prospect of increased customs duties and inadequate supplies of currency naturally aroused merchants' hostility.

It is not surprising that both individual colonists and colonial governments decided to protest the new policies. But, lacking any precedent for a united campaign against acts of Parliament, Americans in 1764 took only hesitant and uncoordinated steps. Eight colonial legislatures sent separate petitions to Parliament requesting repeal of the Sugar Act. They argued that the act placed severe restrictions on their commerce (and would therefore hurt Britain as well), and that they had not consented to its passage. The protests had no effect. The law remained in force and Grenville proceeded with another revenue plan.

THE STAMP ACT CRISIS

The Stamp Act, Grenville's most important proposal, was modeled on a law that had been in effect in England for nearly a century. It touched nearly every colonist by requiring tax stamps on most printed materials, but placed the heaviest burden on merchants and other members of the colonial elite, who used printed matter more frequently than ordinary folk. Anyone who purchased a newspaper or pamphlet, made a will, transferred land, bought dice or playing cards, needed a liquor license, accepted a government appointment, or borrowed money would have to pay the tax. Never before had a revenue measure of such scope been proposed for the colonies. The act would also require that tax stamps be paid for with hard money and that violators be tried in vice-admiralty courts, without juries. Finally, such a law would break decisively with the colonial tradition of self-imposed taxation.

The most important colonial pamphlet protesting the Sugar Act and the proposed Stamp Act was *The Rights of the British Colonies Asserted and Proved*, by James Otis, Jr., a brilliant young Massachusetts attorney. Otis starkly exposed the ideological dilemma that was to confound the colonists for the next decade. How could they justify their opposition to certain acts of Parliament without questioning Parliament's authority over them? On the one hand, Otis asserted that Americans were "entitled to all the natural, essential, inherent, and inseparable rights" of Britons, including the right not to be taxed without their consent. "No man or body of men, not excepting the parliament . . . can take [those rights] away," he declared. On the other hand, Otis was forced to admit that, under the British system established after the Glorious Revolution of 1688 and 1689, "the power of parliament is uncontroulable, but by themselves, and we must obey. . . . Let the parliament lay what burthens they please on us, we must, it is our duty to submit and patiently bear them, till they will be pleased to relieve us."

Otis's Rights of the British Colonies

Otis's first contention, drawing on colonial notions of representation, implied that Parliament could not constitutionally tax the colonies because Americans were not represented in its ranks. Yet his second point both acknowledged political reality and accepted the prevailing theory of British government—that Parliament was the sole, supreme authority in the empire. Even unconstitutional laws enacted by Parliament had to be obeyed until Parliament decided to repeal them. According to orthodox British political theory, there could be no middle ground between absolute submission to Parliament and a frontal challenge to its authority. Otis tried to find such a middle ground by proposing colonial representation in Parliament, but his idea was never taken seriously on either side of the Atlantic. The British believed that the colonists were already virtually represented in Parliament, and the Americans quickly realized that a handful of colonial delegates to London would simply be outvoted.

Otis wrote his pamphlet before the Stamp Act was passed. When Americans learned of its adoption in the spring of 1765, they did not at first know how to react. Few colonists publicly favored the law; opposition to it was nearly universal, even among appointed government officials. But colonial petitions had already failed to prevent its adoption, and further lobbying appeared futile. Perhaps Otis was right, and the only course open to the Americans was to pay the stamp tax, reluctantly but loyally. Acting on that assumption, colonial agents in London sought the appointment of their American friends as stamp distributors, so that the law would at least be enforced equitably.

Not all the colonists were resigned to paying the new tax without a fight. Just such a man was a twenty-nine-year-old lawyer serving his first term as a member of the Virginia House of Burgesses. Patrick Henry later recalled that he was at the time "young, inexperienced, unacquainted with the forms of the House and the members that composed it," and appalled by his fellow legislators' unwillingness to oppose the Stamp Act openly. Henry decided to act. "Alone, unadvised, and unassisted, on a blank leaf of an old law book," he wrote the Virginia Stamp Act Resolves.

Patrick Henry and the Virginia Stamp Act Resolves

Little in Henry's earlier life foreshadowed his success in the political arena he entered so dramatically. The son of a prosperous Scottish immigrant to western Virginia, Henry had had little formal education. After marrying at eighteen, he failed at both farming and storekeeping before turning to the law as a means of supporting his wife and their six children. Henry lacked legal training, but his oratorical skills made him an effective advocate, first for his clients and later for his political beliefs. As a prominent Virginia lawyer said of him, "He is by far the most powerful speaker I ever heard. Every word he says not only engages, but commands the attention; and your passions are no longer your own when he addresses them."

Patrick Henry introduced his proposals in late May, near the end of the legislative session; many members of the House of Burgesses had already departed for home. Henry's fiery speech in support of his resolutions led the Speaker of the House to accuse him of treason. (Henry quickly denied the charge, contrary to the nineteenth-century myth that had him exclaiming in reply, "If this be treason, make the most of it!") The small number of burgesses remaining in Williamsburg adopted five of Henry's resolutions by a bare majority. Though they repealed the most radical resolution the next day, their action had far-reaching effects. Some colonial newspapers printed Henry's seven original resolutions as if they had been uniformly passed by the House, even though one had been rescinded and two others were evidently never debated or voted on at all.

The four propositions adopted by the burgesses repeated the arguments James Otis had already advanced. The colonists had never forfeited the rights of British subjects, they declared, and consent to taxation was one of the most important of those rights. The other three resolutions went much further. The one that was repealed claimed for the burgesses "the only exclusive right" to tax Virginians. The final two asserted that residents of the colony did not have to obey tax laws passed by other legislative bodies (namely Parliament) and termed any opponent of that opinion "an Enemy to this his Majesty's Colony."

The burgesses' decision to accept only the first four of Henry's resolutions accurately predicted the position most Americans would adopt throughout the following decade. Though willing to contend for their rights, the colonists did not seek independence. They merely wanted some measure of self-government. Accordingly, they backed away from the assertions that they owed Parliament no obedience and that their own assemblies alone could tax them. Indeed, declared the Maryland lawyer Daniel Dulany, whose *Considerations on the Propriety of Imposing Taxes on the British Colonies* was the most widely read pamphlet of 1765, "The colonies are dependent upon Great Britain, and the supreme authority vested in the king, lords, and commons, may justly be exercised to secure, or preserve their dependence." But, warned Dulany, a superior did not have the right "to seize the property of his inferior when he pleases"; there was a crucial distinction between a condition of "dependence and *inferiority*" and one of "absolute *vassalage* and *slavery*."

Over the course of the next ten years, America's political leaders searched for a formula that would enable them to control their internal affairs, especially taxation, but remain within the British Empire. The chief difficulty lay in British officials' inability to compromise on the issue of parliamentary power. The notion that Parliament could exercise absolute authority over all colonial possessions was basic to the British theory of government. Even the harshest British critics of the ministries of the 1760s and 1770s questioned only the wisdom of specific policies, not the principles on which they were based. In effect, the Americans wanted British leaders to revise their fundamental understanding of the workings of their government. That was simply too much to expect, given the circumstances.

The ultimate effectiveness of Americans' opposition to the Stamp Act did not rest on ideological arguments over parliamentary power. What gave the resistance its primary force were the decisive and inventive actions of some colonists during the late summer and fall of 1765.

In August the Loyal Nine, a Boston social club of printers, distillers, and other artisans, organized a demonstration against the Stamp Act. Hoping to show that people of all social and **Loyal Nine** economic ranks opposed the act, they approached the leaders of the city's rival laborers' associations, one based in the North End and one in the South End. The two gangs, composed of unskilled workers and poor tradesmen, often battled with each other, but the Loyal Nine convinced them to lay aside their differences and participate in the demonstration. After all, the stamp taxes would have to be paid by all colonists, not just affluent ones.

Early in the morning of August 14, the demonstrators hung an effigy of Andrew Oliver, the province's stamp distributor, from a tree on Boston Common. That night a large crowd led by a group of about

This woodcut, produced half a century after the event, shows a crowd parading the effigy of the New Hampshire stamp distributor through the streets of Portsmouth in 1765. The procession is led by men carrying a coffin to symbolize the death and burial of the Stamp Act.   The Metropolitian Museum of Art, Bequest of Charles Allen Munn.

fifty well-dressed tradesmen paraded the effigy around the city. The crowd tore down a small building they thought was intended as the stamp office and built a bonfire with the wood near Oliver's house. They then beheaded the effigy and added it to the flames. Members of the crowd broke most of Oliver's windows and threw stones at officials who tried to disperse them. In the midst of the melee, the North End and South End leaders drank a toast to their successful union. The Loyal Nine's demonstration achieved its objective when Oliver publicly promised not to fulfill the duties of his office. One Bostonian jubilantly told a relative, "I believe people never was more Universally pleased not so much as one could I hear say he was sorry, but a smile sat on almost every ones countinance."

But another crowd action twelve days later, aimed this time at Oliver's brother-in-law Lieutenant Governor Thomas Hutchinson, drew no praise from the respectable citizens of Boston. On the night of August 26, a mob reportedly led by the South End leader, Ebenezer MacIntosh, attacked the homes of several customs officers. The crowd then completely destroyed Hutchinson's elaborately furnished townhouse in one of Boston's most fashionable districts. The lieutenant governor reported that by the next morning "one of the best finished houses in the Province had nothing remaining but the bare walls and floors." His trees and garden were ruined as well, and the mob had "emptied the house of every thing whatsoever except a part of the kitchen furniture." But Hutchinson took some comfort in the fact that "the encouragers of the first mob never intended matters should go this length and the people in general express the utmost detestation of this unparalleled outrage."

The differences between the two Boston mobs of August 1765 exposed divisions that would continue to characterize colonial protests in the years that followed. Although few residents of the colonies sided with Great Britain during these early years of protest,

Americans' Divergent Interests

the various colonial interest groups often had divergent goals that caused splits in their ranks. The skilled craftsmen who composed the Loyal Nine and members of the educated elite like merchants and lawyers preferred orderly demonstrations confined to political issues. For the city's laborers, by contrast, economic grievances may well have been paramount; certainly, their "hellish Fury" as they wrecked Hutchinson's house suggests a resentment against his ostentatious display of wealth.

The colonies, like the mother country, had a long tradition of crowd action, in which disfranchised people took to the streets to redress deeply felt local grievances (such as the high cost of food during a depression or the operation of a house of prostitution in a residential neighborhood). But the Stamp Act controversy drew ordinary urban folk into the vortex of imperial politics for the first time. Matters that had previously been of concern only to genteel folk, or to members of colonial legislatures, were now discussed on every street corner. Sally Franklin observed as much when she wrote to her father, Benjamin, who was then serving as a colonial agent in London, that "nothing else is talked of, the Dutch [Germans] talk of the stompt act the Negroes of the tamp, in short every body has something to say."

The entry of lower-class whites, blacks, and women into the realm of imperial politics both threatened and afforded an opportunity to the well-to-do white men who wanted to mount effective opposition to British measures. On the one hand, crowd action could have a stunning impact (see map). Anti–Stamp Act demonstrations occurred in cities and towns stretching from Halifax, Nova Scotia, in the north, to the Caribbean island of Antigua. They were so successful that by November 1, when the law was scheduled to take effect, not a single stamp distributor was willing to carry out the duties of his office. As a result, the act could not be enforced. But at the same time, since the goals of the crowd were not always identical to the goals of its nominal leaders (as the Boston experience so clearly showed), members of the elite recognized that mobs composed of the formerly powerless could potentially endanger their own dominant position in society. What would happen, they wondered, if the "hellish Fury" of the crowd were turned against them?

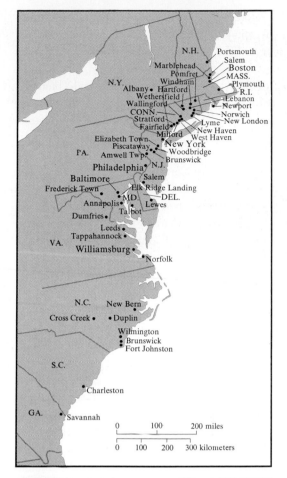

Sites of Major Demonstrations Against the Stamp Act

Therefore, they attempted to channel resistance into acceptable forms by creating an intercolonial association, the Sons of Liberty. The first such group was created in New York City in early November, and branches spread rapidly through the colonies. Largely composed of merchants, lawyers, prosperous tradesmen, and the like, the Sons of Liberty linked resistance leaders in cities from Charleston, South Carolina, to Portsmouth, New Hampshire, by early 1766.

Sons of Liberty

But the Sons of Liberty could not control all reactions in the new climate of protest. In Charleston in late October 1765 an organized crowd shouting "Liberty Liberty and stamp'd paper" forced the resignation of the South Carolina stamp distributor. The event was celebrated a few days later in the largest demonstration the city had ever known, at which was displayed a British flag with the word LIBERTY written across it. But white resistance leaders were horrified when in January 1766 local slaves paraded through the streets similarly crying "Liberty." The local militia was mustered, messengers were sent to outlying areas with warnings of a possible plot, and one black was banished from the colony.

In Philadelphia, resistance leaders were dismayed when an angry mob threatened to attack Benjamin Franklin's house. The city's laborers believed Franklin to be partly responsible for the Stamp Act, since he had obtained the post of stamp distributor for a close friend. But Philadelphia's artisans—the backbone of the opposition movement there and elsewhere—were fiercely loyal to Franklin, one of their own who had made good. They gathered to protect his home and family from the crowd. The house was saved, but the resulting split between the better-off tradesmen and the common laborers prevented Philadelphians from establishing a successful workingmen's alliance like that of Boston.

During the fall and winter of 1765 and 1766, opposition to the Stamp Act proceeded on three separate fronts. The colonial legislatures petitioned Parliament to repeal the hated law and sent delegates to an intercolonial congress, the first since 1754. In October the Stamp Act Congress met in New York to draft a unified but relatively conservative statement of protest. At the same time, the Sons of Liberty held mass meetings in an effort to win public support for the resistance movement. Finally, American merchants organized nonimportation associations to put economic pressure on British exporters. By the 1760s one-quarter of all British exports were being sent to the colonies, and American merchants reasoned that London merchants whose sales had suffered severely would lobby for repeal. Since times were bad and American merchants were finding few customers for imported goods in any case, a general moratorium on future purchases would also help to reduce their bloated inventories.

In March 1766, Parliament repealed the Stamp Act. The nonimportation agreements had had the anticipated effect, creating allies for the colonies among wealthy London merchants. But boycotts, formal protests, and crowd actions were less important in winning repeal than was Grenville's replacement as prime minister in summer 1765. Lord Rockingham, the new minister, had opposed the Stamp Act, not because he believed Parliament lacked power to tax the colonies but because he thought the law unwise and divisive. Thus, although Rockingham proposed repeal, he linked it to passage of the Declaratory Act, which asserted Parliament's ability to tax and legislate for Britain's American possessions "in all cases whatsoever."

Repeal of the Stamp Act

News of the repeal arrived in Newport, Rhode Island, in May, and the Sons of Liberty quickly transmitted the welcome tidings to all parts of the colonies. They also organized many celebrations commemorating the glorious event, all of which stressed the Americans' unwavering loyalty to Great Britain. Their goal achieved, the Sons of Liberty dissolved. Few colonists saw the ominous implications of the Declaratory Act.

RESISTANCE TO
THE TOWNSHEND ACTS

The colonists had accomplished their immediate aim, but the long-term prospects were unclear. Another change in the ministry, in the summer of 1766, revealed how fragile their victory had been.

BRITISH MINISTRIES AND THEIR AMERICAN POLICIES	
Head of Ministry	Major Acts
George Grenville	Sugar Act (1764)
	Currency Act (1764)
	Stamp Act (1765)
Lord Rockingham	Stamp Act repeal (1766)
	Declaratory Act (1766)
William Pitt/Charles Townshend	Townshend Acts (1767)
Lord North	Townshend duties repealed (all but tea tax) (1770)
	Coercive Acts (1774)
	Quebec Act (1774)

Charles Townshend, a Grenvillite, was named chancellor of the exchequer in a new administration headed by the ailing William Pitt. Pitt was ill much of the time, and Townshend became the dominant force in the ministry. He decided to renew the attempt to obtain additional funds from the colonies.

The taxes Townshend proposed in 1767 were to be levied on trade goods like paper, glass, and tea, and thus seemed on the surface to be nothing more than extensions of the existing Navigation Acts. But the Townshend duties differed from previous customs taxes in two ways. First, they were levied on items imported into the colonies from Britain, not from foreign countries. Thus they were at odds with mercantilist theory (see page 61). Second, they were designed, like the Sugar Act, to raise money. The receipts, moreover, would pay the salaries of royal officials in the colonies. That posed a direct challenge to the colonial assemblies, which derived considerable power from threatening to withhold officials' salaries. In addition, Townshend's scheme provided for the establishment of an American Board of Customs Commissioners and for the creation of vice-admiralty courts at Boston, Philadelphia, and Charleston. Both moves angered merchants, whose profits would be threatened by more vigorous enforcement of the Navigation Acts. Lastly, Townshend proposed the appointment of a secretary of state for American affairs and the suspension of the New York legislature for refusal to comply with an act requiring colonial governments to supply certain items (like firewood and candles) to British troops stationed permanently in America.

Unlike 1765, when months passed before the colonists began to protest the Stamp Act, the passage of the Townshend Acts drew a quick response. One series of essays in particular, *Letters from a Farmer in Pennsylvania* by the prominent lawyer John Dickinson, expressed a broad consensus. Eventually all but four colonial newspapers printed Dickinson's essays; in pamphlet form they went through at least seven American editions. Dickinson contended that Parliament could regulate colonial trade, but could not exercise that power for the purpose of raising revenues. By drawing a distinction between the acceptable regulation of trade and unacceptable commercial taxation, Dickinson entirely avoided the sticky issue of consent and how it affected the extent of colonial subordination to Parliament. But his argument created a different, and equally knotty, problem. In effect it forced the colonies to assess Parliament's motives in passing any law pertaining to imperial trade before deciding whether to obey it. That was clearly an unworkable position.

The Massachusetts assembly responded to the Townshend Acts by drafting a circular letter to the

John Dickinson, as painted by Charles Willson Peale in 1770. Dickinson was then at the height of his popularity as a spokesman for the colonial cause; this portrait was commissioned by an English admirer of his work.   The Historical Society of Pennsylvania.

The figure 45 became a symbol of resistance to Great Britain when John Wilkes, a radical Englishman sympathetic to the American cause, was jailed for libel because of his publication of the essay *The North Briton No. 45*. After the events in Massachusetts, 92, the number of votes cast against recalling the circular letter, assumed ritual significance as well. In Boston, for example, the silversmith Paul Revere made a punchbowl weighing 45 ounces, which held 45 gills (half-cups) and was engraved with the names of the 92 legislators; James Otis, John Adams, and others publicly drank 45 toasts from it.

Pleasant social occasions though they were, such public rituals served important educational functions. Just as the pamphlets by Otis, Dulany, Dickinson, and others acquainted literate colonists with the issues raised by British actions, so the public rituals taught illiterate Americans about the reasons for resistance and familiarized them with the terms of the argument. When Boston's revived Sons of Liberty invited hundreds of the city's residents to dine with them each August 14 to commemorate the first Stamp Act uprising, and the Charleston Sons of Liberty held their meetings in public, crowds gathered to watch and listen. The participants in such events were openly expressing their commitment to the cause of resistance and encouraging others to join them.

Rituals of Resistance

During the two-year campaign against the Townshend duties, the Sons of Liberty and other American leaders made a deliberate effort to involve ordinary folk in the formal resistance movement, not just in occasional crowd actions. In a June 1769 Maryland nonimportation agreement, for instance, the signers (who were identified as "Merchants, Tradesmen, Freeholders, Mechanics [artisans], and other Inhabitants") agreed not to import or consume items of British origin. Such tactics helped to increase the number of colonists who were publicly aligned with the protest movement.

Women, who had previously regarded politics as outside their proper sphere, now took a part in resisting British policy. In towns throughout America, young women calling themselves Daughters of Liberty met to spin in public, in an effort to spur other women to make homespun and end the colonies' depen-

Daughters of Liberty

other colonial legislatures, calling for unity and suggesting a joint petition of protest. It was less the letter itself than the ministry's reaction to it that united the colonies. When Lord Hillsborough, the first secretary of state for America, learned of the circular letter, he ordered Governor Francis Bernard of Massachusetts to insist that the assembly recall it. He also directed other governors to prevent their assemblies from discussing the letter. Hillsborough's order gave the colonial assemblies the incentive they needed to forget their differences and join forces to meet the new threat to their prerogatives. In late 1768 the Massachusetts legislature met, debated, and resoundingly rejected recall by a vote of 92 to 17. Bernard immediately dissolved the assembly, and other governors followed suit when their legislatures debated the circular letter.

Massachusetts Assembly Dissolved

dence on English cloth. These symbolic displays of patriotism served the same purpose as the male rituals involving the numbers 45 and 92. When young ladies from well-to-do families sat publicly at spinning wheels all day, eating only American food and drinking local herbal tea, and afterwards listening to patriotic sermons, they were serving as political instructors. Many women took great satisfaction in their new-found role. When a New England satirist hinted that women discussed only "such triffling subjects as Dress, Scandal and Detraction" during their spinning bees, three Boston women replied angrily: "Inferior in abusive sarcasm, in personal invective, in low wit, we glory to be, but inferior in veracity, sincerity, love of virtue, of liberty and of our country, we would not willingly be to any."

Women also took the lead in promoting nonconsumption of tea. In Boston more than three hundred matrons publicly promised not to drink tea, "Sickness excepted." The women of Wilmington, North Carolina, burned their tea after walking through town in a solemn procession. Housewives throughout the colonies exchanged recipes for tea substitutes or drank coffee instead. The best known of the protests (because it was satirized by a British cartoonist), the so-called Edenton Ladies Tea Party, actually had little to do with tea; it was a meeting of prominent North Carolina women who pledged formally to work for the public good and to support resistance to British measures.

But the colonists were by no means united in support of nonimportation. If the Stamp Act protests had occasionally (as in Boston and Philadelphia) revealed a division between artisans and merchants, on the one hand, and common laborers, on the other, resistance to the Townshend Acts exposed new splits in the American ranks. The most important divided the former allies of 1765 and 1766, the urban artisans and merchants, and it arose from a change in economic circumstances. The Stamp Act boycotts had helped to revive a depressed economy. In 1768 and 1769, by contrast, merchants were enjoying boom times and had no financial incentive to support a boycott. As a result, merchants signed the agreements only reluctantly. And, as John Mein revealed, they often secretly violated those agreements. Artisans, on the other hand, supported nonimportation enthusiastically, re-

Divided Opinion over Boycotts

MADE at the Subscriber's Glass-Works, and now on Hand, to be sold at his House in Market-Street, opposite the Meal-Market, either wholesale or retail between Three and Four Hundred BOXES of WINDOW GLASS, consisting of the common Sizes, 10 by 12, 9 by 11, 8 by 10, 7 by 9, 6 by 8, &c. Lamp Glass, or any uncommon Sizes, under 16 by 18, are cut upon a short Notice. Where also may be had, most Sorts of Bottles, Gallon, Half Gallon, and Quart, full Measure Half Gallon Case Bottles, Snuff and Mustard, Receivers and Retorts of various Sizes; also electrifing Globes and Tubes, &c, As the abovementioned Glass is of American Manufactory, it is consequently clear of the Duties the Americans so justly complain of, and at present it seems peculiarly the Interest of America to encourage her own Manufactories, more especially those upon which Duties have been imposed, for the sole Purpose of raising a Revenue,

N B. He also continues to make the Philadelphia Brass Buttons, well noted for their Strength, such as were made by his deceased Father, and are warranted for seven Years.

Philadelphia, August 10.   RICHARD WISTAR.

At the peak of the nonimportation movement in the summer of 1769, the Philadelphia glassmaker Richard Wistar placed this advertisement in the New York Journal. *In addition to listing his wares, he appealed for customers by arguing that Americans should patronize local glassmakers instead of paying the hated Townshend duties on imported glass. Thus could patriotic pleas serve to increase an artisan's business at the expense of merchants dealing in imported goods.* The Historical Society of Pennsylvania.

cognizing that the absence of British goods would create a ready market for their own manufactures. Thus tradesmen formed the core of the crowds that coerced both importers and their customers by picketing stores, publicizing offenders' names, and sometimes destroying property.

Such tactics were effective: colonial imports from England dropped dramatically in 1769, especially in New York, New England, and Pennsylvania. But they also aroused significant opposition, creating a second major division among the colonists. Some Americans who supported resistance to British measures began to question the use of violence to force others to join the boycott. In addition, wealthier and more conservative colonists were frightened by the threat to private property inherent in the campaign. Moreover, political activism on the part of ordinary colonists challenged the ruling elite's domination, just as they had feared in 1765. Thus a Charleston essayist warned in 1769 that "the industrious mechanic [is] a useful and essential part of society . . . in his own sphere," but "when he steps out of it, and sets up for a statesman! believe me he is in a fair way

A Society of Patriotic Ladies, *painted by Philip Dawes (?) in 1775. A disapproving Briton produced this grotesque caricature of female patriots. At left the women empty their tea cannisters into a chamber pot. The cartoon bears no resemblance to the actual event, the signing of an anti-British petition by female residents of Edenton, North Carolina.*
Library of Congress.

to expose himself to ridicule, and his family to distress, by neglecting his private business." Pretending concern for tradesmen's welfare, the author obviously feared for his own position in society.

Americans were relieved when the news arrived in April 1770 that a new prime minister, Lord North, had persuaded Parliament to repeal the Townshend duties, except the tea tax, on the grounds that duties on trade within the empire were bad policy. Although some political leaders argued that nonimportation should be continued until the tea tax was repealed, merchants quickly resumed importing. The rest of the Townshend Acts remained in force, but repeal of the taxes made the other laws appear less objectionable. In addition, John Mein's widely circulated disclosure that leading patriots like John Hancock were themselves violating

Repeal of the Townshend Duties

the nonimportation agreement caused dissension in the ranks of the boycotting merchants. That too hastened the end of nonimportation.

GROWING RIFTS

At first the new ministry did nothing to antagonize the colonists. Yet on the very day Lord North proposed repeal of the Townshend duties, a clash between civilians and soldiers in Boston led to the death of five Americans. The origins of the event patriots called the Boston Massacre lay in repeated clashes between customs officers and the people of Massachusetts. The Townshend Acts' creation of an American Board of Customs Commissioners had been error enough, but a decision to base it in Boston severely compounded the mistake.

From the day of their arrival in November 1767, the customs commissioners were frequent targets of mob action. In June 1768, their seizure of the patriot leader John Hancock's sloop *Liberty* on suspicion of smuggling caused a riot in which prominent customs officers' property was destroyed. The riot in turn helped to convince the ministry in London that troops were needed to maintain order in the unruly port. The assignment of two regiments of regulars to their city confirmed Bostonians' worst fears; the redcoats were a constant reminder of the oppressive potential of British power.

Bostonians, accustomed to leading their lives with a minimum of interference from government, now found themselves hemmed in at every turn. Guards on Boston Neck, the entrance to the city, checked all travelers and their goods. Redcoat patrols roamed the city day and night, questioning and sometimes harassing passers-by. Military parades were held on Boston Common, accompanied by loud martial music and often the brutal public whipping of deserters and other violators of army rules. Parents began to fear for the safety of their daughters, who were subjected to the soldiers' coarse sexual insults when they ventured out on the streets. But the greatest potential for violence lay in the uneasy relationship between the soldiers and Boston laborers. Many redcoats sought

Paul Revere's engraving of the Boston Massacre, a masterful piece of propaganda. At right the British officer seems to be ordering the soldiers to fire on a peaceful, unresisting crowd. The Customs House has been labeled Butcher's Hall, and smoke drifts up from a gun barrel sticking out of the window. Library of Congress.

employment in their off-duty hours, competing for unskilled jobs with the city's ordinary workingmen, and members of the two groups brawled repeatedly in taverns and on the streets.

On March 2, 1770, workers at a ropewalk (a ship-rigging factory) attacked some redcoats seeking jobs; a pitched battle resulted when both groups acquired reinforcements. Three days later, the tension exploded. Early on the evening of March 5, a crowd began throwing hard-packed snowballs at sentries guarding the Customs House. Goaded beyond endurance, the sentries fired on the crowd against express orders to the contrary, killing four and

Boston Massacre

wounding eight, one of whom died a few days later. Resistance leaders idealized the dead rioters as martyrs for the cause of liberty, holding a solemn funeral three days later and commemorating March 5 annually with patriotic orations. The best-known engraving of the massacre, by Paul Revere, was itself a part of the propaganda campaign. It depicts a peaceful crowd, an officer ordering the soldiers to fire, and shots coming from the window of the Customs House.

The leading patriots wanted to make certain the soldiers did not become martyrs as well. Furthermore, despite the political benefits the patriots derived from the massacre, it is unlikely that they approved of the crowd action that provoked it. Ever since August

1765 the men allied with the Sons of Liberty had supported orderly demonstrations and expressed distaste for uncontrolled riots, of which the Boston Massacre was a prime example. Thus when the soldiers were tried for the killings in November, they were defended by John Adams and Josiah Quincy, Jr., both unwavering patriots. All but two of the accused men were acquitted, and those convicted were released after having been branded on the thumb. Undoubtedly the favorable outcome of the trials prevented London officials from taking further steps against the city.

For more than two years after the Boston Massacre and the repeal of the Townshend duties, a superficial calm descended on the colonies. Local incidents, like the burning of the customs vessel *Gaspée* in 1772 by Rhode Islanders, marred the relationship of individual colonies and the mother country, but nothing caused Americans to join in a unified protest. Even so, the resistance movement continued to gather momentum. The most outspoken colonial newspapers, such as the *Boston Gazette*, the *Pennsylvania Journal*, and the *South Carolina Gazette*, published essays drawing on Real Whig ideology and accusing Great Britain of a deliberate plan to oppress America. After repeal of the Stamp Act, the patriots had praised Parliament; following repeal of the Townshend duties, they warned of impending tyranny. What had seemed to be an isolated mistake, a single ill-chosen stamp tax, now appeared to be part of a plot against American liberties. Among other things, essayists pointed to Parliament's persecution of the English radical John Wilkes, the stationing of troops in Boston, and the growing number of vice-admiralty courts as evidence of a plan to enslave the colonists. Indeed, patriot writers played repeatedly on the word *enslavement.* Most white colonists had direct knowledge of slavery (either being slaveholders themselves or having slave-owning neighbors), and the threat of enslavement by Britain must have hit them with peculiar force.

Still, no one yet advocated complete independence from the mother country. Though the patriots were becoming increasingly convinced that they should seek freedom from parliamentary authority, they continued to acknowledge their British identity and to pledge their allegiance to George III. They began, therefore, to try to envision a system that would enable them to be ruled largely by their own elected legislatures while remaining loyal to the king. But any such scheme was totally alien to Britons' conception of the nature of their government, which was that Parliament held sole undivided sovereignty over the empire. Furthermore, in the British mind, Parliament encompassed the king as well as the House of Lords and the Commons, and so separating the monarch from the legislature was impossible. Conservative colonists recognized the dangers inherent in the patriots' new mode of thinking. The former stamp distributor Andrew Oliver, for example, predicted in 1771 that "serious consequences" would follow from the fact that "the leaders of the people were never [before] so open in asserting our independence of the British Legislature," even though "there is an intermission of Acts of violence at present."

Oliver's prediction proved correct when, in the fall of 1772, the North ministry began to implement the portion of the Townshend Acts that provided for governors and judges to be paid **Committees of** from customs revenues. In early **Correspondence** November, voters at a Boston town meeting established a Committee of Correspondence to publicize the decision by exchanging letters with other Massachusetts towns. Heading the committee was the man who had proposed its formation, Samuel Adams. A year earlier, Adams had described the benefits of organizing an official communications network within and among the separate colonies. "If conducted with a proper spirit," Adams had asked, "would it not afford reason for the Enemies of our common Liberty, to tremble?"

Samuel Adams was fifty-one years old in 1772, thirteen years the senior of his distant cousin John and a decade older than most other leaders of American resistance. He had been a Boston tax collector, a member and clerk of the Massachusetts assembly, and an ally of the Loyal Nine (though evidently not a member). Unswerving in his devotion to the American cause, Adams drew a sharp contrast between a corrupt Britain and the virtuous colonies. His primary forum was the Boston town meeting. An experienced political organizer, Adams continually stressed the necessity of prudent collective action. His Committee of Correspondence thus undertook to create an informed consensus among all the citizens of Massachusetts.

Such committees, which were soon established

throughout the colonies, represented the next logical step in the organization of American resistance. Until 1772, the protest movement was largely confined to the seacoast, and primarily to major cities and towns (see map, page 113). Adams realized that the time had now come to widen the movement's geographic scope, to attempt to involve the residents of the interior in the struggle that had hitherto enlisted chiefly the residents of urban areas. Accordingly, the Boston town meeting directed the Committee of Correspondence "to state the Rights of the Colonists and of this Province in particular," to list "the Infringements and Violations thereof that have been, or from time to time may be made," and to send copies to the other towns in the province. In return, Boston requested "a free communication of their Sentiments on this Subject."

Samuel Adams, James Otis, Jr., and Josiah Quincy, Jr., prepared the statement of the colonists' rights. Declaring that Americans had absolute rights to life, liberty, and property, the committee asserted that the idea that "a British house of commons, should have a right, at pleasure, to give and grant the property of the colonists" was "irreconcileable" with "the first principles of natural law and Justice . . . and of the British Constitution in particular." The list of grievances, drafted by another group of prominent patriots, was similarly sweeping. It complained of taxation without representation, the presence of unnecessary troops and customs officers on American soil, the use of imperial revenues to pay colonial officials, the expanded jurisdiction of vice-admiralty courts, and even the nature of the instructions given to American governors by their superiors in London.

The entire document, which was printed as a pamphlet for distribution to the towns, exhibited none of the hesitation that had characterized colonial claims against Parliament in the 1760s. No longer were patriots—at least in Boston—concerned about defining the precise limits of parliamentary authority. No longer did they mention the necessity of obedience to Parliament. They were committed to a course that placed American rights first, loyalty to Great Britain a distant second.

The response of the Massachusetts towns to the committee's pamphlet must have caused Samuel Adams to rejoice. Some towns disagreed with Boston's assessment of the state of affairs, but most aligned themselves with the city. From Braintree came the assertion that "all civil officers are or ought to be Servants to the people and dependent upon them for their official Support, and every instance to the Contrary from the Governor downwards tends to crush and destroy civil liberty." The town of Holden declared that "the People of New England have never given the People of Britain any Right of Jurisdiction over us." The citizens of Petersham commented that resistance to tyranny was "the first and highest social Duty of this people." And Pownallborough warned, "allegiance is a relative Term and like Kingdoms and commonwealths is local and has its bounds." It was beliefs like these that made the next crisis in Anglo-American affairs the final one.

THE BOSTON TEA PARTY

The only one of the Townshend duties still in effect by 1773 was the tax on tea. In the years since 1770 some Americans had continued to boycott English tea, while others had resumed drinking it either openly or in secret. Tea had long been an important component of the Anglo-American diet, and the possession of tea-drinking equipment (teapots and matched sets of cups) indicated high status (see page 76). Well-to-do Americans, women and men alike, socialized frequently at private tea parties, so that observing the tea boycott required colonial elites not only to change the beverage they habitually drank but also to alter their lifestyles. Tea thus retained an explosively symbolic character even though the boycott was less than fully effective after 1770.

In May 1773, Parliament passed an act designed to save the East India Company from bankruptcy by changing the way British tea was sold in the colonies.

Tea Act   Resistance leaders were immediately suspicious. Under the Tea Act, certain duties paid on tea were to be returned to the company. Furthermore, tea was to be sold only by designated agents, which would enable the East India Company to avoid colonial middlemen and undersell any competitors, even smugglers. The

The Able Doctor, or America Swallowing the Bitter Draught. Paul Revere engraved this cartoon for the Royal American Magazine *of June 1774. Lord North, a copy of the Boston Port Act in his pocket, is forcing tea down the throat of America, represented as an Indian woman. While Britannia weeps, a Frenchman and a Spaniard comment on the proceedings. In the background, the British fleet bombards Boston.   Library of Congress.*

net result would be cheaper tea for American consumers. But many colonists interpreted the new measure as a pernicious device to make them admit Parliament's right to tax them, since the less expensive tea would still be taxed under the Townshend law. Others saw the Tea Act as the first step in the establishment of an East India Company monopoly of all colonial trade. Residents of the four cities singled out to receive the first shipments of tea accordingly prepared to respond to what they perceived as a new threat to their freedom.

In New York City, the tea ships failed to arrive on schedule. In Philadelphia, the captain was persuaded to turn around and sail back to England. In Charleston, the tea was unloaded, stored under the direction of local tradesmen, and later destroyed. The only confrontation occurred in Boston, where both sides—the town meeting, joined by participants from nearby towns, and Governor Thomas Hutchinson, two of whose sons were tea agents—rejected compromise.

The first of three tea ships, the *Dartmouth,* entered Boston harbor on November 28. Under the customs laws, a cargo had to be landed and the appropriate duty paid within twenty days of a ship's arrival. If that was not done, the cargo would be seized by customs officers. After a series of mass meetings, Bostonians voted to prevent the tea from being unloaded and to post guards on the wharf. Hutchinson, for his part, refused to permit the vessels to leave the harbor.

On December 16, 1773, one day before the cargo would have to be confiscated, more than five thousand people (nearly a third of the city's population) crowded into Old South Church. The meeting, chaired by Samuel Adams, made a final attempt to persuade Hutchinson to send the tea back to England. But Hutchinson remained adamant. At about 6 p.m., Adams reportedly announced "that he could think of nothing further to be done—that they had now done all they could for the Salvation of their Country." As if his statement were a signal, cries rang out from the back of the crowd: "Boston harbor a tea-pot night! The Mohawks are come!" Small groups pushed their way out of the meeting. Within a few minutes, about sixty men crudely disguised as Indians assembled at the wharf, boarded the three ships, and dumped the cargo into the harbor. By 9 p.m. their work was done: 342 chests of tea worth approximately £10,000 floated in splinters on the ebbing tide.

Among the "Indians" were many representatives of Boston's artisans. Five masons, eleven carpenters and builders, three leatherworkers, a blacksmith, a hatter, three coopers, two barbers, a coachmaker, a silversmith, and twelve apprentices have been identified as participants. Their ranks also included four farmers from outside Boston, ten merchants, two doctors, a teacher, and a bookseller. The next day John Adams exulted in his diary that the Tea Party was "so bold, so daring, so firm, intrepid and inflexible" that "I can't but consider it as an epocha in history."

The North administration reacted with considerably less enthusiasm when it learned of the Tea Party. In March 1774, after failing in an attempt to charge the Boston resistance leaders with high treason, the ministry proposed the first of the four laws that became known as the Coercive, or Intolerable, Acts. It called for closing the port of Boston until the tea was paid for and prohibiting all but coastal trade in food and firewood. Colonial sympathizers in Parliament were easily outvoted by those who wished to punish the city that had been the center of opposition to British policies. Later in the spring, Parliament passed three further punitive mea-

Coercive and Quebec Acts

sures. The Massachusetts Government Act altered the province's charter, substituting an appointed council for an elected one, increasing the powers of the governor, and forbidding special town meetings. The Justice Act provided that a person accused of committing murder in the course of suppressing a riot or enforcing the laws could be tried outside the colony where the incident had occurred. Finally, the Quartering Act gave broad authority to military commanders seeking to house their troops in private dwellings.

After passing the last of the Coercive Acts in early

IMPORTANT EVENTS

1754	Albany Congress French and Indian War begins
1760	American phase of war ends George III becomes king
1763	Treaty of Paris Pontiac's uprising Proclamation of 1763
1764	Sugar Act
1765	Stamp Act Sons of Liberty formed
1766	Repeal of Stamp Act Declaratory Act
1767	Townshend Acts
1770	Lord North becomes prime minister Repeal of Townshend duties except tea tax Boston Massacre
1772	Boston Committee of Correspondence formed
1773	Tea Act Boston Tea Party
1774	Coercive Acts

June, Parliament turned its attention to much-needed reforms in the government of Quebec. The Quebec Act, though unrelated to the Coercive Acts, thus became linked with them in the minds of the patriots. Intended to ease the strains that had arisen since the British conquest of the formerly French colony, the Quebec Act granted greater religious freedom to Catholics—alarming the Protestant colonists, who regarded Roman Catholicism as a mainstay of religious and political despotism. It also reinstated French civil law, which had been replaced by British procedures in 1763, and established an appointed council (rather than an elected legislature) as the governing body of the colony. Finally, in an attempt to provide the northern Indian tribes some protection against white settlement, the act annexed to Quebec the area east of the Mississippi River and north of the Ohio River. Thus that region, parts of which were claimed by individual seacoast colonies, was removed from their jurisdiction.

Members of Parliament who voted for the punitive legislation believed that the acts would be obeyed, that at long last they had solved the problem posed by the troublesome Americans. But the patriots showed little inclination to bow to the wishes of Parliament. In their eyes, the Coercive Acts and the Quebec Act proved what they had feared since 1768: that Great Britain had embarked on a deliberate plan to oppress them. If the port of Boston could be closed, why not those of Philadelphia or New York? If the royal charter of Massachusetts could be changed, why not that of South Carolina? If certain people could be removed from their home colonies for trial, why not all violators of all laws? If troops could be forcibly quartered in private houses, did not that pave the way for the occupation of all of America? If the Roman Catholic church could receive favored status in Quebec, why not everywhere? It seemed as though the full dimensions of the plot against American rights and liberties had at last been revealed.

The Boston Committee of Correspondence urged all the colonies to join in an immediate boycott of British goods. But the other provinces were not yet ready to take such a drastic step. Instead, they suggested that another intercolonial congress be convened to consider an appropriate response to the Coercive Acts. Few people wanted to take hasty action; even the most ardent patriots still hoped for reconciliation

with Great Britain. Despite their objections to British policy, they continued to see themselves as part of the empire. Americans were approaching the brink of confrontation, but they had not committed themselves to an irrevocable break. And so the colonies agreed to send delegates to Philadelphia in September.

Over the preceding decade, momentous changes had occurred in the ways politically aware colonists thought about themselves and their allegiance. Once linked unquestioningly to Great Britain, they had begun to develop a sense of their own identity as Americans. They had started to realize that their concept of the political process differed from that held by people in the mother country. They also had come to understand that their economic interests did not necessarily coincide with those of Great Britain. In the late summer of 1774, they were committed to resistance, but not to independence. Even so, they had started to sever the bonds of empire. During the next decade, they would forge the bonds of a new American nationality to replace those rejected Anglo-American ties.

SUGGESTIONS FOR FURTHER READING

General

Ian R. Christie, *Crisis of Empire: Great Britain and the American Colonies 1754–1783* (1966); Ian R. Christie and Benjamin W. Labaree, *Empire or Independence, 1760–1776: A British-American Dialogue on the Coming of the American Revolution* (1976); Lawrence Henry Gipson, *The Coming of the Revolution 1763–1775* (1954); Merrill Jensen, *The Founding of a Nation: A History of the American Revolution, 1763–1776* (1968); Robert Middlekauff, *The Glorious Cause: The American Revolution, 1763–1783* (1982); Edmund S. Morgan, *The Birth of the Republic, 1763–1789* (1956).

Colonial Warfare and the British Empire

Lawrence Henry Gipson, *The British Empire Before the American Revolution*, 15 vols. (1936–1970); Robert C. Newbold, *The Albany Congress and Plan of Union of 1754*

(1955); Howard H. Peckham, *The Colonial Wars, 1689–1762* (1963); William Pencak, *War, Politics, and Revolution in Provincial Massachusetts* (1981); Alan Rogers, *Empire and Liberty: American Resistance to British Authority, 1755–1763* (1974); John Shy, *Toward Lexington: The Role of the British Army in the Coming of the American Revolution* (1965).

British Politics and Policy

George L. Beer, *British Colonial Policy 1754–1765* (1907); John Brewer, *Party Ideology and Popular Politics at the Accession of George III* (1976); John Brooke, *King George III* (1972); John L. Bullion, *A Great and Necessary Measure: George Grenville and the Genesis of the Stamp Act, 1763–1765* (1981); Bernard Donoughue, *British Politics and the American Revolution: The Path to War, 1773–1775* (1965); Michael Kammen, *A Rope of Sand: The Colonial Agents, British Politics, and the American Revolution* (1968); Lewis B. Namier, *England in the Age of the American Revolution*, 2nd ed. (1961); P. D. G. Thomas, *British Politics and the Stamp Act Crisis* (1975); Carl Ubbelohde, *The Vice-Admiralty Courts and the American Revolution* (1960).

Indians and the West

Thomas P. Abernethy, *Western Lands and the American Revolution* (1959); John R. Alden, *John Stuart and the Southern Colonial Frontier: A Study of Indian Relations, War, Trade, and Land Problems in the Southern Wilderness, 1754–1775* (1944); Richard Aquila, *The Iroquois Restoration: Iroquois Diplomacy on the Colonial Frontier 1701–1754* (1983); David H. Corkran, *The Cherokee Frontier: Conflict and Survival, 1740–1762* (1962); David H. Corkran, *The Creek Frontier, 1540–1783* (1967); Georgiana C. Nammack, *Fraud, Politics, and the Dispossession of the Indians: The Iroquois Land Frontier in the Colonial Period* (1969); Howard H. Peckham, *Pontiac and the Indian Uprising* (1947); Jack M. Sosin, *Whitehall and the Wilderness: The Middle West in British Colonial Policy, 1760–1775* (1961).

Political Thought

Bernard Bailyn, *The Ideological Origins of the American Revolution* (1967); Edwin G. Burrows and Michael Wallace, "The American Revolution: The Ideology and Psychology of National Liberation," *Perspectives in American History*, 6 (1972), 167–302; Jay Fliegelman, *Prodigals & Pilgrims: The American Revolution Against Patriarchal Authority 1750–1800* (1982); J. G. A. Pocock, "Machiavelli, Harrington, and English Political Ideologies in the Eighteenth Century," *William and Mary Quarterly*, 3rd ser., 22 (1965), 547–583; Caroline Robbins, *The Eighteenth-Century Commonwealthman: Studies in the Transmission, Development, and Circumstance of English Liberal Thought from the Restoration of Charles II until the War with the Thirteen Colonies* (1959); Clinton Rossiter, *Seedtime of the Republic: The Origin of the American Tradition of Political Liberty* (1953).

American Resistance

David Ammerman, *In the Common Cause: American Response to the Coercive Acts of 1774* (1974); Richard Beeman, *Patrick Henry: A Biography* (1974); Richard D. Brown, *Revolutionary Politics in Massachusetts: The Boston Committee of Correspondence and the Towns, 1772–1774* (1970); Joseph Albert Ernst, *Money and Politics in America, 1755–1775: A Study in the Currency Act of 1764 and the Political Economy of Revolution* (1973); Dirk Hoerder, *Crowd Action in Revolutionary Massachusetts, 1765–1780* (1977); Rhys Isaac, *The Transformation of Virginia, 1740–1790* (1982); Benjamin W. Labaree, *The Boston Tea Party* (1964); Pauline R. Maier, *From Resistance to Revolution: Colonial Radicals and the Development of American Opposition to Britain, 1765–1776* (1972); Pauline R. Maier, *The Old Revolutionaries: Political Lives in the Age of Samuel Adams* (1980); Edmund S. Morgan and Helen M. Morgan, *The Stamp Act Crisis: Prologue to Revolution* (1953); Gary B. Nash, *The Urban Crucible: Social Change, Political Consciousness, and the Origins of the American Revolution* (1979); Richard Ryerson, *The Revolution Is Now Begun: The Radical Committees of Philadelphia, 1765–1776* (1978); Arthur M. Schlesinger, *The Colonial Merchants and the American Revolution 1763–1776* (1918); Peter Shaw, *American Patriots and the Rituals of Revolution* (1981); Richard Walsh, *Charleston's Sons of Liberty: A Study of the Artisans, 1763–1789* (1959); John J. Waters, Jr., *The Otis Family in Provincial and Revolutionary Massachusetts* (1968); Alfred H. Young, ed., *The American Revolution: Explorations in the History of American Radicalism* (1976); Hiller B. Zobel, *The Boston Massacre* (1970).

A Revolution, Indeed
1775–1783

Chapter 5

One April morning in 1775, Hannah Winthrop awoke with a start to drumbeats, bells, and the continuous clang of the Cambridge fire alarm. She and her husband, a professor at Harvard, soon learned that redcoat troops had left Boston late the evening before, bound for Concord. A few hours later they watched British soldiers march through Cambridge to reinforce the first group. The Winthrops quickly decided to leave home and seek shelter elsewhere. Along with seventy or eighty other refugees, mostly wives and children of patriot militiamen, they made their way to an isolated farmhouse near Fresh Pond. But it was no secure haven. They were, Mrs. Winthrop later wrote, "for some time in sight of the Battle, the glistening instruments of death proclaiming by an incessant fire that much blood must be shed, that many widowd and orphand ones be left as monuments of that persecuting Barbarity of British Tyranny."

Afraid to abandon their refuge even after the sounds of battle ceased, the Winthrops and their companions remained in the farmhouse overnight, sleeping in chairs and on the floor. The next morning, warned that Cambridge was still unsafe, the couple headed north toward Andover. The roads were filled with other frightened families, some carrying all their belongings. Their route took them through Menotomy (now Arlington), scene of some of the bloodiest fighting the day before. The battlefield, Mrs. Winthrop recorded, was "strewd with the mangled bodies." Along the way they encountered a farmer gathering the corpses of his neighbors and searching for the body of his son, who had reportedly been killed in battle. As she walked toward Andover, Hannah Winthrop mentally compared herself with Eve expelled from the Garden of Eden; lines from John Milton's *Paradise Lost*, she later told a friend, had echoed repeatedly in her mind. She was convinced that nothing would be the same again.

In that expectation, Hannah Winthrop was wrong. She and her husband soon returned to their Cambridge home and resumed their normal lives. But their experience in 1775 was typical of that of thousands of other Americans over the next eight years. The Revolution, one of only two major conflicts ever fought on American soil—the other was the Civil War—was more than just a series of clashes between British and patriot armies. It also uprooted thousands of civilian families, disrupted the economy, reshaped society by forcing many colonists into permanent exile, and led Americans to develop new conceptions of politics. Indeed, even before the shooting began the patriots had established functioning revolutionary governments throughout the colonies.

The struggle for independence required revolutionary leaders to accomplish three separate but closely related tasks. The first was political and ideological. They had to transform the 1760s consensus favoring loyal resistance into a coalition supporting independence: a different goal entirely. They took a variety of steps ranging from persuasion to coercion to enlist all whites in the patriot cause. In the case of blacks and Indians, America's elected leaders hoped for cooperation at best, neutrality at worst. Still, they had good reason to fear that Indians, blacks, and the English would unite against them.

The second task was diplomatic. To win their independence, the patriot leaders knew they needed international recognition and aid, particularly assistance from France. Thus they dispatched to Paris Benjamin Franklin, the most experienced American diplomat (he had served for years as a colonial agent in London). Franklin skillfully negotiated the Franco-American alliance of 1778, which was to prove crucial to the winning of independence.

Only the third task directly involved the British. George Washington, commander-in-chief of the American army, quickly realized that his primary goal should be not to win battles but rather to avoid losing them decisively. He understood that, as long as his army survived to fight another day, the outcome of any individual battle was more or less irrelevant (although at times victories were necessary, if only to bolster morale). Accordingly, the story of the Revolutionary War reveals British action and American reaction, British attacks and American defenses. The American war effort was aided by British military planners' failure to analyze accurately the problem confronting them. Until it was too late, they treated the war against the colonists as they did wars against other Europeans; that is, they concentrated on winning battles and did not consider the difficulties inherent in achieving their main goal, retaining the colonies' allegiance. In the end, the Americans' triumph owed more to their own endurance and to Britain's mistakes than to their military prowess.

GOVERNMENT BY CONGRESS AND COMMITTEE

First Continental Congress

When the fifty-five delegates to the First Continental Congress convened in Philadelphia in September 1774, they knew that any measures they adopted were likely to enjoy support among many of their fellow countrymen and women. During the summer of 1774, open meetings held in towns, cities, and counties throughout the colonies had endorsed the idea of another nonimportation pact. Participants in such meetings had promised (in the words of the freeholders of Johnston County, North Carolina) to "strictly adhere to, and abide by, such Regulations and Restrictions as the Members of the said General Congress shall agree to, and judge most convenient." The committees of correspondence that had been established in many communities publicized these popular meetings so effectively that Americans everywhere knew about them. Most of the congressional delegates were selected by extralegal provincial conventions whose members were chosen at such local gatherings, since the royal governors had forbidden the regular assemblies to conduct formal elections. Thus the very act of designating delegates to attend the congress involved Americans in open defiance of British authority.

The colonies' leading political figures—most of them lawyers, merchants, or planters—were sent to the Philadelphia congress. The Massachusetts delegation included both Samuel Adams, the experienced organizer of the Boston resistance, and his younger cousin John, an ambitious lawyer. Among others

New York sent John Jay, a talented young attorney. From Pennsylvania came the conservative Joseph Galloway, speaker of the assembly, and his long-time rival John Dickinson. Virginia elected Richard Henry Lee and Patrick Henry, both noted for their patriotic zeal, as well as the stolid and reserved George Washington. Most of these men had never met, but in the weeks, months, and years that followed they were to become the chief architects of the new nation.

The congressmen faced three tasks when they convened at Carpenters Hall on September 5, 1774. The first two were explicit: defining American grievances and developing a plan for resistance. The third was implicit—outlining a theory of their constitutional relationship with England—and proved troublesome. The delegates readily agreed on a list of the laws they wanted repealed (notably the Coercive Acts) and chose as their method of resistance an economic boycott coupled with petitions for relief. But they could not reach a consensus on the constitutional issue. Their discussion of this crucial question was rendered all the more intense by events in Massachusetts.

On the second day of the meeting, word arrived that the British had attacked the Massachusetts countryside and were bombarding Boston from land and sea. This rumor was proven false two days later, but it nevertheless lent a sense of urgency to the congressmen's discussions. That thousands of militiamen had gathered in Cambridge to repel the rumored attack demonstrated how close to the brink of war Great Britain and the colonies had already come. The congressmen accordingly set about their work with particular fervor and commitment.

Since the colonists' resistance was based on the claim that their constitutional rights had been violated, it seemed necessary to define what the colonies' constitutional relationship with England was. But the delegates held widely differing views on that subject. The most radical congressmen, like Lee of Virginia and Roger Sherman of Connecticut, agreed with the position published a few weeks earlier by Thomas Jefferson—who was not a delegate—in his *Summary View of the Rights of British America.* Jefferson argued that the colonists owed allegiance only to George III, and that Parliament was nothing more than "the legislature of one part of the empire." As such, he declared, it could not exercise legitimate authority

EXTRACTS

From the

VOTES and PROCEEDINGS

Of the AMERICAN CONTINENTAL

CONGRESS,

Held at PHILADELPHIA on the
5th of *September* 1774.

CONTAINING

The BILL of RIGHTS, a Lift of GRIEV-
ANCES, Occafional Refolves, the
Affociation, an *Addrefs* to the PEOPLE
of GREAT-BRITAIN, and a *Memorial*
to the INHABITANTS of the BRITISH
AMERICAN COLONIES.

Publifhed by order of the CONGRESS.

PHILADELPHIA:

Printed by WILLIAM and THOMAS BRADFORD,
October 27th, M,DCC,LXXIV.

The First Continental Congress publicized its actions in this pamphlet, which was widely reprinted in the colonies. It informed Americans of the various steps their representatives had taken to protest the Coercive Acts.   Library of Congress.

over the American provinces, which had historically been governed by their own assemblies.

Meanwhile the conservative Joseph Galloway and his ally James Duane of New York insisted that the congress should acknowledge Parliament's supremacy over the empire and its right to regulate American trade. Galloway embodied these ideas in a formal plan of union. His plan proposed the establishment of an American legislature, its members chosen by individual colonial assemblies, which would have to consent to laws pertaining to America. After a heated debate, the delegates rejected Galloway's proposal. But they were not prepared to go as far as Jefferson had.

Finally, they accepted a compromise position worked out by John Adams. The crucial clause Adams drafted in the congress's Declaration of Rights and Grievances read in part: "From the necessity of the case, and a regard to the mutual interest of both countries, we cheerfully consent to the operation of such acts of the British parliament, as are bona fide, restrained to the regulation of our external commerce." Note the key phrases. "From the necessity of the case" indicated Americans' abandonment, once and for all, of the unquestioning loyalty to the mother country that had so bedeviled James Otis, Jr., just a decade earlier. The colonists were now declaring that they owed obedience to Parliament only because they had decided it was in the best interest of both countries. "Bona fide, restrained to the regulation of our external commerce" resonated with overtones of the Stamp Act controversy and Dickinson's arguments in his *Farmer's Letters*. The delegates intended to make clear to Lord North that they would continue to resist taxes in disguise, like the Townshend duties. Most striking of all was that such language, which only a few years before would have been regarded as irredeemably radical, could be presented and accepted as a compromise in the fall of 1774. The Americans had come a long way since their first hesitant protests against the Sugar Act (see page 109).

Once the delegates had resolved the constitutional issue, they discussed the tactics by which to force another British retreat. They adopted an agreement known as the Continental Association, which called for nonimportation of all goods from Great Britain and Ireland, as well as tea and molasses from other British possessions and slaves from any source, effective December 1. An end to the consumption of British products was also readily accepted, to become effective on March 1, 1775. Nonexportation, on the other hand, generated considerable debate. The Virginia delegation adamantly refused to accept a ban on exports to England until after its planters had had a chance to market their 1774 tobacco crop, which needed to be dried and cured before it could be sold. As a result, the congress provided that nonexportation would not begin until September 10, 1775.

Declaration of Rights and Grievances

Chapter 5: A REVOLUTION, INDEED, 1775–1783

More influential than the details of the Continental Association was the method the congress recommended for its enforcement: the election of committees of observation and inspection in every county, city, and town in America. Such committees were officially charged only with overseeing enforcement of the association, but over the next six months they became de facto governments. Since the congress specified that committee members be chosen by all persons qualified to vote for members of the lower house of the colonial legislatures, the committees were guaranteed a broad popular base. Furthermore, their numbers ensured that many new men would be incorporated into the resistance movement. In some places the committeemen were former local officeholders; in other places they were obscure men who had never before held office. Everywhere, however, these committeemen—perhaps seven to eight thousand of them in the colonies as a whole—found themselves increasingly linked to the cause of American resistance.

Committees of Observation

At first the committees confined themselves to enforcing the nonimportation clause—examining merchants' records and publishing the names of those who continued to import or sell British goods. But the Continental Association also promoted home manufactures and encouraged Americans to adopt simple modes of dress and behavior. Wearing homespun garments became a sign of patriotism, just as it had been in the late 1760s. Since expensive leisure-time activities were symbols of vice and corruption, the congress urged Americans to forgo dancing, gambling, horse racing, cock fighting, and other forms of "extravagance and dissipation." In enforcing these injunctions, sometimes even by jailing offenders, the committees gradually extended their authority over nearly all aspects of American life.

Some committees forbade public and private dancing, extracted apologies from people caught gambling or racing, prohibited the slaughter of lambs (because of the need for wool), and offered prizes for the best locally made cloth. The Baltimore County committee even advised citizens not to attend the upcoming town fair, which they described as nothing more than an occasion for "riots, drunkenness, gaming, and the vilest immoralities."

The committees also attempted to identify opponents of American resistance. Although seeking to protect American rights—which presumably included freedom of speech and thought—the patriots saw no reason to grant those rights to people who disagreed with them. They viewed the resistance movement as a collective endeavor that would succeed only if all colonists supported it. Consequently, the committees developed elaborate spy networks, circulated copies of the association for signatures, and investigated reports of dissident remarks and activities. Suspected dissenters were first urged to convert to the colonial cause; if that failed, the committees had them watched or restricted their movements. Sometimes people engaging in casual political exchanges with friends one day found themselves charged with "treasonable conversation" the next. Committees cooperated with each other, too. In 1775, for example, the Northampton, Massachusetts, committee told its counterpart in nearby Hadley that a townsman had been heard to call the congress "a Pack or Parcell of Fools" that was "as tyrannical as Lord North and ought to be opposed & resisted." The Hadley committee examined the accused man, who admitted his statements and refused to recant. The committee thereafter had him watched.

While the committees were expanding their power during the winter and early spring of 1775, the established governments of the colonies were collapsing. Only in Connecticut, Rhode Island, Delaware, and Pennsylvania did regular assemblies continue to meet without encountering patriot challenges to their authority. In every other colony, popularly elected provincial conventions took over the task of running the government, sometimes entirely replacing the legislatures and at other times holding concurrent sessions. In late 1774 and early 1775, these conventions approved the Continental Association, elected delegates to the Second Continental Congress (scheduled for May), organized militia units, and gathered arms and ammunition. The British-appointed governors and councils, unable to stem the tide of resistance, watched helplessly as their authority crumbled.

Provincial Conventions

The frustrating experience of Governor Josiah Martin of North Carolina is a case in point. When a provincial convention was called to meet at New Bern on April 4, 1775—the same day the legislature was to convene—Martin proclaimed that "the Assembly of this province duly elected is the only true and lawful representation of the people." He asked all citizens to "renounce disclaim and discourage all such meetings cabals and illegal proceedings . . . which can only tend to introduce disorder and anarchy." Martin's proclamation had no visible effect, and when the convention met at New Bern its membership proved to be virtually identical to that of the colonial legislature. The delegates proceeded to act alternately in both capacities and even passed some joint resolves. Continuing the farce, the exasperated Martin delivered a speech to the assembly denouncing the election of the convention. On April 7, Martin admitted to Lord Dartmouth, the American Secretary in North's ministry, that his government was "absolutely prostrate, impotent, and that nothing but the shadow of it is left."

Royal officials in the other colonies suffered the same frustrations. Courts were prevented from holding sessions; taxes were paid to agents of the conventions rather than provincial tax collectors; sheriffs' powers were questioned; and militiamen refused to muster except by order of the local committees. In short, during the six months preceding the battles at Lexington and Concord, independence was being won at the local level, but without formal acknowledgment and for the most part without shooting or bloodshed. Not many Americans fully realized what was happening. The vast majority of colonists still proclaimed their loyalty to Great Britain and denied that they sought to leave the empire. Among the few Americans who did recognize the trend toward independence were those who opposed it.

CHOOSING SIDES: LOYALISTS, BLACKS, AND INDIANS

The first protests against British measures, in the mid-1760s, had won the support of most colonists. Only in the late 1760s and early 1770s did a significant number of Americans begin to question

both the aims and the tactics of the resistance movement. In 1774 and 1775 such people found themselves in a difficult position. Like their more radical counterparts, most of them objected to parliamentary policies and wanted some kind of constitutional reform. (Joseph Galloway, for instance, was a conservative by American standards, but his plan for restructuring the empire was too novel for Britain to accept.) Nevertheless, if forced to a choice, these colonists sympathized with Great Britain rather than with an independent America. The events of the crucial year between the passage of the Coercive Acts and the outbreak of fighting in Massachusetts crystallized their thinking. Their doubts about violent protest, their desire to uphold the legally constituted colonial governments, and their fears of anarchy combined to make them especially sensitive to the dangers of resistance.

In 1774 and 1775 some conservatives began to publish essays and pamphlets critical of the congress and its allied committees. In New York City, a group of Anglican clergymen jointly wrote pamphlets and essays arguing the importance of maintaining a cordial connection between England and America. In Pennsylvania, Joseph Galloway published *A Candid Examination of the Mutual Claims of Great Britain and the Colonies*, attacking the Continental Congress for rejecting his plan of union. In Massachusetts, the young attorney Daniel Leonard, writing under the pseudonym Massachusettensis, engaged in a prolonged newspaper debate with Novanglus (John Adams). All the conservative authors stressed the point that Leonard put so well in his sixth essay in January 1775: "There is no possible medium between absolute independence and subjection to the authority of parliament." Leonard and his fellows realized that what had begun as a dispute over the extent of American subordination within the empire had now raised the question of whether the colonies would remain linked to Great Britain at all. "Rouse up at last from your slumber!" the Reverend Thomas Bradbury Chandler of New Jersey cried out to Americans. "There is a set of people among us . . . who have formed a scheme for establishing an independent government or empire in America."

Some colonists heeded the conservative pamphleteers' warnings. About one-fifth of the white American population remained loyal to Great Britain, actively

Loyalists, Patriots, and Neutrals

opposing independence. Unlike their fellow countrymen and women, loyalists remained true to the colonial self-conception once held by most eighteenth-century white Americans. In other words, it was the patriots who changed their allegiance, not the loyalists. What is therefore surprising is that there were so few active loyalists, not that there were so many.

With notable exceptions, most people of the following types remained loyal to the crown: British-appointed government officials; merchants whose trade depended on imperial connections; Anglican clergy everywhere and lay Anglicans in the North—where their denomination was in the minority—since the king was the head of their church as well as the state; former officers and enlisted men from the British army, many of whom had settled in America after 1763; non-English ethnic minorities, especially Scots; tenant farmers, particularly those whose landlords sided with the patriots; members of persecuted religious sects; and many of the backcountry southerners who had rebelled against eastern rule in the 1760s and early 1770s. All these people had one thing in common: the patriot leaders were their long-standing enemies, though for different reasons. Local and provincial disputes thus helped to determine which side a person chose in the imperial conflict.

The active patriots, who accounted for about two-fifths of the population, came chiefly from the groups that had dominated colonial society, either numerically or politically. Among them were yeoman farmers, members of dominant Protestant sects (both Old and New Lights), Chesapeake gentry, merchants dealing mainly in American commodities, city artisans, elected officeholders, and people of English descent. Wives usually but not always adopted their husbands' political beliefs. Although all these patriots supported the Revolution, many pursued different goals within the broader coalition, as they had done in the 1760s. Some sought limited political reform, others extensive political change, and still others social and economic reforms. (The ways in which their concerns interacted will be discussed in Chapter 6.)

There remained in the middle perhaps two-fifths of the white population. Some of those who tried to avoid taking sides were sincere pacifists, such as Pennsylvania Quakers. Others opportunistically shifted

Connecticut imprisoned many of its loyalists in notorious Newgate prison, a converted copper mine. The offenders were housed in caverns below the large structure left of center. Some prominent loyalists (like Benjamin Franklin's son William, the last royal governor of New Jersey) were held in private homes.   The Connecticut Historical Society.

their allegiance depending on which side happened to be winning at the time. Still others simply wanted to be left alone to lead their lives; they cared little about politics and normally obeyed whichever side controlled their area. But such colonists also resisted the British and the Americans alike when the demands made on them seemed too heavy—when taxes became too high, for example, or when calls for militia service came too often. Their attitude might best be summed up in the phrase "a plague on both your houses." Such persons made up an especially large proportion of the population in the southern backcountry, where the Scotch-Irish settlers had little love for either the patriot gentry or the English authorities.

To American patriots, that sort of apathy or neutrality was a crime as heinous as loyalism. Those who were not for them were against them; in their minds, there could be no conscientious objectors. By the winter of 1775 and 1776, less than a year after Lexington and Concord, the Continental Congress was recommending to the states that all "disaffected" persons be disarmed and arrested. The state legislatures quickly passed laws prescribing severe penalties for suspected loyalists. Many began to require all voters (or, in some cases, all free adult males) to take oaths of allegiance; the punishment for refusal was usually banishment or extra taxes. In 1778 and thereafter, many states formally confiscated the property of banished loyalists.

During the war, loyalists tended to congregate in cities held by the British army. When those posts were evacuated at the end of the war, the loyalists scattered to different parts of the British Empire— England, the West Indies, and especially Canada. In the provinces of Nova Scotia, New Brunswick, and Ontario they recreated their lives as colonists, laying the foundations of British Canada. All told, perhaps as many as 100,000 white Americans preferred to leave their homeland rather than to live in a nation independent of British rule. That fact speaks volumes about the depth of their loyalty to an Anglo-American definition of their identity.

The patriots' policies helped to ensure that the weak, scattered, and persecuted loyalists could not band together to threaten the Revolutionary cause. But loyalists were not the patriots' only worry. They had reason to believe that Indians and enslaved blacks might join the forces arrayed against them.

Afro-American slaves faced a dilemma at the beginning of the Revolution: how could they best achieve their goal of escaping perpetual servitude? Should they fight with or against their white **The Blacks'** masters? The correct choice was not **Dilemma** immediately apparent, and so blacks made different decisions. Some joined the revolutionaries, others the British. In the early days of the war, those who decided to join the American side were primarily free blacks from New England, men to whom the issue of slavery or freedom did not apply. They were already free men, even if few of them owned property and none of them could vote. They made choices about their allegiance in the same way as their white neighbors.

For blacks who were still enslaved, alliance with the British held out more promise. Not surprisingly, therefore, news of slave conspiracies surfaced in different parts of the colonies in late 1774 and early 1775. All shared a common element: a plan to assist the British in return for freedom. A group of blacks petitioned General Thomas Gage, the commander-in-chief of the British army in Boston, promising to fight for the redcoats if he would liberate them. The

governor of Maryland authorized the issuance of extra guns to militiamen in four counties where slave uprisings were expected. The most serious incident occurred during the summer of 1775 in Charleston, where Thomas Jeremiah, a free black harbor pilot, was brutally executed after being convicted of attempting to foment a slave revolt.

A fear of acts such as these made white residents of the British West Indian colonies far more cautious in their opposition to parliamentary policies than their counterparts on the mainland. On most of the Caribbean islands, blacks outnumbered whites by six or seven to one. The planters simply could not afford to risk opposing Britain, their chief protector, with the ever-present threat of black revolt hanging over their heads. The Jamaica assembly agreed with the mainland colonial legislatures that citizens should not be bound by laws to which they had not consented. Nevertheless its members assured the king in 1774 that "it cannot be supposed, that we now intend, or ever could have intended Resistance to Great Britain." They cited as reasons Jamaica's "weak and feeble" condition, "its very small number of white inhabitants, and . . . the incumbrance of more than Two hundred thousand Slaves."

Racial composition affected politics in the continental colonies as well. In the North, where whites greatly outnumbered blacks, revolutionary fervor was at its height. In Virginia and Mary-**Racial** land, where whites constituted a safe **Composition** majority of the population, there **and Patriotic** was occasional alarm over potential **Fervor** slave revolts but no disabling fear. But in South Carolina, which was over 60 percent black, and Georgia, where the racial balance was nearly even, whites were noticeably less enthusiastic about resistance. Georgia, in fact, sent no delegates to the First Continental Congress, and reminded its representatives at the Second Continental Congress to consider its circumstances, "with our blacks and tories within us," when voting on the question of independence.

The whites' worst fears were realized in November 1775, when Lord Dunmore, the governor of Virginia, offered to free any slaves and indentured servants who would leave their patriot masters to join the British forces. Dunmore hoped to use blacks in his fight against the revolutionaries, and to disrupt the

An advertisement for a runaway slave suspected of joining Lord Dunmore—a common sight in Virginia and Maryland newspapers during the fall and winter of 1775 and 1776. Virginia State Library.

economy by depriving white Americans of their labor force. But fewer blacks than expected rallied to the British standard in 1775 and 1776 (there were at most two thousand). Many of those who did perished in a smallpox epidemic that raged through the naval vessels housing them in Norfolk harbor. Even so, Dunmore's proclamation led Congress in January 1776 to modify its previous policy prohibiting the enlistment of blacks in the Continental Army (the first New England black patriots served only in local militias).

Though black Americans did not pose a serious threat to the revolutionary cause in its early years, the patriots managed to turn rumors of slave uprisings to their own advantage. In South Carolina in particular, they won adherents by promoting white unity under the revolutionary banner. The Continental Association was needed, they argued, to protect whites from blacks at a time when the royal government was unable to muster adequate defense forces. Undoubtedly many wavering Carolinians were drawn into the revolutionary camp by fear that an overt division among the colony's whites would encourage a slave revolt.

A similar factor—the threat of Indian attacks—helped to persuade some reluctant westerners to support the struggle against Great Britain. In the years since the Proclamation of 1763, British officials had won the trust and respect of the interior tribes by attempting to protect them from land-hungry whites. The British-appointed superintendents

Indian Neutrality

of Indian affairs, John Stuart in the South and Sir William Johnson in the North, lived among and sympathized with the Indians. In 1768, Stuart and Johnson negotiated separate agreements modifying the proclamation line and attempting to draw realistic defensible boundaries between tribal holdings and white settlements. The two treaties—signed respectively at Hard Labor Creek, South Carolina, in October and at Fort Stanwix, New York, in November—supposedly established permanent borders for the colonies. But just a few years later, in the treaties of Lochaber (1770) and Augusta (1773), the British pushed the southern boundary even farther west to accommodate the demands of whites in western Georgia and Kentucky.

By the time of the Revolution, the Indians were impatient with white Americans' aggressive pressure on their lands. The relationship of the tribes and frontier whites was filled with acrimony, misunderstanding, and occasional bloody encounters. In combination with the tribes' confidence in Stuart and Johnson, such grievances predisposed most Indians toward an alliance with the British. Even so, the latter hesitated to make full and immediate use of their potential Indian allies. The superintendents were well aware that the tribes might prove a liability, since their aims and style of fighting were not necessarily compatible with those of the British. Accordingly, John Stuart and Guy Johnson (who became northern superintendent following his uncle's death) sought nothing more from the tribes than a promise of neutrality. The superintendents even helped to prevent a general Indian uprising in the summer of 1774. Through clever maneuvering they ensured that the Shawnee attracted few Indian allies for an attack on frontier villages in Kentucky. Lord Dunmore's War, between the Shawnee and the Virginia militia, ended with Kentucky being opened to white settlement but with hunting and fishing rights still being reserved to the Shawnee.

The patriots, recognizing that their standing with the tribes was poor, also sought the Indians' neutrality. In 1775 the Second Continental Congress sent a general message to the tribes describing the war as "a family quarrel between us and Old England" and requesting that they "not join on either side," since "you Indians are not concerned in it." A branch of the Cherokee tribe, led by Chief Dragging Canoe, nevertheless decided that the whites' "family quarrel" would allow them to settle some old scores. They attacked white settlements along the western borders of the Carolinas and Virginia in the summer of 1776. But a coordinated campaign by Carolina and Virginia militia destroyed many Cherokee towns, along with crops and large quantities of supplies. Dragging Canoe and his diehard followers fled west to the Tennessee River, where they established new outposts, while the rest of the Cherokee agreed to a treaty that ceded more of their land to the whites.

The fate of the Shawnee and Cherokee—each forced to fight alone without other Indian allies, and more easily defeated as a result—foreshadowed much of the history of Indian involvement in the American Revolution. During the eighteenth century the Iroquois had forcefully established their dominance over neighboring tribes. But the basis of their power had started to disintegrate with the British victory over France in 1763, and their subsequent friendship with Sir William Johnson could not prevent the erosion of their position during the years before 1775. Tribes long resentful of Iroquois power (and of the similar status of the Cherokee in the South) saw little reason to ally themselves with those from whose dominance they had just escaped, even to achieve the goal of preventing white encroachment on their lands. Consequently, during the Revolution most tribes pursued a course that aligned them with neither side, but which (as the American leaders wanted) for the most part kept them out of active involvement in the war.

Thus, although the patriots could never completely ignore the threats posed by loyalists, blacks, neutrals, and Indians, only rarely did fear of these groups seriously hamper the revolutionary movement. Occasionally frontier militia refused to turn out for duty on the seaboard because they feared Indians would attack in their absence. Sometimes southern troops refused to serve in the North because they (and their political leaders) were unwilling to leave the South unprotected against a slave insurrection. But the practical impossibility of a large-scale slave revolt, coupled with tribal feuds and the patriots' successful campaign to disarm and neutralize loyalists, ensured that the revolutionaries would remain firmly in control as they fought for independence.

WAR BEGINS

On January 27, 1775, the secretary of state for America, Lord Dartmouth, addressed a fateful letter to General Thomas Gage in Boston. Expressing his belief that American resistance was nothing more than the response of a "rude rabble without plan," Dartmouth ordered Gage to arrest "the principal actors and abettors in the provincial congress." If such a step were taken swiftly and silently, Dartmouth observed, no bloodshed need occur. Opposition could not be "very formidable," Dartmouth wrote, and even if it were, "it will surely be better that the Conflict should be brought on, upon such ground, than in a riper state of Rebellion."

Because of poor sailing weather, Dartmouth's letter did not reach Gage until April 14. The major patriot leaders had by then already left Boston, and in any

Battles of Lexington and Concord

event Gage did not believe that arresting them would serve a useful purpose. The order nevertheless spurred him to action: he decided to send an expedition to confiscate provincial military supplies stockpiled at Concord. Bostonians dispatched two messengers, William Dawes and Paul Revere (later joined by a third, Dr. Samuel Prescott), to rouse the countryside. Thus when the

British vanguard of several hundred men approached Lexington at dawn on April 19, they found a straggling group of seventy militiamen—approximately half the adult male population of the town—drawn up before them on the town common. The Americans' commander, Captain John Parker, ordered his men to withdraw, realizing that they were too few to halt the redcoat advance. But as they began to disperse, a shot rang out; the British soldiers then fired several volleys. When they stopped, eight Americans lay dead and another ten had been wounded. The British moved on to Concord, five miles away (see map).

There the contingents of militia were larger; the men of Concord had been joined by groups from Lincoln, Acton, and other nearby towns. The Americans allowed the British to enter Concord unopposed, but later in the morning they attacked the British infantry companies guarding the North Bridge. The brief exchange of gunfire there spilled the first British blood of the Revolution: three men were killed and nine (including four officers) wounded. On their retreat to Boston, the British were attacked by thousands of militiamen, firing from behind trees, bushes, and houses along the road. By the end of the day, the redcoats had suffered 272 casualties, 70 of whom were dead. Only the arrival of reinforcements from the city and the militia's lack of coordination prevented much heavier British losses. The patriots suffered just 93 casualties.

By the evening of April 20, perhaps as many as twenty thousand American militiamen had gathered around Boston, summoned by local committees that spread the alarm across the New England countryside. Many did not stay long, since they were needed at home for spring planting, but those who remained dug in along siege lines encircling the city. For nearly a year the two armies sat and stared at each other across those lines. During that period the redcoats attacked their besiegers only once, on June 17, when they drove the Americans from trenches atop Breed's Hill in Charlestown. In that misnamed Battle of Bunker Hill, the British incurred their greatest losses of the entire war: over 800 wounded and 228 killed. The Americans, though forced to abandon their position, lost fewer than half that number. During the same eleven-month period, the patriots captured Fort Ticonderoga, a British post on Lake Champlain, acquiring much-needed cannon. In the hope of bringing

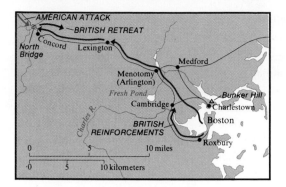

Lexington and Concord, April 19, 1775

Canada into the war on the American side, they also mounted an uncoordinated northern campaign that ended in disaster at Quebec in early 1776. But the chief significance of the first year of the war lay in the long lull in fighting between the main armies at Boston. The delay gave both sides a chance to regroup, organize, and plan their strategies.

Lord North and his new American secretary, Lord George Germain, made three major assumptions about the war they faced. First, they concluded that patriot forces could not withstand the assaults of trained British regulars. They and their generals were convinced that the campaign of 1776 would be the first and last of the war. Accordingly, they dispatched to America the largest single force Great Britain had ever assembled anywhere: 370 transport ships carrying 32,000 troops and tons of supplies, accompanied by 73 naval vessels and 13,000 sailors. Such an extraordinary effort would, they thought, ensure a quick victory. (Among the troops were thousands of mercenaries from the German state of Hesse; eighteenth-century armies were largely composed of such professional soldiers who hired out to the highest bidder.)

British Strategy

Second, British officials and army officers persisted in comparing this war to wars they had fought successfully in Europe. Thus they adopted a conventional strategy of capturing major American cities and defeating the rebel army decisively without suffering serious casualties themselves. Third, they assumed that a clear-cut military victory would automatically bring about their goal of retaining the colonies' allegiance.

All these assumptions proved false. North and Germain, like Lord Dartmouth before them, vastly underestimated the Americans' commitment to armed resistance. Defeats on the battlefield did not lead the patriots to abandon their political aims and sue for peace. The ministers also failed to recognize the significance of the American population's dispersal over an area 1,500 miles long and more than 100 miles wide. Although at one time or another during the war the British would control each of the most important American ports, less than 5 percent of the population lived in those cities. And the coast offered so many excellent harbors that essential commerce was easily rerouted. In other words, the loss of the cities did little to damage the American cause, while the desire for such ports repeatedly led redcoat generals astray.

Most of all, the British did not at first understand that a military victory would not necessarily bring about a political victory. Securing the colonies permanently would require hundreds of thousands of Americans to return to their original allegiance. The conquest of America was thus a far more complicated task than the defeat of France twelve years earlier. The British needed not only to overpower the patriots, but also to convert them. After 1778, they adopted a strategy designed to achieve that goal through the expanded use of loyalist forces and the restoration of civilian authority in occupied areas. But the new policy came too late. The British never fully realized that they were not fighting a conventional European war at all, but rather an entirely new kind of conflict: the first modern war of national liberation.

The British at least had a bureaucracy ready to supervise the war effort. The Americans had only the Second Continental Congress, originally intended merely as a brief gathering of colonial representatives to consider the British response to the Continental Association. Instead, the delegates who convened in Philadelphia on May 10, 1775, found that they had to assume the mantle of intercolonial government. "Such a vast Multitude of objects, civil, political, commercial and military, press and crowd upon us so fast, that we know not what to do first," John Adams wrote a close friend early in the session. Yet as the summer passed, the congress slowly organized the colonies for war. It

Second Continental Congress

authorized the printing of money with which to purchase necessary goods, established a committee to supervise relations with foreign countries, and took steps to strengthen the militia. Most important of all, it created the Continental Army and appointed its generals.

Until the congress met, the Massachusetts provincial congress had taken responsibility for organizing the massive army of militia encamped at Boston. But that army, composed of men from all the New England states, was a heavy drain on limited local resources. Consequently, on May 16 Massachusetts asked the Continental Congress to assume the task of directing the army. First, congress had to choose a commander-in-chief. Since the war had thus far been a wholly northern affair, many delegates recognized the importance of naming a non–New Englander to command the army. There seemed only one obvious candidate: they unanimously selected their fellow delegate, the Virginian George Washington.

Washington was no fiery radical, nor was he a reflective political thinker. He had not played a prominent role in the prerevolutionary agitation, but his devotion to the American cause was unquestioned. He was dignified, conservative, respectable, and a man of unimpeachable integrity. The younger son of a Virginia planter, Washington had not expected to inherit substantial property and had planned to make his living as a surveyor. But the early death of an older brother and his marriage to the wealthy widow Martha Custis had made him a rich man. Though unmistakably an aristocrat, Washington was unswervingly committed to representative government. And he had other desirable traits as well. His stamina was remarkable: in more than eight years of war Washington never had a serious illness and took only one brief leave of absence. Moreover, he both looked and acted like a leader. Six feet tall in an era when most men were five inches shorter, his presence was stately and commanding. Other patriots praised his judgment, steadiness, and discretion, and even a loyalist admitted that Washington could "atone for many demerits by the extraordinary coolness and caution which distinguish his character."

George Washington: A Portrait of Leadership

Washington needed all the coolness and caution he could muster when he took command of the army outside Boston in July 1775. It took him months to impose hierarchy and discipline on the unruly troops and to bring order to the supply system. But by March 1776, when the arrival of cannon from Ticonderoga enabled him at last to put direct pressure on the redcoats in the city, the army was prepared to act. As it happened, an assault on Boston proved unnecessary. Sir William Howe, who had replaced Gage, had been considering an evacuation for some time; he wanted to transfer his troops to New York City. The patriots' bombardment of Boston early in the month decided the matter. On March 17, the British and more than a thousand of their loyalist allies abandoned Boston forever.

That spring of 1776, as the British fleet left Boston for the temporary haven of Halifax, Nova Scotia, the colonies were moving inexorably toward the act the Massachusetts loyalists on board the ships feared most: a declaration of independence. Even months after fighting had begun, American leaders still denied they sought a break with the empire. Then in January 1776 there appeared a pamphlet by a man who not only thought the unthinkable but advocated it.

Thomas Paine's *Common Sense* exploded on the American scene like a bombshell. Within three months of publication, it sold 120,000 copies. The author, a radical English printer who had lived in America only since 1774, called stridently and stirringly for independence. More than that: Paine challenged many common American assumptions about government and the colonies' relationship to England. Rejecting the notion that a balance of monarchy, aristocracy, and democracy was necessary to preserve freedom, he advocated the establishment of a republic. Instead of acknowledging the benefits of a connection with the mother country, Paine insisted that Britain had exploited the colonies unmercifully. In place of the frequent assertion that an independent America would be weak and divided, he substituted an unlimited confidence in America's strength when freed from European control. These striking statements were clothed in equally striking prose. Scorning the polite, rational style of his classically educated predecessors, Paine adopted a furious, raging tone. Although a printed work, the pamphlet reflected the oral culture of ordinary folk. It was couched in everyday language

Thomas Paine's *Common Sense*

George Washington (1732–1799), painted in his uniform. His stalwart bearing, so vividly conveyed in this portrait, was one of his prime assets as a leader. *Washington-Custis-Lee Collection, Washington and Lee University, Virginia.*

and relied heavily on the Bible—the only book familiar to most Americans—as a primary source of authority. No wonder the pamphlet had a wider distribution than any other political publication of its day.

There is no way of knowing how many people were converted to the cause of independence by reading *Common Sense*. But by late spring 1776 independence had clearly become inevitable. On May 10, the Second Continental Congress formally recommended that individual colonies "adopt such governments as shall, in the opinion of the representatives of the people, best conduce to the happiness and safety of their constituents in particular, and America in general." From that source grew the first state constitutions. Perceiving the trend of events, the few loyalists still connected with the congress severed their ties to that body.

Then on June 7 came the confirmation of the movement toward independence. Richard Henry Lee

After listening to the first formal reading of the Declaration of Independence in New York City on July 9, 1776, a crowd of soldiers and civilians spontaneously pulled down a statue of George III that stood on the Bowling Green in the heart of the city. Most of the statue was later melted down and made into bullets, but some pieces of it were found a few years ago in Connecticut. Library of Congress.

of Virginia, seconded by John Adams of Massachusetts, introduced the crucial resolution: "that these United Colonies are, and of right ought to be, free and independent States, that they are absolved of all allegiance to the British Crown, and that all political connection between them and the State of Great Britain is, and ought to be, totally dissolved." The congress debated but did not immediately adopt Lee's resolution. Instead, it postponed a vote until early July, to allow time for consultation and public reaction. In the meantime, a committee composed of Thomas Jefferson, John Adams, Benjamin Franklin, Robert R. Livingston of New York, and Roger Sherman of Connecticut was directed to draft a declaration of independence.

Declaration of Independence

The committee in turn assigned primary responsibility for writing the declaration to Jefferson, who was well known for his apt and eloquent style. Years later John Adams recalled that Jefferson had modestly protested his selection, suggesting that Adams prepare the initial draft. The Massachusetts revolutionary recorded his frank response: "You can write ten times better than I can."

Thomas Jefferson was at the time thirty-four years old, a Virginia lawyer educated at the College of William and Mary and in the law offices of the prominent attorney George Wythe. He had read widely in history and political theory and had been a member of the House of Burgesses. His broad knowledge was evident not only in the declaration but also in his draft of the Virginia state constitution, completed just a few days before his appointment to the committee. Jefferson, an intensely private man, loved his home and family deeply. This early stage of his political career was marked by his beloved wife Martha's repeated difficulties in childbearing. While he wrote and debated in Philadelphia during the summer of 1776, she suffered a miscarriage at their home, Monticello. Not until after her death in 1782, from complications following the birth of their sixth (but only third surviving) child in ten years of marriage, did Jefferson fully commit himself to public service.

The draft of the declaration was laid before congress on June 28. The delegates officially voted for independence four days later, then debated the wording of the declaration for two more days, adopting it with some changes on July 4. Since Americans had long since ceased to see themselves as legitimate subjects of Parliament, the Declaration of Independence concentrated on George III (see Appendix). That focus also provided a single identifiable villain on whom to center the charges of misconduct. The document accused the king of attempting to destroy representative government in the colonies and of oppressing Americans through the unjustified use of excessive force. But the declaration's chief long-term importance did not lie in its lengthy catalogue of grievances against George III (including, in a section omitted by congress, Jefferson's charge that the British monarchy had introduced slavery into America). It lay instead in the ringing statements of principle that have served ever since as the ideal to which Americans aspire. "We hold these truths to be self-evident: That all men are created equal; that they are endowed by their Creator with certain unalienable rights; that among these are life, liberty and the pursuit of happiness; that, to secure these rights, governments are instituted among men, deriving their just powers from the consent of the governed; that whenever any form of government becomes destructive of these ends, it is the right of the people to alter or to abolish it, and to institute new government." These phrases have echoed down through American history like no others.

The delegates in Philadelphia who voted to accept the Declaration of Independence did not have the advantage of our two hundred years of hindsight. When they adopted the declaration, they risked their necks: they were committing treason. Thus when they concluded the declaration with the assertion that they "mutually pledge[d] to each other our lives, our fortunes, and our sacred honor," they spoke no less than the truth. The real struggle still lay before them, and few of them had Thomas Paine's boundless confidence in success.

THE LONG STRUGGLE
IN THE NORTH

In late June 1776, the first of the ships carrying Sir William Howe's troops from Halifax appeared off the coast of New York. On July 2, the day the congress voted for independence,

Battle for New York City the redcoats landed on Staten Island. But Howe waited until mid-August, after the arrival of troop transports from England, to begin his attack on the city. The delay gave Washington sufficient time to march his army south to meet the threat. To defend New York, Washington had approximately seventeen thousand soldiers: ten thousand Continentals who had promised to serve until the end of the year, and seven thousand militiamen who had enlisted for shorter terms. Neither he nor most of his men had ever fought a major battle against the British, and their lack of experience led to disastrous mistakes. The difficulty of defending New York City only compounded the errors.

Washington's problem was as simple as the geography of the region was complex (see map, page 142). To protect the city adequately, he would have to divide his forces among Long Island, Manhattan Island, and the mainland. But the British fleet under Admiral Lord Richard Howe, Sir William's brother, controlled the harbors and rivers that separated the American forces. The patriots thus constantly courted catastrophe, for swift action by the British navy could cut off the possibility of retreat and perhaps even communication. But despite these dangers, Washington could not afford to surrender New York to the Howes without a fight. Not only did the city occupy a strategic location, but the region that surrounded it was known to contain many loyalist sympathizers. A show of force was essential if the revolutionaries were to retain any hope of persuading waverers to join them.

On August 27, Sir William Howe's forces attacked the American positions on Brooklyn Heights, pushing the untried rebel troops back into their defensive entrenchments. But he failed to press his advantage, even neglecting to send his brother's ships into the

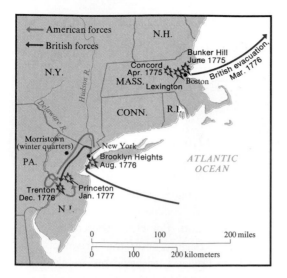

The War in the North, 1775–1777

East River to cut off a retreat. Consequently, the Americans were able to escape; a troop of Marblehead fishermen ferried nine thousand men to the southern tip of Manhattan Island in less than twelve hours on the night of August 29. Washington then moved north along the island, retreating onto the mainland but leaving behind nearly three thousand men in the supposedly impregnable Fort Washington on the west shore of Manhattan. Howe slowly followed him into Westchester County, then turned back to focus his attention on the fort. Its defenses collapsed, and the large garrison surrendered in early November. Only when Charleston fell to the British in May 1780 did the Americans lose more men on a single occasion.

George Washington had defended New York, but he had done a bad job of it. He had repeatedly broken a basic rule of military strategy: never divide your force in the face of a superior enemy. In the end, though, the Howe brothers' failure to move quickly prevented a decisive defeat of the Americans. Although Washington's army had been seriously reduced by battlefield casualties, the surrender of Fort Washington, and the loss of most of the militiamen (who had returned home for the harvest), its core remained. Through November and December, Washington led his men in a retreat across New Jersey. Howe followed at a leisurely pace, setting up a string of outposts manned mostly by Hessian mercenaries. After Washington crossed the Delaware River into Pennsylvania,

the British commander turned back and settled into comfortable winter quarters in New York City.

The British now controlled most of New Jersey. Hundreds of Americans accepted the pardons offered by the Howes. Among them were Joseph Galloway, a delegate to the First Continental Congress, and Richard Stockton, a signer of the Declaration of Independence. Occupying troops met little opposition, and the Revolutionary cause appeared to be in disarray. "These are the times that try men's souls," wrote Thomas Paine in his pamphlet *The Crisis*. "The summer soldier and the sunshine patriot will, in this crisis, shrink from the service of his country; . . . yet we have this consolation with us, that the harder the conflict, the more glorious the triumph."

In the aftermath of battle, as at its height, the British generals let their advantage slip away. The redcoats stationed in New Jersey went on a rampage of rape and plunder. Because loyalists and patriots were indistinguishable to the British and Hessian troops, families on both sides suffered nearly equally. Livestock, crops, and firewood were seized for use by the army. Houses were looted and burned, churches and public buildings desecrated. But nothing was better calculated to rally doubtful Americans to the cause of independence than the wanton murder of innocent civilians and rape of women.

The soldiers' marauding alienated potentially loyal New Jerseyites and Pennsylvanians whose allegiance the British could ill afford to lose. It also spurred Washington's determination to strike back. The enlistments of most of the Continental troops were to expire on December 31, and Washington also wanted to take advantage of short-term Pennsylvania militia who had recently joined him. He moved quickly and attacked the Hessian encampment at Trenton early in the morning of December 26, while the redcoats were still reeling from their Christmas celebration. The patriots captured more than nine hundred Hessians and killed another thirty; only three Americans were wounded. A few days later, after persuading many of his men to stay on beyond the term of their enlistments, Washington attacked again at Princeton. Having gained command of the field and buoyed American spirits with the two swift victories, Washington set up winter quarters at Morristown, New Jersey.

Battle of Trenton

Jean Baptiste Antoine de Verger, a sublieutenant in the French army in America, painted this watercolor of revolutionary soldiers in his journal. They are, left to right, a black light infantryman, a musketman, a rifleman, and an artilleryman. Brown University Library.

The campaign of 1776 established patterns that were to persist throughout much of the war, despite changes in British leadership and strategy. British forces were usually more numerous and often better led than the Americans. But their ponderous style of maneuvering, lack of familiarity with the terrain, and inability to live off the land without antagonizing the populace helped to offset those advantages. Furthermore, although Washington always seemed to lack regular troops—the Continental Army never numbered more than 18,500 men—he could usually count on the militia to join him at crucial times. American militiamen did not like to sign up for long terms of service or to fight far from home, but when their homes were threatened they would rally to the cause. Washington and his officers frequently complained about the militia's habit of disappearing during planting or harvesting. But time and again their presence, however brief, enabled the Americans to launch an attack or counter an important British thrust.

As the war dragged on, the Continental Army and the militia took on decidedly different characters. State governments, responsible for filling military quotas, discovered that most men willing to enlist for long periods in the regular army were young, single, and footloose. Farmers with families tended to prefer short-term militia duty. As the supply of whites willing to sign up for the Continentals diminished, recruiters in the northern states turned increasingly to blacks, both slave and free. (White southerners continued to resist this approach.) Perhaps as many as five thousand blacks eventually served in the Revolutionary army, and most of them won their freedom as a result. They commonly served in racially integrated units, often being assigned tasks that whites wanted to avoid (such as cooking, foraging for food, or driving wagons).

Also attached to the American forces were a number of women, mostly wives and widows of poor soldiers. Such camp followers worked as cooks, nurses, and launderers, performing vital services for the army in return for rations and low wages. The presence of the women, as well as the militiamen who floated in and out of the American camp at irregular intervals, made for an unwieldy army that its officers found difficult to manage. Yet the army's shapelessness also reflected its greatest strength: an almost unlimited reservoir of man and woman power.

Deborah Sampson (1760–1827), who disguised herself as a man and enlisted in the Continental Army as Robert Shurtleff. She served from May 1782 to October 1783, when her sex was discovered and she was discharged. In later years she gave public lectures describing her wartime experiences. After her death her husband became the only man to receive a pension as the "widow" of a revolutionary soldier. Courtesy of the Rhode Island Historical Society.

In 1777, the chief British effort was planned by the flashy "Gentleman Johnny" Burgoyne, a playboy general as much at home at the gaming tables of London as on the battlefield. Burgoyne, a subordinate of Howe, had spent the winter of 1776 to 1777 in London, where he gained the ear of Lord George Germain. Burgoyne convinced Germain that he could lead an invading force of redcoats and Indians down the Hudson River from Canada, cutting off New England from the rest of the states. He proposed to rendezvous near Albany with a similar force that would move east from Niagara along the Mohawk River valley. The combined force would then pre-

sumably link up with that of Sir William Howe in New York City.

That Burgoyne's scheme would give "Gentleman Johnny" all the glory and relegate Howe to a supporting role did not escape the latter's notice. While Burgoyne was plotting in London, Howe was laying his own plans in New York City. Joseph Galloway and other Pennsylvania loyalists persuaded Howe that Philadelphia could be taken easily and that his troops would be welcomed by many residents of the region. Just as Burgoyne left Howe out of his plans, Howe left Burgoyne out of his. Thus the two major British armies in America would operate independently in 1777, and the result would be a disaster (see map).

Howe accomplished his objective: he captured Philadelphia. But he did so in an inexplicable fashion, delaying for months before beginning the campaign,

Howe Takes Philadelphia

then taking six weeks to transport his troops by sea to the head of Chesapeake Bay instead of marching them overland. That maneuver cost him at least a month, debilitated his men, and depleted his supplies. Incredibly, he was only forty miles closer to Philadelphia at the end of the lengthy voyage than when he started. Two years later, when Parliament formally inquired into the conduct of the war, Howe's critics charged that his errors were so extraordinary he must have deliberately committed treason. Even today, historians have not been able to explain his motives adequately. In any event, by the time Howe was ready to move on Philadelphia, Washington had had time to prepare its defenses. Twice, at Brandywine Creek and again at Germantown, the two armies clashed near the rebel capital. Though the British won both engagements, the Americans handled themselves well. The redcoats took Philadelphia in late September, but to little effect. The campaign season was nearly over; the Revolutionary army had gained confidence in itself and its leaders; few welcoming loyalists had materialized; and, far to the north, Burgoyne was going down to defeat.

Burgoyne and his men had set out from Montreal in mid-June, floating down Lake Champlain into New York in canoes and flat-bottomed boats. In early June they had easily taken Fort Ticonderoga from its outnumbered and outgunned defenders. But trouble

Burgoyne's Campaign in New York began as Burgoyne started his overland march. His clumsy artillery carriages and baggage wagons foundered in the heavy forests and ravines. Patriot militia felled giant trees across the army's path. As a result, Burgoyne's troops took twenty-four days to travel the twenty-three miles to Fort Edward, on the Hudson River. Short of supplies, the general dispatched eight hundred German mercenaries to forage the countryside. On August 16, American militia companies nearly wiped out the Germans near Bennington. Yet Burgoyne failed to recognize the seriousness of his predicament and continued to dawdle, giving the Americans more than enough time to prepare for his coming. By the time he finally crossed the Hudson in mid-September, bound for Albany, Burgoyne's fate was sealed. After several bloody clashes with the American force commanded by Horatio Gates, Burgoyne was surrounded near Saratoga, New York. On October 17, 1777, he surrendered his entire force of more than six thousand men.

Long before, the 1,400 redcoats and Indians marching along the Mohawk River toward Albany had also been turned back. Under the command of Colonel Barry St. Leger, they had advanced easily until they reached the isolated American outpost at Fort Stanwix in early August. After they had laid siege to the well-fortified structure, they learned that a patriot relief column was en route to the fort. Leaving only a small detachment at Fort Stanwix, the British ambushed the Americans at Oriskany on August 6. The British claimed victory in the ensuing battle, one of the bloodiest of the war, but they and their Indian allies lost their taste for further fighting. The Americans tricked them into believing that another large patriot force was on the way, and in late August the British abandoned the siege and returned to Niagara.

The battle of Oriskany marked a split of the Iroquois Confederacy. In 1776 the Six Nations had formally pledged to remain neutral in the Anglo-American struggle. But two influential Mohawk leaders, Joseph and Mary Brant, worked tirelessly to persuade their fellow Iroquois to join the British. Mary Brant, a powerful tribal matron, was also the widow of the respected Indian

Split of the Iroquois Confederacy

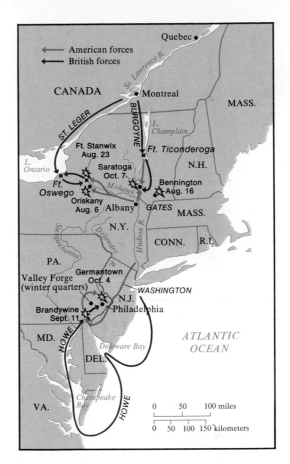

Campaign of 1777

superintendent Sir William Johnson. Her younger brother Joseph, a renowned warrior, was convinced that the Six Nations should ally themselves with the British in order to prevent American encroachment on their lands. As an observer said of Mary, "one word from her goes farther with them [the Iroquois] than a thousand from any white man without exception." The Brants won over to the British the Seneca, Cayuga, and Mohawk, all of whom contributed warriors to St. Leger's expedition. But the Oneida preferred the American side, bringing the Tuscarora with them. (The remaining Iroquois tribe, the Onondaga, split into three factions, one on each side and one supporting neutrality.) At Oriskany, some Oneidas and Tuscaroras joined the patriot militia to fight their Iroquois brethren; thus a league of friendship that had survived over three hundred years was torn apart by the whites' family quarrel.

The Mohawk chief Joseph Brant (1742–1807), painted in London in 1786 by Gilbert Stuart.   New York State Historical Association, Cooperstown.

The collapse of Iroquois unity and the confederacy's abandonment of neutrality had important consequences for both whites and Indians in subsequent years. In 1778, Iroquois warriors allied with the British raided the New York frontier villages of Wyoming and Cherry Valley; to retaliate, in the late summer of 1779 the whites dispatched an expedition under General John Sullivan to burn Iroquois crops, orchards, and settlements. The destruction was so thorough that many bands had to leave their ancestral homeland to seek food and shelter with the British north of the Great Lakes during the winter of 1779 to 1780. A large number of Iroquois people never returned to New York, but settled permanently in British Canada.

For the Indians, Oriskany was the most significant battle of the northern campaign; for the whites, it was Saratoga. The news of Burgoyne's surrender brought joy to patriots, discouragement to loyalists and Britons. In exile in London, Thomas Hutchinson wrote of the "universal dejection" among loyalists there. "Everybody in a gloom," he commented; "most of us expect to lay our bones here." The disaster prompted Lord North to authorize a peace commission to offer the Americans everything they had requested in 1774—in effect, a return to the imperial system of 1763. It was, of course, far too late for that: the patriots rejected the overture and the peace commission sailed back to England empty-handed in mid-1778.

Most important of all, the American victory at Saratoga drew France formally into the conflict. Ever since 1763, the French had sought to avenge their defeat in the French and Indian War, and the American Revolution provided them with that opportunity. Even before Benjamin Franklin arrived in Paris in late 1776, France was covertly supplying the revolutionaries with military necessities. Indeed, 90 percent of the gunpowder the Americans used in the first two years of the war came from France.

The Franco-American Alliance of 1778

Franklin worked tirelessly to strengthen the ties between the two nations. Although he was not a Quaker, he deliberately affected a plain style of dress that made him stand out amid the luxury of the court of King Louis XVI. He cleverly presented himself as a representative of American simplicity, playing on the French image of Americans as virtuous yeomen. Franklin's efforts culminated in February 1778 when the countries signed two treaties. In the first, France recognized American independence; the second provided for a formal alliance between the two nations until the war was won. The most visible symbol of Franco-American cooperation in the years that followed was the Marquis de Lafayette, a young nobleman whose father had been killed by the British in King George's War. He volunteered for service with George Washington in 1777 and fought with the American forces until the conflict ended.

The French alliance had two major benefits for the patriot cause. First, France began to aid the Americans openly, sending troops and naval vessels in addition to supplies of arms, ammunition, clothing, and blankets. Second, the British could no longer focus their attention on the American mainland alone, for they had to fight the French in the West Indies and elsewhere. Spain's entry into the war in 1779 as an ally of France (but not the United States) further magnified Britain's problems. Throughout the war, French assistance was important to the Americans, but in the last years of the conflict that aid was especially vital.

The Long Struggle
in the South

In the aftermath of the Saratoga disaster, Lord George Germain and the military officials in London reassessed their strategy. Maneuvering in the North had done them little good; perhaps shifting the field of battle southward would bring success. The many loyalist exiles in England encouraged this line of thinking. They argued that loyal southerners would welcome the redcoat army as liberators, and that once the region had been pacified and returned to civilian control it could serve as a base for attacking the North.

In early 1778 Sir William Howe was replaced by Sir Henry Clinton. As commander-in-chief, Clinton was also afflicted with sluggishness and lack of resolution. Still, he oversaw the regrouping of British forces in America, ordering the evacuation of Philadelphia in June 1778 and dispatching a small expedition to Georgia at the end of the year. When Savannah and then Augusta fell easily into British hands, Clinton became convinced that a southern strategy would work. In late 1779 he sailed down the coast with 8,500 troops to attack Charleston, the most important American city in the South (see map).

Although the Americans worked hard to bolster Charleston's defenses, the city fell to the British on May 12, 1780. General Benjamin Lincoln surrendered the entire southern army—5,500 men—to the invaders. In the weeks that followed, the redcoats spread through South Carolina, establishing garrisons at key points in the interior. As in New Jersey in 1776, hundreds of South Carolinians renounced allegiance to the United States and proclaimed their loyalty to the crown. Clinton organized loyalist regiments and the process of pacification began.

Fall of Charleston

Yet the British triumph was less complete and secure than it appeared. The success of the southern campaign depended on British control of the seas, for only by sea could the widely dispersed British armies remain in communication with one another.

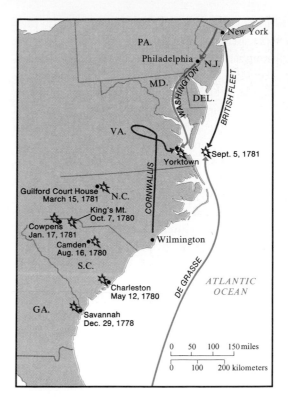

The War in the South

For the moment the Royal Navy safely dominated the American coastline, but French naval power posed a threat to the entire southern enterprise. Moreover, the redcoats never managed to establish full control of the areas they seized. As a result, patriot bands operated freely throughout the state, and loyalists could not be guaranteed protection against their enemies. Last but not least, the fall of Charleston did not dishearten the patriots; instead, it spurred them to greater exertions. As one Marylander declared confidently, "The Fate of America is not to be decided by the Loss of a Town or Two." Patriot women in four states formed the Ladies Association, which collected money to purchase shirts for needy soldiers. Recruiting efforts were stepped up.

Throughout most of 1780, though, the war in South Carolina went badly for the patriots. In August, a reorganized southern army under the command of Horatio Gates was crushingly defeated at Camden by the forces of Lord Cornwallis, who had been placed in charge of the southern campaign. The British army was joined wherever it went by hundreds, even thousands, of blacks seeking freedom on the basis of

Lord Dunmore's proclamation. Slaves ran away from their patriot masters individually and as families, in such numbers that they seriously disrupted planting and harvesting in 1780 and 1781. More than fifty-five thousand blacks were lost to their owners as a result of the war. Not all of them joined the British or won their freedom if they did, but their flight had just the effect Dunmore wanted. Many served the British well as scouts, guides, and laborers.

After the defeat at Camden, Washington (who had to remain in the North to oppose the British army occupying New York) gave command of the southern campaign to General Na-

Greene Rallies South Carolina
thanael Greene of Rhode Island. Greene was appalled by what he found in South Carolina. As he wrote to a friend, "the word difficulty when applied to the state of things here . . . is almost without meaning, it falls so far short" of reality. His troops needed clothing, blankets, and food, but "a great part of this country is already laid waste and in the utmost danger of becoming a desert." The constant guerrilla warfare had, he commented, "so corrupted the principles of the people that they think of nothing but plundering one another." Under such circumstances, Greene had to move cautiously. He adopted a conciliatory policy toward loyalists and neutrals, persuading the governor of South Carolina to offer complete pardons to those who had fought for the British if they would join the patriot militia. He also ordered his troops not to loot loyalist property and to treat captives fairly. Greene recognized that the patriots could win only by convincing the people that they could bring stability to the region. He thus helped the shattered provincial congresses of Georgia and South Carolina to begin re-establishing civilian authority in the interior—a goal the British were never able to accomplish, even along the coast.

Greene also took a conciliatory approach to the southern Indians. With his desperate need for soldiers, he could not afford to have frontier militia companies occupied in defending their homes against Indian attacks. Since he had so few regulars (only 1,600 when he took command), Greene had to rely on western volunteers. Therefore, he negotiated with the Indians.

His policy eventually met with success, although at first royal officials cooperating with the British invasion forces won allies among a number of southern tribes, especially Dragging Canoe's Cherokee band. But the southern Indians, recalling the disastrous defeat the Cherokee had suffered in 1776, never committed themselves wholeheartedly to the British. In 1781 the Cherokee began negotiations with the patriots, and the next year the other tribes too sued for peace. By the end of the war only the Creek remained allied to the redcoats. A group of Chickasaw chiefs explained their reasoning to American agents in July 1782, after Greene's battlefield successes had forced the British to withdraw into Savannah and Charleston: "The English put the Bloody Tomahawk into our hands, telling us that we should have no Goods if we did not Exert ourselves to the greatest point of Resentment against you, but now we find our mistake and Distresses. The English have done their utmost and left us in our adversity. We find them full of Deceit and Dissimulation."

Even before Greene took command of the southern army in December 1780, the tide had begun to turn. At King's Mountain in October, a force of "over-mountain men" from the settlements west of the Appalachians had defeated a large party of redcoats and loyalists. Then in January 1781 Greene's trusted aide, Brigadier General Daniel Morgan, brilliantly defeated the crack British regiment Tarleton's Legion at Cowpens, near the border between North and South Carolina. Greene himself confronted the main body of British troops under Lord Cornwallis at Guilford Court House, North Carolina, in March. Cornwallis controlled the field at the end of the day, but his army had been largely destroyed. He had to retreat to Wilmington, on the coast, to receive supplies and fresh troops from New York by sea. In the meantime Greene returned to South Carolina, where, in a series of swift strikes, he forced the redcoats to abandon their posts in the interior and quickly retire to Charleston.

Cornwallis had already ignored explicit orders not to leave South Carolina unless the state was safely in British hands. Evidently bent on his own destruc-

Surrender at Yorktown
tion, he now headed north into Virginia, where he joined forces with a detachment of redcoats commanded by the American traitor Benedict Arnold. (Arnold had fought heroically with the patriots early in the war, but defected to the

In 1781 Charles Willson Peale traveled to Yorktown to commemorate the great victory by the combined American and French forces. That he was present in the immediate aftermath of the battle is indicated by his portrayal of sunken ships in the river and dead horses on the beach. On the right stands Washington with (from left to right) the Marquis de Lafayette, Count Rochambeau, and Tench Tilghman, one of Washington's aides.   Maryland Historical Society.

British in 1780 in the belief that the Americans did not fully appreciate him.) Instead of acting decisively with his new army of 7,200 men, Cornwallis withdrew to the tip of the peninsula between the York and James rivers, where he fortified Yorktown and in effect waited for the end. Seizing the opportunity, Washington quickly moved over seven thousand troops south from New York City. When a French fleet under the Comte de Grasse arrived from the West Indies in time to defeat the Royal Navy vessels sent to rescue Cornwallis, the British general was trapped (see map, page 147). On October 19, 1781, four years and two days after Burgoyne's defeat at Saratoga, Cornwallis surrendered to the combined American and French forces while his military band played "The World Turned Upside Down."

When news of the surrender reached England,

Lord North's ministry fell. Parliament voted to cease offensive operations in America and authorized peace negotiations. But guerrilla warfare between patriots and loyalists continued to ravage the Carolinas and Georgia for more than a year, and in the North vicious retaliatory raids by Indians and whites kept the frontier aflame. Indeed, the single most brutal massacre of the war occurred in March 1782, at Gnadenhuetten in the Ohio country. A group of white militiamen, seeking the Indians who had killed a frontier family, encountered a peaceful band of Delawares. The Indians, who had been converted to both Christianity and pacifism by Moravian missionaries, were slaughtered unmercifully. Ninety-six men, women, and children died that day, some burned at the stake, others tomahawked. Two months later, hostile members of the Delaware tribe captured three

IMPORTANT EVENTS

1774	First Continental Congress
1775	Battles of Lexington and Concord
	Lord Dunmore's Proclamation
	Second Continental Congress
1776	Thomas Paine, *Common Sense*
	British evacuate Boston
	Declaration of Independence
	New York campaign
1777	British take Philadelphia
	Burgoyne surrenders at Saratoga
1778	French alliance
	British evacuate Philadelphia
1779	Sullivan expedition against Iroquois villages
1780	British take Charleston
1781	Cornwallis surrenders at Yorktown
1782	Peace negotiations begin
1783	Treaty of Paris

white militiamen and subjected them to gruesome tortures in reprisal. The persistence of conflict between whites and Indians after Yorktown, all too often overlooked in accounts of the Revolution, serves to underline the degree to which the Indians were the real losers in the war initiated by whites.

The fighting finally ended when Americans and Britons learned of the signing of a preliminary peace treaty at Paris in November 1782. The American negotiators—Benjamin Franklin, **Treaty of Paris** John Jay, and John Adams—ignored their instructions to be guided by France and instead struck a separate agreement with Great Britain. Their instincts were sound: the French government was more an enemy to Britain than a friend to the United States. In fact, French ministers worked secretly behind the scenes to try to prevent the establishment of a strong, unified, independent government in America. The new British ministry, headed by Lord Shelburne (formerly a persistent critic of Lord North's harsh American policies), was weary of war and made numerous concessions—so many, in fact, that Parliament ousted the ministry shortly after the peace terms were approved.

Under the treaty, signed formally on September 3, 1783, the Americans were granted unconditional independence and unlimited fishing rights off Newfoundland. The boundaries of the new nation were generous: to the north, approximately the current boundary with Canada; to the south, the thirty-first parallel; to the west, the Mississippi River. Florida, which the British had acquired in 1763, was returned to Spain. In ceding so much land unconditionally to the Americans, the British entirely ignored the territorial rights of their Indian allies. Once again, the tribes' interests were sacrificed to the demands of European power politics. Loyalists and British merchants were also poorly served by the British negotiators. The treaty's ambiguously worded clauses pertaining to the payment of prewar debts and the postwar treatment of loyalists caused trouble for years to come and proved impossible to enforce.

The long war finally over, the victorious Americans could look back on their achievement with satisfaction and awe. In 1775, with an inexperienced ragtag army, they had taken on the greatest military power in the world—and eight years later they had won. They had accomplished their goal more through persistence and commitment than through brilliance on the battlefield. Actual victories had been few, but their army had always survived defeat and stand-offs to fight again. Ultimately, the Americans had simply worn their enemy down.

SUGGESTIONS FOR FURTHER READING

General

Edward Countryman, *The American Revolution* (1985); Larry Gerlach, ed., *Legacies of the American Revolution* (1978); *Journal of Interdisciplinary History,* 6, No. 4 (spring 1976),

Interdisciplinary Studies of the American Revolution; Stephen G. Kurtz and James H. Hutson, eds., *Essays on the American Revolution* (1973); Library of Congress, *Symposia on the American Revolution*, 5 vols. (1972–1976); Edmund S. Morgan, *The Challenge of the American Revolution* (1976); *William and Mary Quarterly*, 3rd ser., 33, No. 3 (July 1976), *The American Revolution*; Alfred Young, ed., *The American Revolution: Explorations in the History of American Radicalism* (1976).

Military

John Richard Alden, *The American Revolution 1775–1783* (1964); John C. Dann, ed., *The Revolution Remembered: Eyewitness Accounts of the War for Independence* (1980); Ira Gruber, *The Howe Brothers and the American Revolution* (1972); Richard J. Hargrove, *General John Burgoyne* (1983); Don Higginbotham, *The War of American Independence: Military Attitudes, Policies, and Practice, 1763–1789* (1971); Ronald Hoffman and Peter Albert, eds., *Arms and Independence: The Military Character of the American Revolution* (1984); Piers Mackesy, *The War for America, 1775–1783* (1964); James K. Martin and Mark Lender, *A Respectable Army: The Military Origins of the Republic 1763–1789* (1982); Charles Royster, *A Revolutionary People at War: The Continental Army and American Character, 1775–1783* (1980); John Shy, *A People Numerous & Armed: Reflections on the Military Struggle for American Independence* (1976); William Willcox, *Portrait of a General: Sir Henry Clinton in the War of Independence* (1964).

Local and Regional

Richard V. W. Buel, *Dear Liberty: Connecticut's Mobilization for the Revolutionary War* (1980); Edward Countryman, *A People in Revolution: The American Revolution and Political Society in New York, 1760–1790* (1981); Jeffrey Crow and Larry Tise, eds., *The Southern Experience in the American Revolution* (1978); Robert A. Gross, *The Minutemen and Their World* (1976); Ronald Hoffman, *A Spirit of Dissension: Economics, Politics, and the Revolution in Maryland* (1973); Ronald Hoffman, Thad W. Tate, and Peter Albert, eds., *An Uncivil War: The Southern Backcountry During the American Revolution* (1985); Robert J. Taylor, *Western Massachusetts in the Revolution* (1954).

Indians and Blacks

Barbara Graymont, *The Iroquois in the American Revolution* (1972); Isabel T. Kelsey, *Joseph Brant, 1743–1807: Man of Two Worlds* (1984); Duncan J. MacLeod, *Slavery, Race, and the American Revolution* (1974); James H. O'Donnell, III, *Southern Indians in the American Revolution* (1973);

Benjamin Quarles, *The Negro in the American Revolution* (1961); Anthony F. C. Wallace, *The Death and Rebirth of the Seneca* (1969).

Loyalists

Bernard Bailyn, *The Ordeal of Thomas Hutchinson* (1974); Robert McCluer Calhoon, *The Loyalists in Revolutionary America 1760–1781* (1973); William H. Nelson, *The American Tory* (1961); Mary Beth Norton, *The British-Americans: The Loyalist Exiles in England, 1774–1789* (1972); Paul H. Smith, *Loyalists and Redcoats: A Study in British Revolutionary Policy* (1964); James W. St. G. Walker, *The Black Loyalists: The Search for a Promised Land in Nova Scotia and Sierra Leone 1783–1870* (1976).

Women

Linda Grant DePauw and Conover Hunt, *"Remember the Ladies": Women in America 1750–1815* (1976); Linda K. Kerber, *Women of the Republic: Intellect & Ideology in Revolutionary America* (1980); Mary Beth Norton, "Eighteenth-Century American Women in Peace and War: The Case of the Loyalists," *William and Mary Quarterly*, 3rd ser., 33 (1976), 386–409; Mary Beth Norton, *Liberty's Daughters: The Revolutionary Experience of American Women, 1750–1800* (1980).

Foreign Policy

Samuel F. Bemis, *The Diplomacy of the American Revolution* (1935); Felix Gilbert, *To the Farewell Address* (1961); Ronald Hoffman and Peter Albert, eds., *Diplomacy and Revolution: The Franco-American Alliance of 1778* (1981); James H. Hutson, *John Adams and the Diplomacy of the American Revolution* (1980); Lawrence Kaplan, ed., *The American Revolution and a "Candid World"* (1977); Richard B. Morris, *The Peacemakers: The Great Powers and American Independence* (1965); Richard W. Van Alstyne, *Empire and Independence: The International History of the American Revolution* (1965).

Patriot Leaders

Fawn M. Brodie, *Thomas Jefferson: An Intimate History* (1974); Verner W. Crane, *Benjamin Franklin and a Rising People* (1954); Marcus Cunliffe, *George Washington: Man and Monument* (1958); James T. Flexner, *George Washington*, 4 vols. (1965–1972); Eric Foner, *Tom Paine and Revolutionary America* (1976); Claude A. Lopez and Eugenia Herbert, *The Private Franklin: The Man and His Family* (1975); Dumas Malone, *Jefferson and His Time*, 6 vols. (1948–1981); Peter Shaw, *The Character of John Adams* (1976); Garry Wills, *Inventing America: Jefferson's Declaration of Independence* (1977).

Forging a National Republic

1776–1789

Chapter 6

"*In the new* Code of Laws which I suppose it will be necessary for you to make I desire you would Remember the Ladies," Abigail Adams wrote her congressman husband John on March 31, 1776. "Remember all Men would be tyrants if they could," she continued. "If perticuliar care and attention is not paid to the Laidies we are determined to foment a Rebelion, and will not hold ourselves bound by any Laws in which we have no voice, or Representation."

With these words, Abigail Adams took a step that was soon to be duplicated by other disfranchised Americans. She deliberately employed the ideology that had been developed to combat Great Britain's claims to political supremacy, but applied it to purposes white male leaders had never intended. Since men were "Naturally Tyrannical," she argued, America's new legal code should "put it out of the power of the vicious and the Lawless to use us with cruelty and indignity." Thus she called for reformation of the American law of marriage, which made wives wholly subordinate to their husbands.

John Adams failed to take his wife's suggestion seriously. Two weeks later he replied, "As to your extraordinary Code of Laws, I cannot but Laugh. We have been told that our Struggle has loosened the bands of Government every where"—that children, apprentices, slaves, Indians, and college students had all become "disobedient" and "insolent." Her letter was the first sign that "another Tribe more numerous and powerfull than all the rest were grown discontented." But women, he insisted, had little reason for complaint. "In Practice you know We are subjects. We have only the Name of Masters, and rather than give up this, which would compleatly subject Us to the Despotism of the Peticoat, I hope General Washington and all our brave Heroes would fight."

Abigail Adams's famous words have often been cited as the first stirrings of feminism in America. Whether or not such an interpretation is accurate, her comments were, as John Adams recognized, a sign of the impact the Revolution and its ideology had had on American society. Few aspects of American life remained untouched by the Revolution: during and after the war Americans reshaped their political structures, their intellectual world, and their social interactions.

At the core of the changes lay their new commitment to republicanism: the notion that the government should be based wholly on the consent of the people. When they left the British Empire, Americans abandoned the idea that the best system of government balanced monarchy, aristocracy, and democracy. Instead they substituted a belief in the superiority of republicanism, in which the people, not Parliament, were sovereign. Americans disagreed, however, on such critical issues as how to define "the people" and how fully and frequently to obtain their consent. Although almost all white men agreed that women and blacks should be excluded from formal participation in politics, they found it difficult to reach a consensus on how many of their own number should be included. And when should consent be sought: semiannually? annually? at intervals of two or more years? Further, how should governments be structured so as to reflect the people's consent most accurately? Americans replied to these questions in different ways.

Republican political ideas carried with them a host of implications for other areas of American life. Because it was widely believed that the citizens of a republic had to be especially virtuous or the republic would not survive, America's political and intellectual leaders worked hard to inculcate virtue in their fellow countrymen and women. After 1776 American literature, theater, art, and architecture all had moral goals. Each in its own way was intended to inspire its audience to behave virtuously. Women too played a particularly important role in the preservation of virtue. As the mothers of the republic's children, they were primarily responsible for ensuring their nation's future. For the first time America's leaders became concerned about the nature and content of women's education. If the United States was to endure, they concluded, the mothers of the rising generation had to be properly educated.

Other elements of republicanism had more troublesome connotations. Should a republic conduct its dealings with Indian tribes, or with foreign countries,

In the mid-1780s Abigail Adams (1744–1818) and her husband John (1735–1826) sat for these portraits in London. John Adams was then American ambassador to Great Britain.   Left, Boston Athenaeum; right: New York State Historical Association, Cooperstown.

any differently from other types of governments? Did republics, in other words, have an obligation to negotiate fairly and honestly at all times? Even more bothersome were Thomas Jefferson's words in the Declaration of Independence: "all men are created equal." Given that bold statement of principle, how could white republicans justify holding Afro-Americans in perpetual bondage? Some answered that question by freeing their slaves or by voting for state laws that abolished slavery. Others responded by denying that blacks were "men" in the same sense as whites.

The most important task facing Americans in these years was the construction of a national government. Before 1765, the English mainland colonies had rarely cooperated on common endeavors. Many things separated them: their diverse economies, varying religious traditions and ethnic compositions, competing land claims (especially in the west), and the differences in their political systems (see Chapters 2 and 3). But fighting the Revolutionary war brought them together and created a new nationalistic spirit, especially in

the ranks of those men who served in the Continental Army or the diplomatic corps. Wartime experiences broke down at least some of the boundaries that had previously divided Americans, replacing loyalties to state and region with loyalties to the nation.

Still, forging a *national* republic (as opposed to a set of loosely connected state republics) was neither easy nor simple. America's first such government, the Articles of Confederation, proved to be inadequate. But the nation's political leaders learned from their experiences and tried another approach when they drafted the Constitution in 1787. Some historians have argued that the Articles of Confederation and the Constitution reflected opposing political philosophies, the Constitution representing an "aristocratic" counterrevolution against the "democratic" Articles. The two documents are more accurately viewed as separate and successive attempts to solve the same problems. Both in part applied theories of republicanism to practical problems of governance; neither was entirely successful in resolving those difficulties.

CREATING A VIRTUOUS REPUBLIC

Many years after the Revolution, John Dickinson recalled that in 1776, when the colonies declared their independence from Great Britain, "there was no question concerning forms of Government, no enquiry whether a Republic or a limited Monarchy was best. . . . We knew that the people of this country must unite themselves under some form of Government and that this could be no other than the Republican form." But what, precisely, was a republic? And what role would be played in it by previously disfranchised white men? by the white women who displayed a new political consciousness and activism during the 1760s and 1770s? by blacks? During and after the war Americans offered varying answers to these and other related questions.

Three different definitions of republicanism emerged in the new United States. The first, held chiefly by members of the educated elite (for example, the Adamses of Massachusetts), was **Varieties of Republicanism** based directly on ancient history and political theory. It insisted that republics were especially fragile forms of government that risked chronic instability. The histories of popular governments in such places as Greece and Rome seemed to prove that republics could succeed only if they were small in size and homogeneous in population. Furthermore, unless the citizens of a republic were especially virtuous, willing to sacrifice their own private interests for the good of the whole, the government would inevitably collapse. In return for sacrifices, though, a republic offered its citizens equality of opportunity. Under such a government, rank would be based on merit rather than inherited wealth and status. Society would be ruled by members of a "natural aristocracy," men of talent who had risen from what might have been humble beginnings to positions of power and privilege. Rank would not be abolished but instead would be placed on a different footing.

A second definition of republicanism, also advanced by members of the elite but in addition by some skilled craftsmen, drew more on economic than political thought. Instead of perceiving the nation as an organic whole, composed of people sacrificing to the common good, this version of republicanism emphasized individuals' pursuit of rational self-interest. The nation could only benefit from aggressive economic expansion, such men as Alexander Hamilton (see page 186) argued. When republican men sought to improve their own economic and social circumstances, the entire nation would benefit. Republican virtue would be achieved through the advancement of private interests, rather than through their subordination to some communal ideal.

The third notion of republicanism was less influential, because it was popular primarily with people who were illiterate or barely literate, and who thus wrote little to promote their beliefs. But it certainly involved a more egalitarian approach to governance than did either of the other two, both of which contained considerable potential for inequality. In other words, some late-eighteenth-century Americans (like Thomas Paine) can be termed democrats in more or less the modern sense. They emphasized the importance of widespread participation in political activities, wanted government to be responsive to their needs, and openly questioned the gentry's ability to speak for them.

Despite the differences, it is important to recognize that the three strands of republicanism were part of a unified whole, and that they shared many of the same assumptions. For example, all three contrasted a virtuous, industrious America to the corrupt luxury of England and Europe. In the first version, that virtue manifested itself in frugality and self-sacrifice; in the second, it would prevent self-interest from becoming vice; in the third, it was the justification for including even propertyless white men in the ranks of voters. "Virtue, Virtue alone . . . is the basis of a republic," asserted Dr. Benjamin Rush of Philadelphia, an ardent patriot, in 1778. His fellow Americans fully concurred, even if they defined virtue in divergent ways.

As the citizens of the United States set out to construct their republic, then, they believed they were embarking on an unprecedented enterprise. With great pride in their new nation, they wanted to exchange the vices of monarchical Europe for the virtues of republican America. They wanted to embody republican principles not only in their governments (see page 161) but also in their society and their culture. They looked to painting, literature, drama, and architecture to convey messages of nationalism and virtue to the public.

But Americans faced a crucial contradiction at the very outset of their efforts. To some republicans, the fine arts were themselves manifestations of vice. Their

Virtue and the Arts

appearance in a virtuous society, many contended, signaled the arrival of luxury and corruption. What need did a frugal yeoman have for a painting—or, worse yet, a novel? Why should anyone spend hard-earned wages to see a play in a lavishly decorated theater? The first American artists, playwrights, and authors were thus trapped in a dilemma from which escape was nearly impossible. They wanted to produce works embodying virtue, but those very works, regardless of their content, were viewed by many as corrupting.

Still, they tried. William Hill Brown's *The Power of Sympathy* (1789), the first novel written in the United States, was a lurid tale of seduction intended as a warning to young women, who made up a large proportion of America's fiction readers. In Royall Tyler's *The Contrast* (1787), the first successful American play, the virtuous conduct of Colonel Manly was contrasted (hence the title) with the reprehensible behavior of the fop Billy Dimple. The most popular book of the era, Mason Locke Weems's *Life of Washington*, published in 1800 shortly after its subject's death, was, the author declared, designed to "hold up his great Virtues . . . to the imitation of Our Youth." Weems could hardly have been accused of being subtle. The famous tale he invented—six-year-old George bravely admitting cutting down his father's favorite cherry tree—ended with George's father exclaiming, "Run to my arms, you dearest boy. . . . Such an act of heroism in my son, is worth more than a thousand trees, though blossomed with silver, and their fruits of purest gold."

Painting, too, was expected to embody high moral standards. The major artists of the republican period—Gilbert Stuart and John Trumbull—studied in London under Benjamin West and John Singleton Copley, the first great American-born painters, both of whom had emigrated to England before the Revolution. Stuart and Charles Willson Peale (an American-

In the 1780s, this fabric was manufactured in England specifically for the American market. At top left, two cherubs hold a map of America; at top right, Benjamin Franklin and Liberty display a scroll proclaiming, "Where Liberty Dwells There is My Country." Below them George Washington drives a chariot in which an allegorical figure of America carries a sign noting "American Independence 1776," and an Indian carries a banner with Franklin's segmented snake "Unite or Die" motto. Douglas Political Americana Collection, Cornell University.

trained artist) painted innumerable portraits of upstanding republican citizens—the political, economic, and social leaders of the day. Trumbull's vast canvases depicted such milestones of American history as the Battle of Bunker Hill, Burgoyne's surrender at Saratoga, and Cornwallis's capitulation at Yorktown. Both portraits and historical scenes were intended to arouse patriotic virtues in their viewers.

Architects likewise hoped to convey in their buildings a sense of the young republic's ideals, and most of them consciously rejected British models. When the Virginia government asked Thomas Jefferson, then ambassador to France, for advice on the design of a state capitol in Richmond, Jefferson unhesitatingly recommended copying a Roman building, the Maison Carrée at Nîmes. "It is very simple," he explained, "but it is noble beyond expression." Jefferson set forth ideals that would guide American architecture for a generation to come: simplicity of line, harmonious proportions, a feeling of grandeur. Nowhere were these rational goals of republican art manifested more clearly than in Benjamin H. Latrobe's plans for the majestic domed United States Capitol in Washington, built shortly after the turn of the century.

Despite the artists' efforts, or perhaps, some would have said, because of them, some Americans were beginning to detect signs of luxury and corruption by the mid-1780s. The end of the war and resumption of European trade brought a return to fashionable clothing styles for both men and women and abandonment of the simpler homespun garments patriots had once worn with such pride. Balls and concerts resumed in the cities and were attended by well-dressed elite families. Parties no longer seemed complete without gambling and card-playing. Social clubs for young people multiplied; Samuel Adams worried in print about the possibilities for corruption lurking behind innocent plans for tea drinking and genteel conversation among Boston youths. Especially alarming to fervent republicans was the establishment in 1783 of the Society of the Cincinnati, a hereditary organization of Revolutionary War officers and their descendants. Many feared that the group would become the nucleus of a native-born aristocracy. All these developments directly challenged the United States's image as a virtuous republic.

Their deep-seated concern for the future of the infant republic focused Americans' attention on their children, the "rising generation." Education acquired new significance in the context of

Educational Reform

the republic. Since the early days of the colonies, education had been seen chiefly as a private means to personal advancement, and thus of concern only to individual families. Now, though, it would serve a public purpose. If young people were to resist the temptation of vice, they would have to learn the lessons of virtue at home and at school. In fact, the very survival of the nation depended on it. The early republican period was thus a time of major educational reform.

The 1780s and 1790s brought two significant changes in American educational practice. First, some states began to be willing to use tax money to support public elementary schools. Nearly all education in the colonies, at whatever level, had been privately financed. In the republic, though, schools could lay claim to tax dollars. In 1789 Massachusetts became one of the first states to require towns to supply their citizens with free public elementary education.

Second, schooling for girls was improved. Americans' recognition of the importance of the rising generation led to the realization that mothers would have to be properly educated if they were to be able to instruct their children adequately. Therefore Massachusetts insisted in its 1789 law that town elementary schools be open to girls as well as boys. Throughout the United States, private academies were founded to give teenage girls from well-to-do families an opportunity for advanced schooling. No one yet proposed opening colleges to women, but a few fortunate girls could now study history, geography, rhetoric, and mathematics. The academies also trained female students in fancy needlework—the only artistic endeavor open to women.

The chief theorist of women's education in the early republic was Judith Sargent Murray, of Gloucester, Massachusetts. In a series of essays published in

Judith Sargent Murray on Education

the 1780s and 1790s, Murray argued that women and men had equal intellectual capacities, though women's inadequate education might make them seem to be less intelligent. "We can only reason from what we know," she declared, "and if an opportunity of acquiring knowledge hath been denied us, the inferiority of our sex cannot fairly be deduced from thence." Therefore, concluded Murray, boys and girls should be offered equivalent scholastic training. She further contended that girls should be taught to support themselves by their own efforts: "Independence should be placed within their grasp." Because she rejected the prevailing notion that a young woman's chief goal in life should be finding a husband, Judith Sargent Murray deserves the title of the first American feminist. (That distinction is usually accorded to better-known nineteenth-century women like Margaret Fuller or Sarah Grimké.)

Judith Sargent (1751–1820), later Mrs. John Murray, painted by John Singleton Copley when she was in her late teens. Although her steady gaze suggests clear-headed intelligence, there is little in the stylized portrait—typical of Copley's work at the time—to suggest her later emergence as the first notable American feminist theorist.   Frick Art Reference Library.

Murray's direct challenge to the traditional colonial belief that (as one man put it) girls "knew quite enough if they could make a shirt and a pudding" was part of a general rethinking of women's position that occurred as a result of the Revolution. Male patriots who enlisted in the army or served in Congress were away from home for long periods of time. In their absence their wives, who had previously handled only the "indoor affairs" of the household, had to shoulder the responsibility for "outdoor affairs" as well. As the wife of a Connecticut militiaman later recalled, her husband "was out more or less during the remainder of the war [after 1777], so much so as to be unable to do anything on our farm. What was done, was done by myself."

In many households, the necessary shift of re-sponsibilities during the war taught men and women that their notions of proper sex roles had to be re-thought. Both John and Abigail

Women's Role in the Republic

Adams took great pride in Abigail's developing skills as a "farmeress," and John praised her courage repeatedly. "You are really brave, my dear, you are an Heroine," he told her in 1775. Abigail Adams, like her female contemporaries, stopped calling the farm "yours" in letters to her husband, and began referring to it as "ours"—a revealing change of pronoun. Both men and women realized that female patriots had made a vital contribution to winning the war through their work at home. Thus, in the years after the Revolution, Americans began to develop new ideas about the role women should play in a republican society.

Only a very few thought that role should include the right to vote. Abigail Adams did not press for female suffrage, believing that women's influence was best exerted in the privacy of their homes, through their impact on their husbands and children, especially their sons. But some women thought differently, as events in New Jersey proved. The men who drafted the state constitution in 1776 defined voters loosely as "all free inhabitants" who met certain property qualifications. They thereby unintentionally gave the vote to property-holding white spinsters and widows, as well as to free blacks. In the 1780s and 1790s women successfully claimed the right to vote in New Jersey's local and congressional elections. They continued to exercise that right until 1807, when women and blacks were disfranchised by the state legislature on the grounds that their votes could be easily manipulated. Yet the fact that they had voted at all was evidence of their altered perception of their place in political life.

Such dramatic episodes were unusual. On the whole the re-evaluation of women's position had its greatest impact on private life. The traditional colonial view of marriage had stressed the sub-

Marriage and Motherhood

ordination of wife to husband. But in 1790 a female "Matrimonial Republican" asserted that "marriage ought never to be considered as a contract between a superior and an inferior, but a reciprocal union of interest. . . . The obedience between man and wife is, or ought to be mutual." This new understanding of the marital relationship seems to have contributed to a rising divorce rate after the war. Dissatisfied wives proved less willing to remain in unhappy marriages than they had been previously. At the same time, state judges became more sympathetic to women's desires to be freed from abusive or unfaithful husbands. Even so, divorces were still rare; most marriages were for life. And married women continued to suffer serious legal disabilities. Like John Adams, most political leaders failed to heed calls for reform. It was not until the 1830s that legislators began to change the statutes governing the legal status of married women.

The republican decades witnessed an ever-increasing emphasis on the importance of mothers. In 1790 one woman even argued publicly for female superiority, resting her claim on woman's maternal role. Men, she said, had assumed primacy in the past "on the vain presumption of their being assigned the most important duties of life." But God had clearly intended otherwise, since to women He had "assigned the care of making the first impressions on the infant minds of the whole human race, a trust of more importance than the government of provinces, and the marshalling of armies."

Other Americans did not go that far. To be sure, they were more willing than before to expand the meaning of the phrase "all men are created equal" to apply to women, but they still viewed woman's role in traditional terms. Most eighteenth-century white Americans assumed that women's place was in the home and that their primary function was to be good wives and mothers. They accepted the notion of equality, but within the context of men's and women's separate spheres. Whereas their forebears had seen women as inferior and subordinate to men, members of the revolutionary generation regarded the sexes and their roles as more nearly equal in importance. However, equality did not mean sameness.

Indeed, the differences they perceived between the male and female characters eventually enabled Americans to resolve the conflict between the two most influential strands of republican thought. Because married women could not own property or participate directly in economic life, women in general came to be seen as the embodiment of self-sacrificing, disinterested republicanism. Through female-run char-

itable and other social welfare groups, they assumed responsibility for the welfare of the community as a whole. Yet because they worked chiefly with women and children in familial settings, women continued to be seen primarily as private beings. Thus men were freed from any naggings of conscience as they pursued their economic self-interest (that other republican virtue), secure in the knowledge that their wives and daughters were fulfilling the family's obligation to the common good. The ideal republican man, therefore, was an individualist, seeking advancement for himself and his family; the ideal republican woman, by contrast, always put the well-being of others ahead of her own.

Together white men and women established the context for the creation of a virtuous republic. But nearly 20 percent of the American population was black. How did approximately 700,000 Afro-Americans fit into the developing national plan?

EMANCIPATION AND THE GROWTH OF RACISM

Revolutionary ideology exposed one of the primary contradictions in American society. Just as Abigail Adams pointed out to her husband his failure to apply revolutionary doctrines to the status of women, so too both blacks and whites recognized the irony of slaveholding Americans claiming that one of their aims in taking up arms was to prevent Britain from "enslaving" them.

As early as 1764, James Otis, Jr., had identified the basic problem in his pamphlet *The Rights of the British Colonies Asserted and Proved* (see page 110). If according to natural law all people were born free and equal, that meant *all* humankind, black and white. "Does it follow that 'tis right to enslave a man because he is black?" Otis asked. "Can any logical inference in favor of slavery be drawn from a flat nose, a long or short face?" The same theme was later voiced by other revolutionary leaders. In 1773 the Philadelphia doctor Benjamin Rush called slavery "a vice which degrades human nature," warning ominously that "the plant of liberty is of so tender a nature that it cannot thrive long in the neighborhood of slavery." Common folk too saw the contradiction. When Josiah Atkins, a Connecticut soldier marching south, saw George Washington's plantation, he observed in his journal: "Alas! That persons who pretend to stand for the *rights of mankind* for the *liberties of society*, can delight in oppression, & that even of the worst kind!"

Afro-Americans themselves were quick to recognize the implications of revolutionary ideology. In 1779 a group of slaves from Portsmouth, New Hampshire, asked the state legislature "from what authority [our masters] assume to dispose of our lives, freedom and property," and pleaded "that the name of slave may not more be heard in a land gloriously contending for the sweets of freedom." That same year several black residents of Fairfield, Connecticut, petitioned the legislature for their freedom, characterizing slavery as a "dreadful Evil" and "flagrant Injustice." Surely, they declared pointedly, "your Honours who are nobly contending in the Cause of Liberty, whose Conduct excited the Admiration, and Reverence, of all the great Empires of the World; will not resent, our thus freely animadverting, on this detestable Practice."

Both legislatures responded negatively. But the postwar years did witness the gradual abolition of slavery in the North. Vermont abolished slavery in its 1777 constitution. Massachusetts courts decided in the 1780s that the clause in the state constitution declaring that "all men are born free and equal, and have certain natural, essential, and unalienable rights" prohibited slavery in the state. Pennsylvania passed an abolition law in 1780; four years later Rhode Island and Connecticut provided for gradual emancipation, followed by New York (1799) and New Jersey (1804). Although New Hampshire did not formally abolish slavery, only eight slaves were reported on the 1800 census and none remained a decade later.

Gradual Emancipation

No southern state adopted similar general emancipation laws, but the legislatures of Virginia (1782), Delaware (1787), and Maryland (1790 and 1796) did decide to change laws that had restricted masters' ability to free their slaves. South Carolina and Georgia never considered adopting such acts, though, and North Carolina insisted that all manumissions

(emancipations of individual slaves) be approved by county courts.

Thus revolutionary ideology had limited impact on the well-entrenched economic interests of large slaveholders. Only in the North, where there were few slaves and where little money was invested in human capital, could state legislatures vote to abolish slavery with relative ease. Even there, legislators' concern for property rights—the Revolution was, after all, fought for property as well as life and liberty—led them to favor gradual emancipation over immediate abolition. Most states provided only for the freeing of children born after passage of the law, not for the emancipation of adults. And even those children were to remain slaves until ages ranging from eighteen to twenty-eight. As a result, some northern states still had a few legally held slaves at the time of the Civil War.

Despite the slow progress of abolition, the free black population of the United States grew dramatically in the first years after the Revolution. Before the war there had been few free blacks in America. (According to a 1755 Maryland census, for example, only 4 percent of the Afro-Americans in the colony were free.) Most prewar free blacks were mulattoes, born of unions between white masters and enslaved black women. But wartime disruptions radically changed the size and composition of the free black population. Slaves who had escaped from plantations during the war, others who had served in the American army, and still others who had been emancipated by their owners or by state laws were now free. Because most of them were not mulattoes, dark skin was no longer an automatic sign of slave status. By 1790 there were nearly 60,000 free people of color in the United States; ten years later they numbered more than 108,000 and represented nearly 11 percent of the total black population. The effects of postwar manumissions were felt most sharply in the Chesapeake, where they were fostered by such economic changes as declining soil fertility and the shift from tobacco to grain production. (Since grain cultivation was less labor-intensive than tobacco growing, planters began to complain about "excess" slaves. They often solved that problem by freeing the most favored or least productive of their bondspeople.) The free Negro population of Virginia more

Growth of the Free Black Population

The Reverend Lemuel Haynes was one of the best-known black clergymen of the late eighteenth and early nineteenth centuries. He attacked the institution of slavery both in print and from the pulpit. Here he is shown preaching to an attentive congregation. Rhode Island School of Design.

than doubled between 1790 and 1810, and by the latter year nearly a quarter of Maryland's black population was no longer in legal bondage.

In the 1780s and thereafter, freed people often made their way, as had landless colonists decades before them, to the port cities of the North. They moved to Boston and Philadelphia in particular, where slavery was abolished sooner than it was in New York City. Women outnumbered men among the migrants by a margin of three to two. Like female whites, black women found more opportunities for employment, particularly as domestic servants, in the cities than in the countryside. Some black men also worked in domestic service, but larger numbers were employed as unskilled laborers or seamen. A few of the women and a sizable proportion of men (nearly a third of those in Philadelphia in 1795) were skilled workers or retailers. These freed people chose new names for

themselves, exchanging the surnames of their former masters for names like Newman or Brown, and as soon as possible they established independent two-parent nuclear families instead of continuing to live in white households. They also began to cluster their residences in certain neighborhoods, probably as a result of both discrimination by whites and a desire for black solidarity.

Emancipation did not bring equality, though. Even whites who recognized Afro-Americans' right to freedom were unwilling to accept them as equals. Laws discriminated against emancipated blacks as they had against slaves—South Carolina, for example, did not permit free blacks to testify against whites in court. Public schools often refused to educate the children of free black parents. Freedmen found it difficult to purchase property and find good jobs. And though in many areas Afro-Americans were accepted as members—even ministers—of evangelical churches, whites rarely allowed them an equal voice in church affairs.

Gradually free blacks developed their own separate institutions, often based in the neighborhoods in which they lived. In Charleston, mulattoes formed the Brown Fellowship Society, which provided insurance coverage for its members, financed a school for free children, and helped to support black orphans. In 1787 blacks in Philadelphia and Baltimore founded churches that eventually became the African Methodist Episcopal (AME) denomination. AME churches later sponsored schools in a number of cities and, along with African Baptist and African Presbyterian churches, became cultural centers of the free black community. Freed people quickly learned that if they were to survive and prosper they would have to rely on their own collective efforts rather than on the benevolence or goodwill of their white compatriots.

Development of Black Institutions

Their endeavors were all the more important because the postrevolutionary years ironically witnessed the development of a coherent racist theory in the United States. Whites had long regarded blacks as inferior, but the most influential writers on race had attributed that inferiority to environmental, rather than hereditary, factors. That is, they argued that blacks' seemingly debased character derived from their enslavement, instead of enslavement being the consequence of genetic inferiority. In the aftermath of the Revolution, white southerners needed to defend their holding other human beings in bondage against the notion that "*all* men are created equal." Consequently, they began to argue that blacks were less than fully human, that the principles of republican equality applied only to whites. To avoid having to confront the contradiction between their practice and the egalitarian implications of revolutionary theory, in short, they redefined the theory, making it inapplicable to blacks.

Development of Racist Theory

Their racism had several intertwined elements. First was the insistence that, as Thomas Jefferson suggested in 1781, blacks were "inferior to the whites in the endowments both of body and mind." Second came the belief that blacks were congenitally lazy, dishonest, and uncivilized (or uncivilizable). Third,

A woodcut portrait of Benjamin Banneker adorned the cover of his almanac for 1795.   Maryland Historical Society.

and of crucial importance, was the notion that all blacks were sexually promiscuous and that black men lusted after white women. The specter of interracial sexual intercourse involving black men and white women haunted early American racist thought. The reverse situation, which occurred with far greater frequency (as white masters sexually exploited their female slaves), aroused little comment.

Afro-Americans did not allow these developing racist notions to pass unnoticed. Benjamin Banneker, a free black surveyor, astronomer, and mathematical genius, directly challenged Thomas Jefferson's belief in blacks' intellectual inferiority. In 1791 Banneker sent Jefferson a copy of his latest almanac (which included his astronomical calculations), as an example of blacks' mental powers. Jefferson's response admitted Banneker's capabilities but implied that he regarded Banneker as an exception. The future president insisted that he needed more evidence before he would abandon his previous position.

At its birth, then, the republic was defined as an exclusively white enterprise. Indeed, some historians have argued that the subjection of blacks was a necessary precondition for equality among whites. They have pointed out that identifying a common racial antagonist helped to create white solidarity and to lessen the threat to gentry power posed by the enfranchisement of poorer whites. It was less dangerous to allow whites with little property to participate formally in politics than to open the possibility that they might combine with freed blacks to question the rule of the "better sort." That was one reason why, in the postrevolutionary years, the division of American society between slave and free was transformed into a division between black —some of whom were free—and white. The white male wielders of power ensured their continued dominance in part by making certain that race replaced enslavement as the primary determinant of Afro-Americans' status.

A Republic for Whites Only

DESIGNING REPUBLICAN GOVERNMENTS

On May 10, 1776, even before passage of the Declaration of Independence, the Continental Congress directed the states to devise new republican governments to replace the provincial congresses and committees that had met since 1774. Thus Americans initially concentrated on drafting state constitutions and devoted little attention to their national government— an oversight they were later forced to remedy. At the state level, they immediately faced the problem

Drafting of State Constitutions

of defining just what a constitution was. The British constitution could not serve as a model because it was an unwritten mixture of law and custom; Americans wanted tangible documents specifying the fundamental structures of government. Several years passed before the states agreed that their constitutions could not be drafted by regular legislative bodies, like ordinary laws. Following the lead established by Massachusetts in 1780, they began to call conventions for the sole purpose of drafting constitutions. Thus the states sought direct authorization from the people— the theoretical sovereigns in a republic—before establishing new governments. After the new constitutions had been drawn up, delegates submitted them to the people for ratification.

Those who wrote the state constitutions concerned themselves primarily with outlining the distribution of and limitations on governmental power. Both questions were crucial to the survival of republics. If authority was improperly distributed among the branches of government or not confined within reasonable limits, the states might become tyrannical, as Britain had. Indeed, Americans' experience with British rule affected every provision of their new constitutions.

Under their colonial charters, Americans had learned to fear the power of the governor—in most cases the appointed agent of the king or the proprietor—and to see the legislature as their defender. Accordingly, the first state constitutions typically provided for the governor to be elected annually (usually by the legislature), limited the number of terms any one governor could serve, and gave him little independent authority. At the same time the constitutions expanded the powers of the legislature. They redrew the lines of electoral districts to reflect population patterns more accurately and increased the number of members in both the upper and lower houses. Finally, most states lowered property qualifications for voting. As a result the legislatures came to include some men who before the war would not even have been eligible to vote. Thus the revolutionary era witnessed the first deliberate attempt to broaden the base of American government, a process that has continued into our own day.

But the authors of the state constitutions knew that governments designed to be responsive to the people would not necessarily provide sufficient protection should tyrants be elected to office. Consequently, they included limitations on governmental authority in the documents they composed. Seven of the constitutions contained formal bills of rights, and the others had similar clauses. Most of them guaranteed citizens freedom of the press and of religion, the right to a fair trial, the right of consent to taxation, and protection against general search warrants. An independent judiciary was charged with upholding such rights.

In sum, the constitution-makers put far greater emphasis on preventing state governments from becoming tyrannical than on making them effective wielders of political authority. Their approach to the process of shaping governments was understandable, given the American experience with Great Britain. But establishing such weak political units, especially in wartime, practically ensured that the constitutions would soon need revision. As early as the 1780s some states began to rewrite the constitutions they had drafted in 1776 and 1777. Invariably, the revised versions increased the powers of the governor and reduced the scope of the legislature's authority. Only then, a decade after the Declaration, did Americans start to develop a formal theory of checks and balances as the primary means of controlling governmental power. Once they realized that legislative supremacy did not in itself guarantee good government, Americans attempted to achieve their goal by balancing the powers of the legislative, executive, and judicial branches against one another. The national constitution they drafted in 1787 would embody that principle.

Pennsylvania's Constitutional Debate

The most heated constitutional debate took place in Pennsylvania. There the adherents of the third— or democratic—philosophy of republicanism early gained the upper hand. They dominated the Pennsylvania Assembly that in spring 1776 drafted the state's first constitution. It abolished the office of governor (replacing the single executive with an executive council) and established a one-house (unicameral) legislature. The constitution extended the right of suffrage to a much larger proportion of the male population than did any other state at the time. It defined voters as men who met minimum age, residency, and tax-paying (but not property-holding) requirements. Believing that the people should have a real and continuing impact on government policies, the constitution-drafters also limited the number of terms officials could serve and ordered that all meetings of the assembly be open to the public. Even more important, they provided that, in order to allow time for public comment, any bill would have to be passed by two separate legislative sessions before it became law.

The Pennsylvania Constitution of 1776 represented such a break with the previous form of government that it immediately aroused intense opposition, chiefly among the educated elite. The critics, who included adherents of both the other two definitions of republicanism, primarily focused on the lack of an upper house and an effective governor. As the debate progressed, both sides appealed to the people, each claiming to be more republican than the other. Each argued that its brand of republicanism would better preserve the people's rights by more effectively limiting the reach of government. The Constitutionalists praised the provisions for frequent rotation of offices and weakening the executive; the Republicans (as the elite critics termed themselves) called for the establishment of another house to represent the people's wishes and stressed the need for a balance of powers among governmental branches. In 1790, when Pennsylvania revised its constitution, the Republicans won the prolonged struggle. Pennsylvania's experiment in direct democracy had proved to be out of step with developing American notions of proper political structure.

The constitutional theories that Americans applied at the state level did not at first influence their conception of the nature of a national government. The powers and structure of the Continental Congress evolved by default early in the war, since Americans had little time to devote to legitimizing their de facto government while organizing the military struggle against Britain. Not until late 1777, after Burgoyne's defeat at Saratoga, did Congress send the Articles of Confederation to the states for ratification.

The articles by and large wrote into law the arrangements that had developed, unplanned and largely unheeded, in the Continental Congress. The chief organ of national government was a unicameral leg-

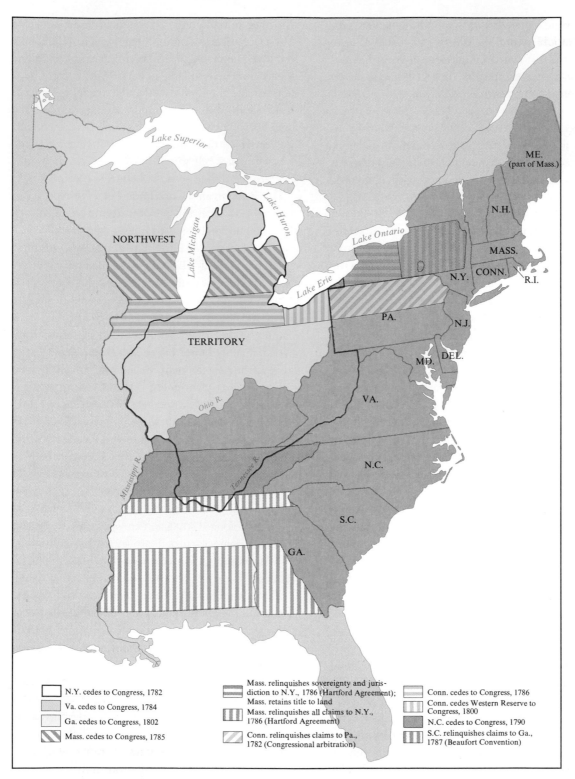

Lake Superior

Lake Huron

Lake Michigan

NORTHWEST

Lake Ontario

Lake Erie

ME.
(part of Mass.)

N.H.

MASS.

CONN.

N.Y.

R.I.

PA.

N.J.

TERRITORY

MD. DEL.

Ohio R.

VA.

N.C.

Mississippi R.

Tennessee R.

S.C.

GA.

	N.Y. cedes to Congress, 1782		Mass. relinquishes sovereignty and juris-diction to N.Y., 1786 (Hartford Agreement); Mass. retains title to land		Conn. cedes to Congress, 1786
	Va. cedes to Congress, 1784		Mass. relinquishes all claims to N.Y., 1786 (Hartford Agreement)		Conn. cedes Western Reserve to Congress, 1800
	Ga. cedes to Congress, 1802		Conn. relinquishes claims to Pa., 1782 (Congressional arbitration)		N.C. cedes to Congress, 1790
	Mass. cedes to Congress, 1785				S.C. relinquishes claims to Ga., 1787 (Beaufort Convention)

Western Land Claims and Cessions, 1782–1802

Articles of Confederation islature in which each state had one vote. Its powers included the conduct of foreign relations, the settlement of disputes between states, control over maritime affairs, the regulation of Indian trade, and the valuation of state and national money. The articles did not give the national government the ability to tax effectively or to enforce a uniform commercial policy. The United States of America was described as "a firm league of friendship" in which each state "retains its sovereignty, freedom and independence, and every Power, Jurisdiction and right, which is not by this confederation expressly delegated to the United States, in Congress assembled."

The articles required the unanimous consent of the state legislatures for ratification or amendment, and a clause concerning western lands turned out to be troublesome. The draft accepted by Congress allowed the states to retain all land claims derived from their original colonial charters. But states with definite western boundaries in their charters (like Maryland, Delaware, and New Jersey) wanted the other states to cede the lands west of the Appalachian Mountains to the national government. Otherwise, they feared, states with large claims could expand and overpower their smaller neighbors. Maryland absolutely refused to accept the articles until 1781, when Virginia finally promised to surrender its western holdings to national jurisdiction (see map).

The fact that a single state could delay ratification for three years was a portent of the fate of American government under the Articles of Confederation. The unicameral legislature, whether it was called the Second Continental Congress (until 1781) or the Confederation Congress (thereafter), was too inefficient and unwieldy to govern effectively. The authors of the articles had not given adequate thought to the distribution of power within the national government or to the relationship between the Confederation and the states. The congress they created was simultaneously a legislative body and a collective executive, but it had no independent income and no authority to compel the states to accept its rulings. What is surprising, in other words, is not how poorly the Confederation functioned in the following years, but rather how much the government was able to accomplish.

TRIALS OF THE CONFEDERATION

During and after the war the most persistent problem faced by the American governments, state and national, was finance. Because legislators at all levels were understandably reluctant to levy taxes on their fellow countrymen, both Congress and the states tried to finance the war by simply printing currency. Even though the money was backed by nothing but good faith, it circulated freely and without excessive depreciation during 1775 and most of 1776. Demand for military supplies and civilian goods was high, stimulating trade (especially with France) and local production. Indeed, the amount of money issued in those years was probably no more than what a healthy economy required as a medium of exchange.

But in late 1776, as the American army suffered major battlefield reverses in New York and New Jersey, prices began to rise and inflation set in. The value of the currency rested on Americans' faith in their government, a faith that was sorely tested in the years that followed, especially during the dark days of the early British triumphs in the South (1779 and 1780). Some state governments fought inflation by controlling wages and prices, requiring acceptance of paper currency on an equal footing with hard money, borrowing, and even levying taxes. Their efforts were futile. So too was Congress's attempt to stop printing currency altogether and to rely solely on state contributions. By early 1780 it took forty paper dollars to purchase one in silver. A year later Continental currency was worthless.

Monetary Problems

The severe wartime inflation seriously affected people on fixed incomes—including many soldiers and civilian leaders of the Revolution. Common laborers, small farmers, clergymen, and poor folk in general could do nothing to stop the declining value of their incomes. Yet there were people who benefited from such economic conditions. Military contractors could make sizable profits. Large-scale farmers who produced surpluses of meat, milk, and grains could sell their goods at high prices to the army or to civilian merchants. People with money could invest in lucrative trading voyages. More risky, but potentially even more profitable, was privateering against enemy shipping—an enterprise that attracted venturesome sailors and wealthy merchants alike.

Such accumulations of private wealth did nothing to help Congress with its financial problems. In 1781, faced with the total collapse of the monetary system, the delegates undertook major reforms. After establishing a department of finance under the wealthy Philadelphia merchant Robert Morris, they asked the states to amend the Articles of Confederation to allow Congress to levy a duty on imported goods. Morris put national finances on a solid footing, but the customs duty was never adopted. First Rhode Island, then New York refused to agree to the tax. The states' resistance reflected genuine fear of a too-powerful central government. As one worried citizen wrote in 1783, "If permanent Funds are given to Congress, the aristocratical Influence, which predominates in more than a major part of the United States, will fully establish an arbitrary Government."

Congress also faced major diplomatic problems at the close of the war. Chief among them were issues involving the peace treaty itself. Article 4, which promised the repayment of prewar **Failure to** debts (most of them owed by Amer- **Enforce the** icans to British merchants), and **Treaty of Paris** Article 5, which recommended that states allow loyalists to recover their confiscated property, aroused considerable opposition. States passed laws denying British subjects the right to sue for recovery of debts or property in American courts, and town meetings decried the loyalists' return. As residents of Norwalk, Connecticut, put it, few Americans wanted to permit the "Tory Villains" to return "while filial Tears are fresh upon our Cheeks and our Murdered Brethren scarcely cold in their Graves." The state governments also had reason to oppose enforcement of the treaty. Sales of loyalists' land, houses, and other possessions had helped to finance the later stages of the war; since most of the purchasers were prominent patriots, the states had no desire to raise questions about the legitimacy of their property titles.

The failure of state and local governments to comply with Articles 4 and 5 gave Britain an excuse to maintain posts on the Great Lakes long after its troops were supposed to be withdrawn. Furthermore, Congress's inability to convince the states to implement the treaty pointed up its lack of power, even in an area—foreign affairs—in which it had been granted specific authority by the Articles of Confederation. Concerned nationalists argued publicly that enforcement of the treaty, however unpopular, was a crucial test for the republic. "Will foreign nations be willing to undertake anything with us or for us," asked Alexander Hamilton, "when they find that the nature of our governments will allow no dependence to be placed on our engagements?"

Congress's weakness was especially evident in the realm of trade, because the Articles of Confederation specifically denied it the power to establish a national commercial policy. Immediately following the war, Britain, France, and Spain restricted American trade with their colonies. Americans, who had hoped independence would bring about free trade with all nations, were outraged but could do little to change matters. Members of Congress watched helplessly as British manufactured goods flooded the United States while American produce could no longer be sold in the British West Indies, once its prime market. The South Carolina indigo industry, deprived of the British bounty that had supported it, suffered a setback. Though Americans began trading with northern European countries like the Netherlands and opened a profitable trade with China in 1784, neither substituted for access to closer and larger markets.

Congress also had difficulty dealing with the threat posed by Spain's presence on the southern and western borders of the United States. Determined to prevent the new nation's expansion, Spain in 1784 closed the Mississippi River to American navigation. It thus deprived the growing settlements west of the Appalachians of their major access route to the rest of the nation and the world. If Spain's policy were not reversed, westerners might have to accept Spanish sovereignty as the necessary price for survival. Congress opened negotiations with Spain in 1785, but even John Jay, one of the nation's most experienced diplomats, could not win the necessary concessions on navigation. The talks collapsed the following year after Congress divided sharply on the question of whether agreement should be sought on other issues. Southerners, voting as a bloc, insisted on navigation rights on the Mississippi, while northerners were willing to abandon that claim in order to win commercial concessions. The impasse raised doubts about the possibility of a national consensus on foreign affairs.

Diplomatic problems of another sort confronted congressmen when they considered the status of the land on the United States's western borders. Although

Encroachment on Indian Lands

tribal claims were not discussed by British and American diplomats at the end of the war, the United States assumed that the Treaty of Paris (1783) cleared its title to all land east of the Mississippi except the areas still held by Spain. But recognizing that some sort of land cession should be obtained from the major tribes, Congress initiated negotiations with both northern and southern Indians. At Fort Stanwix, New York, in 1784, and at Hopewell, South Carolina, in late 1785 and early 1786, American representatives signed treaties of questionable legality with the Iroquois and with Choctaw, Chickasaw, and Cherokee chiefs respectively (see map). The United States took the treaties as final confirmation of its sovereignty over the Indian territories, and authorized white settlers to move onto the land. Whites soon poured over the southern Appalachians, provoking the Creek tribe—which had not agreed to the Hopewell treaties—to defend its territory by declaring war. Only in 1790, when the Creek chief Alexander McGillivray traveled to New York to negotiate a treaty, did the tribe finally come to terms with the United States.

In the North, meanwhile, the Iroquois Confederacy was in disarray. The members of the Six Nations who had not fled to Canada in 1779 soon found that they had little bargaining power left. In 1786 they formally repudiated the Fort Stanwix treaty and threatened new attacks on frontier settlements, but both whites and Indians knew the threat was an empty one. The flawed treaty was permitted to stand by default. At intervals during the remainder of the decade the state of New York purchased large amounts of land from individual Iroquois tribes. By 1790 the once-proud Iroquois Confederacy was confined to a few scattered reservations.

Western tribes like the Shawnee, Chippewa, Ottawa, and Potawatomi had once allowed the Iroquois to speak for them. After the collapse of Iroquois power, they formed their own confederacy and de-

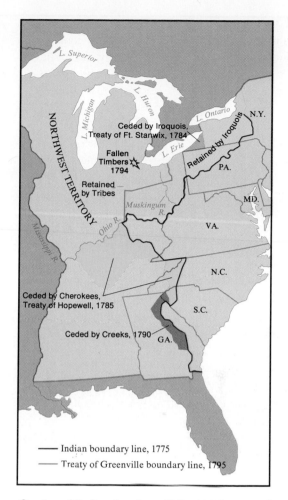

Cession of Indian Lands to U.S., 1775–1790 *Source: Reprinted by permission of Princeton University Press.*

manded direct negotiations with the United States. Their aim was to present a united front, so as to avoid the piecemeal surrender of land by individual tribes.

At first the national government ignored the western Indian confederacy. Shortly after the state land cessions were completed, Congress began to organize the

Northwest Ordinances

Northwest Territory, bounded by the Mississippi River, the Great Lakes, and the Ohio River. Ordinances passed in 1784, 1785, and 1787 outlined the process through which the land could be sold to settlers and formal governments organized. To ensure orderly development, Congress directed that the land be surveyed into townships six miles square, each divided into thirty-six sections of 640

General Anthony Wayne accepting the surrender of the Indian leader Little Turtle after the United States Army's victory in the Battle of Fallen Timbers, August 1794. Chicago Historical Society.

acres (one square mile). Revenue from the sale of the sixteenth section of each township was to be reserved for the support of public schools—the first instance of federal aid to education in American history. The minimum price per acre was set at one dollar, and the minimum sale was to be 640 acres. Congress was not especially concerned about helping the small farmer: the minimum outlay of $640 was beyond the reach of most Americans (except, of course, veterans who had received part of their army pay in land warrants). The proceeds from the land sales were the first independent revenues available to the national government.

The most important ordinance was the third, passed in 1787. The Northwest Ordinance contained a bill of rights guaranteeing settlers in the territory freedom of religion and the right to a jury trial, prohibiting cruel and unusual punishments, and abolishing slavery. It also specified the process by which residents of the territory could eventually organize state governments and seek admission to the union "on an equal footing with the original States." Early in the nation's history, therefore, Congress laid down a policy of admitting new states on the same basis as the old and assuring residents of the territories the same rights as citizens of the original states. Having suffered under the rule of a colonial power, congressmen understood the importance of preparing the United States's first "colony" for eventual self-government. Nineteenth- and twentieth-century Americans were to be less generous in their attitudes toward residents of later territories, many of whom were nonwhite or non-Protestant.

But the nation never fully lost sight of the egalitarian principles of the Northwest Ordinance.

In a sense, though, the ordinance was purely theoretical at the time it was passed. The Miami, Shawnee, and Delaware refused to acknowledge American sovereignty and insisted on their right to the land. They opposed white settlement violently, attacking unwary pioneers who ventured too far north of the Ohio River. In 1788 the Ohio Company, to which Congress had sold a large tract of land at reduced rates, established the town of Marietta at the juncture of the Ohio and Muskingum rivers. But the Indians prevented the company from extending settlement very far into the interior. After General Arthur St. Clair, the first governor of the Northwest Territory, failed to negotiate a meaningful treaty with the tribes in early 1789, it was apparent that the United States could not avoid a clash with a western confederacy, composed of eight tribes and led by the Miami.

Little Turtle, the able war chief of the Miami confederacy, defeated first General Josiah Harmar (1790) and then St. Clair himself (1791) in major battles near the present border between Indiana and Ohio. More than six hundred of St. Clair's men were killed and scores more wounded; it was the whites' worst defeat in the entire history of the American frontier. In 1793 the Miami confederacy declared that peace could be achieved only if the United States recognized the Ohio River as the boundary between white and Indian lands. But the national government refused to relinquish its claim to the Northwest Territory. A new army under the command of General Anthony Wayne, a Revolutionary War hero, attacked and defeated the tribesmen in August 1794, at the Battle of Fallen Timbers (near Toledo, Ohio). This victory made it possible for serious negotiations to begin.

War in the Northwest

By the summer of 1795, Wayne had reached agreement with delegates from the Miami confederacy. The Treaty of Greenville gave each side a portion of what it wanted. The United States gained the right to settle much of what was to become the state of Ohio, the tribes retaining only the northwest corner of the region. The Indians received the acknowledgment they had long sought: American recognition of their rights to the soil. At Greenville, the United States formally accepted the principle of Indian sovereignty, by virtue of residence, over all lands the tribes had not yet ceded. Never again would the United States government claim that it had acquired Indian territory solely through negotiation with a European or American country.

The problems the United States encountered in ensuring safe settlement of the Northwest Territory pointed up, once again, the basic weakness of the Confederation government. Not until after the Articles of Confederation were replaced with a new constitution could the United States muster sufficient force to implement all the provisions of the Northwest Ordinance. Thus, although the ordinance is often viewed as one of the few major accomplishments of the Confederation Congress, it must be seen within a context of political impotence.

FROM CRISIS TO A CONSTITUTION

The Americans most deeply concerned about the inadequacies of the Articles of Confederation were those involved in overseas trade and foreign affairs. It was in those areas that the articles were most obviously deficient: Congress could not impose its will on the states to establish a uniform commercial policy or to ensure the enforcement of treaties. The problems involving trade were particularly serious. Less than a year after the end of the war, the American economy slid into a depression; both exporters of staple crops (especially tobacco and rice) and importers of manufactured goods were adversely affected by the postwar restrictions on American commerce imposed by European powers. Although recovery had begun by 1786, the war's effects proved impossible to erase entirely, particularly in the Lower South.

The war, indeed, had wrought permanent change in the American economy. The near-total cessation of commerce in nonmilitary items during the war years proved a great stimulus to domestic manufacturing. Consequently, despite the influx of European goods after 1783, the postwar period witnessed the

A woodcut of Daniel Shays and one of his chief officers, Job Shattuck, in 1787. National Portrait Gallery, Smithsonian Institution, Washington, D.C.

stirrings of American industrial development—for example, the first American textile mill began production in Pawtucket, Rhode Island, in 1793. Because of continuing population growth, the domestic market assumed greater relative importance in the overall economy. Moreover, foreign trade patterns shifted from Europe and toward the West Indies, continuing a trend that had begun before the war. Foodstuffs shipped to the French and Dutch Caribbean islands became America's largest single export, replacing tobacco (thus accelerating the Chesapeake's conversion from tobacco to grain production; see page 78).

Recognizing the Confederation Congress's inability to deal with commercial matters, Virginia invited the other states to a conference at Annapolis, Maryland, to discuss trade policy. Although eight states named representatives to the meeting in September 1786, only five delegations attended. Those present realized that they were too few in number to have any real impact on the political system. They issued a call for another convention, to be held in Philadelphia in nine months, "to devise such further provisions as shall . . . appear necessary to render the constitution of the federal government adequate to the exigencies of the Union."

That fall an incident in western Massachusetts helped to convince other Americans that broad changes were necessary in their national government.

Shays' Rebellion

Crowds of farmers angered by high taxes and the low supply of money halted court proceedings in which the state was trying to seize property for nonpayment of taxes. The insurgents were led by Daniel Shays, a farmer who had risen to the rank of captain in the Revolutionary army; many of them were respected war veterans, described as "gentlemen" in contemporary accounts of the riots. Clearly the episode could not be dismissed as the work of an unruly rabble. What did the uprising mean for the future of the republic? Was it a sign of impending anarchy? Those were the questions that worried the nation's political leaders.

The protesters explained their position in an address to the governor and council of Massachusetts. They proclaimed their loyalty to the nation but objected to the state's fiscal policies, which, they said, prevented them from providing adequately for their families. Referring to their experience as revolutionary soldiers, they asserted that they "esteem[ed] one moment of Liberty to be worth an eternity of Bondage."

To residents of eastern Massachusetts and other citizens of the United States, the most frightening aspect of the uprising was the rebels' attempt to forge direct links with the earlier struggle for independence. The state legislature issued an address to the people, asserting that "in a republican government the majority must govern. If the minor part governs it becomes aristocracy; if every one opposed at his pleasure, it is no government, it is anarchy and confusion." Thus Massachusetts officials insisted that the crowd actions that had once been a justifiable response to British tyranny were no longer legitimate. In a republic, reform had to come about through the ballot box rather than by force. If the nation's citizens refused to submit to legitimate authority, the result would be chaos and collapse of the government.

Consequently, Shays' Rebellion symbolically seemed to challenge the existence of the entire United States, though it never seriously threatened even the state of Massachusetts. (The rebels were easily dispersed by militia early in 1787.) Of the major American political thinkers, only Thomas Jefferson could view the Massachusetts incidents without alarm. "What country can preserve its liberties, if its rulers are not warned from time to time that their people preserve the spirit of resistance?" Jefferson wrote from Paris, where he was serving as American ambassador. "What signify a few lives lost in a century or two? The tree of liberty must be refreshed from time to time, with the blood of patriots and tyrants. It is its natural manure."

But Jefferson was clearly exceptional. Shays' Rebellion unquestionably hastened the movement toward comprehensive revision of the Articles of Confederation. In February 1787, after most

Calling of the Constitutional Convention

of the states had already appointed delegates, the Confederation Congress belatedly endorsed the convention. In mid-May, fifty-five men, representing all the states but Rhode Island, assembled in Philadelphia to begin their deliberations.

The vast majority of the delegates were men of property and substance, and they all favored reform; otherwise they would not have come to Philadelphia. Most wanted to invigorate the national government, to give it new authority to solve the problems besetting the United States. Among their number were merchants, planters, physicians, generals, governors, and especially lawyers—twenty-three had studied the law. Most had been born in America, and many came from families that had arrived in the seventeenth century. In an era when only a tiny proportion of the population had any advanced education, more than half had attended college. A few had been educated in Britain, but most were graduates of American institutions: Princeton (ten), William and Mary (four), Yale (three), Harvard and Columbia (two each). The youngest delegate was twenty-six, the oldest—Benjamin Franklin—eighty-one. Like George Washington, whom they elected chairman, most were in their vigorous middle years. A dozen men did the bulk of the convention's work: Oliver Ellsworth and Roger Sherman of Connecticut; Elbridge Gerry and Rufus King of Massachusetts; William Paterson of New Jersey; Gouverneur Morris of New York; James Wilson of Pennsylvania; John Rutledge and Charles Pinckney of South Carolina; and Edmund Randolph, George Mason, and James Madison of Virginia. Of those leaders, Madison was by far the most important; he truly deserves the title Father of the Constitution.

The frail, shy, slightly built James Madison was thirty-six years old in 1787. Raised in the Piedmont country of Virginia, he had attended Princeton, served on the local committee of safety,

James Madison: His Early Life

and been elected successively to the Virginia provincial convention, the state's lower and upper houses, and finally the Continental Congress (1780–1783). Although Madison returned to Virginia to serve in the state legislature in 1784, he remained in touch with national politics, partly through his continuing correspondence with his close friend Thomas Jefferson. A promoter of the Annapolis convention, he strongly supported its call for further reform.

Madison was unique among the delegates in his systematic preparation for the Philadelphia meeting. Through Jefferson in Paris he bought more than two hundred books on history and government, and carefully analyzed their accounts of past confederacies and republics. In April 1787, a month before the convention began, he summed up the results of his research in a lengthy paper entitled "Vices of the Political System of the United States." After listing the eleven major flaws he perceived in the current structure of the government (among them "en-

James Madison (1751–1836), the youthful scholar and skilled politician who earned the title Father of the Constitution.   Collection of Albert E. Leeds.

croachments by the states on the federal authority" and "want of concert in matters where common interest requires it"), Madison revealed the conclusion that would guide his actions over the next few months. What the government most needed, he declared, was "such a modification of the sovereignty as will render it sufficiently neutral between the different interests and factions, to controul one part of the society from invading the rights of another, and at the same time sufficiently controuled itself, from setting up an interest adverse to that of the whole Society."

Thus Madison set forth the principle of checks and balances. The government, he believed, had to be constructed in such a way that it could not become tyrannical or fall wholly under the influence of a particular interest group. He regarded the large size of a potential national republic as an advantage in that respect. Rejecting the common assertion that republics had to be small to survive, Madison argued that a large, diverse republic was in fact to be preferred.

Because the nation would include many different interest groups, no one of them would be able to control the government. Political stability would result from compromises among the contending parties.

Madison's conception of national government was embodied in the so-called Virginia plan, introduced on May 29 by his colleague Edmund Randolph. The

Virginia and New Jersey Plans

plan provided for a two-house legislature with proportional representation in both houses, an executive elected by Congress, a national judiciary, and congressional veto over state laws. It gave Congress the broad power to legislate "in all cases to which the separate states are incompetent." Had the Virginia plan been adopted intact, it would have created a government in which national authority reigned unchallenged and state power was greatly diminished.

But the convention included many delegates who, while recognizing the need for change, believed that the Virginians had gone too far in the direction of national consolidation. After Randolph's proposal had been debated for several weeks, the disaffected delegates united under the leadership of William Paterson. On June 15 Paterson presented an alternative scheme, the New Jersey plan, calling for modifications in the Articles of Confederation rather than a complete overhaul of the government. Even before introducing his proposals, Paterson had made his position clear in debate. On June 9 he asserted that the articles were "the proper basis of all the proceedings of the convention," and warned that if the delegates did not confine themselves to amending the articles they would be charged with "usurpation" by their constituents. All that was needed, Paterson contended, was "to mark the orbits of the states with due precision and provide for the use of coercion" by the national government. Although the delegates rejected Paterson's narrow interpretation of their task, he and his allies won a number of major victories in the months that followed.

The delegates began their work by discussing the structure and functions of Congress. They readily concurred that the new national government, like the states, should have a two-house (bicameral) legislature. But then they discovered that they differed widely in their answers to three key questions: Should there be representation proportional to population in both houses of Congress? How was that representation in either or both houses to be apportioned among the states? And, finally, how were the members of the two houses to be elected?

The last issue was the easiest to resolve. In the words of John Dickinson, the delegates thought it "essential" that members of one branch of Congress be elected directly by the people and "expedient" that members of the other be chosen by the state legislatures. Since the legislatures had selected delegates to the Confederation Congress, they would expect a similar privilege in the new government. Had the convention not agreed to allow state legislatures to elect senators, the Constitution would have aroused significant opposition among political leaders at the state level.

Considerably more difficult was the matter of proportional representation in the Senate. The delegates accepted without much debate the principle of proportional representation in the lower house. But the smaller states, through their spokesman Luther Martin of Maryland, argued for equal representation in the Senate, while large states like Pennsylvania supported a proportional plan for the upper house. Martin argued that "an equal vote in each state was essential to the federal idea," but James Wilson responded with the query, are we forming a government "for *men*, or for the imaginary beings called *states*?" For weeks the convention was deadlocked on the issue, neither side being able to obtain a majority. A committee appointed to work out a compromise recommended equal representation in the Senate, coupled with a proviso that all appropriation bills had to originate in the lower house. But not until the convention accepted Roger Sherman's suggestion that a state's two senators vote as individuals rather than as a unit was a breakdown averted.

Another critical question remained, one that divided the nation along sectional rather than population lines: How was representation in the lower house to be apportioned among the states? Delegates from states with large numbers of slaves wanted all people, black and white, to be counted equally; delegates from states with few slaves wanted only free people to be counted. The issue was resolved by using a formula developed by the Confederation Congress in 1783 to allocate taxation among the states: three-fifths of the slaves would be included in the population

totals. (The formula reflected the delegates' judgment that slaves were less efficient producers of wealth than free people, not that they were 60 percent human and 40 percent property.) After the three-fifths compromise was linked to a clause allowing Congress to stop the slave trade after twenty years (thereby preventing the indefinite increase of the slave population), it was unanimously accepted. Only two delegates, Gouverneur Morris and George Mason, spoke out against the institution of slavery itself.

Once agreement was reached on the knotty problem of representation, the delegates had little difficulty achieving consensus on the other major issues confronting them. Instead of giving Congress the nearly unlimited scope proposed in the Virginia plan, the delegates enumerated congressional powers and then provided for flexibility by granting all authority "necessary and proper" to carry out those powers. Discarding the legislative veto contained in the Virginia plan, the convention implied a judicial veto instead. The Constitution plus national laws and treaties would constitute "the supreme law of the land; and the judges in every state shall be bound thereby." The convention placed primary responsibility for the conduct of foreign affairs in the hands of the president, who was also designated commander-in-chief of the armed forces. The delegates established an elaborate mechanism, the electoral college, to select the president, in order to ensure that the executive would be independent of the national legislature. They also agreed that the chief executive should serve a four-year term but be eligible for re-election.

The final document still showed signs of its origins in the Virginia plan, but compromises had created a system of government less powerful at the national level than Madison and Randolph had envisioned. The key to the Constitution was the distribution of political authority—separation of powers among the executive, legislative, and judicial branches of the national government, and division of powers between states and nation. The branches were balanced against one another, their powers deliberately entwined to prevent them from acting independently. The president was given a veto over congressional legislation, but his treaties and major appointments required the consent of the Senate. Congress could impeach the president and the federal

Separation of Powers

judges, but the courts appeared to have the final say on interpretation of the Constitution. As Madison had intended, the system of checks and balances would make it difficult for the government to become tyrannical. At the same time, though, the elaborate system would sometimes prevent the government from acting quickly and decisively. Furthermore, the line between state and national powers was so ambiguously and vaguely drawn that the United States had to fight a civil war in the next century before the issue was fully resolved. (See Appendix for the full text of the Constitution.)

The convention held its last session on September 17, 1787. Of the forty-two delegates present, only three refused to sign the Constitution. (Two of the three, George Mason and Elbridge Gerry, declined, in part, because of the lack of a bill of rights.) Benjamin Franklin had written a speech calling for unity; because his voice was too weak to be heard, James Wilson read it for him. "I confess that there are several parts of this constitution which I do not at present approve," Franklin admitted. Yet he urged its acceptance "because I expect no better, and because I am not sure, that it is not the best." Only then was the Constitution made public. The convention's proceedings had been entirely secret—and remained so until the delegates' private notes were published in the nineteenth century.

OPPOSITION AND RATIFICATION

Later that same month the Confederation Congress submitted the Constitution to the states but did not formally recommend approval. The ratification clause of the Constitution provided for the new system to take effect once it was approved by special conventions in at least nine states. The delegates to each state convention were to be elected by the people. Thus the national constitution, unlike the Articles of Confederation, would rest directly on popular authority (and the presumably hostile state legislatures would be circumvented).

As the states began to elect delegates to the special conventions, debate over the proposed government grew more heated. Newspapers were filled with essays questioning various clauses of the Constitution, and pamphlets attacked or defended the convention's decisions. It quickly became apparent that the disputes within the Constitutional Convention had been minor compared with the divisions of opinion within the country as a whole. After all, the delegates at Philadelphia had agreed on the need for basic reforms in the American political system. Many citizens, though, not only rejected that conclusion but believed that the proposed government, despite its built-in safeguards, held the potential for tyranny.

Antifederalists

Critics of the Constitution, who became known as Antifederalists, fell into two main groups: those who emphasized the threat to the states embodied in the new national government, and those who stressed the dangers to individuals posed by the lack of a bill of rights. Ultimately, though, the two positions were one. The Antifederalists saw the states as the chief protectors of individual rights, and their weakening as the onset of arbitrary power.

Fundamentally the Antifederalists were traditionalists, fearful of a too-powerful government. Their arguments against the Constitution often consisted largely of lists of potential abuses of the national government's authority. They were the heirs of the Real Whig ideology of the late 1760s and early 1770s, which stressed the need for the people's constant vigilance to avert oppression (see page 109). Indeed, in some instances the Antifederalists were the very men who had originally promulgated those ideas; for example, Samuel Adams and Richard Henry Lee were both leaders of the opposition to the Constitution. Antifederalist ranks were heavily peopled not only by such older Americans (whose political opinions had been shaped prior to the more centralizing, nationalistic Revolution) but also by small farmers, who jealously guarded their property against excessive taxation by either state or nation.

As the months passed and public debate continued, the Antifederalists focused more sharply on the Constitution's lack of a bill of rights. Even if the states were weakened by the new system, they believed, the people could still be protected from tyranny if their rights were specifically guaranteed. The Constitution did contain some prohibitions on congres-

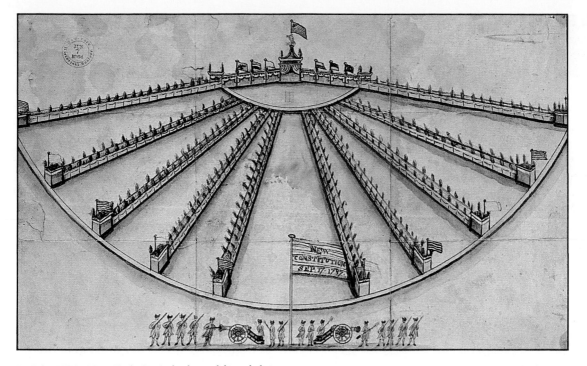

In July 1788, New York City's leaders celebrated their state's ratification of the Constitution at an elaborate banquet served in a pavilion erected for the occasion. Their hopes for an orderly government were symbolized by the orderly arrangement of the tables, separate but linked into a semicircle by the central structure displaying flags and banners. *The New-York Historical Society.*

sional power—for example, the writ of habeas corpus, which prevented arbitrary imprisonment, could not be suspended except in dire emergencies—but the Antifederalists found these provisions inadequate. Nor were they reassured by the Federalists' assertion that, since the new government was one of limited powers, it had no authority to violate the people's rights. *Letters of a Federal Farmer,* perhaps the most widely read Antifederalist pamphlet, listed the rights that should be protected: freedom of the press and of religion, the right to trial by jury, and guarantees against unreasonable search warrants.

From Paris, Thomas Jefferson added his voice to the chorus. Replying to Madison's letter conveying a copy of the Constitution, Jefferson wrote: "I like much the general idea of framing a government which should go on of itself peaceably, without needing continual recurrence to the state legislatures." He also approved of the separation of powers among the three branches of government and declared himself "captivated" by the compromise between the large and small states. Nevertheless, he added, he did not like "the omission of a bill of rights. . . . A bill of rights is what the people are entitled to against every government on earth, general or particular, and what no just government should refuse, or rest on inference."

As the state conventions met to consider ratification, the lack of a bill of rights loomed larger and larger as a flaw in the new form of government. Four of the first five states to ratify did so unanimously, but serious disagreements then began to surface. Massachusetts ratified by a majority of only 19 votes out of 355 cast; in New Hampshire the Federalists won by a majority of 57 to 47. When New Hampshire ratified, in June 1788, the requirement of nine states had been satisfied. But New York and Virginia had not yet voted, and everyone realized

Ratification of the Constitution

which governs best governs least," by the late 1780s many had changed their minds. These were the drafters and supporters of the Constitution, who had concluded from the republic's vicissitudes under the Articles of Confederation that the United States needed a more powerful central government. They won their point when the Constitution was adopted, however narrowly. They contended during the ratification debates that their proposed solution to the nation's problems was just as "republican" in conception (if not more so) as the articles. While disagreeing about details, both sides concurred in their general adherence to republican principles.

White males wholly dominated the new United States. The era that saw the formation of the union also witnessed the systematic formulation of American racist thought, and the two processes were intimately linked. One way to preserve the freedom of all whites was to ensure the continued subjection of all blacks, slave or free. Likewise, one way to preserve the un-challenged economic independence of white men was to ensure the economic and political dependence of white women on their husbands, fathers, and brothers. Even if the leaders of the United States were not consciously aware of adopting such strategies, their decisions had similar effects. Independence had been fought for and won by many Americans—white, black, and red, male and female—but in the new republic only white males would hold political power.

the new constitution could not succeed unless those key states accepted it. In Virginia, despite a valiant effort by the Antifederalist Patrick Henry, the pro-Constitution forces won 89 to 79. In New York James Madison, John Jay, and Alexander Hamilton cam-paigned for ratification by publishing *The Federalist*, a political tract that explained the theory behind the Constitution and masterfully answered its critics. Their reasoned arguments, coupled with the promise that a bill of rights would be added to the Constitution, helped win the battle. On July 26, 1788, New York ratified the Constitution by the slim margin of 3 votes. The new government was a reality, even though the last state (Rhode Island, which had not participated in the convention) did not formally join the union until 1790.

The experience of fighting a war and of struggling for survival as an independent nation in the 1780s had altered the political context of American life. Whereas at the outset of the war most politically aware Americans believed that "that government

SUGGESTIONS FOR FURTHER READING

General

Joyce Appleby, "The Social Origins of American Revo-lutionary Ideology," *Journal of American History*, 64 (1978), 935–958; Staughton Lynd, *Class Conflict, Slavery, & the United States Constitution: Ten Essays* (1967); Forrest McDonald, *E Pluribus Unum: The Formation of the American Republic 1776–1790* (1965); Jackson Turner Main, *The Social Structure of Revolutionary America* (1965); Curtis P. Nettels, *The Emergence of a National Economy, 1775–1815* (1962); Robert R. Palmer, *The Age of the Democratic Rev-*

Chapter 6: FORGING A NATIONAL REPUBLIC, 1776–1789

olution: A Political History of Europe and America 1760–1800, 2 vols. (1959, 1964); Gordon S. Wood, *The Creation of the American Republic, 1776–1787* (1969).

Continental Congress and Articles of Confederation

E. James Ferguson, *The Power of the Purse: A History of American Public Finance, 1776–1790* (1961); H. James Henderson, *Party Politics in the Continental Congress* (1974); Merrill Jensen, *The Articles of Confederation: An Interpretation of the Social-Constitutional History of the American Revolution, 1774–1781*, 2nd ed. (1959); Merrill Jensen, *The New Nation: A History of the United States During the Confederation, 1781–1789* (1950); Jack N. Rakove, *The Beginnings of National Politics: An Interpretive History of the Continental Congress* (1979).

State Politics

Willi Paul Adams, *The First American Constitutions: Republican Ideology and the Making of the State Constitutions in the Revolutionary Era* (1980); Edward Countryman, *A People in Revolution: The American Revolution and Political Society in New York, 1760–1790* (1981); Ronald Hoffman and Peter Albert, eds., *Sovereign States in an Age of Uncertainty* (1981); Donald Lutz, *Popular Consent and Popular Control: Whig Political Theory in the Early State Constitutions* (1980); Jackson Turner Main, *Political Parties Before the Constitution* (1973); Jackson Turner Main, *The Sovereign States, 1775–1783* (1973); Jackson Turner Main, *The Upper House in Revolutionary America, 1763–1788* (1967); Stephen E. Patterson, *Political Parties in Revolutionary Massachusetts* (1973); J. R. Pole, *Political Representation in England and the Origins of the American Republic* (1966); Marion L. Starkey, *A Little Rebellion* (1955); David P. Szatmary, *Shays' Rebellion: The Making of an Agrarian Insurrection* (1980).

The Constitution

Douglass Adair, *Fame and the Founding Fathers* (1974); Charles A. Beard, *An Economic Interpretation of the Constitution of the United States* (1913); Irving Brant, *James Madison*, 6 vols. (1941–1961); Forrest McDonald, *We the People: The Economic Origins of the Constitution* (1958); Jackson Turner Main, *The Anti-Federalists: Critics of the Constitution, 1781–1788* (1961); Frederick W. Marks, III, *Independence on Trial: Foreign Affairs and the Making of the Constitution* (1973); Clinton Rossiter, *1787: The Grand Convention* (1973); Robert A. Rutland, *The Ordeal of the Constitution: The Antifederalists and the Ratification Struggle of 1787–88* (1966); Abraham Sofaer, *War, Foreign Affairs, and Constitutional Power*, vol. 1: *The Origins* (1976); Carl

Van Doren, *The Great Rehearsal: The Story of the Making and Ratifying of the Constitution of the United States* (1948); Garry Wills, *Explaining America: The Federalist* (1981).

Education and Culture

Lawrence A. Cremin, *American Education: The National Experience, 1783–1876* (1981); Joseph J. Ellis, *After the Revolution: Profiles of Early American Culture* (1979); Carl F. Kaestle, *Pillars of the Republic: Common Schools and American Society, 1780–1860* (1983); Russel B. Nye, *The Cultural Life of the New Nation: 1776–1803* (1960); Kenneth Silverman, *A Cultural History of the American Revolution* (1976).

Women

Charles Akers, *Abigail Adams: An American Woman* (1980); Ruth Bloch, "American Feminine Ideals in Transition: The Rise of the Moral Mother, 1785–1815," *Feminist Studies*, 4, No. 2 (June 1978), 100–126; Nancy F. Cott, "Divorce and the Changing Status of Women in Massachusetts," *William and Mary Quarterly*, 3rd ser., 33 (1976), 586–614; Linda K. Kerber, *Women of the Republic: Intellect & Ideology in Revolutionary America* (1980); Mary Beth Norton, *Liberty's Daughters: The Revolutionary Experience of American Women, 1750–1800* (1980); Lynn Withey, *Dearest Friend: A Life of Abigail Adams* (1980).

Blacks and Slavery

Ira Berlin, *Slaves Without Masters: The Free Negro in the Antebellum South* (1974); Ira Berlin and Ronald Hoffman, eds., *Slavery and Freedom in the Age of the American Revolution* (1983); David Brion Davis, *The Problem of Slavery in the Age of Revolution, 1770–1823* (1975); Carol V. R. George, *Segregated Sabbaths: Richard Allen and the Emergence of Independent Black Churches 1760–1840* (1973); Winthrop Jordan, *White over Black: American Attitudes Toward the Negro, 1550–1812* (1968); Duncan J. Macleod, *Slavery, Race, and the American Revolution* (1974); Donald L. Robinson, *Slavery in the Structure of American Politics 1765–1820* (1971); Arthur Zilversmit, *The First Emancipation: The Abolition of Slavery in the North* (1967).

Indians

Dorothy Jones, *License for Empire: Colonialism by Treaty in Early America* (1982); Francis Paul Prucha, *American Indian Policy in the Formative Years: The Indian Trade and Intercourse Acts 1790–1834* (1962); Bernard Sheehan, *Seeds of Extinction: Jeffersonian Philanthropy and the American Indian* (1973); Anthony F. C. Wallace, *The Death and Rebirth of the Seneca* (1969).

POLITICS AND SOCIETY IN THE EARLY REPUBLIC

1790–1800

CHAPTER 7

Charles Thomson, secretary to Congress, arrived at Mount Vernon, Virginia, around noon on April 14, 1789. He brought momentous news: the first electoral college convened under the new Constitution had unanimously elected George Washington president of the United States, and Congress had confirmed the choice.

Washington had been expecting the summons to New York City, the nation's capital. Two days later he and Thomson began the journey north. The new president, who disliked pomp, hoped in vain for an uneventful trip. After being honored at formal dinners in Alexandria, Baltimore, and Wilmington, he arrived on April 20 at a bridge across the Schuylkill River. Charles Willson Peale, the painter and naturalist, had turned the crude bridge into a triumphal avenue, beginning and ending with laurel-bedecked arches twenty feet high and flanked on both sides by flags. As Washington rode a white horse beneath the first arch, Peale's daughter Angelica operated a machine that placed a laurel wreath on his head. In Philadelphia, on the other side of the river, more than twenty thousand people lined the streets for a glimpse of the first president of the new republic.

Entering Trenton the next day, Washington rode under another triumphal arch, this one emblazoned with the words, "The Defender of the Mothers will be the Protector of the Daughters." The women of New Jersey had not forgotten that Washington's victories at Princeton and Trenton had put an end to the epidemic of rape they endured when the British occupied the state. A group of girls dressed in white threw flowers in his path while singing an ode composed for the occasion.

Each New Jersey town Washington passed through greeted him with speeches, music, pealing bells, and military salutes. Finally, at Elizabeth on April 23, he was met by a congressional committee sent to escort him to Manhattan. The official party traveled up the Hudson on a specially constructed fifty-foot barge draped in red. When the barge arrived at the foot of Wall Street, church bells rang and thirteen guns fired a salute. On the night of Washington's inauguration one week later, New York City was illuminated by lanterns and the festivities ended with a spectacular two-hour fireworks display.

The United States formally honored its first president with an outpouring of affection and respect that has rarely been equaled since. Washington's inauguration allowed the people to express their pride in the Revolution, the new Constitution, and most of all in the nation itself. The struggle against Britain had nurtured in Americans an intense nationalism. They believed their republican experiment placed them in the vanguard of political reform, and they optimistically expected a future of prosperity, expansion, national unity, and independence from Europe.

Yet Americans were unsuccessful in their quest for unity and unqualified independence during the 1790s. Nowhere was their failure more evident than in the realm of national politics. The fierce battle over the Constitution foreshadowed an even wider division over the major political issues the republic had to confront. To make matters worse, Americans' belief in the efficacy of republicanism prevented them from fully anticipating the political disagreements that characterized the 1790s. They believed that the Constitution would resolve the problems that had arisen during the Confederation period, and they expected the new government to rule largely by consensus. Accordingly, they found it difficult to understand and deal with partisan tensions that developed out of disputes over such fundamental questions as the extent to which authority, especially fiscal authority, should be centralized in the national government; the formulation of foreign policy in an era of continual warfare in Europe; and the limits of dissent within the republic. As the decade closed they still had not come to terms with the implications of partisan politics.

Prosperity and expansion too were not easily attained. The United States economy still depended on the export trade, as it had throughout the colonial era. When warfare between England and France resumed in 1793, Americans found their commerce disrupted once again, with consequent fluctuations in their income and profits. Moreover, the strength of the Miami confederacy blocked the westward expansion of white settlement north of the Ohio River

The Federal Plan Most Solid is Sacred
And Gave Their Freedom Will Endure
All Arts Shall Flourish in Columbia's Land
And All Her Sons Join as One Social Band

SOCIETY of PEWTERERS

SOLID AND PURE.

This flag of the New York Society of Pewterers was carried in the New York City Constitution ratification parade in July 1788.   The New-York Historical Society.

until after the Treaty of Greenville in 1795 (see page 171). South of the Ohio, settlements were established west of the mountains as early as the 1770s, but the geographical barrier of the Appalachians tended to isolate them from the eastern seaboard. Not until the last years of the century did the frontier settlements become more fully integrated into American life through the vehicle of the Second Great Awakening, a religious revival that swept both east and west.

BUILDING A WORKABLE GOVERNMENT

I n 1788 Americans celebrated the ratification of the Constitution with a series of parades, held in many cities on the Fourth of July. The processions were carefully planned to symbolize the unity of the new nation and to recall its history to the minds of the watching throngs. The parades, like prerevolutionary protest meetings, served as political educators for literate and illiterate Americans alike. Men and women who could not read were thereby informed of the significance of the new Constitution in the life of the nation. They were also instructed about political leaders' hopes for industry and frugality on the part of a virtuous American public.

The Philadelphia parade, planned largely by Charles Willson Peale, was filled with symbols related to those goals. About five thousand people participated in the procession, which stretched for a mile and a half and lasted three hours. Twelve costumed "axemen" representing the first pioneers were followed by a mounted military troop and a group of men with flags symbolizing independence, the peace treaty, the French alliance, and other revolutionary events. A band played a "Federal March" composed for the occasion. There followed a Constitution float, displaying a large framed copy of the Constitution and a thirteen-foot-high eagle. A number of local dignitaries marched in front of the next float, "The Grand Federal Edifice," a domed structure supported by thirteen columns (three of which were left unfinished to signify the states that had not yet ratified).

The remainder of the parade consisted of groups of artisans and professionals marching together and dramatizing their work. One of the farmers scattered seed in the streets; on the manufacturers' float, cloth was being made; the printers operated a press, distributing copies of a poem written to honor the Constitution. More than forty other groups of tradesmen, such as barbers, hatters, and clockmakers, sponsored similar floats. The artisans were followed by lawyers, doctors, clergymen of all denominations, and congressmen. Bringing up the rear was a symbol of the nation's future, a contingent of students from the University of Pennsylvania and other city schools. Marching with their teachers, they carried a flag labeled "The Rising Generation."

The nationalistic spirit expressed in the ratification processions carried over into the first session of Congress. In the congressional elections, held late in 1788, only a few Antifederalists had run or been elected to office. Thus the First Congress was composed chiefly of men who were considerably more inclined toward a strong national government than had been the delegates to the Constitutional Convention. Since the Constitution had deliberately left many key issues undecided, the nationalists' domination of Congress meant that their views on those points quickly prevailed.

First Congress

Congress faced four immediate problems when it convened in April 1789: raising revenue to support the new government, responding to the state ratification conventions' calls for the addition of a bill of rights to the Constitution, setting up executive departments, and organizing the federal judiciary. The latter task was especially important. The Constitution established a Supreme Court but left it to Congress to decide whether to have other federal courts as well.

The Virginian James Madison, who had been elected to the House of Representatives, soon became as influential in Congress as he had been at the Philadelphia convention. Only a few months into the session, he persuaded Congress to impose a tariff on certain imported goods. Consequently, the First Congress quickly achieved what the Confederation Congress never had: an effective national tax law. The new government would have problems, but lack of revenue in its first years was not one of them.

Madison also took the lead on the issue of constitutional amendments. At the convention and thereafter, he had consistently opposed additional limitations on the national government on the grounds that it was unnecessary to guarantee the people's rights when the government was one of limited, delegated powers. But Madison recognized that public opinion, as expressed by the state ratifying conventions, was against him, and accordingly placed nineteen proposed amendments before the House. Congress eventually sent twelve amendments to the states for ratification. Two, having to do with the number of congressmen and their salaries, were not accepted by a sufficient number of states. The other ten amendments officially became part of the Constitution on December 15, 1791. Not for many years, though, did they become known collectively as the Bill of Rights (see Appendix).

Bill of Rights

The first amendment specifically prohibited Congress from passing any law restricting the people's right to freedom of religion, speech, press, peaceable assembly, or petition. The next two arose directly from the former colonists' fear of standing armies as a threat to freedom. The second amendment guaranteed the people's right "to keep and bear arms" because of the need for a "well-regulated Militia." Thus the constitutional right to bear arms was based on the expectation that most able-bodied men would serve the nation as citizen soldiers, and there would be no need for a standing army. The third amendment defined the circumstances in which troops could be quartered in private homes. The next five pertained to judicial procedures. The fourth amendment prohibited "unreasonable searches and seizures"; the fifth and sixth established the rights of accused persons; the seventh specified the conditions for jury trials in civil, as opposed to criminal, cases; and the eighth forbade "cruel and unusual punishments." Finally, the ninth and tenth amendments reserved to the people and the states other unspecified rights and powers. In short, the authors of the amendments made clear that in listing some rights explicitly they did not mean to preclude the exercise of others.

While debating the proposed amendments, Congress also concerned itself with the organization of the executive branch. It was readily agreed to continue the three administrative departments established under the Articles of Confederation: War, Foreign Affairs (renamed State), and Treasury. Congress also instituted two lesser posts: the attorney general—the nation's official lawyer—and the postmaster general, who would oversee the Post Office. The only serious controversy was whether the president alone could dismiss officials whom he had originally appointed with the consent of the Senate. After some debate, the House and Senate agreed that he had such authority. Thus was established the important principle that the heads of the executive departments are responsible solely to the president. Though it could not have been foreseen at the time, this precedent paved the way for the development of the president's cabinet.

Aside from the constitutional amendments, the most far-reaching piece of legislation enacted by the First Congress was the Judiciary Act of 1789. That

Judiciary Act of 1789

act was largely the work of Senator Oliver Ellsworth of Connecticut, a veteran of the Constitutional Convention who in 1796 would become the third chief justice of the United States. The Judiciary Act provided for the Supreme Court to have six members: a chief justice and five associate justices. It also defined the jurisdiction of the federal judiciary and established thirteen district courts and three circuit courts of appeal.

The act's most important provision may have been Section 25, which allowed appeals from state courts to the federal court system when certain types of constitutional issues were raised. This section was intended to implement Article VI of the Constitution, which stated that federal laws and treaties were to be considered "the supreme Law of the Land." If Article VI was to be enforced uniformly, the national judiciary clearly had to be able to overturn state court decisions in cases involving the Constitution, federal laws, or treaties. Yet nowhere did the Constitution explicitly permit such action by federal courts. The nationalistic First Congress accepted Ellsworth's argument that the right of appeal from state to federal

courts was implied in the wording of Article VI. Eventually, however, judges and legislators committed to the ideal of states' rights were to challenge that interpretation.

During the first decade of its existence, the Supreme Court handled few cases of any importance. Indeed, for its first three years it heard no cases at all. John Jay, the first chief justice, served only until 1795, and only one of the first five associate justices remained on the bench in 1799. But in a significant 1796 decision, *Ware* v. *Hylton,* the Court—acting on the basis of section 25 of the Judiciary Act of 1789— for the first time declared a state law unconstitutional. That same year it also reviewed the constitutionality of an act of Congress, upholding its validity in the case of *Hylton* v. *US.* The most important case of the decade, *Chisholm* v. *Georgia* (1793), established that states could be freely sued in federal courts by citizens of other states; this decision, unpopular with the states, was overruled five years later by the Eleventh Amendment to the Constitution (See Appendix for the text of the Constitution and all amendments.)

DOMESTIC POLICY UNDER WASHINGTON AND HAMILTON

George Washington did not seek the presidency. When he returned to Mount Vernon in 1783, he was eager for the peaceful life of a Virginia planter. He rebuilt his house, redesigned his

Election of the First President

gardens, experimented with new agricultural techniques, improved the breeding of his livestock, and speculated in western lands. Yet his fellow countrymen never regarded Washington as just another private citizen. Although he took little part in the political maneuverings that preceded the Constitutional Convention, he was unanimously elected its presiding officer. As a result, he did not participate in debates, but he consistently voted for a strong national government. Once the proposed structure of the government was presented to the public, Americans concurred that only George Washington had sufficient

The inauguration of George Washington as first president of the United States occurred on the balcony of Federal Hall in New York City. This engraving of the event was printed the following year; it was purchased by many patriotic Americans who wanted personal reminders of the momentous occasion. Library of Congress.

prestige to serve as the republic's first president. The vote of the electoral college was just a formality.

Washington was reluctant to return to public life, but knew he could not resist his country's call. Awaiting the summons to New York, he wrote to an old friend, "My movements to the chair of Government will be accompanied by feelings not unlike those of a culprit who is going to the place of his execution. . . . I am sensible, that I am embarking the voice of my Countrymen and a good name of my own, on this voyage, but what returns will be made for them, Heaven alone can foretell."

During his first months in office Washington acted cautiously, knowing that whatever he did would set precedents for the future. He held weekly receptions at which callers could pay their respects and toured different areas of the country in turn. When the title

by which he should be addressed aroused a good deal of controversy (Vice President John Adams favored "His Highness, the President of the United States of America, and Protector of their Liberties"), Washington said nothing; the accepted title soon became a plain "Mr. President." He used the heads of the executive departments collectively as his chief advisors and thus created the cabinet. As the Constitution required, he sent Congress an annual "State of the Union" message (though he did not deliver it in person, as presidents do today). Washington also concluded that he should exercise his veto power over congressional legislation very sparingly—only, indeed, if he was convinced a bill was unconstitutional.

Washington's first major task as president was to choose the men who would head the executive departments. For the War Department he selected an old comrade-in-arms, Henry Knox, who had been his reliable general of artillery during much of the Revolution. His choice for the State Department was his fellow Virginian Thomas Jefferson, who had just returned to the United States from his post as ambassador to France. Finally, for the crucial position of secretary of the treasury, the president chose the brilliant, intensely ambitious Alexander Hamilton.

The illegitimate son of a Scottish aristocrat and a woman divorced by her husband for adultery and desertion, Hamilton was born in the British West Indies in 1757. His early years were spent in poverty; after his mother's death when he was eleven, he worked as a clerk for a mercantile firm. In 1773 Hamilton enrolled in King's College (later Columbia University) in New York City; only eighteen months later the precocious seventeen-year-old contributed a major pamphlet to the prerevolutionary publication wars of late 1774. Devoted to the patriot cause, Hamilton volunteered for service in the American army, where he came to the attention of George Washington. In 1777 Washington appointed the young man as one of his aides-de-camp, and the two developed great affection for one another. Indeed, in some respects Hamilton became the son Washington never had.

The general's patronage enabled the poor youth of dubious background to marry well. At twenty-three he took as his wife Elizabeth Schuyler, the daughter of a wealthy New York family. After the

Alexander Hamilton: His Early Life

war, Hamilton practiced law in New York City and served as a delegate first to the Annapolis Convention in 1786 and the following year to the Constitutional Convention. Though he exerted little influence at either convention, his contributions to *The Federalist* in 1788 revealed him to be one of the chief political thinkers in the republic.

In his dual role as secretary of the treasury and one of Washington's major advisors, two traits distinguished Hamilton from most of his contemporaries. First, he displayed an undivided, unquestioning loyalty to the nation as a whole. As a West Indian who had lived on the mainland only briefly before the war, Hamilton had no ties to an individual state. He showed little sympathy for, or understanding of, demands for local autonomy. Thus his fiscal policies aimed always at consolidation of power at the national level. Furthermore, he never feared the exercise of centralized executive authority, as did his older counterparts who had clashed repeatedly with colonial governors.

Second, he regarded his fellow human beings with unvarnished cynicism. Perhaps because of his difficult early life and his own overriding ambition, Hamilton believed people to be motivated primarily, if not entirely, by self-interest—particularly economic self-interest. He placed absolutely no reliance on people's capacity for virtuous and self-sacrificing behavior. That outlook set him apart from those republicans who foresaw a rosy future in which public-spirited citizens would pursue the common good rather than their own private advantage. Although other Americans (like Madison) also stressed the role of private interests in a republic, Hamilton went beyond them in his nearly exclusive emphasis on self-interest as the major motivator of human behavior. And those beliefs significantly influenced the way in which he tackled the monumental task before him: straightening out the new nation's tangled finances.

In 1789 Congress ordered the new secretary of the treasury to study the state of the public debt and to submit recommendations for supporting the government's credit. Hamilton discovered

National Debt that the country's remaining war debts fell into three categories: those owed by the United States to foreign governments and investors, mostly to France (about $11 million); those owed by the national government to merchants,

Alexander Hamilton (1737–1804), painted by John Trumbull in 1792. Hamilton was then at the height of his influence as secretary of the treasury, and his haughty, serene expression reveals his supreme self-confidence. Trumbull, an American student of the English artist Benjamin West, painted the portrait at the request of John Jay. National Gallery of Art, Gift of the Avalon Foundation.

former soldiers, holders of revolutionary bonds, and the like (about $27 million); and, finally, similar debts owed by state governments (roughly estimated at $25 million). With respect to the national debt, there was little disagreement: politically aware Americans recognized that if their new government was to succeed it would have to pay the obligations the nation had incurred while winning independence.

The state debts were quite another matter. Some states—notably Virginia, Maryland, North Carolina, and Georgia—had already paid off most of their war debts. They would oppose the national government's assumption of responsibility for other states' debts, since their citizens would be taxed to pay such obligations in addition to their own. Massachusetts, Connecticut, and South Carolina, on the other hand, still had sizable unpaid debts and would welcome a system of national assumption. The possible assumption of state debts also had political implications. Consolidation of the debt in the hands of the national government would unquestionably help to concentrate both economic and political power at the national level. A contrary policy would reserve greater independence of action for the states.

Hamilton's "Report on Public Credit," sent to Congress in January 1790, reflected both his national loyalty and his cynicism. It proposed that Congress assume outstanding state debts, combine them with national obligations, and issue new securities covering both principal and accumulated unpaid interest. Current holders of state or national debt certificates would have the option of taking a portion of their payment in western lands. Hamilton's aims were clear: he wanted to expand the financial reach of the United States government and reduce the economic power of the states. He also wanted to ensure that the holders of public securities—many of them wealthy merchants and speculators—would have a significant financial stake in the survival of the national government.

Hamilton's "Report on Public Credit"

Hamilton's plan stimulated lively debate in Congress. The opposition coalesced around his former ally James Madison. Madison opposed the assumption of state debts, since his own state of Virginia had already paid off most of its obligations. As a congressman tied to agrarian rather than moneyed interests, he opposed the notion that only current holders of public securities should receive payments. Believing with some reason that speculators had purchased large quantities of debt certificates at a small fraction of their face value, Madison proposed that the original holders of the debt also be compensated by the government. But Madison's plan, though probably more fair than Hamilton's—in that it would have directly rewarded those people who had actually supplied the revolutionary governments with goods or services—was exceedingly complex and perhaps impossible to administer. The House of Representatives rejected it.

At first, however, the House also rejected the assumption of state debts. Since the Senate, by contrast, adopted Hamilton's plan largely intact, a series of compromises followed. Hamilton agreed to changes in the assumption plan that would benefit Virginia in particular. The assumption bill also became linked in a complex way to the other major controversial issue of that congressional session: the location of the permanent national capital. Northerners and southerners both wanted the capital in their region. The traditional story that Hamilton and Madison agreed over Jefferson's dinner table to exchange assumption of state debts for a southern site is not supported by the surviving evidence, but a political deal was undoubtedly struck. The Potomac River was designated as the site for the capital. Simultaneously, the four congressmen from Maryland and Virginia whose districts contained the most likely locations for the new city switched from opposition to support for assumption. As a result, the first part of Hamilton's financial program became law in August 1790.

Four months later Hamilton submitted to Congress a second report on public credit, recommending the chartering of a national bank. Like his proposal for assumption of the debt, this recommendation too aroused considerable opposition. Unlike the earlier debate, which involved matters of policy, this one focused on constitutional issues. It also arose primarily after Congress had already adopted the bank proposal.

Hamilton modeled his bank on the Bank of England. The Bank of the United States was to be capitalized at $10 million, with only $2 million coming from public funds. The rest would be supplied by private investors. Its charter was to run for twenty years, and one-fifth of its directors were to be named by the government. Its bank notes would circulate as the nation's currency; it would also act as the collecting and disbursing agent for the treasury, and lend money to the government. Most people recognized that such an institution would benefit the country, especially because it would solve the problem of America's perpetual shortage of an acceptable medium of exchange. But there was another issue: did the Constitution give Congress the power to establish such a bank?

First Bank of the United States

James Madison, for one, answered that question with a resounding no. He pointed out that the delegates at the Philadelphia convention had specifically rejected a clause authorizing Congress to issue corporate charters. Consequently, he argued, that power could not be inferred from other parts of the Constitution.

Washington was sufficiently disturbed by Madison's contention that he decided to request other opinions before signing the bill. Edmund Randolph, the attorney general, and Thomas Jefferson, the secretary of state, agreed with Madison that the bank was unconstitutional. Jefferson referred to Article I, Section 8, of the Constitution, which gave Congress the power "to make all Laws which shall be necessary and proper for carrying into Execution the foregoing Powers." *Necessary* was the key word, Jefferson argued: Congress could do what was needed but it could not do what was merely desirable without specific constitutional authorization. Thus Jefferson formulated the strict-constructionist interpretation of the Constitution.

Washington asked Hamilton to reply to these negative assessments of his proposal. Hamilton's "Defense of the Constitutionality of the Bank," presented to Washington in February 1791, was a brilliant exposition of what has become known as the broad-constructionist view of the Constitution. Hamilton argued forcefully that Congress could choose any means not specifically prohibited by the Constitution to achieve a constitutional end. In short, if the end was constitutional and the means was not *un*constitutional, then the means was also constitutional.

Washington was convinced. The bill became law; the bank proved successful. So did the scheme for funding and assumption: the new nation's securities became desirable investments for its own citizens and for wealthy foreigners. But two other aspects of Alexander Hamilton's wide-ranging financial scheme did not fare so well.

In December 1791, Hamilton presented to Congress his "Report on Manufactures," the third and last of his prescriptions for the American economy. In it he outlined an ambitious plan for encouraging and protecting the United States's infant industries, like shoemaking and textile manufacturing. Hamilton argued that the nation could never be truly independent as long as it had to rely heavily on Europe for its manufactured goods. He thus urged Congress to promote the immigration of technicians and laborers, enact protective tariffs, and support industrial development. Although many of Hamilton's ideas were implemented in later decades, few congressmen in 1791 could see much merit in his proposals. They firmly believed that America's future was agrarian. The mainstay of the republic was the virtuous yeoman farmer. Therefore, Congress rejected the report.

That same year Congress did accept the other part of Hamilton's financial program, an excise tax on whiskey, because of the need for additional government revenues and because of the congressmen's desire to reduce the nation's consumption of distilled spirits. (Eighteenth-century Americans were notorious for their heavy drinking habits; annual per capita consumption of alcohol then was about double today's rate.) The import duties adopted in 1789 had raised the price of rum (which was made from imported molasses); the excise tax increased the price of domestically produced whiskey. The new tax most directly affected western farmers, who sold their grain crops in the form of distilled spirits as a means of avoiding the high costs of transporting wagonloads of bulky corn over the mountains.

News of the excise law set off immediate protests in frontier areas of Pennsylvania and the Carolinas. But matters did not come to a head until the summer

Whiskey Rebellion

of 1794, when western Pennsylvania farmers tried to stop a federal marshal from arresting some men charged with violating the law. The only person killed in the disturbances was a leader of the rioters, but President Washington was determined to prevent a recurrence of Shays' Rebellion. On August 7, he issued a proclamation calling on the insurgents to disperse by September 1, and he summoned more than twelve thousand militia from Pennsylvania and neighboring states. By the time the federal forces marched westward in October and November (headed some of the time by Washington himself), the riots had long since ended. The troops, who met no resistance, arrested a number of suspects. Only two were ever convicted of treason, and Washington pardoned both. The rebellion, such as it was, ended almost without bloodshed.

The chief importance of the Whiskey Rebellion was not military victory over the rebels—for there was none—but rather the message it forcefully conveyed to the American public. The national government, Washington had demonstrated, would not allow violent organized resistance to its laws. In the new republic, change would be effected peacefully, by legal means. Those who were dissatisfied with the law should try to amend or repeal it, not take extralegal action.

An American artist painted this view of President Washington, in army uniform once again, as he (on October 18, 1794) reviewed the troops that had been summoned to suppress the Whiskey Rebellion. Metropolitan Museum of Art, Gift of Edgar William and Bernice Chrysler Garbisch, 1963.

By 1794, a group of Americans had already begun to seek change systematically within the confines of electoral politics, even though traditional political theory regarded organized opposition—especially in a republic—as illegitimate. The leaders of the opposition were Thomas Jefferson and James Madison, who became convinced as early as 1792 that Hamilton and his supporters intended to impose a corrupt, aristocratic government on the United States. Jefferson and Madison justified their opposition to Hamilton and his policies by contending that they were the true heirs of the Revolution, whereas Hamilton was actually plotting to subvert republican principles. To emphasize their point, they and their followers in Congress began calling themselves *Republicans.* Hamilton in turn accused Jefferson and Madison of the

same crime: attempting to destroy the republic. To legitimize their claim to being the rightful interpreters of the Constitution, Hamilton and his supporters called themselves *Federalists.* In short, each group accused the other of being an illicit faction that was working to destroy the republican principles of the Revolution. (A faction was, in the traditional sense of the term, by definition opposed to the public good.)

At first, President Washington tried to remain aloof from the political dispute that divided his chief advisors, Hamilton and Jefferson. Even so, the controversy helped to persuade him to seek a second term of office in 1792 in hopes of promoting political unity. But in 1793 and thereafter, a series of developments in foreign affairs magnified the disagreements.

PARTISAN POLITICS AND FOREIGN POLICY

The first years under the Constitution were blessed by international peace. Eventually, however, the French Revolution, which began in 1789, brought about the resumption of hostilities between France, America's wartime ally, and Great Britain, America's most important trading partner.

At first, Americans welcomed the news that France was turning toward republicanism. The French people's success in limiting, then overthrowing, the monarchy seemed to vindicate the United States's own revolution. Now more than ever, Americans could see themselves as being in the vanguard of an inevitable historical trend that would reshape the world for the better. But by the early 1790s the reports from France were disquieting. Outbreaks of violence continued, ministries succeeded each other with bewildering rapidity, and executions were commonplace. The king himself was beheaded in early 1793. Although many Americans, including Jefferson and Madison, retained their sympathy for the French revolutionaries, others began to view France as a prime example of the perversion of republicanism. As might be expected, Alexander Hamilton fell into the latter group.

At that juncture, France declared war on Britain, Spain, and Holland. The Americans thus faced a dilemma. The 1778 treaty with France bound them to that nation "forever," and a mutual commitment to republicanism created ideological bonds. Yet the United States was connected to Great Britain as well. Aside from sharing a common history and language, America and England were economic partners. Americans still purchased most of their manufactured goods from Great Britain and sold their own produce chiefly in British and British colonial markets. Indeed, since the Hamiltonian financial system depended heavily on import tariffs as a source of revenue, and America's imports came primarily from Britain, the nation's economic health in effect required uninterrupted trade with the former mother country.

The political and diplomatic climate was further complicated in April 1793, when Citizen Edmond

Citizen Genet

Genet, a representative of the French government, landed in Charleston. As Genet made his leisurely way northward to New York City, he was wildly cheered and lavishly entertained at every stop. En route, he recruited Americans for expeditions against British and Spanish possessions in the Western Hemisphere and distributed privateering commissions with a generous hand. Genet's arrival raised a series of key questions for President Washington. Should he receive Genet, thus officially recognizing the French revolutionary government? Should he acknowledge an obligation to aid France under the terms of the 1778 treaty? Or should he proclaim American neutrality in the conflict?

For once, Hamilton and Jefferson saw eye to eye. Both told Washington that the United States could not afford to ally itself firmly with either side. Washington agreed; thus he received Genet officially, but also issued a proclamation informing the world that the United States would adopt "a conduct friendly and impartial toward the belligerent powers." In deference to Jefferson's continued support for France, the word *neutrality* did not appear in the declaration— but its meaning was nevertheless clear.

Genet himself was removed as a factor in Franco-American relations at the end of the summer. His faction fell from power in Paris, and instead of returning

Democratic-Republican Societies

home to face almost-certain execution he sought political asylum in the United States. But his disappearance from the diplomatic scene did not lessen the continuing impact of the French Revolution in America. The domestic divisions Genet helped to widen were perpetuated by clubs called Democratic-Republican societies, formed by Americans sympathetic to the French Revolution and worried about trends in the Washington administration. The societies thus expressed grassroots concern about the same developments that troubled Jefferson and Madison.

More than forty Democratic-Republican societies were organized between 1793 and 1800, in both rural and urban areas. Their members saw themselves as heirs of the Sons of Liberty, seeking the same goal as their predecessors: protection of the people's liberties against encroachments by corrupt and evil rulers. To that end, they publicly protested government policies and published "addresses to the people" warning of impending tyranny. The societies repeatedly proclaimed their belief in "the equal rights of man," stressing in particular the rights to free speech, free press, and assembly. Like the Sons of Liberty, the Democratic-Republican societies were composed chiefly of artisans and craftsmen of various kinds, although professionals, farmers, and merchants also joined.

The rapid growth of such groups, outspoken in their criticism of the Washington administration for its failure to come to the aid of France and for its domestic economic policies, deeply disturbed Hamilton and eventually Washington himself. Newspapers sympathetic to the Federalists charged that the societies were subversive agents of a foreign power. Their "real design," one asserted, was "to involve the country in war, to assume the reins of government and tyrannize over the people." The climax of the attack came in the fall of 1794, when Washington accused the societies of having fomented the Whiskey Rebellion.

In retrospect, Washington's and Hamilton's reaction to the Democratic-Republican societies seems hysterical, overwrought, and entirely out of proportion to whatever challenge they may have posed to the administration. But it must be kept in mind that "faction" was believed to be dangerous to the survival of a republic. In a monarchy, opposition groups were to be expected, even encouraged. In a government of the people, though, serious and sustained disagreement was taken as a sign of corruption and subversion. The Democratic-Republican societies were the first formally organized political dissenters in the United States. As such, they aroused the fear and suspicion of elected officials who had not yet accepted the idea that one component of a free government was an organized loyal opposition.

That same year George Washington decided to send Chief Justice John Jay to England to try to reach agreement on four major unresolved questions affecting Anglo-American affairs. Jay's diplomatic mission had important domestic consequences. The first point at issue was recent British seizures of American merchant ships trading in the French West Indies. The United States wanted to establish the principle of freedom of the seas and to assert its right, as a neutral nation, to trade freely with both sides. Second, Great Britain had not yet carried out its promise in the Treaty of Paris (1783) to evacuate its posts in the American Northwest. Western settlers believed that the British were responsible for the renewed Indian warfare in the region (see pages 169–171), and they wanted that threat removed. Third and fourth, the Americans hoped for a commercial treaty and sought compensation for the slaves who had left with the British army at the end of the war.

The negotiations in London proved difficult, since Jay had little to offer Britain in exchange for the concessions he wanted. In the end, Britain did agree to evacuate the western forts and ease the restrictions on American trade to England and the West Indies. (Some limitations were retained, however, violating the Americans' stated commitment to open commerce.) No compensation for lost slaves was agreed to, but Jay accepted a provision establishing an arbitration commission to deal with the matter of prewar debts owed to British creditors. A similar commission was to handle the question of compensation for the seizures of American merchant ships. Under the circumstances, Jay had done remarkably well: the treaty averted war with England at a time when the United States, which lacked an effective navy, could not have hoped to win a conflict with its former mother country. Nevertheless, most Americans, including the president, were dissatisfied with at least some parts of the treaty.

Jay Treaty

At first, however, potential opposition was blunted, because the Senate debated and ratified the treaty in secret. Not until after it was formally approved by a vote of 20 to 10 on June 24, 1795, was the public informed of its provisions. The Democratic-Republican societies led protests against the treaty, which were especially intense in the South. Planters criticized Jay's failure to obtain compensation for runaway slaves as well as the commitment to repay prewar debts. Once President Washington had reluctantly signed the treaty, though, there seemed to be little the Republicans could do to prevent it from taking effect. Just one opportunity remained: Congress had to appropriate funds to carry out the treaty provisions, and according to the Constitution money bills had to originate in the House of Representatives.

When the House took up the issue in March 1796, opponents of the treaty tried to prevent approval of the appropriations. To that end, they called on Washington to submit to the House all documents pertinent to the negotiations. In successfully resisting the House's request, Washington established the doctrine of executive privilege—that is, the power of the president to withhold information from Congress if he believes circumstances warrant doing so. Although the treaty's opponents initially appeared to be in the majority, pressure for approval built as time passed. Frontier residents were eager for evacuation of the British posts, fearing a new outbreak of Indian war despite the signing of the Treaty of Greenville the previous year (see page 171). Merchants wanted to reap the benefits of widened trade with the British Empire. Furthermore, Thomas Pinckney of South Carolina had negotiated a treaty with Spain giving the United States navigation privileges on the Mississippi, which would be an economic boost to the West and South. Its popularity (the Senate ratified Pinckney's Treaty unanimously) helped to overcome opposition to the Jay Treaty. For all these reasons the House on April 30, 1796, voted the necessary funds by the narrow margin of 51 to 48.

Analysis of the vote reveals both the regional nature of the division and the growing cohesion of the Republican and Federalist factions in Congress. Voting

Republicans and Federalists in favor of the appropriations were 44 Federalists and 7 Republicans; voting against were 45 Republicans and 3 Federalists. The final tally was also split by region. The vast majority of votes against the bill were cast by southerners (including the three Federalists, who were Virginians). The bill's supporters were largely from New England and the middle states, with the exception of two South Carolina Federalists. The seven Republicans who voted for the appropriations were from commercial areas in New York, Pennsylvania, and Maryland.

The small number of defectors revealed a new force at work in American politics: partisanship. Voting statistics from the first four congresses show the ever-increasing tendency of members of the House of Representatives to vote as coherent groups, rather than as individuals. If factional loyalty is defined as voting together at least two-thirds of the time on national issues, the percentage of nonaligned congressmen dropped from 42 percent in 1790 to just 7 percent in 1796. Also, the majority slowly shifted from Federalist to Republican. Federalists controlled the first three congresses, through spring 1795; Republicans

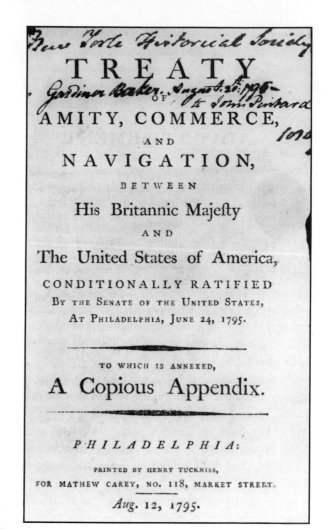

Title page of the Jay Treaty. Publication of the document after its secret ratification by the Senate aroused widespread protest against its terms. The House of Representatives tried but failed to halt its implementation. The New-York Historical Society.

gained the ascendancy in the Fourth Congress; Federalists returned to power with slight majorities in the Fifth and Sixth Congresses; and the Republicans took over in the Seventh Congress in 1801.

To describe these shifts is easier than to explain them. The growing division cannot be accurately explained in the terms used by Jefferson and Madison (aristocrats versus the people) or by Hamilton and Washington (true patriots versus subversive rabble). Simple economic differences between agrarian and commercial interests do not provide the answer either, since more than 90 percent of Americans in the

1790s lived in rural areas. Moreover, Jefferson's vision of a prosperous agrarian America was based on commercial, not self-sufficient, farming. Yet certain distinctions can be made. Republicans tended to be self-assured, confident, and optimistic about both politics and the economy. They did not fear instability, at least among the white population, and they sought to widen the people's participation in government. They foresaw a prosperous future, and looked first to the United States's own resources, second to its position in the world. Republicans also remained sympathetic to France in international affairs.

Federalists, on the other hand, were insecure, uncertain of the future. They stressed the need for order, authority, and regularity in the political world. Unlike Republicans, they had no grassroots political organization and put little emphasis on involving ordinary people in government. The nation was, in their eyes, perpetually threatened by potential enemies, both internal and external, and best protected by a continuing alliance with Great Britain. Their vision of international affairs may have been more accurate, given the warfare in Europe, but it was also narrow and unattractive. Since it held out little hope of a better future to the voters of any region, it is not surprising that the Republicans eventually became dominant.

If the factions' respective attitudes are translated into economic and regional affiliations, the pattern is clear. Northern merchants and commercially oriented farmers, well aware of the uncertainties of international trade, tended to be Federalists. Since New England's soil was poor and agricultural production could not be expanded, northern subsistence farmers also gravitated toward the more conservative party, which wanted to preserve the present (and past) rather than look to the future.

Republican southern planters, on the other hand, firmly in control of their region and of a class of enslaved laborers, could anticipate unlimited westward expansion. Many planters had successfully shifted from the cultivation of soil-draining tobacco to grains and other foodstuffs. The invention of the cotton gin in 1793 allowed southerners to plant many more acres of cotton (see Chapter 11). For their part, small farmers in the South found the Republicans' democratic rhetoric (despite aristocratic leadership) more congenial than the Federalist viewpoint. So too urban artisans,

who stressed their role as independent producers of necessary goods, supported the Republican position.

Finally, the two sides drew supporters from different ethnic groups. Americans of English stock tended to be Federalists, while those of Irish or Scots origin were more likely to be Republicans. Another large group, the Germans, was split fairly evenly at first but eventually moved into the Republican camp. To what degree ethnic antagonisms contributed to the growing political split is impossible to say. But since patterns of migration to and within America (see pages 73–75) rendered regional and ethnic lines largely parallel, it is conceivable that ethnicity was as important as other factors in determining political alignments.

The presence of the two organized groups, not yet parties in the modern sense but nonetheless active contenders for office, made the presidential election of 1796 the first that was seriously contested. George Washington, tired of the criticism to which he had been subjected, decided to retire from office. (Presidents had not yet been limited to two terms by constitutional amendment.) In September Washington published his famous "Farewell Address," most of which was written by Hamilton. Washington outlined two principles that guided American foreign policy at least until the late 1940s: maintain commercial but not political ties to other nations and enter no permanent alliances. He also drew a sharp distinction between the United States and Europe, stressing America's uniqueness and the need for unilateralism (independent action in foreign affairs).

Domestically, Washington lamented the existence of factional divisions among his fellow countrymen. His call for an end to partisan strife has often been interpreted by historians as the statement of a man who could see beyond political affiliations to the good of the whole. But it is more accurately read in the context of its day as an attack on the legitimacy of the Republican opposition. What Washington wanted was unity behind the Federalist banner, which he saw as the only proper political stance. The Federalists (like the Republicans) continued to see themselves as the sole guardians of the truth, the only true heirs of the Revolution, and they perceived their opponents as misguided, unpatriotic troublemakers.

To succeed Washington, the Federalists in Congress put forward the candidacy of Vice President John

Election of 1796 Adams, with the diplomat Thomas Pinckney of South Carolina as his vice-presidential running mate. Congressional Republicans caucused and chose Thomas Jefferson as their candidate; the lawyer, revolutionary war veteran, and active Republican politician Aaron Burr of New York agreed to run for vice president.

That the election was contested did not mean that its outcome was decided by the people. Voters could cast their ballots only for electors, not for the candidates themselves. Many voters did not even have that opportunity, since more than 40 percent of the members of the electoral college that year were chosen by state legislatures, some even before the presidential candidates had been selected. Furthermore, the method of voting prescribed for the electoral college by the Constitution tended to work against the new factions, which was not surprising, since the authors of the Constitution had not foreseen the development of opposing national political organizations. Members of the electoral college were required to vote for two persons, without specifying the office. The man with the highest total became president; the second highest became vice president. In other words, there was no way an elector could explicitly support one person for president and another for vice president.

This procedure proved to be the Federalists' undoing. Adams won the presidency with 71 votes, but a number of Federalist electors (especially those from New England) failed to cast ballots for Pinckney. Thomas Jefferson won 68 votes, 9 more than Pinckney, and became vice president. The incoming administration was thus politically divided. The next four years were to see the new president and vice president, once allies and close friends, become bitter enemies.

JOHN ADAMS AND POLITICAL DISSENT

John Adams took over the presidency peculiarly blind to the partisan developments of the previous four years. As president he never abandoned the outdated notion George Washington had discarded as early as 1794: that the president should be above politics, an independent and dignified figure who did not seek petty factional advantage. Thus Adams kept Washington's cabinet intact, despite its key members' allegiance to his chief rival, Alexander Hamilton. He often adopted a passive posture, letting others (usually Hamilton) take the lead, when he should have acted decisively. As a result his administration gained a reputation for inconsistency. When Adams's term ended, the Federalists were severely divided and the Republicans had won the presidency. But at the same time Adams's detachment from Hamilton's maneuverings enabled him to weather the greatest international crisis the republic had yet faced: the so-called Quasi-War with France.

The Jay Treaty improved America's relationship with England, but it provoked retaliation from France. Angry that the United States had, in effect, abandoned the 1778 French-American treaty, the Directory (the coalition then in power in Paris) ordered French vessels to seize American ships carrying British goods. In response, Adams appointed three special commissioners to try to reach a settlement with France: Elbridge Gerry, an old friend from Massachusetts; John Marshall, a Virginia Federalist; and Charles Cotesworth Pinckney of South Carolina, Thomas's older brother. At the same time Congress increased military spending, authorizing the building of ships and the stockpiling of weapons and ammunition.

For months, the American commissioners futilely sought to open negotiations with Talleyrand, the French foreign minister. But Talleyrand's agents demanded a bribe of $250,000 before **XYZ Affair** talks could begin. The Americans retorted, "No, no; not a sixpence," and reported the incident in dispatches that President Adams received in early March 1798. Adams informed Congress of the impasse and recommended increased appropriations for defense.

Convinced that Adams had deliberately sabotaged the negotiations, congressional Republicans insisted that the dispatches be turned over to Congress. Aware that releasing the reports would work to his advantage, Adams complied. He withheld only the names of the French agents, referring to them as X, Y, and Z. The revelation that the Americans had been treated with utter contempt by the Directory stimulated a wave of anti-French sentiment in the United States. A journalist's version of the commissioners' reply, "Millions for defense, but not a cent for tribute," became the national slogan. Cries for war filled the air. Congress formally abrogated the 1778 treaty and authorized American ships to seize French vessels.

Thus began the United States's first undeclared war. The Quasi-War with France was fought in the West Indies, between French privateers seeking to capture American merchant vessels and warships of the United States Navy. Although initial American losses of merchant shipping were heavy, by early 1799 the navy had established its superiority in Caribbean waters. Its ships captured a total of eight French privateers and naval vessels, easing the threat to America's vital West Indian trade.

The Republicans, who opposed war and continued to sympathize with France, could do little to stem the tide of anti-French feelings. Since Agent Y had boasted of the existence of a "French party in America," Federalists flatly accused the Republicans of traitorous designs. A New York newspaper declared that anyone who remained "lukewarm" after reading the XYZ dispatches was a "criminal—and the man who does not warmly reprobate the conduct of the French must have a soul black enough to be *fit* for *treason Strategems* and *spoils.*" John Adams wavered between calling the Republicans traitors and acknowledging their right to oppose administration measures. His wife was less tolerant: "Those whom the French boast of as their Partizans," Abigail Adams told her older sister, deserved to be "adjudged traitors to their country." If Jefferson had been president, "we should all have been sold to the French."

The Federalists saw this climate of opinion as an opportunity to deal a death blow to their Republican opponents. Now that the country seemed to see the truth of what they had been saying ever since the Whiskey Rebellion in 1794—that the Republicans were subversive foreign agents—the Federalists sought to codify that belief into law. In the spring and summer of 1798, the Federalist-controlled Congress adopted a set of four laws known as the Alien and Sedition Acts, intended to suppress dissent and prevent further growth of the Republican party.

Three of the acts were aimed at immigrants, whom the Federalists quite correctly suspected of being Republican in their sympathies. The Naturalization Act

Alien and Sedition Acts lengthened the residency period required for citizenship from five to fourteen years and ordered all resident aliens to register with the federal government. The Alien Enemies Act provided for the detention of enemy aliens in time of war. The Alien Friends Act, which was to be in effect for only two years, gave the president almost unlimited authority to deport any alien he deemed dangerous to the nation's security. (Adams never used that authority. The Alien Enemies Act was not implemented either, since war was never formally declared.)

The fourth law, the Sedition Act, sought to control both citizens and aliens. It outlawed conspiracies to prevent the enforcement of federal laws and set the maximum punishment for such offenses at five years in prison and a $5,000 fine. The act also tried to control speech. Writing, printing, or uttering "false, scandalous and malicious" statements "against the government of the United States, or the President of the United States, with intent to defame . . . or to bring them or either of them, into contempt or disrepute" became a crime punishable by as much as two years imprisonment and a fine of $2,000. Today the Supreme Court would declare unconstitutional any such law punishing speech alone. But in the eighteenth century, when organized political opposition was regarded with suspicion, the Sedition Act was legally acceptable.

In all, there were fifteen indictments and ten convictions under the Sedition Act. Most of the accused were outspoken Republican newspaper editors who failed to mute their criticism of the administration in response to the law. But the first victim—whose story may serve as an example of the rest—was a Republican congressman from Vermont, Matthew Lyon. The Irish-born Lyon, a former indentured servant who had purchased his freedom and fought in the Revolution, was indicted for declaring in print that John Adams had displayed "a continual grasp for power" and "an unbounded thirst for ridiculous pomp, foolish adulation, and selfish avarice." Though convicted, fined $1,000, and sent to prison for four months, Lyon was not silenced. He conducted his re-election campaign from jail, winning an overwhelming majority. The fine, which he could not afford, was ceremoniously paid by contributions from leading Republicans around the country.

Matthew Lyon, the congressman convicted of violating the Sedition Act, had a fiery temper. In January 1798, before his arrest and trial, he engaged in this brawl with a congressman from Connecticut in the chamber of the House of Representatives.   Library of Congress.

Faced with the prosecutions of their major supporters, Jefferson and Madison sought an effective means of combating the Alien and Sedition Acts.

Virginia and Kentucky Resolutions

Petitioning the Federalist-controlled Congress to repeal the laws would clearly do no good. Furthermore, Federalist judges refused to allow accused persons to question the Sedition Act's constitutionality. Accordingly, the Republican leaders turned to the only other possible mechanism for protest: the state legislatures. Carefully concealing their own role (it would hardly have been desirable for the vice president to be indicted for sedition), Jefferson and Madison each drafted a set of resolutions. Introduced into the Kentucky and

Virginia legislatures respectively in the fall of 1798, the resolutions differed somewhat but their import was the same. Since the Constitution was created by a compact among the states, they contended, the people speaking through their states had a legitimate right to judge the constitutionality of actions by the federal government. Both sets of resolutions pronounced the Alien and Sedition Acts null and void and asked other states to join in the protest.

Although no other state replied positively to the Virginia and Kentucky resolutions, they nevertheless had major significance. In the first place, they were superb political propaganda, rallying Republican opinion throughout the country. They placed the opposition party squarely in the revolutionary tradition

This handpainted banner, ca. 1800, celebrating Thomas Jefferson's victory over John Adams, was found in the early 1960s in Massachusetts. The eagle carries a streamer that reads, "T. Jefferson/President of the United States of America/John Adams no more." Ralph E. Becker Collection, Smithsonian Institution.

of resistance to tyrannical authority. Second, the theory of union they proposed was expanded on by southern states'-rights advocates in the 1830s and thereafter. Jefferson and Madison had identified a key constitutional issue: how far could the states go in opposing the national government? How could a conflict between the two be resolved? These questions were not to be definitively answered until the Civil War.

Ironically, just as the Sedition Act was being implemented and northern state legislatures were rejecting the Virginia and Kentucky resolutions, Federalists split badly over the course of action the United States should take toward France. Hamilton and his supporters still called for a declaration legitimizing the undeclared naval war the two nations had been waging for months. But Adams had received a number of private signals that the Directory now regretted its treatment of the three American commissioners. Acting on these assurances, he dispatched the envoy William Vans Murray to Paris. The United States asked two things of France: nearly $20 million in compensation for ships the French had seized since 1793, and abrogation of the Treaty of 1778. The Convention of 1800, which ended the Quasi-War, included the latter but not the former. Still, it freed the United States from its only permanent alliance, thus allowing it to follow the independent diplomatic course George Washington had outlined in his Farewell Address (see page 194).

The results of the negotiations were not known in the United States until after the presidential election of 1800. Even so, Adams's decision to seek a peaceful settlement probably cost him re-election because of the divisions it caused in Federalist ranks.

In sharp contrast, the Republicans entered the

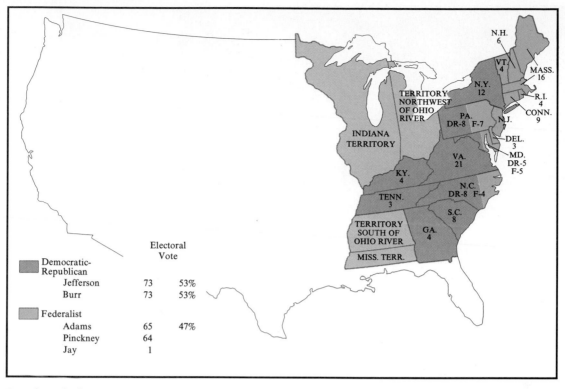

Democratic-Republican

	Electoral Vote	
Jefferson	73	53%
Burr	73	53%

Federalist

Adams	65	47%
Pinckney	64	
Jay	1	

Presidential Election, 1800

1800 presidential race firmly united behind the Jefferson-Burr ticket. Though they won the election, their lack of foresight almost cost them dearly. The problem was caused by the system of voting in the electoral college, which the Federalists understood more clearly than the Republicans. The Federalists arranged in advance for one of their electors to fail to vote for Charles Cotesworth Pinckney, their vice-presidential candidate. John Adams thus received the higher number of Federalist votes (65 to Pinckney's 64). The Republicans failed to make the same distinction between their candidates, and all 73 cast ballots for both Jefferson and Burr (see map). Because neither Republican had a plurality, the Constitution required that the contest be decided in the House of Representatives, with each state's congressmen voting as a unit. Since the new House, dominated by Republicans, would not take office for some months, Federalist congressmen decided the election. It took them thirty-five ballots to decide that Jefferson would be a lesser evil than Burr. As a result of the tangle, the twelfth amendment to the

Election of 1800

Constitution (1804) changed the method of voting in the electoral college to allow for a party ticket.

WESTWARD EXPANSION, SOCIAL CHANGE, AND RELIGIOUS FERMENT

I n the postrevolutionary years, the United States experienced a dramatic increase in internal migration. As much as 5 to 10 percent of the population moved each year, half of them relocating in another state. Young white men were the most mobile segment of the populace, but all groups moved with approximately equal frequency. The major population shifts were from east to west (see map, page 200): from New England to upstate New York, from New Jersey to western Pennsylvania, from the Chesapeake to

Western Expansion, 1785–1805

Chapter 7: Politics and Society in the Early Republic, 1790–1800

the new states of Kentucky and Tennessee, which entered the union in 1792 and 1796, respectively. Very few people moved north or south, the largest proportion being southerners (perhaps yeomen farmers escaping the expansion of slavery) seeking new homes farther north.

Some of these migrants moved west of the Appalachian Mountains. The first permanent white settlements beyond the mountains were established in

White Settlement in the West

western North Carolina in 1771, along the Holston and Wautauga rivers. But not until after the defeat of the Shawnee in 1774 and the Cherokee in 1776 (see pages 135–136) was the way cleared for a more general migration. Small groups of families filtered through the Cumberland Gap into Kentucky, following the Wilderness Road carved out by Daniel Boone in 1775. Once the war had ended, Americans streamed over the mountains in considerably larger numbers. In 1783, only about twelve thousand people lived west of the mountains and south of the Ohio River; less than a decade later, the 1790 census counted more than 100,000 residents of the future states of Kentucky and Tennessee.

North of the Ohio River, white settlements grew more slowly because of the strength of the Miami confederacy. But once the Treaty of Greenville was signed in 1795, Ohio too grew rapidly. Whites migrating to Ohio traveled by land to Pittsburgh, then floated down the river on flatboats and rafts to Marietta or another Ohio River town, where they either stayed or moved farther inland onto farms surveyed under the terms of the land ordinance of 1785 (see pages 169–170).

The westward migration of slaveholding whites, first to Kentucky and Tennessee and then later into the rich lands of western Georgia and eventually the

Blacks in the West

Gulf Coast, had a major adverse impact on Afro-Americans. The web of family connections built up over several generations of residence in the Chesapeake was torn apart by the population movement. Even those few large planters who moved their entire slave force west could not have owned all the members of every family on their plantations. Far more commonly the white migrants were younger sons of eastern slaveholders, whose inheritance in-

cluded only a portion of the family's slaves, or small farmers who owned just one or two blacks. In the early years of American settlement in the West, the population was widely dispersed; accordingly, Chesapeake blacks who had been raised in the midst of large numbers of kin had to adapt to lonely lives on isolated farms, far from their parents, siblings, or even spouses and children. The approximately 100,000 Afro-Americans forcibly moved west by 1810 had to begin to build new families there to replace those unwillingly left behind in the East. They succeeded well, as will be seen in Chapter 11.

The mobility of both blacks and whites created a volatile population mix in frontier areas. Everyone was new to the region and few had relatives nearby. Since most of the migrants were young single men just starting to lead independent lives, western society was at first unstable. Like the seventeenth-century Chesapeake (see page 27), the late-eighteenth-century American West was a society in which single women married quickly. One genteel Connecticut girl, reluctantly moving to Ohio with relatives in 1810 after the death of her parents, was dismayed to find that other travelers assumed she was going west to find a husband after failing to wed in the East. (She did marry within a year.) The other side of the same coin was that the few women among the migrants lamented their lack of congenial female friends. Isolated, far from familiar surroundings, women and men both strove to create new communities to replace those they had left behind.

Perhaps the most meaningful of the new communities was that supplied by evangelical religion. Among the migrants to Kentucky and Tennessee were clergymen and committed lay

Second Great Awakening

members of the evangelical sects that arose in America after the First Great Awakening: Baptists, Presbyterians, and Methodists. The Awakening had flourished in the southern backcountry much later than it had in New England (see pages 94–96), and therefore the Second Great Awakening, which began around 1800 in the West, can in one sense be seen as simply an extension of the first colonial revival to that region. Laymen and clerics alike spread the doctrine of evangelical Christianity through the countryside, carrying the message of salvation to the rootless and largely uneducated frontier folk.

In the early nineteenth century, a French artist traveling in America drew this picture of Methodists en route to a camp meeting. They carry bundles of food and clothing with them. Note the large proportion of women in the crowd. Library of Congress.

At camp meetings, sometimes attended by thousands of people and usually lasting from three days to a week, clergymen exhorted their audiences to repent their sins and become genuine Christians. They stressed that salvation was open to all, downplaying the doctrine of predestination that had characterized orthodox colonial Protestantism. The emotional nature of the conversion experience was emphasized far more than the need for careful study and preparation. Such preachers thus brought the message of religion to the people in more ways than one. They were in effect "democratizing" American religion, making it available to all rather than to a preselected and educated elite.

The most famous camp meeting took place at Cane Ridge, Kentucky, in 1801. At a time when the largest settlement in the state had no more than two thousand inhabitants, attendance at Cane Ridge was estimated at between ten and twenty-five thousand. One witness, a Presbyterian cleric, marveled that "no sex nor color, class nor description, were exempted from the pervading influence of the spirit; even from the age of eight months to sixty years, there were evident subjects of this marvellous operation." He went on to recount how people responded to the preaching with "loud ejaculations of prayer, . . . some struck with terror, . . . others, trembling, weeping and crying out . . . fainting and swooning away, . . . others surrounding them with melodious songs, or fervent prayers for their happy resurrection, in the love of Christ." Such scenes were to be repeated many times in the decades that followed. Revivals swept across different regions of the country until nearly the middle of the century, leaving an indelible legacy of evangelism to American Protestant churches.

The sources of the Second Great Awakening, which revitalized Protestant Christianity in the United States during the nineteenth century, were embedded in late-eighteenth-century American society in the East as well as the West. From the 1760s through the 1780s, religious concerns had been subordinated to secular affairs, as clergymen and lay people of all denominations had concentrated their energies on war and politics. Indeed, clerics had created a kind of "civil religion" for the nation, in which the fervor of the veneration for the republic sometimes surpassed the fervor of religious worship. Moreover, the orthodox churches, showing the influence of Enlightenment thought, had for decades stressed reason more than revelation. Circumstances were thus ripe for a movement of spiritual renewal that would appeal to the emotional side of people's natures.

In addition, America's largest Protestant denominations had to find new sources of financial and membership support after the Revolution. In the colonial period, most of the provinces had had established, or state-supported, churches. In Massachusetts, for example, the Congregational church had been financed by taxes levied on all residents of the state, not just the members of that church. The same was true of the Church of England in such southern colonies as Virginia and South Carolina. Before the war, the protests of religious dissenters, like Baptists, had fallen on deaf ears. Yet they too—like other disadvantaged groups in American society—learned to use revolutionary ideology for their own purposes. Isaac Backus, a New England Baptist, pointed out forcefully that "many, who are filling the nation with the cry of LIBERTY and against *oppressors* are at the same time themselves violating that dearest of all rights, LIBERTY OF CONSCIENCE." Legislators could not resist the logic of such arguments. Many states dissolved their ties to churches during or immediately after the war, and others vastly reduced state support for established denominations.

These changes meant that congregations could no longer rely on tax revenues and that all churches were placed on the same footing with respect to the government. Church membership was now entirely

Disestablishment of Religion

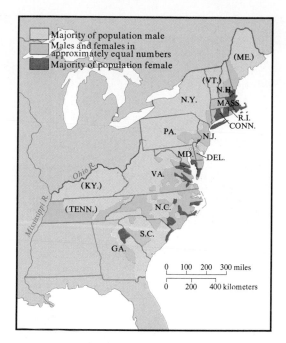

Sex Ratio of White Population, 1790

voluntary, as were monetary contributions from members. If congregations were to survive, they had to generate new sources of support, by increasing their number of enthusiastic members; revivals proved a convenient means of doing so. The revivals represented genuine outpourings of religious sentiment, but their more mundane function must not be overlooked.

An analysis of secular society can help to explain the conversion patterns of the Second Awakening. Unlike the First Great Awakening, when converts were evenly divided by sex, more women than men—particularly young women—answered the call of Christianity during the Second Awakening. The increase in female converts seems to have been directly related to major changes in women's circumstances at the end of the eighteenth century. In some areas of the country, especially New England (where the revival movement flourished), women outnumbered men after 1790, since many young men had migrated westward (see map). Thus eastern girls could no longer count on finding marital partners. The uncertainty of their social and familial position seems to have led them to seek spiritual certainty in the church.

Young women's domestic roles changed dramatically

Women and the Second Awakening

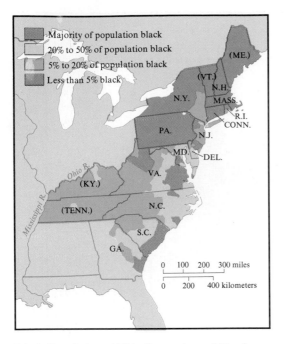

Black Population, 1790: Proportion of Total Population *Source: Reprinted by permission of Princeton University Press.*

at the same time, as cloth production began to move from the household to the factory (see page 254). Deprived of their chief household role as spinners and weavers, New England daughters found in the church a realm where they could continue to make useful contributions to society. Church missionary societies and charitable associations provided an acceptable outlet for their talents. One of the most striking developments of the early nineteenth century was the creation of hundreds of female associations to aid widows and orphans, collect money for foreign missions, or improve the quality of maternal care. Thus American women collectively assumed the role of keepers of the nation's conscience, taking the lead—via their churches—in charitable enterprise, and freeing their husbands from concern for such moral issues.

The religious ferment among both blacks and whites in frontier regions of the Upper South contributed to racial ferment as well. People of both races attended the camp meetings, and sometimes black preachers exhorted whites in addition to members of their own race. When revivals spread eastward

Blacks and the Second Awakening

into more heavily slaveholding areas, white planters became fearful of the egalitarianism implied in the evangelical message of universal salvation and harmony. At the same time, revivals created a group of respected black leaders—preachers—and provided them with a ready audience for a potentially revolutionary doctrine.

Recent events in the West Indies gave whites ample reason for apprehension. In the 1790s, over the course of several years, mulattoes and blacks in the French colony of Saint Domingue (Haiti) overthrew European rule under the leadership of a mulatto, Toussaint L'Ouverture. The revolt was bloody, vicious, prolonged, and characterized by numerous atrocities committed by both sides. In an attempt to prevent the spread of such unrest to their own slaves, southern state legislators passed laws forbidding white Haitian refugees from bringing their slaves with them. But North American blacks learned about the revolt anyway. Furthermore, the preconditions for racial upheaval did not have to be imported into the South from the West Indies: they already existed on the spot.

The Revolution had caused immense destruction in the South, especially in the states south of Virginia. The heavy losses of slaves and constant guerrilla warfare, not to mention the changes in American trading patterns brought about by withdrawal from the British Empire, wreaked havoc on the southern economy. After the war Lower South planters rushed to replace their lost work force; the postwar decades therefore witnessed the single most massive influx of Africans into North America since the beginnings of the slave trade. Before the legal trade was halted in 1808, more than ninety thousand new Africans had been imported into the United States.

The vast postwar increase in the number of free blacks severely strained the system of race relations that had evolved during the eighteenth century. Color, caste, and slave status no longer coincided, as they had when the few free blacks were all mulattoes (see map). Furthermore, like their white compatriots, blacks (both slave and free) had become familiar with notions of liberty and equality. They had also witnessed the benefits of fighting collectively for freedom, rather than resisting individually or running away. The circumstances were ripe for an explosion, and the Second Awakening was the match that lit the fuse in both Virginia and North Carolina.

The Virginia revolt was planned by Gabriel Prosser, a blacksmith who argued that blacks should fight to obtain the same rights as whites, and who explicitly placed himself in the tradition of the French and Haitian revolutions.

Gabriel's Rebellion At revival meetings led by his brother Martin, a preacher, Gabriel recruited other blacks like himself—artisans who moved easily in both black and white circles and who lived in semifreedom under minimal white supervision. The artisan leaders then enlisted rural blacks in the cause. The conspirators planned to attack Richmond on the night of August 30, 1800, setting fire to the city, seizing the state capitol, and capturing the governor. Their plan showed considerable political sophistication, but heavy rain made it impossible to execute the plot as scheduled. Several whites then learned of the plan from their slaves and spread the alarm. Gabriel avoided capture for some weeks, but most of the other leaders of the rebellion were quickly arrested and interrogated. The major conspirators, including Prosser himself, were hanged, but in the months that followed other insurrectionary scares continued to frighten Virginia slaveowners.

Two years later a similar wave of fear swept North Carolina and the bordering counties of Virginia. A slave conspiracy to attack planters' homes, kill all whites except small children, and seize the land was uncovered in Bertie County. Similar plots were rumored elsewhere. Again, slave artisans and preachers played prominent roles in the planned uprisings. Nearly fifty blacks were executed as a result of the whites' investigations of the rumors. Some were certainly innocent victims of the planters' hysteria, but there can be no doubt about the existence of most of the plots.

Significantly, the Iroquois were affected by a religious revival at the same time as American whites and blacks were experiencing the Second Great Awakening. Led by their prophet, Handsome Lake, the remaining American Iroquois, who were scattered on small reservations, embraced the traditional values of their culture and renounced such destructive white customs as drinking alcohol and playing cards. At the same time, though, they began abandoning their ancient way of life. With Handsome Lake's approval, Quaker missionaries taught the Iroquois Anglo-American styles of agricultural subsistence; men were

IMPORTANT EVENTS	
1789	George Washington inaugurated Judiciary Act of 1789 French Revolution begins
1790	Alexander Hamilton's first "Report on Public Credit"
1791	First ten amendments (Bill of Rights) ratified
1793	France declares war on Britain, Spain, and Holland Neutrality Proclamation Democratic-Republican societies founded
1794	Whiskey Rebellion
1795	Jay Treaty
1796	First contested presidential election: John Adams elected president, Thomas Jefferson vice president
1798	XYZ affair Alien and Sedition Acts Virginia and Kentucky resolutions
1798–99	Quasi-War with France
1800	Franco-American Convention Jefferson elected president, Aaron Burr vice president Second Great Awakening begins Gabriel's Rebellion

now to be cultivators rather than hunters and women housekeepers rather than cultivators. Since the tribes had lost their hunting territories to white farmers, Iroquois men accepted the changes readily. But many women—especially the powerful tribal matrons—resisted the shift in the gender division of labor. They realized that when they surrendered control over food production they would jeopardize their status in the tribe. But Handsome Lake branded as "witches" any women who opposed the changes too vigorously, and eventually he triumphed. A division of work by sex continued to characterize Iroquois economic organization, but the specific tasks assigned to men and women changed completely. In order to maintain some cultural autonomy, the Iroquois had to adopt an economic system resembling that of the dominant whites.

Their plight may be taken as symbolic of that of tribes located west of the Appalachians, for they too would have to find ways of accommodating themselves to the dominant Anglo-American culture. Although most had yet to feel the full force of the whites' westward thrust, the weapon that had served the Iroquois and other interior tribes so well—the countervailing presence of England, France, and Spain—was not available to them. Now that the United States had established its independence, western tribes had no alternative but to confront directly the problems posed by land-hungry whites. They would delay but not halt the expansion of the United States.

As the new century began, then, white, red, and black inhabitants of the United States were moving toward an accommodation to their new circumstances. The United States was starting to take shape as a free nation no longer dependent on England. In domestic politics, the Jeffersonian interpretation of republicanism had prevailed over the Hamiltonian approach. As a result, the country would be characterized by a decentralized economy, minimal government (especially at the national level), and maximum freedom of action and mobility for individual white males.

But that freedom would be purchased at the expense of white females and black men, women, and children. In the decades to come, both groups would be subject to further control. To prevent a recurrence of outbreaks of violence like those of 1800 through 1802, slaveholders increased the severity of the slave codes, further restricting their human property. Before long, all talk of emancipation (gradual or otherwise) ceased, and slavery became even more firmly entrenched as an economic institution and way of life. Likewise, the Revolution's implicit promise for women was never fully realized. Woman's place was still in the home; in the first half of the nineteenth century an unprecedented outpouring of books and magazine articles asserted that conclusion with ever greater force

and fervor. Jeffersonian Republicans, like almost all Americans before them, failed to extend to women the freedom and individuality they recognized as essential for men.

SUGGESTIONS FOR FURTHER READING

National Government and Administration

Ralph Adams Brown, *The Presidency of John Adams* (1975); John R. Howe, *The Changing Political Thought of John Adams* (1966); Richard H. Kohn, *Eagle and Sword: The Federalists and the Creation of the Military Establishment in America, 1783–1802* (1975); Stephen G. Kurtz, *The Presidency of John Adams: The Collapse of Federalism, 1795–1800* (1957); Forrest McDonald, *Alexander Hamilton: A Biography* (1979); Forrest McDonald, *The Presidency of George Washington* (1974); John C. Miller, *The Federalist Era, 1789–1801* (1960); Merrill D. Peterson, *Thomas Jefferson & The New Nation: A Biography* (1970); Carl E. Prince, *The Federalists and the Origins of the U.S. Civil Service* (1978); Leonard D. White, *The Federalists: A Study in Administrative History* (1948); Garry Wills, *Cincinnatus: George Washington and the Enlightenment* (1984).

Partisan Politics

Leland D. Baldwin, *The Whiskey Rebels* (1939); Lance Banning, *The Jeffersonian Persuasion: Evolution of a Party Ideology* (1978); Richard Beeman, *The Old Dominion and the New Nation, 1788–1801* (1972); Richard W. Buel, Jr., *Securing the Revolution: Ideology in American Politics, 1789–1815* (1972); William Nisbet Chambers, *Political Parties in a New Nation: The American Experience, 1776–1809* (1963); Joseph Charles, *The Origins of the American Party System* (1956); Noble E. Cunningham, *The Jeffersonian Republicans: The Formation of Party Organization, 1789–1801* (1957); Manning J. Dauer, *The Adams Federalists* (1953); Paul Goodman, *The Democratic Republicans of Massachusetts* (1964); Richard Hofstadter, *The Idea of a Party System: The Rise of Legitimate Opposition in the United States, 1780–1840* (1970); Adrienne Koch, *Jefferson and Madison: The Great Collaboration* (1950); Eugene P. Link, *Democratic-*

Republican Societies, 1790–1800 (1942); Norman K. Risjord, *Chesapeake Politics, 1781–1800* (1978); Patricia Watlington, *The Partisan Spirit: Kentucky Politics, 1779–1792* (1972); Alfred F. Young, *The Democratic-Republicans of New York: The Origins, 1763–1797* (1967); John Zvesper, *Political Philosophy and Rhetoric: A Study of the Origins of American Party Politics* (1977).

Foreign Policy

Harry Ammon, *The Genet Mission* (1973); Samuel F. Bemis, *Jay's Treaty*, 2nd ed. (1962); Samuel F. Bemis, *Pinckney's Treaty*, 2nd ed. (1960); Jerald A. Combs, *The Jay Treaty* (1970); Alexander DeConde, *Entangling Alliance: Politics and Diplomacy under George Washington* (1958); Alexander DeConde, *The Quasi-War: Politics and Diplomacy of the Undeclared War with France, 1797–1801* (1966); Felix Gilbert, *To the Farewell Address: Ideas of Early American Foreign Policy* (1961); Reginald Horsman, *The Diplomacy of the New Republic, 1776–1815* (1985); Bradford Perkins, *The First Rapprochement: England and the United States, 1795–1805* (1967); Charles Ritcheson, *Aftermath of Revolution: British Policy Toward the United States, 1783–1795* (1969); William Stinchcombe, *The XYZ Affair* (1981); Paul A. Varg, *Foreign Policies of the Founding Fathers* (1963).

Civil Liberties

Leonard W. Levy, *Origins of the Fifth Amendment* (1968); Leonard W. Levy, *Legacy of Suppression: Freedom of Speech and Press in Early American History* (1960); Robert A. Rutland, *The Birth of the Bill of Rights, 1776–1791* (1955); James Morton Smith, *Freedom's Fetters: The Alien and Sedition Laws and American Civil Liberties* (1956).

Women and Blacks

Ira Berlin and Ronald Hoffman, eds., *Slavery and Freedom in the Age of the American Revolution* (1983); Nancy F. Cott, *The Bonds of Womanhood: "Woman's Sphere" in New England, 1780–1835* (1977); Nancy F. Cott, "Young Women in the Second Great Awakening in New England," *Feminist Studies*, 3, No. 1/2 (1975), 15–29; Jeffrey J. Crow, "Slave Rebelliousness and Social Conflict in North Carolina, 1775 to 1802," *William and Mary Quarterly*, 3rd ser., 37 (1980), 79–102; Gerald W. Mullin, *Flight and Rebellion: Slave Resistance in Eighteenth-Century Virginia* (1972).

Social Change and Westward Expansion

Mary H. Blewett, "Work, Gender, and the Artisan Tradition in New England Shoemaking, 1780–1860," *Journal of Social History*, 17 (1983), 221–248; Reginald Horsman, *The Frontier in the Formative Years 1783–1815* (1970); Howard Rock, *Artisans of the New Republic: The Tradesmen of New York City in the Age of Thomas Jefferson* (1979); Malcolm Rohrbough, *The Trans-Appalachian Frontier: Peoples, Societies, and Institutions, 1775–1850* (1979); W. J. Rorabaugh, *The Alcoholic Republic: An American Tradition* (1979); Charles G. Steffen, *The Mechanics of Baltimore: Workers and Politics in the Age of Revolution, 1763–1812* (1984); Sean Wilentz, *Chants Democratic: New York City and the Rise of the American Working Class, 1788–1850* (1984).

Religion

Sydney Ahlstrom, *A Religious History of the American People* (1972); Catharine Albanese, *Sons of the Fathers: The Civil Religion of the American Revolution* (1976); Fred J. Hood, *Reformed America 1783–1837* (1980); William McLoughlin, *Revivals, Awakenings, and Reform* (1978).

THE EMPIRE OF LIBERTY
1801–1824

CHAPTER 8

"*I have this* morning witnessed one of the most interesting scenes a free people can ever witness," Margaret B. Smith, a Philadelphian, wrote on March 4, 1801, to her sister-in-law. "The changes of administration, which in every government and in every age have most generally been epochs of confusion, villainy and bloodshed, in this our happy country take place without any species of distraction, or disorder." On that day, Thomas Jefferson strolled from his New Jersey Avenue boardinghouse in the new federal capital of Washington, D.C., to be sworn in as president at the Capitol building. The precedent of an orderly and peaceful change of government had been established.

Jefferson's inauguration marked a change of style in government, at the beginning of a period when Americans were struggling to assert and define their nationalism amid challenges, both foreign and domestic. Almost overnight the formality of the Federalist presidencies of Washington and Adams was significantly altered as Jefferson set the tone for the Republican government. Gone were the aristocratic wigs and breeches (knee-length trousers) the first two presidents had favored; Jefferson wore plainer garb. Though personally richer and with more luxurious tastes than Adams, Jefferson rejected the aristocratic and wealthy pretensions he associated with the Federalists. Republican virtue would be restored.

Ordinary folk who had come to celebrate Jefferson's inaugural overran Washington, causing Federalists to cluck their tongues at the seeming collapse of authority and order. For two weeks following the inauguration, Jefferson still lived and worked at his modest lodgings a few blocks from the Capitol. He ran the presidency from the parlor next to his bedroom and continued to eat at the communal dining table. Not until March 19 did he move to the president's mansion.

The government had moved to Washington from Philadelphia in November 1800, and its unfinished federal buildings seemed to symbolize the unfinished nation. Augustus John Foster, a British diplomat, lamented the move. The diplomatic corps, he reported, found it "difficult to digest" moving from "agreeable," urban Philadelphia "to what was then scarce any better than a mere swamp." Abigail Adams found it "the very dirtyest Hole," its streets "a quagmire after every rain." On the other hand, Washington offered amusements unlike any other Atlantic capital. "Excellent snipe shooting and even partridge shooting was to be had on each side of the main [Pennsylvania] avenue and even close under the wall of the Capitol," Foster recalled. But the simpler lifestyle seemed to suit the change from the formality of the Federalist government to the less pretentious Republican administration.

The new district, carved out of Maryland and Virginia, had been chosen because of its central location. Washington was thus beholden to neither the colonial past nor any single state. Few buildings were needed to house the government, which essentially collected tariffs, delivered mail, and defended the nation's borders. But a small government suited the republic. Even for the Federalists, the adoption of the Constitution and their holding power in the 1790s had been more a result of dissatisfaction with the Articles of Confederation than a sign of their confidence in central government. The election of the Republican Thomas Jefferson in 1800 began the Virginia dynasty and a swing back to state authority that lasted until 1825. In an age when it took some congressmen more than a week to reach the capital, most Americans favored government closer to home.

The transfer of power to the Republicans from the Federalists intensified political conflict and voter interest. Republican presidents sought, in the Revolutionary War tradition, to limit government and decentralize authority. Federalists prized a stronger national government with more order and authority in a centralized system. With both parties competing for adherents and popular support, the basis was laid for the evolution of democratic party politics. But factionalism and the partisanship of personal disputes within each party prevented the development of true political parties, and the Federalists, unable to build a popular base, slowly disappeared as an organized opposition party.

Events abroad both encouraged and threatened the expansionism of the young nation. Seizing one opportunity, the United States purchased the Louisiana Territory, pushing the frontier further west. But then from the high seas came war. Caught between the British and the French, the United States found itself a victim of European conflict with its shipping rights as a neutral, independent nation ignored and violated. When the humiliation became too great, Americans took up arms in the War of 1812 both to defend their rights as a nation and to expand farther to the west and north. Although unprepared for combat, the United States fought Great Britain to a standstill. The peace treaty merely restored the prewar status quo, but the war and the treaty nevertheless reaffirmed American independence and determination to steer clear of European conflicts, and led to growing accommodation with Great Britain.

The War of 1812 unleashed a wave of nationalism and self-confidence. The disruption of trade with Europe during the war promoted the development of manufacturing in the United States. The war also pointed up the need for better transportation within the country. Following the war, the government became the champion of business and promoted the building of roads and canals. The new spirit encouraged economic growth and western expansion at home and assertiveness throughout the hemisphere, as was evident in the Monroe Doctrine. By the 1820s the United States was no longer an experiment; a new nation had emerged. Free of its colonial past, the country began energetically shaping its own identity.

Growth and expansion did generate new problems, however. A financial panic brought hardship and conflict in 1819, which sowed the seeds for the Jacksonian movement in the 1830s. More ominously, sectional differences and the presence of slavery created divisions that would widen in the wake of further westward expansion during the 1840s and 1850s.

JEFFERSON IN POWER

Jefferson delivered his inaugural address in the Senate chamber, the only part of the Capitol that had been completed. Nearly a thousand people strained to hear his barely audible voice. "We are

Jefferson's Inaugural Address all Republicans, we are all Federalists," he told the assembly in an appeal for unity. Confidently addressing those with little faith in the people's ability to govern themselves, he called America's republican government "the world's best hope." If "man cannot be trusted with the government of himself," Jefferson argued, "can he, then, be trusted with the government of others? Or have we found angels in the forms of kings to govern him? Let history answer this question."

The new president went on to outline his own and his party's republican goals:

A wise and frugal government, which shall restrain men from injuring one another, which shall leave them otherwise free to regulate their own pursuits. . . .

Equal and exact justice to all men, of whatever state or persuasion, religious or political. . . .

The support of the state governments in all their rights, as the most competent administrators for our domestic concerns and the surest bulwarks against antirepublican tendencies.

At the same time, he assured Federalists that he shared some of their concerns as well:

The preservation of the general government in its whole constitutional vigor. . . .

The honest payment of our debts and sacred preservation of the public faith. . . .

Encouragement of agriculture and of commerce as its handmaid.

Yet Jefferson and his fellow Republicans distrusted the Federalists. They considered them to be antidemocratic and antirepublican at heart and accused them of imitating the court society of England. One of Jefferson's first acts was to extend the grasp of Republicanism over the federal government. Virtually all appointed officials were loyal Federalists: of the six hundred or so appointed under Washington and Adams, only six were known Republicans. To counteract Federalist power and restore government to those who shared his vision of an agrarian republic, Jefferson refused to recognize Adams's last-minute "midnight appointments" to local offices in the District of Columbia. Next he dismissed Federalist customs collectors from New England ports. Vacant treasury and judicial offices were awarded to Republicans,

Trumbull's formal portrait of Thomas Jefferson. Increasingly Jefferson came to disdain wearing a wig and preferred plainer garb. At his inaugural he was simply dressed as he spoke to his fellow citizens of republican virtue and reconciliation. The Metropolitan Museum of Art.

until by July 1803 only 130 of 316 presidentially controlled offices were held by Federalists. Jefferson, in restoring political balance in government, used patronage to reward his friends, to build a party organization, and to compete with the Federalists.

The Republican Congress similarly proceeded to affirm its republicanism. Guided by Secretary of the Treasury Albert Gallatin and John Randolph of Virginia, Jefferson's ally in the House, the federal government went on a diet. Congress repealed all internal taxes, even the whiskey tax. Gallatin cut the army budget in half, to just under $2 million, and reduced the navy budget from $3.5 to $1 million in 1802. Moreover, Gallatin laid plans to reduce the national debt—Alexander Hamilton's engine of economic growth—from $83 to $57 million, as part of a plan

to retire it altogether by 1817. Jefferson even closed two of the nation's five diplomatic missions abroad—the Hague and Berlin—to save money.

More than frugality, however, separated Republicans from Federalists. Opposition to the Alien and Sedition laws of 1798 had helped unite Republicans before Jefferson's election (see pages 196–199). Now as president, Jefferson forswore using the acts against his opponents, as President Adams had, and Congress let them expire in 1801 and 1802. Congress also repealed the Naturalization Act of 1798, which had required fourteen years of residency for citizenship. The 1802 act that replaced it required only five years of residency, acceptance of the Constitution, and the forsaking of foreign allegiance and titles. The new act would remain the basis of naturalized American citizenship into the twentieth century.

The Republicans turned next to the judiciary, the last stronghold of unchecked Federalist power. During the 1790s not a single Republican had been appointed to the federal bench. Moreover, the

Attacks on the Judiciary Judiciary Act of 1801, passed in the last days of the Adams administration, had created fifteen new judgeships (which Adams filled in his midnight appointments, signing appointments until his term was just hours away from expiring) and would reduce by attrition the number of justices on the Supreme Court from six to five. Since that reduction would have denied Jefferson any Supreme Court appointments until two vacancies had occurred, the new Republican-dominated Congress repealed the 1801 act as one of its first moves.

Republicans also targeted opposition judges for removal. Federalist judges had refused to review the Sedition Act, and Federalists had prosecuted critics of the administration under the act. At Jefferson's suggestion, the House impeached (indicted) Federal District Judge John Pickering of New Hampshire; in 1804 the Senate removed him from office. Although he was an alcoholic and emotionally disturbed, Pickering had not committed any crime.

The same day Pickering was convicted, the House impeached Supreme Court Justice Samuel Chase for judicial misconduct. Chase, an arch-Federalist and leader in pressing convictions under the Sedition Act, had repeatedly denounced Jefferson's administration from the bench. The Republicans, however, failed to muster the two-thirds majority necessary to convict him; they had gone too far. Their failure to remove Chase preserved the Court's independence and established a precedent for narrow interpretation of the grounds for impeachment (criminal rather than political). Time soon cured Republican grievances; by the year Jefferson left office, he had appointed three new Supreme Court justices. Nonetheless, under Chief Justice John Marshall, the Court remained a Federalist stronghold.

Marshall was an astute lawyer with keen political sense. A Virginia Federalist who had served under George Washington in the Revolutionary War, he had been minister to France and **John Marshall** then secretary of state under President Adams before being named chief justice. Jefferson considered Marshall a midnight appointment, believing that any appointment after Adams learned of his defeat in the electoral college on December 12, 1800, was wrong and immoral, if not illegal. But Congress approved the appointment in January 1801 before Jefferson was sworn in as president.

Although he was an autocrat by nature, Marshall possessed a grace and openness of manner well suited to the new Republican political style. Under Marshall's domination, the Supreme Court retained a Federalist viewpoint even after Republican justices achieved a majority in 1811. Throughout his tenure (from 1801 until 1835), the Court upheld federal supremacy over the states and protected the interests of commerce and capital.

More important, Marshall made the Court an equal branch of government in practice as well as theory. First, he made a place on the Court a coveted honor. Prior to Marshall it had been difficult to keep the Court filled. Fifteen justices had served on the six-member Court during its first twelve years; after Marshall's appointment it took forty years for fifteen new members to be appointed. Marshall's presence had made the Court worthy of ambitious and talented men. Second, he unifed the Court, influencing the justices to issue single majority opinions rather than individual concurring judgments. Marshall himself became the voice of the majority. From 1801 through 1805 he wrote 24 of the Court's 26 decisions; through 1810 he wrote 85 percent of the 171 opinions, including every important decision.

John Marshall (1755–1835), chief justice of the Supreme Court from 1801 to 1835. This portrait shows the strength of personality that enabled Marshall to make the Court into a Federalist stronghold. Supreme Court of the United States.

Finally, Marshall increased the Court's power. *Marbury* v. *Madison* (1803) was the landmark case that enabled Marshall to strengthen the Court. William Marbury had been designated **Marbury v.** a justice of the peace in the District **Madison** of Columbia as part of Adams's midnight appointments of March 2, 1801. He now sued the new secretary of state, James Madison, for failing to certify his appointment so that Jefferson could appoint a Republican. In his suit Marbury requested a writ of mandamus (a court order compelling Madison to appoint him).

At first glance, the case presented a political dilemma. Even if the Supreme Court ruled in favor of Marbury and issued a writ of mandamus, the president might not comply. After all, why should the president, sworn to uphold the Constitution, allow the Court to decide for him what was constitutional? On the other hand, if the Court refused to issue the writ, it would be handing the Republicans a victory. Marshall avoided both alternatives. Speaking for the Court, he ruled that Marbury had a right to his commission but that the Court could not compel Madison to honor it, because the Constitution did not grant the Court power to issue a writ of mandamus. Thus Marshall declared unconstitutional Section 13 of the Judiciary Act of 1789, which authorized the Court to issue such writs. Marbury lost his job and the justices denied themselves the power to issue writs of mandamus, but the Supreme Court claimed its power to judge the constitutionality of laws passed by Congress.

In succeeding years Marshall fashioned the theory of judicial review. Since the Constitution was the supreme law, he reasoned, any act of Congress contrary to the Constitution must be null and void. And since the Supreme Court was responsible for upholding the law, it had a duty to decide whether or not a conflict existed between a legislative act and the Constitution. If such a conflict did indeed exist, the Court would declare the congressional act unconstitutional.

Marshall's decision rebuffed Republican criticism of the Court as a partisan instrument. He avoided a confrontation with the Republican-dominated Congress by not ruling on its repeal of the 1801 Judiciary Act. And he enhanced the Court's independence by claiming the power of judicial review.

While President Jefferson fought with the Federalist judiciary and struggled to reduce federal spending, he kept a wary eye on the Louisiana Territory. Louisiana, France's largest colony in the

Louisiana Purchase

New World, defined the western United States border along the Mississippi from the Gulf of Mexico to present-day Minnesota. It had been ceded to Spain in 1762 at the end of the French and Indian War (see page 105). Jefferson shared with other Americans the belief that the United States was destined to expand its "empire of liberty." Since the first days of American independence, Louisiana had held a special place in the young nation's expansionist dreams. By 1800, hundreds of thousands of Americans in search of land had trekked into the rich Mississippi and Ohio valleys to settle, often intruding on Indian lands. Down the Mississippi and Ohio rivers to New Orleans they floated their farm goods for export.

Thus, whoever controlled the port of New Orleans had a hand on the throat of the American economy. As long as Spain owned Louisiana, Americans did not fear. But in 1802 Napoleonic France acquired the vast territory in an ambitious bid to rebuild its empire in the New World. The transfer, moaned Jefferson, "works most sorely" on the United States. Fears intensified even more in October 1802, when Spanish officials, on the eve of ceding control to the French, violated Pinckney's Treaty (see page 193), by denying Americans the privilege of storing their products at New Orleans prior to transshipment to foreign markets. Western farmers and eastern merchants thought a devious Napoleon had closed the port; they grumbled and talked war.

To relieve the pressure for war and to prevent westerners from joining Federalists in opposition to his administration, Jefferson simultaneously prepared for war and accelerated talks with the French. In January 1803 he sent James Monroe to France to help the American minister Robert Livingston in negotiating to buy New Orleans. Meanwhile, Congress authorized a call-up of eighty thousand militia if it proved necessary. Arriving in Paris in April, Monroe was astonished to learn that France had already offered to sell all 827,000 square miles of Louisiana to the United States for $15 million. On April 30 Monroe and Livingston signed a treaty to purchase the vast territory, whose borders were left undefined at that time (see map).

The Louisiana Purchase doubled the size of the nation and opened the way for westward expansion across the continent. The acquisition was the single most popular achievement of Jefferson's presidency. Yet for Jefferson, the purchase presented a dilemma. It promised fulfillment of the dream of a continental nation reaching to the Pacific Coast, "with room enough for our descendants to the hundredth and thousandth generation," as he put it. And it offered a solution to Indian-settler conflict in the frontier by providing land to which eastern tribes, North and South, could be removed. But its legality was questionable. The Constitution gave him no clear authority to acquire new territory and incorporate it into the nation. Jefferson considered requesting a constitutional amendment to allow the purchase, but in the end he justified it on the grounds that it was part of the

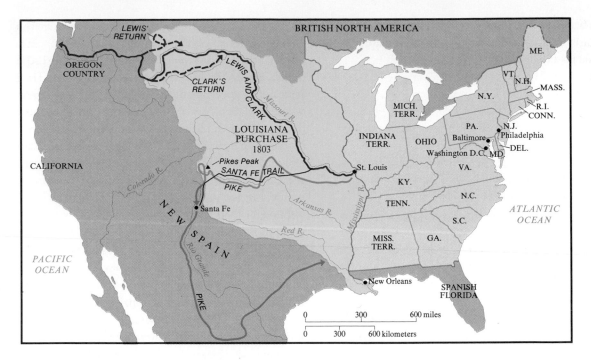

Louisiana Purchase

president's implied powers to protect the nation. The people, he knew, would accept or reject the purchase on election day in 1804.

The president had had a long-standing interest in Louisiana and the West. As early as 1782, as an American envoy in France, Jefferson had suggested sending an exploratory mission across the continent to California. As secretary of state ten years later he commissioned a French emigré, André Michaux, to explore the Missouri River. Allegations of Michaux's complicity in the Genet Affair (see page 191) aborted this mission. In 1803 Jefferson renewed Michaux's

Lewis and Clark

instructions when he sent Meriwether Lewis and William Clark to the Pacific Ocean via the Missouri and Columbia rivers. Lewis and Clark, from 1804 to 1806, headed the nearly fifty-strong "Corps of Discovery," which was aided by trappers and American Indians along the way. A French-Canadian trader and his young Shoshone wife, Toussaint Charbonneau and Sacajawea, joined the expedition. Sacajawea interpreted both the terrain and the languages of the West to the wanderers in a strange land.

The Lewis and Clark expedition, planned in secrecy before the Louisiana Purchase, reflected both Jefferson's scientific curiosity and his interest in western commercial development, especially the prospects of the fur and China trades. Other explorers soon followed them, led in 1805 and 1806 by Lieutenant Zebulon Pike in search of the source of the Mississippi. A year later Pike attempted to find a navigable path to the Far West and sought the headwaters of the Arkansas River. He reached the Rocky Mountains in present-day Colorado, though he never made it to the top of the peak that bears his name. Pike and his men wandered into Spanish territory to the south, where the Spanish arrested them and held them captive for several months in Santa Fe. After his release, Pike wrote an account of his experiences that set commercial minds spinning. He described a potential commercial market in southwestern Spanish cities as well as the bounty of furs and precious minerals to be had. The vision of the road to the Southwest became a reality with the opening of the Santa Fe Trail in the 1820s. Over the next few decades Americans avidly read published accounts of western exploration. Expansion and the West had caught their imagination, and Jefferson considered the acquisition of Louisiana and the opening of the West among his greatest presidential accomplishments.

REPUBLICANS VERSUS FEDERALISTS

Campaigning for re-election in 1804, Jefferson claimed credit for western expansion and the restoration of republican values. He removed the
1804 Election Federalist threat to liberty by allowing the Alien and Sedition and Judiciary Acts to expire. At the same time he reduced the size and cost of government by cutting spending. And despite his opponents' charges, he proved that Republicans supported commerce. He removed major obstacles to American commercial growth by purchasing the Louisiana Territory, including New Orleans, and by having Congress repeal the Federalist excise and property taxes. And further American trade with Europe flourished. Unwisely, Federalists who had earlier criticized Jefferson for not seizing Louisiana now attacked the president for paying too much for the territory or for exceeding his powers. Charles Cotesworth Pinckney, a wealthy South Carolina lawyer and former Revolutionary War aide to General George Washington, carried the opposition standard against Jefferson. Pinckney had been Adams's vice-presidential candidate in 1800 and inherited the Federalist party leadership. Jefferson and his running mate, George Clinton of New York, swamped Pinckney and Rufus King in the electoral college by 162 votes to 14, carrying fifteen of the seventeen states.

Jefferson's re-election was both a personal and a party triumph. The political dissenters of the 1790s had turned their Democratic-Republican societies into a political party—an organization for the purpose of winning elections. More than anything else, opposition to the Federalists had molded and unified them. Indeed, it was where the Federalists were strongest— in commercial New York and Pennsylvania in the 1790s and in New England in the 1800s—that the Republicans had organized most effectively.

Until the Republican successes in 1800 and 1804, Federalists had disdained popular campaigning. They believed in government by the "best" people—those whose education, wealth, and experience marked them as leaders. For candidates to debate their qualifications before their inferiors—the voters—was unnecessary and undignified. The direct appeals of the Republicans therefore struck them as a subversion of the natural political order.

But after their resounding defeat in 1800, a younger generation of Federalists began to imitate the Republicans. They organized statewide and, led by men
Younger Federalists like Josiah Quincy, a young congressman from Massachusetts, they began to campaign for popular support. Quincy cleverly identified the Federalists as the people's party, attacking Republicans as autocratic planters. "Jeffersonian Democracy," Quincy satirized in 1804, was "an indian word, signifying '*a great tobacco planter who had herds of black slaves.*'" In attacking frugal government, the self-styled Younger Federalists played on fears of a weakened army and navy. Merchants depended on a strong navy to protect ocean trade while westerners, encroaching on Indian tribes, looked for federal support.

In the states where both parties organized and ran candidates, participation in elections increased markedly. In some states more than 90 percent of the eligible voters—nearly all of whom were white males— cast ballots between 1804 and 1816. People became more interested in politics generally, especially at the local level; and as participation in elections increased, the states expanded suffrage. Nevertheless, the popular base of the parties was still restricted. Property qualifications for voting and holding office remained common and in six states the legislatures still selected presidential electors in 1804. Even Republicans were restrained in committing themselves to party organization. Most leaders, fearing the divisiveness of partisanship, were suspicious of cohesive political movements.

Yet party competition, spurred on by a vigorous press which saw its primary role as political advocacy, led to grassroots campaigning. The political barbecue symbolized the new style as the parties responded to

Citizens gather at the State House in Philadelphia to whip up support for their candidates and parties. This picture, drawn on Election Day in 1816, suggests the overwhelmingly white, exclusively male composition of the electorate. Library of Congress.

increasing voter involvement in politics. In New York they roasted oxen; on the New England coast they baked clams; in Maryland they served oysters. The guests washed down their meals with beer and punch and sometimes competed in corn shuckings or horse pulls. During the barbecue, candidates and party leaders spoke from the stump. Oratory was a popular form of entertainment, and the speakers delivered lengthy and uninhibited speeches. They often made wild accusations, which—given the slow speed of communications—might not be answered until after the election. In 1808, for example, a New England Republican accused the Federalists of causing the Boston Massacre.

Soon both parties were using barbecues to appeal directly to voters. But although the Younger Federalists adopted the political barbecue, the Federalist party never fully mastered the art of wooing voters. Older Federalists still opposed such blatant campaigns. And though they were strong in a few states like Connecticut and Delaware, the Federalists never offered the Republicans sustained competition. Divisions between Older and Younger Federalists often hindered them, and the extremism of some Older Federalists tended to discredit the party. A case in point was Timothy Pickering, a Massachusetts congressman and former secretary of state who opposed the Louisiana Purchase, feared Jefferson's re-election, and urged the secession of New England in 1803 and 1804. Pickering won some support among the few Federalists in Congress, but others opposed his plan for a northern confederacy. When Vice President Aaron Burr lost his bid to become governor of New York in 1804, the plan collapsed. Burr, more an opportunist than a loyal Republican, was to have led New York into secession, with the other states to follow.

Both political parties suffered from factionalism and individuals' personal ambitions, which undermined party loyalty and cohesiveness. For a long time, for instance, Aaron Burr and Alexander Hamilton had crossed swords in political conflict. Burr had an affinity for conspiracies and it seemed to him that Hamilton always blocked his path. Hamilton had thwarted Burr's attempt to steal the 1800 election from Jefferson (see page 199) and in the 1804 New York gubernatorial race the Federalist Hamilton backed a rival Republican faction against Burr. Burr, his political career in ruins, turned his resentment on Hamilton and challenged him to a duel. The specific insult was Hamilton's description of Burr as dangerous and unfit to hold office. With his honor at stake, Hamilton accepted Burr's challenge, although he found dueling repugnant. They withdrew to New Jersey since New York had outlawed dueling. On July 11, 1804, at Weehawken, New Jersey, Hamilton deliberately fired astray. He paid for that decision with his life. Burr was indicted for murder in New York and New Jersey and faced immediate arrest if he returned to either state.

Hamilton-Burr Duel

With his political career over in the United States, Burr plotted to build an empire in the Southwest, using Louisiana as a base from which to launch an attack against Spanish lands. He planned to raise a private army, but the United States commander in the Mississippi Valley, General James Wilkinson, informed President Jefferson of Burr's plans. In 1807 Burr was tried and acquitted of treason but fled to Europe to avoid further prosecution.

The Burr-Hamilton conflict highlights some of the limitations of the early party system. Personal animosities often prompted the crossing of party lines and the appearance of new, temporary factions. Moreover, although politicians appealed for voter support and participation in politics broadened, the electoral base remained narrow. As the election of 1804 revealed, the Federalists could offer only weak competition at the national level. And where Federalists were too weak to be a threat, Republicans succumbed to the temptation to fight among themselves.

Thus, although this period is commonly called the era of the first party system, parties as such never fully developed. Competition encouraged party organization, but personal ambition, personality clashes, and local, state, and regional loyalties worked against it. Increasingly, external events intruded, and these would occupy most of Jefferson's time in his second administration.

PRESERVING AMERICAN NEUTRALITY IN A WORLD AT WAR

"Peace, commerce, and honest friendship with all nations, entangling alliance with none," President Jefferson had sensibly proclaimed in his first inaugural address. And Jefferson's efforts to stand clear of European conflict worked until 1805. Thereafter he found peace and undisturbed commerce an elusive goal, though pursuit of it occupied nearly his entire second administration.

After the Senate ratified the Jay Treaty in 1795 (see pages 192–193), the United States and Great Britain had appeared to reconcile their differences. Britain withdrew from its western forts and interfered less in American trade with France. More importantly, trade between the United States and Britain increased: the republic became Britain's best customer, and the British Empire in turn bought the bulk of American exports.

But renewal of the Napoleonic wars in May 1803—two weeks after Napoleon sold Louisiana to the United States—again trapped the nation between the two unfriendly superpowers. For two years American commerce actually benefited from the conflict. As the world's largest neutral carrier, the United States became the chief supplier of food to Europe. American merchants also gained control of most of the West Indian trade, which was often transshipped through American ports to Europe.

Meanwhile, the United States victory over Tripolitan pirates on the north coast of Africa (the Barbary states) provided Jefferson with his one clear success in protecting American trading rights. In 1801 Jefferson had refused the demands of the Sultan of Tripoli for payment of tribute to exempt American ships from seizure by Barbary Coast pirates. Instead he sent a naval squadron to the Mediterranean to protect American merchant ships. In 1803 and 1804, under Lieutenant Stephen Decatur, the navy blockaded Tripoli harbor while marines marched overland from Egypt to seize the port of Derna. The United States signed a peace treaty with Tripoli in 1805, but continued to pay tribute to other Barbary states.

That same year American merchants became victims of Anglo-French enmity. First Britain tightened its control over the high seas with its victory over the French and Spanish fleets at the Battle of Trafalgar in October 1805. Two months later Napoleon defeated the Russian and Austrian armies at Austerlitz. Stalemated, the two powers waged commercial war, blockading and counterblockading each other's trade. As a trading partner of both countries, the United States paid a high price.

The British navy at the same time stepped up impressments of American sailors. Britain, whose navy was the world's largest, was suffering a severe shortage of sailors. Few enlisted, and those already in service frequently deserted, discouraged by poor food and living conditions and brutal discipline. The Royal Navy resorted to stopping American ships and forcibly removing British deserters, British-born naturalized American seamen, and other unlucky sailors mistakenly suspected of being British. It is estimated that six to eight thousand Americans were drafted in this manner between 1803 and 1812.

Impressment of American Sailors

Americans saw impressment as a direct assault on their new republic. It violated America's rights as a neutral nation, and the British principle of "once a British subject, always a British subject" ignored American citizenship and sovereignty. Moreover, the practice exposed the weakness of the new nation;

the United States was in effect unable to protect its citizens from impressment.

In February 1806 the Senate denounced British impressment as aggression and a violation of neutral rights. To protest the insult Congress passed the Non-Importation Act, prohibiting importation from Great Britain of a long list of cloth and metal articles. In November Jefferson suspended the act temporarily while William Pinckney, a leading Baltimore lawyer, joined James Monroe in London in an attempt to negotiate a settlement. But the treaty Monroe and Pinckney carried home violated their instructions—it did not mention impressment—and Jefferson never submitted it to the Senate for ratification.

Less than a year later the *Chesapeake* Affair exposed American military weakness and revealed the emotional impact of impressment on the public. In June 1807 the forty-gun frigate U.S.S. *Chesapeake* left Norfolk, Virginia, on a mission to protect American ships trading in the Mediterranean. About ten miles out, still inside American territorial waters, it met the fifty-gun British frigate *Leopard.* When the *Chesapeake* refused to be searched for deserters, the *Leopard* repeatedly emptied its guns broadside into the American ship. Three Americans were killed and eighteen wounded, including the ship's captain, Commodore James Barron. Four sailors were impressed—three of them American citizens, all of them deserters from the Royal Navy. Wounded and humiliated, the *Chesapeake* crept back into port.

Chesapeake Affair

Had the United States been better prepared militarily, the howl of public indignation that resulted might have brought about a declaration of war. But the United States was ill equipped to defend its neutral rights with force; it was no match for the British navy. Fortunately, Congress was not in session at the time of the *Chesapeake* Affair, and Jefferson was able to avoid hostilities. The president responded instead by strengthening the military and putting economic pressure on Great Britain: in July Jefferson closed American waters to British warships to prevent similar incidents and soon thereafter he increased military and naval expenditures. On December 14, 1807, Jefferson again invoked the Non-Importation Act, followed eight days later by a new measure, the Embargo Act.

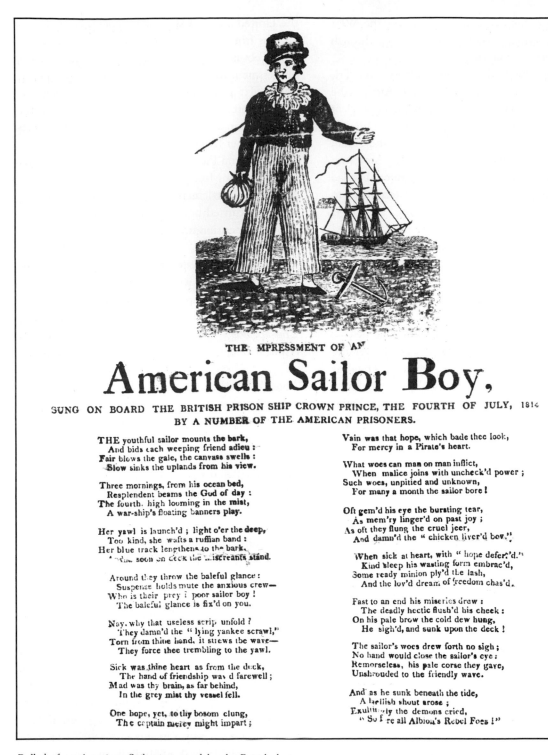

THE IMPRESSMENT OF AN

American Sailor Boy,

SUNG ON BOARD THE BRITISH PRISON SHIP CROWN PRINCE, THE FOURTH OF JULY, 1814
BY A NUMBER OF THE AMERICAN PRISONERS.

THE youthful sailor mounts the bark,
  And bids each weeping friend adieu :
Fair blows the gale, the canvass swells :
  Slow sinks the uplands from his view.

Three mornings, from his ocean bed,
  Resplendent beams the God of day :
The fourth, high looming in the mist,
  A war-ship's floating banners play.

Her yawl is launch'd ; light o'er the deep,
  Too kind, she wafts a ruffian band :
Her blue track lengthens to the bark,
  And soon on deck the miscreants stand.

Around they throw the baleful glance :
  Suspense holds mute the anxious crew—
Who is their prey ? poor sailor boy !
  The baleful glance is fix'd on you.

Nay, why that useless scrip unfold ?
  They damn'd the " lying yankee scrawl,"
Torn from thine hand, it strews the wave—
  They force thee trembling to the yawl.

Sick was thine heart as from the deck,
  The hand of friendship wav'd farewell ;
Mad was thy brain, as far behind,
  In the grey mist thy vessel fell.

One hope, yet, to thy bosom clung,
  The captain mercy might impart ;

Vain was that hope, which bade thee look,
  For mercy in a Pirate's heart.

What woes can man on man inflict,
  When malice joins with uncheck'd power ;
Such woes, unpitied and unknown,
  For many a month the sailor bore !

Oft gem'd his eye the bursting tear,
  As mem'ry linger'd on past joy ;
As oft they flung the cruel jeer,
  And damn'd the " chicken liver'd boy."

When sick at heart, with " hope defer'd,"
  Kind sleep his wasting form embrac'd,
Some ready minion ply'd the lash,
  And the lov'd dream of freedom chas'd.

Fast to an end his miseries drew :
  The deadly hectic flush'd his cheek :
On his pale brow the cold dew hung,
  He sigh'd, and sunk upon the deck !

The sailor's woes drew forth no sigh ;
  No hand would close the sailor's eye :
Remorseless, his pale corse they gave,
  Unshrouded to the friendly wave.

And as he sunk beneath the tide,
  A hellish shout arose ;
Exultingly the demons cried,
  " So fare all Albion's Rebel Foes !"

Ballad of an American Sailor impressed by the British during the War of 1812. References to the British captain as a "Pirate" and the British crew as "demons" reveal the intense indignation felt by the American public.   The New-York Historical Society.

Intended as a short-term measure, the Embargo Act forbade virtually all exports from the United

Embargo Act

States to any country. Imports came to a halt as well, since foreign ships delivering goods would have to leave American ports with empty holds. Smuggling blossomed overnight.

Few American policies were as well intentioned but as unpopular and unsuccessful as Jefferson's embargo. Although the notion of "peaceable coercion" was an enlightened concept in international affairs, some Republicans felt uneasy about using coercive federal power. Federalists felt no unease; commercially minded and generally pro-British, they opposed the embargo vociferously. Some feared its impact internationally; "If England sink," Rufus King said in 1808, "her fall will prove the grave of our liberties." For mercantile New Englanders, it dug another grave. Their region, the heart of Federalist opposition to the Virginian presidents, felt the brunt of the resulting depression. Shipping collapsed as exports fell by 80 percent from 1807 to 1808. In the winter of 1808 to 1809, talk of secession spread through New England port cities. Although unemployment soared, some benefited. Merchants with ships abroad at the time of the embargo or those willing to trade illegally and risk the weak and lax enforcement could garner enormous profits. Similarly, United States manufacturers received a boost, since the domestic market was theirs exclusively.

Great Britain, in contrast, was only mildly affected by the embargo. Those British citizens hurt most—West Indians and English factory workers—had no voice in policy. English merchants actually gained, since they took over the Atlantic carrying trade from the stalled American merchant marine. Moreover, because the British blockade of Europe had already ended most trade with France, the embargo had little practical effect on the French. Indeed, it gave France an excuse to privateer against American ships that had managed to escape the embargo by avoiding American ports. The French argued that such ships must be British ships in disguise, since the embargo barred American ships from the seas.

In the election of 1808, the Republicans faced the Federalists, the embargo, and factional dissent in their own party. Jefferson followed Washington's example, renouncing a third term and supporting James Madison, his secretary of state, as the Republican standard-bearer. Madison won the endorsement of the congressional caucus, but Virginia Republicans put forth James Monroe (who later withdrew), and some eastern Republicans supported Vice President George Clinton. This was the first time the Republican nomination had been contested.

Charles Cotesworth Pinckney and Rufus King again headed the Federalist ticket, but with new vigor. The Younger Federalists, led by Harrison Gray Otis and other Bostonians, pounded away at the widespread disaffection with Republican policy, especially the embargo. Although Pinckney received only 47 electoral votes to Madison's 122, the Federalists did manage to make the election a race. Pinckney carried all of New England except Vermont, and won Delaware and some electoral votes in two other states as well. Federalists also gained seats in Congress and captured the New York state legislature. For the Younger Federalists, the future looked promising.

As for the embargo, it eventually collapsed under the pressure of domestic opposition. Jefferson felt the weight of his failure; "never did a prisoner, released

Non-Intercourse Act

from his chains," Jefferson wrote on leaving office, "feel such relief as I in shaking off the shackles of power." In his last days in office he had tried to lighten the burden by working to replace the embargo with the Non-Intercourse Act of 1809. The act reopened trade with all nations except Britain and France and authorized the president to resume trade with either country if it ceased to violate neutral rights. But the new act solved only the problems that had been created by the embargo; it did not convince Britain and France to change their policies. For one brief moment it appeared to work: President Madison reopened trade with England in June 1809 after the British minister to the United States assured him that Britain would offer the concessions he sought. His Majesty's government in London, however, repudiated the minister's assurances, and Madison renewed nonintercourse.

When the Non-Intercourse Act expired in spring 1810, Congress created a variant, relabeled Macon's Bill Number 2. The bill reopened trade with both Great Britain and France, but provided that if either nation ceased to violate American rights, the president could shut down American commerce with the other. Madison, eager to use the bill rather than go to war, was tricked at his own game. When Napoleon declared that French edicts against United States shipping would be lifted, Madison declared nonintercourse against Great Britain in March 1811. But Napoleon did not keep his word. The French continued to seize American ships, and nonintercourse failed a second time.

Britain, not France, was the main target of American hostility, since the Royal Navy controlled the Atlantic. New York harbor was virtually blockaded by the British, so reopening trade with any nation had little practical effect. Angry American leaders tended to blame even Indian resistance in the West on British agitation, ignoring the Indians' legitimate protests against white encroachment and treaty violations. Frustrated and having exhausted all efforts to alter British policy, the United States in 1811 and 1812 drifted into war with Great Britain.

Meanwhile, unknown to the president and Congress, Great Britain was changing its policy. The Anglo-French conflict had ended much of British commerce with the European continent, and exports to the United States had fallen 80 percent. Depression had hit the British Isles. On June 16, 1812, Britain opened the seas to American shipping. But two days later, before word had crossed the Atlantic, Congress declared war.

The War of 1812 was the logical outcome of United States policy after the renewal of war in Europe in 1803. The grievances enumerated in President Madison's message to Congress on June 1, 1812, were old ones: impressment, interference with neutral commerce, and the British alliances with western Indians. Unmentioned was the resolve to defend American independence and honor—and the thirst of expansionists for British Canada. Yet Congress and the country were divided. Much of the sentiment for war came from the War Hawks, land-hungry southerners and westerners led by Henry Clay of Kentucky and John C. Calhoun of South Carolina. They were concerned equally with national honor and expansion. Most representatives from the coastal states opposed war, since armed conflict with the great naval power threatened to close down all Amer-

ican shipping. The vote for war—79 to 49 in the House, 19 to 13 in the Senate—reflected these sharp regional differences. The split would also be reflected in the way Americans fought the war.

THE WAR OF 1812

War was a foolish adventure for the United States in 1812; despite six months of preparation, American forces remained ill equipped. Because the army had neither an able staff nor an adequate force of enlisted men, the burden of fighting fell on the state militias—and not all the states cooperated. The navy did have a corps of well-trained, experienced officers who had proven their mettle in protecting American merchantmen from Mediterranean pirates. But next to the Royal Navy, the ruler of the seas, the U.S. Navy was minuscule. Jefferson's warning that "our constitution is a peace establishment—it is not calculated for war" proved a wise one. Fortunately for the United States, the war consisted mostly of scuffles and skirmishes; full-scale battles were rare.

For the United States, the only readily available battlefront on which to confront Great Britain was Canada. The mighty Royal Navy was useless on the waters separating the United States

Invasion of Canada

and Canada, since no river afforded it access from the sea. Invasion of Canada, thousands of miles from British supply sources, therefore might give the United States an edge. And England, preoccupied with fighting Napoleon on the European continent, was unlikely to reduce its continental forces to defend Canada.

Begun with high hopes, the invasion of Canada ended as a disaster. The American strategy was to concentrate on the West, splitting Canadian forces and isolating the Shawnee, Potawatomi, and other tribes who supported the British. General William Hull, governor of Michigan Territory, marched his troops into Lower Canada, near Detroit. More experienced as a politician than a soldier, Hull surrounded himself with newly minted colonels equally politically

Major Campaigns of the War of 1812

astute and militarily ignorant. The British anticipated the invasion, mobilized their Indian allies, moved troops into the area, and demanded Hull's surrender. When a pro-British, mostly Potawatomi, contingent captured Fort Dearborn, near Detroit, Hull capitulated (see map). Farther to the west, other American forts surrendered. By the winter of 1812 and 1813, the British controlled about half the Old Northwest (Ohio, Indiana, Illinois, Michigan, and Wisconsin).

The United States had no greater success on the Niagara front, where New York borders Canada. At the Battle of Queenstown, north of Niagara, the United States regular army met defeat because the New York state militia refused to leave the state. This scene was repeated near Lake Champlain, where American plans to attack Montreal were foiled when the militia declined to cross the border.

The navy provided the only bright note in the

first year of the war: the U.S.S. *Constitution*, the U.S.S. *Wasp*, and the U.S.S. *United States* all bested British warships on the Atlantic. But their victories gave the United States only a brief advantage. In defeat the British lost just 1 percent of their strength; in victory the Americans lost 20 percent. The British admiralty simply shifted its fleet away from the American ships, and by 1813 the Royal Navy again commanded the seas.

In 1813 the two sides also vied for control of the Great Lakes, the key to the war in the Northwest. The contest was largely a shipbuilding race. Under **Great Lakes Campaign** Master Commandant Oliver Hazard Perry and shipbuilder Noah Brown, the United States outbuilt the British on Lake Erie and defeated them at the bloody Battle of Put-in-Bay on September 10. The ships fought fiercely and at close range; of 103 men on duty on the U.S.S. *Lawrence*, 21 were killed and 63 wounded. With this costly victory, the Americans gained control of Lake Erie.

General William Henry Harrison then began the march that proved to be the United States's most successful moment in the war. Harrison's 4,500-man force, mostly Kentucky volunteers, crossed Lake Erie and pursued the British, Shawnee, and Chippewa forces into Canada, defeating them at the Battle of the Thames on October 5. The Shawnee and Chippewa warriors continued to fight after the British had surrendered in the battle; defeat came when the great Shawnee chief Tecumseh died, ending the Indian confederacy he had formed to resist American expansion (see pages 285–286). Harrison's campaign gave the United States virtual control of the Old Northwest.

The American success on Lake Erie could not be repeated on Lake Ontario. After the Battle of the Thames, both sides seemed to favor petty victories over strategic goals in the Northwest. The Americans raided York (now Toronto), the Canadian capital, and looted and burned the Parliament before withdrawing, too few in number to hold the city.

Outside the Old Northwest the British set Americans back. In December 1812 the Royal Navy blockaded the Chesapeake and Delaware bays. By May **British Naval Blockade** 1813 the blockade had closed nearly all southern and Gulf of Mexico ports, and by November it had reached north to Long Island Sound. By 1814 all New England ports were closed. American trade had declined nearly 90 percent since 1811, and the decline in revenues from customs duties threatened to bankrupt the federal government.

Following their defeat of Napoleon in April 1814, the British stepped up the land campaign against the United States, concentrating their efforts in the Chesapeake. In retaliation for the burning of York—and to divert American troops from Lake Champlain, where the British planned a new offensive—royal troops occupied Washington and set it to the torch, leaving the Executive Mansion scarred by fire. The attack on the capital was, however, only a raid. The major battle occurred at Baltimore, where the Americans held firm. Although the British inflicted heavy damages both materially and psychologically, they achieved no more than a stalemate. The British offensive at Lake Champlain proved equally unsuccessful. An American fleet forced a British flotilla to turn back at Plattsburgh on Lake Champlain, and the offensive was discontinued.

The last campaign of the war was waged in the South, along the Gulf of Mexico. It began when Tennessee militia general Andrew Jackson defeated the Creek Indians at the Battle of Horseshoe Bend in March 1814. The battle ended the year-long Creek War, which had begun after a series of skirmishes between Indians and settlers. As a result, the Creek nation ceded two-thirds of its land and withdrew to southern and western Alabama. Jackson became a major general in the regular army and continued south toward the Gulf. To forestall a British invasion at Pensacola Bay, which provided an overland route to New Orleans, Jackson seized Pensacola—in Spanish Florida—on November 7, 1814. After securing Mobile, he marched on to New Orleans and prepared for a British attempt to capture the city.

The Battle of New Orleans was the final military engagement. Early in December the British fleet landed 1,500 men east of New Orleans, hoping to gain control of the Mississippi River. **Battle of New Orleans** They faced an American force of regular army troops, plus a larger contingent of Tennessee and Kentucky frontiersmen and two companies of free black volunteers from New Orleans. For three weeks the

Oliver Hazard Perry's victory at Put-in-Bay (1813), in which the United States gained control of Lake Erie. New York State Historical Association, Cooperstown.

British under Sir Edward Pakenham and the Americans under Jackson played cat-and-mouse, each trying to gain a major strategic position. Finally, on January 8, 1815, the two forces met head on. Jackson and his mostly untrained army held their ground against two frontal assaults and a reinforced British contingent of 6,000. It was a massacre. More than 2,000 British soldiers lay dead or wounded at the day's end; the Americans suffered only 21 casualties. Andrew Jackson emerged a national hero. Ironically, the Battle of New Orleans was fought two weeks after the end of the war; unknown to Jackson, a treaty had been signed in Ghent, Belgium, on December 24, 1814.

The United States government had gone to war only reluctantly and during the conflict had continued to probe for a diplomatic end to hostilities. In 1813, for instance, President Madison had eagerly accepted a Russian offer to mediate, but Great Britain had refused it. Three months later, British Foreign Minister Lord Castlereagh suggested opening peace talks. It took over ten months to arrange meetings, but in August 1814 a team of American negotiators, including John Quincy Adams and Henry Clay, began talks with the British in Ghent.

The Ghent treaty made no mention of the issues that had led to war. The United States received no satisfaction on impressment, blockades, or other maritime rights for neutrals. Likewise,

Treaty of Ghent

British demands for an Indian buffer state in the Northwest and territorial cessions from Maine to Minnesota went unmet. Essentially, the Treaty of Ghent restored the prewar status quo. It provided for an end to hostilities, release of prisoners, restoration of conquered territory, and arbitration of boundary disputes. Other questions—notably compensation for losses and fishing rights—would be negotiated by joint commissions.

Why did the negotiators settle for so little? Events in Europe had made peace and the status quo acceptable at the end of 1814, as they had not been in 1812. Napoleon's fall from power allowed the United States to abandon its demands, since peace in Europe made impressment and interference with American commerce moot questions. Similarly, war-weary Britain, its treasury nearly depleted, gave up pressing for a military victory.

The War of 1812 reaffirmed the independence of the young American republic. Although conflict with Great Britain continued, it never again led to war.

Effects of War of 1812

The experience strengthened America's resolve to steer clear of European politics, for it had been the British-French conflict that had drawn the United States into war. For the rest of the century the nation would shun involvement in European political issues and wars.

The war had disastrous results for most Indian tribes. With the death of Tecumseh, they lost their most powerful political and military leader; with the withdrawal of the British, they lost their strongest ally. Although in the peace treaty the United States agreed to return Indian lands seized after 1811, the collapse of Indian leadership and British withdrawal made this provision moot. The Shawnee, Potawatomi, Chippewa, and other midwestern tribes had lost most of the resources with which they could have resisted American expansion (see pages 284–290).

Domestically, the war exposed weaknesses in defense and transportation, which were vital for westward expansion. American generals had found American roads inadequate to move an army and its supplies among widely scattered fronts. In the Northwest, General Harrison's troops had depended on homemade cartridges and gifts of clothing from Ohio residents, and in Maine troops had melted down spoons to make bullets. Clearly, improved transportation and a well-equipped army were major priorities. In 1815 President Madison responded by centralizing control of the military, and Congress voted a standing army of 10,000 men, one-third of the army's wartime strength but three times the size it was during Jefferson's administration.

Possibly most important of all, the war stimulated economic change. The embargo, the Non-Importation and Non-Intercourse Acts, and the war itself had spurred the production of manufactured goods—cloth and metal—to replace banned imports. And in the absence of commercial opportunities abroad, New England capitalists had begun to invest in manufactures. The effects of these changes were to be far-reaching (see Chapter 9).

And, finally, the war sealed the fate of the Federalist party. Realizing that their chances of winning a presidential election in wartime were slight, the Federalists had joined dissatisfied Republicans in supporting De Witt Clinton of New York in 1812. This was the high point of Federalist organization at the state level, and the Younger Federalists campaigned hard. Clinton nevertheless lost to President Madison by 128 to 89 electoral votes; areas that favored the war (the South and West) voted solidly Republican. The Federalists did, however, gain some congressional seats, and they carried many local elections.

But once again extremism undermined the Federalists. During the war Older Federalists had revived talk of secession, and from December 15, 1814, to

Hartford Convention

January 5, 1815, Federalist delegates from New England met in Hartford, Connecticut. With the war in a stalemate and trade in ruins, they plotted to revise the national compact or pull out of the republic. Moderates prevented a resolution of secession, but convention members condemned the war and the embargo, and endorsed radical changes in the Constitution. In particular, they wanted constitutional amendments restricting the presidency to one term and requiring a two-thirds congressional vote to admit new states. They also hoped to abolish the three-fifths compromise, whereby slaves were counted in the apportionment of congressional representatives, and to forbid naturalized citizens from holding office. These proposals were aimed at the growing West and South—the heart of Republican electoral strength—and at Irish immigrants.

If nothing else, the timing of the Hartford Convention proved fatal. The victory at New Orleans and news of the peace treaty made the Hartford Convention, with its talk of secession and proposed constitutional amendments, look ridiculous, if not treasonous. Rather than harassing a beleaguered wartime administration, the Federalists now retreated before a rising tide of nationalism. Though it remained strong in a handful of states until the 1820s, the Federalist party began to dissolve. The war, at first a source of revival as opponents of war flocked to the Federalist banner, helped kill the party.

POSTWAR NATIONALISM AND DIPLOMACY

With peace came a new sense of American nationalism. Self-confidently, the nation asserted itself at home and abroad as Republicans aped Federalists in encouraging economic development and commerce. In his last message to Congress in December 1815, President Madison embraced Federalist doctrine by recommending military expansion and a program to stimulate economic growth. Wartime experiences had, he said, demonstrated the need for a national bank (the first bank had expired) and for better transportation. To raise government revenues and perpetuate the wartime growth in manufacturing, Madison called for a protective tariff—a tax on imported goods. Yet in straying from Jeffersonian Republicanism, Madison did so within limits. Only a constitutional amendment, he argued, could give the federal government authority to build roads and canals that were less than national in scope.

The congressional leadership pushed Madison's nationalist program energetically. Congressman John C. Calhoun and Speaker of the House Henry Clay, who named the program the American System, believed it would unify the country. They looked to the tariff on imported goods to stimulate industry. New mills would purchase raw materials; new millworkers would buy food from the agricultural South and West. New roads would make possible the flow of produce and goods, and tariff revenues would provide the money to build them. Finally, a national bank would facilitate all these transactions.

American System

Indeed, Hamilton's original plan for a Bank of the United States became fundamental to the new Republican policy. Fearing the concentration of economic power in a central bank, the Republicans had allowed the charter of the first Bank of the United States to expire in 1811. State banks, however, proved inadequate to the nation's needs. Their resources had been insufficient to assist the government in financing the War of 1812. Moreover, people distrusted currency issued by banks in distant localities. Because many banks issued notes without gold to back them up, and counterfeit notes were common, merchants hesitated to accept strange currency. Republicans therefore came to favor a national bank. In 1816 Congress chartered the Second Bank of the United States for twenty years, with its headquarters, like those of the first Bank of the United States, in Philadelphia. The government provided $7 million of the $35 million capital and appointed one-fifth of the directors, and the bank opened its doors on January 1, 1817.

Congress did not share Madison's reservations about the constitutionality of using federal funds to build local roads. "Let us, then, bind the republic together," Calhoun declared, "with a perfect system of roads and canals." But Madison vetoed Calhoun's internal improvements bill, which provided for the construction of roads of mostly local benefit, adamantly insisting that it was unconstitutional. Internal improvements were the province of the states and of private enterprise. (Madison did, however, approve funds for the continuation of the National Road to Ohio, on the grounds that it was a military necessity.)

This watercolor by George Tattersall shows the primitive state of American roads in the early nineteenth century. Museum of Fine Arts, Boston, M. and M. Karolik Collection.

Protective tariffs completed Madison's nationalist program. Though the embargo and the war had stimulated domestic industry, especially cloth and iron manufacturing, resumption of trade after the war brought competition from abroad. Americans charged that British firms were dumping their goods on the American market at below cost to stifle American manufacturing. To aid the new industries, Madison recommended and Congress passed the Tariff of 1816, the first protective tariff in American history. The act levied taxes on imported woolens and cottons, especially inexpensive ones, and on iron, leather, hats, paper, and sugar. In effect it raised the cost of these imported goods. Some New England representatives viewed the tariff as interference in free trade, and southern representatives (except Calhoun and a few others) opposed it because it raised the cost of

imported goods to southern farmers. But the western and Middle Atlantic states backed it, and the tariff passed.

James Monroe, Madison's successor as president, retained Madison's domestic program, supporting the bank and tariffs and vetoing internal improvements on constitutional grounds. Monroe was the third member of the Virginia dynasty that held the presidency from 1801 through 1825. A former United States senator, twice governor of Virginia and an experienced diplomat, he served under Madison as secretary of state and of war. As secretary of state he received the nomination of the Republican congressional caucus in 1816. Later that year he easily defeated Rufus King, the last Federalist nominee, sweeping all the states except the Federalist strongholds of Massachusetts, Connecticut, and Delaware. Monroe optimistically declared that "discord does not belong to our system." The American people were, he said, "one great family with a common interest." A Boston newspaper dubbed the one-party period the "Era of Good Feelings." And for Monroe's first term that seemed true.

Under Chief Justice John Marshall, the Supreme Court during this period also became the bulwark of a nationalist point of view. In *McCulloch* v. *Maryland* (1819), the Court struck down a

McCulloch v. Maryland

Maryland law taxing the federally chartered Second Bank of the United States. Maryland had adopted the tax in an effort to destroy the bank's Baltimore branch. The issue was thus one of state versus federal power. Speaking for a unanimous Court, Marshall asserted the supremacy of the federal government over the states. "The Constitution and the laws thereof are supreme," he declared; "they control the constitution and laws of the respective states and cannot be controlled by them."

Having established federal supremacy, the Court in *McCulloch* v. *Maryland* went on to consider whether Congress could issue a bank charter. No such power was specified in the Constitution. But Marshall noted that Congress had the authority to pass "all laws which shall be necessary and proper for carrying into execution" the enumerated powers of the government (Article I, Section 8). Therefore Congress could legally exercise "those great powers on which the welfare of the nation essentially depends." If the ends were legitimate and the means were not prohibited, Marshall ruled, a law was constitutional. The Constitution was, in Marshall's words, "intended to endure for ages to come, and consequently, to be adapted to the various causes of human affairs." The bank charter was declared legal.

In *McCulloch* v. *Maryland* Marshall combined Federalist nationalism with Federalist economic views. By asserting federal supremacy he was protecting the commercial and industrial interests that favored a national bank. This was Federalism in the tradition of Alexander Hamilton. The decision was only one in a series. In *Fletcher* v. *Peck* (1810) the Court voided a Georgia law that violated individuals' right of contract. Similarly, in the famous *Dartmouth College* v. *Woodward* (1819), the Court nullified a New Hampshire act altering the charter of Dartmouth College, which Marshall ruled constituted a contract. In protecting such contracts, Marshall thwarted state interference in commerce and business.

John Quincy Adams, Monroe's secretary of state, matched the self-confident Marshall Court in nationalism and assertiveness. From 1817 to 1825 he

John Quincy Adams as Secretary of State

managed the nation's foreign policy brilliantly. He was the son of John and Abigail Adams, an experienced diplomat who had served abroad and negotiated the Treaty of Ghent.

Adams stubbornly pushed for expansion, fishing rights for Americans in Atlantic waters, political distance from the Old World, and peace. An ardent expansionist, he nonetheless placed limits on expansion: it must come through negotiations, not war, and newly acquired territories must not permit slavery. In appearance a small, austere man, once described by a British official as a "bulldog among spaniels," Adams was a superb diplomat who knew six languages.

Despite being an Anglophobe, Adams worked to strengthen the peace with Great Britain. In April 1817 the two nations agreed in the Rush-Bagot Treaty to limit their Great Lakes naval forces to one ship each on Lakes Ontario and Champlain and two vessels each on the other lakes. This first disarmament treaty of modern times led to the demilitarization of the United States–Canadian border.

Adams then pushed for the Convention of 1818 which fixed the United States–Canadian border from the Lake of the Woods in Minnesota west to the Rockies along the 49th parallel. When agreement could not be reached on the territory west of the mountains, Britain and the United States settled on joint occupation of Oregon for ten years, which was renewed for another ten years in 1827. Adams wanted to fix the border along the 49th parallel right through to the Pacific Ocean, which would gain the important inland waterways of Juan de Fuca Strait and Puget Sound for the United States. He hoped for a better negotiating position when the treaty lapsed.

Adams's next move was to settle long-term disputes with Spain. Although the 1803 Louisiana Treaty had omitted reference to Spanish-ruled West Florida, the United States claimed the territory as far as the Perdido River (the present-day Florida-Alabama border), but only occupied a small finger of that area. During the

War of 1812 the United States seized Mobile and the remainder of West Florida. Afterward it took advantage of Spain's preoccupation with domestic and colonial troubles to negotiate for the purchase of East Florida. Talks took place in 1818, while General Andrew Jackson's troops occupied much of Florida on the pretext of suppressing Seminole raids against American settlements across the border. Adams was furious with Jackson, but defended his brazen act. The following year, on behalf of Spain, Don Luís de Onís, Spanish minister to the United States, agreed to cede Florida to the United **Adams-Onís** States without payment. In this **Treaty** Transcontinental, or Adams-Onís Treaty, the United States also defined the southern boundary of the Louisiana Purchase. The border zigzagged across the West from Texas to the Pacific Ocean (see map, page 232). In return, the United States government assumed $5 million worth of claims by American citizens against Spain and gave up its dubious claim to Texas. Expansion had thus been achieved at little cost and without war, and American territorial claims now stretched from the Atlantic to the Pacific.

While the Rush-Bagot Treaty, the Convention of 1818, and the Adams-Onís Treaty temporarily resolved conflict between the United States and European nations, events to the south still threatened United States interests. John Quincy Adams's desire to insulate the United States and the Western Hemisphere from European conflict led to his greatest achievement: the Monroe Doctrine.

Specifically, the thorny issue of the recognition of new governments in Latin America had to be confronted. The United Provinces of the Río de la Plata (present-day northern Argentina, Paraguay, and Uruguay), Chile, Peru, Columbia, and Mexico had all broken free from Spain between 1808 and 1822. Many Americans wanted to recognize the independence of these former colonies because they seemed to be following the United States's revolutionary tradition. But Monroe and Adams moved cautiously. They sought to avoid conflict with Spain and its allies and to assure themselves of the stability of the revolutionary regimes. But in 1822, shortly after the Adams-Onís Treaty with Spain was safely signed and ratified, the United States became the first nation outside Latin America to recognize the new states.

Soon events in Europe again threatened the stability of the New World. Spain suffered a domestic revolt, and France occupied Spain in an attempt to bolster the weak monarchy against the rebels. The United States feared that France would seek to restore the new Latin American states to Spanish rule. Similarly distrustful of France, Great Britain proposed a joint United States–British declaration against European intervention in the hemisphere and a joint disavowal of British and American territorial ambitions in the region. But Adams rejected the British overture; he insisted that the United States act independently in accordance with the principle of avoiding foreign entanglements.

Determined to thwart joint action with Great Britain, the unbending Adams tenaciously outargued other cabinet members. Those who favored joint action believed that the United States needed British naval power to prevent French or Russian intervention. They were supported by former president Jefferson, then in retirement at Monticello. Adams, however, won. "It would be more candid, as well as more dignified," he argued, "to avow our principles explicitly to Russia and France, than to come in as a cockboat in the wake of the British man-of-war." Moreover, he rejected the British proposal to abdicate territorial ambitions as a deliberate attempt at preventing further American expansion.

President Monroe presented the American position—the Monroe Doctrine—in his last message to Congress on December 2, 1823. He called for, first, *noncolonization* of the Western **Monroe** Hemisphere by European nations, **Doctrine** a principle that expressed American anxiety not only about Latin America but also about Russian expansion on the West Coast. Second, he demanded *nonintervention* by Europe in the affairs of independent New World nations. Finally, Monroe pledged *noninterference* by the United States in European affairs, including those of Europe's existing New World colonies.

The Monroe Doctrine proved popular at home as an anti-British, anti-European assertion of American nationalism, and it eventually became the foundation of American policy in the Western Hemisphere. Monroe's words, however, carried no force. Indeed, the policy could not have succeeded without the support of the British, who were already committed

John Quincy Adams (1767–1848), secretary of state from 1817 to 1825 and architect of the Monroe Doctrine, in an early daguerreotype taken by Southworth and Hawes shortly before his death. This famous photograph suggests Adams's bulldog tenacity. The Metropolitan Museum of Art, Gift of I. N. Phelps Stokes, Edward S. Hawes, Alice Mary Hawes, Marion Augusta Hawes, 1937.

to keeping other European nations out of the New World. Europeans ignored the doctrine; it was the Royal Navy they respected, not American policy.

THE PANIC OF 1819 AND RENEWED SECTIONALISM

Monroe's domestic achievements could not match the diplomatic successes that John Quincy Adams brought to his administration. By 1819 postwar nationalism and confidence had eroded,

and financial panic darkened the land. (Neither panic nor the resurgence of sectionalism hurt Monroe politically; without a rival political party to rally opposition, he won a second term in 1820 unopposed.)

But hard times spread. The postwar expansion had been built on loose money and widespread speculation. State banks extended credit and printed notes too freely, fueling a speculative western land boom. When it slowed, the manufacturing depression that had begun in 1818 deepened, and prices spiraled downward. The Second Bank of the United States, in order to protect its assets, reduced loans, thus accelerating the contraction in the economy. Distressed urban workers lobbied for relief and began to take a more active role in politics. Farmers clamored for lower tariffs. Hurt by a sharp decline in the price of cotton, southern planters railed at the protective Tariff of 1816, which had raised prices at the same time their incomes were falling sharply. The Virginia Agricultural Society of Fredericksburg, for example, argued that the tariff violated the very principles on which the nation had been founded. In a protest to Congress in January 1820, the society called the tariff an unequal tax that awarded exclusive privileges to "oppressive monopolies, which are ultimately to grind both us and our children after us 'into dust and ashes.'" Manufacturers, on the other hand, demanded greater tariff protection—and eventually got it in the Tariff of 1824.

Economic Depression

Western farmers suffered too. Those who had purchased public land on credit could not repay their loans. To avoid mass bankruptcy, Congress delayed payment of the money, and western state legislatures passed "stay laws" restricting mortgage foreclosures. Many westerners blamed the panic on the Second Bank of the United States for tightening the money supply. Many state banks, in debt to the national bank, folded, and westerners bitterly accused the bank of saving itself while the nation went to ruin. Although the economy recovered in the mid-1820s, the seeds of the Jacksonian movement (see pages 335–339) had been sown.

Even more divisive was the question of slavery. Ever since the drafting of the Constitution, political leaders had largely avoided the issue. The one exception was the 1807 act closing the slave trade after January 1, 1808, which passed without much op-

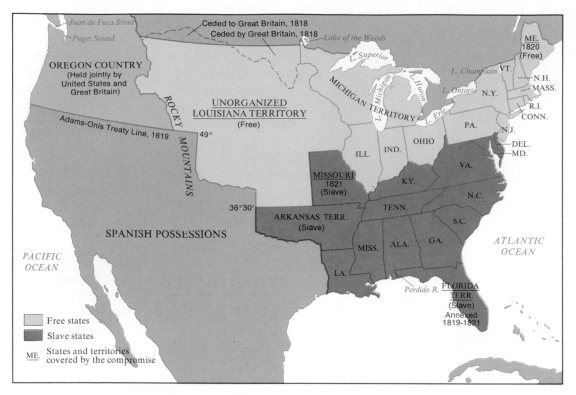

The Missouri Compromise and the State of the Union, 1820

position. It had been taken for granted that once the Constitutional ban (Article I, Section 9) on closing the slave trade expired in 1808, Congress would act. In February 1819, however, slavery finally crept onto the political agenda when Missouri residents petitioned Congress for admission to the Union as a slave state. For the next two-and-one-half years the issue dominated all congressional action. "This momentous question," Thomas Jefferson wrote, fearful for the life of the Union, "like a fire bell in the night, awakened and filled me with terror."

Slavery Question

The debate transcended slavery in Missouri. At stake was the undoing of the compromises that had kept the issue quarantined since the Constitutional Convention. Five new states had joined the Union since 1812—Louisiana (1812), Indiana (1816), Mississippi (1817), Illinois (1818), and Alabama (1819)—and of these, Louisiana, Mississippi, and Alabama were slave states. Missouri was on the same latitude as free Illinois, Indiana, and Ohio (a state since

1803), and its admission as a slave state would thus thrust slavery further northward. It would also tilt the political balance toward the states committed to slavery. In 1819 the Union consisted of an uneasy balance of eleven slave and eleven free states. If Missouri entered as a slave state, the slave states would have a two-vote edge in the Senate.

But what made the issue so divisive was not the politics of admission to statehood, but white people's emotional attitudes toward slavery. The settlers of Missouri were mostly Kentuckians and Tennesseeans who had grown up with slavery. But in the North, slavery was slowly dying out, and many northerners had come to the conclusion that it was evil. During the Second Great Awakening, there arose a groundswell for reform, including abolition, especially among women (see Chapter 12). Thus when Representative James Tallmadge, Jr., of New York introduced an amendment providing for gradual emancipation in Missouri, it led to passionate and sometimes violent debate on moral grounds. The House, which had a northern majority, passed the Tallmadge amendment, but the Senate rejected it. The two sides were deadlocked.

A compromise emerged in 1820 under pressure from House Speaker Henry Clay: the admission of free Maine, carved out of Massachusetts, was linked with that of slave Missouri. In the

Missouri Compromise

rest of the Louisiana Territory north of 36°30′ (Missouri's southern boundary), slavery was prohibited forever (see map). The compromise carried, but the agreement almost came apart in November when Missouri submitted a constitution that barred free blacks from settling in the state. Opponents contended that the proposed state constitution violated the federal Constitution's provision that "the citizens of each State shall be entitled to all privileges and immunities of citizens in the several States." Advocates argued that restrictions on free blacks were common in state law both North and South. In 1821 Clay produced a second compromise: Missouri guaranteed that none of its laws would discriminate against citizens of other states. (Once admitted to the Union, however, Missouri twice adopted laws banning free blacks.)

Although political leaders had successfully removed slavery from the congressional agenda, sectional issues undermined Republican unity and ended the reign of the Virginia dynasty. The Republican party would come apart in 1824 as presidential candidates from different sections of the country scrambled for caucus support (see pages 336–337).

Sectionalism and the question of slavery would ultimately threaten the Union itself. Still, the first decades of the nineteenth century were a time of nationalism and growth for the young republic. Political parties channeled and limited partisan divisions, and a tradition of peaceful transition of power through presidential elections was established. A second war with Britain—the War of 1812—had to be fought to reaffirm American independence; thereafter the nation was able to settle many disputes at the bargaining table. The foreign policy problems confronting the infant republic from the turn of the century through the mid-1820s strikingly resemble those faced today by the newly established nations of the Third World. The mother country often treated its former colony as if it had not won its independence. And

ENUMERATION OF THE INHABITANTS OF THE STATE OF MISSOURI.

COUNTIES	Free white males	Free white females	Free persons of color	Slaves	Persons bound to service for a term of years	Total	Representatives
Boone,	1679	1486	1	576		3692	3
Cooper,	1612	1419	12	440		3483	3
Callaway,	712	642		443		1797	1
Cole	582	444		53		1028	1
Chariton,	883	541	7	290	5	1416	1
Cape Girardeau	5526	3200	44	1089		7859	6
Franklin	880	853	9	186		1928	2
Gasconade	650	463	1	60		1174	1
Howard	3219	2690	2	1400	3	7321	5
Jefferson	875	749	4	200	1	1833	2
Lincoln	893	636	2	211	2	1674	1
Lillard	695	515		130		1340	1
Montgomery	928	802		302		2032	2
Madison	858	715	5	344	3	1907	1
New madrid	1155	972	7	310		2444	2
Pike	1286	1014	2	495		2677	2
Perry	740	623	1	229	6	1599	1
Ralls	749	581	1	358	2	1694	1
Ray	912	730	2	141	2	1730	2*
St. Louis	3564	2858	141	1608	24	8190	5
St. Charles	1856	1453	11	738	5	4055	3
St. Genevieve	1317	1081	62	717	4	3181	2
Saline	519	446	2	172	1	1115	1
Washington	1816	1302	2	550		4---	3
Wayne	720	645	1	246	2	1614	1
	32120	26003	321	11254	60	70647	54

*County divided.   County of St. Francois   1

55

With the Missouri Compromise of 1820, Missouri and Maine joined the Union as slave and free states respectively. The first census of the new state (1821) enumerated the large slave population and the small number of free blacks whom many Missourians wished to bar from settlement. Library of Congress.

like Third World nations today, the young United States steered clear of alliances with superpowers, preferring neutrality and unilateralism. The War of 1812 and diplomatic assertiveness brought a sense of national security and confidence.

After the war, all branches of the government, responding to the popular mood, pursued a more vigorous national policy. The Supreme Court further advanced national unity by extending federal power over the states and encouraging commerce and economic growth. In spite of Jefferson's vision of an agrarian society of independent farmers and artisans, the country was gradually changing to a market economy in which people produced goods not just for their own use but to sell to others (see Chapter 9).

IMPORTANT EVENTS

1801	John Marshall becomes Chief Justice
	Jefferson inaugurated
1801–05	Tripoli War
1803	*Marbury v. Madison*
	Louisiana Purchase
1804	Jefferson re-elected
1804–06	Lewis and Clark expedition
1807	*Chesapeake* Affair
	Embargo Act
1808	Madison elected president
1812–15	War of 1812
1814	Treaty of Ghent
1814–15	Hartford Convention
1815	Battle of New Orleans
1816	Monroe elected president
	Second Bank of the United States chartered
1817	Rush-Bagot Treaty
1819	*McCulloch v. Maryland*
	Adams-Onís Treaty
1819–23	Financial panic; depression
1820	Missouri Compromise
	Monroe re-elected
1823	Monroe Doctrine

Disruption of trade during the war had promoted the manufacturing of goods in the United States, instead of dependence on imports from Europe. The development of faster transportation further promoted the economy, and old cities expanded in the market-oriented North as new ones sprouted up in the West on trade and transportation routes (see Chapter 10).

But along with the nationalism and growth of the country came the problem of sectionalism. While the manufacturers and commercial interests in the North were becoming increasingly connected with the agricultural producers in the West through transportation and trade, the South was developing its own economy and culture based on cotton crops, export markets, a plantation system, and slavery (see Chapter 11). Politicians kept the question of slavery off the national agenda as long as possible and worked out the Missouri Compromise as a stopgap measure. But new land acquisitions and further westward expansion in the 1840s and 1850s, combined with a rising tide of reform impulse, eventually made the question of slavery unavoidable (see Chapters 12 and 13). Americans would finally settle the issue in the Civil War.

SUGGESTIONS FOR FURTHER READING

General

Henry Adams, *History of the United States of America During the Administration of Thomas Jefferson and of James Madison*, 9 vols. (1889–1891); George Dangerfield, *The Awakening of American Nationalism, 1815–1828* (1965); George Dangerfield, *The Era of Good Feelings* (1952); John Mayfield, *The New Nation, 1800–1845* (1981); Glover Moore, *The Missouri Compromise, 1819–1821* (1953); Murray N. Rothbard, *The Panic of 1819* (1962); Marshall Smelser, *The Democratic Republic, 1801–1815* (1968).

Party Politics

James M. Banner, *To the Hartford Convention: The Federalists and the Origins of Party Politics in the Early Republic, 1789–1815* (1967); James Broussard, *The Southern Federalists 1800–1816* (1978); Noble E. Cunningham, Jr., *The Jeffersonian Republicans in Power: Party Operations, 1801–1809* (1963); David Hackett Fischer, *The Revolution of American Conservatism: The Federalist Party in the Era of Jeffersonian Democracy* (1965); Linda K. Kerber, *Federalists in Dissent* (1970);

Shaw Livermore, *Twilight of Federalism: The Disintegration of the Federalist Party, 1815–1830* (1962); Milton Lomask, *Aaron Burr*, 2 vols. (1979, 1983); Richard P. McCormick, *The Presidential Game. The Origins of American Presidential Politics* (1982); James Sterling Young, *The Washington Community, 1800–1828* (1966).

The Virginia Presidents

Harry Ammon, *James Monroe: The Quest for National Identity* (1971); Irving Brant, *James Madison*, 6 vols. (1941–1961); Irving Brant, *The Fourth President: A Life of James Madison* (1970); Noble E. Cunningham, Jr., *The Process of Government Under Jefferson* (1978); James Ketcham, *James Madison* (1970); Forrest McDonald, *The Presidency of Thomas Jefferson* (1976); Dumas Malone, *Jefferson and His Time*, 6 vols. (1948–1981); Merrill D. Peterson, *The Jefferson Image in the American Mind* (1960); Merrill D. Peterson, *Thomas Jefferson and the New Nation* (1970).

The Supreme Court and the Law

Leonard Baker, *John Marshall: A Life in Law* (1974); Albert Beveridge, *The Life of John Marshall*, 4 vols. (1916–1919); Richard E. Ellis, *The Jeffersonian Crisis: Courts and Politics in the Young Republic* (1971); Charles G. Haines, *The Role of the Supreme Court in American Government and Politics, 1789–1835* (1944); Morton J. Horowitz, *The Transformation of American Law, 1780–1860* (1977); R. Kent Newmyer,

The Supreme Court Under Marshall and Taney (1968); Francis N. Stites, *John Marshall: Defender of the Constitution* (1981).

Expansion and the War of 1812

Roger H. Brown, *The Republic in Peril: 1812* (1964); A. L. Burt, *The United States, Great Britain, and British North America* (1940); Harry L. Coles, *The War of 1812* (1965); Alexander De Conde, *This Affair of Louisiana* (1976); Clifford L. Egan, *Neither Peace nor War: Franco-American Relations, 1803–1812* (1983); Reginald Horsman, *The War of 1812* (1969); Donald Jackson, ed., *Letters of the Lewis and Clark Expedition with Related Documents, 1783–1854* (1962); Bradford Perkins, *Prologue to War: England and the United States, 1805–1812* (1961); Julius W. Pratt, *Expansionists of 1812* (1925); Burton Spivak, *Jefferson's English Crisis: Commerce, Embargo, and the Republican Revolution* (1974); J. C. A. Stagg, *Mr. Madison's War. Politics, Diplomacy, and Warfare in the Early Republic, 1783–1830* (1983).

The Monroe Doctrine

Samuel F. Bemis, *John Quincy Adams and the Foundations of American Foreign Policy* (1949); Walter LaFeber, ed., *John Quincy Adams and American Continental Empire* (1965): Ernest R. May, *The Making of the Monroe Doctrine* (1976); Dexter Perkins, *The Monroe Doctrine 1823–1826* (1927); Dexter Perkins, *Hands Off: A History of the Monroe Doctrine* (1941).

A MARKET AND INDUSTRIAL ECONOMY

1800–1860

CHAPTER 9

John Jervis suffered from canal fever and railroad fever nearly all his life. He first contracted the obsession in 1817, when at age twenty-two he left his father's upstate New York farm to clear a cedar swamp for the Erie Canal. Like the other laborers, as well as the men directing the project, Jervis had no experience in canal construction. Indeed, he had never built anything according to a plan or diagram.

Together the directors and workers learned enough on the job to construct 363 well-engineered miles of canal. Jervis's education began his first day. Though he was an expert axeman, he had never downed a line of trees along an exact path. With ingenuity, he learned to hew with precision. Jervis learned new skills each year, advancing from axeman to surveyor to engineer to superintendent of a division. He was the most famous engineer to have received his training from the Erie Canal "School of Engineering."

When the Erie Canal was completed in 1825, Jervis signed on as second-in-command of the Delaware and Hudson Canal project. To reduce costs, he substituted a railroad line for the last seventeen miles of the canal. Since there was not a single locomotive in the United States in 1828, Jervis had one sent from England. The engine that was delivered, however, was heavier than the one he had ordered, and on both tests it crushed the hemlock rails.

Undaunted, the self-trained engineer left the Delaware canal company to supervise construction of another early rail experiment, the Mohawk and Hudson Railroad from Albany to Schenectady. In building the railroad Jervis redesigned the locomotive's wheel assembly, and his design became standard throughout America.

Jervis spent the next two decades building the 98-mile Chenango Canal and the fresh-water supply for New York City—consisting of the Croton Reservoir, a 33-mile aqueduct, and pumping system. Later he built other railroads, including the Michigan Southern, the Rock Island, and the Nickel Plate. In 1864, at age sixty-nine, Jervis returned home to Rome, New York, and organized an iron mill. He had spent his life constructing the mechanisms—canals and railroads—that would change America.

John Jervis's life bridged the old and the new. His roots lay in the rural farm country that was typical of the United States at the beginning of the nineteenth century. Born at Huntington, Long Island, in 1795, he was taken to western New York in 1798 by his carpenter father, who moved to the frontier to farm. He learned to read and write during occasional attendance at common school, and to farm and handle an axe from his father. But in 1817 he left behind much of that tradition and became involved in undertakings that would lead to a new, far different nation. He had to acquire skills not used on the farm: the ability to follow and create construction plans, to calculate weight stresses, and to work precisely in tandem with others. A religious man, he extolled the pioneer virtues of hard work and independence, and he prided himself on his rise from farm boy to world-class engineer. Yet, by the time of his death in 1885 engineering leadership had passed to the university-trained.

The canals and railroads that John Jervis and others built were the most visible signs of economic development and the best-known links in the growing national economy from 1800 through 1860. The canal boat, the steamboat, the locomotive, and the telegraph all helped to open up the frontier and to encourage greater farm production for markets at home and abroad. They made it possible for New England mill girls to turn slave-produced southern cotton into factory-made cloth that was purchased by women in New York, Cincinnati, San Francisco, and thousands of smaller towns across America. Increasingly, farmers grew more for market while urban producers worked for wages. Thus, if transportation was the most visible change, less tangible but equally significant was the increased specialization in agriculture, manufacturing, and finance that eventually brought about a national, capitalist market economy.

The dramatic transformation of the United States between 1800 and 1860 was manifest nearly everywhere. In 1800 most of the 5.3 million Americans earned a living working the land and serving those who did. Except in Kentucky and Tennessee, settlement had not stretched far to the west. By 1860,

31.4 million Americans had spread across the continent; in the Midwest some farms were 1500 miles from the Atlantic; and on the Pacific Slope, settlement boomed. A continental nation had been forged. Though still primarily agricultural, the economy was being transformed by an enormous commercial and industrial expansion.

Promotion of economic growth became the hallmark of government, especially in the nationalist mood after the War of 1812. Government sought to encourage individual freedom and choice by furthering an environment in which farming and industry could flourish. New financial institutions amassed the capital for large-scale enterprises like factories and railroads. Mechanization took root; factories and precision-made machinery began to replace home workshops and handmade goods, while reapers and sowers revolutionized farming.

New problems and tensions accompanied the rewards of economic expansion. Not everyone profited, as John Jervis did, in wealth and opportunity. The journeyman tailor who was replaced by new retailers and cheaper labor had a far different experience from the new merchant princes. New England farm daughters found their world changing no less radically. Moreover the cycles of boom and bust became part of the fabric of ordinary life. Whatever the benefits and drawbacks, however, economic development and change were irreversible.

THE MARKET ECONOMY

Most farmers in the early nineteenth century geared production to family needs. They lived in interdependent communities and kept detailed account books of labor and goods exchanged with neighbors. Farm families tended to produce much of what they needed—foodstuffs, clothing, candles, soap, and the like—but traded agricultural surpluses for or purchased items they could not produce, such as cooking pots, shoes for animals, coffee, tea, and white sugar. On most such farms, men selling cordwood and women selling eggs, butter, cheese, and poultry produced the family's only cash. By the Civil War,

however, the United States had an industrializing economy in which an increasing number of men and women worked in factories or offices for a wage, and in which most citizens—farmers and workers alike—had become dependent on store-bought necessities.

In the market economy crops were grown and goods were produced for sale in the marketplace, at home or abroad. The money received in market transactions, whether from the sale of goods or of a person's labor, purchased items produced by other people—such as the candles and soap no longer made at home. Such a system encouraged specialization. Formerly self-sufficient farmers, for example, began to grow just one or two crops, or to concentrate on raising only cows, pigs, or sheep for market. Farm women gave up spinning and weaving at home and purchased fabric produced by wage-earning farm girls in Massachusetts textile mills.

Definition of a Market Economy

Sustained growth was the result of this economic evolution. Improvements in transportation and technology, the division of labor, and new methods of financing all fueled expansion of the economy—that is, the multiplication of goods and services. In turn, this growth prompted new improvements. The effect was cumulative; by the 1840s the economy was growing more rapidly than in the previous four decades. Per capita income doubled between 1800 and 1860.

The Ohio dairy industry illustrates this process. In the first decades of the century, Ohio farm women made whatever cheese they needed for their own tables. Some made cheese to sell elsewhere, but only because they had a surplus of milk. However, the development of canals and railroads in the 1830s and 1840s changed Ohio farming. Farmers began to specialize, finding it more profitable to invest in better tools and spend all their time on one product. Some chose to grow wheat or tobacco for market, and to purchase whatever dairy products they needed. Others, especially in northeastern Ohio, decided to devote themselves full time to dairy farming. Beginning in 1847, entrepreneurs built cheese factories in rural towns and contracted to buy curd from these local dairy farmers. In 1851 one such factory in Gustavus, Ohio, produced a daily average of 5,000 pounds of cheese from the milk of 2,500 cows. The cheese was shipped by canal and railroad to cities and eastern

Traditionally cheese making was a woman's chore. The work was physically arduous and continuous, requiring daily attention to the curds. Evan Jones, The World of Cheese, Knopf, 1976.

ports. In Boston and New York, some merchants turned to handling cheese and other dairy products exclusively, selling to consumers as far away as California, England, and China. By 1860 Ohio dairymen were producing 21.6 million pounds of cheese a year for market—a huge leap in production over the early 1800s.

The changes in Ohio dairy husbandry altered farm life. Traditionally the making of cheese was a family industry in which men fed and tended the cows, men or women milked them, and women made the cheese. As cheese production increased, women's work on family-run dairy farms intensified as they added cheese-making to their regular tasks. The work was physically arduous and continuous, requiring daily attention both to the new day's curds and to the previous days' cheese, which needed to be pressed and turned. The *Ohio Cultivator* in 1848 noted that "the condition of women in dairies is frequently little better than servitude." In large, commercial dairies, however, where making cheese was a male task, gender roles had shifted under the pressure of market demands.

Though economic change and growth were sustained, their pace was uneven. Prosperity reigned during two long periods, from 1823 to 1835 and from 1843 to 1857. But there were long stretches of economic contraction as well. During the time from

Boom-and-Bust Cycles Jefferson's 1807 embargo through the War of 1812, the interruption in trade contributed to a negative growth rate—that is, fewer goods and services were produced. Contraction and deflation occurred again during the depressions of 1819 through 1823, 1839 through 1843, and 1857. These periods were characterized by the collapse of banks, business bankruptcies, and a decline in wages and prices. Workers faced increasing insecurity as a result of these cycles; on the down side, they suffered not only lower incomes but also unemployment.

Working people, a Baltimore physician noted during the depression of 1819, felt hard times "a thousand fold more than the merchants." Yet even during good times wage earners could not build up sufficient financial reserves to get them through the next depression; often they could not make it through the winter without drawing on charity for food, clothing, and firewood. In the 1820s and 1830s, free laborers in Baltimore found steady work from March through October and unemployment and hunger from November through February.

If good times were hard on workers and their families, depressions devastated them. In 1839 in Baltimore, small manufacturers for the local market closed their doors; tailors, shoemakers, milliners, and shipyard and construction workers lost their jobs. Ninety miles to the north, Philadelphia took on an eerie aura. "The streets seemed deserted," Sidney George Fisher observed in 1842; "the largest [merchant] houses are shut up and to rent, there is no business . . . no money, no confidence." Only auctions boomed, as the sheriff sold off seized property at a quarter of predepression prices. Elsewhere in the city, soup societies fed the hungry. In New York, breadlines and beggars crowded the sidewalks. In smaller cities like Lynn, Massachusetts, the poor who did not leave became scavengers, digging for clams and harvesting dandelions.

In 1857 hard times struck again. The Mercantile Agency recorded 5,123 bankruptcies in 1857—nearly double the number in the previous year. The bankrupt firms had a total debt of $300 million, only half of which would be paid off. Contemporary reports estimated 20,000 to 30,000 unemployed in Philadelphia, and 30,000 to 40,000 in New York City. Female benevolent societies expanded their soup kitchens and distributed free firewood to the needy. In Chicago, charities reorganized to meet the needs of the poor; in New York, the city hired the unemployed to fix streets and develop Central Park. And in Fall River, Massachusetts, a citizens' committee disbursed public funds on a weekly basis to nine hundred families. The soup kitchen, the breadline, and public aid had become fixtures in urban America.

What caused the cycles of boom and bust that brought about such suffering? In general, they were a direct result of the new market economy. Prosperity inevitably stimulated greater demand for staples and finished goods. In-

Cause of Boom-and-Bust Cycles

creased demand led in turn to higher prices and still higher production, to speculation in land, and to the flow of foreign currency into the country. Eventually production surpassed demand, leading to lower prices and wages; and speculation outstripped the true value of land and stocks. The inflow of foreign money led first to easy credit and then to collapse when unhappy investors withdrew their funds.

Some economists considered this process beneficial—a self-adjusting cycle in which unprofitable economic ventures were eliminated. In theory, people concentrated on the activities they did best, and the economy as a whole became more efficient. Advocates of the system argued also that it furthered individual freedom, since ideally each seller, whether of goods or labor, was free to determine the conditions of the sale. But in fact the system put workers on a perpetual rollercoaster; they had become dependent on wages—and the availability of jobs—for their very existence.

Many also felt a distinct loss of status. For Joseph T. Buckingham, foreman of the Boston printing shop of West & Richardson, wage labor represented failure. Buckingham had been a master printer, running the shop of Thomas & Andrews on commission and doing some publishing of his own. In 1814 he purchased the shop, but did not get enough work to pay his debts. Without the capital to sustain his losses or to compete with larger shops, Buckingham had to sell his presses at auction. He became a wage earner, albeit a foreman. Though his wages were about the equal of an ordinary printer's income, Buckingham was unhappy. In his own words, he was "nothing more than a journeyman, except in responsibility."

GOVERNMENT PROMOTES ECONOMIC GROWTH

The eighteenth-century political ideas which had captured the imagination of the Revolutionary War generation and found expression in the ideal of republican virtue were paralleled in economic thought by the writings of Adam Smith, a Scottish political economist. Smith's *The Wealth of Nations* first appeared in 1776, the year of the Declaration of Independence; both works emphasized individual liberty, one economic, the other political. Both were reactions against forceful government: Jefferson attacked monarchy and distant government while Smith attacked mercantilism, government regulation of the economy to benefit the state (see page 61). They believed that virtue was lodged in individual freedom and that the entire community would benefit most from individuals pursuing their own self-interest. As president, Jefferson put these political and economic beliefs into action by reducing the role of government.

Jefferson, influenced by the economic and egalitarian ideas of republicanism (see pages 156–157), recognized that government was nonetheless a necessary instrument in promoting individual freedom. Freedom, he believed, thrived where individuals had room for independence, creativity, and choices; individuals fettered by government, monopoly, or economic dependence could not be free. Committed to the idea that a republican democracy would flourish best in a nation of independent farmers and artisans and an atmosphere of widespread political participation, Jefferson worked to realize those ideals. Beginning with the purchase of Louisiana in 1803, Republican party policy, no less than that of the Federalists, turned to using government as an active promoter of the economy. Belief in a limited government was not an end in itself, but only a means to greater individual freedom.

Once Louisiana had been acquired, the federal government played an active role in promoting economic growth and in fulfilling the spirit of manifest destiny by encouraging westward expansion and settlement and by promoting agriculture. The Lewis and

Clark expedition from 1804 to 1806 (see page 215) was the beginning of a continuing federal interest in geographic and geologic surveying and the first step in the opening of western lands to exploitation and settlement.

New steps followed quickly. In 1817 and 1818 Henry Rowe Schoolcraft explored the Missouri and Arkansas region, reporting on its geologic features and mineral resources. In 1819 and 1820 Major Stephen Long explored the Great Plains, mapping the area between the Platte and Canadian rivers. Between 1827 and 1840 the government surveyed about fifty railroad routes. The final door to western settlement was opened in 1843 and 1844 by John C. Frémont's expedition, which followed the Oregon Trail to the Pacific, then traveled south to California and returned east by way of the Great Salt Lake. Frémont, later a California senator and 1856 Republican presidential candidate, gained fame as a soldier-surveyor of the West. His report of his journey dispelled a long-standing myth that the center of the continent was a desert.

To encourage western agriculture, the federal government offered public lands for sale at reasonable prices (see page 263) and evicted Indian tribes from their traditional lands. And because transportation was crucial to development of the frontier, the government financed roads and subsidized railroad construction through land grants. Even the State Department aided agriculture: its consular offices overseas collected horticultural information, seeds, and cuttings and published technical reports in an effort to improve American farming.

The federal government played a key role in technological and industrial growth. Federal arsenals pioneered new manufacturing techniques and helped to develop the machine-tool industry. The United States Military Academy at West Point, founded in 1802, emphasized technical and scientific subjects in its curriculum. And the U.S. Post Office stimulated interregional trade and played a brief but crucial role in the development of the telegraph: the first telegraph line, from Washington to Baltimore, was constructed under a government grant, and during 1845 the Post Office ran it, employing inventor Samuel F. B. Morse as superintendent. Finally, to create an atmosphere conducive to economic growth and individual creativity, the government protected inventions and do-mestic industries. Patent laws gave inventors a seventeen-year monopoly on their inventions, and tariffs protected American industry from foreign competition.

The federal judiciary validated government promotion of the economy and encouraged business enterprise. In *Gibbons* v. *Ogden* (1824), the Supreme Court overturned a New York state law that had given Robert Fulton and Robert Livingston a monopoly on the New York–New Jersey steamboat trade. Ogden, their successor, lost his monopoly when Chief Justice John Marshall ruled that the trade fell under the sway of the commerce clause of the Constitution. Thus Congress, not New York, had the controlling power. Since the federal government issued such licenses on a nonexclusive basis, the decision ended monopolies on waterways throughout the nation. Within a year, forty-three steamboats were plying Ogden's route.

Legal Foundations of Commerce

In defining interstate commerce broadly, the Marshall Court expanded federal powers over the economy while limiting the ability of states to control economic activity within their borders. Its action was consistent with its earlier decision in *Dartmouth College* v. *Woodward* (1819), which protected the sanctity of contracts against interference by the states (see page 229). "If business is to prosper," Marshall wrote, "men must have assurance that contracts will be enforced."

Federal and state courts, in conjunction with state legislatures, also encouraged the proliferation of corporations—groups of investors that could hold property and transact business as one person. In 1800 the United States had about 300 incorporated firms; in 1817 about 2,000. By 1830 the New England states alone had issued 1,900 charters, one-third to manufacturing and mining firms. At first each firm needed a special legislative act to incorporate, but after the 1830s applications became so numerous that incorporation was authorized by general state laws. Though legislative action created corporations, the courts played a crucial role in defining their status, extending their powers, and protecting them.

A further encouragement to economic development, corporate development, and free enterprise was the Supreme Court's ruling in *Charles River Bridge* v. *Warren Bridge* (1837) that new enterprises could not be restrained by implied privileges under old charters.

The Marshall Court encouraged business competition by ending the state-licensed monopolies on inland waterways. Gibbons v. Ogden (1824) opened up the New York-New Jersey trade to new lines, and within a short time dozens of steamboats ferried passengers and freight across the Hudson River. The New-York Historical Society.

The case involved issues of great importance: should a new interest be able to compete against existing, older privileges, and should the state protect existing privilege or encourage innovation to benefit all? In 1785 the Massachusetts legislature chartered the Charles River Bridge Company, and in 1791 extended its charter to a seventy-year term. In return for the risk of building the bridge between Charlestown and Boston, the owners received the privilege of collecting tolls. In 1828 the legislature chartered another company to build the Warren Bridge across the Charles, with the right to collect tolls for six years, after which the bridge would be turned over to the state and be toll-free. With the terminus of the new bridge only ninety yards away from its own, the Charles River Bridge Company sued in 1829, claiming that the new bridge breached the earlier charter and contradicted the principles in *Dartmouth College* v. *Woodward*. Justice Roger Taney, speaking for the Court majority, noted that the original charter did not confer the privilege of monopoly and therefore exclusivity could not be implied. Focusing on the question of corporate privilege rather than the right of contracts, Taney ruled that charter grants should be interpreted narrowly and that ambiguities would be decided in favor of the public interest. New enterprises should not be restricted under old charters, and economic growth would best be served by narrowing the application of the *Dartmouth College* decision. Thus, the judiciary supported economic expansion and individual economic opportunity.

State governments far surpassed the federal government in promoting the economy. From 1815 through 1860, for example, 73 percent of the $135 million invested in canals was gov-

State Promotion of the Economy ernment money, mostly from the states. In the 1830s the states shifted their investments to rail construction. Even though the federal government played a larger role in building railroads than canals, state and local governments provided more than half of southern rail capital. In the nineteenth century, railroads received 131 million acres in land subsidies, 48 million of which was provided by the states. State governments also invested in corporation and bank stocks, providing those institutions with much-needed capital. Pennsylvania, probably the most active of the states in promoting its economy, invested a total of $100 million in canals, railroads, banks, and manufacturing firms; its appointees sat on more than 150 corporate boards of directors.

States actually equaled or surpassed private enterprise in their investments. But they did more than invest in industry. By establishing bounties for agricultural prizes, they stimulated commercial agriculture, especially sheep raising and wool manufacture (see page 258). Through special acts and general incorporation laws, states regulated the nature and activities of both corporations and banks. They also used their licensing capacity to regulate industry; in Georgia, for example, grading and marketing of tobacco was regulated by the state.

From the end of the War of 1812 until 1860 the United States experienced uneven but sustained economic growth largely as a result of these government efforts. Though political controversy raged over questions of state versus federal activity—especially with regard to internal improvements and banking—all parties agreed on the general goal of economic expansion (see Chapters 8 and 12). Indeed, the major restraint on government action during these years was not philosophical but financial: both the government and the public purse were small. As the private sector grew stronger, entrepreneurs looked less to government for financial support and states played less of an investment role. In either case, government provided an atmosphere conducive to business and economic growth.

TRANSPORTATION AND REGIONALIZATION

From 1800 through 1860 the North, South, and West followed distinctly different paths economically. Everywhere agriculture remained the foundation of the American economy. Nevertheless, industry, commerce, and finance came to characterize the North, plantations and subsistence farms the South, and commercialized family farms, agricultural processing, and implement manufacturing the West. Paradoxically, this tendency toward regional specialization made the sections at once more different and more dependent on each other.

The revolution in transportation and communications was probably the single most important cause of these changes. It was the North's heavy investment in canals and railroads that made it the center of American commerce; its growing seaboard cities distributed western produce and New England textiles. New York financial and commercial houses linked the southern cotton-exporting economy to the North and Europe. The South, with most of its capital invested in slave labor, built fewer canals, railroads, and factories and remained largely rural and undeveloped (see Chapter 11).

Before the canal fever of the 1820s and 1830s and the railroad fever of the 1830s and after became epidemic, it was by no means self-evident that New England and the Middle Atlantic

Change in Trade Routes states would dominate American economic life. In fact, the natural orientation of the 1800 frontier— Tennessee, Kentucky, and Ohio—was to the South. The southward-flowing Ohio and Mississippi rivers were the lifelines of early western settlement. Flatboats transported western grain and hogs southward for consumption or transfer to oceangoing vessels at New Orleans. Southern products—first tobacco, then lumber and cotton—flowed directly to Europe. Settlement of southern Illinois and Indiana and the appearance of steamboats on western rivers only intensified this pattern.

But the pattern changed in the 1820s and 1830s. New roads and turnpikes opened up east-west travel. The National Road, a stone-based, gravel-topped highway beginning in Cumberland, Maryland, reached Wheeling (then in Virginia) in 1818 and Columbus, Ohio, in 1833. More important, the Erie Canal, completed in 1825, forged an east-west axis from the Hudson River to Lake Erie, linking the Greak Lakes with New York City and the Atlantic Ocean. The canal carried easterners and then immigrants to settle the Old Northwest and the frontier beyond; in the opposite direction, it bore western grain to the large and growing eastern markets. Railroads and later the telegraph would solidify these east-west links. By contrast, only at one place—Bowling Green, Kentucky—did a northern railroad actually connect with a southern one. Although trade still continued southward along the Ohio and Mississippi rivers, the bulk of western trade flowed eastward by 1850. Thus, by the eve of the Civil War, the northern and Middle Atlantic states were closely tied to the former frontier of the Old Northwest.

Construction of the 363-mile-long Erie Canal was a visionary enterprise. When the state of New York authorized it in 1817, the longest existing American canal was only 28 miles long. Vigorously promoted by Governor De Witt Clinton, the Erie cost $7 million, much of it raised by loans from British investors. The canal shortened the journey between Buffalo and New York City from twenty to six days and reduced freight charges from $100 to $5 a ton. By 1835 traffic was so heavy that the Erie had to be widened from forty to seventy feet and deepened from four to seven feet. The skeptics who had called the canal "Clinton's big ditch" had long since been silenced by the success of the enterprise.

The Erie triggered an explosion of canal building. Other states and cities, sensing the advantage New York had gained, rushed to follow suit. By 1840 canals crisscrossed the Northeast and Midwest, and canal mileage in the United States had reached 3,300—an increase of more than 2,000 miles in a single decade. Unfortunately for investors, none of these canals enjoyed the financial success achieved by the Erie. The high cost of construction and economic contraction after 1837 lowered profitability.

Canals

A mid-nineteenth-century poster boasts of the superior services of the New York Central Railroad.   American Antiquarian Society.

As a result, investment in canals began to slump in the 1830s. By 1850 more miles were being abandoned than built, and the canal era had ended.

Meanwhile, railroad construction was on the upswing, and visionaries like John Jervis left canals for railroads. The railroad era began in 1830 when Peter Cooper's locomotive *Tom Thumb* first steamed along 13 miles of track constructed by the Baltimore and Ohio Railroad. In 1833 a second railroad ran 136 miles from Charleston to Hamburg, South Carolina. By 1850 the United States had nearly 9,000 miles of railroad; by 1860, roughly 31,000 (see map, page 246). Canal fever stimulated this early railroad construction. Promoters of the Baltimore and Ohio had turned to the railroad in an effort to compete with the canal. Similarly, the line between Boston and Worcester, Massachusetts, was intended as the first link in a line to Albany, at the eastern end of the Erie Canal.

Railroads

The earliest railroads connected two cities or one city and its surrounding area. Not until the 1850s would railroads offer long-distance service at reasonable rates. And the early lines also had technical problems

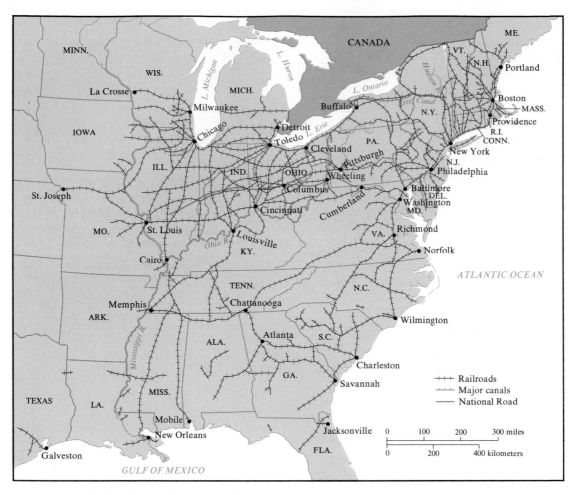

Major Railroads, Canals, and Roads in 1860

to contend with. As John Jervis had discovered, locomotives heavy enough to climb steep grades and pull long trains required strong rails and resilient roadbeds. Engineers met those needs by replacing wooden track with iron rails and by supporting the rails with ties embedded in gravel. John Jervis's wheel alignment—called the swivel truck—removed another major obstacle by enabling engines to hold the track on sharp curves. Other problems persisted, though: notably the continued use of hand brakes, which severely restricted speed, and the lack of a standard gauge for track. The Pennsylvania and Ohio railroads, for instance, had no fewer than seven different track widths. Thus a journey from Philadelphia to Charleston, South Carolina, involved eight changes in gauge.

In the 1850s technological improvements, competition, and economic recovery prompted the de-velopment of regional and later national rail networks. The West too experienced a railroad boom. By 1853 rail lines linked New York to Chicago, and a year later track had reached the Mississippi River. By 1860 rails stretched as far west as St. Joseph, Missouri—the edge of the frontier. In that year the railroad network east of the Mississippi approximated its physical pattern for the next century, but the process of corporate integration had only begun. In 1853 seven short lines combined to form the New York Central system, and the Pennsylvania Railroad was unified from Philadelphia to Pittsburgh. Most lines, however, were still independently run, separated by gauge, scheduling, differences in car design, and a commitment to serve their home towns first and foremost.

Railroads did not completely replace water transportation. Steamboats, introduced in 1807 when

Steamboats   Robert Fulton's *Clermont* paddled up the Hudson from New York City, still plied the rivers. They had proven their value on western rivers in 1815 when the *Enterprise* first carried cargo upstream on the Mississippi and Ohio rivers. Until the 1850s, when western rail development blossomed, steamboats outdid railroads in carrying freight. Great Lakes steamers managed to hold their own even into the 1850s, for the sealike lakes permitted the construction of giant ships and the widespread adoption of propellers in place of paddle wheels. These leviathans were especially well suited to carrying heavy bulk cargoes like lumber, grain, and ore.

Gradually steamboats replaced sailing vessels on the high seas. In days gone by, sailing ships—whalers, sleek clippers, and square-rigged packets—had been the pride of American commerce. But sailing ships were dependent on prevailing winds and weather, and thus could not schedule regular crossings. In 1818 steam-powered packets made four round trips a year between New York and Liverpool, sailing on schedule rather than waiting for a full cargo as had ships before then. The breakthrough came in 1848, though, when Samuel Cunard introduced regularly scheduled steamships to the Atlantic run between Liverpool and New York, reducing travel time from twenty-five days eastbound and forty-nine days westbound to ten to fourteen days each way. Sailing ships quickly lost first-class passengers and light cargo to these swift steamships. For the next decade they continued to carry immigrants and bulk cargo, but by 1860 only the freight trade remained to them.

By far the fastest spreading technological advance of the era was the magnetic telegraph. Samuel F. B. Morse's invention freed messages from the restraint of traveling no faster than the messenger; instantaneous communication became possible even over long distances. By 1853, only nine years after construction of the first experimental line, 23,000 miles of telegraph wire spread across the United States; by 1860, 50,000. In 1861 the telegraph bridged the continent, connecting the east and west coasts. The new invention revolutionized news-gathering, provided advance information for railroads and steamships, and altered patterns of business and finance. Rarely has innovation had so great an impact so quickly.

Telegraph

The changes in transportation and communications from 1800 to 1860 were revolutionary. Railroads reduced the number of loadings and unloadings, were cheap to build over difficult terrain, and remained in use all year, unlike water transport which was frozen out in winter. But time was the key. In 1800 it took four days to travel from New York City to Baltimore, and nearly four weeks to reach Detroit. By 1830 Baltimore was only a day-and-a-half away and Detroit only a two-week journey. By 1857 Detroit was but an overnight trip; in a week one could reach Texas, Kansas, or Nebraska. This reduced travel time saved money and facilitated commerce. During the first two decades of the century, wagon transportation cost 30 to 70 cents per ton per mile. By 1860, railroads in New York State carried freight at an average charge of 2.2 cents per ton per mile; wheat moved from Chicago to New York for 1.2 cents a ton-mile. In sum, the transportation revolution had transformed the economy—and with it the relationships of the North, West, and South.

THE RISE OF MANUFACTURING AND COMMERCE

The McCormick reaper, ridiculed the London *Times*, looked like "a cross between a flying-machine, a wheelbarrow, and an Astley chariot." In one continuous motion, the horse-drawn reaper used a revolving drum to position the stalks before a blade, with the cut grain falling onto a platform. Put to a competitive test through rain-soaked wheat, the Chicago-made reaper alone passed, to the cheers of the skeptical English spectators. The reaper and hundreds of other American products made their international debut at the 1851 London Crystal Palace Exhibition, the first modern world's fair. There the design and quality of American machines and wares—from familiar farm tools to such exotic devices as an ice-cream freezer and the reaper—astonished observers. American manufacturers returned home with dozens of medals, including all three prizes for piano making. Most impressive to the Europeans were three simple machines: Alfred C. Hobb's unpickable padlocks, Samuel Colt's revolvers, and Robbins and Lawrence's six rifles with completely interchangeable parts. All were machine- rather than hand-tooled, products of what the British called the American system of manufacturing.

So impressed were the British—the leading industrial nation of the time—that in 1853 they sent a parliamentary commission to study the American system. A year later a second committee returned to examine the firearms industry in detail. In their report, the committee described an astonishing experiment performed at the federal armory in Springfield, Massachusetts. To test the interchangeability of machine-made muskets, they selected rifles made in each of the previous ten years. While the committee watched, the guns were dismantled "and the parts placed in a row of boxes, mixed up together." The Englishmen "then requested the workman, whose duty it is to 'assemble' the arms, to put them together, which he did—the Committee handing him the parts, taken at hazard—with the use of a turnscrew only, and as quickly as though they had been English muskets, whose parts had carefully been kept separate." Britain's Enfield arsenal subsequently converted to American equipment. Within the next few years other nations followed Great Britain's lead, sending delegations across the Atlantic to bring back American machines.

The American system of manufacturing used precision machinery to produce interchangeable parts that needed no filing or fitting. In 1798 Eli Whitney had used a primitive system of interchangeable parts when he contracted with the federal government to make ten thousand rifles in twenty-eight months. By the 1820s the Connecticut manufacturer Simeon North, the Springfield, Massachusetts, Arsenal, and the Harpers Ferry, Virginia, Armory were all producing machine-made interchangeable parts for firearms. From the arsenals the American system spread, giving birth to the machine-tool industry—the mass manufacture of specialized machines for other industries. One by-product was an explosion in consumer goods: since the time and skill involved in manufacturing had been greatly reduced, the new system permitted mass production at low cost. Waltham watches, Yale locks,

American System of Manufacturing

and Singer sewing machines became household items, inexpensive yet of uniformly high quality.

Interchangeable parts and the machine-tool industry were uniquely American contributions to the industrial revolution. Both paved the way for America's swift industrialization following the Civil War. The process of industrialization began, however, in a simple and traditional way, not unlike that of other nations. In 1800 manufacturing was relatively unimportant to the American economy. What manufacturing there was took place mostly in small workshops or homes, where journeymen and apprentices worked with and under master craftsmen, or women spun thread and wove cloth alone at home. Tailors, shoemakers, and blacksmiths made articles by hand for a specific customer.

The clothing trades illustrate well the nineteenth-century changes in manufacturing and distribution. In the eighteenth century, most men wore clothes made by their mothers, wives, or daughters, or occasionally bought used clothing. Wealthy men had clothing made by tailors who cut and sewed unique garments to fit them. A tailor was a master craftsman whose journeymen and apprentices worked with him to produce goods made to order. By the 1820s and 1830s, clothiers and clothing manufacturers had replaced most, though not all, of the old craftsmen and journeymen. In the 1820s clothiers appeared with stocks of ready-made clothes. T. S. Whitmarsh of Boston advertised in 1827 that "he keeps constantly for Sale, from 5 to 10,000 Fashionable ready-made Garments." In 1830, J. T. Jacobs of New York boasted that "Gentlemen can rely upon being as well fitted from the shelves as if their measures were taken—their stock being very extensive and their sizes well assorted."

Clothing Trades

The early mass-produced clothes, crude and limited to a variety of loose-fitting sizes, were mainly produced for men. They sold to men who lived in city boarding and rooming houses, away from the female kin who would previously have made their clothes. Most women made their own clothes, since nearly all girls were expected to acquire sewing skills, but those women who could afford it employed seamstresses to make their tailored garments.

Upon entering Whitmarsh's or Jacobs's emporium

L. J. Levy and Company, exclusively a dry goods retail store, sold ready-to-wear clothing and helped make Chestnut Street a fashionable shopping street in Philadelphia. The Free Library of Philadelphia.

a customer found row after row of ready-made goods without a sign of tailors or a workshop. Unlike the eighteenth-century tailor, the nineteenth-century ready-to-wear clothier was exclusively a retailer. The merchant most likely bought the goods wholesale; if he manufactured them himself, it would not be in his retail shop. Nor were the goods made under the master-journeyman-apprentice system. The former master tailor, now often an entrepreneur, might employ a journeyman to cut out fabric panels, but most of the sewing was put out at piece rates to unskilled or semiskilled labor. In 1832 Boston tailors employed 300 journeymen tailors at $2.00 per day and 100 boys and 1,300 women at 50 cents a day. Most of the women worked in their own homes sewing straight seams. Apprentices, if used at all, were no longer learning a trade but were a permanent source of cheap labor. Sewing skills were learned within a different type of master-apprentice system; they were passed down from mother to daughter.

Essential to this change in the clothing industry was the rise of the cotton textile mill. First in England, then in the United States, mills insatiably processed the increasing supply of cotton grown in the slave South. At the same time, the expanding market economy, fed by the population boom, bought the manufactured cotton goods. The first American textile mill, built in Pawtucket, Rhode Island, in 1790, used water-powered spinning machines constructed from British models by the English immigrant Samuel Slater. Slater employed women and children as cheap labor and sold manufactured thread from Maine to Maryland. Soon other mills sprang up, stimulated by the embargo on British imports from 1807 through 1815. From

1809 through 1813 alone, 151 cotton and woolen companies incorporated.

Early mills also used the putting-out system. Traditionally women had spun their own thread and woven it into cloth for their own families; now many women received thread from the mills and returned finished cloth. The change was subtle but significant: although the work itself was familiar, women now operated their looms for piece-rate wages and produced cloth for the market, not for their own use.

Textile manufacturing was radically transformed in 1813 by the construction of the first American power loom and the chartering of the Boston Manufacturing Company. The corpo-

Waltham (Lowell) System

ration was capitalized at $400,000—ten times the amount behind the Rhode Island mills—by Francis Cabot Lowell and other Boston merchants. Its goal was to eliminate problems of timing, shipping, coordination, and quality control inherent in the putting-out system. The owners erected their factories in Waltham, Massachusetts, combining all the manufacturing processes at a single location. They also employed a resident manager to run the mill, thus separating ownership from management. The company produced cloth suitable for the mass market so inexpensively that most women began to purchase rather than make their own cloth. Nonetheless, spinning and weaving remained women's work in many rural homes. And not until the end of the century would a majority of women purchase ready-made clothing (see page 542).

In the rural setting of Waltham not enough hands could be found to staff the mill, so the managers recruited New England farm daughters, accepting responsibility for their living conditions and their virtue. To persuade young women to come, they offered cash wages, company-run boardinghouses, and such cultural events as evening lectures—none of which were available on the farm. This paternalistic approach, called the Waltham or Lowell system, was adopted in other mills erected alongside New England rivers. The Hamilton Corporation (1825), the Appleton and Lowell corporations (1828), and the Suffolk, Tremont, and Lawrence firms (1831) all followed.

By 1860 a cotton mill resembled a modern factory. A majority of the mill work force by this time were immigrant Irish women, who lived at home; the mills did not provide subsidized housing for them. New England farm girls continued to stay in the remaining boardinghouses, but they had become few in number. Technological improvements in the looms and other machinery made the work tasks less skilled and more alike. The mills could thus pay lower wages, and with increased immigration during the nineteenth century, they always had a reservoir of unskilled labor to draw from. The factory had radically altered work relationships in America.

Textile manufacturing changed New England. Lowell, the famous "city of spindles" that came to symbolize early American industrialization, grew from 2,500 people in 1826 to 33,000 in 1850. The textile industry became the most important in the nation before the Civil War, employing 115,000 workers in 1860, more than half of whom were women and immigrants. The key to its success was that the machines, not the women, spun the thread and wove the cloth. The workers watched the machines and intervened to maintain smooth operation. When a thread broke, for instance, the machine stopped automatically; the worker would find the break, piece the ends together, and restart the machine. The mills used increasingly specialized machines, relying heavily on advances in the machine-tool industry. Here was the American system of manufacturing applied.

Though textile mills were in the vanguard of industrialization, manufacturing grew in many areas. Woolen textiles, farm implements, machine tools, iron, glass, and finished consumer goods all became major industries. "White coal"—water power—was widely used to run the machines. Yet by 1860, the United States was still predominantly an agricultural nation; just over one-half of the work force was engaged in agriculture. Manufacturing accounted for only a third of total production, even though that percentage had doubled in twenty years.

To a great extent, industrialization in this period can be seen as flowing from other changes in American life rather than the agent of change. Ever since Alexander Hamilton's report on manufactures (see page 189), national self-consciousness and pride had emphasized the development of American industry. Contrary to Hamilton's hopes, however, more money flowed into the merchant marine than into industry between 1789 and 1808. In the early republic, greater profits could be made by transporting British products to the United States than by producing the same items at home. But the embargo and the War of 1812 reversed the situation, and merchants began to shift their capital from shipping to manufacturing (see pages 221–226). It was in this new economic environment that the Waltham system took root.

Other factors also helped to stimulate industry. Population growth, especially in urban areas and the Old Northwest, created a large domestic market for finished goods (see maps, page 252). The rise of commercial agriculture brought farmers more fully into the market economy. Specialty merchants and new modes of transportation speeded up the development of these new markets. And the relative scarcity of skilled craftsmen encouraged mechanization—as more workers moved westward than entered the factories, merchants had to find some way to produce more goods with less labor. Finally, beginning with the Tariff of 1816 and culminating in the Tariff of Abominations of 1828, Congress passed tariffs more to protect the market for domestic manufactures than to increase government revenue.

Essential to the rise of manufacturing was the growth of, and specialization in, commerce. Cotton, for instance, had once been traded by plantation agents who handled all the goods produced and bought by the owners, extending credit where needed. As cotton became a great staple export following the invention of the cotton gin in 1793, exports rose from half a million pounds in that year to 83 **Specialization** million pounds in 1815. Gradually **of Commerce** some agents came to specialize in finance alone: cotton brokers appeared, men who for a commission brought together buyers and sellers. Similarly, wheat and hog brokers sprang up in the West—in Cincinnati, Louisville, and St. Louis. The supply of finished goods also became more specialized. Wholesalers bought large quantities of a particular item from manufacturers, and jobbers broke down the wholesale lots for retail stores and country merchants.

In small towns the general merchant persisted for a longer time. Such merchants continued to sell some goods through exchange with farm women—trading flour or pots and pans for eggs or other local produce. They left the sale of finished goods, such as shoes and clothing, to local craftsmen. In rural areas and on the frontier, peddlers acted as general merchants.

But as transportation improved and towns grew, even small-town merchants began to specialize.

Commercial specialization made some traders in the big cities, especially New York, virtual merchant princes. New York had emerged as the dominant port in the late 1790s, outstripping Philadelphia and Boston. When the Erie Canal opened, the city became a standard stop on every major trade route—from Europe, the ports of the South, and the West. New York traders were the middlemen in southern cotton and western grain trading; in fact, New York was the nation's major cotton-exporting city. Merchants in other cities played a similar role within their own regions.

These newly rich traders invested their profits in processing and then manufacturing, further stimulating the growth of northern cities. Some cities became leaders in specific industries: Rochester became a milling center and Cincinnati—"Porkopolis"—the first meat-packing center.

To support their complex commercial transactions, many merchants required large office staffs. In an age before typewriters and carbon paper, much of the office staff—all male—worked **Counting** on high stools laboriously copying **House** business forms and correspondence. **and Credit** The scratch of their pens was the **Systems** early-nineteenth-century equivalent of the typewriter's clatter. At the bottom of the office hierarchy were messenger boys, often pre-teenagers, who delivered documents. Above them were the ordinary copyists, who hand-copied documents in ink as many times as needed. Clerks handled such assignments as customs-house clearances and duties, shipping papers, and translations. Above them were the bookkeeper and the confidential chief clerk. Those seeking employment in such an office, called a counting house, could take a course from a writing master to acquire a "good hand." All hoped to rise to the status of partner.

Banking and other financial institutions played a significant role in the expansion of commerce and manufacturing and were themselves an important industry. The new financial institutions (banks, insurance companies, and corporations) linked savers—those who put money in the bank—with **Banking and** producers or speculators—those who **Credit Systems** wished to borrow money for equip-

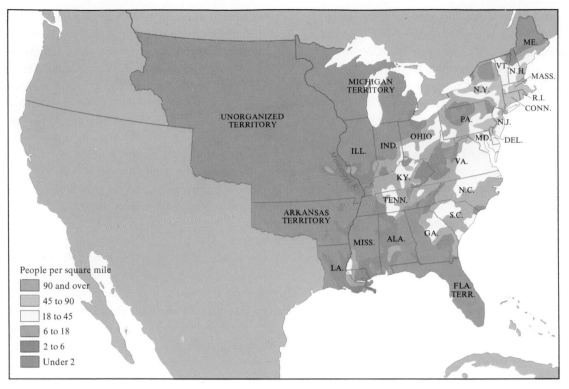

United States Population, 1820

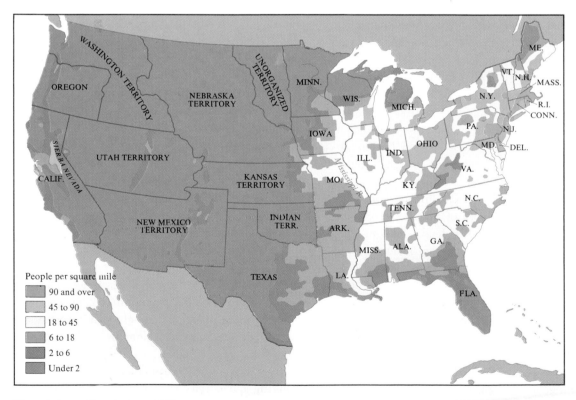

United States Population, 1860

Chapter 9: A MARKET AND INDUSTRIAL ECONOMY, 1800–1860

ment. The expiration of the first Bank of the United States in 1811 after Congress refused to renew its charter acted as a stimulus to state-chartered banks, and in the next five years the number of banks more than doubled. Nonetheless, state banks proved inadequate to spur national growth, and in 1816 Congress chartered the Second Bank of the United States (see page 227). From then until 1832, however, many farmers, local bankers, and politicians denounced the bank as a monster, and they finally succeeded in killing it (see page 341).

The closing of the Second Bank in 1836 caused a nationwide credit shortage that, along with the Panic of 1837, stimulated major reforms in banking. Michigan and New York introduced charter laws promoting what was called *free banking.* Previously every new bank had required a special legislative charter, which made each bank incorporation a political decision. Under the new laws, any proposed bank that met certain minimum conditions—amount of money, notes issued, and types of loans to be made—would automatically receive a state charter. Although banks were thus freer to incorporate, more restrictions were placed on their practices, slightly reducing the risk of bank failure. Other states soon followed suit.

Free banking proved a significant stimulus to the economy in the late 1840s and 1850s. New banks sprang up everywhere, providing merchants and manufacturers with the credit they needed. The free banking laws also served as a precedent for general incorporation statutes, which allowed manufacturing firms to receive state charters without special acts. Investors in corporations, called shareholders, were granted *limited liability,* or freedom from responsibility for the company's debts. An attractive feature to potential investors, limited liability thus encouraged people to back new business ventures.

Business itself became more sophisticated. Merchants learned to evaluate their customers carefully before shipping them goods on credit. One response to the need to minimize risk was Lewis Tappan's mercantile agency, founded in 1841. The forerunner of Dun and Bradstreet, Tappan furnished his subscribers with confidential credit reports on country merchants. One such report read:

James Samson is a peddler, aged 30; he comes to Albany to buy his goods, and then peddles them out along the canal from Albany to Buffalo. He is worth $2,000; owns a wooden house at Lockport . . . has a wife and three children . . . drinks two glasses cider brandy, plain, morning and evening— never more; drinks water after each; chews fine cut; never smokes; good teeth generally; has lost a large double tooth on lower jaw, back, second from throat on left . . . purchases principally jewelry and fancy articles.

Changes in insurance firms also promoted industrialization. In the course of business, insurance companies accumulated large amounts of money as reserves against future claims. Then as now, their greatest profits came from investing those reserves. Beginning in the 1840s and 1850s, insurance companies lent money for longer periods than banks, and they bought shares in corporations. They were able to do so by persuading customers to buy whole-life policies rather than annual term insurance. They also took advantage of improvements in communications to establish networks of local agencies, thus expanding the number of customers they served.

In the 1850s, with credit and capital both more easily obtainable, the pace of industrialization increased. In the North, industry began to rival agriculture and commerce in dollar volume. Meanwhile commercial farming, financed by the credit boom, integrated the early frontier into the northern economy. By 1860 six northern states—Massachusetts, New York, Pennsylvania, Connecticut, Rhode Island, and Ohio—were highly industrialized. The clothing, textile, and shoe industries employed more than 100,000 workers each, lumber 75,000, iron 65,000, and woolens and leather 50,000. Although agriculture still predominated even in these states, industrial employment would soon surpass it.

MILL GIRLS AND MECHANICS

Oh, sing me the song of the Factory Girl!
So merry and glad and free!
The bloom in her cheeks, of health how it speaks,
Oh! a happy creature is she!
She tends the loom, she watches the spindle,

And cheerfully toileth away,
Amid the din of wheels, how her bright eyes
   kindle,
And her bosom is ever gay.

Oh, sing me the song of the Factory Girl!
Whose fabric doth clothe the world.
From the king and his peers to the jolly tars
With our flag o'er all seas unfurled.
From the California's seas, to the tainted breeze
Which sweeps the smokened rooms,
Where "God save the Queen" to cry are seen
The slaves of the British looms.

This idyllic portrait of factory work was an anachronism when it appeared in the Chicopee, Massachusetts, *Telegraph* in 1850. But it was a fitting song for the teenage, single women who first left the villages and farms of New England to work in the mills. The mill owners, believing that the degradation of English factory workers arose from their living conditions and not from the work itself, designed a model community offering airy courtyards and river views, secure dormitories, prepared meals, and cultural activities. Housekeepers enforced strict curfews, banned alcohol, and reported to the corporations on workers' behavior and church attendance.

Kinship ties, the promise of steady work, and good pay at first lured rural young women into the mills. Many pairs of sisters and cousins worked in the same mill and lived in the same boardinghouse. They helped each other adjust, and letters home brought other kin to the mills. Girls then had few opportunities for work outside their own homes, and at the same time their families had less need for their labor. The commercial production of thread and cloth had reduced a good part of the work done in farm households by New England daughters, whereas sons were still needed to assist their fathers. Moreover, the mills paid better wages than did farm work, domestic service, or sewing. Yet the New England daughters, who averaged sixteen and one-half years of age when they entered the mills, usually stayed there only about five years. Few intended to stay longer. Mill earnings brought a special satisfaction: feelings of independence and of freedom of choice in spending or saving their money. That satisfaction was not sufficient, however, to change their life's ambitions to be wives and mothers, not mill girls. Most left the mills to marry, only to be replaced by other women.

In the 1840s factory girls rebelled against the mill and mill town. They expressed their feelings in many ways, as in the song "The Factory Girl's Come-All-Ye" (about 1850):

No more I'll take my bobbins out,
No more I'll put them in,
No more the overseer will say
"You're weaving your cloth too thin!"

No more will I eat cold pudding,
No more will I eat hard bread,
No more will I eat those half-baked beans,
For I vow! They're killing me dead!

I'm going back to Boston town
And live on Tremont Street;
And I want all you fact'ry girls
To come to my house and eat!

What had happened to dash the hopes of these young women? The corporation's goal of building an industrial empire had taken precedence over its concern for workers' living conditions. In the race for profits, owners had lengthened hours, cut wages, and tightened discipline. Eliza R. Hemingway, a six-year veteran of the Massachusetts mills, told an 1845 state House of Representatives committee that the worker's hours were too long, "her time for meals too limited. In the summer season, the work is commenced at 5 o'clock, A.M., and continued 'til 7 o'clock, P.M., with half an hour for breakfast and three quarters of an hour for dinner." When Hemingway worked evenings—which was compulsory—lamps provided dim light in the room. There was no bloom of health in her cheeks.

New England mill workers responded to their deteriorating working conditions by organizing and striking. In 1834, in reaction to a 25-percent wage cut, they unsuccessfully "turned out" (struck) against the Lowell mills. Two years later, when boardinghouse rates were raised, they turned out again. Following the period from 1837 to 1842, when most mills ran only part-time because of a decline in demand for cloth, managers applied still greater pressures on workers. The speedup, the stretch-out, and the premium system became common methods of increasing production. The speedup increased the speed of the machines; the stretch-out increased the number of machines each worker had to operate.

**Mill Girl
Protests**

Premiums were paid to overseers whose departments produced the most cloth. The result was that in Lowell between 1836 and 1850, the number of spindles and looms increased 150 and 140 percent respectively, while the number of workers increased by only 50 percent. Some mill workers began to think of themselves as slaves.

As conditions worsened, workers changed their methods of resistance. In the 1840s strikes gave way to a concerted effort to shorten the workday. Massachusetts mill women joined forces with other workers to press for legislation mandating a ten-hour day. They aired their complaints in worker-run newspapers—the *Factory Girl* appeared in New Hampshire and the *Wampanoag and Operatives' Journal* in Massachusetts, both in 1842. Two years later the *Factory Girl's Garland* and the *Voice of Industry*, nicknamed "the factory girl's voice," were founded. Even the *Lowell Offering*, the owner-sponsored paper that was the pride of mill workers and managers alike, became embroiled in controversy when some workers charged that articles critical of working conditions had been suppressed.

But not all the militant native-born mill workers stayed on to fight the managers and owners, and gradually fewer New England daughters entered the mills. The immigrant women, mostly Irish, who constituted a majority of mill workers by the end of the 1850s were driven to the mills by the need to support their families. Most could not afford to complain about their working conditions.

What happened in the New England mills occurred in less dramatic fashion throughout the nation. Work tasks and workplaces changed, as did relations between workers and supervisors. In the traditional workshops and households, work relationships were intensely personal. People worked within family settings and shared a sense of unity and purpose; men and women had a feeling of control over the quality, value (wages), and conditions of their labor.

But textile mills, insurance companies, wholesale stores, canals, and railroads were the antithesis of the old workshop and household production tradition.

Changes in the Workplace Factories and counting houses lacked the reciprocity that had characterized earlier relationships. Workers lost their sense of autonomy, and impersonal market forces seemed to dominate. Stiff

This 1853 timetable from the Lowell Mills illustrates the regimentation workers had to submit to in the new environment of the factory. Note that workers frequently began before daylight, finished after sunset, and were given only half an hour for meals. Merrimack Valley Textile Museum.

competition among mills in the growing textile industry of the 1820s and 1830s led to layoffs and replacement of operatives with cheaper, less-skilled workers or children. The formal rules of the factory contrasted sharply with the conditions in workshops or farm households. Supervisors separated the workers from the owners. The division of labor and the use of machines reduced the skills required of workers. And the coming and going of the large work forces was governed by the bell, the steam whistle, or the clock. In 1844 the *Factory Girl's Garland* published a poem describing how the ringing of the factory bell controlled when the workers awoke, ate, began and ended work, and went to sleep. The central problem, of course, was the quickening of the work between the bells. Since owners and managers no longer shared the workers' tasks, it was easier for them to expect faster and faster performance.

Like the mill women, most workers at first welcomed the new manufacturing methods; new jobs and higher wages seemed adequate compensation. But later wage reductions, speedups, and stretch-outs changed their minds. Other adjustments were difficult too. Young women in the mills had to tolerate the roar of the looms, and all workers on power machines risked accidents that could kill or maim. Most demoralizing of all, they had to accept that their future was relatively fixed. Opportunities to become an owner or manager in the new system were virtually nil.

Changes in the workplace transformed workers. Initially, mill girls used kinship, village, and gender ties to build supportive networks in factories. In the 1840s and after, as Irish women came to predominate, more workers were strangers before they entered the mills, so that what they had in common, the bases for friendship and mutual support, were their work and job experiences. Yet as a sense of distance from their employers increased, so did deep-seated differences among workers. Nationality, religion, education, and future prospects separated Irish and Yankee mill workers. For many Irish women, mill work was not a stage in their lives; it would be permanent. Unlike their Yankee sisters, they could not risk striking and loss of their jobs; they and their families were dependent upon their earnings. With legions of unskilled immigrants looking for work, Irish mill girls and women considered themselves fortunate to hold on to their jobs, even though the mills cut wages three times in the 1850s and continued the speedups and stretch-outs. Many of the New England women resented the immigrants who came to the mill villages, and management set one against the other through selective hiring and promotions. Though the Irish workers assisted one another as much as possible, formal action was limited.

Eroded too were the republican virtues that artisans shared with the revolutionary war generation. Thomas Jefferson had hoped to preserve these values with the purchase of the Louisiana Territory, but the market economy, in which artisans and household workers were transformed into wage workers, undermined the Jeffersonian hopes with accumulating force and rapidity. Those who stayed in the master-journeyman-apprentice system or remained on farms after the 1830s saw themselves as distinct from the new wage workers. So too did many Yankee mill workers, for whom factory work remained merely a stage in their lifecycle before marriage.

One response to these changes was the active participation of workers in reform politics. In the 1820s labor parties arose in Pennsylvania, New York, and Massachusetts; they eventually spread to a dozen states. These parties advocated free public education, abolition of imprisonment for debt, revision of the militia system (in which workers bore the greatest burden) and opposition to banks and monopolies. Workers' reform often crossed paths with middle-class benevolent movements, since the two groups shared a concern not only for public education but also for public morals: temperance, observance of the Sabbath, and suppression of vice (see Chapter 12). Ironically, however, reform politics tended to divide workers. Many of the reforms—moral education, temperance, Sabbath closings—served merchants and industrialists seeking a more disciplined work force. Others broadened the divisions between native-born and immigrant workers. Anti-immigrant and anti-Catholic movements spread.

Emergence of a Labor Movement

Because of these divisions and economic upheaval, organized labor was not a strong force during this period. Labor unions tended to be local in nature; the strongest resembled medieval guilds. The first unions arose among urban journeymen in printing, woodworking, shoemaking, and tailoring. These craftsmen sought to protect themselves against the competition of inferior workmen by regulating apprenticeship and establishing minimum wages. In the 1820s and 1830s craft unions—unions organized by occupation—forged larger umbrella organizations in the cities, including the National Trades Union (1834). But in the depression of 1839 through 1843, the movement fell apart amidst wage reductions and unemployment. In the 1850s the deterioration of working conditions strengthened the labor movement again. Workers won a reduction in hours, and the ten-hour day became standard. Though the Panic of 1857 wiped out the umbrella organizations, some of the new national unions for specific trade groups—notably printers, hat finishers, and stonecutters—survived. By 1860 five more national unions had been organized by the painters, cordwainers, cotton spinners, iron molders, and machinists.

Organized labor's greatest achievement during this

Women shoe workers strike for higher wages at Lynn, Massachusetts, in 1860.   Library of Congress.

period was in gaining recognition of its right to exist. When journeymen shoemakers organized in the first decade of the century, employers **Right to Strike** turned to the courts, charging criminal conspiracy. The cordwainers' conspiracy cases, which involved six trials from 1806 through 1815, left labor organizations in a tenuous position. Although the journeymen's right to organize was recognized, the courts ruled unlawful any coercive action that harmed other businesses or the public. In effect strikes were illegal. Eventually a Massachusetts case, *Commonwealth* v. *Hunt* (1842), effectively reversed the decision when Chief Justice Lemuel Shaw ruled that Boston journeymen bootmakers could combine and strike "in such manner as best to subserve their own interests."

The impact of economic and technological change, however, fell more heavily on individual workers than on their organizations. As a group, the workers' share of the national wealth declined after the 1830s. Individual producers—craftsmen, factory workers, and farmers—had less economic power than they had had a generation or two before. And workers were increasingly losing control over their own work.

COMMERCIAL FARMING

Beyond the town and city limits, agriculture remained the backbone of the economy. Although urban areas were growing quickly, so too were rural districts, and America was still overwhelmingly rural; even in 1860 rural residents far outnumbered urban dwellers. Indeed, it was rural population growth that transformed so many farm villages into bustling small cities. And it was the ability of farmers to feed the growing town and village populations that made possible the concentration of population and the development of commerce and industry.

New England and Middle Atlantic farmers in 1800 worked as their fathers and mothers had. They tilled relatively small plots of land centered around a household economy in which the needs of the family and the labor it supplied mostly determined what was produced and in what amounts. Most of their implements were homemade—wooden plows, rakes, shovels, and yokes. For iron parts, they turned to the local blacksmith.

But then canals and railroads began transporting grains, especially wheat, eastward from the fertile Old Northwest. And at the same time, northeastern agriculture developed some serious **Northeastern** problems. Northeastern farmers had **Agriculture** already cultivated all the land they could; expansion was impossible. Moreover, these small New England farms with their uneven terrain did not lend themselves to the new labor-saving farm implements introduced in the 1830s—mechanical sowers, reapers, threshers, and balers. Many northeastern farms also suffered from soil exhaustion: the worn-out land produced lower yields while requiring a greater investment in seed.

In response to these problems and to competition from the West, many northern farmers either went west or gave up farming for jobs in the merchant houses and factories. For eastern farm sons and daughters, western New York was the first frontier. After the Erie Canal was completed, these Yankees and Yorkers settled on more fertile, cheaper land in Ohio and Illinois, and then in Michigan, Indiana, and Wisconsin. Farm daughters who did not go west flocked to the early textile mills. Still other New Englanders—urban, better educated, and often experienced in trade—entered the counting houses of New York and other cities.

Neither the counting house nor the factory, however, depleted New England agriculture. The farmers who remained proved as adaptable at farming as their children did at copy desks and water-powered looms. By the 1850s New England and Middle Atlantic farmers were successfully adjusting to competition from western agricultural products. They abandoned commercial production of wheat and corn and stopped tilling poor land. Instead they improved their livestock, especially cattle, and specialized in vegetable and fruit production and dairy farming. They financed these changes through land sales or borrowing. In fact, their greatest profit was made from increasing land values, not from farming itself.

Yet many could not buy farm land. Indeed, the growing division between worker and owner was mirrored in commercial agriculture by the gap between hired hands or tenants and farm owners. Though the United States was still primarily an agricultural nation—and many saw the frontier farm as the antidote to commerce and industrialization—not all farmers were yeomen. Farm laborers, once scarce in the United States, had become commonplace. In the North in 1860 there was one hired hand for every 2.3 farms. Given the high cost of land and of farming by that time, hired hands had little opportunity to acquire farms of their own. By the 1850s it took from ten to twenty years for a rural laborer to save enough money to farm for himself. For the same reason, the number of tenant farmers increased.

Nonetheless, state governments still energetically promoted commercial agriculture in order to spur economic growth and sustain the values of an agrarian-based republic. Massachusetts in 1817 and New York in 1819 subsidized agricultural prizes and county fairs. New York required contestants to submit written descriptions of how they grew their prize crops; the state then published the best essays to encourage the use of new methods and to promote specialization. Farm journals also helped to familiarize farmers with developments in agriculture. By 1860 there were nearly sixty journals with a combined circulation of from 250,000 to 300,000.

Even so, the Old Northwest gradually and inevitably replaced the northeastern states as the center of American family agriculture. Farms in the Old Northwest were much larger than **Mechanization** northeastern ones and better suited **of Agriculture** to the new mechanized farming implements. The farmers of the region bought machines such as the McCormick reaper on credit and paid for them with the profits from their high yields. By 1847 Cyrus McCormick was selling a thousand reapers a year. Using interchangeable

Chapter 9: A MARKET AND INDUSTRIAL ECONOMY, 1800–1860

parts, he expanded production to five thousand a year, but still demand outstripped supply. Similarly, John Deere's steel plow, invented in 1837, replaced the inadequate iron plow; steel blades kept the soil from sticking and were tough enough to break the roots of prairie grass. By 1856, Deere's sixty-five employees were making 13,500 plows a year.

These machines eased the problem of scarce farm labor and permitted a 70-percent surge in wheat production in the 1850s alone. By that time the area that had been the western wilderness in 1800 had become one of the world's leading agricultural regions. Midwestern farmers fed an entire nation and a generation of immigrants, and had food to export.

THE WESTERN FRONTIER

Between 1800 and 1860 the frontier moved westward at an incredible pace. In 1800 the edge of settlement formed an arc from western New

Movement of the Frontier

York through the new states of Kentucky and Tennessee, south to Georgia. Twenty years later it had shifted to Ohio, Indiana, and Illinois in the North and Louisiana, Alabama, and Mississippi in the South. By 1860 settlement had reached the West Coast; the 1800 frontier was long-settled, and once-unexplored regions were dotted with farms and mines, towns and villages. Unsettled land remained— mostly between the Mississippi River and the Sierra Nevada—but essentially the frontier and its native inhabitants, the Indians, had given way to white settlement (see pages 287–290). All that remained for whites was to people the plains and mountain territories.

The legal boundaries of the country also changed rapidly during this period. Between 1803 and 1853 the United States pushed its original boundaries to their present continental limits (except for Alaska). The Louisiana Purchase roughly doubled the nation's size, and the acquisition of Florida from Spain in 1819 secured the Southeast. In the 1840s the United States annexed the Republic of Texas, defined its northern border with Canada, and acquired through

war California, Nevada, Utah, and most of Arizona from Mexico (see pages 349, 357). In the 1850s the Gadsden Purchase added southern Arizona and New Mexico.

The lore of the vanishing frontier forms part of the mythology of America. It includes fur trappers, explorers, and pioneers braving an unknown environment and hostile Indians; settlers crossing the arid plains and snow-covered Rockies by Conestoga wagon to bring civilization to the wilderness; Mormons finding Zion in the Great American Desert; forty-niners sailing on clipper ships to California in search of gold.

Americans have only recently come to recognize that there are other sides to these familiar stories. Women, Indians, and blacks as well as white men were pioneers. Explorers and pioneers did not discover North America by themselves, nor did the wagon trains fight their way across the plains—Indians guided them along traditional paths and led them to food and water. And rather than civilizing the frontier, settlers at first brought a rather primitive economy and society, which did not compare favorably with the well-ordered Indian civilizations. In the South, frontier settlement carried with it slavery. The Mormons who sought a new Jerusalem by Salt Lake were fleeing the gehenna (hell) imposed on them by intolerant, violent frontier folk farther east (see page 329). And all those who sought furs, gold, and lumber spoiled the natural landscape in the name of progress and development.

This was the ironic contrast between the ideal and the reality of the frontier. If pioneers were attracted by the beauty and bounty of the American wilderness, if they were lured by the opportunity to live a simple, rewarding life close to the soil, they were also destroying the natural landscape in the process. It was almost as if the vast forests, prairies, and lakes were enemies to be conquered and bent to their will. Millions of trees were felled to make way for farms. Michigan lumbermen denuded the land. And farther west, miners in search of gold leveled the hills.

No figure has come to symbolize the frontier more aptly than the footloose, rugged fur trapper, who roamed thousands of unmapped miles in search of

Fur Trade

pelts. The trapper, with his backpack, rifle, and kegs of whiskey, spearheaded America's manifest destiny (see page 346), extending the United States

*Spring rendezvous at Green River, Wyoming, painted by
W. H. Jackson. United States Department of the Interior,
National Park Service.*

presence to the Pacific Slope. Fur trading, especially
for beaver, had been economically important since
the early colonial period. Traders were the link in
an elaborate network that reached from beyond the
settled frontier to sophisticated European shops. But
after 1800 American investors organized to compete
with foreign trading companies such as Hudson's Bay.
The German immigrant John Jacob Astor, for instance,
became a millionaire through his American Fur Trading Company. And Americans also changed the
method by which furs were acquired. In 1825 the
St. Louis merchant William Henry Ashley pioneered
the rendezvous system. Instead of buying beaver furs
from Indians, Ashley sent out non-Indian trappers
to roam the Rockies and farther west; at a meeting
on the Green River, in present-day Wyoming, at
season's end, the trappers exchanged their pelts for
goods Ashley had brought in from St. Louis. This
annual spring rendezvous was the hallmark of the
American fur-trading system through the late 1830s,
when silk hats replaced beaver ones and trapping
declined. In many areas the beaver had been virtually
trapped out of existence.

Throughout the West trappers sought the cooperation of neighboring tribes in their territory, and
nearly 40 percent wed Indian women. Most often
the trapper or trader followed the tribe's custom,
negotiating with her parents for the match. When
a chief's daughter wed a fur merchant, separate cultures
convened to celebrate, as when Archibald McDonald
of the Hudson's Bay Company and Koale-xoa, daughter
of a Chinook chief, were married in traditional ceremonies at the mouth of the Columbia River. Since
in Indian and white frontier societies there was little
distinction between public and private spheres, an
Indian wife played an important "public" role in
bridging trapper culture and economy and Indian
society. Moreover, Indian women brought special
trading privileges as well as family ties and experiences
of life on the frontier. Over time, Métis or mixed
bloods (Indian-white offspring) and white women
replaced Indian women as trappers' wives; not only
did this change trapper culture but in itself it was a
sign of the decline of the fur trade. It signaled the
coming of settled, agrarian society.

The history of trapping was in essence the history

The gold rush brought treasure seekers—men and women, white and black, native and foreign born—to California. Few found their fortune in gold, but most stayed to settle the West Coast. California State Library.

of the frontier. Early fur traders exploited friendly Indian tribes; then pioneers (mountain trappers) monopolized the trade through the systematic organization and financial backing of trading companies. Soon settlements and towns sprang up along the trappers' routes. With the decline in the fur trade, some trappers settled down. In Oregon in 1843 former trappers helped organize the first provisional government and pressured for United States statehood. In the mountain states the mining and cattle frontiers were to continue for another half-century, following the development of the fur-trading frontier.

But not all regions followed this pattern. By contrast, California was settled almost overnight. In January 1848 James Marshall, a carpenter, spotted a few gold-

California Gold Rush

like particles in the millrace at Sutter's Mill (now Coloma, California). Word of the discovery spread, and other Californians rushed to garner instant fortunes. When John C. Frémont reached San Francisco in June 1848, he found that "all, or nearly all, its male inhabitants had gone to the mines." The town, "which a few months before was so busy and thriving, was then almost deserted."

By 1849 the news had spread eastward; hundreds of thousands of fortune-seekers flooded in. Most forty-niners never found enough gold to pay their expenses. "The stories you hear frequently in the States," one gold-seeker wrote home, "are the most extravagant lies imaginable—the mines are a humbug. . . . the almost universal feeling is to get home." But many stayed, unable to afford the passage back home, or tempted by the growing labor shortage in California's cities and agricultural districts. San Francisco, the gateway from the coast to the interior, became an instant city, ballooning from 1,000 people in 1848 to 35,000 just two years later.

Although those who came produced almost nothing, they had to be fed. Thus began the great California agricultural boom, centered along the natural waterways in the fertile interior of the state. Wheat was the great staple; it required minimal investment, was easily planted, and offered a quick return at the end of a relatively short growing season. California farmers became eager importers of machinery, since wages were high in the labor-scarce district and the extensive flat, treeless plains were well suited to horse-drawn machines. By the mid-1850s, California was exporting wheat. In its growing cities, merchant princes arose to supply, feed, and clothe the new settlers. One such merchant was Levi Strauss, whose tough mining pants became synonymous with American jeans.

Still food had to be cooked and clothes washed. In the western frontier women were relatively few in number. Unlike the Midwest, where family farms were the basic unit of production **Frontier** and life, in California gold and ore **Women** mining, grazing, and large-scale wheat farming were overwhelmingly male occupations. The women who comprised about one-seventh of the travelers on the overland trails found that their domestic skills were therefore in great demand. They received high fees for cooking, laundering, and sewing, and inevitably the boardinghouses and hotels were run by women, as men shunned domestic work. Not all women were entrepreneurs. Some found their domestic skills offered free by over-hospitable husbands. Abigail Scott Duniway, a leading western crusader for women's suffrage and a veteran of the Overland Trail to Oregon, wrote of one woman's experience. "It was a hospitable neighborhood composed chiefly of bachelors," she wrote in 1859, "who found comfort in mobilizing at meal time at the homes of the few married men of the township, and seemed especially fond of congregating at the hospitable cabin home of my good husband, who was never quite so much in his glory as when entertaining men at this fireside, while I,

if not washing, scrubbing, churning, or nursing the baby, was preparing their meals in our lean-to kitchen."

Gold altered the pattern of settlement along the entire Pacific Coast. Before 1848 most overland traffic flowed north over the Oregon Trail; fewer pioneers turned south to California or used the Santa Fe Trail. But by 1849 a pioneer observed that the Oregon Trail "bore no evidence of having been much traveled this year." Traffic was instead flowing south, and California was becoming the new population center of the Pacific Slope. One measure of the shift was the overland mail routes. In the 1840s the Oregon Trail had been the major communications link between the Pacific and the Midwest. But the Post Office officials who organized mail routes in the 1850s terminated them in California; there was no route farther north than Sacramento.

By 1860 California, like the Great Plains and prairies farther east, had become a farmers' and merchants' frontier. Though the story of these settlers is less dramatic than that of the trappers **Farming** and forty-niners, it is nevertheless **Frontier** the story of the overwhelming majority of westerners before 1860. The farming frontier started first on the western fringes of the eastern seaboard states and in the Old Northwest, then moved to the edge of the Great Plains and California. Pioneer families cleared the land of trees or prairie grass, hoed in corn and wheat, fenced in animals, and constructed cabins of logs or sod. If they were successful—and many were not—they slowly cleared more land. As settled areas expanded, farmers built roads to carry their stock and produce to market and bring back supplies they could not produce themselves. Growth brought specialization; as western farmers shifted from self-sufficiency to commercial farming, they too tended to concentrate on one crop. By this time the area was no longer a frontier, and families seeking new land had to go farther west. In John Jervis's time a farmer from Rome, New York, might have gone to Michigan via the Erie Canal and Lake Erie. A later generation would go farther west to Iowa, Nebraska, or even California.

What made farm settlement possible was the availability of land and credit. Some public lands were granted as a reward for military ser- **Land Grants** vice: veterans of the War of 1812 **and Sales** received 160 acres; veterans of the

The greatest wealth was to be found in supplying, feeding, and clothing the gold seekers. Men and women opened stores for and provided services to the miners; overnight towns like Marysville, California, sprang up in the gold district.   Library of Congress.

Mexican War (see Chapter 13) could purchase land at reduced prices. And until 1820, civilians could buy government land at $2 an acre (a relatively high price) on a liberal four-year payment plan. More important, from 1800 to 1817 the government successively reduced the minimum purchase from 640 to 80 acres. However, when the availability of land prompted a flurry of land speculation that ended in the Panic of 1819, the government discontinued credit sales. Instead it reduced the price further, to $1.25 an acre.

Some eager pioneers settled land before it had been surveyed and put up for sale. Such illegal settlers, or squatters, then had to buy the land they lived on at auction, and faced the risk of being unable to purchase it. In 1841, to facilitate settlement, simplify

land sales, and end property disputes, Congress passed the Pre-emption Act, which legalized settlement prior to surveying.

Since most settlers, squatters or not, needed to borrow money, private credit systems arose. Banks, private investors, country storekeepers, and speculators all extended credit to farmers. Railroads also sold land on credit—land they had received from the government as construction subsidies. (The Illinois Central, for example, received 2.6 million acres in 1850.) Indeed, nearly all economic activity in the West involved credit, from land sales to the shipping of produce to railroad construction. And again in 1836, 1855, and 1856 easy credit helped to boost land prices. When the speculative bubbles burst, much land fell into the hands of speculators, and as a

spearheaded settlement farther west. Steamboats connected eastern markets and ports with these river and lake cities, carrying grain east and returning with finished goods. As in the Northeast, these western cities eventually developed into manufacturing centers when merchants shifted their investments from commerce to industry. Chicago became a center for the manufacture of farm implements, Louisville of textiles, and Cleveland of iron. Smaller cities specialized in flour mills, and all produced consumer goods for the hinterlands.

Urban growth in the West was so spectacular that by 1860 Cincinnati, St. Louis, and Chicago had populations exceeding 100,000, and Buffalo, Louisville, San Francisco, Pittsburgh, Detroit, Milwaukee, and Cleveland had surpassed 40,000. Thus commerce, urbanization, and industrialization overtook the farmers' frontier, wedding the Old Northwest and areas beyond to the Northeast.

For the nation as a whole, the period from 1800 through 1860 was one of sustained growth. Population increased sixfold. Settlement, once restricted to the Atlantic seaboard and the eastern rivers, extended more than a thousand miles inland by 1860 and was spreading east from the Pacific Ocean as well. Whereas agriculture had completely dominated the nation at the turn of the century, by midcentury farming was being challenged by a booming manufacturing sector. And agriculture itself was becoming mechanized.

Economic development changed the American landscape and the way people lived. Canals, railroads, steamboats, and telegraph lines linked together economic activities hundreds and thousands of miles apart. The market economy brought both sustained growth and cycles of boom and bust. Hard times and unemployment became frequent occurrences.

At the same time, commercial and industrial growth altered production and consumption. Manufactured goods changed farm work as farmers began to purchase goods produced formerly by wives and daughters. Many New England farm daughters left the farms to become the first factory workers in the new textile industry. As factories grew larger and as factory production replaced the master-journeyman-apprentice system, workplace relations became more impersonal and conditions harsher. Immigrants began to form a new industrial group, and some workers organized labor unions.

consequence tenancy became more common in the West than it had been in New England.

Towns and cities were the lifelines of the agricultural West. Cities along the Ohio and Mississippi rivers—Pittsburgh, Louisville, Cincinnati, and St. Louis—preceded most of the settlement of the early frontier.

Frontier Cities A generation later the lake cities of Cleveland, Detroit, and Chicago

The American people too were changing. Immigration and western expansion made the people and society more diverse. Urbanization, commerce, and industry produced significant divisions among Americans. And their reach extended deeply into the home as well as the workshop.

SUGGESTIONS FOR FURTHER READING

General

Stuart Bruchey, *The Roots of American Economic Growth, 1607–1861: An Essay in Social Causation* (1965); David Klingaman and Richard Vedder, eds., *Essays in 19th Century History* (1975); Susan Previant Lee and Peter Passell, *A New Economic View of American History* (1979); Otto Mayr and Robert C. Post, eds., *Yankee Enterprise. The Rise of the American System of Manufactures* (1981); Douglass C. North, *Economic Growth of the United States, 1790–1860* (1966); Nathan Rosenberg, *Technology and American Economic Growth* (1972).

Transportation

Robert G. Albion, *The Rise of New York Port, 1815–1860* (1939); Albert Fishlow, *American Railroads and the Transformation of the Ante-Bellum Economy* (1965); Carter Goodrich, *Government Promotion of American Canals and Railroads, 1800–1890* (1960); Louis C. Hunter, *Steamboats on the Western Rivers* (1949); Harry N. Scheiber, *Ohio Canal Era: A Case Study of Government and the Economy, 1820–1861* (1969); Ronald E. Shaw, *Erie Water West: Erie Canal, 1797–1854* (1966); George R. Taylor, *The Transportation Revolution, 1815–1860* (1951).

Commerce and Manufacturing

Alfred D. Chandler, Jr., *The Visible Hand: Managerial Revolution in American Business* (1977); Thomas C. Cochran, *Frontiers of Change: Early Industrialization in America* (1981); H. J. Habakkuk, *American and British Technology in the Nineteenth Century* (1962); Louis Hartz, *Economic Policy and Democratic Thought: Pennsylvania, 1776–1860* (1954); David J. Jeremy, *Transatlantic Industrial Revolution: The Diffusion of Textile Technologies Between Britain and America, 1790s–1830s* (1981); Stanley I. Kutler, *Privilege and Creative Destruction. The Charles River Bridge Case* (1971); James D. Norris, *R. G. Dun & Co. 1841–1900* (1978); Merritt Roe Smith, *Harpers Ferry Armory and the New Technology* (1977); Caroline F. Ware, *Early New England Cotton Manufacturing* (1931).

Agriculture

Percy Bidwell and John Falconer, *History of Agriculture in the Northern United States 1620–1860* (1925); Allan G. Bogue, *From Prairie to Corn Belt: Farming on the Illinois and Iowa Prairies in the Nineteenth Century* (1963); Clarence Danhof, *Change in Agriculture: The Northern United States, 1820–1870* (1969); Paul W. Gates, *The Farmer's Age: Agriculture, 1815–1860* (1962); Benjamin H. Hibbard, *A History of Public Land Policies* (1939); Robert Leslie Jones, *History of Agriculture in Ohio to 1880* (1983); Edward C. Kendall, *John Deere's Steel Plow* (1959).

The Western Frontier

Ray A. Billington, *The Far Western Frontier, 1830–1860* (1956); Ray A. Billington and Martin Ridge, *Westward Expansion*, 5th ed., (1982); John Mack Faragher, *Women and Men on the Overland Trail* (1979); William H. Goetzmann, *Exploration and Empire: The Explorer and the Scientist in the Winning of the American West* (1966); Leroy R. Hafen, ed., *The Mountain Men and the Fur Trade of the Far West*, 10 vols. (1965–1972); John A. Hawgood, *America's Western Frontier: The Exploration and Settlement of the Trans-Mississippi West* (1967); Julie Roy Jeffrey, *Frontier Women. The Trans-Mississippi West 1840–1880* (1979); Theodore J. Karamanski, *Fur Trade and Exploration. Opening the Far Northwest 1821–1852* (1983); John D. Unruh, Jr., *The Overland Emigrants and the Trans-Mississippi West, 1840–1860* (1979); David J. Wishart, *The Fur Trade of the American West, 1807–1840* (1979).

Workers

Alan Dawley, *Class and Community: The Industrial Revolution in Lynn* (1977); Thomas Dublin, *Women at Work: The Transformation of Work and Community in Lowell, Massachusetts, 1826–1860* (1979); Thomas Dublin, ed., *Farm to Factory. Women's Letters, 1830–1860* (1981); Susan E. Hirsch, *Roots of the American Working Class: The Industrialization of Crafts in Newark, 1800–1860* (1978); Alice Kessler-Harris, *Out to Work. A History of Wage-Earning Women in the United States* (1982); Bruce Laurie, *Working People of Philadelphia, 1800–1850* (1980); Norman Ware, *The Industrial Worker, 1840–1860* (1924); Sean Willentz, *Chants Democratic: New York City and the Rise of the American Working Class, 1788–1850* (1984).

Toward Greater Diversity:
The American People
1800–1860

Chapter 10

For twenty years actors Edwin Forrest and his English rival William Charles Macready had vied for the favor of American audiences. Literary and intellectual circles lionized Macready; artisans and mechanics preferred Forrest, an American who stressed his love of flag, country, and democracy. When the two actors appeared simultaneously in New York City in May 1849, posters went up challenging Macready.

WORKING MEN,
shall
AMERICANS OR ENGLISH RULE
in this city?

Macready's opening night was ruined by noise and a barrage of objects, including four chairs, thrown from the gallery. Later in his run a crowd gathered outside the theater, protesting Macready's appearance as a symbol of "English *ARISTOCRATS!!* and Foreign Rule!" Adding to the fray were Anglophobic Irish immigrants, recently escaped from famine and English rule. As Macready left the theater under police protection, the mob surged. The militia, on guard to maintain order, fired in the air, missing the rioters but felling dozens of bystanders. Twenty-two people were killed, thirty-six injured.

This incident was an extreme version of the chaos typical of theaters. The Englishwoman Frances Trollope, in her *Domestic Manners of the Americans* (1832), described the audience at a Cincinnati theater: "The spitting was incessant," accompanied by "the mixed smell of onions and whiskey. . . . The noises, too, were perpetual, and of the most unpleasant kind." An 1830 theater poster forbade "personal altercations in any part of the house," "the uncourteous habit of throwing nut shells, apples, etc., into the Pit," and "clambering over the balustrade into the Boxes, either during or at the end of the Performance." Indeed, theater regularly evoked the strongest of passions among Americans. "When a patriotic fit seized them, and 'Yankee Doodle' was called for," Trollope observed, "every man seemed to think his reputation as a citizen depended on the noise he made."

The theater, a pre-eminent institution in American life, reflected the class, race, ethnic, gender, and patriotic divisions and conflicts of the times. On the floor of the theater were the benches of the pit, where the mass of mechanics and artisans sat. In the tiers of boxes beyond the pit were the most expensive seats, where merchants, professionals, and ladies gathered. The third tier of boxes was generally reserved for less respectable women—boardinghouse keepers and other gainfully employed women. Above these boxes, farthest from the stage, was the gallery (balcony). If the theater permitted blacks, they sat in the gallery, along with prostitutes and those of the working class unable to afford a seat in the pit.

As the American scene changed, so did the theater. As cities and towns grew larger, they boasted more than one or two theaters, and different houses began to cater to different classes. In New York, the Park Theater enjoyed the patronage of the carriage trade, the Bowery drew the middle class, and the Chatham attracted workers. The opera house generally became the upper-class playhouse. Again, the theater mirrored society, for with the increasing pace of urbanization and industrialization, the gap between the sexes and classes yawned wider. It was economic hardship as much as patriotism that sent Edwin Forrest's admirers into the streets of New York in 1849. The theater was the stage for their much larger drama.

Indeed, as the United States grew, its society became at once more diverse and more turbulent. Communities changed as they grew larger everywhere, and, with increased mobility, one year's frontier became the next year's settled town. More and more people lived in cities, where poverty, overcrowding, and crime set them against each other. Opulent mansions existed within sight of notorious slums, and both wealth and poverty reached extremes unknown in traditional agrarian America.

Private space—the family—underwent changes too. With increasing industrialization, the home began to lose its function as a workplace. Especially among the middle and upper classes, it became woman's domain, a refuge from man's world. At the same time, birth control was more widely practiced and families were smaller.

Immigration further increased social diversity.

Within large cities and in the countryside, whole districts became European enclaves. In hiring themselves out to build transportation and industry, immigrants reshaped American culture in the process.

The position of free blacks and Indians within this society was uncertain. Their very presence disturbed many Americans. Free people of color were second-class citizens at best, struggling to better their lot against overwhelming legal and racial barriers. Eastern Indians, forced to abandon their lands for resettlement beyond the Mississippi River, fared no better.

To a great degree, many Americans were uncomfortable with the new direction of American life. Antipathy toward immigrants was common among native-born Americans, who feared competition for jobs. Blacks fought unceasingly for equality, and Indians tried unsuccessfully to resist forced removal. And some women began to raise their voices against the restrictions they faced. In a society growing ever more diverse and complex, conflict became common.

COUNTRY LIFE, CITY LIFE

Communities, and life within them, changed significantly in the first half of the nineteenth century. Within a generation many frontier settlements became sources rather than recipients of migration. Villages in western New York State lured the sons and daughters of New England in the first two decades of the century. Yet in the 1820s and 1830s, after the best land was settled and tilled and the Erie Canal opened (1825), young people moved from New York villages to the new frontier in the Old Northwest. Later, Ohio and Michigan towns and farms would send their young people further west. Similarly, migrants from the Upper South went to Illinois and Ohio as people on the move further south settled the Gulf states.

Widespread settlement and the development of towns rapidly overtook the frontier so that the isolated pioneers of the 1840s and 1850s—the hunter, the trapper, the homesteader—were more than one thousand miles from where their counterparts had been in the 1800s and 1810s. For all the romance of pioneering, many longed for a sense of community. In the late 1820s Mrs. Trollope visited a farm family living near Cincinnati. The family grew or produced all their necessities except for coffee, tea, and whiskey, which they got by sending butter or chickens to market. But until other settlers came to live near them, they lacked the human contact that a community offered. For their inexpensive land and self-sufficiency they paid the price of isolation and loneliness. " 'Tis strange to us to see company," lamented the mother. "I expect the sun may rise and set a hundred times before I shall see another *human* that does not belong to the family."

Throughout the United States, however, the farm community rather than the isolated family dominated rural America. The farm village was the center of rural life—the farmers' link with religion, politics, and the outside world. But rural social life was not limited to trips to the village; families gathered on each other's farms to do as a community what they could not do individually. Barn-raising was among the activities that regularly brought people together. In preparation for the event, the farmer and an itinerant carpenter built a platform and cut beams, posts, and joists. When the neighbors arrived by buggy and wagon, they put together the sides and raised them into position. After the roof was up, everyone celebrated with a communal meal, and perhaps with singing and dancing. Similar gatherings took place at harvest time and on special occasions.

Farm Communities

Rural women met more formally than did men. Farm men had frequent opportunities to mix at general stores, markets, and taverns. Women had to prearrange their regular work and social gatherings: after-church dinners; sewing, quilting, and corn-husking bees; and preparations for marriages and baptisms. These were times to exchange experiences and thoughts, offer each other support, and swap letters, books, and news.

Irene Hardy, who spent her childhood in rural southwestern Ohio in the 1840s, left a record of the gatherings she attended as a girl. Most vivid in her memory fifty years later were the apple bees, when neighbors gathered to make apple butter or preserves. "Usually invitations were sent about by word of mouth," she recalled. " 'Married folks' came and

Country people looked forward to combining work and play in communal bees. At the annual fall apple bee, depicted above, young and old gathered to socialize, gossip, play, eat, court, and make apple preserves.   Library of Congress.

worked all day or afternoon." A dinner feast followed, for which the visiting women made biscuits, vegetables, and coffee. After cleaning up, "the old folks went home to send their young ones for their share of work and fun." The elders gossiped to pass the time; the youngsters joked and teased each other in a comic-serious precourting ritual. "Then came supper, apple and pumpkin pies, cider, doughnuts, cakes, cold chicken and turkey," Hardy wrote, "after which games, 'Forfeits,' 'Building a Bridge,' 'Snatchability,' even 'Blind Man's Buff' and 'Pussy Wants a Corner.' "

Traditional country bees had their town counterparts. Fredrika Bremer, a Swedish visitor to the United States, described a sewing bee in 1849 in Cambridge, Massachusetts, at which neighborhood women made clothes for "a family who had lost all their clothing by fire." Yet these town bees were not the all-day family affairs typical of the countryside, and when the Hardy family moved to the town of Eaton in 1851, young Irene missed the country gatherings. The families of Eaton seldom held bees; they purchased their goods at the store.

Everywhere cities were growing, especially in the North. The transportation revolution and the ex-pansion of commerce and manufacturing, fed by immigration and internal migration, caused cities to burst their colonial boundaries. Between 1800 and 1860, the number of Americans increased sixfold to 31.4 million. As the population grew, the frontier receded, and rural settlements became towns. In 1800 the nation had only 33 towns with 2,500 or more people and only 3 with more than 25,000. By 1860, 392 towns exceeded 2,500 in population and 35 had more than 25,000.

In the Northeast, the percentage of people living in urban areas grew from 9 to 35 percent from 1800 to 1860. Significantly, most of this growth occurred in northern and western communities located along the new transportation routes, where increased commerce created new jobs and opportunities. Kingston, New York, ninety miles north of New York City on the Hudson River, was one example. The Delaware and Hudson Canal, which extended from the Hudson Valley to the coalfields of Pennsylvania, rapidly transformed Kingston from a sleepy farm village of 1,000 in the 1820s to an urban community of more than 10,000 in 1850.

Growth of Cities

The hundreds of small new cities like Kingston were surpassed by stars of even greater magnitude: the great metropolitan cities. In 1860 twenty-one cities exceeded 40,000 in population and nine exceeded 100,000 (see maps, page 272). By 1810 New York City had overtaken Philadelphia as the nation's most populous city, and major port and commercial center; its population soared thereafter, reaching 1,174,779 in 1860. Baltimore and New Orleans dominated the South, and San Francisco became the leading West Coast city. In the Midwest the new lake cities (Chicago, Detroit, and Cleveland) began to overtake the frontier river cities (Cincinnati, Louisville, and Pittsburgh) founded a generation earlier. These cities formed a nationwide urban network, linked by canals, roads, and railroads, connecting the great metropolises of the North (see Chapter 9).

Rapid urban growth in turn brought about a radical change in American commerce and trade. In 1800 most merchants performed the functions of retailer, wholesaler, importer and exporter, and banker. But in New York and Philadelphia in the 1790s, and increasingly in all large cities after the War of 1812, the general merchant gave way to the specialist. As a result, the distribution of goods became more systematic. By the 1830s and 1840s, urban centers had been transformed into a pattern we would recognize today: retail shops featured such specialized lines as shoes, wines and spirits, dry goods, and hardware. Within the downtown area importers and exporters, wholesalers, bankers, and insurance brokers clustered on particular streets, near transportation and the merchant exchanges that catered to specialized trades.

Thus Kingston in the 1850s differed from Kingston in the 1820s not just in size and population density but also in the complexity of its institutions. In the small rural village of the 1820s, homes and workplaces were often combined; thirty years later Kingston had separate commercial and residential districts. By 1858 Kingston's downtown boasted china shops, clothing stores, fancy-goods outlets, and dry-goods stores, as well as other retail shops, doctors' and lawyers' offices, and financial firms. Beyond the commercial center, two small industrial zones housed nearly all of the city's manufacturing.

Other city institutions became more complex as well. As the workplace and home grew apart, there were fewer opportunities to turn work into festivals

City Life or family gatherings as rural folk did in barn-raisings and sewing bees. In cities, amusements were more organized than in the country. Entertainment became part of specialized commerce; one purchased a ticket—to the theater, the circus, or P. T. Barnum's American Museum; or in the 1840s, to the racetrack; or a decade later, to the baseball park. The concentration of population in cities supported this diversity of activities.

Though population density and cultural diversity animated city life, they also became problems in themselves. Sporting events became so crowded that one New Yorker doubted whether it was worth battling the mobs of people to attend the racetrack. The "crowd and the dust and the danger and the difficulty of getting on and off the course with a carriage," Philip Hone wrote in 1842, "are scarcely compensated by any pleasure to be derived from the amusement." Everywhere there seemed to be mobs of people. When P. T. Barnum brought Jenny Lind, the famous Swedish soprano, to New York in September 1850, twenty thousand people mobbed the hotel entrance for a glimpse of her.

As cities grew in size, public transportation made it easier to get around. Horse-drawn buses appeared in New York in 1827, and the Harlem Railroad, completed in 1832, ran the length of Manhattan. By the 1850s all big cities had streetcars. And they needed them. Cities grew so fast, they seemed to leap overnight into the countryside. George Templeton Strong, a New York lawyer and devoted diarist, recorded in 1856 that he had attended a party at a Judge Hoffman's "in thirty-seventh!!!—it seems but the other day that thirty-seventh Street was an imaginary line running through a rural district and grazed over by cows."

Strong and other upper-class New Yorkers found the density and diversity of the city repugnant. He especially disliked mixing with the masses on the city railroad. One day in 1852, suffering from a "splitting headache," Strong expressed his disgust at the immigrant population that crowded the city's public transportation. In "the choky, hot railroad car," he gagged on the "stale, sickly odors from sweaty Irishmen in their shirt sleeves." The other people repelled him as well: "German Jew shop-boys in white coats, pink faces, and waistcoats that looked like virulent prickly heat; fat old women, with dirty-nosed babies; one

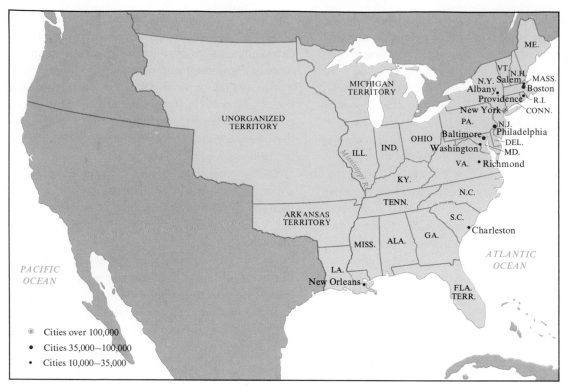

Major American Cities, 1820

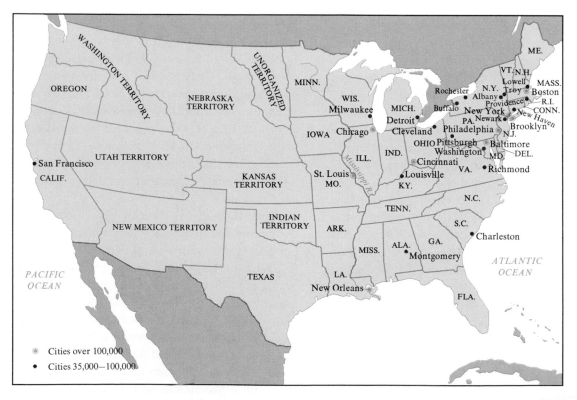

Major American Cities, 1860

Chapter 10: TOWARD GREATER DIVERSITY: THE AMERICAN PEOPLE, 1800–1860

sporting man with black whiskers, miraculously crisp and curly, and a shirt collar insulting stiff, who contributed a reminiscence of tobacco smoke—the spiritual body of ten thousand bad cigars."

Strong's prejudices reflect one man's responses to immigration and city life in the period. Yet, by twentieth-century standards, early-nineteenth-century cities were certainly disorderly, unsafe, and unhealthy. Expansion occurred so suddenly that few cities could handle the problems it brought. For example, migrants from rural areas were used to relieving themselves and throwing refuse in any vacant area. But in the city waste spread disease, created water pollution, and gave off obnoxious odors. New York City solved part of the problem in the 1840s by abandoning wells in favor of reservoir water piped into buildings and outdoor fountains. In some districts scavengers and refuse collectors carted away garbage and human waste, but in much of the city it just lay on the ground until it rotted.

Crime was another problem. To keep order and provide for public safety, Boston supplemented (1837) and New York replaced (1845) their colonial watchmen and constables with paid policemen. Nonetheless, middle-class men and women did not venture out alone at night, and during the day they stayed clear of many city districts. And the influx of immigrants to the cities compounded social tensions by pitting people of different backgrounds against each other in the contest for jobs and housing. Ironically, in the midst of the dirt, the noise, the crime, and the conflict, as if to tempt those who struggled to survive, rose the opulent residences of the very rich.

EXTREMES OF WEALTH

Some observers, notably the young French visitor Alexis de Tocqueville, saw the United States before the Civil War as a place of equality and opportunity. Over a nine-month period in 1831 and 1832, Tocqueville and his companion Gustave de Beaumont traveled four thousand miles and visited all twenty-four states. He later introduced *Democracy in America,* his classic analysis of the American people and nation, with the statement: "No novelty in the United States struck me more vividly during my stay there than the equality of conditions."

Tocqueville believed American equality—the relative fluidity of the social order in the United States—derived from its citizens' geographic mobility. Migration offered people opportunities to start anew regardless of where they came from or who they were. Prior wealth or family mattered little; a person could be known by deeds alone. And indeed, ambition for security and success drove Americans on; sometimes they seemed unable to stop. "An American will build a house in which to pass his old age," Tocqueville wrote, "and sell it before the roof is on; he will plant a garden and rent it just as the trees are coming into bearing; he will clear a field and leave others to reap the harvest; he will take up a profession and leave it, settle in one place and soon go off elsewhere with his changing desires."

Talent and hard work, many Americans believed, found their just reward in such an atmosphere. It was common advice that anyone could advance by working hard and saving money. A local legend from Newburyport, Massachusetts, sounded this popular theme. Tristram Dalton, a Federalist lawyer, wanted his carriage repaired. Moses Brown, an energetic mechanic, refused to wait for Dalton's servants to tow the carriage to his shop; he sought out the vehicle and fixed it on the spot. After Dalton's death his heirs squandered the family fortune, but Brown's industriousness paid off. Through hard work the humble carriage craftsman became one of Massachusetts' richest men. Eventually he bought the Dalton homestead and lived out his life there. The message was clear: "Men succeed or fail . . . not from accident or external surroundings," as the *Newburyport Herald* put it in 1856, but from "possessing or wanting the elements of success in themselves."

But other observers recorded the rise of a new aristocracy based on wealth and power, and growing class and ethnic divisions. Among those who disagreed with the egalitarian view of American life was *New York Sun* publisher Moses Yale Beach, author of twelve editions of *Wealth and Biography of the Wealthy Citizens of New York City.* In 1845 Beach listed a thousand New Yorkers with assets of $100,000

Differences in Wealth

or more. (John Jacob Astor led with a $25-million fortune.) Combining gossip-column tidbits with often erroneous guesses at people's wealth, Beach's book nevertheless suggests the enormous wealth of New York's upper class. Tocqueville himself, ever sensitive to the conflicting trends in American life, had described the growth of an American aristocracy based on industrial wealth. The rich and well educated "come forward to exploit industries," Tocqueville wrote, and become "more and more like the administrators of a huge empire. . . . What is this if not an aristocracy?"

Wealth throughout the United States was becoming concentrated in the hands of a relatively small number of people. In Brooklyn in 1810 two-thirds of the families owned only 10 percent of the wealth; by 1841 their share had decreased to almost nothing. In New York City between 1828 and 1845, the wealthiest 4 percent of the city's population increased their holdings from an estimated 63 percent to 80 percent of all individual wealth. By 1860 the top 5 percent of American families owned more than half the nation's wealth; the top tenth owned over 70 percent.

Inequality, urbanization, and immigration contributed to the renewal of urban conflict as rioting and sporadic incidents of violence became frequent.

Urban Riots The colonial tradition of crowd action, in which disfranchised people took to the streets (see Chapter 4), had diminished in the first three decades of the nineteenth century. In the 1830s riots again became commonplace as professionals and merchants, skilled craftsmen, and ordinary laborers vented their rage against their opponents. "Gentlemen of property and standing," unnerved by the abolitionist attack on American society and traditional leadership, sacked abolitionist newspapers and offices and attacked antislavery advocates throughout the nation. In the 1840s "respectable" citizens waged war against the Mormons, driving them from Illinois and Missouri. Skilled workers raged against new migrants to the cities and other symbols of the new industrial order. In Philadelphia, for instance, native-born workers fought Irish weavers in 1828; whites and blacks rioted on the docks in 1834 and 1835. And in North Philadelphia from 1840 to 1842, residents took to the streets continuously until the construction of a railroad

through their neighborhood was abandoned. These disturbances climaxed in the great riots of 1844, in which mostly Protestant skilled workers fought Irish Catholics. In the 1850s nativist riots peaked. By 1840 more than 125 people had died in urban riots, and by 1860 more than 1,000.

A cloud of uncertainty hung over working men and women. Many were afraid that in periods of economic depression they would become part of the urban flotsam and jetsam of able-bodied men and women, white and black, who could not find steady work. They feared the competition of immigrant and slave labor. They feared the insecurities and indignities of poverty, chronic illness, disability, old age, widowhood, and desertion. And they had good reason.

Indeed, poverty and squalor stalked the urban working class as cities grew. Cities were notorious for the dilapidated districts where newly arrived immigrants, indigent blacks, working **Urban Slums** poor and thieves, beggars, and prostitutes lived. Five Points in New York City's Sixth Ward became the worst slum in pre–Civil War America. Dominated by the Old Brewery, which in 1837 had been converted to housing for hundreds of adults and children, the neighborhood was equally divided between Irish and blacks. Ill-suited to human habitation and lacking such amenities as running water and sewers, it exemplified the worst of urban life.

In New York and other large cities lived "street rats," children and young men who earned their living off the streets by bootblacking or petty thievery. They slept on boats, in haylofts, or in warehouses. Charles Loring Brace, a founder of the Children's Aid Society (1853), described the street rats in his *Dangerous Classes of New York* (1872): "Like the rats, they were too quick and cunning to be often caught in their petty plunderings, so they gnawed away at the foundations of society undisturbed." To Brace and others, such rootless persons threatened American society. They represented a threat far different from Shay's Rebellion, Burr's conspiracies, or the Hartford Convention. "They will vote—they will have the same rights as we ourselves," warned the first report of the Children's Aid Society in 1854, "though they have grown up ignorant of moral principle, as any savage or Indian." Moreover, "they will perhaps be embittered at the wealth and luxuries they never

The infamous Five Points section of New York City's Sixth Ward, probably the worst slum in pre-Civil War America. Immodestly dressed prostitutes cruise the streets or gaze from windows, while a pig roots for garbage in their midst. Courtesy of the New-York Historical Society.

share. Then let society beware, when the vicious, reckless multitude of New York boys, swarming now in every foul alley and low street, come to know their power and *use it!*"

A world apart from Five Points and the people of the streets was the upper-class elite society of Philip Hone, one-time mayor of New York. Hone's diary, meticulously kept from 1826 until his death in 1851, records the activities of an American aristocrat. On February 28, 1840, for instance, Hone attended a masked ball at the Fifth Avenue mansion of Henry Breevoort, Jr., and Laura Carson Breevoort. The ball began at the fashionable hour of 10 P.M., and the five hundred ladies and gentlemen who filled the mansion wore costumes adorned with ermine and gold. For more than a week, Hone believed, the

Urban Elite

affair "occupied the minds of the people of all stations, ranks, and employments." Few balls attained such grandeur, but at one time or another similar parties were held in Boston, Philadelphia, Baltimore, and Charleston.

At a less rarefied level, Hone's social calendar was filled with elegant dinner parties featuring fine cuisine and imported wines. The New York elite who filled the pages of Hone's diary—the 1 percent of the population who owned 50 percent of the city's wealth—lived in large townhouses and mansions, attended by a corps of servants. They comprised the "carriage trade" for whom Broadway merchants filled their shop windows with luxuries from around the world. In the summer, country estates, ocean resorts, mineral spas, and grand tours of Europe offered them relief from the winter and spring social seasons.

A world apart from the slums was the upper-class society. This lithograph depicts Boston's elite dancing the quadrille at a fashionable Tremont House ball around 1840. The American Antiquarian Society.

The basis of this new wealth tended to be inherited. For every John Jacob Astor who made his millions in the western fur trade, or George Law who left a farm to become a millionaire contractor and investor in railroads and banks, there were ten who built additional wealth on money they inherited or married. Andrew H. Mickle, a poor Irish immigrant, became a millionaire and mayor of New York City, but his fortune came from marrying the daughter of his employer. Many of the wealthiest bore the names of the colonial commercial elite—Beekman, Breevoort, Roosevelt, Van Rensselaer, and Whitney. Yet these men were not an idle class; they devoted energy to increasing their fortunes and power. Urban capitalists like Philip Hone profited enormously from the transportation, commercial, and manufacturing revolutions; hardly a major canal, railroad, bank, or mill venture lacked the names and investments of the fashionable elite. Wealth begat wealth, and family ties through inheritance and marriage were essential in that world.

More modest in wealth though hard working were those in the expanding middle class. The growth and specialization of trade had rapidly increased their numbers, and they were a distinct part of the urban scene. The men were businessmen or professionals, the women homemakers. They were the backbone of the rich associational life that Tocqueville had discovered in America. They filled the family pews in church on Sundays; their children pursued whatever educational opportunities were available. Often they dreamed of Philip Hone's world while mindful that the gulf between them and manual workers was narrow.

WOMEN AND THE FAMILY

Economic change transformed women and families too, and made them more diverse. What had been fairly similar backgrounds of native-born white women began to splinter and to show differences by class, life cycle, and place of residence. Families too varied greatly, and change affected them at different rates and in varying ways.

Increasingly, women's and men's work grew apart, as men left their homes to "go to work." On farms, there was still an overlap, but in the new shops, offices, and factories, tasks diverged. Specialization in business and production accompanied specialization in work tasks; men acquired new, narrower skills which were applied in set ways with purposefully designed tools and systems. Authority within the work environment, removed from the household, became more formal and impersonal.

Some women shared these experiences for brief periods in their lives. New England farm daughters who were the first textile-mill workers left home to perform new, specialized work tasks.

Working Women In the 1840s the new urban department stores hired young women as clerks and cash runners. Others worked in the expanding needle trades. Paid employment represented merely a stage in their life cycle, a brief period between their parental and marital households.

Working-class women—the poor, widows, free blacks—worked for wages most of their lives. Leaving their parental homes as early as twelve or thirteen, they earned wages most of their lives, with only short respites for bearing children and rearing infants. Unlike men, however, most of these women did not work in the new shops and factories. Instead they sold their domestic skills for wages outside of their own households. Unmarried girls and women worked as domestic servants in other women's homes; married and widowed women worked as laundresses, seamstresses, cooks, and boardinghouse keepers.

Increasingly work took on greater gender meaning and segregation. Most women's work centered, as it always had, on the home. As the family lost its importance in the production of goods, household upkeep and childrearing continued to magnify in importance, requiring women's full-time attention. Education, religion, morality, domestic arts, and culture began to overshadow the productive functions of the family. These roles became associated for many with ideal female characteristics, what has come to be called woman's sphere or the cult of domesticity of the nineteenth century.

Many American women and men placed great im-

A watercolor-and-ink portrait of a scrubwoman, made in 1807. Domestic work was still the most common job held by women working outside the home in the early nineteenth century.   The New-York Historical Society.

portance on the family. The role of the mother in the early republic was to ensure the nation's future by rearing her children and providing her husband with a spiritual and virtuous environment. The family was to be a moral institution where selflessness and cooperation ruled. Thus women were idealized as the embodiment of self-sacrificing republicanism. This contrasted with the world outside the home, one increasingly identified with men. The world of work—the market economy—was seen as one of conflict, dominated by base self-interest. Amidst a rapidly changing world in which single men and women left their parental homes and villages, in which factories and stores replaced traditional production and distribution, the family was supposed to be a rock of stability and traditional values.

The domestic ideal limited the paying jobs middle-class women could hold outside of the home. Most paid work was viewed with disapproval since it conflicted with the ideal of domesticity. One occupation did come to be recognized as consistent with the genteel female nature: teaching. In 1823 Catharine

While sensitive to the changing life cycles of women, the above lithograph emphasizes the domestic ideal to which most women aspired. But in depicting the roles of daughter, wife, and mother, it neglects woman's paid employment.   Library of Congress.

Beecher established a female academy with her sister Mary. Their Hartford Female Seminary added philosophy, history, and science to the traditional women's curriculum of domestic arts and religious education. In the 1830s Catharine Beecher campaigned to establish schools for girls and training seminaries for female teachers. Viewing formal education as an extension of women's nurturing role, Beecher had great success in spreading her message. By the 1850s schoolteaching became a major woman's vocation, with women teachers in the majority in most large cities. The employment of female teachers served to enlarge the work opportunities open to educated women. Not only did many consider education an appropriate nurturing role for women, but men shunned it because of the low pay. Even then, women were often hired at half the wages paid to male teachers. For society, it was a bargain that worked as long as talented, educated women had relatively limited opportunities to use their education in other occupations.

While woman's work outside the home remained limited, family size was shrinking. In 1800 an American woman bore, on the average, six children; in 1860 she would bear five, and by 1900 four. This decline occurred even while many immigrants with large-family traditions were settling in the United States; thus the birth rate for native-born women declined even more sharply. Although rural families were larger than urban ones, birth rates in both areas declined to the same degree.

Decline in the Birth Rate

A number of factors reduced family size. Increasingly, small families were viewed as desirable. Children would have greater opportunities in smaller families; parents could pay more attention to them and would be better able to educate them and help them financially. Also, contemporary marriage manuals stressed the harmful effects of too many births on a woman's health; too many children weakened women physically and overworked them as mothers.

All this evidence suggests that wives and husbands made deliberate decisions to limit the size of families. In those areas where farm land was relatively expensive, families were smaller than in other agricultural districts. It appears that parents who foresaw difficulty setting up their children as independent farmers chose to have fewer children. Similarly, in urban areas children were more an economic burden than an asset. As the family lost its role as a producer of goods, the length of time during which children were only consumers grew, as did the economic costs to parents.

How did men and women limit their families in the early nineteenth century? Many married later, thus shortening the period of childbearing. And women had their last child at a younger

Birth Control age, dropping from around forty in the mid-eighteenth century to around thirty-five in the mid-nineteenth century. More important, however, was the widespread use of birth control. The popular marriage guide by the physician Charles Knowlton, *Fruits of Philosophy; or, the Private Companion of Young Married People* (1832), provides us with a glimpse of contemporary birth control methods. Probably the most widespread practice was *coitus interruptus,* or withdrawal of the male before completion of the sexual act. But medical devices were beginning to compete with this ancient folk practice. Although animal-skin condoms imported from France were too expensive for popular use, cheap rubber condoms were widely adopted when they became available in the 1850s. Some couples used the rhythm method—attempting to confine intercourse to a woman's infertile periods. Knowledge of the "safe period," however, was uncertain even among physicians. Another method was abstinence, or less frequent sexual intercourse.

If all else failed, abortion was widely available, especially after 1830. Ineffective folk remedies for self-induced abortion had been around for centuries, but in the 1830s surgical abortions became common. Abortionists advertised their services in large cities, and middle-class and elite women asked their doctors to perform abortions. One sign of the upswing in abortions was the increase in legislation against it. Between 1821 and 1841, ten states and one territory prohibited abortions; by 1860, twenty states had outlawed it. Only three of those twenty punished the mother, however, and the laws were rarely enforced.

Significantly, the birth-control methods women themselves controlled—douching, the rhythm method, abstinence, and abortion—were the ones that were increasing in popularity. For the new emphasis on women's domesticity encouraged women's autonomy in the home and gave them greater control over their own bodies. According to the cult of domesticity, the refinement and purity of women ruled the household, including the bedroom; as one woman put it, "woman's duty was to subdue male passions, not to kindle them."

In turn, smaller families and fewer births changed the position and living conditions of women. At one time birth and infant care had occupied the entire span of women's adult lives, and few mothers had lived to see their youngest child reach maturity. But after the 1830s many women had time for other activities. Smaller families also allowed women to devote more time to their older children, and slowly childhood came to be perceived as a distinct part of the life span. The beginnings of public education in the 1830s (see page 331) and the policy of grouping school children by age tended to reinforce this trend.

Sarah Ripley of Massachusetts, an eighteenth-century young girl and a nineteenth-century adult, revealed in her diaries the changes American society

Sarah Ripley Stearns was experiencing. Daughter of a Greenfield shopkeeper, her childhood was a privileged one both at home and boarding school. After completing school she returned home to work as a shop assistant in her father's store. In 1812, after a five-year courtship, she married Charles Stearns of Shelburn. "I have now acquitted the abode of my youth, left the protection of my parents and given up the name I have always borne," she recorded in her diary. "May the grace of God enable me to fulfill with prudence and piety the great and important duties which now evolve on me." Yet she missed the bustle of the shop, as she confessed in her diary.

Sarah Ripley Stearns's life was not a settled one; change was everywhere. Motherhood occupied her, as she bore three children within four years. Her brother moved west; after marriage she left her parents' home and village; she moved with her family three times during her marriage; and in 1818 she became a widow. Amidst all, Sarah Ripley Stearns found religion an anchor. When a revival visited her village in the 1810s, Stearns declared her faith. Rather than leading to introspection, religion promoted social interaction. With her neighbors she formed a "little band of associated females" and sponsored a school society and juvenile home.

Revival and reform had come early to Sarah Ripley Stearns in northwestern Massachusetts, but it was an experience many other women shared during this period. The ideal of domesticity, however, did not confine these middle-class women to their homes. Visits and meetings in parlors and churches led women into a public sphere that was an extension of their domestic concerns. Stearns's benevolent society work not only aided poor children but also provided its female participants with experience and opportunities in organizing, chairing meetings, raising funds, and cultivating an extended network of other women. Thus religion and charity stimulated new directions for women's roles (see pages 325–327).

At the same time, working women were pioneering new roles for women beyond the home. Many found teaching a rewarding profession and preferred it to marriage and domesticity. Mill girls forged new roles for women, as did the women who assembled at Seneca Falls, New York, in 1848. Modeling their protest on the Declaration of Independence, they called for political, social, and economic equality for women (see page 332). Free black women, however, had little choice between paid employment and maintaining households and rearing children. Their different tasks had to be accomplished simultaneously. Immigrant women, too, often had to combine many roles at the same time and, like black women, they found that gender and class were but part of the burdens they carried; ethnic and religious differences created a separate set of problems.

IMMIGRANT LIVES IN AMERICA

No less than gender, ethnic and religious differences divided Americans. In numbers alone immigrants drastically altered the United States. The 5 million immigrants who settled in the states between 1820 and 1860 outnumbered the entire population of the country at the first census in 1790. They came from all continents, though Europeans made up the vast majority. The peak period of pre–Civil War immigration was from 1847 through 1857; in that eleven-year period, 3.3 million immigrants entered the United States, 1.3 million from Ireland and 1.1 million from the German states. By 1860, 15 percent of the white population was foreign-born.

This massive migration had been set in motion decades earlier. In Europe around the turn of the nineteenth century, the Napoleonic wars had begun one of the greatest population shifts in history, which was to last more than a century. One part of the movement, increasingly significant as time went on, was emigration of Europeans to the United States. War, revolution, famine, industrialization, and religious persecution oppressed weary Europeans. Meanwhile, the United States beckoned. Millions of unplowed acres there awaited Europeans, offering them economic opportunity and religious freedom.

European Immigration

Large construction projects and mines needed strong young laborers. Textile mills and city homes recruited young women workers. Europeans' awareness of the United States heightened as employers, states, and shipping companies advertised the opportunities to be found across the Atlantic. Often the message was stark: work and prosper in America or starve in Europe. With regularly scheduled sailing ships commuting across the ocean, the cost of transatlantic travel was within easy reach of millions of Europeans.

So they came, enduring the hardships of travel and of settling in a strange land. The journey was difficult. The average crossing took six weeks; in bad weather it could take three months. Disease spread unchecked among people huddled together like cattle

In 1855, New York State established Castle Garden, in the background above, as an immigrant center. There at the tip of Manhattan Island, many immigrants first touched American soil. The painting depicts immigrants ending their long sea voyage from Ireland. Museum of the City of New York.

in steerage. More than 17,000 immigrants, mostly Irish, died from "ship fever" in 1847. On disembarking, immigrants became fair game for the con artists and swindlers who worked the docks. Agents greeted them and tried to lure them from their chosen destinations. In 1855, in response to the immigrants' plight, New York State's commissioners of emigration established Castle Garden as an immigrant center. There, at the tip of Manhattan Island, the major port of entry, immigrants were somewhat sheltered from fraud. Authorized transportation companies maintained offices in the large rotunda and assisted immigrants with their travel plans.

Most immigrants gravitated toward the cities, since only a minority had farming experience or the means to purchase land and equipment. Many stayed in New York itself. By 1845, 35 percent of the city's 371,000 people were of foreign birth. Ten years later 52 percent of its 623,000 inhabitants were immigrants, 28 percent from Ireland and 16 percent from Germany. In the Sixth Ward, home of Five Points, no fewer than 70 percent of the residents were immigrants. Boston, an important entry point for the Irish, took on a European tone. Throughout the 1850s the city was about 35 percent foreign-born, of whom more than two-thirds were Irish. In the South, too, major cities had large immigrant populations. In 1860 New Orleans was 44 percent foreign-born, Savannah 33 percent, and the border city of St. Louis, 61 percent. On the West Coast, San Francisco had a foreign-born majority.

Some immigrants, however, did settle in rural areas. In particular, German, Dutch, and Scandinavian farmers gravitated toward the Midwest. Greater percentages of Scandinavians and Netherlanders took up farming than other nationalities; both groups came mostly as religious dissenters and migrated in family units. The Dutch who founded the American Holland in Michigan and Wisconsin, for instance, had seceded from the official Reformed Church of the Netherlands. Under such leaders as Albertus C. Van Raalte, they fled persecution in their native land to establish new and more pious communities—Holland and Zeeland, Michigan, among them.

Success in America bred further emigration. "I wish, and do often say that we wish you were all in this happy land," wrote shoemaker John West of Germantown, Pennsylvania, to his kin in Corsley, England, in 1831.

Promotion of Immigration

"A man nor woman need not stay out of employment one hour here," he advised. John Down, a weaver from Frome, England, settled in New York City without his family. Writing to his wife in August 1830, he described the bountiful meal he had shared with a farmer's family: "They had on the table puddings, pyes, and fruit of all kind that was in season, and preserves, pickles, vegetables, meats, and everything that a person would wish, and the servants [farm hands] set down at the same table with their masters." Though Down missed his family dearly, he wrote, "I do not repent of coming, for you know that there was nothing but poverty before me, and to see you and the dear children want was what I could not bear. *I would rather cross the Atlantic ten times than hear my children cry for victuals once.*" To those skeptics who claimed the United States was filling up, he advised, "There is plenty of room yet, and will be for a thousand years to come." These letters and others were widely circulated in Europe to advertise the success of pauper immigrants in America.

American institutions, both public and private, actively recruited European emigrants. Western states lured potential settlers in the interest of promoting their economies. In the 1850s, for instance, Wisconsin appointed a commissioner of emigration, who ad-vertised the state's advantages in American and European newspapers. Wisconsin also opened a New York office and hired European agents to compete with other states and with firms like the Illinois Central Railroad for immigrants' attention.

Before the potato blight hit Ireland, tens of thousands of Irish were lured to America by recruiters. They came to swing picks and shovels on American canals and railroads, to dig the foundations of mills and factories. The popular folksong "Working on the Railroad" records their story:

Oh in eighteen hundred and forty-three
I sailed away across the sea,
I sailed away across the sea,
To work upon the railway, the railway.
I'm weary of the railway;
Oh poor Paddy works on the railway!

. . .

Oh in eighteen hundred and forty-six
I changed my trade to carrying bricks,
I changed my trade to carrying bricks,
From working on the railway, the railway . . .

Oh in eighteen hundred and forty-seven
Poor Paddy was thinking of going to Heaven,
Poor Paddy was thinking of going to Heaven,
After working on the railway, the railway,
He was weary of the railway;
Oh poor Paddy worked on the railway!

But as other verses reveal, not all the Irish immigrants were successful; tens of thousands of them returned to their homeland. Among them was Michael Gaugin, who had the misfortune to

Immigrant Disenchantment

arrive in New York City during the financial panic of 1837. Gaugin, for thirteen years an assistant engineer in the construction of a Dublin canal, had been attracted to the United States by the promise that "he should soon become a wealthy man." The Dublin agent for a New York firm convinced Gaugin to quit his job, which included a house and an acre of ground, in order to emigrate to the United States. Within two months of arriving in the United States, Gaugin had become a pauper. In August 1837 he declared he was "now without means for the support of himself and his family, and has no employment, and has already suffered great deprivation since he arrived in this country; and is now soliciting means to enable him to return with his family home to Ireland." Many of those who had come with the Gaugins had already returned home.

Such experiences did not deter Irish men and women from coming to the United States. Ireland was the most densely populated European country, and among the most impoverished. From 1815 on, small harvests prompted a steady stream of Irish to emigrate to America. Then in 1845 and 1846 potatoes—the basic Irish food—rotted in the fields. From 1845 to 1849, death in the form of starvation, malnutrition, and typhus spread. In all, 1 million died and about 1.5 million fled, two-thirds of them to the United States. People became Ireland's major export.

Irish Immigrants

In the 1840s and 1850s a total of 1.7 million Irish men and women entered the United States. At the peak of Irish immigration, from 1847 to 1854, 1.2 million came. By the end of the century there would be more Irish in the United States than in Ireland.

The new Irish immigrants differed greatly from those who had left Ireland to settle in the American colonies. In the eighteenth century, the Scotch-Irish predominated (see pages 74–75), and their journey had involved moving from one part of the British Empire to another. The nineteenth-century Roman Catholic Irish travelers to America, however, moved from still-colonial Ireland to an independent republic, and the political and religious differences made their cultural adaptation that much more difficult. In comparison with the Scotch-Irish, the newer immigrants from Ireland tended to be younger, increasingly female, and mostly from the rural provinces. With eldest sons heirs to the family farms and with eldest daughters staying home to care for parents, the younger children who came alone to the United States were expendable in Ireland's declining economy. Farmers' daughters could find work only as domestic servants, and poverty-stricken Ireland could not absorb all of them. In American cities they found work in factories and households. If they married, they would marry late, as did their sisters in Ireland. They helped support their families still at home and built Catholic churches and organizations in United States cities.

In the urban areas where they clustered in poverty, most Irish immigrants met growing anti-immigrant,

Anti-Catholicism

anti-Catholic sentiment. Everywhere "No Irish Need Apply" signs appeared. During the colonial period, white Protestant settlers had feared "popery" as a system of tyranny and had discriminated against the few Catholics in America. Following the Revolution, anti-Catholicism receded. But in the 1830s the trend reversed, and anti-Catholicism appeared wherever the Irish did. Attacks on the papacy and the church circulated widely in the form of libelous texts like *The Awful Disclosures of Maria Monk* (1836), which alleged sexual orgies among priests and nuns. Nowhere was anti-Catholicism more open and nasty than in Boston, though such sentiments were widespread. Anti-Catholic riots were almost commonplace. In Charlestown, Massachusetts, a mob burned a convent (1834); a Philadelphia crowd attacked priests and nuns and vandalized churches (1844); and in Lawrence, Massachusetts, a mob leveled the Irish neighborhood (1854).

The native-born who embraced anti-Catholicism were motivated largely by anxiety. They feared that a militant Roman church would subvert American society, that unskilled Irish workers would displace American craftsmen, and that the slums inhabited in part by the Irish were undermining the nation's values. Every American problem from immorality and the evils of alcohol to poverty and economic upheaval was blamed on immigrant Irish Catholics. Impoverished workers complained to the Massachusetts legislature that the Irish displaced "the honest and respectable laborers of the State . . . and from their manner of living . . . work for much less per day . . . being satisfied with food to support the animal existence alone." American workers, on the other hand, "not only labor for the body but for the mind, the soul, and the State." Friction increased as Irish-American men fought back against anti-Irish and anti-Catholic prejudice; in the 1850s they began to vote and to become active in politics.

Though potato blight also sent many Germans to the United States in the 1840s, other hardships contributed to the steady stream of German immigrants.

German Immigrants

Many came from areas where small landholdings made it hard to eke out a living and to pass on land to their sons. Others were craftsmen displaced by the industrial revolution. These refugees were joined by middle-class Germans who had sought to unify the three dozen or so German states in a liberal republic. Frustration with abortive revolutions like one that occurred in 1848 led them to emigrate to the United States. For some, the only other choice was jail.

Unlike the Irish, who tended to congregate in towns and cities, Germans settled everywhere. Many came on German cotton boats, disembarked at New Orleans, and traveled up the Mississippi. In the South they became peddlers and merchants; in the North and West they worked as farmers, urban laborers, and businessmen. Also unlike the Irish, they tended to migrate in families. A strong desire to maintain the German language and culture prompted them to colonize areas as a group.

German immigrants transplanted their Old World institutions in the New World, creating New Germanies in rural areas and transforming the tone and culture of established cities like Cincinnati and Milwaukee. *Turnvereine*—German physical-culture clubs—sprouted in villages and cities; by 1853 sixty such societies were hosting exercise groups and German-language lectures.

In adhering to German traditions, German-Americans too met with antiforeign attitudes. More than half the German immigrants were Catholic, and their Sabbath practices were different from the Protestants'. On Sundays German families typically gathered at beer gardens to eat and drink beer, to dance, sing, and listen to band music, and sometimes to play cards. Protestants were outraged by such violations of the Lord's day. In Chicago riots broke out when Protestants enforced the Sunday prohibition laws.

Their persistence in using the German language and their different religious beliefs set them apart. Besides the Catholic majority, a significant number of German immigrants were Jewish. And even the Protestants—mostly Lutherans—founded their own churches and often educated their children in German-language schools. Not all Germans, however, were religious. The failure of the revolution of 1848 had sent to the United States a whole generation of liberals and freethinkers, some of whom were socialists, communists, and anarchists. The freethinkers entered politics with a loud voice, embracing abolitionism and the Republican party.

The conflict between the immigrants and the society they joined paralleled the inner tensions most immigrants experienced. On the one hand they felt impelled to commit themselves wholeheartedly to their new country, to learn the language and adapt themselves to American ways. On the other hand they were rooted in their own cultural traditions—the comfortable, tested customs of the country of their birth, the familiar ways and words that came intuitively and required no education.

For immigrants, conflict centered around their desire to be part of American society, albeit for some on their own terms. Once here, they claimed their right to a fair economic and political share. Indians, on the other hand, had to defend what they conceived of as prior rights. Their land, their religion, their way of life came under constant attack as they were most often viewed as an obstacle to expansion and economic growth.

INDIAN RESISTANCE AND REMOVAL

The clash between Indians and the larger society had been inherited from the colonial past. Population growth, westward expansion, the transportation revolution, and invigorated capitalism underlay the designs and demands on Indian land. At best Indians could hope for mutual understanding, but when that rare event occurred, it was only on a personal level. Whatever good intentions motivated the leaders of the republic, they were subordinated to the desire for Indian land. Indian resistance proved incapable of protecting either their land or their traditional culture, and the great Indian nations were removed to lands west of the Mississippi.

As the colonial powers in North America had done, the United States treated Indian tribes as sovereign nations until Congress ended the practice in 1871. In its relations with tribal leaders, the government followed the ritual of international protocol. Indian chiefs and delegations who visited Washington were received with the appropriate pomp and ceremony. Leaders exchanged presents as tokens of

The Shawnee Chiefs Prophet (left) and Tecumseh (right). The two brothers led a revival of traditional Shawnee culture and preached Indian federation against white encroachment. In the War of 1812, they allied themselves with the British, but Tecumseh's death at the Battle of Thames (1813) and British indifference thereafter caused Indian resistance and unity to collapse. Prophet: National Museum of American Art; Tecumseh: Field Museum of Natural History, Chicago.

friendship, and commemorative flags and silver medals with presidents' likenesses became prized possessions among Indian chiefs. Agreements between a tribe and the United States were signed, sealed, and ratified as was any international pact.

In practice, however, Indian sovereignty was a fiction. Though protocol seemed to acknowledge independence and mutual respect, treaty negotiations exposed the fiction. Essentially, treaty-making was a process used to acquire Indian land. Differences in power made it less than the bargaining of two equal nations. Treaties were often made between victors and vanquished. In a context of coercion, old treaties often gave way to new ones in which the Indians ceded their traditional holdings in return for different lands in the West. Beginning with President Jefferson,

the government withheld payments due to tribes for previous land cessions to pressure them to sign new treaties.

The War of 1812 snuffed out whatever realistic hopes Indian leaders might have had of resisting American expansion by warfare. Armed resistance persisted, and it was bloody on both sides, as in the Seminole Wars, but only the revived idea of pan-Indian federation offered any hope to counter the military might of the United States. The Shawnee chiefs Prophet and Tecumseh attempted to build such a movement, taking advantage of Anglo-American friction in the decade before the War of 1812, but in the end it failed. And with it died the most significant resistance to the federal government's treaty-making tactics.

Prophet's early experiences mirror the fate that befell many frontier tribes. Born in 1775, a few months after his father had died in battle, Prophet was afterward abandoned by his mother, who rejoined her native tribe further west. He was raised by his sister and called Lalawethika (noisemaker) as a young man. He was among the defeated Shawnee at the Battle of Fallen Timbers and among the Indians expelled under the 1795 Treaty of Greenville (see page 171). He joined a small band of his tribe in Ohio, then moved with them to Indiana. Within the shrunken territory granted to them under the treaty, game became scarce and Lalawethika found it difficult to feed his family. Encroachment by whites and the periodic ravages of disease brought further misery to Indian villages and tribes; economic and social instability went hand in hand. Like other Indians, Lalawethika turned to whiskey. He was befriended by a local shaman, who shared his traditional folk knowledge of medicine and Indian lore. When the medicine man died in 1804, he was succeeded by his young disciple. But Lalawethika was a failure; his medicine could not stop the white man's viral illnesses from ravaging his village.

Prophet

Lalawethika emerged from his own battle with illness in 1805 as a new man, called Prophet. Claiming to have died and been resurrected, he told a visionary tale of this experience and warned of damnation for those who drank whiskey. In the following years, Prophet traveled widely in the Northwest as a holy man, attacking the decline of moral values among Indians, condemning intertribal battles, and stressing harmony and respect for elders. In essence he preached the revitalization of traditional Shawnee culture. Return to the old ways, he told the Indians of the Old Northwest, abandon white customs. Hunt with bows and arrows, he said, not guns; release domestic animals and discard the wearing of hats; refrain from eating bread and cultivate corn and beans.

Prophet's message was a reassuring one to the Shawnee, Potawatomi, and other Indians of the Old Northwest who felt unsettled and threatened by whites. Prophet won converts by performing miracles—he darkened the sun by coinciding this act with an eclipse—and used opposition to federal Indian policy to draw others into his camp.

The government and white settlers were alarmed by the religious revival led by Prophet. With his brother, Tecumseh, who was seven years older, he refused to leave lands claimed by the government. In 1808 Prophet and his brother began to turn from a message of spiritual renewal to one of resistance to white aggression. In repudiating land sales to the government under the Treaty of Fort Wayne (1809), Tecumseh told Indiana's Governor William Henry Harrison at Vincennes in 1810 that "the only way to check and stop this evil is, for all the red men to unite in claiming a common and equal right in the land, as it was at first, and should be yet; for it never was divided, but belongs to all, for the use of each. . . . No part has a right to sell, even to each other, much less to strangers."

Tecumseh

At that point Tecumseh, the towering six-foot warrior and magnetic orator, replaced Prophet as Shawnee leader. Prophet's medicine could not stop white encroachment, so the young warriors looked to Tecumseh for political leadership. Convinced that only a federation of tribes could stop the advance of white settlement, Tecumseh sought to unify northern and southern Indians. He warned Harrison that the Indians would resist white occupation of the 2.5 million acres on the Wabash that they had ceded in the Treaty of Fort Wayne.

A year later, using a Potawatomi raid on an Illinois settlement as an excuse, Harrison attacked and demolished Prophet's Town, Tecumseh's headquarters on Tippecanoe Creek in Indiana Territory. Losses on both sides were heavy. Indian warriors throughout the Midwest came to Tecumseh's side; Harrison appealed for help to President Madison. When the War of 1812 started, Tecumseh joined the British in return for a promise of an Indian country in the Great Lakes region. But he was killed in the Battle of the Thames in October 1813, and with his death Indian unity collapsed (see pages 224 and 226).

After Tecumseh's death, Prophet attempted to rally the remnants of the movement, but he lacked the political and military skills of his brother. Prophet remained under British protection in Canada after the War of 1812 even though most of his followers returned to the United States. Finally he came back to the United States in 1825 and worked for the emigration of the remaining Shawnee to Indian territory in Kansas. He made the trip west, but it was a bitter and miserable one since the promised government assistance never came. Prophet died in Kansas in 1836, all but forgotten.

By 1820 Indians in Ohio, southern Indiana and Illinois, southwestern Michigan, most of Missouri, central Alabama, and southern Mississippi had been

Indian Policy

forced to cede their lands. They had given up nearly 200 million acres for pennies an acre. But white settlers' appetites were insatiable; the expansion of commercial farming in the Midwest and of cotton plantations in the South increased demands for Indian land and for Indians to assimilate. One instrument that served both purposes was the Indian agency system, which monopolized trade with Indians in a designated locality and paid out the rations, supplies, and annuities that Indians received in exchange for abandoning their land. The tribes became dependent on these government payments—a dependency intended to make them more docile in treaty negotiations.

At the same time, reformers sought to assimilate Indians into American society by educating and Christianizing them. Motivated by a sincere concern for Indians and influenced by the Second Great Awakening, female missionary and benevolent societies assisted in founding four Christian schools for Indians by 1819. In that year, under missionary lobbying, Congress appropriated $10,000 annually for the "civilization of the tribes adjoining the frontier settlements." This "civilization act" was a means to teach Indians to live like white settlers. Within five years thirty-two schools appeared, scattered throughout the country, and government financial support rose. The new boarding schools, unlike the earlier ones, substituted English for native Indian languages and taught agricultural techniques in addition to the Gospel.

To settlers eyeing Indian land, assimilation through education was too slow a process, and Indians themselves questioned the instruction. There were never more than one thousand students at any one time in all the schools; at that rate it would take centuries to assimilate all Indians. And after 1826, when Congress reduced its annual appropriations to $10,000, missionary societies failed to make up the deficit. Some Indian tribes found the missionary message repugnant. The Creek nation permitted the schools

only after being assured that there would be no preaching. Zealous missionaries violated the agreement, preaching to the Creek and their black slaves. With no other recourse available, a band of Creek sacked the school. Similarly, the Passamaquoddy tribe of New England, many of whom were Catholics, opposed teachers' efforts to make them Episcopalians. Even the vocational aspects seemed unpromising; graduates who returned to their tribal villages had no way of applying the commercial agricultural skills acquired in the schools.

It became apparent in the 1820s that neither economic dependency nor education could force Indians voluntarily to cede much more land to meet the demands of expansionists. Attention focused on the Cherokee, Creek, Choctaw, Chickasaw, and Seminole tribes in the South because much of their land remained intact after the War of 1812 and because they aggressively resisted white encroachment. They had more formal political institutions than the northern Indians and thus were better organized to resist.

In his last annual message in December 1824, President James Monroe suggested to Congress that all Indians settle beyond the Mississippi River. Sec-

Indian Removal

retary of War John C. Calhoun agreed, and three days later the president sent a special message to Congress advocating removal. Stressing the positive aspects, Monroe believed his proposal an "honorable" one that would protect Indians from invasion, and provide them with independence for "improvement and civilization." Monroe felt that force would be unnecessary; the promise of a home free from white encroachment would be sufficient to win Indian acceptance.

The southern tribes unanimously rejected Monroe's offer. The Cherokee, Creek, Choctaw, and Chickasaw tribes to whom the program was directed wanted to be left alone. Between 1789 and 1825 they had negotiated a total of thirty individual treaties with the United States; they had reached their limits. They wished to remain on what was left of their ancestral land.

Pressure from Georgia had prompted Monroe's policy. Most Cherokee and some Creek lived in northwestern Georgia, and in the 1820s the state accused the federal government of not fulfilling its 1802 promise to remove the Indians in return for the state's re-

The French genre painter Alfred Boisseau recorded the passage of the Choctaw through Louisiana from Mississippi to Indian Territory. With dignity they made the forced march. Isaac Delgado Museum of Art, New Orleans.

nunciation of its claim to western lands. Georgia sought complete removal and was not satisfied by Monroe's removal messages nor by further Creek cessions. Although in 1826 the Creek nation, under federal pressure, ceded all but a small strip of its Georgia lands, Governor George M. Troup wanted all their land. Troup sent surveyors to the one remaining strip; President John Quincy Adams then threatened to send the army to protect the Indians' claims, and Troup countered with his own threats. Only the eventual removal of the Georgia Creek to the west in 1826 prevented a clash between the state and the federal government. For the Creek the outcome was a devastating defeat. In attempting to hold fast to the remainder of their traditional lands, they had significantly altered their political structure. In 1829 they centralized tribal authority, strengthening their national council at the expense of traditional village autonomy, and had forbidden any chief from negotiating land cessions. In 1827 the Cherokee tried

to resist forced removal by adopting a written constitution modeled after the United States system and by organizing themselves officially as an independent nation. But in 1828 the Georgia legislature annulled the constitution, extended state sovereignty over the Cherokee, and ordered the seizure of tribal lands.

In 1829 the Cherokee, with the support of sympathetic whites but without the support of the new president, Andrew Jackson, turned to the federal courts to defend their treaty with the United States and prevent Georgia's seizure of their land. In *Cherokee Nation* v. *Georgia* (1831), Chief Justice John Marshall ruled that under the federal Constitution an Indian tribe was neither a foreign nation nor a state, and therefore had no standing in federal courts. Nonetheless, said Marshall, the Indians had an unquestioned right to their lands; they could lose title only by voluntarily giving it up. A year later, in *Worcester* v. *Georgia*,

Cherokee Nation v. Georgia

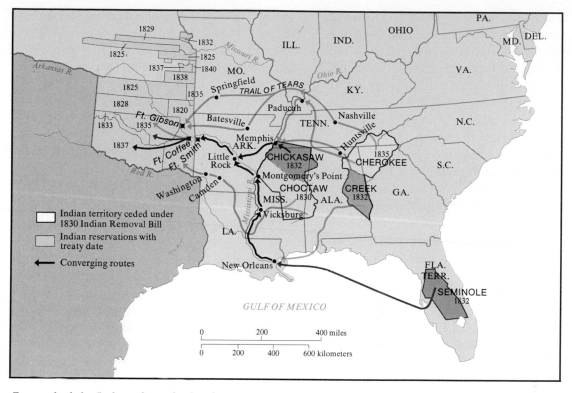

Removal of the Indians from the South, 1820–1840
Source: Redrawn by permission of Macmillan Publishing
Company, Inc. From American History Atlas by Martin
Gilbert, cartography by Peter Kingsland. Copyright © 1968
by Martin Gilbert.

Marshall defined the Cherokee position more clearly.
The Indian nation was, he declared, a distinct political
community in which "the laws of Georgia can have
no force" and into which Georgians could not enter
without permission or treaty privilege.

President Andrew Jackson, who as a general had
led the expedition against the Seminole in Spanish
Florida in 1818, had little sympathy for the Indians
and ignored the Supreme Court's ruling. Keen to
open up new lands for settlement, he was determined
to remove the Cherokee at all costs. In the Removal
Act of 1830 Congress provided Jackson the funds he
needed to negotiate new treaties and resettle the

Trail of Tears   resistant tribes west of the Mississippi. The Choctaw were the first
to go; in the winter of 1831 and
1832, they made the forced journey from Mississippi
and Alabama to the West (see map). Alexis de Tocqueville was visiting Memphis when they arrived
there, "the wounded, the sick, newborn babies, and

the old men on the point of death. . . . I saw them
embark to cross the great river," he wrote, "and the
sight will never fade from my memory. Neither sob
nor complaint rose from that silent assembly. Their
afflictions were of long standing, and they felt them
to be irremediable."

Soon other tribes were forced west. The Creek in
Alabama delayed removal until 1836, when the army
pushed them westward. A year later the Chickasaw
followed. The Cherokee, having fought through the
courts to stay, found themselves divided. Some recognized the hopelessness of further resistance and
accepted removal as the only chance to preserve their
civilization. The leaders of this minority signed a
treaty in 1835 in which they agreed to exchange
their southern home for western land. But when the
time for evacuation came in 1838, most Cherokee
refused to move. President Martin Van Buren then
sent federal troops to round up the Indians. About
twenty thousand Cherokee were evicted, held in de-

tention camps, and marched to Oklahoma under military escort. Nearly one-quarter died of disease and exhaustion on the infamous Trail of Tears. When it was all over, the Indians had traded about 100 million acres of land east of the Mississippi for 32 million acres west of the river plus $68 million. Only a few scattered remnants of the tribes, among them the Seminole, remained in the East and South.

A small band of Seminole successfully resisted removal and remained in Florida. In the 1832 Treaty of Payne's Landing, tribal chiefs agreed to relocate to the West within three years. Un-
Seminole War   der Osceola, however, a minority refused to vacate their homes, and from 1835 on they waged a fierce guerrilla war against the United States. The army in turn attempted, ruthlessly but unsuccessfully, to exterminate the Seminole. In 1842 the United States finally abandoned the Seminole War; it had cost 1,500 soldiers' lives and $20 million. Osceola's followers remained in Florida.

To open up the West to white settlement, Commissioner of Indian Affairs William Medill in 1848 proposed gathering the western Indians into two great reservations, one northern and one southern. The Kansas and Platte valleys separated the two areas, creating a wide corridor for white settlers to use on their way westward. In 1853, however, the government took back most of the northern lands in a new round of treaties, and Kansas and Nebraska were opened to white settlement.

A complex set of attitudes drove whites to force Indian removal. Most merely wanted Indian lands; they had little or no respect for the rights or culture of the Indians. Manifest destiny and westward migration justified bulldozing Indians aside. Others were aware of the injustice, but believed the Indians must inevitably give way to white settlement. Some, like John Quincy Adams, believed the only way to preserve Indian civilization was to remove the tribes and establish a buffer zone between Indians and whites. Others, including Thomas Jefferson, doubted that white civilization and Indian "savagery" could coexist. Supported by missionaries and educators, they hoped to "civilize" the Indians and assimilate them slowly into American culture. Whatever the source of white behavior, the outcome was the same: the devastation of Native American people and their culture.

Another minority experienced insecurity and struggled for recognition and legal rights. Like most Indians, they too were involuntarily a part of American society. Unlike Indians, however, they wished to be fully a part of the American people.

FREE PEOPLE OF COLOR

No black person was safe, wrote the abolitionist and former slave Frederick Douglass after the Philadelphia riot of 1849. "His life—his property—and all that he holds dear are in the hands of a mob, which may come upon him at any moment—at midnight or mid-day, and deprive him of his all." Between 1832 and 1849 five major antiblack riots occurred in Philadelphia. Mobs stormed black dwellings and churches, set them to the torch, and killed the people inside. For free people of color, mobs could take many forms. They could come in the shape of slave hunters, seeking fugitive slaves but as likely to kidnap a free black as a slave. Or they could take the form of civil authority, as in Cincinnati in 1829, when city officials, frightened by the growing black population, drove one to two thousand blacks from the city by enforcing a law requiring cash bonds for good behavior. In whatever form, free blacks faced insecurity daily.

Under federal law, blacks held an uncertain position. The Bill of Rights seemed to apply to free blacks; the Fifth Amendment specified that "no person shall . . . be deprived of life, liberty, or property, without due process of law." Yet the racist theory of the eighteenth century that defined a republic as being only for whites seemed to exclude blacks (see pages 163–164). This exclusion was reflected in early federal legislation. In 1790 naturalization was limited to white aliens, and in 1792 the militia was limited to white male citizens. Moreover, Congress approved the admission to the Union of states whose constitutions restricted the rights of blacks. Following the admission of Missouri in 1821, every new state admitted until the Civil War banned blacks from voting. And when the Oregon and New Mexico territories were organized, public land grants were limited to whites.

In the North blacks faced legal restrictions nearly

everywhere; Massachusetts was the major exception. Many states barred entry to free blacks or required bonds of $500 to $1,000 to guarantee their good behavior, as in Ohio (1804), Illinois (1819), Michigan (1827), and Oregon (1857). Although seldom enforced, these laws clearly indicated the less-than-free status of blacks. Only in Massachusetts, New Hampshire, Vermont, and Maine could blacks vote on an equal basis with whites throughout the pre–Civil War period. Blacks gained the right to vote in Rhode Island in 1842, but they had lost it earlier in Pennsylvania and Connecticut. No state but Massachusetts permitted blacks to serve on juries; four midwestern states and California did not allow blacks to testify against whites. In Oregon blacks could not own real estate, make contracts, or sue in court.

Legal status was important, but practice and custom were crucial. Although Ohio repealed its law barring black testimony against whites in 1849, the exclusion persisted as custom in southern Ohio counties. Throughout the North free people of color were either excluded from or segregated in public places.

Exclusion and Segregation of Blacks

Abolitionist Frederick Douglass was repeatedly turned away from public facilities during a speaking tour of the North in 1844. A doorkeeper refused him admission to a circus in Boston, saying "We don't allow niggers in here." He met the same reply when he tried to attend a revival meeting in New Bedford. At a restaurant in Boston and on an omnibus in Weymouth, Massachusetts, he heard the familiar words. Hotels and restaurants were closed to blacks, as were most theaters and churches.

Probably no practice inflicted greater injury than the general discrimination in hiring. The counting houses, retail stores, and factories that characterized the expanding economy refused to hire black men other than as janitors and general handymen. New England mills hired only white women. Other than a small professional and commercial and skilled elite, northern free black men found steady work difficult to obtain; most toiled as unskilled daily laborers. Black women more easily found jobs as their domestic skills were in great demand in the burgeoning urban society, and they worked as domestic servants, cooks, laundresses, and seamstresses. Unlike their white counterparts, however, these women did not view paid employment as a distinct period in their life

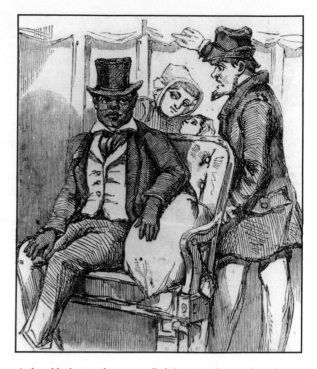

A free black man being expelled from a whites-only railway car in Philadelphia. Prior to the Civil War, blacks were commonly segregated or excluded from public places in the North. Library of Congress.

cycle; around 40 percent of black women worked for wages during marriage and the childrearing years. Given the lower wages black workers received, not many black families could survive on one income.

Free people of color faced more severe legal and social barriers in the southern slave states, where their presence was often viewed as an incentive to insurrection. Indeed, southern states responded to fear of mass rebellion by tightening the restrictions on free blacks and forcing them to leave small towns and interior counties. After a successful slave rebellion in Haiti in the 1790s and Gabriel Prosser's Virginia slave revolt in 1800 (see page 205), southern states barred the entry of free blacks for two decades. And in 1806 Virginia required newly freed blacks to leave the state. Following Nat Turner's slave uprising in Southampton County in 1831, the position of free blacks weakened further. Within five years nearly all the southern states prohibited the freeing of any slaves without legislative or court approval, and by the 1850s Texas, Mississippi, and Georgia had banned manumission altogether.

BLACK POPULATION OF THE UNITED STATES, 1800–1860

Year	Total Black Population	Percentage of Total U.S. Population	Free People of Color	Free Blacks as a Percentage of Black Population
1800	1,002,000	18.9	108,000	10.8
1810	1,378,000	19.0	186,000	13.5
1820	1,772,000	18.4	234,000	13.2
1830	2,329,000	18.1	320,000	13.7
1840	2,874,000	16.8	386,000	13.4
1850	3,639,000	15.7	435,000	11.9
1860	4,442,000	14.1	488,000	11.0

To restrict free blacks and encourage them to migrate north, southern states adopted elaborate "black codes." Blacks were required to have licenses for certain occupations and were barred from others (for example, Virginia and Georgia banned black river captains and pilots). Some states forbade blacks to assemble without a license; some prohibited blacks from being taught to read and write. In the late 1830s, when these black codes were enforced with vigor for the first time, free blacks increasingly moved northward, even though northern states discouraged the migration.

Black Codes

In spite of these obstacles, the free black population rose dramatically in the first part of the nineteenth century, from 108,000 in 1800 to almost 500,000 in 1860 (see table). Nearly half lived in the North, occasionally in rural settlements like Hammond County, Indiana, but more often in cities like Philadelphia, New York, or Cincinnati. Baltimore had the largest free black community; sizable free black populations also existed in New Orleans, Charleston, and Mobile (see pages 305–306).

The ranks of free blacks were constantly increased by ex-slaves. Some, like Frederick Douglass and Harriet Tubman, were fugitives. Douglass had hired himself out as a ship caulker in Baltimore, paying $3 monthly to his owner.

Fugitive Slaves

Living among free workers made him yearn to escape slavery. By masquerading as a free black with the help of borrowed seaman's papers, he bluffed his way to Philadelphia and freedom. Tubman, a slave on the eastern shore of Maryland, escaped to Philadelphia in 1849 when her master's death led to rumors that she would be sold out of the state. Within the next two years she returned twice to free her two children, her sister, her mother, and her brother and his family. Other slaves were voluntarily freed by their owners. Some, like a Virginia planter named Sanders who settled his slaves as freedmen in Michigan, sought to cleanse their souls by freeing their slaves in their wills. Some freed elderly slaves after a lifetime of service rather than support them in old age. The parents of the slave Isabella (Sojourner Truth) were freed when whites who inherited the family would not support the father, who was too old to work.

Sojourner Truth's experience in New York reveals that the gradual emancipation laws of northern states had little effect as long as slavery existed elsewhere. In 1817 New York State adopted an emancipation plan whereby all slaves over forty years old were freed, and young slaves would serve ten more years. But owners tried to thwart the law by selling their slaves into other states. In 1826, fearing sale to the South, Sojourner Truth found refuge with a nearby

Sojourner Truth (about 1797–1883), the spellbinding preacher, abolitionist, and crusader for women's rights. Sophia Smith Collection, Smith College.

industry, and morality, thus equipping their members to improve their lot. But no amount of effort could counteract white prejudice. Blacks remained second-class in status.

The network of societies among urban free black men and women provided a base for black protest. From 1830 to 1835, and thereafter irregularly, free blacks held national conventions with delegates drawn from ad hoc city and state organizations. Under the leadership of the small black middle class, which included the Philadelphia sail manufacturer James Forten and the orator Reverend Henry Highland Garnet, the convention movement served as a forum to attack slavery and agitate for equal rights. The militant new black newspapers joined the struggle. *Freedom's Journal,* the first black weekly, appeared in March 1827; in 1837 the *Weekly Advocate* began publication in New York City. Both papers circulated throughout the North, spreading black thought and activism.

Although abolitionism and civil rights remained at the top of the blacks' agenda, the mood of free blacks began to shift in the late 1840s and 1850s.

Black Nationalism Many were frustrated by the failure of the abolitionist movement and by the passage of the Fugitive Slave Law of 1850 (see page 361). Some black leaders became more militant, and a few joined John Brown in his plans for rebellion. But many more were swept up in the tide of black nationalism, which stressed racial solidarity and unity, self-help, and a growing interest in Africa. Before this time, efforts to send Afro-Americans "back to Africa" had originated with whites seeking to solve racial problems by ridding the United States of blacks. But in the 1850s blacks held emigrationist conventions of their own under the leadership of Henry Bibb and Martin Delany. In 1859 Delany led a Niger Valley exploration party as the emissary of a black convention. He signed a treaty with Yoruba rulers allowing him to settle American blacks in that African kingdom (the plan was never carried out). Nothing better illustrates the ironic position of free blacks in the United States than the flight of blacks to Canada and Africa, in search of freedom, while millions of European migrants were coming to the United States for liberty and opportunity. With the coming of the Civil War and emancipation, however, the status of blacks, free and

abolitionist couple. With their help she sued successfully for the freedom of her son Peter, who had been sold unlawfully to an Alabaman. One can only guess how many blacks did not receive such help and were permanently deprived of their freedom.

In response to their oppression, free blacks founded strong, independent self-help societies to meet their unique needs and fight their less-than-equal status.

Founding of Black Institutions Revival and reform influenced blacks as well. In every black community there appeared black churches, fraternal and benevolent associations, literary societies, and schools. In Philadelphia in the 1840s, more than half the black population belonged to mutual beneficiary societies, and female benevolent societies and schools flourished. The black Masons grew to more than fifty lodges in seventeen states by 1860. Many black leaders believed that these mutual aid societies would encourage thrift,

IMPORTANT EVENTS

1805	Prophet emerges as Shawnee leader
1810	New York surpasses Philadelphia in population
1813	Death of Tecumseh
1819	Indian "Civilization Act"
1823	Beechers' Hartford Female Seminary established
1824	Monroe proposes Indian removal
1827	*Freedom's Journal* first published
1830s–1850s	Urban riots
1831	*Cherokee Nation* v. *Georgia*
1831–38	Trail of Tears
1835–42	Seminole War
1837	Boston employs paid policemen
1845	Start of Irish potato famine
1848	Abortive German revolution
1849	New York theater riot

to insulate their homes from the competition of the market economy. Many women found fulfillment in the domestic ideal, although others found it confining. More and more, urban women became associated with nurturing roles, first in homes and schools, then in churches and reform societies.

In Europe, famine and religious and political oppression sent millions of people across the Atlantic. They were drawn to the United States by the promise of jobs and of political and religious toleration. Yet most found the going rough even though conditions were often better than in their native lands. In the process they changed the profile of the American people; Americans differed from each other more and more and shared common traditions and experiences less and less. Competition and diversity bred intolerance and prejudice. None were to feel that more painfully than Indians and free blacks, who were most often made to feel as aliens in their own land. Indians were expelled from their traditional lands while free people of color were second-class citizens.

But change was not limited to the North and West. The agrarian, slave South too was undergoing a transformation.

SUGGESTIONS FOR FURTHER READING

Communities and Inequality

Stuart M. Blumin, *The Urban Threshold: Growth and Change in a Nineteenth-Century American Community* (1976); Don H. Doyle, *The Social Order of a Frontier Community: Jacksonville, Illinois, 1825–1870* (1978); Roger W. Lotchin, *San Francisco, 1846–1856: From Hamlet to City* (1974); Raymond A. Mohl, *Poverty in New York, 1783–1825* (1971); Edward Pessen, *Riches, Class and Power Before the Civil War* (1973); Jonathan Prude, *The Coming of Industrial Order. Town and Factory Life in Rural Massachusetts, 1810–1860* (1983); Edward K. Spann, *The New Metropolis. New York City, 1840–1857* (1981); Stephan Thernstrom, *Poverty and Progress: Social Mobility in a Nineteenth Century City* (1964); Alexis de Tocqueville, *Democracy in America,* 2 vols. (1835–1840); Richard C. Wade, *The Urban Frontier: 1790–1830*

slave, would move back onto the national political agenda, and Afro-Americans would focus with renewed intensity on their position at home.

The United States in 1860 was a far more diverse and complex society than it had been in 1800. Industrialization, specialization, urbanization, and immigration had altered the ways people lived and worked. Economic growth not only created new jobs in towns and cities but also caused clearer distinctions in wealth and status. Inequality increased everywhere, and competition and insecurity produced resentments and conflict. Increasingly, cities housed ostentatious wealth and abject poverty, and violence and disorder became commonplace.

Amidst these changes, middle-class families sought

(1957); Anthony F. C. Wallace, *Rockdale: The Growth of an American Village in the Early Industrial Revolution* (1978).

Women and the Family

Nancy F. Cott, *The Bonds of Womanhood: "Woman's Sphere" in New England, 1780–1835* (1977); Carl N. Degler, *At Odds: Women and the Family in America from the Revolution to the Present* (1980); Hasia R. Diner, *Erin's Daughters in America. Irish Immigrant Women in the Nineteenth Century* (1983); Linda Gordon, *Woman's Body, Woman's Rights: A Social History of Birth Control in America* (1976); James C. Mohr, *Abortion in America: The Origins and Evolution of National Policy, 1800–1900* (1978); James Reed, *From Private Vice to Public Virtue: The Birth Control Movement and American Society Since 1830* (1978); Mary P. Ryan, *Cradle of the Middle Class. The Family in Oneida County, New York, 1790–1865* (1981); Kathryn Kish Sklar, *Catharine Beecher: A Study in American Domesticity* (1973); Maris A. Vinovskis, *Fertility in Massachusetts from the Revolution to the Civil War* (1981); Robert V. Wells, *Revolutions in Americans' Lives* (1982); Barbara Welter, "The Cult of True Womanhood, 1820–1860," *American Quarterly*, 18 (Summer 1966), 151–174.

Immigrants

Rowland Berthoff, *British Immigrants in Industrial America* (1953); Theodore C. Blegen, *Norwegian Migration to America, 1825–1860* (1931); Kathleen Neils Conzen, *Immigrant Milwaukee: 1836–1860* (1976); Jay P. Dolan, *The Immigrant Church: New York's Irish and German Catholics, 1815–1865* (1975); Charlotte Erickson, *Invisible Immigrants* (1972); Robert Ernst, *Immigrant Life in New York City, 1825–1863* (1949); Oscar Handlin, *Boston's Immigrants: A Study in Acculturation*, rev. ed. (1959); Harold Runblom and Hans Norman, *From Sweden to America* (1976); Philip Taylor, *The Distant Magnet: European Emigration to the United States of America* (1971); Mark Wyman, *Immigrants in the Valley.*

Irish, Germans and Americans in the Upper Mississippi, 1830–1860 (1984).

Native Americans

Robert F. Berkhofer, Jr., *The White Man's Indian* (1978); Arthur De Rosier, *Removal of the Choctaw Indians* (1970); R. David Edmunds, *The Shawnee Prophet* (1983); Grant Foreman, *Indian Removal: The Emigration of the Five Civilized Tribes of Indians*, rev. ed. (1953); Michael D. Green, *The Politics of Indian Removal. Creek Government and Society in Crisis* (1982); Charles Hudson, *The Southeastern Indians* (1976); John K. Mahon, *History of the Second Seminole War, 1835–1842* (1967); Francis P. Prucha, *American Indian Policy in the Formative Years* (1962); Ronald N. Satz, *American Indian Policy in the Jacksonian Era* (1975); Herman J. Viola, *Thomas L. McKenney. Architect of America's Early Indian Policy: 1816–1830* (1974); Wilcomb E. Washburn, *The Indian in America* (1975); Thurman Wilkin, *Cherokee Tragedy* (1970).

Free People of Color

Ira Berlin, *Slaves Without Masters: The Free Negro in the Antebellum South* (1974); Leonard P. Curry, *The Free Black in Urban America 1800–1850* (1981); James Horton and Lois Horton, *Black Bostonians: Family Life and Community Struggle in the Antebellum North* (1979); Luther Porter Jackson, *Free Negro Labor and Property Holding in Virginia, 1830–1860* (1942); David M. Katzman, *Before the Ghetto: Black Detroit in the Nineteenth Century* (1973); Rudolph M. Lapp, *Blacks in Gold Rush California* (1977); Leon Litwack, *North of Slavery: The Negro in the Free States, 1790–1860* (1961); Floyd J. Miller, *The Search for a Black Nationality: Black Colonization and Emigration 1787–1863* (1975); Emma Lou Thornbrough, *The Negro in Indiana* (1957); Juliet E. K. Walker, *Free Frank. A Black Pioneer on the Antebellum Frontier* (1983); Arthur Zilversmit, *The First Emancipation: The Abolition of Slavery in the North* (1967).

SLAVERY AND THE GROWTH OF THE SOUTH

1800–1860

CHAPTER 11

He was weeping, sobbing. In a humble voice he had begged his master not to give him to Mr. King, who was going away to Alabama, but it had done no good. Now his voice rose and he uttered "an absolute cry of despair." Raving and "almost in a state of frenzy," he declared that he would never leave the Georgia plantation that was home to his father, mother, wife, and children. He twisted his hat between clenched fists and flung it to the ground; he would kill himself, he said, before he lost his family and all that made life worth living.

To Fanny Kemble, watching from the doorway, it was a horrifying and disorienting scene. One of the most famous British actresses ever to tour America, Fanny had grown up breathing England's antislavery tradition as naturally as the air. In New England she had become friends with such enlightened antislavery thinkers as William Ellery Channing, the liberal Boston minister who founded Unitarianism; Catharine Maria Sedgwick, America's foremost woman novelist; and Elizabeth Dwight Sedgwick, an educator and Catharine's sister-in-law. Amid such company, Fanny understandably assumed that attitudes in America were advanced and civilized. Then the man she married took her away from New England to a Georgia rice plantation, where hundreds of dark-skinned slaves produced the white grain that was his source of wealth.

Pierce Butler, Fanny's husband, was all that a cultured Philadelphia gentleman should be. He had lived all his life in the North, though part of his family's fortune had always sprung from southern slavery. When Fanny chose him from dozens of suitors, he had seemed an attractive exemplar of American culture. Yet now he shattered his slave's hopes without hesitation. Quietly "leaning against a table with his arms folded," Butler advised the distraught black man not to "make a fuss about what there was no help for."

Fanny wondered what America was really like. In the South, the northerner she thought she knew seemed a different man. Only with tears and vehement pleas was she able to convince Butler to keep the slave family together. He finally agreed as a favor to her, not on principle or because she had a right to be consulted.

This incident, which occurred in 1839, illustrates both the similarities between South and North and the differences that were beginning to emerge. Though racism existed in the North, its influence was far more visible on southern society. And though some northerners, like Pierce Butler, were undisturbed by the idea of human bondage, a growing number considered it shocking and backward. In the years after the Revolution, these northerners, possessing few slaves and influenced by the revolutionary ideal of natural rights, had adopted gradual emancipation laws (see page 161). At the same time they had developed a widening market economy and embarked on an industrial revolution. These changes increased production, spurred mechanization, and rendered forced labor obsolete.

In the South too, the years from 1800 to 1860 were a time of growth and prosperity; new lands were settled and new states peopled. But as the North grew and changed, economically the South merely grew; change there only reinforced existing economic patterns. Steadily the South emerged as the world's most extensive and vigorous slave economy. Its people were slaves, slaveholders, and nonslaveholders rather than farmers, merchants, mechanics, and manufacturers. Its well-being depended on agriculture alone, rather than agriculture plus commerce and manufacturing. Its population was almost wholly rural rather than rural and urban.

These facts meant that the social lives of southerners were unavoidably distinct from those of northerners. Nonslaveholders operated their family farms in a society dominated by slaveholding planters. A handful of planters developed an aristocratic lifestyle, while slaves—one-third of the South's people—lived without freedom, struggling to develop a culture that sustained hope. The influence of slavery spread throughout the social system, affecting not just southern economics but southern values, customs, and laws. It created a society that was noticeably different from the society of the north.

The South Remains Rural

The South in the early 1800s was the product of precisely the kind of resource-exploiting commercial agriculture that most of the early colonies had aspired to develop. Only there, nonmechanized agriculture remained highly profitable, as it did not in the Northeast. Southern planters were not sentimentalists who held onto their slaves for noneconomic reasons even in the face of the industrial revolution. Like other Americans, they were profit-oriented. But circumstances allowed them to continue to profit from a plantation economy.

At the time of the Revolution, slave-based agriculture was not exceedingly lucrative. Debt hung heavily over most of Virginia's extravagant and aristocratic tobacco growers, prodding them to consider the disadvantages of slavery. Cotton was a lucrative export crop only for sea-island planters, who grew the luxurious long-staple variety. The short-staple cotton that grew readily in the interior was unmarketable because its sticky seeds lay tangled in the fibers. But in spite of the limited usefulness of slavery, much wealth was tied up in it. Social inertia and fear of slave revolts prevented its abolition.

Then England's burgeoning textile industry changed the southern economy. English mills needed more and more cotton. Sea-island cotton was so profitable between 1785 and 1795 that thousands of farmers in the interior experimented with the short-staple variety; by the early 1790s southern farmers were growing 2 to 3 million pounds of it each year. Some of this cotton was meant for domestic use, but most was grown in the hope that some innovation would make the crop salable to the English. In such circumstances the invention of a cotton gin was almost inevitable, and Eli Whitney responded in 1793 with a simple machine that removed the seeds from the fibers. By 1800 cotton was spreading rapidly westward from the seaboard states.

So the antebellum South, or Old South, became primarily a cotton South. Tobacco continued to be grown in Virginia and North Carolina, and rice and sugar were still very important in certain coastal areas,

Rise of the Cotton South especially in South Carolina, Georgia, and Louisiana. But cotton was the largest crop, the most widespread, and the force behind the South's hunger for new territory. Ambitious cotton growers poured across the Appalachians into the West, pushing the Indians off their fabulously fertile Gulf lands (see pages 287–290). The boom in the cotton economy came in the 1830s in Alabama and Mississippi. But not until the 1850s did the wave of cotton expansion cross Louisiana and pour into Texas (see maps, page 300).

Thus the Old South was not old at all; in 1860 it was young and still growing. For although prices plunged sharply at least once a decade after 1820, overall demand for cotton soared. Since English mills would buy virtually all the cotton a planter could grow, eager southerners bought more slaves and more land. Soon they were exporting more than three-quarters of their crop and supplying almost the same proportion of England's purchases. In just a few decades some of these planters amassed great personal fortunes and rose to an aristocratic position in society. Though some old Virginia and South Carolina families were represented among the proud new "cotton snobs," most of the wealthy were newly rich.

To the hard-working and lucky, riches came quickly. A good example is the family of Jefferson Davis. Like Abraham Lincoln, Davis was born in humble circumstances. His father was one of **Jefferson Davis: His Early Life** the thousands of American farmers on the frontier who moved frequently, unwisely buying land when prices were high and selling when they were low, never making his fortune. Luckily for Davis, his older brother migrated to Mississippi and became successful. Settling on rich bottomlands next to the Mississippi River, Joseph Davis made profits, expanded his holdings of land and slaves, and made more profits. Soon he was an established figure in society, and he used his position to arrange an education at West Point for his younger brother. A large plantation awaited Jefferson's resignation from the army. Thus the Davis family became aristocrats in one generation.

A less-fortunate consequence of the cotton boom was the relative indifference of farmers to the long-term fertility of the soil. In an expanding economy,

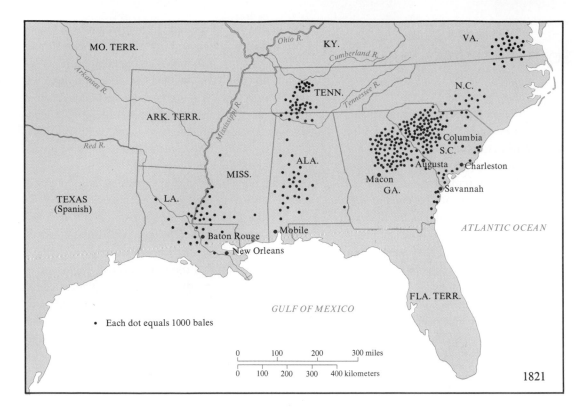

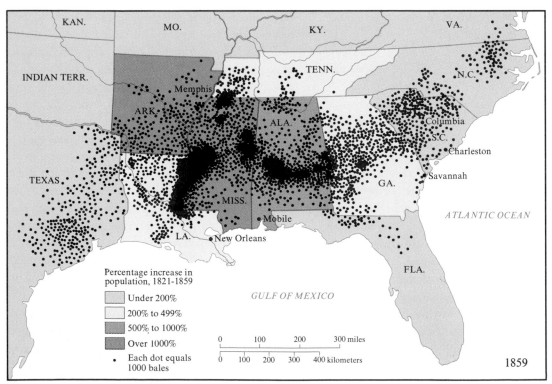

Cotton Production in the South

Chapter 11: SLAVERY AND THE GROWTH OF THE SOUTH, 1800–1860

Jefferson Davis became a stiff and formal aristocrat. Varina Howell Davis, despite her glum expression here, was lively and clever, a social asset to her husband.   Library of Congress.

with cheap and superior land available farther west, most people preferred to exhaust the land and move on rather than invest heavily in preserving it. Only in the older states of the Upper South, where the major landholders stayed behind, and where the cotton boom had less impact, did serious interest in diversified farming develop.

An even more important consequence of the boom was thin population distribution. Producers spread out over as large an area as possible in order to maximize production and income. Because farms were far apart, southern society remained predominantly rural. Population density, low even in the older plantation states, was especially so in the frontier areas being brought under cultivation. In 1860 there were only 2.3 people per square mile in Texas, 15.6 in Louisiana, and 18.0 in Georgia. By contrast, population density in the nonslaveholding states east of the Mississippi River was almost three

Population Distribution

times higher. The Northeast had an average of 65.4 persons per square mile, and in some places the density was much higher. Massachusetts had 153.1 people per square mile, and New York City, where overcrowding reached epic proportions, compressed 86,400 people into each square mile.

Even in the 1850s, much of the South seemed almost uninhabited, a virtual wilderness. Frederick Law Olmsted, a northerner who later became famous as a landscape architect, made several trips through the South in the 1850s as a reporter. He found that the few trains and stagecoaches available to travelers offered only rough accommodations and kept their schedules poorly. Indeed, he had to do most of his traveling on horseback along primitive trails. Passing from Columbus, Georgia, to Montgomery, Alabama, Olmsted observed "a hilly wilderness, with a few dreary villages, and many isolated cotton farms." Alabama, of course, had been frontier as recently as 1800, but Olmsted encountered the same conditions

John Blake White's painting, Perspective of Broad Street *(1836), which depicts the arrival of the mail, suggests the excitement of an urban world in Charleston, one of the South's few cities.* The City of Charleston, South Carolina, City Hall Collection.

in parts of eastern Virginia: "For hours and hours one has to ride through the unlimited, continual, all-shadowing, all-embracing forest, following roads in the making of which no more labor has been given than was necessary to remove the timber which would obstruct the passage of wagons; and even for days and days he may sometimes travel and see never two dwellings of mankind within sight of each other."

Society in such rural areas was characterized by relatively weak institutions, for it takes people to create and support organized activity. Where the concentration of people was low, it was difficult to finance and operate schools, churches, libraries, or even hotels, restaurants, and other urban amenities. Southerners were strongly committed to their churches, and some believed in the importance of universities, but all such institutions were far less developed than those in the North.

The few southern cities were likewise smaller and less developed than those in the North. As exporters, southerners did not need large cities; a small group of merchants working in connection with northern brokers sufficed to ship their cotton overseas and to import necessary supplies and luxuries. As planters, southerners invested most of their capital in slaves; they had little money left to build factories—another source of urban growth. A few southerners did invest in iron or textiles on a small scale. But the largest southern "industry" was lumbering and the largest factories were cigar factories, where slaves finished tobacco products. As a result, in 1860 only 49,000 out of 704,000 South Carolinians lived in towns with 2,500 or more residents. Less than 3 percent of Mississippi's population lived in places of comparable size. In 1860 the population of Charleston was only 41,000, Richmond 38,000, and Mobile 29,000. New Orleans, by far the largest southern city, had only 169,000 residents, and it was being left behind because it was not part of the national railroad network.

Weak Urban Sector

Thus, although it was economically attuned to an international market, the South was only semideveloped in comparison with other sections of the country. Its people prospered, but neither as rapidly nor as independently as residents of the North. There commerce and industry brought unprecedented advances in productivity, widening the range of affordable goods and services and raising the average person's standard of living. In the South, change was quantitative rather than qualitative; farming techniques remained essentially the same. To prosper, southern planters increased their acreage and hoped for continued high demand from foreign customers—decisions that worked to the ultimate disadvantage of the region. Subsistence farmers merely worked harder and hoped to grow a bit more.

The society that developed in this largely agrarian economy was a society of extremes. The social distance between a wealthy planter and a small slaveholder was as great as the distance between a slaveholder and a nonslaveholder, to say nothing of the distance between whites and slaves. And, contrary to popular belief, planters were neither the most numerous nor the most typical group. The typical white southerner was a yeoman farmer.

Yeoman Farmers

More than two-thirds of white southern families owned no slaves. Some of them lived in towns and ran stores or businesses, but most were farmers who owned their own land and grew their own food. Independent and motivated by a hearty share of frontier individualism, these people lived a self-sufficient farming life. They had little connection with the market or its type of progress. Families might raise a small surplus to trade for needed items or spending cash, but they were far from major market networks and therefore not particularly concerned about a larger cash income. They valued instead their self-reliance and freedom from others' control. Absorbed in their isolated but demanding rural life, they formed an important, though sometimes silent, part of southern society. If their rights were threatened, however, they could react strongly.

Yeomen pioneered the southern wilderness as herders of livestock and then as farmers. In successive waves they moved down the southern Appalachians into new Gulf lands following the War of 1812. The herdsmen grazed their cattle and pigs on the abundant natural vegetation in the woods. Before long, however, the next wave of settlers arrived and broke ground for crops. These yeoman farmers forced many herdsmen farther west, and eventually across the Mississippi.

Migration became almost a way of life for some yeoman families. Lured by stories of the good land over the horizon, men often uprooted their families repeatedly. They worked hard in each new place to clear fields and establish a farm, while their wives performed their tasks in the household economy and patiently recreated a few social ties—to relatives, neighbors, church members—that enriched experience. "We have been [moving] all our lives," recalled one woman. "As soon as ever we git comfortably settled, it is time to be off to something new." Maria Lides's father took the family from South Carolina to Alabama, but "his having such a good crop" there, lamented Maria, "seems to make him more anxious to move." She almost wished he would decide on California, because "he would be obliged to stop then for he could go no farther."

Some yeomen acquired large tracts of level land and became wealthy planters. Others clung to the beautiful mountainous areas they loved, or pressed farther into the wilds because they "couldn't stand the sound of another man's axe." As they moved, they tended to stick to the climate and soils they knew best. Yeomen could not afford the richest bottomlands, which were swampy and required expensive draining, but they owned land almost everywhere else.

Observers sometimes concluded that these people were poor and idle, especially the herdsmen who sat on their cabin porches while their stock foraged in the woods. It is more accurate to say that they were frontiersmen and farmers who did not manage to become rich. They worked hard, as farmers do everywhere, and enjoyed a folk culture based on family, church, and community. They spoke with a drawl and their inflections were reminiscent of their Scottish and Irish backgrounds. Once a year they flocked to religious revivals called protracted meetings or camp meetings, and in between they enjoyed events such as house-raisings, logrollings, quilting bees, and corn-shuckings. These combined work with fun and provided a fellowship that was especially welcome to isolated rural dwellers. There was food in abundance and often some liquor. The men did most of the farming; though the women occasionally helped in the fields, they commonly spent their time preserving and preparing food, making clothes, blankets, and candles, and tending to household matters. Both sexes worked hard for the family economy, continuing the colonial tradition of outdoor work for men and indoor work for women.

Folk Culture of the Yeoman

Beyond these basic facts, historians know little about the yeomen. Because their means were modest, they did not generate the voluminous legal papers, such as contracts, wills, and inventories of estates, that document the activities of the rich. Only a few letters have found their way into libraries and archives. It is reasonable to suppose, though, that yeomen held a variety of opinions and pursued individual goals. Some envied the planters and strove to be rich; others were content with their independence, recreation, family life, and religion.

At the first extreme was a North Carolinian named John F. Flintoff, whose rare diary records the ambitions

Like the figures in George Caleb Bingham's painting, The Squatters (1850), *southern yeomen were tough, independent people who tamed the frontier.   Museum of Fine Arts, Boston.*

of a nonslaveholder who hungered to be rich. Flintoff was born in 1823 and at age eighteen went to Mississippi to seek his fortune. Like other aspiring yeomen, he worked as an overseer, but often found it impossible to please his employers. At one time he gave up and returned to North Carolina, where he married and lived in his parents' house. But Flintoff was "impatient to get along in the world," so he tried Louisiana next and then Mississippi again.

For Flintoff, the fertile Gulf region had its disadvantages. "My health has been very bad here," he noted; "chills and fever occasionally has hold of me." "First rate employment" alternated with "very low wages." Moreover, as a young man working on isolated plantations, Flintoff often felt "all alone." Even a revival meeting in 1844 proved "an extremely cold time" with "little warm feeling." His uncle and other

employers found fault with his work, and in 1846 Flintoff concluded in despair that "managing negroes and large farms is soul destroying."

Still, a desire to succeed kept him going. At twenty-six, before he owned a foot of land, Flintoff bought his first slave, "a negro boy 7 years old." Soon he had purchased two more children, the cheapest slaves available. Conscious of his status as a slaveowner, Flintoff resented the low wages he was paid and complained that his uncle offered him *"hand pay,"* the wages of a day laborer rather than a slaveowner and manager. In 1853, with nine young slaves and a growing family, Flintoff faced "the most unhappy time of my life." He was fired by his uncle, "treated shamefully." Finally he said, "I will have to sell some of my negroes to buy land. This I must have. I want *a home."*

Returning to North Carolina, Flintoff purchased 124 acres with help from his in-laws. He grew corn, wheat, and tobacco and earned extra cash hauling wood in his wagon. By 1860 he owned 3 horses, 26 hogs, 10 cattle, and several slaves, and was paying off his debts. Eventually Flintoff owned 217 acres and became a fairly prosperous tobacco and grain farmer. He was able to send his sons to college, and prided himself that he had freed his wife from much of the labor of yeoman women, so that she "lived a *Lady*." But the struggle upward had not been easy, and Flintoff never became the cotton planter he had aspired to be.

Probably more typical of the southern yeoman was Ferdinand L. Steel. As a young man Steel moved from North Carolina to Tennessee to work as a hatter and river boatman, but he eventually settled down to farming in Mississippi. He rose every day at five and worked until sundown. With the help of his family he raised corn, wheat, pork, and vegetables for the family table. Cotton was his cash crop: like other yeomen he sold five or six bales a year to obtain money for sugar, coffee, salt, calico, gunpowder, and a few other store-bought goods.

Steel picked his cotton himself (never exceeding 120 pounds per day—less than many slaves averaged) and regretted that cotton cultivation was so arduous and time-consuming. He was not tempted to grow more of it. The market fluctuated, and if cotton prices fell, a small grower like himself could be driven into debt and lose his farm. Steel, in fact, wanted to grow less cotton. "We are too weak handed" to manage it, he noted in his diary. "We had better raise small grain and corn and let cotton alone, raise corn and keep out of debt and we will have no necessity of raising cotton."

Steel's life in Mississippi in the 1840s retained much of the flavor of the frontier. He made all the family's shoes; his wife and sister sewed dresses, shirts, and "pantiloons." The Steel women also rendered their own soap, and spun and wove cotton into cloth; the men hunted for game. House-raisings and corn-shuckings provided entertainment, and Steel doctored his illnesses with boneset tea and other herbs.

The focus of Steel's life was his family and his religion. The family prayed together every morning and night, and he prayed and studied Scripture for an hour after lunch. Steel joined a temperance society and looked forward to church and camp meetings. "My Faith increases, & I enjoy much of that peace which the world cannot give," he wrote in 1841. Seeking to improve himself and be "ready" for judgment, Steel borrowed histories, Latin and Greek grammars, and religious books from his church. Eventually he became a traveling Methodist minister. "My life is one of toil," he reflected, "but blessed be God that it is as well with me as it is."

Toil, with even less security, was the lot of two other groups of free southerners: landless whites and free blacks. From 25 to 40 percent of the white workers in the South were laborers who owned no land. Their property consisted of a few household items and some animals—usually pigs—that could feed themselves on the open range. These animals were a major economic asset, for good, steady employment was uncertain in a region whose large producers relied on slave labor. In addition to unskilled laborers in the countryside and towns, the landless included some immigrants, especially Irish, who did heavy and dangerous work such as building railroads and digging ditches.

The white farm laborers were people struggling to become yeomen. They faced low wages or, if they rented, they were dependent on the unpredictable market price for their crops. Some fell into debt and were frequently sued; others, by scrimping and saving and finding odd jobs, managed to climb into the ranks of yeomen. When James and Nancy Bennitt of North Carolina succeeded in their ten-year struggle to buy land, they decided to avoid the unstable market as much as possible; thereafter they raised extra corn and wheat as sources of cash.

There were nearly a quarter of a million free blacks in the South in 1860, people whose conditions were worse than the yeoman's and often little better than the slave's. The free blacks of the

Free Blacks Upper South were usually decendants of men and women emancipated by their owners in the 1780s and 1790s, a period of postrevolutionary idealism that coincided with a decline in tobacco prices. They had few material advantages; most did not own land and had to labor in someone else's field, frequently beside slaves. By law they could not own a gun or liquor, violate curfew, assemble except in church, testify in court, or (everywhere after 1835) vote. Despite these obstacles, a minority bought land, and others found jobs as artisans, draymen, boatmen, and fishermen. A few owned slaves, who were almost always their wives and children, purchased from bondage.

Farther south, in the cotton and Gulf regions, a large proportion of free blacks were mulattoes, the privileged offspring of wealthy planters. Some received good educations and financial backing from their fathers, who recognized a moral obligation to them. In a few cities such as New Orleans and Mobile, extensive interracial sex had produced a mulatto population that was recognized as a distinct class. These mulattoes formed a society of their own and sought a status above slaves and other freedmen, if not equal to planters. But outside New Orleans, Mobile, and Charleston such groups were rare, and most mulattoes encountered disadvantages more frequently than they enjoyed benefits from their light skin tone. (For a more detailed discussion of free blacks during this period, see Chapter 10).

SLAVEHOLDING PLANTERS

At the opposite end of the spectrum from free blacks were the slaveholders. As a group slaveowners lived well, on incomes that enabled them to enjoy superior housing, food, clothing, and luxuries. But most did not live on the opulent scale that legend suggests. A few statistics tell the story: 88 percent of southern slaveholders had fewer than twenty slaves; 72 percent had fewer than ten; 50 percent had fewer than five. Thus the average slaveholder was not a man of great wealth but an aspring farmer. Nor was he a polished aristocrat, but more usually a person of humble origins, with little formal education and many rough edges to his manner. In fact, he probably had little beyond a degree of wealth and a growing ambition to distinguish him from a nonslaveholder.

Even wealthy slaveowners often lacked the refined manner of aristocrats. Many in the Gulf states were new to wealth, and their desire to plant more cotton and buy more slaves often caused them to postpone the enjoyment of luxuries. First-generation planters often lived for decades in their original log cabin,

improved only by clapboards or a frame addition. A Mississippi gentleman admitted, "If you wish to see people worth millions living as they were not worth hundreds, come down here." Yet the planters' wealth put ease and refinement within their grasp.

A Louisiana planter named Bennet Barrow, to take an example, was neither especially polished nor unusually coarse. Barrow's plantation lay in a wealthy parish in Louisiana, but his wealth was new and Barrow was preoccupied with moneymaking. He worried constantly over his cotton crop, filling his diary with tedious weather reports and gloomy predictions of his yields. Yet Barrow also strove to appear above such worries, and in boom times he grandly endorsed notes for men who left him saddled with debt.

Barrow hunted frequently, and he had a passion for racing horses and raising hounds. Each year he set aside several weeks to attend the races in New Orleans, where he entered stallions brought from as far away as Tennessee. Barrow could report the loss of a slave without feeling, but emotion shattered his laconic manner when misfortune struck his sporting animals. "Never was a person more unlucky than I am," he complained; "My favorite pup never lives." His strongest feelings surfaced when his horse Jos Bell—equal to "the best Horse in the South"—"broke down in running a mile . . . ruined for Ever." That same day the distraught Barrow gave his field hands a "general Whipping." Barrow was rich, but his wealth had not softened his rough, direct style of life.

The wealth of the greatest planters gave ambitious men like Barrow something to aspire to. If most planters lived in spacious, comfortable farmhouses, some did live in mansions. If most slaveowners sat down at mealtimes to an abundance of tempting country foods—pork and ham, beef and game, fresh vegetables and fruits, tasty breads and biscuits, cakes and jams—the sophisticated elite consumed such delights as "gumbo, ducks and olives, *supreme de volaille*, chickens in jelly, oysters, lettuce salad, chocolate cream, jelly cake, claret cup, etc." On formal and business occasions such as county court days, a traveler in Mississippi would see gentlemen decked out in "black cloth coats, black cravats and satin or embroidered silk waistcoats; all, too, sleek as if just from a barber's hands, and redolent of perfumes."

The ladies wore the latest fashions to parties and balls and made many other occasions sources of mer-

The North Carolina planter Duncan Cameron (1776–1853) built this spacious and comfortable farmhouse for his bride, Rebecca Bennehan, in 1804. The house, called Fairntosh, is more typical of the average planter's home than the elaborate Greek-revival-style mansions of popular legend.   Library of Congress.

riment. Relations and friends often visited each other for several days or weeks at a time, enjoying good food and good company. Courtship was a major attraction at the larger parties or dances. Between social occasions women and many men kept up their close friendships through constant letter-writing.

Among the wealthiest and oldest families, slaveholding men dominated through a paternalistic ideology. Instead of stressing the acquisitive aspects of commercial agriculture, they focused on *noblesse oblige*. They saw themselves as custodians of the welfare of society as a whole and of the black families who depended on them. The paternalistic planter saw himself not as an oppressor but as the benevolent guardian of an inferior race. He developed affectionate feelings toward his slaves (as long as they kept in their place) and was genuinely shocked at outside criticism of his behavior.

Southern Paternalism

The letters of Paul Carrington Cameron, North Carolina's largest slaveholder, illustrate this mentality. After a period of sickness among his one thousand North Carolina slaves (he had hundreds more in Alabama and Mississippi), Cameron wrote, "I fear the Negroes have suffered much from the want of proper attention and kindness under this late distemper . . . no love of lucre shall ever induce me to be cruel, or even to make or permit to be made any great exposure of their persons at inclement seasons." On another occasion he described to his sister the sense of responsibility he felt: "I cannot better follow the example of our venerated Mother than in doing my duty to her faithful old slaves and their descendants. Do you remember a cold & frosty morning, during her illness, when she said to me 'Paul my son the people ought to be shod' this is ever in my ears, whenever I see any ones shoes in bad order; and in my ears it will be, so long as I am master."

There is no doubt that the richest southern planters saw themselves in this way. It was comforting to do so, and slaves, accommodating themselves to the realities of power, encouraged their masters to think their benevolence was appreciated. Paternalism also provided a welcome defense against abolitionist criticism. Still, for most planters, paternalism affected the manner and not the substance of their behavior. It was a matter of style. Its softness and warmth covered harsher assumptions: blacks were inferior; planters should make money. As discussion of owners' duties increased, theories about the complete and permanent inferiority of blacks also multiplied.

Even Paul Cameron's concern vanished with changed circumstances. Following the Civil War he bristled at their efforts to be free and made sweeping economic decisions without regard to their welfare. Writing on Christmas Day, 1865, Cameron showed little Christian charity (but a healthy profit motive) when he expressed his desire to get "free . . . of the negro. I am convinced that the people who gets rid of the free negro first will be the first to advance in improved agriculture. Have made no effort to retain any of mine [and] will not attempt a crop beyond the capacity of 30 hands." With that he turned out nearly a thousand black agriculturalists, rented his lands to several white farmers, and invested in industry.

Relations between men and women in the planter class were similarly paternalistic. An upper-class southern woman typically was raised and educated to be the subordinate companion **Woman's Role** of men. Her proper responsibility was home management. She was not to venture into politics and other worldly affairs. In a social system based on the coercion of an entire race, no woman could be allowed to challenge society's rules. If she defied or questioned the status quo, she risked universal condemnation.

Within the domestic circle the husband reigned supreme. For the fortunate woman, like North Carolina diarist Catherine Devereux Edmondston, whose marriage joined two people of shared tastes and habits, the husband's authority weighed lightly or not at all. But other women, even some who considered themselves happily married, were acutely conscious of that authority. "He is master of the house," wrote South Carolina's Mary Boykin Chesnut. "To hear is to obey

. . . all the comfort of my life depends upon his being in a good humor." In a darker mood Chesnut once observed that "there is no slave . . . like a wife." Unquestionably there were some, possibly many, close and satisfying relationships between men and women in the planter class, but many women were dissatisfied.

The upper-class southern woman had to clear several barriers in the way of happiness. Making the right choice of a husband was especially important. With this decision a young woman moved from the rather narrow experience that society had permitted her into a restricted lifetime role. After spending her early years within the family circle, a planter's daughter usually attended one of the South's rapidly multiplying academies or boarding schools. There she formed friendships with other girls and received an education that emphasized grammar, composition, penmanship, geography, literature, and languages, but much less of science and mathematics. As she developed some sense of herself, the young woman typically maintained dutiful and affectionate ties with her parents. But very soon she had to commit herself for life to a man whom she generally had known for only a brief time.

Once married, she lost most of her legal rights to her husband, became part of his family, and was expected to get along with numerous in-laws during extended visits. Most of the year, she was isolated on a large plantation, where she had to learn a host of new duties. Although free from much of the labor of yeoman women, the plantation mistress was not free from care. She had to supervise many tasks: overseeing the cooking and preserving of food, managing the house, caring for the children, and attending sick slaves. As a woman she was forbidden to travel and visit unless accompanied by men. All the circumstances of her future life depended on the man she chose.

It is not surprising that the intelligent and perceptive young woman sometimes approached marriage with a feeling akin to dread. Lucy Breckinridge, a wealthy Virginia girl, sensed how much autonomy she would have to surrender on her wedding day. She realized that thereafter her life would depend on men, who though chivalrous in manner, expected to be the center of attention. In her diary she recorded this unvarnished observation on marriage: "If [husbands] care for their wives at all it is only as a sort of servant, a being made to attend to their comforts and to keep the children out of the way. . . . A woman's life after she is married, unless there is an immense amount of love, is nothing but suffering and hard work."

Lucy loved young children but knew that child-bearing often involved grief and sorrow. On learning of a relative's death, Lucy said, "It is a happy release for her, for her married life has been a long term of suffering. She has been married about seven years and had five children." This case was not too unusual, for in 1840 the birthrate for southern women in their fertile years was almost 20 percent higher than the national average. At the beginning of the nineteenth century, the average southern woman could expect to bear eight children; by 1860 the figure had decreased only to six, and one or more miscarriages were likely among so many pregnancies. The high birthrate took a toll on women's health, for complications of child-birth were a major cause of death.

Moreover, a mother had to endure the loss of many of the infants she bore. Infant mortality in the first year of life exceeded 10 percent and remained high during the next few years. In the South in 1860 almost five out of ten children died before age five, and among South Carolinians younger than twenty, fewer than four in ten survived to reach the twenty- to sixty-year-old category. For those women who wanted to plan their families, methods of contraception were not always reliable. And doctors had few remedies for infection or irritation of the reproductive tract.

Slavery was another source of trouble, a nasty sore that women sometimes had to bandage but were not supposed to notice. "Violations of the moral law . . . made mulattoes as common as blackberries," protested a woman in Georgia, but wives had to play "the ostrich game." "A magnate who runs a hideous black harem," wrote Mrs. Chesnut, "under the same roof with his lovely white wife, and his beautiful accom-plished daughters . . . poses as the model of all human virtues to these poor women whom God and the laws have given him. From the height of his awful majesty, he scolds and thunders at them, as if he never did wrong in his life."

In the early 1800s, some southern women, especially Quakers, had spoken out against slavery. Even when they did not criticize the "peculiar institution," white women approached it differently than men, seeing it less as a system and more as a series of relationships with individuals. Perhaps southern men sensed this, for they wanted no discussion by women of the slavery issue. In the 1840s and 1850s, as national and in-ternational criticism of slavery increased, southern men published a barrage of articles stressing that women should restrict their concerns to the home. A writer in the *Southern Literary Messenger* bemoaned "these days of Women's Rights." Disapproving of women with political opinions, the *Southern Quarterly Review* declared, "The proper place for a woman is at home. One of her highest privileges, to be politically merged in the existence of her husband." Thomas Dew, one of the nineteenth century's first proslavery theorists, advised that "women are precisely what the men make them," and another writer promoted "affection, reverence, and duty" as a woman's proper attitudes.

But southern women were beginning to chafe at their customary exclusion from financial matters. A study of women in Petersburg, Virginia, has revealed behavior that amounted to an implicit criticism of the institution of marriage and the loss of autonomy it entailed. During several decades before 1860 the proportion of women who had not married, or not remarried after the death of a spouse, grew to exceed 33 percent. Likewise the number of women who worked for wages, controlled their own property, or even ran businesses increased. In managing property these women benefited from legal reforms, beginning with Mississippi's Married Women's Property Act of 1839, that were not designed to increase female in-dependence. Rather, to offset business panics and recessions, the law gave women some property rights in order to protect families from ruin caused by the husband's indebtedness. But some women saw the resulting opportunity and took it. In the countryside southern women had fewer options, but Petersburg's women were seeking to use the talents they had and the education they had gained.

Restrictions on freedom and the use of education were not limited to upper-class women. For a large category of southern men and women, freedom was wholly denied and education in any form was not allowed. Male or female, slaves were expected to accept bondage and ignorance as their condition.

Slaves and the Conditions of Their Servitude

For Afro-Americans, slavery was a curse that brought no blessings other than the strengths they developed to survive it. Slaves knew a life of poverty, coercion, toil, heartbreak, and resentment. They had few hopes that were not denied; often they had to bear separation from their loved ones; and they were despised as an inferior race. That they endured and found loyalty and strength among themselves is a tribute to their courage, but it could not make up for a life without freedom or opportunity.

Southern slaves enjoyed few material comforts beyond the bare necessities. Their diet was plain and limited, though generally they had enough to eat.

Slave Diet, Clothing, and Housing The basic ration was cornmeal, fat pork, molasses, and occasionally coffee. Many masters allowed slaves to tend gardens, which provided the variety and extra nutrition of greens and sweet potatoes. Fishing and hunting benefited some slaves. "It was nothin' fine," recalled one woman, "but it was good plain eatin' what filled you up."[1] Most slaveowners were innocent of the charge that they starved their slaves, but there is considerable evidence that slaves often suffered the effects of beriberi, pellagra, and other dietary-deficiency diseases.

Clothing too was plain, coarse, and inexpensive. Children of both sexes ran naked in hot weather and wore long cotton shirts in cool. When they were big enough to go to the fields, the boys received a work shirt and a pair of breeches and the girls a simple dress. On many plantations slave women made their own clothing of osnaburg, a coarse cotton fabric known as "nigger cloth." Probably few received more than one or two changes of clothing for hot and cold seasons and one blanket each winter. Those who could earn a little money by doing extra work often bought additional clothing. Many slaves had to go without shoes until December, even as far north as Virginia. The shoes they received were frequent objects of complaint—uncomfortable brass-toed brogans or stiff wraparounds made from leather tanned on the plantation.

Summer and winter, slaves lived in small one-room cabins with a door and possibly a window opening, but no glass. Logs chinked with mud formed the walls, dirt was the only floor, and a wattle-and-daub or stone chimney vented the fireplace that provided heat and light. Bedding consisted of heaps of straw, straw mattresses, or wooden bedframes lashed to the walls with rope. A few crude pieces of furniture and cooking utensils completed the furnishings of most cabins. More substantial houses survive today from some of the richer plantations, but the average slave lived in crude accommodations. The gravest drawback of slave cabins was not their appearance and lack of comfort but their unhealthfulness. In each small cabin lived one or two whole families. Crowding and lack of sanitation fostered the spread of infection and contagious diseases. Many slaves (and whites) carried worms and intestinal parasites picked up from fecal matter or the soil. Lice were widespread among both races, and flies and other insects spread such virulent diseases as typhoid fever, malaria, and dysentery.

Hard work was the central fact of the slaves' existence. In Gulf-coast cotton districts long hours and large work gangs suggested factories in the field rather than the small-scale, isolated work patterns of slaves in the eighteenth-century Chesapeake. Overseers rang the morning bell before dawn, so early that some slaves remembered being in the fields "before it was light enough to see clearly . . . holding their hoes and other implements—afraid to start work for fear that they would cover the cotton plants with dirt because they couldn't see clearly." And, as one woman testified, when interviewed by workers in the Federal Writers' Project of the 1930s, "it was way after sundown 'fore they could stop that field work. Then they had to hustle to finish their night work in time for supper, or go to bed without it." Except in urban settings and on some rice plantations, where

Slave Work Routines

---

[1]Accounts by ex-slaves are quoted from *The American Slave: A Composite Autobiography,* edited by George P. Rawick (Westport, Conn.: Greenwood Press, First Reprint Edition 1972, Second Reprint Edition 1974), from materials gathered by the Federal Writers' Project and originally published in 1941. The spelling in these accounts has been standardized.

slaves were assigned daily tasks to complete at their own pace, working from "sun to sun" became universal in the South. These long hours and hard work were at the heart of the advantage of slave labor. As one planter put it, slaves were the best labor because "you could command them and *make* them do what was right." White workers, by contrast, were few and couldn't be *driven;* "they wouldn't stand it."

Planters aimed to keep all their laborers busy all the time. Profit took precedence over paternalism's "protection" of women: slave women did heavy field work, often as much as the men and even during pregnancy. Old people—of whom there were few—were kept busy caring for young children, doing light chores, or carding, ginning, or spinning cotton. Children had to gather kindling for the fire, carry water to the fields, or sweep the yard. But slaves had a variety of ways to keep from being worked to death. It was impossible for the master to supervise every slave every minute, and slaves slacked off when they were not being watched. Thus travelers frequently described lackadaisical slaves who seemed "to go through the motions of labor without putting strength into them," and owners complained that slaves "never would lay out their strength freely . . . it was impossible to make them do it." Stubborn misunderstanding and literal-mindedness was another defense. One exasperated Virginia planter exclaimed, "You can make a nigger work, *but you cannot make him think.*"

Of course the slave could not slow his labor too much, because the owner enjoyed a monopoly on force and violence. Whites throughout the South believed that Negroes "can't be governed except with the whip." One South Carolinian frankly explained to a northern journalist that he had whipped his slaves occasionally, "say once a fortnight; . . . the Negroes knew they would be whipped if they didn't behave themselves, and the fear of the lash kept them in good order." Evidence suggests that whippings were less frequent on small farms than on large plantations, but the reports of former slaves show that a large majority even of small farmers plied the lash. These beatings symbolized authority to the master and tyranny to the slaves, who made them a benchmark for evaluating a master. In the words of former slaves, a good owner was one who did not "whip too much,"

Physical and Mental Abuse of Slaves

To maximize the return on their investment, slaveowners put young and old to work, especially at harvest. This family of slaves was picking cotton outside Savannah in 1855. *The New-York Historical Society.*

whereas a bad owner "whipped till he'd bloodied you and blistered you."

As this testimony suggests, terrible abuses could and did occur. The master wielded virtually absolute authority on his plantation, and courts did not recognize the word of a chattel. Pregnant women were whipped, and there were burnings, mutilations, tortures, and murders. Yet the physical cruelty of slavery may have been less in the United States than elsewhere in the New World. In sugar-growing or mining regions of the Western Hemisphere in the 1800s, slaves were regarded as an expendable resource to be replaced after seven years. Treatment was so poor and families so uncommon that death rates were high and the heavily male slave population did not replace itself, and rapidly shrank in size. In the United States, by contrast, the slave population showed a steady natural increase, as births exceeded deaths, and each generation grew larger.

The worst evil of American slavery was not its physical cruelty but the fact of slavery itself: coercion, loss of freedom, belonging to another person. Recalling their days in bondage, some former slaves emphasized the physical abuse—those were "bullwhip days" to one woman; another said, "What I think 'bout slavery? Huh—nigger get back cut in slavery time, didn't he?" But their comments focused on the tyranny of whipping as much as the pain. A woman named Delia Garlic cut to the core when she said, "It's bad to belong to folks that own you soul an' body. I could tell you 'bout it all day, but even then you couldn't guess the awfulness of it." And a man named Thomas Lewis put it this way: "There was no such thing as being good to slaves. Many people were better than others, but a slave belonged to his master and there was no way to get out of it."

As these comments show, American slaves retained their mental independence and self-respect despite their bondage. They hated their oppression, and contrary to some whites' perceptions, they were not grateful to their oppressors. Although they had to be subservient and speak honeyed words in the presence of their masters, they talked quite differently later on among themselves. The evidence of their resistant attitudes comes from their actions and from their own life stories.

Former slaves reported some kind feelings between masters and slaves, but the overwhelming picture was one of antagonism and resistance. Slaves mistrusted kindness from whites and suspected self-interest in their owners. A woman whose mistress "was good to us Niggers" said her owner was kind " 'cause she was raisin' us to work for her." A man recalled that his owners "always thought lots of their niggers and Grandma Maria say, 'Why shouldn't they—it was their money.' " Christmas presents of clothing from the master did not mean anything, observed another, " 'cause he was going to [buy] that anyhow."

Slaves' Attitudes Toward Whites

Slaves also saw their owners as people who used human beings as beasts of burden. "Master was pretty good," said one man. "He treated us just about like you would a good mule." Another said that his master "fed us reg'lar on good, 'stantial food, just like you'd tend to your horse, if you had a real good one." A third recalled his master saying, " 'A well-fed, healthy nigger, next to a mule, is the best propersition a man can invest his money in.' "

Slaves were sensitive to the thousand daily signs of their degraded status. One man recalled the general rule that slaves ate cornbread and owners ate biscuits. If blacks did get biscuits, "the flour that we made the biscuits out of was the third-grade shorts." A woman reported that on her plantation "Old Master hunted a heap, but us never did get none of what he brought in." "Us catch lots of 'possums, but mighty few of 'em us Niggers ever got a chance to eat or rabbits neither," said another. "They made Niggers go out and hunt 'em and the white folks ate 'em." If the owner took slaves' garden produce to town and sold it for them, the slaves suspected him of pocketing part of the profits.

Suspicion and resentment often grew into hatred. According to a former slave from Virginia, "the white folks treated the nigger so mean that all the slaves prayed God to punish their cruel masters." When a yellow fever epidemic struck in 1852, many slaves saw it as God's retribution. As late as the 1930s an elderly woman named Minnie Fulkes cherished the conviction that God was going to punish white people for their cruelty to blacks. She described the whippings that her mother had had to endure and then exclaimed, "Lord, Lord, I hate white people and the flood waters goin' to drown some more." A young slave girl who had suffered abuse as a house servant admitted that she took cruel advantage of her mistress when the woman had a stroke. Instead of fanning the mistress to keep flies away, the young slave struck her in the face with the fan whenever they were alone. "I done that woman bad," the slave confessed, but "she was so mean to me."

The bitterness between blacks and whites was vividly expressed by a former slave named Savilla Burrell, who visited her former master on his deathbed long after the Civil War. Sitting beside him, she reflected on the lines that "sorrow had plowed on that old face and I remembered he'd been a captain on horseback in the war. It come into my remembrance the song of Moses: 'the Lord had triumphed glorily and the horse and his rider have been throwed into the sea.' " She felt sympathy for a dying man, but she also felt satisfaction at God's revenge.

On the plantation, of course, slaves had to keep such thoughts to themselves. Often they expressed one feeling to whites, another within their own race and culture.

The Old Plantation. *Slaves do the Juba, a dance of Yoruba origin, to the music of a stringed* molo *and a gudu-gudu (drum). The women's colorful headscarves recall African styles and customs, as does the man's use of a cane in his dance. Drawn in the late eighteenth century on a plantation between Charleston and Orangeburg.   The Abby Aldridge Rockefeller Folk Art Center, Williamsburg, Virginia.*

SLAVE CULTURE AND EVERYDAY LIFE

The force that helped slaves to maintain such defiance was their culture. They had their own view of the world, a body of beliefs and values born of both their past and their present, as well as the fellowship and support of their own community. With power overwhelmingly in the hands of whites, it was not possible for slaves to change their world. But drawing strength from their culture, they could resist their condition and struggle on against it.

Slave culture changed significantly after the turn of the century. Between 1790 and 1808, when Congress banned further importation of slaves, there was a rush to import Africans. After that the proportion of native-born blacks rose steadily, reaching 96 percent in 1840 and almost 100 percent in 1860. (For this reason blacks can trace their American ancestry back further than many white Americans.) Meanwhile, more and more slaves adopted Christianity. With time the old African culture faded further into memory as an Afro-American culture matured.

In one sense African influences remained primary. For African practices and beliefs reminded the slaves that they were and ought to be different from their oppressors, and thus encouraged them to resist. The most visible aspects of African culture were the slaves'

Remnants of African Culture

dress and recreation. Some slave men plaited their hair into rows and fancy designs; slave women often wore their hair "in string"— tied in small bunches with a string or piece of cloth. A few men and many women wrapped their heads in kerchiefs following the styles and colors of West Africa.

For entertainment slaves made musical instruments with carved motifs that resembled some African stringed instruments. Their drumming and dancing clearly followed African patterns; whites marveled at them. One visitor to Georgia in the 1860s described a ritual dance of African origin: "A ring of singers is formed. . . . They then utter a kind of melodious chant, which gradually increases in strength, and in noise, until it fairly shakes the house, and it can be heard for a long distance." This observer also noted the agility of the dancers and the call-and-response pattern in their chanting.

Many slaves continued to see and believe in spirits. Whites also believed in ghosts, but the belief was more widespread among slaves. It closely resembled the African concept of the living dead—the idea that deceased relatives visited the earth for many years until the process of dying was complete. Slaves also practiced conjuration, voodoo, and quasi-magical root medicine. By 1860 the most notable conjurers and root doctors were reputed to live in South Carolina, Georgia, Louisiana, and other isolated coastal areas of heavy slave importation.

These cultural survivals provided slaves with a sense of their separate past. Black achievement in music and dance was so exceptional that whites felt entirely cut off from it; in this one area some whites became aware that they did not "know" their slaves and that the slave community was a different world. Conjuration and folklore also directly fed resistance; slaves could cast a spell or direct the power of a hand (a bag of articles belonging to the person to be conjured) against the master. Not all masters felt confident enough to dismiss such a threat.

In adopting Christianity, slaves fashioned it too into an instrument of support and resistance. Theirs was a religion of justice quite unlike that of the propaganda their masters pushed at them. Former slaves scorned the preaching arranged by their masters. "You

Slave Religion

ought to have heard that preachin'," said one man. " 'Obey your master and mistress, don't steal chickens and eggs and meat,' but nary a word about havin' a soul to save." To the slaves, Jesus cared about their souls and their present plight. They rejected the idea that in heaven whites would have "the colored folks . . . there to wait on em." Instead, when God's justice came, the slaveholders would be "broilin' in hell for their sin." "God is punishin' some of them ol' suckers and their children right now for the way they used to treat us poor colored folks," said one woman.

For slaves Christianity was a religion of personal and group salvation. Devout men and women worshipped and prayed every day, "in the field or by the side of the road," or in special "prayer grounds" such as a "twisted thick-rooted muscadine bush" that afforded privacy. Beyond seeking personal guidance, these worshippers prayed "for deliverance of the slaves." Some waited "until the overseer got behind a hill" and then laid down their hoes and called on God to free them. Others held fervent secret prayer meetings that lasted far into the night. From such activities many slaves gained the unshakable belief that God would end their bondage. As one man asserted, "it was the plans of God to free us niggers." This faith and the joy and emotional release that accompanied their worship sustained blacks.

Slaves also developed a sense of racial identity. The whole experience of southern blacks taught them that whites despised their race. White people, as one ex-slave put it, "have been and are now and always will be against the Negro." Even "the best white woman that ever broke bread wasn't much," said another, " 'cause they all hated the poor nigger." Blacks naturally drew together, helping each other in danger, need, and resistance. "We never told on each other," one woman declared. Former slaves were virtually unanimous in denouncing those who betrayed the group or sought personal advantage through allegiance to whites.

Of course, different jobs and circumstances created natural variations in attitude among slaves. But for most slaves, there was no overriding class system within the black community. Only one-quarter of all slaves lived on plantations of fifty blacks or more, so few knew a wide chasm between exalted house servants and lowly field hands. In fact, many slaves did both housework and field work, depending on their age and the season. Their primary loyalty was to each other.

The main source of support was the family. Slave families faced severe dangers. At any moment the master could sell a husband or wife, give a slave child away as a wedding present, **Slave Family** or die in debt, forcing a division of **Life** his property. Many families were broken in such ways. Others were uprooted in the trans-Appalachian expansion of the South, which caused a large interregional movement of the black population. Between 1810 and 1820 alone, 137,000 slaves were forced to move from North Carolina and the Chesapeake states to Alabama, Mississippi, and other western regions. An estimated 2 million persons were sold between 1820 and 1860. When the Union Army registered thousands of black marriages in Mississippi and Louisiana in 1864 and 1865, 25 percent of the men over forty reported that they had been forcibly separated from a previous wife. A similar proportion of former slaves later recalled that slavery had destroyed one of their marriages. Probably a substantial minority of slave families suffered disruption of one kind or another.

But this did not mean that slave families could not exist. American slaves clung tenaciously to the personal relationships that gave meaning to life. For although American law did not protect slave families, masters permitted them. In fact, slaveowners expected slaves to form families and have children. As a result, even along the rapidly expanding edge of the cotton kingdom, where the effects of the slave trade would have been most visible, there remained a normal ratio of men to women, young to old.

Following African kinship taboos, Afro-Americans avoided marriage between cousins (a frequent occurrence among aristocratic slaveowners). Adapting to the circumstances of their captivity, they did not condemn unwed mothers, although they did expect a young girl to form a stable marriage after one pregnancy, if not before. By naming their children after relatives of past generations, Afro-Americans emphasized their family histories. If they chose to bear the surname of a white slaveowner, it was often not their current master's but that of the owner under whom their family had begun.

Slaves abhorred interference in their family lives.

Some of their strongest protests sought to prevent the breakup of a family. Indeed, some individuals refused to accept such separations and struggled for years to maintain or re-establish contact. Rape was a horror for both men and women. Some husbands faced death rather than permit their wives to be sexually abused, and women sometimes fought back. In other cases slaves seethed with anger at the injustice but could do nothing except soothe each other with human sympathy and understanding. Significantly, blacks condemned the guilty party, not the victim.

Slave men did not dominate their wives in a manner similar to white husbands, but it is misleading to say that slave women enjoyed equality of power in sex roles and family life. The larger truth is that all black people, men *and* women, were denied the opportunity to provide for or protect their families. Slavery's cruelties put black men and women in the same dilemma. Under the pressures of bondage they had to share the responsibilities of parenthood. Each might have to stand in for the other and assume extra duties. Similarly, uncles, aunts, and grandparents sometimes raised the children of those who had been sold away.

In two other respects, however, distinct gender roles remained very important in slave families and experience. First, after work in the fields was done, men's activities focused on tradi-**Sex Roles** tional "outdoor" tasks while women did "indoor" work. Slave men hunted and fished for the family stewpot, fashioned a rough piece of furniture, or repaired implements; women cooked the food, mended garments, and cleaned house. It is clear, too, that slave families resembled white families in the fact that black men held a respected place in their homes.

Second, the life cycle and pattern of work routines frequently placed slave women in close associations with each other that heightened their sense of sisterhood. On plantations young girls worked together as house servants, nursing mothers shared opportunities to feed and care for their children, adults worked together in many common tasks from soapmaking to quilting, and old women were assigned to spin thread or supervise a nursery. Female slaves thus lived significant portions of their lives as part of a group of women, a fact that emphasized the gender-based element of their experience.

Although slave marriage ceremonies were often brief, usually involving jumping over a broomstick in the master's presence, partners "stuck lots closer then," in one woman's words. "[When] they marries they stayed married," said another. When husbands and wives lived on neighboring plantations, visits on Wednesday and Saturday nights included big dinners of welcome and celebration. Christmas was a similarly joyous time " 'cause husbands is coming home and families is getting united again."

Slaves brought to their efforts at resistance the same common sense, determination, and practicality that characterized their family lives. American slavery produced some fearless and implac-

Resistance to Slavery

able revolutionaries. Gabriel's conspiracy apparently was known to more than a thousand slaves when it was discovered in 1800, just before it was put into motion (see page 205). A similar conspiracy in Charleston in 1822, headed by a free black named Denmark Vesey, involved many of the most trusted slaves of leading families. But the most famous rebel of all, Nat Turner, rose in violence in Southampton County, Virginia, in 1831.

The son of an African woman who passionately hated her enslavement, Nat was a precocious child who learned to read very young. Encouraged by his first owner to study the Bible, he enjoyed some special privileges but also knew changes of masters and hard work. His father, who successfully ran away to freedom, stood always before him as an example of defiance. In time young Nat became a preacher, an impressive orator with a reputation among whites as well as blacks. He also developed a tendency toward mysticism, and he became increasingly withdrawn. After nurturing his plan for several years, Turner led a band of rebels from house to house in the predawn darkness of August 22, 1831. The group severed limbs and crushed skulls with axes or killed their victims with guns. Before they were stopped, Nat Turner and his followers had slaughtered sixty whites of both sexes and all ages. Nat and perhaps two hundred blacks, including many innocent victims of marauding whites, lost their lives as a result of the rebellion.

But most slave resistance was not violent, for the odds against revolution were especially poor in North America. The South had the highest ratio of whites to blacks in the hemisphere; at the same time plantations were relatively small, which meant that whites had ample opportunity to supervise the slaves' activities. There was thus literal truth to one slave's remark that "the white man was the slave's jail." Moreover, the South lacked vital geographic and demographic features that had aided revolution elsewhere. The land offered relatively few jungles and mountain fastnesses to which rebels could flee. And compared with South America, southern slave importations were neither large nor prolonged. The South therefore lacked a preponderance of young male slaves. Nor were its military forces weak and overtaxed, like those of many Latin American nations and colonies.

Thus the scales weighed heavily against revolution, and the slaves knew it. Consequently they directed their energies toward creating means of survival and resistance within slavery. A desperate slave could run away for good, but as often or probably more often slaves simply ran off temporarily to hide in the woods. There they were close to friends and allies who could help them escape capture in an area they knew well. Every day that a slave "lay out" in this way the master lost a day's labor. Most owners chose not to mount an exhaustive search and sent word instead that the slave's grievances would be redressed. The runaway would then return to bargain with the master. Most owners would let the matter pass, for, like the owner of a valuable cook, they were "glad to get her back."

Other modes of resistance had the same object: to resist but survive under bondage. Appropriating food (stealing, in the master's eyes) was so common that even whites sang humorous songs about it. Blacks were also alert to the attitudes of individual whites, and learned to ingratiate themselves or play off one white person against another. Field hands frequently tested a new overseer to intimidate him or win more favorable working conditions. Other blacks fought with patrollers. Some slaves engaged in verbal arguments and even physical violence to deter or resist beatings. The harshest masters were the most strongly resisted. "Good masters had good slaves 'cause they treated 'em good," but "where the old master was mean an' ornery," his slaves were ornery too.

Harmony and Tension in a Slave Society

Not only for blacks but for whites too, slave labor stood at the heart of the South's social system. A host of consequences flowed from its existence, from the organization of society to an individual's personal values.

For blacks, the nineteenth century brought a strengthening and expansion of the legal restrictions of slavery. In all things, from their workaday movements to Sunday worship, slaves fell under the supervision of whites. Courts held that a slave "has no civil right" and could not even hold property "except at the will and pleasure of his master." When slaves revolted, legislators tightened the legal straitjacket: after the Nat Turner insurrection in 1832, for example, they prohibited owners from teaching their slaves to read.

The weight of this legal and social framework fell on nonblacks as well. All white male citizens bore an obligation to ride in patrols to discourage slave movements at night. Whites in strategic positions, such as ship captains and harbor masters, were required to scrutinize the papers of blacks who might be attempting to escape bondage. White southerners who criticized the slave system out of moral conviction or class resentment were intimidated, attacked, or legally prosecuted. (Some, like James Birney, went north to join the antislavery movement, and two sisters from Charleston, Angelina and Sarah Grimké, became leading advocates of both abolition and women's rights—see pages 331–332.) Urban residents who did not supervise their domestic slaves as closely as planters found themselves subject to criticism. And the South's few manufacturers felt pressure to use slave rather than free labor.

Slavery had a deep effect on southern values because it was the main determinant of wealth in the South. Ownership of slaves guaranteed the labor to produce cotton and other crops on a large scale—labor otherwise unavailable in a rural society. Slaves were therefore vital to the acquisition of a fortune. Beyond

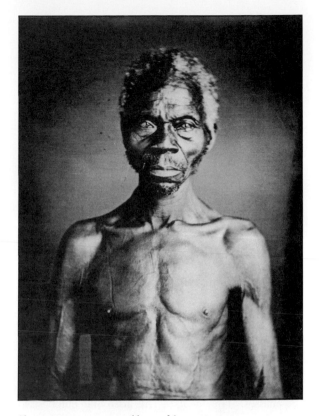

Slave property was tangible wealth—an investment—to whites. Increasingly they tried to deny that slaves were people who suffered, as this rare photograph of Renty, an elderly "Congo" field hand, reminds us. Harvard University.

Slavery as the Basis of Wealth and Social Standing that, slaves were a commodity and an investment, much like gold; people bought them on speculation, hoping for a steady rise in their value. In fact, for southern society as a whole, slaveholding indicated wealth in general with remarkable precision. Important economic enterprises not based on slavery were so rare that the correspondence between geographic variations in wealth and variations in slaveholding was nearly one-to-one.

It was therefore natural that slaveholding should be the main determinant of a man's social position, with women deriving high status from their husband's or father's ownership of slaves. Wealth in slaves was also the foundation on which the ambitious built their reputations. Ownership of slaves brought political power: a solid majority of political officeholders were slaveholders, and the most powerful of them were generally large slaveholders. Though lawyers and newspaper editors were sometimes influential, they did not hold independent positions in the economy or society. Dependent on the planters for business and support, they served planters' interests and reflected their outlook.

As slavery became entrenched, its influence spread throughout the social system until even the values and mores of nonslaveholders bore its imprint. For one thing, the availability of slave labor tended to devalue free labor. Where strenuous work under another was reserved for an enslaved race, few free people relished working "like a nigger." Nonslaveholders therefore preferred to work for themselves rather than to hire out. Whites who had to sell their labor tended to resent or reject tasks that seemed degrading. This kind of thinking engendered an aristocratic value system ill-suited to a newly established democracy.

In modified form the attitudes characteristic of the planter elite gained a considerable foothold among the masses. The ideal of the aristocrat emphasized lineage, privilege, power, pride, and refinement of person and manner. Some of those qualities were in short supply in the recently settled, expanding cotton kingdom, however; they mingled with and were modified by the tradition of the frontier. In particular, independence, and defense of one's honor were highly valued by planter and frontier farmer alike.

Aristocratic Values and Frontier Individualism

Fights and even duels over personal slights were not uncommon in southern communities. This custom sprang from both frontier lawlessness and aristocratic tradition. Throughout the sparsely settled regions of America in the early nineteenth century, pugnacious people took the law into their own hands. Thus it was not unusual for a southern slaveowner who had warned patrollers to stay off his property to shoot at the next group of trespassers. But instead of gradually disappearing, as it did in the North, the code duello, which required men to defend their honor through the rituals of a duel, hung on in the South and gained an acceptance that spread throughout the society.

An incident that occurred in North Carolina in 1851 will illustrate. A wealthy planter named Samuel Fleming responded to a series of disputes with the rising lawyer William Waightstill Avery by whipping or "cowhiding" him on a public street. According to the code, Avery had two choices: to redeem his honor through violence or to brand himself a coward through inaction. Three weeks later Avery shot Fleming dead at pointblank range during a session of Burke County Superior Court, with Judge William Battle and numerous spectators looking on. A jury took just ten minutes to find Avery not guilty, and the spectators gave him a standing ovation. Some people, including Judge Battle, were troubled by the victory of the unwritten code over the law, but most white males seemed satisfied.

Other aristocratic values that marked the planters as a class were less acceptable to the average citizen. Simply put, planters believed they were better than other people. In their pride, they expected not only to wield power but to receive special treatment. By the 1850s, some planters openly rejected the democratic creed, vilifying Jefferson for his statement that all men were equal.

These ideas shaped the outlook of the southern elite for generations, but they were never acceptable to the individualistic members of the yeoman class. Independent and proud of their position, yeomen resisted any infringement of their rights. They believed that they were as good as anyone, and many belonged to evangelical faiths that exalted values far removed from the planters' love of wealth. They were conscious, too, that they lived in a nation in which democratic ideals were gaining strength. Thus there were occasional conflicts between aristocratic pretensions and democratic zeal. As Mary Boykin Chesnut pointed out, a wealthy planter who sought public office could not announce his status too haughtily. She described the plight of Colonel John S. Preston, a South Carolinian with great ambitions. Preston, a perfect aristocrat, carried his high-flown manners too far; he refused to make the necessary gestures of respect toward the average voter—mingling with the crowd, exchanging jokes and compliments. Thus his highest aspiration, political leadership, could never be fulfilled. The voters would not accept him.

Such tensions found significant expression in the western parts of the seaboard states during the 1820s and 1830s. There yeoman farmers and citizens resented their underrepresentation in state legislatures, corruption in government, and undemocratic control

Democratic Reform Movements

over local government. After vigorous debate, the reformers won most of their battles. Five states—Alabama, Mississippi, Tennessee, Arkansas, and Texas—adopted what was for that time a thoroughly democratic system: popular election of governors; white manhood suffrage; legislative apportionment based on the white population; and locally chosen county government. Kentucky was democratically governed except in its counties. Georgia, Florida, and Louisiana were not far behind, and reformers won significant concessions in Maryland and some adjustments in North Carolina. Only South Carolina and Virginia effectively defended property qualifications for office, legislative malapportionment, appointment of county officials, and selection of the governor by the lawmakers. Democracy had expanded with the cotton kingdom.

Even in Virginia, nonslaveholding westerners raised a basic challenge to the slave system. Following the Nat Turner rebellion, advocates of gradual abolition forced a two-week legislative debate on slavery, arguing that it was injurious to the state and inherently dangerous. When the House of Delegates finally voted, the motion favoring abolition lost by just 73 to 58. This was the last major debate on slavery in the antebellum South.

With such tension in evidence, it was perhaps remarkable that slaveholders and nonslaveholders did not experience frequent and serious conflict. Why were class confrontations among whites so infrequent? Historians who have considered this question have given many answers. In a rural society, family bonds and kinship ties are valued, and some of the poor nonslaveholding whites were related to the rich new planters. The experience of frontier living must also have created a relatively informal, egalitarian atmosphere. And there is no doubt that the South's racial ideology, which stressed whites' superiority to blacks and race, not class, as the social dividing line, tended to reduce conflict among whites.

Also, it is important to remember that the South was a new and mobile society. Many people had risen in status, and far more were moving away geographically. Yeomen often moved several times during a lifetime of farming, and many slaveowners did too. Even in cotton-rich Alabama in the 1850s, fewer than half the richest families in a county belonged

to its elite category ten years later. Most had not died or lost their wealth; they had merely moved on to some new state. This constant mobility meant that southern society had not settled into a rigid, unchanging pattern.

But two other factors, social and economic, were probably more important. First, the South was rural and uncrowded. Travel was difficult, and people stayed much to themselves. Consequently slaveowners and nonslaveowners rarely collided or confronted each other as groups. Classes, as collective, competing objects, were rarely visible. Second, the two groups functioned quite independently of each other. The yeomen farmed for themselves; planters farmed for themselves and for the market. The complementary growing patterns of corn and cotton allowed planters to raise food for their animals and laborers without lowering cotton production: from spring through December, cotton and corn needed attention alternately, but never at the same time. Thus the planter did not need to depend on the nonslaveholder, and yeomen needed nothing from the planters. In politics, too, national issues that affected planters economically often had less meaning to yeomen who stayed largely outside the market economy.

There were signs, however, that the relative lack of conflict between slaveholders and nonslaveholders was coming to an end. As the region grew older, nonslaveholders saw their opportunities beginning to narrow; meanwhile wealthy planters enjoyed an expanding horizon. The risks of cotton production were becoming too great and the cost of slaves too high for many yeomen to rise in society. Thus from 1830 to 1860 the percentage of white southern families holding slaves declined steadily from 36 to 25 percent. At the same time, the monetary gap between the classes was widening. Although nonslaveholders were becoming more prosperous, slaveowners' wealth was increasing much faster. And though slaveowners made up a smaller portion of the population in 1860, their share of the South's agricultural wealth remained at between 90 and 95 percent. In fact, the average slaveholder was almost fourteen times as rich as the average nonslaveholder.

Hardening of Class Lines

Urban artisans and mechanics felt the pinch acutely. Their numbers were few, their place in society was hardly recognized, and in bad times they were often the first to lose work. Moreover, they faced stiff competition from urban slaves, whose masters wanted them to hire their time and bring in money by practicing a trade. White workers in Charleston, Wilmington, and elsewhere staged protests and demanded that economic competition from slaves be forbidden. This demand was always ignored—the powerful slaveowners would not tolerate interference with their property or the income they derived from it. But the angry protests of white workers resulted in harsh restrictions on *free* black workers and craftsmen, who lacked any powerful allies to stand behind them. In Charleston on the eve of the Civil War, many successful free blacks actually felt compelled to leave the city.

Pre–Civil War politics reflected these tensions. Facing the prospect of a war to defend slavery, slaveowners expressed growing fear about the loyalty of nonslaveholders and discussed schemes to widen slave ownership, including reopening of the African slave trade. In North Carolina, a prolonged and increasingly bitter controversy over the combination of high taxes on land and low taxes on slaves erupted, and a class-conscious nonslaveholder named Hinton R. Helper denounced the slave system. Convinced that slavery had impoverished many whites and retarded the whole region, Helper attacked the institution in his book *The Impending Crisis*, published in New York in 1857. Discerning planters knew that such fiery controversies lay close at hand in every southern state.

But for the moment slaveowners stood secure. They held from 50 to 85 percent of the seats in state legislatures and a similarly high percentage of the South's congressional seats. In addition to their near-monopoly on political office, they had established their point of view in all the other major social institutions. Professors who criticized slavery had been dismissed from colleges and universities; schoolbooks that contained "unsound" ideas had been replaced. And almost all the Methodist and Baptist clergy, some of whom had criticized slavery in the 1790s, had given up preaching against the institution. In fact, except for a few obscure persons of conscience, southern clergy had become its most vocal defenders. Society as southerners knew it seemed stable, if not unthreatened.

Elsewhere in the nation, however, society was anything but stable. Change had become one of the major characteristics of the northern economy and society, and social conflict was an increasingly common phenomenon. Throughout the North, in a variety of ways, people were trying to cope with change.

SUGGESTIONS FOR FURTHER READING

Southern Society

Edward L. Ayers, *Vengeance and Justice* (1984); W. J. Cash, *The Mind of the South* (1941); Avery O. Craven, *The Growth of Southern Nationalism, 1848–1861* (1953); Clement Eaton, *The Growth of Southern Civilization, 1790–1860* (1961); Clement Eaton, *Freedom of Thought in the Old South* (1940); Alison Goodyear Freehling, *Drift Toward Dissolution* (1982); William W. Freehling, *Prelude to Civil War* (1965); Eugene D. Genovese, "Yeoman Farmers in a Slaveholders' Democracy," *Agricultural History*, 49 (April 1975), 331–342; Eugene D. Genovese, *The World the Slaveholders Made* (1964); William Sumner Jenkins, *Pro-Slavery Thought in the Old South* (1935); Donald G. Mathews, *Religion in the Old South* (1977); Robert McColley, *Slavery and Jeffersonian Virginia* (1964); Frederick Law Olmsted, *The Slave States*, ed. Harvey Wish (1959); Edward Phifer, "Slavery in Microcosm: Burke County, North Carolina," *Journal of Southern History*, XXVIII (May 1962), 137–165; Charles S. Sydnor, *The Development of Southern Sectionalism, 1819–1848* (1948); Ralph A. Wooster, *Politicians, Planters, and Plain Folk* (1975); Ralph A. Wooster, *The People in Power* (1969); Gavin Wright, *The Political Economy of the Cotton South* (1978); Bertram Wyatt-Brown, *Southern Honor* (1982).

Slaveholders and Nonslaveholders

Bennet H. Barrow, *Plantation Life in the Florida Parishes of Louisiana, as Reflected in the Diary of Bennet H. Barrow*, ed. Edwin Adams Davis (1943); Ira Berlin, *Slaves Without Masters* (1974); William J. Cooper, *The South and the Politics of Slavery, 1828–1856* (1978); Everett Dick, *The Dixie Frontier* (1948); Clement Eaton, *The Mind of the Old South* (1967); Drew Faust, *James Henry Hammond and the Old South* (1982); Drew Faust, *A Sacred Circle: The Dilemma of the Intellectual in the Old South* (1977); John Hope Franklin, *The Militant South, 1800–1861* (1956); John Hope Franklin, *The Free Negro in North Carolina, 1790–1860* (1943); Luther P. Jackson, *Free Negro Labor and Property Holding in Virginia*,

1830–1860 (1942); Michael P. Johnson and James L. Roark, *Black Masters* (1984); Frances Anne Kemble, *Journal of a Residence on a Georgian Plantation in 1838–1839* (1863); Robert Manson Myers, ed., *The Children of Pride* (1972); James Oakes, *The Ruling Race* (1982); Frank L. Owsley, *Plain Folk of the Old South* (1949); J. Mills Thornton, III, *Politics and Power in a Slave Society* (1978); C. Vann Woodward, ed., *Mary Chesnut's Civil War,* (1981).

Southern Women

Carol Bleser, *The Hammonds of Redcliffe* (1981); Jane Turner Censer, *North Carolina Planters and Their Children, 1800–1860* (1984); Catherine Clinton, *The Plantation Mistress* (1982); Jacqueline Jones, *Labor of Love, Labor of Sorrow* (1985); Suzanne Lebsock, *Free Women of Petersburg* (1983); Elisabeth Muhlenfeld, *Mary Boykin Chesnut* (1981); Mary D. Robertson, ed., *Lucy Breckinridge of Grove Hill* (1979); Ann Firor Scott, *The Southern Lady* (1970); Deborah G. White, *Arn'n't I a Woman?* (1985); C. Vann Woodward and Elisabeth Muhlenfeld, eds., *The Private Mary Chesnut* (1985).

Conditions of Slavery

Kenneth F. Kiple and Virginia H. Kiple, "Black Tongue and Black Men," *Journal of Southern History*, XLIII (August 1977), 411–428; Ronald L. Lewis, *Coal, Iron, and Slaves* (1979); Richard G. Lowe and Randolph B. Campbell, "The Slave Breeding Hypothesis," *Journal of Southern History*, XLII (August 1976), 400–412; Leslie Howard Owens, *This Species of Property* (1976); Willie Lee Rose, ed., *A Documentary History of Slavery in North America* (1976); Todd L. Savitt, *Medicine and Slavery* (1978); Kenneth M. Stampp, *The Peculiar Institution* (1956); Robert S. Starobin, *Industrial Slavery in the Old South* (1970).

Slave Culture and Resistance

Herbert Aptheker, *American Negro Slave Revolts* (1943); John W. Blassingame, *The Slave Community* (1972); Judith Wragg Chase, *Afro-American Art and Craft* (1971); Jeffrey J. Crow, *The Black Experience in Revolutionary North Carolina* (1977); Dena J. Epstein, *Sinful Tunes and Spirituals* (1977); Paul D. Escott, *Slavery Remembered* (1979); Eric Foner, ed., *Nat Turner* (1971); Eugene D. Genovese, *From Rebellion to Revolution* (1979); Eugene D. Genovese, *Roll, Jordan, Roll* (1974); Herbert G. Gutman, *The Black Family in Slavery and Freedom, 1750–1925* (1976); Vincent Harding, *There Is a River* (1981); Charles Joyner, *Down by the Riverside* (1984); Lawrence W. Levine, *Black Culture and Black Consciousness* (1977); Gerald W. Mullin, *Flight and Rebellion* (1972); Stephen B. Oates, *The Fires of Jubilee* (1975); Albert J. Raboteau, *Slave Religion* (1978); Robert S. Starobin, *Denmark Vesey* (1970); Peter H. Wood, *Black Majority* (1974).

REFORM, POLITICS, AND EXPANSION

1824–1844

CHAPTER 12

The gaunt, bearded New Englander Henry David Thoreau was skeptical of the value of the artifacts of a changing economy and society: railroads, steamboats, the telegraph, factories, and cities. "There is an illusion about" such improvements, he wrote in *Walden, or Life in the Woods* (1854). "There is not always a positive advance. . . . Men think that it is essential that the *Nation* have commerce, and export ice, and talk through a telegraph, and ride thirty miles an hour . . . but whether we should live like baboons or like men, is a little uncertain."

Thoreau was seeking to escape the marketplace, to forgo the world of cities and factories, to live simply in the landscape that existed before the plow and the engine, when he retreated to the wilderness shores of Walden Pond in Concord, Massachusetts. Yet for all his idealization of the simple life, Thoreau did not withdraw from the world, much less from Concord. While at Walden he dined with townsfolk, joined the men congregating around the grocery-store stove, and hosted picnics. In reality his everyday life was infused with all those modern improvements he seemed to spurn. Thoreau even raised a cash crop—beans—and sold it to support himself at Walden. As he said in his own journal, he loved "society as much as most." But he was caught up in a basic ambivalence toward industrialization and urbanization that he shared with millions of other Americans. They were lured on the one hand by the simplicity and beauty of pastoral days gone by, pulled on the other by their belief in progress and the promise of machine-generated prosperity and happiness.

In the early nineteenth century, reformers of all kinds sought to find or impose harmony on a society in which economic change and discord had reached a crescendo. Prompted by the evangelical ardor of the Second Great Awakening and convinced of the perfectibility of the human race, they crusaded for individual improvement. Some withdrew from the everyday competitive world to seek perfection in utopian communities. Others sought to improve themselves by renouncing alcohol. Inevitably the personal impulse to reform oneself led to the creation and reshaping of institutions. Schools, penitentiaries, and other institutions all underwent scrutiny and reform. Women were prominent in the reform movement, and the role of women in public life became an issue in itself.

Eventually one concern overrode all others: antislavery. No single issue evoked the depth of passion that slavery did. On a personal level it pitted neighbor against neighbor, settler against settler, section against section. Territorial expansion in the 1840s and 1850s would make it politically explosive as well.

Once reformers of various causes became a cohesive group, they naturally turned to the state as an effective instrument of social and economic change. The line between social reform and politics was not always distinguishable. Their opponents were no less concerned with social problems. What set them apart from reformers was their skepticism about human perfectibility and their distrust of institutions and power, both public and private. To them, coercion was the greater evil. They sought to reverse, not shape, change.

In the late 1820s the opponents of reform found a champion in Andrew Jackson and a home in the Democratic party. Jackson reversed the emphasis of previous presidents on an activist national government, believing that a strong federal government restricted individual freedom by favoring one group over another. In response, reformers rallied around the new Whig party, which became the vehicle for humanitarian reform. The two parties competed energetically in the second party system, a system marked by strong organizations, intensely loyal followings, and religious and ethnic differences.

During the economically prosperous 1840s, both Democrats and Whigs eagerly promoted westward expansion to further their goals. Democrats saw the agrarian West as an antidote to urbanization and industrialization; Whigs focused on new commercial opportunities. The idea of expansion from coast to coast seemed to Americans to be the inevitable manifest destiny of the United States. The politics of territorial expansion would collide with the antislavery movement with explosive results in the 1850s and 1860s.

The Lackawanna Valley (1855) by George Inness. Hired by the Lackawanna Railroad to paint a railroad scene, Inness blended landscape and machine into an organic whole. American industrialism, Inness seemed to say, belonged to the landscape; it would neither overpower nor obliterate the land. *National Gallery of Art, Washington, Gift of Mrs. Huttleston Rogers.*

REFORM AND RELIGIOUS REVIVAL

While the South was becoming more entrenched in a plantation system and slave society, the vast changes taking place in the rest of the country were having an unsettling effect. Population growth, immigration, internal migration, loosening family and community ties, the advancing frontier, and territorial expansion all contributed to the remaking of the United States. But the undisputed symbol of change was the machine—that fine-tooled, power-driven substitute for men's and women's own hands, stamping out interchangeable parts for other machines. Some feared it would turn America into a giant factory, in which everything would be viewed as a commodity to be sold at the marketplace.

Many people felt they were no longer masters of their own fate. Change was occurring so rapidly that people had difficulty keeping up with it. An apprentice tailor could find his trade obsolete by the time he became a journeyman; a student could find himself lacking sufficient arithmetic to enter a counting house when he graduated; a young rural woman could find her tasks unneeded on her family's farm. Americans had fought the Revolution to make themselves independent; poverty and obsolescent trades and education made them dependent. Other aspects of change were simply unpleasant or culturally alien. Respectable citizens found their safety threatened by urban mobs and paupers, and the Protestant majority feared the growing Catholic minority, with their distinctive customs and beliefs. Protestants had waged war to preserve the rights they claimed as Englishmen, not to protect alien cultures and religions. To many, all these changes seemed to undermine republican virtues.

Disturbed by change, yet convinced that the world could be improved, and confident that they could do something about it, various reformers and reform movements began to emerge and coalesce during the 1820s. Basically, reformers sought to restore order to a society made disorderly by economic, social, and cultural change. They were so active from 1820 through the 1850s that the period became known as an age of reform.

Reform was at its core an attempt to impose more direction on society. The movement encompassed both individual improvement (religion, temperance, health) and institutional reform (antislavery, women's rights, and education). Some reformers were motivated more by fear than by hope—Antimasonic, nativist, and anti-Catholic. Not all the problems that reformers addressed were new to the nineteenth century; some were generations old. Slavery had existed in the United States for two centuries, and alcohol had been a colonial problem; yet neither became a national issue until the 1820s and after, when the reformist ferment prompted action.

Though reform movements played an important role in all sections of the country, most were northern. In the South, slavery and the complex issues surrounding that institution tended to suppress the reform impulse. Fear of educating blacks, for instance, led even antislavery southerners to ignore the movement for educational reform.

The prime motivating force behind organized reform was probably religion. Starting in the late 1790s, a tremendous religious revival, the Second Great Awakening, galvanized Protestants, especially women (see pages 201–204). The Awakening began in small villages in the East, intensified in the 1820s in western New York, and continued

Second Great Awakening

through the late 1840s. Under its influence, Christians in all parts of the country tried to right the wrongs of the world.

Evangelical Christianity was a religion of the heart, not the head. In 1821 Charles G. Finney, "the father of modern revivalism," experienced a soul-shaking conversion, which, he said, brought him "a retainer from the Lord Jesus Christ to plead his cause." Finney, a former teacher and lawyer, immediately began his career as a converter of souls, preaching that salvation could be achieved through spontaneous conversion or spiritual rebirth like his own. In everyday language, he told his audiences that "God has made man a moral free agent." In other words, evil was avoidable; Christians were not doomed by original sin. Hence anyone could achieve salvation. Finney's brand of revivalism transcended sects, wealth, and race. Presbyterians, Baptists, and Congregationalists became evangelists, as did some Methodists.

The Second Great Awakening also raised people's hopes for the Second Coming of the Christian messiah and the establishment of the Kingdom of God on earth. Revivalists set out to speed the Second Coming by creating a heaven on earth. They joined the forces of good and light—reform—to combat those of evil and darkness. Some revivalists even believed that the United States had a special mission in God's design, and therefore a special role in eliminating evil.

Regardless of theology, all shared a belief in individual perfection as a moving force. In this way the Second Great Awakening bred reform, and evangelical Protestants became missionaries for both religious and secular salvation. Wherever they preached, voluntary societies arose. Evangelists organized an association for each issue—temperance, education, Sabbath observance, antidueling, and later antislavery; collectively these groups formed a national web of benevolent and moral reform societies.

As social change accelerated in the 1830s and 1840s, so did reform. In western New York and Ohio, Charles G. Finney's preaching was a catalyst to reform. Western New York experienced such continuous and heated waves of revivalism that it became known as the "burned-over" district. The opening of the Erie Canal and the migration of New Englanders carried the reform ferment farther westward. There, revivalist institutions—Ohio's Lane Seminary and Oberlin

College were the most famous—sent committed graduates out into the world to spread the gospel of reform. Evangelists also organized grassroots political movements. In the late 1830s and 1840s they rallied around the Whig party in an attempt to use government as an instrument of reform. Their efforts stirred nonevangelical Protestants, Catholics, and Jews as well as evangelical Christians.

Women were the earliest converts, and they tended to sustain the Second Great Awakening. When Finney led daytime prayer meetings in Rochester, New York, for instance, pious middle-class women visited families while the men were away at work. Slowly they brought their families and husbands into the churches and under the influence of reform. Women more than men tended to feel personally responsible for the increasingly secular orientation of the expanding market economy. Many women felt guilty for neglecting their religious duties, and the emotionally charged conversion experience set them on the right path again.

At first, revival seemed to reinforce the cult of domesticity since piety and religious values were associated with the domestic sphere (see Chapter 10). In the conversion experience, women declared their submissiveness to the will of Providence, vowing to purge themselves and the world of wickedness. Yet the commitment to spread the word, to become evangelicals, led to new, public roles for women. The organized prayer groups and female missionary societies that preceded and accompanied the Second Great Awakening were soon surpassed by greater organized reform and religious activity. Thus revival prompted and legitimized woman's public role, providing a path of certainty and stability amidst a rapidly changing economy and society.

From Revival to Reform

The establishment and work of female reform societies were not merely responses to inner voices; they were reactions to the poverty and wretched urban conditions found in the growing cities. At the turn of the nineteenth century, most of the expanding cities had women's societies to help needy women and orphans, as did Salem, Massachusetts, with its Female Charitable Society. The spread of poverty and vice that accompanied urbanization increasingly affected women, especially those caught up in the fervor of revival.

An 1830 exposé of prostitution in New York City revealed the diverging concerns and responses of men and women and demonstrated the convergence of urban problems, revival, and reform. John R. McDowall, a divinity student, detailed how prostitution had taken hold on New York City. Philip Hone, one of the city's leaders (see page 275), called McDowall's *Magdalen Report* "a disgraceful document," and he and other New York men united to defend the city's good name against "those base slanders." Their condemnation led the male-run New York Magdalen Society to cease its work. Women, on the other hand, moved by the plight of "fallen women," responded by forming two new societies concerned with prostitutes and prostitution. In revival and reform, women acted in the face of men's opposition and indifference.

The Female Moral Reform Society, in particular, led the crusade against prostitution. Over the next decade, the New York–based association expanded its activities and geographical scope as the American Female Moral Reform Society. By 1840, it had 555 affiliated female societies among the converted across the nation. These women not only fought the evils of prostitution but also assisted poor women and orphans and entered the political sphere. In New York State in the 1840s the movement fostered public morality by successfully crusading for criminal sanctions against seducers and prostitutes.

Another response to change was the interest in utopian communities. Such settlements offered an antidote to the market economy and to the untamed growth of large urban communities, and an opportunity to restore tradition and social cohesion. Whatever their particular philosophy, utopians sought order and regularity in their daily lives and a cooperative rather than competitive environment. Some experimented with communal living and nontraditional work, family, and gender roles.

America's earliest utopian experiments were organized by the Shakers, who derived their name from the way they danced and swayed at worship services.

Shakers

An offshoot of the Quakers, their sect was established in America in 1774 by the English Shaker Ann Lee. Shakers believed that the end of the world was near, and that sin entered the world through sexual intercourse. They regarded existing churches as too

Etching of a Shaker dance during worship. *Library of Congress.*

worldly and considered the Shaker family the instrument of salvation.

After the death of Mother Ann Lee in 1784, the Shakers turned to communal living to fulfill their mission. In 1787 they "gathered in" at New Lebanon, New York, to live, worship, and work communally. Other colonies soon followed. At its peak, between 1820 and 1860, the sect had about six thousand members in twenty settlements in eight states. Shaker communities emphasized agriculture and crafts; most managed to become self-sufficient, profitable enterprises. In particular, Shaker furniture became famous for its excellent construction, utility, and beauty of design.

Though economically conservative, the Shakers were social radicals. They abolished individual families, practiced celibacy, and treated men and women equally in their communities. Each colony was one large family. The Shaker ministry was headed by a woman, Lucy Wright, during its period of greatest growth. Celibacy, however, led to the withering away of the communities. Unable to reproduce naturally, the colonies succumbed to death by attrition in the twentieth century.

Not all utopian communities were founded by re-

ligious groups. Robert Owen's New Harmony was a short-lived attempt to found a socialist utopia in Indiana. A wealthy Scottish industrialist, Owen established the cooperative community in 1825. According to his plan, its nine hundred members were to exchange their labor for goods at a communal store. Handicrafts (hat- and boot-making) flourished at New Harmony. But the economic base of the community, its textile mill, failed after Owen gave it to the community to run. Turnover in membership was too great for the community to develop any cohesion, and by 1827 the experiment had ended.

More successful were the New Englanders who lived and worked at the Brook Farm cooperative in West Roxbury, Massachusetts. Inspired by the transcendental philosophy that the **Brook Farm** spiritual rises above the worldly, its members rejected materialism and sought satisfaction in a communal life combining spirituality, work, and play. Founded in 1841 by the Unitarian minister George Ripley, Brook Farm attracted not only farmers and skilled craftsmen but teachers and writers, among them Nathaniel Hawthorne. Indeed, the fame of Brook Farm rested on the intellectual achievements of its members. Its school

Chapter 12: REFORM, POLITICS, AND EXPANSION, 1824–1844

drew students from outside the community, and its residents contributed regularly to the *Dial*, the leading transcendentalist journal. In 1845 Brook Farm's hundred members organized themselves into model phalanxes (work-living units) in keeping with the philosophy of the French utopian Charles Fourier. Rigid regimentation replaced individualism, and membership dropped. Following a disastrous fire in 1846, the experiment collapsed.

Though short-lived, Brook Farm played a significant part in the Romantic movement. During these years Hawthorne, Emerson, and the *Dial*'s editor Margaret Fuller joined Thoreau, James Fenimore Cooper, Herman Melville, and others in creating what is known today as the American Renaissance—the flowering of a national literature. In poetry and prose these Romanticists praised individualism and intuition, rejecting or modifying the ordered world of the Enlightenment in favor of the mysteries of nature. Rebelling against convention, both social and literary, they probed and celebrated the American character and the American experience. Cooper, for instance, wrote of the frontier in the Leatherstocking Tales, and Melville wrote of great spiritual quests in the guise of seafaring adventures. Their themes were universal, their settings and people, American.

Ralph Waldo Emerson was the "high priest" of the American Renaissance and the center of the transcendental movement. He had followed his father and grandfather into the ministry, but quit his Boston Unitarian pulpit in 1831. He returned from a two-year pilgrimage in Europe to lecture and write, preaching individualism and self-reliance. His message stressed that each person could experience God directly and intuitively through the "Oversoul." What gave Emerson's writings such force was his simple, direct prose. Others admired him, and he influenced Thoreau, Margaret Fuller, Nathaniel Hawthorne, and the members of Brook Farm. They followed his advice in *Nature* (1836) and "The American Scholar" (1837), turning to American themes and reform.

Far and away the most successful communitarians were the Mormons, who originated in the burned-over district of western New York. Organized by **Mormon Community of Saints** Joseph Smith in 1830 as the Church of Jesus Christ of Latter-day Saints, the church established communities dedicated to Christian cooperation.

Fleeing persecution in Ohio, Illinois, and Missouri because of their claims of divine sanction and their newly adopted practice of polygamy (having more than one wife at the same time), the Mormons trekked across the continent in 1846 and 1847 to found a New Zion in the Great Salt Lake Valley. There, under Brigham Young, head of the Twelve Apostles (their governing body), they established a cohesive community of Saints—a heaven on earth. The Mormons created agricultural settlements and distributed land according to family size. An extensive irrigation system, constructed by men who contributed their labor according to the quantity of land they received and the amount of water they expected to use, transformed the arid valley into a rich oasis. As the colony developed, its cooperative principles gradually gave way to benevolent corporate authority, and the church elders came to control water, trade, industry, and even the territorial government of Utah. As the Mormon experience demonstrates, revival and reform could pursue and combine many diverse directions.

TEMPERANCE, PUBLIC EDUCATION, AND FEMINISM

One of the most successful reform efforts was the campaign against the consumption of alcohol, which was more widespread in the early nineteenth century than it is today. As a group, American men liked to drink alcoholic spirits—whiskey, rum, and hard cider. They gathered in public houses, saloons, and rural inns to gossip, discuss politics, play cards, escape work and home pressures, and drink. Men drank on all occasions: contracts were sealed with a drink; celebrations were toasted with spirits; barn-raisings and harvests ended with liquor. And though respectable women did not drink in public, many regularly tippled alcohol-based patent medicines promoted as cure-alls. Moreover, immigration brought more people for whom drinking was part of everyday life.

Why then did temperance become such a vital issue? And why were women specially active in the movement? As with all reform, temperance had a strong religious base. "The Holy Spirit," a temperance pamphlet proclaimed, "will not visit, much less dwell with him who is under the polluting, debasing effects of intoxicating drink." To evangelicals, the selling of whiskey was a chronic symbol of Sabbath violation, for workers commonly labored six days a week, then spent Sunday at the public house drinking and socializing. Alcohol was seen as a destroyer of families as well, since men who drank heavily either neglected their families or could not adequately support them. Temperance literature was laced with domestic images—abandoned wives, prodigal sons, drunken fathers. Outside the home, the habit of drinking could not be tolerated in the new world of the factory. Employers complained that drinkers took "St. Monday" as a holiday to recover from Sunday. Whatever they felt about other reforms, industrialists supported temperance as part of the new work habits needed for factory work. Timothy Shay Arthur dramatized all these evils in *Ten Nights in a Barroom* (1853), a classic American melodrama.

Demon rum thus became a major target of reformers. As the movement gained momentum, they shifted their emphasis from temperate use of spirits to voluntary abstinence and finally to a crusade

Temperance Societies to prohibit the manufacture and sale of spirits. The American Society for the Promotion of Temperance, organized in 1826 to urge drinkers to sign a pledge of abstinence, shortly thereafter became a pressure group for state prohibition legislation. By the mid-1830s there were some five thousand state and local temperance societies, and more than a million people had taken the pledge. By the 1840s the movement's success was reflected in a sharp decline in alcohol consumption in the United States. Between 1800 and 1830, annual per capita consumption of alcohol had risen from three to more than five gallons; by the mid-1840s, however, it had dropped below two gallons. Success bred more victories. In 1851 Maine prohibited the manufacture and sale of alcohol except for medicinal purposes, and by 1855 similar laws had been enacted throughout New England, the Old Northwest, and in New York and Pennsylvania.

Even though consumption of alcohol was declining, opposition to it did not weaken. Many reformers believed that alcohol was an evil introduced and perpetuated by Catholic immigrants. From the 1820s

This certificate of membership in a temperance society, for display, announced the virtues of the household to all visitors. In the illustration, the man signs with the support of wife and child; demon rum and its accompanying evils were banished from this home.   Library of Congress.

on, antiliquor reformers based much of their argument on this false prejudice. The Irish and Germans, the *American Protestant Magazine* complained in 1849, "bring the grog shops like the frogs of Egypt upon us." Rum and immigrants defiled the Sabbath; rum and immigrants brought poverty; rum and immigrants supported the feared papacy. Some Catholics did join with nonevangelical Protestant sects like the Lutherans to oppose temperance legislation. But other Catholics took the pledge of abstinence and formed their own temperance organizations, such as the St. Mary's Mutual Benevolent Total Abstinence Society in Boston. Even nondrinking Catholics tended to oppose state regulation of drinking, however; temperance seemed to them a question of individual choice, not state coercion. They favored self, not societal, control.

Another important part of the reform impulse was the development of new institutions to meet the social needs of citizens. The list of organizations founded during this era is a long one— Protestant denominations, Catholic orders, reform Judaism; schools and colleges, hospitals, asylums, orphanages, and penitentiaries; new political parties; and myriad reform societies. Many of these institutions experimented with new techniques for handling old problems. New York State's penitentiary at Auburn, for example, placed prisoners in rehabilitative cooperative labor programs during the day, confining them only at night. Other states soon followed New York's lead.

Public education was one of the more lasting results of the age of institution building. In 1800 there were no public schools outside New England; by 1860 every state had some public education. Massachusetts took the lead, especially under Horace Mann, secretary of the state board of education from 1837 to 1848. Under Mann, Massachusetts established a minimum school year of six months, increased the number of high schools, formalized the training of teachers, and emphasized secular subjects and applied skills rather than religious training. In the process, teaching became a woman's profession.

Horace Mann on Education

Horace Mann was an evangelist of public education and school reform; his preaching on behalf of free state education changed schooling throughout the nation. "If we do not prepare children to become good citizens," Mann prophesied, "if we do not develop their capacities, . . . imbue their hearts with the love of truth and duty, and a reverence for all things sacred and holy, then our republic must go down to destruction." The abolition of ignorance, Mann claimed, would end misery, crime, and suffering. "The only sphere . . . left open for our patriotism," he wrote, "is the improvement of our children,—not the few, but the many; not a part of them but all."

In laying the basis of free public schools, Mann also broadened the scope of education. Previously, education had focused exclusively on literacy, religious training, and discipline. Thus most parents were indifferent to whether or not their children continued their schooling. Under Mann's leadership, the school curriculum became more secular and appropriate for future clerks, farmers, and workers. Students now studied geography, American history, arithmetic, and science. Moral education was retained, but direct religious indoctrination was dropped.

Many traditionalists, including New England Congregationalists, fought to maintain the old ties between education and religion. Some feared secular public education was a sign of the decline of American morality and virtue. But others, including many deeply religious people reborn in the Second Great Awakening, believed that public education would strengthen religious and family values. Mann's ideals and motives—the general betterment of society—were similar to theirs, and they saw merit in a democratic school system available to all, rich and poor. They noted, furthermore, that the Bible remained the centerpiece of elementary school education. And free public education would enable Sunday schools to devote full time to their students' religious needs without having to teach reading and writing as well. Thus Sunday-school teachers became Mann's allies.

A more controversial reform movement was the rise of American feminism in the 1840s. Ironically, it was women's traditional image as pious and spiritual that brought them into the public sphere. Revivalism, with its emphasis on conversion through the heart, served to elevate women; they were thought to be more emotional than men, and emotion was the most important element in being reborn. Organized into groups like the American Female Moral Reform Society, women slowly entered the public arena.

Reaction to the growing involvement of women in reform movements led many women to re-examine their position in society. In 1837 two antislavery lecturers, Angelina and Sarah Grimké, became particular objects of controversy. Natives of Charleston, South Carolina, they moved north in the 1820s to speak and write more openly and forcefully against slavery. They received a hostile reception for speaking before mixed groups of men and women. Some New England Congregationalists and even abolitionists joined in the criticism; as one pastoral letter put it, women should obey, not lecture, men. This reaction turned the Grimkés' attention from slavery to women's condition. The two attacked the concept of "subordination to man," insisting that both men and women had the "same rights and same duties." Sarah Grimké's *Letters on the Condition of Women and the Equality of the Sexes* (1838) and her sister's *Letters to Catharine E. Beecher*, published the same year, were the opening volleys in the war against the legal and social inequality of women.

Angelina and Sarah Grimké

In arguing against slavery, some women noticed the similarities between their own position and that of slaves. They saw parallels in their legal disabilities—

inability to vote or control their own property, except in widowhood—and their social restrictions—exclusion from advanced schooling and from most occupations. "The investigation of the rights of the slave," Angelina Grimké confessed, "has led me to a better understanding of my own." Some of the women who worked in the Lowell mills came to the same conclusion in the 1840s.

Unlike other reform movements, which succeeded in building a broad base of individual and organizational support, the movement for women's rights was limited. Some men joined the ranks, notably abolitionist William Lloyd Garrison and ex-slave Frederick Douglass, but most were actively opposed. In the 1840s the question of women's rights split the antislavery movement, the majority declaring themselves opposed. At a Woman's Rights Convention at Seneca Falls, New York, in 1848, led by Elizabeth Cady Stanton and Lucretia Mott, a much-published indictment of the injustices suffered by women was issued. If women had the vote, these reformers argued, they would be able both to protect themselves and to realize their potential as moral and spiritual leaders. Their argument won few over to their cause. By the 1850s feminists were focusing more and more on the single issue of suffrage. But another cause would eclipse their movement, at least for a time.

THE ANTISLAVERY MOVEMENT

Antislavery began as one among many reform movements. But, sparked by territorial expansion, the issue of slavery eventually became so overpowering that it consumed all other reforms. Passions would become so heated that they would threaten the nation itself. Above all else, those opposed to slavery saw it as a moral issue, evidence of the sinfulness of the American nation. When territorial questions in the 1850s forced the issue of slavery to center stage, the antislavery forces were well prepared (see Chapter 13).

Prior to the 1820s antislavery had played on the conscience of the individual slaveholder. Quakers had led the first antislavery movement in the eigh- teenth century, freeing their slaves and preaching that bondage was a Christian sin. But in the North, where most states had abolished slavery by 1800, whites took little interest in an issue that did not concern them directly. It was in the Upper South that antislavery sentiment was strongest, at least until the 1820s. But the movement there seemed to be as much concerned with preparing society for the natural death of slavery as with the plight of the slaves themselves.

Through the 1820s only free people of color demanded an immediate end to slavery. By 1830 there were at least fifty black antislavery societies in major black communities. These associations assisted fugitive slaves, attacked slavery at every turn, and reminded the nation that its mission as defined in the Declaration of Independence remained unfulfilled. A free black press helped to spread their word. Black abolitionists Frederick Douglass, Sojourner Truth, and Harriet Tubman then joined forces with white reformers in the American Anti-Slavery Society. These crusaders also stirred European support for their militant and unrelenting campaign. "Brethren, arise, arise, arise!" Henry Highland Garnet commanded the 1843 National Colored Convention. "Strike for your lives and liberties. Now is the day and hour. Let every slave in the land do this and the days of slavery are numbered. Rather die freemen than live to be slaves."

Black Antislavery Movement

In the 1830s a small minority of white reformers made antislavery their primary commitment and made abolitionism a crusade. The most prominent and uncompromising abolitionist, though clearly not the most representative, was William Lloyd Garrison, who demanded "immediate and complete emancipation." Garrison had begun his career in the late 1820s editing the *National Philanthropist*, a weekly paper devoted to general reform, but especially to prohibition. It was in 1828, when Benjamin Lundy recruited him to another journal, *The Genius of Universal Emancipation*, that Garrison entered the ranks of the abolitionists. But Lundy favored colonization and sought to end slavery through persuasion, a position Garrison came to reject. In January 1831 Garrison broke with gradualists like Lundy and published the first issue of the *Liberator*, which was to be his

William Lloyd Garrison

major weapon against slavery for thirty-five years. "I am in earnest—I will not equivocate—I will not excuse—I will not retreat a single inch—and *I will be heard*," he wrote in the first issue.

Garrison's refusal to work with anyone who even indirectly delayed emancipation left him isolated. He even forswore political action, on the grounds that it was governments that permitted slavery. (On July 4, 1854, Garrison burned a copy of the Constitution, proclaiming, "So perish all compromises with tyranny.") Through sheer force of rhetoric, Garrison helped to make antislavery the prevailing issue. His "immediatism" is probably best defined as tolerating no delay in ending slavery; he had no specific plan for abolishing it. In essence, Garrison called for an antislavery revival—all those who held slaves or cooperated with institutions supporting slavery should cast off their sins, repent, and do battle against evil.

Garrison alone could not have made antislavery a central issue. By the 1830s many northern reformers were recognizing the evils of slavery and preparing to act. Moral and religious ferment in the burned-over district and the Old Northwest had primed evangelists to enter the fray. And the reform activities of the 1820s, including antislavery, had built a network of interrelated organizations. In Michigan, for example, reformers convened one day as a temperance group and reconvened the next day as an antislavery society.

Ironically, it was in defense of the constitutional rights of abolitionists, not slaves, that many whites entered the struggle. Wherever they went, abolitionists found their civil rights in danger, especially their right of free speech. Unruly audiences found their rhetoric dangerous and a threat to the preservation of the Union. Using the new steam press, the American Anti-Slavery Society had increased its distribution of antislavery propaganda tenfold between 1834 and 1835, sending out 1.1 million pieces in 1835. But southern mobs seized and destroyed much of the mail, and South Carolina intercepted and burned abolitionist literature that entered the state (with the approval of the postmaster general). President Andrew Jackson even proposed a law prohibiting the mailing of antislavery tracts.

Another civil rights confrontation developed in Congress. Exercising their constitutional right to petition Congress, abolitionists mounted a campaign to abolish slavery and the slave trade in the District

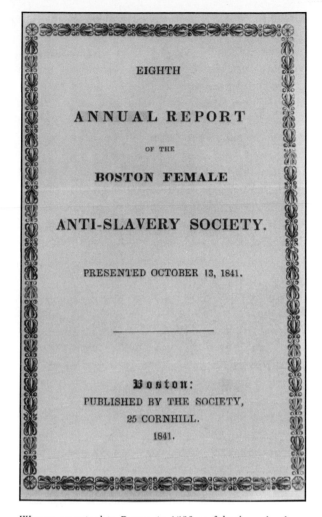

Women organized in Boston in 1833 to fight the evils of slavery. This annual report of their society was published in 1841. Sophia Smith Collection, Smith College.

of Columbia. (Since the district was under federal rule, states'-rights arguments against interfering with slavery did not apply there.) But Congress responded in 1836 by adopting the so-called gag rule, which automatically tabled abolitionist petitions, effectively preventing debate on them. In a dramatic defense of the right of petition, ex-president John Quincy Adams, then a Massachusetts representative, took to the floor repeatedly to defy the gag rule and eventually succeeded in getting it repealed (1844).

Gag Rule

Antislavery speakers often faced hostile crowds, and their presses were under constant threat of attack. The martyrdom of Elijah P. Lovejoy at the hands of a mob in Alton, Illinois, in 1837, drew attention to proslavery violence. Lovejoy, who had been driven out of slaveholding Missouri, had re-established his printing plant just across the river in Illinois. A mob sacked his office, with the cooperation of local authorities, and killed the abolitionist editor. Public outrage at Lovejoy's murder, as with the gag rule and censorship of the mails, only served to broaden the base of antislavery support in the North.

Frustration with the federal government also fed northern support for antislavery. By and large, politicians and government officials sought to avoid the question of slavery. The Missouri Compromise of 1820 had been an effort to quarantine the issue by adopting a simple formula—banning slavery north of 36°30′, Missouri's southern boundary—that would make debate on the slave or free status of new states unnecessary. Censorship of the mails and the gag rule were similar attempts to keep the issue out of the political arena. Yet the more national leaders, especially Democrats, sought to avoid the matter, the more they hardened the resolve of the antislavery forces.

The effect of the unlawful, violent, and obstructionist tactics used by proslavery advocates cannot be overestimated. Antislavery was not at the outset a unified movement. It was splintered and factionalized, and its adherents fought each other as often as they fought the defenders of slavery. They were divided over Garrison's emphasis on "moral suasion" versus the more practical political approach of James G. Birney, the Liberty party's candidate for president in 1844 (see page 349). They were split over support of other reforms, especially the rights of women. And they disagreed over the place of free black people in American society. Even so, abolitionists eventually managed to unify and make antislavery a major issue in the politics of the 1850s.

ANTIMASONRY

Antimasonry did not have the lasting appeal that antislavery had, but for a brief time it matched the intensity of abolitionism. The Antimasonry movement appeared like a comet in the burned-over district of western New York in 1826, and it stirred political activity before disappearing in the 1840s. As in antislavery, the line between reform and politics faded. The political arena quickly absorbed Antimasonry, but its short life illustrates the close tie between politics and reform from the 1820s through the 1840s.

Antimasonry was a reaction to Freemasonry, which had come to the United States from England in the eighteenth century. Freemasonry was a secret middle- and upper-class fraternity that attracted the sons of the Enlightenment, such as Benjamin Franklin and George Washington, with its emphasis on the Deity as opposed to organized religion and on brotherhood as opposed to one church. In the early nineteenth century it spread in the growing towns, attracting many commercial and political leaders. For ambitious young men, the Masons offered access to and fellowship with community leaders.

The Morgan affair was the catalyst for Antimasonry as an organized movement. In 1826, William Morgan, a disillusioned Mason, wrote an exposé of Masonry,

Morgan Affair *The Illustration of Masonry, By One of the Fraternity Who Has Devoted Thirty Years to the Subject,* to which his printer David Miller had added a scathing attack on the order. On September 12, 1826, prior to the book's appearance, a group of Masons abducted Morgan outside the Canandaigua, New York, jail. It was widely believed that the Masons had murdered Morgan, whose body was never found.

What energized the Antimasonry crusade was that its worst fears and charges seemed to be confirmed. Many of the officeholders in western New York, especially prosecutors, were Masons and they appeared to obstruct the investigation of Morgan's abduction. Public outcry and opposing political factions pressed for justice, and a series of notorious trials from 1827 through 1831 led many to suspect a conspiracy at work. The cover-up became as much the issue as Masonry itself, and the movement spilled over from the burned-over district to other states. In the Morgan affair, Antimason claims of a secret conspiracy seemed to be justified. Opponents of Masonry charged that the order's secrecy was antidemocratic and antirepublican, as was its elite membership and its use of regalia and such terms as knights and priests. As

In this contemporary Antimason cut, Freemasonry is represented as a Hydra-headed monster, with its tail strangling the Tree of Liberty. William Morgan, at the far right with an open book, is unmasking the monster, assisted by Antimasons. The winged figures are the Angels of Light and Truth with a holy mandate to finish off the monster. Library of Congress.

church leaders took up the moral crusade against Masonry, evangelicals labeled the order satanic.

As a moral crusade, however, Antimasonry crossed over into politics almost immediately. The issue itself was a political one since obstruction of justice was a signal element. Antimasonry attracted the lower and middle classes, pitting them against higher-status Masons and exploiting the general public's distrust and envy of local political leaders. And always there were factional leaders like Governor DeWitt Clinton of New York, willing to join the public outrage and pit his faction against others.

Unwittingly the Masons stoked the fires of Antimasonry. The silence of the order seemed to condone the murder of Morgan, and the construction of monumental lodges, like the one in Boston, advertised their determination to remain a public force. When editors who were Masons ignored the crusade against Masonry, the Antimasons started their own newspapers. The struggle, carried out within and without political parties, aroused public interest in politics.

Antimasonry spread as a popular movement and introduced the convention system for choosing political candidates. In defense of public morality and the republic, the Antimasons held conventions in 1827 **Convention System** to oppose Masons running for public office. In 1828 the conventions supported the National Republican candidate, John Quincy Adams, and opposed Andrew Jackson because he was a Mason. In 1831 the Antimasons held the first national political convention in Baltimore, and a year later nominated in convention William Wirt as their presidential candidate. Thus the Antimasons became one rallying point for those opposed to President Andrew Jackson.

By the mid-1830s Antimasonry had lost force as a moral and political movement. Most Antimasons found a comfortable anti-Jackson vehicle in the Whig party. Yet the movement left an indelible mark on the politics of the era. As a moral crusade concerned about public officeholders, it inspired and welcomed wider participation in the political process. In the burned-over district, wherever religious fervor appeared, and wherever families entered the market economy, Antimasonry arose. The revivalist and reform impulses in movements like Antimasonry further stimulated and awakened disagreements over values and ideology that were reinforced by conflicts over wealth, religion, and status. These differences helped polarize politics and shape parties as organizations to express those differences. The Antimasons contributed specifically to party development by pioneering the convention system and by stimulating greater grassroots involvement.

Jacksonianism and the Beginnings of Modern Party Politics

The distinction between reform and politics eroded in the 1820s and after as reform inched its way into politics. The Antimasons, and then the abolitionists, appealed directly to voters. Although their means often differed, party leaders too sought to deal with the problems created by an expanding, urbanizing, market-oriented nation. President John

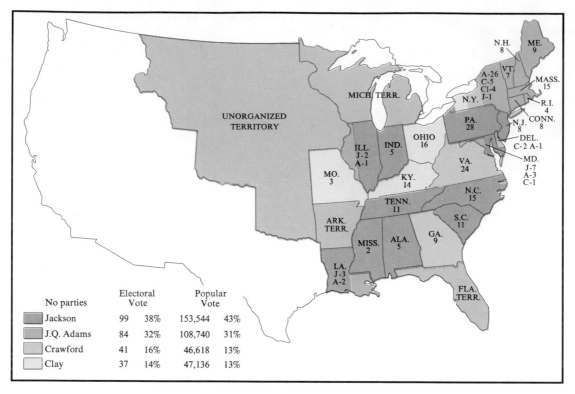

Presidential Election, 1824

No parties	Electoral Vote		Popular Vote	
Jackson	99	38%	153,544	43%
J.Q. Adams	84	32%	108,740	31%
Crawford	41	16%	46,618	13%
Clay	37	14%	47,136	13%

Quincy Adams advocated a nationalist program and an activist federal government; Andrew Jackson and his followers adhered to the Jeffersonian ideal of a more limited federal government.

The election of 1824, in which Adams and Jackson faced each other for the first time, signaled the beginning of a new, more open political system. The Federalist party had died out after the election of 1816, and Monroe had run unopposed in 1820 as the Republican candidate. In 1824, however, the Republicans were unable to agree on a candidate. From 1800 through 1820 a caucus in the House of Representatives had chosen the Republican presidential nominees: Jefferson, Madison, and Monroe. Jefferson and Madison had both indicated to the caucus that their secretaries of state should succeed them, and the system had worked efficiently. Of course, such a system restricted voter involvement—but this was not a real drawback at first, since in 1800 only five of sixteen states selected presidential electors by popular vote. (In most, legislatures designated the electors.) In 1816, however, ten out of

End of the Caucus System

nineteen states chose electors by popular vote, and in 1824, eighteen out of twenty-four did so.

Moreover, President Monroe never designated an heir apparent. Without direction from the president, therefore, the caucus in 1824 chose William H. Crawford, secretary of the treasury. But other Republicans, encouraged by the opportunity to appeal directly to the voters in most states, challenged Crawford. Secretary of State John Quincy Adams drew support from New England, and westerners backed Speaker of the House Henry Clay of Kentucky. Secretary of War John C. Calhoun looked to the South for support, and hoped to win Pennsylvania as well. Andrew Jackson, a popular military hero whose political views were unknown, was nominated by resolution of the Tennessee legislature and won support everywhere. But Crawford, who had declined to oppose Monroe in 1816 and 1820, had the most widespread support in Washington. Since his choice by the caucus was a foregone conclusion, the other four candidates joined in attacking the caucus system as undemocratic. When their supporters boycotted the deliberations, Crawford's victory became hollow,

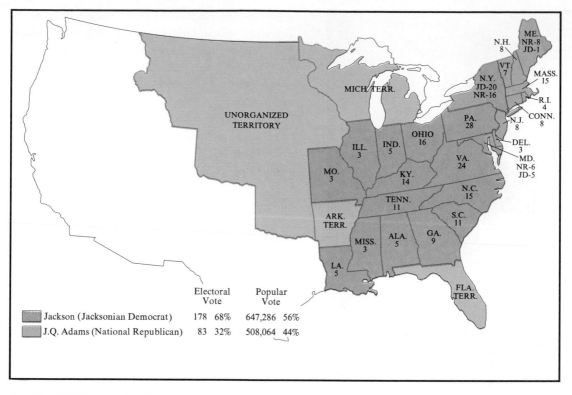

	Electoral Vote		Popular Vote	
▮ Jackson (Jacksonian Democrat)	178	68%	647,286	56%
▯ J.Q. Adams (National Republican)	83	32%	508,064	44%

Presidential Election, 1828

based on a minority vote. The role of the congressional caucus in nominating presidents ended.

Though Andrew Jackson led in both popular and electoral votes in the four-way presidential election of 1824, no one received a majority (see map). Adams finished second, and Clay and Crawford trailed far behind. (Calhoun dropped out of the race before the election.) Under the Constitution, the selection of a president in such circumstances fell to the House of Representatives, which would vote by state delegation, one vote to a state. Crawford, a stroke victim, never received serious consideration; Clay, who had received the fewest votes, was dropped. But Clay, as Speaker of the House and leader of the Ohio Valley states, backed Adams, who received the votes of thirteen out of twenty-four state delegations. Clay was rewarded with the position of secretary of state in the Adams administration—the traditional stepping-stone to the presidency. Angry Jacksonians denounced the arrangement as a "corrupt bargain" that had stolen the office from the clear frontrunner.

As president, John Quincy Adams took a strong nationalist position emphasizing Henry Clay's Amer-ican System of protective tariffs, a national bank, and internal improvements (see page 227). Adams believed the federal government should take an activist role not only in the economy but in education, science, and the arts; accordingly, he proposed a national university in Washington, D.C.

Brilliant as a diplomat and secretary of state, Adams was sadly inept as president. He underestimated the lingering effects of the Panic of 1819 and the ensuing bitter opposition to a national bank and protective tariffs. Meanwhile, supporters of Andrew Jackson sabotaged Adams's administration at every opportunity.

The 1828 campaign between Adams and Jackson was an intensely personal conflict. Whatever principles the two men stood for were obscured by the mud-slinging both sides indulged in. Jackson's supporters claimed that the presidency had been stolen from the general in 1824. Adams, son of John Adams and a former Federalist, distrusted party organization, and as president he did not use his patronage power to aid his policies or his re-election. Though Adams won the same states as in 1824, the opposition was unified, and Jackson swamped him (see map).

Andrew Jackson in 1832, at the peak of his success and power. Library of Congress.

Jackson polled 56 percent of the popular vote and won in the electoral college, 178 to 83. For him and his supporters, the election of 1828 was the culmination of a long-fought, well-organized campaign based on party organization. Through a lavishly financed coalition of state parties, political leaders, and newspaper editors, a popular movement had elected a president. An era had ended, and the Democratic party became the first truly modern political party in the United States. The future belonged to well-organized political parties and leaders who engaged in party politics.

Andrew Jackson was nicknamed "Old Hickory," after the toughest American hardwood. A rough-and-tumble, ambitious man, he rose from humble

Andrew Jackson birth to become a wealthy planter and slaveholder. Jackson was the first American president not born into comfortable circumstances, a self-made man at ease among both frontiersmen and southern planters.

Few Americans have been celebrated in myth and legend as has Andrew Jackson. As a general in the Tennessee militia, Jackson had led the battle to remove the Creek from the Alabama and Georgia frontier. He burst onto the national scene as the great hero of the War of 1812, and in 1818 enhanced his glory in an expedition against the Seminole in Spanish Florida. Jackson also served as a congressional representative and senator from Tennessee, as a judge in his home state, and as the first territorial governor of Florida (1821) before running for president in 1824. He was an active presidential aspirant until he won the office in 1828.

Jackson and his supporters offered a distinct alternative to the strong national government Adams had advocated. They and their party, the Democratic-Republicans (shortened to Democrats), represented a wide range of

Democrats beliefs but shared some common ideals. Fundamentally, they sought to foster the Jeffersonian concept of an agrarian society, harkening back to the belief that a strong central government was the enemy of individual liberty, a tyranny to be feared. Thus, like Jefferson, they favored limited government and emphasized state sovereignty.

Jacksonians were as fearful of the concentration of economic power as they were of political power. They saw government intervention in the economy as benefiting special-interest groups and creating corporate monopolies, and thus rejected an activist economic program as favoring the rich. Jacksonians sought to restore the independence of the individual—the artisan and the yeoman farmer—by ending federal support of banks and corporations and restricting the use of paper currency. Their concept of the proper role of government tended to be negative, and Jackson's political power was largely expressed in negative acts; he used the veto more than all previous presidents combined.

Finally, Jackson and his supporters were hostile to reform as a movement and an ideology. Reformers were increasingly calling for an activist and interventionist government as they organized to turn their programs into legislation. But Democrats tended to oppose programs like educational reform and the establishment of public education. They believed, for instance, that public schools restricted individual liberty by interfering with parental responsibility, and undermined freedom of religion by replacing church schools. Nor did Jackson share reformers' humanitarian concerns. He showed little sympathy for the Indians, ordering their removal from the Southeast to make way for white agricultural settlement (see page 289).

Yet Jackson and the Jacksonians considered themselves reformers in a different way. In following Jefferson's notion of restraint in government and in emphasizing individualism, Jackson and his followers sought to restore old republican virtues. Individual traits such as industriousness, prudence, sobriety, and economy were highly prized. No less than reformers he favored human goodness. He believed that his party, headed by a politically sensitive and astute leader, was the best instrument to restore those traditional values.

Like Jefferson, Jackson strengthened the executive branch of government at the same time as he tended to weaken the federal role. Given his popularity and the strength of his personality, this concentration of power in the presidency was perhaps inevitable; but his deliberate policy of combining the roles of party leader and chief of state centralized even greater power in the White House. Enamored of power, Jackson never hesitated to confront his opponents with all the weapons at his command. Among his followers he commanded enormous loyalty, and he rewarded them handsomely. Invoking the principle that rotating officeholders would make government more responsive to the public will, Jackson used the spoils system to reward loyal Democrats with appointments to office. Though he removed fewer than one-quarter of federal officeholders in his two terms, his use of patronage nevertheless strengthened party organization and loyalty.

Among Jackson's opponents animosity grew year by year. "When he comes," Daniel Webster wrote in 1829 of the soon-to-be-inaugurated Jackson, "he will bring a breeze with him. Which way it will blow I cannot tell . . . , but my *fear* is greater than my hope." Once in office, Jackson was mocked as King Andrew I for his quick and firm actions. Critics attempted to undermine his claim of restoring republican virtue and of inheriting the mantle of Jefferson. They charged him with recklessly and impulsively destroying the economy.

Jackson invigorated the philosophy of limited government. In 1830 he vetoed the Maysville Road bill, which would have provided a federal subsidy to construct a sixty-mile turnpike from Maysville to Lexington, Kentucky. Jackson insisted that an internal improvement confined to one state was unconstitutional, and that such projects were properly a state responsibility. The veto undermined Henry Clay's American System and personally embarrassed Clay, since the project was in his home district.

THE NULLIFICATION AND BANK CONTROVERSIES

Jackson had to face more directly the question of the proper division of sovereignty between state and central government. The growing reform crusades, especially antislavery, had made the southern states fearful of federal power—and none more so than South Carolina, where the planter class was strongest and slavery most concentrated. Having watched the growth of abolitionist sentiment in Great Britain, which resulted in 1833 in emancipation in the West Indies, South Carolinians feared the same thing would happen at home. Hard hit by the Panic of 1819, from which they never fully recovered, they also resented the high prices of imported goods created by protectionist tariffs.

To protect their interests, South Carolinian political leaders developed the doctrine of *nullification,* according to which a state had the right to overrule, or nullify, federal legislation that conflicted with its own. The act that directly inspired this doctrine was the passage in 1828 of the Tariff of Abominations. In his unsigned *Exposition and Protest,* John C. Calhoun argued that in any disagreement between the federal government and a state, a special state convention—like those called to ratify the Constitution—would decide the conflict by either nullifying or accepting the federal law. Only the power of nullification could protect the minority against the tyranny of the majority, Calhoun asserted.

In public, John C. Calhoun let others take the lead in advancing nullification. As Jackson's running mate in 1828, he avoided publicly identifying with nullification and thus embarrassing the ticket. And as vice president, he hoped to win Jackson's support as Democratic presidential nominee over Martin Van Buren. Thus a silent Calhoun presided over the Senate and its packed galleries when Senators Daniel Webster (New Hampshire) and Robert Y. Hayne (South Carolina) debated nullification in January 1830. The debate explored North-South grievances and the question of the nature of the Union. With Calhoun nodding agreement in the chair, Hayne charged that the Hartford Convention at the end of the War of 1812 had been an act of disunity (see page 226). Over two days Webster defended the New England states and his beloved republic in eloquent rhetoric. Though debating Hayne, he aimed his remarks at Calhoun as he depicted the nation as a compact of people, not merely states. In the climax of his career as a debator, he invoked two images. One, which he hoped he would not see, was the outcome of nullification: "states dissevered, discordant, belligerent; on a land rent with civil feuds, or drenched . . . in fraternal blood!" The other was a patriotic vision of a great nation flourishing under the motto "Liberty *and* Union, now and forever, one and inseparable."

Webster-Hayne Debate

Though sympathetic to states' rights, Jackson shared Webster's dread and distrust of nullification. Soon after the Webster-Hayne debate, the president made his position clear at a Jefferson Day dinner, with the toast: "Our Federal Union, it *must* and *shall be* preserved." Calhoun, when it came to his turn, offered: "The Federal Union—next to our liberty the most dear." Calhoun, torn between devotion to the Union and loyalty to his state, had revealed his preference for states' rights. Politically and personally Calhoun and Jackson grew apart, and it soon became apparent that Jackson favored Secretary of State Martin Van Buren, not Calhoun, as his successor.

South Carolina first invoked its theory of nullification against the tariff of 1832. Though this tariff had the effect of reducing some duties, it retained high taxes on imported iron, cottons, and woolens. A majority of southern representatives supported the new tariff, but South Carolinians refused to go along. In their view, their constitutional right to control their own destiny had been sacrificed to the demands of northern industrialists. They feared

Nullification Crisis

the consequences of accepting such an act; it could set a precedent for congressional legislation on slavery. In November 1832 a South Carolina state convention nullified the tariff, making it unlawful for officials to collect duties in the state after February 1, 1833. Immediately recruiters began to organize a volunteer army to ensure nonenforcement of the tariff.

"Old Hickory" responded with toughness. Privately, he threatened to invade South Carolina and hang Calhoun, his vice president; publicly, he sought to avoid the use of force. On December 10, 1832, Jackson issued his own proclamation nullifying nullification. He moved troops to federal forts in South Carolina and prepared United States marshals to collect the required duties. At Jackson's request, Congress passed the Force Act, which supposedly renewed Jackson's authority to call up troops; it was actually a scheme to avoid the use of force by collecting duties before ships reached South Carolina. At the same time, Jackson extended the olive branch by recommending tariff reductions. Calhoun, disturbed by South Carolina's drift toward separatism, resigned as vice president and became a South Carolina senator. In the Senate he worked with Henry Clay to draw up the compromise tariff of 1833. Quickly passed by Congress and signed by the president, the revision lengthened the list of duty-free items and reduced duties over the next nine years. Satisfied, South Carolina's convention repealed its nullification law, and in a final salvo nullified Jackson's Force Act. Jackson ignored the gesture.

Although fought over the practical issue of tariffs (and the unspoken issue of slavery), the nullification controversy did represent a genuine debate on the true nature and principles of the republic. Each side believed it was upholding the Constitution. Both felt they were fighting special privilege and subversion of republican values. South Carolina was fighting the tyranny of the federal government and the manufacturers who sought tariff protection; Jackson was fighting the tyranny of South Carolina, whose refusal to bow to federal authority threatened to split the republic. Neither side won a clear victory, though both claimed to have done so. Another issue, that of a central bank, would define the powers of the federal government more clearly.

At stake was the rechartering of the Second Bank of the United States, whose twenty-year charter expired in 1836. Like its predecessor, the bank served

Second Bank of the United States

as a depository for federal funds, on which it paid no interest; and it served the republic in many other ways. Its bank notes circulated as currency throughout the country; they could be readily exchanged for gold, and the federal government accepted them as payment in all transactions. Through its twenty-five branch offices, the bank acted as a clearing-house for state banks, keeping them honest by refusing to accept their notes if they had insufficient gold in reserve.

But the bank had enemies. Most state banks resented the central bank's police role; by presenting state bank notes for redemption all at once, the Second Bank could easily ruin a state bank. Moreover, state banks, with less money in reserve, found themselves unable to compete on an equal footing with the Second Bank. Many state governments regarded the national bank, with its headquarters in Philadelphia, as unresponsive to local needs. Westerners and urban workers remembered with bitterness the bank's conservative credit policies during the Panic of 1819—and there was some truth to their complaints. Though the Second Bank served some of the functions of a central bank, it was still a private profit-making institution, and its policies reflected the self-interest of its owners. Its president, Nicholas Biddle, controlled the bank completely. Conservative and anti-Jacksonian, Biddle symbolized all that westerners found wrong with the bank. Moreover, the bank had great political influence. Many members of Congress and business leaders were beholden to it, and the only check on that power was at rechartering time.

Although the bank's charter would not expire until 1836, Biddle, aware of Jackson's hostility and encouraged by the National Republican presidential candidate, Henry Clay, sought to make it an issue in the campaign of 1832. His strategy backfired. Biddle's success with Congress did not deter Jackson; in July 1832 Jackson vetoed the rechartering bill, and the Senate failed to override the veto. Jackson's veto message was an emotional attack on the undemocratic nature of the bank. "It is to be regretted," he said, "that the rich and powerful too often bend the acts of government to their selfish purposes." Rechartering would grant "exclusive privileges, to make the rich richer and the potent more powerful."

The bank became the major symbol and issue in the presidential campaign of 1832. Jackson ignored its constitutionality and its functions; instead he denounced special privilege and economic power. The Jacksonians had organized a highly effective party, and they used it in the election. Operating in a system in which all the states but South Carolina now chose electors by popular vote, the Jacksonians mobilized voters by advertising the presidential election as the focal point of the political system. The Antimasons adopted a party platform, the first in the nation's history. The Democrats and the major opposition party, the National Republicans, quickly followed suit. Jackson and Martin Van Buren were nominated at the Democratic convention, Clay and John Sergeant at the National Republican. John Floyd ran as South Carolina's candidate. Jackson was reelected easily in a Democratic party triumph.

After his victory and second inauguration in 1833, Jackson moved not only to dismantle the Second Bank of the United States but to ensure that it would not be resurrected. He deposited federal funds in favored state-chartered ("pet") banks; without federal money, the bank shriveled. When its federal charter expired in 1836, it became just another Pennsylvania-chartered private bank. In 1841 it closed its doors.

As part of the coup de grâce delivered to the Bank of the United States, Congress, with Jackson's support, passed the Deposit Act of 1836. Under this act, the secretary of the treasury designated one bank in each state and territory to provide the services formerly performed by the Bank of the United States. The act provided that the federal surplus in excess of $5 million be distributed to the states as interest-free loans beginning in 1837, and these loans were never recalled—a fitting Jacksonian hold on the federal purse.

Jackson was worried about more than just restraining the government. The surplus had derived from wholesale speculation in public lands. Purchasers bought public land on credit, borrowed from banks against the land to purchase additional acreage, and repeated the cycle. Between 1834 and 1836 federal receipts from land sales rose from $5 to $25 million. Banks issued bank notes in providing loans, and Jackson, an opponent of paper money, feared that the speculative craze threatened the state banks while closing the door to settlers, who could not compete with speculators in bidding for the best land.

When New York state banks stopped redeeming bank notes for gold or silver during the Panic of 1837, Whigs blamed the crisis on Jackson's opposition to the Second Bank of the United States. This satirical six-cent note drawn on the Humbug Glory Bank ridicules Jackson and Van Buren. Notice the Democratic donkey and the hickory leaf on the face of the paper. The New-York Historical Society.

Following his hard-money instinct and his opposition to paper currency, President Jackson ordered Treasury Secretary Levi Woodbury to issue the Specie Circular.

Specie Circular It provided that after August 15, 1836, only specie—gold or silver— or Virginia land scrip would be accepted as payment for federal lands. The circular stated that it sought to end "the monopoly of the public lands in the hands of speculators and capitalists" and the "ruinous extension" of bank notes and credit. By ending credit sales, the circular reduced significantly public land purchases and forced a halt to the distribution of the surplus to the states; the final payments were never made since the surplus evaporated.

The policy was a disaster on many fronts. Although federal land sales were sharply reduced, speculation still continued as available land for sale became a scarce commodity. The ensuing increased demand for specie squeezed banks, and many suspended specie payment (the redemption of bank notes for specie). This led to further credit contraction, as banks issued fewer notes and gave less credit. Equally damaging was the way Jackson attacked the problem. He pursued a tight money policy instinctively, and was indifferent to the impact of his policies. More important, the Specie Circular, issued in July 1836, was similar to a bill defeated in the Senate nearly three months earlier. His opponents saw King Andrew at work. Congress voted to repeal the circular in the waning days of Jackson's administration, but the president pocket-vetoed the bill. Finally in May 1838, a joint resolution of Congress overturned the circular.

Jackson used the veto power more often than did all his predecessors combined. From Washington to John Quincy Adams, presidents had vetoed nine bills; Jackson vetoed twelve. And he was the first to use the pocket veto—refusing to sign or veto a bill at the end of a congressional session, thus killing it. Previous presidents believed that vetoes were justified only on constitutional grounds, but Jackson, as in the veto of the Second Bank of the United States, negated bills merely because he disagreed with them. He made the veto an important weapon in controlling Congress, since representatives and senators had to consider the possibility of a presidential veto on any bill. In effect, he made the executive power equal to that of two-thirds of both houses of Congress.

The Whig Challenge and the Second Party System

Once historians described the 1830s and 1840s as the Age of Jackson, and the personalities of the leading political figures dominated history books. Increasingly, however, historians have viewed these years as an age of popularly based political parties and reformers. For it was only when the passionate concerns of evangelicals and reformers spilled into politics that party differences became important again and party loyalties solidified. For the first time grassroots political groups, organized from the bottom up, set the tone of political life.

In the 1830s the Democrats' opponents, including remnants of the now-disorganized National Republican party, found shelter under a common umbrella, the Whig party. Resentful of Jackson's domination of Congress, the Whigs borrowed their name from the British party that had opposed the tyranny of Hanoverian monarchs in the eighteenth century. From the congressional elections of 1834 through the 1840s, they and the Democrats competed nearly equally; only a few percentage points separated the two parties in national elections. They fought at every level—city, county, and state—and achieved a stability previously unknown in American politics. Both parties built strong organizations, commanded the loyalty of legislators, and attracted mass popular followings.

The two parties emphasized responsiveness to their supporters, a priority that reflected significant changes in the electoral process. At the local level, direct voting had replaced nomination and election by legislators and electors. And though many states still permitted only taxpayers to vote in local elections, by the 1830s only a handful significantly restricted adult white male suffrage in nonlocal elections. Some even allowed immigrants who had taken out their first citizenship papers to vote. The effect of these changes was a sharp increase in the number of votes cast in presidential elections. Between 1824 and 1828 the number of votes cast for president increased threefold, from 360,000 to over 1.1 million. In 1840, 2.4 million men cast votes. The proportion of eligible voters who cast ballots also increased. In 1824 an estimated 27 percent of those eligible voted; from 1828 through 1836, about 55 percent, in 1840, more than 80 percent.

On the political agenda during these years were numerous fundamental issues. At the national level, officials struggled with the question of the proper constitutional roles of the federal and state governments, national expansion, and Indian policy. Also during this period, many state conventions were drafting new constitutions and deliberating over such basic issues as the rights of individuals and corporations; the rights of labor and capital; government aid to business; currency and sources of revenue; and public education, temperance, and antislavery.

Increasingly the two parties differed in their approaches to these issues. Though both favored economic expansion, the Whigs sought it through an activist government, the Democrats through limited central government.

Whigs

Thus the Whigs supported corporate charters, a national bank, and paper currency; the Democrats were opposed. The Whigs also favored more humanitarian reforms than did the Democrats—public schools, abolition of capital punishment, temperance, and prison and asylum reform.

In general, Whigs were simply more optimistic than Democrats, and more enterprising. They did not hesitate to help one group if doing so would promote the general welfare. The chartering of corporations, they argued, expanded economic opportunity for everyone, providing work for laborers and increasing demand for food from farmers. Meanwhile the Democrats, distrustful of the concentration of economic power and of moral and economic coercion, held fast to their Jeffersonian principle of limited government.

For all the rank economic inequality that characterized the era, it was not the major issue that divided the parties. Nor were the conflicts over the bank and government or the issuing of corporate charters battles between the haves and have-nots. Although the Whigs attracted more of the upper and middle class, both sides drew support from manufacturers, merchants, laborers, and farmers. Instead, it was religion and ethnicity that determined party membership. In the North, the Whigs' concern for energetic government and humanitarian and moral reform won the favor of native-born and British-American evangelical Protestants, especially those involved in religious revival. These Presbyterians, Baptists, and Congregationalists were overwhelmingly Whigs, as were the relatively small number of free black voters. Democrats, on the other hand, tended to be foreign-born Catholics and nonevangelical Protestants, both groups that preferred to keep religious and secular affairs separate.

The Whig party thus became the vehicle of evangelical Christianity. In many locales, the membership of reform societies overlapped that of the party. Indeed,

Whigs and Reformers

Whigs practiced a kind of political revivalism. Their rallies resembled camp meetings; their speeches echoed evangelical rhetoric; their programs embodied the perfectionist beliefs of reformers. This potent blend of religion and politics—which, as Tocqueville noted, were "intimately united" in America—greatly intensified political loyalties.

In unifying evangelicals, the Whigs alienated members of other faiths. The evangelicals' ideal Christian state had no room for Catholics, Mormons, Unitarians, Universalists, or religious freethinkers. Sabbath laws, temperance legislation, and Protestant-inspired public education threatened the religious freedom and individual liberty of these groups, which generally opposed state interference in moral and religious questions. As a result, more than 95 percent of Irish Catholics, 90 percent of Reformed Dutch, and 80 percent of German Catholics voted Democratic.

Vice President Martin Van Buren headed the Democratic ticket in the presidential election of 1836. Hand-picked by Jackson, Van Buren was a shrewd politician who had built the Democratic party in New York. The Whigs, who had not yet coalesced into a national party, entered three sectional candidates: Daniel Webster of New England, Hugh White of the South, and William Henry Harrison of the West. By splintering the vote, they hoped to throw the election into the House, but Van Buren squeaked through with a 25,000-vote edge out of a total of 1.5 million. No vice-presidential candidate received a majority of electoral votes, though, and for the only time in American history the Senate chose a vice president: the Democratic candidate, Richard M. Johnson.

Van Buren took office just weeks before the Amer-ican credit system collapsed. The economic boom of the 1830s was over. In May 1837 New York banks

Martin Van Buren and Hard Times

stopped redeeming paper currency in gold, and soon all banks suspended payments in hard coin. As confidence faded, banks curtailed loans. The credit contraction only made things worse; after a brief recovery, full-scale depression set in, and persisted from 1839 to 1843.

Not surprisingly, economic issues were paramount during these years. Unfortunately, Van Buren followed Jackson's hard-money policies. He curtailed federal spending, thus accelerating deflation, and opposed the Whigs' advocacy of a national bank, which would have expanded credit. Even worse, Van Buren proposed a new treasury system under which the government would keep its funds in regional treasury offices rather than banks. The treasury branches would accept and pay out only gold and silver coin; they would not accept paper currency or checks drawn on state banks. Van Buren's independent treasury bill was passed in 1840. By creating a constant demand for hard coin, it deprived banks of gold and added to the general deflation.

Undaunted, the Whigs fought the Democrats at the state level over these issues, since great economic advantages were at stake. The Whigs favored new banks, more paper currency, and more corporations. As the party of hard money, the Democrats favored eliminating paper currency altogether and using only gold or silver coin. Increasingly the Democrats became distrustful even of state banks, and by the mid-1840s a majority favored eliminating all bank corporations. The Whigs, riding the wave of economic distress into office, made banking and corporate charters more readily available.

With the nation in a depression, the Whigs confidently prepared for the election of 1840. Their strategy was simple: keep their loyal supporters and win

Election of 1840

over independents distressed by hard times. The Democrats renominated President Van Buren in a somber convention. The Whigs rallied behind the military hero General William Henry Harrison, conqueror of Prophet Town or Tippecanoe Creek in 1811. Harrison and his running mate, John Tyler of Virginia, ran a "log cabin and hard cider" campaign—a people's crusade against the aristocratic president in the Palace, as the Whigs called the White House. Using many of the techniques of twentieth-century politics—huge rallies, parades, songs, posters, and campaign hats—the Whigs wooed supporters and independents alike. Harrison stayed carefully above the issues, earning the nickname General Mum, but party hacks bluntly blamed the depression on the Democrats. In a huge turnout in which 80 percent of eligible voters cast ballots, Harrison won the popular vote by a narrow margin but swept the electoral college 234 to 60.

Immediately after taking office in 1841, President Harrison called a special session of Congress to enact the Whig economic program: repeal of the independent treasury system; a new national bank; and a higher protective tariff. Unfortunately for the Whigs, Harrison died within a month of his inauguration. His successor, John Tyler, a former Democrat who had left the party in opposition to Jackson's nullification proclamation, turned out to be more of a Democrat than a Whig. Tyler consistently opposed the Whig congressional program. He repeatedly vetoed Henry Clay's protective tariffs, bills promoting internal improvements, and bills aimed at reviving the Bank of the United States. The only important measures that became law under his administration were the repeal of the independent treasury and a higher tariff. Two days after Tyler's second veto of a bank bill, the entire cabinet except Secretary of State Daniel Webster resigned. Webster, involved in negotiating a new treaty with Great Britain, left shortly thereafter. Tyler became a president without a party, and the Whigs lost the presidency without an election.

Virtually expelled from the Whig party and at war with them over domestic policy, Tyler tended to territorial questions. During the late 1830s, Anglo-American relations, friendly since the War of 1812, again became tense. Southern alarm over West Indian emancipation; northern comercial rivalry with Britain; the default of state governments and corporations on British-held debts during the Panic of 1837; rebellion in Canada; boundary disputes; and American expansionism—all fueled Anglo-American tensions.

Anglo-American Tensions

One of the most troublesome of these disputes arose from the *Caroline* affair, in which a United States citizen, Amos Durfee, had been killed when

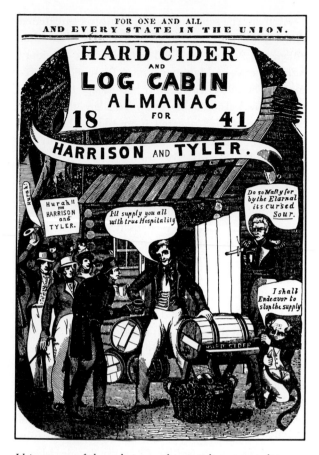

Using many of the techniques of twentieth-century politics, General William Henry Harrison ran a "log cabin and hard cider" campaign—a popular crusade—against Jackson heir, President Martin Van Buren. The almanac cover shows a victorious Harrison receiving the people's acclaim while Jackson's cider—popularity—has turned sour and Van Buren is unable to stem the Whig's appeal. Library of Congress.

Canadian militia set the privately owned steamer *Caroline* afire in the Niagara River. (The *Caroline* had supported an unsuccessful uprising against Great Britain in Upper Canada in 1837.) Britain refused to apologize for its revenge, and patriotic Americans seethed with rage. Fearing that popular support for the Canadian rebels would ignite war, President Van Buren posted troops at the border to discourage border raids. Tensions subsided in November 1840 when Alexander McLeod, a Canadian deputy sheriff, was arrested in New York for the murder of Durfee. McLeod was eventually acquitted; had he been found guilty and executed, Lord Palmerston, the British foreign minister, might have sought war.

At about the same time another quarrel threatened Anglo-American relations. The Treaty of Ghent that ended the War of 1812 had not solved the boundary dispute between Maine and New Brunswick. Moreover, although Great Britain had accepted an 1831 arbitration decision fixing a new boundary, the United States Senate had rejected it in 1832. Thus when Canadians began to log the disputed region in the winter of 1838 and 1839, the citizens of Maine attempted to expel them. Soon the lumbermen had captured the Maine land agent and posse; both sides had mobilized their militia; and Congress had authorized a call-up of fifty thousand men. No blood was spilled, though. General Winfield Scott, who had patrolled the border during the *Caroline* affair, was dispatched to Aroostook, Maine. Scott arranged a truce between the warring state and province, and the two sides compromised on their conflicting claims in the Webster-Ashburton Treaty (1842).

These border disputes with Great Britain prefigured an issue that became prominent in national politics in the mid- to late 1840s: the westward expansion of the United States. Tyler's succession to power in 1841 and a Democratic victory in the presidential election of 1844 ended activist, energetic government on the federal level for the rest of the decade. Meanwhile economic issues were eclipsed by debate over the nation's destiny to stretch from coast to coast. Reform, however, was not dead. Its passions would resurface in the 1850s in the debate over slavery in the territories.

MANIFEST DESTINY

The belief that American expansion westward and southward was inevitable, divinely ordained, and just was first called *manifest destiny* by a Democrat, the newspaperman John L. O'Sullivan. The annexation of Texas, O'Sullivan wrote in 1845, was "the fulfillment of our manifest destiny to overspread the continent allotted by Providence for the free development of our yearly multiplying millions." Americans had thought similarly for decades, but during the 1840s they used such rhetoric to hurry the inexorable

process along and to justify war and threats of war in the quest for more territory.

Americans had been hungry for new lands ever since the colonists first turned their eyes westward. There lay fertile soil, valuable minerals, and the chance for a better life or a new beginning. Acquisition of the Louisiana Territory and the Floridas had set the process in motion (see map). Agrarian Democrats saw the West as an antidote to urbanization and industrialization. Enterprising Whigs looked to the new commercial opportunities the West offered. No wonder that between 1833 and 1860 the proportion of Americans living west of the Appalachians grew from one-quarter to one-half.

A fierce national pride also spurred the quest for western land. Dampened during times of depression, it reasserted itself during recoveries and booms, as in the 1840s. North or South, Whig or Democrat, Americans were convinced that theirs was the greatest country on earth, with a special role to play in the world. What better evidence of such a role could there be than expansion from coast to coast?

Americans also idealistically believed that westward expansion would extend American freedom and democracy. The acquisition of new territory would, they reasoned, bring the benefits of America's republican system of government to less fortunate people. Of course such idealism was self-serving, and it contained an undercurrent of racism as well. Indians were perceived as savages best removed from their homes east of the Mississippi and confined to small areas in the West. Mexicans and Central and South Americans were also seen as inferior peoples, fit to be controlled or conquered. Thus the same racism that justified slavery in the South and discrimination in the North supported expansion in the West.

Finally, the expansionist fever of the 1840s was fed by the desire to secure the nation from perceived external enemies. The internal enemies of the 1830s—a monster bank, corporations, paper currency, alcohol, Sabbath violation—seemed to pale before the threats Americans found on their borders in the 1840s. Expansion, some believed, was necessary to preserve American independence.

Among the long-standing objectives of expansionists was the Republic of Texas, which included parts of present-day Oklahoma, Kansas, Colorado, Wyoming, and New Mexico as well as all of Texas. This territory

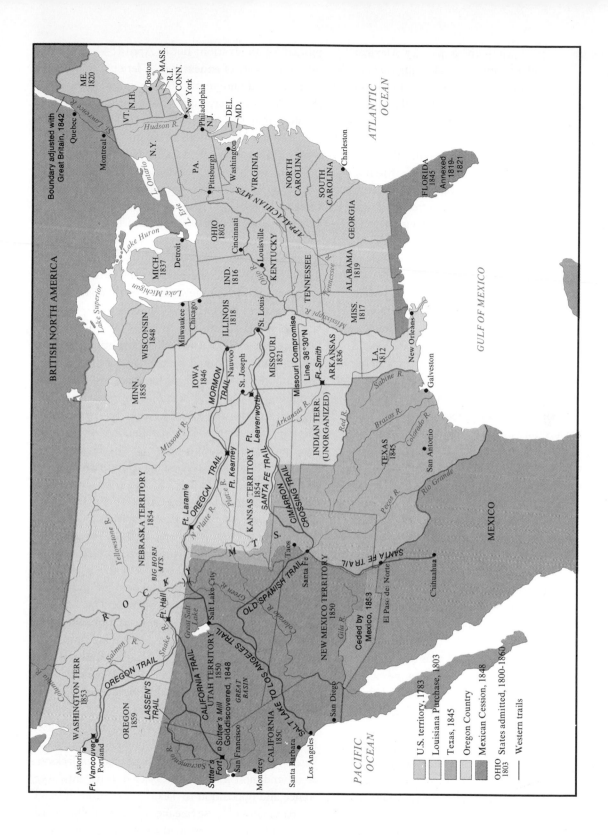

Westward Expansion, 1800–1860

Republic of Texas was originally a part of Mexico. After winning its independence from Spain in 1821, the government of Mexico encouraged the development of these rich but remote northern provinces, offering large tracts of land to certain settlers called *empresarios* who agreed to bring two hundred or more families into the area. Americans like Moses and Stephen Austin, who had helped to formulate the policy, responded eagerly, for Mexico was offering land virtually free in return for settlers' promises to become Mexican citizens and adopt the Catholic religion.

By 1835, 35,000 Americans, including many slaveholders, lived in Texas. These new settlers ignored local laws and oppressed native Mexicans, and when the Mexican government attempted to tighten its control over the region, a rebellion erupted. At the Alamo in San Antonio in 1836, fewer than 200 Texans made a heroic stand against 3,000 Mexicans under General Santa Anna. All the defenders of the fort, including Davy Crockett and Colonel James Bowie, died in the battle, and "Remember the Alamo" became the Texans' rallying cry. By the end of the year the Texans had won independence, delighting most Americans, some of whom saw the victory as a triumph of white Protestantism over Catholic Mexico.

Although they established an independent republic, Texans soon sought annexation to the United States. To many white Texans, an independent republic was but a means to joining the Union. President Sam Houston opened negotiations with Washington, but the issue became politically explosive. Southerners favored annexing the proslavery territory; antislavery forces, many northerners, and most Whigs opposed it. In view of the political dangers, President Jackson delayed recognition of Texas until after the election of 1836, and President Van Buren ignored annexation.

Rebuffed by the United States, Texans talked about developing close ties with the British and extending their republic all the way to the Pacific Coast. Faced with the specter of a rival republic to the south, and with British colonies already entrenched to the north, some Americans feared encirclement. If Texas reached the ocean and became an English ally, would not American independence be threatened?

Now President Tyler—committed to expansion, fearful of the Texans' talk of ties with the British, and eager to build political support in the South—pushed for annexation. But in April 1844 the Senate rejected a treaty of annexation. A letter from Secretary of State Calhoun to the British minister justifying annexation as a step in protecting slavery so outraged senators that the treaty was defeated 16 to 35.

Just as southerners sought expansion to the Southwest, northerners looked to the Northwest. In 1841 "Oregon fever" struck thousands. Lured by the glowing reports of missionaries, who seemed **Oregon Fever** to show as much interest in the Northwest's richness and beauty as in the conversion of the Indians, migrants organized hundreds of wagon trains and embarked on the Oregon Trail. The two-thousand-mile journey took six months or more, but within a few years five thousand settlers had arrived in the fertile Willamette Valley south of the Columbia River.

Since the Anglo-American convention of 1818, Britain and the United States had jointly occupied the disputed Oregon Territory (see page 229). Beginning with the administration of President John Quincy Adams, the United States had tried to fix the boundary at the 49th parallel, but Britain was determined to maintain access to the Puget Sound and the Columbia River. Time only increased the American appetite. In 1843 a Cincinnati convention demanded that the United States obtain the entire Oregon Territory, up to its northernmost border of 54°40'. Soon "Fifty-four Forty or Fight" had become the rallying cry of American expansionists.

The expansion into Oregon and the rejection of annexation of Texas, both favored by antislavery forces, heightened southern pessimism. Thus southern leaders became anxious about their **Election of 1844** diminishing ability to control the debate over slavery. Calhoun persuaded the 1844 Democratic convention to adopt a rule that the presidential nominee receive two-thirds of the convention votes. In effect, the southern states acquired a veto, and they used it to block Van Buren as the nominee. Calhoun had hated Van Buren since their days as rivals for Jackson's favor, and most southerners objected to his antislavery stance and opposition to Texas annexation. Instead, the party chose House Speaker James K. Polk, a hard-money Jacksonian and avid expansionist from Tennessee. The Whig leader Henry Clay, who opposed annexation, won his party's unanimous designation.

"Oregon Fever" lured thousands of men, women, and children to make the six-month, two-thousand-mile journey across the plains and mountains. They both succumbed to and fueled the spirit of Manifest Destiny. National Park Service.

The main plank of the Democratic platform called for occupation of the entire Oregon Territory and annexation of Texas. The Whigs, though they favored expansion, argued that the Democrats' belligerent nationalism would lead the nation to war with Great Britain or Mexico or both. Clay favored expansion through negotiation, not force.

But few militant expansionists supported Clay, and Polk and the Democrats captured the White House by 170 electoral votes to 105 (they won the popular vote by just 38,000 out of 2.7 million). Polk carried New York's 36 electoral votes by just 6,000 votes; abolitionist James G. Birney, the Liberty party candidate, drew almost 16,000 votes away from Clay, handing the state and the election to Polk. Thus abolitionist forces had influenced the choice of a president.

Interpreting Polk's victory as a mandate for annexation, President Tyler proposed in his last days in office that Texas be admitted by joint resolution of Congress. (The usual method of annexation, by treaty negotiation, required a two-thirds vote in the Senate—which expansionists clearly did not have. Joint resolution required only a simple majority in both houses.) Proslavery and antislavery congressmen debated the extension of slavery into the territory, and the resolution passed the House 120 to 98 and the Senate 27 to 25. Three days before leaving office, Tyler signed the measure. Mexico immediately broke relations with the United States; war loomed.

Politics, the reform spirit, and expansionism commingled in the 1830s and 1840s. Reform imbued with revivalism sought to bring order in a rapidly changing society. But reformers had no monopoly on claims of republican virtue; their opponents too claimed descent from the revolutionary values that held dear individual liberty. Once reform entered politics, it sparked a broader-based interest. Political organization and conflict stimulated even greater interest in campaigns and political issues. Eventually, however, one issue absorbed nearly all attention and created a crisis in the Union: slavery.

1790s–1840s	Second Great Awakening	1836	Republic of Texas established Specie Circular Van Buren elected president
1825	House of Representatives elects John Quincy Adams president	1837	Financial panic
1826	American Society for the Promotion of Temperance founded Morgan affair	1837–39	U.S.–Canada border tensions
		1837–48	Horace Mann heads Massachusetts Board of Education
1828	Tariff of Abominations Jackson elected president	1839–43	Depression
1830	Webster–Hayne debate	1840	Whigs under Harrison win presidency
1830s–1840s	Second party system	1841–47	Brook Farm
1831	*Liberator* begins publication First national Antimason Convention	1841	Tyler assumes the presidency Oregon fever
		1844	Polk elected president
1832	Veto of Second Bank of the United States recharter Jackson re-elected	1845	Texas admitted to the Union
		1846–47	Mormon trek to the Great Salt Lake
1832–33	Nullification crisis	1848	Woman's Rights Convention, Seneca Falls, New York

SUGGESTIONS FOR FURTHER READING

Religion and Revivalism

Leonard J. Arrington and Davis Bitton, *The Mormon Experience. A History of the Latter-day Saints* (1979); Whitney R. Cross, *The Burned-Over District* (1950); Leon A. Jick, *The Americanization of the Synagogue, 1820–1870* (1976); Charles A. Johnson, *The Frontier Camp Meeting* (1955); Paul E. Johnson, *A Shopkeeper's Millennium: Society and Revivals in Rochester, New York, 1815–1837* (1978); William G. McLoughlin, *Revivals, Awakenings, and Reform: An Essay on Religion and Social Change in America, 1607–1977* (1978); Perry Miller, *The Life of the Mind in America: From the Revolution to the Civil War* (1966); Timothy L. Smith, *Revivalism and Social Reform in Mid-Nineteenth Century America* (1957); William W. Sweet, *Revivalism in America* (1949).

Reform

Ray Allen Billington, *The Protestant Crusade, 1800–1860: A Study of the Origins of American Nativism* (1938); Henri Desroche, *The American Shakers from Neo-Christianity to Pre-Socialism* (1971); Lawrence Foster, *Religion and Sexuality: Three American Communal Experiments of the Nineteenth Century* (1981); Clifford S. Griffin, *The Ferment of Reform, 1830–1860* (1967); Clifford S. Griffin, *Their Brother's Keepers: Moral Stewardship in the United States, 1800–1865* (1960); Raymond Muncy, *Sex and Marriage in Utopian Communities:*

19th Century America (1973); Russel B. Nye, Society and Culture in America, 1830–1860 (1974); David J. Rothman, The Discovery of the Asylum: Social Order and Disorder in the New Republic (1971); Mary P. Ryan, Cradle of the Middle Class. The Family in Oneida County, New York, 1790–1865 (1981); Wallace Stegner, The Gathering of Zion: The Story of the Mormon Trail (1964); Alice Felt Tyler, Freedom's Ferment (1944); Ronald G. Walter, American Reformers, 1815–1860 (1978).

Temperance, Education, and Feminism

Barbara J. Berg, The Remembered Gate: Origins of American Feminism. The Woman and the City, 1800–1860 (1977); Lawrence A. Cremin, American Education: The National Experience, 1783–1876 (1980); Ellen C. Du Bois, Feminism and Suffrage: The Emergence of an Independent Woman's Movement in America 1848–1869 (1978); Barbara Leslie Epstein, The Politics of Domesticity. Women, Evangelism, and Temperance in Nineteenth-Century America (1981); Carl Kaestle, Pillars of the Republic: Common Schools and American Society, 1780–1860 (1982); Michael Katz, The Irony of Early School Reform (1968); Jonathan Messerli, Horace Mann (1972); W. J. Rorabaugh, The Alcoholic Republic: An American Tradition (1979); Ian R. Tyrrell, Sobering Up: From Temperance to Prohibition in Antebellum America, 1800–1860 (1979).

Antislavery and Abolitionism

Frederick Douglass, Life and Times of Frederick Douglass (1881); Martin Duberman, ed., The Anti-Slavery Vanguard (1965); Aileen S. Kraditor, Means and Ends in American Abolitionism: Garrison and His Critics on Strategy and Tactics (1967); Gerda Lerner, The Grimké Sisters of South Carolina (1967); William H. Pease and Jane H. Pease, They Would Be Free: Blacks' Search for Freedom, 1830–1861 (1974); Lewis Perry and Michael Fellman, eds., Antislavery Reconsidered (1979); Benjamin Quarles, Black Abolitionists (1969); Leonard L. Richards, "Gentlemen of Property and Standing": Anti-Abolition Mobs in Jacksonian America (1970); John L. Thomas, The Liberator: William Lloyd Garrison (1963); Ronald G. Walters, The Antislavery Appeal: American Abolitionism After 1830 (1976); Bertram Wyatt-Brown, Lewis Tappan and the Evangelical War Against Slavery (1969).

Andrew Jackson and the Jacksonians

Lee Benson, The Concept of Jacksonian Democracy: New York as a Test Case (1964); Richard B. Latner, The Presidency of Andrew Jackson (1979); Marvin Meyers, The Jacksonian Persuasion (1960); John Niven, Martin Van Buren (1983); Edward Pessen, Jacksonian America: Society, Personality, and Politics, rev. ed. (1979); Robert V. Remini, Andrew Jackson and the Course of American Democracy (1984); Robert V. Remini, Andrew Jackson and the Course of American Freedom, 1822–1832 (1981); Robert V. Remini, Andrew Jackson and the Bank War (1967); Arthur M. Schlesinger, Jr., The Age of Jackson (1945); John William Ward, Andrew Jackson: Symbol for an Age (1955); Harry L. Watson, Jacksonian Politics and Community Conflict. The Emergence of the Second American Party System in Cumberland County, North Carolina (1981); Major L. Wilson, The Presidency of Martin Van Buren (1984).

Democrats and Whigs

Ronald P. Formisano, The Transformation of Political Culture. Massachusetts Parties, 1790s–1840s (1983); Ronald P. Formisano, The Birth of Mass Political Parties: Michigan, 1827–1861 (1971); William W. Freehling, Prelude to Civil War: The Nullification Controversy in South Carolina (1966); Daniel Walker Howe, The Political Culture of the American Whigs (1979); Kathleen Smith Kutolowski, "Antimasonry Reexamined: Social Bases of the Grass-Roots Party," Journal of American History, 71 (September 1984), 269–293; Richard P. McCormick, The Second American Party System: Party Formation in the Jacksonian Era (1966); James Roger Sharp, The Jacksonians Versus the Banks. Politics in the States After the Panic of 1837 (1970); William Preston Vaughn, The Antimasonic Party in the United States 1826–1843 (1983).

Manifest Destiny and Foreign Policy

Norman B. Graebner, ed., Manifest Destiny (1968); Reginald Horsman, Race and Manifest Destiny (1981); Frederick Merk, Manifest Destiny and Mission in American History (1963); David M. Pletcher, The Diplomacy of Annexation: Texas, Oregon, and the Mexican War (1973); Charles G. Sellers, Jr., James K. Polk: Continentalist, 1843–1846 (1966); Paul A. Varg, United States Foreign Relations, 1820–1860 (1979); Albert K. Weinberg, Manifest Destiny (1935).

Territorial Expansion and Slavery: The Road to War

1845–1861

Chapter 13

"*Our people have* filled the eastern valley of the Mississippi, adventurously ascended the Missouri to its headsprings, and are already engaged in establishing the blessings of self-government in valleys of which the rivers flow to the Pacific. Our title to the country of Oregon," continued James K. Polk, "is 'clear and unquestionable.'" With these words, spoken in 1845, a new president made territorial expansion the centerpiece of his administration's agenda and pledged his support for Americans' expansionist energies. Many shared President Polk's enthusiasm and rejoiced when the nation obtained a vast western domain through war with Mexico. But expansion stirred conflict along with celebration, as Polk had reason to know. One year before, as a dark-horse candidate for the presidential nomination, Polk had little chance until that issue divided the Democratic party's convention. From the deadlocked convention he eventually emerged, victorious.

Fifteen years later the nation's territories figured prominently in another political gathering. In 1860 tense and angry Democrats gathered at Charleston for another nominating convention. Again the convention deadlocked, but this time there was no successful resolution. Charging that southern rights in the territories were being denied, delegates from six deep-South states walked out of the meeting amid cheers and applause from the Charleston gallery. That walkout destroyed the last remaining national party and began the destruction of the Union. Americans' fascination with new land had brought Texas, the West Coast, and the Southwest into the nation and launched the settling of the Great Plains, but ultimately it disrupted the Union.

Some experienced politicians had foreseen just such a result, because slavery lay at the root of territorial controversies. Each time the nation expanded it confronted a thorny issue—whether new territories and states should be slave or free. Over this question there were disagreements too violent to compromise. Sensing that fact, John C. Calhoun called Mexico "the forbidden fruit; the penalty of eating it would be to subject our institutions to political death." A host of political leaders, including Henry Clay, Lewis Cass, Stephen A. Douglas, and Presidents Jackson and Van Buren, labored from the 1830s through the 1850s to postpone or compromise disagreements about slavery in the territories. But repeatedly these disputes injected the bitterness surrounding slavery into national politics. If slavery was the sore spot in the body politic, territorial disputes were like salt rubbed into the sore.

Moreover, as Americans fought over slavery in the territories, the conflict broadened to encompass many other issues. The United States had always been a heterogeneous, diverse society, not a cohesive unit, but now various concerns became linked to one divisive issue instead of balancing each other off. Northerners came to believe that their liberties, political rights, and economic interests were under attack by an aggressive South. Southerners began to fear that their safety, rights, and prosperity were in peril from a hostile North. Citizens in both sections, North and South, worried that opportunity, a precious social commodity for themselves and their children, was at stake.

Battles over slavery in the territories broke the second party system apart and then shaped a realigned system that emphasized sectional enmity. Sectional parties replaced nationwide organizations. No matter how diverse the following of these sectional parties was, their rise was alarming; it seemed to confirm the trend toward disunion. In addition, it removed intraparty pressures for compromise and strengthened the hand of intransigent elements.

As parties clamored for support, and as citizens reflected on events, the feeling grew that North and South were too different to thrive within the same country. A northern ideology advanced by the new Republican party suggested that progress depended on the free labor, civil liberties, and economic change that the South opposed. A southern ideology depicted northern society as unstable, lacking in respect for the Constitution, and prone to interfere with slavery, which southerners claimed was the foundation of white equality and republicanism. Some concluded that the two sections had to separate.

Not all Americans were obsessed with these conflicts. In fact, the results of the 1860 presidential election strongly suggested that most voters wanted neither disunion nor civil war. Yet within six months they had both. By 1860 the cloud over the territories had grown into a storm. Both sections felt threatened and anxious, and an area of disagreement that once had been limited to a small minority of extremists now engaged two powerful groups: the victorious Republican party and defensive southern slaveholders. These groups were on a collision course, and they chose not to accept any of the desperate, last-minute compromises offered to resolve their differences. Because neither side gave in, conflict was inevitable. Because thousands who disagreed with the antagonists shared many of their fears, a vast Civil War began.

James K. Polk was an effective president who achieved his goals. But territorial expansion led to sectional conflict. Painting by George Peter Alexander Healy in the Collection of the Corcoran Gallery of Art.

CONFLICT BEGINS:
THE MEXICAN WAR

The Mexican War evoked enthusiasm and conflict, national pride and sectional suspicions. Americans learned of bold advances in the military theater and key victories by their soldiers. In the political theater Americans found themselves embroiled in serious and long-lasting divisions. The war introduced other, broader issues and entangled politicians in a growing number of problems related to slavery.

James K. Polk's territorial ambitions pushed events in the direction of war. Despite his claim, the United States's title to Oregon was not "clear and unquestionable." Since 1818 America and Britain had jointly occupied the disputed territory, and for over twenty years the British had refused to accept a boundary dividing the two nations' jurisdictions at the 49th parallel. But when he entered office, Polk found that Texas was the more pressing crisis. Congress's annexation of Texas had outraged Mexican leaders. They had severed relations with the United States, yet American ambitions in that region remained undiminished. Observers knew that war could break out at any time (see page 349).

Faced with imminent war in the Southwest, President Polk decided to use diplomacy to avoid a second conflict with Great Britain in the Northwest. Dropping the demand for a boundary at 54°40′, he kept up pressure on the British to accept the 49th parallel. Eventually, in 1846 Great Britain agreed. In the Oregon Treaty, the United States gained all of present-day Oregon, Washington, and Idaho and parts of Wyoming and Montana (see map, page 356).

Determined to acquire California and New Mexico in addition to all the land claimed by Texas, Polk charted a firm course in regard to Mexico. He ordered American troops to defend the border claimed by Texas but disputed by Mexico, and he attempted to buy a huge tract of land in the Southwest from the resentful Mexicans. After purchase failed Polk resolved to ask Congress for a declaration of war and set to work compiling a list of grievances. This task became unnecessary when word arrived that Mexican forces had engaged a body of American troops in disputed territory. American blood had been shed. Eagerly Polk declared that "war exists by the act of Mexico itself" and summoned the nation to arms.

Congress voted to recognize a state of war between

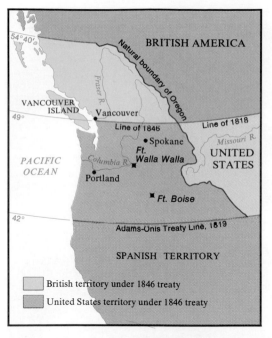

American Expansion in Oregon

Mexico and the United States in May 1846, but controversy rapidly grew. Public opinion about the war was sharply divided, with southwesterners enthusiastic and New Englanders strenuously opposed. In Congress Whigs charged that Polk had "literally provoked" an unnecessary war and "usurped the power of Congress by making war upon Mexico." The aged John Quincy Adams passionately opposed the war, dying after delivery of a powerful speech against it, and a tall young Whig from Illinois named Abraham Lincoln questioned its justification. Moreover, a small minority of antislavery Whigs agreed with abolitionists—the war was no less than a plot to extend slavery. Joshua Giddings of Ohio charged on the floor of the House that Polk's purpose was "to render slavery secure in Texas" and to extend the slave domain to vast expanses of new territory.

These charges fed fear of the Slave Power. Abolitionists long had warned that there was a Slave Power—a slaveholding oligarchy in control of the South and intent on controlling the **Idea of a** nation. In the South these dangerous **Slave Power** aristocrats had gained power by persecuting critics of slavery and suppressing their ideas. The Slave Power's assault on northern liberties, abolitionists argued, had begun in

1836, when Congress passed the gag rule (see page 333). Many white northerners, even those who saw nothing wrong with slavery, had viewed John Quincy Adams's stand against the rule as a defense of free speech and the right to petition. The fight over the gag rule increased the influence of the largely unpopular abolitionists. Anxieties about free speech and civil liberties first made the idea of a Slave Power credible.

Now the Mexican War increased fears of this sinister power. Sectional acrimony took a marked turn for the worse as Congress debated the conduct of the war. A Democratic representative **Wilmot** from Pennsylvania, David Wilmot, **Proviso** rose to offer an amendment to an appropriations bill in support of the war. Wilmot's Proviso added a simple but fateful condition: "neither slavery nor involuntary servitude shall ever exist" in any territory gained from Mexico. The proviso did not pass, and some observers did not immediately sense its significance. But within a few years the Wilmot Proviso became a rallying cry for abolitionists and Free-Soilers, and eventually fourteen northern legislatures endorsed it.

David Wilmot, significantly, was neither an abolitionist nor a Free-Soiler. He denied having any "squeamish sensitiveness upon the subject of slavery" or "morbid sympathy for the slave" and explained that his goal was to defend "the rights of white freemen." Wilmot wanted California "for free white labor"; he was fighting for opportunity for "the sons of toil, of my own race and own color." His involvement in antislavery controversy showed the alarming ability of the slavery issue to broaden through territorial questions.

Like Wilmot, most northerners were racists, not abolitionists. But fear of the Slave Power was transforming the abolitionist impulse into a broader and more potent antislavery movement, which terrified southern spokesmen. Northern voters, even antiblack voters, were becoming opponents of slavery. Their concern was to protect themselves, not southern blacks, from the Slave Power. As the issues of the day broadened, they excited larger numbers of people: more northerners cared about the Slave Power than about the extension of slavery, and more cared about slavery extension than about abolition. In the form of territorial controversies, issues that had at first alarmed only a few claimed the attention of many.

Despite this dissension at home, events on the battlefield went well for American troops, who as in previous wars were mainly volunteers furnished by the states. General Zachary Taylor's forces attacked and occupied Monterrey, securing northeastern Mexico (see map, page 359.) Polk then ordered Colonel Stephen Kearny and a small detachment to invade the remote and relatively unpopulated provinces of New Mexico and California. Taking Santa Fe without opposition, Kearney pushed into California, where he joined forces with rebellious American settlers, led by Captain John C. Frémont, and a couple of United States naval units. A quick victory was followed by reverses, but American soldiers soon re-established their dominance in distant and thinly populated California.

Meanwhile, General Winfield Scott led fourteen thousand men from Veracruz, on the Gulf of Mexico, toward Mexico City. This daring invasion was the decisive campaign of the war. After a series of hard-fought battles, Scott's men captured the Mexican capital and brought the war to an end. On February 2, 1848, representatives of both countries signed the Treaty of Guadalupe Hidalgo. The United States gained California and New Mexico (including present-day Nevada, Utah, and Arizona) and recognition of the Rio Grande as the southern boundary of Texas. In return, the American government agreed to settle the claims of its citizens against Mexico and to pay Mexico a mere $15 million.

Treaty of Guadalupe Hidalgo

The cost of the war included thirteen thousand Americans and fifty thousand Mexicans dead, plus Mexican-American enmity lasting into the twentieth century. But the domestic cost may have been even higher. The acquisition of new territory only fed sectional distrust and acrimony. Northerners and southerners disagreed with each other more frequently, and under the pressure of sectional issues, party unity for both Democrats and Whigs began to loosen.

Hoping to stem growing factionalism among Democrats, Polk had renounced a second term early in his administration. He also offered regular Democrats nearly all they could ask for in the way of traditional Jacksonian economic policy. He persuaded Congress to reinstitute the independent treasury system and to remove protectionist features from the tariff, and he vetoed internal improvements. But slavery in the

ANTI-TEXAS MEETING
AT FANEUIL HALL!

Friends of Freedom!

A proposition has been made, and will soon come up for consideration in the United States Senate, to annex Texas to the Union. This territory has been wrested from Mexico by violence and fraud. Such is the character of the leaders in this enterprise that the country has been aptly termed "that valley of rascals." It is large enough to make *nine* or *ten* States as large as Massachusetts. It was, under Mexico, a free territory. The freebooters have made it a slave territory. The design is to annex it, with its load of infamy and oppression, to the Union. The immediate result may be a war with Mexico—the ultimate result *will be* some 18 or 20 more slaveholders in the Senate of the United States, a still larger number in the House of Representatives, and the balance of power in hands of the South! And if, when in a minority in Congress, slaveholders browbeat the North, demand the passage of gag laws, trample on the Right of Petition, and threaten, in defiance of the General Government, to hang every man, caught at the South, who dares to speak against their "domestic institutions,"'what limits shall be set to their intolerant demands and high handed usurpations, when they are in the majority ?

All opposed to this scheme, of whatever sect or party, are invited to attend the meeting at the Old Cradle of Liberty, to-morrow, (Thursday Jan. 25,)at 10 o'clock, A. M., at which time addresses are expected from several able speakers.

Bostonians ! Friends of Freedom!! Let your voices be heard in loud remonstrance against this scheme, fraught with such ruin to yourselves and such infamy to your country.
January 24, 1838.

As this broadside shows, suspicion that the Slave Power sought additional territory and influence preceded the Mexican War and was deeply rooted. Library of Congress.

territories was one issue beyond solution by him or anyone else. When Polk recommended that Oregon be a free territory, southerners felt anew the old fear that congressional power would be used against slavery. Some northern expansionists, on the other hand, thought that Texas had received priority over Oregon due to a Slave Power plot.

In the presidential election of 1848 slavery in the territories was the one overriding issue. Both parties tried to push this question into the background, but it dominated the conventions, the campaign, and the election. The Democrats tried to avoid sectional conflict by nominating General Lewis Cass of Michigan for president and General William Butler of Kentucky for vice president. Cass devised the idea of "popular sovereignty" for the territories—letting residents in the territories decide the question of slavery for themselves. His party's platform declared that Congress did not have the power to interfere with slavery and criticized those who pressed the question. The Whigs nominated General Zachary Taylor, who was a southern slaveholder as well as a military hero, along with Millard Fillmore for vice president. Their convention similarly refused to assert

Election of 1848 and Popular Sovereignty

There was more to the Mexican War than romance and glory. Several fierce battles took place along the route of General Scott's invasion. West Point Museum.

that Congress had power over slavery in the territories. But the issue would not stay in the background.

Antislavery Whigs in the North were not satisfied with their party's stand, and many southern Democrats apparently voted for Taylor because he was a slaveholder. Some northern Democrats broke with their party and nominated former president Van Buren, who received support from the Liberty party and abolitionist Whigs and became the Free-Soil candidate. This new party, whose slogan was "Free soil, free speech, free labor, and free men," drew many northern votes away from Cass. In New York support for Free-Soil pulled enough votes away from the Democrat, Cass, to put Zachary Taylor in the White House. Sectional concerns were fragmenting the parties, and antislavery forces again had influenced the outcome of the election.

The election of 1848 and the conflict over slavery in the territories shaped politics in the 1850s. At the national level, all issues would be seen through the prism of sectional conflict over slavery in the

territories. The nation's uncertain attempts to deal with economic and social change would give way to more pressing questions about the nature of the Union itself. And the second party system would itself succumb to crisis.

TERRITORIAL PROBLEMS ARE COMPROMISED BUT RE-EMERGE

The first sectional battle of the decade involved the territory of California. More than eighty thousand Americans flooded into California in 1849. President Taylor, seeing a simple solution to the challenge of governing lands acquired from Mexico, urged the settlers to apply for admission to the Union. They promptly did so, submitting a proposed state

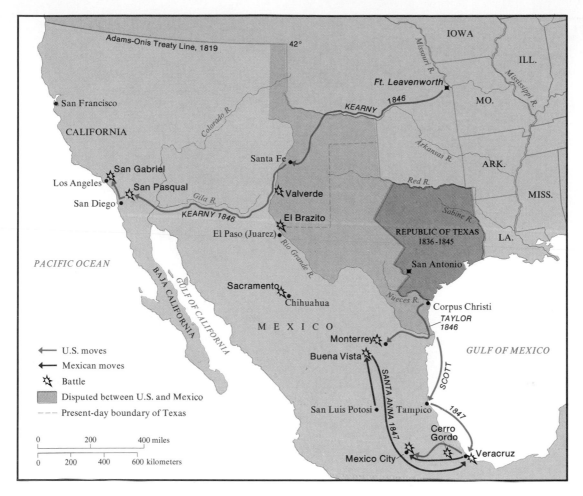

The Mexican War

constitution that did not allow for slavery. But southern politicians wanted to make California slave territory, or at least to extend the Missouri Compromise line west through California. Representatives from nine southern states met in an unofficial convention in Nashville to assert the South's right to part of the territory.

Sensing that the Union was in peril, the venerable Whig leader Henry Clay marshalled his energies once more. Twice before, in 1820 and 1833, the "Great Pacificator" had taken the lead in shaping sectional compromise; now he labored one last time to preserve the nation. To hushed Senate galleries Clay presented a series of compromise measures. Over the weeks that followed, Clay and Senator Stephen A. Douglas of Illinois steered their omnibus bill, or package of compromises, through debate and amendment.

The problems to be solved were thorny indeed. Would California or a part of it become a free state? How should the land acquired from Mexico be organized? Texas, which allowed slavery, claimed large portions of the new land as far west as Santa Fe, so that claim too had to be settled. And in addition to southern complaints that fugitive slaves were not being returned, as the Constitution required, and northern objections to the sale of human beings in the nation's capital, the lawmakers had to deal with competing theories of settlers' rights in the territories. It was these theories that proved most troublesome in the continuing debate over the territories.

Clay and Douglas hoped to avoid a specific formula and preserve the ambiguity that existed about settlers' rights in the territories. Lewis Cass's idea of popular sovereignty, for example, had both an attractive ring

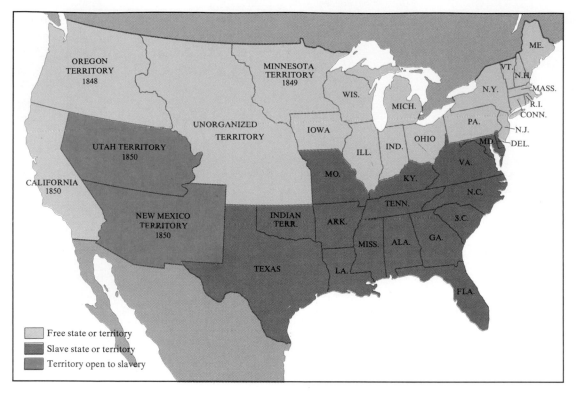

The Compromise of 1850

to it and a useful vagueness. Cass had observed that Congress could stay out of the territorial wrangle. Ultimately it would have to approve statehood for a territory, but Congress should "in the meantime," Cass said, allow the people living there "to regulate their own concerns in their own way." These few words, seemingly clear, proved highly ambiguous, disagreement centering on the meaning of "meantime."

When could settlers bar slavery? Southerners claimed that they had equal rights in the territories as well as in the nation. Therefore neither Congress nor a territorial legislature could bar slavery. Only when settlers framed a state constitution could they take that step. Northerners, meanwhile, argued that Americans living in a territory were entitled to local self-government, and thus could outlaw slavery at any time, if they allowed it at all. To avoid dissension within their party, northern and southern Democrats had explained Cass's statement to their constituents in these two incompatible ways. Their conflicting interpretations caused strong disagreement in the debate on Clay's proposals.

After months of labor, Clay and Douglas finally brought their package to a vote, and met defeat. But the determined Douglas had not given up. With Clay sick and absent from Washington, Douglas brought the compromise measures up again, one at a time. Congress lacked a majority to approve the package, but Douglas shrewdly realized that different majorities might be created for each of the measures. The strategy worked, and Douglas's resourcefulness salvaged a positive result from six months of congressional effort. The Compromise of 1850, as it was called, became law.

Under the terms of its various measures, California was admitted as a free state, and the Texan boundary was set at its present limits (see map). The United States paid Texas $10 million in **Compromise of 1850** consideration of the boundary agreement. And the territories of New Mexico and Utah were organized with power to legislate on "all rightful subjects . . . consistent with the Constitution." A stronger fugitive slave law and an act to suppress the slave trade in the District of Columbia completed the compromise.

Chapter 13: TERRITORIAL EXPANSION AND SLAVERY, 1845–1861

Jubilation greeted passage of the Compromise of 1850; in Washington, crowds celebrated the happy news. "On one glorious night," records a modern historian, "the word went abroad that it was the duty of every patriot to get drunk. Before the next morning many a citizen had proved his patriotism," and several prominent senators "were reported stricken with a variety of implausible maladies—headaches, heat prostration, or overindulgence in fruit."

In reality, there was less cause for celebration than citizens thought. Fundamentally, the Compromise of 1850 was not a settlement of sectional disputes. It was at best an artful evasion. Douglas had found a way to pass his proposals without getting northerners and southerners to come to agreement on them; neither side had given up anything. Though this compromise bought time for the nation, it did not create guidelines for the settlement of future territorial questions. It merely put them off.

Furthermore, the compromise had two basic flaws. The first pertained to popular sovereignty. What were "rightful subjects of legislation, consistent with the Constitution"? During debate, southerners asserted that this meant there would be no prohibition of slavery during the territorial stage; northerners declared that settlers could bar slavery whenever they wished. After passage of the compromise, legislators from the two sections went home and explained the act in these different ways, as if there were two different compromises. (In fact, the compromise admitted the disagreement by providing for the appeal of a territorial legislature's action to the Supreme Court. But no such case ever arose.) Thus, in the controversy over popular sovereignty, nothing had been settled. In one politician's words, the legislators seemed to have enacted a lawsuit instead of a law.

The second flaw lay in the Fugitive Slave Act, which stirred up controversy instead of laying it to rest. The new law empowered slaveowners to go into court in their own states and present

Fugitive Slave Act

evidence that a slave who owed them service had escaped. The transcript of such a proceeding, including a description of the fugitive, was to be taken as conclusive proof of a person's slave status, even in free states and territories. Legal authorities had to decide only whether the black person brought before them was the person described, not whether

he or she was indeed a slave. Fees and penalties encouraged U.S. marshals to assist in apprehending fugitives and discouraged citizens from harboring them. (Authorities were paid $10 if the alleged fugitive was turned over to the slaveowner, $5 if he was not.)

Abolitionist newspapers quickly attacked the fugitive slave law as a violation of the Bill of Rights. Why were alleged fugitives denied a trial by jury before being sent to bondage in a slave state? Why did suspected fugitives have no right to present evidence or cross-examine witnesses? Did not the law give authorities a financial incentive to turn prisoners over to slaveowners? These arguments convinced some northerners that free blacks could be sent into slavery, mistakenly or otherwise, with no means to defend themselves. Protest meetings were held in Massachusetts, New York, Pennsylvania, northern Ohio, northern Illinois, and elsewhere. In Boston in 1851, a mob grabbed a runaway slave from a U.S. marshal and sent him to safety in Canada.

At this point a relatively unknown writer dramatized the plight of the slave in a way that captured the sympathies of millions of northerners. Harriet Beecher

Uncle Tom's Cabin

Stowe, daughter of a religious New England family that had produced many prominent ministers, wrote *Uncle Tom's Cabin* out of deep moral conviction. Her book, published in March 1852, showed how slavery brutalized the men and women who suffered under it. Stowe also portrayed slavery's evil effects on slaveholders, indicting the institution itself more harshly than the southerners caught in its web. In nine months the book sold over 300,000 copies; by mid-1853, over a million. Countless people saw *Uncle Tom's Cabin* performed as a stage play or read similar novels inspired by it. Stowe had brought the issue of slavery home to many who had never before given it much thought.

The popularity of *Uncle Tom's Cabin* alarmed and appalled many southerners, who had long been sensitive about slavery. Southern leaders were intelligent men who were fully aware of the worldwide movement away from slavery and the forces gathering against it within the United States. They were also men who tended to see the world from the perspective of their plantations. Human bondage was so central to their world that life without slavery was almost unimaginable to them. They had built their fortunes

Holy Bible.
Thou shalt not deliver unto the master his servant that has escaped from his master unto thee. He shall dwell with thee. Even among you in that place which he shall choose in one of thy gates where it liketh him best. Thou shalt not oppress him.
Deut XXIII 15.16

Effects of the Fugitive-Slave-Law.

Declaration of independence.
We hold that all men are created equal: that they are endowed by their Creator with certain unalienable rights, that among these are life, liberty and the pursuit of happiness.

Despite their racial prejudice, many northerners disapproved of slavery and viewed summary proceedings that could send a man into slavery as contrary to the Bill of Rights. Library of Congress.

and their society on the institution of slavery, and they wanted to keep the world they knew. Accordingly, they fought every battle in the sectional crisis with a white-hot intensity. In so doing, they developed a variety of proslavery arguments.

Some southerners tried to prove the necessity of expanding slavery into the territories. Expansion was essential to the welfare of the Negro, they declared, for prejudice lessened as the concentration of blacks decreased. It was necessary to the prosperity of the South, they argued, for rich opportunities lay waiting in the territories, while older areas of declining fertility had surplus slave populations. Yet there was a noticeable absence of huge migrations of slaveholders into the territories. A more likely cause of southern concern over the territories was the fear that if nearby areas became free soil, they would be used as bases from which to spread abolitionism into the slave states. Jefferson Davis of Mississippi voiced such a concern when he wrote in 1855 that "abolitionism would gain but little in excluding slavery from the territories, if it were never to disturb that institution in the States."

To counter indictments of slavery as a moral wrong, proslavery theorists elaborated numerous arguments based on partially scientific or pseudoscientific data.

Proslavery Theories

At a moment's notice southern writers or politicians could discuss anthropological evidence for the separate origin of the races; physicians' views on the inferiority of the black body; and sociological arguments for the superiority of the slave-labor system. Writers explained the history of ancient races or the new "science" of phrenology. Its data on the external dimensions of human skulls and the volume of the cranial cavity "proved" that blacks were a separate and inferior race. One southern sociologist, a Virginian named George Fitzhugh, focused on relations between management and labor in both the North and the South. He concluded that wage labor in industry was more inhumane than slavery because employers cared nothing about wage laborers as people and turned them out when they grew old or sick, in contrast to paternalistic slaveowners. From these points Fitzhugh drew an extreme conclusion—slavery ought to be practiced in all societies, whatever their racial composition.

But in private and in their hearts, most of these men fell back on two rationales: a belief that blacks were inferior and biblical accounts of slaveholding. Among friends, Jefferson Davis ignored all the latest racist theories and reverted to the eighteenth-century argument that southerners were doing the best they could with a situation they had inherited. "Is it well to denounce an evil for which there is no cure?" he asked. On another occasion, repeating the widespread belief that living with a sizable free black population was impossible, he protested to a friend that Congress never discussed "any thing but that over which we have no control, slavery of the negro."

To try to control Congress, southern leaders relied on their chief tool in defending slavery: constitutional theory. They developed an interpretation of the Constitution and the principles of American government that linked them to the founding fathers and the original purposes of the nation. Drawing on Thomas Jefferson's concept of strict construction, they emphasized that the nation arose from a compact among sovereign states; that the states were primary and the central government secondary; that the states retained all powers not expressly granted to the central government; and that the states were to be treated equally. Along with these theories went the philosophy that the power of the federal government should be kept to a minimum. By keeping government close to home, southerners hoped to maintain slavery.

Many of them hoped that slavery would be secure and allowed to expand under the administration of a new president. Franklin Pierce, a Democrat from New Hampshire, won a smashing victory in 1852 over the Whig presidential nominee, General Winfield Scott. Pierce's victory derived less from his strengths than from his opponents' weaknesses. The Whigs had been a congressional party that was competitive with the Democrats in the states and strong in the nation's legislature, but lacked commanding presidents in an era of strong leaders like Jackson and Polk. Sectional discord was steadily splitting the party up into southern and northern

Election of 1852

wings that cooperated less and less. The deaths of President Taylor (1850), Daniel Webster (1852), and Henry Clay (1852) deprived the party of the few dominant personalities it had, and no new leaders emerged to solve its problems. The Whig party in 1852 ran on little but its past reputation, and many politicians were predicting its demise.

But southerners were pleased that Pierce made no secret of his belief that the defense of each section's rights was essential to the nation's unity. Americans hoped that Pierce's firm support for the Compromise of 1850 might end sectional divisions. By comparison Scott's views on the compromise were unknown, and the Free-Soil candidate, John P. Hale of New Hampshire, openly repudiated it. Thus Pierce's victory seemed to confirm most Americans' support for the Compromise of 1850.

But Pierce did not seem able to avoid sectional conflict. His proposal for a transcontinental railroad ran into congressional dispute over where it should be built, North or South. His attempts to acquire foreign territory stirred up more trouble. An annexation treaty with Hawaii failed because southern senators would not vote for another free state, and Pierce's efforts to annex Cuba angered antislavery northerners. Pierce tried to purchase Cuba from Spain in 1854. When publication of a government document, the Ostend Manifesto, revealed that three administration officials had rashly talked of "wresting" Cuba from Spain, some northerners concluded that Pierce was determined to acquire more slave territory. The new president's efforts to avoid slavery controversies were heading toward failure when another territorial bill threw Congress, and the nation, into a bitter conflict that had significant results.

TERRITORIAL PROBLEMS SHATTER THE PARTY SYSTEM

The new controversy began in a surprising way. Stephen A. Douglas, one of the architects and manager of the Compromise of 1850, introduced a bill to establish the Kansas and Nebraska territories.

Although Douglas had no reason to attack the compromise, which lent him fame, he did have other concerns and goals. Douglas was from Illinois, a state whose economy benefited from settlement on the Great Plains. A midwestern transcontinental railroad would accelerate this process, but a necessary precondition for such a railroad was the organization of the territory it would cross. Thus it was probably in the interest of building such a railroad that Douglas introduced a bill that inflamed sectional passions, completed the destruction of the Whig party, damaged the northern wing of the Democratic party, gave birth to the Republican party, and injured his own ambitions for national office.

The Kansas-Nebraska bill exposed the first flaw of the Compromise of 1850, and conflict over popular sovereignty erupted once more. Douglas's bill clearly left "all questions pertaining to slavery in the Territories . . . to the people residing therein," but northerners and southerners still disagreed violently over what territorial settlers could constitutionally do. Moreover, the Kansas-Nebraska bill opened a new Pandora's box. The new territories lay within the Louisiana Purchase, and under the Missouri Compromise all that land from 36°30′ north to the Canadian border was off-limits to slavery. Thus, if popular sovereignty were to mean anything in Kansas or Nebraska, it had to mean that the Missouri Compromise no longer was in force. If settlers were to have a choice, they could choose slavery.

Kansas-Nebraska Bill

Southern congressmen, anxious to establish the slaveholders' right to take their slaves into any territory, pressed Douglas to concede this point. He needed southern votes to win passage of his bill, and southerners demanded an explicit repeal of the 36°30′ limitation as the price of their support. During a carriage ride with Senator Archibald Dixon of Kentucky, Douglas debated the point at length. Finally he made an impulsive decision: "By God, Sir, you are right. I will incorporate it in my bill, though I know it will raise a hell of a storm."

Douglas did not regard his bill as a proslavery measure, for he believed that conditions of climate and soil would effectively keep slavery out of Kansas and Nebraska. But the fact remained that his bill threw land open to slavery where it had been prohibited before. This fact immediately generated opposition from free-soil and antislavery forces. The struggle in Congress was titanic and lasted three and one-half months. Douglas obtained the support of President Pierce, and eventually he prevailed: the bill became law in May 1854 (see map). Unfortunately the storm—far more violent than Douglas had imagined—was just beginning. The Kansas-Nebraska Act inflamed fears and angers that had only simmered before. Abolitionists charged that the act was sinister aggression by the Slave Power, its most brazen yet. Concern over the fugitive slave law deepened: between 1855 and 1859 Connecticut, Rhode Island, Massachusetts, Michigan, Maine, Ohio, and Wisconsin passed personal liberty laws designed to interfere with the swift action of the Fugitive Slave Act. These laws, which provided counsel for alleged fugitives and sought to guarantee trial by jury, revealed the strength of northern fear of the Slave Power. To the South, they were outrageous signs of bad faith, a refusal to honor the Compromise of 1850. Even more important, however, was the devastating impact of the Kansas-Nebraska Act on political parties.

The Kansas-Nebraska Act cemented the division of the Whig party into northern and southern wings so irrevocably that it ceased to exist as a national organization and could no longer compete politically. One of the two great parties in the second party system was now gone. The Democrats survived, but their support in the North fell drastically in the 1854 elections. Northern Democrats lost sixty-six of the ninety-one congressional seats they had won in free states in 1852.

Moreover, anger over the territorial issue created a new political party. During debate on the Kansas-Nebraska bill, six congressmen had published an "Appeal of the Independent Democrats," attacking Douglas's legislation as "a gross violation of a sacred pledge" (the Missouri Compromise) and a "criminal betrayal of precious rights" that would make free territory a "dreary region of despotism." This appeal sparked other protests. In the summer and fall of 1854, antislavery Whigs and Democrats, Free-Soilers, and other reformers throughout the Northwest met to form a new Republican party, dedicated to keeping slavery out of the territories. The Republicans' influence rapidly spread to the East, and they won a stunning victory

The New Republican Party

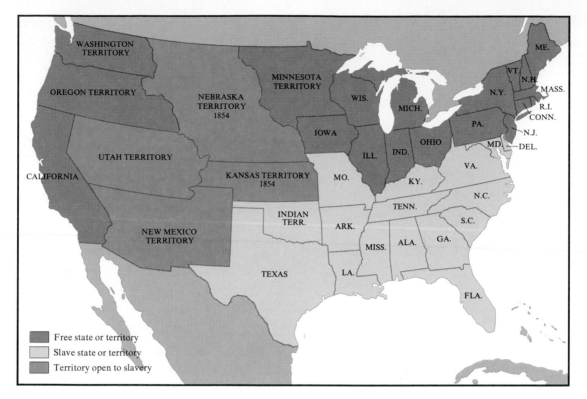

The Kansas-Nebraska Act, 1854

Free state or territory
Slave state or territory
Territory open to slavery

in the 1854 elections. In the party's first appearance on the ballot, Republicans captured a majority of House seats in the North.

For the first time, a sectional party based on a sectional issue had gained significant power in the political system. In the second party system, Whigs and Democrats had been strong in both the North and the South. The national base of support enjoyed by each had moderated sectional conflict, as party leaders compromised to achieve unity. To compete more effectively for national office, the two parties had always papered over their own sectional differences. But now the Whigs were gone, and politics in the 1850s would never be the same. Henceforth, Democrats would struggle to maintain a national following while the new Republican party flourished in a sectional context by exploiting sectional concerns.

Nor were Republicans the only new party. An anti-immigrant organization, the American party, also seemed likely for a few years to replace the Whigs.

Know-Nothings
This party, popularly known as the Know-Nothings (because its members at first kept their purposes se-

cret, answering all queries with the words "I know nothing"), exploited nativist fear of foreigners. Between 1848 and 1860, nearly 3.5 million immigrants came to the United States—proportionally the heaviest influx of foreigners in American history (see pages 280–284). The Democratic party diligently ministered to the needs of these new citizens and relied on their votes in elections. But native-born Americans harbored serious misgivings about them. The temperance movement gained new strength early in these years, promising to stamp out the evils associated with liquor and immigrants. It was in this context that the Know-Nothings became prominent, campaigning to reinforce Protestant morality and restrict voting and office-holding to the native-born.

By the mid-1850s the American party was powerful and growing; in 1854 so many new congressmen won office with anti-immigrant as well as antislavery support that Know-Nothings could claim they outnumbered Republicans. But like the Whigs, the Know-Nothings could not keep their northern and southern wings together, and they melted away after 1856. That left the field to the Republicans, who wooed the nativists

POLITICAL SUCCESSORS TO THE WHIG PARTY

Party	Period of Influence	Area of Influence	Outcome
Free-Soil party	1848–1854	North	Merged with Republican party
Know-Nothings (American party)	1853–1856	Nationwide	Disappeared, freeing some northern voters to join Republican party
Republican party	1854–present	North (later nationwide)	Became rival of Democratic party in third party system

and in several states passed temperance ordinances and laws postponing suffrage for naturalized citizens (see table).

Republicans, Know-Nothings, and Democrats were all scrambling to attract former Whig voters. The death of that party insured a major realignment of the political system. For practical politicians the grand prize was the old Whig following, a magnificent block of voters that once had accounted for approximately half the electorate. To woo these homeless Whigs, the remaining parties stressed a variety of issues chosen to appeal for one reason or another. Immigration, temperance, homestead bills, the tariff, internal improvements—all played an important role in attracting voters during the 1850s. For many Americans it was these issues, not the controversy over slavery, that were the real stuff of politics.

Realignment of Political System

The Republicans appealed strongly to groups interested in the economic development of the West. Commercial agriculture was booming in the Ohio–Mississippi–Great Lakes area, but residents of that region needed more canals, roads, and river and harbor improvements to reap the full benefit of their labors. Because credit was scarce, there was also widespread interest in a federal land-grant program: its proponents argued that western land should be

Republican Appeals

made available free to those who would use it. The Whigs had favored all these things before their party collapsed, but the Democrats resolutely opposed them. Following long-standing party principles, Democratic presidents vetoed internal improvements bills and a homestead bill as late as 1859. Seizing their opportunity, the Republicans added internal improvements and land-grant planks to their platform. They also backed higher tariffs as an enticement to industrialists and businessmen, whose interest in tariffs was quickened by a panic, or recession, in 1857.

Another major feature of the realigned political system was ideology, and ideological appeals had a significant impact on the sectional crisis. In the North, Republicans attracted many voters through effective use of ideology. They spoke to the image that northerners had of themselves, their society, and their future when they preached "Free Soil, Free Labor, Free Men." These phrases resonated with traditional ideals of equality, liberty, and opportunity under self-government—the heritage of republicanism. Use of that heritage also undercut charges that the Republican party was radical and unreliable.

"Free Soil, Free Labor, Free Men" seemed to fit with a northern economy that was energetic, expanding, and prosperous. Untold thousands of farmers had moved west to establish productive farms and growing communities. Midwestern farmers were using machines that multiplied their yields. Railroads were

Republican support for roads, canals, river and harbor improvements, and free homesteads appealed powerfully to those who were settling the thriving states of the upper Middle West. Copyright © 1971, The R. W. Norton Art Gallery, Shreveport, La. Used by permission.

carrying their crops to market. And industry was beginning to perform wonders of production, making available goods that had hitherto been beyond the reach of the average person. As northerners surveyed the general growth and prosperity, they thought they saw a reason for it.

The key to progress seemed, in the eyes of many, to be free labor. People believed in the dignity of labor and the incentive of opportunity. Any hardworking, virtuous person, it was thought, could improve his condition and gain economic independence by applying himself to opportunities that the country had to offer. Republicans pointed out that the South, which relied on slave labor and was not industrializing, appeared backward

Republican Ideology

and retrograde in comparison. Praising both laborers and opportunity, the Republican party projected an ideology that captured much of the spirit of the age in the North.

In the tradition of Republicanism the virtuous citizen, unhindered by aristocrats and strong by virtue of his liberty, character, and aspirations, was the backbone of the country. As a contemporary symbol of the tradition, Republicans held up Abraham Lincoln as an example of a person of humble origins who had improved his lot and became a successful lawyer and political leader. They portrayed their party as the guardian of economic opportunity, working to ensure that individuals could continue to apply their energies to the land's resources and attain success. In the words of an Iowa Republican, the United

The Republicans had to appeal to various reformers and interests in order to build a winning coalition. This Democratic cartoon tries to ridicule the new party as a collection of dangerous and selfish cranks. Library of Congress.

States was thriving because its "door is thrown open to all, and even the poorest and humblest in the land, may, by industry and application, gain a position which will entitle him to the respect and confidence of his fellow-men."

Thus the Republican party picked up support from a variety of sources. Opposition to the extension of slavery had brought the party together, but party members carefully broadened their appeal by adopting the causes of other groups, whether or not those groups were alarmed by slavery. They were wise to do so. As the newspaper editor Horace Greeley wrote in 1856, "It is beaten into my bones that the American people are not yet anti-slavery." Four years later Greeley observed again, "An Anti-Slavery man *per se* cannot be elected." But, he added, "a Tariff, River-and-Harbor, Pacific Railroad, Free Homestead man, *may* succeed *although* he is Anti-Slavery."

Greeley's last remark was insightful. The Republican party was an amalgam of many interests, but functionally it had only one stand in the North-South controversy. Since a high proportion of the original activist Republicans were strongly opposed to slavery, the party's position on slavery and the territories was immune to change. Thus all Republicans, whatever their reasons for joining the coalition, weighed as antislavery voters in the minds of nervous southerners. Republican strength was antislavery strength. The process of party building was linking voters to the sectional conflict, whether the issue of slavery seemed important to them or not.

A similar process was under way in the South. The disintegration of the Whig party had left many southerners at loose ends politically, including a good number of wealthy planters, small-town businessmen,

Southern Democrats

and slaveholders. Some of these people gravitated to the American party, but not for long. In the increasingly tense atmosphere of sectional crisis, they were highly susceptible to strong states'-rights positions, which provided a handy defense for slavery. Democratic leaders markedly increased their use of such appeals during the 1850s and managed to convert most of the formerly Whig slaveholders. Democrats spoke to the class interests of slaveholders, and the slaveholders responded.

Most Democrats south of the Mason-Dixon line, however, were not slaveholders. Since Andrew Jackson's day, small farmers had been the heart of the Democratic party. Democratic politicians, though often slaveowners themselves, had lauded the common man and argued that their policies advanced his interests. According to the southern version of republicanism, white citizens in a slave society enjoyed liberty and social equality because the black race was enslaved. Slavery supposedly prevented the evil of aristocracy by making all white men equal. As Jefferson Davis put it in 1851, other societies undermined the status of the common white because in them social distinctions were drawn "by property, between the rich and the poor." In the South, however, slavery elevated every white person's status and allowed the non-slaveholder to *stand upon the broad level of equality with the rich man.* To retain the support of ordinary whites, southern Democrats emphasized this argument and appealed to racism. The issue in the sectional crisis, they warned, was "shall negroes govern white men, or white men govern negroes?"

Southern leaders also portrayed sectional controversies as matters of injustice and insult to all southerners. The rights of all southerners, they argued, were in jeopardy because antislavery and Free-Soil forces were undermining the principle of self-government. They were attacking an institution protected by the Constitution, and thus northern agitators were damaging rights precious to southerners. Although the stable, well-ordered South was the true defender of constitutional principles, runaway change in the North was subverting the government.

These arguments had their effect, and racial fears and traditional political loyalties helped keep the political alliance between yeoman farmers and planters intact through the 1850s. No viable party emerged in the South to replace the Whigs. The result was a one-party system there that emphasized sectional issues. No one raised potential conflicts of interest between slaveholders and nonslaveholders. Instead, in the South as in the North, political realignment obscured support for the Union and made sectional divisions seem even sharper and deeper than they really were.

In both sections political leaders were arguing that opportunity was threatened. The *Montgomery (Alabama) Mail* blatantly claimed that the aim of the Republicans was "to free the negroes and force amalgamation between them and the children of the poor men of the South. The rich will be able to keep out of the way of the contamination." Republicans likewise were charging that if slavery entered the territories, the great reservoir of opportunity for decent people without means would be poisoned. The North's free labor system had to be extended to the territories if coming generations were to prosper. These claims and counterclaims aroused anxieties and fears and made the gap between the sections even wider.

Like successive hammer blows, events also continued to drive North and South further apart. Controversy over Kansas did not subside; it grew. For among the settlers in the territory were partisans of both sides, each determined to make Kansas free or slave. Abolitionists and religious groups sent Free-Soil settlers to save the territory from slavery; southerners sent their own reinforcements, fearing that "northern hordes" were about to steal Kansas away. Clashes between the two groups led to violence, and soon the whole nation was talking about "Bleeding Kansas."

Indeed, political processes in the territory resembled war more than democracy. When elections for a territorial legislature were held in 1855, thousands of proslavery Missourians invaded the polls and ran up a large but unlawful majority for slavery candidates. The legislature that resulted promptly legalized slavery, and in response Free-Soilers called an unauthorized convention and created their own government and constitution. A proslavery posse sent to arrest the Free-Soil leaders sacked the town of Lawrence; in revenge, John Brown, a fanatic who saw himself as God's instrument to destroy slavery, murdered five proslavery settlers. Soon armed bands of guerrillas roamed the state, battling over land claims as well as slavery.

Bleeding Kansas

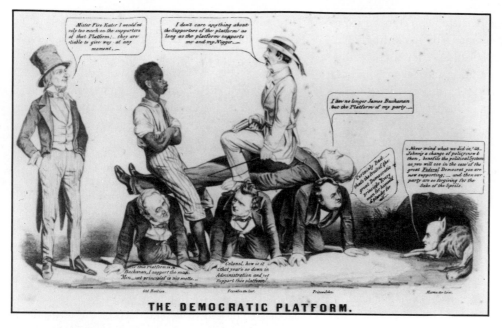

THE DEMOCRATIC PLATFORM.

Growing divisions within the Democratic party provided the opportunity for this Republican cartoon, which suggests that violent slaveholders run a party held together only by Buchanan's unknown views and the lust for spoils. Library of Congress.

The passion generated by this conflict erupted in the chamber of the United States Senate in May 1856, when Charles Sumner of Massachusetts denounced "the Crime against Kansas." Idealistic and radical in his antislavery views, Sumner censored the president, the South, and Senator Andrew P. Butler of South Carolina. Soon thereafter Butler's nephew, Representative Preston Brooks, approached Sumner at his Senate desk and beat him brutally with a cane. Voters in Massachusetts and South Carolina seethed; the country was becoming polarized.

The election of 1856 showed how far the polarization had gone. When Democrats met to select a nominee, they shied away from prominent leaders whose views on the territories were well known. Instead they chose James Buchanan of Pennsylvania, whose chief virtue was that he had been in Britain for four years, serving as ambassador, and thus had not been involved in territorial controversies. This anonymity and superior party organization helped Buchanan win 1.8 million votes and the election, but he owed his victory to southern support. Eleven of sixteen free states voted against him, and Democrats did not regain

power in those states for decades. The Republican candidate, John C. Frémont, won those eleven free states and 1.3 million votes; Republicans had become the dominant party in the North. The Know-Nothing candidate, Millard Fillmore, won almost 1 million votes, but this election was his party's last hurrah. The future battle was between a sectional Republican party and an increasingly divided Democratic party.

CONTROVERSY DEEPENS INTO CONFRONTATION

For years the issue of slavery in the territories had convulsed Congress, and for years the members of Congress had tried to settle the issue with vague formulas. In 1857 a different branch of government stepped onto the scene with a different approach. The Supreme Court addressed this emotion-charged subject and attempted to lay controversy to rest with a definitive verdict.

A Missouri slave named Dred Scott had sued his owner for his freedom. Dred Scott based his suit on the fact that his former owner, an army surgeon,

Dred Scott Case had taken him for several years into Illinois, a free state, and into the Wisconsin Territory, from which slavery had been barred by the Missouri Compromise. Scott first won and then lost his case as it moved on appeal through the state courts, into the federal system, and finally after eleven years to the Supreme Court.

Normally this was the type of case that the Supreme Court avoided. Its justices were reluctant, as a rule, to inject themselves into political battles, and it seemed likely that the Court would stay out of this one. An 1851 decision had declared that state courts had the last word in determining the status of Negroes who lived within their jurisdiction. The Supreme Court had only to follow this precedent to avoid ruling on substantive, and very controversial, matters.

The case raised an array of potentially disturbing questions: Was a Negro like Dred Scott a citizen and eligible to sue? Had residence in free territory made him free? And did Congress have the power to prohibit slavery in a territory or to delegate that power to a territorial legislature? Behind that last question lay all the disagreement that Lewis Cass, Henry Clay, Stephen Douglas, and others had tried to paper over.

For a long time it appeared that the Supreme Court would dispose of *Dred Scott* v. *Sanford* by following the 1851 precedent. At its conference the Court had even assigned one justice the task of writing such an opinion. Then the Court suddenly decided to change its plan and to rule on the Missouri Compromise. The change occurred for a number of reasons. Two northerners on the Court indicated that they would dissent from the planned ruling and argue for Scott's freedom and for the constitutionality of the Missouri Compromise. Their action pressured those who disagreed with them to answer their arguments. Southern members of the Court also had some desire to declare the 1820 compromise unconstitutional, and many of the justices felt the Court should try to resolve an issue whose uncertainties had caused so much strife.

Thus, on March 6, 1857, Chief Justice Roger B.

Roger B. Taney, Chief Justice of the Supreme Court from 1836 to 1864, presided over many major cases. But his decision in Dred Scott v. Sanford fanned the fires of sectional conflict. Supreme Court of the United States.

Taney delivered the majority opinion of a divided Court. Taney declared that Scott was not a citizen either of the United States or Missouri; that residence in free territory did not make Scott free; and most important, that Congress lacked the power to bar slavery from a territory, as it had done in the Missouri Compromise. Not only did the decision overturn a sectional compromise that had been venerated for years, it also said that the basic ideas of the Wilmot Proviso, and probably popular sovereignty, were not valid. In addition to being controversial in content, the decision had been reached in a manner that aroused sectional suspicions. The majority of the justices were southern; only one northerner had agreed with them. Three northern justices actively dissented or refused to concur in crucial parts of the decision.

A storm of angry reaction broke in the North. The decision alarmed a wide variety of northerners—abolitionists, would-be settlers in the West, and those who hated black people but feared the influence of the South. Every charge against the aggressive Slave Power seemed now to be confirmed. "There is such a thing as THE SLAVE POWER," warned the *Cincinnati Daily Commercial*. "It has marched over and annihilated the boundaries of the states. We are now one great homogenous slaveholding community." And the *Cincinnati Freeman* asked, "What security have the Germans and Irish that their children will not, within a hundred years, be reduced to slavery in this land of their adoption?" Echoed the *Atlantic Monthly*, "Where will it end? Is the success of this conspiracy to be final and eternal?" The poet James Russell Lowell both stimulated and expressed the anxieties of poor northern whites when he had his Yankee narrator, Ezekiel Biglow, say,

> Wy, it's jest ez clear ez figgers,
>   Clear ez one an' one make two,
> Chaps thet make black slaves o' niggers,
>   Want to make wite slaves o' you.

Republican politicians capitalized on these fears, building their coalition of abolitionists, who opposed slavery on moral grounds, and racists, who feared that slavery jeopardized their interests. Indeed, Abraham Lincoln's greatest achievement in the 1850s, one historian has pointed out, was as a Republican political propagandist against slavery. Lincoln cloaked the crudest charges against the Slave Power in language of biblical majesty, chilling thousands of voters. The South threatened democracy, he argued, and slavery threatened all whites.

Abraham Lincoln on the Slave Power

At the crux of the matter was the self-interest of whites. Pointing to the southern obsession with the territories, Lincoln had declared as early as 1854 that "the whole nation is interested that the best use shall be made of these Territories. We want them for homes of free white people. This they cannot be, to any considerable extent, if slavery shall be planted within them." The territories must be reserved, he now insisted, "as an outlet for *free white people everywhere*" so that immigrants could come to America and "find new homes and better their condition in life." After the Dred Scott decision, Lincoln charged that the next step in the unfolding Slave Power conspiracy would be a Supreme Court decision "declaring that the Constitution does not permit a State to exclude slavery from its limits. . . . We shall lie down pleasantly, dreaming that the people of Missouri are on the verge of making their State free; and we shall awake to the reality instead, that the Supreme Court has made Illinois a slave State." The proslavery argument's denigration of freedom and southerners' harping on the inferiority of blacks, Lincoln warned, were signs of a desire "to make *things* out of poor white men."

Lincoln's most eloquent statement against the Slave Power was his famous House Divided speech. In it Lincoln declared: "I do not expect the Union to be dissolved—I do not expect the House to fall—but I do expect it to cease to be divided. It will become all one thing or all the other. Either the opponents of slavery will arrest the further spread of it, and place it where the public mind shall rest in the belief that it is in the course of ultimate extinction; or its advocates will push it forward, till it shall become alike lawful in all the States, old as well as new, North as well as South. Have we no tendency to the latter condition?" The concluding question was the key element of the passage, for it drove home the idea that slaveholders were trying to extend bondage over the entire nation.

The brilliance of Republican tactics offset the difficulties the Dred Scott decision posed for them. By endorsing southern constitutional arguments, the Court had invalidated the central position of the Republican party: no extension of slavery. Republicans could only repudiate the decision, appealing to a "higher law," or hope to change the personnel of the Court. They did both, and by charging that the Supreme Court had become part of the Slave Power they probably gained politically.

For northern Democrats like Stephen Douglas, however, the Court's decision posed an awful dilemma. Northerners were alarmed by the prospect that the territories would be opened up to slavery. To retain support in the North, therefore, Douglas had to find some way to hedge, to reassure voters. Yet he had to do so without alienating southern Democrats. Douglas's task was problematic even at best; given the emotions of the time, it proved impossible.

Douglas chose to stand by his principle of popular sovereignty, which encountered a second test in Kansas in 1857. There, after Free-Soil settlers boycotted an election, proslavery forces met at Lecompton and wrote a constitution that permitted slavery. New elections to the territorial legislature, however, returned an antislavery majority, and the legislature promptly called for a popular vote on the new constitution, which was defeated by more than ten thousand votes. Despite this overwhelming evidence that Kansans did not want slavery, President Buchanan tried to force the Lecompton constitution through Congress. Douglas threw his weight against a document the people had rejected; he gauged their feelings correctly, and in 1858 Kansas voters rejected the constitution a third time. But his action infuriated southern Democrats.

In his well-publicized debates with Abraham Lincoln, his challenger for the Illinois Senate seat in 1858, Douglas further alienated the southern wing of his party. Speaking at Freeport, Illinois, he attempted to revive the notion of popular sovereignty with some tortured extensions of his old arguments. Asserting that the Court had not ruled on the powers of a *territorial* legislature, Douglas claimed that a territorial legislature could bar slavery either by passing a law against it or by doing nothing. Without the patrol laws and police regulations that support slavery, he reasoned, the institution could not exist. This argument, called the Freeport Doctrine, temporarily shored up Douglas's crumbling position in the North. But it gave southern Democrats further evidence that Douglas was unreliable, and some turned viciously against him. A few southerners, like William L. Yancey of Alabama, studied the trend in northern opinion and concluded that southern rights would be safe only in a separate southern nation.

Stephen Douglas Proposes the Freeport Doctrine

A growing number of slaveholders were similarly deciding that slavery could not be safe within the Union. Such concern was not new. As early as 1838, the Louisiana planter Bennet Barrow had written in his diary, "Northern States medling with slavery . . . openly speaking of the sin of Slavery in the southern states . . . must eventually cause a separation of the Union." And in 1856, a calmer, more polished Georgian named Charles Colcock Jones, Jr., rejoiced at the Democrat James Buchanan's defeat of Republican John C. Frémont for the presidency. The result guaranteed four more years of peace and prosperity, wrote Jones, but "beyond that period . . . we scarce dare

expect a continuance of our present relations." Increasingly slaveowners agreed with Jones and Barrow.

The immediate problem, however, was that the Dred Scott decision had hardened the position of southerners dramatically. Most southerners, probably most slaveowners, were not ready to decide that slavery could be safe only in a southern nation. But after Dred Scott they *were* ready to demand what they saw as their rights. Through years of controversy southern political leaders had fought for the rights flowing from Calhoun's theory of the Constitution and the territories. Now the Supreme Court had affirmed those rights, and southern leaders determined to demand them, both from the nation and from their party.

Thus the territorial issue continued to generate wider and more dangerous conflict, even though it had diminishing practical significance. By 1858 even Jefferson Davis had given up on agricultural development in the Southwest and admitted his uncertainty that slavery could succeed in Kansas. In territories outside Kansas the number of settlers was small, and everywhere the number of blacks was negligible— less than 1 percent of the population in Kansas and New Mexico. Nevertheless, men like Davis and Douglas spent many hours attacking each other's theories on the floor of the Senate. And the general public, both North and South, moved from anxiety to alarm and anger. The situation had become explosive.

THE BREAKUP OF THE UNION

Again, events gave the nation no rest from the growing sectional confrontation. One year before the 1860 presidential election, violence inflamed passions further when John Brown led a small band in an attack on Harpers Ferry, Virginia, hoping to trigger a slave rebellion. Brown failed miserably, and was quickly captured, tried, and executed. It came to light, however, that Brown had had the financial backing of several prominent abolitionists, and northern intellectuals such as Emerson and Thoreau praised him as a hero and a martyr. Since slave rebellion excited the deepest fears in the white South, these disclosures multiplied southerners' fear and anger many times over. The unity of the nation was now in peril.

Many observers feared that the election of 1860 would decide the fate of the Union. An ominous occurrence at the beginning of the campaign did nothing to reassure them. The baneful effects of the Dred Scott decision came to rest on the Democratic party. With southern Democrats intent on their territorial rights and northern Democrats eager to remain competitive in an increasingly free-soil North, the results for the party—and the nation were bitter.

For several years, the Democratic party had been the only remaining organization that was truly national in scope. Even religious denominations had split into northern and southern wings during the 1840s and 1850s. "One after another," wrote a Mississippi newspaper editor, "the links which have bound the North and the South together, have been severed . . . [but] the Democratic party looms gradually up, its nationality intact, and waves the olive branch over the troubled waters of politics." At its 1860 convention, however, the Democratic party broke in two.

Stephen A. Douglas wanted the party's presidential nomination, but could not afford to alienate northern opinion by accepting a strongly southern position on the territories. Southern Democrats like William L. Yancey, on the other hand, were determined to have their rights recognized, and they moved to block Douglas's nomination. When Douglas nevertheless marshalled a majority for his version of the platform, delegates from the five Gulf states plus South Carolina, Georgia, and Arkansas walked out of the convention hall in Charleston. Efforts at compromise failed, so the Democrats presented two nominees: Douglas for the northern wing, Vice President John C. Breckinridge of Kentucky for the southern. The Republicans nominated Abraham Lincoln; a Constitutional Union party, formed to preserve the nation but strong only in Virginia and the Upper South, nominated John Bell of Tennessee.

Splintering of the Democratic Party

In the ensuing campaign three of the candidates stressed their support for the Union. Bell's only issue was the need to preserve the Union intact. Douglas clearly preferred saving the Union to endangering it, and Breckinridge quickly backed away from any appearance of extremism. His supporters in several states declared that he was not a threat to the Union. Then the *New Orleans Bee* charged that every disunionist in the land was enthusiastic for Breckinridge, and a Texas paper made an earthy reference to his association with radicals: "Mr. Breckinridge claims that he isn't a disunionist. An animal not willing to pass for a pig shouldn't stay in the stye." Frightened by such criticism, Breckinridge went even further to disavow secession. He altered his plan to do no speaking during the campaign and delivered one address in which he flatly denied that his aim was secession. Thereafter his supporters stressed his loyalty and even went so far as to ridicule the possibility of secession in case of a Republican victory.

The results of the balloting were sectional in character, but, if one judges by the candidates' stands, they clearly indicated that most voters were satisfied in the Union. Douglas, Breckinridge, and Bell together received far more votes than Lincoln. Douglas had broad-based support but won few states; Breckinridge carried nine southern states, with his strength concentrated in the Deep South; Bell won pluralities in Virginia, Kentucky, and Tennessee. Lincoln prevailed in the North, but in the states that ultimately remained loyal to the Union he won only a plurality, not a majority (see table). Lincoln's victory was won in the electoral college.

Election of 1860

Given the heterogeneous nature of Republican voters, it is likely that most of even Lincoln's supporters did not view the issue of slavery in the territories as paramount. Thus the majority of voters had not cast ballots for extreme action. In such circumstances, partisan leaders had an opportunity either to work for compromise or to accentuate the conflict.

Determined minorities, however, also had an opportunity to exert pressure and bend the situation toward their goals. They did so, in both North and South. Abolitionists and free-soilers in the North worked through the press and the party to keep the Republicans from compromising on their territorial stand. Proslavery advocates and secessionists whipped up public opinion in the South and shrewdly manipulated state conventions.

Perhaps the most crucial decision was made by

PRESIDENTIAL VOTE IN 1860

	Lincoln	Other Candidates
Entire United States	1,866,452	2,815,617
North plus border and southern states that rejected secession prior to war[1]	1,866,452	2,421,752
North plus border states that fought for union[2]	1,864,523	1,960,842

Note the large vote for other candidates in the righthand column.

[1]Kentucky, Missouri, Maryland, Delaware, Virginia, North Carolina, Tennessee, Arkansas

[2]Kentucky, Missouri, Maryland, Delaware

Source: David Potter, *Lincoln and His Party in the Secession Crisis* (New Haven and London: Yale University Press, 1942, 1967), p. 189.

Lincoln, who decided not to soften his party's position on the territories. In his inaugural address he spoke of the necessity of maintaining the bond of faith between voter and candidate, of declining to set "the minority over the majority." But Lincoln's party was *not* the majority. His refusal to compromise probably had more to do with the unity of the Republican party than with the integrity of the democratic process. For though many conservative Republicans—eastern businessmen and former Whigs who did not feel strongly about slavery—hoped for a compromise, the original and strongest Republicans—antislavery voters and "conscience Whigs"—would not abandon Free Soil. To preserve the unity of his party, then, Lincoln had to take a position that endangered the Union.

Southern leaders in the Senate were willing, conditionally, to accept a compromise formula drawn up by Senator John J. Crittenden of Kentucky. Crittenden, hoping to don the mantle of Henry Clay and avert disaster, had suggested that the two sections divide the territories between them at 36°30'. But the southerners would agree to this *only* if the Republicans did too, for they wanted no less and knew that extremists in the South would demand much more. When Lincoln rejected the possibility that Republicans would make concessions on the territorial issue, Crittenden's peacemaking effort collapsed. Virginians called for a special convention in Washington, to which several states sent representatives. But this gathering, too, failed to find a magical formula or to reach unanimity on disputed questions.

Political leaders in the North and the South had communicated clearly with each other about the Crittenden proposal, but in a larger sense they tragically misjudged each other. As the historian David Potter has shown, Lincoln and other prominent Republicans believed that southerners were bluffing when they threatened secession; they expected a pro-Union majority in the South to assert itself. Therefore Lincoln determined not to yield to threats, but to call the southerners' bluff. On their side, moderate southern leaders had become convinced, with more accuracy, that northerners were not taking them seriously, and that a posture of strength was necessary to win respect for their position. "To rally the men of the North, who would preserve the government as our fathers found it, we . . . should offer no doubtful or divided front," wrote Jefferson Davis. Thus southern leaders who hoped to avert disaster did not offer compromise, for fear of inviting aggression. Nor did northern leaders who loved the Union, believing compromise would be unnecessary and unwise. With such attitudes controlling leaders' actions, the prospects for a solution were dim.

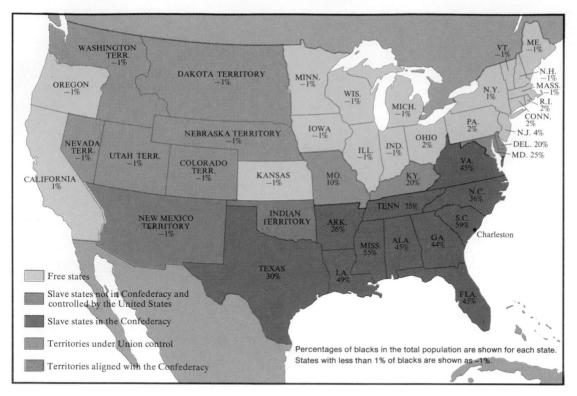

The Divided Nation—Slave and Free Areas, 1861

Meanwhile the Union was being destroyed. On December 20, 1860, South Carolina passed an ordinance of secession amid jubilation and cheering.

Secession of South Carolina This step marked the inauguration of a strategy known as separate-state secession. Foes of the Union, despairing of persuading all the southern states to challenge the federal government simultaneously, had concentrated their hopes on the most extreme proslavery state. With South Carolina out of the Union, they hoped other states would follow suit and momentum would build toward disunion.

The strategy proved effective. By reclaiming its independence, South Carolina had raised the stakes in the sectional confrontation. No longer was secession an unthinkable step; the Union was broken. Now, argued extremists, other states should secede to support South Carolina. Those who wanted to compromise would surely be able to make a better deal outside the Union than in it. Moderates found it difficult to dismiss such arguments, since most of them—even those who felt deep affection for the Union—were committed to defending southern rights and the southern way of life.

In these circumstances, southern extremists soon got their way. Overwhelming their opposition, they quickly called conventions and passed secession or-

Confederate States of America dinances in six other states: Mississippi, Florida, Alabama, Georgia, Louisiana, and Texas. By February 1861 these states had joined with South Carolina to form a new government in Montgomery, Alabama: the Confederate States of America. Choosing Jefferson Davis as their president, they began to function independently of the United States.

Yet this apparent unanimity of action was deceiving. Confused and dissatisfied with the alternatives, many voters who had cast a ballot for president stayed home rather than vote for delegates who would consider secession. In some conventions the vote to secede had been close, the balance tipped by the overrepresentation of plantation districts. Furthermore, the conventions were noticeably reluctant to seek ratification of their acts by the people. Four states in the Upper South—Virginia, North Carolina, Tennessee, and Arkansas—flatly rejected secession, and did not join the Confederacy until after the fighting had started. In Kentucky and Missouri popular sentiment was too divided for decisive action; these states remained under Union control, along with Maryland and Delaware (see map).

Misgivings about secession were not surprising, since it posed new and troubling issues for southerners, not the least of them the possibility of war and the question of who would be sacrificed. A careful look at election returns indicates that slaveholders and nonslaveholders were beginning to part company politically. Heavily slaveholding counties drew together in strong support of secession. But nonslaveholding areas that had been willing to support Breckinridge proved far less willing to support secession. Many counties with few slaves took an antisecession position or were staunchly Unionist. Large numbers of yeomen also sat out the election. In other words, nonslaveholders were beginning to consider their class interests, as planters had been doing for some time. With the threat of war on the horizon, nonslaveholders began to ask themselves how far they would go to support slavery and the slaveowners.

Finally, there was still considerable love for the Union in the South. Some opposition to secession was fervently pro-Union, as is apparent in the comment of a northern Alabama delegate after his convention had approved secession: "Here I sit & from my window see the nasty little thing flaunting in the breeze which has taken the place of that glorious banner which has been the pride of millions of Americans and the boast of freemen the wide world over." Such sentiments presented problems for the Confederacy, though they were not sufficiently developed to prevent secession.

The dilemma facing President Lincoln on inauguration day in March 1861 was how to maintain the authority of the federal government without provoking war in the states that had left the Union. He decided to proceed cautiously; by holding onto federal fortifications, he reasoned, he could assert federal sovereignty while waiting for a restoration of relations. But Jefferson Davis, who could not claim to lead a sovereign nation if its ports and military facilities were under foreign control, would not cooperate. A collision was inevitable.

It came in the early morning hours of April 12,

After a fierce bombardment, the Confederate flag replaced the Stars and Stripes over Fort Sumter. The nation's bloodiest war had begun.   National Archives.

1861, at Fort Sumter in Charleston harbor. A federal garrison there was running low on food. Lincoln had decided to send a supply ship and had notified the South Carolinians of his intention. For the Montgomery government, the only alternative to an attack on the fort was submission to Lincoln's authority. Accordingly, orders were sent to obtain surrender or attack the fort. Under heavy bombardment for two days, the federal garrison finally surrendered. The Confederates permitted the soldiers to sail away on unarmed vessels while the residents of Charleston celebrated. Thus the bloodiest war in the nation's history began in a deceptively gala spirit.

Attack on Fort Sumter

Throughout the 1840s and 1850s many able leaders had worked diligently to avert this outcome. North and South, most had hoped to keep the nation together. As late as 1858 even Jefferson Davis had declared, "This great country will continue united." He had explained sincerely that the United States "is my country and to the innermost fibers of my heart I love it all, and every part." Secession dismayed northern editors and voters, but it also plunged some planters into depression. Paul Cameron, the largest slaveowner in North Carolina, confessed that he was "very unhappy. I love the Union." Why, then, had the war occurred? Why had all the efforts to prevent it failed?

Slavery was an issue that could not be compromised. The conflict over slavery was fundamental and beyond adjustment. Too many powerful emotions were engaged in attacking or defending it. Too many important economic and social interests were involved in maintaining or destroying it. It was entwined with a host of other issues that mattered deeply to people. Ultimately each section regarded slavery as too important to the future to ignore.

Even after extreme views were put aside, the North and the South had different approaches to the institution. The logic of Republican ideology tended in the direction of abolishing slavery, though Republicans denied any such intention. Similarly, the logic of arguments by southern leaders led toward establishing slavery everywhere, though southerners also denied that they sought any such thing. Lincoln put the problem succinctly. Soon after the 1860 election he assured his old friend, Alexander Stephens of Georgia, that the Republican party would not attack slavery in the states where it existed. But Lincoln continued, "You think slavery is *right* and ought to be extended; while we think it is *wrong* and ought to be restricted. That I suppose is the rub."

Fundamental disagreements have not always led to war. It is possible for a nation to encounter unresolvable issues yet manage to get past them. New events can capture people's attention. Time can alter interests and attitudes—if in the intervening years conflict is contained or restricted. That is precisely what America's compromisers sought to achieve. They tried to soothe passions and buy time for the nation, to avoid a conflict that could not be settled and conserve the many areas of consensus among Americans. Their efforts were well intentioned and patriotic, but they were doomed to failure.

The issue of slavery in the territories made conflict impossible to avoid. Territorial expansion generated disputes so frequently that the nation never gained a breathing space. And as the conflict recurred it spread to other questions that were broader and therefore more dangerous. The possibility of sectional

peace receded swiftly as abolitionism broadened into antislavery, as criticism of slaveholding expanded into the idea of the Slave Power, and as alarmed slaveholders became more insistent in their demands.

By 1860 fear added an irrational and complicating element. Its effect was visible in the ironies that prevailed on the eve of war. A vigorous, industrializing, rapidly growing North saw itself as the victim of southern domination. A frightened, defensive, and increasingly isolated South issued belligerent demands and ultimatums. Each section accused the other of violating its rights. Mutual suspicions poisoned trust and carried both sections away from values they held in common. In the end even those who did not want war could find no way to prevent it.

In the profoundest sense, slavery was tied up with the war. Concerns about slavery had driven all the other conflicts, but the fighting began with this, its central issue, shrouded in confusion. How would the Civil War affect slavery, its place in the law, and black people's place in society? The answers to those questions, and the degree to which answers were sought, would be matters of fateful import.

SUGGESTIONS FOR FURTHER READING

Politics: General

Thomas B. Alexander, *Sectional Stress and Party Strength* (1967); Ray Allen Billington, *The Protestant Crusade, 1800–1860* (1938 and 1964); Stanley W. Campbell, *The Slave Catchers* (1968); Avery O. Craven, *The Coming of the Civil War* (1942); Don E. Fehrenbacher, *The Dred Scott Case* (1978); George M. Fredrickson, *The Black Image in the White Mind* (1971); Holman Hamilton, *Prologue to Conflict* (1964); Michael F. Holt, *The Political Crisis of the 1850s* (1978); Stephen E. Maizlish and John J. Kushma, eds., *Essays on American Antebellum Politics, 1840–1860* (1982); Paul D. Nagle, *One Nation Indivisible* (1964); Roy F. Nichols, *The Disruption of American Democracy* (1948); Russell B. Nye, *Fettered Freedom* (1949); Stephen B. Oates, *To Purge This Land with Blood,* 2nd ed. (1984); David M. Potter, *The Impending Crisis, 1848–1861* (1976); James A. Rawley, *Race and Politics* (1969); Joel H. Silbey, *The Transformation*

IMPORTANT EVENTS

1846	War with Mexico Wilmot Proviso
1847	Lewis Cass proposes idea of popular sovereignty
1848	Taylor elected president
1849	California applies for admission to Union as free state
1850	Compromise of 1850
1851	Mob rescues fugitive slave in Boston
1852	Harriet Beecher Stowe, *Uncle Tom's Cabin* Pierce elected president
1854	Kansas-Nebraska bill "Appeal of the Independent Democrats" Republican party formed Democrats lose ground in congressional elections
1856	Preston Brooks attacks Charles Sumner in Senate chamber Bleeding Kansas Buchanan elected president
1857	*Dred Scott* v. *Sanford* Lecompton Constitution
1858	Voters reject Lecompton Constitution Lincoln-Douglas debates Freeport Doctrine
1859	John Brown raids Harpers Ferry
1860	Democratic party splits in half Lincoln elected president Crittenden Compromise fails South Carolina secedes from Union
1861	Six more southern states secede Confederacy established Attack on Fort Sumter

of *American Politics, 1840–1860* (1967); Kenneth M. Stampp, *And the War Came* (1950); Gerald W. Wolff, *The Kansas-Nebraska Bill* (1977).

The South and Slavery

William L. Barney, *The Secessionist Impulse* (1974); Drew G. Faust, *The Ideology of Slavery* (1981); Drew G. Faust, *A Sacred Circle: The Dilemma of the Intellectual in the Old South* (1978); Eugene D. Genovese, *The World the Slaveholders Made* (1969); Eugene D. Genovese, *The Political Economy of Slavery* (1967); William Sumner Jenkins, *Pro-Slavery Thought in the Old South* (1935); David M. Potter, *The South and the Sectional Conflict* (1968); William R. Stanton, *The Leopard's Spots* (1960); J. Mills Thornton, III, *Politics and Power in a Slave Society* (1978).

The North and Antislavery

Eugene H. Berwanger, *The Frontier Against Slavery* (1967); Louis Filler, *The Crusade Against Slavery, 1830–1860* (1960); Eric Foner, *Free Soil, Free Labor, Free Men* (1970); William E. Gienapp, *The Origins of the Republican Party, 1852–1856* (1986); Henry V. Jaffa, *Crisis of the House Divided* (1959); Aileen S. Kraditor, *Means and Ends in American Abolitionism* (1969); Lewis Perry and Michael Fellman, eds., *Antislavery Reconsidered* (1979); Jeffrey Rossbach, *Ambivalent Conspirators* (1982); Alice Felt Tyler, *Freedom's Ferment* (1944); Ronald G. Walters, *American Reformers* (1978).

The Mexican War and Foreign Policy

Reginald Horsman, *Race and Manifest Destiny* (1981); Ernest M. Lander, Jr., *Reluctant Imperialists: Calhoun, the South Carolinians, and the Mexican War* (1980); Robert E. May, *The Southern Dream of a Caribbean Empire, 1854–1861* (1973); Frederick Merk, *The Oregon Question* (1967); David M. Pletcher, *The Diplomacy of Annexation: Texas, Oregon, and the Mexican War* (1973); John H. Schroeder, *Mr. Polk's War* (1973); Otis A. Singletary, *The Mexican War* (1960).

Transforming Fire:
The Civil War
1861–1865

Chapter 14

They came from many different places. They held many different points of view. Perhaps the only thing that united them was the fact that they were caught in a gigantic struggle. Each felt dwarfed by the immense force of the Civil War, a vast and complex event beyond any individual's control.

Moncure Conway, a Virginian who had converted to abolitionism and settled in New England, saw the Civil War as a momentous opportunity to bring justice to human affairs. The progress of reform in the North, Conway wrote in an earnest pamphlet, heralded the dawn of "Humanity's advancing day." Before this dawn, "Slavery, hoary tyrant of the ages," cried out " 'Back! back . . . into the chambers of Night!' " Conway urged northerners to accept slavery's challenge and defeat it, so that "the rays of Freedom and Justice" could shine throughout America. Then the United States would stand as a beacon not only of commercial power but of moral righteousness.

Conway's lofty idealism was far removed from the motives that drove most federal soldiers to march grimly to their death. Though slaves believed they were witnessing God's "Holy War for the liberation of the poor African slave people," Union troops often took a different perspective. When a Yankee soldier ransacked a slave family's cabin and stole their best quilts, the mother exclaimed, "Why you nasty, stinkin' rascal. You say you come down here to fight for the niggers, and now you're stealin' from em." The soldier replied, "You're a G-- D--- liar, I'm fightin' for $14 a month and the Union."

Southerners too acted from limited and pragmatic motives, fighting in self-defense or out of regional loyalty. A Union officer interrogating Confederate prisoners noticed the poverty of one captive. Clearly the man was no slaveholder, so the officer asked him why he was fighting. "Because y'all are down here," replied the Confederate.

The great suffering and frustration of the war were apparent in the bitter words of another southerner, a civilian. Impoverished by the conflict, this farmer had endured inflation, taxes, and shortages to support the Confederacy. Then an impressment agent arrived to take from him still more—grain and meat, horses and mules and wagons. In return the agent offered only a certificate promising repayment sometime in the future. Angry and fed up, the farmer bluntly declared, "the sooner this damned Government falls to pieces, the better it will be for us."

In contrast, many northern businessmen looked to the economic effects of the war with optimism and anticipation. The conflict ensured vast government expenditures, a heavy demand for products, and lucrative government contracts. *Harper's Monthly* reported that an eminent financier expected a long war, the kind of war that would mean huge purchases, paper money, active speculation, and rising prices. "The battle of Bull Run," predicted the financier, "makes the fortune of every man in Wall Street who is not a natural idiot."

For each of these people and millions of others, the Civil War was a life-changing event. It obliterated the normal circumstances of life, sweeping millions of men into training camps and battle units. Armies numbering in the hundreds of thousands marched over the South, devastating once-peaceful countrysides. Families struggled to survive without their men; businesses tried to cope with the loss of workers. Women, North and South, faced added responsibilities in the home and moved into new jobs in the work force. Nothing seemed untouched.

Change was most drastic in the South, where the leaders of the secession movement had launched a revolution for the purpose of keeping things unchanged. Never were men more mistaken: their revolutionary means were fundamentally incompatible with their conservative purpose. Southern whites had feared that a peacetime government of Republicans would interfere with slavery and upset the routine of plantation life. Instead their own actions led to a war that turned southern life upside down and imperiled the very existence of slavery. The Civil War forced changes in every phase of southern society, and the leadership of Jefferson Davis resulted in policies more objectionable to the elite than any proposed by Lincoln. The Confederacy proved to be a shockingly unsouthern experience.

War altered the North as well, but not as deeply.

Since the bulk of the fighting took place on southern soil, most northern farms and factories remained physically unscathed. The drafting of workers and the changing needs for products slowed the pace of industrialization somewhat, but factories and businesses remained busy. Though workers lost ground to inflation, the economy hummed. And a new probusiness atmosphere dominated Congress, where southern representatives no longer filled their seats. To the discomfort of many, the powers of the federal government and the president increased during the war.

The war strained society, both North and South. Disaffection was strongest in the Confederacy, where the sufferings of ordinary citizens were greatest. There poverty and class resentment fed a lower-class antagonism to the war that threatened the Confederacy from within as federal armies assailed it from without. But dissent also flourished in the North, where antiwar sentiment occasionally erupted into violence.

Ultimately, the Civil War forced new social and racial arrangements on the nation. Its greatest effect was to compel leaders and citizens to deal with an issue they had often tried to avoid: slavery. This issue had, in complex and indirect ways, given rise to the war; now the scope and demands of the war forced reluctant Americans to deal with it.

THE SOUTH GOES TO WAR

In the first bright days of the southern nation, few foresaw the changes that were in store. Lincoln's call for troops to put down the Confederate insurrection stimulated an outpouring of regional loyalty that unified the classes. Though four border slave states—Missouri, Kentucky, Maryland, and Delaware—and western Virginia refused to secede, the rest of the Upper South promptly joined the Confederacy. From every quarter southerners flocked to defend their region against Yankee aggression. In the first few months of the war half a million men volunteered to fight; there were so many would-be soldiers that the government could not arm them all.

This ground swell of popular support for the Confederacy generated a mood of optimism and gaiety.

Women sewed dashing, colorful uniforms for men who would before long be lucky to wear drab gray or butternut homespun. Confident recruits boasted of whipping the Yankees and returning home in time for dinner. And the first major battle

Battle of Bull Run

of the war only increased such cockiness. On July 21, 1861, General Irvin McDowell and thirty thousand federal troops attacked General P. G. T. Beauregard's twenty-two thousand southerners at a stream called Bull Run, near Manassas Junction, Virginia. Both armies were ill-trained, and confusion reigned on the battlefield. But nine thousand Confederate reinforcements and a timely stand by General Thomas Jackson (thereafter known as "Stonewall" Jackson) won the day for the South. Union troops fled back to Washington in disarray, and shocked northern picnickers who had expected to witness a victory suddenly feared their capital would be taken.

As 1861 faded into 1862, however, the North undertook a massive buildup of troops in northern Virginia. In the wake of Bull Run, Lincoln had given command of the army to General George B. McClellan, an officer who had always been better at organization and training than at fighting. McClellan devoted the fall and winter to readying a formidable force of a quarter of a million men. "The vast preparation of the enemy," wrote one Confederate soldier, produced a "feeling of despondency" among southerners.

The North also moved to blockade southern ports in order to choke off the Confederacy's avenues of commerce and supply. At first the handful of available steamers proved woefully inadequate to the task of patrolling 3,550 miles of coastline. But the Union Navy gradually increased the blockade's effectiveness, though it never bottled up southern commerce completely.

In the fall of 1861 Union naval power came ashore in the South. Federal squadrons captured Cape Hatteras and Hilton Head, part of the

Union Naval Campaign

Sea Islands off Port Royal, South Carolina. A few months later, similar operations secured Albemarle and Pamlico sounds, Roanoke Island, and New Bern in North Carolina, as well as Fort Pulaski, which defended Savannah. Then in April 1862 ships commanded by Admiral David Farragut smashed through log booms on the Mississippi River and

After the tension of the secession crisis, both sides welcomed action and military preparations. Thomas Nast captured the festive atmosphere at a parade of New York's Seventh Regiment on April 19, 1861. Seventh Regiment National Guard Armory, New York.

fought their way upstream to capture New Orleans (see map).

The coastal victories off South Carolina foreshadowed another major development in the unraveling of the southern status quo. At the gunboats' approach, frightened planters abandoned their lands and fled. Their slaves, who thus became the first to escape slavery through military action, greeted what they hoped to be freedom with rejoicing and destruction of the cotton gins, symbols of their travail. Their jubilation and the constantly growing stream of runaways who poured into the Union lines removed any doubt about which side the slaves would support, given the opportunity. Ironically the federal government, unwilling at first to wage a war against slavery, did not acknowledge the slaves' freedom—though it

did set to work finding ways to use them in the national cause.

With the approach of spring 1862, the military outlook for the Confederacy darkened again, this time in northern Tennessee. There a hard-drinking, hitherto unsuccessful general named **Grant's** Ulysses S. Grant recognized the **Campaign in** strategic importance of Forts Henry **Tennessee** and Donelson, the Confederate outposts guarding the Tennessee and Cumberland rivers. Grant saw that if federal troops could capture these forts, two prime routes into the heartland of the Confederacy would lie open. In the space of ten days he seized the forts, using his forces so well that he was able to demand unconditional surrender of Fort Donelson's defenders. A path into

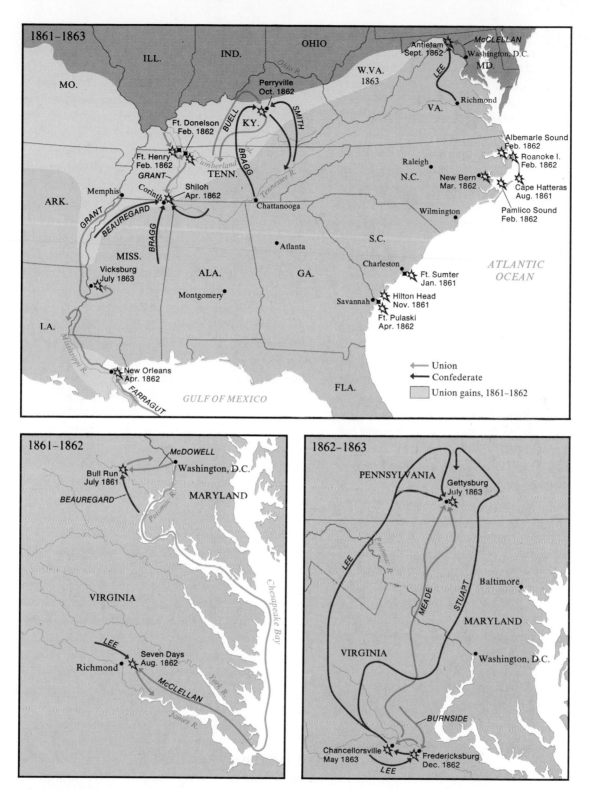

The Civil War, 1861–1863

Tennessee, Alabama, and Mississippi now lay open before the Union army.

On April 6, Confederate General Albert Sidney Johnston caught Grant's army in an undesirable position at Pittsburg Landing in southern Tennessee. The Confederates inflicted heavy damage in fierce fighting. Close to victory, however, General Johnston was struck by a ball that severed an artery in his thigh; within minutes he was dead. Deprived of their leader, southern troops faced a reinforced Union army the next day, and the tide of battle turned. After ten hours of heavy combat, Grant's men forced the Confederates to withdraw to Corinth, Mississippi. Though the Battle of Shiloh was a Union victory, destruction reigned. Northern troops lost 13,000 of 63,000 men; southerners sacrificed 11,000 out of 40,000.

Both soldiers and civilians were beginning to recognize the enormous costs of this war. Never before in Europe or America had such massive forces pummeled each other with weapons of such destructive power. Yet the Civil War's armies seemed virtually indestructible. Even in the bloodiest engagements the losing army was never destroyed—only men died. Many citizens, like soldier (later Supreme Court Justice) Oliver Wendell Holmes, wondered at "the butcher's bill." The improved range of modern rifles multiplied casualties. Since medical knowledge was rudimentary, even minor wounds often led to death through infection.

The slaughter was most vivid, of course, to the soldiers themselves, who saw the blasted bodies of their friends and comrades. "Any one who goes over a battlefield after a battle," wrote one Confederate, "never cares to go over another . . . again. . . . It is a sad sight to see the dead and if possible more sad to see the wounded—shot in every possible way you can imagine."

Troops learned the hard way that soldiering was far from glorious. "The dirt of a camp life knocks all its poetry into a cocked hat," wrote a North Carolina volunteer in 1862. One year later he marveled at his earlier innocence. Fighting had taught him "the realities of a soldier's life. We had no tents after the 6th August, but slept on the ground, in the woods or open fields, without regard to the weather. . . . I learned to eat fat bacon raw, and to like it. . . . Without time to wash our clothes or our persons, and sleeping on the ground all huddled together, the whole army became lousy more or less with body lice. It was a necessary and unavoidable incident to our arduous campaign."

The scope and duration of the conflict began to have unexpected effects. As the spring of 1862 approached, southern officials worried about the strength of their armies. Tens of thousands of Confederate soldiers had volunteered for just one year's service, planning to return home in the spring to plant their crops. To keep southern armies in the field, the War Department offered bounties and furloughs to all who would reenlist. Officials then called for new volunteers; but, as one admitted, "the spirit of volunteering had died out." Three states threatened or instituted a draft. Finally, still faced with a critical shortage of troops, the Confederate government enacted the first national conscription law in American history. The war had forced an unprecedented change on the states that had seceded for fear of change.

Confederacy Resorts to a Draft

With their ranks reinforced, southern armies moved into heavier fighting. Early in 1862 most of the combat centered on Virginia, where the Confederacy had relocated its capital. General McClellan sailed his troops to the York peninsula and advanced on Richmond from the east. By May and June the sheer size of the federal armies outside the South's capital was highly threatening. But when McClellan sent his legions into combat, Generals Jackson and Lee managed to stave off his attacks. First, Jackson maneuvered into the Shenandoah Valley, behind Union forces, and threatened Washington, drawing some of the federals away from Richmond to protect their own capital. Then, in a series of engagements culminating in the Seven Days' battles, Lee held McClellan off. On August 3 McClellan withdrew to the Potomac, and Richmond was safe for almost two more years.

Buoyed by these results, Jefferson Davis conceived an ambitious plan to turn the tide of the war and compel the United States to recognize the Confederacy. He ordered a general offensive, sending Lee north to Maryland and Generals Kirby Smith and Braxton Bragg to Kentucky. The South would abandon the defensive and take the war north. Davis and his commanders issued a proclamation to the people of Maryland and Kentucky asserting

Davis Orders an Offensive

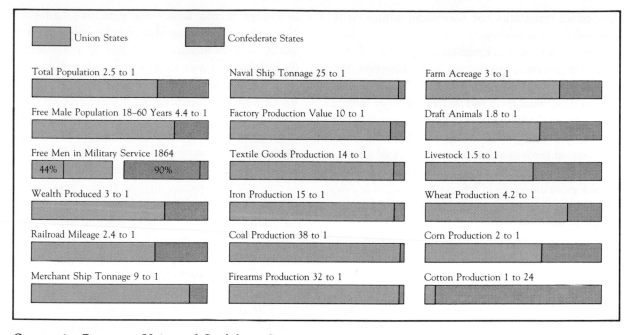

Union States		Confederate States			
Total Population 2.5 to 1		Naval Ship Tonnage 25 to 1		Farm Acreage 3 to 1	
Free Male Population 18–60 Years 4.4 to 1		Factory Production Value 10 to 1		Draft Animals 1.8 to 1	
Free Men in Military Service 1864 — 44% / 90%		Textile Goods Production 14 to 1		Livestock 1.5 to 1	
Wealth Produced 3 to 1		Iron Production 15 to 1		Wheat Production 4.2 to 1	
Railroad Mileage 2.4 to 1		Coal Production 38 to 1		Corn Production 2 to 1	
Merchant Ship Tonnage 9 to 1		Firearms Production 32 to 1		Cotton Production 1 to 24	

Comparative Resources, Union and Confederate States, 1861. Source: Times Atlas of World History. *Times Books, London, 1978.*

that the Confederates sought only the right of self-government. Lincoln's refusal to grant them independence forced them to attack "those who persist in their refusal to make peace." Davis urged invaded states to make a separate peace with his government and invited the Northwest, whose trade followed the Mississippi to New Orleans, to leave the Union.

The plan was promising, and Davis rejoiced that his outnumbered forces were ready to take the initiative. Every part of the offensive failed, however. In the bloodiest single day of fighting, September 17, 1862, McClellan turned Lee back in the Battle of Antietam near Sharpsburg, Maryland. Smith and Bragg had to withdraw from Kentucky just one day after Bragg had attended the inauguration of a provisional Confederate governor. The entire effort had collapsed.

But southern arms were not exhausted. Jeb Stuart executed a daring cavalry raid into Pennsylvania on October 10 through 12, and Lee decimated General Ambrose Burnside's soldiers as they charged his fortified positions at Fredericksburg, Virginia, on December 13. The Confederate Army of Northern Virginia performed so bravely and controlled the engagement so thoroughly that Lee, a restrained and humane man, was moved to say, "It is well that war is so terrible. We should grow too fond of it."

Nevertheless, the Confederacy had marshalled all its strength for a breakthrough and failed utterly. Outnumbered and disadvantaged in resources (see figure), the South could not continue its offensive. Meanwhile the North still had reserves of every kind on which to draw. Profoundly disappointed, Davis admitted to a committee of Confederate representatives that southerners had entered "the darkest and most dangerous period we have yet had." Tenacious defense and stoical endurance now seemed the South's only long-range hope. Perceptive southerners shared their president's despair.

WAR TRANSFORMS THE SOUTH

E ven more than the fighting itself, changes in civilian life robbed southerners of their gaiety and nonchalance. The war altered southern society beyond all expectations and with astonishing speed. One of the first traditions to fall was the southern preference for local government.

The South had been an area of little government. States' rights had been its motto, but even the state governments were weak and sketchy affairs by modern standards. To withstand the massive power of the North, however, the South had to centralize; like the colonial revolutionaries, southerners faced a choice of join or die. No one saw the necessity of centralization more clearly than Jefferson Davis. If the states insisted on fighting separately, said Davis, "we had better make terms as soon as we can."

From the outset, Davis pressed to bring all arms, supplies, and troops under his control. He advocated conscription when the states failed to enroll enough new soldiers. And he took a strong

Centralization of Power in the South

leadership role toward the Confederate congress, which raised taxes and later passed a tax-in-kind—a levy not on money but on wheat, corn, oats, rye, cotton, peas, and other farm products. Almost three thousand agents dispersed to collect the tax, assisted by almost fifteen hundred appraisers. Where opposition arose, the government suspended the writ of habeas corpus and imposed martial law. In the face of a political opposition that cherished states' rights, Davis proved unyielding.

To replace the food that soldiers would have grown, Davis exhorted farmers to switch from cash crops to food crops; he encouraged the states to require that they do so. But the army was still short of food and labor. In emergencies the War Department resorted to impressing slaves for labor on fortifications, or took meat and grain in lieu of forced labor. After 1861, the government relied heavily on food impressment to feed the armies. Officers swooped down on farms in the line of march and carted away grain, meat, and other food, plus wagons and draft animals to carry it.

Soon the Richmond administration was taking virtually complete direction of the southern economy. Because it controlled the supply of labor through conscription, the administration could regulate industry, compelling factories to work on government contracts to supply government needs. In addition, the Confederate congress passed laws giving the central government almost full control of the railroads; and

later shipping, too, came under extensive regulation. New statutes even limited corporate profits and dividends. A large bureaucracy sprang up to administer these operations: over seventy thousand civilians were needed to run the Confederate war machine. By the war's end the southern bureaucracy was proportionally larger than its northern counterpart.

The mushrooming bureaucracy expanded the cities. Clerks and subordinate officials, many of them women, crowded the towns and cities where Confederate departments had their offices. These

Effects of War on Southern Cities and Industry

sudden population booms stretched the existing housing supply and stimulated new construction. The pressure was especially great in Richmond, whose population increased two-and-a-half times. Before the war's end Confederate officials were planning the relocation of entire departments to diminish crowding in that city. Mobile's population jumped from 29,000 to 41,000; Atlanta began to grow; and 10,000 people poured into war industries in little Selma, Alabama.

Another prime cause of urban growth was industrialization. Because of the Union blockade, which interrupted imports of manufactured products, the traditionally agricultural South became interested in industry. Davis exulted that southerners were manufacturing their own goods, thus "becoming more and more independent of the rest of the world." Many planters shared his expectations, remembering their battles against tariffs and hoping that their agrarian nation would industrialize enough to win "deliverance, full and unrestricted, from all commercial dependence" on the North. And indeed, though the Confederacy started from scratch, it achieved tremendous feats of industrial development. Chief of Ordnance Josiah Gorgas was able to increase the capacity of the Tredegar Iron Works and other factories to the point that his Ordnance Bureau was supplying all Confederate small arms and ammunition by 1865.

As a result of these changes southerners adopted new values. Women, sheltered in the patriarchal antebellum society, gained substantial new responsibilities. The wives and mothers of soldiers became

Change in the Southern Woman's Role

heads of households and undertook what had previously been considered men's work. To them fell the added tasks of raising crops and tending

Male doctors often resisted women as nurses, yet the women took real risks. This photograph of a nurse and her patients was taken on the front lines right after the battle of Fredericksburg. Armed Forces Institute of Pathology.

animals. Though wives of nonslaveowners had a harder time cultivating their fields than women whose families owned slaves, the latter had to struggle with the management of field hands unused to feminine oversight. Only among the very rich were there enough servants to take up the slack and leave a woman's routine undisturbed. In the cities, white women, who had been virtually excluded from the labor force, found a limited number of new, respectable, paying jobs. Clerks had always been males, but now the war changed that, too. "Government girls" staffed the Confederate bureaucracy, and female schoolteachers became a familiar sight for the first time. Such experiences, though restricted in scope, undermined the image of the omnipotent male and gave thousands of women new confidence in their abilities.

One of those who acquired such confidence as a result of the war was a young North Carolinian named Janie Smith. Raised in a rural area by prosperous parents, she had faced few challenges or grim realities. Then suddenly the war reached her farm, and the troops turned her home into a hospital. "It makes me shudder when I think of the awful sights I witnessed that morning," she wrote to a friend. "Ambulance after ambulance drove up with our wounded. . . . Under every shed and tree, the tables were carried for amputating the limbs. . . . The blood lay in puddles in the grove; the groans of the dying and complaints of those undergoing amputation were hor-

rible." But Janie Smith learned to cope with crisis. She helped to nurse the wounded and ended her account with the proud words "I can dress amputated limbs now and do most anything in the way of nursing wounded soldiers."

The Confederate experience introduced and sustained many other new values. Legislative bodies yielded power to the executive branch of government, which could act more decisively in time of war. The traditional emphasis on aristocratic lineage gave way to respect for achievement and bravery under fire. Thus many men of ordinary background, such as Josiah Gorgas, Stonewall Jackson, and General Nathan Bedford Forrest, gained distinction in industry and on the battlefield that would have been beyond their grasp in time of peace. Finally, sacrifice for the cause discouraged the pursuit of pleasure; hostesses gave "cold water parties" (at which water was the only refreshment) to demonstrate their patriotism.

For the elite such sacrifice was symbolic, but for millions of ordinary southerners it was terrifyingly real. Mass poverty descended on the South, afflicting for the first time a large minority of the white population. The crux of the problem was that many yeoman families had lost their breadwinners to the army. As a South Carolina newspaper put it, "The duties of war have called away from home the sole supports of many, many families. . . . Help must be given, or the poor will suffer." The poor sought such help from relatives, neighbors, friends, anyone. Sometimes they took their cases to the Confederate government, as did an elderly Virginian who pleaded, "If you dount send [my son] home I am bound to louse my crop and cum to suffer. I am eaighty one years of adge." One woman wrote: "I ask in the name of humanity to discharge my husband he is not able to do your government much good and he might do his children some good and thare is no use in keeping a man thare to kill and leave widows and poor little orphen children to suffer . . . my poor children have no home nor no Father."

Other factors aggravated the effect of the labor shortage. The South was in many places so sparsely populated that the conscription of one skilled craftsman could work a hardship on the people of an entire county. Often they begged in unison for the exemption or discharge of the local miller or the neighborhood

Human Suffering in the South

The war separated many young lovers forever. Probably some girl treasured the photo on the left of Private Edwin Francis Jennison of Georgia, killed at Malvern Hill shortly after the picture was taken. The portrait on the right was found beside the body of a Confederate who fell on the battlefield at Chancellorsville. Left: Library of Congress; right: Museum of the Confederacy.

tanner, wheelwright, or potter. Physicians were also in short supply. Most serious, however, was the loss of a blacksmith. As a petition from Alabama explained, "our Section of County [is] left entirely Destitute of any man that is able to keep in order any kind of Farming Tules, Such as the few aged Farmers and families of Those that is gone to defend their rites is Compeled to have to make a Support With."

The blockade created further shortages of common but important items—salt, sugar, coffee, nails—and speculation and hoarding made them worse. Avaricious businessmen moved to corner the supply of some commodities; prosperous citizens tried to stock up on food. The *Richmond Enquirer* criticized one man for hoarding seven hundred barrels of flour; another man, a planter, purchased so many wagonloads of supplies that his "lawn and paths looked like a wharf covered with a ship's loads." Some people bought up the entire stock of a store and held the goods to sell later at higher prices. "This disposition to speculate upon the yeomanry of the country," lamented the *Richmond Examiner*, "is the most mortifying feature of the war." North Carolina's Governor Zebulon Vance asked where it would all stop: "the cry of distress comes up from the poor wives and children of our soldiers. . . . What will become of them?"

Inflation raged out of control until prices had increased almost 7,000 percent. This fact imperiled urban dwellers and the many who could no longer provide for themselves. As early as 1861 and 1862, newspapers were reporting that "the poor of our . . . country will be unable to live at all" and that "want

Hoarding and Runaway Inflation in the South

Chapter 14: TRANSFORMING FIRE: THE CIVIL WAR, 1861–1865

and starvation are staring thousands in the face." Officials warned of "great suffering next year," predicting that "women and children are bound to come to suffering if not starvation."

Some concerned citizens tried to help. "Free markets," which dispersed goods as charity, sprang up in various cities; some families came to the aid of their neighbors. But there were other citizens who would not cooperate: "It is folly for a poor mother to call on the rich people about here," raged one woman. "Their hearts are of steel they would sooner throw what they have to spare to their dogs than give it to a starving child." The need was so vast that it overwhelmed private charity. A rudimentary relief program organized by the Confederacy offered hope, but was soon curtailed to supply the armies. Southern yeomen sank into poverty and suffering.

As their fortunes declined, these people of once-modest means looked around them and found abundant evidence that all classes were not sacrificing equally. They saw that the wealthy curtailed only their luxuries, while many poor families went without necessities. They saw that the government contributed to these inequities through policies that favored the upper class. Until the last year of the war, for example, prosperous southerners could avoid military service by furnishing a hired substitute. Prices for substitutes skyrocketed, until it was common for a man of means to pay $5,000 or $6,000 to send someone to the front. Well over fifty thousand upper-class southerners purchased such substitutes; Mary Boykin Chesnut knew of one young aristocrat who had "spent a fortune in substitutes. Two have been taken from him [when *they* were conscripted], and two he paid to change with him when he was ordered to the front. He is at the end of his row now, for all able-bodied men are ordered to the front. I hear he is going as some general's courier."

As Chesnut's last remark indicates, the rich also traded on their social connections to avoid danger. "It's a notorious fact," complained an angry Georgian, that "if a man has influential friends—or a little money to spare he will never be enrolled." The Confederate senator from Mississippi, James Phelan, informed Jefferson Davis that apparently "nine tenths of the youngsters of the land whose relatives are

Inequities of the Confederate Draft

conspicuous in society, wealthy, or influential obtain some safe perch where they can doze with their heads under their wings."

Anger at such discrimination exploded when in October 1862 the Confederate congress exempted from military duty anyone who was supervising at least twenty slaves. This "twenty nigger law" became notorious. "Never did a law meet with more universal odium," observed one representative. "Its influence upon the poor is most calamitous." Immediately protests arose from every corner of the Confederacy, and North Carolina's legislators formally condemned the law. Its defenders argued, however, that the exemption preserved order and aided food production, and the statute remained on the books.

Dissension spread as growing numbers of citizens concluded that the struggle was "a rich man's war and a poor man's fight." Alert politicians and newspaper editors warned that class resentment was building to a dangerous level; letters to Confederate officials during this period contained a bitterness that suggested the depth of the people's anger. "If I and my little children suffer [and] die while there Father is in service," threatened one woman, "I invoke God Almighty that our blood rest upon the South." Another woman swore to the secretary of war that

an allwise god . . . will send down his fury and judgment in a very grate manar [on] all those our leading men and those that are in power if thare is no more favors shone to . . . the wives and mothers of those who in poverty has with patrootism stood the fence Battles. . . . I tell you that with out some grate and speadly alterating in the conduckting of afares in this our little nation god will frown on it.

Trouble was brewing in the Confederacy.

THE NORTHERN ECONOMY COPES WITH WAR

With the onset of war, a tidal wave of change rolled over the North, just as it had over the South. Factories and citizens' associations geared up to support the war, and the federal government and its executive branch gained power they had never had before. Civil liberties were restricted; social values were influenced by both personal sacrifice and wartime riches. Idealism and greed flourished together.

But there was an important difference between North and South: the war did not destroy the North's prosperity. Northern factories ran overtime, and unemployment was low. Furthermore, northern farms and factories came through the war unscathed, whereas most areas of the South suffered extensive destruction. To Union soldiers on the battlefield, sacrifice was a grim reality; but northern civilians experienced only the bustle and energy of wartime production.

Initially, the war was a shock to business. With the sudden closing of the southern market, firms could no longer predict the demand for their goods; many companies had to redirect their activities in order to remain open. And southern debts became uncollectible, jeopardizing not only merchants but many western banks. In farming regions, families struggled with an aggravated shortage of labor. For reasons such as these, the war initially caused an economic slump.

Initial Slump in Northern Business

A few enterprises never pulled out of the tailspin: cotton mills lacked cotton; construction declined; shoe manufacturers sold fewer of the cheap shoes planters had bought for their slaves. Overall the war slowed industrialization in the North. But historians have shown that the war's economic impact was not all negative. Certain entrepreneurs, such as wool producers, benefited from shortages of competing products, and soaring demand for war-related goods swept some businesses to new heights of production. To feed the voracious war machine the federal government pumped unprecedented amounts of money into the economy. The treasury issued $3.2 billion in bonds and paper money called greenbacks, while the War Department spent over $360 million in tax revenues. Government contracts soon totaled more than $1 billion.

Secretary of War Edwin M. Stanton's list of supplies for the Ordnance Department indicates the scope of government demand: "7,892 cannon, 11,787 artillery carriages, 4,022,130 small-arms . . . 1,022,176,474 cartridges for small-arms, 1,220,555,435 percussion caps . . . 14,507,682 cannon primers and fuses,

12,875,294 pounds of artillery projectiles, 26,440,054 pounds of gunpowder, 6,395,152 pounds of niter, and 90,416,295 pounds of lead." Stanton's list covered only weapons; the government also purchased innumerable quantities of uniforms, boots, food, camp equipment, saddles, ships, and other necessaries.

War-related spending revived business in many northern states. In 1863, a merchants' magazine examined the effects of the war in Massachusetts: "Seldom, if ever, has the business of Massachusetts been more active or profitable than during the past year. . . . Labor has been in great demand . . . trade is again in a high state of prosperity. Wealth has flowed into the State in no stinted measure, despite war and heavy taxes. In every department of labor the government has been, directly or indirectly, the chief employer and paymaster." Government contracts had a particularly beneficial impact on the state's wool, metal, and shipbuilding industries, and saved shoe manufacturers there from ruin.

War production also promoted the development of heavy industry in the North. The output of coal rose substantially. Iron makers improved the quality of their product while boosting the production of pig iron from 920,000 tons in 1860 to 1,136,000 tons in 1864. And although new railroad construction slowed, the manufacture of rails increased. Of considerable significance for the future were the railroad industry's adoption of a standard gauge for track and foundries' development of new and less expensive ways to make steel.

Effects of War on Northern Industry and Agriculture

Another strength of the northern economy was the complementary relationship between agriculture and industry. The mechanization of agriculture had begun well before the war. Now, though, wartime recruitment and conscription gave western farmers an added incentive to purchase labor-saving machinery. This shift from human labor to machines had a doubly beneficial effect, creating new markets for industry and expanding the food supply for the urban industrial work force.

The boom in the sale of agricultural tools was tremendous. Cyrus and William McCormick built an industrial empire in Chicago from their sale of reapers. Between 1862 and 1864 the manufacture of mowers and reapers doubled to 70,000 yearly; manufacturers

Chapter 14: TRANSFORMING FIRE: THE CIVIL WAR, 1861–1865

HARPER'S WEEKLY.
A JOURNAL OF CIVILIZATION.

VOL. V.—No. 238.]   NEW YORK, SATURDAY, JULY 20, 1861.   [SINGLE COPIES SIX CENTS.
$2.50 PER YEAR IN ADVANCE.

Entered according to Act of Congress, in the Year 1861, by Harper & Brothers, in the Clerk's Office of the District Court for the Southern District of New York.

FILLING CARTRIDGES AT THE UNITED STATES ARSENAL AT WATERTOWN, MASSACHUSETTS.—[SEE NEXT PAGE.]

*In both North and South women entered the factories to
boost wartime production. This* Harper's Weekly *cover
shows women filling cartridges in the United States arsenal
at Watertown, Massachusetts.   Library of Congress.*

THE NORTHERN ECONOMY COPES WITH WAR

could not supply the demand. By the end of the war, there were 375,000 reapers in use, triple the number in 1861. Large-scale commercial agriculture had become a reality. As a result, farm families whose breadwinners had gone to war did not suffer as they did in the South. "We have seen," one magazine observed, "a stout matron whose sons are in the army, cutting hay with her team . . . and she cut seven acres with ease in a day, riding leisurely upon her cutter."

Northern industrial and urban workers did not fare as well. Though jobs were plentiful following the initial slump, inflation took much of a worker's paycheck. By 1863 nine-cent-a-pound beef was selling for eighteen cents. The price of coffee had tripled; rice and sugar had doubled; and clothing, fuel, and rent had all climbed. Studies of the cost of living indicate that between 1860 and 1864 consumer prices rose at least 76 percent; meanwhile daily wages rose only 42 percent. To make up the difference, workers' families had to do without.

As their real wages shrank, industrial workers also lost job security. To increase production, some employers were replacing workers with labor-saving machines. Other employers urged the government to liberalize immigration procedures so they could import cheap labor. Workers responded by forming unions and sometimes by striking. Skilled craftsmen organized to combat the loss of their jobs and status to machines; women and unskilled workers, excluded by the craftsmen, formed their own unions. And in recognition of the increasingly national scope of business activity, thirteen occupational groups—including tailors, coalminers, and railway engineers—formed national unions during the Civil War. Because of the tight labor market, unions were able to win many of their demands without striking; but still the number of strikes rose steadily.

New Militancy Among Northern Workers

Employers reacted negatively to this new spirit among workers—a spirit that William H. Sylvis, leader of the iron molders, called a "feeling of manly independence." Manufacturers viewed labor activism as a threat to their property rights and freedom of action, and accordingly they too formed statewide or craft-based associations to cooperate and pool information. These employers compiled blacklists of union members and required new workers to sign "yellow dog" contracts, or promises not to join a union. To put down strikes, they hired strikebreakers from the ranks of the poor and desperate—blacks, immigrants, and women—and sometimes received additional help from federal troops.

Troublesome as unions were, they did not prevent many employers from making a profit. The highest profits were made in profiteering on government contracts. Unscrupulous businessmen took advantage of the sudden immense demand for goods for the army by selling clothing and blankets made of "shoddy"— wool fibers reclaimed from rags or worn cloth. The goods often came apart in the rain; most of the shoes purchased in the early months of the war were worthless too. Contractors sold inferior guns for double the usual price and tainted meat for the price of good. Corruption was so widespread that it led to a year-long investigation by the House of Representatives. One group of contractors that had demanded $50 million for their products had to reduce their claims to $17 million as a result of the findings of the investigation.

Legitimate enterprises also turned a neat profit. The output of woolen mills increased so dramatically that dividends in the industry nearly tripled. Some cotton mills, though they reduced their output, made record profits on what they sold. Brokerage houses worked until midnight and earned unheard-of commissions. And railroads carried immense quantities of freight and passengers, increasing their business to the point that railroad stocks doubled or even tripled. Erie Railroad stock skyrocketed from $17 to $126 a share.

Wartime Benefits to Northern Business

In fact, railroads were a leading beneficiary of government largesse. Congress had failed in the 1850s to resolve the question of a northern versus a southern route for the first transcontinental railroad. But with the South out of Congress, the northern route quickly prevailed. In 1862 and 1864 Congress chartered two corporations, the Union Pacific Railroad and the Central Pacific Railroad, and assisted them financially in connecting Omaha, Nebraska, with Sacramento, California. For each mile of track laid, the railroads received a loan of $16,000 to $48,000 plus twenty square miles of land along a free four-hundred-foot-

Like the Union volunteers boarding this large group train, soldiers North and South found that they were entering bureaucratic organizations whose scale, though suggestive of the future, was comparatively unknown in the past. Free Library of Philadelphia.

wide right of way. Overall, the two corporations gained approximately 20 million acres of land and nearly $60 million in loans.

Other businessmen benefited handsomely from the Morrill Land Grant Act (1862). To promote public education in agriculture, engineering, and military science, Congress granted each state 30,000 acres of public land for each of its congressional representatives. The states were free to sell the land as they saw fit, as long as they used the income for the purposes Congress had intended. Though the law eventually fostered sixty-nine colleges and universities, one of its immediate effects was to enrich a few prominent speculators. Hard-pressed to meet wartime expenses, some states sold their land cheaply to wealthy entrepreneurs. Ezra Cornell, for example, purchased 500,000 acres in the Midwest.

Higher tariffs also pleased many businessmen. Northern businesses did not uniformly favor high import duties; some manufacturers desired cheap imported raw materials more than they feared foreign competition. But northeastern congressmen tradi-

tionally supported higher tariffs, and after southern lawmakers left Washington, they had their way: the Tariff Act of 1864 raised tariffs generously. According to one scholar, manufacturers had only to mention the rate they considered necessary and that rate was declared. And, as one would expect, some healthy industries made artificially high profits by raising their prices to a level just below that of the foreign competition. By the end of the war, tariff rates averaged 47 percent, more than double the rates of 1857.

WARTIME SOCIETY IN THE NORTH

The frantic wartime activity, the booming economy, and the Republican alliance with business combined to create a new atmosphere in Washington.

The balance of opinion shifted against consumers and wage earners and toward large corporations; the notion spread that government should aid businessmen but not interfere with them. This was the golden hour of untrammeled capitalism, and railroad builders and industrialists—men such as Leland Stanford, Collis P. Huntington, John D. Rockefeller, John M. Forbes, and Jay Gould—took advantage of it. Their enterprises grew with the aid of government loans, grants, and tariffs.

Wartime Powers of the U.S. Executive

As long as the war lasted, the powers of the federal government and the president continued to grow. Abraham Lincoln found, as had Jefferson Davis, that war required active presidential leadership. At the beginning of the conflict, Lincoln launched a major shipbuilding program without waiting for Congress to assemble. The lawmakers later approved his decision, and Lincoln continued to act in advance of Congress when he deemed it necessary. In one striking exercise of executive power, Lincoln suspended the writ of habeas corpus for all people living between Washington and Philadelphia. The justification for this action was practical rather than legal; Lincoln was ensuring the loyalty of Maryland. Later in the war, with congressional approval, Lincoln repeatedly suspended the writ and invoked martial law. Roughly ten to twenty thousand United States citizens were arrested on suspicion of disloyal acts.

On occasion Lincoln used his wartime authority to bolster his political power. He and his generals proved adept at arranging furloughs for soldiers who could vote in close elections. Needless to say, the citizens in arms whom Lincoln helped to vote usually voted Republican. In another instance, when the Republican governor of Indiana found himself short of funds because of Democratic opposition, Lincoln generously supplied eight times the amount of money the governor needed to get through the emergency situation.

Among the clearest examples of the wartime expansion of federal authority were the National Banking Acts of 1863, 1864, and 1865. Prior to the Civil War the nation did not have a uniform currency. Banks operating under a variety of state charters issued no fewer than seven thousand different kinds of notes, which had to be distinguished from a variety of forgeries. Now, acting on the recommendations of Secretary of the Treasury Salmon Chase, Congress established a national banking system empowered to issue a maximum number of national bank notes. At the close of the war in 1865, Congress laid a prohibitive tax on state bank notes and forced most major institutions to join the system. This process led to a sounder currency and a simpler monetary system, but also to an inflexibility in the money supply and an eastern-oriented financial structure.

Soldiers may have sensed the increasing scale of things better than anyone else. Most federal troops were young; eighteen was the most common age, followed by twenty-one. Many soldiers went straight from small towns and farms into large armies supplied by extensive bureaucracies. By December 1861 there were 640,000 volunteers in arms, a stupendous increase over the regular army of 20,000 men. The increase occurred so rapidly that it is remarkable the troops were supplied and organized as well as they were. But many soldiers' first experiences with large organizations were unfortunate.

Blankets, clothing, and arms were often inferior. Vermin were commonplace. Hospitals were badly managed at first. Rules of hygiene in large camps were badly written or unenforced; latrines were poorly made or carelessly used. One investigation turned up "an area of over three acres, encircling the camp as a broad belt, on which is deposited an almost perfect layer of human excrement." Water supplies were unsafe and typhoid fever epidemics common. About 57,000 army men died from dysentery and diarrhea.

The situation would have been much worse but for the U.S. Sanitary Commission. A voluntary civilian organization, the commission worked to improve conditions in camps and to aid sick and wounded soldiers. Still, 224,000 Union troops died from disease or accidents, far more than the 140,000 who died in battle.

Self-indulgence Versus Sacrifice in the North

Such conditions would hardly have predisposed the soldier to sympathize with changing social attitudes on the home front. Amid the excitement of money-making, a gaudy culture of vulgar display flourished in the largest cities. A visitor to Chicago commented that "so far as lavish display is concerned, the South Side in some portions has no rival in Chicago, and perhaps not outside New York." Its new residences boasted "marble fronts and expensive ornamentation" that created "a glittering, heartless appearance." As William Cullen Bryant, the distinguished editor of the *New York Evening Post,* observed sadly, "Extravagance, luxury, these are the signs of the times. . . . What business have Americans at any time with such vain show, with such useless magnificence? But especially how can they justify it . . . in this time of war?"

The newly rich did not bother to justify it. *Harper's Monthly* reported that "the suddenly enriched contractors, speculators, and stock-jobbers . . . are spending money with a profusion never before witnessed in our country, at no time remarkable for its frugality. . . . The ordinary sources of expenditure seem to have been exhausted, and these ingenious prodigals have invented new ones. The men button their waistcoats with diamonds . . . and the women powder their hair with gold and silver dust." The *New York Herald* summarized that city's atmosphere:

All our theatres are open . . . and they are all crowded nightly. . . . The most costly accommodations, in both hotels and theatres, are the first and most eagerly taken. . . . The richest silks, laces and jewelry are the soonest sold. . . . Not to keep a carriage, not to wear diamonds, not to be attired in a robe which cost a small fortune, is now equivalent to being a nobody. This war has entirely changed the American character. . . . The individual who makes the most money—no matter how—and spends the most—no matter for what—is considered the greatest man. . . .

The world has seen its iron age, its silver age, its golden age, and its brazen age. This is the age of shoddy.

Yet strong elements of idealism coexisted with ostentation. Abolitionists, after initial uncertainty over whether to fight the South or allow division of the Union to separate the North from slavery, campaigned to turn the war into a war against slavery. Free black communities and churches both black and white responded to the needs of slaves who flocked to the Union lines. They sent clothing, ministers, and teachers in generous measure to aid the runaways in every possible way.

Northern women, like their southern counterparts, took on new roles. Those who stayed home organized over ten thousand soldiers' aid societies, rolled innumerable bandages, and raised $3 million. Thousands served as nurses in front-line hospitals, where they pressed for better care of the wounded. The professionalization of medicine since the Revolution had created a medical system dominated by men; thus dedicated and able female nurses had to fight both military regulations and professional hostility to win the chance to make their contribution. In the hospitals they quickly proved their worth, but only the wounded welcomed them. Even Clara Barton, the most famous female nurse, was ousted from her post during the winter of 1863.

The poet Walt Whitman, who became a daily visitor to wounded soldiers in Washington, D.C., left a record of his experiences as a volunteer nurse. As he dressed wounds and tried to

Walt Whitman comfort suffering and lonely men, Whitman found "the marrow of the tragedy concentrated in those Army Hospitals." But despite "indescribably horrid wounds . . . the groan that could not be repress'd . . . [the] emaciated face and glassy eye," he also found in the hospitals inspiration and a deepening faith in American democracy. Whitman admired the "incredible dauntlessness" and sacrifice of the common soldier who fought for the Union. "The genius of the United States is not best or most in its executives or legislatures," he had written in the Preface to his great work *Leaves of Grass* (1855), "but always most in the common people." Whitman worked this idealization of the common man into his poetry, rejecting the lofty meter and rhyme characteristic of European verse and striving instead for a "genuineness" that would appeal to the masses.

Thus northern society embraced strangely contradictory tendencies. Materialism and greed flourished alongside idealism, religious conviction, and self-sacrifice. While wealthy men purchased 118,000 substitutes and almost 87,000 commutations at $300 each to avoid service in the Union army, other soldiers risked their lives out of a desire to preserve the Union or extend freedom. It was as if there were several different wars under way, each of them serving different motives.

THE STRANGE ADVENT OF EMANCIPATION

At the very highest levels of government there was a similar lack of clarity about the purpose of the war. Through the first several months of the struggle, both Davis and Lincoln studiously avoided references to slavery, the crux of the matter. For his part, Davis was intelligent enough to realize that emphasis on the issue might increase class conflict in the South. Earlier in his career he had struggled on occasion to convince nonslaveholders that defense of the planters' slaves was in their interest. Rather than face that challenge again, Davis articulated a conservative ideology. He told southerners they were fighting for constitutional liberty: northern betrayal of the founding fathers' legacy had necessitated secession. As long as Lincoln also avoided making slavery an issue, Davis's line seemed to work.

Lincoln had his own reasons for refraining from mention of slavery. For some time he clung to the hopeful but mistaken idea that a pro-Union majority would assert itself in the South. Perhaps it would be possible, he thought, to coax the South back into the Union and end the fighting. Raising the slavery issue would effectively end any such possibility of compromise.

Powerful political considerations also dictated that Lincoln remain silent. The Republican party was a young and unwieldy coalition. Some Republicans burned with moral outrage over slavery, while others were frankly racist, dedicated to protecting free whites from the Slave Power and the competition of cheap slave labor. Still others saw the tariff or immigration or some other issue as paramount. A forthright stand by Lincoln on the subject of slavery could split the party, pleasing some groups and alienating others. Until a consensus developed among the party's various wings, or until Lincoln found a way to appeal to all the elements of the party, silence was the best approach.

The president's hesitancy ran counter to some of his personal feelings. Lincoln was a sensitive and compassionate man whose self-awareness, humility, and moral anguish during the war were evident in his speeches and writings. But as a politician, Lincoln kept his moral convictions to himself. He distinguished between the personal and the official; he would not let his feelings determine his political acts. As a result, his political positions were studied and complex, calculated for maximum advantage. Frederick Douglass, the astute and courageous black protest leader, sensed that Lincoln the man was without prejudice toward black people. Yet Douglass judged him "preeminently the white man's president."

Lincoln first broached the subject of slavery in a major way in March 1862, when he proposed that the states consider emancipation on their own. He asked Congress to pass a resolution promising aid to any state that decided to emancipate, and he appealed to border-state representatives to give the idea of emancipation serious consideration. What Lincoln was talking about was gradual emancipation, with compensation for slaveholders and colonization of the freed slaves outside the United States. To a delegation of free blacks he explained that "it is better for us both . . . to be separated." Until well into 1864 Lincoln steadfastly promoted an unpromising and in national terms wholly impractical scheme to colonize blacks in some region like Central America. Despite Secretary of State William H. Seward's care to insert phrases such as "with their consent," the word *deportation* crept into one of Lincoln's speeches in place of *colonization.* Thus his was as conservative a scheme as could be devised. Moreover, since the states would make the decision voluntarily, no responsibility for it would attach to Lincoln.

Lincoln's Plan for Gradual Emancipation

But others wanted to go much further. A group of congressional Republicans known as the Radicals had dedicated themselves to seeing that the war was prosecuted vigorously. They had been instrumental in creating a joint committee on the conduct of the war, which investigated Union reverses, sought to increase the efficiency of the war effort, and prodded the executive to take stronger measures. Early in the war these Radicals, with support from other representatives, turned their attention to slavery.

In August 1861, at the Radicals' instigation, Congress passed its first confiscation act. Designed to punish the Confederate rebels, the law confiscated

Confiscation Acts all property used for "insurrectionary purposes." That is, if the South used slaves in a hostile action, those slaves were declared seized and liberated from their owners' possession. A second confiscation act (July 1862) was much more drastic: it confiscated the property of all those who supported the rebellion, even those who merely resided in the South and paid Confederate taxes. Their slaves were "forever free of their servitude, and not again [to be] held as slaves." The logic behind these acts was that the insurrection—as Lincoln always termed it—was a serious revolution requiring strong measures. Let the government use its full powers, free the slaves, and crush the revolution, urged the Radicals.

Lincoln chose not to go that far. He stood by his proposal of voluntary gradual emancipation by the states and made no effort to enforce the second confiscation act. His stance brought a public protest from Horace Greeley, editor of the powerful *New York Tribune*. In an open letter to the president entitled "The Prayer of Twenty Millions," Greeley wrote, "We require of you . . . that you execute the laws. . . . We think you are strangely and disastrously remiss . . . with regard to the emancipating provisions of the new Confiscation Act. . . . We complain that the Union cause has suffered from mistaken deference to Rebel Slavery." Reaching the nub of the issue, the influential editor went on, "On the face of this wide earth, Mr. President, there is not one disinterested, determined, intelligent champion of the Union cause who does not feel that all attempts to put down the Rebellion and at the same time uphold its inciting cause are preposterous and futile."

Lincoln's letter in reply was an explicit statement of his complex and calculated approach to the question. He disagreed, he said, with all those who would make the saving or destroying of slavery the paramount issue of the war. "I would save the Union," announced Lincoln. "If I could save the Union without freeing *any* slave I would do it, and if I could save it by freeing *all* the slaves I would do it; and if I could save it by freeing some and leaving others alone I would also do that. What I do about slavery, and the colored race, I do because I believe it helps to save the Union." Lincoln closed with a personal disclaimer: "I have here stated my purpose according to my view of *official* duty; and I intend no modification of my oft-expressed *personal* wish that all men everywhere could be free."

When he wrote those words, Lincoln had already decided to take a new step: issuance of the Emancipation Proclamation. On the advice of the cabinet, however, he was waiting for a major Union victory before announcing it, so the proclamation would not appear to be an act of desperation. Yet the letter to Greeley was not simply an effort to stall; it was an integral part of Lincoln's approach to the future of slavery, as the text of the Emancipation Proclamation would show.

On September 22, 1862, shortly after the Battle of Antietam, Lincoln issued the first part of his two-part proclamation. Invoking his powers as commander-in-chief of the armed forces, he announced that on January 1, 1863, he would emancipate the slaves in states whose people "shall then be in rebellion against the United States." The January proclamation would designate the areas in rebellion based on the presence or absence of bona fide representatives in Congress.

Emancipation Proclamations

The September proclamation was less a declaration of the right of slaves to be free than it was a threat to southerners to end the war. "Knowing the value that was set on the slaves by the rebels," said Garrison Frazier, a black Georgian, "the President thought that his proclamation would stimulate them to lay down their arms . . . and their not doing so has now made the freedom of the slaves a part of the war." Lincoln may not actually have expected southerners to give up their effort, but he was careful to offer them the option, thus putting the onus of emancipation on them.

Lincoln's designation of the areas in rebellion on January 1 is worth noting. He excepted from his list every Confederate county or city that had fallen under Union control. Those areas, he declared, "are, for the present, left precisely as if this proclamation were not issued." And in a telling omission, Lincoln neglected to liberate slaves in the border slave states that remained in the Union.

"The President has purposely made the proclamation inoperative in all places where . . . the slaves [are] accessible," complained the antiadministration *New York World*. "He has proclaimed emancipation only where he has notoriously no power to execute it."

Black troops soon proved to doubters that they could fight, and 186,000 black men (approximately 150,000 of whom were former slaves) made a vital contribution to the Union armies and navies. Ohio Historical Society.

The exceptions, said the paper, "render the proclamation not merely futile, but ridiculous." Partisanship aside, even Secretary of State Seward, a moderate Republican, said sarcastically that, "we show our sympathy with slavery by emancipating slaves where we cannot reach them and holding them in bondage where we can set them free." A British official, Lord Russell, commented on the "very strange nature" of the document, noting that it did not declare "a principle adverse to slavery."

Furthermore, by making the liberation of the slaves "a fit and necessary war measure," Lincoln raised a variety of legal questions. How long did a war measure have force? Did its power cease with the suppression of a rebellion? The proclamation did little to clarify the status or citizenship of the freed slaves. And a reference to garrison duty in one of the closing par-

agraphs suggested that slaves would have inferior duties and rank in the army. (For many months, in fact, their pay and treatment were inferior.)

Thus the Emancipation Proclamation was a puzzling and ambiguous document that said less than it seemed to say. Physically it freed no bondsmen, and major limitations were embedded in its language. But if as a moral and legal document it was wanting, as a political document it was nearly flawless. Because the proclamation defined the war as a war against slavery, liberals could applaud it. Yet at the same time it protected Lincoln's position with conservatives, leaving him room to retreat if he chose and forcing no immediate changes on the border slave states. The president had not gone as far as Congress had, and he had taken no position he could not change later if necessary.

In June 1864, however, Lincoln gave his support to the constitutional end of slavery. On the eve of the Republican national convention, he called the party's chairman to the White House and instructed him to have the party "put into the platform as the keystone, the amendment of the Constitution abolishing and prohibiting slavery forever." It was done; the party called for a new constitutional amendment, the thirteenth. Although Republican delegates probably would have adopted such a plank without his urging, Lincoln showed his commitment by lobbying Congress for quick approval of the measure. He succeeded, and the proposed amendment went to the states for ratification or rejection. Lincoln's strong support for the Thirteenth Amendment—an unequivocal prohibition of slavery—constitutes his best claim to the title Great Emancipator.

Yet Lincoln soon clouded that clear stand, for in 1865 the newly re-elected president considered allowing the defeated southern states to re-enter the Union and delay or defeat the amendment. In February he and Secretary of State Seward met with three Confederate commissioners at Hampton Roads, Virginia. The end of the war was clearly in sight, and southern representatives angled vainly for an armistice that would allow southern independence. But Lincoln was doing some political maneuvering of his own, apparently contemplating the creation of a new and broader party based on a postwar alliance with southern Whigs

Hampton Roads Conference

and moderates. The cement for the coalition would be concessions to planter interests.

Pointing out that the Emancipation Proclamation was only a war measure, Lincoln predicted that the courts would decide whether it had granted all, some, or none of the slaves their freedom. Seward observed that the Thirteenth Amendment, which would be definitive, was not yet ratified; re-entry into the Union would allow the southern states to vote against it and block it. Lincoln did not contradict him, but spoke in favor of "prospective" ratification—ratification with a five-year delay. He also promised to seek $400 million in compensation for slaveholders and to consider their position on such related questions as confiscation. Such financial aid would provide an economic incentive for planters to rejoin the Union, and capital to ease the transition to freedom for both races.

These were startling propositions from a president who was on the verge of military victory. Most northerners opposed them, and only the opposition of Jefferson Davis, who set himself against anything short of independence, prevented discussion of the proposals in the South. They indicated that even at the end of the war, Lincoln was keeping his options open, maintaining the line he had drawn between "*official* duty" and "*personal* wish." Contrary to legend, then, Lincoln did not attempt to lead public opinion on race, as did advocates of equality in one direction and racist Democrats in the other. Instead he moved cautiously, constructing complex and ambiguous positions. He avoided the great risks inherent in challenging, educating, or inspiring national conscience.

Before the war was over, the Confederacy too addressed the issue of emancipation. Ironically, a strong proposal in favor of liberation came from Jefferson Davis. Though emancipation was far less popular in the South than in the North, Davis did not flinch or conceal his purpose. He was dedicated to independence, and he was willing to sacrifice slavery to achieve that goal. After considering the alternatives for some time, Davis concluded in the fall of 1864 that it was necessary to act.

Davis's Plan for Emancipation

Reasoning that the military situation of the Confederacy was desperate, and that independence with emancipation was preferable to defeat with emancipation, Davis proposed that the central government purchase and train forty thousand male Negro laborers. The men would work for the army under a promise of emancipation and future residence in the South. Later Davis upgraded his proposal, calling for the recruitment and arming of slave soldiers. The wives and children of these soldiers, he made plain, must also receive freedom from the states. Davis and his advisors did not favor full equality—they envisioned "an intermediate stage of serfage or peonage." Thus they shared with Lincoln and their whole generation a racial pessimism and blindness that tried to ignore the massive changes underway.

Still, Davis had proposed a radical change for the conservative, slaveholding South. Bitter debate resounded through the Confederacy, but Davis stood his ground. When the Confederate congress approved enlistments without the promise of freedom, Davis insisted on more. He issued an executive order to guarantee that owners would cooperate with the emancipation of slave soldiers, and his allies in the states started to work for emancipation of the soldiers' families. Some black troops started to drill as the end of the war approached.

Confederate emancipation began too late to revive southern armies or win diplomatic advantages with antislavery Europeans. But Lincoln's Emancipation Proclamation stimulated a vital infusion of forces into the Union armies. Beginning in 1863 slaves shouldered arms for the North. Before the war was over, 150,000 of them had fought for freedom and the Union. Their participation was crucial to northern victory, and it discouraged recognition of the Confederacy by foreign governments. Lincoln's policy, despite its limitations and its lack of clarity, had great practical effect.

THE DISINTEGRATION OF CONFEDERATE UNITY

During the final two years of fighting, both northern and southern governments waged the war in the face of increasing opposition at home. Dissatisfaction that had surfaced earlier grew more intense and sometimes even violent. The unrest was connected to the military stalemate: neither side was close to victory in 1863, though the war had become gigantic in scope and costly in lives. But protest also arose from fundamental stresses in the social structures of the North and the South.

The Confederacy's problems were both more serious and more deeply rooted than the North's. Vastly disadvantaged in terms of industrial capacity, natural resources, and labor, southerners felt the cost of the war more quickly, more directly, and more painfully than northerners. But even more fundamental were the Confederacy's internal problems; crises that were integrally connected with the southern class system threatened the Confederate cause.

One ominous development was the increasing opposition of planters to their own government, whose actions often had a negative effect on them. Not only did the Richmond government impose high taxes and a tax-in-kind, Confederate military authorities also impressed slaves to build fortifications. And when Union forces advanced on plantation areas, Confederate commanders sent detachments through the countryside to burn stores of cotton that lay in the enemy's path. Such interference with plantation routines and financial interests was not what planters had expected of their government, and they resisted. Many taxes went unpaid, and many planters continued to grow and ship cotton, despite the government's desire to withhold it from world markets as a diplomatic weapon.

Nor were the centralizing policies of the Davis administration popular. Many planters agreed with the *Charleston Mercury* that the southern states had seceded because the federal government had grown and "usurped powers not granted—progressively trenched upon State Rights." The increasing size and power of the Richmond administration therefore startled and alarmed them.

The Confederate constitution, drawn up by the leading political thinkers of the South, had in fact granted substantial powers to the central government, especially in time of war. But for many planters, states' rights had become virtually synonymous with complete state sovereignty. R. B. Rhett, editor of the *Charleston Mercury*, wishfully (and inaccurately) described the Confederate constitution: "[It] leaves the States untouched in their Sovereignty, and com-

mits to the Confederate Government only a few simple objects, and a few simple powers to enforce them." Governor Joseph E. Brown of Georgia took a similarly exalted view of the importance of the states. During the brief interval between Georgia's secession from the Union and its admission to the Confederacy, Brown sent an ambassador to Europe to seek recognition for the sovereign republic of Georgia from Queen Victoria, Napoleon III, and the King of Belgium. His mentality harkened back to the 1770s and the Articles of Confederation, not to the Constitution of 1789 or the Confederate constitution.

In effect, years of opposition to the federal government within the Union had frozen southerners in a defensive posture. Now they erected the barrier of states' rights as a defense against change, hiding behind it while their capacity for creative statesmanship atrophied. Planters sought a guarantee that their plantations and their lives would remain untouched; they were deeply committed neither to building a southern nation nor to winning independence. If the Confederacy had been allowed to depart from the Union in peace and continue as a semideveloped cotton-growing region, they would have been content. When secession revolutionized their world, they could not or would not adjust to it.

Confused and embittered, southerners struck out instead at Jefferson Davis. Conscription, thundered Governor Brown, was "subversive of [Georgia's] sovereignty, and at war with all the principles for the support of which Georgia entered into this revolution." Searching for ways to frustrate the law, Brown bickered over draft exemptions and ordered local enrollment officials not to cooperate with the Confederacy. The *Charleston Mercury* told readers that "conscription . . . is . . . the very embodiment of Lincolnism, which our gallant armies are today fighting." And in a gesture of stubborn selfishness, planter Robert Toombs of Georgia, a former U.S. Senator, defied the government, the newspapers, and his neighbors' petitions by continuing to grow large amounts of cotton. His action bespoke the inflexibility and frustration of the southern elite at a crucial point in the Confederacy's struggle to survive.

The southern courts ultimately upheld Davis's power to conscript. He continued to provide strong leadership and drove through the legislature measures that gave

A southern family flees its home as the battle lines draw near. Photographed by Matthew Brady.   National Archives.

the Confederacy a fighting chance. Despite his cold formality and inability to disarm critics, Davis possessed two important virtues: iron determination and total dedication to independence. These qualities kept the Confederacy afloat, for he implemented his measures and enforced them. But his actions earned him the hatred of most influential and elite citizens.

Meanwhile, at the bottom of southern society, there were other difficulties. Food riots occurred in the spring of 1863 in Atlanta, Macon, Columbus, and Augusta, Georgia; and in Salisbury and High Point, North Carolina. On April 2, a crowd assembled in the Confederate capital of Richmond to demand relief from Governor Letcher. A passerby, noticing the excitement, asked a young girl, "Is there some celebration?" "There is," replied the girl. "We celebrate our right to live. We are starving. As soon as enough of us get together we are going to the bakeries and each of us will take a loaf of bread." Soon they did just

Food Riots in Southern Cities

that, sparking a riot that Davis himself had to quell at gunpoint. Later that year, another group of angry rioters ransacked a street in Mobile, Alabama.

Throughout the rural South, ordinary people resisted more quietly— by refusing to cooperate with impressments of food, conscription, or tax collection. "In all the States impressments are evaded by every means which ingenuity can suggest, and in some openly resisted," wrote a high-ranking commissary officer. Farmers who did provide food refused to accept certificates of credit or government bonds in lieu of cash, as required by law. And conscription officers increasingly found no one to draft—men of draft age were hiding out in the forests. "The disposition to avoid military service," observed one of Georgia's senators in 1864, "is general." In some areas tax agents were killed in the line of duty.

Davis was ill-equipped to deal with such discontent. Austere and private by nature, he failed to communicate with the masses. For long stretches of time he buried himself in military affairs or administrative details, until a crisis forced him to rush off on a speaking tour to revive the spirit of resistance. His class perspective also distanced him from the sufferings of the common people. While his social circle in Richmond dined on duck and oysters, ordinary southerners leached salt from the smokehouse floor and went hungry. State governors who saw to the common people's needs won the public's loyalty, but Davis failed to reach out to them and thus lost the support of the plain folk.

Such civil discontent was certain to affect the Confederate armies. "What man is there that would stay in the army and no that his family is sufring at home?" an angry citizen wrote anonymously to the secretary of war. An upcountry South Carolina newspaper agreed, asking, "What would sooner make our soldiers falter than the cry from their families?" Spurred by concern for their loved ones and resentment of the rich man's war, large numbers of men did indeed leave the armies, supported by their friends and neighbors. Mary Boykin Chesnut observed a man being dragged back to the army as his wife looked on. "Desert agin, Jake!" she cried openly. "You desert agin, quick as you kin. Come back to your wife and children."

Desertions from the Confederate Army

Desertion did not become a serious problem for the Confederacy until the summer of 1862, and stiffer policing solved the problem that year. But from 1863 on, the number of men on duty fell rapidly as desertions soared. By the summer of 1863, John A. Campbell, the South's assistant secretary of war, wondered whether "so general a habit" as desertion could be considered a crime. Campbell estimated that 40,000 to 50,000 troops were absent without leave and that 100,000 were evading duty in some way. Liberal furloughs, amnesty proclamations, and appeals to return had little effect; by November 1863, Secretary of War James Seddon admitted that one-third of the army could not be accounted for. And the situation was to worsen.

The gallantry of those who stayed on in Lee's army and the daring of their commander made for a deceptively positive start to the 1863 campaign. On May 2 and 3 at Chancellorsville, Virginia, 130,000 members of the Union Army of the Potomac bore down on fewer than 60,000 Confederates. Acting as

Battle of Chancellorsville

if they enjoyed being outnumbered, Lee and Stonewall Jackson boldly divided their forces, ordering 30,000 men under Jackson on a day-long march westward and to the rear for a flank attack. Jackson arrived at his position late in the afternoon to witness unprepared Union troops "laughing, smoking," playing cards, and waiting for dinner. "Push right ahead," Jackson said, and his weary but excited corps swooped down on the Federals and drove their right wing back in confusion. The Union forces left Chancellorsville the next day defeated. Though Stonewall Jackson had been fatally wounded, it was a remarkable southern victory.

But two critical battles in July 1863 brought crushing defeats to the Confederacy. General Ulysses S. Grant, after months of searching through swamps and bayous, had succeeded in finding an advantageous approach to Vicksburg, and promptly laid siege to that vital western fortification. If Vicksburg fell, U.S. forces would control the Mississippi, cutting the Confederacy in half and gaining an open path into the interior. Meanwhile, with no serious threat to Richmond, General Robert E. Lee proposed a Confederate invasion of the North, to turn the tables on the Union and divert attention from Vicksburg. Both movements drew toward conclusion early in July.

In the North, Lee's troops streamed through western Maryland and into Pennsylvania, threatening both Washington and Baltimore. The possibility of a major victory before the Union capital became more and more likely. But along the Mississippi, Confederate prospects darkened. Davis and Secretary of War Seddon repeatedly wired General Joseph E. Johnston to concentrate his forces and attack Grant's army. "Vicksburg must not be lost, at least without a struggle," they insisted. Johnston, however, either failed in imagination or did not understand the possibilities of his command. "I consider saving Vicksburg hopeless," he telegraphed at one point, and despite prodding he did nothing to relieve the garrison. In the meantime, Grant's men were supplying themselves by drawing on the agricultural riches of the Mississippi River valley. With such provisions, they could continue their siege indefinitely. In fact, their rich meat-and-vegetables diet had become so tiresome to them that one day, as Grant rode by, a private looked up and muttered, "Hardtack" (pilot biscuit). Soon a line

These dead Union soldiers helped to repulse Confederate troops who charged valiantly but futilely up Gettysburg's gentle hills. Library of Congress.

of soldiers was shouting "Hardtack! Hardtack!" demanding respite from turkey and sweet potatoes.

In such circumstances the fall of Vicksburg was inevitable, and on July 4, 1863, its commander surrendered. That same day a battle that had been raging since July 1 concluded at Gettysburg, Pennsylvania. On July 1 and 2, the Union and Confederate forces had both made gains in furious fighting. Then on July 3 Lee ordered a direct assault on Union fortifications atop Cemetery Ridge. Full of foreboding, General James Longstreet warned Lee that "no 15,000 men ever arrayed for battle can take that position." But Lee, hoping success might force the Union to accept peace with independence, stuck to his plan. His brave troops rushed the position, and a hundred momentarily breached the enemy's line. But most fell in heavy slaughter. On July 4 Lee had to withdraw, having suffered almost 4,000 killed and approximately 24,000 missing and wounded. The Confederate general reported to Jefferson Davis that "I am alone to blame," and tendered his resignation. Davis replied that to find a more capable commander was "an impossibility."

Battle of Gettysburg

Though southern troops had displayed a courage and dedication that would never be forgotten, the results had been disastrous. Josiah Gorgas, the genius of Confederate ordnance operations, confided to his diary, "Today absolute ruin seems our portion. The Confederacy totters to its destruction." In desperation President Davis and several state governors resorted to threats and racial scare tactics to drive southern whites to further sacrifice. Defeat, Davis warned, would mean "extermination of yourselves, your wives, and children." Governor Charles Clark of Mississippi predicted "elevation of the black race to a position of equality—aye, of superiority, that will make them your masters and rulers." Abroad, British officials held back the delivery of badly needed warships, and diplomats postponed any thought of recognizing the Confederate government.

From this point on, the internal disintegration of the Confederacy quickened. A few newspapers and a few bold politicians began to call openly for peace. "We are for peace," admitted the *Raleigh* (North Carolina) *Daily Progress,* "because there has been enough of blood and carnage, enough of widows and orphans." A neighboring journal, the *North Carolina*

Standard, vowed to "tell the truth," tacitly admitted that defeat was inevitable, and called for negotiations. Similar proposals were made in several state legislatures, though they were presented as plans for independence on honorable terms. But more important, Confederate leaders had begun to realize that they were losing the support of the common people. A prominent Texan noted in his diary that secession had been the work of political leaders operating without the firm support of "the mass of the people without property." Governor Zebulon Vance of North Carolina, who agreed, wrote privately that independence would require more "blood and misery . . . and our people will not pay this price I am satisfied for their independence. . . . The great popular heart is not now & never has been in this war."

In North Carolina a peace movement grew under the leadership of William W. Holden, a popular Democratic politician and editor. In the summer of

Southern Peace Movements

1863 over one hundred public meetings took place in support of peace negotiations; many established figures believed that Holden had the majority of the people behind him. In Georgia early in 1864, Governor Brown and Alexander H. Stephens, vice president of the Confederacy, led a similar effort. Ultimately, however, these movements came to naught. The lack of a two-party system threw into question the legitimacy of any criticism of the government; even Holden and Brown could not entirely escape the taint of dishonor and disloyalty. That the movement existed despite the risks suggested deep disaffection.

The results of the 1863 congressional elections continued the tendency toward dissent. Everywhere secessionists and supporters of the administration lost seats to men who were not identified with the government. Many of the new representatives, who were often former Whigs, openly opposed the administration or publicly favored peace. In the last years of the war, Davis depended heavily on support from Union-occupied districts to maintain a majority in the congress. Having secured the legislation he needed, he used the bureaucracy and the army to enforce his unpopular policies. Ironically, as the South's situation grew desperate, former critics such as the *Charleston Mercury* became supporters of the administration. They and a solid core of courageous and determined

soldiers kept the Confederacy alive in the face of disintegrating popular support.

By 1864 much of the opposition to the war had moved entirely outside politics. Southerners were simply giving up the struggle, withdrawing their co-operation from the government, and forming a sort of counter-society. Deserters joined with ordinary citizens who were sick of the war to dominate whole towns and counties. Secret societies dedicated to reunion, such as the Heroes of America and the Red Strings, sprang up. Active dissent spread throughout the South but was particularly common in upland and mountain regions. "The condition of things in the mountain districts of North Carolina, South Carolina, Georgia, and Alabama," admitted Assistant Secretary of War John A. Campbell, "menaces the existence of the Confederacy as fatally as either of the armies of the United States." Confederate officials tried using the army to round up deserters and compel obedience, but this approach was only temporarily effective. The government was losing the support of its citizens.

ANTIWAR SENTIMENT IN THE NORTH

In the North opposition to the war was similar in many ways, but not as severe. There was concern over the growing centralization of government, and war-weariness was a frequent complaint. Discrimination and injustice in the draft sparked protest among poor citizens, just as they had in the South. But the Union was so much richer than the South in human resources that none of these problems ever threatened the stability of the government. Fresh recruits were always available, and food and other necessaries were not subject to severe shortages.

What was more, Lincoln possessed a talent that Davis lacked: he knew how to stay in touch with the ordinary citizen. Through letters to newspapers and to soldiers' families, he reached the common people and demonstrated that he had not forgotten them. Their grief was his also, for the war was his personal tragedy. After scrambling to the summit of political ambition, Lincoln had seen the glory of the presidency turn to horror. The daily carnage, the tortuous political problems, and the ceaseless criticism weighed heavily on him. In moving language, this president with the demeanor of a self-educated man of humble origins was able to communicate his suffering. His words helped to contain northern discontent, though they could not remove it.

Much of this wartime protest sprang from politics. The Democratic party, though nudged from its dominant position by the Republican surge of the late

Peace Democrats

1850s, remained strong. Its leaders were determined to regain power, and they found much to criticize in Lincoln's policies: the carnage and length of the war, the expansion of federal powers, inflation and the high tariff, and the improved status of blacks. Accordingly, they attacked the continuation of the war, calling for reunion on the basis of "the Constitution as it is and the Union as it was." The Democrats denounced conscription and martial law, and defended states' rights and the interests of agriculture. They charged repeatedly that Republican policies were designed to flood the North with blacks, depriving white males of their status, jobs, and women. Their stand appealed to southerners who had settled north of the Ohio River, to conservatives, to many poor people, and to some eastern merchants who had lost profitable southern trade. In the 1862 elections, the Democrats made a strong comeback. And during the war, peace Democrats influenced New York State and won majorities in the legislatures of Illinois and Indiana.

Led by outspoken men like Clement L. Vallandigham of Ohio, the peace Democrats were highly visible. Vallandigham criticized Lincoln as a dictator who had suspended the writ of habeas corpus without congressional authority and arrested thousands of innocent citizens. Like other Democrats, he condemned both conscription and emancipation and urged voters to use their power at the polling place to depose "King Abraham." Vallandigham stayed carefully within legal bounds, but his attacks were so damaging to the war effort that military authorities arrested him after Lincoln suspended habeas corpus. Fearing that Vallandigham might gain the stature of a martyr, the president decided against a jail term and exiled

him to the Confederacy. Thus Lincoln rid himself of a troublesome critic, in the process saddling puzzled Confederates with a man who insisted on talking about "our country." Eventually Vallandigham returned to the North through Canada.

Lincoln believed that antiwar Democrats were linked to secret organizations, such as the Knights of the Golden Circle and the Order of American Knights, that harbored traitorous ideas. These societies, he feared, stimulated draft resistance, discouraged enlistment, sabotaged communications, and plotted to aid the Confederacy. Likening such groups to a poisonous snake striking at the government, Republicans sometimes branded them—and by extension the peace Democrats—as Copperheads. Though Democrats were connected with these organizations, most engaged in politics rather than treason. And though some saboteurs and Confederate agents were active in the North, they never effected any major demonstration of support for the Confederacy. Whether Lincoln overreacted in arresting his critics and suppressing opposition is still a matter of debate, but it is certain that he acted with a heavier hand and with less provocation than Jefferson Davis.

More violent opposition to the government came from ordinary citizens facing the draft, especially the urban poor. Conscription was a massive but poorly organized affair. Federal enrolling officers made up the list of eligibles, a procedure open to personal favoritism and ethnic or class prejudice. Lists of those conscripted reveal that poor men were called more often than rich, and that disproportionate numbers of immigrants were called. (Approximately 200,000 men born in Germany and 150,000 born in Ireland served in the Union Army.) And rich men could furnish substitutes or pay a commutation to avoid service.

As a result, there were scores of disturbances and melees. Enrolling officers received rough treatment in many parts of the North, and riots occurred in

New York City Draft Riot

Ohio, Indiana, Pennsylvania, Illinois, and Wisconsin, and in such cities as Troy, Albany, and Newark. By far the most serious outbreak of violence, however, occurred in New York City in July 1863. The war was unpopular in that Democratic stronghold, and ethnic and class tensions ran high. Shippers had recently broken a longshoremen's strike

These photographers capture the very different personal styles of Grant (left) and Lee (right). Their costly battles stimulated war weariness in 1864 but eventually made the end of the war more clear.   Left: Library of Congress; right: National Archives.

Chapter 14: TRANSFORMING FIRE: THE CIVIL WAR, 1861–1865

by hiring black strikebreakers who worked under police protection. Working-class New Yorkers feared an influx of such black labor from the South and regarded blacks as the cause of an unpopular war. Irish workers, often recently arrived and poor themselves, resented being forced to serve in the place of others. And indeed, local draft lists certified that the poor foreign-born were going to have to bear the burden of service.

The provost marshal's office came under attack first. Then mobs crying "Down with the rich" looted wealthy homes and stores. But blacks proved to be the rioters' special target. Luckless blacks who happened to be in the rioters' path were beaten; soon the mob rampaged through black neighborhoods, destroying an orphans' asylum. At least seventy-four people died during the violence, which raged out of control for three days. Only the dispatch of army units fresh from Gettysburg ended the episode.

Once inducted, northern soldiers felt many of the same anxieties and grievances as their southern counterparts. Federal troops too had to cope with loneliness and concern for their loved ones, disease, and the tedium of camp life. Thousands of men slipped away from authorities. Given the problems plaguing the draft and the discouragement in the North over lack of progress in the war, it is not surprising that the Union Army struggled with a desertion rate as high as the Confederates'.

Discouragement and war-weariness neared their peak during the summer of 1864. At that point the Democratic party nominated the popular General George B. McClellan for president and put a qualified peace plank into its platform. The plank, written by Vallandigham, condemned "four years of failure to restore the Union by the experiment of war" and called for an armistice. Lincoln concluded that it was "exceedingly probable that this Administration will not be re-elected."

Then, during a publicized interchange with Confederate emissaries in Canada, Lincoln insisted that the terms for peace include reunion and "the abandonment of slavery." A wave of protest rose in the North, for many voters were weary of war and unready to demand terms beyond preservation of the Union. Lincoln quickly backtracked, denying that his offer meant "that nothing *else* or *less* would be considered, if offered." He would insist on freedom only for those slaves (about 150,000) who had joined the Union army under his promise of emancipation. Thus Lincoln in effect acknowledged the danger that he would not be re-elected. The fortunes of war, however, soon changed the electoral situation.

NORTHERN PRESSURE AND SOUTHERN WILL

Northern Diplomatic Strategy

The year 1864 brought to fruition the North's long-term diplomatic strategy. From the outset, the North had pursued one paramount diplomatic goal: to prevent recognition of the Confederacy by European nations. Foreign recognition would damage the North's claim that it was fighting an illegal rebellion, not a separate nation. But more important, recognition would open the way to the foreign military and financial aid that could assure Confederate independence. Among the British elite, there was considerable sympathy for southern planters, whose aristocratic values were similar to their own. And in terms of power politics, both England and France stood to benefit from a divided America, which would necessarily be a weaker rival. Thus Lincoln and Secretary of State Seward faced a difficult task. To achieve their goal, they needed to avoid both major military defeats and unnecessary controversies with the European powers.

Southerners aided them by an overconfident reliance on "King Cotton" diplomacy. Knowing that the textile industry, directly or indirectly, employed one-fifth of the British population, southern leaders declared that "Cotton is King." They believed that the British government, concerned to obtain cotton for the country's mills, would *have* to recognize the Confederacy. But though cotton was a good card to play, it was not a trump. At the beginning of the war British mills had a 50-percent surplus of cotton on hand. New sources of supply in India, Egypt, and Brazil helped to fill their needs later on, and some southern cotton continued to reach Europe, despite the Confederacy's recommendation that its citizens plant and ship no cotton. The British government, refusing to be stampeded into recognition, kept its eye on the battlefield. France, though sympathetic to the South, was unwilling to act without the British. Confederate agents were able to purchase valuable arms and supplies in Europe and obtained some loans from European financiers, but they never achieved a diplomatic breakthrough.

More than once the Union strategy nearly broke down. A major crisis occurred in 1861 when the overzealous commander of an American frigate stopped the British steamer *Trent* and abducted two Confederate ambassadors. The British reacted strongly, but Lincoln and Seward were able to delay until a less-excited public opinion allowed them to back down and return the ambassadors. In a series of confrontations, the United States protested against the building and sale of warships to the Confederacy. A few ships built in Britain, notably the *Alabama*, reached open water to serve the Confederacy. Over twenty-two months, without entering a southern port, the *Alabama* destroyed or captured more than sixty northern ships. But soon the British government began to bar delivery to the Confederacy of warships such as the Laird rams, formidable vessels whose pointed prows were designed to break the Union blockade.

Back on American battlefields, the northern victory was far from won. Most engagements had demonstrated the advantages enjoyed by the defense and the extreme difficulty of destroying an opposing army. As General William Tecumseh Sherman recognized, the North had to "keep the war South until they are not only ruined, exhausted, but humbled in pride and spirit." Yet the world's recognized military authorities agreed that deep invasion was extremely difficult and risky. The farther an army penetrated enemy territory, the more vulnerable its own communications and support became. Moreover, noted the Prussian expert Karl von Clausewitz, if the invader encountered a "truly national" resistance, his troops would be "everywhere exposed to attacks by an insurgent population." Thus, if southerners were determined enough to mount a "truly national" resistance, their defiance and the vast size of their country would make a northern victory virtually impossible.

General Grant decided to test these obstacles—and southern will—with an innovation of his own: the strategy of raids. Raids were not new, but what

Grant had in mind was on a massive scale. He proposed to use whole armies, not just cavalry, to destroy Confederate railroads, thus denying the enemy rail transportation and damaging the South's economy. Federal armies, abandoning their lines of support, would live off the land while they laid waste all resources useful to the Confederacy. After General George H. Thomas's troops won the Battle of Chattanooga in November 1863 by ignoring orders and charging up Missionary Ridge, the heartland of the South lay open. Moving to the Virginia theater, Grant entrusted General Sherman with 100,000 men for such a raid deep into the South, toward Atlanta.

Jefferson Davis countered by placing the army of General Johnston in Sherman's path. Davis's entire political strategy for 1864 depended on the demonstration of Confederate military strength and a successful defense of Atlanta. With the federal elections of 1864 approaching, Davis hoped that a display of strength and resolution by the South would defeat Lincoln and elect a president who would sue for peace. When Johnston slowly but steadily fell back toward Atlanta, Davis grew anxious and pressed his commander for information and assurances that Atlanta would be held. From a purely military point of view, Johnston was conducting the defense skillfully, but Jefferson Davis could not take a purely military point of view. When Johnston remained uninformative and continued to drop back, Davis replaced him with the one-legged General John Hood, who knew his job was to fight. "Our all depends on that army at Atlanta," wrote Mary Boykin Chesnut. "If that fails us, the game is up."

And for southern morale, the game was up. Hood attacked but was beaten, and Sherman's army occupied Atlanta on September 2, 1864. The victory buoyed northern spirits and assured Lincoln's re-election. Mary Chesnut moaned, "There is no hope," and a government clerk in Richmond wrote, "Our fondly-cherished visions of peace have vanished like a mirage of the desert." Though Davis exhorted southerners to fight on and win new victories before the federal elections, he had to admit that "two-thirds of our men are absent . . . most of them absent without leave." Hood's army marched north to cut Sherman's supply lines and force him to retreat, but Sherman, planning to live off the land, marched the greater

Sherman's march demonstrated, as nothing before had, the enormous destructiveness and total, economic character of modern war. The ordnance trains and rolling mill above were blown up at Atlanta. Library of Congress.

part of his army straight to the sea, destroying Confederate resources as he went (see map, page 412.)

As he moved across Georgia Sherman cut a path fifty to sixty miles wide; the totality of the destruction was awesome. A Georgia woman described the "Burnt Country" this way: "The fields were trampled down and the road was lined with carcasses of horses, hogs, and cattle that the invaders, unable either to consume or to carry away with them, had wantonly shot down to starve our people and prevent them from making their crops. The stench in some places was unbearable." Such devastation diminished the South's material resources, but, more importantly, it was bound to impact on the faltering southern will to resist.

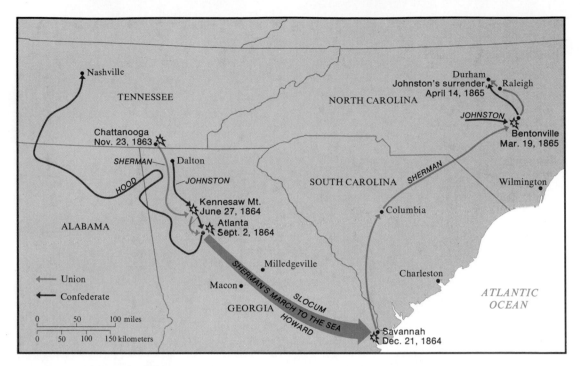

Sherman's March to the Sea

After reaching Savannah in December, Sherman turned north and marched his armies into the Carolinas. Wreaking great destruction as he moved through South Carolina into North Carolina, Sherman encountered little resistance. The opposing army of General Johnston was small, but Sherman's men should have been prime targets for guerrilla raids and harassing attacks by local defense units. The absence of both led South Carolina's James Chesnut, Jr., to write that his state "was shamefully and unnecessarily lost. . . . We had time, opportunity and means to destroy him. But there was wholly wanting the energy and ability required by the occasion." Southerners were reaching the limit of their endurance.

Sherman's march brought additional human resources to the Union cause. In Georgia alone as many as nineteen thousand slaves gladly took the opportunity to escape bondage and join the Union army as it passed through the countryside. Others held back to await the end of the war on the plantations, either from an ingrained wariness of whites or from negative experiences with the federal soldiers. The destruction of food harmed slaves as well as white rebels; many blacks lost blankets, shoes, and other valuables to their liberators. In fact, the brutality of Sherman's troops shocked these veterans of the whip. "I've seen them cut the hams off of a live pig or ox and go off leavin' the animal groanin'," recalled one man. "The master had 'em kilt then, but it was awful."

It was awful, too, in Virginia, where the preliminaries to victory proved to be protracted and ghastly. Throughout the spring and summer Grant hurled his troops at Lee's army and suffered appalling losses: almost 18,000 casualties in the Battle of the Wilderness, more than 8,000 at Spotsylvania, and 12,000 in the space of a few hours at Cold Harbor (see map). Before the last battle, Union troops pinned scraps of paper bearing their names and addresses to their backs, certain that they would be mowed down as they rushed Lee's trenches. In four weeks in May and June, Grant lost as many men as were enrolled in Lee's entire army. Undaunted, Grant remarked, "I propose to fight it out along this line if it takes all summer." And the heavy fighting did prepare the way for eventual victory: Lee's army shrank to the point that offensive action was no longer possible, while the Union army kept replenishing its forces with new recruits.

Chapter 14: TRANSFORMING FIRE: THE CIVIL WAR, 1861–1865

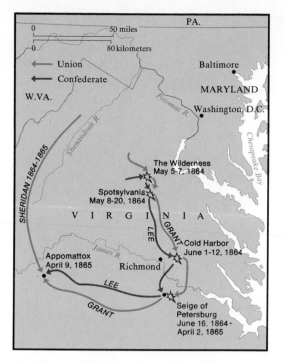

The War in Virginia, 1864–1865

COSTS AND EFFECTS

The end finally came in the spring of 1865. Grant kept battering at Lee, who tried but failed to break through the federal line east of Petersburg on March 25. With the numerical superiority of Grant's army now upwards of two-to-one, Confederate defeat was inevitable. On April 2 Lee abandoned Richmond and Petersburg. On April 9, hemmed in by federal troops, short of rations, and with fewer than 30,000 men left, Lee surrendered to Grant. At Appomattox Courthouse the Union general treated his rival with respect and paroled the defeated troops. Within weeks Jefferson Davis was captured, and the remaining Confederate forces laid down their arms and surrendered. The war was over at last.

Heavy Losses Force Lee's Surrender

Lincoln did not live to see the last surrenders. On the evening of Good Friday, April 14, he went to Ford's Theatre in Washington, where an assassin named John Wilkes Booth shot him at pointblank range. Lincoln died the next day. The Union had lost its wartime leader, and to many, relief at the war's end was tempered by uncertainty about the future.

The costs of the Civil War were enormous. Although precise figures on enlistments are impossible to obtain, it appears that during the course of the conflict the Confederate armies claimed the services of 700,000 to 800,000 men. Far more, possibly 2.3 million, served in the Union armies. Northern reserves were so great that more men were legally subject to the draft at the end of the war than at the beginning.

Statistics on casualties are more precise and more appalling. Approximately 364,222 federal soldiers died, 140,070 of them from wounds suffered in battle. Another 275,175 Union soldiers were wounded but survived. On the Confederate side, an estimated 258,000 lost their lives, and even a conservative estimate of Confederate wounded brings the total number of casualties on both sides to more than 1 million—a frightful toll for a nation of 31 million people. More men died in the Civil War than in all other American wars before Vietnam combined.

Casualties

Such carnage seems a terrible price to pay over a disagreement in which some possibilities of compromise—such as a national convention—were never tried. But any democratic system requires an underlying degree of consensus in order to function. That consensus had failed in 1860 and 1861. Although most voters in 1860 had not wanted war, and surely not a bloody war like this, the disagreements between North and South had become too deep and too great to manage. Powerful interests had refused to compromise. A fundamental clash of wills, which would continue to trouble Reconstruction, had caused unprecedented loss of life.

Property damage and financial costs were also enormous, though difficult to tally. Federal loans and taxes during the conflict totaled almost $3 billion, and interest on the war debt was $2.8 billion. The Confederacy borrowed over $2 billion but lost far more in the destruction of homes, fences, crops, livestock, and other property. To give just one example of the wreckage that attended four

Financial Cost of the War

Lincoln's face betrays the strain of four years of war. Compare his youthful appearance in Springfield, Illinois, on August 13, 1860, left, with the photograph on the right, taken in Washington, April 10, 1865, four days before his assassination.   Library of Congress.

years of conflict on southern soil, the number of hogs in South Carolina plummeted from 965,000 in 1860 to approximately 150,000 in 1865. Thoughtful scholars have noted that small farmers lost just as much, proportionally, as planters whose slaves were emancipated.

Estimates of the total cost of the war exceed $20 billion—five times the total expenditure of the federal government from its creation to 1865. The northern government increased its spending by a factor of seven in the first full year of the war; by the last year its spending had soared to twenty times the prewar level. By 1865 the federal government accounted for over 26 percent of the gross national product.

These changes were more or less permanent. In the 1880s, interest on the war debt still accounted for approximately 40 percent of the federal budget, and soldiers' pensions for as much as 20 percent. Thus, although many southerners had hoped to separate government from the economy, the war made such separation an impossibility. And although federal expenditures shrank after the war, they stabilized at twice the prewar level, or 4 percent of the gross national product. Wartime emergency measures had brought the banking and transportation systems under federal control, and the government had put its power behind manufacturing and business interests through tariffs, loans, and subsidies. In political terms too, national power increased. Extreme forms of the states' rights controversy were dead, though Americans continued to favor a state-centered federalism.

Yet despite all these changes, one crucial question remained unanswered: what was the place of black men and women in American life? The Union victory provided a partial answer: slavery as it had existed before the war could not persist. But what would replace it? About 186,000 black soldiers had rallied to the Union cause, infusing it with new strength. Did their sacrifice entitle them to full citizenship? They and other former slaves eagerly awaited an answer, which would have to be found during Reconstruction.

SUGGESTIONS FOR FURTHER READING

The War and the South

Thomas B. Alexander and Richard E. Beringer, *The Anatomy of the Confederate Congress* (1972); Robert F. Durden, *The Gray and the Black* (1972); Clement Eaton, *A History of the Southern Confederacy* (1954); Paul D. Escott, *Many Excellent People* (1985); Paul D. Escott, *After Secession* (1978); Paul D. Escott, " 'The Cry of the Sufferers': The Problem of Poverty in the Confederacy," *Civil War History*, XXIII (September 1977), 228-240; Archer Jones et al., *Why the South Lost the Civil War* (1985); J. B. Jones, *A Rebel War Clerk's Diary*, 2 vols., ed. Howard Swiggett (1935); Stanley Lebergott, "Why the South Lost," *Journal of American History*, 70 (June, 1983), 58–74; Ella Lonn, *Desertion During the Civil War* (1928); Larry E. Nelson, *Bullets, Ballots, and Rhetoric* (1980); Harry P. Owens and James J. Cooke, eds., *The Old South in the Crucible of War* (1983); Frank L. Owsley, *State Rights in the Confederacy* (1925); Charles W. Ramsdell, *Behind the Lines in the Southern Confederacy*, ed. Wendell H. Stephenson (1944); James L. Roark, *Masters Without Slaves* (1977); Georgia Lee Tatum, *Disloyalty in the Confederacy* (1934); Emory M. Thomas, *The Confederate Nation* (1979); Emory M. Thomas, *The Confederacy as a Revolutionary Experience* (1971); Emory M. Thomas, *The Confederate State of Richmond* (1971); Bell Irvin Wiley, *The Life of Johnny Reb* (1943); Bell Irvin Wiley, *The Plain People of the Confederacy* (1943); W. Buck Yearns, ed., *The Confederate Governors* (1985); W. Buck

Yearns and John G. Barrett, *North Carolina Civil War Documentary* (1980).

The War and the North

Ralph Andreano, ed., *The Economic Impact of the American Civil War* (1962); Robert Cruden, *The War That Never Ended* (1973); Wood Gray, *The Hidden Civil War* (1942); Frank L. Klement, *The Copperheads in the Middle West* (1960); Susan Previant Lee and Peter Passell, *A New Economic View of American History* (1979); George Winston Smith and Charles Burnet Judah, *Life in the North During the Civil War* (1966); George Templeton Strong, *Diary*, 4 vols., ed. Allan Nevins and Milton Halsey Thomas (1952); Paul Studenski, *Financial History of the United States* (1952); Bell Irvin Wiley, *The Life of Billy Yank* (1952).

Women

John R. Brumgardt, ed., *Civil War Nurse: The Diary and Letters of Hannah Ropes* (1980); Beth Gilbert Crabtree and James W. Patton, eds., *"Journal of a Secesh Lady": The Diary of Catherine Ann Devereux Edmondston, 1860–1866* (1979); Jacqueline Jones, *Labor of Love, Labor of Sorrow* (1985); Mary D. Robertson, ed., *Lucy Breckinridge of Grove Hill: The Journal of a Virginia Girl, 1862–1864* (1979); C. Vann Woodward and Elisabeth Muhlenfeld, eds., *The Private Mary Chesnut* (1984); C. Vann Woodward, ed., *Mary Chesnut's Civil War* (1981).

Blacks

Ira Berlin, ed., *Freedom: A Documentary History of Emancipation, 1861–1867*, Series II, *The Black Military Experience* (1982); Dudley Cornish, *The Sable Arm* (1956); James M. McPherson, *The Negro's Civil War* (1965); James M. McPherson, *The Struggle for Equality* (1964); Benjamin Quarles, *The Negro in the Civil War* (1953).

Military History

Bern Anderson, *By Sea and by River* (1962); Bruce Catton, *Grant Takes Command* (1969); Bruce Catton, *Grant Moves South* (1960); Thomas L. Connelly and Archer Jones, *The Politics of Command* (1973); Burke Davis, *Sherman's March* (1980); William C. Davis, ed., *The Image of War*, multivolume (1983–1985); Shelby Foote, *The Civil War, a Narrative*, 3 vols. (1958–1974); William A. Frassanito, *Grant and Lee: The Virginia Campaigns, 1864–1865* (1983); Douglas Southall Freeman, *Lee's Lieutenants*, 3 vols. (1942–1944);

Douglas Southall Freeman, *R. E. Lee*, 4 vols. (1934–1935); Herman Hattaway and Archer Jones, *How the North Won* (1983); Archer Jones *et al.*, *Why the South Lost the Civil War* (1986); Archer Jones, *Confederate Strategy from Shiloh to Vicksburg* (1961); Thomas L. Livermore, *Numbers and Losses in the Civil War in America* (1957); James Lee McDonough, *Chattanooga* (1984); James Lee McDonough and Thomas L. Connelly, *Five Tragic Hours* (1984); Grady McWhiney and Perry D. Jamieson, *Attack and Die* (1982); J. B. Mitchell, *Decisive Battles of the Civil War* (1955); Frank E. Vandiver, *Rebel Brass* (1956).

Diplomatic History

Stuart L. Bernath, *Squall Across the Atlantic: American Civil War Prize Cases and Diplomacy* (1970); Kinley J. Brauer, "The Slavery Problem in the Diplomacy of the American Civil War," *Pacific Historical Review*, XLVI, no. 3 (1977), 439–469; David P. Crook, *Diplomacy During the American Civil War* (1975); David P. Crook, *The North, the South, and the Powers, 1861–1865* (1974); Charles P. Cullop, *Confederate Propaganda in Europe* (1969); Norman A. Graebner, "Northern Diplomacy and European Neutrality," in David Donald, ed., *Why the North Won the Civil War* (1960); Frank J. Merli, *Great Britain and the Confederate Navy* (1970); Frank L. Owsley and Harriet Owsley, *King Cotton Diplomacy* (1959); Gordon H. Warren, *Fountain of Discontent: The Trent Affair and Freedom of the Seas* (1981); Gordon H. Warren, "The King Cotton Theory," in Alexander DeConde, ed., *Encyclopedia of American Foreign Policy*, 3 vols. (1978).

Abraham Lincoln and the Union Government

Fawn Brodie, *Thaddeus Stevens* (1959); LaWanda Cox, *Lincoln and Black Freedom* (1981); Richard N. Current, *The Lincoln Nobody Knows* (1958); David Donald, *Charles Sumner and the Rights of Man* (1970); Ludwell H. Johnson, "Lincoln's Solution to the Problem of Peace Terms, 1864–1865," *Journal of Southern History*, XXXIV (November 1968); 441-447; Peyton McCrary, *Abraham Lincoln and Reconstruction* (1978); Stephen B. Oates, *Our Fiery Trial* (1979); Stephen B. Oates, *With Malice Toward None* (1977); James G. Randall, *Mr. Lincoln* (1957); Benjamin F. Thomas, *Abraham Lincoln* (1952); Hans L. Trefousse, *The Radical Republicans* (1969); Glyndon G. Van Deusen, *William Henry Seward* (1967); T. Harry Williams, *Lincoln and His Generals* (1952); T. Harry Williams, *Lincoln and the Radicals* (1941).

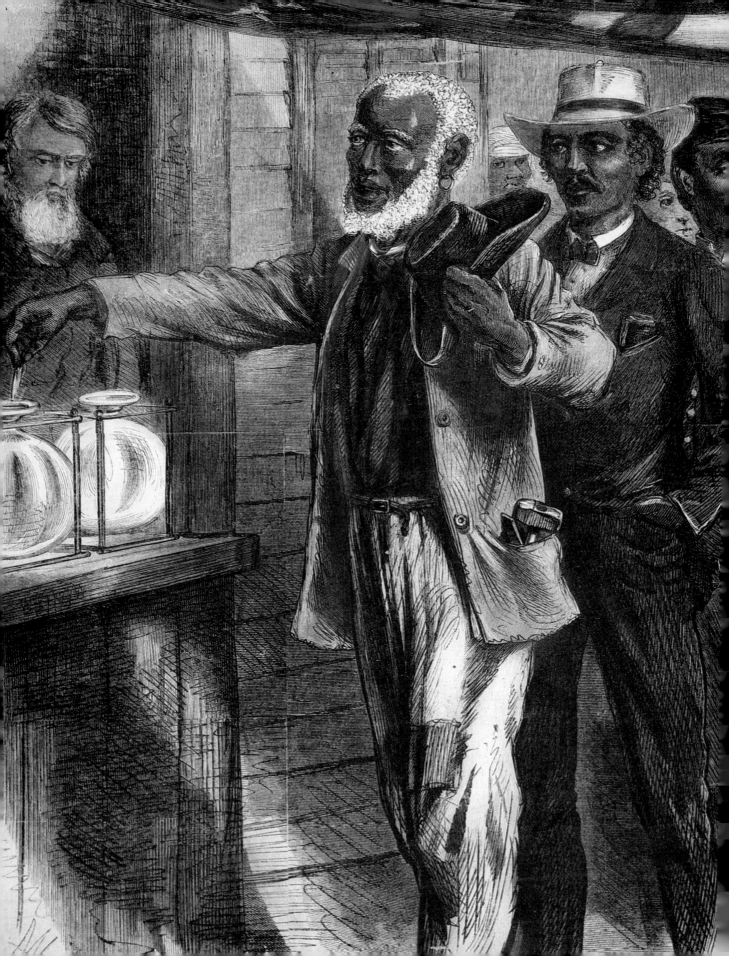

Reconstruction by Trial and Error

1865–1877

Chapter 15

It was a beautiful spring day in 1868. Sunlight and balmy weather bathed the nation's capital on Saturday, May 16, but few people paused to relax or enjoy their surroundings. All of Washington was tense with excitement. Professional gamblers had flooded into the city, outnumbered perhaps only by the reporters who leapt upon every rumor or scrap of information. As the morning passed, a crowd gathered around the Senate chamber. Foreign dignitaries filled the diplomatic box, and spectators packed the Senate galleries. Outside the chamber thousands milled about, choking the hallways and spilling onto the terraces and streets outside.

Precisely at noon the Chief Justice of the United States entered the Senate. Managers and counsel stood ready. Soon two senators who were seriously ill slowly made their way into the chamber, bringing the number of senators present to its full fifty-four. All principals in this solemn drama were present before the High Court of Impeachment except the accused: Andrew Johnson, President of the United States. Johnson, who never appeared to defend himself in person, waited anxiously at the White House as Chief Justice Salmon Chase ordered the calling of the roll. To each senator he put the questions, "How say you? Is the respondent, Andrew Johnson, President of the United States, guilty or not guilty of a high misdemeanor, as charged in this article?" Thirty-five senators answered, "Guilty," nineteen, "Not guilty." The total was one short of a two-thirds majority. The nation had come within one vote of removing its president from office.

How had this extraordinary event come about? What had brought the executive and legislative branches of government into such severe conflict? An unprecedented problem—the reconstruction of the Union—furnished the occasion, and deepening differences over the proper policy to pursue had led to the confrontation. Obviously, by 1868 president and Congress had reached a point of bitter antagonism, with some congressmen charging that the president was siding with traitors.

In 1865, at the end of the war, such a result seemed most unlikely. Although he was a southerner from Tennessee, Johnson had built his career upon criticizing the wealthy planters and championing the South's small farmers. When an assassin's bullet thrust him into the presidency, many former slaveowners shared the worries of a North Carolina lady who wrote, "Think of Andy Johnson [as] the president! What will become of us—'the aristocrats of the South' as we are termed?" Northern Radicals who sounded out the new president on his views also felt confident that he would deal sternly with the South. When one of them suggested the exile or execution of ten or twelve leading rebels to set an example, Johnson had vigorously replied, "How are you going to pick out so small a number? Robbery is a crime; rape is a crime; *treason* is a crime; and *crime* must be punished."

Moreover, fundamental change was already under way in the South. During his army's last campaign, General William T. Sherman had issued Special Field Order No. 15, which set aside for Negro settlement the Sea Islands and all abandoned coastal lands thirty miles to the interior, from Charleston to the Saint John's River in northern Florida. Black refugees quickly poured into these lands; by the middle of 1865, forty thousand freed people were living in their new homes. One former slaveowner who visited his old plantation in Beaufort, South Carolina, received friendly and courteous treatment. But his ex-slaves "firmly and respectfully" informed him that "we own this land now. Put it out of your head that it will ever be yours again."

Before the end of 1865, however, these signs of change were reversed. Although Jefferson Davis was imprisoned for two years, no Confederate leaders were executed, and southern aristocrats soon came to view Andrew Johnson not as their enemy but as their friend and protector. Johnson pardoned rebel leaders liberally, allowed them to take high offices, and ordered government officials to reclaim the freedmen's land and give it back to the original owners. One man in South Carolina expressed blacks' dismay: "Why do you take away our lands? You take them from us who have always been true, always true to the Government! You give them to our all-time enemies! That is not right!"

The unexpected outcome of Johnson's program led Congress to examine his policies and design new plans for Reconstruction. Out of negotiations in Congress and clashes between the president and the legislators, there emerged first one, and then two, new plans for Reconstruction. Before the process was over, the nation had adopted the Fourteenth and Fifteenth Amendments and impeached its president.

Racism did not disappear. During the war the federal government had been reluctant to give even black troops fair treatment, and in Congress northern Democrats continued to oppose equality. Republicans were often divided among themselves, but a mixture of idealism and party purposes drove them forward. Ultimately, fear of losing the peace proved decisive with northern voters. The United States enfranchised the freedmen and gave them a role in reconstructing the South.

Blacks benefited from greater control over their personal lives and took the risks of voting and participating in politics. But they knew that the success of Reconstruction also depended on the determination and support of the North. Southern opposition to Reconstruction grew steadily. By 1869 a secret terrorist organization known as the Ku Klux Klan had added large-scale violence to southern whites' repertoire of resistance. Despite federal efforts to protect them, black people were intimidated at the polls, robbed of their earnings, beaten, or murdered. Prosecution of Klansmen rarely succeeded, and Republicans lost their offices in an increasing number of southern states. By the early 1870s the failure of Reconstruction was apparent. Republican leaders and northern voters had to decide how far they would persist in their efforts to reform the South.

As the 1870s advanced, other issues drew attention away from Reconstruction. Industrial growth accelerated, creating new opportunities and raising new problems. Interest in territorial expansion revived. Political corruption became a nationwide scandal and bribery a way of doing business. North Carolina's Jonathan Worth, an old-line Whig who had opposed secession as strongly as he now fought Reconstruction, deplored the atmosphere of greed. "Money has become the God of this country," he wrote in disgust, "and men, otherwise good men, are almost compelled to worship at her shrine." Eventually these other forces triumphed, politics moved on to new concerns, and the courts turned their attention away from civil rights. Even northern Republicans gave up on racial reform in 1877.

Thus the nation stumbled, by trial and error, toward a policy that attempted to reconstruct the South. Congress insisted on equality before the law for black people and gave black men the right to vote. It took the unprecedented step of impeaching the president. But more far-reaching measures to advance black freedom never had much support in Congress, and when suffrage alone proved insufficient to remake the South, the nation soon lost interest. Reconstruction proclaimed anew the American principle of human equality but failed to secure it in reality.

EQUALITY:
THE UNRESOLVED ISSUE

For America's former slaves, Reconstruction had one paramount meaning: a chance to explore freedom. A southern white woman admitted in her diary that the black people "showed a natural and exultant joy at being free." Former slaves remembered rejoicing and singing far into the night after federal troops reached their plantations. The slaves on one Texas plantation jumped up and down and clapped their hands as one man shouted, "We is free—no more whippings and beatings."

A few blacks gave in to the natural desire to do what had been impossible before. One grandmother who had long resented her treatment "dropped her hoe" and ran to confront the mistress. "I'm free!" she yelled at her. "Yes, I'm free! Ain't got to work for you no more! You can't put me in your pocket [sell me] now!" Another man recalled that he and others "started on the move" and left the plantation, either to search for family members or just to exercise their new-found freedom of movement. As he traveled, one man sang about being free as a frog, " 'cause a frog had freedom to get on a log and jump off when he pleases."

Most freedmen reacted more cautiously and shrewdly, taking care to test the boundaries of their

In the changed circumstances after emancipation, former slaves and former slaveowners had to work out the terms of a new relationship. Winslow Homer suggested some of the complexity of their encounters in A Visit from the Old Mistress *(1876). National Museum of American Art, Smithsonian Institution, Washington, D.C., Gift of William T. Evans.*

new condition. "After the war was over," explained one man, "we was afraid to move. Just like tarpins or turtles after emancipation. Just stick our heads out to see how the land lay." As slaves they had learned to expect hostility from white people, and they did not presume it would instantly disappear. Life in freedom, they knew, might still be a matter of what was allowed, not what was right. "You got to say master?" asked a freedman in Georgia. "Naw," answered his fellows, but "they said it all the same. They said it for a long time."

One sign of this shrewd caution was the way freedmen evaluated potential employers. "Most all the niggers that had good owners stayed with 'em, but the others left. Some of 'em come back and some

didn't," explained one man. If a white person had been relatively considerate to blacks in bondage, blacks reasoned that he might prove a desirable employer in freedom. Other blacks left their plantation all at once, for, as one put it, "that master am sure mean and if we doesn't have to stay we shouldn't, not with that master."

Even more urgently than a fair employer, the freedmen wanted land of their own. Land represented their chance to farm for themselves, to have an independent life. It represented compensation for their generations of travail in bondage. A northern observer noted that freedmen made "plain, straight-forward" inquiries as they settled the

Blacks' Desire for Land

land set aside for them by Sherman. They wanted to be sure the land "would be theirs after they had improved it." Not just in the Sea Island region but everywhere, blacks young and old thirsted for homes of their own. One southerner noted with surprise in her diary that

> Uncle Lewis, the pious, the honored, the venerated, gets his poor old head turned with false notions of freedom and independence, runs off to the Yankees with a pack of lies against his mistress, and sets up a claim to part of her land!

Lewis simply wanted a new beginning. Like millions of other freedmen, he hoped to leave slavery behind.

But no one could say how much of a chance the whites, who were in power, would give to blacks. During the war the federal government had refused to arm black volunteers. Many whites agreed with Corporal Felix Brannigan of the Seventy-fourth New York Regiment. "We don't want to fight side and side with the nigger," he said. "We think we are a too superior race for that." In September 1862 Abraham Lincoln said, "If we were to arm [the Negroes], I fear that in a few weeks the arms would be in the hands of the rebels."

Necessity forced a change in policy; because the war was going badly the administration authorized black enlistments. By spring 1863 black troops were proving their value. One general reported that his "colored regiments" possessed "remarkable aptitude for military training," and another observer said, "They fight like fiends." Lincoln came to see "the colored population" as "the great *available* and yet *unavailed of* force for restoring the Union," and recruitment proceeded rapidly.

Black leaders hoped that military service would secure equal rights for their people. Once the black soldier had fought for the Union, wrote Frederick Douglass, "there is no power on earth which can deny that he has earned the right of citizenship in the United States." If black soldiers turned the tide, asked another man, "Would the nation refuse us our rights . . .? Would it refuse us our vote?"

Wartime experience seemed to prove it would. Despite their valor, black soldiers faced persistent discrimination. In Ohio, for example, a mob shouting "Kill the nigger" attacked an off-duty soldier; on duty, blacks did most of the "fatigue duty," or heavy labor. Moreover, black soldiers were expected to accept inferior pay as they risked their lives. The government paid white privates $13 per month plus a clothing allowance of $3.50. Black troops earned $10 per month less $3 deducted for clothing. Blacks resented this injustice so deeply that in protest two regiments refused to accept any pay, and eventually Congress remedied the discrimination.

Still, this was only a small victory over prejudice; the general attitude of northerners on racial questions was mixed. Abolitionists and many Republicans helped black Americans fight for equal rights, and they won some victories. In 1864 the federal courts accepted black testimony, and New York City desegregated its streetcars. The District of Columbia did the same in 1865, the year the Thirteenth Amendment won ratification. One state, Massachusetts, enacted a comprehensive public accommodations law. On the other hand, there were many more signs of resistance to racial equality. The Democratic party fought against equality, charging that Republicans favored race-mixing and were undermining the status of the white worker. Voters in three states—Connecticut, Minnesota, and Wisconsin—rejected black suffrage in 1865. The racial attitudes of northerners seemed mixed and uncertain.

This was a significant fact, for the history of emancipation in the British Caribbean indicated that, if equality were to be won, the North would have to take a strong and determined stand. In 1833 Great Britain had abolished slavery in its possessions, providing slaveowners with £20 million in compensation plus the benefit of a six-year apprenticeship over all former agricultural slaves. Despite such generosity to the slaveowners, the transition to free labor had not been easy.

Everywhere in the British Caribbean planters fought tenaciously to maintain control over their laborers. Retaining control of local government, the planters fashioned laws, taxes, and administrative decisions with an eye to keeping freedmen on the plantations. With equal determination, the former slaves attempted to move onto small plots of land and raise food crops instead of sugar. They wanted independence and were not interested in raising export crops for the world market. The British, even abolitionists, however,

These schoolteachers were part of Gideon's Band, volunteers sent by northern religious organizations to aid the freed people in Beaufort and Port Royal, South Carolina. Thousands followed their example during Reconstruction. Western Reserve Historical Society, Cleveland, Ohio.

judged the success of emancipation by the volume of production for the market. Their concern for the freedmen soon faded, and before long the authorities assisted planters further by allowing the importation of indentured "coolie" labor from India.

In the United States, some of the same tendencies had appeared on the Sea Islands long before the war ended. The planters had fled and therefore were not present to try to control their former slaves. The freedmen, however, showed a strong desire to leave the plantations and establish small, self-sufficient farms of their own. Northern missionaries, soldiers, and officials brought education and aid to the freedmen but also wanted them to grow cotton. They disapproved of charity and emphasized the values of competitive capitalism. "The danger to the Negro," wrote one worker in the Sea Islands, was "too high wages."

Indeed it would be "most unwise and injurious," declared another worker, to give former slaves free land.

"The Yankees preach nothing but cotton, cotton!" complained one Sea Island black. "We wants land," wrote another, "this very land that is rich with the sweat of we face and the blood of we back." Asking only for a chance to buy land, this man complained that "they make the lots too big, and cut we out." Indeed, the government did sell thousands of acres in the Sea Islands for nonpayment of taxes, but when blacks pooled their earnings to buy almost 2,000 of the 16,749 acres sold in March 1863, 90 percent of the land went to wealthy investors from the North. Thus even among their northern supporters, the former slaves had received only partial support. How much opportunity would freedom bring? That was a major question to be answered during Reconstruction, and the answer depended on the evolution of policy in Washington.

JOHNSON'S RECONSTRUCTION PLAN

Throughout 1865 the formation of Reconstruction policy rested solely with Andrew Johnson, for shortly before he became president Congress recessed and did not reconvene until December. In the nearly eight months that intervened, Johnson devised his own plan and put it into operation. He decided to form new governments in the South by using his power to grant pardons.

Johnson had a few precedents to follow in Lincoln's wartime plans for Reconstruction. In December 1863 Lincoln has proposed a "10-percent" plan for a gov-

Lincoln's Reconstruction Plan

ernment being organized in captured portions of Louisiana. According to this plan, a state government could be established as soon as 10 percent of those who had voted in 1860 took an oath of future loyalty. Only high-ranking Confederate officials would be denied a chance to take the oath, and Lincoln urged that at least a few well-qualified blacks be given the ballot. Radicals bristled, however, at such a mild plan, and a majority of Congress (in the Wade-Davis bill, which Lincoln pocket-vetoed) favored stiffer requirements and stronger proof of loyalty.

Later, in 1865, Lincoln suggested but then abandoned more lenient terms. At Hampton Roads, where he raised questions about the extent of emancipation (see page 401), Lincoln discussed compensation and restoration to the Union, with full rights, of the very state governments that had tried to leave it. Then in April he considered allowing the Virginia legislature to convene in order to withdraw its support from the Confederate war effort. Faced with strong opposition in his cabinet, however, Lincoln reversed himself, denying that he had intended to confer legitimacy

Combative and inflexible, President Andrew Johnson contributed greatly to the failure and rejection of his own reconstruction program. Library of Congress.

on a rebel government. At the time of his death, Lincoln had given general approval to a plan drafted by Secretary of War Stanton that would have imposed military authority and provisional governors as steps toward new state governments. Beyond these general outlines, it is impossible to say what Lincoln would have done had he survived.

Johnson began with the plan Stanton had drafted for consideration by the cabinet. At a cabinet meeting on May 9, 1865, Johnson's advisors split evenly on the question of voting rights for freedmen in the South. Johnson said that he favored black suffrage, but only if the southern states adopted it voluntarily. A champion of states' rights, he regarded this decision as too important to be taken out of the hands of the states.

Such conservatism had an enduring effect on Johnson's policies, but at first it appeared that his old enmity toward the planters might produce a plan for radical changes in class relations among whites. As he appointed provisional governors in the South, Johnson also proposed rules that would keep the wealthy planter class out of power. He required every southern voter to swear an oath of loyalty as a condition of gaining amnesty or pardon. But some southerners would face special difficulties in regaining their rights.

Johnson barred certain classes of southerners from taking the oath and gaining amnesty. Former federal officials who had violated their oaths to support the United States and had aided the Confederacy could not take the oath. Nor could graduates of West Point or Annapolis who had resigned their commissions to fight for the South. The same was true for high-ranking Confederate officers and Confederate political leaders. To this list Johnson added another important group: all southerners who aided the rebellion and whose taxable property was worth more than $20,000. Such individuals had to apply personally to the president for pardon and restoration of political rights, or risk legal penalties, which included confiscation of their land.

Oaths of Amnesty and New State Governments

Thus it appeared that the South's old leadership class would be removed from power, for virtually all the rich and powerful whites of prewar days needed Johnson's special pardon. Many observers, South and North, sensed that the president meant to take his revenge on the haughty aristocrats whom he had always denounced and to raise up a new leadership of deserving yeomen.

Johnson's provisional governors began the Reconstruction process by calling constitutional conventions. The delegates chosen for these conventions had to draft new constitutions eliminating slavery and invalidating secession. After ratification of these constitutions, new governments could be elected, and the states would be restored to the Union with full congressional representation. But no southerners could participate in this process who had not taken the oath of amnesty or who had been ineligible to vote on the day the state seceded. Thus freedmen could not participate in the conventions. Although it was theoretically possible for the white delegates to enfranchise them, such action was at best unlikely.

If Johnson intended to end the power of the old elite, his plan did not work out as he had hoped. The old white leadership proved resilient and influ-ential; prominent Confederates (a few with pardons, but many without) won elections and turned up in various appointive offices. Then, surprisingly, Johnson helped to subvert his own plan. He started pardoning aristocrats and chief rebels, who should not have been in office. By fall 1865 the clerks at the pardon office were straining under the burden, and additional staff had to be hired to churn out the necessary documents. These pardons, plus the return of planters' abandoned lands, put the old elite back in power.

Why did Johnson issue so many pardons? Perhaps vanity betrayed his judgment. Scores of gentlemen of the type who had previously scorned him now waited on him for an appointment. Too long a lonely outsider, Johnson may have succumbed to the attention and flattery of these pardon-seekers. Whether he did or not, he clearly had allowed himself too little time. It took months for the constitution-making and elections to run their course; by the time the process was complete and Confederate leaders had emerged in powerful positions, the reconvening of Congress was near. Johnson faced a choice between admitting failure and scrapping his entire effort or swallowing hard and supporting what had resulted. He decided to stand behind his new governments and declare Reconstruction completed. Thus in December 1865 many Confederate congressmen traveled to Washington to claim seats in the United States Congress, and Alexander Stephens, vice president of the Confederacy, returned to the capital as senator-elect.

Many northerners frowned on the election of such prominent rebels, and there were other results of Johnson's program that sparked negative comment in the North. Some of the state conventions were slow to repudiate secession; others only grudgingly admitted that slavery was dead. Two refused to take any action to repudiate the large Confederate debt. Northerners interpreted these actions as signs of defiance; subsequent legislation defining the status of freedmen confirmed their worst fears. Some legislatures merely revised large sections of the slave codes by substituting the word *freedman* for *slave*, and new laws written from scratch were also very restrictive. In these Black Codes, former slaves who were supposed to be free were compelled to carry passes, observe a curfew, live in housing provided by a landowner, and give up hope of entering many desirable occupations.

Black Codes

Chapter 15: RECONSTRUCTION BY TRIAL AND ERROR, 1865–1877

Finally, observers noted that the practice in state-supported institutions, such as schools and orphanages, was to exclude blacks altogether. To northerners, the South seemed intent on returning black people to a position of servility.

Thus it was not surprising that a majority of northern congressmen decided to take a close look at the results of Johnson's plan. On reconvening, they voted not to admit the newly elected southern representatives, whose credentials were subject under the Constitution to congressional scrutiny. The House and Senate established a joint committee to examine Johnson's policies and advise on new ones. Reconstruction had entered a second phase, one in which Congress would play a strong role.

THE CONGRESSIONAL RECONSTRUCTION PLAN

Northern congressmen disagreed on what to do, but they did not doubt their right to play a role in Reconstruction. The Constitution mentioned neither secession nor reunion, but it did assign a great many major responsibilities to Congress. Among them was the injunction to guarantee to each state a republican government. Under this provision, the legislators thought, they could devise policies for Reconstruction, just as Johnson had used his power to pardon for the same purpose.

They soon found that other constitutional questions had a direct bearing on the policies they followed. What, for example, had the fact of rebellion done to the relationship between southern states and the Union? Lincoln had always insisted that the Union remained unbroken, but not even Andrew Johnson could accept the southern view that the wartime state governments of the South could merely re-enter the nation. Johnson argued that the Union had endured, though individuals had erred; thus the use of his power to grant or withhold pardons. But congressmen who favored vigorous Reconstruction measures tended to argue that war *had* broken the Union. The southern states had committed legal suicide and reverted to the status of territories, they argued, or the South was a conquered nation subject to the victor's will. Moderate congressmen held that the states had forfeited their rights through rebellion, and had thus come under congressional supervision.

These diverse theories mirrored the diversity of Congress itself. Northern legislators fell into four major categories: Democrats, conservative Republicans, moderate Republicans, and Radical Republicans. No one of these groups had decisive power. In terms of ideology the majority of congressmen were conservative. In terms of partisan politics the Republican party had a majority, but there was considerable distance between conservative Republicans, who desired a limited federal role in Reconstruction and were fairly happy with Johnson's actions, and the Radicals. These men, led by Thaddeus Stevens, Charles Sumner, and George Julian, were a minority within their party, but they had the advantage of a clearly defined goal. They believed that it was essential to democratize the South, establish public education, and ensure the rights of freedmen. They favored black suffrage, often supported land confiscation and redistribution, and were willing to exclude the South from the Union for several years if necessary to achieve their goals. Between these two factions lay the moderates, who held the balance of power.

The Radicals

One overwhelming political reality faced all the groups in Congress: the 1866 elections were approaching in the fall. Since Congress had questioned Johnson's program, its members had to develop some modification or alternative program before the elections. The northern public expected them to develop a new Reconstruction plan, and as politicians they knew better than to go before their constituents empty-handed. Thus they had to forge a majority coalition composed either of Democrats and Republicans or various elements of the Republican party. The kind of coalition that formed would determine the kind of plan that Congress developed.

Ironically, it was Johnson and the Democrats that pushed Congress toward Radical rather than conservative policies. The president and the Democrats in Congress refused to cooperate with conservative or moderate Republicans. They insisted, despite evidence of widespread concern, that Reconstruction was over, that the new state governments were legitimate, and that southern representatives should be admitted to Congress. These unrealistic, intransigent positions threw away the Democrats' potential influence and blasted any possibility of bipartisan compromise. Republicans found themselves all lumped together by Democrats; to form a new program, conservative Republicans had to work with the Radicals. Thus bargaining over changes in the Johnson program went on almost entirely within the party.

This development and subsequent events enhanced the influence of the Radicals. But in 1865, Republican congressmen were at first loath to break with the

Congress Struggles for a Compromise
president; he was, for better or worse, the titular head of their party, so they made one last effort to work with him. Early in 1866 many lawmakers thought a compromise had been reached. Under its terms Johnson would agree to two modifications of his program. The life of the Freedmen's Bureau, which fed the hungry, negotiated labor contracts, and started schools, would be extended; and a civil rights bill would be passed to counteract the black codes. This bill, drawn up by a conservative Republican, was designed to force southern courts to recognize equality before the law by giving federal judges the power to remove cases in which blacks were treated unfairly. Its provisions applied to discrimination by private persons as well as government officials. As the first major bill to enforce the Thirteenth Amendment's abolition of slavery, it was a significant piece of legislation, and it became very important in the twentieth century (see page 948).

But in spring 1866, Johnson destroyed the compromise by vetoing both bills (they were later repassed). Denouncing any change in his program, the president condemned Congress's action in inflammatory language. In so doing he questioned the legitimacy of congressional involvement in policymaking and revealed his own racism. Because the Civil Rights Bill defined United States citizens as native-born persons who were taxed, Johnson pronounced it discriminatory toward "large numbers of intelligent, worthy, and patriotic foreigners . . . in favor of the negro." The bill, he said, would "operate in favor of the colored and against the white race."

All hope of working with the president was now gone. But Republican congressmen sensed that their constituents remained dissatisfied with the results of Reconstruction. Violence in the South—notably in Memphis and New Orleans, where police aided brutal raids on black citizens—also convinced Republicans, and the northern public, that more needed to be done. The Republican lawmakers therefore pushed on, and from bargaining among their various factions there emerged a plan. It took the form of a proposed amendment to the Constitution—the fourteenth—and it represented a compromise between radical and conservative elements of the party. The Fourteenth Amendment was Congress's alternative to Johnson's program of Reconstruction.

Of four points in the amendment, there was nearly universal agreement on one: the Confederate debt was declared null and void, the war debt of the United States guaranteed. North-

Fourteenth Amendment
erners uniformly rejected the notion of paying taxes to reimburse those who had financed a rebellion; and business groups agreed on the necessity of upholding the credit of the United States government. There was also fairly general support for altering the personnel of southern governments. In language that harkened back to Johnson's Amnesty Proclamation, the Fourteenth Amendment prohibited political power for prominent Confederates. Only at the discretion of Congress, by a two-thirds vote of each house, could these political penalties be removed.

The section of the Fourteenth Amendment that would have by far the greatest legal significance in later years was the first (see Appendix). On its face, this section was an effort to strike down the black codes and guarantee basic rights to freedmen. It conferred citizenship on freedmen and prohibited states from abridging their constitutional "privileges and immunities." Similarly, the amendment barred any state from taking a person's life, liberty, or property "without due process of law" and from denying "equal protection of the laws." These clauses were phrased broadly enough to become in time powerful guarantees of black Americans' civil rights, indeed, of the rights of all citizens. They also took on added meaning with court rulings that corporations were legally "persons" (see page 487).

The second section of the amendment, which dealt with representation, clearly revealed the compromises

Chapter 15: RECONSTRUCTION BY TRIAL AND ERROR, 1865–1877

and political motives that had produced the document. Northerners, in Congress and out, disagreed whether black citizens should have the right to vote. Commenting on the ambivalent nature of northern opinion, a citizen of Indiana wrote that there was strong feeling in favor of "humane and liberal laws for the government and protection of the colored population." But he admitted to a southern relative that there was prejudice, too. "Although there is a great deal [of] profession among us for the relief of the darkey yet I think much of it is far from being cincere. I guess we want to compell you to do right by them while we are not willing ourselves to do so."

Republican congressmen shied away from confronting this ambivalence, but political reality required them to do something. Under the Constitution, representation was based on population. During slavery each black slave had counted as three-fifths of a person for purposes of congressional representation. Republicans feared that emancipation, which made every former slave five-fifths of a person, might increase the South's power in Congress. If it did, and if blacks were not allowed to vote, the former secessionists would gain seats in Congress.

What a strange result that would seem to most northerners. They had never planned to reward the South for rebellion, and Republicans in Congress were determined not to hand over power to their political enemies. So they offered the South a choice. According to the second section of the Fourteenth Amendment, states did not have to give black men the right to vote. But if they did not do so, their representation would be reduced proportionally. If they did, it would be increased proportionally—but Republicans would be able to appeal to the new black voters. This compromise protected northern interests and gave Republicans a chance to compete if freedmen gained the ballot.

The Fourteenth Amendment dealt with the voting rights of black men but ignored female citizens, black and white. For this reason it elicited a strong reaction from the women's rights movement. Advocates of equal rights for women had worked with abolitionists for decades, often subordinating their cause to that of the slaves. During the drafting of the Fourteenth Amendment, however, female activists demanded to be heard. When legislators defined them as nonvoting citizens, prominent women's leaders such as Elizabeth

Cady Stanton and Susan B. Anthony decided that it was time to end their alliance with abolitionists. Thus the independent women's rights movement grew.

In 1866, however, the major question in Reconstruction politics was how the public would respond to the amendment. Would the northern public support Congress's plan or the president's?

Southern Rejection of the Fourteenth Amendment

Johnson did his best to block the Fourteenth Amendment and to convince northerners to reject it. Condemning Congress's plan and its refusal to seat southern representatives, the president urged state legislatures in the South to vote against ratification. Every southern legislature except Tennessee's rejected the amendment by a large margin. It did best in Alabama, where it failed by a vote of 69 to 8 in the assembly and 27 to 2 in the senate. In three states the amendment received no support at all.

To present his case to northerners, Johnson arranged a National Union convention to publicize his program. The chief executive also took to the stump himself. In an age when active personal campaigning was rare for a president, Johnson boarded a special train for a "swing around the circle" that carried his message far into the Midwest and then back to Washington. In cities such as Cleveland and St. Louis, Johnson castigated the Republicans in his old stump-speaker style. But increasingly audiences rejected his views and hooted and jeered at him.

The election was a resounding victory for Republicans in Congress. Men whom Johnson had denounced won re-election by large margins, and the Republican majority increased as some new candidates defeated incumbent Democrats. Everywhere Radical and moderate Republicans gained strength. The section of the country that had won the war had spoken clearly: Johnson's policies, people feared, were giving the advantage to rebels and traitors. Thus Republican congressional leaders received a mandate to continue with their Reconstruction plan.

But, thanks largely to Johnson, that plan had reached an impasse. All but one of the southern governments created by the president had turned their backs on the Fourteenth Amendment, determined to resist. Nothing could be accomplished as long as those governments existed and as long as the southern electorate was constituted as it was. The newly elected northern Republicans were not going to ignore their constituents' wishes and surrender to the South. To break the deadlock, Republicans had little choice but to form new governments and enfranchise the freedmen. They therefore decided to do both. The unavoidable logic of the situation had forced the majority toward the Radical plan.

The Radicals hoped Congress would do much more. Thaddeus Stevens, for example, argued that economic opportunity was essential to the freedmen. "If we do not furnish them with homesteads from forfeited and rebel property, and hedge them around with protective laws; if we leave them to the legislation of their late masters, we had better left them in bondage," Stevens declared. To provide that opportunity, Stevens drew up a plan for extensive confiscation and redistribution of land. Significantly, only one-tenth of the land affected by his plan was earmarked for freedmen, in 40-acre plots. All the rest was to be sold, to generate money for veterans' pensions, compensation to loyal citizens for damaged property, and payment of the federal debt. By these means Stevens hoped to win support for a basically unpopular measure. But he failed; and in general the Radicals were not able to command the support of the majority of the public. Northerners of that era were accustomed to a limited role for government, and the business community staunchly opposed any interference in private property.

As a result, the Military Reconstruction Act that was passed in 1867 incorporated only a small part of the Radical program. The act called for new governments in the South, with a return to military authority in the interim.

Military Reconstruction Act of 1867 It barred from political office those Confederate leaders listed in the Fourteenth Amendment. It guaranteed freedmen the right to vote in elections for state constitutional conventions and for subsequent state governments. In addition, each southern state was required to ratify the Fourteenth Amendment; to ratify its new constitution; and to submit the new constitution to Congress for approval. Thus black people gained an opportunity to fight for a better life through the political process. The only weapon put into their hands was the ballot, however. The law required no redistribution of land and guaranteed no basic changes in southern social structure. It also permitted an early return to the Union.

Congress's role as the architect of Reconstruction was not quite over, for its quarrels with Andrew Johnson grew more bitter. To restrict Johnson's influence and safeguard its plan, Congress passed a number of controversial laws. First it set the date for its own reconvening—an unprecedented act, since the president had traditionally summoned the legislature to Washington. Then it limited Johnson's power over the army by requiring the president to issue military orders through the General of the Army, Ulysses S. Grant, who could not be sent from Washington without the Senate's consent. Finally, Congress passed the Tenure of Office Act, which gave the Senate power to interfere with changes in the president's cabinet. Designed to protect Secretary of War Stanton, who sympathized with the Radicals, this law violated the tradition that a president controlled his own cabinet.

Johnson took several belligerent steps of his own. He issued orders to military commanders in the South limiting their powers and increasing the powers of the civil governments he had created in 1865. Then he removed army officers who conscientiously enforced Congress's new law, preferring commanders who allowed disqualified Confederates to vote. Finally, in August 1867 he tried to remove Secretary of War Stanton. With this act the confrontation reached its climax.

Twice before, the House Judiciary Committee had considered impeachment, rejecting the idea once and then recommending it by only a 5-to-4 vote. That recommendation had been decisively defeated by the House. After Johnson's last action, however, a third attempt to impeach the president carried easily. In 1868, the angry House was so determined to indict Johnson that it voted before drawing up specific charges. The indictment concentrated on Johnson's violation of the Tenure of Office Act, though modern scholars regard his systematic efforts to impede enforcement of the Military Reconstruction Act as a far more serious offense.

Impeachment of President Johnson

Johnson's trial in the Senate lasted more than three months. The prosecution, led by such Radicals as Thaddeus Stevens and Benjamin Butler, argued that Johnson was guilty of "high crimes and misdemeanors." But they also advanced the novel idea

The confrontation between Congress and Andrew Johnson culminated in the president's impeachment. Here the Senate begins his trial, which ended in acquittal by a margin of one vote.   Library of Congress.

that impeachment was a political matter, not a judicial trial of guilt or innocence. The Senate ultimately rejected such reasoning, which would have transformed impeachment into a political weapon against any chief executive who disagreed with Congress. Though a majority of senators voted to convict Johnson, the prosecution fell one vote short of the necessary two-thirds majority. Johnson remained in office for the few months left in his term, and his acquittal established the precedent that only serious misdeeds merited removal from office.

In 1869, in an effort to write democratic principles and color-blindness into the Constitution, the Radicals succeeded in presenting the Fifteenth Amendment for ratification. This measure forbade

Fifteenth Amendment states to deny the right to vote "on account of race, color, or previous condition of servitude." Ironically, the votes of four uncooperative southern states—

required by Congress to approve the amendment as an added condition to rejoining the Union—proved necessary to impose this principle on parts of the North. Although several states outside the South refused to ratify, the Fifteenth Amendment became law in 1870.

RECONSTRUCTION POLITICS

IN THE SOUTH

From the start, Reconstruction encountered the resistance of white southerners. Their opposition to change appeared in the black codes and other policies of the Johnson governments as well as in

Thomas Nast, in this 1868 cartoon, pictured the combination of forces—southern opposition and northern racism and indifference—that threatened the success of Reconstruction. Library of Congress.

their owners "didn't tell them it was freedom" or "wouldn't let [them] go." Agents of the Freedmen's Bureau in North Carolina agreed. One agent in Georgia concluded, "I find the old system of slavery working with even more rigor than formerly at a few miles distant from any point where U.S. troops are stationed." To hold onto their workers some landowners claimed control over black children and used guardianship and apprentice laws to bind black families to the plantation.

Whites also blocked blacks from acquiring land. Though a few planters divided up plots among their slaves, most condemned the idea of making blacks landowners. One planter in South Carolina refused to sell as little as an acre and a half to each family. Even a Georgian whose family was known for its concern for the slaves was outraged that two property owners planned to "rent their lands to the Negroes!" Such action was "injurious to the best interest of the community." The son of a free black landowner in Virginia who sold nearly two hundred acres to former slaves explained, "White folks wasn't lettin' Negroes have nothing."

Such adamant resistance by propertied whites soon manifested itself in other ways, including violence. In one North Carolina town a local magistrate clubbed a black man on a public street, and bands of "Regulators" terrorized blacks in parts of that state and Kentucky. Such incidents were predictable in a society in which many planters believed, as a South Carolinian put it, that blacks "can't be governed except with the whip."

After President Johnson encouraged the South to resist congressional Reconstruction, many white conservatives worked hard to capture the new state governments. Elsewhere, large numbers of whites boycotted the polls in an attempt to defeat Congress's plans. Since the new constitutions had to be approved by a majority of registered voters, registered whites could defeat them by sitting out the elections. This tactic was tried in North Carolina and succeeded in Alabama, forcing Congress to readjust and base ratification on a majority of those voting.

Very few black men stayed away from the polls. Enthusiastically and hopefully they seized the opportunity to participate in politics, voting solidly Republican. Most agreed with one man who felt that he should "stick to the end with the party that freed

private attitudes. Many whites set their faces against emancipation, and—as was true in

White Resistance

the British Caribbean—the former planter class proved especially unbending. In 1866 a Georgia newspaper frankly declared, "Most of the white citizens believe that the institution of slavery was right, and . . . they will believe that the condition, which comes nearest to slavery, that can now be established will be the best." Unwillingness to accept black freedom would have been a major problem in any circumstances; Andrew Johnson's encouragement of southern whites actively to resist Congress, only intensified the problem.

Fearing the end of their control over slaves, some planters attempted to postpone freedom by denying or misrepresenting events. Former slaves reported that

Chapter 15: RECONSTRUCTION BY TRIAL AND ERROR, 1865–1877

me." Illiteracy did not prohibit blacks (or uneducated whites) from making intelligent choices. Although William Henry could read only "a little," he testified that he and his friends had no difficulty selecting the Republican ballot. "We stood around and watched," he explained. "We saw D. Sledge vote; he owned half the county. We knowed he voted Democratic so we voted the other ticket so it would be Republican."

Zeal for voting spread through the entire black community. Women, who could not vote, encouraged their husbands and sons, and preachers exhorted their congregations to use the franchise. Such community spirit helped to counter white pressure tactics, and the freedmen's enthusiasm showed their hunger for equal rights.

With a large black turnout, and with prominent Confederates barred from politics under the Fourteenth Amendment, a new southern Republican party came to power in the constitutional conventions. Some blacks won seats as delegates, along with northerners who had moved to the South and some native southern whites. Together they brought the South's fundamental law into line with progressive reforms that had been adopted in the rest of the nation. The new constitutions were more democratic—they eliminated property qualifications for voting and holding office, and they made state and local offices elective that had been appointive. They provided for public schools and institutions to care for the mentally ill, the blind, the deaf, the destitute, and the orphaned, and they ended imprisonment for debt and barbarous punishments such as branding.

The conventions also broadened women's rights in possession of property and divorce. Usually, the main goal was not to make women equal but to provide relief to thousands of suffering debtors. In families left poverty-stricken by the war and weighed down by debts, the husband had usually contracted the debts. Thus, giving women legal control over their own property provided some protection to their families. There were some delegates, however, whose goal was to elevate women. Blacks in particular called for women's suffrage but were ignored by their white colleagues.

Under these new constitutions the southern states elected new governments. Again the Republican party triumphed, bringing new men into positions of power.

Triumph of Republican Governments

The ranks of state legislators in 1868 included black southerners for the first time in history. Congress's second plan for Reconstruction was well under way. It remained to be seen what these new governments would do and how much change they would bring to society.

There was one possibility of radical change through these new governments. That possibility depended on the disfranchisement of substantial numbers of Confederate leaders. If the Republican regimes used their new power to exclude many whites from politics, as punishment for rebellion, they would have a solid electoral majority based on black voters and their white allies. Land reform and the assurance of racial equality would be possible. But none of the Republican governments did this, or even gave it serious consideration.

Why did the new legislators shut the door on the possibility of deep and thoroughgoing reform? First, they appreciated the realities of power and the depth of racial enmity. In most states whites were the majority, and former slaveowners controlled the best land and other sources of economic power. James Lynch, a leading black politician from Mississippi, candidly explained why Negroes shunned "the folly of" disfranchisement. Unlike northerners who "can leave when it becomes too uncomfortable," former slaves "must be in friendly relations with the great body of the whites in the state. Otherwise . . . peace can be maintained only by a standing army."

Second, blacks believed in the principle of universal suffrage and the Christian goal of reconciliation. Far from being vindictive toward the race that had enslaved them, they treated leading rebels with generosity and appealed to white southerners to adopt a spirit of fairness and cooperation. Henry McNeil Turner, like other Negro ministers, urged black Georgians to "love whites . . . soon their prejudice would melt away, and with God for our father, we will all be brothers." (Years later Turner criticized his own naiveté, saying that in the constitutional convention his motto had been, "Anything to please the white folks.") Therefore southern Republicans quickly (in come cases immediately) restored the voting rights of former Confederates, as Congress steadily released more individuals from the penalties of the Fourteenth Amendment.

Thus the South's Republican party committed itself

to a strategy of winning white support. To put the matter another way, the Republican party condemned itself to defeat if white voters would not cooperate. In a few short years Republicans were reduced to the embarrassment of making futile appeals to whites while ignoring the claims of their strongest supporters, blacks.

But for a time both Republicans and their opponents, who called themselves Conservatives or Democrats, moved to the center and appealed for support from a broad range of groups. Some propertied whites accepted congressional Reconstruction as a reality and declared that they would try to compete under the new rules. As these Democrats angled for some black votes, Republicans sought to attract more white voters. Both parties found an area of agreement in economic policies.

The Reconstruction governments devoted themselves to stimulating industry. This policy reflected northern ideals, of course, but it also sprang from a growing southern interest in in-

Industrial-ization

dustrialization. Confederates had learned how vital industry was, and many postwar southerners were eager to build up the manufacturing capacity of their region. Accordingly, Reconstruction legislatures designed many tempting inducements to investment. Loans, subsidies, and exemptions from taxation for periods up to ten years helped to bring new industries into the region. The southern railroad system was rebuilt and expanded, coal and iron mining laid the basis for Birmingham's steel plants, and the number of manufacturing establishments nearly doubled between 1860 and 1880. But this emphasis on big business interests also locked Republicans into a conservative strategy. They were appealing to elite whites who never responded, and the alternate possibility of making a strong, class-based appeal to poorer whites was lost.

Policies appealing to black voters never went beyond equality before the law. In fact, the whites who controlled the southern Republican party were reluctant to allow blacks a share of offices proportionate to their electoral strength. Black leaders, aware of

Other Republican Policies

their weakness, did not push for revolutionary economic or social change. In every southern state blacks led efforts to establish public

schools, but most did not press for integrated facilities. Having a school to attend was the most important thing at the time, for the Johnson governments had excluded blacks from schools and other state-supported institutions. As a result, virtually every public school organized during Reconstruction was racially segregated, and these separate schools established a precedent for segregation. By the 1870s segregation was becoming a common practice in theaters, trains, and other public accommodations in the South.

A few black politicians did fight for civil rights and integration. Most were mulattoes from cities such as New Orleans or Mobile, where large populations of light-skinned free blacks had existed before the war. Their experience in such communities had made them sensitive to issues of status, and they spoke out for open and equal public accommodations. But they were a minority. Most elected black officials sought instead to make more limited but essential gains in the face of enormous white hostility.

Economic progress was uppermost in the minds of many of the freed people, especially politicians from agricultural districts. Land above all else had the potential to benefit the former slave, but none of the black state legislators promoted confiscation; freedmen simply lacked the power to make that possible. South Carolina established a land commission, but its purpose was to assist in the purchase of land. Any widespread redistribution of land had to arise from Congress, which never supported such action.

Within a few years, as centrists in both parties met failure, the other side of white reaction to congressional Reconstruction began to dominate. Some conservatives had always favored fierce opposition to Reconstruction through pressure and racist propaganda. They put economic and social pressure on blacks: one black Republican complained that "my neighbors will not employ me, nor sell me a farthing's worth of anything." Charging that the South had been turned over to ignorant blacks, conservatives deplored "black domination." The cry of "Negro rule" now became constant.

Such attacks were gross distortions. Blacks participated in politics but did not dominate or control events. They were a minority in eight out of ten state conventions (northerners were a minority in nine out of ten). Of the state legislatures, only in the lower house in South Carolina did blacks ever constitute a majority; generally their numbers among officials were far inferior to their proportion in the population. Sixteen blacks won seats in Congress before Reconstruction was over, but none was ever elected governor. Freedmen were participating in government, to be sure, but there was no justification for racist denunciations of "Ethiopian minstrelsy, Ham radicalism in all its glory."

Conservatives also stepped up their propaganda against the allies of black Republicans. "Carpetbagger" was a derisive name for whites who had come from

Carpetbaggers and Scalawags the North. It suggested an evil and greedy northern politician, recently arrived with a carpetbag into which he planned to stuff ill-gotten gains before fleeing. The stranger's carpetbag, a popular travel bag whose frame was covered with heavy carpet material, was presumably deep enough to hold all the loot stolen from southern treasuries and filched from hapless, trusting former slaves. Immigrants from the north, who held the largest share of Republican offices, were all tarred with this brush.

In fact most northerners who settled in the South arrived before Congress gave blacks the right to vote. They came seeking business opportunities or a warmer climate, and most never entered politics. Those who did generally wanted to democratize the South and to introduce northern ways, such as industry, public education, and the spirit of enterprise. Hard times and ostracism by white southerners made many of these men dependent on officeholding for a living, a fact that increased Republican factionalism and damaged the party. And although carpetbaggers supported black suffrage and educational opportunities, most opposed social equality and integration.

Conservatives invented the term "scalawag" to stigmatize and discredit any native white southerner who cooperated with the Republicans. A substantial number of southerners did so, including some wealthy and prominent men. Most scalawags, however, were representatives of the yeoman class, men from mountain areas and small farming districts—average white southerners who saw that they could benefit from the education and opportunities promoted by Republicans. Banding together with freedmen, they pursued common class interests and hoped to make headway against the power of long-dominant planters.

A poster celebrating the election of blacks to Congress during Reconstruction. From left to right across the top can be seen portraits of Senator Hiram R. Revels, Representative Benjamin S. Turner, the Reverend Richard Allen, Frederick Douglass, Representatives Josiah T. Walls and Joseph H. Rainy, and the writer William Wells Brown. Library of Congress.

Yet this black-white coalition was always vulnerable to the issue of race, and scalawags shied away from support for racial equality. Except on issues of common interest, scalawags often deserted the other elements of the Republican party.

Besides propaganda, the conservatives had other weapons to use against Reconstruction. Financially the Republican governments, despite their achievements, were doomed to be unpopular. Republicans wanted to continue prewar services, repair war's destruction, and support such important new ventures as public schools. But the Civil War had destroyed much of the South's tax base. One category of valuable property—slaves—was entirely gone. Hundreds of thousands of citizens had lost much of the rest of their real and personal property—money, livestock, fences, and buildings—to the war. Thus an increase

With the rise of the Ku Klux Klan, terrorism against blacks became more organized and purposeful. Note the racist overtones even in this northern illustration of Klan violence. The Bettmann Archive.

in taxes was necessary even to maintain traditional services, and new ventures required much higher taxes.

Corruption was another powerful charge levied against the Republicans. Unfortunately, it was true. Many carpetbaggers and black politicians sold their votes, taking part in what scholars recognize was a nationwide surge of corruption (see page 526). Although white Democrats often shared in the guilt, and despite the efforts of some Republicans to stop it, Democrats convinced many voters that scandal was the inevitable result of a foolish Reconstruction program based on blacks and carpetbaggers.

All these problems damaged the Republicans, but in many southern states the deathblow came through

violence: the murders, whippings, and intimidation of the Ku Klux Klan. Terrorism **Ku Klux Klan** against blacks had occurred throughout Reconstruction, but after 1867 white violence became more organized and purposeful. The Ku Klux Klan rode to frustrate Reconstruction and keep the freedmen in subjection. Nighttime visits, whippings, beatings, and murder became common, and in some areas virtually open warfare developed despite the authorities' efforts to keep the peace.

Although the Klan persecuted blacks who stood up for their rights as laborers or people, its main purpose was political. Lawless nightriders made active Republicans the target of their attacks. Prominent

Chapter 15: RECONSTRUCTION BY TRIAL AND ERROR, 1865–1877

white Republicans and black leaders were killed in several states. After blacks who worked for a South Carolina scalawag started voting, terrorists visited the plantation and "whipped every nigger man they could lay their hands on." Klansmen also attacked Union League Clubs (Republican organizations that mobilized the black vote) and schoolteachers who were aiding the freedmen.

Klan violence was not simply spontaneous; certain social forces gave direction to racism. In North Carolina, for example, Alamance and Caswell counties were the sites of the worst Klan violence. They were in the Piedmont, where slim Republican majorities rested on cooperation between black voters and whites of the yeoman class, particularly yeomen whose Unionism or discontent with the Confederacy had turned them against local Democratic officials. Together these black and white Republicans had ousted officials long entrenched in power. But the Republican majority was a small one, and it would fail if either whites or blacks faltered in their support.

In Alamance and Caswell counties the wealthy and powerful men who had lost their accustomed political control organized the campaign of terror. They brought it into being and used it for their purposes. They were the secret organization's county officers and local chieftains; they recruited members and planned atrocities. They used the Klan to regain political power: by whipping up racism or frightening enough Republicans, the Ku Klux Klan could split the Republican coalition and restore a Democratic majority.

Thus a combination of difficult fiscal problems, Republican mistakes, racial hostility, and terror brought down the Republican regimes, and in most southern states so-called Radical Reconstruction was over after only a few years. But the most lasting failure of Reconstruction governments was not political—it was social. The new governments failed to alter the southern social structure or its distribution of wealth and power. Exploited as slaves, freedmen remained vulnerable to exploitation during Reconstruction. Without land of their own, they were dependent on white landowners, who could use their economic power to compromise blacks' political freedom. Armed only with the ballot, southern blacks had little chance to effect major changes.

Failure of Reconstruction

To reform the southern social order, Congress would have had to redistribute land; and never did a majority of congressmen favor such a plan. Radical Republicans like Albion Tourgée condemned Congress's timidity. Turning the freedman out on his own without advantages, said Tourgée, constituted "cheap philanthropy." Indeed, freedmen who had to live with the consequences of Reconstruction considered it a failure. The North should have "fixed some way for us," said former slaves, but instead it "threw all the Negroes on the world without any way of getting along."

Freedom had come, but blacks knew they "still had to depend on the southern white man for work, food, and clothing," and it was clear that most whites were hostile. Unless Congress exercised careful supervision over the South, the situation of the freedmen was sure to deteriorate. Whenever the North lost interest, Reconstruction would collapse.

THE SOCIAL AND ECONOMIC MEANING OF FREEDOM

Black southerners entered upon life after slavery hopefully, determinedly, but not naively. They had too much experience with white people to assume that all would be easy. As one man in Texas advised his son, even before the war was over, "our forever was going to be spent living among the Southerners, after they got licked." Expecting to meet with hostility, black people tried to gain as much as they could from their new circumstances. Often the most valued changes were personal ones—alterations in location, employer, or surroundings that could make an enormous difference to individuals or families.

One of the first decisions that many took was whether to leave the old plantation or remain. This meant making a judgment about where the chances of liberty and progress would be greatest. Former slaves drew upon their experiences in bondage to assess the whites with whom they had to deal. "Most all the Negroes that had good owners stayed with them," said one man, "but the others left." Not surprisingly, cruel slaveholders usually saw their former

Freed from slavery, blacks of all ages filled the schools to seek the education that had been denied them in bondage. Valentine Museum, Richmond, Virginia.

The federal government and northern reformers assisted this search for education. In its brief life the Freedmen's Bureau founded over four thousand schools, and idealistic men and women from the North established others and staffed them ably. The Yankee schoolmarm—dedicated, selfless, and religious—became an agent of progress in many southern communities. Thus, with the aid of religious and charitable organizations throughout the north, blacks began the nation's first assault on the problems created by slavery. The results included the beginnings of a public school system in each southern state and the enrollment of over 600,000 blacks in elementary school by 1877.

Blacks and their white allies also realized that higher education was essential—colleges and universities to train teachers and equip ministers and professionals for leadership. The American Missionary Association founded seven colleges, including Fisk and Atlanta universities, between 1866 and 1869. The Freedmen's Bureau helped to establish Howard University in Washington, D.C., and northern religious groups, such as Methodists, Baptists, and Congregationalists, supported dozens of seminaries, colleges, and teachers' colleges. By the late 1870s black churches had joined in the effort, founding numerous colleges despite their smaller financial resources. Though some of the new institutions did not survive, they brought knowledge to those who would educate others and laid a foundation for progress.

Even in Reconstruction blacks were choosing many highly educated individuals as leaders. Many blacks who won public office during Reconstruction came from the prewar elite of free people of color. This group had benefited from its association with wealthy whites, who were often blood relatives. Some planters had given their mulatto children outstanding educations. Francis Cardozo, who served in South Carolina's constitutional convention and was later that state's secretary of the treasury and secretary of state, had attended universities in Scotland and England. P. B. S. Pinchback, who became lieutenant governor of Louisiana, was the son of a planter who had sent him to school in Cincinnati at age nine. And the two black senators from Mississippi, Blanche K. Bruce and Hiram Revels, were both privileged in their educations. Bruce was the son of a planter who had

chattels walk off en masse. "And let me tell you," added one man who abandoned a harsh planter, "we sure cussed ole master out before we left there."

On new farms or old the newly freed men and women reached out for valuable things in life that had been denied them. One of these was education.

Education for Blacks

Whatever their age, blacks hungered for the knowledge in books that had been permitted only to whites. With freedom they filled the schools both day and night. On "log seats" or "a dirt floor," many freedmen studied their letters in old almanacs, discarded dictionaries, or whatever was available. Young children brought infants to school with them, and adults attended at night or after "the crops was laid by." Many a teacher had "to make herself heard over three other classes reciting in concert" in a small room, but the scholars kept coming. The desire to escape slavery's ignorance was so great that many blacks paid tuition, typically $1.00 or $1.50 a month, despite their poverty. This seemingly small amount

provided tutoring on his plantation; Revels was the son of free North Carolina mulattoes who had sent him to Knox College in Illinois. These men and many self-educated former slaves brought experience as artisans, businessmen, lawyers, teachers, and preachers to political office.

While elected officials wrestled with the political tasks of Reconstruction, millions of former slaves concentrated on improving life at home, on their farms, and in their neighborhoods. A major goal of black men and women was to gain some living space for themselves and their families. Surrounded by an unfriendly white population, they sought to insulate themselves from white interference and to strengthen the bonds of their own community. Throughout the South they devoted themselves to reuniting their families, moving away from the slave quarters, and founding black churches. Given the eventual failure of Reconstruction, the practical gains that blacks made in their daily lives often proved the most enduring and significant changes of the period.

The search for long-lost family members was awe-inspiring. With only shreds of information to guide them, thousands of black people embarked on odysseys in search of a husband, wife, child, or parent. By relying on the black community for help and information, many succeeded in their quest, sometimes almost miraculously. Others walked through several states and never found their loved ones.

Reunification of Black Families

Husbands and wives who had belonged to different masters established homes together for the first time, and parents asserted the right to raise their own children. Saying "You took her away from me and didn' pay no mind to my cryin', so now I'm takin' her back home," one mother reclaimed a child whom the mistress had been raising in her own house. Another woman bristled when her old master claimed a right to whip her children, promptly informing him that "he warn't goin' to brush none of her chilluns no more." One girl recalled that her mistress had struck her soon after freedom. As if to clarify the new ground rules, this girl "grabbed her leg and would have broke her neck." The freedmen were too much at risk to act recklessly, but as one man put it, they were tired of punishment, and "they sure didn't take no more foolishness off of white folks."

Given the eventual failure of Reconstruction, many blacks, like this elderly couple, probably benefited most from small gains in their daily lives—greater freedom from white supervision, and more living space for themselves and their families. Valentine Museum, Richmond, Virginia.

Black people frequently wanted to minimize all contact with whites. "There is a prejudice against us . . . that will take years to get over," the Reverend Garrison Frazier told General Sherman in January 1865. To avoid contact with intrusive whites, who were used to supervising and controlling them, blacks abandoned the slave quarters and fanned out into distant corners of the land they worked. Some moved away to build new homes in the woods. "After the war my stepfather come," recalled Annie Young, "and got my mother and we moved out in the piney woods." Others described moving "across the creek to [themselves]" or building a "saplin house . . . back in the woods" or " 'way off in the woods." Some rural dwellers established small all-black settlements that still can be found today along the backroads of the South.

Even once-privileged slaves often shared this desire for independence and social separation. One man turned down the master's offer of the overseer's house as a residence and moved instead to a shack in "Freetown." He also declined to let the former owner grind his grain for free, because it "made him feel like a free man to pay for things just like anyone else." One couple, a carriage driver and trusted house servant during slavery, passed up the fine cooking of the "big house" so that they could move "in the colored settlement."

The other side of this distance from whites was closer communion within the black community. Freed from the restrictions and regulations of slavery, blacks could build their own institutions

Founding of as they saw fit. The secret church
Black Churches of slavery now came out into the open; in countless communities throughout the South, "some of the niggers started a brush arbor." A brush arbor was merely "a sort of . . . shelter with leaves for a roof," but the freedmen worshipped in it enthusiastically. "Preachin' and shouting sometimes lasted all day," ex-slaves recalled, for there were "glorious times then" when black people could worship together in freedom. Within a few years independent black branches of the Methodist and Baptist churches had attracted the great majority of black Christians in the South.

This desire to gain as much independence as possible carried over into the freedmen's economic arrangements. Since most former slaves lacked money to buy land, they preferred the next best thing—renting the land they worked. But many whites would not consider renting land to blacks; there was strong social pressure against it. And few blacks had the means to rent a farm. Therefore other alternatives had to be tried.

Northerners and officials of the Freedmen's Bureau favored contracts between owners and laborers. To northerners who believed in "free soil, free labor, free men," contracts and wages seemed the key to progress. For a few years the Freedmen's Bureau helped to draw up and enforce such contracts, but they proved unpopular with both blacks and whites. Owners often filled the contracts with detailed requirements that reminded blacks of their circumscribed lives under

slavery. Disputes frequently arose over efficiency, lost time, and other matters. Besides, cash was not readily available in the early years of Reconstruction; times were hard and the failure of Confederate banks left the South with a shortage of credit facilities.

Black farmers and white landowners therefore turned to a system of sharecropping: in return for use of the land and "furnishing" (tools, mules, seed, a cabin, and food to last until harvest), the

Rise of the farmer paid the landowner a share
Sharecropping of his crop. The cost of food and
System clothing was deducted from the crop before the owner took his share. Naturally, landowners tended to set their share at a high level, but blacks had some bargaining power. By holding out and refusing to make contracts at the end of the year, sharecroppers succeeded in lowering the owners' share to around one-half during Reconstruction.

The sharecropping system originated as a desirable compromise. It eased landowners' problems with cash and credit; blacks accepted it because it gave them a reasonable amount of freedom from daily supervision. Instead of working under a white overseer as in slavery, they were able to farm a plot of land on their own in family groups. But sharecropping later proved to be a disaster, both for blacks and for the South. Part of the problem lay in the fact that an unscrupulous owner in a discriminatory society had many opportunities to cheat a sharecropper. Owners and merchants frequently paid less for blacks' cotton than they paid for whites'. Greedy men could overcharge or manipulate records so that the sharecropper always stayed in debt. But the problem was even more fundamental than that.

Southern farmers were concentrating on cotton, a crop with a bright past and a dim future. During the Civil War, India, Brazil, and Egypt had begun

to supply cotton to Britain; not until
Overdepen- 1878 did the South recover its pre-
dence war share of British cotton pur-
on Cotton chases. This temporary loss of markets reduced per capita income, as did a decline in the amount of labor invested by the average southern farmer. Part of the exploitation of slavery had been the sending of black women and children into the fields. In freedom these people stayed at home, like their white counterparts, when

possible. Black families valued human dignity more highly than the levels of production that had been achieved with the lash.

But even as southerners grew more cotton, matching and eventually surpassing prewar totals, their reward diminished. Cotton prices began a long decline whose causes merely coincided with the Civil War. From 1820 to 1860 world demand for cotton had grown at a rate of 5 percent per year; but from 1866 to 1895 the rate of growth was only 1.3 percent per year. By 1860 the English textile industry, world leader in production, had penetrated all the major new markets, and from that point on increases in demand were slight. As a result, when southern farmers planted more cotton they tended to depress the price.

In these circumstances overspecialization in cotton was a mistake. But most southern farmers had no choice. Landowners required sharecroppers to grow the prime cash crop, whose salability was sure. And due to the shortage of banks and credit in the South, white farmers often had to borrow from a local merchant, who insisted on cotton production to secure his loan. Thus southern agriculture slipped deeper and deeper into depression. Black sharecroppers struggled under a growing burden of debt that reduced their independence and bound them to landowners almost as oppressively as slavery had bound them to their masters. Many white farmers became debtors too and gradually lost their land. All these problems were serious, but few people in the North were paying attention.

THE END OF RECONSTRUCTION

The North's commitment to racial equality had never been total. And by the early 1870s it was evident that even its partial commitment was weakening. New issues were capturing people's attention, and soon voters began to look for reconciliation with southern whites. In the South Democrats won control of one state after another, and they threatened to defeat Republicans in the North as well. Before long the situation had returned to "normal" in the eyes of southern whites.

The Supreme Court, after first re-establishing its power, participated in the northern retreat from Reconstruction. During the Civil War the Court had been cautious and reluctant to assert itself. Reaction to the Dred Scott decision had been so violent, and the Union's wartime emergency so great, that the Court had refrained from blocking or interfering with government actions. The justices, for example, had breathed a collective sigh of relief when legal technicalities prevented them from reviewing the case of Clement Vallandigham, who had been convicted of aiding the enemy by a military court when regular civil courts were open (see page 407).

But in 1866 a similar case, *Ex parte Milligan,* reached the Court through proper channels. Lambdin P. Milligan of Indiana had participated in a plot to free Confederate prisoners of war and overthrow state governments; for these acts a military court had sentenced Milligan, a civilian, to death.

Supreme Court Decisions on Reconstruction

In sweeping language the Court declared that military trials were illegal when civil courts were open and functioning, thus indicating that it intended to reassert itself as a major force in national affairs. This decision could have led to a direct clash with Congress, which in 1867 established military districts and military courts in the initial phase of its Reconstruction program. But Congress altered part of the Court's jurisdiction; it was constitutionally empowered to do so, but had never taken such action before (or since). By altering the Court's jurisdiction, Congress protected its Reconstruction policy and avoided a confrontation.

In 1873, however, an important group of cases, the *Slaughter-House* cases, tested the scope and meaning of the Fourteenth Amendment. In 1869 the Louisiana legislature had granted one company a monopoly on the slaughtering of livestock in New Orleans. Rival butchers in the city promptly sued. Their attorney, former Supreme Court justice John A. Campbell, argued that the Fourteenth Amendment had revolutionized the constitutional system by bringing individual rights under federal protection. Campbell expressed what had been a major Radical goal: to nationalize civil rights and guard them from state interference. Over the years his argument would win acceptance, offering shelter from government regulation to corporate "persons" in the nineteenth century and providing protection for blacks and other minorities in the twentieth.

The Court did not go that far, however, in the *Slaughter-House* decision. In a blow to the hopes of blacks, it refused to accept Campbell's argument. Neither the "privileges and immunities" clause nor the "due process" clause of the amendment guaranteed the great basic rights of the Bill of Rights against state action, the justices said. State and national citizenship remained separate, with the former more important. National citizenship involved only such things as the right to travel freely from state to state and to use the navigable waters of the nation. Thus the Court limited severely the amendment's potential for securing the rights of black citizens.

In 1876 the Court regressed even further, emasculating the enforcement clause of the Fourteenth Amendment and interpreting the Fifteenth in a narrow and negative fashion. In *United States* v. *Cruikshank* the Court dealt with Louisiana whites who were indicted for attacking a meeting of blacks and conspiring to deprive them of their rights. The justices ruled that the Fourteenth Amendment did not extend federal power to cover the misdeeds of private individuals against other citizens; only flagrant state discrimination was covered. And in *United States* v. *Reese* the Court held that the Fifteenth Amendment did not guarantee a citizen's right to vote, but merely listed certain impermissible grounds for denying suffrage. Thus a path lay open for southern states to disfranchise blacks for supposedly nonracial reasons—lack of education, lack of property, or lack of descent from a grandfather qualified to vote before the Military Reconstruction Act. ("Grandfather clauses" became a way of excluding blacks from suffrage, since most blacks were slaves before Reconstruction and hence could not vote.)

The retreat from Reconstruction continued steadily in politics as well. In 1868 Ulysses S. Grant, running as a Republican, defeated Horatio Seymour, a Democrat of New York, in a presidential campaign that revived sectional divisions. Although he was not a Radical, Grant realized that Congress's program represented the wishes of northerners, and he supported a platform that praised congressional Reconstruction and endorsed Negro suffrage in the South. (The platform stopped short of endorsing black suffrage in the North.) The Democrats went in the

Election of 1868

opposite direction; their platform vigorously denounced Reconstruction. By associating themselves with rebellion and with Johnson's repudiated program, the Democrats went down to defeat in all but eight states, though the popular vote was fairly close.

In office Grant sometimes used force to support Reconstruction, but only when he had to. He hoped to avoid confrontation with the South, to erase the image of dictatorship that his military background summoned up. In fact, neither he nor Johnson had imposed anything approaching a military occupation on the South. Rapid demobilization had reduced a federal army of more than 1 million to 57,000 within a year of surrender. Thereafter the number of troops in the South continued to fall, until in 1874 there were only 4,082 in the southern states outside Texas. Throughout Reconstruction the strongest federal units were in Texas and the West, fighting Indians, not white southerners.

In 1870 and 1871 the violent campaigns of the Ku Klux Klan moved Congress to pass two Force Acts and an anti-Klan law. These acts (important precedents for the modern enforcement of civil rights) permitted martial law and suspension of the writ of habeas corpus to combat murders, beatings, and threats by the Klan. Federal troops and prosecutors used them vigorously but unsuccessfully, for a conspiracy of silence frustrated many prosecutions. Possible witnesses were frightened or unwilling to testify and juries unwilling to convict. Thereafter the Klan disbanded officially and went underground. Paramilitary organizations known as Rifle Clubs and Red Shirts often took the Klan's place.

In 1872 a revolt within the Republican ranks foreshadowed the end of Reconstruction. A group calling itself the Liberal Republicans bolted the party and nominated Horace Greeley, the well-known editor of the *New York Tribune*, for president. The Liberal Republicans were a varied group, including civil-service reformers, foes of corruption, and advocates of a lower tariff; they often spoke of a more lenient policy toward the South. That year the Democrats too gave their nomination to Greeley. Though the combination was not enough to defeat Grant, it reinforced his desire to avoid confrontation with white southerners. Grant used troops very sparingly thereafter, and in 1875 refused

Liberal Republicans Revolt

President Grant with wife Julia and his youngest son Jessie. Photographed in 1872. Keystone-Mast Collection, University of California, Riverside.

a desperate request for troops from the governor of Mississippi.

The Liberal Republican challenge revealed the growing dissatisfaction with Grant's administration. Strong-willed but politically naive, Grant made a series of poor appointments. His secretary of war, his private secretary, and officials in the Treasury and Navy departments were all involved in bribery or tax-cheating scandals. Instead of exposing the corruption, Grant defended some of the culprits. As the clamor against dishonesty in government grew, Grant's popularity declined. So did his party's; in the 1874 elections Democrats recaptured the House of Representatives.

Congress's resolve on southern issues weakened steadily. By joint resolution it had already removed the political disabilities of the Fourteenth Amendment from many former Confederates. Then in 1872 it adopted a sweeping Amnesty Act,

Amnesty Act which pardoned most of the re-

maining rebels and left only five hundred excluded from political participation. A Civil Rights Act passed in 1875 purported to guarantee black people equal accommodations in public places, like inns and theaters. But it was weak and contained no effective provisions for enforcement. (The law was later struck down by the Supreme Court; see page 474.)

Democrats regained power in the South rather quickly, winning four states before 1872 and a total of eight by the start of 1876 (see map, page 444). As they did so, northern Republicans worried about their opponents' stress on the failure and scandals of Reconstruction governments. Many Republicans sensed that their constituents were tiring of the same old issues. In fact, a variety of new concerns were catching the public's eye. The Panic of 1873, which threw 3 million people out of work, focused attention on economic and monetary problems. Businessmen were disturbed by the strikes and industrial violence that accompanied the panic; debtors and unemployed

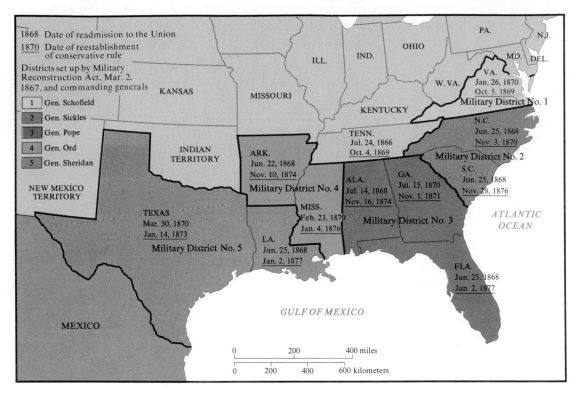

The Reconstruction

sought easy-money policies to spur economic expansion.

The monetary issue aroused strong controversy. Civil War greenbacks had the potential to expand the money supply and lift prices, if they were kept in circulation. In 1872 Democratic farmers and debtors had urged such a policy, but they were overruled by "sound money" men. Now the depression swelled the ranks of "greenbackers"—voters who favored greenbacks and easy money. In 1874 Congress voted to increase the number of greenbacks in circulation, but Grant vetoed the bill in deference to the opinions of financial leaders. The next year sound-money interests prevailed in Congress, winning passage of a law requiring that after 1878 greenbacks be convertible into gold. The law limited the inflationary impact of the greenbacks and aided creditors, not debtors.

Greenbacks Versus Sound Money

Indeed, the government's financial policies were almost perfectly tailored to revive and support industrial growth. Soon after the war Congress had shifted some of the government's tax revenues to pay off the interest-bearing war debt. The debt fell from $2.33 billion in 1866 to only $587 million in 1893, and every dollar repaid was a dollar injected into the economy for potential reinvestment. Thus approximately 1 percent of the gross national product was pumped back into the economy from 1866 to 1872, and only slightly less than that during the rest of the 1870s. Low taxes on investment and high tariffs on manufactured goods also aided industrialists. With such help the northern economy quickly recovered the rate of growth it had enjoyed just before the war.

Another issue that claimed new attention in the 1870s was immigration. After the war the number of immigrants entering the United States began to rise again, along with the ingrained suspicions and hostilities of native Americans. The Mormon question too—how Utah's growing Mormon community, which practiced polygamy, could be reconciled to American law—became prominent.

Renewed pressure for expansion revived interest in international affairs. Secretary of State William H. Seward accomplished the only major addition of territory during these years in 1867. Through ne-

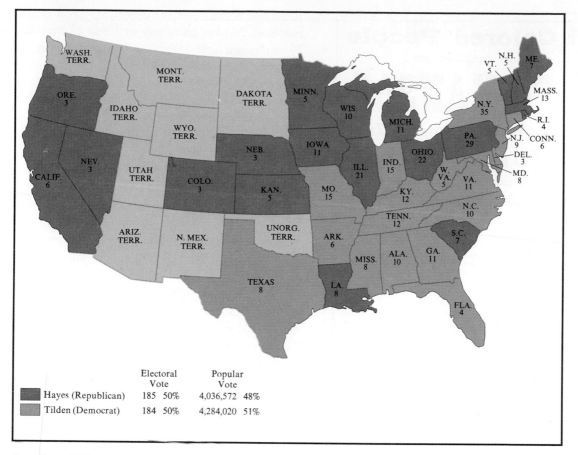

Presidential Election, 1876

	Electoral Vote		Popular Vote	
Hayes (Republican)	185	50%	4,036,572	48%
Tilden (Democrat)	184	50%	4,284,020	51%

gotiation with the Russian government, he arranged the purchase of Alaska for $7.2 million dollars. Opponents ridiculed Seward's venture, calling Alaska Frigidia, the Polar Bear Garden, or Walrussia. But Seward convinced important congressmen of Alaska's economic potential, and other lawmakers favored the dawning of friendship with Russia. In the same year the United States took control of the Midway Islands, a thousand miles from Hawaii, which were scarcely mentioned again until the Second World War. Though in 1870 President Grant tried to annex the Dominican Republic, Senator Charles Sumner blocked the attempt. Seward and his successor, Hamilton Fish, used diplomacy to arrange a financial settlement of claims against Britain for permitting the sale of the *Alabama* and other Confederate cruisers (see page 625).

By 1876 it was obvious to most political observers that the North was no longer willing to pursue the goals of Reconstruction. The results of a disputed presidential election confirmed this fact. Samuel J.

Election of 1876

Tilden, Democratic governor of New York, ran strongly in the South and took a commanding lead in both the popular vote and the electoral college over Rutherford B. Hayes, the Republican nominee. Tilden won 184 electoral votes and needed only one more for a majority. Nineteen votes from Louisiana, South Carolina, and Florida were disputed; both Democrats and Republicans claimed to have won in those states despite fraud on the part of their opponents. One vote from Oregon was undecided due to a technicality (see map).

To resolve this unprecedented situation, on which the Constitution gave no guidance, Congress established a fifteen-member electoral commission. In the interest of impartiality, membership on the commission was to be balanced between Democrats and Republicans. But one independent Republican, Supreme

All Colored People

THAT WANT TO

GO TO KANSAS,

On September 5th, 1877,

Can do so for $5.00

IMMIGRATION.

Whereas, We, the colored people of Lexington, Ky., knowing that there is an abundance of choice lands now belonging to the Government, have assembled ourselves together for the purpose of locating on said lands. Therefore,

Be it Resolved, That we do now organize ourselves into a Colony, as follows:— Any person wishing to become a member of this Colony can do so by paying the sum of one dollar ($1.00), and this money is to be paid by the first of September, 1877, in installments of twenty-five cents at a time, or otherwise as may be desired.

Resolved, That this Colony has agreed to consolidate itself with the Nicodemus Towns, Solomon Valley, Graham County, Kansas, and can only do so by entering the vacant lands now in their midst, which costs $5.00.

Resolved, That this Colony shall consist of seven officers—President, Vice-President, Secretary, Treasurer, and three Trustees. President—M. M. Bell; Vice-President—Isaac Talbott; Secretary—W. J. Niles; Treasurer—Daniel Clarke; Trustees—Jerry Lee, William Jones, and Abner Webster.

Resolved, That this Colony shall have from one to two hundred militia, more or less, as the case may require, to keep peace and order, and any member failing to pay in his dues, as aforesaid, or failing to comply with the above rules in any particular, will not be recognized or protected by the Colony.

Exodusters, southern blacks dismayed by the failure of Reconstruction, left the South by the thousands for Kansas in 1877. This handbill advertised the establishment of a black colony in Graham County, Kansas. Kansas State Historical Society.

Court Justice David Davis, refused appointment in order to accept his election as a senator. A regular Republican took his place, and the Republican party prevailed 8 to 7 on every decision, a strict party vote. Hayes would then become the winner if Congress accepted the commission's findings.

Congressional acceptance, however, was not sure. Democrats controlled the House and had the power to filibuster to block action on the vote. Many citizens worried that the nation had entered a major constitutional crisis and was slipping once again into civil war. But the crisis was resolved when Democrats acquiesced in the election of Hayes. Scholars have found that negotiations went on between some of Hayes's supporters and southerners who were interested in federal aid to railroads, internal improvements, federal patronage, and removal of troops from southern states. But the most recent studies suggest that these negotiations did not have a deciding effect on the outcome. Neither party was well enough organized to implement and enforce a bargain between the sections. Northern and southern Democrats decided they could not win and failed to contest the election. Thus Hayes became president, and southerners looked forward to the withdrawal of federal troops from the South. Reconstruction was unmistakably over.

Southern Democrats rejoiced, but black Americans grieved over the betrayal of their hopes for equality. Tens of thousands of blacks pondered leaving the South, where freedom was no longer

Black Exodusters

a real possibility. "[We asked] whether it was possible we could stay under a people who had held us in bondage," said Henry Adams, who led a migration to Kansas. "[We] appealed to the President . . . and to Congress . . . to protect us in our rights and privileges," but "in 1877 we lost all hopes." Thereafter many southern blacks "wanted to go to a territory by ourselves." In South Carolina, Louisiana, Mississippi, and other southern states, thousands gathered up their possessions and migrated to Kansas. They were known as Exodusters, disappointed people still searching for their share in the American dream. Even in Kansas they met disillusionment, as the welcome extended by the state's governor soon gave way to hostile public receptions.

Thus the nation ended over fifteen years of bloody civil war and controversial reconstruction without establishing full freedom for black Americans. Their status would continue to be one of the major issues facing the nation. A host of other issues would arise from industrialization. How would the country develop its immense resources in a growing and increasingly integrated national economy? How would farmers, industrial workers, immigrants, and capitalists fit into the new social system? Industrialization promised not just a higher standard of living but also a different lifestyle in both urban and rural areas. Moreover, it augmented the nation's power and laid the foundation for an increased American role in international affairs. Again Americans turned their thoughts to expansion and the conquest of new frontiers. As the United States entered its second hundred years of existence, it confronted these serious challenges. The experience of the 1860s and 1870s suggested that the solutions, if any, might not be clear or complete.

IMPORTANT EVENTS

1865	Johnson begins Reconstruction Confederate leaders regain power Black Codes Congress refuses to seat southern representatives Thirteenth Amendment ratified	1870	Force Acts
		1871	Ku Klux Klan Act Treaty with England settles *Alabama* claims

1866	Civil Rights Act
	Congress approves Fourteenth
	  Amendment
	Freedmen's Bureau renewed
	Most southern states reject
	  Fourteenth Amendment
	Ex parte Milligan
		1872	Amnesty Act
			Liberal Republicans organize
			Debtors urge government to keep
			  greenbacks in circulation
			Grant re-elected

		1873	*Slaughter-House* cases

1867	Military Reconstruction Act; Tenure
	  of Office Act
	Purchase of Alaska
	Constitutional conventions called in
	  southern states
		1874	Grant vetoes increase in paper
			  money
			Democrats win House

		1875	Several Grant appointees indicted
			  for corruption
			Civil Rights Act
			Congress requires that after 1878
			  greenbacks be convertible into gold

1868	House impeaches Johnson; Senate acquits him Most southern states readmitted Fourteenth Amendment ratified Ulysses S. Grant elected president	1876	*U.S. v. Cruikshank; U.S. v. Reese* Presidential election disputed
1869	Congress approves Fifteenth Amendment (ratified 1870)	1877	Congress elects Hayes Black Exodusters migrate to Kansas

SUGGESTIONS FOR FURTHER READING

National Policy, Politics, and Constitutional Law

Richard H. Abbott, *The First Southern Strategy* (1986); Herman Belz, *Emancipation and Equal Rights* (1978); Herman Belz, *A New Birth of Freedom* (1976); Herman Belz, *Reconstructing the Union* (1969); Michael Les Benedict, *A Compromise of Principle* (1974); Michael Les Benedict, *The Impeachment and Trial of Andrew Johnson* (1973); Charles S. Campbell, *The Transformation of American Foreign Relations, 1865–1900* (1976); Adrian Cook, *The Alabama Claims* (1975); David Donald, *Charles Sumner and the Rights of Man* (1970); Harold M. Hyman, *A More Perfect Union* (1973); Ronald J. Jensen, *The Alaska Purchase and Russian-American Relations* (1975); William S. McFeely, *Grant* (1981); William S. McFeely, *Yankee Stepfather: General O. O. Howard and the Freedmen* (1968); Eric L. McKitrick, *Andrew Johnson and Reconstruction* (1966); James M. McPherson, *The Abolitionist Legacy* (1975); Kenneth M. Stampp, *Era of Reconstruction* (1965); Mark W. Summers, *Railroads, Reconstruction, and the Gospel of Prosperity* (1984); Glyndon C. Van Deusen, *William Henry Seward* (1967).

The Freed Slaves

Roberta Sue Alexander, *North Carolina Faces the Freedmen* (1985); Ira Berlin, ed., *Freedom* (1984); Edmund L. Drago, *Black Politicians and Reconstruction in Georgia* (1982); Paul D. Escott, *Slavery Remembered* (1979); Eric Foner, "Reconstruction and the Crisis of Free Labor," in *Politics and Ideology in the Age of the Civil War* (1980); Peter Kolchin, *First Freedom* (1972); Leon Litwack, *Been in the Storm So Long* (1979); Howard Rabinowitz, ed., *Southern Black Leaders in Reconstruction* (1982); C. Peter Ripley, *Slaves and Freedmen in Civil War Louisiana* (1976); Willie Lee Rose, *Rehearsal for Reconstruction* (1964); Emma Lou Thornbrough, ed., *Black Reconstructionists* (1972); Okon Uya, *From Slavery to Public Service* (1971); Clarence Walker, *A Rock in a Weary Land* (1982).

Politics and Reconstruction in the South

Jonathan Daniels, *Prince of Carpetbaggers* (1958); W. E. B. Du Bois, *Black Reconstruction* (1935); Paul D. Escott, *Many Excellent People* (1985); W. McKee Evans, *Ballots and Fence Rails* (1966); Eric Foner, *Nothing But Freedom* (1983); William C. Harris, *Day of the Carpetbagger* (1979); Thomas Holt, *Black over White* (1977); Robert Manson Myers, ed., *The Children of Pride* (1972); Elizabeth Studley Nathans, *Losing the Peace* (1968); Lillian A. Pereyra, *James Lusk Alcorn* (1966); Michael Perman, *The Road to Redemption* (1984); Michael Perman, *Reunion Without Compromise* (1973); Lawrence N. Powell, "The Politics of Livelihood," in J. Morgan Kousser and James M. McPherson, eds., *Region, Race and Reconstruction* (1982); Lawrence N. Powell, *New Masters* (1980); George C. Rable, *But There Was No Peace* (1984); James Roark, *Masters Without Slaves* (1977); James Sefton, *The United States Army and Reconstruction, 1865–1877* (1967); Mark W. Summers, *Railroads, Reconstruction, and the Gospel of Prosperity* (1984); J. Mills Thornton III, "Fiscal Policy and the Failure of Radical Reconstruction," in J. Morgan Kousser and James M. McPherson, eds., *Region, Race and Reconstruction* (1982); Albion W. Tourgée, *A Fool's Errand* (1979); Allen Trelease, *White Terror* (1967); Ted Tunnell, *Crucible of Reconstruction* (1984); Sarah Woolfolk Wiggins, *The Scalawag in Alabama Politics, 1865–1881* (1977).

Women and Family History

Ellen Carol Dubois, *Feminism and Suffrage* (1978); Herbert G. Gutman, *The Black Family in Slavery & Freedom, 1750–1925* (1976); Elizabeth Jacoway, *Yankee Missionaries in the South* (1979); Jacqueline Jones, *Labor of Love, Labor of Sorrow* (1985); Jacqueline Jones, *Soldiers of Light and Love* (1980); Rebecca Scott, "The Battle over the Child," *Prologue*, 10, No. 2 (Summer 1978), 101–113.

The End of Reconstruction

Michael Les Benedict, "Southern Democrats in the Crisis of 1876–1877," *Journal of Southern History*, LXVI, No. 4 (November 1980), 489–524; William Gillette, *Retreat from Reconstruction, 1869–1879* (1980); William Gillette, *The Right to Vote* (1969); Keith Ian Polakoff, *The Politics of Inertia* (1973); C. Vann Woodward, *Reunion and Reaction* (1951).

Reconstruction's Legacy for the South

Robert G. Athearn, *In Search of Canaan* (1978); Norman L. Crockett, *The Black Towns* (1979); Stephen J. DeCanio, *Agriculture in the Postbellum South* (1974); Steven Hahn, *The Roots of Southern Populism* (1983); Susan Previant Lee and Peter Passell, *A New Economic View of American History* (1979); Jay R. Mandle, *The Roots of Black Poverty* (1978); Nell Irvin Painter, *Exodusters* (1976); Howard Rabinowitz, *Race Relations in the Urban South, 1865–1890* (1978); Roger L. Ransom and Richard Sutch, *One Kind of Freedom* (1977); Jonathan M. Wiener, *Social Origins of the New South* (1978); Joel Williamson, *After Slavery* (1966); C. Vann Woodward, *Origins of the New South* (1951).

LUNCH BASKETS FILLED FOR 25 CENTS TAKE NOTICE BLACK HILLERS

Transformation of the West and South

1877–1892

Chapter 16

Though shaggy and dressed in buckskins, William F. "Buffalo Bill" Cody earned his nickname for his work, not his looks. Equipped with a powerful rifle, which he dubbed Lucretia Borgia after the scandalous Italian noblewoman, and riding his favorite horse, Brigham, Cody had unequaled hunting skills. Buffalo Bill had such an illustrious reputation by the 1870s that the Kansas Pacific Railroad hired him to supply meat for the company's twelve hundred track layers. For $500 a month, Cody contracted to kill twelve buffalo a day, have them butchered, and deliver them for roasting the same night. In one eight-month stretch he killed over four thousand buffalo.

The millions of buffalo (bison) that roamed the American West helped to feed railroad workers, but they also were bothersome and dangerous. Foraging herds slowed construction, the bulky animals knocked over telegraph poles, and a stampede could derail a train. Railroad operators tried to remove the nuisance and raise money at the same time by sponsoring buffalo hunts for eastern sportsmen. These were hardly sporting events: rifle-toting men sat on slow-moving trains and shot away at the huge targets. Some hunters collected the $1 to $3 offered by tanneries for hides, but others did not even stop to pick up their kill. As a result of these activities, by the 1880s only a few hundred remained of the estimated 13 million buffalo that had existed in the 1850s. Ironically, one of the remaining herds was owned and protected by Buffalo Bill Cody.

The destruction of the buffalo had a more important consequence than facilitating railroad construction: it undermined the culture of Plains Indians, who depended on the animals for almost every essential of life. For centuries natives had cooked and preserved buffalo meat; fashioned hides into clothing, shoes, and blankets; used sinew for thread and bowstrings; carved tools from bones; and made horns into implements. As buffalo became more scarce, the natives were forced to assume a different way of life, where they were more dependent on white traders and the government for their subsistence and where their hunting and territorial claims posed less of a threat to white ambitions for land and profit. Whites were fully aware of these consequences. As one army officer urged during the wars against Plains Indians, "Kill every buffalo you can. Every buffalo dead is an Indian gone."

The buffalo were victims of expansion, and their fate, along with that of the Indians, exemplifies what happened when white Americans transformed the West and South in the late nineteenth century. Settlement of the West proceeded at a furious pace. Between 1870 and 1890 the population living between the Mississippi River and the Pacific Ocean swelled from 7 million to nearly 17 million. Frontiers vanished in the South as well. Shortly after Reconstruction ended, cotton production reached pre–Civil War levels, and people were taking advantage of new opportunities afforded by the region's abundant natural resources.

By 1890 farms, ranches, mines, towns, and cities could be found in almost every region of what was to become the continental United States. That year, the superintendent of the census acknowledged that

> up to and including 1880, the country had a frontier of settlement, but at present the unsettled area has been so broken into by isolated bodies of settlement that there can hardly be said to be a frontier line. In the discussion of its extent and its westward movement, etc., it can not therefore, any longer have a place in the census reports.

What had happened to the frontier and what effect did its disappearance have on the nation?

In popular American thought, the frontier—which has been defined as "the edge of the unused"—has represented the birthplace of American self-confidence and individualism. Taming the continent's vast wilderness and bringing forth foodstuffs and raw materials from it, not to mention building cities in a single generation, filled Americans with a consciousness of power and a belief that anyone eager and persistent enough could succeed. Yet that very self-confidence was easily transformed into an arrogant attitude that Americans were somehow special, and individualism often exerted itself at the expense of racial minorities and the propertyless.

As the continent filled in and the edge of the unused shifted and then faded in the late nineteenth century, Americans exhibited both their best and their worst characteristics. Development of the West was accomplished with courage, creativity, and eagerness that amazed the rest of the world. The optimistic conquerors, however, also displayed a wastefulness, violence, and greed that tarnished the American image. Recovery and growth in the South kindled new optimism, but careless exploitation exhausted the soil and left the lives of poor farmers as downtrodden as ever. Industrialization failed to lessen the dominance of southern staple-crop agriculture, and by 1900 the section was more dependent economically on the North than before the Civil War.

Americans rarely thought about conserving resources because there always seemed to be more territory to exploit. Thus the fading of the frontier, though of great symbolic importance, had little direct impact on people's behavior. Because vast stretches of land remained unsettled, millions of people continued to stream into the West, and more land in the South fell under cultivation. Compared with undeveloped regions in such other parts of the world as Siberia, South America, Africa, and Canada, the American West and South were relatively tame. If American settlers failed in one region, they did not usually perish; they could simply try again somewhere else. Even though life in the West was less romantic and comfortable than settlers might have anticipated, and the unreconstructed South failed to fulfill its potential, the various frontiers left Americans with the feeling that they would always have a second chance. This infinity of second chances, the legacy from the western and southern frontiers, left its imprint on the American character.

EXPLOITATION OF NATURAL RESOURCES

John D. Archbold, an officer of the Standard Oil Corporation, once allegedly offered to drink all the oil ever found outside the state of Pennsylvania.

Luckily for him, no one ever challenged him to make good on his bravado; little did Archbold and others like him dream what vast natural resources lay waiting in the undeveloped regions of the United States. Discovery and use of these resources not only advanced settlement but also primed the revolutions in transportation, agriculture, and industry that swept the United States in the late nineteenth century. At the same time, the search for resources produced a restless, get-rich-quick mentality, reinforced the sexual division of labor, and fed habits of racial oppression.

In the years just before the Civil War, eager prospectors began to comb remote forests and mountains looking for iron, coal, timber, oil, and copper. By 1900, active exploitation of the land's riches, once confined to the Northeast and Appalachian regions, had spread across the continent. Timberlands in the Midwest, South, and Northwest were yielding more lumber than those of New York and Maine. Alabama, Michigan, and Minnesota had become leading sources of iron ore. Montana and Arizona had taken the lead in copper and silver production. And discoveries of oil fields in California and Texas gave the lie to Archbold's faith that Pennsylvania was the only oil-rich state.

The mining frontier advanced rapidly, drawing thousands of people to California, Nevada, Idaho, Montana, and Colorado in the 1850s and 1860s.

Mining and Lumbering

Prospectors tended to be restless optimists, willing to tramp mountains and deserts, searching icy streams for a telltale glint of precious metal. They shot game for food and financed their explorations by convincing merchants to advance credit for equipment in return for a share of the lode yet to be discovered. When their credit ran out, unlucky prospectors took jobs and saved up for another search for riches.

Extracting minerals from the ground involved high expenses for excavation and transportation. Thus individual prospectors who did discover veins of metal seldom mined them. Instead they sold their claims to mining syndicates, lived it up off their new wealth, and then set off on another quest. The mining companies, often financed by eastern investors, had ample capital to bring in engineers, heavy machinery, railroad lines, and work crews. Although discoveries of gold and silver first drew attention to the West and its

Two women stand on a hill overlooking Helena, Montana, a typical mining town of the 1870s. In spite of their small numbers, women exerted a settling influence on frontier towns. Montana Historical Society, Helena.

resources, such companies usually moved into the Rocky Mountain states to exploit less romantic but equally lucrative bonanzas of lead, zinc, tin, quartz, and copper. In Montana, for example, speculator William Clark's Anaconda Mine, opened in 1881, yielded more than $2 billion worth of copper over the next fifty years.

Mineral extraction concentrated intensively on a particular area or mine, but lumber production—another large-scale extractive industry—required vast stretches of land. As lumber companies moved into the thick forests of the Northwest, some not only stripped the land without regard for the future but also grabbed millions of acres fraudulently. To stimulate western settlement, Congress in 1878 passed the Timber and Stone Act; this measure, which applied to land in California, Nevada, Oregon, and Wash-

ington, allowed private citizens to buy at the low price of $2.50 per acre 160-acre plots "unfit for cultivation" and "valuable chiefly for timber." Taking advantage of the act, lumber companies hired thousands of seamen from waterfront boardinghouses to register claims to timberland and turn them over to the companies. By 1900, claimants had bought over 3.5 million acres under Timber and Stone Act provisions, and most of that land belonged to corporations.

While lumbermen were acquiring claims to timberlands in the Northwest, oilmen were beginning to sink wells in the Southwest. In 1900 most of the nation's petroleum still came from fields in the Appalachians and the Midwest, but promising developments were under way in southern California and eastern Texas. The most spectacular strike occurred in 1901 at Spindletop, Texas, where a well shot a stream of oil 160 feet into the air. Although most oil and kerosene were still used for lubrication and lighting, discoveries in the Southwest were to become a vital new source of fuel in the twentieth century.

Much of the natural-resource frontier was a man's world. Mining, general labor, and some farming were the predominant occupations. In 1880, men outnumbered women by more than two

Frontier Society

to one in Colorado, Nevada, and Arizona. Among twenty-to-forty-year-olds, men had a three-to-one majority. In the nation as a whole, by contrast, there were about 97 women for every 100 men; and in the older eastern states, women even frequently outnumbered men.

Yet many western communities had substantial numbers of women. Most women who went to the mining frontier did so for the same reasons men went: to find a fortune. But their independence, on the mining frontier, as elsewhere, was limited. They usually accompanied a husband or father and seldom prospected themselves. Even so, many women realized their own opportunities in the towns, where they provided cooking, laundering, and, in some cases, sexual services for the miners. Some became the family's main breadwinner when their husbands failed to strike it rich. As one wife recalled, "I began at once to figure in my mind how many men I could cook for, if there should be no better way of making money." Women's presence had a settling influence on mining communities. While they pursued new opportunities and freedoms, women also helped to bolster family life and to combat raw materialism and vice by campaigning against drinking, gambling, and whoring. According to one resident of the mining frontier, women of "honest hearts have fallen victim to the peculiar seductions [of] the place," yet "paradoxicaly as the statement may sound, it is rigorously true that these women have improved the morals of the community."

Many of the mining and lumber communities were genuinely heterogeneous, containing small numbers of Chinese, Mexicans, Indians, and blacks. Though most Chinese migrated to work on American railroads (see pages 457–458), some were employed in the camps to do cooking and cleaning. A few blacks also held such jobs. Mexicans and Indians often had been the original settlers of land coveted by whites, and

Chinese gold miners at Auburn Ravine, California, in 1852. Chinese first came to California in the 1850s and 1860s to escape social and economic upheaval at home. They often paid for their transportation by working under a Chinese-operated contract-labor system. California State Library.

some stayed to resist white intruders. Each of these minority groups met with white prejudice, especially when it became evident that the forests and mines would not make everyone rich. California imposed a tax on foreign miners and denied blacks, Indians, and Chinese the right to testify or submit evidence in court. Throughout the West any claims Indians or Mexicans might have had to land sought by white miners were ignored or stolen. Blacks and Chinese who worked in mining camps often suffered abuse and violence. Not all harassment came from whites; in California, for example, Mexican bandits preyed on Chinese even more than on Anglos. Nonwhites defended themselves as best they could against intimidation, but their most common tactic was to pack up and seek jobs and homes in another town or mining camp.

Development of the nation's oil, mineral, and timber resources raised serious questions about what belonged to all the people, as represented by the federal government, and what belonged to private interests whose motive was profit. Two factors worked at cross-purposes. First, most land west of the Mississippi was public domain, and some people believed the federal government, as owner of the land, should receive some return from exploitation of the land. But the government lacked both the motivation and the means to dig mines, sink wells, and cut forests, and therefore sold land to private interests who would take the initiative.

Use of Public Lands

Inevitably, developers of natural resources were more interested in what the land yielded than in the land itself. They wanted trees, not forest land that would become useless once the trees were stripped away. They wanted oil, not the scrubby plain that would be doubly worthless if—as often happened—wells were dug but no oil was found. Thus, to many companies involved in resource production, land purchased at market price was an unnecessary and sometimes prohibitive expense.

To avoid such costs, developers used several ploys, some legal and some not. One method was to purchase or rent limited rights to extract resources. Lumbermen would buy permits to fell a certain number of trees on a given forest tract and share the profits with the landowner. Oilmen and iron miners often leased property from private owners or the government and paid royalties on the minerals extracted. Other practices were corrupt or fraudulent. As they had done since colonial times, some lumbermen simply cut trees on public lands without paying a cent. And, as already noted, lumber companies used trickery to buy land cheaply under the Timber and Stone Act. Even when Congress and the U.S. Land Office tried to prevent fraud by passing tighter legislation and sending out more investigators, many communities resisted in the fear that such crackdowns would slow local economic growth.

Questions about natural resources thus caught Americans between the urge for progress and fear of spoiling the land. By the late 1870s and early 1880s, people concerned about the natural landscape began to coalesce into a conservation movement. The few scientists, artists, and government officials involved in this movement worked chiefly to preserve forests, probably because logging so visibly altered the environment. A leading figure in the conservation movement was the western naturalist John Muir, who helped establish Yosemite National Park in 1890. The next year, under pressure from Muir and others, Congress authorized the president to create forest reserves on public land, protected from cutting by private interests. Such policies met with strong objections. Lumber companies, lumber dealers, and railroads were joined in their opposition by private householders accustomed to cutting timber freely for fuel and building material. Public opinion on conservation also split along sectional lines. Most supporters came from the eastern states, where resources had become less plentiful; opposition was loudest in the West, where people were still eager to take advantage of nature's bounty.

Conquest of the mining and forest frontiers brought western territories to the threshold of statehood. Between 1876 and 1889, jockeying between Democrats and Republicans in Congress prevented the admission of any new states. But in 1889 Republicans seeking to solidify their control of Congress pushed through the Omnibus Bill, granting statehood to North Dakota, South Dakota, Washington, and Montana. Wyoming and Idaho were admitted in 1890, the same year the Census Bureau announced the disappearance of the frontier. Congress balked at granting statehood to Utah because the Mormons, who were a majority of the state's population and controlled its government, practiced polygamy. But the territory's prosperity could not be denied, and when the Mormons agreed to abandon polygamy, Congress voted Utah into the Union in 1896.

Admission of New States

The mining towns and lumber camps in these states spiced American folk culture and fostered the go-getter optimism that distinguished the American spirit. The lawlessness and hedonism of places like Deadwood, in Dakota Territory, and Tombstone, in Arizona Territory, gave the West notoriety and romance. Legends grew up about inhabitants of these towns whose lives both typified and magnified western experience. One such character was Martha Jane Canary, known as Calamity Jane, who in the 1870s worked in eastern Wyoming and the western Dakotas as a scout and wagon driver, freighting supplies to mining camps. Skilled with a rifle and dressed in men's clothes, Calamity Jane acquired a reputation for wild behavior that fiction writers later glorified. Yet she appears simply to have been seeking her place in a hard world. According to an army captain who employed her, Jane was "eccentric and wayward rather than bad and had adopted male attire more to aid her in getting a living than for any improper purpose."

Arizona mining towns, with their free-flowing cash and loose law enforcement, attracted numerous gamblers, thieves, and opportunists whose names stood for the Wild West. Near Tombstone, the infamous Clanton family and their partner John Ringgold, called Johnny Ringo, engaged in smuggling and cattle rustling to supply materials and food to mining camps. Inside the town, the legendary Earp brothers—Wyatt, Jim, Morgan, Virgil, and Warren—and their friends William Barclay "Bat" Masterson and John Henry "Doc" Holliday operated on both sides of the law as gunmen, gamblers, and politicians. A feud between Clanton and Earp factions climaxed on October 26, 1881, in the famous shoot-out at the OK Corral, where three Clantons were killed and Virgil and Morgan Earp were seriously wounded.

Characters like Wild Bill Hickok, Poker Alice, and Bedrock Tom became western folk heroes, and fiction writers like Mark Twain and Bret Harte captured for posterity some of the flavor of mining life. But violence and eccentricity were far from common. Most miners and lumbermen worked seventy hours a week and had neither time, energy, nor money for drinking, gambling, or gunfights. Women worked as long or longer as teachers, cooks, laundresses, storekeepers, and housewives; only a very few were sharpshooters or dance-hall queens. For most westerners, life was a matter of adapting and surviving.

The Age of Railroad Expansion

On May 10, 1869, the whole country knew what was happening at Promontory Point in the mountains of Utah. There, the Central Pacific

Railroad construction camps were peopled by a variety of workers, from Europe and Asia as well as from the United States. Providing food, lodging, and materials for these crews required extensive organization and planning. Library of Congress.

Railroad, built 689 miles eastward from Sacramento, California, was to meet the Union Pacific Railroad, built 1,086 miles westward from Omaha, Nebraska, to form the nation's first transcontinental route. Work crews of six hundred Irish, Chinese, Mexicans, and white and black Americans participated in the ceremony. Though a golden railroad spike was used to commemorate the event, the last spike was actually of steel because it was wired to a telegraph line and when pounded it would signal to the world that the railroad had been completed. Governor Leland Stanford of California was given the honor of driving that final spike. As the crowd hushed, he drew back his silver hammer, swung—and missed the spike. The telegrapher sent the message anyway, and across the nation church bells rang and shouting multitudes celebrated.

Discovery and development of natural riches provided the base on which the nation's economy expanded. But raw wealth would have been of limited use without means of carrying it to factories, marketplaces, and ports. In today's world of trailer trucks,

Railroads hastened development of the West in many ways. Not only did they carry people to new areas of settlement; they also transported manufactured products, such as these thirty stagecoaches ordered by the Wells Fargo Company. The New Hampshire Historical Society, Concord.

cargo planes, and supertankers, a railway train seems almost an anachronism, a relic. But in the half-century following the Civil War, railroads refashioned the American economy, stitching together the nation, supporting new industries, and generating their own romance.

During these years, tens of thousands of laborers built a web of railroad track across the country. Between 1865 and 1890, total track in the United States grew from 35,000 to 200,000 miles. By 1910 the nation had a third of all railroad track in the world. In their haste to lay track, railroad managers recruited large and assorted work crews. The Central Pacific imported seven thousand Chinese to work in the Western mountains, while the Union Pacific used Irish construction gangs. Both companies also hired Civil War veterans. Workers were housed in shacks and tents that could be dismantled, loaded on flatcars, and relocated at intervals of sixty or seventy miles. At one time, the Union Pacific needed forty railcars to supply its crews with rails, ties, bridge materials, and food.

Though construction proceeded erratically, often tainted by stock fraud and mismanagement, by 1900 the country's railroad network was virtually complete (see map). The transcontinental lines were the most awe-inspiring, but regional lines, such as the New York Central in the Northeast, the Louisville and Nashville in the South, and the Burlington in the Midwest, were equally important. These railroads linked major cities and completed formation of a national market system. Henceforth the goods and raw materials of one section could be available in other sections of the country.

The economic consequences of railroads were immense. By 1890 total railroad revenues had topped $1 billion—two-and-one-half times the total revenues of the federal government. After 1880, when more-durable steel rails began to replace iron rails, railroads helped to boost the nation's steel industry to inter-

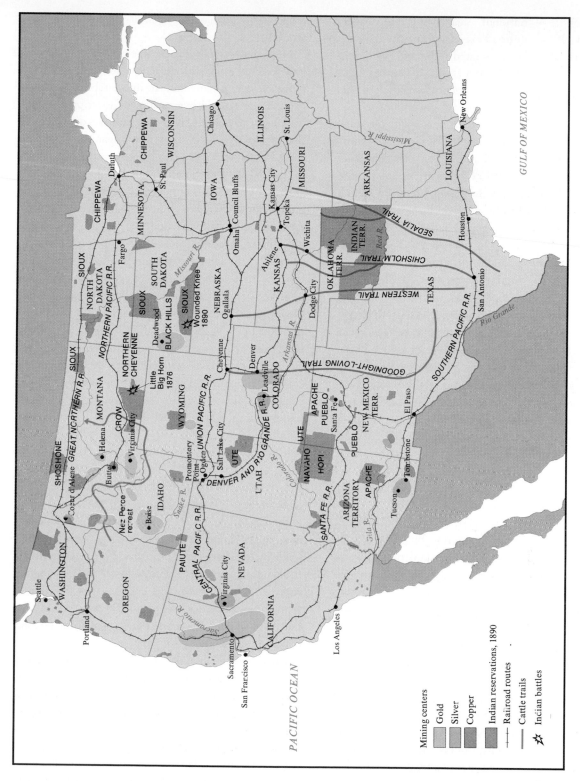

Mining centers
Gold
Silver
Copper
Indian reservations, 1890
Railroad routes
Cattle trails
Indian battles

The American West, 1860–1890

Effects of Railroad Construction

national leadership. Moreover, railroad expansion spawned a number of related industries, including coal production, passenger and freight car manufacture, and depot construction. Finally, railroads altered American conceptions of time and space, and they spurred a movement for standardization. First, by overcoming barriers of distance, railroads transformed space into time. It became easier to measure the separation between places by the amount of time it took to travel from one to the other rather than by the physical distance. Second, railroad scheduling necessitated nationwide agreement on time. Before railroads, each locale had its own time. Community church bells and steeple clocks struck at noon, when the sun was overhead, and people set their own clocks and watches accordingly. But the sun was not overhead at exactly the same moment, so there were variations in time from place to place. For example, clocks in Boston differed from those in New York by almost twelve minutes. To achieve some regularity, railroads set their own time zones, but by 1880 there still were nearly fifty different standards. Finally in 1883 railroads agreed—without consulting Congress, the president, or the courts—to establish four standard time zones for the whole country. Most communities now adjusted their clocks (though Chicago held out briefly) and railroad time became national time.

Third, railroad construction brought about technological and organizational reforms. By the late 1880s, almost all lines had adopted standard narrow-gauge rails so that their tracks could connect with one another. Such devices as the Westinghouse air brake, an automatic car coupler, and standardized handholds on freight cars made rail transportation safer and more efficient. Needs for gradings, tunnels, and bridges helped the American engineering profession to grow. Organizational advances included systems for coordinating complex passenger and freight schedules and the adoption of uniform freight-classification systems.

From other perspectives, however, the effects of railroads were less favorable. For example, the high cost of construction and equipment demanded that new railroads begin operation as soon as possible in order to generate revenues to repay debts and maintain investors' confidence. As a result, many miles of track were laid hastily, without regard for safety or durability.

Nevertheless, railroads became extremely influential and acquired a uniquely American function. European railroads were usually built to link established market centers and to improve or replace existing routes of traffic. In this country, however, railroads often created the very communities they were meant to serve and carried traffic that had never before existed. Particularly in the West and South, railroads accelerated the growth of regional centers such as Omaha, Kansas City, Cheyenne, Los Angeles, Portland, Seattle, Atlanta, and Nashville.

Railroads accomplished these feats with the help of some of the largest government subsidies in American history. Railroad executives argued that their activities were benefiting the public interest and that the government should aid them by giving them land from the public domain. Congress was sympathetic. In order to encourage construction, the government gave railroad companies over 180 million acres, mostly to interstate routes chartered between 1850 and 1871. These grants usually consisted of a right of way plus alternate sections of land in a strip twenty to eighty miles wide along the right of way. Railroad corporations financed construction by using this land as security for bonds or by selling it for cash.

Government Subsidy of Railroads

States and localities heaped further subsidies on new routes. State land was frequently offered to railroads by legislators eager for the advantages railroads could bring—to them personally as well as to the state. Total state grants amounted to about 50 million acres. Counties, cities, and towns also assisted railroads, usually by offering them loans or by purchasing railroad bonds or stocks.

Government subsidies had mixed effects. Capitalists argued against government interference in one breath and accepted government aid in the next. They also pressured public agencies into meeting their needs. The Southern Pacific, for example, threatened to bypass Los Angeles unless the city came up with a bonus and built a depot. Without government help, few railroads could have established themselves sufficiently to attract private investment. Yet public aid was not always salutary. Some laborers and farmers fought subsidies, arguing that companies like the Southern Pacific would become too powerful. During the 1880s, the policy of assistance haunted some communities whose zeal for railroads had prompted them to commit too much to lines that were never built or that defaulted on loans. On the other hand, many communities boomed because they had linked their fortunes to the iron horse.

As the nation's rail network expanded, so did competition and duplication. Shippers sending raw materials or finished products across the country now

Competition and Discriminatory Rate Setting

had several routes to choose from, and railroad operators scrambled for new customers. Lines cut rates to attract more traffic and outmaneuver competitors. In the twenty-five years after the Civil War, freight and passenger rates between New York and Chicago fell by nearly two-thirds. But rate wars soon cut into profits, and several railroads had to reduce or omit dividends to stockholders. Moreover, wild vacillations in rates angered shippers and farmers who missed out on a saving by shipping goods just before a rate reduction or were caught awaiting a reduction when rates were raised. Stability was clearly desirable.

Ironically, while railroad rates generally were falling, complaints about excessively high rates were increasing. Railroads often boosted rates as high as possible on noncompetitive short-distance routes in order to compensate for unprofitably low rates on competitive long-distance routes. For example, it cost twice as much to send wheat from Fargo, North Dakota, to Duluth, Minnesota, as from Minneapolis to Chicago, even though the latter distance was twice as long. Railroad managers justifiably argued that small quantities shipped over short distances involved proportionately higher transportation costs than did bulk goods carried over long distances. But farmers and other shippers continued to believe such rates were illogical and unfair. A spokesman for Michigan farmers in 1886 said he could "hardly imagine a case where it would be right or proper for a railroad to charge more for a shorter than for a longer distance for freight [similar] in kind and quantity and over the same road or roads."

Railroads also devised other forms of rate adjustment. To increase traffic they made special contracts with large shippers, offering rebates and reductions of up to 50 percent of published freight rates. They courted the favor of important shippers and politicians by offering free passenger passes. And to reduce competition, they made agreements among themselves called pools, whose participants shared traffic and earnings and set common rates. Such agreements generally discriminated against small shippers.

These practices upset farmers, retailers, bankers, reform politicians, and even some stockholders. During the 1870s, many of these groups demanded that government regulate railroads, especially

Government Regulation of Railroads

their pricing practices. By 1880, fourteen states had established commissions or other agencies to limit freight and storage rates charged by state-chartered lines. Railroads bitterly fought these laws, arguing that rights of private property superseded public authority. This traditional American belief in the freedom to acquire and use property without government restraint prevented the ultimate step—public ownership of railroads—but did not halt regulation. In 1877 the Supreme Court upheld the principle of railroad regulation in *Munn* v. *Illinois*, saying, "When private property is affected with a public interest it ceases to be *juris privati* only . . . and must submit to be controlled by the public for the common good."

Although the principle of regulation had won acceptance, critics charged that state regulatory commissions were either too weak or too subservient to railroads. Moreover, state commissioners had little control over interstate lines and thus could not affect the largest, most powerful railroads. The Supreme Court affirmed this limitation in 1886 by declaring in the *Wabash* case that only Congress and not the states could regulate rates on interstate commerce. Consequently, reformers called for federal regulation.

Congress responded in 1887 by passing the Interstate Commerce Act. The act prohibited pools, rebates, and long-haul–short-haul rate discriminations; and one of its clauses directed that "all charges . . . shall be reasonable and fair." The law also created the Interstate Commerce Commission (ICC) and gave it power to investigate railroads; to issue "cease-and-desist" orders against illegal practices; and to seek court assistance to enforce compliance with the law.

The Interstate Commerce Act resulted from a political compromise between supporters of regulation and defenders of laissez faire. Its basic provisions quieted the cries of protest from farmers and other interests opposed to railroads' monopolistic practices. It affirmed the principle of regulation, forbade discriminatory practices, and gave the ICC power to investigate on its own initiative as well as in response to specific complaints. But provisions for its enforcement were blurry and left railroads much room for evasion. The ICC could issue cease-and-desist orders, but only the courts could force obedience. In a series of court cases, federal judges chipped away at ICC powers by asserting a right to review ICC orders and by interpreting the Interstate Commerce Act very narrowly. In the *Maximum Freight Rate* case in 1897, the Supreme Court ruled that the act did not grant the ICC power to set rates, and in the *Alabama Midlands* case the same year, the Court shattered prohibitions against long-haul–short-haul discriminations. Between 1887 and 1897, the judiciary overruled 90 percent of ICC rate orders; between 1887 and 1905, the Supreme Court decided against the ICC in fifteen of sixteen cases.

In spite of such setbacks, the era of railroad reform opened new paths for future generations. The right of the federal government to regulate railroads as a public enterprise did gain court support. Regulation at the state level continued, especially with regard to safety and intrastate rates. Finally, establishment of the ICC gave impetus to the movement to eliminate favoritism in society and the economy. Forces of change had begun to gather momentum, but Americans still had to decide whether they desired free competition or cooperation under government regulation.

NATIVE AMERICANS:
CASUALTIES OF EXPANSION

Railroad expansion not only bound the nation together economically, it had a massive impact on previously undeveloped land. The vast domain between the Missouri and the Pacific—the Great Plains and Far West—became more accessible. But much of this land was not empty. It was the home of thousands of native American tribespeople, whose ways of life differed profoundly from those of most white people and whose presence represented a stubborn barrier to whites' exploitation of the land.

As in previous eras, the contact between white and native culture elicited a variety of responses from the Indians. Some tried to adapt to white invaders, by trading with them—usually offering hides in exchange for livestock and guns—and by accepting white alliances as a means of gaining an advantage over rival tribes. Others actively resisted white intrusion, using guerrilla tactics to harass settlers, herders, and troops. Still others alternated between alliance and enmity, depending on their leadership, material needs, and relations with other tribes. In the end, however, though they struggled to retain their culture, Indians faced insurmountable odds and an overwhelming migratory invasion.

Although there was great variety of cultures, most native tribes in the West fit into one of two cultural groups. Some were nomadic or seminomadic, subsisting on food that they hunted or gathered. These tribes included the Shoshone of the Northwest, the Apache in the Southwest, and the Cheyenne, Dakota, and Crow in the Plains. Others were more settled, depending on farming and gardening. These included the Zuni, Hopi, and Navajo tribes in the Southwest, plus Pawnee, Mandan, and Hidatsa tribes in the Plains. Tribal organization often was loose, with leadership only vaguely defined, but almost all Indians had highly formalized cultural systems and religions that regarded their relationship with nature as sacred. Black Elk, an Oglala Sioux, explained one version of this unity:

> Everything an Indian does is in a circle, and that is because the Power of the World always works in circles, and everything tries to be round. . . . The sky is round, and I have heard that the earth is round like a ball, and so are all the stars. The wind, in its greatest power, whirls. Birds make their nests in circles, for theirs is the same religion as ours. The sun comes forth and goes down again in a circle. The moon does the same, and both are round. Even the seasons form a great circle in their changing, and always come back again

A Sioux camp in South Dakota, 1891. The Sioux led a nomadic life, living in harmony with the natural environment; when they packed up and moved on, they left the landscape almost undisturbed. This photograph shows the temporary situation characteristic of their camps. Library of Congress.

to where they were. The life of a man is a circle from childhood to childhood, and so it is in everything where power moves.

Western Indians observed sexual divisions of labor, but their social organization differed greatly from that of white Americans. Generally, men took responsibility for hunting, fishing, and war, and they almost always held the most powerful positions—chief, priest, shaman (medicine man). Women raised children and crops. Often, however, the female side of kinship groups was more influential than the male side, and women had important roles in political, economic, religious, and social affairs. Zuni, Navajo, and Mandan tribes, for example, were matrilineal and matrilocal; that is, family descent was determined by the mother,

and married couples lived with or near the wife's mother. Navajo women controlled most of their family's property, and Apache and Teton Dakota women directed their tribe's most important religious ceremony, the girls' puberty rite. The Navajo and Teton Dakota also valued women for their craft skills.

When white Americans first extensively encountered western Indians in the mid-nineteenth century, they already had two centuries of experience with native tribes (see pages 53–57). Like the British before them, white Americans considered Indians as separate peoples with whom they could make treaties. Thus as white settlers began pressing into native territories, the government made treaties with various tribes, insuring peace and nominally defining boundaries of white and native lands. But the treaties seldom promised the Indians any future land rights; rather, whites assumed that eventually they could settle wherever they wished. Treaties made one week were violated the next, as more settlers streamed into the West. Some Indians acquiesced; others resisted with attacks on settlements, herds, and troops.

Between 1850 and 1877, two factors on the Great Plains accelerated the policy of concentrating Indians on reservations: military conquest and destruction of buffalo herds. Native defense of their homelands against white settlers resulted in a series of bloody battles and massacres. The most legendary battle occurred on June 25, 1876, when 2,500 Sioux, led by Chiefs Rain-in-the-Face, Sitting Bull, and Crazy Horse, annihilated white troops led by the rash Colonel George A. Custer near the Little Big Horn River in southern Montana. Though there were other Indian victories as well, shortage of supplies and relentless pursuit by white troops eventually overwhelmed armed Indian resistance and forced the Native Americans onto reservations, which were usually those parts of their previous territory least desirable to whites (see map, page 459). At the same time, extermination of the buffalo, which had been so vital to native cultures, was even more decisive than government policy in forcing Indians to change their way of life.

Reservation policy had troublesome consequences. In assigning Indians to specific territory, the United States government promised protection from white encroachment and agreed to provide food, clothing, and other necessities, in effect making Indians dependent on the government. As more reservations were created, it became evident that isolation was impossible. White farmers, miners, and herders continually sought even remote Indian lands. Moreover, Indians continued to be restive. During the 1880s violence between whites and Indians broke out on Apache, Sioux, and other reservations. As a result, whites became more intent on "civilizing" the Native Americans—making them accept whites' values, breaking up their tribal organization, and integrating them into the nation. At the same time, humanitarian concern was heightened by Helen Hunt Jackson's popular book, *A Century of Dishonor* (1881), which castigated the government for its unfair treatment of Indians.

In 1887 Congress reversed its reservation policy in the Dawes Severalty Act, which dissolved com-

Dawes Severalty Act munity-owned tribal lands and granted land allotments to individual families. To prevent Indians from selling these plots to speculators, the government retained ownership of the land for twenty-five years. The act also granted citizenship to all who accepted the allotments and authorized the government to sell unallotted land and to set aside the proceeds for the education of Indians. The Dawes Act applied to most western tribes, the major exception being Pueblo peoples who had retained land rights granted to them by the Spanish.

As a result of the Dawes Act, U.S. Indian policy as carried out by the Indian Bureau of the Department of the Interior took on three main features. First and foremost, government officials advocated allotting land to individual families because they believed Indians would become civilized by learning how to manage their own property. Ownership would make them more responsible and industrious. Second, bureau officials believed Indians would lose their "barbaric" habits more quickly if their children could be removed and educated in boarding schools away from the old reservations. Third, the bureau tried to suppress traditional religious ceremonies, such as the Sun Dance, and funded white church groups to establish religious schools among the Indians and teach them to become good Christians.

Indians had no voice in any of these policies, which were carried out by agents of the bureau. These officials lived on the reservations, spent the funds assigned by the bureau, distributed land allotments, secured pupils for the boarding schools, and supervised government farmers and teachers—all without any consultation with Indians themselves. In effect, while reservations were no longer isolated geographically, they remained isolated politically and socially. Increasingly as time went on, antagonisms developed between surrounding white populations and reservation communities, and no local means of resolving disputes existed.

Much of the new Indian policy was ineffective. Land allotment proved to be very complex. In the face of efforts by whites to acquire land titles from Indians who were to receive individual plots, the government simply abandoned the program. In the Southwest, for example, only small parts of the Navajo, Pima, and Colorado River reservations were ever allotted. The boarding school program did affect thousands of children, but rarely did they forsake their culture; most returned to their reservations rather than submit to assimilation into white society. Efforts to suppress native religious observances only forced them under cover. Moreover, whites did not give up their fears and use of violence. Late in 1890, the government sent the Seventh Cavalry, Custer's old regiment, to apprehend some Sioux who were moving north toward Pine Ridge Reservation in South Dakota and who were believed to be armed for revolt. During an encounter at a creek called Wounded Knee, the troups trained newly acquired cannons on the Indians and massacred two hundred sick and hungry men, women, and children in the snow. Although Native Americans retained their culture, the West was won at their expense, and they remained sad casualties of an aggressive age.

THE RANCHING FRONTIER

Railroad construction and Indian removal set the stage for one of the West's most colorful and romantic industries, cattle ranching. Early in the nineteenth century, huge herds of cattle, originally introduced by the Spanish and developed by Mexican ranchers, roamed southern Texas and bred with cattle brought by American settlers. The resulting longhorn breed multiplied and became valuable by the 1860s, when the East's growing population increased demand for food and railroads made transportation of beef more feasible. By 1870 drovers were herding thousands of Texas cattle northward to railroad connections in Kansas, Missouri, and Wyoming. On these long drives, mounted cowboys (as many as 25 percent of whom were blacks) supervised the herds, which fed on open grassland along the way. At the northern terminus— usually Abilene, Dodge City, or Cheyenne—the cattle were loaded onto trains and sent eastward to Chicago and St. Louis for slaughter and distribution.

The long drive gave rise to its own romantic lore, but it was not very efficient. In trekking 1,500 miles, the cattle became sinewy and tough. Herds traveling through Indian lands and farmers' fields were sometimes shot at and later prohibited from such trespass by state laws. The ranchers' only solution was to eliminate long drives by raising herds nearer to railroad routes.

Ranchers soon discovered that crossing sturdy Texas longhorns with heavier Hereford and Angus breeds produced cattle better able to survive northern winters, and cattle raising spread across the Great Plains. Between 1860 and 1880 the cattle population of Kansas, Nebraska, Colorado, Wyoming, Montana, and Dakota increased from 130,000 to 4.5 million.

Cattle raisers were like timber cutters: they needed vast stretches of land where their herds could graze and they wanted to incur as little expense as possible to use such land. Thus they often bought a few acres bordering streams and turned their herds loose on adjacent public domain, which no one would want to own because it lacked water access. By this method, called open-range ranching, a cattle raiser could control thousands of acres by owning only a hundred or so.

Open-range Ranching

Neighboring ranchers often formed associations and allowed their herds to graze together. Herds were distinguished from each other by burning a special mark, or brand, into the hide of every animal. Each ranch had its own brand—an improvised shorthand for documenting title to movable property. Twice each year, cowboy crews rounded up the cattle, to brand new calves in the spring and to drive mature animals to market in the fall.

Roundups provided easterners with colorful images of western life: bellowing cattle, mounted rope-swinging cowboys, the smell of singed hides and smoky campfires. But the roundup was short-lived because it was too successful. By the early 1880s, the profitability of beef raising had lured scores of investors to the industry. As one publication explained:

A good sized steer when it is fit for the butcher market will bring from $45.00 to $60.00. The same animal at its birth was worth but $5.00. He has run on the plains and cropped the grass from the public domain for four or five years, and now, with scarcely any expense to its owner, is worth $40.00 more than when he started on his pilgrimage.

National and international demand for beef kept rising, and ranchers and capital flowed into the Plains. Soon cattle began to overrun the range.

The roundup was one of the most important events on the open range. In the spring, cowboys herded the cattle together and branded calves that followed cows with their owner's insignia. "The Roundup" (detail) by Charles M. Russell, 1913. MacKay Collection, Montana Historical Society.

Fearing depletion of the prairie and loss of control, ranchers began to fence in their pastures with newly invented barbed wire—even though they had no legal title to the land. Fences destroyed the open range and often provoked disputes between competing ranchers, between cattle raisers and sheep raisers, and between ranchers and farmers who claimed use of the same land. In 1885, President Cleveland ordered removal of illegal fences on public lands and Indian reservations. Enforcement was slow, but the order signaled that free use of public domain was ending.

Open-range ranching made beef a staple of the American diet and created a few fortunes, but its extralegal features could not survive the rush of history. By 1890, big businesses were taking over the cattle industry and applying scientific methods of breeding and feeding. The cowboy became just another corporate wage earner, though the myth of his freedom and individualism grew rather than faded. Most cattle ranchers now owned or leased the land they used, though some illegal fencing continued.

Meanwhile, two new groups were contending with cattle ranchers for supremacy on the Plains. From California and New Mexico, sheepherders moved into land east of the Rockies. Ranchers complained that sheep ruined grassland by eating down to the roots and that cattle refused to graze where sheep had been because the "woolly critters" left a repulsive odor. Armed conflict occasionally erupted between cowboys and sheepherders who resorted to violence rather than settle disputes in court, where the judge would discover that both were using the land illegally. More importantly, the farming frontier advanced into the West. From the Missouri to the Pacific there began an agricultural transformation whose social and political ramifications were to affect the entire nation.

FARMING THE PLAINS

I n an 1880 article, *Harper's New Monthly Magazine* marveled at the success of Oliver Dalrymple's farm in Dakota Territory's Red River valley. "You are in a sea of wheat," the writer rhapsodized. "The railroad train rolls through an ocean of grain. . . . We encounter a squadron of war chariots . . . doing the work of human hands. . . . There are 25 of them in this one brigade of the grand army of 115, under the marksmanship of this Dakota farmer." Dalrymple's farm exemplified two important achievements of the late nineteenth century: the taming of wide, windswept prairies so that the land would yield crops to benefit humankind; and the transformation of agriculture into big business by means of mechanization, long-distance transportation, and scientific cultivation.

These achievements did not come easily. The climate and landscape of the Plains presented formidable challenges. And overcoming these challenges did not guarantee success or even provide security. Agricultural development of the West turned the United States into the world's breadbasket, but it also scarred the lives of hundreds of thousands of men and women who made that development possible.

Settlement of the Plains and the West involved the greatest migration in American history. Between 1870 and 1900, more acres were settled and put

Migration to the Plains

under cultivation than in the previous 250 years. Between 1860 and 1910, the number of farms tripled, from 2 million to over 6 million. During the 1870s and 1880s, hundreds of thousands of people streamed into states like Kansas, Nebraska, Texas, and California.

Most, though not all, migrants came from the eastern states or Europe. Several western states opened immigration bureaus in the East and in Europe to lure settlers westward. Land-grant railroads were especially aggressive, advertising cheap land, arranging credit terms, offering reduced fares, and promising instant success. Railroad agents—often former immigrants—greeted newcomers at eastern ports and traveled to Europe to recruit prospective settlers. In California, fruit and vegetable growers imported Japanese and Mexican laborers to work in the fields and canneries.

Most migrants went west because opportunities there seemed to promise a better life. Between 1870 and 1910 the nation's population rose from 40 million to 92 million, and the total urban population swelled by over 400 percent. As a result, demand for farm products grew rapidly. Meanwhile, scientific advances were enabling farmers to use the soil more efficiently. Agricultural experts developed the technique of dry farming, a system of plowing and harrowing that prevented precious moisture from evaporating. Scientists perfected varieties of "hard" wheat whose seeds could withstand northern winters, and millers invented an efficient process for grinding these tougher new wheat kernels into flour. Railroad expansion made remote farming regions more accessible, and grain-elevator construction eased problems of shipping and storage.

In spite of such developments, life on the Plains was much harder than the advertisements suggested. Migrants often encountered scarcities of essentials

Hardships of Life on the Plains

they had taken for granted back home. Vast stretches of land contained little lumber for housing and fuel. Pioneer families were forced to build houses of sod and to burn manure for heat. Water was as scarce as timber. Few families were lucky or wealthy enough to buy land near a stream that did not dry up in summer and freeze in winter. Machinery for drilling wells was scarce until the 1880s, and even then it was very expensive, so that many wells were dug by hand.

Even more formidable than the terrain of the Plains was its climate. The expanse between the Missouri River and the Rocky Mountains divides climatologically along a line running from Minnesota southwest through Oklahoma, then south, bisecting Texas. East of this line, annual rainfall averages about 28 inches, enough for most crops (see map, page 469). West of the line, life-giving rain was never certain; farmers, heartened by adequate water one year, gagged on dust and broke their plows on hardened limestone soil the next.

Weather seldom followed predictable cycles on either side of the line. In summer, weeks of torrid heat and parching winds would suddenly give way to violent storms that washed away crops and property.

A family poses in front of their Kansas prairie home. The background shows the flat, treeless environment of the rural frontier. Western History Collection, University of Oklahoma Libraries.

Winter blizzards piled up mountainous snowdrifts that halted all outdoor movement. In March and April, melting snow swelled streams, and flood waters threatened millions of acres. In the fall, a week without rain could turn dry grasslands into tinder, and the slightest spark could ignite a raging prairie fire.

Even when the climate was better behaved, nature could turn vengeful. Weather that was good for crops was also good for insect breeding. Worms and flying pests ravaged corn and wheat. In the 1870s and 1880s grasshopper plagues virtually ate up entire farms. Heralded only by the rising din of buzzing wings, a cloud of insects a mile long would smother the land and devour everything in sight: plants, seeds, tree bark, and clothes. As one farmer lamented, the "hoppers left behind nothing but the mortgage."

Settlers of the Plains also had to contend with social isolation. The European pattern, whereby farmers lived together in a village and traveled each day to their nearby fields, was rare in the American West. Instead, various peculiarities of land division compelled rural dwellers to live apart from each other.

Social Isolation The Homestead Act of 1862 and other measures adopted to facilitate western settlement offered free or cheap plots to people who would live on and improve their property. Because most homesteads and other plots acquired by small farmers were rectangular—usually encompassing 160 acres—at most four families could live near each other, but only if they congregated around the same four-corner boundary intersection. In practice, farmers usually lived back from their boundary lines, and at least a half-mile separated farmhouses. Often adjacent land was unoccupied, making neighbors even more distant.

Many observers wrote about the loneliness and monotony of life on the Plains. Men escaped the oppressiveness by working outdoors and taking occasional trips to sell crops or buy supplies. But women were more isolated, confined by domestic chores to

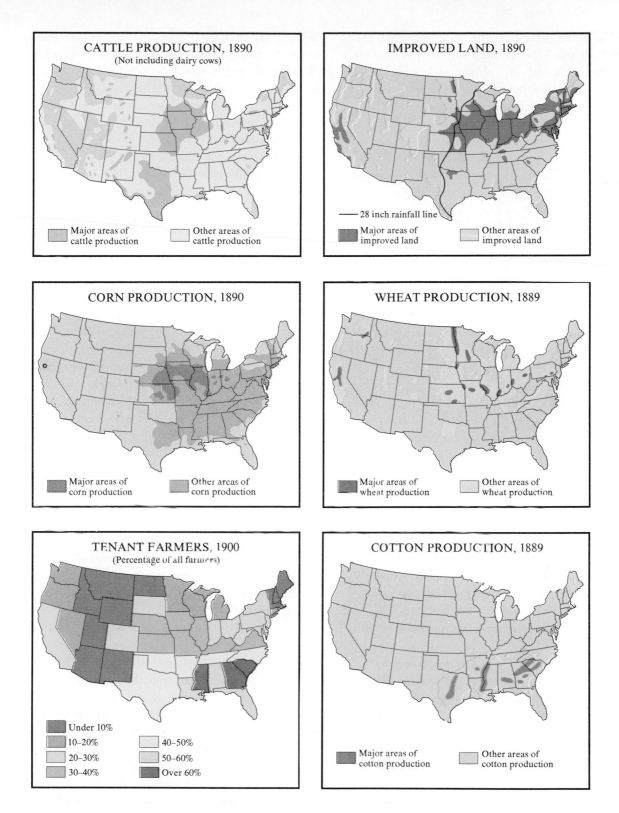

CATTLE PRODUCTION, 1890
(Not including dairy cows)

Major areas of cattle production
Other areas of cattle production

IMPROVED LAND, 1890

—— 28 inch rainfall line

Major areas of improved land
Other areas of improved land

CORN PRODUCTION, 1890

Major areas of corn production
Other areas of corn production

WHEAT PRODUCTION, 1889

Major areas of wheat production
Other areas of wheat production

TENANT FARMERS, 1900
(Percentage of all farmers)

Under 10%
10–20%
20–30%
30–40%
40–50%
50–60%
Over 60%

COTTON PRODUCTION, 1889

Major areas of cotton production
Other areas of cotton production

Agricultural Regions, 1889 and 1900 *Source: Charles O. Paollin, Atlas of the Historical Geography of the United States.*

the household, where, as one writer remarked, they were "not much better than slaves. It is a weary, monotonous round of cooking and washing and mending and as a result the insane asylum is ⅓d filled with wives of farmers."

The letters that Ed Donnell, a young Nebraska homesteader, wrote to his family reveal how time and circumstances could dull optimism. In fall 1885, Donnell wrote his mother in Missouri, "I like Nebr first rate. . . . I have saw a pretty tuff time a part of the time since I have been out here, but I started out to get a home and I was determined to win or die in the attempt. . . . Have got a good crop of corn, a floor in my house and got it ceiled overhead." Already, though, Donnell was lonely. He went on, "There is lots of other bachelors here but I am the only one I know who doesn't have kinfolks living handy. . . . You wanted to know when I was going to get married. Just as quick as I can get money ahead to get a cow." A year and a half later, Donnell's dreams were dissolving, and he was beginning to look for a second chance elsewhere. As he explained to his brother, "The rats eat my sod stable down. . . . I may sell out this summer, land is going up so fast. . . . If I sell I am going west and grow up with the country." By fall, things had worsened, and Donnell wrote his parents, "We have been having wet weather for 3 weeks. . . . My health has been so poor this summer and the wind and the sun hurts my head so. I think if I can sell I will . . . move to town for I can get $40 a month working in a grist mill and I would not be exposed to the weather." Donnell's doubts and hardships, shared by thousands of other people, fed the cityward migration of farm folk that characterized late-nineteenth century urban growth (see pages 512–513).

Most farm families survived by depending on their inner resolve and by organizing churches and clubs where they could socialize a few times a month. And by the early 1900s, two external developments had combined to bring rural settlers into closer contact with modern life (though people in sparsely settled regions beyond the 28-inch rainfall line remained isolated for several more decades). First, starting in the 1870s and 1880s, mail-order houses—Montgomery Ward and Sears Roebuck—expanded and made prod-

Mail-Order Companies and Rural Free Delivery

ucts of the industrial society available to almost everyone. Emphasizing personal attention to customers, Ward's and Sears Roebuck were outlets for sociability as well as material goods. Letters from customers to Mr. Ward often reported family news and sought advice on everything from birthday gifts to child care. A man from Washington State wrote, "As you advertise everything for sale that a person wants, I thought I would write you, as I am in need of a wife, and see what you could do for me." Another wrote: "I suppose you wonder why we haven't ordered anything from you since the fall. The cow kicked my arm and broke it and besides my wife was sick, and there was the doctor bill. But now, thank God, that is paid, and we are all well again, and we have a fine new baby boy, and please send plush bonnet number 29d8077. . . ."

Second, during the 1890s, scores of rural communities petitioned Congress for extension of the postal service, and in 1896 the government made Rural Free Delivery (RFD) widely available. Now farmers no longer lacked news and information; they could receive letters, newspapers, advertisements, and catalogues at home nearly every day. In 1913 the postal service inaugurated parcel post, which enabled people to receive packages, such as orders from Ward's and Sears, more easily. By 1920, rural families had access to industrializing society through the mails.

In the years following the Civil War, the extension of the farming frontier, growing national and international markets for food, and the advent of railroads to ship goods from farm to market brought about an agricultural revolution. But that transformation would not have been possible, nor would the Plains have been conquered, without the expanded use of machinery. When the Civil War drew men away from farms in the upper Mississippi River valley, the women and male laborers who remained behind began using reapers and other implements more extensively to meet demand for grain and to take advantage of high prices. After the war, continued demand and high prices encouraged farmers to depend more on machines, and inventors perfected better implements for farm use. Seeders, combines, binders, mowers, rotary plows, and other machines were introduced to the Plains and California in the 1870s and 1880s.

Mechanization of Agriculture

A squadron of farm machines sweeps across a wheat field in Minnesota's Red River valley. Mechanization multiplied production and turned farming into a big business, enabling the United States to become the breadbasket of the world. Photographed in the 1800s. Montana Historical Society, Helena.

For centuries the acreage of grain a farmer could plant had been limited by the amount that could be harvested by hand. Machines—first driven by animals, then by steam—increased productivity beyond imagination. Before mechanization, a single farmer could harvest about 7.5 acres of wheat. With an automatic binder that cut and tied bundles of grain, the same farmer could harvest 135 acres. Machines dramatically reduced the time and cost of farming a single acre of various other crops as well (see table).

During this period, Congress and scientists were making efforts to improve existing crops and develop new ones. The 1862 Morrill Land Grant Act (see page 395) gave each state public lands to sell in order to finance agricultural and industrial colleges. Although the act discriminated against western states by granting 30,000 acres for each senator and representative—New York thus received about 1 million acres, Kansas

Legislative and Scientific Aid to Farmers

only 90,000—it did promote the establishment of educational institutions that aided agricultural development. The Hatch Act of 1887 provided for agricultural experiment stations in every state, further encouraging the advancement of farming technology.

Farming received a great boost from science in the late nineteenth century. American agriculturists adapted hardy new varieties of wheat from Asia, alfalfa from Mongolia, corn from North Africa, and rice from the Orient. Californian Luther Burbank developed a wide range of new plants by cross-breeding. And Tuskegee Institute's chemist George Washington Carver created hundreds of new products from peanuts, soybeans, sweet potatoes, and cotton wastes and taught methods of soil improvement. Scientists also developed means of combating plant and animal diseases. Though turbulent times for farmers lay just ahead, development of the agricultural hinterland by settlement, science, and technology made America "the garden of the world."

Time and Cost of Farming an Acre of Land by Hand and by Machine, 1890

Crop	Hours Required		Labor Cost	
	Hand	Machine	Hand	Machine
Wheat	61	3	$3.65	$ .66
Corn	39	15	$3.62	$1.51
Oats	66	7	$3.73	$1:07
Loose hay	21	4	$1.75	$ .42

Source: Ray Allan Billington, Westward Expansion: A History of the American Frontier, 2nd ed. (New York: Macmillan, 1960), p. 697.

THE SOUTH AFTER RECONSTRUCTION

In 1880 four times as many farmers lived in the South as on the Plains. Ravaged by a civil war that had killed a third of all draft animals and destroyed half the region's farm equipment, southern agriculture recovered slowly. High prices for seed and implements, declining prices for crops, taxes, and, most of all, debt trapped many white families in perpetual poverty. Conditions were even worse for blacks, who had to endure brutal racial prejudice along with economic hardship. To achieve sectional independence, some southern leaders tried to promote industrialization. Their efforts partially succeeded, but by the early 1900s many southern industries were mere subsidiaries of northern firms. Moreover, southern planters, shippers, and manufacturers depended heavily on northern banks to finance their operations. And while they were striving for progress, many southerners nurtured myths about a romantic prewar era of aristocratic grace, conflict-free race relations, and moral purity.

These fantasies sustained the South's sense of distinctiveness but warped the national image of southern culture.

During and after Reconstruction, a significant shift in the nature of agricultural labor swept the South. Between 1860 and 1880, the total number of farms in southern states more than doubled, from 450,000 to 1.1 million. But the number of landowners did not increase, and the size of the average farm decreased from 347 to 156 acres. Southern agriculture was now dominated by sharecropping and tenant farming (see page 440). Over one-third of the farmers counted in 1880 were sharecroppers and tenants, and the proportion increased to two-thirds by 1920.

This system entangled millions of southerners in a web of humiliation. At its center was the crop lien, which worked in the following way. Currency was scarce, and most farmers were **Crop-Lien** too poor ever to have cash on hand. **System** Forced to borrow in order to buy necessities, they could offer as collateral only what they could grow. Thus a farmer in need of supplies would deal with a nearby "furnishing merchant," who would exchange supplies for a certain portion, or lien, of the farmer's forthcoming crop. In the fall, after the crop had been harvested and brought to market, the merchant collected his debt. But all too often the farmer's debt exceeded his crop's value, and the merchant frequently took advantage of the customer's powerlessness by inflating prices to ensure that such debts could not be paid. Thus the farmer owed the merchant, had received no cash for the crop, and still needed food and supplies. His only choice was to commit the next year's crop to the merchant and sink deeper into debt.

The prices charged to credit customers averaged 30 to 40 percent higher than those charged to cash customers. Credit customers also had to pay interest of 33 to 200 percent on the advances they received. Suppose, for example, a farmer needed a 20-cent bag of seed or a 20-cent slab of bacon and had no cash to pay for it. The furnishing merchant would extend credit for the purchase but would also boost the price to 28 cents. At year's end that 28-cent loan would have accumulated interest, raising the farmer's debt to, say, 42 cents—more than double the item's original cost. The farmer, having pledged more than his crop's worth against scores of such debts, fell behind in payments and never recovered. If he fell too far behind, he could be evicted. As one writer remarked about the crop-lien system, "when one of these mortgages has been recorded against the Southern farmer, he had usually passed into a state of helpless peonage.

The lien system caused serious hardship in former plantation areas where black and white tenants and sharecroppers grew cotton for the same markets that had existed before the Civil War. But in the southern backcountry, which in the antebellum era had contained small farms, relatively few slaves, and diversified agriculture, the problems of crop liens were compounded by other economic changes.

New spending habits of backcountry farmers reflected the most important of these changes. In 1884, for example, Jephta Dickson of Jackson County in the northern Georgia hills bought $53.37 worth of flour, meal, peas, meat, corn, and syrup from one merchant and $2.53 worth of potatoes, peas, and sugar from another. Such expenditures would have been rare in the upcountry before the Civil War, when most farmers grew almost all the supplies they needed. But after the war yeoman farmers like Jephta Dickson shifted from semisubsistence agriculture to more commercialized farming—in the South that

meant cotton-raising—because debts incurred during the war and Reconstruction forced them to grow a crop that would bring in more cash and because railroad expansion enabled them to transport cotton to markets more easily than before. As backcountry yeomen put more acres under cotton cultivation, they raised less of what they needed and were forced more frequently into positions where they were at the mercy of merchants.

At the same time, backcountry farmers suffered from new laws that essentially closed the southern range. This change also resulted from the commercialization of agriculture. Before the 1870s southern farmers had always been able to let their livestock roam freely on other people's land in search of food and water. By custom, farmers who wished to protect their crops from foraging animals were supposed to build fences around those crops. But as commercial agriculture invaded the backcountry, large landowners and merchants induced county and state legislative bodies to require farmers to fence in their animals rather than their crops. Such laws hurt poor farmers who had very little land, because the laws prevented them from letting their animals feed on an open range and caused them to use more of their precious land for pasture. Though the laws accorded with the concept of individual responsibility for private property, they undermined traditional cooperative customs that yeomen cherished. As one farmer asserted, "God makes the grass . . . and corn in the valleys grow, so let's not try to deprive our poor neighbors from receiving his blessing. . . ." Increasingly, yeoman farmers developed antagonisms toward merchants, large landowners, and other supporters of commercialized agriculture. This disaffection would find political expression that eventually coalesced into populism (see Chapter 20).

Closing the Southern Range

Poor whites of the rural South not only faced economic threat from the loss of the open range; they also faced a political threat from newly enfranchised blacks. Wealthy white landowners and merchants would not bend to protests over economic distress, but they did agree with poor farmers on the issue of white supremacy and used their power to reinforce the racial order.

The majority of the nation's black people lived in

In the post-Reconstruction South, black sharecroppers such as these fared little better than under slavery. Tied to crop liens that kept them in perpetual debt, they lived in tiny shacks and struggled against white discrimination. Brown Brothers.

the South and worked in agriculture, where they found that conditions under freedom left them with the same disadvantages they had

Condition of Blacks

borne under slavery. As in the pre-war era, blacks adapted to racial bias by developing and controlling their own social institutions: churches, schools, and family networks. Though abolition of slavery altered their legal status, it did not improve their economic and social opportunities relative to those of whites. In 1880 some 90 percent of all southern blacks depended for a living on farming or personal and domestic service—the same occupations they had had as slaves.

Pushed into sharecropping and burdened with crop liens, blacks also had to contend with new forms of social and political oppression. With slavery dead, white supremacists had to fashion new means of keeping blacks in a position of inferiority. Southern leaders, embittered by northern interference in race

relations during Reconstruction and anxious to reassert their authority after the withdrawal of federal troops (see page 446), instituted racist measures to discourage blacks from voting and legally segregate them from whites.

The overthrow of Reconstruction had not stopped blacks from voting. Although threats and intimidation against them increased, blacks still formed the backbone of the Republican party in the South and some still won elective offices. In North Carolina, for example, forty-three black men were elected to the state house and eleven to the state senate between 1877 and 1890. Yet also, white politicians began more actively to seek ways of reducing the so-called Negro vote by establishing restrictions which appeared neutral but would actually bar blacks from the polls. Beginning with Georgia in 1877, southern states levied taxes of $1 to $2 on all citizens wishing to vote. Though seemingly trivial, these poll taxes were prohibitive to most black voters, many of whom were so deeply in debt to furnishing merchants and landlords that they never had cash for any purpose. Other schemes disfranchised black voters who could not read. For example, voters might be required to deposit ballots for different candidates in different ballot boxes. In order to do so correctly, voters had to be able to read instructions; otherwise, their votes were invalidated.

Racial discrimination also stiffened in social affairs. A widespread informal system of separation had governed race relations in the antebellum South. After the Civil War, this system was codified in law. In

Spread of Jim Crow Laws

a series of cases during the 1870s, the Supreme Court opened the door to discrimination by ruling that the Fourteenth Amendment protected citizens' rights only against infringement by state governments. The federal government, according to the Court, had no control over what individuals or organizations did. If blacks wanted protection under the law, the Court said, they must seek it from the states, which under the Tenth Amendment retained all powers not specifically assigned to Congress.

The climax to these rulings came in 1883, when in the *Civil Rights Cases* the Court struck down the 1875 Civil Rights Act, which had prohibited segregation in public facilities such as streetcars, hotels, theaters, and parks. Again the Court declared that the federal government could not regulate the behavior of private individuals in matters of race relations. Subsequent lower-court cases in the 1880s established the principle that blacks could be restricted to "separate-but-equal" facilities. The Supreme Court upheld the separate-but-equal doctrine in *Plessy* v. *Ferguson* (1896) and officially applied it to schools in *Cummins* v. *County Board of Education* (1899).

Thereafter, segregation laws—known as Jim Crow laws—spread rapidly. Discriminatory legislation piled up throughout the South, confronting black people with countless daily reminders of their inferior status. State laws and local ordinances restricted blacks to the rear of streetcars, to separate drinking and toilet facilities, and to separate sections of hospitals, asylums, and cemeteries. A Birmingham, Alabama, ordinance required that the races be "distinctly separated . . . by well defined physical barriers" in "any room, hall, theatre, picture house, auditorium, yard, court, ball

	IMPORTANT EVENTS
1862	Homestead Act Morrill Land Grant Act
1865–67	War with western Sioux
1869	First transcontinental railroad, the Union Pacific, completed
1873	Major silver discovery of Comstock Lode (Nevada)
1874	Barbed wire fence patented
1876	Gold rush in Black Hills Custer's Last Stand
1878	Timber and Stone Act
1881	Helen Hunt Jackson, *A Century of Dishonor*
1882–83	Transcontinental routes of Santa Fe, Southern Pacific, and Northern Pacific completed
1883	*Civil Rights Cases* Standardization of national time zones
1885–86	Disastrous winters in Plains states
1887	Dawes Severalty Act Interstate Commerce Act Hatch Act
1890	Wounded Knee massacre
1893	Great Northern Railroad completed
1896	*Plessy* v. *Ferguson*
1899	*Cummins* v. *County Board of Education*

park, or other indoor or outdoor place." Local laws defined certain districts or blocks as all-black or all-white. Mobile, Alabama, passed a curfew requiring blacks to be off the streets by 10 P.M. A New Orleans law confined black and white prostitutes to separate districts, and Atlanta required separate Bibles for black witnesses swearing before court. Thus for thousands of black southerners race relations had not changed much since Emancipation, nor would they change until the 1960s when a turbulent civil rights movement overturned many of the old restrictions (see Chapter 33).

In industry, breezes of change were being stimulated by new manufacturing initiatives, but there too a distinctively southern quality prevailed. Two of the South's leading industries in the late

**Industrial-
ization of
the South**

nineteenth century relied on the traditional staple crops, cotton and tobacco. In the 1870s, textile mills began to sprout up in the Cotton Belt-states. Powered by the region's abundant rivers and streams, manned cheaply by poor whites eager to escape crop liens, and fostered by low taxes, such mills grew rapidly. By 1900 the South had four hundred mills with a total of over 4 million spindles, and twenty years later the region was replacing New England in textile manufacturing supremacy. Proximity to raw materials and cheap labor also aided the tobacco industry, and the invention in 1880 of a cigarette-making machine immensely enhanced the marketability of tobacco.

Cigarettes were manufactured in cities by black and white workers; textile mills were concentrated in small towns, and developed their own exploitative labor system. Financed mostly by local investors, mills employed women and children from nearby poor white families and paid them 50 cents a day for twelve or more hours of work. Such wages were barely half what northern workers received. Many companies built squalid villages around their mills and controlled all housing, stores, schools, and churches. Criticism of the company was forbidden, and attempts at union organization were squelched. Mill families soon found that factory jobs changed their status very little. The company store simply replaced the furnishing merchant, and the mill owner replaced the landlord.

Several other industries were launched in the South, but mainly under the sponsorship of northern or European capitalists. Between 1890 and 1900, for example, northern lumber syndicates moved into the pine forests of the Gulf states, boosting production by 500 percent. During the 1880s, northern investors developed southern iron and steel manufacturing, much of which centered in the boom city of Birmingham. Coal mining and railroad construction also expanded rapidly, but New York and London financiers dominated the boards of directors of most companies.

Regardless of outside influence, industrialization prompted southern boosters to herald the emergence of a New South ready to compete economically with other sections. Henry Grady, editor of the *Atlanta Constitution* and the most articulate voice of southern progress, proclaimed, "We have sowed towns and cities in the place of theories, and put business in place of politics. We have challenged your spinners in Massachusetts and your iron-makers in Pennsylvania. . . . We have fallen in love with work." Yet in 1900 the South remained as rural as it had been in 1860. Staple-crop agriculture supported its economy, and white supremacy permeated its social and political relations. Furthermore, the South attracted few immigrants because of its relative lack of industrial jobs, and thus enjoyed little of their energizing influence. A New South would emerge, but not until after a world war and a massive black exodus had jostled old habits and attitudes. Until then, southern society continued to grasp at ways to escape its dependent economic status while holding on to its old racial order.

SUGGESTIONS FOR FURTHER READING

The Western Frontier

Ray A. Billington, *Westward Expansion* (1967); Odie B. Faulk, *Tombstone: Myth and Reality* (1972); William H. Goetzmann, *Exploration and Empire* (1966); William S. Greever, *Bonanza West: Western Mining Rushes* (1963); Robert V. Hine, *The American West* (1973); Julie Roy Jeffrey, *Frontier Women* (1979); Frederick Merk, *History of the Westward Movement* (1978); Ruth Moynihan, *Rebel for Rights: Abigail Scott Duniway* (1983); Rodman W. Paul, *The Frontier and the American West* (1971); Rodman W.

Paul, *Mining Frontiers of the Far West* (1963); Henry Nash Smith, *Virgin Land: The American West as Symbol and Myth* (1950); Roberta B. Sollid, *Calamity Jane* (1958); L. Steckmesser, *The Western Hero in History and Legend* (1965).

Railroads

Alfred D. Chandler, ed., *Railroads: The Nation's First Big Business* (1965); Robert W. Fogel, *Railroads and Economic Growth* (1964); Ari Hoogenboom and Olive Hoogenboom, *A History of the ICC* (1970); Edward C. Kirkland, *Men, Cities, and Transportation* (1948); Gabriel Kolko, *Railroads and Regulation* (1965); George R. Taylor and Irene Neu, *The American Railroad Network* (1956); Alan Trachtenberg, *The Incorporation of America* (1982); O. O. Winther, *The Transportation Frontier* (1964).

Indians and Ranching

Ralph K. Andrist, *The Long Death: The Last Days of the Plains Indians* (1964); Lewis Atherton, *The Cattle Kings* (1961); Joe B. Frantz and Julian Choate, Jr., *The American Cowboy* (1955); Norris Hundley, Jr., ed., *The American Indian* (1974); Francis Paul Prucha, *American Indian Policy in Crisis* (1976); Robert F. Spencer *et al.*, *The Native Americans* (1965); Edward H. Spicer, *Cycles of Conquest: The Impact of Spain, Mexico, and the United States on the Indians of the Southwest* (1962); Robert M. Utley, *The Indian Frontier of the American West, 1846–1890* (1984); Robert M. Utley, *Frontier Regulars: The United States Army and the Indian* (1973); Wilcomb E. Washburn, *Red Man's Land/White Man's Law* (1971).

Settlement of the Plains

Allan G. Bogue, *From Prairie to Corn Belt* (1963); Everett Dick, *The Sod-House Frontier* (1937); Gilbert C. Fite, *The Farmer's Frontier* (1966); Fred A. Shannon, *The Farmer's Last Frontier* (1963); Walter Prescott Webb, *The Great Plains* (1931).

The New South

Orville Vernon Burton and Robert C. McMath, Jr., eds., *Toward a New South?: Post–Civil War Southern Communities* (1982); Thomas D. Clark and Albert D. Kirwan, *The South Since Appomattox* (1967); Vincent P. DeSantis, *Republicans Face the Southern Question, 1877–1897* (1959); Paul Gaston, *The New South Creed* (1970); Dewey Grantham, Jr., *The Democratic South* (1963); Steven Hahn, *The Roots of Southern Populism: Yeoman Farmers and the Transformation of the Georgia Upcountry, 1850–1890* (1983); Stanley P. Hirshson, *Farewell to the Bloody Shirt: Northern Republicans and the Southern Negro* (1962); J. Morgan Kousser, *The Shaping of Southern Politics* (1974); Melton A. McLaurin, *Paternalism and Protest: Southern Cotton Mill Workers and Organized Labor* (1971); Howard N. Rabinowitz, *Race Relations in the Urban South, 1865–1890* (1978); Theodore Saloutos, *Farmer Movements in the South, 1865–1933* (1960); C. Vann Woodward, *The Strange Career of Jim Crow* (1966); C. Vann Woodward, *Origins of the New South* (1951).

THE MACHINE AGE
1877–1920

CHAPTER 17

*C*onrad Carl *tried* to appear calm, but he was understandably nervous. It was spring 1882, and Carl, who for nearly thirty years had been a tailor in New York City, was appearing before a group of U.S. senators in Washington, D.C. The Committee on Education and Labor was conducting an investigation into the causes of recent labor unrest, and Senator James L. Pugh, a former Confederate congressman from Alabama, was asking Carl to explain changing work conditions in the tailoring business.

Admitting that his testimony would probably cost him his job, Carl nevertheless answered candidly. When he first began tailoring, Carl explained, he and his wife and children had pieced together garments by hand. The pace of their work was relaxed, yet he was able to save a few dollars each year. Then, said Carl, "in 1854 or 1855, . . . the sewing machine was invented and introduced, and it stitched very nicely, nicer than the tailor could do; and the bosses said: 'We want you to use the sewing machine; you have to buy one.' "

Carl and his fellow tailors used their meager savings to buy machines, hoping they could earn more by producing more. But their employers cut wages instead of raising them. The tailors "found that we could earn no more than we could without the machine; but the money for the machine was gone now, and we found that the machine was only for the profit of the bosses; that they got their work quicker, and it was done nicer." Moreover, Carl, now old and discouraged, had seen that mechanization had other troubling effects on workers and those around them. "The machine," he said, "makes too much noise and the neighbors want to sleep, and we have to stop sewing earlier, so we have to work faster. We work now in excitement—in a hurry. It is hunting; it is not work at all; it is a hunt."

Conrad Carl's testimony to the Senate committee was one worker's view of the industrialization that was relentlessly overtaking American society. The forces prevailing in the new order were both inspiring and ominous. The factory and the machine broke down manufacturing into minute, routinized tasks and organized work according to dictates of the clock. Corporations merged and amassed frightening power in the quest for productivity and profits. Defenders of the new system devised new social and economic theories to justify it, while critics tried to counteract what they thought were abuses of power. Finally, workers, who had long thought of themselves as valued producers, were caught in the changing modes of production and fought to avoid becoming slaves to the machine.

Industrialization is a process whose complexities defy precise definition. Most simply it is characterized by the production of goods by machine rather than by hand. Factors either related to or resulting from industrialization in America include some of the following:

1. involvement of an increasing proportion of the work force in manufacturing
2. production concentrated in large, intricately organized factories
3. accelerated technological innovation, emphasizing new inventions and applied science
4. expanded markets, no longer merely local and regional in scope
5. growth of a nationwide transportation network based on the railroad, and an accompanying communications network based on the telegraph and telephone
6. increased capital accumulation for investment in expansion of production
7. growth of large enterprises and specialization in all forms of economic activity
8. rapid population increase
9. steady increase in the size and predominance of cities

A few numbers will help illustrate these patterns. In 1860 about a quarter of the American labor force worked in manufacturing and transportation; over half did so in 1920. The number of people gainfully employed rose from 17.4 million in 1880 to 41.6

million in 1920. In 1870 Western Union handled over 9 million telegraph messages on 112,000 miles of wire; by 1900 it processed over 63 million messages on 933,000 miles of wire. And the value of exports increased twelvefold between 1879 and 1920. By the twentieth century, the United States was not only the world's largest producer of raw materials and food, but the most productive industrial nation as well.

Accelerated migration off farms and mass immigration from abroad swelled the industrial work force (see Chapter 18); but machines, more than people, boosted American productivity. Only by using more machines could manufacturers lower production costs and significantly raise each worker's output. Mechanization relied on the use of standardized parts and this brought about more specialization on factory assembly lines.

A spirit of nationalism infused American industrialization. Many industrialists believed that productivity was the key to national welfare. Thus John D. Rockefeller linked his business activities to a nationalistic mission, explaining, "I wanted to participate in the work of making our country great. I had an ambition to build." Yet the accomplishments of industrial expansion, like expansion into natural resources and agricultural frontiers, involved waste and greed. The vigor and creativity that marked the half-century after the end of the Civil War clearly initiated forces that could be considered both constructive and destructive.

These trends weighed most heavily on the industrial work force. Economic growth furnished jobs and income to millions of families who had left American farms and European villages in search of a better existence. But industry's emphasis on productivity and profitability often kept wages at or below subsistence levels and harnessed workers to monotonous routines. Fearful that American industrialism might create a class of helpless proletarians, laborers fought to retain independent work habits and to be paid a living wage. Although the period was not a triumphant one for labor, it did contain a strong undercurrent of worker activism in reforms, cooperatives, and unions in an effort to reconcile new economic realities with the desire to live a life characterized by comfort and dignity.

TECHNOLOGY AND THE QUEST FOR WEALTH

In 1876, Thomas A. Edison and his associates moved into a long wooden shed in Menlo Park, New Jersey, where Edison intended to turn out "a minor invention every ten days and a big thing every six months or so." Here was the brash American spirit adapting itself to a new age. If Americans wanted new products, they could not wait for discoveries; they had to organize and work purposefully to bring about progress. Edison envisioned his Menlo Park laboratory as an invention factory, a place where creative people would pool their ideas and skills to fashion marketable products. Such efforts were part of a process that enlivened American industrialization at the end of the nineteenth century.

The years between 1865 and 1900 were an age of invention. Important devices like the steam engine, dynamo (generator), and sewing machine that had existed since the early nineteenth century now were adapted more fully to the needs of industry and agriculture. Moreover, new late-nineteenth-century inventions and refinements in electricity, internal combustion, and industrial chemistry laid the technical foundations for twentieth-century industrial development. The patent system, created by the Constitution to "promote the Progress of science and useful Arts," testified to an outburst of American inventiveness. Between 1790 and 1860 the U.S. Patent Office had granted a total of 36,000 patents. In 1897 alone, however, it granted 22,000 patents, and in the seventy years after 1860 it granted 1.5 million.

As one of the world's leading pioneers in the electrical industry, Thomas Edison came close to fulfilling the goal he set for his work at Menlo Park. He patented over a thousand inventions, many of which used electrical power to transmit light, sound, and images. Perhaps the biggest of his "big-thing" projects began in 1878 when he formed the Edison Electric Light Company and embarked on a search for a cheap, efficient means

Birth of the Electrical Industry

Thomas Alva Edison (1847–1931) at work in his labora-tory around 1890. Edison developed countless inventions, including the incandescent light bulb, the phonograph, and early forms of motion picture reproduction. He also was a skilled publicist, capable of selling his ideas for commercial purposes. Library of Congress.

of indoor lighting. Gas, candles, and oil lamps had become impractical for lighting streets and large buildings. So Edison turned to light made by an electric current flowing between two carbon rods. His major contribution was perfection of an incandescent bulb, which used a filament in a vacuum. At the same time he worked out a *system* of power production and distribution—an improved dynamo and a parallel circuit of wires—that would provide cheap, convenient lighting to a large number of customers.

Aware that he had to make his ideas marketable, Edison acted as his own publicist. During the 1880

Christmas season he illuminated Menlo Park with forty incandescent bulbs, and in 1882 he built a power plant that would light eighty-five buildings in New York's Wall Street financial district. When this Pearl Street Station began service with great fanfare, a *New York Times* reporter marveled that working in his office at night "seemed almost like writing in daylight." The next year, New Yorkers celebrated Edison's achievement by staging a ballet complete with an electrically lighted model of the Brooklyn Bridge and ballerinas whose costumes were wired so they glowed.

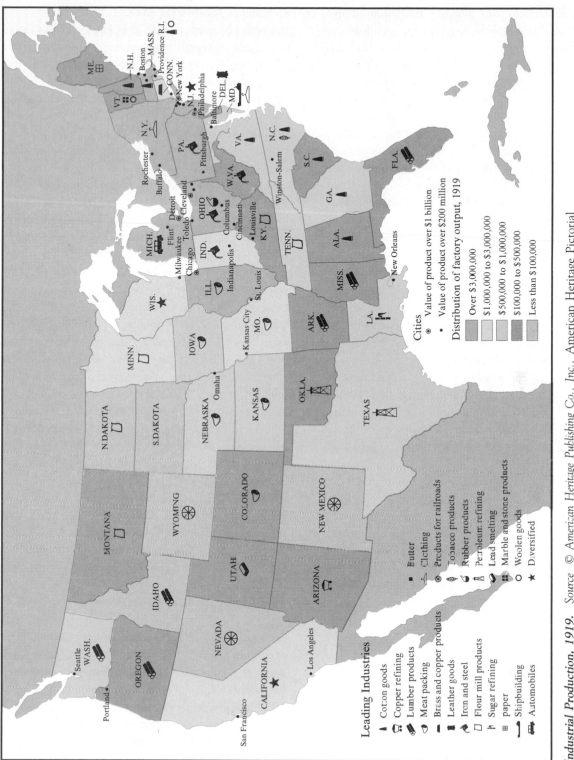

Industrial Production, 1919. *Source © American Heritage Publishing Co., Inc., American Heritage Pictorial Atlas of United States History; data from U.S. Bureau of the Census, Fourteenth Census of the United States, 1920. Vol. IX: Manufacturing (Washington: U.S. Government Printing Office, 1921).*

Cities
⊙ Value of product over $1 billion
• Value of product over $200 million

Distribution of factory output, 1919
Over $3,000,000
$1,000,000 to $3,000,000
$500,000 to $1,000,000
$100,000 to $500,000
Less than $100,000

Leading Industries
Cotton goods
Copper refining
Lumber products
Meat packing
Brass and copper products
Leather goods
Iron and steel
Flour mill products
Sugar refining
paper
Shipbuilding
Automobiles

Butter
Clothing
Products for railroads
Tobacco products
Rubber products
Petroleum refining
Lead smelting
Marble and stone products
Woolen goods
Diversified

Edison's system had a major limitation: it used direct current at low voltage, and could thus send electric power only a mile or two. George Westinghouse, an inventor from Schenectady, New York, who at age twenty-three had become famous for devising an air brake for railroad cars, solved the problem. Westinghouse used alternating current and transformers to reduce high-voltage power to lower voltage levels, thus making transmission over long distances cheaper.

Once Edison and Westinghouse had made their technological breakthroughs, others helped them distribute their inventions to a wide market. Samuel Insull, Edison's private secretary, who later amassed a huge electric-utility empire, deftly attracted investments and organized Edison power plants across the country. In the late 1880s and early 1890s, financiers Henry Villard and J. P. Morgan consolidated patents in electric lighting and merged equipment-manufacturing companies into the General Electric Company. Equally important, General Electric and Westinghouse Electric established research laboratories that paid practical-minded scientists to find new uses for electricity. Under talented scientist and organizer Willis M. Whitney, the General Electric lab pioneered in myriad developments ranging from vacuum tubes for radios through tungsten filaments for light bulbs to atomic theory.

Research laboratories did not eliminate individual dreamers. One such optimist was Henry Ford, who in the 1890s worked as an electrical engineer in Detroit's Edison Company and in his spare time experimented with a gasoline-burning internal combustion engine to power a vehicle. George Selden, a lawyer from Rochester, New York, had been tinkering with internal combustion engines since the 1870s. But Ford's vision and organizational genius spawned a massive industry.

Like Edison, Ford had a scheme as well as an invention. In 1909 he declared, "I am going to democratize the automobile. When I'm through everybody will be able to afford one, and about everyone will have one." The way to do so, according to Ford, was to produce millions of identical cars in exactly the same fashion. The key was mass production, and the watchword was *flow*. Adapting models from the meatpacking and metalworking industries, Ford man-

Mass Production of the Automobile

agers and engineers set up assembly lines that drastically reduced the time and cost of producing cars. Instead of a single worker being responsible for making and assembling the entire automobile, production was broken down so that each worker had responsibility for only one task, constantly repeated, and there was a continuous flow of these tasks from raw materials to finished product. When the Ford Motor Company began operation in 1903, there were only 8,000 autos on the streets of Detroit. In 1908, the first year the famous Model T was built, Ford sold 10,000 cars. By 1914, the year after the first moving assembly line was inaugurated, 248,000 Fords were sold. Many of them cost $490 apiece, only about one-fourth of what they would have cost a decade earlier.

Even this price was beyond the means of many workers, who earned at best $2 a day. In 1914, however, Ford tried to boost buying power and spur worker productivity by offering combined wages and profit sharing of $5 a day. "This is neither charity nor wages," he explained, "but profit sharing and efficiency engineering." Moreover, rising automobile production made for more jobs, higher earnings, and higher profits in such related industries as oil, paint, rubber, and glass. The value of automobiles manufactured, only $6 million in 1900, reached $420 million by 1914. The Model T was indeed replacing the family horse.

The du Ponts did for the chemical industry what Edison and Ford had done for the electrical and automobile industries. The du Pont family had been manufacturing gunpowder and other explosives in America since the early 1800s. In 1902 three du Pont cousins, Alfred, Coleman, and Pierre, took over the family company and began to broaden production. Branching out from explosives research in 1911, the du Pont laboratories began to adapt the flammable substance cellulose to the eventual production of such materials as photographic film, rubber, lacquer, and textile fibers. The company also pioneered in systematic organization, devising efficient methods of executive management, accounting, and earnings investment.

Du Ponts and the Chemical Industry

Although the timing of mechanization varied from one industry to another, a host of other machines and processes helped to alter the nation's economy and everyday life between 1865 and 1900. The tele-

This assembly line at the Ford Motor plant shows how the process of production was broken down into simple, repetitive tasks—here, the fashioning of auto seats. Rather than building the entire product, specialized crews worked on individual parts that later were assembled into the whole automobile.   Ford Motor Company.

phone and typewriter revolutionized communications, making face-to-face conversations less important and facilitating business correspondence and record-keeping. Sewing machines made mass-produced clothing available to almost everyone. Refrigeration changed American dietary habits by making it easier to preserve meat, fruit, vegetables, and dairy products. Streetcars, elevated railroads, and subways extended city limits and enabled people to live farther from their workplaces. Cash registers and adding machines revamped accounting and created new clerical jobs.

All these developments and more thrust the United States into the vanguard of industrial nations. Other effects, however, were less positive. Industrial expansion created countless new jobs, but because most machines and inventions were labor-saving, fewer

workers could produce more in less time— as Conrad Carl knew all too well. Mechanization not only destroyed time-honored crafts but subordinated men and women to rigid schedules and repetitive routines. On another level, the scramble for patents resulted in as much waste as technological advancement. Entrepreneurs spent huge sums hoping to profit from inventing something slightly different from what already existed, or purchased patents on the remote chance they might be profitable. Companies like Bell Telephone and individuals like George Selden clogged the courts with suits alleging patent infringement. To minimize uncertainty, manufacturers pooled patents and tried to monopolize new discoveries by confining research to their own labs. As in farming and mining, bigness and consolidation engulfed the individual.

THE TRIUMPH OF INDUSTRIALISM

I n the industrial sector, profits resulted from higher production at lower costs. As railroads and technological innovations made large-scale production more economical, sizable factories began to replace small ones. Between 1850 and 1900 the average amount of capital invested in a manufacturing firm increased from $700,000 to $1.9 million. Only large factories could afford to buy new machines and operate them at full capacity. And large factories could best take advantage of discount rates for shipping products in bulk and for buying raw materials in quantity. Economists call such advantages *economies of scale.*

Machines and large factories made such efficiencies possible, but profitability was as much a matter of organization as of mechanics. In other words, running
New Emphasis on Efficiency a successful factory depended on how production was *arranged* as well as on the machines that were used. Thus by the 1890s, engineers and managers were working intently to increase output economically and efficiently, putting the primary emphasis on time.

Of the many people who espoused systems of efficient production, the most influential was Frederick W. Taylor. As a foreman and engineer for the Midvale Steel Company in the 1880s, Taylor observed that the only way a company could lessen the impact of fixed costs and thus increase profits was to base production on scientific studies of "how quickly the various kinds of work . . . ought to be done." The "ought" was crucial because it signified the goal of producing more for a lower cost per unit—reducing labor costs by eliminating unnecessary workers. The "how quickly" meant that time and money were equivalent.

In 1898 Taylor took his stopwatch to the Bethlehem Steel Company to illustrate how his principles of scientific management worked. His experiments, he explained, involved identifying the "elementary operations of motions" used by specific workers, selecting better tools, and devising "a series of motions which

Huge machines dwarf workers in the Minneapolis General Electric Company's Main Street Station, symbolizing the way mechanization made many human skills outmoded by the end of the nineteenth century. Minnesota Historical Society; Louis D. Sweet, photographer.

can be made quickest and best." Applying the technique to the shoveling of ore, Taylor designed fifteen kinds of shovel and prescribed the proper motions for using each one. As a result he reduced a crew of 600 men to 140 and cut company costs in half. The remaining shovelers received higher wages.

Taylor's writings helped to make time studies and scientific management a national obsession. Workers' skills became less valued, and managers increasingly controlled the pace and scale of output. Time rather than quality became the measure of acceptable work, and science rather than tradition determined the right ways of doing things. As integral features of the assembly line, where work was divided into specific time-determined tasks, employees had become another kind of interchangeable part.

At the same time, large manufacturers were adding new marketing techniques to their technological and organizational innovations. Meat processor Gustavus Swift used branch slaughterhouses and refrigeration to enlarge the market for fresh meat. James B. Duke, who organized the American Tobacco Company and

New Marketing Techniques made cigarettes a big business, saturated communities with billboards and free samples and offered premium gifts to retailers for selling more cigarettes. Companies like International Harvester and Singer Sewing Machine set up systems for servicing their products and introduced financing schemes to permit customers to buy the machines more easily. In many instances marketing innovations enabled producers to sell directly to retailers, squeezing out wholesalers and eliminating the excess costs wholesaling entailed.

THE CORPORATE CONSOLIDATION MOVEMENT

Neither the wonders of industrial production nor the new techniques of market promotion could mask unsettling factors in the American economy. Competition and the resulting race for higher productivity and new markets had costs as well as benefits. New technology demanded that factories operate at near-capacity in order to produce goods most economically. But the more manufacturers produced, the more they had to sell. And in order to sell more, they had to reduce prices. In order to profit more, they expanded production further and often reduced wages. In order to expand, they had to borrow money. In order to repay the money, they had to produce and sell even more. This circular process strangled small firms that could not keep pace and thrust workers into conditions of constant uncertainty. The same cycle affected trade, banking, and transportation as well as manufacturing.

Such conditions encouraged rapid growth, but optimism could dissolve at the hint that debtors were unable to meet their obligations. In the final third of the nineteenth century, financial panics afflicted the economy at least once a decade, depressing prices, destroying businesses, and putting workers out of jobs. Depressions that began in 1873, 1884, and 1893 each hovered over the nation for several years. Business leaders failed to agree on what caused the declines. Some blamed overproduction; others pointed to underconsumption; still others attributed downturns to lax credit and investment practices. Whatever the reasons—and there were usually several—businessmen began seeking ways to combat the uncertainty of the business cycle. In those years of boom and bust, many turned to more centralized and cooperative forms of economic power, notably corporations, pools, trusts, and holding companies. These new devices of control in turn altered traditional American beliefs in individual effort.

Industrialists, unlike laborers, never questioned the capitalist system or lost faith in entrepreneurial leadership. Instead, they built on the corporate base that had supported economic growth since the early 1800s. The corporation had been given a special American flavor by general incorporation laws passed by the states to encourage commerce and industry (see page 253). Under such laws as they developed in the middle of the nineteenth century, almost anyone could start a company and raise money by selling stock to investors. Full responsibility for company administration was left in the hands of managers. Stockholders could share in profits yet avoid most losses because the laws limited their liability for company debts. Corporations proved to be the best instruments for raising the capital needed for industrial expansion, and by 1900 they were responsible for two-thirds of all goods manufactured in the United States. Moreover, in the 1880s and 1890s corporations received broad judicial protection when the Supreme Court ruled that they, like individuals, were covered by the Fourteenth Amendment. States could not deny corporations equal protection of the laws and could not deprive them of rights or property without due process of law.

As economic disorder and the urge for profits mounted, corporation managers began to seek stability in new and larger forms of economic concentration. Between the late 1880s and early 1900s, an epidemic of consolidation swept the United States, eventually resulting in the massive conglomerates that have dominated the American economy in the twentieth century. At first, however, such efforts were tentative and informal, consisting mainly of cooperative agreements among firms that made the same product or offered the same service. Through these arrangements, called *pools,* competing companies tried to control

The corporate consolidation movement resulted in giant trusts, epitomized by John D. Rockefeller's Standard Oil, which was so powerful that critics warned it could enable Rockefeller to convert the Capitol into an oil refinery and hold the White House and Treasury Department in the palm of his hand.   Library of Congress.

the market by agreeing how much each should produce and what prices should be charged.

Pools, Trusts, and Holding Companies Used by railroads (to divide up traffic), steel producers, and whiskey distillers, pools depended on their members' honesty. Such "gentlemen's agreements" worked during good times when there was enough business for all; but during slow periods, the desire for profits often tempted pool members to evade their commitments by secretly reducing prices or selling more than the agreed quota. The Interstate Commerce Act of 1887 outlawed pools, but by then their usefulness was already fading.

John D. Rockefeller disliked pools, calling them "ropes of sand." In 1879 one of his lawyers, Samuel Dodd, devised a means to overcome the limitations

of pools and still control the market. Dodd adapted an old device called a *trust* whereby companies in the same industry could be lured or forced into turning over control of their stock to a board of trustees, which then supervised all operations. This device allowed Rockefeller to integrate the management of his original Standard Oil Company of Ohio with that of other companies he controlled, thus strengthening his grip on the highly profitable petroleum industry. Then in 1888 New Jersey adopted new incorporation laws allowing corporations chartered there to own property in other states and to own stock in other corporations (trusts provided for trusteeship but not ownership). This liberalization led to the creation of the *holding company*, which controlled a partial or complete interest in other companies.

Holding companies could in turn merge their constituent companies' assets (physical plant, equipment, inventory, cash, and the like) as well as their management. Thus Rockefeller incorporated Standard Oil of New Jersey, merging the assets of forty constituent companies. By 1898, Standard Oil refined 83.7 percent of all the oil produced in the nation, controlled most pipelines, and had moved into natural-gas production and ownership of oil-producing properties.

Standard Oil's expansion into activities besides oil refining exemplified a new form of integration that accompanied the rise of trusts. In an effort to control the market, many companies took over several levels of production and distribution, including control of raw materials and transportation as well as manufacturing. The prime example of this *vertical integration* was Gustavus Swift's meat-processing operation. During the 1880s, Swift boldly invested in livestock, slaughterhouses, refrigerator cars, and a marketing organization of butchers so as to assure sale of his beef without unexpected inconvenience. The device of the holding company aided this kind of consolidation, which fused a broad range of business activities into one entity under unified management.

Originally designed as an arrangement whereby responsible individuals would manage the financial affairs of people unwilling or unable to handle them alone, the trust became the answer to industry's search for order. Between 1889 and 1903, some three hundred combinations were formed, most of them trusts and holding companies. By far the most spectacular was the U.S. Steel Corporation, financed by J. P. Morgan. This new enterprise, made up of iron-ore properties, freight carriers, wire mills, plate and tubing companies, and other firms, was capitalized at over $1.4 billion. Other mammoth combinations included the Amalgamated Copper Company, the American Sugar Refining Company, the American Tobacco Company, and the U.S. Rubber Company, each worth over $50 million.

The merger movement created a new species of businessmen, whose vocation was financial organizing rather than producing a particular good or service. Shrewd operators sought out opportunities for combination, formed corporations, and then persuaded producers to sell their firms to the new company. These businessmen usually raised money by selling stock and borrowing from banks. Unwedded to any

one industry, their attention ranged widely. Thus W. H. Moore organized the American Tin Plate Company, the Diamond Match Company, and the National Biscuit Company. Elbert H. Gary aided consolidation of the barbed-wire industry and the organization of U.S. Steel. And investment bankers like J. P. Morgan and Jacob Schiff piloted the merger movement, inspiring awe with their financial power and organizational skills.

The growth of corporations in the late nineteenth century turned stock exchanges into pulsating centers of activity where investors bought and sold stocks and bonds feverishly. By the end of 1886, trading on the New York Stock Exchange had reached 1 million shares a day. By 1914 the number of industrial stocks traded had reached 511, compared with 145 in 1869. Investment could not have occurred without growth in the capital available for such purposes. Between 1870 and 1900 foreign investment in American companies rose from $1.5 billion to $3.5 billion. More important, personal savings and institutional investment mushroomed: the assets of savings banks, concentrated in the Northeast and on the West Coast, rose by $900 million between 1875 and 1897, to a total of $2.2 billion. States gradually loosened regulations to enable banks to invest in railroads and industrial enterprises. Commercial banks, insurance companies, and corporations also invested heavily. As one journal proclaimed, "Nearly the whole country (including the typical widow and orphan) is interested in the stock market." Though this statement was a gross exaggeration, it reflected what optimistic industrial capitalists wanted to believe.

The Gospel of Wealth

To corporate investors, growth was not only desirable; it was necessary. Profits depended on it, and profits meant everything. Pursuit of wealth had become a struggle for life. As Milton H. Smith of the Louisville and Nashville Railroad put it, "Society, as created, was for the purpose of one man's getting what the other fellow has, if he can, and keep out of the penitentiary."

But the merger movement that resulted in trusts and holding companies upset this philosophical underpinning. J. P. Morgan, whose steely eyes, full mustache, and bulky frame made him a commanding figure among American capitalists, heralded the new order when he told a meeting of railroad directors, "The purpose of this meeting is to cause the members of this association to no longer take the law into their own hands . . . as has been too much the practice heretofore. This is not elsewhere customary in civilized communities, and no good reason exists why such a practice should continue among railroads." Business leaders turned to consolidation under the new corporate forms both to promote growth and to cut down wasteful competition. The monopolistic companies that resulted, however, found it necessary to justify their size and power to a public raised on the ideology of open competition.

Defenders of business thus eagerly embraced the doctrine of Social Darwinism, which seemed to justify aggression in human society. Developed by English philosopher Herbert Spencer and **Social Darwinism** preached in the United States by Yale professor William Graham Sumner, Social Darwinism loosely adapted Charles Darwin's theory of the origin of species to the principles of laissez faire. Human society had evolved naturally, the Social Darwinists reasoned, and any interference with existing institutions would only hamper progress and aid the weak. In a free society operating according to the principle of survival of the fittest, power would flow naturally to the most capable. Property holding and acquisition were therefore sacred rights, and wealth was a mark of well-deserved power and responsibility. Civilization depended on this system, explained Sumner. "If we do not like the survival of the fittest," he wrote, "we have only one possible alternative, and that is survival of the unfittest." Clergymen, journalists, and popular writers also proclaimed the doctrine of Social Darwinism, assuring the public that progress would result only from natural evolution.

This philosophy required that people be left free to accumulate and dispose of wealth. In fact, however, the new corporate forms, with their domination of production and finance, prevented most individuals who did not already have wealth from acquiring it. To compensate for this inconsistency, Social Darwinists reasoned that humanitarian elites could provide for the needs of those less fortunate or less capable. Thus captains of industry strongly believed that their wealth carried moral responsibilities. John D. Rockefeller once stated, "I believe it is my duty to make money and still more money and to use the money I make for the good of my fellow man according to the dictates of my conscience." This belief implied a right to define what was good and necessary for society, and especially for workers. It meant that the wealthy could and should endow churches, hospitals, and schools, since such gifts promoted progress by raising the "moral culture" of all classes. But it also meant that government should not force the rich, through taxation or regulation, to become more humanitarian.

The urge for efficient organization also affected social attitudes of businessmen. Under scientific management, experts determined schedules, production quotas, techniques, and tools. Their rigid principles acquired almost religious certitude: there was only one true way to economic efficiency. Once business leaders had accepted these principles for their own companies, they were only a short step from using them on the rest of society. Scientific management could, it appeared, apply to politics and personal affairs just as easily as it did to factories.

Paradoxically, business executives who exalted individual initiative and independence also pressed for government assistance. They denounced any measures that might aid unions or regulate **Government Assistance to Business** factory conditions; such legislation, they said, thwarted natural economic laws. At the same time, though, they lobbied forcefully for subsidies, loans, and tax relief that would encourage business growth. Tariffs were by far the largest form of government assistance to industry. By putting high import duties on competing goods from abroad, such as kerosene, steel rails, worsted wools, and tin plate, Congress enabled American producers to keep the prices of their goods relatively high. Industrialists argued that tariff protection encouraged the development of new products and the founding of new enterprises. But tariffs also forced consumers to pay artificially high prices for many products.

Railroads and industrial firms also manipulated state and local governments to their own advantage (see pages 460–461). As reformer Henry Demarest Lloyd

Economic expansion in the New South included exploitation of cheap labor. The most extreme example of this exploitation was the employment of prisoners by private companies. Here, convicts are clearing a route for the New Orleans Pacific Railroad. Armed guards supervise the laborers. Culver.

remarked in 1881, Standard Oil "has done everything with the Pennsylvania legislature except refine it." In the South, railroads and mining companies often leased prisoners to work as laborers. Such companies paid the states about 10 cents per prisoner for a day's work, in preference to paying a free laborer $1 a day. Although business executives believed that natural law would lead directly to economic progress, they were not above enlisting help to ensure that natural law would work profitably for them.

Whatever their inconsistencies, business leaders took great pride in the achievements of their era. Many accepted credit for the meteoric rise of the American standard of living—national wealth rose 550 percent between 1860 and 1900, and per capita income increased 150 percent—and they scoffed at charges that only the wealthy were benefiting. Carroll D. Wright, a pioneering social statistician, denied

that the rich were getting richer and the poor poorer. "To the investigator," he testified, "the phrase should be, The rich are growing richer; many more people than formerly are growing rich; and the poor are better off."

The trouble with this materialistic philosophy was that it rested on a shaky foundation. Believers first justified it by invoking natural economic law and the survival of the fittest. But mounting criticism forced them into the illogical position of defending such principles by emphasizing how fragile they were. Thus, they warned, any interference in the business system by labor unions or by government—in the form of regulation, taxation, or support for the underprivileged—would upset everything and stall or even reverse progress. Government interference in the form of tariffs and other aid, however, they considered to be quite another matter.

DISSENTING VOICES

Writers who attacked trusts rarely challenged this reasoning; instead, they based their arguments on traditional American beliefs in independence and opportunity. In doing so, they argued within the same framework of values as did corporate leaders who defended the new economic system. While defenders insisted that trusts were the natural and efficient outcome of economic development, critics charged that trusts were unnatural because they were created by greed and inefficient because they stifled opportunity. Underlying such charges was a deep-seated fear of monopoly. As Charles Francis Adams, a descendant of two presidents, put it, "In the minds of the great majority, and not without reason, the idea of any industrial combination is closely connected with that of monopoly, and monopoly with extortion." Those who feared monopoly believed that large corporations could exploit consumers by fixing prices, demean workers by cutting wages, destroy opportunity by eliminating small businesses, and threaten democracy by corrupting politicians—all of which was not only unnatural but immoral. To critics of trusts, ethics eclipsed economics.

Many believed there was a better way to achieve progress. By the mid-1880s, a number of young professors, troubled by the growing size of industrial and financial organizations, began to challenge Social Darwinism and laissez faire. Some, like pioneering sociologist Lester Ward, attacked the application of evolutionary theory to social and economic relations. In *Dynamic Sociology* (1883), Ward argued that human control of nature, not natural law, accounted for the advance of civilization. To Ward, a system that guaranteed survival only to the fittest was wasteful and brutal; instead, he reasoned, cooperative activity, fostered by planning and government intervention, was the best means to unity and happiness. Economists Richard Ely, John R. Commons, and Edward Bemis agreed that natural forces should be harnessed for the public good. In 1885 they and others of like mind formed the American Economic Association and denounced the laissez-faire system for its "unsound morals." They preferred the positive assistance of the state, which was, Ely declared, "an educational and ethical agency whose positive aid is an indispensable condition of human progress." This sentiment provided a strong rationale for government action during the Progressive era in the early twentieth century (see Chapter 21).

While academics were recommending intervention into natural economic order, others were proposing more utopian schemes for combating monopolies.

Utopian Economic Schemes

Reformer Henry George, whose early life of poverty as a printer and writer had sensitized him to the exploitative power of large enterprises, declared that inequality stemmed from the ability of a few to profit from rising land values. Land values rose, George argued, without effort on the part of owners simply because a growing population increased the demand for living and working space, especially in cities. To restore equality, George proposed to tax the "unearned increment"—the rise in land values caused by increased market demand rather than by owners' improvements—and to eliminate all other taxes. By confiscating undue profits, George insisted, this *single tax* would end monopolistic tendencies and ensure social progress. George's scheme, argued forcefully in his book *Progress and Poverty* (1879), had great popular appeal over the next quarter-century and almost won him the mayoralty of New York in 1886.

Unlike George, who approved of private ownership, novelist Edward Bellamy envisioned a socialist state where government would own and oversee the means of production and distribution and would unite all people under moral laws. Bellamy outlined his vision in the utopian *Looking Backward, 2000–1887*, published in 1888. The novel, which sold over 1 million copies within a few years, warned that catastrophe would result from the extremes of wealth and poverty that characterized American society. The remedy, said Bellamy, was a fully nationalized state free of greedy bankers, industrialists, lawyers, and politicians. A "principle of fraternal cooperation" would replace vicious competition and wasteful monopoly, and a classless society living under the Golden Rule would erase inequality and corruption. Bellamy's system, which he called *Nationalism*, rested on his belief that all people are interested in "breaking the meshes which entangle us, and struggling upward to a higher, nobler plane of existence." His ideas sparked the formation of Nationalist clubs and journals all over the country, and vitalized popular appeals for civil service reform, social welfare measures, and government ownership of railroads and utilities.

Journalist and reformer Henry Demarest Lloyd arrived at a similar conclusion by a different route. His *Wealth Against Commonwealth* (1894) was a quasischolarly indictment of Standard Oil and its monopolistic supremacy. Using his evidence loosely, Lloyd portrayed John D. Rockefeller as a ruthless ogre who trampled widows and invalids as well as competing oil refiners in his rush for profits. Lloyd warned that such unbridled aggression and resulting monopolistic power would lead only to public enslavement. As an alternative, he offered a cooperative commonwealth similar to Bellamy's. Government ownership and operation of the means of production, Lloyd exclaimed, would create a society in which "the organization of processes have become so far developed that the profit-hunting Captains of Industry may be replaced by the public-serving Captains of Industry. . . . We are to have a private life of new beauty. . . . We are to be commoners, travelers to Altruria."

While George, Bellamy, Lloyd, and others grappled with ways to meet what they believed to be a moral crisis of civilization, public clamor against monopolies and trusts began to prod legislators into action. Before 1900, very few people advocated the kind of government ownership Bellamy and Lloyd envisioned, but several state governments did take steps to prohibit monopolies and regulate big business. By the end of the century, fifteen states had constitutional provisions outlawing trusts, and twenty-seven had laws forbidding pools. Most of these were states in the agricultural South and West, responding to antimonopolistic pressure exerted by various farm organizations. But problems of definition and enforcement mounted. State attorneys general lacked the staff and judicial support for a concerted attack on big business, and corporations always found ways to evade restrictions. Consequently, the need for national legislation became more pressing.

Antitrust Legislation

Throughout the 1880s both major parties moved gingerly toward such legislation, and in 1890 Congress passed the Sherman Anti-Trust Act. Introduced by Senator John Sherman of Ohio and rewritten by eastern conservatives in the Senate, the law made illegal "every contract, combination in the form of trust or otherwise, or conspiracy in the restraint of trade." People found guilty of violating the law faced fines and jail terms, and those wronged by illegal combinations could sue for triple damages. However, the law was vague—purposely so, some have said—because that was the only way it could have been passed. It did not define clearly what a restraint of trade was. Moreover, it entrusted interpretation of its provisions to the courts, which at that time were strong allies of business. As one corporate lawyer scoffed, "Legislators madly dashed to the work, threw ink upon paper, and called it a statute and legislation, and they asked the courts to enforce it—enforce a statute based upon doubt and guess and speculation and against the natural laws of trade and business."

The Sherman Anti-Trust Act was intended to encourage free competition by prohibiting unreasonable restraints of trade, but judges—particularly the Supreme Court—blurred distinctions between reasonable and unreasonable. When in 1895 the government prosecuted the so-called Sugar Trust for owning 98 percent of the nation's sugar-refining capacity, eight of nine Supreme Court judges ruled that control of manufacturing did not necessarily mean control of trade (*U.S. v. E. C. Knight Co.*). According to the Court, the Constitution empowered Congress to regulate interstate commerce, but manufacturing, which in the case of sugar took place entirely within the state of Pennsylvania, did not fall under congressional control. The Sugar Trust, said one justice, was attempting to increase its profits from refining, but was innocent of trying to restrain trade.

This interpretation left the antitrust act with only token power to combat industrial bigness. The law, passed to soothe public clamor, found little support among public officials, even those entrusted with enforcing it. Thus Attorney General Richard Olney was prompted to remark, "You will have observed that the Govt has been defeated in the Supreme Court on the trust question. I always supposed it would be & have taken the responsibility of not prosecuting under a law I believed to be no good." Between 1890 and 1900 the federal government prosecuted only eighteen cases under the act. The most successful of these were aimed at railroads directly involved in interstate commerce. Ironically, the Sherman Act did serve government officials as a tool for breaking up labor unions: courts that did not consider monopolistic production a restraint of trade willingly applied antitrust provisions to union strikes that affected trade.

The antimonopoly spirit did not die—in fact, "trustbusting" accelerated between 1900 and the First World War. But the problems of enforcing the Sherman Act reflected the uneven distribution of power among American interest groups. Corporate enterprises had been the first to consolidate, and they controlled great resources of economic and political power. Other groups—farmers, laborers, intellectuals, humanitarians—had numbers and ideas but lacked power. Almost all members of these groups desired the material gains that technology and large-scale production and organization were providing, but they increasingly feared that business was acquiring too much influence. How to rebalance society became the pressing dilemma of industrialism.

MECHANIZATION AND THE CHANGING STATUS OF LABOR

By 1880, when almost 5 million Americans worked in manufacturing, construction, and transportation, the status of labor had shifted dramatically from what it had been a generation earlier when there were only 1.5 million workers in these industries. Most workers could no longer accurately be termed producers—as craftsmen and farmers had traditionally considered themselves. The enlarged working class now consisted mainly of employees—people who worked only when someone else hired them, not when or how they pleased. Whereas producers were paid by consumers according to the quality of what they produced, employees were paid wages based on time spent on the job.

As mass production subdivided manufacturing into minute tasks, workers spent their time repeating one specialized operation. One investigator who looked into the effects of specialization on a typical laborer found that

> he became a mere machine. . . . Take the proposition of a man operating a machine to nail on 40 to 60 cases of heels in a day. That is 2,400 pairs, 4,800 shoes in a day. One not accustomed to it would wonder how a man could pick up and lay down 4,800 shoes in a day, to say nothing of putting them . . . into a machine. . . . That is the driving method of the manufacture of shoes under these minute subdivisions.

No longer was it up to the worker to decide when to begin and end the work day, when to rest, and what tools and techniques to use. Especially as assembly-line production spread, employees lost their sense of independence. As a Massachusetts factory worker complained in 1879, "During working hours the men are not allowed to speak to each other, though working close together, on pain of instant discharge. Men are hired to watch and patrol the shop." And workers were now surrounded by others who, like themselves, worked at the same rate for the same pay, regardless of the quality of their work.

The men and women affected by these changes did not accept them passively. Workers reacted to industrialization by struggling to retain their independence and self-respect in the face of employers' ever-increasing power. As new groups of people encountered the industrial system, they resisted in various ways. Artisans such as cigar makers, glass workers, and coopers, caught in the transition from hand labor to machine production, fought to preserve the pace and quality of their efforts and held on to such customs as appointing a fellow worker to read aloud while they worked. When immigrants went to work in factories, they often succeeded in getting their relatives and friends hired, thus maintaining on-the-job family and village ties they had always known. Off the job, workers continued to get together for traditional leisure-time activities like social drinking and holiday celebrations.

Employers in turn took steps to establish standards that they thought would enhance efficiency and productivity. In order to make workers docile (like machines), they supported temperance and moral reform societies, dedicated to combating supposed drinking

Even as work became more routinized, workers held onto traditional customs. In this photograph a cigar maker reads the newspaper to his fellow workers, according to tradition. International Museum of Photography, George Eastman House.

and debauchery on and off the job. Managers at Ford Motors required workers to meet the company's behavior code before they could earn the profit-sharing segment of the Five-Dollar-Day plan. Other employers established piece rates, paying workers only for the number of items they produced, to encourage maximum use of new machines. And they lowered wages, forcing people to work harder and longer just to maintain the same income.

As machines and assembly-line production reduced the need for skilled workers, employers cut wage costs by hiring more women and children. Between 1880 and 1900, the numbers of employed women grew from 2.6 million to 8.6 million, and their employment patterns underwent major changes (see figure, page 496). First, the proportion of working women engaged in domestic and personal service jobs

Employment of Women

(maids, cooks, laundresses), traditionally the most common form of female employment, dropped dramatically as jobs opened in other economic sectors. Some new jobs were in manufacturing—usually menial positions in textile mills and food-processing plants that paid women as little as $1.56 a week for seventy hours of labor. But though the number of female factory hands tripled, the proportion of women workers in these jobs remained about the same.

Second and more important, a major shift was occurring that set the trend among female workers for much of the twentieth century. The numbers and percentages of women in clerical jobs—clerks, typists, bookkeepers, salespersons—skyrocketed. These workers served the new needs of retail marketing and corporate record-keeping. From the late nineteenth century onward, the invention of numerous machines, such as the typewriter, cash register, adding machine, and

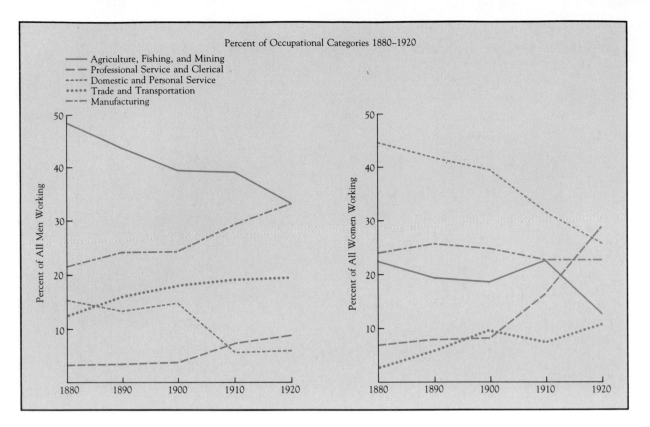

Percent of Occupational Categories, 1880–1920.
Source: U.S. Bureau of the Census, Census of the
United States, 1880, 1890, 1900, 1910, 1920
(Washington: U.S. Government Printing Office).

others, greatly simplified office and sales work. Firms could now increase efficiency by hiring more clerks to operate machines and to replace more expensive managers. An official of a sugar company observed in 1919 that "all the bookkeeping of this company . . . is done by three girls and three bookkeeping machines . . . one operator takes the place of three men."

By 1920 nearly half of all clerical workers were women; only 4 percent had been women in 1880. Analysts often explain the transformation of the clerical sector by asserting that women would work for lower wages than men would and that women's nimble fingers and toleration of boring work suited them for office and sales-floor labor. A more likely explanation, however, is that machines reduced the skills needed for clerical jobs, and companies were willing to hire large numbers of women streaming into the labor market who needed little training for these jobs.

Elementary and high schools were providing basic education in reading and writing and often included courses in typing and shorthand. Thus employers could pay low wages to female workers and not have to invest much in training them, while reserving their resources to train men for higher positions. Sex discrimination characterized the clerical sector, yet the new jobs opened employment opportunities for women.

Although most working children toiled on their parents' farms, the number in nonagricultural occupations tripled between 1870 and 1900. In 1900,

**Employment
of Children**
13 percent of all textile workers were below age sixteen. In other industries too, mechanization created a number of light unskilled tasks (such as running errands and helping machine operators) that children could handle at a fraction of adult wages. Many parents lied about their children's ages to help

Chapter 17: THE MACHINE AGE, 1877–1920

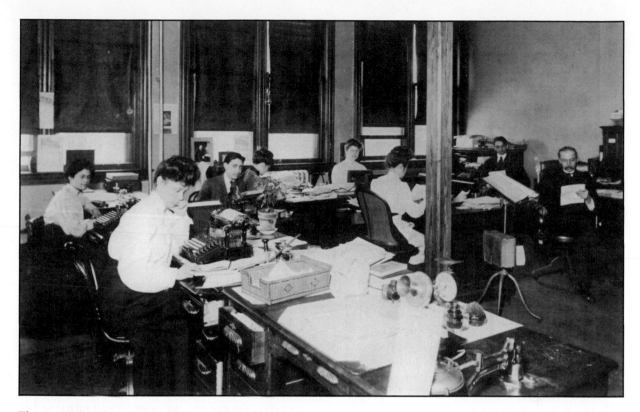

The rise of clerical occupations was one of the most important developments in employment for women at the beginning of the twentieth century. Female typists like these in the Bureau of Chemistry found increasing job opportunities in expanding corporations and bureaucracies. Library of Congress.

them get jobs to supplement the family income. By 1900, child labor laws and further automation had reduced the number of children working in manufacturing, but many more worked in street trades—shining shoes and peddling newspapers—and as helpers in stores.

While working conditions loomed as the major issue laborers had to face, the problem of wages was often the immediate catalyst of worker unrest. Many employers believed in the "iron law of wages," which dictated that employees be paid according to the conditions of supply and demand. Ideally, this principle meant that workers would receive the highest possible wages that would not drive the employer out of business. But in reality it meant that employers did not have to raise wages—and could even lower them—as long as there were people who would accept low pay. Employers justified the system with references to individual freedom: a worker who did not like the

wages being paid was free to quit and find a job elsewhere. Courts reinforced the principle, denying workers the right to bargain collectively and instead saying that whatever wages an employee received should be the result of an individual bargain between employee and employer. Wage earners saw things differently. They believed the wage system trapped and exploited them. As one Massachusetts worker testified in 1879, "The market is glutted, and we have seasons of dullness; advantage is taken of men's wants, and the pay is cut down; our tasks are increased, and if we remonstrate, we are told our places can be filled. I work harder now than when my pay was twice as high."

Moreover, even steady employment was insecure. Repetitive tasks using high-speed machinery dulled workers' concentration, and the slightest mistake could cause serious injury. Industrial accidents rose steadily before 1920, killing or maiming hundreds of thousands

Industrial Accidents of people each year. Even as late as 1913, after factory owners had installed some safety devices, some 25,000 people died in industrial mishaps, and close to 1 million were injured. Each year several sensational disasters, such as explosions, mine cave-ins, and fires, aroused public clamor for better safety regulations. The most notorious of these tragedies was the fire at New York City's Triangle Shirtwaist Company in 1911, which killed 146 workers, most of them women. Equally tragic, however, were the countless accidents that resulted in mangled limbs, infected cuts, chronic illness, and death. A railroad coupler described his own accident in 1888:

> It was four or five months before I "got it." I was making a coupling one afternoon. . . . Just before the two cars were come together, the one behind me left the track. . . . Hearing the racket, I sprang to one side, but my toe caught the top of the rail. I was pinned between the corners of the cars as they came together. I heard my ribs cave in like an old box smashed with an ax.

Families stricken by such accidents suffered acutely, because disability insurance and pensions were almost nonexistent. Nineteenth-century laissez-faire attitudes prevented protective legislation for workers, and employers would not take responsibility for employees' well-being. As one railroad manager told his workers, "The regular compensation of employees covers all risk or liability to accident. If an employee is disabled by sickness or any other cause, the right to claim compensation is not recognized." The only recourse for a stricken family was to sue and prove in court that the killed or injured worker did not realize the risks involved in the job and had not caused the accident.

Reformers in several states passed laws to ease working conditions, but the Supreme Court limited their impact by making narrow interpretations of what jobs were dangerous and which **Courts Restrict Labor Reform** workers needed protection. Initially, in *Holden* v. *Hardy* (1896), the Court decided to uphold a law regulating the working hours of miners because their work was so dangerous that overly long hours would increase the threat of injury. In *Lochner* v. *New York* (1905), however, the Court struck down a law limiting bakery workers to a sixty-hour week and a ten-hour day. In response to the argument that a state had authority to protect workers' health and safety, the Court ruled that baking was not a dangerous enough occupation for the legislature to restrict the right of workers to sell their labor freely. According to the Court, interference with the right of individuals to make contracts for their labor would violate the Fourteenth Amendment's guarantee that no state could "deprive any person of life, liberty, or property without due process of law."

Then, in *Muller* v. *Oregon* (1908), the Court resorted to a different rationale to uphold a law limiting working hours for women to ten a day. In this case, heralded by liberals as a progressive decision, the Court set aside its *Lochner* argument. Labor legislation for women was necessary, the Court asserted, because a woman's health "becomes an object of public interest and care in order to preserve the strength and vigor of the race." As a result, women were barred from many occupations, such as printing and transportation, which required long or nighttime hours, and they thus were confined to the same menial jobs they had always held.

Throughout the nineteenth century, tensions rose and fell as workers confronted mechanization. Adjustments were made in different ways as different groups—rural migrants, foreign immigrants, women, and children—entered the industrial labor force. Some people bent to the demands of the factory, the machine, and the time clock. Some tried to blend old ways of working into the new system. Some never adjusted and wandered from place to place, from job to job. Others, however, turned to organized resistance.

In many ways, the year 1877 was a historical watershed. In July of that year, a series of strikes broke out among railroad workers who were protesting wage **Strikes of 1877** cuts. Violence spread across Pennsylvania and Ohio all the way to Chicago and St. Louis. Venting their anger against corporations rather than against individual employers, rioters attacked railroad property, derailing trains and burning rail yards. Militia companies organized by employers broke up picket lines and fired into threatening crowds. In several areas, factory workers, wives, and even local merchants aided the strikers, while railroads enlisted strikebreakers to replace union men. The

Strikebreaking train operators being dragged from their work in Pittsburgh during the 1877 railroad strikes. Strikers did extensive damage to railroad cars and equipment throughout the country. Library of Congress.

worst violence occurred in Pittsburgh, where on July 21 troops bayoneted and then fired on a crowd of demonstrators, killing ten and wounding many more. Infuriated, the mob drove the soldiers into a railroad roundhouse and set a fire that destroyed 39 buildings, 104 engines, and 1,245 freight and passenger cars. The next day, the troops shot their way out of the roundhouse and killed twenty more citizens before fleeing the city.

After more than a month of unprecedented carnage that reached from Maryland to Illinois, Texas, and California, President Rutherford B. Hayes sent federal troops to restore order and end the strikes. His action marked the first significant use of troops to quell labor unrest.

The immediate cause of these strikes was the squeeze of depression. In the economic slump that followed the Panic of 1873, railroad managers had cut wages, increased workloads, and laid off workers, especially those who had joined a union. Such actions drove workers to strike and riot. Laborers in other industries who suffered the same conditions sympathized with

the strikers, as did other members of their communities. A Pittsburgh militiaman, ordered out to break the 1877 strike by his fellow townsmen, recalled, "I talked to all the strikers I could get my hands on, and I could find but one spirit and one purpose among them—that they were justified in resorting to any means to break down the power of the corporations."

THE UNION MOVEMENT

Anxiety over their loss of independence drove some workers to unionize in protection of their interests. The union movement had precedents but few successes. Craft unions, composed of skilled workers in a particular trade, dated from the early nineteenth century, but their emphasis on exclusive membership left them without broad power. The National Labor Union, which flourished briefly after its founding in 1866, grew to 650,000 members but died during the depression of the 1870s. The only broad-based labor organization to survive that depression was the Knights of Labor. Founded in 1860 by Philadelphia garment cutters, the Knights opened their doors to other workers during the 1870s. In 1879, when the union still had fewer than 10,000 members, it elected Terence V. Powderly, a Catholic machinist, as grand master. Under Powderly's guidance, Knights membership mushroomed, peaking at 730,000 in 1886.

Arising at a time when the factory system was not yet firmly established, the Knights of Labor tried to avert the bleak future that they believed industrialism portended by building an alliance among all workers. Thus the organization recruited women, blacks, immigrants, and unskilled and semiskilled workers, who were excluded from craft unions. Like the farmers' alliances, with which they felt kinship, the Knights believed that all workers could stand together against the forces of monopoly—corporations, banks, and railroads—to create a more harmonious society. The goal, argued Powderly, was to "eventually make every man his own master—every man his own employer. . . . There is no good reason why labor cannot, through cooperation, own and operate mines, factories, and railroads."

Knights of Labor

Technological and economic changes were making it impossible for each worker to be his or her own employer. But like many farmers, the Knights saw producer and consumer cooperatives as preferable alternatives to the forces of greed that surrounded them. They agreed with Edward Bellamy that a society in which all groups lived cooperatively was possible. This view was the source of the organization's strength and of its weakness. The cooperative idea, while attractive in the abstract, did not give laborers much bargaining power with employers. It was simply too vague a concept, and employers held most of the economic leverage. Strikes were a means of seeking immediate goals, but Powderly and other leaders were uncertain: would strikes, which could become violent, help or hinder the long-range goal of peace and cooperation? As strikes began to fail in 1886, as Powderly began to denounce radicalism and violence, and as the more militant craft unions broke away, Knights membership dwindled. The union survived only in a few small towns, where a brief attempt was made to unite with the Populists in the 1890s. The special interests of craft unions overcame the Knights' general appeal, and dreams of labor unity faded.

As the depression of the 1870s subsided and better conditions returned in the early 1880s, a number of labor groups, including the Knights of Labor, began to campaign for an eight-hour workday. This effort by workers to regain control of their work gathered most momentum in Chicago, where radical anarchists as well as various craft unions—perhaps as many as 100,000 workers in all—agitated for the cause. On May 1, 1886, the workers' deadline for achieving their goal, city police were mobilized to prevent possible disorder, especially among striking workers at the huge McCormick reaper factory. The day passed calmly, but two days later police stormed an area near the McCormick plant and broke up a battle between striking unionists and nonunion workers hired as strikebreakers. Police shot and killed two unionists and wounded several others. The next evening, labor groups organized a rally at Haymarket Square, near downtown Chicago, to protest police brutality. As a company of police officers approached the meeting, a bomb exploded near their front ranks, killing seven and injuring sixty-seven. Mass arrests of anarchists and unionists followed. Eventually eight men, all anarchists, were tried and convicted of the bombing, though there was no evidence of their guilt. Four were executed and one committed suicide in prison. The remaining three were pardoned in 1893 by Illinois governor John P. Altgeld, who believed they had been victims of the "malicious ferocity" of the courts.

Haymarket Riot

The Haymarket bombing drew public attention to labor campaigns for better conditions but also revived middle-class fear of radicalism. The fact that strikes had erupted all over the country in 1886, not just in Chicago, and that anarchists and socialists, many of them foreign-born, had participated in some of the agitation, created a sense of crisis, a feeling that forces of law and order had to act swiftly to prevent social turmoil. To protect their city, private Chicago donors helped to establish Fort Sheridan and the Great Lakes Naval Training Station. Elsewhere police forces and armories were strengthened. And employer associations multiplied. These associations of man-

Chapter 17: THE MACHINE AGE, 1877–1920

The Haymarket riot, Chicago, 1886. A bomb explodes among a police brigade trying to break up the labor demonstration. In retaliation, police fired into the crowd of strikers, killing seven men. The caption for the drawing, which appeared in Harper's Weekly, *falsely identified the incident as an "anarchist riot."* Bettmann Archive.

ufacturers in the same industry worked to counter labor militancy by agreeing to resist strikes and by purchasing strike insurance.

The newly formed American Federation of Labor was the major workers' organization to emerge after the 1886 upheavals. A combination of national craft unions, the AFL initially had about 140,000 members, most of whom were skilled native workers. As a federation, it allowed member unions independence in their own areas of interest, but tried to develop a general policy that would suit the self-interest of all members. Led by Samuel Gompers, the pragmatic and opportunistic head of the Cigar Makers' Union, AFL unions avoided

American Federation of Labor

the idealistic rhetoric of worker solidarity (they excluded unskilled industrial workers) to press for specific goals, such as higher wages, shorter hours, and the right to bargain collectively. As Gompers's associate Adolph Strasser explained, "We have no ultimate ends. We are going from day to day. We are fighting only for immediate objects—objects that can be realized in a few years." Thus the AFL, in contrast to the Knights of Labor, accepted industrialism and worked to achieve better conditions within the wage-and-hours system.

Under Gompers the AFL grew to over 1 million members by 1901 and 2.5 million by 1917, when it included 111 national unions and 27,000 local unions. The national organization required all constituent unions to hire organizers to expand membership, and it collected dues for a fund to aid members on strike. The AFL generally refrained from political activity, though it occasionally supported prolabor candidates and prolabor party platforms.

The AFL and the labor movement in general staggered in the early 1890s, when once again labor violence evoked public fears. In July 1892, Henry C. Frick, the stubborn president of the Carnegie Steel Company, closed the company plant in Homestead, Pennsylvania, when the AFL-affiliated Amalgamated Association of Iron and Steelworkers refused to accept pay cuts and went on strike. Shortly thereafter, angry workers attacked and routed three hundred Pinkerton guards hired by Frick to protect the plant. State militia were called in, and after five months the strikers gave in. By then public opinion was against the strike because a young anarchist—who was not a striker—tried to assassinate Frick.

In 1894, workers at the Pullman Palace Car Company walked out in protest over exploitative policies at the company town near Chicago. The paternalistic

Pullman Strike
company head George Pullman tried to do everything for the twelve thousand residents of his so-called model town. His company owned and controlled all land and buildings, the school, the bank, and the water and gas systems. It paid workers' wages, fixed their rents, and employed spies to report on disgruntled workers. One laborer grumbled, "We are born in a Pullman house, fed from the Pullman shop, taught in the Pullman school, catechized in the Pullman church, and when we die we shall be buried in the Pullman cemetery and go to the Pullman hell."

One thing Pullman would not do was negotiate with workers. When the depression that began in 1893 threatened his business, Pullman managed to maintain profits and pay dividends to stockholders by cutting wages 25 to 40 percent but holding firm on rents and prices in the model town. Workers, squeezed into debt and deprivation, sent a committee to Pullman in May 1894 to protest his policies. Pullman reacted by firing three of the committee. The enraged workers, most of whom had joined the American Railway Union, called a strike. Pullman retaliated by shutting down the plant. When the American Railway Union, led by the charismatic young organizer Eugene V. Debs, voted to aid the strikers by boycotting

all Pullman cars, Pullman stood firm and rejected arbitration. The railroad owners' association then enlisted the aid of U.S. Attorney General Richard Olney, who obtained a court injunction to prevent the union from "obstructing the railways and holding up the mails." President Grover Cleveland sent federal troops to Chicago, supposedly to protect the mails but in reality to crush the strike. Within a month the strike was over, and Debs was jailed for six months for contempt of court in defying the injunction. The Supreme Court upheld Debs's sentence on the grounds that the federal government had the power to remove obstacles to interstate commerce.

After the turn of the century, a number of battles occurred between workers and employers in the mining industry. The fledgling United Mine Workers led several strikes in the coal fields of Pennsylvania, Colorado, and West Virginia between 1902 and 1922. Out of the western mining struggles emerged the Industrial Workers of the World (IWW), a radical labor organization, founded in 1905, that fused the Knights of Labor vision of worker solidarity with the tactics of strikes and sabotage. In contrast with the AFL, the IWW hoped to organize workers along industrial, not craft, lines. Using the rhetoric of class conflict—"The final aim is revolution," according to an IWW organizer—the "Wobblies," as they were called, believed that workers should organize and seize the nation's industries and run them without interference from industrialists or politicians. Because of their anticapitalist goals and threatening tactics, the Wobblies attracted considerable attention in spite of their small numbers, and their activities influenced debates on labor reform during the Progressive era (see Chapter 21).

It must be emphasized that during the half-century following the Civil War, only a small fraction of American workers belonged to unions. In 1900 only about 1 million out of a total of 27.6 million workers were unionized. In 1920, total union membership had grown to 5 million—still only 13 percent of the work force. Unionization was strong among workers in the building trades, transportation, communications, and to a lesser extent manufacturing. But organizers took no interest in large segments of the industrial labor force and intentionally excluded others.

Many unions, such as those of the AFL, were openly hostile toward women. Of the 6.3 million

In 1909, thousands of shirtwaist workers in New York, most of whom were women, went on strike and later formed the International Ladies Garment Workers Union. Here, their strike meeting is addressed by Samuel Gompers of the AFL. Brown Brothers.

Women and the Labor Movement

employed women in 1910, only 125,000 were in unions. Male unionists often explained the exclusion of women by saying that women should not be employed. According to one labor leader, "I believe that woman is not qualified for the conditions of wage labor. . . . The mental and physical makeup of woman is in revolt against wage service. She is competing with the man who is her father or husband or is to become her husband." Fear of competition was crucial. Because women were paid less than men, males feared that their own wages would be lowered if women joined them in the workplace. Moreover, men feared that entry of women would transform many jobs from all-male to all-female ones, just as clerical jobs were changing. Male workers, accustomed to sex segregation in employment, could not recognize or accept the possibility of men and women working side by side. Yet female employees could organize and fight employers as bitterly as men could.

Since the early years of industrialization, female workers had organized their own unions; some, such as the Collar Laundry Union of Troy, New York, organized in the 1860s, had been successful in carrying out strikes and achieving higher wages. The first broad-based women's union was the Women's Trade Union League (WTUL), founded in 1903 and patterned after a similar union in England. The WTUL worked for protective legislation for women workers, sponsored educational activities, and joined the cause for women's suffrage. In 1909 it joined with the International Ladies Garment Workers Union in support of a massive strike against New York City sweatshops. Although the WTUL had some forceful working-class leaders—notably Agnes Nestor, a glove maker, Rose Schneiderman, a cap maker, and Mary Anderson, a shoe worker—it was dominated by middle-class women who had humane but generally non-militant purposes in helping working women. In the early 1920s, the WTUL fought a constitutional amendment guaranteeing equal rights to women, arguing that women needed protection from exploitation more than they needed equality. Such reasoning fit the assertion of males who argued that women belonged in their own sphere at home, out of the work force and out of unions. As the WTUL gradually backed away from active union organization, it lost the support of working-class women, and by 1930 it had virtually dissolved.

Organized labor also excluded most immigrant and black workers. Some trade unions welcomed skilled immigrants—in fact, foreign-born craftsmen were prominent leaders of several unions—but only the Knights of Labor and the IWW had firm policies of accepting immigrants and blacks. A few AFL unions included blacks, but the vast majority had exclusion policies. Resentments already fueled by long-held prejudices increased when blacks and immigrants worked as strikebreakers. It is likely that few strikebreakers understood the full effects of such employment when they were recruited to fill the jobs of striking workers; but even for those who did, the lure of employment was too great to resist.

Immigrants, Blacks, and the Labor Movement

The millions of men, women, and children who were not unionized tried in their own ways to cope with the pressures of the new machine age. Increasing numbers of workers, both native-born and immigrants, turned to fraternal societies. These organizations, which for small monthly or yearly contributions provided members with life insurance, sickness benefits, and funeral expenses, became widespread by the early twentieth century. For many workers, issues of wages and hours were meaningless; getting and holding a job was the first priority. Job instability and the seasonal nature of work seriously hindered organizing efforts. Few companies employed a full work force all year round; most employers hired during peak seasons and laid off workers during slack periods. Thus employment rates often fluctuated wildly. The 1880 census showed that in some communities 30 percent or more of adult males had been unemployed at some time during the previous year.

For most American workers, then, the machine age had mixed results. Industrial wages rose between 1877 and 1914, boosting purchasing power and enabling the creation of a mass market for standardized goods (see Chapter 19). Yet in 1900 most employees worked sixty hours a week at wages that averaged 20 cents an hour for skilled work and 10 cents an hour for unskilled work. Moreover, as wages rose, living costs increased even faster. The industrial

---

IMPORTANT EVENTS

1873–78	Depression
1877	Widespread railroad strikes
1879	Henry George, *Progress and Poverty* Edison perfects the incandescent light bulb
1882	Formation of Standard Oil trust
1884–85	Depression
1886	Haymarket riot American Federation of Labor founded
1888	Edward Bellamy. *Looking Backward*
1890	Sherman Anti-Trust Act
1892	Homestead Steel strike
1893–97	Depression
1894	Pullman strike Henry Demarest Lloyd, *Wealth Against Commonwealth*
1901	United States Steel Corporation founded
1902	Reorganization of E. I. du Pont de Nemours and Company
1903	Ford Motor Company founded
1905	*Lochner* v. *New York*
1908	*Muller* v. *Oregon*
1913	First moving assembly line begins operation at Ford

---

transformation had thrust the United States into international leadership in economic capability. But in factories as well as on farms, some people were beginning to question whether a system based on ever-greater profits was the best way for Americans to create a world of peace and prosperity.

SUGGESTIONS FOR FURTHER READING

General

Daniel J. Boorstin, *The Americans: The Democratic Experience* (1973); Thomas C. Cochran and William Miller, *The Age of Enterprise* (1942); Carl N. Degler, *The Age of the Economic Revolution* (1977); Sigmund Diamond, ed., *The Nation Transformed* (1963); Ray Ginger, *The Age of Excess* (1965); Samuel P. Hays, *The Response to Industrialism* (1975).

Technology and Invention

Robert W. Bruce, *Bell: Alexander Graham Bell and the Conquest of Solitude* (1973); Roger Burlingame, *Henry Ford* (1957); George H. Daniels, *Science and Society in America* (1971); Sigfried Giedion, *Mechanization Takes Command* (1948); Matthew Josephson, *Edison* (1959); Leo Marx, *The Machine in the Garden: Technology and the Pastoral Ideal* (1964); Elting E. Morison, *Men, Machines, and Modern Times* (1966); Allan Nevins and Frank E. Hill, *Ford*, 3 vols. (1954–1962); Nathan Rosenberg, *Technology and American Economic Growth* (1972); Harold I. Sharlin, *The Making of the Electrical Age* (1963); Peter Temin, *Steel in Nineteenth Century America* (1964); Frederick A. White, *American Industrial Research Laboratories* (1961).

Industrialism, Industrialists, and Corporate Growth

W. Elliot Brownlee, *Dynamics of Ascent: A History of the American Economy*, 2nd ed. (1979); Stuart Bruchey, *Growth of the Modern Economy* (1973); Alfred D. Chandler, *The Visible Hand: The Managerial Revolution in American Business* (1977); Alfred D. Chandler, *Pierre S. du Pont and the Making of the Modern Corporation* (1971); Alfred D. Chandler, *Strategy and Structure: Chapters in the History of American Industrial Enterprise* (1966); Thomas C. Cochran, *Business in American Life* (1972); Francis L. Eames, *The New York Stock Exchange* (1968); Rendigs Fels, *American Business Cycles, 1865–1897* (1959); David F. Hawkes, *John D.: The Founding Father of the Rockefellers* (1980); Robert Higgs, *The Transformation of the American Economy, 1865–1914* (1971); Matthew Josephson, *The Robber Barons* (1934); Edward C. Kirkland, *Industry Comes of Age* (1961); Harold C. Livesay, *Andrew Carnegie and the Rise of Big Business* (1975); Daniel Nelson, *Managers and Workers: Origins of the New Factory System in the United States, 1880–1920* (1975); Allan Nevins, *Study in Power: John D. Rockefeller*, 2 vols. (1953); Glenn Porter, *The Rise of Big Business* (1973); Joseph Wall, *Andrew Carnegie* (1970).

Attitudes Toward Industrialism

Edward Bellamy, *Looking Backward* (1888); Sidney Fine, *Laissez Faire and the General Welfare State* (1956); Louis Galambos and Barbara Barron Spence, *The Public Image of Big Business in America* (1975); Henry George, *Progress and Poverty* (1879); Richard Hofstadter, *Social Darwinism in American Thought*, rev. ed. (1955); T. Jackson Lears, *No Place of Grace: Antimodernism and the Transformation of American Culture* (1981); Henry Demarest Lloyd, *Wealth Against Commonwealth* (1894); Robert McCloskey, *American Conservatism in the Age of Enterprise* (1951); John L. Thomas, *Alternative America: Henry George, Edward Bellamy, Henry Demarest Lloyd and the Adversary Tradition* (1983).

Work and Labor Organization

Stanley Buder, *Pullman* (1967); Alan Dawley, *Class and Community* (1977); Melvyn Dubofsky, *Industrialism and the American Worker* (1975); Melvyn Dubofsky, *We Shall Be All: A History of the Industrial Workers of the World* (1969); Leon Fink, *Workingmen's Democracy: The Knights of Labor and American Politics* (1982); Philip S. Foner, *The Great Labor Uprising of 1877* (1977); Herbert G. Gutman, *Work, Culture and Society in Industrializing America* (1976); Tamara K. Hareven, *Family Time and Industrial Time: The Relationship Between the Family and Work in a New England Industrial Community* (1982); Stuart Bruce Kaufman, *Samuel Gompers and the Origins of the American Federation of Labor* (1973); Alice Kessler-Harris, *Out to Work: A History of Wage-Earning Women in the United States* (1982); Susan Levine, *Labor's True Women: Carpet Weavers, Industrialization, and Labor Reform in the Gilded Age* (1984); Harold Livesay, *Samuel Gompers and Organized Labor in America* (1978); Milton Meltzer, *Bread and Roses: The Struggle of American Labor, 1865–1915* (1967); Stephen Meyer III, *The Five Dollar Day: Labor Management and Social Control in the Ford Motor Company, 1908–1921* (1981); David Montgomery, *Workers' Control in America: Studies in the History of Work, Technology, and Labor Struggles* (1979); Philip Taft, *Organized Labor in America* (1964); Daniel J. Walkowitz, *Worker City, Company Town* (1978); Barbara Mayer Wertheimer, *We Were There: The Story of Working Women in America* (1977); Leon J. Wolff, *Lockout: The Story of the Homestead Strike of 1892* (1965); Irwin Yellowitz, *Industrialization and the American Labor Movement* (1977).

THE FAME AND SHAME OF THE CITIES

1877–1920

CHAPTER 18

For nearly thirty years, Frank Ventrone had successfully pursued his dream until one night his world literally shattered. In the 1880s, Ventrone had emigrated from Isernia, a town in southern Italy, to Providence, Rhode Island, a bustling city in industrializing America. By saving money and buying property, Ventrone became a prominent businessman in the city's fast-growing Italian immigrant community, many of whose residents had also come from Isernia. Ventrone's biggest success was a pasta business that furnished the community's staple food. But this business was also the source of his trouble.

In the summer of 1914, food prices were rising, and Ventrone followed the trend by increasing the price of his pasta. Angered by the threat to their already overburdened incomes, people of Providence's Italian section vented their frustration against Ventrone. On a warm August weekend, they marched through the neighborhood, broke windows in a block of property owned by Ventrone, entered his business establishment, and dumped his stock of macaroni into the street. When police arrived to quell the disturbance, rioters resisted with catcalls and violence, insisting that the matter was an internal one to be resolved by the community. The next Monday, Ventrone's agent met with community members and agreed to lower his prices. Ventrone had overstepped the bounds of ethnic loyalty and had suffered as a result. "Signor Ventrone . . . owes everything to our colony," declared the neighborhood newspaper. "Our brave colony, when we all stand together, will be given justice."

The Providence "macaroni riot," with its various dimensions—the transfer of immigrant cultures from Old World to New; the mobility of some people from rags to respectability; the continued poverty of others amid economic uncertainty; the eruption of violence—was just one of millions of events that came to characterize city life in America. To be sure, a similar protest might have occurred in Italy, but the American context amplified the event's characteristics. By 1900, Providence was a rapidly growing city, and the United States was the most rapidly urbanizing nation in the western world. The hopes, frustrations, and conflicts that urban growth generated seemed both dazzling and bewildering. In 1914, the same year as the macaroni riot, a student in St. Paul, Minnesota, wrote in her diary: "There is much beauty in a city. Buildings and streets and multitudes of people, and big buildings being built, people building them, smoke, lights dripping and popping out all over; sadness, sordidness, joy, love, pain, badness, goodness all being *swept along together.*" Clanging trolleys, smoky air, crowded streets, a jumble of languages—these sensations and more contrasted with the slow, quiet pace of village and farm life. And as cities grew, they became places of both opportunity and misery.

In the middle third of the nineteenth century, the nation's urban population—those living in places with eight thousand or more people—started to grow much faster than its rural population (see pages 270–272). But not until the 1880s did the United States begin to become a truly urban nation. By 1920 the major milestone of urbanization had been passed: that year's census showed that, for the first time, a majority of Americans (51.4 percent) lived in cities. This new fact of national life was fully as significant as the disappearance of the frontier in 1890. The era of the yeoman farmer was over, and urban growth became the third major theme, along with natural resource development (Chapter 16) and industrialization (Chapter 17), of American expansion in the late nineteenth and early twentieth centuries.

The city became a dominant force by serving as a marketplace, which brought together people, resources, and ideas that were in turn responsible for many of the changes American society was experiencing. By 1900 a network of small, medium, and large cities spanned every section of the country. Only such industrializing states as Rhode Island and Massachusetts had been highly urbanized early in the nineteenth century, but other states' urban populations grew rapidly after the Civil War.

American cities attracted both exuberant admirers and sneering detractors. Some people relished the opportunities cities offered. As one editor wrote, it was "better [to] be the 1/1,000,000,000 of New York than the 1/1 of Aroostook County." Others found the crudeness of cities disquieting. "Having seen it," Rudyard Kipling wrote of Chicago, "I urgently desire never to see it again." But whatever people's personal impressions, the city had become basic to American life. To a large extent, modern American society has been shaped by the ways people built their cities and adjusted to the new urban environment.

THE BIRTH OF THE MODERN CITY

In March 1912, a party of street-railway officials boarded a private trolley car in downtown Boston. Traveling west to Worcester and Springfield in Massachusetts, then south to Hartford, New Britain, New Haven, Bridgeport, and Stamford in Connecticut, the car carried its passengers from one set of tracks to another. The 200-mile journey ended when the car rolled into New York City, having made the entire trip on a continuous route of streetcar—not railroad—tracks. With enough patience and enough nickels for $2.40 in fares and transfers, anyone could have made the same trip. The possibility of such a journey illustrates the extraordinary connection between mass transit and urban growth that occurred at the end of the nineteenth century.

By 1900, the modern American city was reaching maturity. The compact city of the early nineteenth century—where residences were mixed in among shops, factories, and warehouses—had burst open. From Boston to San Francisco, developed areas sprawled outward several miles from the original central core. No longer did walking distance determine a city's size, and no longer did different social groups live physically close together—poor near rich, immigrant near native, black near white. Instead, cities were divided into distinct districts: working-class neighborhoods, black ghettos, a ring of suburbs, business districts. Two forces were responsible for this

New Shape of the City

new arrangement. One was centrifugal, propelling people and enterprises outward from the confines of the old walking city. The other was centripetal, drawing human and economic resources inward. Mass transportation powered the centrifugal force; economic change, the centripetal.

Mass transportation enabled people to move faster and farther. Before the 1870s, horse- and mule-drawn vehicles had been the major means of transport. But they were inefficient. They could carry relatively few riders, and purchasing, feeding, and cleaning up after the animals was costly. In 1880, for example, the 150,000 horses in New York City and Booklyn produced between 1,000 and 1,500 tons of manure daily, about 1.5 pounds per human inhabitant. Though of a different nature than it is today, pollution was a fact of urban life in the nineteenth century too.

Once the technology was developed, entrepreneurs adopted better ways to transport people. Steam-powered commuter railroads had appeared in a few cities during the 1850s and 1860s, but not until the late 1870s did inventors begin to mechanize mass transit. The first power-driven devices were cable cars—carriages that traveled over tracks by clamping onto a moving underground wire. Cheaper than horse cars, cable cars could also haul passengers up and down steep hills. In the 1880s cable-car lines were constructed in Chicago, San Francisco, and many other cities.

Mechanization of Mass Transportation

By the 1890s, however, electric-powered streetcars were replacing the early forms of mass transit. Designed almost simultaneously by Charles J. Van Depele in Montgomery, Alabama, and Frank Sprague in Richmond, Virginia, electric trolleys spread quickly to nearly every large city. Between 1890 and 1902, total mileage of electrified track in American cities grew from 1,300 to 22,000 miles. Meanwhile horse-railway track shrank from 5,700 to 250 miles. "The long-haired mule shall no longer adorn our streets," mused one observer.

In a few cities, trolley companies raised part of their track onto stilts, enabling vehicles to travel through jammed downtown districts without interference from other traffic. And in Boston, New York, and Philadelphia, transit firms dug underground passages for their cars, also to avoid tie-ups and delays.

Sometimes the extension of mass transit preceded residential development. This trolley line in Oak Park, Illinois, a suburb of Chicago, was built in anticipation of the housing construction that eventually filled the lots on either side of the tracks. Photographed in 1903.   Oak Park Public Library.

Elevated railroads and subways were extremely expensive to construct. They thus appeared only in the few cities where companies could amass enough capital to build them and where there were enough riders to make for high profits.

Mass transit lines launched millions of urban dwellers into outlying neighborhoods and created a commuting public. Now those who could afford the fare—usually five cents a ride—could live outside the crowded, dirty central city and still return there for work, shopping, and entertainment. Working-class families, whose incomes rarely topped a dollar a day, found the fare too high and could not take advantage of the streetcars. But for the growing middle class, a home in a quiet, tree-lined neighborhood became a real possibility. Real estate development boomed around the periphery of scores of cities. Between 1890 and 1920, for example, developers in the Chicago area opened 800,000 new lots—enough to house at least three times the city's population in 1890. A

Beginnings of Urban Sprawl

home several miles from downtown was inconvenient, but the benefits seemed to outweigh the costs. As one suburbanite wrote in 1902, "It may be a little more difficult for us to attend the opera, but the robin in my elm tree struck a higher note and a sweeter one yesterday than any *prima donna* ever reached."

Urban sprawl was essentially unplanned. Eager to capitalize on new commuting possibilities, thousands of small investors who bought land in anticipation of settlement paid little attention to the need for parks, traffic control, and public services. Moreover, construction of mass transit was guided by the profit motive and thus served the urban public unevenly. Streetcar lines serviced mainly those neighborhoods that promised the most riders—whose fares, in other words, would provide dividends for stockholders.

Streetcars, elevateds, and subways altered commercial as well as residential patterns. As consumers moved outward, businesses followed. Secondary business centers sprouted at trolley-line intersections and elevated-railway stations. Branches of downtown department stores and banks joined groceries, theaters, drugstores, taverns, and specialty shops to create neighborhood shopping centers, the forerunners of today's shopping malls. Meanwhile, the urban core became the work zone, where offices, stores, warehouses, and factories hulked over streets clogged with traffic. Districts like Chicago's Loop and New York's lower Manhattan concentrated together practically every kind of business and cultural institution.

Cities also became the main arenas for industrial growth, generating and attracting concentrations of economic power. As centers of resources, labor, transportation, and communications, cities provided everything factories needed. Capital accumulated by the cities' commercial enterprises—gathering and distributing raw materials and finished goods—fed industrial investment once mass production became possible. And urban populations furnished consumers for myriad new products. Thus urban growth and industrialization wound together in a mutually beneficial spiral. The further industrialization advanced, the more opportunities it created for work and investment in cities. Increased opportunity drew more people to cities; as workers and as consumers, they in turn fueled further industrialization. By the end of the nineteenth century, urban firms were producing nine-tenths of America's industrial output.

Urban-Industrial Development

Although most cities contained a wide variety of industrial activities, specialization in a single product became common. Some cities used large numbers of workers in the mass production of clothing. The shoe industry became prominent in Philadelphia and Lynn, ready-made garments in New York City, and textiles in several New England cities. Other cities processed products from surrounding agricultural regions: flour in Minneapolis, cottonseed oil in Memphis, beer in Milwaukee. Still others processed natural resources: gold and copper in Denver, fish and lumber in Seattle, coal and iron in Pittsburgh and Birmingham, oil in Houston and Los Angeles. These and countless other activities increased the magnetic attraction of cities.

Urban and industrial growth transformed the national economy and freed the United States from dependence on European capital and manufactured goods. Imports and foreign investments still flowed

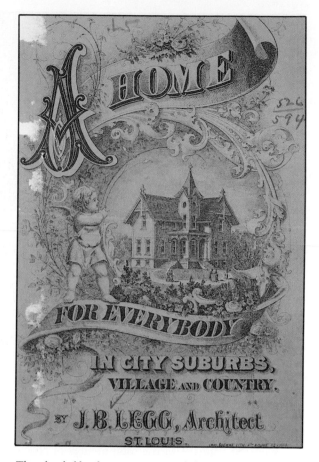

Though ads like this one exaggerated the romantic nature of living in the urban outskirts, a comfortable, detached single-family house surrounded by grass and trees became a realizable ideal in the late nineteenth century. Library of Congress.

into the country. But by the early 1900s, cities and their factories, stores, and banks were converting the United States from a debtor agricultural nation into a major industrial, financial, and exporting power.

PEOPLING THE CITIES: MIGRANTS AND IMMIGRANTS

Economist Edmund J. James had good reason to assert in 1899 that the era he was living in was "not only the age of cities but the age of great cities."

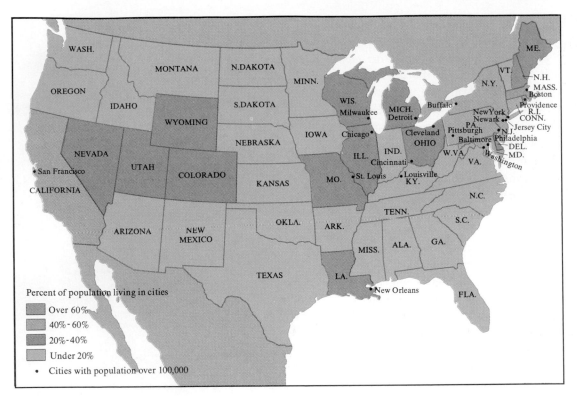

Urbanization, 1880

Between 1870 and 1920, the total number of people living in American cities exploded from 9.9 million to 54.3 million. During the same period, the number of cities with populations over 100,000 grew from fifteen to sixty-eight, and the number with more than 500,000 people swelled from two to twelve (see maps). These figures are dramatic enough by themselves, but they also represent millions of stories of hope and frustration, adjustment and confusion, success and failure.

The population of a given place can grow in three ways: by extension of its borders to include nearby land and people; by natural increase—an excess of births over deaths; and by migration—an excess of in-migrants over out-migrants. Between the Civil War and the early 1900s, many cities annexed nearby suburbs, thereby increasing their populations. The most notable consolidation occurred in 1898 when New York City, which had previously consisted only of Manhattan, merged with four surrounding boroughs and grew overnight from 1.5 million to over 3 million people. Everywhere the thirst for

How Cities Grew

expansion was insatiable. As one observer remarked, "Those who locate near the city limits are bound to know that the time may come when [the city] will extend the limits and take them in." Moreover, many suburbs desired annexation because they needed the services like water, fire protection, and sewer systems that cities had developed. Annexation also added vacant land where new city dwellers could live. Cities like Chicago, Minneapolis, and Cincinnati incorporated hundreds of undeveloped square miles into their borders in the 1880s, only to see them fill up in succeeding decades. Although annexation did increase urban populations, its major effect was to enlarge the physical size of cities.

As death rates declined in the late nineteenth century, the populations of most cities increased naturally. But urban birthrates also fell steadily throughout the nineteenth century. As a result, natural increase did not account for very much of any city's population growth.

Migration and immigration made by far the greatest contribution to urban population growth. In fact, migration to cities nearly matched the migration to

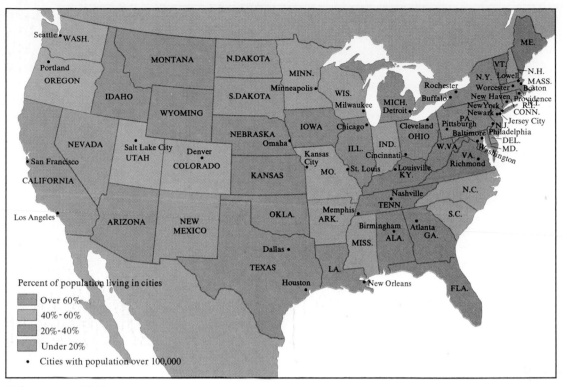

Urbanization, 1920

the West that was occurring at the same time. Each year millions of people were on the move, many of them lured by the cities' promise of opportunity. Urban newcomers arrived from two major sources: the American countryside and Europe. Asia, Canada, and Latin America also supplied immigrants, but in smaller numbers.

In all sections of the country, a variety of factors dashed farmers' hopes and drove them off the land and toward the cities. Rural populations of Vermont, New York, Ohio, Illinois, and other states declined during the 1880s as their urban populations mushroomed. Growth occurred not only in Cleveland, Detroit, and Chicago, but also in scores of secondary cities like Toledo, Indianapolis, Salt Lake City, Birmingham, and San Diego. The thrill and bustle of city life beckoned especially to young people. A character in George Fitch's play *The City* voiced the dreams of many youths when she exclaimed, "Who wants to smell new-mown hay, if he can breathe in gasoline on Fifth Avenue instead! Think of the theaters! the

Major Waves of Migration and Immigration

crowds! *Think* of being able to go out on the street and *see some one you didn't know by sight!*"

An even larger group of newcomers consisted of immigrants who had fled foreign farms and villages for American shores. Many did not intend to stay. They hoped instead to make enough money to return home and live in greater comfort and security. For every hundred foreigners who entered the country, around thirty left. Still, most of the 26 million immigrants who arrived between 1870 and 1920 stayed, and the great majority settled in cities, where they helped to shape modern American culture.

These immigrants were only part of a global movement. Population pressures and economic changes resulting from land reforms and industrialization induced millions to leave Europe and Asia for Canada, Australia, Brazil, Argentina, and other relatively unsettled places as well as the United States. Countless others migrated shorter distances, usually from a rural village or town to an industrial city. Migration always has been a key chapter in human history, but now the telegraph, railroad, and steamship made communications and travel cheaper, quicker, and safer.

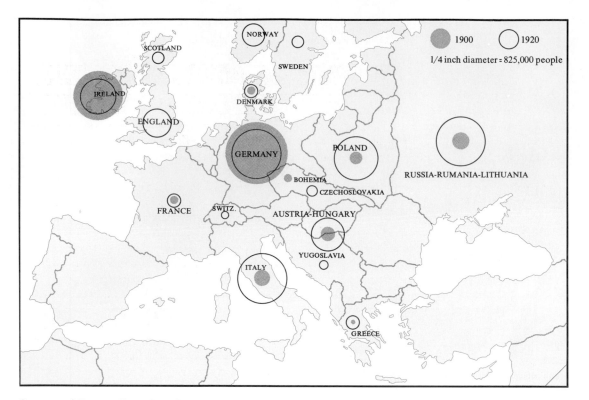

Sources of Foreign-Born Population, 1900 and 1920.

The United States had been the destination of immigrants from northern and western Europe since the 1840s (see pages 280–284), but after 1880 a second wave of mass immigration began from new sources. Though northern and western Europeans continued to arrive, the new wave contained mainly people from eastern and southern Europe, plus smaller contingents from Canada, Mexico, and Japan (see map and figure). For example, two-thirds of the immigrants who arrived in the 1880s were from Germany, England, Ireland, and Scandinavia; between 1900 and 1909, however, two-thirds were from Italy, Austria-Hungary, and Russia. By 1910 arrivals from Mexico were beginning to outnumber arrivals from Ireland; and large numbers of Japanese had moved to the West Coast and Hawaii (see Appendix).

Differences between the two waves of immigrants were in many ways more imagined than real. Many Americans feared that the strange customs, non-Protestant religions, illiteracy, and poverty of the "new" immigrants made them less desirable and as-similable than the "old" immigrants, whose languages and beliefs seemed less alien. This view received sober support from authorities like future president Woodrow Wilson, who wrote in his popular *History of the American People* (1902), "The immigrant new-comers of recent years are men of the lowest class from the South of Italy, and men of the meaner sort out of Hungary and Poland, men out of the ranks where there was neither skill nor energy, nor any initiative or quick intelligence."

In reality, however, the old and new immigrants resembled each other more closely than many Americans wished to believe. The majority of both groups were young—between fifteen and forty-four years old—and male. Both groups settled chiefly in cities, and both lived initially in old districts of the central city vacated by residents who had moved to new outlying neighborhoods.

Perhaps most important, all immigrants brought with them memories of their homelands and adjusted to American life in light of those memories. In new surroundings where the language was a struggle, the workday followed the clock rather than the sun, and

The New Immigration

Chapter 18: THE FAME AND SHAME OF THE CITIES, 1877–1920

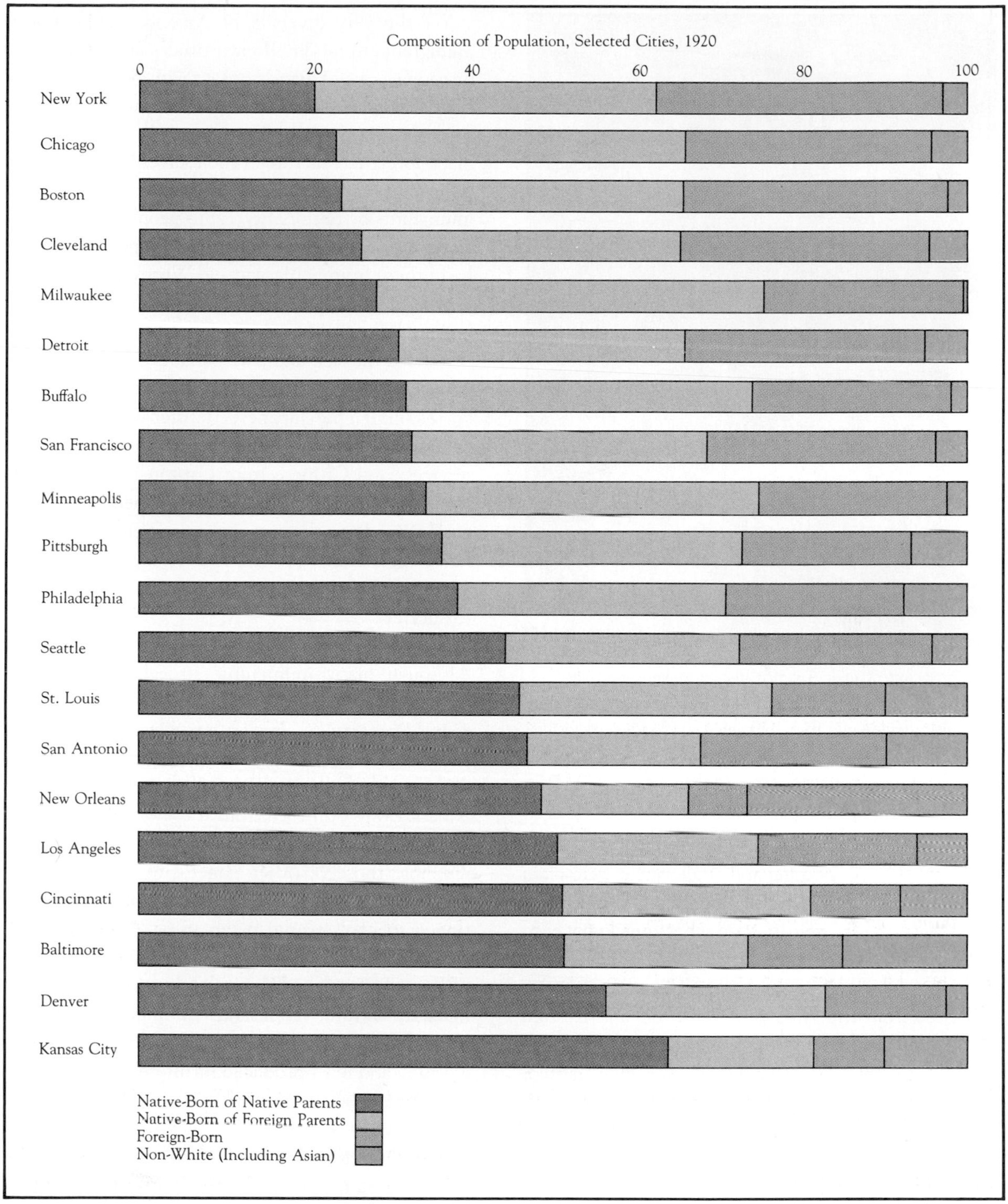

Composition of Population, Selected Cities, 1920

New York
Chicago
Boston
Cleveland
Milwaukee
Detroit
Buffalo
San Francisco
Minneapolis
Pittsburgh
Philadelphia
Seattle
St. Louis
San Antonio
New Orleans
Los Angeles
Cincinnati
Baltimore
Denver
Kansas City

Native-Born of Native Parents
Native-Born of Foreign Parents
Foreign-Born
Non-White (Including Asian)

Composition of Population, Selected Cities, 1920

The first contact with America that most immigrants had was on Ellis Island, just offshore of New York City. Here they were herded into pens, registered, and examined for disease. As this photograph shows, the experience was quite dehumanizing.   Library of Congress.

Immigrant Cultures housing and employment were often uncertain, immigrants anchored their lives on what they knew best: their culture. Many immigrant neighborhoods were made up of enclaves of Italians from the same province, Japanese from the same island district, and Russian Jews from the same *shtetl* (village). In these transplanted communities, Old World customs persisted. People practiced their religions as they always had, held traditional feasts and pageants, married within their group, and pursued old feuds with people from rival villages and provinces. As in eastern Europe, Jewish men grew long sidelocks, women wore wigs, and children were sent to afternoon religious training. Italians transplanted the system whereby a boss, or *padrone,* found jobs for unskilled workers by acting as a kind of broker between an employer and a labor gang.

Yet the very diversity of American cities forced immigrants to modify their attitudes and habits. Few newcomers could avoid contact with people different from themselves, and few could prevent such contacts from altering their traditional ways of life. Although many foreigners identified themselves by their village or region of birth, native-born Americans categorized immigrants by nationality. Thus people from County Cork and County Limerick were lumped together as Irish; those from Schleswig and Wurttemberg became Germans; and those from Calabria and Campobasso became Italians. Mutual benefit and fraternal societies that aided the sick and paid burial expenses continued to be organized along village and provincial lines. For example, the Japanese transferred their *ken* societies, which organized social celebrations and relief services, and Chinese from Canton brought *hui* institutions that raised money to help members acquire businesses. But other immigrant institutions, such as newspapers and churches, found they had to appeal more broadly to the entire nationality group in order to survive.

Still other forces chipped away at old loyalties. Although many immigrants struggled to maintain their native languages and to pass them down to younger generations, English was taught in the schools and needed on the job; it soon penetrated nearly every community. Because the goods available in America often differed from those of the homeland, immigrants were forced to adjust their lifestyles to resemble those of other Americans. Foreigners did not automatically adopt American habits: they continued to cook ethnic meals using American foods and fashioned American fabrics in European styles. Still, convenience and availability influenced their material culture. Thousands of immigrant families had no choice but to buy the American ready-made clothing and mass-produced furniture that were commonplace in the larger society.

The influx of so many immigrants between 1870 and 1920 transformed the United States from a basically Protestant nation into a society of Protestants, Catholics, and Jews. Newcomers from Italy, Hungary, and what would become Czechoslovakia, Yugoslavia, and Poland joined the Irish and Germans to boost the proportion of Catholics in several large cities. In places like Buffalo, Cleveland, Chicago, and Milwaukee, Catholic immigrants and their offspring ap-

An immigrant family at home in their tenement. Though immigrant families were often large and their living conditions difficult, the newcomers displayed resilience and persistence in adapting to a strange environment. The people shown here were poor but proud, with a sense of integrity that shows in their faces.   Bettmann Archive.

proached a majority of the population. Catholic Mexicans comprised over half the population of El Paso. German and eastern European immigrants gave New York one of the largest Jewish populations in the world.

Partly in response to Protestant-based charges that they could not retain Old World religious beliefs and still assimilate into American society, many Catholics and Jews tried to accommodate their faiths to the new environment. A number of Catholic and Jewish leaders—usually from older, more established immigrant groups—supported liberalizing trends such as the use of English in services, the phasing-out of Old World rituals such as saints' feasts, and a preference for public over parochial schooling. As long as new immigrants continued to arrive, however, these tendencies met stiff opposition. Newcomers usually sought to retain familiar religious practices, whether the folk

Catholicism of southern Italy or the orthodox Judaism of eastern Europe; they recoiled from reforms. Catholic immigrants continued to press for ethnically separate parishes in spite of church attempts to make American Catholicism more uniform. Bishops often had to accede to pressures for Polish rather than German-born priests to serve predominantly Polish congregations. Eastern European Jews, believing that Reform Judaism accommodated their faith too much to American ways, established the Conservative branch of their faith, which retained traditional ritual, though it did abolish the segregation of women in synagogues and eased English prayers into the service.

In the 1880s, another group of migrants began to move into American cities. Thousands of rural blacks moved northward and westward, fleeing crop liens, violence, and political oppression and seeking better employment. Although numbers of black urban

Black Migration to the Cities dwellers would grow much larger after 1915, thirty-two cities contained ten thousand or more blacks by 1900, and 79 percent of all blacks outside the South lived in cities. Black migrants resembled foreign immigrants in their peasant backgrounds and economic motivations, but they differed in several important ways. Because few factories would employ blacks, most black workers found jobs in the service sector—cleaning, cooking, carting—rather than the industrial trades. Also, because the majority of jobs in domestic and personal service were traditionally female jobs, black women outnumbered black men in cities such as New York, Baltimore, and New Orleans.

Together the three major migrant groups that peopled American cities—native whites, foreigners, and native blacks—sowed the seeds of modern American culture, to which each group made important contributions. Just as the cities had grown up because they centralized the varied economic functions of commerce, finance, and production, so too they nurtured rich cultural variety: American folk music and literature, Italian and Mexican cuisine, Irish comedy, Yiddish theater, Afro-American jazz and dance, and much more. Like their predecessors, newcomers in the late nineteenth century changed their environment as much as they were changed by it.

LIVING CONDITIONS IN THE
INNER CITY

Population growth created intense pressures on the public and private sectors of the city. Masses of people jammed inner-city districts, where they were known less for their cultural contributions than for the problems they bred. American cities seemed to harbor all the afflictions that plague modern society: poverty, disease, crime, decay, and other unpleasant conditions that result when large numbers of people live close together. City dwellers generally adjusted as best as they could until technology, science, private enterprise, or public authority could alleviate their

problems. Some remarkable successes were achieved. In the late nineteenth century and early twentieth, construction of buildings, homes, streets, sewers, and schools proceeded at a furious pace. American cities set world standards for fire protection and water purification. Yet hardship and other ills await solution.

One of the most persistent shortcomings of American cities has been their failure to provide adequate housing to all who need it. The failure has roots in nineteenth-century urban development. In spite of massive construction in the 1880s and early 1900s, population growth outpaced housing supplies. This condition especially affected working-class families who, because of low-paying jobs, had to rent their living quarters. As cities grew, landlords took advantage of shortages in low-cost rental housing by splitting up existing buildings to house more people, constructing multiple-unit tenements, and hiking rents. Low-income families adjusted to high costs and short supply by sharing space and expenses. Thus it became common in many big cities for a one-family apartment to be occupied by two or three families or by one family plus a number of paying boarders.

Housing Problems

The result was unprecedented crowding. In 1893, there were 702 people per acre in the heart of New York City's immigrant-packed Lower East Side, one of the highest population densities in the world. Low-rent districts had distinctive physical appearances: block after block of six- to eight-story barrackslike buildings in New York; dilapidated row houses in Baltimore and Philadelphia; converted slave quarters in Charleston and New Orleans; and crumbling two- and three-story frame houses in Boston, Chicago, and St. Louis. Everywhere the crowding was acute.

Inside many buildings, living conditions were intolerable. The largest rooms were barely ten feet wide, and interior rooms either had no windows at all or opened onto narrow shafts that bred vermin and rotten odors. "You see," said an immigrant housekeeper describing one such shaft, "it's damp down there, and the families, they throw out garbage and dirty papers and the insides of chickens, and other unmentionable filth. . . . I just vomited when I first cleaned up the air shaft." Few buildings had indoor plumbing, and the only source of heat was coal-burning stoves.

In several places housing problems aroused concerned citizens to mount reform campaigns. New York State took the lead in 1867, 1879, and 1901 by legislating light, ventilation, and safety codes for new tenement buildings. These and similar laws in other states could not remedy the ills of existing buildings, but they did impose government regulation on landlords' property rights. A few reformers, such as Jacob Riis and Lawrence Veiller, advocated housing low-income families in model tenements, with more spacious, airier rooms and better facilities. Model tenements, however, required landlords and investors to accept lower profits—a sacrifice few were willing to make. Neither reformers nor public officials would consider government financing of better housing, fearing such a step would undermine private enterprise. Still, the codes and commissions that resulted from reform campaigns did strengthen the power of local government to regulate housing construction.

Although housing reforms had only limited success, scientific and technological advances enabled city dwellers and the nation in general to live in greater comfort and safety. By the 1890s, most doctors had accepted the germ theory of disease. As a result, cities established more efficient systems of water purification and sewage disposal. Although disease and death rates remained higher in the city than the countryside, and tuberculosis and other respiratory ills continued to plague inner-city districts, public-health regulations helped to control such dread diseases as cholera, typhoid fever, and diphtheria. Street paving, modernized firefighting equipment, and electric street-lighting spread rapidly across urban America. Steel-frame construction, which supported a building by a metal skeleton rather than masonry walls, made possible the construction of skyscrapers—and thus more efficient use of scarce, costly urban land. Electric elevators and steam-heating systems serviced these buildings. Streetcars and subways hastened the pace of urban travel, and steel-cable suspension bridges, developed by John A. Roebling and epitomized by the great Brooklyn Bridge (completed in 1883), linked metropolitan sections more closely.

But none of these improvements lightened the burden of poverty. The urban economy, though generally expanding, advanced erratically. Employment, especially for unskilled workers in manufacturing and construction, rose and fell with business cycles and

Behind the tenements that housed poor working-class families in many cities were even more squalid alley structures such as these in Chicago. In cellars and in these old wooden houses that had been moved back to make room for newer brick buildings lived the poorest of the poor.   Chicago Historical Society.

changing seasons. Often, to make ends meet, more than one member of a working-class

Urban Poverty family had to work. But the wages other family members could earn were minuscule. Thus an ever-increasing number of urban families lived on the margins of survival, where any kind of unlucky occurrence could plunge them into destitution.

Since colonial days, Americans have never agreed on how much responsibility the general public should assume for poor relief. In the late nineteenth and early twentieth centuries, many people held to the traditional beliefs that anyone could escape poverty through hard work and clean living and that poverty was inevitable only because some people were weaker than others. Such reasoning bred fears that assistance to poor people would encourage paupers to depend on public relief rather than self-reliance. As the numbers of poverty cases increased, this attitude hardened, and many city governments discontinued direct grants of food, fuel, and clothing to needy families. Instead, cities either provided relief in return for work on public projects or sent special cases to state-run institutions such as almshouses, orphanages, and homes for the blind, deaf, mentally ill, and handicapped.

Private philanthropic agencies also concerned themselves with helping only the "worthy poor," but their efforts to organize relief more efficiently did foster some change in attitude. Between 1877 and 1892, philanthropists in ninety-two cities formed Charity Organization Societies, an attempt to put social welfare on a more scientific and systematic basis by merging disparate charity groups into a co-ordinated unit. Believing poverty to be the result of personal defects such as alcoholism and laziness, members of these organizations spent most of their time visiting poor families and encouraging them to be thriftier and more virtuous.

Yet close observation of the poor caused some welfare workers to conclude that people's environments, rather than personal failure, caused poverty. That is, they came to believe that the ills of poverty could be cured by improving housing, sanitation, and job opportunities rather than by admonishing the poor to be more moral. This new attitude, which had been gaining ground since the mid-nineteenth century, fueled drives for building codes, factory regulations, and public-health measures. Nevertheless, most middle- and upper-class Americans remained wedded to the belief that in a society of abundance only the unfit were poor, and that relief of poverty should be tolerated but never encouraged. As one charity worker urged, relief "should be surrounded by circumstances that shall . . . repel every one . . . from accepting it."

Even more than crowding and pauperism, crime and disorder alarmed Americans and nurtured fears that urban growth, especially the growth of slums,

Crime and Violence

was corrupting the nation. The more cities grew, it seemed, the more they shook with violence. While homicide rates in other urban-industrial nations like England and Germany declined, those in America rose at an alarming rate: 25 per million people in 1881; 107 per million in 1898. Pickpockets, swindlers, sneak thieves, and holdup men roamed every city. Native whites were quick to blame immigrants and blacks for the so-called crime waves that swept the nation.

Yet it is possible that as a greater proportion of the population was concentrated in cities, crime merely became more conspicuous and sensational rather than more prevalent. To be sure, urban wealth and the mingling of different kinds of people provided new opportunities for organized thievery, petty larceny, vice, and violent grudge-settling. But how do such activities compare to the lawlessness and brutality of backwoods mining camps and southern plantations? Moreover, in spite of distress over Irish bank-robbery gangs, German pickpockets, and Italian Black Hand murderers, there is little evidence that more immigrants than natives populated the rogues' gallery. One investigation of jails in 1900 concluded that "we have ourselves evolved as cruel and cunning criminals as any that Europe may have foisted upon us.

Whatever the extent of criminality, city life in the late nineteenth and early twentieth centuries certainly supported the thesis that there is a tradition of violence in the United States. Cities served as arenas for many of the era's worst riots. As laborers and employers tried to adjust to the uncertainties of industrialization, violence became, in the words of one observer, "a sort of natural and inevitable concomitant." And urban ethnic and racial minorities were often victims of the violent bigotry that was the underside of the American myth of equality. The cityward movement of black people roused white fears, and as the twentieth century dawned, a series of race riots spread across the nation: Wilmington, North Carolina, 1898; Atlanta, Georgia, 1906; Springfield, Illinois, 1908. In cities of the Southwest and Pacific Coast, Chinese and Mexican immigrants often felt the sting of native intolerance. In addition, thousands of minor disruptions made cities scenes of constant turbulence.

Since early in the nineteenth century, city dwellers had increasingly depended on the police to protect life and property. But by the early 1900s law enforcement had become complicated and controversial, because different groups had different interpretations of the law and how it should be enforced. Disadvantaged groups—usually ethnic and racial minorities—could not escape arrest as easily as those with economic or political influence. Individual police officers could apply the law less harshly to members of their own ethnic group (police work was a route of mobility for several immigrant groups) or to people

Chapter 18: THE FAME AND SHAME OF THE CITIES, 1877–1920

The burgeoning cities required large professional police forces to keep order and protect life and property. Station houses like this one became important neighborhood outposts, and the police department an avenue of upward mobility for immigrants.   Library of Congress.

who bought exemptions in the form of bribes. Moreover, political and business leaders often enlisted the government's police power to break up strikes and demonstrations, but not to end or alleviate the exploitative conditions that caused such unrest among workers.

As the public's chief law-enforcement agency, the police were often caught between conflicting pressures for swift and severe action on the one hand and leniency on the other. For when some people clamored for police crackdowns on drinking, gambling, and prostitution, other people privately supported loose law enforcement so they could indulge in these so-called customer crimes. As American society became more diversified, especially in the cities, and as different groups asserted different interests, achieving a balance between the idealistic intentions of criminal law and people's desire for individual freedom became increasingly difficult. It has remained so to this day.

The mounting problems of city life seemed to many Americans to demand greater government action. Thus city governments passed more laws and ordinances that regulated housing, provided poverty relief, and expanded police power. Yet public responsibility always ended at the boundaries of private property. Eventually some advances in housing construction, sanitation, and medical care did reach slum dwellers. But for most people, the only hope was to look to the next generation or to move elsewhere.

PROMISES OF MOBILITY

Between the Civil War and the First World War, Baptist minister Russell Conwell delivered the same sermon more than six thousand times to untold millions across the United States. Titled "Acres of

Diamonds," his immensely popular lecture affirmed the belief that any American could achieve success. People did not have to look very far for riches, Conwell preached; acres of diamonds lay at everyone's feet. Night after night, Conwell would insist to his audience, "the opportunity to get rich, to attain unto great wealth, is here . . . within the reach of almost every man and woman who hears me speak tonight. . . . I say you ought to get rich, and it is your duty to get rich. . . . If you can honestly attain unto riches it is your Christian and Godly duty to do so." Success, then, was not only possible; it was a religious obligation. But how possible was it for people actually to improve their lot and fulfill that duty?

Basically, there were three ways a person could get ahead: occupational advancement (and the higher income that accompanied it); property acquisition (and the potential for greater wealth it represented); and migration to an area of better conditions and greater opportunity. These options were open chiefly to white men. Although many women worked, owned property, and migrated, their social standing was usually defined by the men in their lives—their husbands, fathers, or other kin. Many women did improve their economic status by marrying men with wealth or potential, but other avenues were mostly closed. Men and women who were Afro-American, American Indian, Hispanic-American, or Asian-American had even fewer opportunities for success. Pinned to the bottom of society by prejudice, these groups were expected to accept their inherited station.

To a large number of people, however, the urban and industrial expansion of the late nineteenth century should have offered broad opportunity for occupational mobility. Thousands of small businesses were needed to supply goods and services to burgeoning urban populations. As corporations grew larger and centralized their operations, they required new managerial personnel. Although capital for a large business was hard to obtain, a person could open a saloon or a small store for only $200 or $300. And knowledge of accounting or typing could qualify one for a number of white-collar jobs that sometimes paid better than manual labor. Thus nonmanual work and the higher social status that tended to accompany it were possible.

Occupational Mobility

Such advancement occurred often. To be sure, only a very few traveled the rags-to-riches path that men like Andrew Carnegie and Henry Ford had discovered. Studies of the era's wealthiest businessmen have shown that the vast majority started their careers with distinct advantages: American birth, Protestant religion, better-than-average education, and relatively affluent parents. Yet considerable movement occurred along the path from rags to moderate success as men climbed from manual to nonmanual jobs or saw their children do so. Thus personal successes like that of Meyer Grossman, a Russian immigrant to Omaha, Nebraska, who worked as a teamster before saving enough to open a successful furniture store, were common.

Rates of occupational mobility in late-nineteenth- and early-twentieth-century American communities were slow but steady. In new, fast-growing cities such as Atlanta, Los Angeles, and Omaha, approximately one in five manual workers rose to white-collar or owner's positions within ten years—provided they stayed in the city that long. In older northeastern cities like Boston and Newburyport, upward mobility averaged closer to one in six in ten years. Some people slipped from a higher to a lower rung of the occupational ladder, but rates of upward movement were almost always double the downward rates. Although patterns were far from consistent, immigrants generally experienced lower rates of upward mobility and higher rates of downward mobility than natives did. Still, regardless of birthplace, the chances for a white male to rise occupationally over the course of his career or to have a higher-status job than his father had were relatively good.

It must be remembered, however, that what constitutes a better job depends on an individual's definition of improvement and desires. Many an immigrant artisan, such as a German carpenter or an Italian shoemaker, would have considered an accountant's job demeaning and unproductive. People with long traditions of pride in manual labor neither wanted nonmanual jobs nor enouraged their children to seek them. As one Italian tailor explained, "I learned the tailoring business in the old country. Over here, in America, I never have trouble finding a job because I know my business from the other side [Italy]. . . . I want that my oldest boy learn my trade because I tell him that you could always make at least enough for the family."

Chapter 18: THE FAME AND SHAME OF THE CITIES, 1877–1920

Changing one's place of residence has been one of the most universal experiences of urban dwellers throughout American history. By the end of the nineteenth century, moving companies like this one in Omaha, Nebraska, arose to assist families seeking to improve their living conditions in a new home. Bekins Industries, Inc.

Moreover, business ownership entailed risks. Rates of failure were high among shopkeepers, saloon owners, and the like because business was so uncertain. Thus many manual workers sought security rather than mobility, preferring a steady wage to the risks of ownership. A Sicilian who lived in Bridgeport, Connecticut, observed that "the people that come here they afraid to get in business because they don't know how that business goes. In Italy these people don't know much about these things because most of them work on farms or in [their] trade."

In addition to or instead of advancing occupationally, a person could achieve social mobility by acquiring property. But property was not easy to acquire in turn-of-the-century America. Banks and savings institutions were far stricter in their lending practices than they would become after the 1930s, when the

Acquisition of Property

federal government began to insure real-estate financing. Mortgage loans carried relatively high interest rates and short repayment periods. Thus renting, even of single-family houses, was common, especially in big cities. Nevertheless, a general rise in wage rates enabled many families to build savings accounts, which could be used as down payments on property. Among working-class families who stayed in Newburyport for as long as ten years, a third to a half managed to accumulate some property; two-thirds did so within twenty years. In 1900, 36.3 percent of urban American families owned their homes. That figure may not seem large; yet it was higher than the home ownership rates of all Western nations except Denmark, Norway, and Sweden.

Finally, each year millions of families tried to improve their living conditions by packing up and moving elsewhere. As early as 1847, a foreign visitor, amazed

Residential Mobility by American transiency, wrote, "If God were suddenly to call the world to judgment He would surprise two-thirds of the American population on the road like ants." Americans have always followed the maxim that movement means improvement. This urge to move affected every region, every city. From Boston to San Francisco, from Minneapolis to San Antonio, it became significant that no more than half the families residing in a city at any one time could be found there ten years later.

Some evidence shows that many people who left one place for another, particularly unskilled workers, did not improve their status; they simply floated from one low-paying job to another. Others, however, did find greener pastures. Studies of turn-of-the-century Boston, Omaha, Atlanta, and other cities have revealed that most of the men who rose occupationally had migrated from somewhere else. Thus while cities frustrated the hopes of some, they offered opportunities to others.

In addition to population movement between cities, extraordinary numbers of people moved from one residence to another within the same city. In American communities today, one in every five families moves in a given year. A hundred years ago, the proportion was closer to one in four, or even one in three. In Omaha between 1880 and 1920, for example, nearly 60 percent of those families who remained in the city for as long as fourteen years had lived at three or more addresses during that span of time. Population turnover affected almost every neighborhood, every ethnic and occupational group.

Rapid residential flux undermined the stability of even the most homogeneous neighborhoods. Rarely did a single nationality comprise a clear majority in any large area, even when that area **Ethnic** was known as Little Italy, Jewtown, **Neighborhoods** Over-the-Rhine, or Greektown. **and Ghettos** Even in as heavily ethnic a city as Chicago, a survey of one district found a kaleidoscope of immigrants packed tightly together:

Between Halsted Street and the river live about ten thousand Italians, Neapolitans, Sicilians, and Calabrians. . . . To the South on Twelfth Street are many Germans, and the side streets are given over almost entirely to Polish and Prussian Jews. Further south, three Jewish colonies merge into a huge Bohemian colony. . . . To the north-west are many Canadians . . . and to the north are many Irish.

Moreover, the families inhabiting a certain neighborhood at one point in time were not likely to be living there five or ten years later. Residential change dispersed immigrants from their original areas of settlement into many different neighborhoods. In New York, Boston, and other eastern ports, ethnically homogeneous districts did exist, and people tended to change residences within those districts rather than move away from them. Elsewhere, however, most immigrant families lived dispersed in ethnically mixed neighborhoods rather than in ghettos.

In most places an area's institutions and enterprises, more than the people who actually lived there, identified it as an ethnic neighborhood. A certain part of town, familiar and accessible to a particular group, became the location of its churches, clubs, bakeries, meat markets, and other establishments. Some members of the group lived nearby, while others lived farther away but could travel there on streetcars or on foot. Thus some of the secondary business centers that formed at the intersections of mass transit routes became locations of ethnic business and social activity. A Bohemian Town, for example, received its nickname because it was the location of Swoboda's Bakery, Cermak's Drug Store, Cecha's Jewelry, Knezacek's Meats, St. Wenceslaus Church, and the Bohemian Benevolent Association. Such institutions gave a district an ethnic identity even though the surrounding neighborhoods were mixed and unstable.

If the term *ghetto* is defined as a place of enforced residence from which escape is at best difficult, only nonwhites in this era had a true ghetto experience. Wherever Asians and Mexicans immigrated, they encountered discrimination in housing, occupations, and other areas of public life. Though these groups often preferred to remain separate in Chinatowns and *barrios*, white Americans made every effort to keep them confined. In the 1880s the city of San Francisco, for example, tried to prohibit Chinese laundries from locating in most neighborhoods, and its school board tried to isolate Japanese and Chinese children in Chinatown schools.

Chapter 18: THE FAME AND SHAME OF THE CITIES, 1877–1920

Prejudice and discrimination not only trapped blacks at the bottom of the occupational ladder but operated in housing markets to limit their residential opportunities. Whites organized protective associations that pledged not to sell homes in white neighborhoods to blacks, and occasionally used violence to scare away black families who did move in. Such efforts seldom worked. Whites who lived on the edge of black neighborhoods often fled, leaving their homes and apartments to be sold and rented to black occupants. In almost every city, totally black residential districts expanded while white native and ethnic neighborhoods dissolved. By 1920 ten Chicago census tracts were over 75 percent black. In Detroit, Cleveland, Los Angeles, and Washington, D.C., two-thirds or more of the total black population lived in only two or three wards. Within these districts, blacks nurtured distinct cultural institutions that helped them adjust to urban life: storefront churches, business and educational organizations, social clubs, and saloons. But the ghettos also bred frustration, the result of stunted opportunity and racial bigotry. Color, more than any other factor, made the urban experiences of blacks different from those of whites.

All groups, however, including blacks, could and did move—if not from one part of the city to another, then from one city to another. Americans were always seeking greener pastures, and the hope that things might be better somewhere else acted as a kind of safety valve, relieving some of the tensions and frustrations that simmered inside the city. At times these emotions erupted into violence; more often, people simply left. A railroad ticket from one city to another cost a few dollars; there was little to lose by moving.

Moreover, the possibilities for upward mobility, however limited, seemed to temper people's dissatisfaction. Although the gap between the very rich and the very poor widened, the expanding economies of American cities created more room in the middle of the socioeconomic scale. Few could hope to become another Rockefeller, but many could become respectable merchants, shopkeepers, foremen, clerks, or agents. If advancement was not possible in one generation, it could be possible in the next. Finally, even if migration, occupational mobility, and property acquisition offered little hope of improvement or relief, there was still one sphere to which city dwellers could turn: politics.

THE RISE OF URBAN BOSS POLITICS

Andrew D. White, the American educator and diplomat, was dismayed and disgusted. He wrote in 1890 that he could not accept "the idea that a city is a political body, and therefore that it is to be ruled . . . by a city proletarian mob . . . and . . . that men who carry their ward can control the city." Such an arrangement, White concluded, made American city government "the worst in Christendom." But others characterized the same situation much differently. Referring to Israel Durham of Philadelphia, the very kind of politician whom White despised, one journalist wrote, "Everybody likes him, hundreds love him, and almost everybody calls him 'Iz.' " What provoked such impassioned differences of opinion? It was the urban political machine, one of the most remarkable and notorious of American institutions.

The sudden growth and mounting rivalry among social and economic interest groups that occurred in the late nineteenth century mired cities in a governmental swamp. From suburbs to slums, burgeoning populations, business expansion, and technological change created urgent needs for water, sewers, police and fire protection, schools, parks, and many other services. Such needs strained government institutions beyond their capacities. Furthermore, city governments approached these needs in a disorganized fashion. Legislative and administrative functions were typically dispersed among a mayor, a city council, and independent boards that administered health regulations, public works, poverty relief, and other matters. Philadelphia at one time had thirty different boards plus a mayor and a council to tend to the city's needs. And state governments often imposed their will on city administrations, appointing board members and limiting local prerogatives to levy taxes and sell bonds to raise revenue.

Power thrives on confusion and out of this governmental chaos arose the political machine. Unlike political parties, which ideally exist for higher purposes than merely electing their candidates to office, ma-

Political Machines chines were organizations whose main goal was getting and keeping political power. In order to achieve that goal, a machine had to win popular support. Machine politicians routinely used bribery and graft to further their ends. But they could not have succeeded if they had not provided relief, security, and municipal services to large numbers of people. By doing so, machine politicians alleviated many urban problems and accomplished things that other agencies had been unable or unwilling to attempt.

Machines were also beneficiaries of the new urban conditions. As cities grew larger and economically more complex, business leaders either vied to use government to advance their own interests or withdrew from local affairs to pursue their interests in interurban or interregional economic organizations. At the same time, hordes of newcomers, often unskilled and foreign-born, crowded into the cities. Enfranchised by liberal voting qualifications, the men of these groups became a substantial political force.

These circumstances bred a new kind of leader: the political boss. Conflicting interest groups needed brokers who could bypass governmental stalemates, and urban newcomers had needs that required government attention. Bosses and machines did just that; they established power bases among new urban voters and used politics to solve urban problems. Machines made politics a full-time profession. According to George Washington Plunkett, a small-time boss in New York City who published his memoirs in 1905, "As a rule [the boss] has no business or occupation other than politics. He plays politics every day and night in the year and his headquarters bears the inscription, 'Never closed.' "

Bosses and machines were rarely as dictatorial or corrupt as their critics charged. To be sure, fraud, bribery, and thievery tainted the system. Bosses such as Philadelphia's "Duke" Vare, Kansas City's Tom Pendergast, and New York's Richard Croker lived like kings, though their official incomes were slim. A few bosses had no permanent organization; rather, they were freelance opportunists who bargained for power, sometimes winning and sometimes losing. But from the 1880s onward, most machines evolved into highly organized political structures that wedded accomplishments for the city with personal gain for politicians.

The system rested on a popular base and was held together by loyalty and service. City machines were coalitions of smaller machines that derived their power directly from the neighborhoods, particularly inner-city neighborhoods inhabited by the native and immigrant working classes. In return for votes, bosses provided jobs, built parks and bathhouses, distributed food to the needy, and helped when someone ran afoul of the law. Such personalized service cultivated mass attachment to the boss; never before had government or public leaders assumed such responsibility for people in need.

Moreover, bosses were genuinely public people. They attended weddings and wakes, joined clubs, and held open house in saloons where neighborhood people could contact them person-

Techniques of Bossism ally. Each boss had his own style. Pittsburgh's Christopher Magee gave his city a zoo and a hospital. Brooklyn's Hugh McLaughlin provided free burial services. Boston's James Michael Curley would approach a haggard old woman and tell her that "a woman should have three attributes. She should have beauty, intelligence, and money." Then he would press a silver dollar into her hand, adding, "Now you have all three."

In order to finance their largesse and support their system, bosses exchanged favors for votes or money. Their power over local government enabled machines to control the letting of contracts, the granting of utility or streetcar franchises, and the distribution of city jobs. Recipients of city business and jobs were expected to repay the machine with a portion of their profits or salaries and to cast supporting votes on election day. Bosses called this process gratitude; critics called it graft. Machines constructed public buildings, sewer systems, mass transit lines, and more that otherwise might not have been built; but bribes and kickbacks made such projects costly to taxpayers. Moreover, machines dispensed favors to illegal businesses as well as legitimate ones. Payoffs from gambling, prostitution, and illegal liquor traffic were important sources of machine revenue.

Though there was great variety, between 1880 and 1920, nearly every major city experienced some kind of bossism. Hierarchical machine organization, whereby a city boss presided over neighborhood bosses, was most highly developed in New York City. There,

Political bosses won friends and courted votes through their benevolence. Timothy D. "Big Tim" Sullivan sponsored this huge free barbecue for constituents in a New York City neighborhood. Brown Brothers.

after the downfall of Boss William M. Tweed in the early 1870s, "Honest John" Kelly took over Tweed's Tammany Hall organization and tightened its structure by combining Tammany more thoroughly with the Democratic party. In the late 1880s, Richard Croker assumed control of Tammany Hall and completed Kelly's efforts by making neighborhood bosses more dependent on the city boss for jobs and money and by allying with wealthy business leaders. By contrast, the machine system in Chicago was decentralized, with several ward bosses exercising independent power and cultivating their own special interests.

Medium-sized cities generally had a single boss who used the inner-city districts as his power base. Cincinnati's George Cox and Kansas City's Jim Pendergast (Tom's brother) were downtown saloonkeepers who became powerful political brokers. In the South,

bosses such as New Orleans's Martin Behrman and Memphis's Edward H. Crump drew strength from the region's well-established Democratic party. A few bosses, such as San Francisco's Abe Ruef and Minneapolis's "Doc" Ames, were well educated. But many, including St. Louis's Ed Butler and New York's "Big Tim" Sullivan, never finished grammar school and received their most influential training in city streets and tenements.

Bosses held onto their power because they knew people's needs firsthand and because they tended to the problems of everyday life. Martin Lomasney, boss of Boston's South End, explained, "There's got to be in every ward somebody that any bloke can come to—no matter what he's done—and get help. Help, you understand, none of your law and justice, but help." In an era when unemployment insurance and welfare were virtually unknown, machine politicians believed government existed to aid people in need and to provide services.

The boss system, however, was neither innocent nor fair. Jobs, Christmas turkeys, and funeral money were accompanied by bribery, thievery, and extortion. Moreover, bosses never distributed favors equitably. New immigrant groups such as Italians and Poles, and racial minorities like blacks and Latinos, received only token recognition, if any, from machines. Nevertheless, in an age of economic individualism, bosses were no more guilty of self-interest and discrimination than the respectable business leaders who exploited workers, spoiled the landscape, and manipulated government in pursuit of profits. Sometimes humane and sometimes criminal, bosses were brokers between various sectors of urban society and an uncertain world.

CIVIC REFORM

Machine politics brought some order to city government, met some of the needs of immigrants and other inner-city residents, and lined the pockets of some leaders and their business allies. But the boss system also alarmed the established classes inhabiting the outlying neighborhoods and sensitized many men and women to the problems of urban growth. At the same time the bosses were consolidating their power, a reform movement was organizing to destroy political machines and improve the quality of urban life. This urban reform movement, which paralleled its agrarian counterpart (see pages 572–575) and which laid the foundation for the national reforms of the Progressive era (see Chapter 21), shared the strengths and weaknesses of the American liberal tradition.

In 1885, Congregational minister Josiah Strong wrote, "The city is the nerve center of our civilization. It is also the storm center. . . . It has become a serious threat to our civilization." Strong's sentiments were shared by many middle- and upper-class Americans who feared that immigrant-based political machines menaced the republic and that unsavory alliances between bosses and business undermined municipal finances. Anxious over the mounting poverty, crowding, and disorder that seemed to accompany population expansion, and convinced that urban services were making taxes too high, civic reformers organized to oust bosses and to install more responsible leaders at the helm of urban administration.

Urban reform derived from the industrial system's emphasis on eliminating waste and inefficiency. Business-minded reformers believed government could be made more efficient by running it like a business. They believed that the only way to prevent civic decay was to elect officials who would hold down expenses and prevent corruption. Thus the major goals of reform leaders such as future president Grover Cleveland, mayor of Buffalo in 1881, were to reduce city budgets, make employees work longer, and cut taxes.

As a means of introducing sound business principles to government, civic reformers supported a number of structural changes, such as city-manager and commission forms of government and nonpartisan, citywide election of officials. Each of these reforms was aimed at removing politics from government and placing local decision-making in the hands of experienced experts. Armed with such strategies, reformers believed they could centralize administration under their control and thereby undermine bosses' ward and neighborhood power bases. They rarely realized, however, that bosses succeeded because they used government to meet people's needs. Reformers only noticed the waste and corruption that machines bred.

Structural Reforms in Government

A few reformers did move beyond structural changes to a genuine concern for social problems. Hazen S. Pingree, mayor of Detroit from 1889 to 1896; Samuel "Golden Rule" Jones, mayor of Toledo from 1897 to 1904; and Thomas L. Johnson, mayor of Cleveland from 1901 to 1909, worked to provide jobs for poor people, to reduce charges by transit and utilities companies, and to establish greater governmental responsibility for the welfare of all citizens. Some supported public ownership of gas, electric, and telephone companies—a quasi-socialistic reform that alienated their business allies. But Pingree, Jones, and Johnson were exceptions. Most civic reformers were narrow of vision. Although they achieved temporary success, they could not match the bosses' political savvy and soon found themselves out of power.

Consumer reform originated in many cities at the end of the nineteenth century. Often instigated by reform-minded women, local governments passed laws and created agencies to inspect for adulterated milk and other tainted foods dangerous to health. Culver.

Nevertheless, the seeds of social reform were beginning to sprout outside of politics. Convinced that laissez-faire ideology could no longer work in a complex urban-industrial world and driven **Social Reform** by an urge to identify and address urban problems, a number of men and women—mostly young and middle-class—embarked on campaigns for social betterment. These urban social reformers operated within a variety of fields and sought solutions to a variety of problems. Housing reformers wanted local government to pass building codes to ensure safety in tenements. Protestant reformers influenced by the Social Gospel movement, which emphasized social responsibility as a means to salvation, built churches in slum neighborhoods and urged businesses to be socially responsible. Believing that service to fellow human beings was a Christian

duty, Social Gospel clergymen such as Washington Gladden of Columbus, Ohio, and Walter Rauschenbusch of Rochester, New York, worked to alleviate poverty and to make peace between employers and labor unions. Educational reformers such as William T. Harris of St. Louis saw public schools as a means of preparing immigrants and their children for citizenship by teaching them American values as well as the English language.

Perhaps the most ambitious and inspiring feature of the urban reform movement was the settlement house. Patterned after London's Toynbee Hall, settlements were efforts by young, educated, middle-class men and women to live in slum neighborhoods and bridge the gulf between classes, in hopes that people could learn from each other. Early settlement founders such as Jane Addams, Florence Kelley, and

Graham Taylor wanted to improve the lives of working-class people by helping them to obtain an education, an appreciation of the arts, better jobs, and better housing. Their settlement houses provided neighborhood residents with a wide array of activities, ranging from vocational classes to childcare for working mothers to ethnic art exhibits and pageants. Because of their efforts in areas such as the establishment of school nurses, the passing of building safety codes, the construction of public playgrounds, and the support for labor unions, settlement workers often became reform leaders in cities and in the nation. Though the neighborhood residents they served sometimes mistrusted them because they were outsiders to working-class and immigrant cultures, settlement workers made valuable contributions to urban life.

While settlement-house workers tried to revive neighborhoods, other reformers tried to beautify whole cities. Inspired by the World's Columbian Exposition of 1893, a dazzling world's fair held **Beautification** in the specially built White City **Campaigns** on Chicago's South Side, architects and city planners worked to redesign the urban landscape. Led by architect Daniel Burnham, the City Beautiful movement undertook to build civic centers, parks and boulevards, and transportation systems that would make cities more attractive as well as economically efficient. "Make no little plans," Burnham urged city officials. "Make big plans; aim high in hope and work." This attitude spawned beautifying projects in Chicago, San Francisco, and Washington, D.C., in the first decade of the twentieth century. Yet most big plans turned out to be only big dreams. Neither the public nor the private sector could muster enough money to undertake major projects, and planners disagreed with each other and with social reformers over whether or not beautification would really solve urban problems.

Whether they concentrated on changing government, social services, or city design, urban reformers wanted to save cities, not abandon them. The men and women of the various reform movements believed that they could improve urban life by restoring feelings of service and cooperation among all citizens. They often failed to realize, however, that cities were places of great diversity and that different people had different views of what reform actually meant. Distributing city jobs on the basis of civil service exams rather than political patronage meant progress to governmental reformers, but to working-class men it signified reduced employment opportunities. Moral reformers tried to prohibit the sale of alcoholic beverages to prevent working-class breadwinners from wasting their wages and ruining their health, but European immigrants saw such crusades as interference in their long-held wine- and beer-drinking customs. Planners saw new civic buildings and transportation systems as modern necessities, but such structures often replaced low-cost housing units and displaced the poor. Thus early urban reform merged idealism with naiveté and insensitivity.

THE LEGACY OF URBANISM

Much of what American society has become today originated in the urbanization of the late nineteenth century. American cities may have been less orderly and beautiful than European cities, but they hummed with energy and excitement. When old-fashioned native inventiveness met the traditions of European, African, and Asian cultures, a new kind of society emerged. This new society seldom functioned functioned smoothly; in fact, there really was no coherent urban community, only a collection of subcommunities. Yet its jumble of social classes, ethnic and racial groups, political organizations, and other components left important legacies.

Martin Lomasney, the Boston ward boss, once observed that "one of the strongest human cravings is to be left alone and the uplifter is never liked." By the early 1900s, American cities **Cultural** had become so diverse socially that **Pluralism** immigrant groups were straining to protect their cultures in a changing, bewildering world. Fearful and puzzled native-born Americans tried a host of ways to Americanize and uplift immigrants, but the newcomers stubbornly clung to their religious rituals, languages, family and social organizations, and drinking habits. Optimists had envisioned the American nation as a melting pot where various nationalities would blend into a new, unified people. Instead, many ethnic groups proved

Streets clogged with people and vehicles, canyon walls of tall buildings, a hodge-podge of signs and banners, and a maze of overhead wires gave the modern American city its image of growth and bustling activity.   The New York Historical Society, New York City.

to be unmeltable, and nonwhite racial minorities got burned on the bottom of the pot.

As a result of immigration and urbanization, the United States became a culturally pluralistic society—not a melting pot but a salad bowl. As one immigrant priest told a social worker, "There is no such thing as an American." He meant the same thing literary

critic Randolph Bourne meant when he dubbed the United States "a cosmopolitan federation of national colonies." This kind of reasoning produced hyphenated identifications: people considered themselves Irish-American, Italo-American, Polish-American, and the like.

Pluralism and its attendant interest-group loyalties

IMPORTANT EVENTS

1867	First law passed regulating tenements (New York)
1880s	"New" immigrants from eastern and southern Europe begin to arrive in large numbers
1883	Brooklyn Bridge completed
1886	First settlement house opened
1890s	Electric trolleys replace horse-driven mass transit
1893	World's Columbian Exposition, Chicago
1898	Race riot in Wilmington, North Carolina
1900– 1910	Peak years of immigration
1906	Race riot in Atlanta, Georgia
1920	Majority (51.4 percent) of Americans live in cities

made politics an important institution. If America was not a melting pot, then different groups were competing with each other for power, wealth, and status. When lack of skills, education, capital, and influence closed off paths to success, immigrants turned to politics to protect their interests and to open up new opportunities. American cities became arenas in which different groups formed coalitions to achieve their goals. But such coalitions were fragile, and their membership shifted according to the issue in question.

Adherents of different cultural traditions battled over how much control government should exercise over people's lives (see page 563). The most pro-vocative issue was about the use of leisure time and celebration of Sunday, the Lord's day. In the Puritan tradition, natives supported blue laws (see page 284) designed to prevent the desecration

Cultural-Political Alignments

of the Sabbath by prohibiting various commercial and recreational activities. European immigrants, ac-customed to feasting and playing after church, fought Sunday closings of saloons and other restrictions on the only day they had free for fun and relaxation. Thus in 1913, when the New York General Assembly proposed a law granting cities authority to end re-strictions on Sunday baseball games and liquor sales, both sides argued vehemently. One rural Republican charged that such a measure amounted to "amending Moses' law," while a New York City Democrat of Irish lineage retorted that "Moses was an organization Democrat" who wrote the commandment "Don't covet your neighbor's rights." At about the same time, the Illinois and Ohio legislatures were split over whether or not to legalize boxing, which small-town Repub-licans opposed and urban Democrats favored. Similar splits developed elsewhere over public versus parochial schools and prohibition versus the free availability of liquor.

Such conflicts, plus the ever-growing diversity of the American population illustrate why local and state politics were so heated in the late nineteenth and early twentieth centuries. Some people carried polarization to its extreme and tried to suppress everything new and allegedly un-American. In several communities during the 1890s, the American Pro-tective Association achieved considerable influence by attacking "the diabolical works of the Catholic Church" and demanding an end to immigration. Some of this sentiment influenced national legislation. In 1882, Congress bowed to pressure from West Coast nativists and prohibited Chinese immigration for ten years. In 1902 a new law excluded the Chinese per-manently. And periodic attempts were made to prevent foreign-born citizens from voting by imposing literacy tests on them.

Efforts to enforce homogeneity generally failed, though, because too many people had a stake in the country's cultural diversity. By 1920, immigrants and their offspring outnumbered natives in many cities, and the national economy depended on the new workers and consumers. They had transformed the United States into an urban nation; they had given American culture its rich and varied texture; and they had laid the foundations for the political liberalism and sensitivity to individual liberty that would char-acterize American politics and society in the future.

SUGGESTIONS FOR FURTHER READING

Urban Growth

Howard P. Chudacoff, *The Evolution of American Urban Society*, rev. ed. (1981); Blake McKelvey, *The Urbanization of America* (1963); Arthur M. Schlesinger, *The Rise of the City* (1933); Jon Teaford, *City and Suburb: The Political Fragmentation of Metropolitan America, 1850–1970* (1979); Sam Bass Warner, Jr., *The Urban Wilderness* (1972); Sam Bass Warner, Jr., *Streetcar Suburbs* (1962).

Immigration, Ethnicity, and Religion

Aaron I. Abell, *American Catholicism and Social Action* (1960); Josef J. Barton, *Peasants and Strangers: Italians, Rumanians, and Slovaks in an American City* (1975); John Bodnar, *Immigration and Industrialization* (1977); John Bodnar et al., *Lives of Their Own: Blacks, Italians, and Poles in Pittsburgh, 1900–1960* (1982); John W. Briggs, *An Italian Passage* (1978); Jack Chen, *The Chinese of America* (1980); Leonard Dinnerstein and David Reimers, *Ethnic Americans* (1975); John B. Duff, *The Irish in the United States* (1971); Mario T. Garcia, *Desert Immigrants: The Mexicans of El Paso, 1880–1920* (1981); Nathan Glazer and Daniel P. Moynihan, *Beyond the Melting Pot*, rev. ed. (1970); Caroline Golab, *Immigrant Destinations* (1977); Milton Gordon, *Assimilation in American Life* (1964); Victor Greene, *For God and Country: The Rise of Polish and Lithuanian Ethnic Consciousness in America* (1975); Oscar Handlin, *The Uprooted*, 2nd ed. (1973); Marcus Lee Hansen, *The Immigrant in American History* (1940); John Higham, *Strangers in the Land: Patterns of American Nativism* (1955); Edward R. Kantowicz, *Polish-American Politics in Chicago* (1975); Harry Kitano, *Japanese Americans: The Evolution of a Subculture* (1969); Alan M. Kraut, *The Huddled Masses: The Immigrant in American Society, 1880–1921* (1982); Matt S. Maier and Feliciano Rivera, *The Chicanos: A History of Mexican Americans* (1972); Henry F. May, *Protestant Churches and Industrial America* (1949); Humbert S. Nelli, *The Italians of Chicago* (1970); Moses Rischin, *The Promised City: New York's Jews* (1962); Philip Taylor, *The Distant Magnet: European Emigration to the U.S.A.* (1971); Thomas Wheeler, ed. *The Immigrant Experience* (1972).

Urban Needs and Services

Robert H. Bremner, *From the Depths: The Discovery of Poverty* (1956); James H. Cassedy, *Charles V. Chapin and the Public Health Movement* (1962); Marvin Lazerson, *Origins of the Urban School* (1971); Thomas L. Philpott, *The Slum and the Ghetto* (1978); James F. Richardson, *The New York Police* (1970); Barbara Gutmann Rosencrantz, *Public Health and the State* (1972); Mel Scott, *American City Planning Since 1890* (1969); Selwyn K. Troen, *The Public and the Schools* (1975); Christopher Tunnard and Henry Hope Reed, *American Skyline* (1955); David B. Tyack, *The One Best System: A History of American Urban Education* (1974).

Mobility and Race Relations

Howard P. Chudacoff, *Mobile Americans* (1972); Clyde Griffen and Sally Griffen, *Natives and Newcomers* (1977); David M. Katzman, *Before the Ghetto* (1973); Thomas Kessner, *The Golden Door* (1977); Kenneth L. Kusmer, *A Ghetto Takes Shape* (1976); Gilbert Osofsky, *Harlem: The Making of a Ghetto* (1966); Howard N. Rabinowitz, *Race Relations in the Urban South* (1978); Allan H. Spear, *Black Chicago* (1967); Stephan Thernstrom, *The Other Bostonians: Poverty and Progress in the American Metropolis* (1973); Olivier Zunz, *The Changing Face of Inequality: Urbanization, Industrial Development, and Immigrants in Detroit, 1880–1920* (1982).

Boss Politics

John M. Allswang, *Bosses, Machines and Urban Voters* (1977); Blaine Brownell and Warren E. Stickle, eds., *Bosses and Reformers* (1973); Alexander B. Callow, Jr., ed., *The City Boss in America* (1976); Lyle Dorsett, *The Pendergast Machine* (1968); Zane L. Miller, *Boss Cox's Cincinnati* (1968); Bruce M. Stave, ed., *Urban Bosses, Machines, and Progressive Reformers* (1972).

Urban Reform

John D. Buenker, *Urban Liberalism and Progressive Reform* (1973); James B. Crooks, *Politics and Progress* (1968); Allen F. Davis, *American Heroine: The Life and Legend of Jane Addams* (1973); Allen F. Davis, *Spearheads for Reform* (1967); Michael Ebner and Eugene Tobin, eds., *The Age of Urban Reform* (1977); Melvin Holli, *Reform in Detroit* (1969); C. H. Hopkins, *The Rise of the Social Gospel in American Protestantism* (1940); Roy M. Lubove, *The Progressives and the Slums* (1962); Martin J. Schiesl, *The Politics of Efficiency: Municipal Administration and Reform in America* (1977); John G. Sproat, *The Best Men: Liberal Reformers in the Gilded Age* (1968).

Everyday Life and Culture

1877–1920

Chapter 19

Abigail Roberson was young, sensitive, shy, and beautiful; but none of these qualities inhibited her from suing the Rochester Folding Box Company and one of its customers, the Franklin Mills Company. The Rochester company, it seems, had used Miss Roberson's photograph without her permission on the flour bags it made for Franklin Mills. Hoping that her face would induce consumers to buy the product, the company added the caption "Flour of the Family" above Abigail's image. Miss Roberson claimed that this advertisement brought her ridicule and mental distress, and she sued to prevent unauthorized use of her picture on the flour bags. In 1902 the case reached the New York Court of Appeals, which ruled against Abigail Roberson after heated debate. But public disapproval of the decision was so strong that the next year the New York General Assembly passed one of the nation's first right-to-privacy laws, stipulating that "A person, firm or corporation that uses for advertising purposes or for the purpose of trade the name, portrait or picture of any living person, without having obtained the written consent of such a person . . . is guilty of a misdemeanor."

The Roberson case represents one of many issues that resulted from the changing character of American life. Not only had goods such as Franklin Mills' "Flour of the Family" become widely available, but also companies like Rochester Folding Box strove for new ways to package and advertise their products. In earlier times, before mass markets, mass advertisement, and photography existed, personal privacy and its invasion were not matters that concerned individuals, much less the courts. Suddenly, however, economic, technological, and social changes were affecting everyday life in ways that few had anticipated.

During the half-century between the end of Reconstruction and the end of the First World War, American society began to shift its focus from production to consumption. The nation's farms and industries were producing so much that Americans could afford to reorient their attitudes toward material wants. What had once been accessible only to a few was becoming available to many; what had formerly been dreams were becoming necessities. No trend affected everyday life more decisively than this one. And as Americans tried to adapt to the new values of consumption and its attendant conflicts, they raised questions about themselves that have not been resolved to this day.

Most Americans at the end of the nineteenth century were still relatively isolated. In 1880, seven out of every ten people lived on farms and in small towns. Life in such places was shaped by the dictates of nature and the traditional institutions of family and church. In the fields and in the household, people worked from sunup to sundown—though they could usually control their own work pace and the number of breaks they took. Most foods and clothes were made in the home or nearby. Houses were heated by wood- or coal-burning stoves and lit by oil lamps; most had no bathroom, only basins and tubs indoors and outhouses in the back yard. Families burned what little trash they had, fed their garbage to animals, and poured waste water outside. Besides church, people mingled at the general store and at such special occasions as fairs, circuses, political rallies, and evangelical revivals. Fatigue and pitch-darkness restricted nighttime activities; street lights were rare. People normally went to bed at nine or ten P.M. and rose at four or five A.M.

But such lifestyles were changing rapidly. As the nation's population became increasingly urban (by 1920 the majority lived in cities), there developed a new kind of neighborhood society in which street corners, saloons, shops, and commercial amusements replaced the village church and general store. People tended to spend more time with their peers—members of the same age group—and less with their families. The rapid spread of intercity transportation and of postal, telephone, and electrical service drew even isolated communities into the orbit of a consumer-oriented society. American inventiveness combined with technology, mass production, and mass marketing to produce and make available myriad goods that had not previously existed or had been the exclusive property of the wealthy. This new material well-being, brought about by the advent of such products

Chapter 19: EVERYDAY LIFE AND CULTURE, 1877–1920

A drugstore, complete with soda fountain and showcases of merchandise, symbolizes the new materialism of the late nineteenth century. New mass production and marketing techniques made such materialism possible. Library of Congress.

as ready-made clothes, canned foods, and home appliances had a dual effect. It enabled Americans of differing status to join communities of consumers—communities defined not by place or class but by common possession. But it also accentuated the differences between those who could afford such goods and services and those who could not.

STANDARDS OF LIVING

I f the affluence of a society can be measured by how quickly it converts luxuries into commonplace articles of everyday life, the United States was indeed becoming affluent in the years between 1880 and 1920. In 1880, for example, almost no one smoked cigarettes. (That year a young Virginian named James Bonsack invented a cigarette-making machine.) Only wealthy women could afford silk stockings, and only residents of Florida, Texas, and California could enjoy fresh oranges. The sweets people ate were made at home, and few people ever bought soap. But by 1899, manufactured and perishable products were becoming increasingly common. That year Americans bought 2 billion cigarettes (an average of 27 per person) and 151,000 pairs of silk stockings, consumed oranges at the rate of 100 crates for every 1,000 people, and spent an average of $1.08 per person on store-bought candy and pastries and $.63 on soap. By 1921 the transformation was even more advanced. Americans smoked 43 billion cigarettes that year (403 per person), ate 248 crates of oranges per 1,000 people, bought 217 million pairs of silk stockings, and spent $1.66

per person on confectionery goods and $1.40 on soap. How did Americans afford these goods? How did changes in standards of living come about?

What people can afford depends largely on their resources and incomes. Data for the period from 1880 to 1920 are scattered, but there is no doubt that incomes rose. As always, the rich

Rising Personal Income

got richer. The rapidly expanding economy spawned massive fortunes and created a new industrial elite. The writer of "The Coming Billionaire," an article published in *Forum* magazine in 1891, estimated that there were already 120 Americans worth at least $10 million. By 1920, when income-tax figures made possible the first accurate tabulations of income distribution, the richest 5 percent of the population was receiving almost one-fourth of all income in the country. Returns on investments were even more skewed; the same top 5 percent was receiving almost half of all interest payments and 85 percent of all stock and bond dividends.

But incomes also rose among the middle classes. For example, the average pay for clerical workers rose 36 percent between 1890 and 1910 (see table). After the turn of the century, employees of the federal executive branch were averaging $1,072 a year, and college professors $1,100—not handsome sums, but much more than manual workers received. With these incomes, the middle class could afford relatively comfortable housing. A six- to seven-room house cost around $3,000 to buy or build and $15 to $20 per month to rent.

Wages for industrial workers increased as well, though they varied widely and income figures were deceiving. On the average, the annual wages of industrial workers rose from $486 in 1890 to $630 in 1910. Hourly rates in industries with large female work forces, such as shoe and paper manufacturing, were lower than those in industries with predominantly male work forces, such as coal mining and iron production. Also, regional variations were wide. Nevertheless, wages for all moved upward (see table). Pay for farm laborers followed the same trend, though wages remained relatively low because generally those workers received room and board along with their pay.

Pay scales for industrial and farm workers, however, ignore a vital aspect of living standards. Wage increases

Cost of Living mean little if living costs rise as fast or faster than incomes. In fact, this is what happened in the United States around the turn of the century. According to one economic index, the weekly cost of living for a typical wage earner's family of four rose over 47 percent between 1889 and 1913. In other words, a quantity of food and other items that may have cost $6.78 in 1889 increased, after a slight dip in the mid-1890s, to $10.00 by 1913 (see table for specific food prices). Very rarely did the income for a particular working-class occupation rise at the same rate as the cost of living.

How then could working-class Americans afford the new goods and services that the industrial age offered? Obviously, many could not. The daughter of a textile worker, recalling her school days at the turn of the century, described how "some of the kids would bring bars of chocolate, others an orange. . . . I suppose they were richer than a family like ours. My father used to buy a bag of candy and a bag of peanuts every payday. . . . And that's all we'd have until the next payday. If we asked for something my mother would say, 'Well, we're too poor. We can't afford to buy that.' " Another woman explained how her family coped with high prices and low wages: "My mother made our clothes. People then wore old clothes. My mother would rip them out and make them over."

Still, a working-class family could raise its income and partake at least partially in consumer society by sending children and women into the labor market.

Supplements to Family Income

Thus in a household where the father made $600 a year, the wages of other family members might lift the total income to $800 or $900. Many families also rented household space to boarders and lodgers, a practice that could yield up to $200 a year. These means of increasing family income enabled people to spend more and save more. Between 1889 and 1901, for example, working-class families markedly increased their expenditures for such items as life insurance, amusements, alcoholic beverages, and union dues. Thus workers were able to improve their living standards, but not without sacrifices in their family and home life.

The work people did was part of a more highly developed money economy. Between 1890 and 1920, the American labor force grew from 28 million workers

Chapter 19: EVERYDAY LIFE AND CULTURE, 1877–1920

AMERICAN LIVING STANDARDS, 1880–1920

	1880	1890	1900	1910	1920
Income and earnings					
Annual income:					
clerical worker		$848		$1,156	
public school teacher		$256		$492	
industrial worker		$486		$630	
farm laborer		$233		$336	
Hourly wage:					
soft-coal miner		$0.18[a]		$0.21	
iron worker		$0.17[a]		$0.23	
shoe worker		$0.14[a]		$0.19	
paper worker		$0.12[a]		$0.17	
Labor statistics					
Number of people in labor force	17.4 million	28.5 million			41.7 million
Average workweek, manufacturing		60 hours		51 hours	47.4 hours
Food costs					
10 pounds potatoes		$0.16		$0.17	
Dozen eggs		$0.21		$0.34	
1 pound bacon		$0.12½		$0.25	
Demographic data					
Life expectancy at birth:					
women			48.3 years		54.6 years
men			46.3 years		53.6 years
Death rate per 1,000 people			172		130
Birthrate per 1,000 people	39.8		32.3		27.7
Other					
Number of students in public high schools		203,000			2.3 million
Advertising expenditures	$20 million		$95 million		$500 million
Telephones per 100 people		0.3[b]	2.1[c]		12.6[d]

[a]1892   [b]1891   [c]1901   [d]1921

to 42 million. But these figures are somewhat misleading: in general, they represent a change in the nature of work rather than an increase in the number of available jobs relative to the number of people who could work. In the rural society that the United States was in the nineteenth century, women and children worked at tasks that were important to the family's daily existence—cooking, cleaning, planting, and harvesting. Their jobs were often hard to define, and they seldom appeared in employment figures because they earned no wages. But as the nation industrialized and the agricultural sector's share of the national income and population declined, waged and salaried employment became more common. Jobs in industry and commerce were both easier to define and easier to count. It is probable, then, that the proportion of Americans who were working was not increasing markedly—most Americans, male and female, had always worked. What was new was the increase in paid employment, which also made purchases of consumer goods and services more affordable.

Scientific developments eased some of life's struggles, and their impact on living standards increased after 1900. Advances in medical care and better living conditions sharply reduced death rates and extended the life span. Between 1900 and 1920, for example, life expectancy rose six years, and the death rate dropped by 24 percent (see table, page 539). During the same period there were spectacular declines in the death rates from typhoid, diphtheria, influenza (except for a harsh epidemic in 1918 and 1919), tuberculosis, and intestinal ailments—diseases that had been the scourge of earlier generations. There were, however, significantly more deaths from cancer, diabetes, and heart disease. Americans also found more ways to kill: though the suicide rate remained about the same, homicides and automobile deaths increased dramatically between 1900 and 1920.

Higher Life Expectancy

Not only were amenities and luxuries more readily available in the early 1900s than they had been a half-century earlier, but the means to upward mobility seemed more accessible as well. The spread of public education—particularly high schools—helped equip young people to achieve a higher standard of living than their parents. Between 1890 and 1922 the number of students enrolled in public high schools grew dramatically (see table). And more than ever before, education was becoming the key to success. The creation of new white-collar occupations in the growing service industries helped to stem the downward mobility that resulted when mechanization pushed skilled workers out of their crafts. Yet the United States was not a meritocracy—a society in which the most able individuals rise to the top. The inequality that had pervaded earlier eras remained. A caste system still prevailed: race and sex, more than any other factors, determined one's status. Religion and ethnicity also influenced social relations.

Moreover, the new material abundance and consumerism seemed to make places, things, and experiences too similar. Some people mourned for the more individualistic, self-reliant (and partly mythical) past, when Americans had had to pay more attention to summer heat and winter cold, when they had had to make things for themselves. Critics charged that the new society was creating products and demands that were unnecessary and even harmful. But it was too late to turn back. Americans had set their course toward a future that promised prosperity and comfort.

THE QUEST FOR CONVENIENCE

One of the most representative agents of the revolution in American lifestyles at the end of the nineteenth century was the toilet. The chain-pull, washdown water closet, invented in England around 1870, was adopted in the United States in the 1880s. Shortly after 1900 the flush toilet was developed; thanks to mass production of enamel-coated fixtures, it soon became common in American homes and buildings.

The indoor toilet, suddenly cheaper and easier to install, brought about a shift in habits and attitudes. In the past, people had believed there was no danger in disposing of human waste on or below the ground; only luxury hotels and estates had private bathrooms. By the 1880s, however, acceptance of the germ theory of disease had raised fears about human pollution as a source of infection and water contamination. Much more rapidly than Europeans did, Americans combined a desire for cleanliness with an urge for convenience, and water closets became common, especially in middle-class urban houses. Bodily functions took on a more unpleasant image, and the home bathroom became a place of utmost privacy. Also, the toilet plus the private bathtub gave Americans new ways to use—and waste—water. This process can be seen as part of a broader change that accompanied industrialization and mass production: the democratization of convenience.

The tin can also altered lifestyles. Before the mid-nineteenth century, Americans ate most foods only in season. Drying, smoking, and salting could preserve meat for a short time, but the availability of fresh meat, like that of fresh milk, was very limited; there

A salmon canning factory in Oregon, 1904. Canning preserved food in sealed containers enabled processors to market meats, fruits, and vegetables that formerly had spoiled easily or had been available only at limited times of the year. Factories such as this one also provided expanded employment opportunities for women.   Library of Congress.

was no way to prevent spoilage. But around 1810, a French inventor developed the cooking-and-sealing process of canning. And in the 1850s, an American named Gail Borden developed a means of condensing and preserving milk. Canned goods and condensed milk became more common during the 1860s, but supplies remained low because cans had to be made by hand. By 1880, however, inventors had fashioned stamping and soldering machines that mass-produced cans from tin plate. Suddenly all kinds of foods could be preserved and bought at all times of the year. Americans had acquired still another means of overcoming nature—and littering the landscape.

Other trends and inventions helped make it possible for Americans of all classes to vary their daily diets. Growing urban populations created the demand that encouraged fruit and vegetable farmers to raise more produce. Railroad refrigerator cars enabled growers and meatpackers to ship perishables greater distances and to preserve them for longer periods. Thus by the 1890s, northern city dwellers could enjoy southern and western strawberries, grapes, and tomatoes, previously available for a month at most, for up to six months of the year. In addition, increased use of iceboxes enabled families to store perishables. An easy means of producing ice commercially had been invented in the 1870s, and by 1900 the nation had more than two thousand commercial ice plants, most of which made home deliveries. The icebox became a fixture in the up-to-date middle-class home, and

Processed and Preserved Foods

remained so until the mechanized refrigerator replaced it in the 1920s and 1930s.

Even the working class had a more diversified diet. The lowest-income people still ate what their counterparts in previous eras had eaten: the cheapest foods, heavy with starches and carbohydrates. Southern textile workers, for example, ate corn mush and fatback almost every day. Unskilled urban breadwinners seldom could afford meat. Nevertheless, many families could take advantage of previously unavailable fruits, vegetables, and dairy products, to achieve more varied fare. Workers had to spend a high percentage of their income—almost half the main breadwinner's wages—on food. But they never suffered the severe malnutrition that plagued other developing nations.

Just as tin cans and iceboxes made many foods widely available, the sewing machine brought about a revolution in clothing. In the eighteenth century, almost all the clothes Americans wore were made at home, and a person's social status was indicated largely by what he or she wore. Then in the 1850s the sewing machine (invented in Europe but developed by Americans Elias Howe, Jr., and Isaac M. Singer) came into use for clothing and shoe manufacture. Demand for uniforms during the Civil War boosted the ready-made clothing business, and by 1890 annual retail sales of mass-produced garments had reached $1.5 billion. Through mass production manufacturers could turn out good-quality garments at relatively low cost and develop standard sizes that fit different body shapes. By the turn of the century, only the poorest families could not buy "ready-to-wear" clothes, and tailors and seamstresses, once the originators of fashion, had largely been relegated to repair work.

Ready-made Clothing

The clothing revolution had a socially leveling effect. Rich and poor alike bought their clothes "off the rack." As one merchant crowed, "We have provided not alone abundant clothing at a moderate cost for all classes of citizens, but we have given them at the same time the style and character in dress that is essential to the self-respect of a free democratic people."

By 1900 mass-produced clothing had also enabled a large segment of the population to become concerned with style. Restrictive Victorian fashions still dominated women's clothing, but some of the most burdensome features were beginning to be abandoned. Women's dress design now placed greater emphasis on comfort. Designers used less fabric; by the 1920s a dress required three yards of material instead of ten. Long sleeves and skirt hemlines receded, and high-boned collars disappeared. Petite was still the ideal, however: the most desirable waist measurement was 18 to 20 inches. (Corsets were big sellers at 79 cents apiece, and reformers complained that women often tried to squeeze into dresses, gloves, and shoes that were a size too small.) At the turn of the century, long hair tied at the back of the neck was the most popular style. But by the First World War, when many women worked in hospitals and factories, shorter, more manageable styles had become acceptable.

Men's clothes too became lighter-weight and more stylish. Before 1900, among the middle and more affluent working classes, a man would have had no more than two suits, one for Sundays and special occasions and one for everyday wear. No distinction was made between summer and winter suits. After 1900, however, manufacturers began to produce garments from fabrics of different weights. Men began wearing soft felt hats rather than stiff derbies. Soft collars and cuffs replaced stiff ones, and plain dark-blue serge gave way to softer shades and more intricate weaves. Workingmen's clothes did not change markedly: laborers still needed the most durable, least expensive overalls, shirts, and shoes. But even for those of modest means, clothing was becoming something to be bought rather than to be made and remade at home. It too had become a feature of mass consumerism.

Department stores and chain stores helped to create and serve this new world of consumerism. The great boom in department-store growth occurred between 1865 and 1900, when companies like Macy's, Wanamaker's, Jordan Marsh, and Marshall Field became fixtures of metropolitan America.

Department and Chain Stores

With their open displays of clothing, housewares, and furniture—all available in large quantities to anyone who had the purchase price—department stores effected a merchandising revolution. Not only did they offer wide variety; they added home deliveries, liberal exchange policies, and charge accounts. The Great Atlantic Tea Company, founded in 1859, became the first chain-store system. Renamed

Chapter 19: EVERYDAY LIFE AND CULTURE, 1877–1920

In just a few decades American fashions changed dramatically. Dark, heavy fabrics (left) gave way to lighter, more colorful clothing (right, worn by Governor of New York Al Smith and his wife). Keyston-Mast Collection, University of California, Riverside.

the Great Atlantic and Pacific Tea Company in 1869 and known more familiarly as A&P, the firm's stores sold groceries on a cash-and-carry basis. By buying in volume, the chain could sell to the public at low prices. By 1912 there were almost five hundred A&P stores, and more were being built in communities of all sizes across the nation. Other chains, such as Woolworth's, grew rapidly during the same period.

Though the greatest expansion of chain stores did not occur until after 1920, large-volume, broad-variety food and department stores changed the nature of shopping long before then. They offered personal conveniences (like credit and deliveries) formerly available only at specialty shops that catered to the wealthy, and they provided such services in attractive, sometimes ornate settings. Not only could anyone buy the goods for sale, but anyone who wanted to could enter and just look. No longer were clothes, furniture, and even some foods stocked merely to meet a demand. Now they were displayed in large

quantities, to entice shoppers and create demand. Shopping and consuming had become a thoroughly enjoyable American pastime.

FAMILY LIFE

Though the overwhelming majority of Americans continued to live their lives within a family, this most basic of social institutions underwent considerable strain during the industrial era. As American society became more affluent and complex, it generated new institutions—schools, social clubs, political organizations, and others—that competed with the family to provide nurture, education, companionship, and security. Many popular and scholarly writers warned that rising divorce rates, the growing separation be-

This photograph, titled "The Stork's Visit," epitomizes the new middle-class nuclear family, surrounded by consumer goods and with parents exuding devotion toward their new baby.   Library of Congress.

tween home and work, the entrance of large numbers of women into the work force, and loss of parental control over children spelled peril for home and family. Yet the family retained its fundamental usefulness as a cushion in a hard, uncertain world.

Throughout modern Western history, most people have lived in two overlapping kinds of basic units: the household and the family. A *household* is a residential unit, a group of related and/or unrelated people who live in the same abode. A *family* is a group of people related by kinship, some of whom typically live together. The distinction between household and family is important in describing how Americans lived in the late nineteenth and early twentieth centuries, since the two institutions followed different patterns.

Family and Household Structures

At the most elementary level, Americans between 1877 and 1920 grouped themselves in traditional ways. As in the past, the vast majority (75 to 80 percent) of American households consisted of *nuclear families*—usually a married couple with or without children and including no other relatives. About 15 to 20 percent of households consisted of *extended families*, which might include grandparents, grandchildren, aunts and uncles, in-laws, cousins, or combinations of such relatives. About 5 percent of the population lived alone. Despite slight variations from one ethnic, racial, or socioeconomic group to another, the prevailing pattern held relatively constant among all groups.

Several factors explain this pattern. Because the United States was a nation of immigrants, who tended to be young, the country had a very young population. In 1880 the median age was under twenty-one, and by 1920 it was still only twenty-five. (Presently it is almost thirty-one.) Moreover, fewer people than now lived to old age. In 1900 the death rate among people aged forty-five to sixty-four was over twice what it is today. As a result, there were relatively few old people: in 1900 only 4 percent of the population was sixty-five or older, compared with 12 percent today. Thus few families could form extended three-generation households. Fewer children than today knew their grandparents, and the experience of being a grandparent was rarer. Upward social mobility and migration separated many families, and the ideal of a home of one's own encouraged nuclear household organization.

The relative size of nuclear families did change over time, however. In the nineteenth century almost all of Europe and North America experienced a decline in birthrates. In the United States

Declining Birthrates

the decline began early in the 1800s and accelerated toward the end of the century. In 1880 the birthrate was 39.8 live births per 1,000 people; by 1900 it had dropped to 32.3, by 1920 to 27.7. The reasons for this decline remain unclear. The pattern seems to have been that women in the settled eastern areas of the country were ending childbearing at an earlier age—thus limiting the span during which they bore children—than were women in western areas. Possibly the greater availability of arable land in the West encouraged larger families; differences in a child's economic productivity may also have had an effect.

On farms, where children could work at home or in the fields at an early age, a new child contributed a new set of hands to the family work force. But in the wage-based eastern economy, children could not contribute significantly to the family income for many years; a new child therefore represented another mouth to feed. Throughout the nation, as diet and medical care improved, infant mortality fell, and families did not have to have many children just to ensure that some would survive. It also appears that decisions to limit family size—by abstaining from sex during the wife's fertile period, or by means of other forms of contraception and abortion—resulted from people's growing consciousness that they could improve the quality of life for themselves and their children if their families were smaller than their ancestors' families.

Though fertility among blacks, immigrants, and rural dwellers was consistently higher than among white native urban dwellers, the birthrates of all groups fell. As a result, families with six or eight children became less common; three or four children became more usual. Thus the nuclear family tended to reach its maximum size and then to reduce faster than in earlier eras.

In spite of the predominance of the nuclear family, the household typically expanded and contracted over the lifetime of a given family. First, the size of the family fluctuated as children were born and later left home. Though there were many variations, both male and female children, especially in working-class families, often left home before they were twenty years old, usually to work. Second, the process of leaving home made for huge numbers of young people—and some older people—who lived as boarders and lodgers, especially in cities. Middle- and working-class families commonly took in boarders to help pay the rent or to occupy unused rooms vacated by grown children. Immigrants often lodged newly arrived relatives and fellow villagers until they could establish themselves. Some historians have estimated that there was a 50-percent chance that a city dweller at the end of the nineteenth century would either have lived as a boarder or have taken in boarders at some point during his or her lifetime.

Housing reformers charged that boarding caused

Boarding

overcrowding and loss of privacy. Yet for those who boarded, the practice was highly useful. As one immigrant woman recalled:

> We had four boarders and I had to cook for them. When I first came here I didn't want to do this because everybody want to have their own house. Well, I change my mind because everybody was doing this thing. That time some of the people that came from the other side didn't have no place to stay and we took some of the people in the house that we knew. . . . This is the way that everybody used to do it that time.

Boarding was a transitional stage for immigrants and young people who had left home, providing them with a quasi-family environment until they set up their own households. And it gave the household flexibility, bringing in extra income to meet its needs.

Some households also included extended family members who lived as quasi-boarders. Especially in communities where economic hardship or rapid growth made housing expensive or scarce, newlyweds tended to live with the husband's or wife's parents until they could afford a place of their own. Often a family would take in a widowed parent or unmarried sister or brother who would otherwise have had to live alone. For immigrants and migrants, the family served as a refuge in a strange new place. Having moved from the Old World to the New or from one region to another, they sought out relatives who had preceded them. A Russian Jewish woman prepared for emigration to the United States by writing to relatives in New York. "When I came off the ship," she recalled, "an uncle of mine was supposed to pick me up. . . . But I didn't live with this uncle because I had my mother's sister so I stayed with her."

Kinship, then, had important functions, especially for immigrants and others in need. At a time when welfare and service agencies were rare, the family continued to be the institution to which people could turn. Even when relatives did not live together, they often lived nearby and could help each other with childcare, meals, shopping, advice, consolation, and the like. Family members also obtained jobs for each other. Factory foremen usually had responsibility for hiring, and they often recruited

Importance of Kinship

new workers recommended by their employees. According to one new arrival, "After two days my brother took me to the shop he was working in and his boss saw me and he gave me the job." A woman who worked in an optical factory recalled, "My uncle was foreman there. . . . That was my first job. I worked there with my mother. . . . My sister worked there a while too."

The obligations of kinship, however, were not always welcome or even helpful. Immigrant families often put pressure on last-born children to stay at home and care for aging parents, a practice that stifled opportunities for education, marriage, and economic independence. As an aging Italian-American father confessed, "One of our daughters is an old maid [and] causes plenty of troubles. . . . It may be my fault because I always wished her to remain at home and not to marry for she was of great financial help." Tensions also developed when one relative felt another was not helping out enough. One woman, for example, complained that her brother-in-law "resented the fact that I saved my money in a bank instead of handing it over to him." Nevertheless, kinship, for better or worse, provided people a means of coping with the many stresses caused by an urban industrial society. Social and economic change did not dissolve family ties.

While the family remained resilient and adaptable, subtle but momentous changes began to occur in individual life patterns. Before the twentieth century, the stages of life were less distinct **Stages of Life** than they are today, and generations blended into each other with relatively little separation. Childhood, for instance, was regarded as a period during which young people prepared for adulthood by assuming gradually more adult roles and responsibilities. The subdivisions of childhood—toddlers, schoolchildren, adolescents, and the like—were not nearly as clear-cut as they are today. Because few people lived past sixty-five or left work voluntarily and because homes for the elderly were rare, old people were not treated as separately as in later periods. Married couples had relatively large numbers of children born over a longer time span than is common among twentieth-century couples, so active parenthood occupied most of their adult lives. And older children, who often cared for younger

sisters and brothers, might begin parenting even before reaching adulthood.

By the turn of the century, demographic and social changes had altered these patterns. Decreasing fertility rates reduced the period of parental responsibility, so more middle-aged couples experienced an "empty-nest" stage when all their children had grown up and left home. Longer life expectancy and a tendency on the part of employers, especially in manufacturing, to force the retirement of aged workers further isolated the old from the young. At the same time, work became more specialized and education more formalized—especially after the passage of compulsory-school-attendance laws. Childhood and adolescence therefore became more distinct from adulthood. As a result of these and other trends (including the lower fertility rate, which gave people fewer sisters and brothers to relate to), Americans became more age- and peer-conscious. People's roles in school, in the family, on the job, and in the community came to be defined by age as much as by any other characteristic.

At the turn of the century, family life and its functions were both changing and holding firm. New institutions were assuming tasks formerly performed by the family. Schools were making education more of a community responsibility. Employment agencies, personnel offices, labor unions, and legislatures were beginning to take responsibility for employee recruitment and job security. And age-based peer groups were exerting greater influence over people's values and activities. In addition, migration and a soaring divorce rate seemed to be splitting families apart: 19,633 divorces were granted in the United States in 1880; by 1920, that number had grown to 167,105. Yet in the face of these changes, the family remained a resilient institution. Households and families adjusted, sometimes from one year to the next, by expanding and contracting to meet temporary needs. And kinship remained a dependable, though not always appreciated, institution. In the early 1900s, popular and scholarly writers were predicting the decline of the family just as they are today. But for the majority of people, family life was vital. "As I grew up, living conditions were a bit crowded," one woman reminisced, "but no one minded because we were a family [and we were] thankful we all lived together."

The New Leisure and Mass Culture

On December 2, 1889, as hundreds of workers paraded through Worcester, Massachusetts, in support of shorter working hours, a group of carpenters hoisted a banner that proclaimed, "Eight Hours for Work, Eight Hours for Rest, Eight Hours for What We Will." That last phrase, "for What We Will," was significant, for it marked recognition of a special segment of everyday life that belonged to the individual. Increasingly, leisure activities filled this time segment, among working classes as well as middle and upper classes.

For a nation nurtured on a frontier tradition of hard work and distaste for wasted time, the leisure-time revolution of the late nineteenth century marked a dramatic shift. American inventors **Increase in** and tinkerers had always tried to **Leisure Time** create labor-saving devices, but not until the late nineteenth century did the effects of technological development become truly time-saving. Mechanization and assembly-line production helped to reduce the average workweek for manufacturing workers from sixty-six hours in 1860 to sixty in 1890 and forty-seven in 1920. These reductions not only meant shorter workdays but also freer weekends. Middle-class white-collar workers in the cities spent eight to ten hours a day on the job and often worked only half a day or not at all on weekends. Even on farms, mechanization helped to expand free time. To be sure, many had no time for leisure; thousands still spent twelve- or fourteen-hour shifts in steel mills and sweatshops. Nevertheless, more Americans began to have time for a variety of diversions, and for the first time a substantial segment of the economy began providing for—and profiting from—leisure. By the early 1900s, many Americans were enmeshed in the business of play.

After the Civil War, amusement became an organized activity like production and consumption. The vanguard of this trend was sports. Formerly a fashionable indulgence of the genteel class, organized sports quickly became the most popular pastime of all classes, attracting huge numbers of participants and spectators. Even those who could not play or watch became involved by reading about sports in the newspapers.

The first and most popular organized sport was baseball. Having evolved out of older bat, ball, and base-circling games, baseball was formalized in 1845 **Baseball** when a group of wealthy New Yorkers organized the Knickerbocker Club and codified the rules of the game. By 1860 there were at least fifty baseball clubs, and pick-up games were played on city lots and rural fields across the nation. In 1869 a professional club, the Cincinnati Red Stockings, went on a national tour, and several other clubs quickly followed suit. The National League of Professional Baseball Clubs, founded in 1876, gave the sport a more stable, businesslike structure. By the 1880s, professional baseball was a big business: in 1887, for example, over 51,000 people paid to watch a championship series between St. Louis and Detroit. In 1903, the National League and competing American League (formed in 1901) began a World Series between their championship teams (the Boston Red Socks beat the Pittsburgh Pirates in that first series), further entrenching baseball as the national pastime.

Baseball appealed mostly to men. But croquet, which also swept the nation after the Civil War, attracted both sexes. Across the country, middle- and upper-class people held croquet **Croquet and** parties and even rigged wickets with **Cycling** candles for night games. In an era when the removal of work from the home had begun separating men and women, croquet renewed the opportunity for social contact between the sexes.

Bicycling achieved a popularity rivaling that of baseball—especially after 1885, when the cumbersome velocipede, with its huge front wheel and tall seat, gave way to the safety bicycle with pneumatic tires and wheels of identical size. By 1900 Americans owned over 10 million bicycles, and cycling clubs such as the League of American Wheelmen were pressing state and local governments to build more paved roads. One journal boasted that cycling cured dyspepsia, headaches, insomnia, and sciatica, and

In 1883, the New York Giants began playing their baseball games in a converted six-thousand-seat polo stadium. Within a few years, professional baseball had become so popular that crowds overflowed the stands and had to sit in the outfield. In 1891, a new Polo Grounds was built, enabling the Giants to set an attendance record of over a million fans three years later. Baseball had indeed become the national pastime. Library of Congress.

gave "a vigorous tone to the whole system." Like croquet, bicycling brought men and women together. Especially on the bicycle-built-for-two, it provided a combination of courtship with exercise. Moreover, the bicycle played an influential role in freeing women from the constraints of Victorian fashions. In order to ride bikes, even the dropped-frame female models, women had to wear divided skirts and simple undergarments. Gradually the freer styles of cycling costumes began to have an influence on the style of everyday fashions. As the 1900 census declared, "Few articles . . . have created so great a revolution in social conditions as the bicycle."

Tennis and golf won enthusiasts of both sexes but remained pastimes of the wealthy. Played mostly at private clubs, these sports lacked baseball's team competition and cycling's informality. American football also began as a sport for people of high social rank. At first mainly an intercollegiate sport, football attracted mostly players and spectators wealthy enough to have access to higher education. By the end of the century, however, football was attracting a broader class of supporters. The 1893 Princeton-Yale game drew fifty thousand spectators, and informal football games were being played in the yards and playgrounds of many communities throughout the country.

At the same time, college football was becoming

Football

Chapter 19: EVERYDAY LIFE AND CULTURE, 1877–1920

a national scandal because of its violence and use of "tramp athletes," nonstudents whom colleges hired to play on their teams. Critics charged that football mirrored the worst features of American society. An editor of the *Nation* complained in 1890 that "the spirit of the American youth, as of the American man, is to win, to 'get there,' by fair means or foul; and the lack of moral scruple which pervades the struggles of the business world meets with temptations equally irresistible in the miniature contests of the football field." The scandals climaxed in 1905, when 18 football players were killed and over 150 seriously injured. President Theodore Roosevelt, a strong advocate of athletics, convened a White House conference to discuss ways of eliminating brutality and foul play. The conference founded the Intercollegiate Athletic Association (renamed the National College Athletic Association in 1910) to police college sports. In 1906 the association altered the rules of football to make it less violent and more open. The new rules extended the distance to be gained by the first down from 5 to 10 yards, legalized the forward pass, and tightened player eligibility requirements.

As more women attended college, they began to pursue other forms of physical activity besides croquet, riding, and bicycling. Believing that in order to succeed intellectually they needed to be active and healthy, college women participated in a variety of sports, such as rowing, track, and swimming. Eventually basketball became the most popular sport among college women. Invented in 1891 as a winter sport for men, basketball was given women's rules (that limited dribbling and running and encouraged passing) by Senda Berenson of Smith College in the 1890s, and intercollegiate games became common across the country.

The rise of American show business paralleled the rise of sports, and similarly became a mode of leisure created by and for the common people. Circuses—

Circuses traveling shows of acrobats and animals—had existed since the 1820s. But after the Civil War, railroads enabled circuses to reach more of the country, and the popularity of the big show increased enormously.

Circuses offered two main attractions: so-called freaks of nature, both human and animal, and the temptation and conquest of death. More important, however, was the sheer astonishment aroused by the trapeze artists, lion tamers, high-wire artists, acrobats, and clowns. Writer Hamlin Garland captured the circus's effect on a thousand towns and villages:

> From the time the "advance man" flung his highly colored posters over the fence till the coming of the glorious day, we thought of little else. . . . It was our brief season of imaginative life. In one day—in a part of one day—we gained a thousand new conceptions of the world and of human nature. It was the embodiment of all that was skillful and beautiful in human action. . . . It gave us something to talk about.

Several branches of American show business matured with the growth of cities. Popular drama, musical comedy, and vaudeville all gave Americans a chance

Popular Drama and Musical Comedy to escape from the harsh realities of urban-industrial life into melodrama, adventure, and comedy. The plots were simple, the heroes and villains instantly recognizable. For urbanized people increasingly distant from the frontier, popular plays brought to life the mythical Wild West and Old South through stories of Davy Crockett, Buffalo Bill, and Civil War romances. Virtue, honor, and justice always triumphed in melodramas such as *Uncle Tom's Cabin* and *The Old Homestead*, reinforcing the popular belief that even in an uncertain and disillusioning world, goodness would nevertheless prevail.

Musical comedies raised audiences' spirits with song, humor, and dance. American musical comedy grew out of the lavishly costumed operettas popular in Europe. By introducing American themes (often involving ethnic groups), folksy humor, and catchy tunes and dances, these shows launched the nation's most popular songs and entertainers. George M. Cohan, born into an Irish family of vaudeville entertainers, became the master of American musical comedy after the turn of the century. Drawing on urbanism, patriotism, and traditional values in songs like "Yankee Doodle Boy" and "You're a Grand Old Flag," Cohan helped to reinforce national morale during the First World War. Comic opera too became a fad, and the talented, beautiful, dignified Lillian Russell its most admired performer. The first American comic operas were weak imitations of European musicals, but by the early 1900s, composers like Victor Herbert were writing for American audiences. Shortly

Lavish musical reviews and vaudeville shows became a very popular form of American entertainment. Filled with song, dance, and comedy, these performances reflected the new scale and organization of the American economy and culture. Culver Pictures.

thereafter Jerome Kern began to write more sophisticated musicals, and American musical comedy came into its own.

The French term *vaudeville* first referred to light drama with musical interludes, but in the United States vaudeville became a unique entertainment form.

Vaudeville

Originally staged by saloonkeepers to attract customers, vaudeville variety shows were developed by skilled promoters who used the term to lend respectability to a once-disreputable entertainment. Vaudeville was probably the most popular entertainment in early-twentieth-century America because its variety made it attractive to mass audiences. Shows included magic and animal acts, juggling, stunts, comedy (especially

ethnic humor), and song and dance. Around 1900, the number of vaudeville theaters and troupes skyrocketed. Fostered by sharp promoters who did for entertainment what Edison and Ford did for technology, vaudeville quickly became big business. The most famous promoter, Florenz Ziegfeld, brilliantly packaged popular entertainment in a stylish format—the Ziegfeld follies—and gave the nation a new model of femininity, the Ziegfeld Girl, whose graceful dancing and alluring costumes were meant to suggest a haunting sensuality.

Show business provided new economic opportunities for women, blacks, and immigrants, but also indulged in stereotyping and exploitation. Lillian Russell, vaudeville singer and comedienne Fanny Brice, and burlesque queen Eva Tanguay attracted intensely loyal fans, commanded handsome fees, and won respect for their genuine talents. In contrast to the demure Victorian female, they conveyed pluck and creativity. There was something both shocking and refreshingly confident about Eva Tanguay when she sang earthy songs like "I Want Someone to Go Wild with Me," "It's All Been Done Before But Not the Way I Do It," and her theme song "I Don't Care." But lesser female performers were often exploited by male promoters and theater owners, many of whom wanted only to titillate the public with the sight of scantily clad women.

Before the 1890s, the only form of entertainment open to black performers was the minstrel show. By century's end, however, minstrel shows had given

Blacks and Immigrants in Vaudeville
way to more sophisticated musicals, and blacks had begun to break into vaudeville. As stage sets shifted from the plantation to the city, the music shifted from folk tunes to ragtime. Pandering to the prejudice of white audiences, composers and performers of both races ridiculed blacks. The popularity of songs like "He's Just a Little Nigger, But He's Mine All Mine," and "You May Be a Hawaiian on Old Broadway, But You're Just Another Nigger to Me" is evidence that blacks on the stage suffered in the same way they did elsewhere in society. Even Burt Williams, a highly paid black comedian and dancer who was one of the era's most talented performers, achieved his tormented success mainly by playing the stereotypical roles of darky and dandy.

Much of the uniqueness of American mass entertainment came from its ethnic flavor. Indeed, immigrants were the core of American show business. Vaudeville particularly drew on and embellished ethnic humor, exaggerating its characters' dialects and other national traits. Though countless skits and songs reinforced ethnic stereotypes and made fun of ethnic groups, such distortions were more self-conscious and sympathetic than those directed at blacks. Ethnic humor often focused on the difficulties immigrants faced. A typical scene involving Italians, for example, would revolve around a character's uncertain grasp of English, which caused him to confuse *mayor* with *mare*, *diploma* with *the plumber*, and *pallbearer* with *polar bear*. Such scenes allowed audiences to laugh at the human condition and reminded them that,

deep down, all people—at least white people—were the same. Blacks, however, were never assumed to share the same hopes and frustrations as whites.

Shortly after 1900, live entertainment began to yield to an even more accessible form of amusement: moving pictures. Perfected by Thomas Edison in the

Movies
late 1880s, movies began as slot-machine peepshows in penny arcades and billiard parlors. Eventually images were projected onto a screen so large audiences could view them, and a new medium was born. At first, the subject matter of films was unimportant; it was enough merely to awe viewers with moving pictures of speeding trains, galloping horses, and writhing belly dancers.

Producers soon discovered, however, that a film could tell a story—and tell it with flair. By 1910 motion pictures had become an art form, thanks to creative directors like D. W. Griffith. Griffith's most famous work, *The Birth of a Nation* (1915), an epic film about the Civil War and Reconstruction, fanned racial prejudice by depicting blacks as threatening white moral values; its exaltation of the Ku Klux Klan also helped to revive the hooded empire. But the film's innovative techniques—close-ups, fade-outs, and battle scenes—gave viewers heightened drama and excitement. From the beginning, movies were popular among all classes (admission usually cost a nickel), and audiences idolized such film stars as Mary Pickford, Lillian Gish, and Charlie Chaplin with a passion no stage performer ever enjoyed.

The still camera, modernized by inventor George Eastman, enabled ordinary people to make their own photographic images; and the phonograph, another of Edison's inventions, made possible musical performances at home. The spread of movies, photography, and phonograph records meant that access to live performances no longer limited people's exposure to art and entertainment. Technology had dissolved the uniqueness of experience; now it was possible to mass-produce sound and images. Entertainment had become more widely available than ever before.

To some extent, the new amusements and pastimes had a homogenizing influence, bringing together disparate ethnic and social groups into a common experience. Parks, ball fields, vaudeville shows, and movies were designed for and appealed to everyone; they were nonsectarian and apolitical. Yet various

By the end of the nineteenth century, recreation of all sorts became a value of, and attainable by, almost all classes for the first time in American history. Note the free-spirited relaxation of these bathers on a Coney Island beach; their poses contrast markedly with the stiff formality of people on city streets and the serious concentration of people at work. Library of Congress.

groups adopted leisure institutions in their own way. Even though promoters and entrepreneurs were largely responsible for the spread of amusements, consumers often used them to reinforce their own cultural habits. For example, in some communities working-class immigrant groups used parks and amusement parks as locations for traditional family and ethnic gatherings. Much to the dismay of reformers who hoped that recreation would help assimilate newcomers and teach them habits of restraint, immigrants used picnics and Fourth of July celebrations as occasions for boisterous drinking and sometimes violent behavior. Many early movies intentionally had working-class characters and settings (Charlie Chaplin's films, for instance), reflecting the tastes of their audiences. Thus as Americans learned to play, their leisure—like their work and politics—was shaped by pluralistic forces.

THE TRANSFORMATION OF MASS COMMUNICATIONS

With so many new things to do and buy, how did Americans decide what they wanted? Two new types of communication influenced consumer tastes and mass opinion. Modern advertising molded people's needs and consumption patterns; and popular journalism spread mass culture throughout the country.

A society of scarcity does not need advertising. When demand exceeds the supply of goods and services, producers have no trouble selling what they

Advertising
market. But in a society of abundance such as industrial America, supply frequently outstrips demand. Thus a way of creating or increasing demand becomes necessary. Advertising had existed in the United States long before the late nineteenth century, but it took on a new scale and function in the decades before 1900. In 1865 about $9.5 million was spent on advertising; by 1900 the sum had reached $95 million, and by 1919 nearly $500 million.

The American salesperson's function has traditionally been to respond to a particular need and to convince the customer that a particular product— an insurance policy, a suit of clothes, a home appliance—is uniquely suited to fill that need. Advertisers, on the other hand, aim to *invent* a demand by convincing whole groups that everyone in that group should buy a particular product—a brand of cigarettes, a particular cosmetic, a certain company's canned foods. Indeed, the growth in the late nineteenth century of large companies that mass-produced consumer goods gave advertisers the task of creating "consumption communities"—bodies of consumers loyal to a particular brand name.

In 1881, Congress passed a federal trademark law enabling producers to register and protect brand names. Thousands of companies eventually did so, creating such well-known products as Hires Root Beer, Carter's Little Liver Pills, Uneeda Biscuits, Grape-Nuts, and countless others. Advertising agencies—a new service industry pioneered by N. W. Ayer & Son of Philadelphia—offered expert advice to companies that wished to cultivate brand loyalty. By the turn of the century, advertising techniques had been perfected to such an extent that the French composer Jacques Offenbach observed, "Decidedly the American advertising men play upon the human mind as a musician plays on his piano."

The major vehicle for advertising was the newspaper. Around the mid-nineteenth century, publishers began to pursue greater revenues from advertising by selling more ad space, especially to big urban department stores. In 1879 Wanamaker's placed the first full-page ad, and at about the same time newspapers began to allow advertisers to print pictures of products. Such attention-getting techniques transformed advertising into news. More than ever before, people

As producers exerted themselves to try to lure consumers, advertising became more elaborate, often using personal images and suggestive themes to sell a product. More than ever before, marketing had the function of creating a demand rather than serving a demand that already existed. Library of Congress.

read the newspapers to find out what was for sale as well as what was happening.

Just as advertising became news, news became a form of advertising, or at least of publicity. Canny publishers made people crave news just as they craved amusements and consumer goods. City life and the increase in leisure time seemed to nurture a fascination with the sensational, and from the 1880s onward popular newspapers increasingly whetted and catered to that desire.

Joseph Pulitzer, a Hungarian immigrant who bought the *New York World* in 1883, pioneered the development of journalism as a branch of mass culture. Believing that newspapers should be "dedicated to

Yellow Journalism
the cause of the people rather than to that of the purse potentates," Pulitzer filled the *World* with stories

A newsstand beneath an elevated railway station displays a large variety of popular magazines and newspapers. By the early 1900s these publications were read by millions daily—for their advertisements as well as for their news and sports. Ford Archives.

of disasters, crimes, and scandals. Sensational headlines, set in large bold type like that of advertisements, screamed from every page. Pulitzer's journalists not only reported the news but sought it out—and sometimes even created it. *World* reporter Nellie Bly (real name Elizabeth Cochrane) faked her way into an insane asylum and wrote a sensational exposé of the sordid conditions she found. Other reporters staged stunts and sought out heart-rending human-interest stories. Pulitzer also popularized the comics, and the yellow ink they were printed in gave his emphasis on the sensational the nickname "yellow journalism."

Pulitzer's strategy was immensely successful. In one year he increased the *World's* daily circulation from 20,000 to 100,000, and by the late 1890s it had

reached 1 million. Soon other publishers, such as William Randolph Hearst (who bought the *New York Journal* in 1895 and started an empire of mass-circulation newspapers), adopted Pulitzer's techniques. Yellow journalism became a nationwide phenomenon, enhancing interest in bizarre aspects of the human condition and kindling sentiments for reform.

Pulitzer and his rivals fanned popular interest even further by emphasizing sports and women's news. Newspapers had always reported on sporting events, but the yellow-journalism papers gave such stories far greater prominence by printing separate, expanded sports sections. Such sections did more than anything else to promote sports as a leisure-time attraction. Sports news became a new addiction, recreating a particular game's drama through narrative and statistics. And at the same time they expanded sports news, mostly for male readers, newspapers were adding more women's news. A special section devoted to household tips, fashion, decorum, and women's-club news captured the interest of female readers. Like crime and disaster stories, sports and women's sections helped to make the news a mass commodity.

By the early twentieth century, the communications media, like the mass consumption of goods, were becoming commonplace. Alongside newspapers, mass-circulation magazines were overshadowing the expensive elitist journals of earlier eras. Publications like *McClure's,* the *Saturday Evening Post,* and *Ladies' Home Journal* offered human-interest stories, muckraking exposés (see pages 589–590), titillating fiction, and eye-catching advertisements to a growing mass market. And the total number of books published more than quadrupled between 1880 and 1917. This rising popular consumption of news and books reflected a growing literacy rate. Between 1870 and 1920, the proportion of Americans aged ten or over who could not read or write fell from 20 percent to 6 percent.

Other forms of communication were also expanding. In 1891 there were only 0.3 telephones per 100 people in this country; by 1901 the number had grown to 2.1, and by 1921 it had swelled to 12.6. In 1900 Americans used 4 billion postage stamps; in 1922 they used 14.3 billion stamps. Little wonder, then, that the term *community* took on new dimensions, as people used the media, the mail, and the telephone to extend their horizons far beyond their place of residence. More than ever before, people in different parts of the country knew about and discussed the same staples of mass culture, whether it was a sensational murder, a sex scandal, or the fortunes of a particular entertainer or athlete. America was becoming a mass society.

POPULAR LITERATURE

The same society that celebrated the machine also idolized Tarzan the Ape Man. American culture has long focused one eye on an increasingly complex technological future while casting the other at a sentimentalized, simpler past. These two dispositions shared the popular mind between 1877 and 1920. When modern wonders like telephones, high-speed printing presses, phonographs, and cameras made information and entertainment more accessible, people demanded diversions that reaffirmed the traditional values of optimism, individualism, and freedom. Thus in 1914, just when they were beginning to fully appreciate automobiles, movies, and electricity, Americans made Edgar Rice Burroughs's *Tarzan of the Apes* a best seller.

Popular fiction writers in tune with the times concentrated on the sensational. Such efforts were not exactly new; since the 1840s, low-priced, paperbound adventure novels had circulatd widely among the literate public. After the Civil War such books, called dime novels, became the most widely read variety of American literature, especially among youths. As one man recalled, "I read them at every chance; so did every normal boy of my acquaintance. . . . We swapped them on the basis of two old volumes for every new one; we maintained a clandestine circulating library system which had its branch offices in every stableloft in our part of town." The principal publisher of dime novels was the firm Beadle and Adams, which issued over thirteen hundred titles in the three decades before it went out of business in 1897. Popular magazines like *Tip Top Weekly,* which serialized adventure stories, attracted hundreds of thousands of readers.

Dime Novels

These adventure publications offered three types of stories. The first evoked the Wild West for a population that was seeing the frontier fade into the past. Intertwining fact and fiction, writers like Zane Grey wove adventure stories around famous folk heroes like Buffalo Bill Cody, the Lone Ranger, and Wild Bill Hickok. During the 1880s, however, many authors, recognizing the lure and growing impact of city life, began to give their tales urban settings and themes. Detective thrillers became the leading type of popular urban fiction, and hard-nosed, wily characters like Old Cap Collins and Nick Carter captivated readers of various ages. Just before the end of the century, science fiction and superheroes came to the fore. Influenced by the marvels of new scientific discoveries, such works as the Tom Swift series described

"An ideal publication for the American Youth"

No. 171. Price, Five Cents.

FRANK MERRIWELL'S SECRET
OR TRYING TO STEAL THE DOUBLE SHOOT

BY BURT L. STANDISH

"I WILL GIVE YOU FIVE HUNDRED DOLLARS," SAID CUTTER, "TO SHOW ME HOW TO THROW THE DOUBLE SHOOT."

Frank Merriwell, the fictional hero of hundreds of sports and adventure stories, was a popular character model for young men. In this story, first published in Tip Top Weekly, *an unscrupulous sportsman tries to bribe Frank into teaching him his secret pitch, the "double shoot." Frank not only resists the temptation but teaches a moral lesson in the process. Culver Pictures.*

Alger's heroes begin their lives in poverty and call on ambition, honesty, courage, thrift, and luck to overcome some obstacle and achieve success. But his message was more than an exhortation to morality and frugality. The moral of Alger's stories was that success came to those who were not only virtuous but alert enough to capitalize on a lucky break. Thus Ragged Dick, the hero of Alger's first novel, is clean, honest, and polite, but his opportunity to escape poverty arrives when he rescues the drowning child of a banker. The hero of *Bound to Rise* ministers to a lonely old man who repays him with a bundle of real estate deeds. Thus while the main theme emphasized virtue as the means to overcome poverty, Alger also made his characters models of American resourcefulness.

Just before Alger's death in 1899, one of America's most popular superheroes, Frank Merriwell, was created by Gilbert Patten (using the pen name of Burt Standish), a writer of hack fiction since his teens. Frank Merriwell's adventures had a common theme that accorded with the way many Americans liked to think of themselves and their nation: he attempted and accomplished the impossible. Merriwell's name symbolized American virtues: according to Patten, "I took the three qualities I most wanted him to represent—frank and merry in nature, well in body and mind—and made the name Frank Merriwell."

In a series of fast-paced adventures, Merriwell provided youthful readers with one of the first character models in popular fiction. Whether performing amazing athletic feats or daring rescues, he was a picture of refinement and valor who taught by example, not by preaching. In one story, Frank knocks down a thug hired to break his arm before a big game. Graciously, Frank helps him to his feet and befriends him. The thug exclaims, "Gee, I don't know w'y it is, but jes' bein' wid youse makes me want ter do de square t'ing." Patten wrote 208 Merriwell novels, with titles such as *Frank Merriwell's Trip West, Frank Merriwell at Yale, Frank Merriwell's Air Voyage,* and *Frank Merriwell on Wall Street.*

Young women found escape and inspiration in sentimental tales about growing up and about animals. One of the most widely read was Louisa May Alcott's *Little Women,* published in two parts in 1868 and 1869. This novel, which eventually sold over 2 million copies, recreated the domestic delights and moral

spaceships, gravity nullifiers, and other inventions that surpassed even Edison's imagination.

One popular writer, Horatio Alger, moved beyond the fantasies of dime novels and offered his readers a formula for contending with new social and economic forces. A failed Unitarian clergyman, Alger began writing boys' stories in the 1860s, producing some 130 titles over the next three decades. As Alger's titles attest, each emphasizes the virtues of self-reliance and hard work: *Work and Win, Do and Dare, Struggling Upward, Rise from the Ranks.*

Moral Messages of Popular Fiction

trials of four girls based on Alcott and her sisters. A generation later, Gene Stratton-Porter's romantic novels about animals, like *Freckles* (1904) and *Laddie* (1913), became best sellers. Others in the same vein were Margaret Sidney's *Five Little Peppers* (1880), Anna Sewell's *Black Beauty* (1890), Kate Douglas Wiggins's *Rebecca of Sunnybrook Farm* (1903), and Lucy M. Montgomery's *Anne of Green Gables* (1908).

Popular literature for adults also oozed sentimentality. The best-selling titles of the late nineteenth century included Marie Corelli's *Thelma* (1887) and Charles Majors's *When Knighthood Was in Flower* (1898)—both romances about chivalry and honor—and *Ben Hur* (1880), General Lew Wallace's powerful religious melodrama set in the Roman Empire. Not since *Uncle Tom's Cabin* had a book captured as much attention as *Ben Hur*, which sold 2 million copies by 1933. Self-help and inspiration, both perennial themes in American popular literature, also burgeoned. The style pioneered by *Poor Richard's Almanac* and McGuffey's readers was developed in such works as Samuel Smiles's *Self-Help* (1860), *Character* (1871), *Thrift* (1875), and *Duty* (1880); Andrew Carnegie's *Gospel of Wealth* (1901); and Russell Conwell's published sermon "Acres of Diamonds" (see pages 521–522).

While some popular writers focused on escapism, others were trying to introduce realism into romance. During the 1870s and 1880s, a number of "local-color" writers began producing works

Local Colorists that depicted the people and environment of a particular region more realistically. This movement was largely centered in the South, whose writers felt compelled to rebuild the region's national image. Works by Joel Chandler Harris, who created the popular Uncle Remus stories; Mary Noailles Murfree, who located her tales in Appalachia; and George Washington Cable, who captured the aura of exotic New Orleans, all reproduced authentic characters and dialects. The regional writers of the Far West and Midwest included Bret Harte, who spun tales about the California mining experience; Edward Eggleston, who recreated the life of his native southern Indiana; and Constance Fenimore Woolson, who wrote about the lumbering and fur-trading districts of the Great Lakes. Each of these writers used authentic manners and ways of speech to depict a romantic, rustic past.

One local colorist, Mark Twain (the pen name of Samuel Clemens), moved beyond romance and adventure, and in doing so won recognition from both intellectuals and the masses. A

Literary Classics westerner who had grown up in Hannibal, Missouri, Twain worked as a river pilot on the Mississippi and traveled through the mining towns of the Far West. Though he wrote several works about Europe, such as *Innocents Abroad* (1869) and *A Connecticut Yankee at King Arthur's Court* (1889), he was best known for his books about the American West: *Tom Sawyer* (1876), *Life on the Mississippi* (1883), and *Huckleberry Finn* (1884). These antisentimental novels were realistic portrayals of western life and of human weakness. Twain was sensitive to both the comic and the tragic sides of life, and his writing reflected the dynamic energy and materialism of his era. He once wrote that "my books are mainly autobiographies," and his most famous character, Huck Finn, seemed to represent the daring, hypocrisy, and amiability of both Twain and his nation.

A number of Twain's contemporaries shunned the falseness of escape writing and focused instead on the moral tests life holds. Realists like William Dean Howells, Edith Wharton, and Henry James wrote chiefly about upper-class Americans (James usually wrote about Americans in Europe), but other realists examined the lives of more ordinary folk and in so doing opened new literary vistas. These writers, sometimes called naturalists, often viewed life in terms of the survival of the fittest; they portrayed ruthless struggles for life and power in frank detail. Among the naturalists were Stephen Crane, whose *Maggie: A Girl of the Streets* (1893) shocked readers with its candid description of slum life and sexual immorality; Kate Chopin, who in her novel *The Awakening* (1899) also addressed sensitive topics of sexuality and divorce; Hamlin Garland, whose *Main Traveled Roads* (1891) portrayed a depressing side of rural America, Frank Norris, whose *McTeague* (1899) graphically depicted the brutality of human greed; Jack London, whose stories of the West and Northwest portrayed violence among humans and animals; and Theodore Dreiser, whose *Sister Carrie* (1900) showed that people do not always suffer for their wrongdoings.

The escapism of popular fiction and the realism of serious fiction, though seemingly at odds, offered

others had known. The obstacles to success were not simple, and making one's way in the world required technological skills, organizational know-how, and a lot of capital. More sophisticated and more familiar with the possibilities of a consumption-oriented society, readers craved more from their heroes, such as prowess in the new mass cult of sports (Merriwell), conquest of science (Tom Swift), or abilities to commune with nature (Gene Stratton-Porter's characters).

Meanwhile serious authors, striving to recreate realistically what they saw around them, examined the flaws of progress. Whereas virtue still triumphed in popular and juvenile literature, naturalist writers saw that the new demands the industrial age placed on individuals threatened traditional American values of family, practicality, and moral restraint. The challenges of adjusting to a growing emphasis on consumption would become a major theme of twentieth-century American history.

SUGGESTIONS FOR FURTHER READING

Living Standards and New Conveniences

Daniel J. Boorstin, *The Americans: The Democratic Experience* (1973); James H. Collins, *The Story of Canned Foods* (1924); Richard O. Cummings, *The American and His Food* (1940); Boris Emmet and J. E. Jeuck, *Catalogues and Counters: History of Sears, Roebuck and Company* (1950); *Historical Statistics of the United States*, 2 vols., (1976); T. J. Jackson Lears and Richard W. Fox, eds., *The Culture of Consumption* (1983); Godfrey M. Lebhar, *Chain Stores in America* (1962); Clarence D. Long, *Wages and Earnings in the United States, 1860–1890* (1960); H. Pasadermadjian, *The Department Store* (1954); Peter R. Shergold, *Working Class Life: The "American Standard" in Comparative Perspective, 1899–1913* (1982); Lawrence Wright, *Clean and Decent* (1960).

Family and Individual Life Cycles

W. Andrew Achenbaum, *Old Age in the New Land* (1979); John E. Bodnar *et al.*, *Lives of Their Own: Blacks, Italians, and Poles in Pittsburgh, 1900–1960* (1982); Carl N. Degler, *At Odds: Women and the Family in America* (1980); Michael

similar commentaries on the American society of the early twentieth century. It was no coincidence that Frank Merriwell replaced Horatio Alger's heroes in popular fiction around 1900: by then Americans knew that it took more than honesty, energy, and a timely rescue to become rich. Numberless little-noticed revolutions had transformed the world that Alger and

Gordon, ed., *The American Family in Social-Historical Perspective*, 3rd ed. (1983); Carole Haber, *Beyond Sixty-five: Dilemmas of Old Age in America's Past* (1983); Tamara K. Hareven, *Family Time and Industrial Time: The Relationship Between the Family and Work in a New England Industrial Community* (1981); Tamara K. Hareven, ed., *Transitions: The Family and Life Course in Historical Perspective* (1978); Tamara K. Hareven and Maris Vinovskis, eds., *Family and Population in Nineteenth Century America* (1978); Joseph Kett, *Rites of Passage: Adolescence in America* (1979); David J. Pivar, *Purity Crusade: Sexual Morality and Social Control, 1868–1900* (1973); Richard Sennett, *Families Against the City* (1970); Virginia Yans-McLaughlin, *Family and Community: Italian Immigrants in Buffalo* (1977).

Mass Entertainment and Leisure

Robert Clyde Allen, *Vaudeville and Film, 1895–1915: A Study in Media Interaction* (1977); Gunther Barth, *City People* (1980); Allison Danzig, *History of American Football* (1956); Foster R. Dulles, *America Learns to Play* (1966); Roland Gelatt, *The Fabulous Phonograph* (1965); John F. Kasson, *Amusing the Million: Coney Island at the Turn of the Century* (1978); John A. Lucas and Ronald Smith, *Saga of American Sport* (1978); Donald J. Mrozek, *Sport and American Mentality, 1880–1910* (1983); Joseph A. Musselman, *Music in the Cultured Generation: A Social History of Music in America, 1870–1900* (1971); Beaumont Newhall, *The History of Photography*, rev. ed. (1964); Benjamin G. Rader, *American Sports* (1983); Roy Rosenzweig, *Eight Hours for What We Will! Workers and Leisure in an Industrial City,*

1870–1920 (1983); Harold Seymour, *Baseball*, 2 vols. (1960–1971); Robert Sklar, *Movie-Made America* (1976); Sigmund Spaeth, *History of Popular Music* (1948); Robert C. Toll, *On with the Show: The First Century of Show Business in America* (1976); David Q. Voigt, *American Baseball*, 2 vols. (1966–1970).

Advertising and Journalism

George Juergens, *Joseph Pulitzer and the New York World* (1966); Frank L. Mott, *American Journalism*, 3rd ed. (1962); Frank L. Mott, *A History of American Magazines*, 5 vols. (1930–1968); Daniel Pope, *The Making of Modern Advertising* (1983); W. A. Swanberg, *Citizen Hearst* (1961); Bernard A. Weisberger, *The American Newspaperman* (1961); James P. Wood, *The Story of Advertising* (1958).

Popular Literature

Katharine Anthony, *Louisa May Alcott* (1938); John G. Cawelti, *Apostles of Success in America* (1965); John L. Cutler, *Patten and His Merriwell Saga* (1934); Theodore P. Greene, *America's Heroes: The Changing Models of Success in American Magazines* (1970); Frank L. Mott, *Golden Multitudes: The Story of Best Sellers in the United States* (1947); Edmund L. Pearson, *Dime Novels* (1929); Moses Rischin, ed., *The American Gospel of Success* (1965); Henry Nash Smith, *Mark Twain* (1962); John W. Tebbel, *From Rags to Riches: Horatio Alger, Jr. and the American Dream* (1963); Dixon Wector, *Sam Clemens of Hannibal* (1952); Irvin G. Wyllie, *The Self-Made Man in America* (1954).

Gilded Age Politics
1877–1900

Chapter 20

*T*he *platform written* by the newly organized People's party that met in Omaha, Nebraska, in July 1892 seethed with discontent. Claiming to speak "in the name and on behalf of the people of this country," the platform's preamble charged that the nation had been

> brought to the verge of moral, political, and material ruin. Corruption dominates the ballot-box, the legislatures, the Congress, and touches even . . . the bench. . . . The fruits of the toil of millions are boldly stolen to build up colossal fortunes for a few. . . . From the same prolific womb of governmental injustice we breed the two great classes— tramps and millionaires.

To a modern reader, such rhetoric may seem like the ranting of extremists. Yet to thousands of Americans in the late nineteenth century, these words represented a measured sense of reality.

The transformation of the nation by industrialization, urbanization, and the commercialization of agriculture (see Chapters 16, 17, and 18) introduced disruptive forces that threatened time-honored customs and institutions. Members of the People's party, called Populists, were mostly farmers who believed that new, large-scale modes of production undermined their rights to equality and freedom. Like other protesters, such as labor unions and socialists, the Populists concluded that the economic system was creating irresponsible concentrations of power and wealth that would crush small producers and control government. To Populists, the sense of material ruin, political corruption, and division of society into tramps and millionaires represented the loss of the American dream. Thus they gathered in Omaha to preserve a civilization of cooperation and justice against the greed of market competition and the despotism of big business.

Populists believed that politics and government, the supposed forum for the democratic spirit, had been captured by the forces of monopoly and irresponsibility. In some ways they were right. Corruption and greed tugged at the fabric of democracy, and the venality of the era prompted novelists Mark Twain and Charles Dudley Warner to dub it the Gilded Age. Officeholders used their positions to amass personal fortunes and dispense patronage appointments to their supporters. But more important were the emphases the branches of government seemed to put on cautious policymaking and preserving the status quo. Congress, though split by powerful partisan and regional rivalries, did grapple with important issues, such as the tariff and the currency, and passed some legislation initiating needed reforms. But also, many congressional accomplishments were either weak compromises or favors to special interests. Meanwhile, the judiciary became active in determining public policy. By defending vested rights of property against state and federal regulation, the courts supported the emerging power of big business. The presidency was filled by a series of honest, respectable men who seldom took legislative initiatives; and when they did, they often found themselves beaten back by Congress and the courts.

During the 1870s and 1880s, serious problems were resulting from social and economic change, but the political system seemed slow to respond. The gap between those with political influence and those who were excluded was becoming a chasm, further separating opposing interest groups: farmers versus businesspeople; debtors versus creditors; blacks versus whites; employees versus employers. Then in the 1890s, two developments brought the social and economic turmoil to a boiling point and brought about political change: the climax of rural discontent that had accompanied the transformation of the West and South; and a deep economic depression that had resulted from flaws in the industrial system. In the midst of these crises, a presidential campaign in 1896 stirred Americans as they had not been stirred for a generation. Two candidates, William Jennings Bryan and William McKinley, and three parties, Democrats, Populists, and Republicans, compressed all the symbols of the era into a single election. The nation emerged from the turbulent 1890s with new political alignments, just as it had developed new economic configurations. These alignments prepared the way for the new century and for an era of reform that would

Chapter 20: GILDED AGE POLITICS, 1877–1900

try to overcome the injustices identified in the Omaha platform of the People's party.

POLITICAL EQUILIBRIUM AND EMOTIONAL ISSUES

The historian Henry Adams, grandson and great-grandson of presidents, wrote that in American political history, the period between 1870 and 1895 "was poor in purpose and barren in results." But such a judgment overlooked important characteristics, namely, the spirited competition between major parties and the extensive popular participation in politics.

From the voters' perspective, politics appeared anything but barren. At no other time in the nation's history was public interest in elections higher. Except

High Voter Participation
in the South, where blacks endured growing voting restrictions, 80 to 90 percent of eligible voters cast ballots in local and national elections. (Fewer than 50 percent typically do so today.) Politics was the prime form of mass entertainment, outdistancing even baseball, vaudeville, and circuses. Though only men could vote, campaigns were community events that excited women and children as well. Voting was only the last stage in a process that included rallies, parades, picnics, and speeches, all of which were as much public amusement as civic responsibility. As one observer remarked, "What the theatre is to the French, or the bull fight . . . to the Spanish . . . [election campaigns] and the ballot box are to *our* people." Politics was a personal as well as a community activity. In an era before advertising, polls, and the mass media influenced political choices, people formed strong loyalties to individual politicians, loyalties that often overlooked crassness and corruption.

Allegiances to parties and to individual politicians were usually so evenly distributed that no major faction or party gained lasting supremacy. Between 1877 and 1897, Republicans held the presidency for twelve years, Democrats for eight. The same party controlled the presidency and both houses of Congress for only three two-year spans: the Republicans twice, the Democrats once. Throughout the 1880s and early 1890s elections were extremely close, especially on the national level. The balance persisted despite the admission of six territories to statehood during this period (see map, page 564).

Government appeared to accomplish little in the Gilded Age because little was expected of it. Most Americans wanted an impartial government that did not interfere in social and economic matters. Also, struggles between and within parties stymied passage of effective, lasting legislation. Because the president was rarely of the same party as the majority of Congress, the two branches often blocked rather than supported each other's efforts.

In some ways, the major parties did resemble each other. Both were led by wealthy men, and both tried to appeal to farmers and wage earners as well as merchants and manufacturers. But differences in religious and ethnic values separated voters in the two parties. People who became Republicans were usually *pietistic:* Anglo-Saxon Protestants who believed that salvation was achieved through good works and encouraging others to be moral. They wanted government to legislate moral behavior, as the first Republicans had done in attempting to end slavery. After 1865 the party continued to attract people who supported moral controls such as prohibition of alcoholic beverages, restrictions on Sabbath activities (blue laws), and guidelines for school curricula.

Democrats, by contrast, attracted people whose culture was *ritualistic:* Roman Catholics, Jews, and high Protestants who believed that a person should accept the world as it is and that the way to salvation involved following the beliefs and rituals of the church. They preferred to leave questions of morality to individual conscience, rather than to government, and they preached moderation rather than interference. Thus they opposed government regulation of individual behavior.

These cultural differences—pietism versus ritualism—made for emotional conflicts over social issues, especially on the local level. But at the national level and in Congress, parties split over long-standing political and economic issues, such as sectional controversies, patronage, tariffs, and the currency.

Long after Reconstruction ended, Americans were haunted by the conflicts and disruptions that had

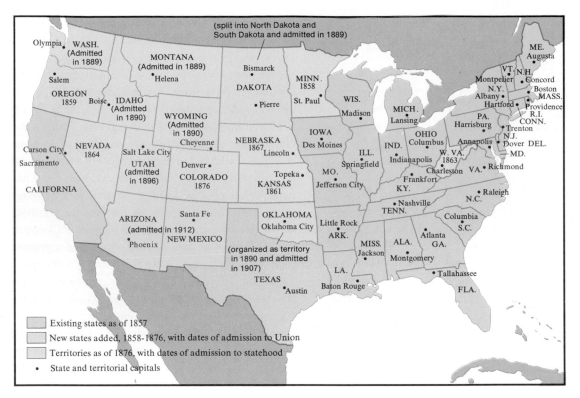

The United States, 1876–1912

followed the Civil War. Republicans capitalized on

Sectional Conflict

the war by "waving the bloody shirt" whenever they faced a Democratic challenge. As one Republican orator harangued in 1876, "Every man that tried to destroy this nation was a Democrat. . . . Soldiers, every scar you have on your heroic bodies was given you by a Democrat." In the South voters also waved the bloody shirt, calling all Republicans traitors. The use of such emotional appeals persisted well into the 1880s.

Politicians were not the only ones who attempted to profit by keeping the memory of the war alive. In the 1880s and 1890s, the Grand Army of the Republic, an organization of Union Army veterans numbering over 400,000, allied itself with the Republican party and pressured Congress into legislating generous pensions for former soldiers and their widows. The bullying tactics of veterans' lobbyists angered some legislators, but few could resist the demands of this huge interest group. "The pension agents who sit around this Capitol," griped one senator, "issue their circulars and decrees . . . and the Senators of

the United States, great and mighty as they may be, bow to the behests . . . and vote the money that they require, and they are afraid not to do it for fear that they would lose political status at home."

Many pensions were well deserved. Union soldiers had been poorly paid, and the war had widowed thousands of women. But for many veterans, the emotional wake of the war provided an opportunity to profit at the public's expense. By the end of the century the federal government was spending $157 million annually for soldiers' pensions, one of the largest welfare commitments it has ever made. No Confederate veterans received any of the largesse, though several southern states did fund small pensions and built old-age homes for ex-soldiers.

Few politicians could afford to oppose Civil War pensions, but a number of reformers attempted to dismantle the spoils system. The practice of awarding

Civil Service Reform

government jobs to party workers, regardless of their qualifications, had taken root in the antebellum years and blossomed after the Civil War in the federal government as well as states and cities.

Before the Pendleton Act of 1883, many government positions were filled by patronage: hat in hand, job seekers beseeched the president to find a place for them. Here a member of Congress presents constituents for office in return for their past political support.   Library of Congress.

As building construction, the postal service, the diplomatic corps, and other government activities expanded, so did the number of jobs on the public payroll. Between 1865 and 1891 federal government positions tripled, from 53,000 to 166,000. Elected officials scrambled to control new appointments as a means of cementing support for themselves and their parties. In return for the relatively short hours and high pay of government jobs, appointees pledged their votes and a portion of their earnings.

A system so susceptible to corruption vexed a growing number of independents, who began advocating appointments and promotions based on merit rather than connections. The movement grew during the 1870s, when scandals in the Grant administration bared the defects of the spoils system. It reached full flower in 1881 with the formation of the National Civil Service Reform League, an organization led by George W. Curtis, editor of *Harper's Weekly,* and E. L. Godkin, editor of the *Nation.* The same year, Charles Guiteau, a frustrated and demented job-seeker, assassinated President James Garfield, and the murder hastened the drive for civil service reform. Late in

1882 Congress passed the Pendleton Civil Service Act, and President Chester Arthur signed it early in 1883.

The law outlawed political contributions by officeholders and created the Civil Service Commission, which would supervise competitive examinations for government positions. The act, however, gave the commission jurisdiction over only about 10 percent of federal jobs—although the president could expand the list. The remaining jobs were subject to the old spoils system. Also, examinations were to apply only to new applicants, not to incumbents. These limitations explain why Republicans, then the majority in Congress, strongly supported the Pendleton Act, while most Democrats opposed it. As one Democratic senator complained, it was simply "a bill to perpetuate in office the Republicans who now control the patronage of the Government."

Civil service reform has often been considered one of the major accomplishments of the Gilded Age; yet its actual impact can be debated. Certainly the system of hiring government workers needed improvement. Under the spoils system, clerical jobs were given to people who could neither read nor write, and because the diplomatic corps contained so many untrained officers (many of whom could not speak the language of the country where they served), the American foreign service was one of the most incompetent in the field. But civil service reformers were not egalitarians who would give all qualified Americans a chance to participate in government. They were conservatives who wanted to restore an era when public servants were chosen from among men whose birth, wealth, and education supposedly fitted them for leadership. Moreover, no one has ever proven that the quality of government employees improved under civil service.

In the 1880s tariffs and money, not government jobs, attracted the most attention in Congress. Through the mid-nineteenth century Congress had

Tariff Policy

raised tariff rates to protect American manufactured goods and some agricultural products from European competition. By the 1880s there were separate tariffs on over four thousand items, and the resulting revenues were making for an embarrassing surplus in the federal treasury. Though a few economics professors and farmers argued for free trade, most Americans still believed high tariffs were necessary to support industry and preserve the jobs of wage earners.

The Republican party, claiming responsibility for economic growth, made protective tariffs a core feature of its policies. Democrats complained that tariffs made prices artificially high, benefiting those interests, such as woolen manufacturers, whose products were protected while hurting farmers whose crops were not protected and consumers who had to buy manufactured goods. Although Democrats generally saw a need for some protection of American goods and raw materials, they favored lower tariff rates to encourage foreign trade and to reduce the treasury surplus.

Privileged interests continued to dominate tariff policy in the 1890s. When in 1894 House Democrats supported by President Grover Cleveland passed a bill to reduce tariff rates, Senate Republicans, aided by southern Democrats eager to protect their region's infant industries, added some six hundred amendments restoring most cuts. In 1897 a new tariff bill, the Dingley Act, raised rates even further, though it greatly expanded reciprocity provisions. Introduced in the McKinley Tariff of 1890 and designed to encourage new foreign trade and to discourage foreign retaliation against high American duties, reciprocity gave the president authority to remove items from the free list if their countries of origin placed unreasonable tariffs on American goods.

The currency controversy was even more tangled than the tariff issue. In brief, it involved opposing reactions to the fall in prices caused by increased industrial and agricultural production after the Civil War (see pages 443–444). Farmers, most of whom were debtors, suffered because they had to pay fixed mortgage and interest payments even while their incomes declined because prices for their crops were dropping. Correctly perceiving that an insufficient money supply had made their debts more expensive relative to other prices, farmers favored schemes like the coinage of silver to increase the amount of currency in circulation. Creditors, on the other hand, believed that overproduction had caused the price decline. They favored a more stable, tightly controlled money supply backed only by gold as a means of maintaining the confidence of native and foreign investors in the American economy.

But the issue involved more than economics. The quantity and quality of money symbolized a whole series of conflicts—social, regional, and emotional. The creditor-versus-debtor conflict translated into haves versus have-nots. It also involved a sectional cleavage, the western silver-mining areas and agricultural regions of the South and West against the more conservative industrial Northeast. Finally, the issue had moral, almost religious, overtones. Gold, the traditional basis of money, was a durable yet malleable metal. Those qualities plus its beauty and rarity gave it a magical potency, a God-given symbol of value. But others considered the gold standard for currency too limiting for the machine age; prosperity, they felt, demanded new attitudes.

By the late 1870s, the currency controversy had become a matter of gold versus silver. Up to that time the government had coined both silver and gold dollars; a silver dollar weighed sixteen times more than a gold dollar, meaning that gold was officially worth sixteen times as much as silver. But gold discoveries since 1848 had increased the supply, lowering gold's market price relative to that of silver. Producers of silver, which was now worth more than one-sixteenth the value of gold, preferred to sell their metal on the open market rather than to the government. As a result, silver dollars disappeared from circulation—owners hoarded them rather than spend them—and in 1873 Congress officially stopped coining silver dollars. At about the same time, European nations also stopped buying silver. Thus the United States and many of its trading partners adopted the gold standard, meaning that their currency was backed chiefly by gold.

Within a few years, however, new mines in the American West began to flood the market with silver, and its price dropped. Gold was now worth more than sixteen times what silver was worth. It became profitable to spend silver dollars—and would have been worthwhile to sell silver to the government in return for gold, but the government was no longer buying it. Debtors, who were suffering from the depression of the mid-1870s in addition to falling prices, and who saw silver as a means of expanding the currency supply, now joined with silver producers to denounce the "Crime of '73" and to press for resumption of coinage at the old sixteen-to-one ratio.

Congress, split into silver and gold factions, tried to neutralize the issue with compromise legislation:

Monetary Policy

the Bland-Allison Act of 1878, which required the treasury to buy $2 to $4 million worth of silver each month; and the Sherman Silver Purchase Act of 1890, which fixed the monthly purchase of silver in weight (4.5 million ounces) rather than in dollars. But neither act satisfied the different interest groups. The Sherman Act, passed partially in response to an economic decline in the mid-1880s, failed to expand the money supply: as the price of silver dropped, the government, now required only to buy a certain weight of silver, could spend less to purchase the stipulated number of ounces. Thus the money supply was not increased as substantially as some had hoped. Not until after a depression in the 1890s and an emotion-filled presidential election would the money issue subside.

While debates over tariffs and money raged, Congress and state legislatures began to face the issue of women's suffrage more squarely than ever before.

Women's Suffrage

After the Civil War, several events mobilized women to pursue the vote. Late in 1869 a Missouri couple, Francis and Virginia Minor, drew up a resolution stating that the Constitution and its amendments had already given women the right to vote. According to the recently adopted Fourteenth Amendment, the Constitution granted citizenship to "all persons born or naturalized in the United States," and no state could abridge the "privileges or immunities" of any citizen, including his—or, said the Minors, her—right to vote. Eventually the Minors, with support from the National Woman Suffrage Association (NWSA), sued a St. Louis registrar who had refused to permit Mrs. Minor to vote. After a series of adverse decisions in lower courts, the case went to the Supreme Court in 1874. The majority opinion written by Chief Justice Morrison R. Waite upheld the lower courts, declaring that suffrage did not automatically accompany citizenship and that states could legally withhold voting rights from certain classes of citizens, such as criminals, the insane—and women.

The Minor decision did not deter the cause of women's suffrage or the NWSA. In 1878 Susan B. Anthony, the indomitable fighter for human rights who also had been rebuffed by the courts when she tried to vote in 1872, convinced Senator A. A. Sargent of California, a strong supporter of women's suffrage, to introduce a constitutional amendment stating that "the right of citizens of the United States to vote shall not be denied or abridged by the United States or by any state on account of sex." (The Women's Suffrage Amendment finally ratified forty-two years later was identical to this "Anthony Amendment.") The bill was killed by a Senate committee, but supporters reintroduced it several times over the next eighteen years. On the few occasions when the bill reached the Senate floor, it was voted down by senators who expressed fears that suffrage would interfere with women's family responsibilities and ruin female virtue.

While the NWSA and others fought for the vote on the national level, the American Woman Suffrage Association worked for constitutional amendments at the state level. (The two suffrage groups joined in 1890 to form the National American Woman Suffrage Association.) Between 1870 and 1910, there were seventeen referenda in eleven states (all but three of which were west of the Mississippi River) to legalize women's suffrage. These attempts seldom succeeded, but they attracted attention from newly formed women's clubs and trained a corps of female leaders in organizing and public speaking. Women did attain partial victories: by 1890 nineteen states allowed women to vote on school issues, and three granted suffrage on tax and bond issues.

The thrust for women's suffrage in the Gilded Age failed because society was still not prepared to accept such reform. Even in the western states where some limited gains were made, male politicians were willing to grant the vote not because women asked for it, but because they believed female voters could help give their communities a more civilized image and thereby attract settlers. Thus in politics, as in other areas of life, women were considered neither similar nor equal to men; instead, they were different and unequal.

Throughout the Gilded Age, legislative leaders did address some of the basic issues, but they failed to agree on clear solutions to pressing economic problems. Congressmen and their constituents were so divided among factions and interest groups that the only passable legislation was the kind, like the Pendleton Civil Service Act, that was ideal to no one but acceptable to most. And while complex problems like the tariff demanded careful study, Congress, and

Sheet music for a late-nineteenth-century song about women's suffrage. Women increased their agitation for the vote until in 1878 a constitutional amendment granting them suffrage was introduced in Congress. The Senate killed the measure that year, but women's groups like the National Woman Suffrage Association continued to fight for the cause. *American Antiquarian Society.*

particularly the Senate, became an oratorical battleground for party and intraparty rivalry over patronage. Between late 1879 and early 1881, for example, the prevailing question was not the nation's economic or social condition, but which member of which Republican faction would be appointed to the patronage-rich post of Collector of the Port of New York. Politics has always been the art of compromise, but in the two decades after Reconstruction, compromise became equated with the postponement of major decisions.

THE DECLINE OF THE PRESIDENCY

In the years between 1877 and 1900, American presidents contrasted sharply with more headstrong predecessors like Jackson and Lincoln. Proper, honorable, and honest, Presidents Hayes, Garfield, Arthur, Cleveland, Harrison, and McKinley won public respect but seldom provoked strong positive or negative emotions. Like other politicians, they used symbols. Hayes served lemonade at the White House to emphasize that, unlike his predecessor Grant, he was no hard drinker. McKinley put aside his cigar in public so photographers would not catch him setting a bad example for youth. But none of the era's six presidents was an inspiring personality, nor could any of them dominate the factional chieftains of their parties.

Thus during the Gilded Age the presidency declined in influence relative to Congress. Until the 1890s no serious crisis threatened the nation, so no president was in a position to assume emergency powers. The nature of domestic issues coupled with the generally nonassertive personalities of the presidents created an atmosphere in which the presidency had little independence. The nation's growing involvement in foreign affairs and the wars and treaties accompanying that involvement did give Presidents Cleveland and McKinley a few opportunities to set policy, but they too had to bow to the pressures of Congress. Cleveland initiated a few pieces of legislation and used the veto to fight some congressional abuses, but he had no

intention of expanding his presidential prerogatives. "I shall keep right on doing executive work," he once stated. "I did not come here to legislate."

Hayes, Garfield, and Arthur

Rutherford B. Hayes (1877 to 1881) personified the belief that the president was a caretaker elected to execute what Congress initiated. Honest and a model of self-control, Hayes had been a Union general and an Ohio congressman and governor before his disputed election to the presidency (see pages 445–446). Once in office, he avoided such controversial issues as the tariff and sectional rivalry. He did, however, take a conservative position on currency, and ordered out troops to quell the 1877 railroad strikes. Hayes pleased civil service advocates by appointing reformer Carl Schurz to the cabinet and battling New York's patronage king, Senator Roscoe Conkling. (He fired Conkling's protégé, Chester Arthur, from the post of New York Customs House Collector.) But Hayes also demanded that his own appointees contribute to Republican coffers for the 1878 elections. He was not a beloved leader. As one reformer wrote, "I have little or no patience with Mr. Hayes. He is a victim of . . . good intentions and his contributions to the pavement of the road to the infernal regions are vast and nefarious."

When Hayes refused to run for re-election in 1880, Republicans selected another Ohio congressman and Civil War hero, James A. Garfield. A husky, serious, and cautious man, Garfield defeated the Democrats' Winfield Scott Hancock, also a Civil War hero, by just 40,000 votes out of over 9 million. By carrying the pivotal states of New York and Indiana, however, Garfield won in the electoral college by a comfortable margin, 214 to 155. Garfield spent most of his brief presidency trying to secure an independent position among party potentates. He appeared to have no relish for his responsibilities, and especially disliked dealing with the hordes of office seekers. "Once or twice," he complained, "I felt like crying out in the agony of my soul against the greed for office and its consumption of my time." He did please civil service reformers by refusing to satisfy Conkling's demands, but Garfield's opportunity to make lasting contributions ended in July 1881 when the crazed Charles Guiteau shot him in a Washington railroad station. Not seriously wounded at first, Garfield lingered for seventy-nine days while doctors tried unsuccessfully to remove a bullet lodged in his back. His condition steadily deteriorated, and he finally succumbed to infection, dying September 19.

Garfield's vice president and successor was New York politician Chester A. Arthur, the spoilsman Hayes had fired in 1878. Arthur had been nominated for vice president only to help the Republicans carry New York State; his elevation to the presidency made reformers shudder. Yet he became a dignified and temperate executive. Arthur lent some support to civil service reform and signed the Pendleton Act. He urged Congress to modify outdated tariff rates, and spoke in favor of federal regulation of railroads. Using the veto as a means to influence Congress, Arthur killed a number of bills that excessively benefited privileged interests. But like his two predecessors, Arthur had no taste for his office. Suffering from illness, he made little effort to run in 1884.

The 1884 presidential campaign magnified the political banalities of the era. The Republicans nominated Senator James G. Blaine of Maine, whose impressive leadership skills and popularity were offset by his practice of using his influence to obtain favorable financial deals for railroads, for which he was paid handsomely. The Democrats named New York's Governor Grover Cleveland, a rotund and righteous bachelor whose respectable reputation was tainted by his having once fathered an illegitimate son—a fact he admitted openly during the campaign. Both parties focused on the sordid side of the opposition, and disapproval of Blaine was so strong that a number of disaffected Republicans called Mugwumps deserted their party for Cleveland. On election day Cleveland beat Blaine by only 23,000 popular votes; his tiny margin of 1,149 votes in New York gave him that state's 36 electoral votes, enough to squeeze a 219-to-182 victory in the electoral college. Cleveland may have won New York because in the last week of the campaign a local Protestant minister publicly equated Democrats with "rum, Romanism, and rebellion" (drinking, Catholicism, and the Civil War). Democrats eagerly publicized the slur among New York's numerous Irish-Catholic population, urging voters to protest by turning out for Cleveland.

Cleveland, the first Democratic president since Buchanan, complained like his Republican predecessors of the "cursed constant grind" of his office and the "want of rest." He did, however, exercise more vigorous leadership. Cleveland used the veto extensively against outrageous pension bills, and he extended the scope of civil service. But his most forceful action was his unsuccessful campaign for tariff reform. Worried about the growing treasury surplus, Cleveland urged Congress to cut duties on raw materials and manufactured goods. When advisers warned him that his stand might weaken his chances for re-election, the president retorted, "What is the use of being elected or re-elected, unless you stand for something?" Cleveland's firmness did not prevail, though. The Mills tariff bill of 1888, passed by the House in response to Cleveland's wishes, was killed by the Senate. Although the Democrats renominated Cleveland for the presidency in 1888, protectionists in the party were soon able to convince Cleveland to temper his attacks on high tariffs.

Cleveland and Harrison

Republicans in 1888 nominated Benjamin Harrison, an intelligent but chilly former senator from Indiana and grandson of President William Henry Harrison. The campaign was less savage than the 1884 campaign had been, but it was far from clean. Some shrewd Republicans manipulated the British minister in Washington into stating that Cleveland's re-election would be good for England. Irish Democrats took offense, as intended, and Cleveland's campaign was weakened. Perhaps more helpful to Harrison was the bribery and multiple voting that helped him to win Indiana by just 2,300 votes and New York by only 14,000. (Democrats also indulged in bribery and vote fraud, but the Republicans were more successful at it.) These crucial states assured Harrison's victory; though Cleveland outpolled Harrison by 90,000 popular votes, Harrison carried the electoral vote by 233 to 168. After the election, Harrison told Matt Quay, the Republican national chairman, "Providence has given us the victory." Quay later quipped to a friend, "Think of the man. He ought to know that Providence hadn't a damned thing to do with it. . . . [He] would never learn how close a number of men were compelled to approach the gates of the penitentiary to make him president."

Harrison was the first president since 1875 whose party controlled both houses of Congress, but he did little to take advantage of this circumstance. Several aspects of his administration were contradictory.

Gilded Age politics was a mass activity, involving both sexes and all age groups. This painting, titled "The Lost Bet," shows a parade in Chicago just after Grover Cleveland won his second term as president in 1892. A local Republican had offered to pull his Democrat friend in a cart if Cleveland won. Here, the Democrat is collecting on the bet to the great enjoyment of a throng of onlookers.   Library of Congress.

Harrison was a fiscal conservative, but under his administration Congress passed the first peacetime budget to exceed $1 billion. At Harrison's urging the House passed a "force bill" to protect blacks' civil rights by allowing federal courts to investigate irregularities in voter registration and jury selection; but Republican senators filibustered and then tabled the bill, causing the president to abandon the cause. And though Harrison supported protective tariff rates and reciprocity agreements to aid business, he agreed to the Sherman Anti-Trust Act and the Sherman Silver Purchase Act (1890), both of which were considered damaging to business. Harrison professed support for civil service and appointed Theodore Roosevelt a civil service commissioner, but the president's lackluster character prompted the reform-minded and impatient Roosevelt to call him a "cold-blooded, narrow-minded, prejudiced, obstinate, timid, old psalm singing Indianapolis politician."

Cleveland and Harrison ran against each other again in 1892. This time Cleveland attracted heavy contributions from business and beat Harrison by 380,000 popular votes (3 percent of the total) and by 277 to 145 electoral votes.

In office once more, Cleveland took bolder steps to meet the problems of currency, tariffs, and labor unrest. But his actions reflected a narrow orientation to the interests of business and bespoke political weakness. In order to protect the nation's gold reserve, which was shrinking during the Panic of 1893, Cleveland enlisted aid from bankers, who bailed out the nation on terms highly favorable to themselves. During the election campaign Cleveland promised sweeping tariff reform, but he made little effort to line up support for such reform in the Senate, where protectionists undercut all efforts to reduce rates. And when 120,000 boycotting railroad workers paralyzed western trade in the 1894 Pullman strike (see page 502), Cleveland bowed to the requests for federal troops from railroad managers and Attorney General Richard Olney. Throughout Cleveland's second term, events—particularly the economic downturn and the Populist ferment—seemed too much for the president. Cleveland's party abandoned him in 1896.

STIRRINGS OF AGRARIAN UNREST

While the political system in Washington faltered, inequities in the new agricultural and industrial systems were creating the first rumblings of a mass democratic movement that was to shake American society in the late nineteenth century. The agrarian revolt—a complex mixture of strident rhetoric, nostalgic dreams, and hard-headed egalitarianism—began when farmers' alliances formed in Texas in the late 1870s, then spread across the Cotton Belt and the Plains in the 1880s. The movement caught on chiefly in areas where farm tenancy, crop liens, furnishing merchants, railroads, banks, weather, and insects threatened the ambitions of hopeful farmers. Once under way, it inspired visions of a truly cooperative, democratic society.

Agricultural expansion in the West and South exposed millions of people to the hardships of rural life (see Chapter 16). Uncertainties might have been more bearable if the rewards had been more promising, but such was not the case. As farmers put more land under cultivation, as mechanization boosted productivity, and as foreign competition increased, supplies exceeded national and worldwide demand for agricultural products. Consequently, prices for staple crops dropped steadily. A bushel of wheat that sold for $1.45 in 1866 brought only $.80 in the mid-1880s and $.49 by the mid-1890s. Meanwhile transportation, storage, and commission fees remained high relative to other prices. Costly seed, fertilizer, manufactured goods, taxes, and mortgage interest combined with social isolation to trap many farm families in disadvantageous and sometimes desperate circumstances. In order to buy necessities and pay bills, farmers had

to produce more. But the spiral only wound more tightly, since the more farmers produced, the lower prices dropped.

Even before the full impact of these developments was felt, farmers had begun to organize to relieve their mounting distress. With aid from Oliver H. Kelley of the Department of Agriculture, farmers founded a network of local organizations called Granges in almost every state during the late 1860s and early 1870s. By 1875 the Grange had nearly twenty thousand local branches and over 1 million members. Strongest in the Midwest and South, Granges served chiefly as social organizations, sponsoring meetings and educational events to help relieve the loneliness of farm life. Family-oriented and open to all, local Granges made explicit provisions for women's participation.

Grange Movement

As membership flourished, Granges moved beyond social functions into economic and political action. At its 1874 national convention, the Grange proposed to avoid high retail prices by forming local cooperatives to buy equipment and supplies directly from manufacturers. Granges also encouraged the formation of sales cooperatives, whereby farmers would pool their grain and dairy products and then divide the profits. In a few instances, Grangers operated implements factories and insurance companies. Most such enterprises failed, however, because farmers lacked cash for cooperative buying and because ruthless competition from large manufacturers and dealers undercut them. In politics, Grangers used their numbers to some advantage, electing sympathetic legislators and pressing for laws to regulate transportation and storage rates.

In spite of their progressive, even radical, efforts, Granges nevertheless declined in the late 1870s. The requirement that cooperatives run on a cash-only basis excluded large numbers of farmers who never had any cash. Efforts to regulate business and transportation withered when corporations won court support against "Granger laws." Politically, Granges disavowed third parties but could not overcome the power of business interests within the established parties. Finally, the Grange's promotion of thrift and hard work was of little value to families already overburdened with both virtues. Thus, after a brief assertion of influence, the Grange reverted to an organization of farmers' social clubs. Its short-lived agrarian campaign served, however, as a precedent for future action.

Rural activism then shifted to the Farmers' Alliances, two networks of organizations—one in the Plains and one in the South—that by 1890 constituted a genuine mass movement. The first

Farmers' Alliances

alliances sprang up in Texas, where hard-pressed farmers rallied against crop liens, furnishing merchants, and railroads in particular, and against money power in general. Adopting an effective system of traveling lecturers to recruit members, alliance leaders extended the movement to other southern states. By 1889 the Southern Alliance boasted over 3 million members, including the powerful Colored Farmers' National Alliance, which claimed over 1 million black members. A similar movement flourished in the Plains, where by the late 1880s 2 million members were organized in Kansas, Nebraska, and the Dakotas.

Alliance members pushed the Grange concept of cooperation to new limits by sponsoring organizational rallies, educational meetings, and cooperative buying and selling agreements. Seeing themselves as laborers battling capitalists in a new age, some alliance members advocated unity with the Knights of Labor and other workers' groups.

Beyond urging democratic cooperation, the alliance movement proposed a scheme to alleviate the most serious rural problems: lack of cash and credit. The

Subtreasury Plan

subtreasury plan, adapted from French and Russian precedents, called for the federal government to construct warehouses in every major agricultural county. At harvest time, farmers could store their crops in these subtreasuries while awaiting higher prices, and the government would loan farmers treasury notes amounting to 80 percent of the market price the stored crops would bring. Farmers could use these subtreasury notes as legal tender to pay debts and make purchases. Once the stored crops were sold, farmers would pay back the loans plus small interest and storage fees.

The subtreasury scheme was meant to replace the crop-lien system and to give farmers greater control over their financial affairs. No longer would merchants be able to take advantage of farmers at harvest time, when market gluts depressed prices. No longer would farmers have to mortgage crops (through crop liens)

The Farmers' Alliance movement organized agrarian unrest into a cogent list of reforms. This cartoon shows how alliance members hoped to protect their mortgages and crops with a series of economic proposals that would make the currency system more flexible. *Library of Congress.*

at high interest. And no longer would they lack cash to buy supplies. Moreover, by issuing subtreasury notes, the government would be injecting more money into the economy and encouraging the kind of inflation agrarian reformers desired: inflation that would raise crop prices without raising the costs of supplies and rents. If government subsidized business, reasoned alliance members, why should it not help farmers earn a decent living too?

Implementation of their plans confronted alliance members with questions of political participation. If the various alliance groups, North and South, had been able to unite, they would have made for a formidable political force. But early attempts at merger were thwarted by sectional differences and personality clashes. At a meeting in St. Louis in 1889, white southerners, fearing reprisals from landowners and objecting to the participation of blacks, rejected proposals that would have ended secrecy in alliance activities and white-only membership rules. Northerners too shied away from amalgamation, fearing they would be dominated by more experienced southern leaders. Differences on issues also prevented unity. Northern farmers, who were mostly Republicans, wanted protective tariffs to keep out foreign grain; white southerners, mostly Democrats, wanted low tariffs. Nevertheless, both alliances favored government control of transportation and communications, liberal credit policies, equitable taxation, prohibition of alien land ownership, and currency reform.

Growing membership and rising confidence drew alliances more deeply into politics. By 1890, farmers had elected a number of officeholders sympathetic to their programs—especially in the

Rise of Populism

South, where alliance members controlled four governorships, eight state legislatures, forty-four seats in the U.S. House of Representatives, and three seats in the U.S. Senate. In the Midwest, alliance candidates often ran on independent third-party tickets, and achieved some success in Kansas, Nebraska, and the Dakotas. Campaigns included spirited rallies and parades that resounded with songs and orations; their banners proclaimed "We Are All Mortgaged But Our Votes." During the summer of 1890, the Kansas Alliance held a "convention of the people" and nominated candidates who swept the fall elections. Formation of this People's party, whose members were called Populists, from *populus*, the Latin word for people, gave a name to alliance political activism.

The 1890 election results energized new efforts to consolidate all alliance groups into a single Populist party. A May 1891 meeting of northern and southern alliances in Cincinnati failed when southerners chose to remain Democrats rather than risk joining a third party. But by early 1892, southern alliance members were ready for independent action. Meeting with northern counterparts in St. Louis, they issued a call for a People's party convention in Omaha on July 4, to draft a platform and nominate a presidential candidate.

The new party's platform, ratified by the 1,300 delegates who gathered in Omaha, was one of the most comprehensive reform documents in American

Mary E. Lease (1850–1933) was a fiery and controversial speaker for the Farmers' Alliance and Populist party in Kansas. Tall and intense, she had a deep, almost hypnotic voice that made her an effective publicist for the farmers' cause. She was one of the founders of the Populist party and gave a seconding speech to the nomination of James B. Weaver at the party convention in 1892. Library of Congress.

history. Declaring in its preamble that "wealth belongs to him that creates it," the Omaha platform presented a host of proposals generated by rural unrest. Most of its planks addressed three central issues: transportation, land, and money. Frustrated with weak state and federal regulation, the Populists demanded government ownership of railroad and telegraph lines. They called on the federal government to reclaim all land owned for speculative purposes by railroads and aliens. The monetary plank called for a flexible currency system based on free and unlimited coinage of silver that would increase the money supply and enable farmers to pay their debts more easily. Other planks advocated a graduated income tax, postal savings banks, the direct election of U.S. senators, and shorter hours for workers. As its presidential candidate, the party nominated James B. Weaver of Iowa, a former Union general and greenback supporter.

The Populist campaign featured colorful personalities and vivid rhetoric. The Kansas plains rumbled with the speeches of Sockless Jerry Simpson, an unschooled but canny rural reformer, and of Mary Lease, a fiery orator who urged farmers to "raise less corn and more hell." The South produced equally forceful but somewhat less flamboyant leaders, such as Charles W. Macune of Texas, Thomas Watson of Georgia, and Leonidas Polk of North Carolina. And there was Minnesota's Ignatius Donnelly, a pseudoscientist and writer of apocalyptic novels who became the chief organizer and ideologue of the northern Plains. Finally, the campaign had its opportunists, like James Hogg of Texas and "Pitchfork Ben" Tillman of South Carolina, who were not genuine Populists but used the rising agrarian fervor for their own political ambitions.

Although Weaver lost badly in 1892, he garnered over 1 million popular votes (8 percent of the total), winning majorities in four states and 22 electoral votes. Not since 1856 had a third party won so many votes in its first national effort. The party's central dilemma—whether to stand by its ideals at all costs or compromise those ideals in order to gain power—still loomed ahead (see pages 580–582). But in the early 1890s, rural dwellers in the South and West foresaw a promising future. The alliance movement had kindled an emotional faith. Although Populists were not perfectly democratic—their mistrust of blacks and foreigners gave them a reactionary vein—they sought change in order to fulfill their version of American ideals. Amid hardship and desperation, millions of people had begun to believe that they could overcome corporate power with a cooperative democracy in which government would act to ensure equal opportunity. A banner hanging above the stage at the Omaha convention summed up the movement's spirit: "We do not ask for sympathy or pity. We ask for justice."

THE DEPRESSION OF THE 1890s

Early in 1893, shortly before Grover Cleveland assumed the presidency for the second time, a seemingly minor but ominous economic event occurred: the Philadelphia and Reading Railroad, once a thriving and profitable line, went bankrupt. Like other railroads, the Philadelphia and Reading had borrowed heavily to lay track and build new stations and bridges. But overexpansion cut into revenues. Profits dwindled, and the company was unable to pay its debts.

The same problem nagged manufacturers. For example, output at the McCormick farm machinery factories was nine times greater in 1893 than it had been in 1879, but revenues had only tripled. To compensate, the company tried to boost profits by automating its plants and squeezing more work out of fewer laborers. But this strategy only enlarged the debt and increased unemployment. And it pushed unemployed workers into the same plight as their employers: they could not pay their creditors.

Banks suffered too. As primary lending agents, their problems compounded when customers defaulted. The failure of the National Cordage Company in May 1893 set off a chain reaction of business and bank closings. During the first four months of 1893, 28 banks failed. By June the number reached 128. In 1894 one adviser warned President Cleveland, "We are on the eve of a very dark night." He was right; between 1893 and 1897, the nation suffered the worst economic depression it had yet experienced.

Personal hardship arrived in the wake of business failures. Although records are sketchy, it appears that about 2.5 million people, or nearly 20 percent of the labor force, were jobless for some time during the depression. Falling demand caused the cost of living to drop between 1892 and 1895, but that decline was more than offset by layoffs and wage cuts. Many people could not afford basic necessities. New York police estimated that twenty thousand homeless and jobless people roamed the city's streets. Surveying the impact of the depression on his own city of Boston, Henry Adams wrote, "Men died like flies under the strain, and Boston grew suddenly old, haggard, and thin."

As the depression deepened, currency problems reached a critical stage. The Sherman Silver Purchase Act of 1890 had committed the government to buy 4.5 million ounces of silver each **Currency** month (see page 567). Payment was **Problems** to be in gold, at the ratio of one ounce of gold for every sixteen ounces of silver. But the western mining boom made silver more plentiful, and its value relative to gold fell. Thus every month the government exchanged gold, whose worth remained fairly constant, for less valuable silver. Fearful that the dollar, which was based on the treasury's holdings in silver and gold, was losing its value, merchants at home and abroad began to exchange paper money and securities for gold. As a result, the nation's gold reserves dwindled, falling below $100 million in April 1893.

The $100-million level was psychologically significant. If business leaders believed that the country's gold reserve was disappearing, they would lose confidence in its economic stability and refrain from investing. For example, British capitalists owned some $4 billion in American stocks and bonds. If the dollar were to depreciate too much, they would stop investing in American economic growth. Yet the lower the gold reserve dropped, the more people rushed to redeem their money and securities—to get their gold before it disappeared. The panic spread, causing further bankruptcies and unemployment.

President Cleveland, promising to protect the gold reserves, called a special session of Congress to repeal the Sherman Silver Purchase Act. But though the repeal was passed in October 1893, the run on the treasury continued through 1894. By early 1895 gold reserves had fallen to only $41 million. In desperation, Cleveland accepted an offer of 3.5 million ounces of gold in return for $62 million worth of federal bonds from a banking syndicate led by J. P. Morgan. When the bankers resold the bonds to the public, they profited handsomely at the nation's expense. Cleveland claimed that the gold reserves had been saved, but discontented farmers, workers, silver miners, and even some members of Cleveland's own party saw only humiliation in the president's actions. "When Judas betrayed Christ," charged South Carolina's Senator "Pitchfork Ben" Tillman, "his heart was not blacker than this scoundrel, Cleveland, in betraying the [Democratic party]."

No one knew what was really happening to the president. At about the time that Cleveland called Congress into special session, doctors discovered a malignant tumor on his palate. The cancer required immediate removal. Fearful that public knowledge of his illness would hasten the run on gold, and intent on preventing Vice President Adlai E. Stevenson, a silver supporter, from gaining influence, Cleveland kept his condition a secret. He announced that he was going sailing with a friend, and doctors removed his cancerous upper left jaw while the yacht sailed up the East River from New York City. Outfitted with a rubber jaw, Cleveland resumed a full schedule five days later, enduring terrible pain to dispel rumors that he was seriously ill. He eventually recovered, but those who knew about his operation believed it had sapped his vitality.

The deal between Cleveland and Morgan did not end the depression. After a slight improvement in 1895, the economy plunged again. Farm income, on the decline since 1887, continued to slide; factories closed; banks that remained open restricted withdrawals and refused to honor checks. Immigration in the mid-1890s dropped to almost 200,000 a year less than in the early 1890s. Economic hardship and reduced immigration depressed housing construction, drying up an important source of jobs. Each night police stations in almost every city became crowded with vagrants who had no place else to stay.

In the final years of the century, new gold discoveries, good harvests, and saner industrial growth brought better times. But the depression had hastened the crumbling of an old system and the emergence of a new one. The processes of industrial development and technological change had been under way for some time. Since the 1850s, railroads had been at the center of American economic development, opening new markets, boosting steel production, spawning numerous subsidiary industries, and expanding banking and finance. But the organizational features of the new business system—consolidation and a trend toward bigness—were just beginning to solidify when the depression hit.

Emergence of New Economic Structures

What had happened was that the national economy had reached the point of interdependence, the point at which the fortunes of a business in one part of the country or the world had repercussions elsewhere. By the 1890s railroads were overextended; their reckless investments inevitably crumbled. And when railroads collapsed, they pulled other industries down with them. In the first half of 1893, for example, thirty-two steel companies failed. In all, five hundred banks and sixteen thousand businesses toppled into bankruptcy that same year. Moreover, European economies also slumped in the 1890s, and more than ever before the fortunes of one country affected those of other countries.

To complicate matters, American farmers had to contend not only with fluctuating transportation rates and falling crop prices at home, but also with Canadian and Russian wheat growers, Argentine cattle ranchers, Indian and Egyptian cotton producers, and Australian wool producers. When farmers fell into debt and lost their purchasing power, their depressed condition in turn affected the economic health of railroads, farm-implements manufacturers, banks, and other businesses. The downward spiral reversed late in 1897, but the depression had left deep scars.

DEPRESSION-ERA PROTESTS

The depression bared a number of problems in the industrial system. For half a century technological and organizational changes had been widening the gap between employers and employees. By the 1890s workers' protests against exploitation threatened economic and political upheaval. In 1894, when the American economy plunged, there were over thirteen hundred strikes and countless riots. Violence reached an alarming pitch, and radical rhetoric escalated. Contrary to the fears of business leaders, all the protesters were not anarchists or communists from Europe come to sabotage American democracy. The disaffected included thousands of men and women who simply wanted a better chance, regardless of how the government was organized.

The era of protest began with the great railroad strikes of 1877 (see pages 498–499). The vehemence of those strikes and the support they drew from other working-class people aroused fears that the United States would repeat what had happened in France six years earlier, when a popular uprising briefly overturned the government and introduced communist principles. Such anxieties were heightened by another railroad strike in 1880, the Haymarket riot of 1886, a general strike in New Orleans in 1891, and the prolonged strike at the Homestead Steel plant in 1892. In the West, too, miners were becoming embittered; in 1892 violence broke out at a silver mine

in Coeur d'Alene, Idaho. Angered by wage cuts and a lockout, strikers seized the mines and battled federal troops sent to subdue them. Such actions prompted some business owners to believe that force was the only effective response to the radical wave, apparently fomented by socialists and anarchists.

Socialists had been involved in these and other incidents, but their numbers were small. Led by Daniel DeLeon, the fiery West Indian–born lawyer and lecturer who dominated the Socialist Labor Party, they agreed with Karl Marx, the father of communism, that whoever controlled the means of production held the power to determine how well people lived. Marx had written that capitalism increased the output of goods by oppressing labor, divorcing workers from the means of production, and pitting classes against each other. No longer did workers have control over how a product would be made; mechanization and the division of labor had demeaned them. Marx predicted that workers throughout the world would become so discontented they would revolt and seize factories, farms, banks, and transportation lines. The governments resulting from this revolution would end exploitation and erase class differences, paving the way for a new order of social justice. Marx's vision appealed to some workers because it promised them independence and abundance, and to intellectuals because it promised an end to class conflict and crude materialism.

Socialism

American socialism suffered from internal disagreements and lack of strong leadership. DeLeon had an antagonistic personality and could not unite the Socialist Labor Party. But events in 1894 triggered changes within the movement. That year the government's quashing of the Pullman strike and of the newly formed American Railway Union created a new and inspiring socialist leader. Eugene V. Debs, the railway union's president, had become a socialist while serving a six-month prison term for defying an injunction against the strike. Once released, the bald, forceful Indianan became the leading spokesperson for American socialism, combining visionary Marxism with Jeffersonian and Populist antimonopolism. Though never good at organizing, Debs attracted huge audiences and captivated them with passionate eloquence. His attacks on the free enterprise system were indignant. "Many of you think you are com-

Coxey's Army. Jacob Coxey (in the foreground, in front of the flag) leads the procession of unemployed workers that became the first of many to march on the capital seeking government relief. In his hand Coxey carries a "war club of peace." Library of Congress.

peting," he would lecture. "Against whom? Against Rockefeller? About as I would if I had a wheelbarrow and competed with the Santa Fe [railroad] from here to Kansas City." Debs's major accomplishments would occur after 1900, but in the late 1890s the group soon to be called the Socialist Party of America was already beginning to unite around him.

In 1894, however, it was not the tall, animated Debs but a short, quiet, frustrated businessman from Massillon, Ohio, who captured public attention. His name was Jacob S. Coxey, and like **Coxey's Army** Debs he had a vision. Coxey had become convinced that, to help debtors, the government should issue paper money unbacked by gold—purposeful inflation, in other words. As the depression spread, Coxey recommended a federal job program financed by an issue of $500 million of this "legal tender" paper money to relieve unemployment and revive consumer spending. He planned to publicize his scheme by leading a march

from Massillon to Washington, D.C., gathering a "commonweal army" of unemployed workers along the way. Coxey was so enthusiastic about his project that he christened his newborn son Legal Tender and proposed that his eighteen-year-old daughter lead the procession in a red-white-and-blue gown on a white horse.

About two hundred strong, Coxey's army left Massillon on March 24, 1894. Moving across Ohio and into Pennsylvania, the army received food, housing, and recruits from a score of depressed industrial towns and rural villages. Many participants succumbed to boredom or the weather and dropped out of the march, but elsewhere in the country similar armies organized and began the trek toward Washington.

Coxey's troops, including women and children, entered the capital on April 30. The next day (May Day, a date that made the police nervous because of its traditional association with socialist demonstrations), the citizen army of some five hundred people marched to the Capitol, armed with "war clubs of peace." When Coxey and a few others vaulted the wall surrounding the Capitol grounds, mounted police moved in and routed the crowd. According to one witness, "Women and children were ruthlessly ridden down. A commonwealer who had in some way escaped from the ranks, stood behind a tree and struck a policeman a terrible blow in the back with his war club of peace. The next officer that came up saw the attack and clubbed the commonwealer into insensibility." Coxey tried to speak from the Capitol steps, but the police arrested him and dragged him away. As the arrests and clubbings continued, Coxey's dreams of a demonstration of 400,000 jobless workers dissolved. Like the strikes, the people's first march on Washington had yielded to police muscle.

Coxey's march was an expression of frustration by people who were seeking relief from the uncertainties of industrialization. Unlike socialists, who believed in altering the whole economic system, the Coxey commonwealers merely wanted more jobs and better living standards. Today, in an age of union contracts, regulation of business, and government-sponsored job relief in times of high unemployment, their goals do not appear radical. Yet the brutal reactions of officials reveal how threatening the dissenters, from Coxey to Debs, must have seemed.

POPULISTS AND THE SILVER CRUSADE

Populists too were part of the activist current of protest. Although they did not experience the same kinds of government suppression that unions and Coxey's army experienced, Populists suffered from problems that surfaced just when their political goals seemed attainable. In 1892 their presidential candidate had received over 1 million votes, and as late as 1894 Populist candidates were making good showings in local and state elections throughout the West and South. Nevertheless, like all third parties, the Populists were underfinanced and underorganized. They had strong and colorful candidates, but not enough of

them to wrest control from the two major parties. Many voters were reluctant to break old loyalties, and the Populists had trouble luring supporters away from the Republicans and Democrats. Moreover, the two major parties fought to destroy Populist voting strength, especially in the South.

By the 1890s, the threat of biracial political dissent posed by the farmers' alliance movement prompted southern white Democrats to take urgent action. During the 1880s southern legislatures had enacted several measures to curtail black voting, including poll taxes and literacy tests (see pages 473–475). Dissatisfied that these measures would thwart a coalition of black and white voters in the Populist party and fearful that northern Republicans might enact federal supervision of elections, southern states in the 1890s tried more directly to prevent all blacks from voting.

Disfranchisement was accomplished in clever and devious ways. In 1876 the Supreme Court had affirmed that the Fifteenth Amendment prohibited states from denying the vote to people "on account of race, color, or previous condition of servitude." But, said the court, Congress had no control over state elections beyond provisions set by the Fifteenth Amendment (*U.S. v. Reese*). Subsequently, state legislatures found ways to exclude black voters without ever mentioning race, color, or previous condition of servitude. In 1890, Mississippi led the way by requiring all voters to prove they could read and interpret the state constitution. Registration officials applied much stiffer standards to blacks than whites, even to the extent of declaring black college graduates ineligible on grounds of illiteracy. In 1898 Louisiana enacted the first "grandfather clause," which excluded from voting anyone whose ancestors were ineligible to vote before 1867, and other southern states soon followed suit. These and other measures proved effective. In South Carolina, for example, 70 percent of eligible blacks had voted in the presidential election of 1880; by 1896 the rate had dropped to 11 percent. By the early 1900s, blacks had effectively lost their political rights in every southern state except Tennessee.

To a large extent, white supremacist fears were unjustified, for fundamental factors impeded acceptance of blacks by white Populists. To be sure, some Populists had sought a coalition of distressed black and white farmers. Tom Watson, Georgia's most prominent

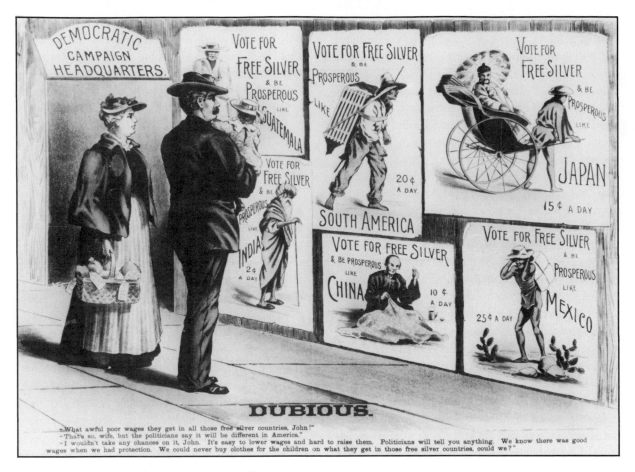

Critics of the free silver policy advocated by Populists and Democrats in 1896 tried to convince voters that such a policy would result in poverty and low wages. The message of this broadside is that free silver would make Americans as downtrodden as peasants of the most backward countries. Smithsonian Institution.

Populist, noted that "the crushing burdens which now oppress both races in the South will cause each to . . . see a similarity of cause and a similarity of remedy." But even poor white farmers could not put aside their racism. Many came from families that had supported the Ku Klux Klan during Reconstruction, some had once even owned slaves, and they considered blacks to be a permanently inferior people who would never be able to do things for themselves. They seemed to take comfort in the belief that there would always be people worse off than they were. Thus Populists seldom addressed needs of black farmers and used white supremacist rhetoric in order to avoid charges that they encouraged racial mingling.

On the national level, the Populist crusade against the "money power" settled on the issue of silver. Though the currency problem was one of the most complex facing American political **Free Silver** leaders, many people saw silver as a simple solution to the nation's ills. To them, free silver meant the end of special privilege for the rich and the return of government to the people. William H. Harvey, author of the immensely popular *Coin's Financial School* (1894), preached that by coining silver "you increase the value of all property by adding to the number of money units in the land. You make it possible for the debtor to pay his debts; business to start anew,

Chapter 20. GILDED AGE POLITICS, 1877–1900

and revivify all the industries of the country, which must remain paralyzed so long as silver as well as all other property is measured by a gold standard."

Using this kind of reasoning, Populists adopted free coinage of silver as their political battle cry. But as the elections of 1896 approached, they faced the dilemma of what strategy to use in order to translate their few previous electoral victories into much greater success. Would they lose their identity by joining with sympathetic factions of the major parties, or would they remain independent as a third party and settle for at best minor successes? Except in the Rocky Mountain states, where free coinage of silver had strong support, the Republicans were unlikely allies. Although Republican politicians could be as moralistic as the Populists, their anti-inflationist conservatism, support for the gold standard, and big-business orientation stood for everything the Populists opposed. In the North and West, alliance with Democrats was more plausible. In many areas the Democratic party retained vestiges of antimonopoly ideology as well as some sympathy for a looser currency system—although gold Democrats like President Grover Cleveland and Senator David Hill of New York did exert powerful opposition. Populists believed they also had links with traditionally Democratic urban workers, who, they assumed, suffered from the same kind of oppression that stifled farmers. In the South, fusion with Democrats seemed less likely, since there the party was the very power structure against which Populists had revolted in the late 1880s. Regardless of their options, the Populists had made certain that the political campaign of 1896 would be like none before it.

THE ELECTION OF 1896

McKinley and Bryan

The presidential campaign of 1896 brought the nation's political wanderings to a climax. Each party was divided. Republicans, under the direction of Marcus Alonzo Hanna, a prosperous Ohio industrialist, had the fewest problems. Since early in 1895, Hanna had been maneuvering to win the nomination for Ohio's governor, William

William Jennings Bryan (1860–1925) in a photograph taken in 1896 when he first ran for president. Bryan was a spellbinding orator who turned agrarian unrest and the issue of free silver into a moral crusade. *Library of Congress.*

McKinley. By the time the party convened in St. Louis in 1896, Hanna had corralled enough delegates to succeed. "He has advertised McKinley," quipped Theodore Roosevelt, "as if he were a patent medicine." The Republicans' only trauma occurred when the party adopted a moderate platform supporting gold, rejecting a prosilver stance proposed by Senator Henry M. Teller of Colorado. Teller, who had been among the party's founders forty years earlier, walked out of the convention in tears, taking a small group of silver Republicans with him.

At the Democratic convention, silver delegates paraded through the Chicago Amphitheatre wearing silver badges and waving silver banners. Observing their tumultuous demonstrations, one eastern delegate

William McKinley (1843–1901) ran for president in 1896 on a platform that linked business prosperity with national prestige and economic well-being.   Library of Congress.

wrote, "For the first time I can understand the scenes of the French Revolution!" "All the silverites need is a Moses," remarked a *New York World* reporter. They found one in William Jennings Bryan.

Bryan had arrived at the Democratic national convention in Chicago in July 1896 as a member of a contested Nebraska delegation. A former congressman whose support for free coinage of silver had annoyed President Cleveland, he was only thirty-six years old, avidly religious, and highly distressed by what the depression had done to midwestern farmers. The convention, as expected, chose to seat Bryan and his colleagues instead of a competing faction that supported the gold standard. Shortly afterward, as a member of the party's resolutions committee, Bryan helped to write a platform calling for free coinage of silver.

When the platform was presented to the full con-

vention, Bryan rose to speak on its behalf. In the heat and humidity of the Chicago summer, Bryan's now-famous closing words gripped the delegates:

> Having behind us the producing masses of this nation and the world, supported by the commercial interests, the laboring interests, and the toilers everywhere, we will answer their [the wealthy classes'] demand for a gold standard by saying to them: You shall not press down upon the brow of labor this crown of thorns, you shall not crucify mankind upon a cross of gold.

The speech could not have been more timely; indeed, Bryan planned it to be so. Friends who had been pushing Bryan for the presidential nomination now had no trouble enlisting support. It took Bryan five ballots to win the nomination, but finally the magnetism of the Boy Orator proved irresistible. In bowing to the silverite will of southerners and westerners and repudiating Cleveland's policies in its platform, the party became more attractive to discontented farmers. But like the Republicans, it too drove away a dissenting minority wing. A group of gold Democrats withdrew and nominated their own candidate.

Bryan's nomination presented the Populist party with a dilemma. Should Populists join Democrats in support of Bryan, or should they nominate their own candidate? Tom Watson of Georgia, expressing strong southern sentiment against fusion with the Democrats, warned that "the Democratic idea of fusion [is] that we play Jonah while they play whale." But others reasoned that supporting a different candidate would split the anti-McKinley vote and allow the Republicans to win. In the end the convention compromised, first naming Watson as its vice-presidential nominee to preserve party identity (the Democrats had nominated Maine shipping magnate Arthur Sewall for vice president) and then nominating Bryan for the presidency.

The campaign, in the words of journalist William Allen White, "took the form of religious frenzy. . . . Far into the night, the voices rose—women's voices, children's voices, the voices of old men, of youths and of maidens, rose on the ebbing prairie breezes, as the crusaders of the revolution rode home, praising the people's will as though it were God's will and cursing wealth for its iniquity." Republicans countered Bryan's moral evangelism and attacks on privilege

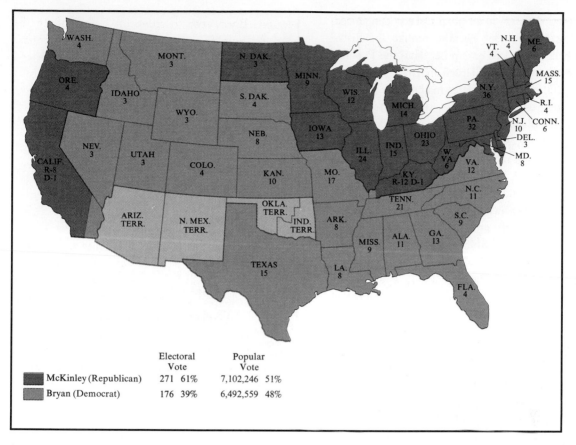

Presidential Election, 1896

(he repeatedly preached that "every great economic question is in reality a great moral question") by predicting chaos if he should win. While Bryan raced around the country giving as many as twenty speeches a day, Mark Hanna invited hundreds of thousands of people to McKinley's home town of Canton, Ohio, where the candidate plied them with speeches on moderation and prosperity. Leaving moralizing to the Democrats, Republican candidates adopted the pragmatic approach of promising something for everyone and a live-and-let-live philosophy for all.

The election results revealed that the political standoff had finally ended. McKinley, the symbol of Republican pragmatism and the new economic order, beat Bryan by over 600,000 popular votes and by 271 to 176 in the electoral college (see map). It was the most lopsided presidential election since 1872.

Election Results

Democrats and Populists had done all they could to rally the nation. Bryan had tried to offset the huge Republican campaign chest, estimated at between $3.5 and $7 million, by traveling 18,000 miles and giving over six hundred speeches, but lean campaign finances and obsession with the silver issue undermined his effort. Silver especially prevented the Populists from building the urban-rural coalition that would have given them political breadth. Reformer Henry Demarest Lloyd summarized the matter succinctly: "Free silver," he wrote, "is the cow bird of the reform movement. It waited till the nest had been built by the sacrifices and labor of others, and then it laid its eggs in it, pushing out the others which it smashed to the ground." Farmers' demands for an expanded currency lacked broad appeal. Urban workers shied away from the silver issue because they feared that high prices would result. Labor leaders like Samuel Gompers of the AFL, though partly sympathetic, would not join with Populists because they were unconvinced that farmers were employees, like industrial workers. And socialists like Daniel DeLeon denounced Populists as "retrograde" because, unlike socialists, they still believed in free enterprise. Thus the Populist crusade for democracy collapsed in 1896. Although Populists and fusion candidates made a few gains in state and congressional elections, the Bryan-Watson ticket polled only 222,600 votes nationwide.

As president, McKinley signed the Gold Standard Act (1900), which required that all paper money be backed by gold. A seasoned politician, personable and attractive, McKinley was best

The McKinley Presidency known for his expertise in crafting high protective tariffs; as a congressman from Ohio, he had guided passage of record high rates in 1890. He accordingly supported the Dingley Tariff of 1897, which raised duties even higher—though it did expand reciprocity provisions. During McKinley's presidency domestic tensions subsided; an upward swing of the business cycle and an increased money supply from new gold discoveries in Alaska, Australia, and South Africa helped to restore prosperity. Good times enabled McKinley to beat Bryan again in 1900, using the slogan "The Full Dinner Pail." Freed from the care of the economy, McKinley spent time on foreign affairs. A strong believer in the need to open new markets abroad, he encouraged imperialistic ventures in Latin America and the Pacific (see Chapter 22).

As a result of the 1896 campaign, political parties learned that in future elections they would have to be sensitive to the pluralism of American society. They would have to satisfy a broad spectrum of interests rather than march under the banner of moral perfection. The reform spirit would survive, but its success would depend on cooperation, not on the sermons of righteous evangelists. Ironically, by 1920 many of the Populists' reform goals would be achieved, including regulation of railroads, banks, and utilities; shorter working hours; a variant of the subtreasury system; a graduated income tax; direct election of senators; the secret ballot, and more. These reforms succeeded because a number of groups united behind them. Immigration, urbanization, and industrialization had transformed the United States into a pluralistic society where compromise among interest groups had become a political fact of life. The election of 1896 and the end of the Gilded Age equilibrium confirmed that transformation.

IMPORTANT EVENTS

1873	Coinage of silver dollars ends
1873–78	Depression
1876	Hayes elected president *U.S.* v. *Reese*
1878	Bland-Allison Act Anthony Amendment defeated in Congress
1880	Garfield elected president
1881	Garfield assassinated; Arthur assumes presidency
1883	Pendleton Civil Service Act
1884–85	Depression
1884	Cleveland elected president
1887	Collapse of farm prices
1888	Harrison elected president
1890	McKinley Tariff Sherman Silver Purchase Act Sherman Anti-Trust Act
1892	Populist convention in Omaha Cleveland elected president
1893	Repeal of Sherman Silver Purchase Act
1893–97	Depression
1894	Wilson-Gorman Tariff Pullman strike; Debs arrested and turns to socialism Coxey's march
1895	Cleveland deals with bankers to save gold reserve
1896	McKinley elected president
1897	Dingley Tariff
1900	Gold Standard Act McKinley re-elected

SUGGESTIONS FOR FURTHER READING

General

Sean Denis Cashman, *America in the Gilded Age* (1984); Harold U. Faulkner, *Politics, Reform, and Expansion, 1890–1900* (1959); Ray Ginger, *The Age of Excess*, 2nd ed. (1975); H. Wayne Morgan, ed., *The Gilded Age* (1970); H. Wayne Morgan, *From Hayes to McKinley* (1969); Paul Studenski and Herman E. Krouss, *Financial History of the United States* (1952); Alan Trachtenberg, *The Incorporation of America: Culture and Society in the Gilded Age* (1982); R. Hal Williams, *Years of Decision: American Politics in the 1890s* (1978).

Parties and Political Issues

John H. Dobson, *Politics in the Gilded Age* (1972); Eleanor Flexner, *Century of Struggle: The Women's Rights Movement in the United States* (1959); Elisabeth Griffith, *In Her Own Right: The Life of Elizabeth Cady Stanton* (1984); J. Rogers Hollingsworth, *The Whirligig of Politics: The Democracy of Cleveland and Bryan* (1963); Ari A. Hoogenboom, *Outlawing the Spoils: The Civil Service Movement* (1961); Richard J. Jensen, *The Winning of the Midwest* (1971); David M. Jordan, *Roscoe Conkling of New York* (1971); Matthew Josephson, *The Politicos* (1938); Morton Keller, *Affairs of State* (1977); Paul Kleppner, *The Third Electoral System, 1853–1892* (1979); Paul Kleppner, *The Cross of Culture* (1970); Robert D. Marcus, *Grand Old Party* (1971); Samuel T. McSeveney, *The Politics of Depression* (1972); Walter T. K. Nugent, *Money and American Society* (1968); A. M. Paul, *Conservative Crisis and the Rule of Law: Attitudes of Bar and Bench, 1887–1895* (1969); David J. Rothman, *Politics and Power: The United States Senate, 1869–1901* (1966); John G. Sproat, *The Best Men: Liberal Reformers in the Gilded Age* (1968); Tom E. Terrill, *The Tariff, Politics, and American Foreign Policy, 1874–1901* (1973).

The Presidency

Kenneth E. Davison, *The Presidency of Rutherford B. Hayes* (1972); Lewis L. Gould, *The Presidency of William McKinley* (1981); Margaret Leech and Harry J. Brown, *The Garfield Orbit* (1978); Horace Samuel Merrill, *Bourbon Leader: Grover Cleveland and the Democratic Party* (1957); H. Wayne Morgan, *William McKinley and His America* (1963); Allan Peskin, *Garfield* (1978); Thomas C. Reeves, *Gentleman Boss: The Life of Chester Alan Arthur* (1975); H. J. Sievers, *Benjamin Harrison*, 3 vols. (1952–1968).

Currents of Protest

William M. Dick, *Labor and Socialism in America* (1972); John P. Diggins, *The American Left in the Twentieth Century* (1973); Ray Ginger, *Bending Cross: A Biography of Eugene Victor Debs* (1969); John Laslett, *Labor and the Left* (1970); Donald L. McMurray, *Coxey's Army* (1929); Nick Salvatore, *Eugene V. Debs: Citizen and Socialist* (1982); David Shannon, *The Socialist Party of America* (1955).

Populism and the Election of 1896

Peter H. Argersinger, *Populism and Politics: William Alfred Peffer and the People's Party* (1974); Paolo Coletta, *William Jennings Bryan: Political Evangelist* (1964); Paul W. Glad, *McKinley, Bryan, and the People* (1964); Paul W. Glad, *The Trumpet Soundeth: William Jennings Bryan and His Democracy* (1964); Lawrence Goodwyn, *Democratic Promise: The Populist Moment in America* (1976); Sheldon Hackney, *Populism to Progressivism in Alabama* (1969); Steven Hahn, *The Roots of Southern Populism* (1983); John D. Hicks, *The Populist Revolt* (1931); Richard Hofstadter, *The Age of Reform: From Bryan to FDR* (1955); Stanley L. Jones, *The Election of 1896* (1964); J. Morgan Kousser, *The Shaping of Southern Politics* (1974); Walter T. K. Nugent, *The Tolerant Populists* (1963); Norman Pollack, ed., *The Populist Mind* (1967); Norman Pollack, *The Populist Response to Industrial America* (1962); Martin Ridge, *Ignatius Donnelly* (1962); Allan Weinstein, *Prelude to Populism: Origins of the Silver Issue* (1970); Charles Morrow Wilson, *The Commoner: William Jennings Bryan* (1970); C. Vann Woodward, *Tom Watson* (1938).

THE PROGRESSIVE ERA

1895–1920

CHAPTER 21

*T*homas Edison, *of* all people, would have known if something was not working properly. He perfected and promoted so many items of modern mass technology—the light bulb, the phonograph, and the motion-picture projector, among others—that he should have had good reason to view his world optimistically. But he did not. With the perceptiveness of the good inventor he was, Edison found American society unsatisfactory and perplexing. Writing to his friend Henry Ford in 1912, Edison observed that

in a lot of respects we Americans are the rawest and crudest of all. Our production, our factory laws, our charities, our relations between capital and labor, our distribution—all wrong, out of gear. We've stumbled along for a while, trying to run a new civilization in old ways, but we've got to start to make this world over.

Americans had always been preoccupied with reforming their society, with "making it over," but between the 1890s and the end of the First World War, an intensified rush of reform swept the country. More and more people who felt as Edison did tried to address the problems of their time directly. Their efforts, inspired by a complicated mixture of calculated self-interest and unselfish benevolence, shaped what can be called the Progressive era.

During the 1890s, a severe depression, frightening labor violence, political upheaval, and foreign entanglements had shaken the nation. Although many of the promises of technology had been fulfilled, great numbers of Americans continued to suffer from poverty and disease. In the minds of many, industrialists had become the nation's new monsters, controlling markets, wages, and prices in order to maximize their profits. And government seemed corroded by bosses and their henchmen, who used politics to enrich themselves.

From this malaise emerged a broad, complex spirit of reform, so many-sided that it is hard to identify the movement's unifying characteristics. By the 1910s many reformers were calling themselves progressives, and a new political party by that name had formed to embody their principles. Since that time historians have used the term *progressivism* to refer to the reform spirit in general, while disagreeing over the movement's meaning and its membership. It is probably most accurate to consider the era between 1895 and 1920 as characterized by a series of movements, each aimed in one way or another at renovating or restoring American society, its values, and its institutions.

The urge toward reform had many causes. Industrialization had brought unprecedented productivity, awesome technology, and a cornucopia of new consumer goods. But it had also included labor problems, wasteful use of natural resources, and abuse of corporate power. The rapidly growing network of cities facilitated the amassing and distribution of goods, services, and cultural amenities but also magnified the problems of poverty, disease, crime, and political corruption. Massive influxes of immigrants and the rise of a new class of managers and professionals shook the foundations of the old social classes. And the debilitating depression that blanketed the nation from 1893 to 1897 made many leading citizens realize what working people had known for some time: the central promise of American life was not being kept. Equality of opportunity—whether economic, political, or social—was a myth.

Progressives tried to surmount these problems by organizing their ideas and actions around three basic themes. First, they would end abuses of power. Attacks on unfair privilege, monopoly, and corruption were not new in 1900; Jacksonians and Populists are only two of many examples of such a tradition. But in the Progressive era, the attacks became more strenuous than ever before. Trustbusting, consumers' rights, and good government became important political issues. Second, progressives aimed to replace corrupt power with the power of reformed social institutions. Though they wanted to protect the individual's rights, they abandoned old individualistic assumptions such as the notion that hard work and good character automatically assured success and that the poor had only themselves to blame for their plight. Instead, progressives acknowledged that society and its institutions had power to help or harm the individual, and they believed these institutions must provide opportunity for everyone. Their revolt against unchanging categories of thought challenged entrenched attitudes toward women's role, race relations, public education, legal and scientific thought, and morality. Third, progressives wanted to apply principles of science and efficiency on a nationwide scale to all economic, social, and political institutions. Their aim was not only to minimize social and economic disorder but to establish cooperation, especially between business and government, that would end wasteful competition.

Befitting their name, progressives had strong faith in the ability of humankind to create a better world. They often used such phrases as "humanity's universal growth" and "the upward spiral of human development." Judge Ben Lindsey of Denver, who spearheaded reform in the treatment of juvenile delinquents, expressed the progressive creed when he wrote, "In the end the people are bound to do the right thing, no matter how much they fail at times." Government, purged of corruption and favoritism to make it the servant of the people, became the instrument of progress. During the Progressive era, a new activism infused the presidency, as well as Congress and state and local governments. More than ever before, Americans looked to government as an agent that could and should intervene in social and economic relations to protect the common good and substitute public interest for self-interest.

WHO WERE THE PROGRESSIVES?

The Progressive era emerged out of the new political atmosphere that formed after the tumultuous election of 1896 (see pages 581–584) and the issues raised by urban reformers in the previous half-century (see pages 528–530). As the twentieth century dawned, the loyalty that political parties had once commanded seriously eroded, and voter turnouts declined considerably. In presidential elections, voter participation dropped from Gilded Age levels of over 80 percent of the eligible electorate to almost 60 percent in northern states and under 30 percent in southern states, where blacks had been excluded from the polls. Parties and elections, it seemed, were losing their functions of providing Americans with a means of influencing government policies.

Instead, the political system was opening up to entry by various and shifting interest groups, many of which supported reform issues related to their activities. First, voluntary associations had been a vital feature of local life since the 1790s, but after the 1890s many organizations became nationwide in scope and began to try to shape government policy. These organizations included professional associations, such as the American Bar Association; women's organizations, such as the National American Woman Suffrage Association; issue-oriented lobbies, such as the National Consumers League; civic associations; and so on. Members of these organizations hoped to advance their own interests and to educate others about their goals. They made politics much more fragmented and issue-focused than in earlier eras.

Second, although a spirit of moral regeneration, political democracy, and antimonopolism lingered from the rural-based Populist movement, the prevailing issues of the Progressive era were urban. The progressive quest for social justice, educational and legal reform, and streamlining of government was actually an extension of the urban-reform goals of the previous half-century. Indeed, between 1890 and 1920 the proportion of the nation's population living in cities rose from 35 percent to over 51 percent; the number of places with fifty thousand or more people rose from 58 to 144. Recognition of the magnitude of such changes, as well as easier communications by mail, telephone, and telegraph, stimulated urban reformers to exchange information and to consolidate their efforts. The formation of the National Municipal League in 1895 and the National Civic Federation in 1900 signaled the beginning of the new reform era. The National Municipal League served as a forum for debate on issues of civic reform, such as bossism versus civil service, revisions of tax laws, nonpartisan elections, and municipal ownership of public utilities. The National Civic Federation broadened discussion of social reforms, such as workers' compensation and arbitration of labor disputes.

Organizations and individuals who accepted the three progressive themes—opposition to abuse of power, reform of social institutions, quest for cooperation and scientific efficiency—could be found

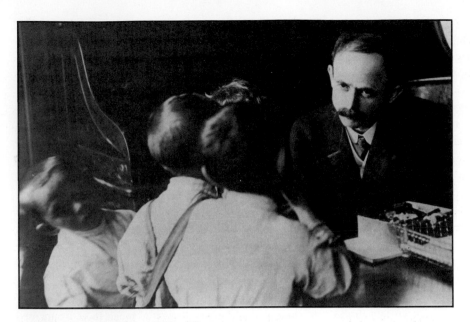

Judge Ben Lindsey (1869–1943) of Denver was a progressive reformer who worked for better legal protection for children. Typical of many reformers of his era, Lindsey had an earnest faith in the ability of humankind to build a better world. Library of Congress

in almost all levels of society. The new middle class, consisting of men and women in the professions of law, medicine, social work, religion, teaching, and business, formed the vanguard of the progressives. Repelled by inefficiency and immorality in business, government, and human relations, these people set out to apply scientific techniques they had learned in their professions to problems of the larger society.

Many middle-class progressive reformers were motivated by personal indignation, if not revulsion, at corruption and injustice. This feeling was expressed by journalists whom Theodore Roosevelt dubbed *muckrakers* (alluding to a character in John Bunyan's *Pilgrim's Progress* who rejected a crown for a muckrake). These writers, unlike journalists who merely reported events, fed the public taste for scandal and sensation by investigating and attacking social, economic, and political wrongs. Their fact-filled articles in *McClure's, Hampton's,* and other popular magazines, as well as books, exposed such offenses as the sale of tainted meat, fraudulent insurance schemes, and prostitution. Lincoln Steffens's articles in *McClure's,* later published as *The Shame of the Cities* (1904), ranked among the highlights of muckraker journalism. Steffens hoped

his surveys of misrule by bosses would inspire mass indignation and ultimately reform. Other well-known muckraking efforts included Upton Sinclair's *The Jungle* (1906), a novel that attacked the meatpacking industry, Burton J. Hendrick's *Story of Life Insurance* (1907), and David Graham Phillips's *Treason of the Senate* (1906).

Middle-class indignation also revealed itself in opposition to party politics, a reflection of the new political system that arose after 1896. Reformers had

Political Reformers

a strong distaste for the bargaining and self-serving they believed permeated boss-ridden parties. They felt, as the journalist William Allen White did, that machines and bosses should "be reduced to mere political scrap iron by the rise of the people." (When reformers referred to "the people," they all too often meant middle-class people like themselves, excluding the native working class, blacks, and immigrants.) To improve the political process, these progressives advocated such reforms as nominating candidates through direct primaries instead of party caucuses and nonpartisan elections to prevent the corruption and bribery that party loyalties seemed to breed.

To involve more people and to make legislators more responsible, they advocated three reform devices: the initiative, which would enable voters to propose new laws on their own; the referendum, which would enable voters to accept or reject a law at the ballot box; and the recall, which would allow voters to remove officials and judges from office before their terms were up. Their goal, like that of the business consolidation movement, was efficiency. The government would be reclaimed by replacing the favoritism of the boss system with rational, accountable management chosen by a responsible electorate.

Middle-class progressive reformers, then, had an aversion to party politics, not to government. They turned to government for aid in achieving most of their goals, for they became convinced that only government had the leverage they needed. Members of the new professions in which systematic investigation and efficient management were of prime importance also believed with the muckrakers that knowledge was the key to progress. Science and scientific method—system, planning, control, predictability—were central to their values. Just as corporations were applying scientific management to achieve economic efficiency, progressives used expertise and planning to achieve social and political efficiency.

The progressive spirit also stirred some elite business leaders. Successful executives like Alexander Cassatt of the Pennsylvania Railroad supported limited government regulation and political re-

Upper-class Reformers forms as means of protecting their interests from more radical political elements. Others, like E. A. Filene, founder of a Boston department store, and Thomas L. Johnson, a wealthy streetcar magnate, were humanitarians who worked unselfishly for social justice. Business leaders guided organizations like the Municipal Voters League and the U.S. Chamber of Commerce, which supported limited political and economic reform. Their aim was to stabilize society by imposing the model of corporate organization on institutions like schools, hospitals, and local government. Women of the elite classes often led reform organizations like the YWCA, which sponsored aid and education for the growing numbers of unmarried working women who had moved away from their families, and the Women's Christian Temperance Union, which was the largest women's organization of its time and which

participated in numerous causes besides those linked with drinking.

But not all progressive reformers had middle- or upper-class standing. During this era vital elements of what would become modern American liberalism grew out of the working-class urban

Working-class Reformers experience. By the close of the nineteenth century, many urban workers were pressing for government intervention to ensure safety and promote welfare. They wanted improvements in housing and health, safe factories, shorter working hours, workers' compensation, and other reforms. Often these were the very people who supported the political bosses, supposedly the enemies of reform. Workers knew that bosses needed to cultivate support among their constituents and would cater to voters' needs. And in fact bossism was not necessarily at odds with humanitarianism. Indeed, when Tammany Hall boss "Big Tim" Sullivan was asked why he supported a law requiring shorter working hours for women, he explained, "I had seen me sister go out to work when she was only fourteen and I know we ought to help these gals by giving 'em a law which will prevent 'em from being broken down while they're still young."

After 1900, voters from inner-city districts populated by migrant and immigrant working-class families elected a number of progressive legislators who had trained in the arena of machine politics. People like New York's Alfred E. Smith and Robert F. Wagner, Massachusetts's David I. Walsh, and Illinois's Edward F. Dunne—all of whom came from immigrant backgrounds—became important reform spokesmen at the state and national levels. They were most successful when they allied with other reformers, particularly those from the middle class, to pass laws aiding labor and social welfare. The chief goal of these legislators was to establish government responsibility for alleviating the hardship that had resulted from urban-industrial growth. They opposed such reforms as prohibition, Sunday closing laws, civil service, and nonpartisan elections, all of which conflicted with their constituents' interests.

Some deeply frustrated workers wanted more than progressive reform. They wanted a different society. These people turned to the socialist movement, a mixture of immigrant intellectuals, industrial workers, disaffected populists, and western miners and lum-

Though their objectives sometimes differed from those of middle-class progressive reformers, socialists also became a more active group in the early twentieth century. Socialist parades on May Day, such as this one in New York in 1910, were meant to express the solidarity of all working people. Library of Congress.

bermen. Some factions had more impact than others. The radical union known as the Industrial Workers of the World—the IWW, or "Wobblies" (see page 502)—organized strife-torn strikes in western lumber and mining camps, in the steel town of McKees Rocks, Pennsylvania (1907), and in the textile mills of Lawrence, Massachusetts (1912). Led by former miner "Big Bill" Haywood, along with the charismatic seventy-five-year-old Mother Jones and the young radical Elizabeth Gurley Flynn, the IWW reached out to unskilled laborers, promising to unite all workers by enabling them to control their own factories. IWW membership probably never exceeded 150,000, however, and the organization faded during the First World War when federal prosecution—and persecution—sent many of its leaders to jail.

Socialists

The majority of socialists united behind Eugene V. Debs (see page 577), the tall, dynamic railroad organizer who drew nearly 100,000 votes in the 1900 presidential election. Though Debs was never able to develop a consistent program beyond his opposition to war and bourgeois materialism, he was a spellbinding speaker for the radical cause. On his speaking tours, he touched increasing numbers of disenchanted workers and intellectuals. As candidate for the Socialist party, Debs won 400,000 votes in his 1904 campaign for the presidency, and in 1912, at the pinnacle of his and his party's career, he polled over 900,000.

With their stinging attacks on exploitation and unfair privilege, Debs and other socialists like Milwaukee's Victor Berger and New York's Morris Hilquit made attractive overtures to reform-minded people. Some, such as settlement-house worker and child-labor reformer Florence Kelley, identified with the socialist cause. But most progressives avoided radical attacks on free enterprise. Municipal ownership of public utilities was as far as they would go toward changing the system. Indeed, progressives had too much at stake in the capitalist system to overthrow it. Thus even in Wisconsin, where progressivism was most highly developed, progressives would not join with Berger's more radical group. California progressives even formed a temporary alliance with reactionaries to prevent socialists from gaining power in Los Angeles. And few humanitarian reformers objected when in 1918 Debs was jailed for giving an antiwar speech.

But it would be a mistake to imagine that the progressive spirit touched all of American society between 1895 and 1920. There were still large numbers of people, heavily represented in Congress, who opposed reform. They disliked government interference in economic affairs—except when it strengthened the tariff—and saw nothing wrong with existing power structures. Outside government, this outlook was represented by business leaders like J. P. Morgan, John D. Rockefeller, and E. H. Harriman, men who insisted that real progress would result from maintaining the profit incentive. Within government, this ideology was expressed by old-guard Republicans like Senator Nelson W. Aldrich of Rhode Island and House Speaker Joseph Cannon of Illinois.

Progressive reformers operated from the center of the ideological spectrum. Moderate, concerned, sometimes contradictory, they believed on the one hand that the laissez-faire system was obsolete and on the other that radical challenges to the fundamentals of capitalism were dangerous. Like the Jeffersonians, they believed in the conscience and will of the people; like the Hamiltonians, they opted for a strong central government to act in the interest of conscience.

The Progressive era, then, was a complex period of multiple, overlapping, and sometimes conflicting reform movements. The era is best characterized by its challenges to almost every aspect of conventional society: politics, social relationships, ideas, institutions, and morality. The goals of progressive reformers were both idealistic and realistic. As minister-reformer Walter Rauschenbusch wrote, "We shall demand perfection and never expect to get it."

GOVERNMENTAL AND LEGISLATIVE REFORM

What were the responsibilities of government? Answers to this question in the early twentieth century were much different from those of the nineteenth century. Traditionally, theorists had held that a democratic government should be small and unobtrusive, interfering in private affairs only in unique circumstances and withdrawing once balance had been restored. In the late nineteenth century this conception eroded. Corporations, though opposed to government regulation of their activities, nevertheless pursued government aid and protection for their enterprises. Discontented farmers organized to seek government regulation of railroads and other monopolistic businesses. City dwellers, accustomed to the favors furnished by local political machines, came to expect government to act positively on their behalf.

By the turn of the century, professionals and intellectuals were accepting the notion that government could and should exert more power to ensure justice and well-being. They were becoming convinced that a simple, inflexible government was ineffective in a complex industrial age, and that public power was needed to counteract corruption and exploitation. But before reformers could use such power in ways they believed to be necessary, they would have to recapture government from the politicians whose greed had soiled the democratic system. Thus an important thrust of progressive activity was the effort to root out corruption in government.

Reformers first attacked this problem in the cities (see pages 528–529). Between 1870 and 1900 opponents of the boss system tried to redirect government through structural reforms such as civil service, nonpartisan elections, and tighter scrutiny of public expenditures. A few reform leaders developed sympathies for poverty relief, housing improvement, and prolabor laws. But most worked chiefly for an efficient—meaning economical—government. After 1900 the momentum for reform brought into being the city manager and city commission forms of government (where urban officials were chosen for their professional expertise, not their political connections) and public ownership of utilities (so that gas, electricity, telephone, and streetcar companies would not profit at the public's expense).

Reformers discovered, however, that the city was too small an arena for the kind of changes they sought. State and federal government offered more promising opportunities for effecting reform through legislation. Because of their faith in a strong, fair-minded executive, progressives looked to governors and other elected officials to extend and protect the reforms that had been achieved at the local level. The reformers' goals varied from one region or state to another. In the Plains and Far West, reformers rallied behind railroad regulation and such governmental reforms as the initiative and referendum. In the South they continued the Populist crusade against big business and autocratic politicians. And in the urban-industrial Northeast and Midwest, reformers directed their attention to corrupt political machines and unsafe labor conditions.

The reform movement produced a number of skillful, influential, and often charismatic governors who used executive power to achieve change. Their ranks included Braxton Bragg Comer of Alabama and Hoke Smith of Georgia, who introduced business regulations and other reforms in the South; Albert Cummins of Iowa and Hiram Johnson of California, who battled the railroads that dominated their states; and Woodrow Wilson of New Jersey, whose administrative reforms were copied by other governors. Such men were not always saints, however. Smith supported the disfranchisement of blacks, and Johnson discriminated against Japanese-Americans.

Progressive Governors

Probably the most notable progressive governor was Wisconsin's Robert M. La Follette. A self-made small-town lawyer whose short, compact build and thick, bristling hair suited his combative personality, La Follette rose through the ranks of the state Republican party to the governorship in 1900. As governor he initiated a multipronged reform program that included direct primaries, more equitable taxes, and regulation of railroad rates. He also established regulatory commissions staffed with experts, whose investigations supplied La Follette with facts and figures that he used in fiery speeches to muster public support for his policies. After three terms as governor, La

Robert M. La Follette (1855–1925) was one of the most dynamic of progressive politicians. As governor of Wisconsin, he sponsored a program of political reform and business regulation known as the Wisconsin Plan. In 1906 he entered the U.S. Senate and continued to champion progressive reform. The National Progressive Republican League, which La Follette founded in 1911, became the core of the Progressive party.   Library of Congress.

Follette was elected senator and carried his progressive ideals into national politics. "Battling Bob" had a rare ability to take a tempered, scientific approach to reform while still appealing to the people with moving rhetoric. His goal, he once asserted, "was not to 'smash' corporations, but to drive them out of politics, and then to treat them exactly the same as other people are treated."

Not all state leaders were as successful as La Follette. To be sure, the crusade against party politics and corruption did accomplish some permanent changes. By 1916 all but three states had direct primaries, and many states had adopted the initiative, referendum, and recall. And political reformers achieved a major goal in 1912 when the states ratified the Seventeenth Amendment, which provided for the direct election of U.S. senators (formerly elected by state legislatures, which often were corrupted by private interests). But political reforms did not always bring about the desired results. Party bosses, better organized and more experienced than reformers, were still able to dominate elections. The initiative, referendum, and recall often failed because special-interest groups could control outcomes by using large funds to lobby the public and organize the voting. Moreover, political reformers found that entrenched power, aided by the courts, many times could counterattack and defeat progressive campaigns.

New state laws aimed at bettering social welfare had greater impact than most political reforms, especially in factories. Broadly interpreting their powers to protect the health and safety of their citizens, many states enacted factory inspection laws, and by 1916 nearly two-thirds of the states had insurance for victims of industrial accidents. A coalition of labor and humanitarian groups supported these laws and even induced some legislatures to grant aid to mothers with dependent children. Under pressure from the National Child Labor Committee, nearly every state established a minimum age for employment (varying from twelve to sixteen), and prohibited employers from working children more than eight or ten hours a day. Such laws, however, were hard to enforce because they seldom provided for the close inspection of factories that full enforcement required. Moreover, families that needed extra income encouraged their children to work and to lie about their ages. Several groups also joined forces to limit working hours for women. After the Supreme Court upheld Oregon's ten-hour limit in 1908, many more states passed laws protecting women workers. Finally, efforts of the American Association for Old Age Security began to succeed in 1914, when Arizona established old-age pensions. Though the law was struck down by the courts, the First World War renewed interest in pensions, and in the 1920s many states enacted laws to provide for needy older people.

Progressive Legislation

These and other social reforms were strongly opposed by people who thought them detrimental to their self-interest or who believed that government interference in such matters would destroy the free enterprise system. Some business associations bitterly fought consumers' efforts to legislate milk and meat inspections. The National Association of Manufacturers coordinated the battle against regulation of business and working conditions. And legislators friendly to special interests connived to weaken the new laws by failing to fund their enforcement.

Reformers themselves were not always certain about what was progressive, especially in terms of human behavior. The main problem seemed to be whether or not it was possible to create a desirable moral climate through legislation. Some reformers, such as the members of the Social Gospel movement (see page 529), believed that only church-based inspiration and humanitarian work, rather than legislation, could transform society. But other people believed state intervention was necessary to achieve purity, especially in drinking habits and sexual behavior.

Moral Reform

The formation of the Anti-Saloon League in 1893 marked a new turn in the long campaign against drunkenness and its effects on society. This organization of reformers joined with the Women's Christian Temperance Union (founded in 1873) to publicize the connections between alcoholism and poverty, unemployment and family breakups and to show that drinking produced liver disease and other health problems. The result was that a large number of states, counties, towns, and city wards restricted the sale and consumption of liquor. By 1900 almost one-fourth of the nation's population lived in communities with such restrictions. But as consumption of alcohol, especially beer, increased after 1900, prohibitionists became convinced that a national law was the only solution. By 1917 they had converted to their cause such notables as Supreme Court Justice Louis D. Brandeis and former president William Howard Taft. And in 1918 they induced Congress to pass the Eighteenth Amendment, prohibiting the manufacture, sale, and transportation of intoxicating liquors. (The amendment was ratified in 1919 and implemented in 1920.) Not all prohibitionists were progressive reformers, and all progressives were not prohibitionists. Yet the Eighteenth Amendment can be seen as an outcome of the progressive urge to change society and elevate morality through reform legislation.

Public outrage boiled over after 1900 when muckraking journalists exposed interstate and international rings that kidnapped young women and forced them to become prostitutes, a practice called white slavery. Middle-class moralists, already alarmed by a perceived link between immigration and prostitution, prodded governments to investigate the problem and recommend corrective legislation. The Chicago Vice Commission, for example, undertook a "scientific" survey and published its findings, called *The Social*

Evil in Chicago, in 1911. The report underscored the poverty, ignorance, and desperation that drove women, especially immigrants and blacks, to prostitution. Above all, however, it asserted that

it is a man and not a woman problem which we face today—commercialized by men—supported by men—the supply of fresh victims furnished by men. . . . So long as there is lust in the hearts of men [the Social Evil] will seek out some method of expression. Until the hearts of men are changed we can hope for no absolute annihilation of the Social Evil.

Nonetheless, reformers believed they could attack prostitution without changing "the hearts of men." By 1915 nearly every state had outlawed brothels and the soliciting of sex. And in 1910 Congress passed the Mann Act, or White Slave Traffic Act, prohibiting interstate and international transportation of women for immoral purposes.

Like prohibition, the Mann Act had reactionary as well as progressive elements. Even so, it reflected growing sentiment that state and national governments could improve human behavior. Reformers believed that the source of evil was not original sin but the social environment. If evil were human-made, then it could be human-destroyed. Thus human intervention, in the form of laws, could help create a heaven on earth.

ASSAULT ON OLD ASSUMPTIONS IN EDUCATION, LAW, AND THE SOCIAL SCIENCES

While legislation anchored the reform impulse, equally important changes were occurring in schools, courts, and settlement houses during the Progressive era. The preoccupation with efficiency and scientific management challenged educators, judges, and social scientists to seek solutions to the problems of modern mass society. Darwin's theory of evolution had upset traditional beliefs; immigration had replaced social uniformity with diverse nationalities; and economic change had shaken old habits of production and consumption. Ways of thinking and acting had to be found that would be meaningful for the new era yet preserve what was best in the past. A new flexibility was needed. Knowledge, as philosopher and educator John Dewey wrote, was "no longer an immobile solid; it has been liquefied. It is actively moving in all the currents of society itself." Such an attitude produced what historians have called a revolt against formalism.

Changing patterns of school attendance encouraged these new ways of thinking. As late as the 1870s, when rural society needed children to do farm work and schools were located far apart, Americans attended school for an average of only four years. By 1900, however, swelling cities contained multitudes of children who were removed from farm work and had more time for school. Also urban taxpayers were providing revenues to make extended mass education possible. Boosted by compulsory-attendance laws, public-school enrollments rose from 6.9 million in 1870 to 17.8 million in 1910. During the same period the number of public high schools grew from five hundred to over ten thousand.

Reformers had long envisioned education as a means of bettering society. As early as 1883, psychologist G. Stanley Hall, whose ideas strongly influenced John Dewey, had noted that the experiences of modern urban schoolchildren were much different from those of their farm-bred parents and grandparents. In the early nineteenth century, school curricula chiefly taught moralistic pieties. *McGuffey's Reader*, used by primary schools throughout the nation, contained homilies such as, "By virtue we secure happiness" and "One deed of shame is succeeded by years of penitence." Hall and Dewey, however, asserted that education had to adjust in order to prepare children for productive citizenship and self-fulfilling lives. Children, not subject matter, should be the focus of school policy, and schools should serve as community centers and instruments of social progress. Above all, said Dewey, education should relate directly to experience. Children should be encouraged to discover things for themselves. Rote memorization

Progressive Education

The objective of progressive education was to free children from the rigid classrooms of the past, where pupils had to sit quietly at attention, and enable them to learn by doing and making things. Rather than make the subject matter the major focus of the learning process, progressives made children the centers of attention.   Library of Congress.

and outdated subjects should be replaced by subjects relevant to students' lives.

Progressive education, based on theories Dewey explored in *The School and Society* (1899) and *Democracy and Education* (1916), was a uniquely American phenomenon. Like American economic theory, it emphasized growth. To Dewey, personal growth, not mastery of a given body of knowledge, was the goal of human existence. Because people grew fastest mentally in their youth, and because the family could no longer perform the educational functions it had fulfilled in an agrarian society, schools had to assume responsibility for cultivating intelligence and creativity. From kindergarten (a new development pioneered by the German educator Friedrich Froebel) through high school, children were supposed to learn through experience. In the Laboratory School that Dewey and his wife Alice directed at the University of Chicago, children were not required to recite lessons as their counterparts had done in the nineteenth century. Instead they examined, built, and discussed things just as they would outside school.

Personal growth also became the driving principle behind college education. The purpose of American colleges and universities had traditionally been that

Growth of Colleges and Universities

of their European counterparts: to train a select few for the professions of law, medicine, teaching, and religion. But in the late nineteenth century, places of higher education multiplied, spurred by public aid and increases in the number of people who could afford tuition. Between 1870 and 1910 the number of colleges and universities grew from 563 to nearly 1,000. Curricula expanded as educators sought to make learning attractive to more students. Harvard University, under President Charles W. Eliot, pioneered in substituting electives for required courses and in experimenting with new teaching techniques.

Much of the expansion in college enrollments,

As part of the progressive impulse to make learning more meaningful to everyday life, textbooks included more illustrations, including "photographs from life." *Library of Congress.*

especially in the Midwest and West, was prompted by the Morrill Land Grant Act of 1862 (see pages 395 and 471). The new land-grant colleges offered a wide variety of courses that ranged from the classics and natural science to carpentry and farming. Many schools considered athletics a vital part of a student's growth, and intercollegiate sports became a central feature of student life, as well as a source of school pride and alumni contributions. Southern states, in keeping with the "separate but equal" policy, set up segregated land-grant colleges for blacks. *Separate* was more descriptive of these institutions than *equal,* however; blacks continued to be constrained by inferior educational institutions.

As colleges and universities expanded, so did their enrollment of women. Between 1890 and 1910 the number of females enrolled in institutions of higher learning swelled from 56,000 to 140,000. By the latter date, 106,000 women attended coeducational institutions (many of which were state universities aided by the Morrill Act), while 34,000 attended women's colleges. By 1920, 283,000 women were attending college, accounting for 47.3 percent of total enrollment. Their numbers alone disproved earlier objections that women were unfit for higher learning because they were mentally and physically inferior to men, but discrimination lingered in admissions and curriculum policies. Most women were encouraged (indeed, they usually sought) to take home economics courses rather than science and mathematics, and most medical schools, including Harvard and Yale, refused to admit women.

At the same time they were developing new approaches to knowledge, American educators adopted the prevailing attitude of business: that more is better. They justifiably congratulated themselves for drawing more people into schools and for making instruction more meaningful. By 1920, fully 78 percent of all children between ages five and seventeen were enrolled in public elementary and high schools; another 8 percent were in private and parochial schools. These figures represented a huge increase over the attendance rate of 1870. And there were 600,000 college and graduate students in 1920, compared with 52,000 in 1870. Yet few people looked beyond the numbers to assess how well schools were doing their job. The faith that schools could promote equality and justice as well as personal growth and responsible citizenship underwent very little critical analysis.

The law, like education, began to exhibit new emphases on experience and scientific principles. An influential proponent of the new point of view was

Progressive Legal Thought

Harvard scholar Roscoe Pound, whose writings urged that social experience influence legal thinking. In practice, Oliver Wendell Holmes, Jr., associate justice of the Supreme Court between 1902 and 1932, led the attack on the old view of law as universal and unchanging—like the Ten Commandments. "The life of the law," said Holmes, sounding like Dewey, "has not been logic; it has been experience." The view that law should reflect society's needs challenged the judicial practice of invoking traditional beliefs and precedents in an inflexible way that often obstructed social legislation. Louis D. Brandeis, a brilliant lawyer who later joined Holmes on the Supreme Court, carried legal reform one step further by insisting that judges' opinions be based on factual, scientifically gathered information about social realities. In the landmark case *Muller v. Oregon* (1908), Brandeis mustered extensive scientific evidence to convince the Supreme Court to uphold Oregon's law limiting women's working hours.

New legal thought, however, met some tough resistance. Judges brought up on laissez-faire economic theory continued to strike down the kind of law progressive lawyers thought necessary for effective reform. Thus in 1905 the Supreme Court overturned a New York law limiting bakers' working hours (*Lochner v. New York*) in spite of Holmes's forceful dissent. As in other cases where it struck down reform, the Court's majority argued that the Fourteenth Amendment protected an individual's right to make contracts without government interference, and that this protection thus superseded reform sentiments. Also, judges weakened federal regulations by invoking the Tenth Amendment, which prohibited the federal government from interfering in matters reserved for state super-

vision. Thus the judiciary's use of constitutional principles governing freedom of contract and the division of government powers continually impeded reform.

The judiciary during the Progressive era was not entirely negative. Courts did sustain some regulatory measures, particularly those affecting the safety of the general public. A string of decisions, beginning with *Holden v. Hardy* in 1898 in which the Supreme Court upheld Utah's mining regulations, supported use of state police powers to protect the health, safety, and morals of their citizens. The judiciary also recognized federal police powers and Congress's authority in interstate commerce in sustaining such federal legislation as the Pure Food and Drug Act, the Meat Inspection Law (see page 607), and the Mann Act (see page 596). In these instances the welfare of citizens took precedence over the Tenth Amendment.

Still, the concept of general welfare posed thorny legal problems. Even if one agreed that law should reflect society's needs, which part of society should be represented? The United States was a mixed nation, and religion and ethnicity deeply influenced law. In many places a native white Protestant majority required Bible reading in public schools (thereby offending Catholics and Jews), stipulated that business establishments close on Sundays, restricted the religious practices of Mormons and other groups, prohibited interracial marriage, and enforced racial segregation. Though Holmes asserted that laws should be made for "people of fundamentally differing views," Americans have always had difficulty creating and applying such laws.

At about the same time, social science—the study of society and its institutions—experienced changes like those overtaking law and education. In economics,

Social Science

for example, a group of young scholars used statistics to argue that laws governing economic relationships were not immutable. Instead, they asserted, economic theory should reflect prevailing social conditions. Richard T. Ely of Johns Hopkins University and the University of Wisconsin, an early spokesman for this point of view, argued that opposition to government interference in social and economic affairs had been outmoded by industrialization. Thus, practical solutions to current problems should be derived through "the united efforts of Church, state, and

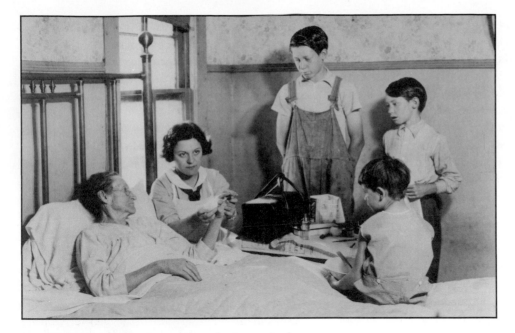

Some of the most lasting of progressive reforms were in the areas of health and welfare. Women often were in the vanguard of these movements. In this photograph, a member of the Visiting Nurses Association provides medical aid to the mother of an immigrant family.   Western Heritage Museum, Omaha, with permission of Visiting Nurses Association.

science." A new breed of sociologists led by Lester Ward, Albion Small, and Edward A. Ross agreed, adding that citizens should engage in planning to cure social ills rather than passively waiting for problems to solve themselves. Meanwhile the progressive historians, Frederick Jackson Turner, Charles A. Beard, and Vernon L. Parrington, were examining the past as a means of explaining current problems in American society and motivating social change. And political scientists like Woodrow Wilson emphasized the practical over the theoretical advocating the expansion of government power as a means to ensure justice and progress.

Social scientists joined with doctors and organizations like the National Consumers League to bring about some of the most far-reaching of progessive reforms: those in the area of public health. Founded by Josephine Shaw, a socially prominent Massachusetts widow, the National Consumers League initially worked to improve wages and conditions of young women employed in department stores. After settlement worker Florence Kelley became the league's general secretary, the organization expanded its activities to include women's suffrage, protection of child laborers, and removal of potential health hazards. Local branches supported such consumer protection measures as the licensing of food vendors and inspection of dairies. They also urged city governments to fund neighborhood clinics that provided health education and medical care to the poor. Their efforts spurred a movement for consumer and health awareness that has continued to the present.

National Consumers League and Public Health Reform

Between the end of the nineteenth century and the First World War, a new breed of men and women pressed for institutional change as well as political reform. Largely middle-class in background, trained by new professional standards, confident that new ways of thinking would bring progress, these people helped to broaden government's role in meeting the needs of a mature industrial society. Their questioning extended beyond their immediate goals and jostled conventional attitudes toward race and sex.

CHALLENGES TO RACIAL AND SEXUAL DISCRIMINATION

W. E. B. Du Bois, the forceful black scholar and teacher, ended an essay in his book *The Souls of Black Folk* (1903) with a call that heralded the twentieth-century civil rights movement: "By every civilized and peaceful method," he wrote, "we must strive for the right which the world accords to men."

By "men" Du Bois meant all human beings, not just one sex. But his statement and its context suggest the dilemma that vexed the two largest groups of underprivileged Americans in the early 1900s: women and nonwhites. Both lived in a society dominated by white males. Both suffered from disfranchisement, discrimination, and humiliation. And for centuries both groups had been striving for "the right which the world accords to men"—freedom and equality. The progressive challenge to old ideas and customs gave impetus to blacks' and women's struggles for their rights, but it posed a dilemma as well. Should women and blacks strive to become just like white men, with white men's values and power as well as their rights? Or was there something unique about racial and sexual identity that should be retained at the risk of sacrificing some gains? Both groups wavered between accepting and rejecting the culture from which they had been excluded.

The problems of blacks in white American society remained regional in scope until well into the twentieth century, though important shifts were beginning to occur. In 1900 only one in ten blacks lived in the North. The rest lived in southern states, where repressive Jim Crow measures had multiplied in the 1880s and 1890s. Southern blacks were not only denied legal and voting rights but were officially segregated in almost all walks of life. They faced constant exclusion and violence. In 1910 only 8,000 out of 970,000 high-school-age blacks in the entire South were enrolled in high schools. Between 1900 and 1914 white mobs lynched over a thousand blacks.

Blacks began to migrate northward in the 1880s, accelerating their rate of departure after 1900. But job and housing discrimination, inferior schools, and segregated neighborhoods characterized northern as well as southern cities. White humanitarians contributed to discrimination by maintaining separate and inferior institutions for blacks, rather than integrating them with whites. A half-century after the abolition of slavery, most whites still agreed with the northern historian James Ford Rhodes that blacks were "innately inferior and incapable of citizenship."

Black leaders differed over how—and whether—to achieve assimilation. In the wake of emancipation, ex-slave Frederick Douglass had urged "ultimate assimilation through self-assertion, and on no other terms." Other blacks, who favored isolation from cruel white society, supported migration back to Africa or establishment of all-black communities in Oklahoma Territory and Kansas. Still others advocated militancy. According to one extremist, "Our people must die to be saved and in dying must take as many along with them as it is possible to do with the aid of firearms and all other weapons."

Most blacks, however, could neither escape nor conquer white society. They thus had to find other routes to improvement. Self-help, a strategy articulated by educator Booker T. Washington, was one of the most popular alternatives. Born in 1856 to slave parents, Washington worked his way through school and in 1881 founded Tuskegee Institute in Alabama, a vocational school for blacks. There he developed the philosophy that blacks' hopes for assimilation lay in at least temporarily accommodating themselves to whites. Rather than fighting for political rights, he said, blacks should work hard, acquire property, and prove they were worthy of their rights. Washington voiced his views in a widely acclaimed speech at the Atlanta Exposition in 1895. "Dignify and glorify common labor," he urged in what became known as the Atlanta Compromise. "Agitation of questions of racial equality is the extremest folly." Envisioning a society where blacks and whites would remain apart but share the same goals, Washington observed that "in all things that are purely social we can be as separate as the fingers, yet one as the hand in all matters essential to mutual progress."

Whites, including progressives, welcomed Washington's policy of accommodation because it urged patience and seemed to remind black people to stay

Booker T. Washington

Black students practicing woodwork at Hampton Institute, Hampton, Virginia. Like Tuskegee Institute, Hampton offered vocational instruction in the belief that by acquiring skills and working hard, blacks could convince whites they were worthy of equal rights.   Library of Congress.

in their place. White businesspeople, reformers, and politicians chose to regard Washington as representative of all blacks, because he said what they wanted to hear. Yet though Washington endorsed the separate-but-equal policy, he projected a subtle racial pride that would find more direct expression in black nationalism later in the twentieth century, when some blacks would urge control of their own businesses and schools. Washington never argued that blacks were inferior to whites; he instead argued that their dignity could be enhanced through self-improvement.

But to some blacks Washington seemed to favor second-class citizenship, which they considered degrading. In 1905 a group of "anti-Bookerites" convened near Niagara Falls and pledged a

W. E. B. Du Bois

more militant pursuit of such rights as unrestricted voting, equal access to economic opportunity, integration, and equality before the law. Spokesperson for the Niagara movement was W. E. B. Du Bois, a vociferous critic of the Atlanta Compromise. A New Englander with a Ph.D. from Harvard, Du Bois had the background of a typical progressive. He had studied in Germany, where he learned about scientific investigation, and he was a professor on the faculty of Atlanta University. Du Bois used scientific methods to compile fact-filled sociological studies of black ghetto dwellers, and he wrote poetically for the cause of civil rights. In his essays and speeches, Du Bois treated Washington politely, but he could not accept Washington's submission to white domination. "The way for a people to gain their reasonable rights," Du Bois asserted, "is not by voluntarily throwing them away." Blacks needed, instead, to agitate for what was indeed rightfully theirs.

Du Bois showed that accommodation was an unrealistic strategy, but his own solution may have been just as fanciful. A blunt elitist, Du Bois believed that an intellectual vanguard of cultivated, highly trained blacks, which he called the Talented Tenth, would save the race by setting an example to whites and uplift other blacks. Inevitably, such sentiments had more attraction for middle-class white liberals than for black sharecroppers. Thus when Du Bois and his allies formed the National Association for the Advancement of Colored People (1909), which aimed to use legal redress in the courts to end racial discrimination, the leadership consisted chiefly of white progressives. Very few working-class black people belonged. By 1914 the NAACP had fifty branch offices and over six thousand members, but rarely did its activities touch sharecropping and laboring families.

Whatever strategy they pursued—accommodation or agitation—black Americans faced continued oppression. In fact, those who managed to acquire property and education encountered increased resentment. And the federal government only aggravated conditions. Under the administration of Woodrow Wilson, segregation within the federal government expanded; southern cabinet members supported racial separation in the rest rooms, restaurants, and offices of government buildings and balked at hiring black workers. Commenting on Wilson's racism in 1913, Booker T. Washington wrote, "I have never seen the colored people so discouraged and so bitter as they are at the present time."

Blacks still sought to fulfill the American dream of success, but many wondered whether membership in a corrupt white society should be part of their quest. Du Bois voiced these doubts poignantly, writing that "one ever feels his twoness—an American, a Negro, two souls, two thoughts, two unreconciled strivings, two warring ideals in one dark body." Somehow blacks would have to reconcile that twoness by combining racial pride with national identity. As Du Bois wrote in 1903, a black

would not Africanize America, for America has too much to teach the world and Africa. He would not bleach his Negro soul in a flood of white Americanism, for he knows that Negro blood has a message for the world. He simply wishes to make it possible for a man to be both a Negro and an American.

That simple wish would haunt the nation for decades to come.

During this time too, the progressive challenge to social relations stirred women to seek liberation from the traditional confines of hearth and home. Their struggle raised questions of identity that resembled those blacks were facing. What tactics should women use to achieve equality, and what should be their role in society? The writer Henry James summed up the dilemma inherent in such questions when he complained that women who wanted to become just like men were disregarding their own uniqueness. Could women achieve equality with men and at the same time change male-dominated society?

The Progressive era included a number of efforts by and on behalf of women to extend their influence beyond domestic bounds. Some of these efforts derived from radical impulses. Feminist Charlotte Perkins Gilman sounded a clarion call in her book *Women and Economics* (1898), declaring that domesticity and female innocence were obsolete and attacking the male monopoly on economic opportunity. This and Gilman's other writings moved some women, but even more were swept up by the women's club movement.

Women's Clubs

Originated as literary and educational organizations, these groups of middle-class women began entering public affairs in the late nineteenth century. Consolidated as the General Federation of Women's Clubs in 1890, they claimed nearly one million members by 1910.

The reform activities of clubs and other women define a particularly female dimension of the Progressive era. Because women were generally excluded from the political arena before 1920 (see page 604), those with reform motivations were drawn less to movements to improve government than to movements for social betterment. Thus rather than press for such reforms as trustbusting, nonpartisan elections, and direct primaries, female reformers tended to work for social goals such as factory inspection, regulation of children's and women's labor, housing reform, and pure food and drug laws. At the same time, college-educated and professionally trained women became active in settlement houses and educational reform movements.

A number of such women joined the birth control movement led by Margaret Sanger. As a visiting

TO THE MALE CITIZEN

IF THIS IS WOMANLY—

WHY NOT THIS?

This cartoon supporting women's rights addressed the illogical attitudes of those who believed women should stay out of public affairs. "No man denies that government is public housekeeping," the caption pointed out. Were women allowed to hold office, the artist's reasoning suggested, they could keep public administration—as well as the streets—clean. The Schlesinger Library, Radcliffe College.

nurse in New York's East Side immigrant neighborhoods, Sanger distributed information about contraception in hopes of preventing unwanted pregnancies and their tragic consequences among poor women. Her crusade, however, captured the attention of middle-class women, who wanted to limit their own families and to control the growth of immigrant masses. It also aroused the opposition of men and women who saw birth control as a threat to family and morality. In 1914 moral purists caused Sanger to be indicted for sending obscene literature (articles on contraception) through the mail, forcing her to flee the country for a year. Sanger persevered and in 1921 formed the American Birth Control League, which enlisted physicians and social workers to convince judges to allow distribution of birth control information. Most states still prohibited the sale of con-

Birth Control

traceptives, but the issue had entered the realm of public discussion.

Except for a few visionaries like Gilman, the women who participated in reform movements seldom thought about effecting a sexual revolution. Many could not decide which aspects of their identity to cultivate and which to drop. Most women opposed birth control, for example, in the belief that contraception threatened women's status as mothers. Others feared that if women became the equals of men they would lose what they considered the special virtues of the female personality.

Ambivalence about the supposed uniqueness of the feminine character pervaded the suffrage movement, which achieved victory in 1920 when enough states ratified the Nineteenth Amendment giving women the vote. The suffrage crusade dated back to the mid-nineteenth century. It had grown out of the abolitionist

Suffragists

crusade's insistence that all Americans, regardless of race or sex, were equal and thus deserved the same rights. Confronted by male resistance, however, some women defended female suffrage by arguing that women's special, even superior, traits would humanize politics. Settlement-house founder Jane Addams, for example, supported the vote for her sex by asking, "If women have in any sense been responsible for the gentler side of life which softens and blurs some of its harsher conditions may not they have a duty to perform in our American cities?"

Suffragists achieved their first successes at the local level; by 1912 nine states, all of them in the West, allowed women to vote. After 1900 women pressed increasingly for the vote on the national level. The suffragists' tactics ranged from the moderate but persistent propaganda campaigns of the National American Women Suffrage Association, led by Carrie Chapman Catt, to the active picketing and marching of the National Women's party, led by Alice Paul. All these activities heightened public awareness of the suffragist cause. More decisive, however, was women's participation on the home front during the First World War as factory laborers, medical volunteers, and municipal workers (see pages 662–664). Their efforts convinced legislators that women could shoulder public responsibilities and gave final impetus to passage of the suffrage amendment.

Although women's clubs and the suffrage movement attracted mostly middle-class women, some efforts were made to encourage feelings of sisterhood among all classes. Since the early nineteenth century, a number of well-to-do women had recognized that all females had common grievances; that feeling gained ground in the early 1900s. Thus Alva Belmont, a wealthy supporter of the shirtwaist workers' strike, said in 1909, "It was my interest in women, in women everywhere and every class that drew my attention and sympathies first to the striking shirtwaist girls." This feeling of sisterhood formed the basis of the feminist movement, for as Mrs. Belmont urged "Women the world over need protection and it is only through the united efforts of women that they will get it."

But women's united efforts failed to create an interest group solid enough or powerful enough to dent political, economic, and social systems run by men.

Like blacks, women knew that voting rights would mean little until people's attitudes could be changed. The Progressive era had helped women to clarify the issues that concerned them, but major reforms would await the future. As the feminist Crystal Eastman, echoing Du Bois, observed in the aftermath of the suffrage crusade,

> Men are saying perhaps, "Thank God, this everlasting women's fight is over!" But women, if I know them, are saying, "Now at last we can begin." . . . Now they can say what they are really after, in common with all the rest of the struggling world, is *freedom*.

THEODORE ROOSEVELT AND THE REVIVAL OF THE PRESIDENCY

The Progressive era's theme of reform—in politics, institutions, and social relations—directed attention to government, especially the federal government, as the ultimate agent of change. At first, however, the federal government seemed incapable of assuming such responsibility. Dominated by two political parties that resembled private clubs more than bodies of impartial statesmen, the government acted mainly for special interests when it acted at all. Then suddenly, in September 1901, the climate changed. The assassination of President William McKinley by an anarchist named Leon Czolgosz vaulted Theodore Roosevelt, the young, vigorous vice president, into the White House.

Political manager Mark Hanna had warned fellow Republicans against nominating Roosevelt for the vice presidency in 1900. "Don't any of you realize," Hanna asked after the nominating convention, "that there's only one life between that madman and the Presidency?" As governor of New York, Roosevelt had angered party bosses by showing sympathy for regulatory legislation. So Republican leaders rid themselves of their pariah by pushing him into national politics. Little did they realize that they were about to present the nation with its most forceful president since Lincoln, a man who would infuse the office with much of its twentieth-century character.

In marked contrast to his predecessors, Theodore Roosevelt lacked the dignified appearance of a president. He stood five-foot-nine but looked shorter.

Theodore Roosevelt: His Early Life Very nearsighted, he was helpless without his metal-rimmed glasses. He had big, prominent teeth and talked in a high-pitched voice. As a youth he had suffered from asthma. Yet throughout his life he was driven by a near-obsession to overcome his physical limitations and exert what he and his contemporaries called manliness. In his teens he practiced diligently to become an expert marksman and horseman. As a Harvard student he competed on the boxing and wrestling teams. In the 1880s he went to live on a Dakota ranch, where he roped cattle and brawled with other cowboys.

A descendant of a Dutch aristocratic family, Roosevelt inherited the wealth to indulge in such pursuits. But he also inherited a sense of civic responsibility that he translated into a career in public office. He served three terms in the New York State Assembly, ran for mayor of New York City in 1886 (finishing third), and served on the federal Civil Service Commission, as New York City's police commissioner, and as assistant secretary of the navy. In this series of offices Roosevelt earned a reputation as a combative, politically crafty leader. He also distinguished himself as a historian with his *The Naval War of 1812* (1882) and *The Winning of the West* (1889).

In 1898 Roosevelt thrust himself into the Spanish-American War by organizing a volunteer cavalry brigade, the Rough Riders, to fight in Cuba (see pages 629–630). His dramatic act excited the public, though it had little impact on the war's outcome. Nevertheless, Roosevelt returned from the war a folk hero (people called him Teddy, a name he disliked) and was elected governor of New York, then vice president.

As president, Roosevelt became a progressive hero. At heart, though, he was a conservative. His impulsive patriotism, admiration for big business, and dislike of anything he considered effeminate recalled the previous era of unbridled expansion when raw power prevailed in social and economic affairs. Yet Roosevelt came to conclusions similar to those reached by pro-

President Theodore Roosevelt (1858–1919) giving one of his typically dynamic speeches. With his broad interests and energetic leadership, Roosevelt revitalized the presidency and gave it much of its twentieth-century character. Library of Congress.

gressives. His sense of history convinced him that the kind of small government Jefferson had hoped for would not suffice in the modern industrial era. Instead, economic development necessitated a Hamiltonian system of government powerful enough to guide national affairs. Like his supporters, Roosevelt believed in the wisdom and talents of a select few, whose superior backgrounds and education qualified them to coordinate public and private enterprise. "A simple and poor society," he observed, "can exist as a democracy on the basis of sheer individualism. But a rich and complex society cannot so exist."

Roosevelt's presidency inaugurated the federal regulation of economic affairs that has characterized twentieth-century American history. Roosevelt first turned his attention to big business, where the com-

Regulation of Trusts

bination movement had produced giant trusts that controlled almost every sector of the economy. Though Roosevelt has a reputation as a trustbuster, he actually believed in consolidation as the most efficient means to achieve material and technological progress. Rather than return to uncontrolled competition, he preferred to distinguish between good and bad trusts, and to prevent the bad ones from manipulating markets. Thus he instructed the Justice Department to use antitrust laws to prosecute the railroad, meatpacking, and oil trusts, which he believed had unscrupulously exploited the public. Roosevelt's policy triumphed in 1904 when the Supreme Court, convinced by the government's arguments, ordered the dissolution of the Northern Securities Company, the huge railroad combination created by J. P. Morgan and his powerful business allies. (Roosevelt chose, however, not to attack other gigantic trusts, such as U.S. Steel, another of Morgan's creations.)

When the prosecution of Northern Securities began, Morgan reportedly collared Roosevelt and offered, "If we have done anything wrong, send your man to my man and they can fix it up." The president refused. But Roosevelt was more sympathetic to such arrangements than his refusal might suggest. He preferred cooperation between business and government. Rather than prosecute, he urged the Bureau of Corporations (part of the newly created Department of Labor and Commerce) to work with companies on mergers and other forms of expansion. Thus through investigation and cooperation the administration exerted pressure on business to regulate itself.

Roosevelt also pushed for regulatory legislation, especially after 1904, when he won a resounding electoral victory by garnering the votes of progressives and businesspeople alike. After a year of wrangling with business lobbyists in Congress, he succeeded in 1906 in getting passage of the Hepburn Act, which imposed stricter control over railroads and expanded the powers of the Interstate Commerce Commission. The act gave the ICC more authority to fix railroad rates, though it did allow the courts to overturn rate decisions. Progressives like Robert La Follette deplored the fact that Roosevelt had compromised with business representatives like Senator Nelson W. Aldrich of Rhode Island to assure the bill's passage. But Roosevelt's aim was to establish at least the principle of government regulation rather than risk defeat over more idealistic objectives.

Roosevelt showed a similar willingness to compromise on legislation to ensure pure food and drugs. For decades reformers had been urging government regulation of patent medicines and processed meat. The outcry against fraud and adulteration heightened in 1906 with the publication of Upton Sinclair's *The Jungle*, a fictionalized exposé of Chicago meatpacking plants. Sinclair, a young socialist more interested in freeing workers from oppression than in muckraking, nevertheless shocked public sensibilities by describing scandalous conditions like the following:

Pure Food and Drug Laws

> There was never the least attention paid to what was cut up for sausage; there would come all the way back from Europe old sausage that had been rejected, and that was mouldy and white—it would be dosed with borax and glycerine, and dumped into the hoppers, and made over again for home consumption. . . . There would be meat stored in great piles in rooms; and the water from the leaky roofs would drip over it, and thousands of rats would race about on it. It was too dark in these storage places to see well, but a man could run his hand over these piles of meat and sweep off handfuls of dried dung of rats. These rats were a nuisance, and the packers would put poisoned bread out for them; they would die, and then rats, bread, and meat would go into the hoppers together.

On reading Sinclair's novel, Roosevelt ordered an investigation. Finding Sinclair's descriptions accurate he supported the Pure Food and Drug Act and the Meat Inspection Act, both passed in 1906. Like the Hepburn Act, these laws reinforced the principle of government regulation. But as part of the compromise to obtain their passage, the government had to pay for inspections, and meatpackers could appeal government decisions in court.

Roosevelt's policy on labor issues resembled his stance toward business. When, for example, the United Mine Workers struck against coal-mine owners in 1902, the president intervened by using the progressive tactics of investigation and arbitration. The mine workers, led by feisty John Mitchell, wanted higher pay and an eight-hour day, but the owners stubbornly refused to recognize the union or arbitrate the grievances. As winter approached and fuel shortages threatened, Roosevelt mustered public opinion. He warned that he would use federal troops to reopen the mines, thereby forcing both sides to accept arbitration of the dispute by a special commission. The commission decided in favor of higher wages and reduced hours, but also declared that the owners did not have to recognize the union. The decision, according to Roosevelt, created a "square deal" for all. The strike settlement illustrated Roosevelt's belief that the president or his agents should have a say in which labor demands were legitimate and which were not—just as he could help to guide business regulation. In Roosevelt's mind there were good and bad labor organizations (socialists, for example, were bad), just as there were good and bad business combinations.

On the issue of conservation, Roosevelt displayed the same mix of flamboyant executive action and quiet compromise that he applied to other domestic matters. He built a reputation as a determined conservationist, warning Congress in 1907, "We are prone to think of the resources of this country as inexhaustible; this is not so." A lover of the outdoors, Roosevelt used presidential authority to add almost 150 million acres to the national forests and to preserve vast areas of water and coal from private plunder. He sympathized with conservationist Gifford Pinchot, who was the government's chief forester, and in 1908 called forty-four governors and five hundred natural-resource experts to a National Conservation Congress. True to the progressive spirit, Roosevelt wanted a "well-conceived plan" for resource management, a plan for ordered growth rather than mere preservation of nature as it was. But compromises and factors beyond his control weakened his scheme. Timber and mining companies shunned supervision of their wasteful practices, and Congress never authorized enough funds to enforce federal regulations.

Roosevelt also had to compromise his principles in the face of economic crisis. In 1907 a financial panic caused by overspeculation forced some New York banks to close to prevent frightened depositors from withdrawing money. J. P. Morgan helped to stem the panic by persuading other financiers to stop dumping their securities. In return for Morgan's aid, Roosevelt approved a deal allowing U.S. Steel to

Conservation

absorb its competitor, the Tennessee Iron and Coal Company—an act that flouted Roosevelt's trustbusting aims.

During his last year in office, Roosevelt moved further away from the Republican party's traditional alliance with big business. He lashed out at irresponsible actions of "malefactors of great wealth" and supported stronger regulation of business and heavier taxation of the rich. Having promised in 1904 that he would not seek re-election, Roosevelt backed his friend Secretary of War William Howard Taft for the nomination in 1908, hoping that Taft would continue to pursue the Roosevelt initiatives. The Democrats nominated William Jennings Bryan for the third time, but the Great Commoner lost again. Aided by Roosevelt, who still had strong popular influence, Taft won by 1.25 million popular votes and a 2 to 1 margin in the electoral college.

Early in 1909 Roosevelt went to Africa to shoot game (he saw no contradiction between hunting and conservation), leaving Taft to face the political problems his predecessor had managed to postpone. Foremost among them were tariff rates, which had risen to excessive levels. Honoring Taft's pledge to cut rates, the House passed a bill sponsored by Representative Sereno E. Payne that provided for numerous downward revisions. As they had in the past, protectionists in the Senate prepared to amend the House bill and revise rates upward. But Senate progressives, led by La Follette, organized a stinging attack on the ways the tariff benefited vested interests. Taft was caught between the reformers, who claimed they were carrying on Roosevelt's antitrust spirit, and the protectionists who still controlled the Republican party. In the end Senator Aldrich and other protectionists restored many of the cuts, and Taft, who was more reluctant than Roosevelt to interfere in the legislative process, signed what became known as the Payne-Aldrich Tariff. To many progressives, Taft had failed the test of filling Roosevelt's shoes.

The progressive and conservative wings of the Republican party were rapidly drifting apart. Soon after the tariff controversy a group of insurgents in the House, led by George Norris of Nebraska, challenged Speaker "Uncle Joe" Cannon of Illinois, whose power over committee assignments and scheduling of debate could make or break a piece of legislation. Taft first

Taft Administration

supported and then abandoned the insurgents, who nevertheless managed to liberalize procedures by enlarging the important rules committee and removing its appointments from Cannon's control. Meanwhile, Taft also angered conservationists by allowing Secretary of the Interior Richard A. Ballinger to remove 1 million acres of forest and mineral land from the reserved list and to fire Gifford Pinchot when he protested a questionable sale of coal lands in Alaska.

In reality Taft was as sympathetic to reform as Roosevelt was. He prosecuted more trusts than Roosevelt; expanded the national forest reserves; signed the Mann-Elkins Act of 1910, which bolstered regulatory powers of the ICC; and supported such labor reforms as the eight-hour day and mine safety legislation. The Sixteenth Amendment, which legalized a federal income tax, and the Seventeenth Amendment, which provided for direct election of U.S. senators, were initiated during Taft's presidency. Like Roosevelt, Taft was forced to compromise with big business, but he lacked Roosevelt's ability to maneuver and to publicize the issues he supported. Roosevelt, who had worked to expand presidential power, had also infused the office with vitality. "I believe in a strong executive," he once asserted. "I believe in power." Taft, on the other hand, believed in the strict restraint of law. He had been a successful lawyer and judge (he returned to the bench as Chief Justice of the United States between 1921 and 1930). His caution and unwillingness to offend disappointed those used to Roosevelt's impetuosity.

Thus in 1910, when Roosevelt returned from Africa boasting over three thousand animal trophies, he found his party torn and tormented. Reformers, angered by Taft's apparent insensitivity to their cause, formed the National Progressive Republican League and rallied behind Robert La Follette for president in 1912—though many hoped Roosevelt would run. Another wing of the party stood loyal to Taft. Roosevelt, disappointed by Taft's performance (particularly his refusal to back Pinchot), began to speak out and to rekindle public attention. He filled his speeches with references to "the welfare of the people" and to stronger regulation of business. When La Follette became ill early in 1912, Roosevelt, proclaiming himself fit as a "bull moose," threw his hat in the ring for the Republican presidential nomination.

Taft's supporters controlled the convention and nominated him for a second term, but Roosevelt forces formed a third party—the Progressive or Bull Moose party—and nominated the fifty-three-year-old former president. Meanwhile, the Democrats endured forty-six ballots before selecting as their candidate New Jersey's progressive governor Woodrow Wilson. The Socialists, by now an organized and growing party, nominated their perennial candidate Eugene V. Debs. The campaign exposed voters to the most thorough evaluation of the American system in nearly a generation.

WOODROW WILSON AND THE EXTENSION OF REFORM

In his acceptance speech before the Progressive party, Theodore Roosevelt had proclaimed, "We stand at Armageddon and we battle for the Lord." But on inauguration day 1913, it was Woodrow Wilson who assumed command of the forces of good. "The Nation," he exhorted,

> has been deeply stirred by a solemn passion, stirred by the knowledge of wrong, of ideals lost, of government too often debauched and made an instrument of evil. The feelings with which we face this new age of right and opportunity sweep across our heartstrings like some air out of God's own presence, where justice and mercy are reconciled and the judge and the brother are one.

The election's outcome illustrated the extent to which the electorate had been swept up by the moral fervor of these pronouncements. Wilson won with 42 percent of the popular vote—he was a minority president, though he did capture 435 out of 531 electoral votes (see map, page 610). Roosevelt received about 27 percent of the popular vote. Taft finished a poor third, polling 23 percent of the popular vote and only 8 electoral votes. Debs won 902,000 votes, 6 percent of the total, but no electoral votes. Thus fully three-quarters of the electorate supported some alternative to the restrained approach to government that Taft represented.

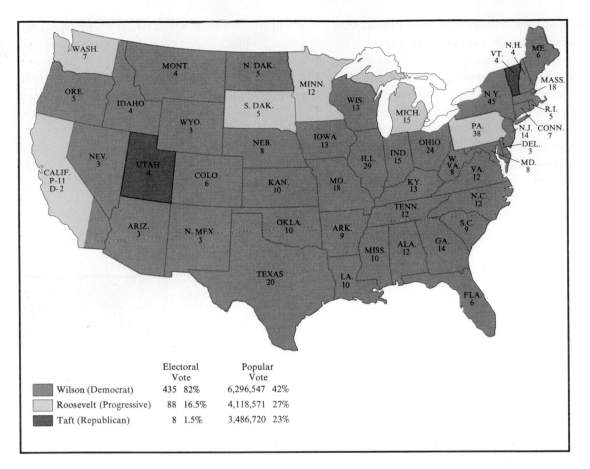

	Electoral Vote		Popular Vote	
Wilson (Democrat)	435	82%	6,296,547	42%
Roosevelt (Progressive)	88	16.5%	4,118,571	27%
Taft (Republican)	8	1.5%	3,486,720	23%

Presidential Election, 1912

The campaign had featured a sharp debate over the fundamentals of progressive government. On one side stood Roosevelt with a system called the New Nationalism, a term coined by reform editor Herbert Croly. Roosevelt foresaw a new era of national unity in which governmental authority would balance and coordinate economic activity. He would not destroy big business, which he saw as an efficient way to organize production. Rather, he would establish regulatory commissions, groups of experts who would protect citizens' interests and ensure the wise use of concentrated economic power. "The effort at prohibiting all combinations has substantially failed," he claimed. "The way out lies . . . in completely controlling them."

The New Nationalism and the New Freedom

Wilson offered a more idealistic scheme in his New Freedom, based on ideas of the progressive lawyer Louis D. Brandeis. Wilson believed that concentration of economic power threatened individual liberty, that monopolies had to be broken so that the marketplace could again become open. But he did not want to restore laissez faire. Like Roosevelt, Wilson would enhance governmental authority to protect and regulate. "Freedom today," he declared, "is something more than being let alone. Without the watchful . . . resolute interference of the government, there can be no fair play between individuals and such powerful institutions as the trusts." But Wilson stopped short of the cooperation between big business and big government inherent in Roosevelt's New Nationalism. In the campaign at least, he spoke in evangelical tones of the need for economic emancipation, the need to "come out of a stifling cellar into the open . . . breathe again and see the free spaces of the heavens."

Roosevelt and Wilson stood closer together than

their rhetoric implied. In spite of his faith in experts as regulators, Roosevelt harbored sentiments for individual freedom as strong as Wilson's. And Wilson was not as hostile to concentrated power as his speeches suggested. Both men strongly supported equality of opportunity, conservation of natural resources, fair wages for workers, and social betterment for all classes. Perhaps more important, both would expand government activity through strong personal leadership and bureaucratic reform. Thus, even though he received a minority of the total vote in 1912, Wilson could interpret the results of the election as a popular mandate to subdue trusts and broaden the federal government's concern for social reform.

Though the public had often fondly referred to Roosevelt as Teddy or TR, no one ever called Thomas Woodrow Wilson Tommy or WW. The son of a

Woodrow Wilson: His Early Career

Presbyterian minister, Wilson was born and raised in the South. His mother, Janet Woodrow, and his first wife, Ellen Axson, were both daughters of Presbyterian ministers. But Wilson chose to become an academic rather than a cleric. He earned a B.A. at Princeton, studied law at Virginia, received a Ph.D. from Johns Hopkins, and became a professor of history, jurisprudence, and political economy. Between 1885 and 1908 he published a number of books on American history and government that established him as a respectable scholar. Wilson's manner and bearing reflected his religious and academic background. Tall, lean, and stiff, he seemed to stare coldly through his pince-nez glasses. He exuded none of Roosevelt's flamboyance, and often spoke self-righteously.

Yet Wilson was an effective and charismatic leader. A superb orator, he could inspire intense loyalty with religious images and an eloquent expression of American ideals. Wilson's convictions had led him early into reform. In 1902 he became president of Princeton, where he upset tradition with his curricular reforms and battles against aristocratic elements in the university. In 1910 New Jersey Democrats, eager for respectability, nominated Wilson for the governorship. After winning the election, Wilson repudiated the party bosses and directed passage of progressive legislation. He was not good at administration, often losing his temper and stubbornly refusing to compromise. But his accomplishments attracted national

Looking like a preacher, Woodrow Wilson (1856–1924) delivers a speech at a campaign rally. Wilson's forceful, carefully crafted speeches, which resembled moral lectures more than political pitches, raised citizens' expectations for the fulfillment of his idealistic promises.   Brown Brothers.

attention and won him the Democratic nomination for president in 1912.

As president, Wilson had to blend his New Freedom ideals with New Nationalism precepts, and in so doing he set the direction of federal economic policy

Wilson's Policy on Business Regulation

for much of the twentieth century. The corporate merger movement had proceeded so far that restoration of free competition was impossible. Thus Wilson could only acknowledge economic concentration and try to prevent its abuse by expanding the government's regulatory powers. His administration moved toward that end with passage in 1914 of the Clayton Anti-Trust Act and a bill creating the Federal Trade Commission (FTC). The Clayton Act extended the Sherman Anti-Trust Act of 1890 by outlawing quasi-monopolistic practices such as price discrimination (whereby a company might try to destroy competition by lowering prices in some regions but not others) and interlocking directorates (management of two or more competing companies by the same executives). The FTC, which replaced the Bureau of Corporations, was to investigate corporations and issue cease-and-desist orders against unfair trade practices. As in ICC rulings, accused companies could appeal FTC orders in the courts. Nevertheless, the FTC represented a further step in the protection of consumers.

Wilson increased federal regulation of finance with the Federal Reserve Act of 1913. The law established the nation's first centralized banking system since Andrew Jackson destroyed the Second Bank of the United States (see pages 340–341). Twelve newly created district banks would hold the reserves of member banks throughout the nation. (The act created many banks rather than one to allay the agrarian fear of a monolithic eastern banking power, which had doomed the bank in Jackson's time.) The district banks would loan money to member banks at a low interest rate, called the *discount rate*. By adjusting this rate (and thus the amount of money a bank could afford to borrow), the district banks could increase or decrease the amount of money in circulation. In other words, depending on the nation's needs, the reserve bank could loosen or tighten credit. Monetary affairs would no longer depend on the supply of gold, and interest rates would be fairer, especially for small borrowers.

Perhaps the only act of Wilson's first administration that promoted free competition was the Underwood Tariff, passed in 1913. For years rising prices had thwarted consumers' desires for the

Tariff and Tax Reform

material benefits of the industrial age. Some prices were unnaturally high because government tariffs had discouraged importation of cheap foreign materials and manufactured products. The Underwood Tariff encouraged imports by drastically reducing or eliminating tariff rates. To recover revenues lost due to the reductions, the act levied a graduated income tax on U.S. residents—an option made possible earlier that year when the Sixteenth Amendment was ratified. The income tax was tame by today's standards. Incomes under $4,000 were exempt; thus almost all factory workers and farmers escaped the tax. People and corporations earning $4,000 to $20,000 had to pay a 1-percent tax, and the rate for higher incomes rose gradually to a maximum of 6 percent on earnings over $500,000. Such rates made no holes in the pockets of the rich. But the income tax did become an institutional feature of American life.

The First World War and the approaching presidential campaign prompted Wilson to support stronger reforms in 1916. Concerned that food shortages might result if farmers could not borrow money to sustain production, the president backed the Federal Farm Loan Act of 1916. The measure created twelve federally supported banks (not to be confused with the Federal Reserve banks) that would lend money at moderate interest rates to farmers who belonged to credit institutions—a watered-down version of something the Populists had agitated for a generation earlier. To stave off railroad strikes that might disrupt transportation at a time of national emergency, Wilson pushed passage of the Adamson Act of 1916, which mandated an eight-hour day and time-and-a-half for overtime for railroad laborers. Early that year, he pleased progressives by appointing Louis D. Brandeis, the "people's advocate," to the Supreme Court. Finally, Wilson courted the support of social reformers by backing laws that outlawed child labor and provided workers' compensation for federal employees who suffered from injury or illness.

In selecting their candidate to oppose Wilson in 1916, the Republicans snubbed Theodore Roosevelt, who wanted the nomination, in favor of Charles

Election of 1916

Evans Hughes, former reform governor of New York and Supreme Court justice. Wilson ran on a platform of peace, progressivism, and preparedness. Many voters were attracted by the Democratic party's campaign slogan: "He Kept Us Out of War." Hughes led a fractured party, and he could not muzzle Roosevelt, whose bellicose speeches suggested that the Republicans would drag Americans into the world war. Wilson received 9.1 million votes to Hughes's 8.5 million, and the president barely won in the electoral college by a 277-to-254 count. The Socialist party, which had earned 902,000 votes four years earlier, dropped to 600,000, largely because Wilson's reforms had attracted some socialists and the ailing Eugene Debs was not the party's standardbearer.

Wilson's second term and the subsequent involvement in the First World War saw a shift away from competition toward interest-group politics and government regulation. During his first term Wilson had been convinced that laws, not regulatory commissions

IMPORTANT EVENTS

1893	Anti-Saloon League founded		1909	NAACP founded
				Payne-Aldrich Tariff
1895	Booker T. Washington's Atlanta Compromise speech		1910	White Slave Traffic Act
				Ballinger-Pinchot controversy
1898	*Holden v. Hardy*		1912	Roosevelt runs for president on Progressive (Bull Moose) ticket
1900	McKinley re-elected			Wilson elected president
1901	McKinley assassinated; Roosevelt assumes presidency		1913	Sixteenth and Seventeenth Amendments ratified
1903	Elkins Act			Underwood Tariff
				Federal Reserve Act
1904	*Northern Securities* case		1914	Federal Trade Commission Act
	Roosevelt elected president			Clayton Anti-Trust Act
1905	Niagara Falls Convention			Sanger indicted
	Lochner v. New York		1916	Wilson re-elected
1906	Hepburn Act			Federal Farm Loan Act
	Pure Food and Drug Act		1919	Eighteenth Amendment ratified
1907	Economic panic		1920	Nineteenth Amendment ratified
1908	Taft elected president			
	Muller v. Oregon			

that could easily fall under the influence of the very interests they were meant to regulate, should govern social and economic behavior. But wartime crisis and the desire for re-election convinced him to adopt a different attitude. The war effort required government coordination of production and cooperation between the public and private sectors. The War Industries Board (see page 661) was one example of this cooperation. The private businesses that were regulated by the board submitted to its direction on the condition that their own profit motives would continue to be satisfied.

After the war the Wilson administration dropped most cooperative and regulatory measures, including farm price supports, guarantees of collective bargaining, and high taxes. This move away from regulation would stimulate a new era of business ascendancy in the 1920s (see Chapter 24).

THE PROGRESSIVE ERA IN PERSPECTIVE

In 1912 Thomas Edison had cautioned uneasily, "We've got to start to make this world over." But by 1920 not many Americans agreed. A quarter-century of reform, climaxing in the nation's participation in a brutal war, had wrought momentous changes. Government, the economy, and society as they had existed in the nineteenth century were gone forever. Public concern over poverty and injustice had been raised to new heights. But for every American who suffered some form of deprivation, three or four enjoyed material comforts unprecedented in human history. This majority simply could not sustain reform indefinitely. Though effects of the Progressive era lingered and in some cases expanded after the First World War, a mass consumer society had begun to refocus people's attention from reform to materialism.

The Progressive era was characterized by a welter of confusing and sometimes contradictory goals. Certainly there was no single progressive movement. On the national level, reform programs ranged from Roosevelt's New Nationalism, with its faith in big government as a coordinator of big business, to Wilson's New Freedom, with its promise to dissolve economic concentrations and legislate open competition. At the state and local levels, reformers pursued causes as varied as neighborhood improvement, government reorganization, public ownership of utilities, betterment of working conditions, and moral revival. Although local organizations and national associations coordinated their efforts on particular issues, reformers with different goals often worked at cross-purposes.

The failure of many progressive initiatives testifies to the strength of opposition to reform as well as ambiguities within the reform movements themselves. By asserting constitutional and liberty-of-contract maxims, the courts struck down some key progressive legislation, most notably the federal law prohibiting child labor. In states and cities, adoption of the initiative, referendum, and recall did not encourage greater participation in government; either those mechanisms were seldom used or they became the tools of special interests. On the federal level, new regulatory agencies rarely had the resources for thorough investigations; they had to obtain their information from the companies they were meant to police. Thus in many respects, progressives failed to redistribute power; in 1920, as in 1900, government remained under the influence of business and industry, a condition which many people considered quite satisfactory.

Yet in spite of all their weaknesses, the numerous reform movements that characterized the Progressive era did refashion the nation's future. Trustbusting, however faulty, had forced industrialists to become more sensitive to public opinion, and reforms initiated by insurgents in Congress had partially diluted the power of dictatorial politicians. Progressive legislation gave government important tools to protect consumers against price-fixing and dangerous products. The income tax was a first step toward building government revenues and redistributing wealth. Social reformers soothed some of the festering sores of urban life. But perhaps most important, progressives challenged old ways of thinking. They raised questions about the quality of American life which, though they remained unresolved, made the nation more aware of its principles and promises.

SUGGESTIONS FOR FURTHER READING

General

Richard Abrams, *The Burden of Progress* (1978); John W. Chambers, *The Tyranny of Change: America in the Progressive Era* (1980); Arthur Ekirch, *Progressivism in America* (1974); Louis Filler, *The Muckrakers*, rev. ed. (1980); Samuel P. Hays, *The Response to Industrialism* (1957); Richard Hofstadter, *The Age of Reform* (1955); William R. Hutchinson, *The Modernist Impulse in American Protestantism* (1976); Gabriel Kolko, *The Triumph of Conservatism* (1963); David W. Noble, *The Progressive Mind*, rev. ed. (1981); James Weinstein, *The Corporate Ideal in the Liberal State, 1900–1918* (1968); Robert Wiebe, *The Search for Order* (1968).

Regional Studies

Dewey Grantham, *Southern Progressivism: The Reconciliation of Progress and Tradition* (1983); Sheldon Hackney, *Populism to Progressivism in Alabama* (1969); Richard L. McCormick, *From Realignment to Reform: Political Change in New York State, 1893–1910* (1981); George E. Mowry, *The California Progressives* (1951); David P. Thelen, *Robert La Follette and the Insurgent Spirit* (1976); David P. Thelen, *The New Citizenship: Origins of Progressivism in Wisconsin* (1972); C. Vann Woodward, *Origins of the New South* (1951).

Legislative Issues and Reform Groups

Norman H. Clark, *Deliver Us from Evil: An Interpretation of American Prohibition* (1976); Allen F. Davis, *Spearheads for Reform: The Social Settlements and the Progressive Movement, 1890–1914* (1967); Ruth Rosen, *The Lost Sisterhood: Prostitution in America, 1900–1918* (1982); James H. Timberlake,

Prohibition and the Progressive Crusade (1963); Walter I. Trattner, *Crusade for the Children* (1970); Irwin Yellowitz, *Labor and the Progressive Movement in New York State* (1965). (For works on socialism, see listings at end of Chapter 20.)

Education, Law, and the Social Sciences

Jerold S. Auerbach, *Unequal Justice: Lawyers and Social Change in Modern America* (1976); Loren P. Beth, *The Development of the American Constitution, 1877–1917* (1971); Lawrence Cremin, *The Transformation of the School: Progressivism in American Education* (1961); Martin S. Dworkin, ed., *Dewey on Education* (1959); Thomas L. Haskell, *The Emergence of Professional Social Science* (1977); David W. Marcell, *Progress and Pragmatism: James, Dewey, Beard, and the American Idea of Progress* (1974); Philippa Strum, *Louis D. Brandeis, Justice for the People* (1984); David Tyack and Elizabeth Hansot, *Managers of Virtue: Public School Leadership in America, 1820–1980* (1982); Lawrence Veysey, *The Emergence of the American University* (1970).

Women

Lois Banner, *Women in Modern America: A Brief History*, 2nd ed. (1984); Ruth Borden, *Women and Temperance* (1980); Carl N. Degler, *At Odds: Women and the Family in America* (1980); Eleanor Flexner, *Century of Struggle: The Women's Rights Movement in the United States* (1959); Linda Gordon, *Woman's Body, Woman's Right: A Social History of Birth Control in America* (1976); David Kennedy, *Birth Control in America: The Career of Margaret Sanger* (1970); Alice Kessler-Harris, *Out to Work: A History of Wage-Earning Women in the United States* (1982); Aileen Kraditor, *The Ideas of the Women's Suffrage Movement* (1965); Ellen Condliffe Lagemann, *A Generation of Women: Education in the Lives of Progressive Reformers* (1979); William L.

O'Neill, *Everyone Was Brave: The Rise and Fall of Feminism in America* (1969); William L. O'Neill, *Divorce in the Progressive Era* (1967); Ross Evans Paulson, *Woman's Suffrage and Prohibition* (1973); Rosalind Rosenberg, *Beyond Separate Spheres: Intellectual Roots of Modern Feminism* (1982); Elyce J. Rotella, *From Home to Office: U.S. Women and Work, 1870–1930* (1981); Sheila M. Rothman, *Woman's Proper Place* (1978).

Blacks

John Dittmer, *Black Georgia in the Progressive Era, 1900–1920* (1977); George Frederickson, *The Black Image in the White Mind* (1971); Louis R. Harlan, *Booker T. Washington: The Wizard of Tuskegee, 1901–1915* (1983); Louis R. Harlan, *Booker T. Washington: The Making of a Black Leader, 1856–1901* (1972); Charles F. Kellogg, *NAACP* (1970); James M. McPherson, *The Abolitionist Legacy: From Reconstruction to the NAACP* (1975); August Meier, *Negro Thought in America, 1880–1915* (1963); Elliot M. Rudwick, *W. E. B. Du Bois* (1969); Donald Spivey, *Schooling for the New Slavery: Black Industrial Education* (1978).

Roosevelt, Taft, and Wilson

John M. Blum, *Woodrow Wilson and the Politics of Morality* (1956); John M. Blum, *The Republican Roosevelt*, 2nd ed. (1954); Paolo E. Coletta, *The Presidency of William Howard Taft* (1973); John Milton Cooper, Jr., *The Warrior and the Priest: Woodrow Wilson and Theodore Roosevelt* (1983); William Harbaugh, *The Life and Times of Theodore Roosevelt* (1961); Arthur S. Link, *Wilson*, 5 vols (1947–1965); Arthur S. Link, *Woodrow Wilson and the Progressive Era* (1954); Edmund Morris, *The Rise of Theodore Roosevelt* (1979); George E. Mowry, *The Era of Theodore Roosevelt* (1958); James Penick, Jr., *Progressive Politics and Conservation: The Ballinger-Pinchot Affair* (1968).

THE QUEST FOR EMPIRE
1865–1914

CHAPTER 22

illiam H. Seward's travels through scenic Alaska in August 1869 revived his enthusiasm for the huge territory he had, as secretary of state, bought from Russia two years earlier. In the colony's abundant marine treasures—whales, sea otters, seals, salmon—Seward foresaw new opportunities for fishing and the fur trade. He remarked effusively on Alaska's thick forests and rich deposits of iron ore, coal, copper, and gold, unaware of the vast petroleum supplies that would be so eagerly tapped in the twentieth century. He told white settlers in Sitka that they were true pioneers in an Indian-populated land. And reinforcements were on the way, he reassured them, for Alaska was destined to become a prosperous "shipyard for the supply of all nations."

Seward's oratory was exaggerated, but it reflected the optimism so characteristic of nineteenth-century Americans, to whom expansion seemed natural, if not preordained. Under the banner of "manifest destiny," they had purchased Louisiana, annexed Florida, Oregon, and Texas, seized California and other western areas from Mexico, and acquired the Gadsden Purchase; and through the export of their products abroad they had developed a foreign trade important to the nation's economic health. "Their destiny is always to expand," remarked the Russian diplomat who negotiated the sale of Alaska—which, he regretted, had not "escaped the lust of Americans."

But the American "lust" for more space, more land, more markets, and more resources was tempered in the late nineteenth century. Although most Americans applauded expansionism, some were uneasy with *imperialism:* the imposition of control over other peoples, denying them the freedom to make their own decisions, undermining their sovereignty. Imperialism could take a variety of forms, both formal (annexation, colonialism, or military occupation) and informal (the threat of intervention or economic manipulation). Many Americans seemed hesitant to become full-fledged participants in the scramble among the great powers for colonies in Asia and Africa. Anti-imperialist critics feared that an overseas American empire would undermine institutions at home, invite perpetual war, and violate honored principles.

The road to trade and empire was strewn with other obstacles. The federal government did not always adequately fund the vehicles of expansion, neglecting the navy until the 1880s and maintaining a foreign service weakened by the political spoils system. Leaders also played politics with foreign policy, complicating the diplomatic process. And most business leaders actually ignored foreign commerce in favor of the bustling domestic marketplace. Still, a pattern of accelerating activity abroad culminated in the tumultuous decade of the 1890s, when the doubters' voices were drowned out by shouts for war and foreign territory, and when American power was sufficient to deliver both.

This chapter is the story of the roots and sources of American expansionism, the tremendous growth of American activity abroad in the late nineteenth century, the building of an overseas empire, and the momentous 1890s debate between imperialists and anti-imperialists over the fundamental course of American foreign policy. After 1900 it is the story of the opportunities opened and the troubles encountered in managing, protecting, and expanding an empire that stretched from Latin America to Asia and that faced threats from restless nationalists, commercial competitors, and other expansive great nations.

EXPANSIONISM REVIVED

The Civil War had temporarily interrupted the country's expansionist course. Once freed from that conflict, however, Americans North and South scouted new frontiers to conquer. Seward eyed Cuba, President Ulysses Grant coveted Santo Domingo, and others envisioned new outposts in the Pacific Ocean. Religious leaders contemplated the conversion of "natives" and "savages" to Christianity. Businesspeople and farmers talked of untapped overseas markets. Nationalists spoke of exporting America's superior political principles and practices to other peoples.

And to ensure the success of these dreams, to protect all these activities, American leaders planned for an enlarged modern navy of the first order. The humorist Finley Peter Dunne captured the American mood near the end of the nineteenth century by putting words in the mouths of his fictional Irish-American characters: " 'We're a gr-reat people,' said Mr. Hennessy, earnestly. 'We ar-re,' said Mr. Dooley. 'We ar-re that. An' th best iv it is, we know we are.' "

After the searing Civil War, American leaders tried to heal sectional wounds with soothing patriotic oratory. The 1876 centennial celebration emphasized

American Nationalism national unity; Confederate and Union soldiers met to exchange captured flags; patriotic societies like the Daughters of the American Revolution (1890) were organized. Civic pride welled up when American machines earned top marks at world fairs. Notions of American exceptionalism and manifest destiny were revived. To the Reverend Josiah Strong, author of the influential book *Our Country* (1885), Americans were a special, God-favored Anglo-Saxon race destined to lead others. "As America goes, so goes the world," he claimed. To Social Darwinists, Americans were a superior people who would surely overcome all competition and thrive. "The rule of the survival of the fittest applies to nations as well as to the animal kingdom," claimed American diplomat John Barrett.

The argument for expansion and empire seemed all the more urgent when Americans anticipated the closing of the frontier at home. In 1893 Professor Frederick Jackson Turner postulated his frontier thesis. Turner argued that an ever-expanding continental frontier had shaped the American character. That "frontier has gone, and with its going has closed the first period of American history." Turner did not explicitly say that a new frontier had to be found overseas. But some thought that was what he meant when he wrote in his famous article "The Significance of the Frontier in American History," that he doubted that "the expansive character of American life has now entirely ceased. Movement has been its dominant fact, and, unless this training has no effect upon a people, the American energy will continually demand a wider field for its exercise."

Foreign policy has always sprung from the domestic setting of a nation—its needs, wants, moods, and

William H. Seward (1801–1872) had a vision of empire matched by few Americans. This ambitious secretary of state added Alaska and Midway Island to the United States domain, but anti-imperialists and political foes thwarted his plans for other territorial acquisitions. Library of Congress.

ideals. The people who guided America's expansionist foreign relations were the same

Domestic Roots of Foreign Policy people who kindled the spirit of national growth at home, who championed the transcontinental railroad, forcefully removed Native Americans from the avenues of white settlement, extolled the wonders of the machine age, and built America's cities and giant corporations. Most Americans, caught up as they were in making a living or exploiting economic opportunities at home, paid scant attention to external issues or to the intense international rivalry of the post–Civil War era. They usually became alive to foreign policy questions only when war threatened. But America's leaders—in politics, business, labor, agriculture, religion, journalism, education, and the military—were alert to the nation's place in world affairs. They believed that the United States could prosper far better in a world in which American influence was exerted. They were aware of the interconnections between domestic developments and foreign events.

The expansionism so evident at home after the Civil War was deeply intertwined with foreign policy. The national network of railroads, for example, made it possible for Iowa farmers to transport their crops to seaboard cities and then on to foreign markets. Their livelihood was thus tied to international market conditions, to the outcomes of foreign wars, and to the time-honored American principle of freedom of the seas, which stood as a reminder to other nations that American goods on American ships should be free to cross the oceans, even in time of foreign war. American cities that burgeoned in the late nineteenth century became centers of foreign commerce and cosmopolitan culture. The products of companies like International Harvester were shipped to distant markets, and new technology was applied to the improved navy required to protect this lucrative commerce. Periodic depressions fostered the belief that the country's surplus production must be sold in foreign markets to restore and sustain economic well-being at home. By promoting economic health, these markets would also contribute to domestic social and political stability. Senator and two-time Secretary of State James G. Blaine put it this way: "With these markets secured new life would be given to our manufactories, the product of the Western farmer would be in demand, the reasons for and inducements to strikers with all their attendant evils would cease."

The tariff too was an issue in both domestic politics and world affairs. Tariff increases (see pages 566, 570, 584) designed to protect American industry and agriculture from foreign competition adversely affected those who sold to America, prompting them to enact retaliatory tariffs on American products. In Cuba and Hawaii, American tariff revisions actually induced economic crises, which fed revolutions that ultimately served American interests. The massive influx of immigrants caused diplomatic problems as well as social upheaval at home. Moreover, notions of racial superiority and Jim Crow practices at home influenced American policies toward Asian and Latin American peoples of color, who were considered inferior. And ambitious politicians were tempted to enhance their political reputations by flexing the national muscle in the world arena. In general, then, the major domestic questions that preoccupied Americans from the Civil War to the First World War were closely linked to the nation's diplomacy. The threads of domestic and foreign policy were densely interwoven.

The spokesmen for expansion and empire belonged to what scholars have labeled the foreign policy elite or opinion leaders. Better read and better traveled than most Americans, more cosmopolitan than provincial in outlook, and politically active, they influenced the making of foreign policy. Unlike domestic policy, foreign policy is seldom shaped by the people. Most Americans simply do not follow international relations or express themselves on its issues. Indeed, studies have demonstrated that no more than 10 to 20 percent of the voting public was alert to world affairs in the late nineteenth century. It was this small group, whom Secretary of State Walter Q. Gresham called "the thoughtful men of the country," whose opinion counted. Increasingly in the late nineteenth century, and especially in the 1890s, they urged an imperialist course. Those members of the political elite who, like President Grover Cleveland, favored economic expansion and United States hegemony (that is, dominance) in South America, but not the annexation of more territory, gradually lost ground to these proempire leaders.

The imperialists in Washington, D.C., were clannish. They met informally to talk about building a bigger navy, about an isthmian canal, and about the need to sell surpluses abroad. They gathered at Henry Adams's house on H Street or at the nearby home of John Hay, who became secretary of state in 1898; they dined together at the Metropolitan Club. Theodore Roosevelt, appointed assistant secretary of the navy in 1897, was among them; so was Brooks Adams, Henry's gloomy brother, a publicist for an American presence in China. Henry Cabot Lodge, who became a member of the Senate Foreign Relations Committee in 1895, often stopped by, and corporate lawyer Elihu Root, who would later serve in the cabinet, joined in as well. These luminaries kept up the drumbeat for empire, and after their elevation to high office in the 1890s they acquired by force much of the empire that earlier Americans had felt would gravitate peacefully to the United States.

With a characteristic mixture of self-interest and

idealism, United States leaders believed that imperialism benefited both Americans and those who came under American control. When they intervened in other lands or lectured weaker states, Americans defended their behavior on the grounds that they were extending the blessings of liberty and prosperity to less fortunate people. For those many imperialists who were also progressive reformers, interventions were necessary to improve foreign societies. To critics at home and abroad, however, American paternalism appeared hypocritical. They charged that the use of coercion to compel resistant foreigners to behave and think like Americans violated cherished American principles. For example, in order to impose on resentful Filipinos an American-style political system theoretically based on democratic tenets, American officials censored the press, jailed some dissidents and killed others, and designated candidates for public office. The persistent American belief that other people cannot solve their own problems and that only the American model of government will work produced what historian William Appleman Williams has called "the tragedy of American diplomacy."

FACTORY, FARM, AND
FOREIGN AFFAIRS

Many business people and farmers were part of the foreign-policy public that savored expansion. There were, of course, profits to be made from foreign sales. "It is my dream," cried the governor of Georgia in 1878, to see "in every valley . . . a cotton factory to convert the raw material of the neighborhood into fabrics which shall warm the limbs of Japanese and Chinese." Fear generated foreign trade as well, for the nation's farms and factories produced more than Americans could consume. Foreign commerce, it was believed, could be a safety valve to avert or relieve economic depression, such as that of the 1890s. Surpluses could be exported.

The tremendous economic growth of the United States after the Civil War stimulated foreign trade, a larger navy to protect this lucrative commerce, a

Growth of Foreign Trade more efficient foreign service, a call for more colonies, and a more activist foreign policy. From the 1860s to 1914, in fact, foreign trade grew faster than the national income. In 1870 United States exports totaled $451 million; in 1900, $1.5 billion. By 1914, at the outbreak of the First World War, American exports had reached $2.5 billion, and European businesspeople complained of the "American export invasion." Beginning in the 1870s the United States began to enjoy a long-term favorable balance of trade (exporting more than it imported). Most of America's products went to Britain, Europe, and Canada, but increasing amounts flowed to new markets in Latin America and Asia. Although exports of manufactured items increased, agricultural goods accounted for about three-quarters of the total in 1870 and about two-thirds in 1900. Manufactured goods led export sales for the first time in 1913, when the United States ranked third behind only Britain and Germany in the export of manufactures.

Breadstuffs, cotton, meat, and dairy products topped the export list in 1900, providing farmers with needed foreign outlets. Over half the annual cotton crop was exported each year. Wisconsin cheesemakers shipped to Britain; the Swift and Armour meat companies exported refrigerated beef to Europe; and wheat farmers became Europe's largest supplier of wheat. James J. Hill of the Great Northern railroad worked hard to sell American grain in Asia. He distributed wheat cookbooks, translated into several Asian languages.

America's ambitious entrepreneurs and large businesses looked to foreign markets, especially in the 1890s, when it became clear that the output of industrial products was outdistancing consumption. Rockefeller's Standard Oil sold abroad, notably in Germany, England, Cuba, and Mexico. In the 1870s and 1880s about two-thirds of all American petroleum was exported, and in succeeding decades the figure was about one-half. Fifteen percent of America's iron and steel, 50 percent of its copper, and 16 percent of its agricultural implements were sold abroad by the turn of the century, making many workers in those industries dependent on exports.

So too with machinery. Thomas Edison and Alexander Graham Bell installed England's telephone network. George Westinghouse marketed his air brakes in Europe; Singer exported about 40 percent of its

Singer sewing machines were exported throughout the globe in the late nineteenth century. Here the King of Ou (the Caroline Islands, in the Pacific) operates the Great Civilizer. The caption for this company-sponsored photograph read: "The Herald of Civilization—Missionary Work of the Singer Manufacturing Company." But the profitable Singer business was interested in more than improving peoples' standard of living; three-quarters of the sewing machines sold in the world in 1890 were Singers. Courtesy, Robert B. Davies, Peacefully Working to Conquer the World.

sewing machines; and Cyrus McCormick's "reaper kings" harvested the wheat of Russian fields. Photography baron George Eastman, whose business operated around the globe, remarked that the growth of foreign sales allowed Americans to "distribute our eggs and pad the basket at the same time." At the 1878 World's Fair in Paris, American exhibitors won more awards than any other country. At the Paris fair in 1889 American agricultural machinery was acclaimed, and at Chicago's Columbian Exposition in 1893 American inventive genius—especially in the application of electricity to machines—dazzled foreign visitors. And direct American investments abroad reached $3.5 billion by 1914, placing the United States among the top four investor countries.

American economic expansion in Latin America was especially impressive and aroused the nation's diplomatic interest in its neighbors to the South.

Economic Expansion in Latin America
United States exports to Latin America, which exceeded $50 million in the 1870s, climbed to over $120 million in 1900 and topped $300 million in 1914. Investments by United States citizens in Latin America amounted to a towering $1.26 billion in 1914. In 1899 two of the largest banana importers merged to form the United Fruit Company. Owning much of the land (over 1 million acres in 1913) and the railroad and steamship lines of Central America, United Fruit became a major economic and political force in the region. It developed transportation, cultivated land, and fought to eradicate yellow fever and malaria. As for Mexico, American capitalists came to own its railroads and mines. By 1910, Americans controlled 43 percent of Mexican property and produced more than half that nation's oil.

Economic expansion abroad became a mechanism for exerting political influence. Dunne's Mr. Dooley put it simply: "I tell ye, th' hand that rocks th' scales in th' grocery store is th' hand that rules th' wurruld." Indeed, by the early twentieth century American economic interests were influencing policies on taxes and natural resources in countries like Cuba and Mexico. American interests were responsible for drawing Hawaii into the American imperial net and for spreading American cultural values abroad. Religious missionaries and Singer executives, for example, joined hands in promoting the "civilizing medium" of the sewing machine. "The world is to be Christianized and civilized," declared Josiah Strong. "And what is the process of civilizing but the creating of more and higher wants. Commerce follows the missionary."

American leaders believed selling, buying, and investing in foreign marketplaces were important to the United States. Why? Because of profits, because the problems of overproduction and unemployment would be relieved at home, because a vigorous foreign trade was a symbol of national power, because economic ties permitted political influence to be exerted abroad, and because economic expansion helped spread the American way of life, creating a world more hospitable to Americans. Most nations engaged in foreign trade and investment, and they signed treaties to govern their exchanges. Most Americans championed economic expansion. But some critics, called anti-imperialists, drew the line between expansionism and imperialism: the first should not lead to the second; mutually beneficial commercial intercourse should not yield to the domination of one nation over another. Profitable and fair trade relationships, yes; exploitation, no. And, others advised, American business activity abroad should not draw the United States into unwanted diplomatic crises and wars. Few Americans sought to stop trade; rather, they wanted to make sure it did not create damaging political problems.

LOOKING OUTWARD, 1860s–1880s

The American empire was built gradually, sometimes haltingly, in the years following the Civil War. One of its chief architects was William H.

William H. Seward

Seward. As senator from New York (1849–1861) and secretary of state (1861–1869), he argued articulately for extension of the American frontier. "There is not in the history of the Roman Empire an ambition for aggrandizement so marked as that which characterized the American people," he once said. Seward envisioned a large, coordinated American empire encompassing Canada, the Caribbean, Cuba, Central America, Mexico, Hawaii, Iceland, Greenland, and certain Pacific islands. This empire would be built not by war but by a natural process of gravitation toward the attractive republican United States. Commerce would hurry the process, he thought, noting that the merchants of Venice and Britain had become "masters of the world."

To ensure the unity of his American empire, Seward appealed for a canal across Central America, a transcontinental American railroad to link up with the markets of Asia, and a telegraph system to speed communications. To Seward economic expansion at home was essential to expansion abroad, and vice versa. Thus he favored an influx of immigrants to provide the labor needed for economic development, and he backed tariffs to protect youthful American factories from foreign competition.

Most of Seward's grandiose plans did not reach fruition during his own tenure as secretary of state. In 1867, for example, he signed a treaty with Denmark to buy the Danish West Indies (the Virgin Islands). Shortly afterward a hurricane and tidal wave wrecked St. Thomas, diminishing its value in the eyes of many senators. (The senators were also reluctant to hand Seward a diplomatic triumph while he was supporting Andrew Johnson during the president's impeachment proceedings.) The treaty was shelved, and the Virgin Islanders, who had voted for annexation, had to wait until 1917 to join the American empire.

Seward desired British-dominated Canada, too, and Canadians feared a United States takeover. Their alarm was intensified by the activities of the Fenian Brotherhood, an Irish-American society organized to agitate for Ireland's independence from Britain. It began raiding Canada from Vermont in 1866. Seward preferred diplomacy over such violence as a means of achieving annexation. When some Canadians petitioned London for a new confederation, and Britain agreed in 1867 to the creation of the Dominion of Canada, hopes of attaching Canada to the United States faded.

Most of Seward's plans for acquiring territory were blocked by a combination of anti-imperialists and political foes. Anti-imperialists like Senator Carl Schurz and E. L. Godkin, editor of the magazine *The Nation,* believed that the country had enough unsettled land, and that creation of a showcase of democracy and prosperity at home was the best way to persuade other peoples to adopt American institutions and principles. Some anti-imperialists, sharing the racism of the times, did not want to annex territory populated by "inferior" dark-skinned people, such as Santo Domingo or slavery-plagued Cuba. And Seward's political antagonists hoped to punish him by denying him his dreams.

Seward did enjoy some successes. When an American naval officer seized the Midway Islands in 1867, Seward laid claim to them for the United States. The same year he paid Russia $7.2 million for the 591,000 square miles of Alaska (see page 445). His

VOL. 15 NO. 382   FEBRUARY 9 1889.   PRICE 10 CENTS.

Judge

ENTERED AT THE POST OFFICE AT NEW YORK AS SECOND-CLASS MATTER.   COPYRIGHT 1889 BY THE JUDGE PUBLISHING CO.

A FRIENDLY ADMONITION.

JOHN BULL—"Don't poke him up, Bizzy—He's a very patient bird, but is almighty nasty when he's roused—I speak from experience!"

The imperial competition for Samoa pitted Britain, Germany, and the United States against one another. In this 1889 Judge magazine cover, the British "John Bull" admonishes German Chancellor Otto von Bismarck to avoid provoking the sometimes menacing American eagle. At the Berlin Conference of that year the great powers defused the crisis by dividing Samoa among themselves.   Library of Congress.

critics ridiculed the purchase, but the Senate voted overwhelmingly for the treaty. Seward also shepherded the Burlingame Treaty with China (1868) through the Senate. The treaty provided for free immigration between the two countries and pledged Sino-American friendship. (A new treaty in 1880 permitted Congress to suspend Chinese immigration to the United States, which it did two years later to satisfy anti-Oriental bias in the Far West.) The secretary's forceful handling of French interference in Mexico also furthered his reputation. In 1861, Napoleon III had placed Archduke Ferdinand Maximilian of Austria on the throne in Mexico. Preoccupied with the Civil War, Seward could do little to help the Mexicans dislodge the intruding Europeans. But in 1866, citing the Monroe Doctrine, he told the French to get out as American troops headed for the Mexican border. Napoleon, troubled at home and now opposed by both Mexicans and Americans, abandoned his venture.

Seward's dream of a world knit together into a giant communications system was satisfied. In 1866, through the persevering efforts of Cyrus Field, an underwater transatlantic cable linked European and American telegraph networks. And, backed by J. P. Morgan's capital, James A. Scrymser strung telegraph lines to Latin America, reaching Chile in 1890. Information about markets, diplomatic crises, and war flowed steadily and quickly. Whereas delivery of surface mail from Washington, D.C., to European capitals often took from ten to twenty-one days, the transatlantic cable enabled the State Department to make same-day contact. In a serious squabble with Spain in 1873 over the Cuban-owned gun-running ship *Virginius*—the Spanish executed some Americans on board—officials made good use of the telegraph system to manage the crisis. In general, drawn closer to one another by improvements in communications and transportation, nations found that far-away events became more important to their prosperity and security. Technology shrank the globe.

Impact of the Telegraph

Seward's successor, Hamilton Fish (1869–1877), inherited the knotty and emotional problem of the *Alabama* claims. The *Alabama* and other vessels built by Great Britain for the Confederacy during the Civil War had marauded Union shipping. Senator Charles Sumner demanded that Britain pay $2 billion in damages or give up Canada, but Fish patiently took the question to the bargaining table.

Anglo-American Relations

In 1871 Britain and America signed the Washington Treaty, whereby the British apologized and agreed to the creation of a tribunal, which later awarded the United States $15.5 million. Disputes over fishing rights along the North Atlantic coast and the hunting of seals in the Bering Sea near Alaska also dogged Anglo-American relations and would continue to do so for decades. Yet the two powers, however competitive, were slowly coming to the conclusion that rapprochement rather than confrontation best served their interests. American politicians still tried to "twist the lion's tail" to score political points at home, but the trend toward Anglo-American accommodation could not be reversed.

Fish also had to deal with President Grant's designs on the Dominican Republic. The president was impressed by the island's raw materials and its potential as a market for American textiles, and the navy eyed the harbor at Samaná Bay. Grant's personal secretary, Orville Babcock, negotiated a treaty of annexation. But Senator Sumner smelled a rat in Babcock, who through private intrigue stood to gain financially from the venture. Furthermore, the Dominican Republic was embroiled in civil war and was nearly at war with its neighbor Haiti. Political rivalry also colored the question. "No wild bull ever dashed more violently at a red rag than he does at anything that he thinks the President is interested in," Fish said of Sumner's political motives. The treaty was defeated in 1870.

Another venture in the Pacific succeeded. In 1878 the United States gained rights to a naval station at the strategic port of Pago Pago in Samoa, several islands four thousand miles from San Francisco on the trade route between Australia and America. The Germans and British also coveted the islands. Year by year tensions grew. To avoid war, Germany, Britain, and the United States met in Berlin in 1889 and, without consulting the Samoans, carved Samoa into three parts. A decade later the United States annexed part of the islands, including Pago Pago.

In Latin America United States interests became extensive. Trade with the region was flourishing, investments were growing, and the navy's presence was conspicuous. The convening of the first Pan-American Conference in Washington, D.C., in 1889

Pan-American Conference

bore witness to growing ties. Sponsored by Secretary of State James G. Blaine, the conference was designed to improve commercial relations. The Latin American conferees toured United States factories and then negotiated several general agreements to promote trade. To improve inter-American cooperation, they founded the Pan American Union, which in 1907 moved into handsome new quarters in Washington, D.C., financed by Andrew Carnegie.

As the United States acquired new territories and markets and extended its influence abroad, the call went out for an improved and enlarged navy. Captain Alfred T. Mahan, who had served on blockade duty during the Civil War and had written a naval history of the conflict, became a major popularizer for the "New Navy." Since foreign trade was vital to the nation's well-being, he argued, the nation required an efficient navy to protect its shipping, and in turn a navy required colonies for bases. "Whether they will or no," Mahan wrote, "Americans must now begin to look outward. The growing production of the country demands it." Mahan became president of the Naval War College in Newport, Rhode Island, founded in 1884, and there gave a series of lectures that was published as *The Influence of Sea Power upon History* (1890). This widely read book sat on every good expansionist's shelf. Theodore Roosevelt and Henry Cabot Lodge consulted Mahan, sharing his belief in the links between trade, navy, and colonies.

Until its modernization the American navy was in a sorry state. Many of its wooden ships were rotting. Its shipyards were havens of political patronage; congressional appropriations were

New Navy

frequently wasted. But in 1883 Congress authorized construction of the first steel warships. American factories went to work to produce steel for hulls, boilers for steam engines, armor plate, high-velocity shells, powerful guns, and precision instruments. Andrew Carnegie, displaying none of the pacifism that would later distinguish him as a champion of world peace, exclaimed "there may be millions for us in armor," and signed a highly profitable naval contract. Businesspeople seeking men-of-war escorts for their commercial vessels and scouts for new trade opportunities cheered the birth of the New Navy.

Gradually, but especially in the 1880s, the navy shifted from sail to steam and from wood to steel. New Navy ships like the *Maine,* the *Oregon,* the *Boston,* and the *Columbia* thrust the United States into naval prominence. The *Columbia* held the naval record for average sea speed, and the other three figured in the imperialist ventures of the 1890s. Incidentally, many of these steel vessels were named for states and cities in a deliberate campaign to kindle patriotism and local support for naval expansion. The enlarged navy provided the United States with the tools to expand and build a greater empire.

CRISES IN THE 1890s: HAWAII, VENEZUELA, AND CUBA

When the United States became engaged in a number of crises in the 1890s, the New Navy warships were put to the test. For decades the Hawaiian Islands had commanded American attention. This major Pacific way station was significant for trade with Asia and had long been a site of missionary work. Its undeveloped but strategic port of Pearl Harbor tempted naval expansionists, and the vast sugar plantations of the islands attracted American entrepreneurs. In 1875 the United States signed a treaty granting Hawaiian sugar duty-free entry to the American market; the Hawaiian sugar industry boomed and became dependent on mainland business. Six years later Secretary Blaine warned other nations away from the islands, declaring them "essentially a part of the American system." In 1887 the United States gained naval rights to Pearl Harbor. When the Congress revised the tariff laws in the early 1890s, however, it eliminated the special protection for Hawaiian sugar and gave American producers a bounty of two cents a pound. Exports of Hawaiian sugar to the United States declined quickly, and American planters in Hawaii were severely hurt. To gain exemption from American tariffs, a group of planters called the Annexation Club plotted a revolution.

In January 1893 the white minority overthrew the native monarch, Queen Liliuokalani. Their success stemmed in part from the support of the chief Amer-

Annexation of Hawaii ican diplomat in Honolulu, John L. Stevens, who saw to it that sailors from the warship *Boston* encircled the royal palace. Stevens informed Washington that the "Hawaiian pear is now fully ripe, and this is the golden hour for the United States to pluck it." Against the protests of Japan, whose nationals accounted for about 40 percent of Hawaii's population (Americans equaled only 5 percent), President Benjamin Harrison sent a treaty of annexation to the Senate. But incoming President Grover Cleveland, an expansionist who disapproved of forced annexation, withdrew it. Five years later, on July 7, 1898, during the Spanish-American-Cuban-Filipino War, President William McKinley successfully maneuvered annexation through Congress. The president, fearing that the Senate lacked the two-thirds majority necessary to pass a treaty, chose the method of a joint resolution, which required only a simple majority. Thus was Hawaii added to the American empire.

The Venezuelan crisis of 1895 also gave the United States an opportunity to express its expansive mood. For decades Venezuela and Great Britain had squabbled

Venezuelan Crisis over the border between Venezuela and British Guiana. The disputed territory contained rich gold deposits and the mouth of the Orinoco River, the commercial gateway to northern South America. Venezuela asked for American help, charging that the imperialist British were violating the Monroe Doctrine. President Cleveland decided that the "mean and hoggish" British had to be warned away. In July 1895, Secretary of State Richard Olney sent the British a brash 12,000-word message that Cleveland compared to a twenty-inch gun—in the naval parlance of the time, a huge weapon. Olney lectured the British that the Monroe Doctrine prohibited European intervention in the Western Hemisphere, whose states "are friends and allies, commercially and politically, of the United States." The spread-eagle words that followed were clearly directed at an international audience: "To-day the United States is practically sovereign on this continent, and its fiat is law upon the subjects to which it confines its interposition."

This statement of United States hegemony did not impress the British, who rejected American interference in what they considered a local issue. American jingoistic nationalists clamored for action. "Let the

"The Real British Lion," according to this 1895 American cartoon, was actually an ugly hog astride the globe. The Venezuelan crisis stimulated this Anglophobic view. *New York Evening World*, 1895.

fight come if it must; I don't care whether our sea coast cities are bombarded or not; we would take Canada," snorted Theodore Roosevelt. But neither London nor Washington wanted war. The British, seeking international friends to counter an intensifying German competition, quietly retreated from the crisis. In 1896 an Anglo-American arbitration board divided the disputed territory. Throughout the deliberations Venezuela was barely consulted. Thus the United States displayed a trait common to imperialists: a disregard for the rights and sensibilities of small nations. This trait characterized American foreign policy thereafter, as did the assertive rhetoric of 1895.

In 1895 another crisis rocked Latin America: the Cuban revolution against Spain. From 1868 to 1878 the Cubans had battled their mother country to no avail. Slavery was abolished but in-

Cuban Revolution dependence denied, and Spanish rule continued to be repressive. The Cuban rebels waited for another chance. José Martí, one of the heroes of Cuban history, collected money, arms, and men in the United States. As in the case of Hawaii, a change in American tariff policy hastened the revolution. The Wilson-Gorman Tariff (1894) imposed a duty on Cuban sugar, which had been entering the United States duty-free under the McKinley Tariff (1890) and a reciprocity agreement with Spain. The Cuban economy, highly dependent on exports, was thrown into turmoil.

From American soil, Martí launched a revolution that became gruesome in its human and material costs. Rebels burned cane fields and razed mills, using guerrilla tactics to avoid head-on clashes with Spanish soldiers. Under the command of Valereano Weyler, soon dubbed the Butcher, Spanish officials instituted a policy of "reconcentration": hundreds of thousands of Cubans were herded into fortified towns and camps to separate them from the insur-

Spanish Reconcentration Policy
gents. Camp conditions were ghastly; hunger, starvation, and killer diseases took a heavy toll. As much as one-quarter of the total Cuban population perished in these reconcentration centers. Weyler's forces ransacked the countryside, Cuba's economy deteriorated badly, and American investments of $50 million were jeopardized. Cuban-American trade in tobacco and sugar further declined. American imports from Cuba, which had amounted to $76 million in 1894, slumped to $15 million in 1898; American exports to the island dropped by half in the same period.

As tragic stories of atrocity and destruction reached the United States—and were played up by the American yellow press (see pages 553–554)—people grew angry with the Spanish and sympathetic toward the insurrectionists. In late 1897 a new government came to power in Madrid. The Spanish modified reconcentration and promised that Cuba would be given some autonomy. Americans waited to see if the new reforms would subdue the rebellious island and restore peace.

When President McKinley came to office he was already an expansionist. He agreed that a large navy was imperative; he recognized that surplus production had to be exported; and he echoed the belief that American supremacy was essential in the Western Hemisphere. The 1896 Republican platform on which McKinley ran demanded both an enlarged American empire and Cuban independence. In his annual message of December 1897, McKinley surveyed the Cuban crisis, ruling out American intervention while Spain

was walking the path of reform. McKinley was by no means the weak leader his critics said he was (Roosevelt once remarked that McKinley did not have the backbone of a chocolate eclair). "He was a man of great power," said Elihu Root, who *"always had his way."* The president, not Congress or public opinion, made the decisions that led to war. But McKinley wanted to avoid war if at all possible.

Events in the first few months of 1898 sabotaged the Spanish reforms and exhausted American patience. Early in January, antireform pro-Spanish loyalists and army personnel rioted in Havana. The Spanish government, it seemed to Americans, could not even maintain discipline within its own ranks. After the riots, Washington officials ordered

Sinking of the *Maine*
the battleship *Maine* to Havana harbor to demonstrate United States concern over the violence and to protect American citizens if need be. On February 15 an explosion ripped the *Maine*, killing 260 American officers and crew. Americans were quick to blame Spain for the disaster.

Spain's image in the United States had been undermined a week earlier when William Randolph Hearst's inflammatory *New York Journal* published a stolen private letter from Enrique Dupuy de Lôme, the Spanish minister in Washington. In the letter de Lôme scorned McKinley as "weak and a bidder for the admiration of the crowd" and revealed Spanish determination to fight on in Cuba. In March the irritated president asked for $50 million in defense funds, and Congress complied unanimously. The naval board created to investigate the sinking of the *Maine* then reported that a mine had caused the explosion. (A report by Admiral Hyman G. Rickover in 1976 refuted that conclusion, blaming the explosion on an internal accident.) The panel did not assign responsibility, but restless Americans blamed Spain— if not for the catastrophe, then at least for creating an atmosphere that permitted it to happen.

McKinley's diplomatic options were greatly reduced by the impact of these events. He decided to send Spain an ultimatum. In late March the United States insisted that Spain accept an armistice, end reconcentration altogether, and designate McKinley as arbiter. The basic American goal was Cuban independence, but the president and his diplomats never

Chapter 22: THE QUEST FOR EMPIRE, 1865–1914

so informed Spain. Yet no Spanish government could have given up Cuba and remained in office.

The Spanish did make concessions. They abolished reconcentration and accepted an armistice on the condition that the insurgents agree first. McKinley had wanted more; he began to write a message to Congress. After completing his speech, however, he received the news that Spain had gone one step further and declared a unilateral armistice. The weary McKinley—who was taking medication in order to sleep—hesitated but chose to go to Congress with a war message nonetheless. He could no longer tolerate the chronic disorder just ninety miles off the American coast. As Senator Lodge explained, "We can not go on indefinitely with this strain, this suspense, and this uncertainty, this tottering upon the verge of war."

In his address on April 11, the president did not ask for a declaration of war against Spain but rather for an authorization to use force, as "an impartial neutral," to effect "a rational compromise between the contestants." McKinley listed American grievances and the reasons why the United States had to end the turmoil. First, the "cause of humanity." Second, the protection of American life and property. Third, the "very serious injury to the commerce, trade, and business of our people." And fourth, referring to the destruction of the *Maine*, the "constant menace to our peace." At the very end of his speech McKinley mentioned Spain's recent concession, but made little of it.

THE SPANISH-AMERICAN-CUBAN-FILIPINO WAR

Congress debated for over a week and then on April 19 declared Cuba free and independent, directing the president to use force to remove Spanish authority from the island. The legislators also passed the Teller Amendment, which disclaimed any American intention to annex Cuba. McKinley beat back a congressional amendment to recognize the rebel

government, for he believed the Cubans were unready for self-government and would first need a period of tutoring by Americans.

Diplomacy had failed. By the time the Spanish concessions were forthcoming, events had already pushed the antagonists to the brink. Washington might have been more patient and Madrid might have faced the fact that its once-grand empire had disintegrated. But the Cuban insurgents would settle for nothing less than independence, which Spain could not easily grant, and which the United States could achieve only through war. What was striking in the Cuban crisis, as in the Venezuelan crisis, was the American insistence that the United States would set the rules for nations in the Western Hemisphere. Great Britain had backed down in 1895, but Spain stood firm in 1898.

The motives of those Americans who favored war were mixed and complex. McKinley's message of April 11 expressed a humanitarian impulse to stop the bloodletting; concern for commerce **Motives** and property; and the psychological **for War** need to end the nightmarish anxiety once and for all. Republican politicians advised McKinley that they would lose the upcoming congressional elections unless the Cuban question was solved. And many businesspeople who had been hesitant before the crisis of early 1898, joined many farmers in the belief that removing Spain from Cuba would open new markets for surplus production—to which the depression of the 1890s had given some urgency.

Inveterate imperialists saw the war as an opportunity to fulfill what Senator Lodge called the "large policy." Naval enthusiasts could prove the worth of the New Navy. Religious leaders too saw merit in war. Social Gospel advocate Washington Gladden remarked that "in saving others we may save ourselves." Some conservatives, alarmed by violent labor strikes and Populism, welcomed war as a national unifier. One senator commented that "internal discord" was disappearing in the "fervent heat of patriotism. . . . You will not see another Debs riot for many years." Sensationalism also figured in the march to war. Assistant Secretary of the Navy Theodore Roosevelt and others too young to remember the inhumanity of the Civil War looked on war as adventure. The yellow press exaggerated

The garrulous Rough Rider Theodore Roosevelt in Cuba during the 1898 war. His ballyhooed role in the battle for San Juan Hill at Santiago earned him a reputation as a war hero, and he went on to become president.   Library of Congress.

no outlet for their vigorous and daring energy, there was always the chance of their fighting one another." The Rough Riders were undisciplined and not always effective warriors, but largely because of Roosevelt's self-serving publicity efforts they got a good press.

The war was hardly splendid. Over 5,400 Americans died, but only 379 of them in combat. The rest fell to malaria and yellow fever. Disease-carrying mosquitos were unrelenting, food was bad, and medical care was unsophisticated. Soldiers were issued heavy woolen uniforms in a tropical climate, and the stench of body odor was sickening. For black troops there was no relief from racism and Jim Crow. Their regiments were segregated and they were constantly insulted with the epithets *coon* and *nigger*. Cafes, saloons, and other public places refused to serve them. Race riots broke out; one in Tampa in early June sent twenty-seven blacks and several whites to the hospital. In Macon, Georgia, black soldiers tore down a park sign reading "No Dogs and Niggers Allowed" and chopped down a persimmon tree famous in the region as a lynching site. Whites in the South, where most troops were stationed, resented the appearance of status the military uniform gave to blacks and used threats and violence to intimidate those who suggested that a war to free the Cubans might help to break down the color line at home. One angry black Iowan announced: "I will not go to war. I have no country to fight for. I have not been given my rights." But most volunteers, black and white, shared the attitude of a soldier who wrote to his parents back in the coal-mining country of Pennsylvania: "The boys are all in good health and spirits, and think they can whip the world."

Before Americans began to fight and die in Cuba, the first news of war came from far-away Asia. It surprised many Americans, who knew little about

stories of atrocities. Anglo-Saxon supremacists like politician Albert Beveridge shouted, "God's hour has struck." But underlying all explanations of American acceptance of war was the spirit and reality of expansionism, which had been moving the nation ever outward in the last half of the nineteenth century.

Author Sherwood Anderson observed that fighting Spain was "like robbing an old gypsy woman in a vacant lot at night after a fair." Indeed, Spain was a weak belligerent, and the war lasted less than four months. But for some there was glory in what John Hay called a "splendid little war." As Roosevelt said of his motley unit of Ivy Leaguers and cowboys, the Rough Riders, they were "children of the dragon's blood, and if they had no outland foe to fight and

Commodore Dewey in the Philippines

the steady United States push into the Pacific, the dreams of farmers and businesspeople for a huge market in China, or the foreign-policy elite's knowledge of the Spanish colony of the Philippines. On May 1 Commodore George Dewey's New Navy ship the *Olympia* steamed into Manila Bay, the Philippines, and wrecked the Spanish fleet. Dewey became an instant hero. His sailors had to be handed volumes of the *Encyclopaedia Britannica* to acquaint them with this strange land, but officials in Washington knew that Manila ranked with Pearl Harbor and Pago Pago as a choice harbor.

Popular accounts still distort the historical record by crediting (or blaming) Theodore Roosevelt for having ordered Dewey to Manila. The story goes that one day in February when the secretary of the navy was away from the office, Assistant Secretary Roosevelt usurped authority and cabled Dewey to take on coal, rest at Hong Kong, and head for Manila upon the outbreak of war. Actually Roosevelt was a member of the McKinley administration following established policy; the president himself approved Roosevelt's instructions to Dewey.

Facing rebels and Americans in both Cuba and the Philippines, Spanish resistance collapsed rapidly. The Spanish Caribbean fleet, trapped in Santiago harbor, made a desperate attempt to escape but was destroyed by American warships on July 3. Several days later, the island of Puerto Rico fell to the invading Americans. Manila surrendered in August under pressure from Americans and Filipino insurgents led by Emilio Aguinaldo. Undermanned and ill-equipped, Spain sued for peace. The combatants signed an armistice on August 12, thus ending a war that should be called—to reflect where it was fought and whose interests were at stake—the Spanish-American-Cuban-Filipino War. "Let's see what we get by this," said Secretary of State William R. Day as he twirled the large globe in his office.

In Paris in December, American and Spanish negotiators agreed on the peace terms: independence for Cuba; cession of the Philippines, Puerto Rico, and Guam to the United States; and American payment of $20 million to Spain for the new territory. Filipino nationalists tried to persuade American officials to set their nation free, but they were rebuffed. The American empire now stretched deep into Asia; and the annexation of Wake Island (1898), Hawaii (1898), and Samoa (1899) gave American traders, missionaries, and naval promoters other steppingstones to China. Puerto Rico provided a long-desired base in the Caribbean which could help protect an American-built isthmian canal. And the United States would soon acquire another naval base at Guantánamo Bay in Cuba.

Treaty of Paris

Taste of Empire: Imperialists and Anti-imperialists Debate

During the war the *Washington Post* detected "a new appetite, a yearning to show our strength. . . . The taste of empire is in the mouth of the people. . . ." But as the debate over the Treaty of Paris intensified in the United States, it became evident that many Americans found the taste sour. Anti-imperialists like Mark Twain, William Jennings Bryan, William Graham Sumner, Andrew Carnegie, Charles Francis Adams, Jr., and Senator George Hoar argued vigorously against annexation of the Philippines. They were disturbed that a war to free Cuba had led to an empire. Their arguments varied. Some appealed to principle, citing the Declaration of Independence and the Constitution: the conquest of people against their will violated the sacred concept of self-determination. Philosopher William James charged that the United States was losing its special place among nations; it was, he warned, about to "puke up its heritage." To those who believed the Filipinos were not yet fit for self-government, former senator and active reformer Carl Schurz mockingly replied that Manila's city council was probably less corrupt than Chicago's. Others protested that the dispatch of troops overseas by the president, as commander-in-chief, greatly increased the power of the presidency and subverted the constitutional checks-and-balances system. Other anti-imperialists argued that the United States could acquire markets without having to subjugate foreign peoples.

Anti-Imperialist Arguments

Reform-minded critics of the treaty emphasized domestic priorities, including the improvement of race relations. "Until our nation has settled the Negro and Indian problems," said Booker T. Washington, "I do not believe that we have a right to assume more social problems." A black politician from Massachusetts—who had just protested a lynching in Georgia watched by two thousand people, followed

"Declined with thanks" reads this 1900 Puck *magazine cartoon. President William McKinley measures Uncle Sam, fattened by a series of territorial meals, as a group of anti-imperialists led by Carl Schurz futilely attempt to administer an antidote. The message was clear: the United States would continue to expand.* Library of Congress.

by mutilation of the black man's body by souvenir hunters—cried that the United States was exhibiting quite a spectacle to the world: "Columbia stands offering liberty to the Cubans with one hand, cramming liberty down the throats of the Filipinos with the other, but with both feet planted upon the neck of the negro." Other anti-imperialists feared the absorption of dark-skinned peoples, who, they warned, would undermine white Anglo-Saxon purity.

Samuel Gompers and other labor leaders worried about the possible undercutting of American labor—and the union movement—by what Gompers called the "half-breeds and semi-barbaric people" of the nation's new colonies. Might not they be imported as cheap contract labor to drive down the wages of American workers? Might not this new empire require a large standing army that would take workers away

from their jobs? Would not exploitation of the weak abroad become contagious and lead to further exploitation of the weak at home? Would not an overseas empire drain interest and resources from pressing domestic problems, delaying reform? Gompers charged, in fact, that imperialism was an attempt "to divert the attention of our people from the ills from which we suffer at home."

The imperialists responded with a mixture of arguments invoking patriotism, destiny, and commerce. They sketched a scenario of American greatness:

The Case for Empire merchant ships plying waters to boundless Asian markets; naval vessels cruising the Pacific to protect American interests; missionaries

uplifting inferior peoples. It was America's duty, they insisted, quoting a then-popular Rudyard Kipling

Chapter 22: THE QUEST FOR EMPIRE, 1865–1914

The missionary Grace Roberts teaches the Bible to Chinese women in Manchuria in 1903. The prominent American flag reveals that Americanism and religious work abroad went hand in hand. And the mission force was feminized; the great majority of missionaries were women.   ABCFM pictures, courtesy of Houghton Library, Harvard University.

poem, to "Take Up the White Man's Burden." Furthermore, insurgents were beginning to resist American rule, and it was cowardly to pull out under fire. Germany and Japan, two major international competitors, were snooping around the Philippine Islands, seemingly ready to seize them if the United States did not. National honor dictated that Americans keep what they had shed blood to take. Senator Beveridge asked what history would say. "Shall it say that, called by events to captain and command the proudest, ablest, purest race of history in history's noblest work, we declined that great commission?"

The anti-imperialists entered the debate with many handicaps. Possession of the Philippines was an accomplished fact; the anti-imperialists' role was thus a negative one. Then, too, they were internally divided, never able to launch an effective campaign. Although many of them belonged to the Anti-Imperialist League, they differed on so many domestic issues that it was difficult for them to speak with one voice on a foreign question. They were also inconsistent: Gompers favored the war but not the postwar annexations; Carnegie would accept colonies if they were not acquired by force; Hoar voted for the annexation of Hawaii but against that of the Philippines. The imperialists sneered that some of their critics

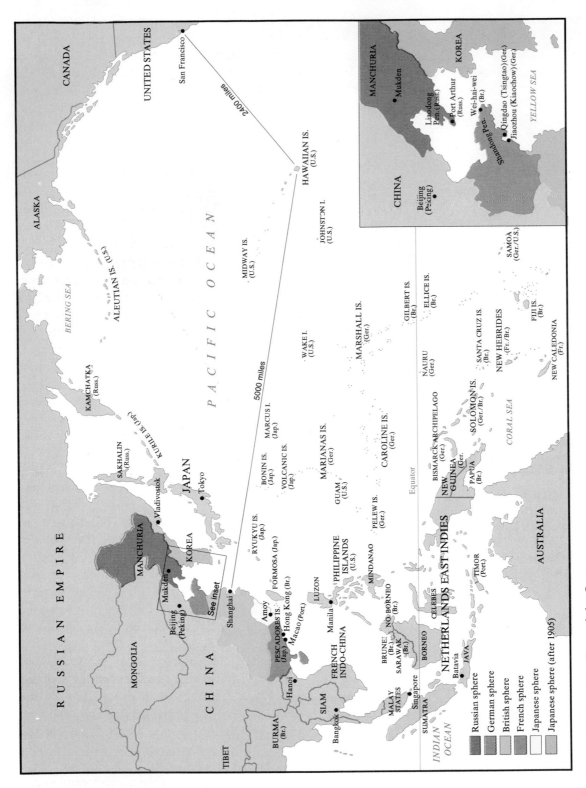

Imperialism in Asia: Turn of the Century

Map legend:
- Russian sphere
- German sphere
- British sphere
- French sphere
- Japanese sphere
- Japanese sphere (after 1905)

Main map labels:

CANADA
UNITED STATES
San Francisco
ALASKA
BERING SEA
ALEUTIAN IS. (U.S.)
PACIFIC OCEAN
2400 miles
5000 miles
HAWAIIAN IS. (U.S.)
JOHNSTON I. (U.S.)
MIDWAY IS. (U.S.)
WAKE I. (U.S.)
MARSHALL IS. (Ger.)
GILBERT IS. (Br.)
ELLICE IS. (Br.)
NAURU (Ger.)
SANTA CRUZ IS. (Br.)
NEW HEBRIDES (Fr./Br.)
FIJI IS. (Br.)
NEW CALEDONIA (Fr.)
SAMOA (Ger./U.S.)
MARCUS I. (Jap.)
BONIN IS. (Jap.)
VOLCANIC IS. (Jap.)
MARIANAS IS. (Ger.)
GUAM (U.S.)
CAROLINE IS. (Ger.)
PELEW IS. (Ger.)
Equator
CORAL SEA
SOLOMON IS. (Ger./Br.)
BISMARCK ARCHIPELAGO (Ger.)
NEW GUINEA (Ger.)
PAPUA (Br.)
AUSTRALIA
RUSSIAN EMPIRE
MONGOLIA
MANCHURIA
Mukden
Beijing (Peking)
CHINA
TIBET
BURMA (Br.)
SIAM
Bangkok
MALAY STATES
Singapore
SUMATRA
FRENCH INDO-CHINA
Hanoi
KAMCHATKA (Russ.)
SAKHALIN (Russ.)
KURILE IS. (Jap.)
Vladivostok
JAPAN
Tokyo
KOREA
RYUKYU IS. (Jap.)
FORMOSA (Jap.)
Amoy
Shanghai
PESCADORES IS. (Jap.)
Hong Kong (Br.)
Macao (Port.)
LUZON
Manila
PHILIPPINE ISLANDS (U.S.)
MINDANAO
NO. BORNEO (Br.)
BRUNEI (Br.)
SARAWAK (Br.)
BORNEO
CELEBES
NETHERLANDS EAST INDIES
JAVA
Batavia
TIMOR (Port.)
INDIAN OCEAN
See inset

Inset map labels:

MANCHURIA
Mukden
Liaodong Pen. (Russ.)
Port Arthur (Russ.)
Wei-hai-wei (Br.)
Qingdao (Tsingtao)(Ger.)
Jiaozhou (Kiaochow)(Ger.)
Shandong Pen.
KOREA
YELLOW SEA
CHINA
Beijing (Peking)

634

were hypocrites, showing more concern for Filipinos than for American Indians, blacks, unskilled workers, or destitute immigrants. John Hay commented privately that Carnegie "does not seem to reflect that the government is in a somewhat robust condition after shooting down several [striking] American citizens in his interest at Homestead."

On February 6, 1899, the Senate passed the Treaty of Paris by a 57-to-27 vote. Republicans, except for Hoar and Senator Eugene Hale of Maine, voted with their president; 22 Democrats voted **Senate Approval** no, but 10 voted for the treaty. The **of Treaty** latter group was probably influenced **of Paris** by Bryan, who had served as a colonel during the war; he urged a favorable vote in order to end the war and then push for Philippine independence. An amendment promising independence as soon as the Filipinos formed a stable government was defeated only by the tie-breaking ballot of the vice president.

The anti-imperialists lost, but Bryan carried the debate into the election of 1900 as the Democratic standard-bearer against McKinley. In that unsuccessful campaign the Nebraskan charged that imperialism benefited only American economic interests. To repudiate the principle of self-government in the Philippines would weaken it at home. "It is not necessary to own people to trade with them," Bryan protested. But McKinley would not apologize for American imperialism. "It is no longer a question of expansion with us," he told a midwestern audience. "If there is any question at all it is a question of contraction; and who is going to contract?"

TROUBLES IN ASIA

In 1895, the same year as the advent of the Cuban revolution and the Venezuelan crisis, Japan claimed victory over China in their war of only eight months. Outsiders had been pecking away at China—known as the Sick Man of Asia—since the 1840s, but the Japanese onslaught intensified the international scramble. The Germans carved out a sphere of interest in Shandong; the Russians moved into Manchuria

and the Liaodong Peninsula; the French grabbed some provinces; and the British drove in stakes too. Japan controlled Formosa and Korea as well as parts of China proper (see map). Within their spheres, the imperial powers built fortified bases, leased territory, and claimed exclusive economic privileges. Religious leaders, whose missions in China had doubled to one thousand in the 1890s, and business interests, who saw trade opportunities threatened, petitioned Washington to halt the dismemberment before they were closed out. What good were the Philippines as steppingstones to China if there was nothing left to step into? asked some.

Secretary of State John Hay recognized that the United States could not force the imperial powers from China. But he was determined to protect American commerce. In September 1899 **Open Door** Hay sent the imperial nations a note **Policy** asking them to offer assurances that they would respect the principle of equal trade opportunity—an Open Door—for all nations in their spheres. Germany, France, and the others sent evasive replies, privately complaining that the United States was seeking for free the trade rights the others had gained and maintained at considerable military and administrative cost. Then in 1900, a secret Chinese society called the Boxers revolted against the foreigners in their midst and laid siege to the foreign legations in Beijing (Peking). The United States joined the imperialists in sending troops to Beijing to lift the siege. And Hay, in a note dated July 3, 1900, again asked for "equal and impartial trade." He also instructed the other nations to preserve China's territorial integrity. Hay's protests notwithstanding, China continued for years to be fertile soil for foreign exploitation, especially for the expansionist Japanese.

Hay's foray into Asian politics settled little, but the Open Door policy thereafter became a central element in United States diplomacy. Actually, the Open Door had long been an American principle, for as a trading nation the United States opposed barriers to international commerce and demanded equal access to markets. After 1900, when the United States began to emerge as the premier world trader, the Open Door policy became an instrument first to pry open markets and then to dominate them, not just in China but in the rest of the world as well.

During the Philippine Insurrection, American soldiers battled Filipino nationalists bent on independence. This United States warrior sits in a Manila churchyard, anticipating action and no doubt wondering what he is doing so far from home. Library of Congress.

But the Open Door was not just a policy; it also became an ideology. The tenets of this ideology were that America's domestic well-being required exports, that foreign trade would suffer interruption unless the United States intervened abroad to implant American principles and keep markets open, and that any area closed to American products, citizens, or ideas threatened the survival of the United States itself.

In the Philippines, meanwhile, the United States antagonized its new colonials, or "wards", as McKinley labeled them. Emilio Aguinaldo, the Philippine nationalist leader, believed that Dewey had promised independence for his country. But after the victory, Aguinaldo was ordered out of Manila and isolated from decisions affecting his nation. Racial slurs like *gugu* and *nigger* infuriated the Filipinos, and they felt betrayed by the Treaty of Paris. Americans' paternalistic attitude toward their new charges grated on Filipino nationalist feelings. Once again Mr. Dooley caught the mood: "In ivry city in this unfair land we will erect schoolhouses an' packin' houses an' houses of correction; and we'll larn ye our language,

Philippine Insurrection

because 'tis aisier to larn ye ours than to larn oursilves yours. An' we'll give ye clothes, if ye pay f'r them; an' if ye don't, ye can go without."

In January 1899, an uncowed Aguinaldo proclaimed an independent Philippine Republic. Soon the Filipinos took up arms. Before the Philippine Insurrection was suppressed in 1901, over 5,000 Americans and over 200,000 Filipinos were dead. The atrocities committed by both sides were abominable. Americans burned villages, tortured people, and introduced a variant of the reconcentration policy. It was the American practice not to take prisoners. Anti-imperialists cried foul, but President Roosevelt remarked that "we haven't a single incident in the Philippines as bad as the massacre at Wounded Knee." This reference to the massacre of Native Americans in South Dakota (see page 465) was appropriate, because Americans stationed at the Philippine front often spoke of the "savage" Filipino insurgents who might "injun up" on them. One soldier from Kansas declared that the Philippines "won't be pacified until the niggers are killed off like the Indians." From 1898 through 1902, twenty-six of thirty U.S. Army generals ordered to the Philippines had had prior experience battling Indians in the American West.

After Aguinaldo's capture in 1901, the United States imposed its regime on the Philippines. Through a policy of "bread and guns," public works programs were introduced, and the architect Daniel Burnham, who led the City Beautiful movement in the United States, planned modern Manila. English was made the official language, American teachers were imported for local schoolhouses, and the University of the Philippines was founded (1908) to train a native American-oriented elite. The Americanization of the Philippines even included the introduction of basketball. Meanwhile a sedition act and political imprisonment silenced critics. The Philippine economy grew as a satellite of the United States economy. In 1916 the Jones Act promised Filipino independence, but not until thirty years later was Aguinaldo's dream realized.

Possession of the Philippines meant American participation in the turbulent politics of Asia. The major contender for influence in the area was Japan, and the Open Door policy was no deterrent to its advances. When competition for Manchuria and Korea led to the Russo-Japanese War (1904–1905), Japan scored quick victories over the stunned Russians. Roosevelt mediated the crisis at the Portsmouth Conference in New Hampshire. The peace settlement, he hoped, would preserve a balance of power in Asia. It did not. In 1905, in the Taft-Katsura Agreement, the United States conceded Japanese

Japanese-American Rivalry

hegemony over Korea in return for Japan's pledge not to undermine the American position in the Philippines. (Roosevelt soon came to think of the vulnerable Philippines as America's Achilles' heel.) To alert Japan to American naval power and to persuade Congress to increase the navy's budget, Roosevelt in 1907 sent the "Great White Fleet" on a world tour, with conspicuous stops in the Pacific. The Japanese were duly impressed, and began to build a bigger navy themselves.

Troubles with Japan boiled to the surface in 1906 when the San Francisco School Board, reflecting the anti-Orientalism of the West Coast, segregated all Chinese, Koreans, and Japanese in a special school. Japan protested this discrimination against its citizens. Because there was little President Roosevelt could do to budge the insistent Californians, he struck a gentleman's agreement with Tokyo restricting Japanese immigration to the United States. Relations with Tokyo were jolted again in 1913 when the California legislature denied Japanese residents the right to own property in the state.

Despite the Root-Takahira Agreement (1908), in which the United States recognized Japan's interests in Manchuria and Japan again pledged the security of American possessions in the Pacific, Japanese-American relations deteriorated. Japan became alarmed by President Taft's ineffective attempt at dollar diplomacy, inducing American bankers to join an international consortium to build a Chinese railway. Dollar diplomacy was an effort to use private funds to serve American diplomatic goals and at the same time to garner profits for American financiers. Realizing neither purpose, Taft's venture seemed only to embolden the Japanese to solidify and extend their holdings in China. When the First World War broke out in Europe, Japan seized the opportunity to grab Shandong and some Pacific islands from the Germans. In 1915 Japan issued its Twenty-One Demands, virtually insisting on hegemony over all of China. The Chinese Revolution of 1911 had brought some unity and strength to the Chinese government, but the aggressive Japanese showed little respect for it. As parts of China passed into the hands of the Japanese, Americans could only protest feebly.

THE FRUITS AND TASKS OF EMPIRE IN LATIN AMERICA

If the United States demonstrated feebleness in Asia, it did not in its own backyard of Latin America (see map, page 638). Although the Teller Amendment (see page 629) had outlawed annexation, it did not rule out American control of postwar Cuba. American troops remained there until 1902. In Washington, officials wrote the Platt Amendment for inclusion in the new Cuban constitution: a frank avowal of United States hegemony, the Platt

Platt Amendment

Amendment provided that Cuba could not make a treaty with another nation that might impair its independence. In short, all treaties had to be approved by the United States. Most important, Cuba granted the United States "the right to intervene" to preserve the island's independence and to maintain domestic order. Cuba was also required to undertake a sanitation program and to lease to the United States a naval base (Guantánamo). These violations of Cuban sovereignty, formalized in 1903, governed Cuban-American relations until 1934. The Cubans, like the Filipinos, resisted their new masters: they marched in the streets against the Platt Amendment, and a revolution in 1906 prompted Roosevelt to send in marines. The marines stayed until 1909, were ordered back for a short time in 1912, and occupied Cuba again from 1917 to 1922. José Martí had warned Cubans from the beginning that the United States posed a threat: "I know the Monster, because I have lived in its lair."

The United States presence left an imprint on Cuban life. Americans helped to improve transportation, expand the public school system, found a national army, and improve sugar production. Walter Reed's experiments, based on the theory of Cuban

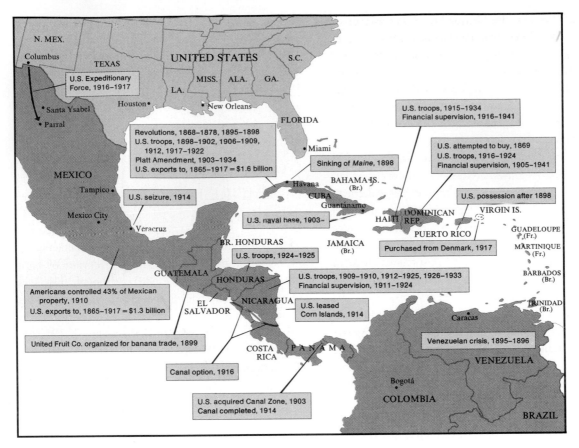

The United States and Latin America

physician Carlos Finlay, proved that the mosquito transmitted yellow fever; American sanitary engineers soon controlled the insect and eradicated the disease from the island. American investments in Cuba grew from $50 million before the revolution to $220 million by 1913, and American exports to the island rose from $26 million in 1900 to $196 million in 1917. But the Cuban nation developed with a colonial mentality, and Cuban nationalists nurtured a resentment that developed into anti-Americanism.

Panama was the site of one of Theodore Roosevelt's boldest expansionist ventures. United States fascination with an isthmian canal in Central America,

Panama Canal

to link the waters of the Pacific and Atlantic, was long-standing. With the opening of the Suez Canal in Egypt in 1869, as well as an abortive attempt by Ferdinand de Lesseps to duplicate that triumph in Panama, American attention heightened.

"A canal under American control, or no canal," snapped President Rutherford B. Hayes. In 1880, he dispatched two warships to the Panamanian coast to demonstrate United States interest. American business interests lobbied for a canal, citing better access to Asian and Latin American markets. But three obstacles had to be overcome. First, the Clayton-Bulwer Treaty with Britain (1850) provided for joint control of a Central American canal. President Theodore Roosevelt persuaded the British, who were cultivating United States friendship and who knew that their influence in the region was diminishing, to step aside (Hay-Pauncefote Treaty of 1901). Second, Colombia was driving a hard bargain in talks over a canal to be cut through its province of Panama. Roosevelt urged Panamanian rebels to declare independence from Colombia, and he sent American warships to the isthmus to ensure the success of the rebellion. In 1903 the United States signed a treaty with the new nation of Panama: the United States was awarded a canal zone and long-term rights to its control; Panama was guaranteed its independence. Colombians would not easily forget this dispoiling of their sovereignty. Third, the cost of constructing a canal was enormous. Roosevelt, having overcome the British and Colombian problems, successfully pressed an obliging Congress for substantial funds.

The completion of the Panama Canal in 1914 marked a major technological achievement. The special bearings and gears used to operate the locks were manufactured by a Wheeling, West Virginia, firm; some fifty Pittsburgh factories and shops made the various bolts and steel girders; and the General Electric Company produced the electrical apparatus. People greeted the canal's opening the way people in the 1960s hailed the landing on the moon. During the canal's first year of operation, over one thousand merchant ships squeezed through its locks. (Ten years later the annual rate was five thousand, equal to the traffic through the Suez Canal.) The United States fortified the zone with conspicuous sixteen-inch guns, the nation's largest.

As for the rest of the Caribbean, it became an American lake. "Speak softly and carry a big stick," said Roosevelt. He did wield a big stick, but he seldom curbed his bombastic rhetoric. In 1904 the president announced his Roosevelt Corollary to the Monroe Doctrine, warning Latin Americans to stabilize their politics and finances to forestall European meddling in their affairs. "Chronic wrongdoing," he lectured, might require "intervention by some civilized nation, and in the Western Hemisphere the adherence of the United States to the Monroe Doctrine may force the United States, however reluctantly, in flagrant cases of such wrongdoing or impotence, to the exercise of an international police power." Roosevelt and his successors were not bluffing. From 1900 to 1917, when the United States entered the First World War, American troops intervened in Cuba, Panama, Nicaragua, the Dominican Republic, Mexico, and Haiti. American officials took over customs houses (as in the Dominican Republic, from 1905 to 1941) to control tariff revenues and thus governmental budgets; they renegotiated foreign debts with American banks; they trained national guards and ran elections.

Roosevelt Corollary

The cruiser Brooklyn *steams out of Havana harbor, Cuba in May 1902. Aboard the warship was General Leonard Wood, the American military governor of the Caribbean island, 1899–1902. Before he departed, Wood had forced the Platt Amendment on the Cubans—a document, he admitted, that left Cuba with "little or no independence."* Library of Congress.

The United States set out to police the Caribbean in the name of order. Whether such order was achieved by the landing of marines, the development of a national guard, a managed electoral process, or a manipulated economy, it was deemed necessary to guarantee United States security and prosperity. After Roosevelt helped to slice off Panama from Colombia and initiated construction of the Panama Canal, Washington would not tolerate disturbances that might threaten the vital waterway. Order was believed essential to American commerce and investment too. Between 1900 and 1917 American exports to Latin America swelled from $132 million to $309 million, and imports from Latin America increased even more. Investments in sugar, tobacco, transportation, and banking also rose impressively. Finally, order seemed imperative to Americans eager to remake Latin American societies in the image of the United States. "When properly directed there is no people not fitted for self-government," Woodrow

The Quest for Order

Wilson remarked. Furthermore, "every nation needs to be drawn into the tutelage of America."

Roosevelt, Taft, and Wilson gave varying expression to this quest for order. The Rough Rider saw world affairs as a constant struggle for international power. The United States, in its own interest, had to lay claim to as much power as possible. The very struggle would ennoble Americans; the result would enrich them. Taft emphasized dollar diplomacy: dollars, not bullets, he predicted, would effect stability and enhance American interests. Wilson was no less a nationalist or pragmatist in desiring to safeguard and expand American prosperity and security. He ordered troops to Haiti, the Dominican Republic, and Mexico, justifying military force by proclaiming it "our peculiar duty" to teach other peoples "order and self-control" and "the drill and habit of law and obedience." Wilson became known for his missionary paternalism, his insistence on liberal capitalism and constitutional government. He spoke of regenerating a benighted world through American salvation. Whether by means of Roosevelt's big stick, Taft's dollars, or Wilson's sermons—in fact, each president used all three methods—United States behavior toward its southern neighbors was imperialistic, because it denied some of them the freedom to make their own choices and thwarted their national sovereignty. The United States possessed few colonies, but developed an empire nonetheless—an informal one largely marked by economic and political control rather than formal annexation.

One of the assumptions that governed United States policy toward Europe was that European nations should not intervene in Western Hemispheric affairs; the Monroe Doctrine, European officials now knew, had power behind it. Another assumption of American policy toward Europe was that the United States should stand outside continental embroilments. And a third was that America's best interests lay in cooperation with Great Britain. The balance of power in Europe was precarious, and seldom did an American president involve the United States directly. At Germany's request, Roosevelt helped to settle a Franco-German clash over Morocco by mediating a settlement at Algeciras, Spain (1906). But the president drew American criticism for entangling the United States in a European problem. Americans endorsed the ultimately futile Hague peace conferences (1899 and

1907) and negotiated various arbitration treaties, but on the whole they stayed outside Europe's embittered arena.

Anglo-American Rapprochement A major offshoot of the German-British rivalry was London's search for American friendship. The makings of the "great rapprochement" had been developing since the late nineteenth century. When the British supported the Americans in the war of 1898, stepped aside in the Hay-Pauncefote Treaty (1901) to permit the building of an American canal, virtually endorsed the Roosevelt Corollary, and withdrew their warships from the Caribbean, Americans warmed toward them. The British overtures paid off in 1917 when the United States threw its arms and men into the First World War on the British side.

From the Civil War to the First World War, expansionism and empire were central to American foreign policy. By 1914 Americans held extensive interests in a world made smaller by modern technology. The outward reach of American policy from Seward to Wilson met opposition from domestic critics, congressional doubters, other nations, and nationalists in subjugated lands, but the trend was never seriously diverted. Ideas of racial supremacy, the belief that the nation needed foreign markets to absorb surplus production so the domestic economy could thrive, a mission to uplift the less fortunate, and emotional appeals to national greatness—all fed the appetite for foreign adventure and commitments. The instruments of expansion and empire were the machines produced by American entrepreneurs and inventors. The underwater cable, the new steel warships, the Panama Canal, the exportation of American products across the globe, and the rifles American soldiers toted into Philippine jungles and into the streets of Latin American capitals—all facilitated the imperial odyssey.

In 1914 Americans braced themselves for the immediate shock of full-scale war in Europe. In the long term, however, their foreign policy would be preoccupied with challenges to United States hegemony from proud and resentful nationalists victimized by American paternalism. And Americans who sincerely believed that they had been helping others to enjoy a better life would feel betrayed and baffled that their foreign clients could be so ungrateful.

IMPORTANT EVENTS

1861–69	Seward is secretary of state
1866	Transatlantic cable completed France withdraws from Mexico
1867	Alaska and Midway acquired
1868	Burlingame Treaty with China
1870	Senate rejects annexation of Dominican Republic
1871	*Alabama* claims settled
1878	U.S. products monopolize awards at Paris World's Fair
1883	Advent of New Navy
1887	U.S. gains naval rights to Pearl Harbor
1889	First Pan-American Conference
1890	Alfred T. Mahan, *The Influence of Sea Power upon History*
1893	Severe depression begins Turner's frontier thesis Hawaiian revolution begins
1895	Crisis over Venezuela Cuban revolution begins Japan defeats China
1896	McKinley elected president
1898	Sinking of the *Maine* Spanish-American-Cuban-Filipino War Hawaii and Wake Island annexed Treaty of Paris
1899	Senate passes Treaty of Paris United Fruit Company founded First Open Door note Outbreak of Philippine Insurrection
1900	Second Open Door note U.S. exports total $1.5 billion McKinley re-elected
1901	Theodore Roosevelt becomes president Aguinaldo captured Hay-Pauncefote Treaty
1903	Panama breaks from Colombia U.S. granted canal rights in Panama Platt Amendment
1904	Roosevelt Corollary
1905	Taft-Katsura Agreement Portsmouth Conference U.S. imposes financial supervision on Dominican Republic
1906	San Francisco segregates Asian schoolchildren U.S. invades Cuba
1907	Great White Fleet Gentleman's agreement with Japan
1908	Root-Takahira Agreement
1910	Mexican Revolution begins
1912	U.S. troops enter Cuba again U.S. troops occupy Nicaragua
1914	U.S. troops invade Mexico First World War begins Panama Canal opens

SUGGESTIONS FOR FURTHER READING

General

"American Empire, 1898–1903," *Pacific Historical Review*, 48 (1979), entire issue; Robert L. Beisner, *From the Old Diplomacy to the New, 1865–1900* (1975); Charles S. Campbell, *The Transformation of American Foreign Relations, 1865–1900* (1976); Richard D. Challener, *Admirals, Generals, and American Foreign Policy, 1889–1914* (1973); James A. Field, Jr., "American Imperialism," *American Historical Review*, 83 (1978), 644–668; John A. S. Grenville and George B. Young, *Politics, Strategy, and American Diplomacy* (1967); David Healy, *U.S. Expansionism* (1970); Ronald J. Jensen, *The Alaska Purchase and Russian-American Relations* (1975); George F. Kennan, *American Diplomacy, 1900–1950* (1951); Walter LaFeber, *The New Empire* (1963); Ernest R. May, *American Imperialism* (1968); H. Wayne Morgan, *America's Road to Empire* (1965); Milton Plesur, *America's Outward Thrust* (1971); David M. Pletcher, *The Awkward Years* (1962); Emily Rosenberg, *Spreading the American Dream* (1982); Rubin F. Weston, *Racisim in United States Imperialism* (1972); William Appleman Williams, *The Tragedy of American Diplomacy*, rev. ed. (1962).

Theodore Roosevelt and Other Expansionists

Howard K. Beale, *Theodore Roosevelt and the Rise of America to World Power* (1956); John M. Blum, *The Republican Roosevelt* (1954); John M. Cooper, Jr., *The Warrior and the Priest: Woodrow Wilson and Theodore Roosevelt* (1983); Lewis L. Gould, *The Presidency of William McKinley* (1981); William H. Harbaugh, *The Life and Times of Theodore Roosevelt* (1975); Frederick Marks, III, *Velvet on Iron: The Diplomacy of Theodore Roosevelt* (1979); Frank Merli and Theodore A. Wilson, eds., *Makers of American Diplomacy* (1974); Edmund Morris, *The Rise of Theodore Roosevelt* (1979); Ernest N. Paolino, *The Foundations of the American Empire* (1973) (on Seward); William C. Widenor, *Henry Cabot Lodge and the Search for an American Foreign Policy* (1980). (For works on Woodrow Wilson, see Chapter 23.)

Economic Expansion

See the works by Beisner, Campbell, and LaFeber cited above; William H. Becker, *The Dynamics of Business-Government Relations* (1982); Robert B. Davies, *Peacefully Working to Conquer the World: Singer Sewing Machines in Foreign Markets, 1854–1920* (1976); David M. Pletcher, "Rhetoric and Results: A Pragmatic View of American Economic Expansionism, 1865–98," *Diplomatic History*, 5 (1981), 93–105; Tom Terrill, *The Tariff, Politics, and American Foreign Policy, 1874–1901* (1973); Mira Wilkins, *The Emergence of the Multinational Enterprise* (1970); William Appleman Williams, *The Roots of the Modern American Empire* (1969).

The American Navy

Benjamin F. Cooling, *Gray Steel and Blue Water Navy* (1979); Kenneth J. Hagan, ed., *In Peace and War*, 2nd ed. (1984); Kenneth J. Hagan, *American Gunboat Diplomacy and the Old Navy, 1877–1889* (1973); Walter R. Herrick, *The American Naval Revolution* (1966); Peter Karsten, *The Naval Aristocracy* (1972); Robert Seager, II, *Alfred Thayer Mahan* (1977); Ronald Spector, *Admiral of the New Empire* (1974) (on Dewey).

The Spanish-American-Cuban-Filipino War

Graham A. Cosmas, *An Army for Empire: The United States Army in the Spanish-American War* (1971); Willard B. Gatewood, Jr., *Black Americans and the White Man's Burden, 1898–1903* (1975); Richard Hofstadter, "Cuba, the Philippines, and Manifest Destiny," in *The Paranoid Style in American Politics*, ed., Richard Hofstadter (1967); Walter LaFeber, "That 'Splendid Little War' in Historical Perspective," *Texas Quarterly*, 11 (1968), 89–98; Gerald F. Linderman, *The Mirror of War: American Society and the Spanish-American War* (1974); Ernest R. May, *Imperial Democracy* (1961); Julius Pratt, *Expansionists of 1898* (1936); David F. Trask, *The War with Spain in 1898* (1981).

Anti-imperialism and the Peace Movement

Robert L. Beisner, *Twelve Against Empire* (1968); Peter Brock, *Pacifism in the United States* (1968); Kendrick A. Clements, *William Jennings Bryan, Missionary Isolationist* (1983); Merle E. Curti, *Peace or War* (1936); Charles DeBenedetti, *Peace Reform in American History* (1980); C. Roland Marchand, *The American Peace Movement and Social Reform, 1898–1918* (1973); Thomas J. Osborne, *"Empire Can Wait": American Opposition to Hawaiian Annexation, 1893–1898* (1981); David S. Patterson, *Toward a Warless World* (1976); E. Berkeley Tompkins, *Anti-Imperialism in the United States* (1970). (See also works in Chapter 23.)

Relations with Cuba and Latin America

Samuel F. Bemis, *The Latin American Policy of the United States* (1943); David Healy, *The United States in Cuba,*

1898–1902 (1963); Walter LaFeber, *Inevitable Revolutions: The United States in Central America* (1983); Walter LaFeber, *The Panama Canal* (1979); Lester D. Langley, *The Banana Wars* (1983); Lester D. Langley, *The United States and the Caribbean, 1900–1970* (1980); Lester D. Langley, *Struggle for the American Mediterranean* (1976); David McCullough, *The Path Between the Seas: The Creation of the Panama Canal, 1870–1914* (1977); Allan R. Millett, *The Politics of Intervention: The Military Occupation of Cuba, 1906–1909* (1968); Dana G. Munro, *Intervention and Dollar Diplomacy in the Caribbean, 1900–1921* (1964); Dexter Perkins, *The Monroe Doctrine, 1867–1907* (1937); Ramon Ruiz, *Cuba* (1968); Karl M. Schmitt, *Mexico and the United States, 1821–1973* (1974); Josefina Vazquez and Lorenzo Meyer, *The United States and Mexico* (1985).

Asia and the Pacific

Charles S. Campbell, *Special Business Interests and the Open Door Policy* (1951); Warren I. Cohen, *America's Response to China*, 2nd ed. (1980); Raymond A. Esthus, *Theodore Roosevelt and Japan* (1966); Michael Hunt, *The Making of a Special Relationship: The United States and China to 1914* (1983); Akira Iriye, *Pacific Estrangement: Japanese and American Expansion, 1897–1911* (1972); Akira Iriye, *Across the Pacific* (1967); Jerry Israel, *Progressivism and the Open Door* (1971); Paul M. Kennedy, *The Samoan Tangle* (1974); Robert McClellan, *The Heathen Chinee: A Study of American Attitudes Toward China, 1890–1905* (1971); Thomas J. McCormick, *China Market* (1967); Charles E. Neu, *The Troubled Encounter* (1975) (on Japan); Merze Tate, *The United States and the Hawaiian Kingdom* (1965); James C. Thomson, Jr., et al., *Sentimental Imperialists* (1981); Paul A. Varg, *The Making of a Myth: The United States and China, 1897–1912* (1968); Paul A. Varg, *Missionaries, Chinese, and Diplomats* (1958); Marilyn Blatt Young, *The Rhetoric of Empire* (1968).

The Philippines: Insurrection and Colony

John M. Gates, *Schoolbooks and Krags: The United States Army in the Philippines, 1898–1902* (1973); Henry F. Graff, ed., *American Imperialism and the Philippine Insurrection* (1969); Glenn A. May, *Social Engineering in the Philippines* (1980); Stuart C. Miller, *"Benevolent Assimilation"* (1982); Julius Pratt, *America's Colonial Experiment* (1950); Daniel B. Schirmer, *Republic or Empire?* (1972); Peter Stanley, *A Nation in the Making: The Philippines and the United States, 1899–1921* (1974); Richard E. Welch, *Response to Imperialism: American Resistance to the Philippine War* (1972); Walter L. Williams, "United States Indian Policy and the Debate over Philippine Annexation," *Journal of American History*, 66 (1980), 810–831; Leon Wolff, *Little Brown Brother* (1961).

Britain and Canada

Kenneth Bourne, *Britain and the Balance of Power in North America, 1815–1908* (1967); Robert C. Brown, *Canada's National Policy, 1883–1900* (1964); Alexander E. Campbell, *Great Britain and the United States, 1895–1903* (1960); Charles S. Campbell, *From Revolution to Rapprochement: The United States and Great Britain, 1783–1900* (1974); Adrian Cook, *The Alabama Claims* (1975); Bradford Perkins, *The Great Rapprochement* (1968).

AMERICA AT WAR
1914–1920

CHAPTER 23

"*Oh, my God,* what am I to do?" murmured Woodrow Wilson. Just moments before he had been holding Ellen Axson Wilson's hand when she died after years of suffering kidney disease. Two days earlier, on August 4, 1914, as he kept vigil at her bedside, the president had drafted a message offering American mediation to end the menacing war the European nations had just begun. Seldom have such painful personal and official burdens fallen on a president at the same time.

In twenty-nine years of marriage Ellen Axson Wilson had been central to his well-being and success. Woodrow Wilson cherished her loyalty, intelligence, and strength in the family. She was a southern woman, born into a Presbyterian minister's family, educated at a small Georgia women's college, and dedicated to making a pleasant home for her husband and daughters. Ellen Axson Wilson was also a painter, avid reader of Shakespeare and Wordsworth, and mother who made her children's clothing, nursed them through scarlet fever, and planned the family budget. A well-managed and serene household mattered to her. "A woman's place is to keep one little spot in the world quiet," she said. She was not, in today's sense, an emancipated woman, although she once complained about having to stay home "like the fixtures." Yet she did not confine herself to the home, often entering her husband's active political world to discuss issues with decision-makers.

Now, at a time of wrenching bereavement, when the partner who had always helped him in times of crisis was gone, Woodrow Wilson faced momentous decisions about America's place in the First World War. In his private grief he found it difficult to concentrate on affairs of state. Wilson had always striven to practice self-control; nations, too, he had long believed, should demonstrate the "dignity of self-control." Yet, as the president entered the era of the First World War, both personal and national self-control, however imperative, seemed elusive. He sought to achieve both, but soon personal and national tragedy, not achievement, would mark his record.

The Great War in Europe shocked Woodrow Wilson and the American people: it seemed a throwing off of civilization. Americans had, of course, witnessed and participated in the years of international competition for colonies, markets, and weapons supremacy. Sporadic military encounters had disturbed the peace, but full-scale war was thought to be a barbarity of the past. "The nineteenth-century view of history as progress," the historian Henry F. May has written, "received a shattering blow." The battle news was gruesome. "We were not used to smelling blood from vast slaughterhouses," recalled William Allen White.

For almost three years President Wilson kept America out of the world war. He sought to protect American interests as a neutral trader and to improve the nation's military posture, all the while lecturing the belligerents to rediscover their humanity and to respect international law. But American neutrality, lives, and property fell victim to British and German naval warfare. In early 1917 the president asked Congress for a declaration of war with his characteristic crusading zeal. America joined the battle not just to win the war but to reform the world that would emerge from it.

The American people in the era of the First World War, even after over a decade of progressive reform, remained heterogeneous and fractious. In 1914 labor-capital confrontations—like the Ludlow Massacre in Colorado, in which two women and eleven children were killed when state militia attempted to break a miners' strike—still claimed headlines. Racial antagonisms were evident in Wilson's decision to segregate federal buildings in Washington, D.C., and by continued lynchings of blacks (fifty-one in 1914). Nativists protested the fast pace of immigration; 1.2 million immigrants entered the United States in 1914 alone. Ethnic groups eyed one another suspiciously. Many women articulated the case for equality among the sexes and for female suffrage, while most men restated the case for traditional subordination.

The war experience accentuated and intensified the nation's social divisiveness. Whites who did not like the migration of southern blacks to work in northern defense plants resisted their new neighbors,

The Wilson family: from left to right, Margaret, Ellen Axson Wilson (1860–1914), Eleanor, Jessie, and President Woodrow Wilson (1856–1924). After his wife's death, the president married again, in the midst of a debate over American preparedness for war.   Library of Congress.

and race riots revealed once again the depth of racial prejudice. German-Americans were denounced as traitors, and war hawks harassed pacifists. The federal government itself trampled on civil liberties to silence critics. And, as communism implanted itself in Soviet Russia, America suffered a postwar Red Scare that did further damage to its reputation as a free and democratic society. In the aftermath of war, groups that sought to consolidate gains made during the war vied with those who sought to restore the prewar status quo.

America's participation in the war also wrought massive changes and accelerated trends already in motion. Wars are emergencies, and during such times the normal way of doing things surrenders to the extraordinary and exaggerated. This period witnessed greater powers for the presidency, the military draft, unprecedented centralization and integration of the economy, increased standardization of products, and unusual cooperation between government and business. Indeed, some historians date the "military-industrial complex"—a term coined years later by President Dwight D. Eisenhower—from the First World War. The war experience also helped cause the splintering and fading of the progressive movement, although reformers did put wartime effort into a few issues, such as prohibition and women's suffrage. But, Jane Addams remarked sadly, "the spirit of fighting burns away all those impulses . . . which foster the will to justice."

The United States came out of the war a major power in a disrupted and economically hobbled world.

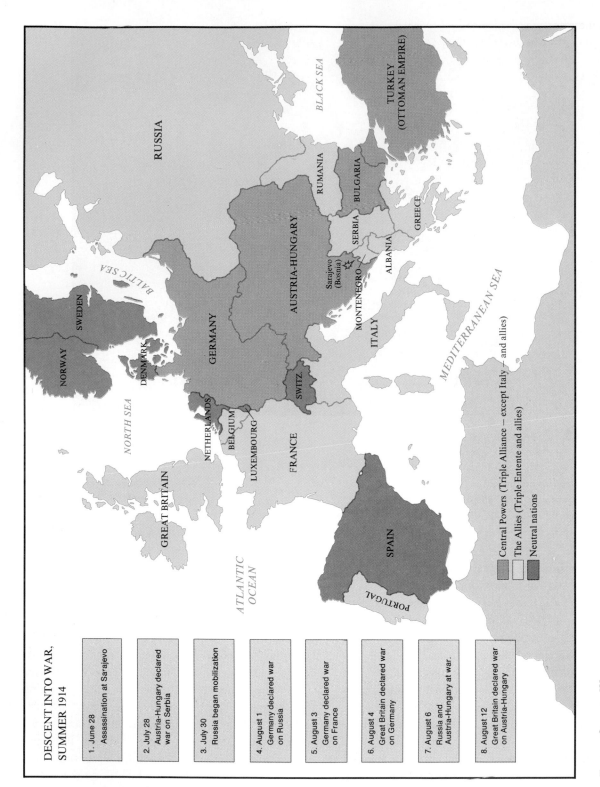

DESCENT INTO WAR,
SUMMER 1914

1. June 28
   Assassination at Sarajevo

2. July 28
   Austria-Hungary declared
   war on Serbia

3. July 30
   Russia began mobilization

4. August 1
   Germany declared war
   on Russia

5. August 3
   Germany declared war
   on France

6. August 4
   Great Britain declared war
   on Germany

7. August 6
   Russia and
   Austria-Hungary at war.

8. August 12
   Great Britain declared war
   on Austria-Hungary

Central Powers (Triple Alliance — except Italy — and allies)

The Allies (Triple Entente and allies)

Neutral nations

RUSSIA

BLACK SEA

TURKEY
(OTTOMAN EMPIRE)

RUMANIA

BULGARIA

GREECE

SERBIA

ALBANIA

AUSTRIA-HUNGARY

Sarajevo
(Bosnia)

MONTENEGRO

ITALY

MEDITERRANEAN SEA

BALTIC SEA

GERMANY

SWITZ.

NORWAY

SWEDEN

DENMARK

NETHERLANDS

BELGIUM

LUXEMBOURG

FRANCE

NORTH SEA

GREAT BRITAIN

ATLANTIC
OCEAN

SPAIN

PORTUGAL

Europe Goes to War

648

Yet Americans who had marched to battle as if on a crusade grew disillusioned. They recoiled from the spectacle of the victors squabbling over the spoils and they chided Wilson for failing to deliver his promised "peace without victory." As in the 1790s, 1840s, and 1890s, Americans engaged in a fundamental national debate about foreign policy. The president appealed for American membership in a new international organization, the League of Nations, which he touted as a vehicle for reforming world politics. But the Senate killed his diplomatic offspring, fearful that it might entangle Americans once again in Europe's problems, impede the growth of the American empire, and compromise the country's traditional unilateralism in international affairs. On many fronts, then, Americans during the era of the First World War were at war with themselves.

THE QUESTION OF NEUTRALITY

The war that erupted in August 1914 grew from tangled roots. Years of imperialist competition over trade, colonies, allies, and armaments had generated two alliance systems. The

European Origins of the First World War

Triple Alliance joined together Germany, Austria-Hungary, and Italy. The Triple Entente combined Britain, France, and Russia. All had economic and territorial ambitions, but Germany seemed particularly bold as it rivaled Britain for world leadership. A series of crises in the Balkans (southeastern Europe) started a chain of events that propelled the European nations into battle.

Slavic nationalists sought to build a Slavic state by adding territories to independent Serbia. Bosnia, part of the Austro-Hungarian Empire, was one of those coveted territories. In June 1914, at Sarajevo, Bosnia, the heir to the Austro-Hungarian throne was assassinated by a Slavic revolutionary linked to Serbia. Austria-Hungary consulted Germany, which urged toughness. Serbia called upon its Slavic friend Russia for help. Russia looked to its ally France. When Austria-Hungary declared war against Serbia in late

July, Russia began to mobilize its armies. Certain that war was coming its way, Germany struck first, declaring war against Russia on August 1 and against France two days later. What would the British do? They hesitated, but when Germany slashed into Belgium to get at France, Britain declared war against Germany on August 4. Eventually Turkey joined the Central Powers of Germany and Austria-Hungary, and Japan and Italy teamed up with the Allies of Britain, France, and Russia. The world was aflame (see map).

President Wilson at first sought to distance America from the conflagration by issuing a proclamation of neutrality. He also asked Americans to refrain from taking sides, to exhibit "fine poise" and "the dignity of self-control." Privately, the president said that "we definitely have to be neutral, since otherwise our mixed populations would wage war on each other." The United States, he fervently hoped, would stand as the pre-eminently sane, civilized nation in a deranged international environment.

Wilson's lofty appeal for American neutrality and unity at home collided with three realities. First, ethnic groups in the United States naturally took

Ethnic Ties to Europe

sides. Many German-Americans and anti-British Irish-Americans (Ireland was then trying to break free from British rule) cheered for the Central Powers. Americans of British and French ancestry applauded the Allies. Anglo-American traditions and slogans like "Remember Lafayette," as well as the sheer number of Americans with roots in the Allied nations, drew a majority to the Allied cause. To them the war was a matter of democracy against autocracy. Germany's attack on neutral Belgium at the start of the war confirmed in many minds that it was the archetype of unbridled militarism, the defiler of innocent women and children.

Second, America's economic links with the Allies also rendered neutrality difficult, if not impossible. England had long been one of the nation's best customers. New war-inspired orders flooded American

Economic Links with the Belligerents

companies and farms, pulling the economy out of its recession. In 1914 American exports to England and France were $753 million; in 1916 the figure spurted to $2.75 billion.

In the same period, however, exports to Germany dropped from $345 million to only $29 million. Much of the American-Allied trade was financed through private American loans, amounting to $2.3 billion during the period of neutrality; in stark contrast, Germany received only $27 million.

The Wilson administration, which at first frowned on the transactions, came to see them as necessary to the economic health of the United States. Without loans to help the Allies pay for American products, one of Wilson's key advisers gloomily told the president, the United States would suffer "restriction of output, industrial depression, idle capital, idle labor, numerous failures, financial demoralization, and general unrest and suffering among the laboring classes." From Germany's perspective, of course, the linkage between the American economy and the Allies meant that the United States had become the quite-unneutral Allied arsenal and bank. Americans, however, were caught in a dilemma that further highlighted the difficulty of maintaining pure neutrality: for the United States to cut its economic ties with Britain would constitute an unneutral act in favor of Germany. That is, under international law the British—who controlled the seas—could buy contraband (war-related goods) and noncontraband from neutrals at their own risk. It was Germany's responsibility, therefore, not America's, to stop the trade in ways that international law prescribed: an effective blockade of the enemy's territory or the seizure of all goods from belligerent (British) ships and contraband from neutral (American) ships.

The third reason neutrality did not work derived from the pro-Allied sympathies of Wilson administration officials. Shortly after Ellen Wilson's death, the president received a note from another man who had lost his wife, British Foreign Secretary Edward Grey. Wilson, moved by the thoughtful message, replied that he felt "that we are bound together by common principle and purpose." He was talking about more than shared bereavement. Indeed, for Wilson, a German victory would destroy government by law and "free industry and enterprise." If Germany won the war, he prophesied, "it would change the course of our civilization and make the United States a military nation." Wilson's chief advisers and diplomats—Colonel Edward House, Sec-

Pro-Allied Sympathies

retary of State Robert Lansing, and Ambassador to London Walter Hines Page among them—also shared these sentiments and were often openly pro-Allied in their viewpoints.

Wilson and his aides also believed that Wilsonian principles stood a better chance of international acceptance if Britain, rather than the Central Powers, sat astride the postwar world. Wilsonianism—the name scholars have given to the body of ideas Wilson espoused—consisted of traditional American diplomatic principles, to which Wilson eloquently gave coherence and currency. His ideal world was to be open in every sense of the word: no barriers to commerce, no impediments to democratic politics, no secret diplomatic deals. Empires were to be opened up in keeping with the principle of self-determination, and armaments were to be reduced. Wilson envisioned free-market, nonexploitative capitalism and political constitutionalism for all nations, to ensure the good society and world peace. His critics complained that Wilson often violated his own tenets in his eagerness to force them upon others.

Wilsonianism

Wilson also articulated the traditional belief in American exceptionalism. America, he believed, had a mission to reform international relations and other societies. American progressivism was to be projected onto the world. "We created this Nation," he intoned, "not to serve ourselves, but to serve mankind." Wilson's missionary zeal blended with a pragmatism that bespoke his understanding of the balance of world power and the intertwining of the American economy with the economies of other countries. His inheritance was the expansionism that characterized American foreign policy before the First World War. And he shared with his predecessors the belief that even unsavory methods—such as military intervention—were sometimes necessary to protect American interests.

To say that American neutrality was never a real possibility, given ethnic loyalties, economic ties, and Wilsonian preferences, is not to say that Wilson sought to enter the war. He emphatically wanted to keep the United States out of the military conflict, and in fact did so for two and a half years. Time and again, Wilson tried to mediate the crisis; he did not wish for one power to crush the other. The president remarked in early 1917 that "we are the only one of the great white nations that is free from war today, and it would be a crime against civilization for us to go in." But go in the United States finally did.

Americans got caught in the Allied–Central Power crossfire. British naval policy was designed to sever neutral trade with Germany in order to cripple the German economy. The British, **British Naval Policy** "ruling the waves and waiving the rules," declared a loose, ineffective, and hence illegal blockade; defined a broad list of contraband (including foodstuffs) which was not supposed to be shipped to Germany by neutrals; mined the North Sea; and harassed neutral shipping by seizing cargoes. American vessels bearing goods for Germany seldom reached their destination. To counter German submarines, the British flouted international law by arming their merchant ships and flying neutral (sometimes American) flags. Wilson frequently protested British violations of neutral rights, pointing out that neutrals had the right to sell and ship noncontraband goods to belligerents without interference. But London often deftly defused American criticism by paying for confiscated cargoes. More than once provocative German actions made British behavior seem comparatively mild or inconsequential.

Germany was determined to lift the injurious blockade and to end American-Allied commerce. Unable to win the war on land, German leaders looked for victory at sea. These ambitious tasks were assigned to the submarine. In February 1915 Berlin announced that it was creating a war zone around the British Isles. All enemy ships in the area would be sunk; neutral vessels were warned to stay out so as not to be attacked by mistake; and passengers from neutral nations like the United States were warned to stay off enemy ships. Writing diplomatic messages on his own typewriter, President Wilson stiffly informed Germany that the United States was holding it to "strict accountability" for any losses of American life and property.

Wilson was interpreting existing international law in the strictest sense. Such law held that an attacker **The Submarine and International Law** had to warn a passenger or merchant ship before attacking, so that passengers and crew could disembark into lifeboats for safety. That rule predated the development of the submarine as a major weapon, but Wilson refused to adjust tradition. The Germans thought him unfair. As they saw it, the slender, frail, and sluggish *unterseebooten* could not surface to warn ships of their imminent destruction: surfacing would deny the U-boats the advantage of surprise. A surfaced submarine was also a sitting target for a British deck gun or hand grenade, and British vessels had standing orders to ram U-boats and sink them. Finally, the time required to evacuate passengers usually gave the distressed ship adequate opportunity to radio for help to a British destroyer in nearby waters. Berlin frequently complained to Wilson that he was denying the Germans the one weapon they could use to break the British economic stranglehold, disrupt the Allies' substantial connection with American producers and bankers, and win the war. To all concerned—British, Germans, and Americans—this naval warfare seemed a matter of life and death, a vital question of national survival.

FROM THE *LUSITANIA* TO WAR

Over the next few months the U-boats sank ship after ship. Then the sinking of the *Lusitania* forced the submarine issue for Wilson. The swift British passenger liner had few rivals for luxurious accommodations. When it left New York City on May 1, 1915, with over twelve hundred passengers, it was carrying a cargo of foodstuffs and contraband, including 4.2 million rounds of ammunition for Remington rifles. Before "Lucy's" departure, the newspapers carried an unusual announcement from the German embassy: travelers on British vessels were warned that a war zone existed and that Allied ships in those waters "are liable to destruction." Few passengers paid attention to the notice; few shifted to an American vessel for the transatlantic trip. On May 7, off the Irish coast, U-20 unleashed torpedoes at the four-stacked vessel. The *Lusitania* exploded, quickly capsized, and carried 1,198 people to their deaths. One hundred twenty-eight Americans died.

Even if the ship carried armaments, argued Wilson, the sinking was a brutal assault on innocent people.

Reaction to the Sinking of the *Lusitania*

But he ruled out a military response. Secretary of State William Jennings Bryan advised that Americans not be permitted to travel on belligerent ships and that passenger vessels not be allowed to carry war goods. "Germany has a right to prevent contraband going to the Allies," wrote Bryan, "and a ship carrying contraband should not rely on passengers to protect her from attack—it would be like putting women and children in front of an army." Bryan also urged that simultaneous protest notes be sent to London and Berlin.

Wilson moved deliberately. He rejected Bryan's counsel, as well as that of Theodore Roosevelt and others who clamored for war. Instead he sent a note to Berlin insisting on the right of Americans to sail on belligerent ships and demanding that Germany cease its inhumane submarine warfare. "Weasel words" from "the word-lover in the White House," shouted Roosevelt. The Germans were not contrite; they asked Wilson to rethink the relationship between international law and the submarine. Wilson fumed. After a stormy White House meeting marked by Bryan's charge that the cabinet was pro-Allied, Wilson dispatched a second letter to Germany reiterating the demand that submarines be kept in port. When the president refused to ban American travelers from belligerent ships, Bryan resigned in protest—an uncommon act for secretaries of state, who usually resign quietly. The pro-Allied Robert Lansing was elevated to the top diplomatic post. For some Americans the *Lusitania* disaster became a rallying cry like the Alamo or the *Maine*. Certainly Wilson's attitude toward Germany hardened. To criticism that he was pursuing a double standard favoring the Allies, Wilson responded that the British were taking cargoes and violating property rights, but the Germans were taking lives and violating human rights.

Germany, seeking to avoid war with America, ordered its U-boat commanders to halt attacks on passenger liners. But in mid-August another British vessel, the *Arabic*, was sunk; two American lives were lost. The Germans hastened to pledge that never again would an unarmed passenger ship be attacked without warning. But the sinking of the *Arabic* fueled the debate over American passengers on belligerent vessels. Why not require Americans to sail on American craft? asked critics. From August 1914 to March 1917 only 3 Americans died on an American ship (the tanker *Gulflight* in May 1915), while about 190 were killed on belligerent ships.

In early 1916 the Gore-McLemore resolution, which would prohibit Americans from traveling on armed merchant vessels or ships carrying contraband, was introduced in Congress. The resolution, it was hoped, would prevent incidents like the *Lusitania* from hurtling the United States into war.

Gore-McLemore Resolution

But Wilson would tolerate no interference in the presidential making of foreign policy (he had just sent Colonel House to Europe to mediate) and no restrictions on American travel. The resolution, he argued, would destroy the "whole fine fabric of international law." After heavy politicking, the House defeated the resolution 276 to 142 and the Senate followed suit 68 to 14. If America's goal was to avoid entry into the First World War, Wilson's critics have pointed out, passage of the Gore-McLemore resolution would have avoided or at least delayed a German-American confrontation over the submarine without undercutting American interests or besmirching national honor.

In March 1916 an attack on the *Sussex*, a French vessel crossing the English Channel, took the United States a step closer to war. Four Americans on that ship, which the U-boat commander mistook for a minelayer, were injured. Stop the marauding submarines, Wilson lectured Berlin, or he would sever diplomatic relations. Again the Germans backed off, pledging not to attack merchant vessels without warning. About the same time, relations with Britain soured. The British crushing of the Irish Easter Rebellion and further restriction of American trade with the Central Powers aroused American ire.

Sentiment for peace remained strong, as evidenced by Wilson's victory on a peace platform in the 1916 election. After his triumph, Wilson futilely labored once again to bring the belligerents to the conference table. In early 1917 he advised them to temper their acquisitive war aims, appealing for a "peace without victory."

In early February 1917, Germany startled the Wilson administration by launching unrestricted submarine warfare. All vessels, belligerent or neutral, warship or merchant, would be attacked if sighted in the declared war zone. This bold decision, reached after extensive debate within the German government, represented a calculated risk that submarines could impede the valuable munitions shipments from America to England and thus defeat the Allies before Americans could be mobilized and ferried across the Atlantic to enter the fight. Wilson quickly broke diplomatic relations with Berlin. Everybody waited for the inevitable collision.

With this German challenge to American neutral rights and economic interests came a German threat to American security. In late February, the British **Zimmermann** intercepted, decoded, and handed **Telegram** to the American government a telegram addressed to the German minister in Mexico from Foreign Secretary Arthur Zimmermann. The minister was instructed to tell the Mexican government that if it joined a military alliance against the United States, Germany would help Mexico to recover the territories it was forced to give up to its northern neighbor in 1848. Zimmermann hoped, as he expressed it to other German officials, to "*set new enemies on America's neck*—enemies which give them plenty to take care of over there."

American officials took the message seriously, since at the time Mexican-American relations were extremely tense. The Mexican Revolution, a bloody civil war with strong anti-American overtones, had spilled across the Rio Grande, and the Mexican government was threatening to nationalize American properties. Wilson had twice ordered American troops onto Mexican soil: in 1914 at Veracruz, to avenge a slight to the American uniform and flag; and again in 1916 in northern Mexico, where General John J. Pershing spent months trying to capture the elusive Pancho Villa after his raid on an American border town. Lansing and Wilson agreed that Zimmermann's telegram constituted "a conspiracy against this country."

Soon after learning of Zimmermann's ploy, Wilson asked Congress for "armed neutrality" to defend American lives and commerce. Specifically he requested the authority to arm American merchant ships, and more generally the power to "employ any other instrumentalities or methods that may be nec-

The cartoonist William A. Rogers of the New York Herald reacted to the German declaration of unrestricted submarine warfare with this drawing. Like many Americans, Rogers saw the Germans as conniving, heartless pirates of the high seas who cared little for the rights of neutrals or human life. Library of Congress.

essary." In the midst of the debate, Wilson released Zimmermann's telegram to the press; the nation was stunned. Still, antiwar Senators Robert M. La Follette and George Norris, among others, saw the armed-ship bill as a blank check for the president to move the country to war and filibustered it to death. Wilson, angrily labeling them a "little group of willful men," proceeded to arm America's commercial vessels anyway. The action came too late to prevent the sinking of several American ships. War cries echoed across the nation. In late March, after a good deal of personal agony and seclusion, Wilson called Congress into special session.

On April 2, 1917, the president stepped before a hushed Congress. Solemnly he chided the Germans

Jeannette Rankin (1880–1973), the first woman to sit in the House of Representatives and the only member of Congress to vote against American entry into both world wars, shown shortly after her election. Elected in 1916, she was defeated in 1918, but ran successfully again in 1940. Born in Montana, Rankin became a social worker, woman's suffrage activist, and devout pacifist.   UPI/Bettmann Newsphotos.

Declaration of War

for "warfare against mankind." Passionately and eloquently Wilson explained American grievances: Germany's violation of the principle of freedom of the seas, disruption of American commerce, attempt to stir up trouble in Mexico, and violation of human rights by killing innocent Americans. The "Prussian autocracy" had to be punished by the "democracies." Russia was now among the latter, he was pleased to report, because the Russian Revolution had ousted the czar just weeks before. Wilson's most famous words rang out: "The world must be made safe for democracy." Congress quickly declared war against Germany, by a vote of 373 to 50 in the House and 82 to 6 in the Senate. The first woman ever to sit in Congress, Montana's Jeannette Rankin, elected in 1916, cast a ringing "no" vote that won her high ranking in the pantheon of American pacifism. "Peace is a woman's job," she believed, "because men have a natural fear of being classed as cowards if they oppose war" and because mothers should protect their children from death-dealing weapons.

For principle, for morality, for honor, for commerce, for security—for all these reasons the United States took up arms against Germany. The submarine was certainly the culprit that drew a reluctant president and nation into the maelstrom. Yet critics like Bryan, Gore, McLemore, La Follette, and Rankin did not think that the U-boat alone was responsible for the American descent into war. They emphasized Wilson's rigid definition of international law, which did not take account of the submarine's tactics. They faulted his contention that Americans could travel anywhere, even on a belligerent ship loaded with contraband, in time of war. But they lost the debate. Although Americans might agree that Wilson's decisions were anti-German, they seemed to accept his view that the Germans had to be checked to ensure an open and orderly world in which American principles and interests would be safe.

In the most general sense, America went to war to reform world politics, not to destroy Germany. That is, by early 1917 Wilson seemed to believe that America could not claim a seat at the peace conference unless it became a combatant. At such a conference, Wilson intended to put into constitutional form the principles he thought essential to a stable world order, to promote democracy and the Open Door, and to outlaw revolution and aggression. If he remained the representative of a neutral nation, he could only "call through a crack in the door" at the postwar peace conference. In the end, Woodrow Wilson decided for war to gain an American-fashioned peace.

TAKING UP ARMS

Even before the war decision, the United States had been preparing for combat. Encouraged by such groups as the National Security League and the Navy League, and by mounting public outrage against Germany's submarine warfare, the president in 1915 began to plan a substantial military buildup. As the debate over preparedness swirled about the nation's capital, Wilson took a new bride, the widowed Edith Bolling Galt, and went on a two-week honeymoon. When the Wilsons returned in early 1916, Senator La Follette and House Majority Leader Claude Kitchin, among others, vowed to block preparedness. Some pacifist progressives, like Jane Addams, Paul Kellogg, and Lillian Wald, had organized in late 1915 an antiwar coalition, the American Union Against Militarism. Addams and suffragist Carrie Chapman Catt founded the Women's Peace party. The businessman Andrew Carnegie, who in 1910 had established the Carnegie Endowment for International Peace with $10 million in U.S. Steel bonds, helped to finance the peace groups. So did Henry Ford, who spent half a million dollars in late 1915 to send a "peace ship" to Europe to propagandize for a negotiated settlement. Socialists like Eugene Debs added their voices to the peace movement.

The various messages of these antiwar advocates were that war drained a nation of its youth, resources, and impulse for reform; that it fostered a repressive spirit at home; that it violated Christian morality; and that wartime business barons reaped huge profits at the expense of the people. Furthermore, Europe's Great War was self-serving. The

Antiwar Sentiment

very outbreak of the war, they argued, proved that an increase in armaments, such as occurred in Europe before the war, only precipitated hostilities. Militarism and conscription, Addams pointed out, were what millions of immigrants had left behind in Europe. Were they now—in the United States—to be forced into the decadent system they had escaped?

But the peace movement was splintered, some of its followers endorsing peace but not pacifism, and it could not prevent passage of the National Defense Act of 1916. This legislation provided for increases in the army and National Guard and for summer training camps modeled on the one in Plattsburg, New York, where a slice of America's social and economic elite had trained in 1915 as "citizen soldiers." The Navy Act, providing for a three-year naval expansion program, soon followed. To pay part of the huge cost of these undertakings, Congress passed the Revenue Act in 1916. Backers of the bill believed that businesspeople should pour back into the national treasury a portion of the profits they were sure to derive from the new defense contracts. The act, which antipreparedness people applauded, raised the surtax on high incomes and corporate profits, imposed a federal tax on large estates, and significantly increased the tax on the gross receipts of munitions manufacturers.

To raise an army after the declaration of war, Congress in 1917 passed the Selective Service Act, requiring the registration of all males between the ages of twenty and thirty (later changed to eighteen and forty-five). National service, proponents believed, would not only prepare the nation for battle but also promote efficiency, order, democracy, personal sacrifice, and nationalism, and, as one general put it, "heat up the melting pot." Where else but in an army tent could a Boston Brahmin, a butcher, a college student, a dairy farmer, and the son of a washerwoman be brought together? Critics, on the other hand, feared that "Prussianism," not democratization, would instead be the likely outcome.

Raising an Army

On June 5, 1917, over 9.5 million men signed up for the "great national lottery." By war's end, 24 million men had been registered by local draft boards. Over 4.8 million served in the armed forces, 2 million

GEE !!
I WISH I WERE
A MAN

I'd JOIN
The NAVY

Howard Chandler Christy

BE A MAN AND DO IT
UNITED STATES NAVY
RECRUITING STATION

Government posters became a popular medium to rally Americans to the armed forces and domestic mobilization. In this poster, the artist Howard Chandler Christy uses the traditional theme of war as masculine enterprise to recruit sailors. National Archives.

of whom fought in France. About 16 percent of the male labor force was drawn into military service; millions of laborers received deferments from military duty because they worked in war industries or had personal dependents. Over 300,000 men evaded the draft by failing to show up when called, and 4,000 were classified as conscientious objectors (many more applied for that classification but failed or changed their minds after induction).

Hundreds of thousands of citizens volunteered to the sound of the popular song "Johnny Get Your Gun." Asked why he joined the army, one soldier replied that he was eager "to see a little of the biggest scrap the world has ever known." Other volunteers gave different answers: "Girls like soldiers," they

wanted to become men, they were homeless, they wanted to "kick the Kaiser." The typical soldier was a draftee between twenty-one and twenty-three years old, white, single, and poorly educated (most had not attended high school). Perhaps as many as 18 percent were foreign-born, and 400,000 were black. Some women became navy clerks; others served in the U.S. Army Signal Corps and Nurse Corps. On college campuses, 150,000 students entered the Student Army Training Corps or similar navy and marine units.

Camp life sapped the fresh recruits of some of their enthusiasm for war. They put in seventeen-hour days. Calisthenics, kitchen duty, target practice, grounds maintenance ("policing the area"), and bayonet drills consumed their regimented time. They ate well but slept on straw mattresses and marched around uncomfortably in olive-drab uniforms and leggings. There were never enough weapons to go around, so some trained without. At officer training camps, the army turned out "ninety-day wonders." Although some soldiers imbibed Wilson's idealism, others were ignorant of the reasons they were going to war. This ignorance of purpose so alarmed Wilson administration officials that they put a copy of the president's war message in every knapsack.

President Wilson, Secretary of War Newton D. Baker, and General John J. "Black Jack" Pershing (head of the American Expeditionary Force) all worried that the young soldiers, once away from their home environments, would turn to vice—especially prostitutes and liquor. They were right. To protect the supposed novices with social armor, the government created the Commission on Training Camp Activities to coordinate the work of the YMCA, the Knights of Columbus, the Salvation Army, the Red Cross, and the Jewish Welfare Board, among others. These organizations dispensed food and provided movies and vaudeville. Athletic contests also kept the soldiers busy, as did the American Library Association's in-camp book depositories. The commission declared five-mile "sin-free" zones around military bases. "Short-arm" inspections became daily routine and prophylactics were distributed to combat venereal disease. Men in uniform were not permitted to drink. "Men must live straight if they would shoot straight," said Secretary of the Navy Josephus Daniels.

Like most black troops in the First World War, these soldiers were assigned to non-combat tasks—here the assembling of coffins in France. Ironically the United States sent a segregated army abroad so that the world, to use President Wilson's words, could be made "safe for democracy." National Archives.

In 1918 a worldwide flu epidemic struck the United States, killing at least 550,000 people. The flu spread quickly to the army. At one time or another during the war, at least one-quarter of the army had influenza. Soldiers had to be quarantined, and training suffered badly. A total of 62,000 soldiers and sailors died of disease during the war, about 52,000 of them from influenza and pneumonia. By comparison, 51,000 lost their lives in battle.

Jim Crow was in the army too. Fearing "arrogant, strutting representatives of black soldiery in every community," as Senator James K. Vardaman of Mis-

sissippi snarled, many southern politicians opposed the drafting of blacks. But the army needed men, white and black. The NAACP and W.E.B. Du Bois urged blacks to join the fight for "world liberty," optimistically thinking that a war to make the world safe for democracy would blur the color line at home. They were greatly disappointed. Military leaders segregated facilities, discouraged blacks from becoming officers, and assigned black recruits to menial labor. Ugly racial slurs echoed through the camps. In Houston, Texas, angry black soldiers

Segregation in the Army

An American soldier of Company K, 110th Infantry Regiment, receives first aid during fighting at Verennes, France. National Archives.

responded to goading from whites by seizing arms and killing thirteen of them. Official white retaliation was immediate and excessive. After brief "trials," thirteen blacks were executed; another six were hanged after an unsuccessful appeal of their death sentences; others were court-martialed and given long prison terms.

In Europe, Pershing wisely refused to submerge American troops in Allied units (officially the United States declared itself an Associated power). Allied commanders had wedded themselves to unimaginative and deadly trench warfare, producing military stalemate and ghastly casualties. Zig-zag trenches fronted by barbed wire and mines stretched across France. Beyond the muddy and stinking trenches lay "no man's land," denuded by artillery fire. When ordered out, soldiers would charge the German lines, also a maze of trenches. Machine guns mowed them down; chlorine gas, first used by Germany in 1915, poisoned them. And so little was gained. At the Battle of the Somme in 1916 the British and French suffered 600,000 dead or wounded to earn only 125 square miles (the Germans lost 500,000 men). Pershing would not commit his clean, fresh "doughboys" to this death-dealing type of warfare.

Firsthand war, the soldiers soon learned, was quite

different from the abstract slogans spoken at home to glorify American participation. They came to know the muck and stink of trench warfare and the horrors of poison gas. Over 230,000 were wounded, and many suffered battle shock: violent tremors, dazed eyes, listless arms and legs. By today's standards army medicine and psychiatry were primitive. Away from the front lines, Red Cross canteens, staffed by women volunteers, served the soldiers as way stations in a strange land, offering haircuts, food, and recreation. American troops might even have met some American literary figures. Early in the war e e cummings, John Dos Passos, Ernest Hemingway, and others had volunteered for ambulance service in Allied countries because they thought it a humane thing to do. But another motive drove them, too, as Dos Passos explained candidly: "What was war like? We wanted to see with our own eyes. . . . I wanted to see the show."

For some young warriors, "the show" played in cafes and brothels—just as officials had feared. It was a common saying in Paris that the British were drunkards, the French whoremongers, and the Americans were both. Despite Pershing's lecture that "sexual intercourse is not necessary for good health, and complete continence is wholly possible," soldiers indulged. Venereal disease became a serious problem. At one point, French Prime Minister Georges Clemenceau offered licensed, supposedly health-inspected prostitutes to the American army. When the generous Gallic offer was received in Washington, Secretary Baker gasped, "For god's sake . . . don't show this to the President or he'll stop the war." Frequent health checks, prophylactics, medical attention, and the threat of court-martial for infected soldiers helped reduce the disease rate.

The influx of American men and material decided the outcome of the First World War. With both sides virtually exhausted, the Americans tipped the balance toward the Allies. Actually the inexperienced Americans did not engage in much combat until after the lull of the severe winter of 1917 and 1918. Then in the spring, after knocking Russia out of the war and closing the eastern front, the Germans launched a major offensive. Kaiser Wilhelm's forces got within

Americans in Combat in France

fifty miles of Paris; American troops helped to blunt their advance at Château-Thierry. In June the U.S. 2nd Division recaptured Belleau Wood; then followed battles at Cantigny, the Marne, the Somme, and St. Mihiel (see map, page 660). In September over 1 million Americans joined British and French troops in the Allied offensive that pushed the Germans back. Its submarine warfare a dismal failure, its ground war a shambles, its troops and cities mutinous, abandoned by Turkey and Austria, Germany sued for peace. The armistice was signed on November 11, 1918.

The armistice was Wilsonian. That is, the president insisted that his Fourteen Points, which he had enunciated in January, be made the general terms for peace negotiations. The Allies balked, but Wilson scared them into acceptance by threatening a separate peace with Germany. The Fourteen Points were a summary of Wilsonianism. The first five called for diplomacy in the "public view," freedom of the seas, lower tariffs, reductions in armaments, and the decolonization of empires. Points 6 through 13 appealed for self-determination for national groups in Europe. For Wilson the last point was the most essential, the vehicle for achieving all the others: "a general association of nations" or League of Nations. Having won the war, the resolute Wilson set out to win the peace.

THE HOME FRONT

"It is not an army that we must shape and train for war," declared the president, "it is a nation." The United States was a belligerent for only nineteen months, but the impact of the war on domestic America was conspicuous. In that comparatively short period the national government quickly geared the economy to war needs and marshaled public opinion for the sacrifices and adjustments belligerency imposed. As never before, the state intervened in American life. An unprecedented concentration of bureaucratic power developed in Washington, D.C. To progressives

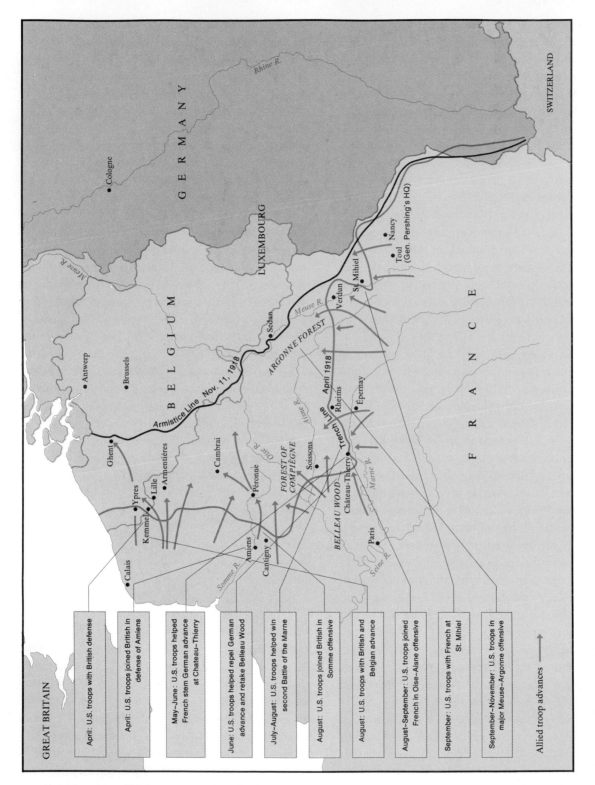

GREAT BRITAIN

GERMANY

Rhine R.

• Cologne

LUXEMBOURG

Meuse R.

• Nancy
(Gen. Pershing's HQ)

• Toul

St. Mihiel

Verdun •

FRANCE

Sedan •

ARGONNE FOREST

Meuse R.

April 1918

Armistice Line Nov. 11, 1918

BELGIUM

• Antwerp

• Brussels

Aisne R.

Rheims •

• Épernay

Ghent •

Cambrai •

Oise R.

FOREST OF
COMPIÈGNE

Soissons •

Trench Line

Marne R.

Ypres •

Lille •

Armentières •

Péronne •

BELLEAU WOOD

Château-Thierry •

Kemmel •

Amiens •

Cantigny •

Paris •

Calais •

Somme R.

Seine R.

April: U.S. troops with British defense

April: U.S. troops joined British in defense of Amiens

May–June: U.S. troops helped French stem German advance at Château–Thierry

June: U.S. troops helped repel German advance and retake Belleau Wood

July–August: U.S. troops helped win second Battle of the Marne

August: U.S. troops joined British in Somme offensive

August: U.S. troops with British and Belgian advance

August–September: U.S. troops joined French in Oise–Aisne offensive

September: U.S. troops with French at St. Mihiel

September–November: U.S. troops in major Meuse–Argonne offensive

→ Allied troop advances

SWITZERLAND

American Troops at the Front, 1918

of the New Nationalist persuasion, the expansion and centralization of governmental power were welcome. To others they seemed an excessive and dangerous development. "War is the health of the state," said radical intellectual Randolph Bourne.

The federal government and private business became partners during the war. Dollar-a-year executives flocked to the nation's capital from major companies; they retained their corporate salaries while serving in administrative and consulting capacities. Early in the war, the government relied on several industrial committees for advice on purchases and prices. But evidence of self-interested businesspeople cashing in on the national interest aroused public protest. The chief of the aluminum advisory committee, for example, was also president of the largest aluminum company in America. The committees were disbanded in July 1917 in favor of the War Industries Board (WIB). The government continued, however, to work closely with business through trade associations, which grew significantly in number. Business-government cooperation was also stimulated by the suspension of antitrust laws; by cost-plus contracts, which guaranteed companies a healthy profit and a means to pay higher wages to head off labor strikes; by the Webb-Pomerene Act (1918), which granted immunity from antitrust legislation to companies that combined to operate in the export trade; by the virtual abandonment of competitive bidding; and by a floor placed under prices to ensure profits.

Business-Government Cooperation

Hundreds of new government agencies, staffed largely by businesspeople, came into being to wage the war. Some of the superagencies placed unprecedented controls on the economy. The Food Administration, led by Herbert Hoover, undertook programs to improve production and conserve food through voluntary action; it also set prices and regulated distribution. Americans were urged to grow "victory gardens" in their backyards and to eat meatless and wheatless meals. The Railroad Administration took over the snarled and financially troubled railway industry. When strikes threatened the telephone and telegraph companies, the federal government seized and ran them.

The largest and potentially most powerful of the wartime agencies was the War Industries Board. Designed as a clearinghouse to coordinate the national economy and headed after early 1918 by millionaire financier Bernard Baruch, the WIB faced the enormous task of satisfying both Allied and domestic needs. It made purchases, allocated supplies, and fixed prices. This usually meant satisfying business requests for price increases. The WIB ordered the standardization of goods to save materials and streamline production. The number of colors of typewriter ribbon, for example, was reduced from 150 to 5. Although the WIB seemed all-powerful, in reality it had to conciliate competing interest groups and compromise with the businesspeople whose advice it so valued.

The performance of the mobilized economy was mixed, but it delivered enough men and materiel to France to ensure the defeat of the Central Powers. About a quarter of all American production was diverted to war needs. Farmers enjoyed boom years as they put more acreage into production and watched prices go up. Induced to produce more at a faster pace, farmers mechanized as never before. From 1915 to 1920 the number of tractors in American fields jumped tenfold. Gross farm income for the period from 1914 to 1919 increased from $7.6 billion to $17.7 billion. Although manufacturing output leveled off in 1918, some industries enjoyed substantial increases because of wartime demand. Steel reached a peak production of 45 million tons in 1917, twice the prewar figure. The cigarette industry profited from the marked wartime increase in the consumption of tobacco, from 26 billion cigarettes in 1916 to 48 billion in 1918. The gross national product in 1920 was 237 percent higher than in 1914.

Massive assignments had to be completed in a hurry, and there were mistakes. Weapons deliveries fell short of demand; the bloated bureaucracy of the War Shipping Board failed to build enough ships. And the severe winter of 1917 and 1918 was a near-disaster for the nation. As the mercury dipped, millions of Americans found that they could not get coal, because the coal companies had held back on production to raise prices and railroads did not have enough coal cars. Harbors froze, closing out coal barges, and the federal government seemed immobilized. People died of pneumonia or freezing: a Brooklyn man went out in the morning to forage for coal and returned to find his two-month-old daughter frozen to death in her crib. In January, blizzards shut down midwestern railroads and factories, impeding the war effort.

If the fuel crisis could be blamed on the weather, inflation was directly attributable to governmental policy. Although inflation was partly caused by demand exceeding supply, due to increases in Allied buying, the government's liberal credit policies and fixing of prices at high levels also encouraged it. As a result, the wholesale price index was 98 percent higher in 1918 than it had been in 1913. By fixing prices on raw materials rather than finished products, the government lost control of inflation. By bowing to the political pressure of southerners who wanted cotton left unregulated, the government permitted runaway cotton prices. Clothing tripled in cost and food prices more than doubled. A quart of milk that cost 9 cents in 1914 had climbed to 17 cents by 1920.

Inflation and Tax Policy

Tax policies during the war months were designed to pull some of the profits reaped from high prices back into the treasury. The Wilson administration believed that wealth as well as labor should be conscripted. Still, the government financed only one-third of the war through taxes. The other two-thirds came from loans, including Liberty Bonds sold to the American people through aggressive campaigns. The War Revenue Act of October 1917 provided for a graduated personal income tax, a corporate income tax, an excess profits tax, and increased excise taxes on alcoholic beverages, tobacco, and luxury items. Although these taxes did curb excessive corporate profiteering, they had several loopholes. Sometimes companies inflated costs to conceal profits or paid high salaries and bonuses to their executives. Four officers of Bethlehem Steel, for example, divided bonuses of $2.3 million in 1917 and $2.1 million the next year. Corporate net earnings for 1913 totaled $4 billion; in 1917 they had risen to $7 billion; and in 1918, after the tax bite and the war's end, they still stood at $4.5 billion. Patriotism and profits had to be partners, the federal government believed, in order for the United States to win the war.

Organized labor sought a partnership with government too, but its gains were far less spectacular.

For unions the war seemed to offer opportunities for recognition and better pay. Samuel Gompers, president of the AFL, threw his loyalty to the Wilson administration, promising to deter strikes. He and other moderate labor leaders were rewarded with appointments to high-level wartime government agencies. The National War Labor Board, created to mediate labor disputes, ruled out strikes and lockouts but fostered the eight-hour day and guaranteed workers the right to organize for collective bargaining. Unionization moved at a fast pace; from roughly 2.7 million in 1916, union membership climbed to over 4 million in 1919. The AFL could not curb strikes by the radical Industrial Workers of the World (IWW) or rebellious AFL locals, especially those with a high proportion of antiwar socialists as members. In the nineteen war months, over six thousand strikes expressed workers' discontent with their wages, working conditions, and inflation. There were some gains: the eight-hour day and forty-eight-hour week became more common, and some companies improved the workers' welfare by installing bathrooms, providing rest periods, and initiating insurance programs. Given the high cost of living, however, workers' earnings rose only slightly.

Wartime Labor Relations

When 16 percent of the male work force trooped off to battle, and when immigration dropped off and some aliens sailed off to fight for their homelands, depriving business of much-needed labor, the call went out to women, blacks, and Mexican-Americans to fill the vacancies. Munitions makers in Bridgeport, Connecticut, for example, dropped leaflets from airplanes urging women to work in their factories. Though the number of women in the work force increased slightly, the real story was that many shifted from one job to another, sometimes into formerly male domains. Some white women left domestic service for factories, moved from clerking in department stores to stenography and typing, and departed textile mills for employment in firearms plants. Twenty percent or more of all workers in the wartime manufacture of electrical machinery, airplanes, and food were women. As white women took advantage of the new opportunities, black women took some of their places in domestic service and in textile factories. For the

Women in the Work Force

Goggled women workers, hired by the Bethlehem Steel Corporation to replace men gone to war, tend their machines. Bethlehem Steel Corporation.

first time department stores employed black women as elevator operators and cafeteria waitresses, though they favored light-skinned blacks for these highly visible positions. Overall, most working women remained concentrated in sex-segregated occupations ("women's jobs") as typists, nurses, teachers, and domestic servants.

The movement of women into jobs that had been the preserve of males generated controversy. Male workers complained that women were destabilizing the work environment with their higher productivity; women answered that they were used to seasonal employment and piecework and hence worked at a

faster pace. Men protested that women were undermining the wage system by working for lower pay; women pointed out that male-dominated companies discriminated against them and unions denied them membership. Finally, male employees resented the spirit of independence evident among women whose labor was now greatly valued. The female workers in a Vermont machine-tool company addressed a crude poem to their harping male cohorts:

We're independent now you see,
Your bald head don't appeal to me,
I love my overalls;

And I would rather polish steel
Than get you up a tasty meal.
Or go with you to balls.
Now, only premiums good and big,
Will tempt us maids to change our rig.
And put our aprons on;
And cook up all the dainty things,
That so delighted men and kings
In days now past and gone.[1]

When the war was over, the gains women made were largely reversed. The attitude that women's proper sphere was the home changed very little. Married working women found their family relationships growing tense; husbands and children resented the disruption of home life. Moreover, reformers complained that working mothers were neglecting their children: keeping older siblings home from school to care for younger ones; leaving their children with neighbors; failing to prepare good meals; and coming home so tired that their housework suffered. Day nurseries were scarce and beyond the means of most working-class families, and few employers provided child-care facilities. Whether married or single—and the great majority of working women were unmarried—they lost their jobs to the returning veterans. "During the war they called us heroines," cried Mary McDowell of the University of Chicago Settlement, "but they throw us on the scrapheap now."

Women who did not join the work force participated in the war effort in other ways. As volunteers they made clothing for refugees and soldiers, rolled bandages, served at Red Cross facilities, and taught French to nurses assigned to the war zone. Many joined the state-level activities of the Women's Committee of the Council of National Defense, whose leaders included Ida Tarbell and Carrie Chapman Catt. This vast network publicized government programs, encouraged home gardens, sponsored drives to sell Liberty Bonds, and continued the push for many social welfare reforms.

Wartime mobilization wrought significant changes for the black community. Wartime jobs in the North provided an escape from southern lynchings, political disenfranchisement, low wages, sharecropping, ten-

---

[1]From the *Springfield Reporter*, December 5, 1917. Reprinted by permission.

Black Migration to the North

ancy, crop liens, floods, and boll-weevil-stricken cotton crops. During the war years, southern blacks undertook a great migration to northern cities to work in railroad yards, packing houses, steel mills, shipyards, and coal mines. In the decade from 1910 to 1920, Cleveland's black population swelled by over 300 percent, Detroit's by over 600 percent, and Chicago's by 150 percent, much of the increase occurring between 1916 and 1919. All told, about a half-million black Americans uprooted themselves to move north. Most were young (twenty to twenty-four years old), skilled or semiskilled, unmarried males seeking economic opportunity. One black man explained in a letter to a friend in Mississippi why he found the North attractive: "I should have been here twenty years ago. I just begin to feel like a man. It's a great deal of pleasure in knowing that you have got some privileges. My children are going to the same school with the whites and I don't have to humble to no one. I have registered. Will vote the next election."

New jobs and improved opportunities could not erase the fact that blacks, North and South, continued to be a minority in a white society. When the United States entered the First World War, there was not one black judge in the entire country and segregation was social custom. The Ku Klux Klan began to revive and racist films like D. W. Griffith's *The Birth of a Nation* (1915) further fed prejudice. Lynching statistics exposed the wide gap between American declarations of humanity in the war and the American practice of inhumanity at home: between 1914 and 1920, 382 blacks were lynched, some of them in military uniform.

Northern whites who resented the "Negro invasion" vented their anger in riots. In East St. Louis, Illinois, in 1917, whites opposed to black employment in a defense plant rampaged through the streets; forty blacks and nine whites lost their lives. In the bloody "Red Summer" of 1919, race riots rocked two dozen cities and towns. The worst race war occurred in Chicago, a favorite destination for migrating blacks. In the very hot days of July 1919, a black youth swimming at a segregated white beach was hit by a thrown rock and drowned. Rumors spread, tempers flared, and soon blacks and whites were battling one another. Stabbings, burnings, and shootings went on for days until state police restored some calm. Thirty-eight

Race Riots

Chapter 23: AMERICA AT WAR, 1914–1920

people died—fifteen whites and twenty-three blacks; over five hundred others were injured.

For some white Americans, this sad record meant that the nation should direct its missionary zeal at the reform not of foreign societies but of its own. Some black leaders spoke out similarly hinting at more militancy than Booker T. Washington, who died in 1915, would have countenanced. Insisting on equality and an end to segregation, W. E. B. Du Bois vowed a struggle: "We return. We return from fighting. We return fighting." The black poet Claude McKay of New York expressed in 1919 a self-assertion and self-defense that prefigured later black protest:

If we must die—let it not be like hogs
Hunted and penned in an inglorious spot,
While round us bark the mad and hungry gods,
Making their mock at our accursed lot.

. . .

Like men we'll face the murderous, cowardly pack,
Pressed to the wall, dying but fighting back![1]

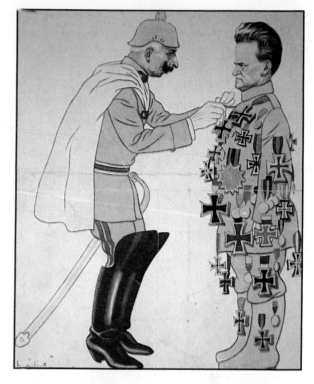

For his opposition to American participation in the First World War, Senator Robert La Follette (1855–1925) was cruelly misrepresented as a traitor. In this cartoon from Life magazine he is decorated by the German Kaiser. La Follette believed a majority of Americans, if given the opportunity in a referendum, would vote his way on the war. "The poor . . . who are the ones called upon to rot in the trenches, have no organized power," he once said. The State Historical Society of Wisconsin.

THE ATTACK ON CIVIL LIBERTIES

"Woe be to the man that seeks to stand in our way in this day of high resolution," warned President Wilson. Dissenters who questioned his war decision and the draft soon faced an official and unofficial campaign to silence them. Jingoists warped truth and incited violence, civil liberties were trampled, and an "Americanization" crusade cut a gaping wound in American democracy. The targets of abuse were the hundreds of thousands of Americans and aliens who refused to support the war: pacifists from all walks of life, conscientious objectors, socialists, the Industrial Workers of the World, the debt-ridden tenant farmers of Oklahoma who staged the Green Corn Rebellion against the draft, the Non-Partisan

[1]From Selected Poems of Claude McKay, Copyright 1981 and reprinted with the permission of Twayne Publishers, a division of G.K. Hall and Co., Boston.

League, reformers like Robert La Follette and Jane Addams, and countless others.

Shortly after the declaration of war in 1917, the president appointed George Creel, a progressive journalist, to head the Committee on Public Information. The CPI was a propaganda agency pure and simple. Employing some of the nation's most talented writers and scholars, the CPI set out to shape and mobilize public opinion by means of anti-German tracts; speeches by "four-minute men," who visited thousands of schools and churches; films like America's Answer (1918); and "self-censorship" of the press. The CPI encouraged people to spy on their neighbors and report any suspicious behavior. "Not a pin dropped in the home of any one with a foreign name," Creel claimed, "but that it rang like thunder on the inner ear of some listening sleuth." Exaggeration, fear-mongering, distortion, half-truths—such were the stuff of the CPI's "mind mobilization."

The Wilson administration also guided through an obliging Congress the Espionage Act (1917) and the Sedition Act (1918). The first statute forbade "false

Espionage and Sedition Acts

statements" designed to impede the draft or promote military insubordination and banned from the mails materials considered treasonous. The Sedition Act made it unlawful to obstruct the sale of war bonds and to use "disloyal, profane, scurrilous, or abusive" language against the government, the Constitution, the flag, and the military uniform. These loosely worded laws gave the government wide latitude to crack down on those with whom it differed. Fair-minded people could disagree over what constituted false or abusive language, but in the feverish home-front atmosphere of the First World War and under the threat of federal prosecution, the Justice Department's definition prevailed. Over two thousand people were prosecuted under the acts and many others were intimidated into silence.

Stories of arrests and an intellectual reign of terror began to fill the newspapers. Three Columbia University students were picked up in mid-1917 for circulating an antiwar petition. The liberal-left journal *The Masses* and Tom Watson's *The Jeffersonian* were denied use of the mails and forced to shut down. Jane Addams was put under Justice Department surveillance, causing her, by her own admission, to moderate her appeals for peace. The producer of *The Spirit of '76*, a film about the American Revolution complete with redcoats shooting minutemen, was given a ten-year prison sentence for, according to the judge, questioning the "good faith of our ally, Great Britain." In the summer of 1918, with a government stenographer present, Socialist party leader Eugene Debs delivered a ringing oration against the war and for free speech. He was given a ten-year sentence. Debs told the court what many dissenters—and later many jurists and scholars—thought of the Espionage Act: it was "a despotic enactment in flagrant conflict with democratic principles and with the spirit of free institutions." Debs remained in jail until late December 1921, when he received a pardon (see page 764).

State and local governments joined the campaign. Because towns had Liberty Bond quotas to fill, they sometimes threatened "slackers" into purchases through public humiliation. Officials banned what they considered "pro-German" books from public schools; the governor of Iowa prohibited the use of any language but English in schools and public places; and Pittsburgh banned Beethoven's music. Everywhere teachers who questioned the war faced dismissal by hostile school boards.

Across the nation, supporters of "Americanization" or "100% Americanism" exploited the emotional wartime atmosphere to urge or compel immigrants to throw off their Old World cultures. The director of the National Security League, conjuring up the image of a nation imperiled by its alien residents, declared that "in the bottom of the melting pot there lies heaps of unfused metal." To fuse a superpatriotic national unity, the CPI set up Loyalty Leagues in ethnic communities. Companies offered English-language and naturalization classes in their factories, and refused jobs and promotions to those who did not make adequate strides toward learning English. What began as education gave way to repression.

Encouraged by official behavior, groups like the American Protective League, the Sedition Slammers, and the American Defense Society took it upon themselves to cleanse the nation through vigilantism. German books were burned in Nebraska and a German-American miner in Illinois was wrapped in a flag and lynched. In Tulsa, a mob whipped IWW members and then poured tar into their bleeding sores. Nor were universities shelters for unorthodox ideas. In a celebrated case, antiwar Professor J. M. Cattell, a distinguished psychologist at Columbia University, was fired. His colleague Charles Beard, an historian with prowar views, resigned in protest: "If we have to suppress everything we don't like to hear, this country is resting on a pretty wobbly basis."

The point was just that: Wilson and his officers tried to crush what they did not like to hear. In particular, the administration concentrated on the

Persecution of Radicals

IWW and the Socialist party. The war emergency and the frank opposition of those two radical organizations gave progressives and conservatives alike an opportunity to throttle their political rivals. Standing for revolution against capitalism and often violent in its tactics, the IWW aroused bitter opposition (see pages 502, 592). Soon after the declaration of war, government agents raided union meetings and arrested IWW leaders. The army was sent into western mining and lumbering regions to put down IWW strikes on the pretense that they were pro-German. Under the immigration acts, alien members of the IWW were deported. Town after town evicted the "Wobblies," and by the end of the war most of the union's leaders were in jail. The Socialist party fared little better: others besides Debs were imprisoned. Although the new Civil Liberties Bureau (forerunner of the American Civil Liberties Union) defended many of the dissenters, it could not stop the rampant suppression. Even the head of the Bureau, Roger Baldwin, was jailed as a conscientious objector.

The Supreme Court, itself attuned to the pulse of the times, upheld the Espionage Act. Justice Oliver Wendell Holmes, in *Schenck* v. *U.S.* (1919), expressed the Court's unanimous opinion that in time of war the First Amendment could be restricted: "Free speech would not protect a man falsely shouting fire in a theater and causing panic." If words "are of such a nature as to create a clear and present danger that they will bring about the substantial evils that Congress has a right to prevent," Holmes went on, free speech could be limited. In another case, *Abrams* v. *U.S.* (1919), the Court voted 7 to 2 (with Holmes and Brandeis in the minority) that the Sedition Act was constitutional. This time Holmes, writing the minority opinion, expressed concern that the "free trade in ideas" was being jeopardized.

THE RED SCARE

The line between wartime suppression of dissent and the postwar Red Scare is not easily drawn. Both were directed against suspected internal enemies, both put on the mask of patriotism to harass radicals and deprive them of their constitutional rights, and both had government sanction. In the last few months of the war, guardians of Americanism began to label dissenters not only pro-German, but pro-Bolshevik.

After the Bolshevik Revolution in the fall of 1917, American hatred for Kaiser Germany was readily transferred to Communist Russia. When the new Russian government under V. I. Lenin made peace with Germany in early 1918, thereby closing the eastern front, Americans felt betrayed. Many lashed out at American radicals, casually applying the term "Red" to people of varying beliefs, such as anarchists, Wobblies, Socialists, pacifists, Communists, union leaders, and reformers.

The ordeal of Victor Berger illustrates the blending of the wartime and postwar suppression of civil liberties. A Socialist of German descent and former congressman from Wisconsin, Berger was indicted under the Espionage Act for denouncing American entry into the European war. Nonetheless, in 1918 the voters of Milwaukee elected him once again to Congress. In early 1919 he was convicted and sentenced to twenty years in federal prison. The House of Representatives thereupon refused to admit him, its members absurdly charging that he was both pro-German and pro-Bolshevik. While out on bail pending an appeal of his conviction, Berger won the special election held to replace him. The House again blocked his admission. Berger's ordeal did not end until 1921 when the Supreme Court reversed his conviction. He was elected to Congress again in 1924; this time he took his seat.

Case of Victor Berger

An early sign of the Wilson administration's anti-Bolshevism was the president's ordering of five thousand American troops to northern Russia in June 1918. Then, a month later, he sent another ten thousand soldiers to Siberia, where they joined other Allied contingents. Wilson did not consult Congress; he announced that the military expeditions were intended to guard Allied supplies and Russian railroads from German seizure, and to rescue a group of Czechs who wished to return to their homeland to fight the Germans. Wilson also worried that the Japanese were building influence in Siberia and closing the Open Door. But he hoped primarily to smash the infant Bolshevik government. The Allied governments were blunter about this goal than Wilson, for they feared that Bolshevism had the potential to spread across Europe. (Indeed, there were short-lived uprisings in Germany and Hungary

Intervention in Russia

A. Mitchell Palmer (1872–1936), the ambitious attorney general who launched raids against suspected radicals during the Red Scare. Palmer ranks as one of the most notorious violators of civil liberties in American history. *Library of Congress.*

in early 1919). Not only did Wilson attempt to subvert Lenin's regime by military means; he participated in an economic blockade of Russia, sent arms to anti-Bolshevik forces, refused to recognize the Bolshevik government, and later blocked Russian participation in the Paris Peace Conference. American troops did not leave Siberia until spring 1920. These interventions in civil war–torn Russia immediately embittered Washington-Moscow relations—a legacy that was to persist deep into the twentieth century.

At home too, the Wilson administration moved against radicals and others imprecisely defined as Bolsheviks or Communists. After the war Americans were edgy: the war had disrupted race relations, the workplace, and the family; it had increased the cost of living; postwar unemployment loomed; and in 1919 the Russian Communists established the Comintern to promote world revolution. Already hardened by wartime violations of civil liberties, legal and illegal, Americans found it easy to blame their postwar troubles on new scapegoats.

Dramatic events sparked the Red Scare. First came a rash of labor strikes in 1919. All told, over 3,300 strikes involving 4 million laborers occurred that year, including a Seattle general strike in January that sent ripples of fear across the nation. America, said Wilson's press secretary with exaggeration, was poised between "organization and anarchy." In May, bombs were sent through the mails to prominent Americans; most of the devices were intercepted and dismantled. Police never captured the conspirators. The common and not-unreasonable assumption was that anarchists and others bent on the destruction of the American way of life were responsible. Next came the Boston police strike in September; some thought it part of a Bolshevik conspiracy. The governor of Massachusetts, Calvin Coolidge, gained fame by proclaiming that nobody had the right to strike against the public safety. State guardsmen were brought in to replace the striking police force.

The strike in the steel industry in September seemed more ominous. Over 350,000 workers walked out. Conservative steel executives, who had long resisted unionization and perpetuated terrible **Steel Strike** working conditions, were determined to roll back wartime concessions to higher wages and unions. Many workers still put in twelve-hour days seven days a week and went home to squalid living quarters. Postwar unemployment in the industry was climbing. The steel barons responded to the strike by sending agents to club strikers, hiring strikebreakers, and deliberately trying to plant in the public mind the belief that it was Bolshevik-inspired and led. When the strike collapsed in 1920, it was evident that the steelworkers' union was severely weakened.

One of the leaders of the steel strike was William

Z. Foster, a radical who joined the Communist party after the strike began. His presence in a labor movement seeking legitimate bread-and-butter goals permitted political and business leaders to dismiss the steel strike as a foreign threat orchestrated by American radicals. There was actually no conspiracy, and the American left was badly splintered. After breaking away from the Socialist party, John Reed and Benjamin Gitlow founded the Communist Labor party in the summer of 1919. That September the Communist party, largely composed of aliens, was launched. Neither Communist party commanded much of a following—perhaps about seventy thousand members total—and in 1919 the harassed Socialist party could muster no more than approximately thirty thousand members.

Although divisiveness among radicals was actually symptomatic of weakness, both progressives and conservatives interpreted the advent of the new parties as a strengthening of the radical menace. That is certainly how the American Legion saw the matter. Organized in May 1919, the veterans' organization soon became a standard-bearer for the Red Scare. The editor of the *London Daily News* visited the United States in 1919 and recalled what he witnessed: the nation was "hag-ridden by the spectre of Bolshevism. . . . 'Radical' covered the most innocent departure from conventional thought with a suspicion of desperate purpose. 'America,' as a wit of the time said, 'is the land of liberty—the liberty to keep in step.'"

Attorney General A. Mitchell Palmer insisted on conformity. A progressive, a Quaker, and an aspirant to the 1920 Democratic presidential nomination, Palmer claimed that the "blaze of revolution" was "eating its way into the homes of the American workmen, its sharp tongues of revolutionary heat . . . licking the altars of the churches, leaping into the belfry of the school bell, crawling into the sacred corners of American homes, burning up the foundations of society." To stamp out the radical fire, Palmer created a new Bureau of Investigation and appointed J. Edgar Hoover to run it. Hoover organized a file of thousands of index cards bearing the names of alleged radical individuals and organizations. In 1919 agents jailed IWW members and deported alien radicals like Emma Goldman.

Titled "Moving Days," this 1919 cartoon credits the newly formed American Legion with frightening away aliens and Bolsheviks. Declaring itself an exponent of "Americanism," the Legion aroused the anti-immigrant and anti-radical feelings so common to the Red Scare.   Library of Congress.

Again, state and local governments took their cue from Washington. The New York State legislature expelled five duly elected Socialist members. States passed peacetime sedition acts under which hundreds of people were arrested. Vigilante groups and mobs flourished once again, their numbers swelled by returning veterans. In November 1919, in Centralia, Washington, a town beset by emotional antiradicalism, four American Legionnaires were shot when they broke from an Armistice Day parade in an apparent attempt to storm the IWW hall. Several Wobblies were arrested and later convicted of murder; one, an exsoldier, was taken from jail by a mob, beaten, castrated, and then shot.

The Red Scare reached a climax in January 1920 when the attorney general staged his Palmer Raids. Using information gathered by Hoover, government **Palmer Raids** agents in thirty-three cities broke into meeting halls, poolrooms, and homes without search warrants. Four thousand people were thrown into overcrowded jails and denied counsel. Of this number, about 550 were deported. In Boston alone, approximately 400 people were kept in detainment on bitterly cold Deer Island; two died of pneumonia, one leaped to his death, and another went insane.

Palmer's disregard for elementary civil liberties soon drew criticism. Civil libertarians and lawyers pointed out that Palmer's blatant tactics ignored the Constitution, that many of the arrested "Communists" had committed no crimes, and that some were not even radicals. Palmer's call for a peacetime sedition act alarmed leaders of many political persuasions. His dire prediction that major violence would mar May Day 1920 proved mistaken. Palmer's exaggerations, his scenarios of Bolshevik conspiracy, simply exceeded the truth so far that he lost credibility. With the steel strike over, the threat of Bolshevism in Europe receding, and the nation settling down into a postwar routine of business as usual, Palmer could no longer count on stampeding the public. Finally, even officials in the Wilson administration refused to cooperate with him. Assistant Secretary of Labor Louis Post and immigration commissioner Frederick Howe blocked Palmer's attempts at wholesale deportations, while charging him with gross violations of human rights.

The campaign against free speech in the period from 1917 through 1920 left casualties. Critics, radical or otherwise, were afraid to speak their minds. Debate, so essential to democracy, was curbed. Reform suffered as reformers either joined in the antiradicalism or became victims of it. The radical movement was badly weakened, the IWW becoming virtually extinct and the Socialist party paralyzed. The government's war on its critics and disrespect for the Bill of Rights left an indelible blot on Wilson's political record. The president made it appear that his critics were attacking the nation itself, when in fact they were questioning the policies of the Wilson administration. Wilson's intolerance of those who disagreed with him seemed to bespeak a distrust of democracy. At the least it illustrated that some progressives would use coercion and authoritarian methods to achieve their goal of a reformed society. Senator La Follette thought the sorry experience demonstrated what was for him

the supreme issue: "the encroachment of the powerful few upon the rights of the many."

THE PEACE CONFERENCE AND LEAGUE FIGHT

As the Red Scare was threatening American democracy, Woodrow Wilson was struggling to make his Fourteen Points a reality. When the president departed for the Paris peace conference in December 1918, he faced obstacles erected by his political enemies, by the Allies, and by himself. Some observers suggested that the ambitious Wilson, confident of his own abilities and religious in his belief that destiny directed his course, underestimated his task.

In the 1918 congressional elections, Wilson had urged a vote for the Democrats as a sign of support for his peace goals. But the American people, probably voting less in response to foreign-policy issues than to domestic questions like inflation, did just the opposite. The Republicans gained control of both houses, signaling trouble for Wilson in two ways. First, any peace treaty would have to be submitted for approval to a potentially hostile Senate; second, Wilson's stature had been diminished in the eyes of foreign leaders. After this setback, Wilson aggravated his political problems by not naming any senator to the American Peace Commission, refusing to take any prominent Republican with him to the conference, and failing to consult with the Senate Foreign Relations Committee before he sailed for Paris. Analysts thought he had lost his political senses.

Another obstacle in Wilson's way was the Allies' determination to impose a harsh, vengeful peace on the Germans. Georges Clemenceau of France, David Lloyd George of Britain, and Vittorio Orlando of Italy—with Wilson, the Big Four—were formidable adversaries. They had signed secret treaties during the war and expected to enlarge their empires at Germany's expense. They scoffed at the headstrong, self-impressed president who wanted to deny them the spoils of war. Sizing up Wilson as a theologian self-consciously wielding United States power, they challenged his blueprint for peace. "God gave us the Ten Commandments, and we broke them," remarked Clemenceau. "Wilson gives us the Fourteen Points. We shall see."

The Paris Conference at the palace of Versailles was a meeting of the titans, "the clearing house of the Fates," as a contemporary put it. Much of the business of the conference was con-

Paris Conference

ducted by the Big Four behind closed doors: critics quickly pointed out that Wilson had thus abandoned the first of his Fourteen Points, which urged diplomacy in the "public view." The victors demanded that Germany pay a huge reparations bill. Wilson called for a small indemnity, fearing that a resentful and economically hobbled Germany might turn to Bolshevism or disrupt the postwar community in some other way. Unable to moderate the Allied position, the president reluctantly gave way, agreeing to a clause blaming the war on the Germans and to the creation of a reparations commission to determine a figure (later set at $33 billion).

As for decolonization (the breaking up of empires) and the principle of self-determination, Wilson only partially overcame the land-grabbing mood of the conference. The conferees placed former German and Turkish colonies under the control of other imperial nations in a League-administered "mandate" system. France and Britain, for example, obtained parts of the Middle East, and Japan gained authority over Germany's colonies in the Pacific. The mandate system was a halfway station between outright imperial domination and independence. In other compromises, Japan was granted influence over China's Shandong Peninsula, and France was permitted occupation rights in Germany's Rhineland. Elsewhere in Europe, however, Wilson's prescriptions fared better. Out of Austria-Hungary and Russia came the new independent states of Austria, Hungary, Yugoslavia, Czechoslovakia, and Poland. Wilson and his colleagues also built a *cordon sanitaire* of new westward-looking nations (Finland, Estonia, Latvia, and Lithuania) around Russia to quarantine the Bolshevik contagion.

Wilson worked harder on the charter for the League of Nations than on anything else. In the long run, he believed, the League would moderate the harshness of the Allied peace terms and temper imperial ambitions. He devised a League that

League of Nations

reflected the power of large nations like the United States: an influential council of five permanent members (great powers) and elected delegates from smaller states; an assembly for discussion; and a World Court. The heart of the League covenant, said Wilson, was Article 10:

> The Members of the League undertake to respect and preserve as against external aggression the territorial integrity and existing political independence of all Members of the League. In case of any such aggression or in case of any threat or danger of such aggression the Council shall advise upon the means by which this obligation shall be fulfilled.

This collective-security provision was the centerpiece of Wilson's international reform program, and with the entire League charter it became part of the peace treaty.

German representatives at first refused to accept the punitive Treaty of Paris, but then signed it in June 1919. In so doing they gave up 13 percent of Germany's territory, 10 percent of its population, all its colonies, and a huge portion of its national wealth. Secretary Lansing and others prophesied that the League could not function in the poisoned atmosphere of revenge and humiliation. But Wilson, filled with America's traditional missionary zeal, was euphoric: "The stage is set, the destiny disclosed. It has come about by no plan of our conceiving, but by the hand of God, who led us into this way."

Americans vigorously debated the merits of the treaty. In March 1919, as the conferees in Paris were hammering out the accord, thirty-nine senators (enough to deny the treaty the nec-

Debate over the Treaty

essary two-thirds vote) signed a petition stating that the League's structure did not adequately protect American interests. Wilson lamented the "pygmy" minds of his antagonists, but persuaded the peace conference to exempt the Monroe Doctrine and domestic matters from League jurisdiction. Having made these concessions to senatorial advice, Wilson would budge no more.

Near the end of his controversial presidency, Woodrow Wilson was a saddened man. A stroke had undercut his health, American voters had repudiated his party and some of his policies in the election of 1920, and the Senate had rejected his pet project—American membership in the League of Nations.   National Archives.

Yet criticism mounted: Wilson had bastardized his own principles; he had conceded Shandong to Japan; he had personally killed a provision affirming the racial equality of all peoples. There was no mention in the treaty of freedom of the seas; there was no reduction in tariffs. Negotiations had been conducted in private, and reparations promised to be punishing. Senator La Follette joined others in complaining that the League was an imperialist assemblage that would perpetuate empire. Conservative critics like Senator Henry Cabot Lodge of Massachusetts feared that the League would limit American freedom of action in world affairs, stymie its expansion, and intrude on domestic questions. Racist nationalists wanted no part of an organization that bestowed the vote on nonwhite peoples. And Article 10 raised serious

questions: Would the United States be obligated to use armed force to ensure collective security? And what about colonial rebellions, such as in Ireland or India? Would they be disturbances of the peace the League would feel compelled to crush?

Wilson pleaded for understanding and lectured his opponents. Did they not realize that compromises were necessary given the awesome, stubborn resistance of the Allies, who had threatened to jettison the conference unless Wilson made concessions? Did they not recognize that the League would rectify wrongs? Could they not see that membership in the League would give the United States "leadership in the world"? Senator Lodge was unimpressed. A Harvard-educated Ph.D. and partisan Republican, he ridiculed Wilson's charter as poor scholarship. Lodge packed the Foreign

Chapter 23: America at War, 1914–1920

Relations Committee with critics of the League and prolonged public hearings. He introduced reservations to the treaty: one stated that the nation's immigration acts could not be subject to League decision; another held that Congress had to approve any obligation under Article 10.

In September 1919, Wilson embarked on a speaking tour of the United States. Growing more exhausted every day, he dismissed his critics as "absolute, contemptible quitters." When he met Irish-American and German-American hecklers, he lashed out in Red Scare language: "I cannot say too often—any man who carries a hyphen about him carries a dagger which he is ready to plunge into the vitals of the Republic." In Colorado, while delivering another passionate speech, the president collapsed. A few days later, in Washington, D.C., he suffered a stroke that paralyzed his left side. Although his mind remained alert, he became grumpy and peevish, fearful of displaying weakness and unable to conduct the heavy business of the presidency. Told by advisers to placate senatorial critics so the treaty would have a chance of passing, Wilson stubbornly refused to "dip [his] colors to dishonorable compromise." From Democrats in the Senate he demanded loyalty—a vote against all reservations.

The Senate first tested the treaty's strength in November. In two votes, one on the treaty with reservations (39–55) and one without (38–53), the Senate rejected it. A group of six-

Senate Rejection of the Treaty

teen "Irreconcilables," determined to defeat any treaty, voted nay each time. Republicans either opposed the treaty altogether or favored reservations; Democrats, on the whole, voted for the treaty without reservations. Eastern and midwestern senators largely voted against an unamended treaty; senators from the South tended to vote aye; western senators were divided. Again in March 1920, the Senate fell short of the necessary two-thirds vote of approval (49–35). Had Wilson permitted Democrats to compromise, he could have achieved his fervent goal of American membership in the infant League of Nations.

Who or what was responsible for the defeat of the treaty? Wilson's stroke incapacitated the president, sapping his energy and the ability to lead effectively; yet, even a healthy Wilson would likely have set his jaw against compromise. Certainly his concessions to a harsh peace at Paris undercut his case in the United States; yet it seems that two-thirds of the Senate were willing to forgive his errors in Versailles if he would accept some reservations. And the bitter personal feud between Wilson and Lodge does not account for enough—it does not, for example, explain the determination of the Irreconcilables.

Wilson's refusal to compromise with his senatorial foes certainly doomed the treaty. Still, this begs the question: why were Wilson's critics so committed to cripple Article 10, and why was the president so adamant against its revision? Because at the core of the debate lay a basic issue of American foreign policy: whether the United States would endorse *collective security* or continue to travel the path of *unilateralism* articulated in Washington's Farewell Address and the Monroe Doctrine. In a world dominated by imperialist states unwilling to subordinate their selfish, acquisitive ambitions to an international organization, Americans preferred their traditional nonalignment and freedom of choice over binding commitments to collective action. Woodrow Wilson failed to create a new world order through reform; he promised more than he could deliver.

THE EXPERIENCE OF WAR

As the war ground to a close in Europe, the historian Albert Bushnell Hart observed that "it is easy to see that the United States is a new country." What had changed? America emerged from the war years an unsettled mix of the old and the new. Above all else the war exposed the heterogeneity of the American people and the deep divisions among them: white versus black, nativist versus immigrant, capital versus labor, dry versus wet, men versus women, radical versus progressive or conservative, pacifist versus interventionist, nationalist versus internationalist. Race riots, labor strikes, the Americanization movement, suppression of civil liberties, the Red Scare, the League fight, and male resentment of female workers—all underscored the distempers of the times. It is no wonder that after 1920 Americans would seek relief in "normalcy" and escape from what John Dewey called the "cult of irrationality."

During the war the federal government intervened in the economy and influenced people's everyday lives as never before. In the period **Enlarged** 1916 to 1919 annual federal ex- **Federal Role** penditures increased 2,500 percent, and war expenses ballooned to $33.5 billion. The total cost of the war was probably triple that figure, since future generations would have to pay veterans' benefits and interest on loans. Centralization of control in Washington, D.C., and mobilization of the home front served as a model for the future. The partnership of government and business in managing the wartime economy contributed to the development of a mass society through the standardization of products and the promotion of efficiency.

The wartime cooperation of government and business also encouraged the growth of trade associations, which numbered about two thousand by 1920. After the war these industry-wide groups would continue to lobby to protect their interests and to minimize competition. Wilsonian wartime policies also nourished the continued growth of big business and of oligopoly through the suspension of antitrust legislation. A 1920 Supreme Court decision not to dissolve the giant U.S. Steel Corporation symbolized the persistent trend toward bigness. After a short postwar recession, business power revived to dominate the next decade. American labor, by contrast, entered what one historian has called its lean years.

America's changed place in world affairs also held significance for later generations. By 1920 the United States was the world's leading economic power, producing 40 percent of its coal, 70 percent of its petroleum, and half its pig iron. It rose to first rank in world trade. During the war years, American companies expanded their overseas operations.

Economic Expansion Abroad

Goodyear went into the Dutch East Indies for rubber; copper interests dug new mines in Chile; and Swift and Armour reached into South America. Preoccupied with the war, competitors like Britain and Germany were outdistanced by American economic expansionists, especially in Latin America. The United States also shifted from a debtor to a creditor nation, becoming the world's leading banker.

The disillusionment common to so many Americans after the disappointment of Versailles did not cause the United States to adopt a policy of isolationist withdrawal (see Chapter 27). Although the League of Nations began to operate without United States membership, Americans became curious onlookers who even occasionally participated in League activities. But in general Americans stood against intervening in European affairs until the Europeans first set their own house in order.

The carnage of the war—10 million people lost their lives—stimulated new appeals for arms control and a revitalized peace movement. At the same time, the military became more professional. The Reserve Officer Training Corps (ROTC) became permanent; military "colleges" provided upper-echelon training; and the Army Industrial College, founded in 1924, pursued business-military cooperation in the area of logistics and planning. The National Research Council, created in 1916 with governmental and Carnegie and Rockefeller funds, continued after the war as an alliance of scientists and businesspeople engaged in research relating to national defense. As before the war, the tendencies toward disarmament on the one hand and preparedness on the other continued to compete.

The international system born in these years was unstable and fragmented. The process of decolonization was set in motion at this time. Nationalist leaders like Ho Chi Minh of Indochina and Mahatma Gandhi of India, taking to heart the Wilsonian principle of self-determination, vowed to achieve independence for their peoples. Communism became a new and disruptive force in world politics, and the Russians bore a grudge against the Allies, who had futilely tried to thwart their revolution. The new states in Central and Eastern Europe proved weak, dependent on outsiders for security. Germans bitterly resented the harsh peace settlement. And the war debts and reparations problems would dog international order for years.

The war experience also changed Americans' mood. The war was grimy and ugly, far less glorious than Wilson's lofty rhetoric had it. People recoiled from the photographs of bodies dangling from barbed wire, poison-gas victims, and battle-shocked faces. American soldiers were eager to return home. Apparently tired of idealism and cynical about their ability to right wrongs, they craved the latest baseball scores. Still, for the doughboys the army years were memorable, a turning point in their lives. They shed some of their parochialism, as the title of a popular song hinted: "How 'Ya Gonna Keep 'Em Down on the Farm, After They've Seen Paree?" And they made lasting friendships that would be cemented by membership in the American Legion. A young soldier from Missouri, Harry S Truman of Battery D, would never lose touch with his wartime buddies, and when he became president in 1945 he would bring some of them into the White House as advisers.

Those progressives who had believed entry into the war would deliver the millennium now marveled at their naiveté. Many lost their enthusiasm for crusades, and many others turned away in disgust from the bickering of the victors. Randolph Bourne commented that progressives felt "like brave passengers who have set out for the Isles of the Blest only to find that the first mate has gone insane and jumped overboard." Some felt betrayed, distraught that the Great War had not proven exceptional. William Allen White angrily wrote to a friend that the Allies "have—those damned vultures—taken the heart out of the peace, taken the joy out of the great enterprise of the war, and have made it a sordid malicious miserable thing like all the other wars in the world."

Woodrow Wilson himself had remarked soon after taking office in 1913, before the Great War, that "there's no chance of progress and reform in an administration in which war plays the principal part." From the vantage point of 1920, looking back on the array of distempers at home and abroad, Wilson would have to agree with his fellow citizens that progress and reform had been dealt blows.

SUGGESTIONS FOR FURTHER READING

General

Randolph Bourne, *War and the Intellectuals*, ed. Carl Resek (1964); John W. Chambers, *The Tyranny of Change* (1980); Allen F. Davis, *American Heroine* (1974) (on Jane Addams); Otis L. Graham, Jr., *The Great Campaigns* (1971); Ellis W. Hawley, *The Great War and the Search for a Modern Order* (1979); Henry F. May, *The End of American Innocence* (1964); Emily S. Rosenberg, *Spreading the American Dream* (1982); Bernadotte Schmitt and Harold E. Vedeler, *The World in the Crucible: 1914–1919* (1984); Ronald Steel, *Walter Lippmann and the American Century* (1980); David P. Thelan, *Robert M. La Follette and the Insurgent Spirit* (1976).

Woodrow Wilson and His Diplomacy

Thomas A. Bailey and Paul B. Ryan, *The Lusitania Disaster* (1975); Edward H. Buehrig, ed., *Wilson's Foreign Policy in Perspective* (1957); John M. Cooper, Jr., *The Warrior and the Priest: Woodrow Wilson and Theodore Roosevelt* (1983); Patrick Devlin, *Too Proud to Fight* (1975); Robert H. Ferrell, *Woodrow Wilson and World War I* (1985); Lloyd C. Gardner, *Safe for Democracy: The Anglo-American Response to Revolution, 1913–1923* (1984); Ross Gregory, *The Origins of American Intervention in the First World War* (1971); Manfred Jonas, *The United States and Germany* (1984); N. Gordon Levin, Jr., *Woodrow Wilson and World Politics* (1968); Arthur S. Link, ed., *Woodrow Wilson and a Revolutionary World, 1913–1921* (1982); Arthur S. Link, *Woodrow Wilson: Revolution, War, and Peace* (1979); Arthur S. Link, *Wilson*, 5 vols. (1947–1965); Ernest R. May, *The World War and American Isolation, 1914–1917* (1959); Walter Millis, *Road to War* (1935); Robert E. Osgood, *Ideals and Self-Interest in American Foreign Relations* (1953); Jeffrey J. Safford, *Wilsonian Maritime Diplomacy* (1977); Frances W. Saunders, *Ellen Axson Wilson* (1985); Daniel M. Smith, *The Great Departure* (1965); Barbara Tuchman, *The Zimmermann Telegram* (1958); Edwin A. Weinstein, *Woodrow Wilson: A Medical and Psychological Biography* (1981).

The American Military and the First World War

Arthur E. Barbeau and Florette Henri, *The Unknown Soldiers: Black American Troops in World War I* (1974); J. Garry Clifford, *The Citizen Soldiers* (1972); Edward M. Coffman, *The War to End All Wars* (1968); Harvey A. DeWeerd, *President Wilson Fights His War* (1968); Marvin E. Fletcher, *The Black Soldier and Officer in the United States Army, 1891–1917* (1974); Thomas C. Leonard, *Above the Battle* (1978); David Trask, *The United States in the Supreme War Council* (1961); Russell F. Weigley, *The American Way of War* (1973).

The Home Front

Valerie Jean Conner, *The National War Labor Board* (1983); Alfred W. Crosby, Jr., *Epidemic and Peace, 1918* (1976); Robert D. Cuff, *The War Industries Board* (1973); Allen F. Davis, "Welfare, Reform, and World War I," *American Quarterly*, 19 (1967), 516–533; Edward R. Ellis, *Echoes of Distant Thunder* (1975); Charles Gilbert, *American Financing of World War I* (1970); Maurine W. Greenwald, *Women, War, and Work* (1980); Frank L. Grubbs, Jr., *The Struggle for Labor Loyalty* (1968); Michael T. Isenberg, *War on Film* (1981); David M. Kennedy, *Over Here* (1980); Paul A. C. Koistinen, "The 'Industrial-Military Complex' in Historical Perspective: World War I," *Business History Review*, 41 (1967), 378–403; Seward W. Livermore, *Politics Is Adjourned* (1966); Frederick C. Luebke, *Bonds of Loyalty: German-Americans and World War I* (1974); John F. McClymer, *War and Welfare: Social Engineering in America, 1890–1925* (1980); Barbara J. Steinson, *American Women's Activism in World War I* (1982); Stephen L. Vaughn, *Holding Fast the Inner Lines: Democracy, Nationalism, and the Committee on Public Information* (1979).

Black Americans

Robert V. Haynes, *A Night of Violence: The Houston Riot of 1917* (1976); Florette Henri, *Black Migration* (1975); Thomas C. Holt, "Afro-Americans," in *Harvard Encyclopedia of American Ethnic Groups*, ed. Stephan Thernstrom (1980); Elliot M. Rudwick, *Race Riot at East St. Louis, July 2, 1917* (1964); William M. Tuttle, *Race Riot: Chicago in the Red Summer of 1919* (1970).

Wartime Dissent, Civil Liberties, and the Red Scare

David Brody, *Labor in Crisis: The Steel Strike of 1919* (1965); Charles Chatfield, *For Peace and Justice: Pacifism in America, 1914–1941* (1971); Stanley Coben, *A. Mitchell Palmer* (1963); Charles DeBenedetti, *Origins of the Modern Peace Movement* (1978); Robert L. Friedheim, *The Seattle General Strike* (1965); Sondra Herman, *Eleven Against War* (1969); Donald Johnson, *The Challenge to American Freedoms* (1963); C. Roland Marchand, *The American Peace Movement and*

Social Reform, 1898–1918 (1973); Paul L. Murphy, *World War I and the Origin of Civil Liberties* (1979); Robert K. Murray, *Red Scare* (1955); H. C. Peterson and Gilbert C. Fite, *Opponents of War, 1917–1918* (1968); William Preston, *Aliens and Dissenters: Federal Suppression of Radicals, 1903–1933* (1966); Francis Russell, *A City in Terror: 1919—The Boston Police Strike* (1975); Harry N. Scheiber, *The Wilson Administration and Civil Liberties, 1917–1921* (1960); James Weinstein, *The Decline of Socialism in America, 1912–1923* (1967).

Hostility Toward Bolshevik Russia

Peter G. Filene, *Americans and the Soviet Experiment, 1917–1933* (1967); John L. Gaddis, *Russia, The Soviet Union, and the United States* (1978); George F. Kennan, *The Decision to Intervene* (1958); George F. Kennan, *Russia Leaves the War* (1956); Christopher Lasch, *The American Liberals and the Russian Revolution* (1962); John Thompson, *Russia, Bolshevism, and the Versailles Peace* (1966); Betty M. Unterberger, ed., *American Intervention in the Russian Civil War* (1969); Betty M. Unterberger, *America's Siberian Expedition, 1918–1920* (1956); William Appleman Williams, *American-Russian Relations, 1781–1947* (1952).

Versailles and the League Fight

Thomas A. Bailey, *Woodrow Wilson and the Great Betrayal* (1945); Thomas A. Bailey, *Woodrow Wilson and the Lost Peace* (1944); Inga Floto, *Colonel House in Paris* (1973); Herbert Hoover, *The Ordeal of Woodrow Wilson* (1958); Warren F. Kuehl, *Seeking World Order* (1969); Arno Mayer, *Politics and Diplomacy of Peacemaking* (1967); Keith Nelson, *Victors Divided* (1973); Ralph A. Stone, *The Irreconcilables* (1970); William C. Widenor, *Henry Cabot Lodge and the Search for an American Foreign Policy* (1980).

Aftermath

Stanley Cooperman, *World War I and the American Mind* (1970); Malcolm Cowley, *Exile's Return* (1951); Paul Fussell, *The Great War and Modern Memory* (1975); Stuart I. Rochester, *American Liberal Disillusionment in the Wake of World War I* (1977); Stephen R. Ward, ed., *The War Generation: Veterans of the First World War* (1975).

THE NEW ERA OF THE 1920s

CHAPTER 24

At 9:39 P. M. on August 6, 1926, a young American woman trudged out of the rough sea onto the English coast. Nineteen-year-old Gertrude Ederle had left France that morning in an attempt to swim the English Channel, a feat that only five men and no women had ever accomplished. She not only succeeded but swam the treacherous thirty-mile stretch in 14 hours 31 minutes, the fastest time yet recorded.

Already known as a swimming champion—she had won a gold medal at the 1924 Olympics—Ederle now became a champion of women. Her conquest of the Channel, wrote the *Literary Digest*, "would be hailed as a battle won for feminism" and the "unanswerable refutation of the masculine dogma that woman is, in the sense of physical power and efficiency, inferior to man." According to a columnist for the *Boston Globe*, "The Channel has been the means of giving to women new physical dignity."

Yet Americans seemed to appreciate that dignity in narrow ways. Along with adulation, Ederle's feat inspired a profusion of swimsuit ads linking physical fitness to sex appeal. Newspapers and magazines not only heralded her swim but increased their coverage of bathing beauties at the Miss America Pageant, a contest begun in 1922, the year Ederle won her first long-distance race. And whatever her accomplishments, the name of Ederle was never as renowned as those of the era's most admired males: Dempsey, Ruth, Lindbergh, or even Capone.

During the 1920s the flower of consumerism reached full bloom. Spurred by advertising and new forms of credit, Americans eagerly bought automobiles, radios, real estate, and stocks. The majority of the population enjoyed an unparalleled standard of living. As in the Gilded Age of the late nineteenth century, government policies supported the interests of business. The most fundamental and perplexing trend of the 1920s was the effect of the new mass consumer culture on individuals and communities. Changes in work habits, family responsibilities, and health care fostered new uses of time and new attitudes about proper behavior.

By the end of the decade, new habits and values had altered American society. Whereas people had once identified with those who believed as they did, they now felt as much, if not more, of a sense of community with fellow consumers of Ford cars, Listerine mouthwash, and Lucky Strike cigarettes. Whereas they had once expressed their individuality in their work and family lives, now they sought vicarious identification with popular heroes like Gertrude Ederle, Charles Lindbergh, and Jack Dempsey.

The 1920s was an era when important reforms occurred at state and local levels of government, and significant advances were made in science and technology. An outburst of creativity occurred in literature, music, and art. Still, the consumer culture predominated in everyday life, causing Americans to ignore rising debts and other increasingly negative economic signs. But poverty dogged small farmers, workers in declining industries, and nonwhites living in slums.

In many ways the Ederle story illustrates the complexities and ironies of the new era of the 1920s. The decade was a time both of great accomplishments—in economic productivity as well as athletics—and of frivolous commercial stunts, contests, and fads. It was a time of swift social change, of frankness and liberation. But the winds of change also stirred up waves of reaction. The new, more liberal values repelled some groups, such as the Ku Klux Klan, immigration restrictionists, and religious fundamentalists. Such groups reacted by trying to restore a society of simpler values, where people knew their place and deviants were not tolerated. Yet in spite of their efforts, material bounty and increased leisure time enticed Americans into a variety of new mass amusements, including games, sports, and movies. In an impersonal world, Americans had turned to mass culture to personalize their lives.

POSTWAR OPTIMISM

Poor Richard's Almanac would have sold poorly in the 1920s. Few Americans of that era had much interest in the virtues of thrift and sobriety that Benjamin Franklin had preached. They saw more attraction in acquisition, amusement, and salesmanship. Instead of traditional homilies like "waste not, want not," they harkened to the advice of an advertising executive: "Make the public want what you have to sell. Make 'em pant for it." With such an attitude Americans attained the highest standard of living they had yet experienced. Though poverty and social injustice still infected the country, many people shared the belief, as journalist Joseph Wood Krutch put it, that "the future was bright and the present was good fun at least."

The decade did not begin very brightly. Besides political wrangling over membership in the League of Nations and ratification of the Treaty of Paris and the Red Scare, the nation suffered a frightening economic decline. For two years after the First World War, consumer spending drove prices up. Then in 1920 people stopped buying, and the export trade and industrial production dropped as wartime orders ended. Net farm income plunged. Unemployment, which had hovered around 2 percent in 1919, passed 12 percent in 1921. The railroad and mining industries suffered declining profits, and layoffs spread through New England as textile companies abandoned outdated factories for the raw materials and cheap labor of the South.

Postwar Economic Recovery

Recovery began in 1922 and continued unevenly until 1929. During this period, industrial output nearly doubled. Electric motors were responsible for much of the rise; by 1929 electricity powered 70 percent of American industry, and thousands of steam engines had been relegated to the scrap heap. The new technique of manufacture by assembly line also contributed, adding countless new consumer products to the market. New metal alloys, chemicals, synthetic materials, and preserved foods became commonplace. As Americans acquired more spending money and as their leisure time expanded, service industries boomed. More people could afford department and specialty stores, restaurants, beauty and barber shops, and movie theaters. This new consumerism was fueled by refined methods of credit, especially the installment or time-payment plan ("a dollar down and a dollar forever," as one critic quipped). Of 3.5 million automobiles sold in 1923, some 80 percent were bought on credit.

Poor Richard would have thrown up his hands in disgust.

Behind the prosperity, an economic revolution was climaxing. First, the consolidation movement that had given birth to trusts and holding companies in the late nineteenth century reached a new stage. Although Progressive-era trustbusting had harnessed big business to some extent, it had not halted *oligopoly*—the control of a whole industry by a few large firms. By the 1920s oligopolies dominated not only production but marketing, distribution, and even financing. In businesses as varied as automobile manufacturing, steel production, meatprocessing, and railroads, a few sprawling integrated companies predominated. Oligopolistic firms, like General Electric, General Motors, and U.S. Steel, developed specialized management techniques to maximize profits and minimize market uncertainties.

The organizational movement that had begun around 1900 also matured in the 1920s. Myriad business and professional associations sprang up to protect their members' interests. Retailers and small manufacturers formed trade associations to pool information and coordinate planning. Farm bureaus and cooperative associations promoted scientific agriculture, lobbied for government protection, and tried to stabilize the market. Lawyers, engineers, and social scientists cooperated with business to promote economic growth.

THE BUSINESS OF GOVERNMENT, THE GOVERNMENT OF BUSINESS

In this outburst of expansion, many Americans shed their fear of big business—swayed in part by the testimonials of probusiness propagandists. "Among the nations of the earth today," one writer proclaimed in 1921, "America stands for one idea: *Business* . . . Thru business, properly conceived, managed and conducted, the human race is finally to be redeemed." Government reflected this outlook. As corporations became more national in scope, they looked increasingly to the federal government for assistance in integrating the economy. Thus during the 1920s a series of Republican administrations extended Theodore Roosevelt's notion of government-business cooperation—though they often made government a passive coordinator rather than the active director Roosevelt had advocated.

All branches of the federal government supported business interests during these years. In 1921 Congress reduced taxes on corporations and wealthy individuals, and in 1922 it raised tariff rates in the Fordney-McCumber Tariff Act. Presidents Harding, Coolidge, and Hoover appointed strong cabinet officers who pursued policies favorable to business. Regulatory agencies such as the Federal Trade Commission and the Interstate Commerce Commission cooperated with corporations more than they regulated them.

The revival of business prompted political analysts to lament the death of progressivism. They were partly right; the concern for social and economic justice that had moved the previous

Extension of Progressive Reforms

generation faded in the 1920s, especially as the image of big business improved. Yet many of the Progressive era's achievements were sustained and consolidated in these years. Although federal trustbusting declined, regulatory commissions and other government agencies still monitored business activities and worked to reduce wasteful practices. And in Congress a sizable corps of reformers, led by George Norris of Nebraska and Robert La Follette of Wisconsin, kept progressive causes alive by supporting labor legislation, federal aid to farmers, and government operation of a federally constructed hydroelectric dam at Muscle Shoals, Alabama. (Business-oriented politicians wanted to sell or lease the dam and its nitrate plant to private interests.) Women's reform organizations marked a major achievement in 1921 when Congress passed the Shepard-Towner Act, which provided federal funds to help set up maternity and pediatric clinics (though the measure was overturned in 1929 when Congress, under pressure from private physicians, cut off funding).

Most reform, however, occurred at the state and local levels. Following initiatives begun before the First World War, thirty-four states instituted or expanded workers' compensation laws in the 1920s. At the same time many states established old-age pensions

and other welfare programs. In hundreds of cities, trained social scientists gathered data and drew maps as part of a systematic effort to identify and solve urban problems. Planning became a common feature of urban government; by 1926 every major city and many smaller ones had planning and zoning commissions that. aimed to harness physical growth to the common good. And social workers continued to strive for justice and economic relief. During the 1920s the nation's state houses, city halls, and universities trained a new generation of reformers who would eventually influence national affairs during the New Deal government of the 1930s.

Organized labor, which had gained ground during the Progressive era, suffered setbacks during the 1920s. Public opinion, influenced by prosperity and pro-business rhetoric, turned against

Suppression of Labor Unions

workers who disrupted everyday life with strikes. The federal government frequently stifled union attempts to exercise power during these years. Early in the decade, for instance, the Justice Department used troops and court injunctions to end strikes by steel, mine, and railroad workers. Meanwhile, large corporations worked to counteract the appeal of unions by promising workers pensions, profit-sharing (which actually amounted to wages withheld for later distribution), and company-sponsored social and sporting events—a policy that became known as *welfare capitalism*. In such a climate, union membership fell from 5.1 million in 1920 to 3.6 million in 1929.

The Supreme Court, led by Chief Justice and former president William Howard Taft, became a powerful policy-making body, exerting its authority as aggressively as in the Gilded Age to protect private property. Its key decisions sheltered business from government regulation and undermined attempts by organized labor to achieve its ends through strikes and legislation. Thus in 1922 Taft ruled in *Coronado Coal Company* v. *United Mine Workers* that a striking union, like a trust, could be prosecuted for illegal restraint of trade. Yet in *Maple Floor Association* v. *U.S.* (1929), the Court gave support to trade associations which had formed to gather and disseminate information within particular industries, by effectively exempting them from antitrust laws. The Court also struck down labor reform in cases such as *Bailey* v. *Drexel Furniture Company* (1922), which voided re-

This photo of President Warren G. Harding (1865–1923) shows both the optimism of the years immediately after the First World War and Harding's affinity for good times with good friends.   Library of Congress.

strictions on child labor, and *Adkins* v. *Children's Hospital* (1923), which overturned a minimum wage law for women because it infringed on liberty of contract.

A symbol of the decade's goodwill toward business was President Warren G. Harding, a Republican elected in 1920 at a time when the populace wanted to avoid national and international crusades. Democrats had nominated Governor James M. Cox of Ohio, who stood behind Woodrow Wilson's fading hopes for United States membership in the League of Nations (see pages 671–673). But the efforts of Cox and his running mate, Franklin D. Roosevelt of New York, failed to attract voters. Harding, who kept his opinion on the League vague, captured 16.1 million popular votes to only 9.1 million for Cox.

A small-town newspaper publisher and senator from Ohio, Harding selected some capable assistants, notably Secretary of State Charles Evans Hughes,

Harding Administration Secretary of Commerce Herbert Hoover, Secretary of the Treasury Andrew Mellon, and Secretary of

Agriculture Henry C. Wallace. Harding also backed some important reforms. He helped streamline the budget, supported antilynching legislation, approved bills assisting farm cooperatives and liberalizing farm credit, and, unlike his predecessor Wilson, was generally tolerant on civil liberties issues.

Harding's problem was that he had too many predatory friends. His father once reputedly remarked, "Warren, it's a good thing you wasn't born a gal. You'd be in the family way all the time—you can't say no." Harding said yes too often, appointing friends to positions from which they infested government with corruption. Charles Forbes of the Veterans Bureau served time in Leavenworth prison after being convicted of fraud and bribery in connection with government contracts. Thomas W. Miller, alien property custodian, was jailed for accepting bribes. Attorney General Harry Daugherty was implicated in a scheme of accepting bribes and in other fraudulent acts; he escaped prosecution only by refusing to testify against himself. In the most notorious case of all, a congressional inquiry in 1923 and 1924 revealed that Secretary of the Interior Albert Fall had accepted bribes to lease government property to private oil companies. For his role in the affair, called the Teapot Dome scandal after a Wyoming oil reserve that had been turned over to the Mammoth Oil Company, Fall was fined $100,000 and spent a year in jail. He was the first cabinet officer to be so disgraced.

In June 1923, few Americans knew how corrupt Harding's administration had become. The president, however, had become disillusioned. Amid rumors of mismanagement and crime, he told journalist William Allen White, "My God, this is a hell of a job. I have no trouble with my enemies. . . . But my friends, my God-damned friends . . . they're the ones that keep me walking the floor nights." On a speaking tour of the West that summer, Harding became ill and died in San Francisco on August 2. Though his death preceded revelation of the Teapot Dome scandal, some people later believed that Harding had committed suicide rather than face the brewing storm. Most evidence, however, points to death from natural causes, probably a heart attack. At any rate, Harding was truly mourned. A warm, dignified-looking man who relished a good joke or an evening of poker and drinking, he seemed right for a nation that had just experienced racking upheaval at home and abroad.

Harding's successor, Vice President Calvin Coolidge, was far more solemn. A dour New Englander (Alice Roosevelt Longworth, Theodore's daughter, once quipped that Coolidge looked as if he had been weaned on a pickle), Coolidge had an undistinguished record as Republican governor of Massachusetts. He had first attracted national attention by his firm stand against striking Boston policemen in 1919, a policy that won him the vice-presidential nomination in 1920. Usually, however, he was content to let events take their course, prompting columnist Walter Lippmann to grumble, "It is a grim, determined, alert inactivity, which keeps Mr. Coolidge occupied constantly."

Coolidge had great respect for private enterprise; he once remarked, "The man who builds a factory builds a temple. The man who works there, worships there." Fortunately for him, his presidency coincided with extraordinary business prosperity. Aided by Andrew Mellon, whom he retained as secretary of the treasury, and other cabinet officers,

Coolidge Prosperity

his administration balanced the budget, reduced government debt, lowered income-tax rates (especially for the rich), and began construction of a national highway system. With his generally tightfisted fiscal policies he won business support. Congress took little initiative during these years and assented to most measures recommended by the cabinet and by business associations such as the U.S. Chamber of Commerce. The only disruptions arose over farm policy. Responding to farmers' complaints of falling prices, Congress twice passed bills to establish government-backed price supports for staple crops (the McNary-Haugen bills of 1927 and 1928). But Coolidge exercised his executive privilege and vetoed the measure both times.

"Coolidge prosperity" was the determining issue in the presidential election of 1924. That year both major parties ran candidates who accepted business supremacy. The Republicans nominated Coolidge with little dissent. At their national convention the Democrats first debated heatedly whether or not to condemn the Ku Klux Klan, voting 542 to 541 against condemnation. Then they endured 103 ballots before breaking a deadlock between southern prohibitionists who favored former Secretary of the Treasury William G. McAdoo and antiprohibition easterners who backed New York's Governor Alfred E. Smith. They finally settled on John W. Davis, a corporation lawyer from New York. Remnants of the progressive movement, along with various farm, labor, and socialist groups, formed a new Progressive party and nominated Robert M. La Follette, the aging reformer from Wisconsin. The new party revived issues unresolved in previous generations: public ownership of utilities; aid to farmers; decreased restraint on organized labor; increased regulation of business.

The election results resembled those of 1912 in reverse: the two probusiness candidates captured most of the votes. Coolidge beat Davis by 15.7 million to 8.4 million popular votes, 382 to 136 electoral votes. Like Taft in 1912, La Follette finished a poor third, receiving a respectable but ineffective 4.8 million popular votes and only 13 electoral votes. Though the trend of low voter turnout begun in the Progressive era continued (to the dismay of feminists, even newly enfranchised women voted in small numbers), those who did vote seemed satisfied with the general prosperity.

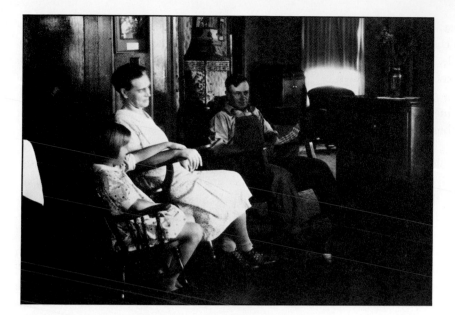

The age of electrical appliances dawned in the 1920s. Here, a family gathers around a radio, one of the most popular electrical innovations of the age. The radio not only popularized modern music and folksy drama but also created new schedules in family life. *National Archives.*

MATERIALISM UNBOUND

"One day," Henry Ford recalled, "someone brought to us a slogan which read: 'Buy a Ford and Save the Difference.' I crossed out the 'save' and inserted 'spend'—'Buy a Ford and Spend the Difference.' It is the wiser thing to do. Society lives by circulation and not by congestion." Ford had a way of making new values sound like old truths. His ardent consumerism was a major theme of the 1920s, to which he contributed materially as well as philosophically. By 1925 the assembly line at Ford's Highland Park plant produced a motor car every ten seconds.

Indeed, between 1919 and 1929 the gross national product—the total value of all goods and services produced in the United States—swelled by 40 percent. Wages and salaries also increased

Expansion of the Consumer Society (though not as much) while the cost of living remained relatively stable. The result was that people

had more purchasing power. And they spent as Americans had never spent. In an article in *Survey* magazine in 1928, Eunice Fuller Barnard contrasted family expenditures in 1900 with those of 1928:

1900

2 bicycles	$ 70
wringer and washboard	$ 5
brushes and brooms	$ 5
sewing machine (mechanical)	$ 25
Total	$105

1928

automobile	$700
radio	$ 75
phonograph	$ 50
washing machine	$150
vacuum cleaner	$ 50
sewing machine (electric)	$ 60
other electrical equipment	$ 25
telephone (year)	$ 35
Total	$1,145[1]

[1]From Paul Carter, *Another Part of the Twenties,* © 1977, Columbia University Press. By permission.

Barnard added that certain items, such as education and medical care, had become costlier. Yet she felt the change had been worthwhile. She would rather pay more for a quart of milk knowing it was safer and purer than the product of a generation earlier. "When some of us bewail the higher cost of living we may be talking about the higher cost of *better* living," Barnard concluded.

The benefits of modern technology were reaching more people than ever before. By 1929 two-thirds of all Americans lived in dwellings that had electricity, compared with one-sixth in 1912. In 1929 one-fourth of all families owned electric vacuum cleaners and one-fifth had electric toasters. Many could afford these and other items such as radios, washing machines, and movie tickets only because more than one family member worked or because the breadwinner took a second job. Nevertheless, new products and services were available to more than just the rich.

Of all the era's technological and economic wonders, the automobile was the vanguard. During the 1920s automobile registrations soared from 8 million to 23 million. Mass production and competition had brought down prices, making cars affordable even to some working-class families. By 1926 a Ford Model T cost under $300 and a Chevrolet sold for $700—at a time when workers in manufacturing earned around $1,300 a year and clerical workers about $2,300. The car had become a source of pride as well as a means of transportation; no sacrifice was too great to obtain one. Thus when an interviewer asked a rural housewife why her family owned a car but not a bathtub, the woman retorted, "Bathtub? You can't go to town in a bathtub."

Effects of the Automobile

The motor car altered society as much as the railroad had seventy-five years earlier. Public officials were forced to pay more attention to safety regulations and traffic control. (In 1924 the General Electric Company responded to the needs with the first timed stop-and-go traffic light.) Changes in car design provided new opportunities for youths to escape watchful parents. By 1927, five-sixths of all autos were enclosed (in 1919 most had had open tops), making for a privacy that bred fears of "houses of prostitution on wheels." The growing choice of models (there were 108 different automobile manufacturers in 1923) and colors allowed automobile owners to suit their personal tastes in a growing mass society. But most important, the car was the ultimate symbol of social equality. As one writer observed in 1924, "It is hard to convince Steve Popovich, or Antonio Branca, or plain John Smith that he is being ground into the dust by Capital when at will he may drive the same highways, view the same scenery, and get as much enjoyment from his trip as the modern Midas."

Americans' newly acquired taste for driving necessitated extensive construction of roads and abundant supplies of fuel. Since the late 1800s farmers and bicyclists had been pressing for improved roads; after the First World War motorists joined the campaign, prompting cities and states to improve local arteries. The important advances came in 1921 when Congress passed the Federal Highway Act, which provided federal aid for state roads; and in 1923 when the Bureau of Public Roads planned a national highway system.

The oil industry, already vast and powerful, shifted its emphasis from products providing illumination and lubrication to products providing propulsion. In 1920 the United States was producing about 65 percent of the world's oil, much of it controlled by the Standard Oil trust. But already Americans were tasting a bitter future (see pages 976–979) as corporate and government officials warned of fuel shortages and shrinking reserves. Early in 1920 a U.S. Geological Survey report stated that "unless our consumption is checked, we shall by 1925 be dependent on foreign oilfields." In some parts of the country companies limited the amount of gasoline people could buy and doubled the price. But the crisis had a dubious flavor. Just after the shortages and price hikes occurred, the State Department persuaded the British to grant Standard Oil a share in British-controlled Iraqi oilfields. Immediately thereafter, the crisis abated.

Advertising

More than ever, Americans' taste for automobiles and other goods and services was whetted by advertising. By 1929 total advertising earnings reached $3.4 billion, more than was spent on all types of formal education. For many, advertising became the language of a new gospel. In his best-selling *The Man Nobody Knows* (1925), advertising executive Bruce Barton called Jesus "the founder of modern business" because he "picked up twelve men from the bottom ranks of business and forged them into an organization

Chapter 24: THE NEW ERA OF THE 1920s

"Everyone owns a car but us"~

You, too, can own an automobile without missing the money, and *now*, is the time to buy it—through the easiest and simplest method ever devised:

Ford Weekly Purchase Plan

Thousands of families, who thought a car was out of the question because of limited incomes, found that they could easily, quickly and surely buy a car of their own under this remarkable plan

You *can* own an automobile, and you *should*. It will mean so much to you. It will add much to the happiness of your family that is worth while. It will bring the most glorious pleasures into your life. It will increase your chances for success. It will give you and your family a social and business prestige that will be invaluable—and which you, and every family, should enjoy. A car is a symbol of success—a mark of achievement, and it brings opportunities to you that you would probably never secure otherwise. You should have a car of your own, and *you can*.

The Ford Plan makes it possible for anyone to own an automobile. It is so easy, simple and practical that many who could easily pay "spot cash" take advantage of it—and buy their car from weekly earnings. The plan is simply wonderful! Before you realize it, you are driving your own automobile. If you have felt that you did not make enough to buy a car, you must read The Ford Plan Book. Send for it. See how easy it is to get a car of your own, *now*, and pay for it without missing the money. It seems almost too good to be true, doesn't it? *But it is true*. Get the book—at once. Simply mail the coupon. *Mail it today!*

Give your family the advantages which others have. Get a car of your own. The Ford Plan Book tells you "how" you can buy a car and pay for it without missing the money. Get it! Read it!

Mail Coupon Now. This Book Will be Sent by Return Mail.

Ford Motor Company
Detroit

IT IS EASY TO OWN A CAR BY USING THIS PLAN

COUPON

FORD MOTOR COMPANY
Dept. B-3   Detroit, Michigan
Please send me your book, "The Ford Plan" which fully explains your easy plan for owning an automobile.

Name ——————————

R. F. D. Box or St. & No. ——————

Town —————— *State* ——————

By the 1920s, not only was an automobile affordable, especially through installment payments such as the "Ford Weekly Purchase Plan," but also there was strong social pressure on families to own one. As this advertisement so vividly illustrates, Americans were made to feel that they needed an automobile for the pleasure and status it would bring them.   Library of Congress.

that conquered the world." About the same time, a pamphlet titled *Moses, Persuader of Men* declared, "Moses was one of the greatest salesmen and real-estate promoters that ever lived"—demonstrating that advertising could be ecumenical. Advertising theorists also adopted psychological principles and practical cynicism in asserting that, with proper environmental influences, any person's tastes could be manipulated.

Although daily newspaper circulation declined during the 1920s, other media assumed vital advertising functions. By 1929 over 10 million families owned radios, which bombarded them almost continuously with advertisements. Station KDKA in Pittsburgh pioneered in commercial radio broadcasting beginning in 1920; by 1922 there were 508 such stations. By 1929 Americans were spending $850 million a year on radio equipment, and the National Broadcasting Company, which had begun to assemble a network of radio stations three years earlier, was charging advertisers $10,000 to sponsor an hour-long show. Commercial intermissions at movie houses and highway billboards also reminded viewers to buy. Packaging and product display became sciences, with the object of creating demand.

Though poor people could not afford many of the products and services, some of the new trends touched working-class groups, especially those in the cities. Indoor plumbing and electricity became more common in private residences, and canned foods, varied diets, ready-made clothes, and mass-produced shoes became more affordable. A little cash and a lot of credit enabled many to purchase an automobile. And even if a family could not afford a radio, vacuum cleaner, or vacation, there was always hope. Spending became a national pastime. No wonder many people wanted Henry Ford to run for president in 1924.

CITIES, MIGRANTS, AND SUBURBS

The expansion of consumerism bespoke not only an economically mature nation but an urbanized one. In 1920 for the first time the federal census

Continuing Urbanization revealed that a majority of Americans, 51.4 percent, lived in urban areas (places with 2,500 or more people)—a sign that the city had become the locus of national experience. Indeed, the growth of services and industry both derived from and responded to urbanization. Industries such as steel, oil, and auto production boosted cities like Detroit, Birmingham, and Houston; service and retail trades accounted for expansion in Atlanta, Minneapolis, and Seattle. The most explosive growth occurred in areas of warm climate—Miami and San Diego—where promises of comfort and profit attracted thousands of speculators.

The trend toward urbanization continued during the 1920s, as an estimated 6 million Americans left their farms for nearby or distant cities. Midwestern migrants, particularly young single people, moved to regional centers or to California. A steady stream of southerners moved into burgeoning industrial cities of the South or followed railroad lines north.

Blacks accounted for a sizable portion of the migrants. Crushed by tenant farming and lured by industrial jobs, 1.5 million blacks moved cityward during the 1920s, accelerating a trend begun a decade earlier (see pages 517–518). The black populations of New York, Chicago, Detroit, and Houston doubled during these years. Forced by necessity and discrimination to seek the cheapest housing, the newcomers squeezed into ghettos—low-rent districts from which escape was difficult at best. For unlike white migrants, who were free to move away from inner-city districts if and when they could afford to do so, blacks found better housing closed to them. The only way they could expand their housing opportunities was to spill into nearby neighborhoods, a process that sparked resistance and violence. Fears of such expansion prompted white neighborhood associations to adopt restrictive covenants, whereby homeowners pledged not to sell their property to blacks.

In response partly to their new urban experiences and partly to race riots and threats, thousands of blacks in northern cities joined movements that glorified black independence. The most **Marcus Garvey** influential of these black nationalist groups was the Universal Negro Improvement Association (UNIA), headed by Marcus Garvey, a Jamaican immigrant who believed blacks

During and after the First World War, thousands of southern blacks migrated northward, taking railroad routes into cities like Chicago, New York, and St. Louis. In these cities blacks found new job opportunities and better housing but also racial tension and occasional violence. The Phillips Collection, Washington.

should separate themselves from a corrupt white society. Proclaiming "I am the equal of any white man," Garvey cultivated race pride through militant mass meetings and parades. He also promoted black capitalism to demonstrate blacks' management skills. His newspaper, the *Negro World,* refused to publish ads for hair straighteners and skin-lightening cosmetics, and his Black Star shipping line was intended to help blacks emigrate to Africa.

The UNIA declined in the mid-1920s when the Black Star line went bankrupt (unscrupulous dealers had sold the line dilapidated ships) and when antiradical fears prompted government prosecution (ten of the organization's leaders were arrested on charges of anarchism and Garvey was deported for mail fraud). Black middle-class leaders like W. E. B. Du Bois opposed the UNIA. Nevertheless, the organization

had attracted a huge following (contemporaries estimated it at 500,000; Garvey claimed 6 million) in New York, Chicago, Detroit, and other cities. And Garvey's speeches had served notice that blacks had their own aspirations, which they could and would translate into action.

The newest immigrants to American cities came from Mexico and Puerto Rico. As in the nineteenth century, many Mexicans moved north to work as agricultural laborers in the Southwest, but in the 1920s a large number also flowed into growing cities like Denver, San Antonio, Los Angeles, and Tucson. Like other immigrant groups, Mexicans generally lacked resources and skills, and men greatly outnumbered women. Victims of white discrimination, Mexicans crowded

Mexican and Puerto Rican Immigrants

During the 1920s, a housing boom occurred in many suburbs. The automobile facilitated commuting to the nearby city and enabled middle-class families to live in "bedroom communities" such as Tarrytown, New York, pictured above. The Bettmann Archive.

into low-rent, inner-city districts where they often were deprived of decent city services, such as sanitation, schools, and police protection. Yet their communities, called *barrios,* provided an environment in which the immigrants could sustain customs and values of the homeland and develop institutions to help them adapt to American society.

The 1920s also saw a great influx of Puerto Ricans to the mainland (Puerto Rico had been a U.S. possession since 1898; see page 631). A shift in the island's economy from sugar to coffee production had created a surplus population willing to move and attracted by contracts from American employers seeking cheap labor. Most Puerto Rican migrants moved to New York City where they formed *barrios* in parts of Brooklyn and Manhattan. Besides manufacturing, Puerto Ricans found jobs in hotels, res-

taurants, and domestic service. As with Mexicans, Puerto Rican communities contained some educated elites—doctors, lawyers, business owners—who served as ethnic leaders. The *barrios,* which contained nearly equal numbers of women and men, also developed their own consumer institutions, such as *bodegas* (grocery stores), restaurants and boardinghouses.

As urban growth peaked, suburban growth accelerated. Although towns had existed around the edges of urban centers since the nation's earliest years, prosperity and easier transportation—mainly the automobile—made the urban fringe more accessible in the 1920s. Between 1920 and 1930, suburbs of Chicago (such as Oak Park and Evanston), Cleveland (such as Shaker Heights), and Los Angeles (such as Burbank and Inglewood) grew

Growth of the Suburbs

five to ten times as fast as the central cities. Most such suburbs were middle- and upper-class bedroom communities, though they included industrial suburbs like Highland Park (near Detroit) and East Chicago.

With their own police, fire protection, and water and gas services, many suburbs resisted annexation to core cities. Suburbanites wanted to escape big-city crime, dirt, and taxes, and they fought to preserve local control. "Under local government," one suburban editor reasoned, "we can absolutely control every objectionable thing that may try to enter our limits— but once annexed we are at the mercy of city hall." Particularly in the Northeast and Midwest, the fierce independence of growing suburbs choked off expansion by the central city and divided metropolitan areas in ways that would cause problems for future generations.

The bulging cities and suburbs fostered the new mass culture that gave the decade its character. Most of the consumers who jammed retail establishments, movie houses, and sporting arenas and who embraced fads like crossword puzzles, miniature golf, and marathon dancing were city and suburb dwellers. Cities and suburbs were the places where people flouted law and morality by patronizing speakeasies (illegal saloons), wearing outlandish clothes, and listening to jazz. They were also the places where women, ethnic and racial minorities, and religious denominations strained hardest to adjust to the new era. And yet the ideal of small-town society survived. While millions thronged cityward and intellectuals carped that small towns stifled personal growth, Americans still reminisced about the innocence and simplicity of a world gone by. This was the dilemma of a modern nation: how could one anchor oneself in a world of rampant material and social change?

New Rhythms
of Everyday Life

Amid all the change, Americans developed new social values and new ways of using time. Increasingly, people were splitting their daily lives into three distinct compartments: work, family, and leisure. Each type of time was altered in the 1920s. For many people, time on the job shrank. Among industrial workers the five-and-one-half-day workweek (half a day on Saturday) was becoming common. Many white-collar employees enjoyed two days off and worked a forty-hour week. Annual vacations were becoming a standard job benefit for white-collar workers, whose numbers grew by 40 percent during the decade.

Family time is harder to measure, but certain figures suggest important changes. As birth control became more widely accepted, birthrates dropped noticeably between 1920 and 1930. As a result, family size decreased. Among American women who married in the 1870s and 1880s, well over half who survived to fifty had had five or more children; of those who married in the 1920s, however, just 20 percent had five or more children. Over the same period the divorce rate rose. In 1920 there was one divorce in every 7.5 marriages; in 1929 the national ratio was 1 in 6, and in many cities it was 2 in 7. Lower birthrates, more divorce, plus longer life expectancy meant that adults were devoting a smaller portion of their lives to parental and other family tasks.

At the same time the availability of ready-to-wear clothes, preserved foods, and mass-produced furniture meant that family members spent less time producing household necessities. Wives still

Household Management spent most of their day cleaning, cooking, mending, and otherwise maintaining the home, but new machines lightened some of their tasks. Especially in middle-class households, electric irons and washing machines made the most tedious chores less burdensome. Central heating and hot-water heaters eliminated the hauling of wood, coal, and water, the upkeep of a kitchen fire, and the removal of ashes.

As a result, housewives filled their time differently from their forebears. In some ways the new technology made new demands on them. By eliminating servants, who had formerly helped with cleaning, cooking, and childcare, machines shifted the entire job of household management and childraising onto the wife herself. And instead of being a producer of food and clothing as women had been, the wife now became chief consumer, doing the shopping and making sure the family spent its money wisely.

The ready availability of washing machines, hot

$1000.00 PRIZE CONTEST—(INQUIRE WITHIN)

Life

Commuters' Number

Suburbanization and the demands of white collar work created new schedules and roles in the middle class family. Here the housewife, now the chief consumer and household manager, sews a button on the sleeve of the breadwinner husband while he gulps coffee and reads his paper before rushing to catch his commuter train.   Library of Congress.

water, and commercial soap put greater pressure on wives to keep everything clean. Advertisers tried to coax women into buying products by making them feel guilty for not giving enough attention to cleaning the home, caring for the children, and tending to personal hygiene. "Are you unpopular with your own children?" asked the makers of Listerine mouthwash. If so, the ad continued, "More often than you would imagine . . . halitosis is at fault. Children are quick to resent it. . . . Realizing this, [intelligent people] eliminate any risk of offending by the systematic use of Listerine in the mouth. Every morning. Every night." Thus, while the industrial and service sectors became more specialized as a result of technological advances, housewives retained a wide variety of responsibilites and added new ones as well.

While family time shifted and work time decreased, nonwork, nonfamily activities were expanding. More people spent more years in school. High school en-rollment quadrupled between 1910 and 1929; by 1929 over a third of all high school graduates went on to college. And as the use of electricity spread, people stayed up later at night to read or listen to the radio. They filled their expanding leisure time with automobile rides, sports events, motion pictures, shopping, and other forms of amusement.

In general, more rest and better diets were making Americans healthier. Between 1920 and 1930 life expectancy at birth increased from fifty-four to sixty years, and infant mortality decreased by two-thirds. Sanitation and medical research in bacteriology and immunology combined with better nutrition to reduce the risks of life-threatening diseases such as tuberculosis and diphtheria. Medical progress did not benefit all groups equally, however. Rates of stillbirth and infant mortality were 50 to 100 percent higher among blacks than among whites, and the incidence of tuberculosis in urban slums remained alarmingly high. Moreover, the death rate from automobile accidents rose 150 percent, and deaths from heart disease and cancer, diseases of old age, increased about 15 percent. Nevertheless, Americans in general were living longer: the total number of people age sixty-five and over grew 35 percent between 1920 and 1930, while the rest of the population increased only 15 percent.

Growing numbers and worsening economic conditions of the elderly stirred interest in old-age pensions and other forms of assistance. Old people increasingly faced poverty due to forced retirement and reduced income, for the industrial system put a premium on youth and agility. Realizing the needs of their aging citizens, most European countries had established state-supported pension systems in the early 1900s. But many Americans still believed that people should prepare for old age by saving in their youth; pensions, they felt, smacked of socialism. As late as 1923 the Pennsylvania Chamber of Commerce labeled old-age assistance "unAmerican and socialistic . . . an entering wedge of communistic propaganda."

Old Age and Retirement

Yet something had to be done. During the decade, a large majority of all inmates in state pauper institutions were old people, and almost one-third of all Americans sixty-five and older were financially dependent on someone else. Only a few companies had retirement plans; most, including the federal government, did not take care of retired employees. Noting that the government fed retired horses until they died, one postal worker complained, "For the purpose of drawing a pension, it would have been better had I been a horse than a human being." Resistance to pensions finally broke at the state level in the 1920s. Led by Isaac Max Rubinow and Abraham Epstein, reformers persuaded voluntary associations, labor unions, and legislators to accept the principle of old-age support through pensions, insurance programs, and retirement homes. By 1933 almost every state provided at least minimal assistance to the needy elderly, and the way had been opened for a national program of old-age insurance.

With more people spending time away from work and family, new values were inevitable. Especially among the middle class but among the working class too, clothes became a means to per-

Social Values sonal expression and freedom. Both men and women wore more casual and more gaily colored styles than their parents would have considered. The line between inappropriate and acceptable behavior blurred as smoking, swearing, and frankness about sex became more common. Thousands who had never read psychoanalyst Sigmund Freud's theories were certain that he prescribed an uninhibited sex life as the key to mental health. Birth-control advocate Margaret Sanger, who a decade earlier had been accused of promoting race suicide and forced to flee the country, now gained a large following in respectable circles. Newspapers, magazines, motion pictures, and popular songs (such as "Hot Lips" and "Burning Kisses") made certain that Americans did not suffer from "sex starvation." A typical movie ad announced "brilliant men, beautiful jazz babies, champagne baths, midnight revels, petting parties in the purple dawn, all ending in one terrific smashing climax that makes you gasp."

Still other trends contributed to the breakdown of traditional values. Because child-labor laws and compulsory-school-attendance laws kept children in school longer than was common in earlier generations, schools and peer groups now played a greater role in socializing children. In earlier times, different age groups had common activities; for example, children worked with older people in the fields, and young apprentices worked with older journeymen and craftsmen. Now, however, graded school classes, sports, clubs, and

By obtaining jobs, many young women of the 1920s could afford the latest fashions. These three modishly dressed black women from Harlem were part of the swelling numbers of female secretaries, store clerks, waitresses, and hairdressers. The Schomburg Collection, New York Public Library.

other activities constantly brought together children who were the same age, separating them from the company and influence of adults. In addition, parents tended to rely less on family tradition and more on childcare manuals in raising their children. Old-age homes, public health clinics, and workers' compensation reduced the family's responsibilities even further.

Although the home remained a female domain, and in spite of the closing off of employment opportunities the First World War had created, women

Jobs for Women continued to stream into the labor force during the 1920s. By 1930 10.8 million women worked, an increase of over 2 million since the war's end. The sex segregation that had long characterized occupations continued; most female workers could be found in jobs where few men worked. More than a million women were teachers and nurses. Some 2.2 million were typists, bookkeepers, and office clerks, a tenfold increase since 1920; another 736,000 were salespeople in stores. Increasingly large numbers of women took jobs as waitresses and hairdressers. Almost 2 million women worked in factories, though their numbers grew very little over the decade.

Women's foray into work outside the home reflected an extension of their family roles. Although they worked for a combination of reasons, the economic needs of their families shaped the job experiences of most women. The consumerism of the 1920s prompted working-class and middle-class families to satisfy their wants either by living beyond their means or by sending women and children into the labor force. In previous eras, most of these extra wage earners were young and single. But in the 1920s, married women joined the group, a trend that has increased down to the present. Between 1920 and 1930, the proportion of the work force that contained married women rose by 30 percent, and the numbers of married women working swelled from 1.9 million to 3.1 million. Pressures of poverty gave many of these women no choice but to work; yet others did so because they wanted to increase their family's material comforts. They still justified their work on the basis of need, but this definition of need reflected the new consumer values—the family "needed" a radio and a car as well as food and clothing. The vast majority of married women remained out of the work force (only 12 percent were employed in 1930), but they did so because social pressures and demands of housework and child-care prevented them. (Black women were the exception; their proportions in the work force were twice those of white women, indicating both greater economic burdens and family arrangements that enabled them to balance housework along with their outside jobs.)

Married Women in the Labor Force

Feminists in the 1920s directed their concern to the issue of married women in the labor force, but they did not fully understand the motivations of married working women. Building on the ideas of Charlotte Perkins Gilman (see page 603), a number of female writers pushed for greater economic opportunity for women, especially married women. They believed that the separation of place of work from place of residence had left women at

Economic Feminism

home to tend household chores that few men would do. Women's earlier functions as economic producers of food and clothes, said feminists, had lapsed into passive roles as child nurturers and homemakers; the result was economic dependency. The way to restore married women's sense of worth in a money-oriented society was for them to have gainful employment. A job, asserted *Harper's* editor Dorothy Bromley, would make a married woman "a full-fledged individual who is capable of molding her own life."

But because feminists tried to separate the notion of career from domestic roles, they had little appeal to women who placed family needs, not individual needs, above all else regardless of whether or not they held jobs. Thus few women heeded the call for equal pay and equal opportunity voiced by Alice Paul, leader of the new National Women's party, who in 1922 supported an equal rights amendment to the Constitution. Indeed, after obtaining the vote in 1920, many women seemed to turn their backs on politics. The National American Women Suffrage Association disbanded, and the League of Women Voters which followed it, avoided party politics and controversial issues.

Whether they worked or not, all types of women were exposed to alternative images of femininity. Short skirts and bobbed hair, regarded as signs of sexual freedom, became common among office workers and store clerks as well as among middle-class college coeds. Several studies claimed that sexual experimentation, including premarital sex, increased among young women during the decade. The most popular models of female behavior were not chaste, sentimental heroines but movie vamps like Clara Bow, the "It Girl," and Gloria Swanson, who specialized in torrid love affairs on and off the screen. And though not everyone was a flapper, as the young independent-minded woman was called, many women were clearly asserting their equality with men. As one observer described the "new woman":

Alternative Images of Femininity

> She takes a man's point of view as her mother never could. . . . She will never make you a hat-band or knit you a necktie, but she'll drive you from the station . . . in her own little sports car. She'll don knickers and go skiing with you . . . she'll dive as well as you, perhaps better, she'll

dance as long as you care to, and she'll take everything you say the way you mean it. . . .

These new social trends represented a sharp break with the more restrained culture of the nineteenth century. But social change, as always, did not proceed smoothly. As the decade wore on, various groups prepared to defend against the threat to older, more familiar values.

LINES OF DEFENSE

I n the spring of 1920 the leader of a newly formed organization decided to hire two public-relations experts to recruit members. Using modern advertising techniques, the promoters, Edward Clarke and Elizabeth Tyler, canvassed cities and towns in the South, Southwest, and Midwest, where they found thousands of men eager to pay $10 to join and another $6 for a uniform made of white cloth. For their efforts, Clarke and Tyler pocketed $2.50 out of each membership fee. No one could argue with their success. By 1923 the organization claimed 5 million members. But this was no ordinary civic club like the Lions or Kiwanis; it cultivated a very special kind of social consciousness. It was the Ku Klux Klan, a revived version of the hooded order that had terrorized southern communities following the Civil War, and its appeal was based largely on fear. As one of the pamphlets distributed by Clarke and Tyler put it, "Every criminal, every gambler, every thug, every libertine, every girl ruiner, every home wrecker, every wife beater, every dope peddler, every moonshiner, every white slaver, every Rome-controlled newspaper, every black spider—is fighting the Klan. Think it over, which side are you on?"

The Klan was the most sinister reactionary movement of the 1920s. Founded in 1915 by William J. Simmons, an Atlanta evangelist and insurance salesman who wanted to purify southern

Ku Klux Klan culture, the new Invisible Empire revived the hoods, intimidating tactics, and mystical terms of its forerunner. (Local societies were *klaverns*, its leader the Imperial Wizard,

its book of rituals the *kloran*.) But the new Klan was broader in membership and in objectives than the old. Its chapters fanned outward from the deep South and for a time wielded frightening power in all other regions of the country. And unlike the first Klan, which terrorized mostly emancipated blacks, the new Klan directed its venom toward a variety of groups.

One brief phrase expressed the Klan's objectives: "Native, white, Protestant supremacy." *Native* meant no immigration, no "mongrelization" of white Protestant culture. According to Imperial Wizard Hiram Wesley Evans, *white* supremacy was a matter of survival. "The world," he warned, "has been so made so that each race must fight for its life, must conquer, accept slavery, or die. The Klansman believes the whites will not become slaves, and he does not intend to die before his time." Evans praised *Protestantism* for permitting "unhampered individual development." The Catholic Church, on the other hand, prevented immigrants from assimilating and suppressed free conscience by subordinating people to priests and a foreign pope.

Using threatening assemblies, violence, and political pressure, Klan members made their presence felt in many communities in the early 1920s. Assuming the role of moral protector, they meted out vigilante justice to bootleggers, wife beaters, and adulterers; forced schools to adopt Bible readings and stop teaching the theory of evolution; and campaigned against Catholic and Jewish political candidates. By the mid-1920s, however, the Invisible Empire was on the wane, outnumbered by its foreign-stock opponents and rocked by scandal. (In 1925 Indiana Grand Dragon David Stephenson allegedly kidnapped and raped a woman who later died either from taking poison or from an infection caused by bites on her body; Stephenson was convicted of second-degree murder on the grounds that he was responsible for her suicide.) The Klan's negative, exclusive brand of patriotism and purity could not compete in a pluralistic society.

The Ku Klux Klan had no monopoly on bigotry. The 1920s bared the pervasiveness of intolerance in American society. Since the 1880s a number of groups had been urging an end to free immigration. Huge influxes of Catholic and Jewish immigrants, these nativists charged, clogged inner-city slums, upset traditional norms with their drinking habits, and stubbornly held to alien religious and political beliefs.

Bartolomeo Vanzetti and Nicola Sacco, painted by Ben Shahn. The trial and execution of the two immigrant anarchists touched the consciences of many artists and writers, prompting them to incorporate social themes in their work. Collection, The Museum of Modern Art, New York. Gift of Abby Aldrich Rockefeller. Tempera on paper over composition board, 10½ × 14½".

As self-styled expert Madison Grant wrote in *The Passing of the Great Race* (1916): "These immigrants adopt the language of the native American, they wear his clothes, they steal his name and they are beginning to take his women, but they seldom adopt his religion or understand his ideals."

Fear of radicalism, left over from the Red Scare of 1919, fueled these antiforeign sentiments. The most notorious outburst of hysteria occurred in 1921, when a court convicted Nicola

Sacco and Vanzetti

Sacco and Bartolomeo Vanzetti, two immigrant anarchists, of murdering a guard and paymaster during a robbery in South Braintree, Massachusetts. But Sacco and Vanzetti's main offenses seem to have been their political beliefs and Italian origins, since evidence failed to prove their involvement in the robbery.

Judge Webster Thayer nevertheless openly sided with the prosecution, privately calling the defendants "those anarchist bastards." Appeals by protesters failed to win a new trial, and the two Italians, who remained calm and dignified throughout their ordeal, were executed in August 1927. Their deaths chilled those who had looked to the United States as the land that nurtured freedom of belief.

Meanwhile, the move to restrict immigration was gathering support. Labor leaders warned that a flood of aliens would depress wages and raise unemployment. Business executives who had formerly opposed restrictions because immigrant laborers were easy to exploit changed their minds when they discovered that mechanization and the hiring of native black workers could enable them to keep labor costs low. Drawing support from these groups as well as other

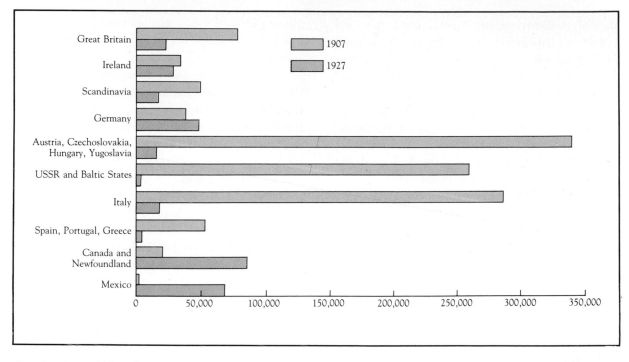

Immigration, 1907 and 1927

nativists, Congress established yearly immigration quotas for each nationality.

These quotas favored northern and western Europeans, reflecting the prejudices of natives against newer immigrant groups from southern and eastern Europe. The Emergency Quota, or Johnson, Act of 1921 provided that the annual immigration of any given nationality could not exceed 3 percent of the number of immigrants from that nation residing in the United States in 1910. But this law, meant to be temporary, did not satisfy restrictionists' aims, so Congress replaced it with the National Origins Act of 1924. The new law set the quota at 2 percent of each nationality residing in the United States in *1890*, further limiting the influx of southern and eastern Europeans, since far fewer of these groups lived in the United States in 1890 than in 1910. The National Origins Act was amended in 1927, at which time Congress moved the base year to 1920 and set a limit of 150,000 immigrants a year—including 65,721 from Great Britain and 25,957 from Germany, but only 5,802 from Italy and 2,712 from Russia. These laws virtually excluded Asians, but left the

Immigration Quotas

door open to peoples from the Western Hemisphere. Soon Canadians, Mexicans, and Puerto Ricans became the largest groups of newcomers (see figure).

The impulse to insure moral purity also stirred religious fundamentalists. Millions of Americans sought certainty in a rapidly changing world by following the evangelical branches of Protestantism that accepted a literal interpretation of the Bible. For them unquestioning faith was not only a means to salvation but a traditional and highly comforting defense against the skepticism and irreverence of a materialistic, hedonistic society.

In 1925 fundamentalist Christianity clashed with new scientific theory in a celebrated case in Dayton, Tennessee. Early that year the Tennessee legislature passed a law forbidding public school instructors to teach the theory that humans had evolved from lower forms of life rather than from Adam and Eve. Shortly thereafter, high school teacher John Thomas Scopes was arrested for violating the law (he had volunteered to serve in a test case). Scopes's trial that summer became a headline event, with William Jennings Bryan, former secretary of state and three-time pres-

Scopes Trial

idential candidate, arguing for the prosecution, and a team of civil-liberties lawyers headed by Clarence Darrow arguing for the defense. Hordes of news correspondents crowded into town, and radio stations broadcast the trial.

Although Scopes was convicted—clearly he had broken the law—modernists claimed victory; the testimony, they believed, had shown fundamentalism to be at odds with secular social trends. Indeed, the trial's climax occurred when Bryan agreed to take the witness stand as an expert on religion and science. Responding to Darrow's probing, Bryan asserted that Eve had truly been created from Adam's rib; that a big fish had swallowed Jonah; and that God had created the world in six days—though Bryan noted that a "day" might have lasted a million years. The liberal press mocked Bryan's uncritical faith; humorist Will Rogers quipped, "I see you can't say that man descended from the ape. At least that's the law in Tennessee. But do they have a law to keep a man from making a jackass of himself?" Nevertheless, fundamentalists nursed their wounds and steadfastly pursued their cause of faith and salvation.

Ku Klux Klan rallies, immigration restriction, and fundamentalist protests might be seen as last gasps of a rural society yielding to modern urban-industrial values. Yet city dwellers swelled the ranks of these defensive movements. Nearly half the Klan's members lived in cities, especially in native white working-class neighborhoods, where fear of invasion by blacks and foreigners was strong. Even urban reformers backed laws limiting immigration, seeing them as a means of controlling poverty and quickening the assimilation of foreign groups. Cities also housed hundreds of pentecostal churches, which attracted whites struggling between the middle and lower classes. Such people were swayed by the pageantry and closeness to God these churches offered. Using elaborately staged services, radio broadcasts, and modern advertising techniques, cult leaders such as Aimee Semple McPherson of Los Angeles stirred revivalist fervor. Finally, many urban dwellers supported prohibition. Middle-class Protestants and even some Catholics and Jews believed that by eliminating the temptation of drink they could win the battle against poverty, vice, and corruption.

The emotional responses Americans made to events during the 1920s were part of a larger attempt to sustain old, local values in a fast-moving, materialistic world. Occasionally Americans lashed out at minority cultures and seemingly hedonistic trends in behavior. Millions of otherwise decent Americans firmly believed that nonwhites and immigrants were inferior people who threatened existing values. And evangelists who preached against evolution were rare compared to the number of clergy and teachers of all faiths who condemned drinking, dancing, new styles of dress, and new sexual habits.

Even as they worried about losing old values, most Americans tried to adjust to the new order in one way or another. Few refrained from attending motion pictures or listening to the radio, activities that proved less corrupting than critics feared. Radio featured harmless music, news, and homey drama. And the movie industry bowed to pressure from legislatures in 1927 and instituted self-censorship, forbidding nudity, rough language, and plots that did not end with justice triumphant. More than ever, Americans sought fellowship in civic organizations. Membership swelled in Rotary, Kiwanis, Lions, Elks, and women's clubs, and the number of community chests—associations that coordinated civic and welfare projects—grew from 12 in 1919 to 361 in 1930. But perhaps most important, more and more people were finding release in a world of leisure.

THE AGE OF PLAY

During the 1920s Americans developed an almost insatiable thirst for recreation. In 1919 they spent about $2.5 billion on leisure activities; by 1929 such expenditures topped $4.3 billion, a figure that would not again be equaled until after the Second World War. Spectator amusements—movies, theater, sports, and the like—accounted for about 21 percent of the figure for 1929. Individual recreation, from participation sports to reading, hobbies, music, and travel, took up the remainder.

Entrepreneurs responded quickly. The decade marked the flowering of fads, frivolities, and what contemporaries called ballyhoo, a blitz of publicity that lent exaggerated importance to some person or event. New games and fancies were particularly attractive to middle-class families with large spendable incomes. In the early 1920s the Chinese tile game of mahjongg was the rage. Merchants could not import enough of the games, so dozens of American manufacturers began to produce them. By the mid-1920s people were turning to crossword puzzles, which mass-circulation newpapers and magazines had begun printing a decade earlier. In 1924 the new publishing firm of Simon and Schuster brought out a book of crossword puzzles with a pencil attached—anyone who did a crossword puzzle in pen was labeled a foolish optimist—and the volume became an instant best seller. A few years later fun seekers adopted miniature golf as their new craze. By 1930 some thirty thousand miniature golf courses featuring tiny castles, windmills, and waterfalls dotted cities and towns across the country. And throughout the decade dance crazes like the Charleston riveted public attention, aided by radio music and the growing popularity of jazz.

In addition to their active participation in leisure activities, Americans were avid spectators, particularly of movies and sports. In terms of total capital investment, motion pictures became

Movies

one of the nation's leading industries. Nearly every community had at least one theater, whether it was a hundred-seat Bijou on Main Street or a big-city picture palace with ornate walls, fountains in the lobby, and thousands of cushioned seats. In 1922 movies attracted 40 million viewers a week; by 1930 the number had reached 100 million—at a time when total population was just over 120 million and total weekly church attendance was under 60 million. The introduction of sound in *The Jazz Singer* in 1927 and of color a few years later made movies even more attractive and realistic. Movie producers provided the public fantasy and vicarious escape more than they did a serious new art form. The most popular films were mass spectacles such as Cecil B. DeMille's *The Ten Commandments* (1923) and *The King of Kings* (1927); lurid titles such as *Souls for Sale* (1923) and *A Woman Who Sinned* (1924); and slapstick comedies starring Fatty Arbuckle, Harold Lloyd, Buster Keaton, and Charlie Chaplin. Ironically, the comedies, with their often poignant satire of the human condition, carried the most thought-provoking messages.

Spectator sports also boomed. Each year millions packed stadiums, arenas, and parks to watch athletic events. By the late 1920s gate receipts from college football alone had surpassed $21 million. In an age when technology and mass production had robbed experiences and objects of their uniqueness, sports provided the unpredictability and drama that people craved. Newspapers and radio captured and exaggerated this drama, feeding news to an eager public and often overpromoting events with unrestrained narrative. Thus in 1920 the otherwise staid *New York Times* resorted to wild hyperbole to summarize a tennis match between William Tilden, the national champion, and challenger William Johnston:

> The Tilden-Johnston struggle will go down on the records as the most astounding exhibition of tennis, the most nervewracking battle that the courts have ever seen. . . . Tilden and Johnston played five acts of incredible melodrama, with a thrill in every scene, with horrible errors leading suddenly to glorious achievements with skill and courage and good and evil fortune. . . . Tilden's victory was a triumph for supertennis.

With reporting like this, sports promoters did not need to buy advertisements.

Baseball, with its drawn-out suspense, infinite variety of plays, and potential for statistics-keeping, attracted a huge following. After the World Series scandal of 1919, in which eight members of the Chicago White Sox were accused of taking bribes to lose games (they were acquitted in 1921), the two major professional leagues appointed Kenesaw Mountain Landis, a federal district judge, as baseball commissioner. Landis gave the game renewed respectability by rooting out alleged dishonest players. At the same time, the nature of the game changed. Discovering that home runs aroused excitement, the leagues redesigned the ball to make it livelier. Thereafter, attendance at major-league games skyrocketed. In 1921 a record 300,000 people attended the six-game World Series between the New York Giants and the New York Yankees. That same year millions more gathered regularly to watch their local teams take on nearby rivals.

Sports, movies, and the news gave Americans a galaxy of heroes. As society became more anonymous and the individual less significant, people clung to heroic personalities as a means of identifying with the unique. Though names such as Tilden in tennis,

The first million-dollar fight. Close to 90,000 people jammed an arena in Jersey City, New Jersey, on July 2, 1921, to witness heavyweight boxing champion Jack Dempsey knock out Georges Carpentier in the fourth round. The fight grossed $1.8 million, more than twice as much as any previous match. Brown Brothers.

Sports Heroes Ederle in swimming and Bobby Jones in golf became household words, boxing, football, and baseball produced the biggest sports heroes. Heavyweight champion Jack Dempsey, a powerful brawler from Manassa, Colorado, attracted the first of many million-dollar gates in his fight with Georges Carpentier in 1921. Harold "Red" Grange, running back for the University of Illinois football team, thrilled thousands and became the idol of sportswriters. During his senior year in 1925 Grange was offered huge contracts by real-estate and motion-picture companies, collected $42,000 for his first two games as a professional with the Chicago Bears, and received a petition from admirers who wanted him to run for Congress.

Baseball's major hero was George Herman "Babe" Ruth, who began his career as a pitcher but found he could use his prodigious strength to better advantage hitting home runs. Ruth hit 29 of them in 1919, 54 in 1920, the year he moved from the Boston Red Sox to the New York Yankees, 59 in 1924, and 60 in 1927—each year a record. His exaggerated gestures on the field, defiant life style, and boyish grin endeared him to millions, and he became a national legend. Known for overindulgence in food, drink, and women, Ruth missed almost two months of the 1925 season when he was hospitalized with "the stomach ache that was heard round the world." But he usually made fans forget his excesses by appearing at public events and making special efforts to visit children in hospitals.

If Americans identified with the physical exploits of sports stars, they fulfilled a yearning for romance and adventure through adulation of movie stars. The films and personal lives of Douglas Fairbanks, Gloria

Rudolph Valentino in The Sheik, *his most famous movie. With flashing eyes and wanton smile, Valentino carries a swooning woman to his tent. This immensely popular movie earned a million dollars for Paramount Pictures.   Museum of Modern Art Film Still Archive.*

Movie Stars and Public Heroes

Swanson, Charlie Chaplin, and scores of others were discussed in parlors and pool halls across the country. Perhaps the decade's most ballyhooed personality was Rudolph Valentino, whose Latin machismo made women swoon and prompted men to copy his pomaded hairdo and slick sideburns. Valentino's films exploited the era's new-found sexual liberalism and flirtation with evil. Playing a sheik who passionately snatched women into his arms and carried them into his tent, he combined the roles of seducer and abductor. When Valentino died of complications from ulcers and appendicitis at the age of thirty-one, the press turned his funeral into a public extravaganza. Crowds lined up for over a mile to file past his coffin.

News promoters created their own heroes outside the worlds of athletics and entertainment. For two weeks in 1925, newspapers kept readers on edge with reports on the plight of Floyd Collins, trapped in a Kentucky cave. Rescuers eventually found Collins dead, but not before the entire country had idolized him as a hero battling nature. Flagpole sitters, marathon dancers, and other record seekers regularly occupied the front pages. The most notable news hero was Charles A. Lindbergh, the pilot whose daring nonstop solo flight across the Atlantic in 1927 was cheered by millions. A modest, independent midwesterner whom writers dubbed the Lone Eagle, Lindbergh accepted fame but did not try to profit from it. Because his quiet personality contrasted so starkly with the ballyhoo that surrounded him, Americans honored him even more fervently. A few months after Lindbergh returned from Paris to a mammoth reception, columnist Mary B. Mullett wrote in *American Magazine:*

We shouted ourselves hoarse. Not because a man had flown across the Atlantic! Not even because he was an American! But because he was as clean in character as he was strong and fine in body; because he put "ethics" above any desire for wealth; because he was as modest as he was courageous; and because—as we know beyond any shadow of doubt—*these are the things which we honor most* in life.

In part the adulation of Lindbergh may have reflected guilt over betrayal of the virtues Mullett extolled. For in their quest for fun and individual expression—liberties that prohibi-

Prohibition

tion seemed to deny—Americans became lawbreakers and supporters of crime. The constitutional amendment and federal law that prohibited the manufacture, sale, and transportation of alcoholic beverages (see page 595) worked very well at first. Per capita consumption of liquor dropped, arrests for drunkenness diminished, and the price of illegal booze rose higher than the average worker could afford. But beyond passing supportive laws, legislators saw little need to enforce prohibition. In 1922 Congress gave the Prohibition Bureau only three thousand employees and less than $7 million for nationwide enforcement.

Prohibition was especially effective in regions where temperance movements had historically been successful. In fact, some people believe that, had it applied only to hard liquor, not beer or wine, it might have succeeded more widely. But after about 1925 the noble experiment broke down in the cities, where the desire for personal freedom overwhelmed the weak means of enforcement. The law allowed the manufacture of beer for dilution into near-beer and the sale of alcohol for medicinal and sacramental purposes, but bootleggers cleverly obtained and sold such spirits for other purposes. Smuggling and home manufacture of liquor were rampant. Hundreds of thousands of people made their own wine and bathtub gin, and illegal importation along the country's long borders and shorelines was beyond the reach of the few patrols that attempted to curb it.

Local officials realized it was impractical to devote their scarce resources to strict enforcement of Prohibition. For drinking, like gambling and prostitution, was a business that had willing cus-

Al Capone

tomers. Criminal organizations were quick to recognize the possibilities of the situation. The most notorious of such mobs belonged to Al Capone, a burly tough who seized control of illegal liquor and vice organizations in Chicago and exercised his influence through bribery, intimidation, and violence. With his armed force of gangsters, Capone was able to influence local politics as well as vice operations until 1931, when the federal government convicted and imprisoned him for income-tax evasion.

It is important to recognize that Prohibition and its weak enforcement did not create organized crime. Gangs like Capone's had provided illegal goods and services long before the 1920s. As Capone explained it, "Prohibition is a business. All I do is supply a public demand. I do it in the least harmful way I can." Americans wanted their liquor and their freedom; Capone took advantage of these desires.

Thus during the 1920s Americans were caught between two value systems. On the one hand, the Puritan tradition of hard work, sobriety, and restraint—"waste not, want not"—still prevailed, especially in rural areas where new diversions were unavailable. On the other hand, a liberating age of play beckoned. At no previous time in American history had so many opportunities for recreation presented themselves. Not just mass entertainment such as nightclubs, movies, sports, and radio, but individual amusements such as stamp collecting, puzzle working, and playing and listening to music became commonplace. Most of these activities were not illegal or immoral, but many people were increasingly willing to break the law or shun moral tradition if such restrictions interfered with their personal quest for pleasure. As Walter Lippmann wrote in 1931, "The high level of lawlessness is maintained by the fact that Americans desire to do so many things which they also desire to prohibit."

CULTURAL CURRENTS

This tension between value systems pulled artists and intellectuals in new directions. Rejection of old beliefs energized an experimental movement in literature, art, and music. Fear that materialism and conformity were being fostered by mass society gave this movement a bitterly critical tinge. Yet critics seldom voiced a radical message; they had no urge to destroy modern society, only to protect the individual from dehumanizing forces.

Many of the era's leading literary figures, finding the vulgar materialism of the time hostile to their art, succumbed to disillusionment and became known

Literature of Alienation

as the Lost Generation. A number of them, including the novelist Ernest Hemingway and the poets Ezra Pound and T. S. Eliot, moved to Europe. Others, such as the novelists William Faulkner and Sinclair Lewis, remained, but assailed what they saw happening around them. Along with innovative forms of expression and the realistic portrayal of emotions, these writers also produced biting social commentary.

The dominant themes of their social criticism were middle- and upper-class materialism and the impersonality of modern society. F. Scott Fitzgerald's *This Side of Paradise* (1920) and *The Great Gatsby* (1925); Lewis's *Babbitt* (1922), *Arrowsmith* (1925), and *Elmer Gantry* (1927); and Eugene O'Neill's plays exposed Americans' overemphasis on money. The powerful antiwar sentiments of John Dos Passos's *Three Soldiers* (1921) and Hemingway's *A Farewell to Arms* (1929) were skillfully interwoven with passionate critiques of the impersonality of modern relationships.

Perhaps the most trenchant social criticism flowed from the pen of H. L. Mencken. A Baltimore newspaperman and founder of the *American Mercury*, Mencken jabbed at prevailing customs with stinging cynicism. No group, no individual was too sacred to escape his satire. He jeered at the inane quest for status of the middle-class "booboisie," labeled Woodrow Wilson a "self-bamboozled presbyterian," and scorned political reformers as "saccharine liberals" and "jitney messiahs." A man with a unique flair for language, Mencken could not stomach its misuse. He once charged that President Harding

> writes the worst English I have ever encountered. It reminds me of a string of wet sponges; it reminds me of tattered wash on the line, it reminds me of stale bean soup, of college yells, of dogs barking idiotically through endless nights. . . . It drags itself out of the dark abyss . . . of pish and crawls insanely up to the topmost pinnacle of posh.

A spiritual discontent quite different from that of white writers inspired the work of a new generation of young black artists. Largely middle-class and well-educated, these writers often rejected

Harlem Renaissance

the amalgamation of black and white cultures, exalting the militantly assertive "New Negro," proud of his or her African heritage. Most of them lived in Harlem, the black section of upper Manhattan. In this "Negro Mecca" black intellectuals and artists, aided by a few white patrons, celebrated modern black culture in what became known as the Harlem Renaissance.

Harlem in the 1920s fostered a number of gifted writers, among them Langston Hughes, who wrote forceful and sometimes humorous poems, stories, and essays; Countee Cullen, a poet with moving lyrical skills; and Claude McKay, whose militant verses sounded a clarion call for rebellion against bigotry. Jean Toomer's novels and poems portrayed black life with passionate realism, and Alain Locke's essays gave direction to the artistic renaissance. Much of this group's writing addressed issues of identity. For though black intellectuals took pride in African culture, they also realized that black Americans had to assert themselves and come to terms with themselves as Americans. Thus Locke urged that the New Negro should "lay aside the status of beneficiary and ward for that of a collaborator and participant in American civilization." Simultaneously, Hughes wrote, "We younger Negro artists who create now intend to express our individual dark-skinned selves without fear or shame. If white people are pleased we are glad. If they are not, it doesn't matter. We know we are beautiful."

Although black authors did not reach many people (Jean Toomer's stirring novel *Cane* sold only five hundred copies when it was first published), black

Jazz

musicians had considerable influence. The Jazz Age, as the decade is sometimes called, owed its name to the music that grew out of black urban culture. Evolving from African and black American folk music, early jazz communicated unrestrained freedom that black people seldom knew in their public, working, or political lives. With its emotional rhythms and emphasis on improvisation, jazz blurred the distinction between composer and performer and created a new intimacy between performer and audience.

Jazz, a music form that was originated and developed by black artists such as those posing in this photograph, became America's most distinctive art form in the first half of the twentieth century. Its unrestrained improvisational qualities reflected the joys and sorrows of life and the freedom that blacks were denied in white society.   The New York Public Library.

As blacks moved north from the Mississippi Delta, they brought jazz with them. By the 1920s dance halls and bars featured jazz, sometimes popularized by white musicians such as Paul Whiteman and Bix Biederbecke. Gifted black performers like trumpeter Louis Armstrong, trombonist Kid Ory, and singer Bessie Smith enjoyed widespread fame. Phonograph records and radio, better suited than sheet music to the spontaneity of jazz, helped to popularize it. In fact, jazz boosted the recording industry immensely, and music recorded by black artists and bought by millions of black purchasers (sometimes called race records) gave black Americans a distinctive place in the new consumer culture. More important, jazz endowed America with its most distinctive art form.

In many ways the 1920s were the most creative years the nation had yet experienced. Influenced by jazz and by experimental writing, painters such as Georgia O'Keeffe and John Marin tried to forge a distinctively American style of painting. And although European composers and performers still dominated classical music, Americans such as Henry Cowell, who pioneered electronic music, and Aaron Copland, who built orchestral and vocal works around native folk motifs, began careers that later won wide acclaim. George Gershwin gave popular music increased respectability by blending jazz, classical, and folk musical forms in his serious compositions (*Rhapsody in Blue,* 1924 and *Concerto in F,* 1925), musical dramas (*Funny Face,* 1927), and numerous hit tunes. In architecture the skyscraper boom drew worldwide attention, and Frank Lloyd Wright's "prairie-style" houses, churches, and schools reflected the magnificence of the American landscape. At the beginning of the decade, essayist Harold Stearns had complained that "the most . . . pathetic fact in the social life of America today is emotional and aesthetic starvation." By 1929 such a contention was hard to support.

Chapter 24: THE NEW ERA OF THE 1920s

THE ELECTION OF 1928

Whatever doubts intellectuals may have had about materialism in the 1920s faded before the confident rhetoric of politics. Herbert Hoover epitomized that confidence in his speech accepting the Republican nomination for president in the summer of 1928. "We in America today," Hoover boasted, "are nearer to the final triumph over poverty than ever before in the history of any land. . . . We have not yet reached the goal, but, given a chance to go forward with the policies of the last eight years, we shall soon, with the help of God, be in sight of the day when poverty will be banished from this nation."

Hoover was an apt candidate for the Republicans in 1928 (Coolidge chose not to run for re-election), because he blended old values of success through individual hard work with the new **Herbert Hoover** emphasis on collective action. A Quaker from West Branch, Iowa, who was orphaned at the age of ten, Hoover worked his way through Stanford University and became a wealthy mining engineer. During and after the First World War, he distinguished himself as U.S. food administrator and as head of food relief for Europe. As secretary of commerce under Harding and Coolidge, Hoover expanded Theodore Roosevelt's New Nationalism. Recognizing the extent to which large nationwide associations had come to dominate commerce and industry, Hoover mounted a campaign calculated to stimulate cooperation between business and government. He took every opportunity to make his department a center for the promotion of business, encouraging formation of trade associations, holding conferences, sponsoring studies, and issuing reports, all aimed at improving production, marketing, and profitability. His active leadership prompted one observer to quip that Hoover was "Secretary of Commerce and assistant secretary of everything else."

As Hoover's opponent, the Democrats chose Governor Alfred E. Smith of New York, whose career contrasted markedly with that of Hoover. Whereas Hoover had rural, native, Protestant, business roots and had never run for public office, **Al Smith** Smith was an urbane, gregarious

politician of immigrant stock whose career was rooted in New York City's Tammany Hall. Smith was also the first Roman Catholic to run for president on a major party ticket. As such, he had considerable appeal among urban ethnic groups, who were voting in increasing numbers, but he lost southern and rural votes for the same reason. During his governorship, Smith had compiled a strong record as a promoter of progressive reforms and civil rights, but his campaign failed to build a reform coalition of farmers and city dwellers because he stressed issues that were not likely

IMPORTANT EVENTS	
1919	Eighteenth Amendment ratified
1920	Nineteenth Amendment ratified
	Harding elected president
	First commercial radio broadcast
1920–21	Postwar deflation and depression
1921	Federal Highway Act
	Immigration quotas established
	Sacco and Vanzetti convicted
1922	Economic recovery
1923	Harding dies; Coolidge assumes presidency
	Peak of Ku Klux Klan activity
	Equal Rights Amendment introduced
1923–24	Exposure of government scandals
1924	National Origins Act
	Coolidge elected president
1925	Scopes trial
1927	Sacco and Vanzetti executed
	Lindbergh's transatlantic flight
	Babe Ruth hits sixty home runs
	The Jazz Singer first sound movie
1928	Stock market soars
	Hoover elected president

to unite these groups. That is, he openly opposed prohibition, and he struck back at charges that his Catholicism made him a servant of the Pope.

Though Smith waged a dynamic campaign, Hoover, who stressed the nation's prosperity, won the popular vote by 21 million to 15 million, the electoral vote by 444 to 87. But Smith's candidacy had important effects on the Democratic party. Smith carried the nation's twelve largest cities, which formerly had given majorities to Republican candidates, and lured millions of foreign-stock voters to the polls for the first time. From 1928 onward, the Democratic party would solidify this urban base, which when combined with its traditional strength in the South made the party a formidable force in national elections.

Democrats and Republicans both had reasons to be encouraged in 1928. But a few people had begun to grow uneasy over the nation's economic climate. Just before Hoover stood in front of his party and predicted the conquest of poverty, a banker surveyed the soaring stock market and observed,

> Stocks look dangerously high to me. This bull market has been going on for a long time and although prices have slipped a bit recently, they might easily slip a good deal more. Business is none too good. Of course if you buy the right stock you'll probably be all right in the long run and you may even make a profit. But if I were you I'd wait awhile and see what happens.

Little did the banker know how sound his advice was. In the next several years the era of expansion and frivolity would end, and the economy would have to be rebuilt.

SUGGESTIONS FOR FURTHER READING

Overviews of the 1920s

Frederick Lewis Allen, *Only Yesterday* (1931); John Braeman et al., eds., *Change and Continuity in Twentieth Century America: The 1920s* (1968); Paul A. Carter, *Another Part of the Twenties* (1977); Ellis Hawley, *The Great War and*

the Search for a Modern Order (1979); John D. Hicks, *Republican Ascendancy* (1960); William E. Leuchtenburg, *The Perils of Prosperity* (1958); Robert Lynd and Helen Lynd, *Middletown* (1929); Donald R. McCoy, *Coming of Age* (1973); George Soule, *Prosperity Decade* (1947).

Business and the Economy

Irving L. Bernstein, *The Lean Years: A History of the American Worker, 1920–1933* (1960); Alfred D. Chandler, *Strategy and Structure* (1962); James J. Flink, *The Car Culture* (1975); Allan Nevins, *Ford*, 2 vols. (1954–1957); J. W. Prothro, *The Dollar Decade* (1954); John Rae, *The Road and the Car in American Life* (1971); Robert Zieger, *Republicans and Labor, 1919–1929* (1969).

Politics and Law

David Burner, *Herbert Hoover* (1979); David Burner, *The Politics of Provincialism* (1968); Paula Elder, *Governor Alfred E. Smith: The Politician as Reformer* (1983); J. Joseph Huthmacher, *Massachusetts People and Politics* (1959); Matthew Josephson and Hannah Josephson, *Al Smith* (1970); Allan J. Lichtman, *Prejudice and the Old Politics: The Presidential Election of 1928* (1979); Richard Lowitt, *George W. Norris* (1971); Samuel Lubell, *The Future of American Politics* (1952); Donald R. McCoy, *Calvin Coolidge* (1967); Alpheus Mason, *The Supreme Court from Taft to Warren* (1958); Robert K. Murray, *The Harding Era* (1969); Andrew Sinclair, *The Available Man* (1965); George Tindall, *The Emergence of the New South* (1967); James Weinstein, *The Decline of Socialism in America, 1912–1925* (1967); Joan Hoff Wilson, *Herbert Hoover: The Forgotten Progressive* (1975).

Blacks and Hispanics

Rodolfo Acuna, *Occupied America: A History of Chicanos* (1980); E. D. Cronon, *Black Moses: The Story of Marcus Garvey* (1955); Kenneth Kusmer, *A Ghetto Takes Shape* (1976); Matt S. Meier and Feliciano Rivera, *The Chicanos* (1972); Gilbert Osofsky, *Harlem: The Making of a Ghetto* (1965); Mark Reisler, *By the Sweat of Their Brows* (1976) (on Mexican-Americans); Alan Spear, *Black Chicago* (1967); Theodore Vincent, *Black Power and the Garvey Movement* (1971).

Women and the Family

W. Andrew Achenbaum, *Shades of Gray: Old Age, American Values, and Federal Policies Since 1920* (1983); William H. Chafe, *The American Woman: Her Changing Social, Economic, and Political Role* (1972); Ruth Schwartz Cowan, *More Work for Mother* (1983); David H. Fischer, *Growing Old in America* (1977); Linda Gordon, *Woman's Body, Woman's*

Right: A Social History of Birth Control in America (1976);
J. Stanley Lemons, The Woman Citizen: Social Feminism in
the 1920s (1973); Sheila Rothman, Woman's Proper Place
(1978); Lois Scharf, To Work and to Wed (1980); Susan
Strasser, Never Done: A History of American Housework
(1982); Winifred D. Wandersee, Women's Work and Family
Values, 1920–1940 (1981).

Lines of Defense

David M. Chalmers, Hooded Americanism: The History of
the Ku Klux Klan (1965); Norman F. Furnis, The Funda-
mentalist Controversy (1954); Joseph R. Gusfeld, Symbolic
Crusade (1963); John Higham, Strangers in the Land: Patterns
of American Nativism (1955); Kenneth T. Jackson, The Ku
Klux Klan and the City (1967); G. L. Joughin and E. M.
Morgan, The Legacy of Sacco and Vanzetti (1948); William
G. McLoughlin, Modern Revivalism (1959); Andrew Sinclair,
Prohibition: The Age of Excess (1962).

Mass Culture

Erik Barbouw, A Tower of Babel: A History of Broadcasting
in the United States to 1933 (1966); Robert Creamer, Babe
(1974); Kenneth S. Davis, The Hero, Charles A. Lindbergh
(1959); Paula Fass, The Damned and the Beautiful: American
Youth in the 1920s (1977); Fred J. MacDonald, Don't Touch
That Dial (1979); Otis Pease, The Responsibilities of American
Advertising (1958); Randy Roberts, Jack Dempsey, The
Manassa Mauler (1979); Philip T. Rosen, The Modern Sten-
tors: Radio Broadcasting and the Federal Government, 1920–
1933 (1980); Robert Sklar, Movie-made America (1976).

Literature and Thought

Robert Crunden, From Self to Society: Transition in American
Thought, 1919–1941 (1972); George H. Douglas, H. L.
Mencken (1978); Robert Elias, Entangling Alliances with
None: An Essay on the Individual in the American Twenties
(1973); Nathan I. Huggins, Harlem Renaissance (1971);
David L. Lewis, When Harlem Was in Vogue (1981); Roderick
Nash, The Nervous Generation: American Thought, 1917–
1930 (1969); Marvin K. Singleton, H. L. Mencken and
the American Mercury Adventure (1962); Kenneth M. Wheller
and Virginia L. Lussier, eds., Women and the Arts and the
1920s in Paris and New York (1982).

THE SHAKEN DREAM

1929–1933

CHAPTER 25

"*Anything wrong with* my work for company?" asked an autoworker of Slavic descent who had just been fired by the Ford Motor Company after fourteen years of employment. No, his work had been good, but cars were not selling. "I have no money now . . . lose my home quick, what I do children, what I do doctor?" When two of his daughters went to work to support the family and their sick mother, he cried, "I ain't man now."

People like John Boris were among the three thousand men and women who gathered on March 7, 1932, for a hunger march to Ford's huge River Rouge plant in Dearborn, just outside Detroit, Michigan. Most of the marchers were unemployed Ford workers. Dearborn-Detroit authorities nonetheless blamed the march on the Communist party, which had in fact helped to plan the protest and to prepare the list of demands for jobs, food, medical aid, and the right to organize.

At the Dearborn line, the marchers, shivering from the near-zero temperature, were blocked by a phalanx of police. Ordered to disperse, they refused to retreat. When the police volleyed tear gas, the marchers hurled back rocks. Firefighters soon hosed down the demonstrators and Ford's stern-faced private police assembled. Suddenly shots rang out, killing two marchers. A policeman shouted, "Get your gats and let them have it." By the end of the skirmish, four marchers were dead, more than twenty wounded. Twenty-five police officers had to be treated for wounds from rocks and other objects.

The fundamental source of this trouble was not the Communist party, not the marchers, not the Dearborn police, not Henry Ford himself, but a nationwide disaster called the Great Depression. Detroit was especially hard hit; by fall 1932, 350,000 workers, or about half the city's wage earners, were unemployed. At the River Rouge plant, employment of hourly workers fell from 98,337 to 28,915 during Herbert Hoover's administration (1929–1933). The Ford Hunger March was just one of the many desperate American cries for relief from the pain of this very human tragedy.

Only three years earlier, optimism, not tragedy, marked the nation's mood. Hoover administration officials knew that the economy suffered weaknesses and that society seethed with divisiveness, but they were confident men who believed they could solve or isolate the problems. What a shock the stock market crash of fall 1929 was to these leaders. Slowly but steadily cascading tremors rolled through the economy, and the nation moved from economic downturn to Great Depression. Many Americans watched their incomes dwindle or disappear and their health decline. Unemployment placed strains on relations within the family. Blacks and other minorities sank deeper into destitution. Working women, still located in sex-segregated jobs, some of which contracted less than those of men, heard renewed calls for their return to the home in order to open places for males in the labor market. Overall, the economic catastrophe aggravated old tensions: labor versus capital, white versus black, male versus female.

Americans tried to puzzle out the many interrelated causes of the depression, but to little avail. Questions of underconsumption and international trade, after all, bedeviled even the experts. Americans found it especially difficult to understand how people could be hungry when farmers' bins were overflowing or how workers could be unemployed when they remained able-bodied and eager and the factories stood in place. Only one thing was certain: too many Americans did not have enough money to buy the goods stocked in their local stores. Stunned by the magnitude of their plight, Americans' faith in themselves and in their dream of success was shaken. But they did not turn to violent revolt or political extremism. Their rootedness in the past—their traditionalism—would not let them. Instead, they improvised to survive, and they looked to their governments for help.

Although President Hoover activated the federal government more than any of his predecessors had done in an economic crisis, he opposed direct relief. When he refused to take measures strong enough to relieve their hardship, Americans peacefully resorted to a traditional method of voicing disapproval: they turned Hoover out of office in the election of 1932. They replaced the somber Hoover with smiling

Franklin D. Roosevelt, who had promised vigorous action and who projected hope in a time of despair.

THE NEW DAY

There was little sense of impending tragedy in 1928, when 62 percent of Wayne County (Detroit and Dearborn) voters cast their ballots for Republican presidential candidate Herbert Hoover. (In 1932 they would give him only 39 percent.) And in early 1929, when Hoover entered the White House, the byword was optimism. In his inaugural address the president proclaimed a New Day, telling his listeners that the future "is bright with hope."

The new president, known popularly as the Great Engineer, was a proven administrator who promised to bring efficiency to the federal government and harmony to society. He believed that America's economic growth would persist, that the country's problems were manageable. Yet privately Hoover worried that his reputation was being oversold. "They expect the impossible of me and should there arise in the land conditions with which the political machinery is unable to cope, I will be the one to suffer." Hoover's uneasiness also prompted him to sell all his common stock just a few months after taking office because "possible hard times [are] coming."

Hoover's government was a mixture of the old and the new. Sitting in the cabinet, composed largely of businessmen, were six millionaires. Andrew Mellon stayed on as secretary of the treasury.

Hoover Administration This vastly wealthy man's aluminum monopoly, petroleum and banking interests, and prized art collection marked him as one of the most successful practitioners of the American success story. With his icy and aloof personality and his heartlessness toward human suffering, Mellon contrasted sharply with Hoover, who had gained a reputation for compassion when he managed food relief for destitute Europeans during and after the First World War. On the whole, Hoover's appointees to high office were, like Mellon, smug devotees of the existing order, champions of a capitalist utopia. Innovation was not expected from them. In

Herbert Hoover (1874–1964), the wealthy mining engineer and businessman, headed a relief program during the First World War and served as Secretary of Commerce in the 1920s. His reputation for brilliance and compassion was tarnished when as president he faced the Great Depression. Library of Congress.

the lower ranks, on the other hand, Hoover brought in the New Patriots, mostly young professionals who agreed with the president that scientific methods could be applied to government to solve its problems. The New Patriots, called such because they seemed willing to pass up opportunities for personal wealth to serve their nation, emphasized modernization of operations, collection of data, and rational decision-making. In time, Hoover and his experts believed, they could establish a stable social order based on cooperation between government and various civic groups.

If Hoover and his advisers were optimistic about the future, so were most Americans. To them American achievements seemed boundless. The new era of the 1920s had given birth to such exciting gadgets as radios and refrigerators. Americans owned 23 million automobiles, roughly three-quarters of the world's

This Judge *magazine cartoon titled "There is a Santa Claus," published in December 1929, captured well President Herbert Hoover's initial response to the Great Depression: build up business confidence. Then the economy—and the people—would enjoy once again the benefits of the American system. But confidence-building proved impossible as businesses and banks closed their doors and workers lost their jobs. Library of Congress.*

total. Conquests of new frontiers seemed inevitable, and promoters strove to outdo each other in grandiose displays. As businesspeople in Chicago laid plans for the World's Fair, a huge celebration of material progress, Al Smith and Democratic party chairman John J. Raskob were organizing a company to build the tallest structure in the world, the Empire State Building. When this monument to the new era was completed, it stood 102 stories high on fashionable Fifth Avenue in New York and had through accidents cost the lives of forty-eight workers. Yet

Business Optimism

many of its offices were vacant in 1931 when Hoover pushed the button that turned on the building's innumerable lights—sad evidence that dreams could be undermined by economic realities. After walking its marbled hallways, critic Edmund Wilson remarked that it was tragic that the regal building "is advertised now as a triumph in the hour when the planless competitive society, the dehumanized urban community, of which it makes the culmination, is bankrupt."

Still, before the Great Depression sapped the national spirit, reverence for what Hoover called "the American system" ran high. The belief that individuals were responsible for their own condition, that unemployment or poverty suggested personal failing, was widespread. "It is as if we set a race," said Hoover. The individual, seizing the ever-present opportunity, had to demonstrate will power and ambition in the face of competition. The government provided the competitors with an equal start through public education and served as referee to ensure fairness. The winners were the people with the best training, ability, and character.

Prevailing thought also held that changes in the business cycle were natural and therefore not to be tampered with. Depressions were to be weathered stoically until the economy inevitably wound its way back to prosperity. As for the government, its job was limited: to ensure equal opportunity and to stimulate the economy through judicious advice and public works projects. "The spread of government," concluded Hoover, "destroys initiative and thus destroys character." He implored people to regulate themselves, to join voluntary associations (such as farm cooperatives and private charities) to right wrongs, but not to expect the federal government to bail them out of their difficulties.

Much of this thinking was, of course, shallow, self-serving, or utopian. Self-interested businesspeople had often tinkered with the system. Government had long played favorites or neglected to blow the referee's whistle. A few companies dominated each industry, squeezing out smaller firms. Equal opportunity was denied to Americans who were nonwhite or female. Educational programs were segregated and unequal. Both government and business were hostile to labor unions (in 1929 only 10 percent of the nonagricultural work force was unionized). Discriminatory wages for women and minorities, the stretch-out (more work for the same pay), automation, and safety hazards also plagued workers. In Waterbury, Connecticut, for example, clock workers risked death from radium poisoning. At least one-third of the nation's farmers were tenants or sharecroppers—dependent, propertyless, and unable even to join the race. Because of these conditions, income and wealth were maldistributed.

Hoover himself knew that not all was well. "The only trouble with capitalism is capitalists," he complained. "They're too damned greedy." Hoover's ideal capitalist was one who tempered his self-interest to advance the general welfare, who cooperated with others to build a progressive, nonexploitative society. He later admitted that most businesspeople did not approach this ideal.

Evidence that there was quite a difference between the optimistic spirit and rhetoric of the New Day and the reality of everyday life came in March 1929 in Elizabethton, Tennessee. In that **Elizabethton Textile Strike** textile town, where 40 percent of the rayon mill laborers were young women earning 16 to 18 cents an hour for a fifty-six-hour week, workers went on strike for better wages. The state militia marched in to break the strike, and employees who had joined the United Textile Workers found themselves blacklisted. By 1931, wrote one observer, what remained were a "few hundred unemployed ex-strikers, half-starved and disillusioned, cynical and justly bitter." Just a few months before the strike erupted, Hoover had addressed a large crowd in Elizabethton, extolling the progress of southern industry and its "great reserve of labor."

On the eve of the Great Depression, then, America seemed tangled in contradictions: optimism and pessimism; prosperity and hardship; individualism and mass culture; competition and cooperation; progress and deterioration; opportunity and inequality; strength and weakness. But the shortcomings of American life received far less attention than the dramatic accomplishments of the New Era. Then came the Great Depression to deflate the boom mentality, expose infirmities, prompt reanalysis, and redefine the role of the federal government.

THE GREAT CRASH AND THE GREAT DEPRESSION

The gloom and economic woe that people in mining towns, textile mills, and agricultural communities suffered at the end of the 1920s hardly penetrated the elegant offices of Wall Street. There, all seemed magical; glamour stocks such as General Electric, International Harvester, and Radio Corporation of America soared in value. By late 1928 one share of RCA cost $400, the equivalent of several months' income for many people. The bull market attracted millions of buyers, many of whom joined the speculative binge by buying their shares on margin (paying only a portion of the cost in cash and borrowing the rest) or investing their savings. By October 1929 brokers' loans to stock purchasers amounted to a staggering $8.5 billion. John J. Raskob, a member of General Motors' board of directors as well as chairman of the Democratic party, was so enthusiastic about the boom that he proclaimed that "anyone not only can be rich, but ought to be rich" by speculating in the stock market.

The get-rich-quick mentality was jolted in September and early October when stock prices dropped. Analysts attributed the dip to "shaking out the lunatic fringe." But on October 24, Black **Wall Street Crash** Thursday, a record number of shares was traded; many stocks sold at low prices, and some could find no takers. Stunned crowds gathered outside the frantic New York Stock Exchange, buzzing about the apparent seriousness of the decline. At noon, banking leaders met at the headquarters of J. P. Morgan and Company to halt the skid and restore confidence. They put up $20 million, told everybody about it, and ceremoniously began by buying ten thousand shares of United States Steel. The mood changed and some stocks rallied. The bankers, it seemed, had preserved the dream of success.

But the nation gradually succumbed to panic. News of Black Thursday spread across the country, and trouble ("sell!") ricocheted back to New York via

Reginald Marsh's sketch of the New York Stock Exchange on the day of the Great Crash revealed the more-than-usually hectic, noisy, and intense activity of trading in shares. *Library of Congress.*

telephone. Another bolt struck on Black Tuesday (October 29) when stock prices plunged again. The market settled into a grim pattern of declines and weak rallies. Hoover, who had never approved of what he called the "fever of speculation," assured Americans that the economy was sound. He shared the popular assumption that the stock market's ills could be quarantined from a generally healthy economy. Businesspeople, schooled in the credo of progress, comforted themselves with the thought that the stock market would soon right itself. Although their boosterism seems terribly misguided or deceptive today, it was sincerely, if blindly, believed at the time. Anyway, said the secretary of labor, "one doesn't improve the condition of a sick man by constantly telling him how ill he is."

The crash ultimately helped to unleash a devastating depression. The economic downturn did not come suddenly; it was more like a leak in a punctured tire than a blowout. There were several interrelated causes of the Great Depression. The first was the increasing weakness of the economy in the 1920s. Had the economy of the new era been strong, it would have stood

Economic Weaknesses

a better chance of weathering the crash on Wall Street. In fact, some historians suggest that the stock market collapse merely moved an ongoing recession into depression. Throughout the 1920s the agricultural sector was plagued with overproduction, declining prices for farm products, mounting debts, bankruptcies, and small bank failures. Some industries, like coal, railroads, and textiles, were in distress long before 1929, and two mainstays of economic growth, autos and construction, also declined early (see pages 685–686). What all these weaknesses meant by 1929 was that major sectors of the economy were not expanding; businesspeople were not investing funds to build new plants, hire more workers, and produce more goods. Indeed, the opposite was true: unsold inventories were stacking up in warehouses, investments were shrinking, laborers were being sent home, and consumer purchases were dropping off.

Second and related, the onset and severity of the depression can be attributed to underconsumption. That is, production (supply) had outstripped consumption (demand). Wages and mass purchasing power had lagged behind the industrial surge of the 1920s; the workers who produced the new consumer products

Under-consumption ultimately could not afford to buy them. Why did purchasing decline? Laborers and farmers constituted the great majority of consumers. Yet, as we have seen, farmers suffered economic distress and had to trim their purchases. And as industries like coal, autos, and construction declined, they laid off men and women who then lacked the money to sustain buying. Other laborers lost their jobs because machines displaced them. In Hartford and New Haven in 1929, for example, the installation of more efficient machinery threw 1,190 rubber workers out of their jobs. And 35,000 orchestra musicians were unemployed in mid-1929 because "machine music" had been installed in the nation's theaters. Overall, then, a sizable nonconsuming group had grown in America before the Great Depression hit.

Another important aspect of underconsumption was the unequal distribution of income. In the 1920s the rich got much richer while others made only modest gains. Average per capita **Unequal** disposable income (income after **Distribution** taxes) rose about 9 percent from **of Wealth** 1920 to 1929, but the income of the wealthiest 1 percent rose 75 percent. In 1929 experts estimated that about 60 percent of America's families lived on or below the subsistence level ($2,000 a year), despite a 29 percent increase in the number of employed married women over the decade. The Federal Trade Commission reported that 1 percent of the American people owned 59 percent of the country's wealth; 87 percent owned only 10 percent. Income and wealth, in other words, were concentrated at the top of America's economic ladder. Why did this uneven distribution contribute to underconsumption and depression? Because much of the accumulating income was put into luxuries, savings, investments, and stock-market speculation instead of being spent on consumer goods. Put another way, more money in the hands of workers and farmers and less money building up in the vaults of the wealthy would probably have meant more consumption and hence more stable economic growth.

Third, the American business system was shaky, for a few large corporations in each industry—oligopolies—unbalanced it. In 1929 **Large** the top two hundred nonfinancial **Corporations** corporations controlled 49 percent of corporate wealth. The old cliché "The bigger they are, the harder they fall" was literally true. Many companies speculated dangerously on the stock market and built pyramidlike businesses based on shady, if legal, manipulation of assets through holding companies. If one part of the edifice collapsed, the entire structure crumbled. Such was the case with Samuel Insull's mighty electrical empire based in Chicago. Insull built a utilities network that produced one-eighth of America's electrical power and operated in thirty-nine states. Within this vast system one company held the stock of another company, which held the stock of another company, and so on. Sometimes Insull's various companies bought stock from one another, each showing an artificially high profit from the transactions. Even Insull admitted that he was not sure how it all worked; his sixty-five chairmanships, eighty-five directorships, and seven presidencies confused him as much as anybody else. When his interlocking network collapsed in 1932, he fled to Europe to escape arrest for fraud. Found in Turkey, he returned to the United States, hired advertising agencies to improve his public image, and in 1934 was acquitted.

The depression derived, fourth, from pell-mell, largely unregulated, speculation on the stock market. Corporations and banks invested large sums in stocks; some speculated in their own issues. **Speculation** Brokers sold stocks to buyers who **on the Stock** put up little cash, borrowed in order **Market** to purchase, and then used the stocks they bought as collateral for their loans. When the stocks came tumbling down, so did brokers, bankers, and companies. Brokers called up buyers to ask for more cash. Some buyers drained their savings from banks, but when others could not come up with the money, the brokers sold the stock for the little it would command. Bankers, meanwhile, were calling up brokers and other speculators, searching for cash. The domino effect was crushing, and the whole economic system tottered as obligations went unmet. From 1930 to 1933 stock-market losses climbed to $85 billion. A new byword circulated: "Trust God, not stocks."

International economic troubles constitute a fifth explanation for the coming of the depression. As the world's leading creditor and trader, the United States was deeply involved with the world economy. Billions of dollars in loans had flowed to Europe during the

International Economic Troubles First World War and then during postwar reconstruction. Yet in the late 1920s American investors were beginning to keep their money at home, to invest it in the more exciting and lucrative stock market. Europeans, unable to borrow more funds and unable to sell their goods easily in the American market because of high tariffs, began to buy less from America and to default on their debts. Pinched at home, they raised their own tariffs, further crippling international commerce, and withdrew their investments from America. It was Hoover's view that "the European disease had contaminated the United States." He would have been more accurate had he said that the European and American illnesses were mutually infectious.

Finally, government policies and practices contributed to the crash and depression. The federal government failed to regulate the **The Failure of** wild speculation, contenting itself **Federal Policies** with occasional scoldings of bankers and businesspeople. It neither checked corporate power nor raised income taxes to encourage a more equitable distribution of income. Indeed, it lowered taxes, thus promoting the uneven distribution. And the Federal Reserve Board pursued easy-credit policies, charging low discount rates, or interest rates, on its loans to member banks, even though it knew the easy money was paying for the speculative binge. The "Fed" blundered again after the crash, in 1931. This time the board drastically raised the rate, tightening the money market at a time when just the opposite was needed: loosening to spur borrowing and spending.

Today, in an era of computerized data, daily economic forecasts, and the watchdog Council of Economic Advisers (see page 833), it is difficult to recall that in 1929 the state of economic analysis and statistics-gathering was comparatively primitive. The several explanations for the onset of depression were not easily grasped in 1929, especially while people were absorbed in a headlong rush to make as much money as possible as fast as possible. And the conventional wisdom, based on the experience of previous depressions, was that little could be done to correct economic problems. So in 1929 people waited for the deflation to bottom out.

DESPAIRING AMERICANS

As the economy limped into the 1930s, statistics began to tell the story of a human tragedy. Between 1929 and 1933 a hundred thousand businesses failed; corporate profits fell from $10 billion to $1 billion; and the gross national product was cut in half. What happened to America's banks—and savings—illustrates especially well the cascading nature of the Great Depression. Banks tied into the stock market or foreign investments were badly weakened; some failed. When nervous Americans made runs on banks to salvage their threatened savings, a powerful momentum—panic—took command. In 1929, 659 banks folded; in 1930 the number of failures climbed to 1,350. The next year proved worse, 2,293 banks shutting their doors, and another 1,453 ceased to do business in 1932. By 1933 9 million savings accounts had been lost, amounting to $2.5 billion in losses. Americans who believed that saving was a virtue, a path to material fulfillment, discovered that their deposits had disappeared with the banks.

Americans lost savings—and jobs. Although most people remained employed, day after day thousands of men and women received severance slips. At the beginning of 1930 the number of jobless had reached at least 4 million; by November it had jumped to 6 million. When President Hoover left office in 1933, about one-fourth of the labor force was idle—13 million workers—and millions more were underemployed, working only part-time. Hoover asked businesspeople not to cut wages, but labor income dropped by 40 percent during his presidency. Half the workers in Cleveland went off payrolls; in Lowell, Massachusetts, two-thirds of the labor force was unemployed.

Blacks and the unskilled lost their jobs first; whites and managerial personnel were let go last. Black women were more likely to lose jobs than white women. In Cleveland, for example, one-half of black female workers were unemployed, compared with one-sixth of white female laborers. Desperate whites proved willing to take menial jobs once held largely by blacks, and because white employers preferred to hire whites, blacks were pushed out of the labor force. Thus many whites displaced blacks as domestic servants, and Atlanta fired its black sanitation workers to replace them with whites.

In 1930 over 10.5 million women were in the work force, composing 22 percent of all workers. Despite these statistics, most Americans believed that

Women Workers

women should not work outside the home, that they should strive instead to be good wives and mothers, and that women who worked were doing so for "pin money" to buy frivolous things. Moreover, the depression invigorated the longstanding charge that women in the labor force necessarily displaced male breadwinners. One Chicago civic group protested that women "are holding jobs that rightfully belong to the God-intended providers of the household." Married women workers received the most criticism; some states even passed laws forbidding the hiring of married women for civil service positions. Such thinking missed the point, for two reasons. First, women were heavily concentrated in certain occupations or "women's jobs," including clerical positions (49 percent of all employees were women), teachers (81 percent), telephone operators (95 percent), and nurses (98 percent). Men rarely sought these "feminized" jobs and probably would not have been hired had they applied for such work. Second, most women workers (72 percent in 1930) were single, not married. Many were self-supporting or were keeping their families from slipping into poverty. Work was thus a necessity for them. Although married women, because of depression-induced hardship, entered the labor force in greater numbers, they do not seem to have displaced men.

The depression thus affected women workers in different ways from their male counterparts. Women suffered the stings of popular antagonism toward their employment. The depression retarded the movement of women into professional occupations. But the rate of unemployment for women was lower than that for men. Why? Because "men's jobs" (in manufacturing, for example) were harder hit by the depression than were women's sex-typed occupations; because, given traditional wage discrimination, women were cheaper to hire than men; and because men did not think of competing for feminized secretarial or nursing jobs.

The experience of teachers provides an example. Because women accounted for four-fifths of all teachers in 1930, the depression's damage to school systems particularly alarmed women. Some towns failed to meet payrolls. To save money, others shortened terms, released teachers, increased class loads, eliminated kindergartens and art and music classes, or shut down schools altogether. In 1931–1932, about 5,000 rural schools closed across the nation. Of the 1,500 urban school systems surveyed by the National Education Association in 1930–1931, 77 percent refused to hire married women as teachers and 63 percent fired female teachers who married while employed. Still, fewer jobs were lost in teaching than in occupations more associated with males. By fall 1933 only 8 percent of the teaching force was unemployed, whereas the figure for the entire American work force had reached 25 percent.

How could a nation of such abundance and high production, with its factories intact and its workers eager to work, find itself saddled with such utter hardship? men and women asked themselves. It was difficult for Americans raised on the philosophy of hard work and self-help to understand the contradiction of poverty amidst plenty. "Why," asked one man, "must they wear shabby clothes? Because we have too much cotton, too much wool, too many mills, and too many hands." Humorist Will Rogers quipped, "We are the first nation in the history of the world to go to the poorhouse in an automobile."

Actually people were putting their cars up on blocks and using other means to search for work. In Detroit auto workers roamed from plant to plant, only to discover padlocked gates. "A worker's got no right to have kids any more," cried one. Western apple growers sent their surplus to the cities, where a new class of street-corner entrepreneurs peddled the fruit at five cents each. A reporter portrayed a New York City unemployment office: "The room is almost silent. A slight, despairing hum from the job seekers. Patient, stretched on the rack of a social system that compels this degradation, they stand quite mute. The suspense is painful." A Minneapolis woman described her futile daily vigil at the city unemployment department: "So we sit in this room like cattle waiting for a nonexistent job, willing to work to the farthest atom of energy, unable to work, unable to get food and lodging,

In Chicago in 1930 the gangster Al Capone's soup kitchen attracted hungry men eager for a free meal.   Library of Congress.

unable to bear children. Here we must sit in this shame looking at the floor, worse than beasts at a slaughter."

People's diets deteriorated, malnutrition became common, and the undernourished fell victim more easily to disease. Some people quietly lined up at

Deterioration of Health

Red Cross and Salvation Army soup kitchens or queued in breadlines. Others ate only potatoes, crackers, or dandelions, stole dog biscuits from the local dog pound, or scratched through garbage cans for bits of food. Milk consumption decreased to such an extent that Kentucky miners called it medicine. Pregnant women went without essential foods like eggs and vegetables. Because of inadequate diets doctors witnessed an increase in tuberculosis, typhoid, dysentery, and heart and stomach disorders. Lillian Wald of the Henry Street Settlement House in New York City saw semistarved parents trembling

uncontrollably: what food they had they had given to their children. In that city in 1932, hospitals reported 95 deaths from starvation. The nation's suicide rate also climbed, though the overall death rate continued its long-term trend downward.

Millions of Americans were not only hungry and ill; they were cold. Unable to afford fuel, some huddled in unheated tenements and shacks. Families doubled up in crowded apartments, but some who were unable to pay the rent were evicted, furniture and all. Urban jungles sprouted up, constructed from packing boxes and other debris usually carted away as junk. Several hundred women took to sleeping in Chicago's Lincoln and Grant parks; in Oakland, California, hundreds of people lived in the leftover concrete waste ducts of Sewer-Pipe City.

In the countryside, hobbled long before the depression struck, economic hardship deepened. Between 1929 and 1933 farm income was cut in half. Though

Chapter 25: THE SHAKEN DREAM, 1929–1933

farm prices dropped 60 percent, production decreased only 6 percent as individual farmers struggled to make up for lower prices by producing more, thereby creating an excess. And the surplus that so depressed agricultural prices could not be exported, since foreign demand had shrunk. Drought, foreclosure, clouds of hungry grasshoppers, and bank failures further plagued the American farmer. A Missouri man who could not pay his taxes or his mortgage, nor afford to truck his corn and barley to market, appealed for help: "I have no horses, no car am 73 yrs old, born on this farm but don't seem like I can hold it much longer." On southern cotton plantations, black sharecroppers barely subsisted on an income of less than $300 a year; whites fared little better with $400.

Plight of the Farmers

Native Americans descended further into malnutrition and disease. In Oklahoma, where the Choctaw, Cherokee, and Seminole lived with over twenty other tribes on infertile soil, three-fourths of all Indian children were undernourished. Tuberculosis swept through the reservations. Told to grow gardens to feed themselves, the Indians lacked seed. At the heart of the problem was a 1929 ruling by the U.S. comptroller general that landless tribes were ineligible for federal aid. Not until 1931 did the Indian Bureau take steps to relieve the suffering. A federal relief program was launched to provide flour from the Red Cross, surplus clothing from the War Department, and seed from the Department of Agriculture. Yet, when Congress substantially increased the bureau's budget that year, much of the money went to raise the salaries of white employees and to hire more bureaucrats. The bureau thus had an average of about one supervisor for every thirty-six Indians.

Native Americans

Some Americans became transients in search of jobs or food. Desperate tenant farmers—husbands, wives, and children—walked the roads of the South. The California Unemployment Commission reported in 1932 that an "army of homeless" had trooped into the state and moved constantly from place to place, forced by one town after another to move on. Hundreds of thousands jumped aboard freight trains—"rode the rods"—or hitchhiked. Some boys and girls wandered on their own, living in hobo jungles usually populated

Going West—1933, *painted by Robinson Boardman. This stark rendering of anxious migrants searching for work and a happier life is typical of art produced during the depression era. National Museum of American Art, Smithsonian Institution, Washington, D.C.*

by adults. Congressman Maury Maverick of Texas, who wanted to find out for himself what it was like, was stunned by his hobo tour: "There was promiscuity, filth, degradation. . . . Men and families slept in jails, hot railroad urinals, cellars, dugouts, tumbledown shacks." Routes south were the most popular, for there the weather was less cruel.

During these years many Mexicans and Mexican-Americans moved south of the border, sometimes willingly, sometimes deported by immigration officials or forced out by California officials eager to purge them from the relief rolls. As an inducement, the government offered free one-way train tickets to Mexico. From 1929 through 1934, about 425,000, mostly from Texas, California, Indiana, and Illinois, returned to Mexico.

Across America economic woe and geographical mobility changed marriage patterns and family life. People postponed marriage, and married couples postponed having children. Demographers estimate

Marriage and the Family

that 800,000 marriages that would normally have occurred in the years 1930 through 1933 did not occur because of the depression. The birthrate fell from 21.3 live births per 1,000 population in 1930 to 18.4 in 1933. Divorces also declined, from 206,000 in 1929 to 164,000 in 1932. Couples may not have been able to afford a divorce, or they may have decided they could face hardship better by sticking together. Families made other adjustments, too. Maybe they moved to a less expensive house or apartment; maybe they sold the car or sacrificed the telephone; maybe sons and daughters were denied a college education.

With less opportunity for outside recreation, family members were forced to spend more time together. This enforced closeness did not cause difficulty for happy, well-integrated, and stable families, but it did create unpleasantness and disorder in families suffering unemployment and crowded living quarters. Out-of-work fathers felt ashamed, resenting their diminished role. "A child who was playing irritated him," recalled the son of an unemployed Waterloo, Iowa, tool-and-die maker. "It wasn't just my own father. They all got shook up." The self-esteem of fathers and husbands was further undermined by a reversal of sex roles caused when the wage-earning work of wives and daughters supported the family. Some women made all their children's clothing and canned vegetables and fruits, becoming in essence the family's provider. Yet in most families the husband still remained the dominant partner.

Some men and women tried to massage their despair with humor. Even the president asked comedians to tell jokes to lighten people's burdens. Hoover himself bore the brunt of much of the comedy. "What? You say business is better? You mean Hoover died?" Jackrabbits shot by hungry farmers were "Hoover hogs"; makeshift shanty towns in vacant urban lots were "Hoovervilles"; and newspapers were "Hoover blankets". Even home run–hitter Babe Ruth got into the act. When he was negotiating his salary for 1930 ($80,000) with the New York Yankees, the Babe was criticized for asking for more money than the president of the United States made. He shot back: "What the hell has Hoover got to do with it? Besides, I had a better year than he did." Eddie Cantor drew laughs when he imitated a hotel clerk asking a stockbroker whether he wanted a room for sleeping or jumping. Others joked about two men who had jumped to their deaths hand in hand because they had a joint account.

Although a third of the nation's movie theaters shut down in the early years of the depression, millions of Americans still paid to see Hollywood's latest offerings. Movies were a form of escape from economic troubles. One studio put it this way: "There's a Paramount Picture probably around the corner. See it and you'll be out of yourself, living someone else's life." The "someone elses" included gangsters (played by Edward G. Robinson and James Cagney) whose lives were success stories in a disordered society, and comedians like the horseplaying Marx brothers, who in *Animal Crackers* (1930) and *Duck Soup* (1933) poked fun at convention. Seductive Mae West, who demonstrated that woman could be the hunter as well as the hunted, and whose line "Come up and see me sometime" became a legend, rose to stardom. And the role of the "fallen woman" who offered sex for personal survival (played by Tallulah Bankhead and Marlene Dietrich) became popular. There were also musicals like the popular *Gold Diggers* (1933) and horror films like *Dracula* (1932) and *Frankenstein* (1932). And then there was the giant monster in *King Kong* (1933) who scaled the Empire State Building and smashed his way through New York City. King Kong, wrote the historian Robert Sklar, "may have given the audiences precisely the proper combination of fear for the survival of their society and pleasure at seeing someone, if only a doomed gorilla, vent his rage at it."

Movies as an Escape from Hardship

THE AGGRAVATION OF RACIAL TENSIONS

The depression sank the vast majority of blacks deeper into an already precarious mire of fear, political disfranchisement, Jim Crow segregation, and privation. "It was a frightening time," Susie W. Walker of Canton, Mississippi, recalled. "A lot of people didn't know where their next meal was coming from." In 1931, when her daughter was born, "I couldn't even produce breast milk for the baby because we weren't getting enough to eat."

In 1930 about three-quarters of all blacks lived in the South. Most were not permitted to vote; were excluded from juries; could not be treated at the local hospital; were not hired except for the least desirable, most menial jobs; could not enroll at universities; and were denied access to public parks and swimming pools. Blacks living in rural areas (in 1930, 56.9 percent) were propertyless share-croppers, tenants, or wage hands caught in a cycle of poverty, disease, and illiteracy. The infant mortality rate for blacks in 1930 was double that of whites; pneumonia, tuberculosis, and venereal disease were far more prevalent among black Americans as well. In 1929 black life expectancy was more than ten years lower than white life expectancy (46.7 years versus 57.1). And the specter of the lynch mob's noose—the unspeakable torture, the crowd shouting for death, the utter lawlessness—was ever before black men. In 1929 seven blacks were lynched; in 1930, twenty; the following year, twelve. In 1932 the figure was comparatively low at six, but in 1933, when the depression was at its worst, twenty-four blacks were lynched.

Blacks in the Depression

Southern blacks continued to migrate to the cities and to the North, as they had since the First World War, but they found conditions not much better. Both employers and unions discriminated against them. Black unemployment rates ran high; in Pittsburgh, 48 percent of black workers were jobless in 1933, compared with 31 percent of white laborers. And in the movie theaters, blacks appeared on the screen only as yea-saying domestics, jungle natives, plump mammies, or gospel singers. For black Americans, then, the depression made for no dramatic shift in status. They had been stereotyped, segregated, and poor long before 1929. Now, though, they lost jobs to whites and were discriminated against even on the breadlines.

Blacks were aware that Herbert Hoover shared prevailing white racial attitudes; what was more, they knew he was attempting to push them out of the Republican party in order to attract white southern Democrats. Hoover sought, as a saying of the time put it, a lily-white GOP. He appointed few blacks to federal office, disbanded the Negro division of the Republican National Committee, rejected appeals for an antilynching law, and continued the segregation of the army and federal buildings in the nation's capital. Hoover's philosophy of individualism, opportunity, and fair play was, like the signs posted across the country, "For Whites Only."

In 1930, the president showed his insensitivity to blacks by nominating Judge John J. Parker of North Carolina to a position on the Supreme Court. Ten years earlier Parker had endorsed the disfranchisement of blacks; the NAACP remembered the speech and protested the nomination. Because Judge Parker had also decided in favor of the yellow-dog contract—a contract in which employees agree not to join a union—and the use of the injunction in labor disputes, the American Federation of Labor joined the protest. This combined pressure plus liberal votes in the Senate defeated Parker's nomination, 41 to 39. Unmoved, Hoover stood by his nominee throughout.

Then came Scottsboro, a celebrated civil-liberties case that symbolized the ugliness of race relations in the depression era. One afternoon in March 1931 a freight train pulled into the yard at Paint Rock, near Scottsboro, Alabama. Aboard were some youthful transients traveling in the boxcars. When the train stopped, armed sheriff's deputies arrested nine blacks, charging them with roughing up some white hobos and throwing them off the train earlier in the day. When two white women who were removed from the same freight claimed that the blacks had raped them, an angry white mob gathered. Within two weeks eight of the "Scottsboro boys" had been convicted of rape by all-white juries and sentenced to death. The ninth, only twelve years old, was favored by a hung jury. But because court-appointed lawyers had offered little defense for the homeless, illiterate, poorly clad, and sickly youths, the Supreme Court in 1932 overturned the convictions on the grounds that the accused had not been granted adequate legal counsel.

Scottsboro Trials

New trials opened in 1933, again with all-white juries. This time, however, the Scottsboro blacks

The nine Scottsboro youths in jail in Decatur, Alabama.
Seated with the attorney Samuel Leibowitz is Haywood
· Patterson.   Brown Brothers.

were defended by Samuel Leibowitz, a talented attorney hired by the Communist-sponsored International Labor Defense. To a crowded courtroom, the local prosecutor sneered at Leibowitz, announcing that "Alabama justice cannot be bought and sold with Jew money from New York." Medical evidence showed that the women had not had intercourse on the train. Ruby Bates and Victoria Price had lied, perhaps because they feared arrest as prostitutes. Nevertheless, the first defendant up for retrial, Haywood Patterson, was once again found guilty. Judge James Horton, who had stated that under American law "we know neither black nor white. . . . It is our duty to mete out even-

handed justice," was convinced that Patterson was an innocent victim of racial hatred. The courageous Horton overturned the jury's decision.

A new judge was found, a new trial held, and for the third time Patterson was ordered to die. But another Supreme Court ruling intervened, this time because it was evident that in Alabama blacks were systematically excluded from juries. Patterson faced a fourth trial in 1936. Found guilty again, he was given a seventy-five-year jail sentence. Four of the other youths were sentenced to life imprisonment, and the state dropped charges against the remaining four. Not until 1950 were all five out of jail—four by parole and Patterson by escaping from his work gang. Scottsboro's constitutional implications were important for the future: for the first time the Supreme Court used the Fourteenth Amendment as a vehicle to apply the criminal protection procedures of the Bill of Rights against the states (previously they had been applied only against the federal government).

Blacks coped with their white-circumscribed environment and fought back against racism in a variety of ways during the depression. Black Baptist and African Methodist Episcopal churches articulated black concerns; black newspapers like the *Amsterdam News* (New York), the *Chicago Defender*, and the *Pittsburgh Courier* cultivated racial consciousness. Black Renaissance poets and writers like Langston Hughes promoted civil rights. And Howard University, Tuskegee Institute, and Atlanta University, among others, trained a generation of black leaders. The NAACP, although internally divided, lobbied quietly against a long list of injustices, and A. Philip Randolph's Brotherhood of Sleeping Car Porters defended the rights of black workers. In Cleveland and New York, black doctors protested discriminatory practices at municipal hospitals. In Harlem the militant Harlem Tenants League fought rent increases and evictions, and in some cities black consumers began to boycott white merchants. But America's white leaders made few concessions. Only the Supreme Court, which declared the Texas "white primary" law unconstitutional and attempted to check the abuses in the Scottsboro trials, provided a measure of protection for black Americans in the thirties.

THE TEMPERED PROTEST

Most Americans—black or white—met the new crisis not with violence, protest, or political extremism, but with bewilderment and an inability to fix the blame. They scorned businesspeople, of course, but often they blamed themselves as well, as the traditional ideology of the self-made man had taught them to do. There were some grocery-store robberies, an increase in homicides, a few nasty strikes and protest marches, and flirtations with radicalism on the left and right, but they were usually scattered, unconnected, and spontaneous. Nothing like the extreme political convulsions that rocked Europe hit the United States. Robert Hutchins, president of the University of Chicago, thought about why Americans responded so temperately to the catastrophe: "How could there be a revolt against a system in which everybody believed, including those who were starving to death because of it?" The few protests sought immediate relief—jobs, food, housing—not long-term radical social change. In the words of a depression-era song:

I don't want your millions, mister,
I don't want your diamond ring.
All I want is the right to live, mister;
Give me back my job again.
I don't want your Rolls-Royce, mister,
I don't want your pleasure yacht.
All I want is food for my babies;
Give me my old job back.[1]

Despair, sullenness, demoralization, and shock cut deeply into the American psyche. When the novelist Sherwood Anderson picked up hitchhikers along the road, he found many of them to be apologetic about their plight. A psychiatrist describing unemployed miners wrote, "They hung around street corners and in groups. They gave each other solace. They were loath to go home because they were indicted, as if it were their fault for being jobless. A jobless man was a lazy good-for-nothing. . . . They felt despised, they were ashamed of themselves." This was the stuff not of revolution, but of self-hatred and melancholy.

Scattered protests did, however, raise the specter of popular revolt. In Iowa's Cow War of 1931, angry farmers assailed state tuberculin inspectors who condemned diseased cattle but gave farmers little compensation for their losses. Soon the National Guard was escorting veterinarians on their rounds, arresting uncooperative farmers. In Nebraska, Iowa, and Minnesota, farmers protesting low prices put up barricades, stopped trucks, and dumped milk and vegetables on the road. Some of these demonstrations were organized by the Farmers' Holiday Association. Its leader, Milo Reno, argued that the propertied farmer was the

[1]From "I Don't Want Your Millions Mister" by Jim Garland. © Copyright 1947 by Stormking Music, Inc. All Rights Reserved. Used by permission.

Farmers' Holiday Association

backbone of society and the economy; lift up the farmer and the nation would be lifted out of depression. Reno encouraged farmers to take a holiday—to keep their products off the market until they commanded a better price. The Sioux City milk strike in the summer of 1932 was the association's most dramatic effort, but like others it failed to improve significantly the economic position of farmers. The following year a Wisconsin dairy farmers' strike ended unsuccessfully after National Guardsmen tossed tear gas and charged with fixed bayonets into a crowd of rock-throwing farmers.

Like their forebears in Shays' Rebellion (1786), farmers were more effective in slowing foreclosures on farm properties. By harassing sheriffs, judges, and lawyers, they sometimes prevented evictions; and they conspired at auctions to bid very low on foreclosed land and then turned over the property to its relieved former owners. Their protests contributed to the passage of state laws that inhibited foreclosure.

Isolated protests also sounded in cities and in mining regions. In Chicago, Los Angeles, and Philadelphia, the unemployed marched on city halls. Chicago schoolteachers, protesting drastic budget cuts, pulled down the 1933 World's Fair flag and stormed the city hall. And in Harlan County, Kentucky, miners struck against wage reductions (1931). Mine owners responded with strikebreakers, bombs, the National Guard, the closing of relief kitchens, and evictions from company-owned housing. "The law," grumbled one woman, "is a gun thug in a big automobile." Though Theodore Dreiser, Lincoln Steffens, and other socially conscious writers traveled to the poor Kentucky county to draw national attention to the struggle, the strike failed nonetheless.

The most spectacular confrontation shook Washington, D.C., in summer 1932. Congress was considering a bill authorizing immediate issuance of bonuses of $2.4 billion already allotted to First World War veterans, but not due for payment until 1945. To lobby for the bill, fifteen thousand unemployed veterans and their families converged on the tense nation's capital, calling themselves the Bonus Expeditionary Force (BEF). They camped in crude shacks on vacant lots and in empty government buildings. Blacks mingled with

Bonus Expeditionary Force

whites; Jim Crow was "absent with leave," said Roy Wilkins of the NAACP.

Though President Hoover threw his weight against the bonus bill, the House passed it. The showdown came in the Senate, which voted "no" after much debate. One BEF member shouted: "We were heroes in 1917, but we're bums today." Many of the bonus marchers then left Washington, but several thousand stayed on. Hoover grew impatient, carelessly labeled them "insurrectionists" and Communists, and refused to meet with them.

In July General Douglas MacArthur, assisted by Majors Dwight D. Eisenhower and George S. Patton, met the veterans and their families with cavalry, tanks, and bayonet-bearing soldiers. The BEF hurled back stones and bricks. What followed shocked the nation. Men and women were chased down by horsemen; children were teargassed; shacks were set afire. As smoke wafted above the capital's stately buildings, a United Press correspondent commented on the ugly scene: "So all the misery and suffering had finally come to this—soldiers marching with their guns against American citizens." Although one might argue whether ex-servicemen deserved special legislative favor, there can be no question that the answer to their predicament was not violence but food. Hoover's image as a humanitarian was badly tarnished, even though he thought MacArthur had gone too far in using force. When presidential hopeful Franklin D. Roosevelt heard about the attack on the Bonus Army, he turned to his friend Felix Frankfurter and said: "Well, Felix, this will elect me."

With capitalism on its knees, American Communist leaders anticipated large gains for their party. Across the nation they organized "unemployed councils" to arouse class consciousness and to agitate for jobs and food. In March 1930 they conducted urban demonstrations, some of which ended in violent clashes with local police. And with the slogan "Fight—Don't Starve," they led a hunger march on Washington, D.C., in 1931. Their tangles with authority publicized the real human tragedy of the depression.

Still, the Communist party gained few followers. Workers shunned it, blacks responded without enthusiasm to its recruiting drives, and farmers, although attracted to its call for debt relief and federal aid, rejected the party's appeal that they abandon the in-

Communist Party

Their lobbying having failed, these members of the Bonus Expeditionary Force buried not only the bonus they so ardently sought from an unobliging Senate, but also President Hoover and former Secretary of the Treasury Andrew Mellon, both of whom had opposed payment of the bonus. One message was surely that the veterans intended to bury politically the Republican president in the forthcoming election of 1932. Within a month, these BEFers and others would be driven violently from their makeshift houses by American troops   Library of Congress.

dividual ownership of property for collectivization. Ordinary Americans, the journalist Gerald Johnson commented, "have no more idea of turning communistic than they have of turning Mohammedan." Some intellectuals were attracted to Marxism and saw the party as one vehicle for social change, economic planning, and antifascism. Theodore Dreiser, Lincoln Steffens, Jack Conroy, John Dos Passos, and Erskine Caldwell were among them. But many of these writers became disenchanted with the Communists' rigid discipline and dogma and attachment to the Soviet Union. The hero of Conroy's *The Disinherited* (1933) grows critical of the party's abstractions: "Why don't they talk about beans and potatoes, land and bacon instead of 'ideology,' 'agrarian crisis,' and 'rationalization.' " Total party membership in 1930 was only six thousand; by 1932 it remained small at twelve thousand.

The Socialist party, which argued with both Communists and capitalists, fared little better. More reformist than radical, more evolutionary than revolutionary, the Socialists ran well in municipal elections after the stock market crash but scored few victories. In the 1932 presidential election, Socialist candidate Norman Thomas received 884,000 votes, a mere 2 percent of the total. (Communist candidate William Z. Foster won only 103,000 votes.) Party membership consisted mostly of older Jewish trade-union leaders, Protestant pacifists, students, and teachers; workers and labor unions gave the party little support. In 1930 the membership rolls listed 9,700 persons; by 1932 the figure had grown to 17,000, fewer than in 1903. Thomas found it "amazing that the workers were so comparatively quiet." Indeed, few despairing Americans looked to left-wing parties and doctrines, protest marches, or violence for relief from their misery. They turned instead to institutions of considerable longevity and stability: their local, state, and federal governments.

HOOVER HOLDS THE LINE

When urgent daily appeals for government relief for the jobless reached the White House, Hoover at first became defensive, if not hostile. "We cannot legislate ourselves out of a world depression; we can and will work ourselves out," he replied. Hoover rejected direct relief—derisively called the dole—because he believed it would undermine character and individualism. "It is a reassuring thought, in the cold weather," the critic Edmund Wilson wrote sarcastically, "that the emaciated men in the bread lines, the men and women beggars in the streets, and the children dependent on them, are all having their fibre hardened." Indeed, to a growing number of Americans, Hoover seemed heartless and inflexible at a time when humanitarianism and activity were called for. Rather than deal with the quarter of the work force that was jobless, he emphasized the many who were still on payrolls. The president did not help his public image by brooding and conveying indifference. "This is not a showman's job," he snapped. "You can't make a Teddy Roosevelt out of me." And he made the mistake of being photographed on the White House lawn—feeding his dog.

True to his beliefs, the president urged people to help themselves and their neighbors. He applauded private voluntary relief through charitable agencies such as the Community Chest and the Red Cross. Yet when the need was greatest, donations declined. State and urban officials found their treasuries drying up too. Philadelphia, after hiring the unemployed to paint city buildings, exhausted its relief funds by 1931, leaving 57,000 families without assistance. The "demands of suffering humanity," cried the mayor, required federal action. He got no sympathy from Secretary of the Treasury Andrew Mellon, who with a mixture of conventional wisdom and callousness advised the president to "let the slump

Reliance on Private Relief

liquidate itself. Liquidate labor, liquidate stocks, liquidate the farmers, liquidate real estate. . . . It will purge the rottenness out of the system." Will Rogers cast the problem in a different light. "We got more wheat, more corn, more food, more cotton, more money in the banks, more than any nation that ever lived ever had, yet we are starving to death." "It's simply a case," Rogers advised, "of getting it fixed."

Hoover did try to fix the economy. As the depression intensified, his opposition to federal action diminished. He rejected Mellon's insensitive counsel, hesitantly and gradually energizing the White House and federal agencies to take action—more action than the government had taken before. He met with business and labor leaders, winning pledges from them to maintain wages and production and to avoid strikes. He urged state governors to increase their expenditures on public works. And he created the President's Organization on Unemployment Relief (POUR) to generate private contributions for relief of the destitute. Unfortunately, the chairman, president of the American Telephone and Telegraph Company Walter Gifford, seemed a man of limited concern and vision. Asked by a senator to specify the nation's relief requirements, Gifford said he had no precise information. The incredulous senator leaned forward: "Do you know what the relief needs are in the rural districts of the United States?" Gifford answered simply, "No."

If POUR proved ineffective, Hoover's spurring of federal public works projects (including the Boulder, or Hoover, and Grand Coulee dams) did provide some jobs. Help also came from the Federal Farm Board, created before the depression under the Agricultural Marketing Act of 1929. An outcome of Hoover's emphasis on cooperation among individuals, groups, and government, the Farm Board supported agricultural prices by lending money to cooperatives to buy products and keep them off the market. But the board soon found itself short of money, and unsold surplus commodities jammed warehouses. And though the federally sponsored and privately funded National Credit Corporation assisted faltering banks, it barely slowed the number of bank failures. To retard the collapse of the international monetary system, Hoover announced a moratorium on the payment of First World War debts and reparations (1931).

The president also reluctantly asked Congress to charter the Reconstruction Finance Corporation

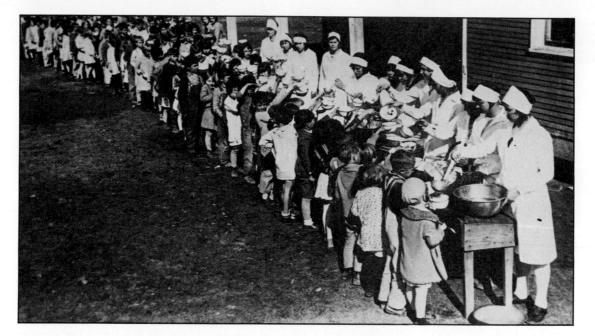

In early 1931 needy children in El Paso, Arkansas, lined up for soup dispensed free by Red Cross workers. Soup lines and bread lines became conspicuous features of American life during the Great Depression, but declining contributions put restraints on the activities of voluntary, charitable associations like the Red Cross. National Archives.

Reconstruction Finance Corporation

(RFC). Created in 1932 and eventually empowered with $2 billion, the RFC was designed to make loans to banks, insurance companies, and railroads and later to state and local governments. The theory behind the RFC was that it would lend money to large entities at the top of the economic system, and benefits would trickle down to people at the bottom through a sort of percolation process. Liberal Republican Representative Fiorello La Guardia of New York labeled the plan a "millionaires' dole." It did not work; banks continued to collapse and small companies to go into bankruptcy.

Despite warnings from prominent economists, Hoover also signed the Hawley-Smoot Tariff (1930). A congressional compromise serving special interests, the tariff raised duties by about one-third. Besides wishing to fulfill a Republican party pledge, Hoover argued that the tariff would help farmers and manufacturers by keeping foreign goods off the market. Actually, the tariff further weakened the economy by making it even more difficult for foreign nations

to sell their products and thus earn the money to buy American products and pay off their First World War debts.

Like most of his contemporaries, Hoover believed that a balanced budget was sacred, and deficit spending sinful. In 1931 he appealed for a decrease in federal expenditures and an increase in taxes. The following year he supported a sales tax on manufactured goods, which liberal Democrats charged was an attempt to avoid higher income and corporate taxes. The sales tax was defeated, but the Revenue Act of 1932 raised corporate, excise, and personal income taxes. Hoover seemed caught in a contradiction: he urged people to spend to spur recovery, but his tax policies deprived them of spending money. He never did balance the budget. Nor did he seek repeal of the legal loopholes that permitted the partners of J. P. Morgan and other wealthy Americans to escape paying any income taxes in 1931 and 1932.

Although Hoover expanded public works projects and approved loans to some institutions, he vetoed a variety of relief bills presented to him by the

an ideologue who, when faced with problems of unprecedented magnitude, failed to take bold steps to meet them. Hoover once said that nobody was starving, and in late 1931 he remarked, "Our people have been protected from hunger and cold." Such a statement arose not from heartlessness but from faith in the status quo. Whatever one's interpretation, Hoover's restrained and cautious response to the depression did not mean that he was weak. "Weak Presidents are ignored or brushed aside," the historian Albert Romasco has written. "Hoover remained a formidable, effective obstacle to new ideas and innovations until he was blasted away by the presidential election returns."

Hoover's traditionalism was well demonstrated by his handling of prohibition. Despite the Eighteenth Amendment, Americans were producing and drinking liquor with grand illegality and hypocrisy. The law was not and could not be enforced. Yet Hoover resisted the mounting public pressure for repeal. Opponents argued not only that prohibition encouraged crime, but that its repeal would stimulate economic recovery in Milwaukee and St. Louis, increase demand for grain, and revive the nation's old beer, liquor, and pretzel factories. But the president would not, he said, tamper with the Constitution, and the liquor industry, having no socially redemptive value, was best left depressed. Instead, Hoover pushed for better enforcement of the Eighteenth Amendment. And during the presidential election campaign of 1932, he stood firm against repeal. As on other issues, Hoover held the line.

Democratic Congress. "Prosperity," he intoned, "cannot be restored by raids upon the public treasury." He also vetoed a multipurpose development project for the Tennessee River, arguing that its cheap electricity would compete with power from private companies. Clinging to his old viewpoints, Hoover stretched government activities as far as he thought he could without violating his cherished principles.

Because Hoover mobilized the resources of the federal government as never before, some historians have depicted him as a bridge to the New Deal of the 1930s. If nothing else, he pre-

Hoover Assessed
pared the way for massive federal activity by giving private enterprise the opportunity to solve the depression—and to fail. They point out, moreover, that Hoover was a progressive trapped by unprecedented events, and that few leaders of the time were sure what to do. But others have argued that Hoover was

TRADITION IN TIME OF CRISIS: THE ELECTION OF 1932

Herbert Hoover and the Republican party faced dreary prospects in 1932. The tired and sullen president grumbled at reporters, banks continued to close, and memories of the Bonus March persisted. Hoover kept pointing to international causes for the economic crisis, when Americans were less concerned with abstract explanations than with tomorrow's meal. He grew impatient with critics who held him responsible for the depression. "Is it my fault," he asked a reporter, "that cheap politicians and selfish men over the whole world have refused to see the folly of their policies until it was too late?" His critics replied that as secretary of commerce during the 1920s Hoover shared responsibility for the depression. But what soured public opinion most was that Hoover seemed not to lead at a time when innovative generalship was required, that he refused to budge. "No president," Hoover told a friend, "must ever admit he has been wrong."

In 1932 Republicans who did not want to be associated with a loser ran independent campaigns; Progressive Republicans like Senator George Norris deserted Hoover; W. E. B. Du Bois urged blacks to vote Democratic. The president made few major speeches, rarely left Washington, and when he did venture out was frequently jeered and booed. On the final day of the campaign, when Hoover returned to California to vote, his motorcade was interrupted by stink bombs.

Franklin D. Roosevelt, on the other hand, enjoyed a different reputation. The smiling, ingratiating governor of New York appealed to the American penchant

Democratic Candidate Franklin D. Roosevelt

for optimism. "I figure out that if we can get rid of Old Gloom and put in a feller that can laugh and act human," a cab driver remarked, "the Depression will be half over."

As governor of New York, Roosevelt had launched relief programs and an unemployment commission. In 1932 he outmaneuvered try-again Al Smith and Speaker of the House John Nance Garner to gain the top spot on the Democratic ticket. Accepting the nomination in person, the fifty-year-old Roosevelt called for a "new deal for the American people."

The two party platforms differed little, but the Democrats were willing to abandon prohibition and to launch federal relief. Roosevelt, playing the political game superbly, promised to help everybody—a Santa Claus campaign, one critic called it. Hoover complained that his opponent was a chameleon on plaid. Indeed, Roosevelt's speeches, pieced together by ghostwriters, seemed contradictory. He would agree with Hoover that the budget had to be balanced,

A gloomy Hoover and a buoyant Roosevelt ride to the inauguration in 1933. This magazine cover was actually never published, apparently because the editors of the New Yorker magazine thought it inappropriate after an attempted assassination of the president-elect. *Franklin D. Roosevelt Library.*

then appeal for costly new programs. When Roosevelt spoke of the forgotten man and declared himself ready to provide direct relief to individuals, Hoover boiled: "This campaign is more than a contest between two men," he said. "It is more than a contest between two parties. It is a contest between two philosophies of government." Roosevelt seemed to agree, explaining his liberalism with a metaphor:

Say that civilization is a tree which, as it grows, continually produced rot and dead wood. The radical says: "Cut it down." The conservative says: "Don't touch it." The liberal compromises: "Let's prune, so that we lose neither the old trunk nor the new branches." This campaign is waged to teach the country to march upon its appointed course . . ., avoiding alike the revolution of radicalism and the revolution of conservatism.

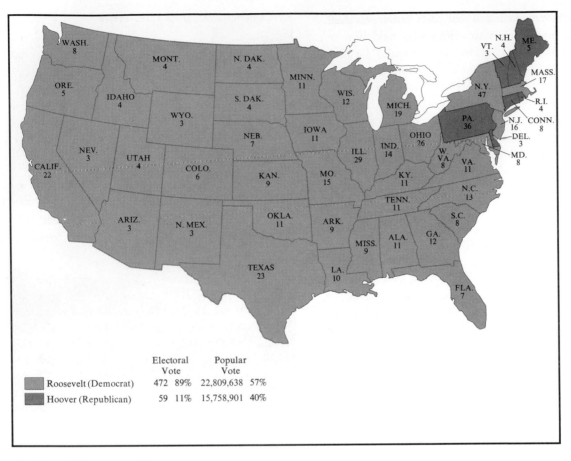

Presidential Election, 1932

More people went to the polls in 1932 than in any election since the First World War. In a crisis-ridden moment Americans quietly, calmly, even routinely followed tradition and peacefully exchanged one government for another. Roosevelt's 22.8 million popular votes far outdistanced Hoover's 15.8 million: 57 percent of the popular vote went to the Democrat, 40 percent to the Republican, and **1932 Election Results** 3 percent to minor party candidates. Hoover won only Vermont, New Hampshire, Maine, Connecticut, Delaware, and Pennsylvania, giving him a paltry 59 electoral votes to Roosevelt's 472 (see map). Cities continued the trend, begun in 1928, of voting Democratic. But although Hoover was in trouble with some black leaders, two-thirds of the black vote remained Republican in 1932. Roosevelt had appealed to southern whites as Hoover had, and he held racial views that seemed to differ little from Hoover's.

Democrats also won overwhelming control of the Senate and the House. From November to March, a lame-duck president, a lame-duck Congress (158 of whose members had been defeated), and a hesitant president-elect took little positive action, and the depression continued to cut its debilitating path. Americans wondered what would happen next. Might not radicals make gains? Some thought Roosevelt would reform the American system enough to forestall radical solutions. Others envisioned demagogues, splinter parties, or violence. Hoover feared Roosevelt would implant "collectivism" in the nation, smothering individualism and destroying the American system. But Hoover exaggerated his differences with Roosevelt, who hardly sought the destruction of capitalism. The two parted ways largely on the extent to which the federal government should intervene in economic and social affairs. And the majority of Americans had spoken for more intervention. How strikingly

Chapter 25: THE SHAKEN DREAM, 1929–1933

different from their mood four years earlier was their mood on inauguration day 1933.

SUGGESTIONS FOR FURTHER READING

Hoover and His Administration

David Burner, *Herbert Hoover* (1979); Carl N. Degler, "The Ordeal of Herbert Hoover," *Yale Review*, 52 (1963), 563–583; Martin L. Fausold, *The Presidency of Herbert C. Hoover* (1985); Martin L. Fausold and George T. Mazuzan, eds., *The Hoover Presidency* (1974); Ellis W. Hawley, *The Great War and the Search for a Modern Order* (1979); Richard Hofstadter, *The American Political Tradition* (1949); Barry D. Karl, "Presidential Planning and Social Science Research: Mr. Hoover's Experts," *Perspectives in American History*, 3 (1969), 347–409; William E. Leuchtenberg, *The Perils of Prosperity, 1914–1932* (1958); James S. Olson, *Herbert Hoover and the Reconstruction Finance Corporation, 1931–1933* (1977); Edgar E. Robinson and Vaughn D. Bornet, *Herbert Hoover* (1975); Albert V. Romasco, *The Poverty of Abundance: Hoover, The Nation, The Depression* (1965); Elliot A. Rosen, *Hoover, Roosevelt, and the Brains Trust* (1977); Jordan A. Schwarz, *Interregnum of Despair* (1970); Richard N. Smith, *An Uncommon Man* (1984); Harris G. Warren, *Herbert Hoover and the Great Depression* (1959); Joan Hoff Wilson, *Herbert Hoover: Forgotten Progressive* (1975).

The Great Depression and Its Causes

W. Elliot Brownlee, *Dynamics of Ascent*, 2nd ed. (1979); Lester V. Chandler, *America's Greatest Depression, 1929–1941* (1970); Milton Friedman and Anna Schwartz, *The Great Contraction, 1929–1933* (1965); John K. Galbraith, *The Great Crash*, 50th anniv. ed. (1979); Robert L. Heilbroner and Aaron Singer, *The Economic Transformation of America*, 2nd ed. (1984); Susan Kennedy, *The Banking Crisis of 1933* (1973); Charles Kindleberger, *The World in Depression, 1929–1939* (1973); Broadus Mitchell, *Depression Decade* (1947); Jim Potter, *The American Economy Between the Wars* (1974); George Soule, *Prosperity Decade* (1947); Peter Temin, *Did Monetary Forces Cause the Great Depression?* (1976); Gordon Thomas and Max Morgan-Witts, *The Day the Bubble Burst* (1979).

The American People in Hard Times

Francisco E. Balderrama, *In Defense of La Raza: The Los Angeles Mexican Consulate and the Mexican Community, 1929–1936* (1982); Andrew Bergman, *We're in the Money: Depression America and Its Films* (1971); Caroline Bird, *The Invisible Scar* (1965); Sidney Fine, *Frank Murphy: The Detroit Years* (1975); Milton Meltzer, *Brother, Can You Spare a Dime?* (1969); Cabel Phillips, *From the Crash to the Blitz, 1929–1939* (1969); Robert Sklar, *Movie-made America* (1975); Bernard Sternsher, ed., *Hitting Home: The Great Depression in Town and Country* (1970); Studs Terkel, *Hard Times* (1970); David Tyack et al., *Public Schools in Hard Times* (1984); Dixon Wecter, *The Age of the Great Depression, 1929–1941* (1948); Edmund Wilson, *The American Earthquake* (1958).

Workers

Irving Bernstein, *The Lean Years: A History of the American Worker, 1920–1933* (1960); John W. Hevener, *Which Side Are You On? The Harlan County Coal Miners, 1931–1939* (1978); Lois Scharf, *To Work and to Wed: Female Employment, Feminism, and the Great Depression* (1980); Winifred D. Wandersee, *Women's Work and Family Values, 1920–1940* (1981).

Farmers

Lowell K. Dyson, *Red Harvest: The Communist Party and American Farmers* (1982); Theodore Saloutos and John D. Hicks, *Twentieth Century Populism: Agricultural Discontent in the Middle West, 1900–1939* (1951); John L. Shover, *Cornbelt Rebellion: The Farmers' Holiday Association* (1965).

Protest

Roger Daniels, *The Bonus March* (1971); John P. Diggins, *The American Left in the Twentieth Century* (1973); Harvey Klehr, *The Heyday of American Communism* (1984); Donald J. Lisio, *The President and Protest: Hoover, Conspiracy, and the Bonus Riot* (1974); Mark Naison, *Communists in Harlem During the Depression* (1983); David Shannon, *The Socialist Party of America* (1955).

Race Relations

Dan T. Carter, *Scottsboro*, rev. ed. (1979); Harvard Sitkoff, *A New Deal for Blacks* (1978); Bernard Sternsher, ed., *The Negro in Depression and War* (1969); Raymond Wolters, *Negroes and the Great Depression* (1970); Robert L. Zangrando, *The NAACP Crusade Against Lynching, 1909–1950* (1980).

THE GREAT DEPRESSION AND THE NEW DEAL

1933–1941

CHAPTER 26

*F*ranklin D. Roosevelt loved the sea. So in August 1921, when a business associate with a yacht offered a cruise to Roosevelt's summer home on Campobello Island, off the coast of New Brunswick, he happily accepted. Sailing into the frigid waters of the Bay of Fundy between New Brunswick and Nova Scotia, the two encountered rough water, and Roosevelt stood for hours at the helm until the boat was in harbor.

The next day Roosevelt went fishing and fell overboard. "I never felt anything so cold as that water!" he said later, "so cold it seemed paralyzing." Roosevelt was exhausted, but he did not slacken his pace. There was a forest fire to be fought, followed by another dip in the cold waters. Finally, he was too tired to stand up. When Roosevelt awoke the next morning, his left leg ached. He also had a fever. Soon he had no feeling in either leg. A doctor diagnosed polio. Just a year before, in 1920, he had been the robust vice-presidential candidate of the Democratic party. Now he was crippled, totally paralyzed in both legs.

What should Roosevelt do next? Should he retire from public life, a rich invalid? His answer and his wife Eleanor's was no. Throughout the 1920s Franklin and Eleanor contended with his new handicap. Rejecting self-pity even though he at times experienced intense pain, Roosevelt worked to rebuild his body. People who had known him before commented that polio had made him a "twice-born man," that his "fight against that dread disease had evidently given him new moral and physical strength." As Roosevelt explained it: "If you had spent two years in bed trying to wiggle your big toe, after that anything would seem easy."

For her part, Mrs. Roosevelt learned to do things for herself, such as driving a car; and she began to shape her own career in public life, giving speeches and participating in the activities of the League of Women Voters, the Women's Trade Union League, and the Democratic party. Two of her strongest commitments came to be equal opportunity for women and for Afro-Americans, and she especially wanted to help the poor and suffering.

In 1933 Franklin D. Roosevelt became president, and the source of strength for a nation troubled by the Great Depression. The qualities of character he and Eleanor had discovered and nurtured in the 1920s would prove invaluable assets in the years to come.

From the first days of his presidency Roosevelt displayed a buoyancy and a willingness to experiment that helped to restore public confidence in the government and the economy. He acted not only to reform such economic institutions as banks and stock exchanges, but also to provide relief to the suffering. After shoring up the banking system, Roosevelt proposed a succession of laws to aid landowning farmers, blue-collar workers, businesses and local governments facing bankruptcy, the unemployed, the elderly, and even impoverished writers and artists. This sweeping legislation was based on the unorthodox concept of "pump priming," or deficit financing, to stimulate consumer buying power, business enterprise, and ultimately employment by pouring billions of federal dollars into the economy.

Roosevelt's New Deal inspired opposition from both the left and right. Businesspeople and economic conservatives found it fiscally irresponsible; demagogues and left-wing politicians thought it too conservative. Ultimately Roosevelt prevailed, however, revitalizing the progressive movement, vastly expanding both the scope of the federal government and the popularity of the Democratic party, and in the process establishing America's welfare state.

During these years several million workers seized the chance to organize for better wages and working conditions. The new Congress of Industrial Organizations (CIO) established unions in major industries like automobiles, steel, and meatpacking. Nonwhites registered political and economic gains too, though in general they benefited less from the New Deal than did whites. Some federal agencies actually worked against blacks; on the other hand, black advisers took posts in the White House, and Native Americans discovered that New Dealers respected their culture and tribal rights.

Two-and-a-half million additional women workers joined the labor force during the 1930s. But female

Chapter 26: THE GREAT DEPRESSION AND THE NEW DEAL, 1933–1941

workers were segregated in low-income jobs, and the New Deal excluded many women from Social Security coverage and minimum-wage protection.

Roosevelt was re-elected in 1936, but soon thereafter his fortunes began to wane. In 1937 the nation sank into a severe economic recession, and Congress rejected Roosevelt's attempt to increase the number of sympathetic judges on the federal bench. In 1938 the spate of relief and reform legislation came to an end. But by that time the New Deal had transformed the United States; although the New Deal was not a revolution, its legacy is still with us today. Farmers still plant according to federal crop allotments. The elderly and disabled still collect Social Security payments. The Federal Deposit Insurance Corporation still insures bank deposits. And the Securities and Exchange Commission still monitors the stock exchange. One goal the New Deal did not accomplish—putting back to work all the people who wanted jobs. That would await the nation's entry into the Second World War.

FRANKLIN DELANO ROOSEVELT

Franklin D. Roosevelt was born into privilege, the only child of doting parents who heaped on him all sorts of advantages. He was graduated from Harvard in 1903, and in fall 1904 he entered the School of Law at Columbia University. He soon announced his engagement to his fifth cousin once-removed, Anna Eleanor Roosevelt, the niece of President Theodore Roosevelt. The next spring they were married.

Roosevelt began the practice of law, but he had other ambitions—political ones. In 1910 he ran for the New York State Assembly and won. In 1912 he accepted President Wilson's offer of the post of assistant secretary of the navy. For eight years Roosevelt supervised the navy's relations with business and labor unions. He learned lessons about the emergence of the United States as a world power and the need for decisive presidential leadership in times of crisis.

Roosevelt's Early Career

In November 1930 Franklin D. Roosevelt (1882–1945) read the good news. Re-elected governor of New York by 735,000 votes, he immediately became a leading contender for the 1932 Democratic presidential nomination. Note Roosevelt's leg braces, rarely shown in photographs because of an unwritten agreement by photographers to shoot him from the waist up. UPI/Bettmann Newsphotos.

In 1920 the Democratic party nominated Roosevelt for the vice presidency. Campaigning on the need for the League of Nations and continued domestic reform, he and Governor James M. Cox of Ohio were roundly defeated by Republicans Harding and Coolidge. But Roosevelt suffered his most devastating loss the next year, when he was struck by polio. After deciding to fight his polio rather than succumb to it, Roosevelt practiced law and pursued various business ventures. And he returned to politics, nominating New York's Governor Al Smith for president at both the 1924 and 1928 Democratic conventions and becoming a spokesperson for progressive Democrats. Also in 1928 Roosevelt agreed to run for governor of New York; in November he won by 25,000 votes. Smith, in contrast, not only lost the election, but failed to carry his home state of New York, losing it by 100,000 votes. Right away Roosevelt became an obvious prospect for the 1932 Democratic presidential nomination. "You are," Virginia's Senator Harry Byrd wrote to Roosevelt, "the hope of the Democratic party."

Roosevelt's governorship coincided with Hoover's presidency, and both coincided with the onset of the Great Depression. But whereas Hoover appeared hardhearted and unwilling to help the jobless, Roosevelt seemed just the opposite. He urged unemployment insurance and direct relief payments for the jobless. Under his leadership New York's Temporary Emergency Relief Administration (1931) became the first state agency to mobilize on behalf of the poor. Aid to the unemployed, Roosevelt declared, "must be extended by Government, not as a matter of charity, but as a matter of social duty."

Roosevelt as Governor of New York

Roosevelt was also more willing than Hoover to experiment. As governor of New York, he advocated creating jobs in publicly funded reforestation, land reclamation, and hydroelectric power projects. He also endorsed and worked for old-age pensions and protective legislation for labor unions. Roosevelt warned people not to dismiss such experimentation "with the word radical. Remember the radical of yesterday is almost [always] the reactionary of today." After he was re-elected in 1930 by a record-setting plurality of 735,000 votes, politicians had to take a serious look at his vote-getting ability.

To prepare a national political platform, Roosevelt surrounded himself with a "brain trust" of lawyers and university professors. Foremost among these advisers were Columbia University professors Rexford G. Tugwell, Raymond Moley, and Adolf A. Berle, Jr. Bigness was unavoidable in the modern American economy, these experts reasoned; thus the cure for the nation's ills was not to go on a rampage of trustbusting, but to place large corporations, monopolies, and oligopolies under effective government regulation. "We are no longer afraid of bigness," declared Tugwell, speaking in the tradition of Theodore Roosevelt's New Nationalism. "We are resolved to recognize openly that competition in most of its forms is wasteful and costly; that larger combinations in any modern society must prevail."

Roosevelt's "Brain Trust"

Roosevelt and his brain trust agreed that it was essential for the government to restore purchasing power to farmers, blue-collar workers, and the middle classes, and that the way to do so was to cut production. If the demand for a product remained constant and the supply were cut, they reasoned, the price would rise. Producers would make higher profits, and workers would earn more money. This method of combating a depression has been called the economics of scarcity. Unlike Hoover, Roosevelt also advocated immediate and direct relief to the unemployed. Finally, Roosevelt and his advisers rejected Hoover's explanation that the depression was international, not domestic, in origin. They demanded that the federal government engage in centralized economic planning and experimentation to bring about recovery.

The presidential election of 1932 had never been much of a contest (see page 730). But once elected, Roosevelt had to wait until his inauguration on March 4 to act.[1] It was a troubled four months. Almost 13 million unemployed people walked the streets, some participating in hunger riots and job protest marches. Prices for agricultural and manufactured goods continued to plummet, forcing the bankruptcy of countless farms, small businesses, railroads, and even local governments. Industrial production sank to new depths. And while farmers in the Farm Holiday movement

---

[1] As a result of that crucial loss of time, the Twentieth Amendment to the Constitution—the Lame Duck Amendment—was ratified. It moved all future inaugurations forward to January 20.

poured milk into ditches and threatened to hang foreclosing judges, another kind of holiday was observed in some states: the bank holiday. Throughout the United States, depositors lined up in front of banks demanding their money. Banks with insufficient funds on hand to pay depositors had to close their doors and declare themselves insolvent. In February, Michigan and Maryland suspended banking operations, and by March 4, thirty-six other states, including New York, had followed suit.

On the afternoon of March 2, 1933, President-elect Roosevelt and his family and friends boarded a train for Washington, D.C., and the inauguration ceremony. Roosevelt was carrying with him rough drafts of two presidential proclamations, one summoning a special session of Congress, the other declaring a national bank holiday, suspending banking transactions throughout the nation.

RESTORING CONFIDENCE

"First of all," declared the newly inaugurated president, "let me assert my firm belief that the only thing we have to fear is fear itself—nameless, unreasoning, unjustified terror." In his inaugural address Roosevelt scored his first triumph as president, instilling hope and courage in the rank and file. Roosevelt attacked the nation's bankers, accusing them of having "fled from their high seats in the temple of our civilization." He invoked "the analogue of war," proclaiming that, as in the First World War, the American people must march forward "as a trained and loyal army willing to sacrifice for the good of a common discipline." And if need be, he asserted, "I shall ask the Congress for the one remaining instrument to meet the crisis—broad Executive power to wage a war against the emergency, as great as the power that would be given to me if we were in fact invaded by a foreign foe."

On March 5, Roosevelt declared a four-day national bank holiday and summoned Congress to an emergency session. Congress convened on March 9 to begin what observers would call the Hundred Days. Roosevelt's initial legislative requests were cautious; por-

Beginning of the Hundred Days
tions had even been drafted by Hoover's advisers before leaving office. The first measure, the Emergency Banking Relief Bill, was introduced on March 9, passed sight unseen by unanimous House vote, approved 73 to 7 in the Senate, and signed by the president that evening. The act confirmed Roosevelt's emergency actions and provided for the reopening, under Treasury Department license, of banks that were solvent and the reorganization and management of those that were not. It also prohibited gold hoarding and export. But it was a conservative law that upheld the status quo, leaving the nation's banking system essentially unchanged, with the same people in charge. This was a special disappointment to those who had taken seriously the antibanker rhetoric of Roosevelt's inaugural address. Complained one representative, "The President drove the money-changers out of the Capitol on March 4th—and they were all back on the 9th."

On the next day, March 10, another conservative New Deal bill was introduced in Congress; ten days later it became law. Called the Economy Act, its purpose was to balance the federal budget by chopping veterans' benefits and allowances by $400 million and reducing by $100 million the pay of federal employees. Under Roosevelt, the budget balancers had won a battle that could not have been won under Hoover. Despite the deflationary effects of this legislation, the important point was that Roosevelt had acted and had done so boldly.

On Sunday evening, March 12, the president broadcast the first of his fireside chats, and 60 million people heard his comforting voice on their radios.

First Fireside Chat
His message: banks were once again safe places for depositors' savings. On Monday morning the banks opened their doors, but instead of queuing up to withdraw their savings, people were waiting outside to deposit their money. "The people trust this administration," a wealthy woman jotted in her diary, "as they distrusted the other." The bank runs were over; people had regained confidence in their political leadership, their banks, even their economic system.

So far, the New Deal had embraced a drastically deflationary economic policy that decreased rather than increased the amount of money in circulation.

Roosevelt next pursued a measure, the Beer-Wine Revenue Bill, that was not only deflationary but would actually take money out of people's pockets. The bill was designed to generate revenues by legalizing the sale of low-alcohol wines and beers and levying a tax on them. (Repeal of prohibition had been proposed by Congress in the Twenty-first Amendment in February 1933; it would be ratified by the states in December 1933.) To many, levying new taxes seemed a strange way to restore purchasing power to people who could not afford to buy what they needed. Roosevelt knew that. "I realize well," he wrote a friend, "that thus far we have actually given more of deflation than of inflation. . . . It is simply inevitable that we must inflate." He added that his "banker friends may be horrified" by the large-scale federal spending that was to come. And beginning in mid-March, Roosevelt did seek congressional authorization to spend.

LAUNCHING THE NEW DEAL

(supported Big Business)

The New Deal seemed to promise something for everybody—farmers, businesspeople, workers, homeowners. Roosevelt was the artful broker, weighing the claims of these competing in-

Agricultural Adjustment Act

terest groups. On March 16, he sent to Congress the Agricultural Adjustment Bill, his plan to restore farmers' purchasing power. If overproduction was the cause of farmers' problems—falling prices and mounting surpluses—then the government had to encourage farmers to grow less food. Under the domestic allotment plan, as it was called, the government would pay farmers to reduce their acreage or plow under crops already in the fields. Farmers would receive payments based on *parity*, a system of regulated prices for corn, cotton, wheat, rice, hogs, and dairy products that would allow them the same purchasing power they had had during the prosperous period of 1909 through 1914. In effect, the government was making up the difference between the actual market value of farm products and the income farmers needed to

make a profit. The funds for the subsidies would come from taxes levied on the processors of agricultural commodities.

Roosevelt's farm plan immediately encountered vehement opposition. How, people asked, could there be crop surpluses and overproduction when some Americans were hungry and even starving? Underconsumption, they argued, was the result of a maldistribution of wealth and power as well as of goods and services. Some politicians wanted to stimulate inflation by coining silver, printing greenbacks, altering the gold content of the dollar, or taking the nation off the gold standard altogether. Cheap money, they contended, was the farmers' panacea, for it would make it easier for them to repay their debts. On May 12 Congress finally overcame opposition to the domestic allotment plan and passed the Agricultural Adjustment Act (AAA). A month later the Farm Credit Act also became law. By providing short- and medium-term loans to farmers—more than $100 million worth in seven months—the Farm Credit Act enabled many farmers to refinance their mortgages and hang on to their homes and land.

Meanwhile, other relief measures became law. On March 21 the president requested massive infusions of relief of three kinds: a job corps called the Civilian

Civilian Conservation Corps (CCC)

Conservation Corps (CCC); direct cash grants to the states to provide relief payments for needy citizens; and public works projects. Ten days later Congress approved the CCC. Within four months 1,300 camps were in operation and 300,000 young men between the ages of eighteen and twenty-five went to work planting trees, clearing camping areas and beaches, and building bridges, dams, reservoirs, fish ponds, and fire towers. More than 2.5 million young men eventually lived and worked in CCC camps. Then on May 12 Congress passed the Federal Emergency Relief Act, which authorized $500 million in aid to state and local governments.

Roosevelt's proposed plan for public works became Title II of the National Industrial Recovery Act (NIRA). Passed on June 16, it established in the Public Works Administration (PWA) a fund of $3.3 billion to build roads, sewage and water systems, public buildings, and a host of other projects, including

Under the Agricultural Adjustment Act, farmers received government payments for not planting crops or for destroying crops that had already been planted. These farmers in Kaufman County, Texas, are lined up for their checks. National Archives.

ships and naval aircraft. The purpose of the PWA was to prime the economic pump to spur economic recovery.

Pump priming was an unorthodox concept in 1933, and Roosevelt resorted to it only as a last-ditch measure. He remained orthodox in his views, anxious to return to a balanced budget at the earliest opportunity. Not until 1936 was the masterwork on pump priming, John Maynard Keynes's *General Theory of Employment, Interest and Money*, published. Roosevelt met with Keynes after the book's publication, but claimed he could not make heads or tails of the British economist's advice to spend massively.

If the AAA was the agricultural cornerstone of the New Deal, the National Industrial Recovery Act was the industrial cornerstone. The NIRA was a testimony to the New Deal belief

Economic Planning under the NIRA

in national planning as opposed to an individualistic, intensely competitive, laissez-faire economy. It was essential, the planners argued, for

businesses to end cutthroat competition and raise prices by limiting production. Like the War Industries Board (WIB) during the First World War (see page 661), the NIRA exempted businesses from antitrust laws through the National Recovery Administration (NRA). The NRA adopted a symbol, the Blue Eagle, and rallied popular support through motorcades and mass meetings. Also under the NRA, competing businesses met with representatives of workers and consumers to draft codes of fair competition, which limited production and established prices.

With businesses enjoying new concessions, workers wanted a share of the pie too. Congress guaranteed their right to unionize and to bargain collectively in Section 7(a) of the NIRA, which called for industrywide codes establishing minimum wages and maximum hours.

One of the boldest programs that Congress enacted during this period concerned the badly depressed Tennessee River valley, which ran through Tennessee, North Carolina, Kentucky, Virginia, Mississippi,

NEW DEAL ACHIEVEMENTS

	Labor	Agriculture	Business and Industrial Recovery	Relief	Reform
1933	Section 7A of NIRA	Agricultural Adjustment Act Farm Credit Act	Emergency Banking Act Economy Act Beer and Wine Revenue Act Banking Act of 1933 (guaranteed deposits) National Industrial Recovery Act	Civilian Conservation Corps Federal Emergency Relief Act Home Owners Refinancing Act Public Works Administration Civil Works Administration	TVA Federal Securities Act
1934	National Labor Relations Board				Securities Exchange Act
1935	National Labor Relations (Wagner) Act	Resettlement Administration Rural Electrification Administration		Works Progress Administration and National Youth Administration	Banking Act of 1935 Social Security Act Public Utilities Holding Company Act Revenue Act (wealth tax)
1937		Farm Security Administration			
1938	Fair Labor Standards Act	Agricultural Adjustment Act of 1938			

Source: Adapted by permission from Charles Sellers, Henry May, and Neil R. McMillen, *A Synopsis of American History*, 5th ed., pp. 296–297. Copyright © 1981 by Houghton Mifflin Company.

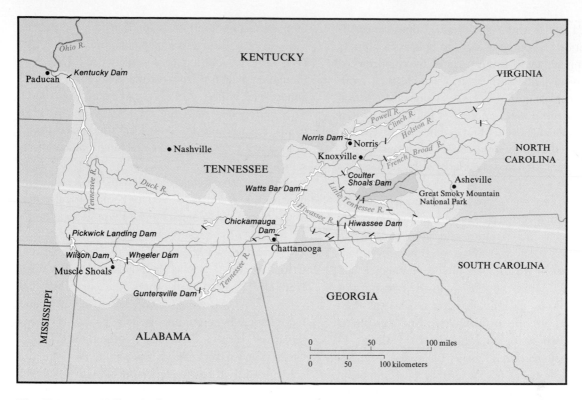

The Tennessee Valley Authority

Georgia, and Alabama. For years progressives led by Senator George Norris of Nebraska had advocated government operation of the Muscle Shoals electric power and nitrogen facilities on the Tennessee River. But Roosevelt's Tennessee Valley Authority (TVA), as finally established in May 1933, was a much broader program than the progressive plan. Its dams would not only serve to control floods, but they could also generate hydroelectric power, reclaim and reforest land, and prevent soil erosion. The TVA also would produce and sell nitrogen fertilizers to private citizens and nitrate explosives to the government; dig a 650-mile navigation channel from Knoxville to Paducah; and construct public power facilities as a yardstick for determining fair rates for privately produced electric power. The goal of the TVA was nothing less than enhancement of the economic well-being of the entire Tennessee River valley (see map).

Congress finally adjourned on June 16, its Hundred Days completed. Roosevelt had delivered fifteen messages to Congress, and fifteen significant laws had been enacted (see table). Notable among these laws

End of the Hundred Days

were the Federal Securities Act, to compel brokers to tell the truth about new securities issues, and the Banking Act of 1933, which set up the Federal Deposit Insurance Corporation for insuring bank deposits. Finally, on April 19 the United States abandoned the gold standard by announcing that it would no longer guarantee the gold value of the dollar abroad. Freed from the gold standard, Roosevelt's monetary policy became another tool for economic recovery.

Within a few months of Roosevelt's taking office, the United States had rebounded from shock, hysteria, and near-collapse. Columnist Walter Lippmann wrote that at the time of the inauguration, the country was a collection of "disorderly panic-stricken mobs and factions. In the hundred days from March to June we became again an organized nation confident of our power to provide for our own security and to control our own destiny."

Throughout the remainder of 1933 and the spring and summer of 1934, more New Deal bills became law. The beneficiaries of many of the new recovery acts were property-owning farmers. In October 1933, for example, the Commodity Credit Corporation was organized under the Agricultural Adjustment Administration. Its purposes were to bolster crop prices by lending money to farmers against their underpriced crops, and to allow farmers to withhold their crops from the market until prices rose. Nonfarm legislation designated additional hundreds of millions of dollars for unemployment relief and public works. Finally, in 1934 legislation established the Securities and Exchange Commission and the National Labor Relations Board.

The New Deal represented interest-group democracy at work, with government benefits accruing not only to business but to agriculture and labor; to farm and

Broker State Democracy

homeowners; to corporations, railroads, and city governments; and to the jobless. In the midst of this coalition of all interests was President Roosevelt, the artful broker. And this broker state appeared to be working. In 1933 almost 13 million people had been jobless. Following New Deal legislation the figure fell steadily to 11.4 million in 1934, 10.6 million in 1935, and 9 million in 1936. Net farm income rose from $2.5 billion in 1932 to just over $3 billion in 1933, almost $3.5 billion in 1934, and $5.85 billion in 1935. And manufacturing salaries and wages also increased, jumping from $6.25 billion in 1933 to over $9.5 billion two years later and almost $13 billion in 1937.

There was no doubt about the popularity of either the New Deal or Roosevelt. In the 1934 congressional elections, the Democrats gained ten seats in the House and ten in the Senate. The New Deal, according to Arthur Krock of the *New York Times,* had won "the most overwhelming victory in the history of American politics." And as for Roosevelt, "he has been all but crowned by the people," wrote William Allen White.

REACTIONS AGAINST
THE NEW DEAL

Yet there was more than one way to read employment and income statistics and election returns. For example, though unemployment had dropped from a high of 13 million (25 percent) in 1933 to 9 million (16.9 percent) in 1936, it had been only 1.5 million (3.2 percent) in 1929. And though manufacturing wages and salaries had reached almost $13 billion in 1937, that figure was almost $1.5 billion less than the total for 1929. In other words, regardless of the New Deal's successes, it had a long way to go before reaching predepression standards.

With the arrival of partial economic recovery, many businesspeople and conservatives became vocal critics of the New Deal. Some charged there was too much taxation and government regulation.

Conservative Critics of the New Deal

Others criticized the deficit financing of relief and public works. According to still others, the New Deal had subverted individual initiative and self-reliance by providing welfare payments. Conservatives hinted darkly of totalitarianism. This "maelstrom of centralized order-giving," wrote the columnist David Lawrence, "more strongly resembles the dictatorships of the Fascistic and Communistic states of Europe than it does the American system."

If businesspeople felt the government was their enemy, others thought the government favored business too much. Critics argued that business leaders had dominated the drafting of NRA codes, which, they claimed, favored industry's needs over those of workers and consumers. In addition, a major debate developed between the trustbusters and probusiness planners in the NRA. For a while, government propaganda urging Americans to support the NRA quieted the debate, particularly during the business recovery of 1933. In time, however, criticism grew. Farmers, labor unions, individual entrepreneurs, and antitrust critics complained that the NRA set prices too high and favored large-scale producers over small businesses. And the federal courts began to scrutinize the constitutionality of the legislation in cases brought by critics.

The AAA came under attack as well because of its encouragement of cutbacks in production. In 1933 farmers had plowed under 10.4 million acres of cotton and slaughtered 220,000 sows and 6 million pigs—at a time when people were ill-clothed and ill-fed. Though for landowning farmers the program was successful, the average person found such waste to be shocking. And what about tenant farmers and sharecroppers? They too were supposed to receive government payments for taking crops out of cultivation, but very few of them, especially if they were black, received what they were entitled to. Furthermore, the AAA's hopes that landlords would keep their tenants on the land even while cutting production were not fulfilled. In the South the number of sharecropper farms dropped from 776,278 in 1930 to 541,291 in 1940. The result was a homeless population, some of whom, known in the folklore of the times as "Okies" and "Arkies," packed up and took off for California.

As dissatisfaction mounted, so too did the appeal of various demagogues. Father Charles Coughlin, the Roman Catholic priest whose weekly radio sermons offered a curious combination of

Demagogic Attacks on the New Deal

anti-Communism, anticapitalism, and anti-Semitism, was one of the more famous. According to Coughlin, the worst abuses of capitalism had been inflicted by the Jews. Such anti-Semitism also was popular among some farm leaders (for example, Milo Reno of the Farm Holiday Association, who referred to the New Deal as the "Jew Deal") and some urban Catholics. For a while Coughlin supported the New Deal, calling it "Christ's deal." But he was critical of the AAA's plowing-under of crops and slaughtering of livestock. In late 1934, declaring "these old parties are all but dead," Coughlin organized the National Union for Social Justice and began to criticize the New Deal for having "out-Hoovered Hoover."

Another challenge to the New Deal came from Dr. Francis E. Townsend, who had conceived what he called an Old Age Revolving Pensions plan. Under Townsend's scheme the government would pay monthly pensions of $200 to all citizens over age sixty, on condition that they spent the money in the same month they received it. Townsend claimed his plan would not only aid the aged but cure the depression by pumping enormous purchasing power into the economy. Though the plan was fiscally impossible, it addressed a real need. Many old people suffered extreme deprivation in the 1930s, a time when local relief for the elderly was nonexistent in many places and Social Security had not yet been established.

And then there was Huey Long, "the Kingfish," perhaps the most successful demagogue in American history. In 1928 Long was elected governor of Louisiana

Plagued by dust storms, evictions, and the unsympathetic policies of the Agricultural Adjustment Administration, thousands of tenant farmers and sharecroppers were forced to leave their land during the Great Depression. Known as "Okies" and "Arkies," they took off for California with their few belongings. This woman and her two children were photographed by Dorothea Lange near Tulelake, California, in 1939. Library of Congress.

with the slogan "Every Man a King, But No One Wears a Crown." Highly intelligent, aggressive, and at times brutal, Long adopted the methods of a dictator, especially after defeating an effort to remove him from office in 1929. At first Long supported the New Deal; but he found the Economy Act and the NRA too conservative, and began to believe that Roosevelt had fallen captive to big business and big money. Long countered in 1934 with the Share Our Wealth Society, which advocated the seizure by taxation of all incomes over $1 million and all inheritances over $5 million. With those funds, the government would furnish each family a homestead allowance of $5,000 and an annual income of $2,000, along with free college education, government storage of crops and control of planting, and limitations on working hours. By mid-1935 Long's movement claimed 7 million members, and few doubted that Long aspired to the presidency. Though an assassin's bullet extinguished

Senator Huey Long of Louisiana (center) had a mass following in the 1930s, and he had presidential ambitions. But he was assassinated in 1935, the same evening this photograph was taken. Long fell into the arms of James O'Connor (left), a political crony, while Louisiana's Governor O. K. Allen (right) seized a pistol and dashed into a corridor after the murderer, shouting, "If there's shooting, I want to be in on it." National Archives.

his ambition in September 1935, the Share Our Wealth movement persisted under a new leader, the vitriolic anti-Semite Gerald L. K. Smith.

Some politicians of the 1930s, like Floyd Olson, governor of Minnesota, declared themselves socialists. Olson sought a third party that would "preach the gospel of government and collective ownership of the means of production and distribution." In neighboring Wisconsin the left-wing Progressive party re-elected Robert La Follette, Jr., to the Senate in 1934, sent seven of the state's ten representatives to Washington, and placed La Follette's brother Philip in the governorship. And the old muckraker Upton Sinclair almost won the Democratic gubernatorial nomination in California

Left-wing Critics of the New Deal

in 1934 on the platform End Poverty in California (EPIC).

Perhaps the most controversial alternative to the New Deal was the Communist party of the United States of America (CPUSA). In the early days of the depression Communists had organized hunger marches and helped to establish labor unions among auto and electrical workers, seamen, and longshoremen (see pages 724–725). And in 1932 a number of distinguished writers had endorsed the Communist presidential candidate, William Z. Foster. But membership in the CPUSA remained small until 1935, when the party leadership changed its strategy. Proclaiming "Communism is Twentieth Century Americanism," the CPUSA disclaimed any intention of overthrowing the United States government and began to cooperate with left-wing labor unions, student groups, and writers' organizations.

Russia's response to the Spanish Civil War also encouraged some Americans to join the CPUSA. Only Russia seemed determined to stem the tide of fascism that had washed over Germany and Italy and in 1936 threatened Spain (see Chapter 27). One convert to the CPUSA, writer and editor Whittaker Chambers, explained that Communism offered "what nothing else in the dying world had power to offer at the same intensity—faith and a vision." Still, at its high point for the decade in 1938, the CPUSA had only 55,000 members.

In addition to challenges from the right and the left, the New Deal was threatened by the Supreme Court. Many New Deal laws had been hastily drafted and enacted, and the majority of the justices feared that this legislation had vested too much power in the presidency. In January 1935, in *Panama Refining Co. v. Ryan*, the Court struck down part of the NIRA. By granting the president power to prohibit interstate and foreign shipment of oil, the Court ruled, Congress had unconstitutionally delegated legislative power to the executive branch. Then on May 27 the Court unanimously struck down the whole NIRA (*Schechter v. U.S.*) on the grounds that it gave excessive legislative power to the White House, and that the commerce clause of the Constitution did not give the federal government authority to regulate intrastate businesses. Roosevelt's industrial recovery program was dead. In January 1936 his farm program met a similar fate when the Court invalidated the AAA (*U.S. v. Butler*), deciding that agriculture was a local problem and thus, under the Tenth Amendment, subject to state, not federal, action.

Supreme Court Decisions Against the New Deal

As Roosevelt looked ahead to the presidential election of 1936, he saw that he was in danger of losing his capacity to lead and to govern. His coalition of all interests was breaking up; radicals and demagogues were offering Americans alternative programs; and the Supreme Court was dismantling the New Deal. In the spring and summer of 1935, Roosevelt took the initiative once more, and the New Deal scored some of its biggest victories. So impressive was the new legislation that some historians have called it the Second New Deal.

THE SECOND NEW DEAL

There was an important difference between the First and Second New Deals. In 1933 and 1934 Roosevelt had cooperated with business. Beginning in 1935, however, he denounced business leaders for placing their selfish interests above the national welfare. Roosevelt also was being pushed left by the liberal Congress that had been elected in 1934 and by the unions' militancy and growing ranks.

The first triumph of the Second New Deal was an innocuous-sounding but momentous law called the Emergency Relief Appropriation Act, which Congress passed and Roosevelt signed in April 1935. The act authorized the president to issue executive orders establishing massive public works programs for the jobless, including the Works Progress Administration (WPA).

Emergency Relief Appropriation Act

Later renamed the Work Projects Administration, the WPA ultimately employed more than 8.5 million people on a total of 1.4 million projects. By the time it was terminated in 1943, the WPA had built over 650,000 miles of highways, streets, and roads, 125,000 public buildings, and 8,000 parks, as well as numerous bridges, airports, and other structures. But WPA did more than lay bricks. Its Federal Theatre Project brought plays, vaudeville shows, and circuses to cities and towns across the country, and WPA artists painted murals in post offices and other public buildings. The Federal Music Project and the WPA Dance Theatre sponsored laboratories for young composers and choreographers. And the Federal Writers' Project hired writers like Conrad Aiken, John Cheever, Claude McKay, John Steinbeck, and Richard Wright to write local guidebooks and regional, ethnic, and folk histories.

Besides the WPA, the Emergency Relief Appropriation Act funded other relief and public works measures. The Resettlement Administration (RA) resettled destitute families and organized rural homestead communities and suburban greenbelt towns for low-income workers. The Rural Electrification Administration (REA) distributed electricity to isolated

During the Great Depression the Works Progress Administration (WPA) employed artists to decorate public buildings and record its public works projects for posterity. Harold Lehman's painting of a burly, determined driller was one product of the federally sponsored employment program. National Museum of American Art, Transfer from the Newark Museum.

rural areas. And the National Youth Administration (NYA) sponsored work relief programs for young adults and provided jobs for the part-time employment of students.

As significant as these achievements were, Roosevelt wanted new legislation, some of it aimed at controlling the activities of big business. The Supreme Court had condemned the government-business cooperation that had been the foundation of the First Hundred Days. And businesspeople had become increasingly critical of Roosevelt and the New Deal. Now Roosevelt determined that if big business would not cooperate with government, government should "cut the giants down to size" through antitrust suits and heavy corporate taxes. In June he asked Congress to enact five major bills: a labor bill sponsored by Senator Robert Wagner; a Social Security bill; a banking bill; a measure to regulate public-utilities holding companies; and a "soak-the-rich" tax bill.

These were the Second Hundred Days; when they were over, the president would have everything he had requested. On July 5 the National Labor Relations

Roosevelt's Second Hundred Days

(Wagner) Act granted workers something for which they had long struggled: the right to unionize and to bargain collectively with management. When the Supreme Court struck down the NIRA, labor unions had lost their federal protection. But the new Wagner Act was stronger than its predecessor. It empowered the National Labor Relations Board to supervise the democratic election of bargaining agents and to issue cease-and-desist orders against unfair labor practices by employers, such as the firing of workers for union membership. Now employers had no legal way to resist unionization of their plants.

On August 15 Roosevelt signed the Social Security Act, which established a cooperative federal-state system of unemployment compensation and old-age

Social Security Act

and survivors' insurance. According to the law, workers who paid social security taxes out of their wages would receive retirement benefits at age sixty-five. The benefits would be paid for partially by their own contributions and partially by their employers. Social Security was a conservative measure: the government did not pay for old-age benefits; workers and their bosses did. The tax was also regressive—the more workers earned, the less they were taxed proportionately—and deflationary—it took money out of people's pockets that it did not repay for years. Finally, many people were ineligible for coverage under the law, including farm workers, domestic servants, and many hospital and restaurant workers. Large numbers of women and nonwhites were excluded from coverage. But although the act was far from inclusive, it was still a milestone in American history. It acknowledged the government's responsibility to establish a system of insurance for the aged, the dependent, the disabled, and the temporarily unemployed.

In the next two weeks Roosevelt gained the remainder of what he had asked for, including the Banking Act of 1935, the Public Utilities Holding Company (Wheeler-Rayburn) Act, and the Revenue (Wealth Tax) Act of 1935. None of these laws contained everything Roosevelt had requested. The Wealth Tax Act, which some critics saw as the president's attempt to "steal Huey's thunder," did not result in a redistribution of income, for instance, though it did increase the income taxes paid by the wealthy. It also increased taxes on inheritances, large gifts, and profits from the sale of property.

The Second Hundred Days indicated not only that the president was once again in charge, but that he was set to run for re-election. The campaign was less heated than might have been expected, however. Naturally the Republican nominee, Governor Alf Landon of Kansas, criticized Roosevelt, condemning him for threatening the free enterprise system with regulated monopolies, unconstitutional laws, and deficit spending. But Republicans conceded the need for government action, and they did not advocate wholesale repeal of the New Deal. The followers of Father Coughlin, Dr. Townsend, and the late Senator Long banded together in the Union party and nominated Representative William Lemke of North Dakota. The Socialists nominated Norman Thomas; the Communists, Earl Browder.

Election of 1936

The president and the Democratic party swept to a landslide victory. Roosevelt polled 27.8 million votes to Landon's 16.7 million; Lemke, Thomas, and Browder together received slightly over 1 million. The Democrats carried every state but Maine and Vermont and won huge majorities in the House and Senate. Some observers worried that the two-party system was about to collapse.

Political analysts have suggested that demographic shifts lay behind the Democratic triumph at the polls. In the 1920s and 1930s the sons and daughters of 13 million southern and eastern European immigrants were reaching voting age and swelling the ranks of their parents' traditional party. In addition, the 6 million Americans who had migrated from farms to cities in the 1920s looked to the government for rent control and food purity laws, regulation of working hours and conditions, and welfare for the unemployed. Before long they too had gravitated to the Democratic party. In 1920 the nation's twelve largest cities gave the Republicans 1.6 million more votes than the Democrats. In 1924 the Republican plurality dropped to 1.25 million, and in 1928 it disappeared. But that was just the beginning of the Democratic groundswell, which in 1932 jumped to 1.9 million and in 1936 to 3.6 million more big-city votes than the Republicans.

By 1936 Roosevelt and the Democrats had forged what observers have called the "New Deal coalition." The growing strength of the party in the cities, the suffering wrought by the Great Depression, and the New Deal response to social distress had converged to make Roosevelt the champion of the urban masses, as well as of farmers and the elderly. Labor, especially the new unions of the Congress of Industrial Organizations (CIO), was an indispensable member of the coalition (see pages 749–751). These unions fused the interests of millions of workers, native and foreign-born, black and white, male and female, skilled and unskilled. And black voters in northern cities, most of whom had been Republicans prior to the 1930s, now cast their lot with the Democratic party (see pages 752–753). Finally, many lifelong Socialists began to vote Democratic. In 1932 Norman Thomas, the Socialist party candidate, had polled 884,000 votes; in 1936 his total slipped to just 187,000. The Democratic party had become the dominant half of the two-party system.

New Deal Coalition

ROOSEVELT'S SECOND TERM: THE UNREALIZED PROMISE

Despite the bold and unprecedented steps of his first term, Roosevelt faced a darkening horizon during his second term. The economy faltered again between 1937 and 1939, bringing renewed unem-

ALL I SAID WAS "GIMME SIX MORE JUSTICES!"

President Roosevelt's court-packing plan provoked an outcry from Democrats as well as Republicans. Roosevelt's miscalculation resulted in a major defeat for his administration. Library of Congress.

ployment and suffering. And Europe drew closer to war, threatening to drag the United States into the conflict (see Chapter 27). To gain support for his foreign and military policies, Roosevelt began to court conservative politicians who had been long-time opponents of his domestic reforms. The eventual result was the demise of the New Deal.

In several instances Roosevelt caused his own defeat. The Supreme Court had invalidated much of the work of the First Hundred Days; now Roosevelt feared it would do the same with the fruits of the Second Hundred Days. So in February 1937 the president sent to Congress his Judiciary Reorganization Bill. What the federal judiciary needed, he claimed, was a more enlightened and progressive world view. Four of the justices steadfastly opposed the New Deal; three generally approved of it; and two were swing votes: Chief Justice Charles Evans Hughes and Associate Justice Owen J. Roberts. Although the justices had overturned some New Deal legislation on unanimous votes, they had also declared some other laws unconstitutional by such narrow margins as 5 to 4 and 6 to 3.

What Roosevelt requested was the authority to add a federal judge whenever an incumbent who had already served at least ten years failed to retire within six months of reaching age seventy. He wanted the

Roosevelt's Court-packing Plan

power to name up to fifty additional federal judges, including six to the Supreme Court. Though Roosevelt spoke of understaffed courts and aged and feeble judges, it was obvious that he envisioned using the bill to create a Supreme Court sympathetic to the New Deal.

Opposition to Roosevelt's attempt to pack the Court was widespread and vocal. Naturally, Republicans and some conservative Democrats opposed the bill, but liberals resisted as well. In many ways Roosevelt had only himself to blame. Had he made the bill an issue during the 1936 presidential election and won a great victory nevertheless, he could have sent his plan to Congress as the mandate of the people. Instead he had to concede defeat. The bill Roosevelt signed in August made pensions available to retiring judges, but it denied him the power to increase the number of judges.

This episode had an ironic final twist. During the public debate over court packing, the two swing-vote justices, Hughes and Roberts, began to vote in favor of liberal, pro-New Deal rulings. In March 1937, for example, the Court upheld a Washington State minimum-wage statute 5 to 4 (*West Coast Hotel* v. *Parrish*). Just a year before, in a case almost indistinguishable from this one, the Court had invalidated a similar New York State law. Then in April the Court upheld the Wagner Act 5 to 4 (*N.L.R.B.* v. *Jones & Laughlin Steel Corp.*), ruling that Congress's power to regulate interstate commerce involved also the power to regulate production of goods for interstate commerce. And in May the Court upheld the Social Security Act 5 to 4.

Roosevelt had lost the legislative battle but won the war for a more progressive judicial outlook. Encouraged by the new pensions, judges past the age of seventy did begin to retire, and the president was able to appoint seven new associate justices in the next four years, including such notables as Hugo Black, Felix Frankfurter, and William O. Douglas. Overwhelmingly, the new justices voted to sustain Roosevelt's policies and actions, and they continued to have a progressive influence for decades.

Another New Deal defeat, the renewed economic recession of 1937 through 1939, had no unexpected payoffs. Roosevelt had never abandoned his commitment to the balanced budget. In 1937, confident

Recession of 1937–1939 that most of the problems of the depression had been solved, he began to order drastic cutbacks in government spending. Between January and August 1937 the WPA cut its job rolls in half, from 3 million to 1.5 million people, and the government slashed other relief programs as well. To reduce the inflation rate of 3.6 percent, the Federal Reserve System increased the reserve requirements of member banks. The sudden tightening of credit sent the economy into a tailspin: unemployment soared from 14.3 percent in 1937 to 19.1 percent the next year.

In response to the new recession Roosevelt eventually revived deficit financing, and Congress appropriated billions more for the WPA, the CCC, and other programs. But even with sudden infusions of relief in 1938, unemployment still stood at 17.2 percent in 1939. Not until the end of that year did the economy return to 1937 levels. Many people wondered whether they had lived through two years of unnecessary recession and hardship.

Roosevelt's personal campaign against three conservative southern Democrats in the off-year elections of 1938 further revealed his desperation. Senators Walter George of Georgia, "Cotton Ed" Smith of South Carolina, and Millard Tydings of Maryland, all critics of the New Deal, won re-election despite Roosevelt's campaigning against them. As it turned out, Roosevelt would soon need the support of these conservatives for his programs of military rearmament and preparedness.

In spring 1938, with conflict over events in Europe commanding more and more of the nation's attention, the New Deal came to an end. The last significant laws enacted were a new Agricultural Adjustment Act and the Fair Labor Standards Act, which established minimum wages and maximum hours for many but by no means all workers.

THE RISE OF THE CIO

As governor of New York, Franklin Roosevelt had expressed his belief in the right of workers to organize and bargain with their bosses through representatives of their own choosing. Yet he arrived at the White House with no specific program for guaranteeing this right. Section 7(a) of the NIRA had not been his idea; when he signed the bill into law he did not appreciate what it meant or how it could be enforced.

On its enactment in June 1933, Section 7(a) inspired the organization of new unions and the vigorous recruitment of members. "Millions of workers throughout the nation," recalled American Federation of Labor (AFL) President William Green, "stood up for the first time in their lives to receive their charter of industrial freedom." Organizers for the United Mine Workers (UMW) told coal miners, "President Roosevelt wants you to join the union," and many thousands did. By October 1933 an additional 1.5 million workers had enlisted in unions, bringing total membership to 4 million. With passage of the Wagner Act in mid-1935, labor union recruiting received another big boost; within three years total membership surpassed 7 million.

But these gains did not always come easily. Management put up determined resistance in the 1930s, hiring armed thugs to intimidate workers and break up strikes. Violence surfaced in the **Rivalry Between Craft and Industrial Unions** steel, automobile, and textile industries and among the dock workers of the West Coast, the lumber workers of the Pacific Northwest, and the teamsters in Minneapolis. Labor confronted yet another obstacle in the AFL craft unions' traditional skepticism and hostility toward industrial unions. Craft unions typically consisted of skilled workers in a particular trade, such as carpentry, plumbing, or typography. Industrial unions, on the other hand, represented all the workers in a given industry, skilled and unskilled. The UMW, the United Brewery Workers, and the International Ladies' Garment Workers Union were all industrial rather than craft unions. Ever since its establishment in 1886, the AFL had been dominated by craft unions. But organizing gains in the 1930s were far more impressive in industrial unions than in craft unions, with hundreds of thousands of workers joining unions in such industries as autos, garments, rubber, and steel. What resulted was a struggle for control of the labor movement between craft and industrial union leaders.

Personifying this power struggle were the leaders

Like many pickets at this time, these men and women proclaimed their New Deal support and their "Americanism." Singing union songs and hymns, these pickets met outside of a textile mill in Greensboro, Georgia, in 1941. Library of Congress.

of the two sides, William Green, leader of the AFL, and John L. Lewis of the UMW. Lewis was probably the most colorful and tenacious labor leader in the nation's history, a fighter with a flair for the dramatic. William Green, on the other hand, was dull. But he was president of the entire AFL, whereas Lewis represented only one of the many unions within the AFL.

Attempts to reconcile the craft and industrial union movements failed, and in late 1935 Lewis resigned as vice president of the AFL. He and other industrial unionists within the AFL formed the Committee for Industrial Organization (CIO). When the AFL's Executive Council demanded that the CIO disband, Lewis replied: "The American Federation of Labor is standing still, with its face toward the dead past." In 1938 the AFL expelled the CIO unions, and the CIO reorganized itself as the Congress of Industrial Organizations. By that time CIO membership stood at 3.7 million, more than the AFL's 3.4 million.

The CIO, which in the 1930s evolved into a pragmatic, bread-and-butter labor organization, had organized millions of workers who had never before had an opportunity to join a union.

Sit-down Strikes One of these unions, the United Auto Workers (UAW), scored a major victory in late 1936. The union, thirty thousand strong, demanded recognition from General Motors, Chrysler, and Ford. When GM refused, the UAW launched a new kind of strike: the sit-down. Beginning in the Fisher Body plants in Flint, Michigan, workers refused to leave the plants. To discourage the strikers, GM managers turned off the heat; when that tactic failed, they called the police, who were met by a barrage of missiles—iron bolts, coffee mugs, and pop bottles. When the police resorted to tear gas, the strikers turned the plant's water hoses on them, and the police retreated in what the high-spirited strikers called the Battle of the Running Bulls.

The strike lasted for weeks, GM obtained a court order to evacuate the plant, but the strikers continued, risking imprisonment and fines. With the support of their families and neighborhoods, the workers stuck

On Memorial Day 1937, Chicago police used guns, clubs, and tear gas to break up a peaceful picket line at a Republic Steel plant. Ten people were killed and forty wounded in the Memorial Day Massacre. Wide World Photos.

to their rigid discipline. Community women organized an "emergency brigade" to picket and deliver food and supplies to the strikers. In 1937 the UAW prevailed: GM agreed to recognize the union. Chrysler signed a similar agreement, but Ford held out for four more years, a time of bloody encounters between the UAW and union-busting hoodlums hired by the Ford Service Department.

What made the sit-down strike significant was that it spread to all kinds of workers: textile, glass, and rubber workers, dime store clerks, janitors, dressmakers, and pie bakers began using the technique. Some people condemned the sit-down as a trespass on private property; others endorsed it, including muckraker Upton Sinclair, who wrote that "for 75 years big business has been sitting down on the American people, and now I am delighted to see the process reversed."

In 1937 too the Steel Workers Organizing Com-

mittee (SWOC) signed a contract with the nation's largest steelmaker, U.S. Steel, that guaranteed an eight-hour day and a forty-hour week. Other steel companies refused to go along, however. Confrontations between these so-called little steel companies and the SWOC led to violence. On Memorial Day in Chicago, strikers and their families had joined with sympathizers in a peaceful picket line in front of the Republic Steel plant. Suddenly and without provocation the police opened fire. They continued to shoot into the crowd even as people turned away and began to run. Of the ten fatalities, none had been shot in the front of the body; of the forty gunshot wounds, only four were frontal.

Memorial Day Massacre

As senseless as the Memorial Day Massacre was, its occurrence was not surprising. During the 1930s industries had hired private police agents and accumulated large stores of arms and ammunition for use in deterring workers from organizing and joining unions. A Senate committee headed by Robert La Follette, Jr., found that companies had spent millions of dollars in the process. Republic Steel, for example, was the nation's largest single purchaser of tear and sickening gas. Youngstown Sheet and Tube owned 8 machine guns, 369 rifles, 190 shotguns, 450 revolvers, and thousands of rounds of ammunition. All told, companies had hired almost four thousand private detectives to infiltrate unions, provoke discontent, impede organization, and report on union activities.

Through it all, the CIO continued to enroll new members. By 1938 industrial unions had enlisted 600,000 miners, 375,000 steelworkers, 400,000 auto workers, 300,000 textile workers, 250,000 ladies' garment workers, and 100,000 agricultural and packinghouse workers. By the end of the decade the CIO had succeeded in organizing most of the nation's mass-production industries.

MIXED PROGRESS FOR NONWHITES

For another segment of the New Deal coalition, black Americans, Franklin D. Roosevelt had become the most appealing president since Abraham Lincoln. Part of the reason was the courageous way he bore his physical disability. Blacks, who suffered from a handicap of their own—racism—knew what courage was. Moreover, Roosevelt seemed a decided improvement over Herbert Hoover, who had nominated a white supremacist to the Supreme Court (see page 721) and appeared hardhearted in the face of extreme suffering. Blacks suffered more than whites during the depression, and Roosevelt, in his fireside chats and through his personal magnetism and buoyancy, spoke directly to them. When they saw pictures of black visitors at the White House and read about Roosevelt's Black Cabinet, they were heartened.

The Black Cabinet, or black brain trust, was unique in United States history. Never before had there been so many black advisers at the White House, and never had they been highly trained professionals.

Black Cabinet There were black lawyers, journalists, and doctors of philosophy; black experts on housing, labor, and social welfare. William H. Hastie and Robert C. Weaver, both of whom held advanced degrees from Harvard, served in the Department of the Interior. Mary McLeod Bethune, a college president, was director of the Division of Negro Affairs of the National Youth Administration. Eugene Kinckle Jones, executive secretary of the National Urban League, and Lawrence A. Oxley, a professional social worker, served in comparable posts in the Departments of Commerce and Labor. Black social scientists, among them Ralph Bunche, Abram L. Harris, and Rayford W. Logan, acted as government consultants.

There were also among the New Dealers some whites who had committed themselves to first-class citizenship for Afro-Americans. Foremost among these people was Eleanor Roosevelt. In 1939, when the acclaimed black contralto Marian Anderson was barred from performing in Washington's Constitution Hall by its owners, the Daughters of the American Revolution, Mrs. Roosevelt arranged for Anderson to sing on Easter Sunday at the Lincoln Memorial.

The president himself, however, remained uncommitted to black civil rights. Fearful of alienating southern whites, he never endorsed two key goals of the civil rights struggle: a federal **Antiblack** law against lynching and abolition **Effects of the** of the poll tax. Furthermore, some **New Deal** New Deal programs functioned in ways that were definitely hostile to black Americans. The AAA, rather than benefiting black tenant farmers and sharecroppers, actually forced many of them off the land. The Federal Housing Administration (FHA) refused to guarantee mortgages on houses purchased by blacks in white neighborhoods. The CCC was racially segregated, as was much of the TVA, which constructed all-white towns and handed out skilled jobs to whites first. Finally, waiters, cooks, hospital orderlies, janitors, farm workers, and domestics, many of whom were black, were excluded from Social Security coverage and from the minimum-wage provisions of the Fair Labor Standards Act of 1938. In short, though blacks benefited, they did not get their fair share.

Despite these shortcomings, blacks overwhelmingly supported Roosevelt's New Deal. As Nancy J. Weiss, the historian, has written: "Meager though the Negro's share may have been, it came in the form of tangible benefits that touched the lives of millions of black Americans." And at election time, black voters showed their gratitude by giving Roosevelt large majorities.

Confronted with the mixed message of the New Deal, some blacks concluded that ultimately they could depend only on themselves and organized self-help and direct-action movements. Black tenant farmers and sharecroppers joined with poor whites to form the Southern Tenant Farmers' Union. In the North blacks boycotted stores in Don't Buy Where You Can't Work campaigns, launched Jobs for Negroes movements, and started tenants' unions to fight high rents. More and more they criticized the NAACP for ignoring the economics of second-class citizenship and for being too middle-class and legalistic in its war on racism. Although the NAACP had scored notable victories in opening up graduate and professional schools to black students, critics charged that these gains benefited only the black bourgeoisie, not the masses who above all needed jobs.

Nowhere was the trend toward direct action more evident than in the March on Washington Movement of 1941. In that year billions of federal dollars flowed into American industry as the nation prepared for the possibility of another world war. The government funds generated many thousands of new jobs, but discrimination deprived blacks of their fair share. One executive in the aircraft industry notified black job applicants that "the Negro will be considered only as janitors and in other similar capacities." So in early 1941, A. Philip Randolph, president of the Brotherhood of Sleeping Car Porters, proposed that blacks march on the nation's capital to demand equal access to jobs in defense industries.

March on Washington Movement

The idea was a popular one, and by midsummer thousands of blacks were ready to march. Roosevelt and other government officials feared that the march might provoke riots and that Communists might infiltrate the movement. The president announced that if the march were cancelled, he would issue an executive order with "teeth in it" prohibiting discrimination in war industries and in the government. The result was Executive Order No. 8802, issued on June 25, 1941, which established the Fair Employment

In 1938 Eleanor Roosevelt presented the NAACP's Spingarn Medal to the black opera star Marian Anderson. A year later when the Daughters of the American Revolution refused to let Anderson perform in Washington's Constitution Hall, Roosevelt arranged for her to sing before a much larger crowd at the Lincoln Memorial. Metropolitan Opera Archives.

Practices Committee (FEPC). The March on Washington Movement anticipated future trends in the civil rights movement. It was all-black; its tactic was direct action—a threat by the masses to take to the streets; and the beneficiaries of the movement were the urban working classes, not the black bourgeoisie.

Native Americans benefited more directly than blacks from the New Deal. In recent years they had suffered from governmental neglect (see page 719), but in 1933 with the New Deal, federal policy changed. Roosevelt appointed John Collier commissioner of Indian affairs. In the 1920s, as founder of the American Indian Defense Association, Collier had crusaded for Indian landownership; now he championed the Indian Reorganization (Wheeler-Howard) Act of 1934, which

Indian Reorganization Act

Violence erupted in October 1933 in California's San Joaquin Valley. When Mexican farm workers struck, the growers evicted them and their families. The growers also fired upon workers holding strike meetings at Pixley and Arvin, killing three. This group of Mexican women was bound for the picket line to protest for food relief for the hungry families.   Library of Congress.

ended the allotment policy of the Dawes Severalty Act of 1887 (see pages 464–465).

"The allotment act," Collier wrote in 1934, "contemplates total landlessness for the Indians of the third generation of each allotted tribe." First the tribal lands had been divided among the tribal members, many of whom then sold their holdings to white ranchers, miners, and farmers. Indeed, since 1887, Indian landholdings had dropped from 138 million acres to 48 million acres, 20 million of which were arid or semiarid. The Indian Reorganization Act sought to reverse the process by restoring lands to tribal ownership and forbidding future division of Indian lands into individual parcels. Other provisions of the act enabled tribes to obtain loans for economic development and to establish self-government. Collier also encouraged the perpetuation of Indian religions and cultures. One of his orders stated: "No interference with Indian religious life or expression will hereafter be tolerated. The cultural history of Indians is in all respects to be considered equal to that of any non-

Indian group. And it is desirable that Indians be bilingual." Collier's reforms would stand until 1953 (see page 857).

Mexican-Americans also suffered extreme hardship during the depression, but no government programs benefited them. Indeed, due to a variety of government discouragements (see page 719), many Mexican-Americans packed up their belongings and left the United States. According to the federal census, the Mexican-born population dropped from 617,000 in 1930 to 377,000 in 1940. One reason for this sharp decline was that many employers had changed their minds about the desirability of hiring Mexican-American farm workers. In the 1920s farmers had boasted that Mexican-Americans were a cheap, docile labor supply and would not join unions. But in the 1930s Mexican-Americans belied their image by engaging in prolonged and sometimes bloody strikes. During one protest in the strawberry fields of El Monte, California, workers established their own union, the Confederación de Uniones de Campesinos y Obreros

Mexicanos (CUCOM), which waged a couple of dozen strikes from 1933 to 1936. In united action in the San Joaquin valley in October 1933, eighteen thousand cotton pickers walked off their jobs and set up a "strike city" after being evicted from the growers' camps. Shortly after, their union hall was riddled with bullets and two strikers died.

The New Deal offered little help to these Mexican-Americans. The AAA was created to assist property-owning farmers, not migratory farm workers. The Wagner Act did not cover farm workers' unions, nor did the Social Security Act or the Fair Labor Standards Act cover farm laborers. One New Deal agency, the Farm Security Administration (FSA), was established in 1937 to help farm workers, in part by setting up migratory labor camps. But the FSA came too late to help Mexican-Americans, most of whom had by that time been replaced by dispossessed white farmers. Between 1935 and 1940 more than 350,000 Okies and Arkies fled to California from Oklahoma, Arkansas, Texas, and other drought-stricken "Dust Bowl" states. As early as 1936 they made up 85 to 90 percent of the state's migratory work force, compared to less than 20 percent before the depression.

In just a few years, however, Mexican-Americans would be back. With the onset of the Second World War, the United States would again need Mexican-Americans to work in the fields and on the railroads. In 1942 the United States and Mexico would agree to the *bracero* program, whereby Mexicans would be admitted to the United States on short-term work contracts, with guarantees of minimum wages, inspected housing, and return transportation.

WOMEN, WORK, AND THE
DEPRESSION

During the depression women had to work over-time to maintain themselves and their families. In *It's Up to the Women* (1933), Eleanor Roosevelt wrote that during such periods, wives and mothers often had to bear a heavier responsibility than husbands and fathers. "The women know," she asserted, "that

life must go on and that the needs of life must be met. . . ."

With families experiencing severe income reductions, wives and mothers followed the maxim, "Use it up, wear it out, make it do, or do without." Making do, Eleanor Roosevelt wrote, meant "endless little economies and constant anxiety for fear of some catastrophe such as accident or illness which may completely swamp the family budget." Women bought day-old bread and cheap cuts of meat; they relined old coats with blankets and saved string, rags, and broken crockery for possible future use. In short, many families with reduced incomes were able to maintain their standard of living only because of astute women shoppers or because women substituted their own labor in the home for goods and services they used to purchase. Husbands and fathers shared these financial concerns, but it was usually women's responsibility to do the family budgeting; it was estimated that wives and mothers in the 1930s allocated over 80 percent of all family income.

Wives and Mothers Face the Depression

An irony of the 1930s was that women's assistance with family expenses did not improve their status. As the sociologists Robert and Helen Lynd observed at the time: "The men, cut adrift from their usual routine, lost much of their sense of time and dawdled helplessly and dully about the streets; while in the homes the women's world remained largely intact and the round of cooking, housecleaning, and mending became if anything more absorbing." But even while women were making increased contributions to the family, their husbands, including those without jobs, still exercised authority over the family. In her 1940 book, *The Unemployed Man and His Family*, Mirra Komarovsky found that in only 25 percent of the families she studied did unemployment undermine the man's predominant role as family decision-maker. Regardless of circumstances, the father was still in charge.

What added to this irony was that during the 1930s more women than ever left the home to become paid workers in the labor force. In 1930 over 10.5 million women were paid workers; ten years later, the female labor force topped 13 million. These women obtained and held onto their jobs despite widespread hostility to their working, particularly if they were married.

Some people in the 1930s argued that male unemployment stemmed directly from women working. Norman Cousins, the magazine editor, wrote that there was an easy solution to the depression: "Simply fire the women, who shouldn't be working anyway, and hire the men. Presto! No unemployment. No relief rolls. No depression." And when a Gallup poll in 1936 asked whether wives should work if their husbands had jobs, 82 percent of the respondents (including 75 percent of the women) answered no. Severe job discrimination resulted from these attitudes. A 1939 survey showed that most insurance companies, banks, and public utilities had policies against married women working. From 1932 to 1937 federal law prohibited more than one family member from working for the civil service, and because wives usually earned less than their husbands, they were the ones who quit their government jobs.

Still, married women constituted 35 percent of the female work force in 1940, an increase from 29 percent in 1930 and 15 percent in 1900. Many women had no choice; necessity forced them into the labor market. But how did they find work? One explanation is that the occupations in which women were concentrated, such as clerical and sales positions and nursing, shrank less than those in manufacturing, where men had held most of the jobs. Just as important, the economy had become so segregated into "men's jobs" and "women's jobs" that men rarely competed for work performed by women. The problem for women in this labor market was that, on balance, their wages lagged far behind those for men.

Women were active participants in the New Deal. Susan Ware, the historian, has written that there was in Washington a "women's network" of government and Democratic party officials who were united by their attitudes toward social reform and the role of women in politics and government. Many were long-time personal friends and professional allies who had worked together in the National Consumers' League, Women's Trade Union League, and other organizations. Most were "social feminists" who believed that working women needed protective laws for their health and safety on the job. At the center of the network was Eleanor Roosevelt, who was her husband's valued adviser. Frances Perkins, the secretary of labor, was the nation's first

The "Women's Network"

woman cabinet officer. Other historic New Deal appointments included the first woman federal appeals judge and the first women ambassadors. Molly Dewson, head of the Democratic party's Women's Division, noted with pride: "The change from women's status in government before Roosevelt is unbelievable."

The New Deal did take into account women's needs, but only if reminded forcefully to do so. The maximum-hour and minimum-wage provisions mandated by the NRA, for example, won women's applause. Women workers in the lowest-paying jobs, many of them laboring under sweatshop conditions, had the most to gain from these standards. At the same time, some NRA codes mandated pay differentials based on gender, so that women's minimum wages were lower than those for men. Federal relief agencies, such as the Civil Works Administration and the Federal Emergency Relief Administration, put only one woman to work for every eight to ten men placed in relief jobs. A popular New Deal program, the Civilian Conservation Corps, was limited by law to young men, and women who were low-income workers, especially in agriculture and domestic service, were not protected by the 1935 Social Security Act or the 1938 Fair Labor Standards Act.

THE ELECTION OF 1940 AND THE LEGACY OF THE NEW DEAL

As the presidential election of 1940 approached, many people wondered whether Roosevelt would run for a third term (no president had ever served more than two terms). Roosevelt himself seemed undecided until May 1940, when Hitler's military advances apparently convinced him to stay on. He confided his decision to no one, however, and even sent a message to the Democratic convention that he did not want to be renominated. But at a timely moment, loudspeakers broadcast the chant "We want Roosevelt!" throughout the convention hall, and delegates began to snake dance up and down the aisles. Roosevelt wanted the nomination, but he also wanted the appearance of a draft. He was nominated

IMPORTANT EVENTS

1932	Franklin D. Roosevelt elected president
1933	13 million Americans unemployed National Bank Holiday Agricultural Adjustment Act Tennessee Valley Authority →National Industrial Recovery Act Twentieth (Lame Duck) Amendment Twenty-first Amendment repeals Eighteenth (Prohibition) Amendment
1934	Townsend's Old Age Revolving Pensions plan Huey Long's Share Our Wealth Society Indian Reorganization (Wheeler-Howard) Act Democratic victories in congressional elections Coughlin's National Union for Social Justice
1935	Emergency Relief Appropriation Act Works Progress Administration *Schechter* v. *U.S.* invalidates NIRA

	→National Labor Relations (Wagner) Act Social Security Act Huey Long assassinated Committee for Industrial Organization (CIO) established
1936	*U.S.* v. *Butler* invalidates AAA Roosevelt defeats Landon
1937	United Auto Workers' sit-down strikes "Court-packing" plan *N.L.R.B.* v. *Jones & Laughlin* upholds Wagner Act Memorial Day Massacre Farm Security Administration
1937–39	Business recession
1938	AFL expels CIO unions Fair Labor Standards Act 10.4 million Americans unemployed
1939	Marian Anderson's concert at the Lincoln Memorial
1940	Roosevelt defeats Willkie
1941	March on Washington Movement Fair Employment Practices Committee (FEPC) established

on the first ballot and selected Secretary of Agriculture Henry A. Wallace as his running mate.

The Republican candidate was Wendell Willkie, a utilities executive who had been an anti–New Deal Democrat throughout most of the 1930s. As president of the Commonwealth and Southern Corporation, Willkie had battled the Tennessee Valley Authority, condemning it as socialistic, but as a politician he was an unknown. As late as April 1940 he did not have a single delegate to the Republican convention, which was scheduled to open in two months. In May, however, with the Nazi invasion of the Low Countries

and France, Willkie's support mounted in public opinion polls. Other anti–New Deal Democrats joined with eastern Republicans to boost his candidacy, painting him as an internationalist who would halt the Nazi advance before it reached England. On the sixth ballot Willkie defeated the early leader at the convention, New York County's District Attorney Thomas E. Dewey.

Willkie campaigned against the New Deal, contending that its meddling in the affairs of business had failed to return the nation to prosperity. He also criticized the government's lack of military preparedness. But Roosevelt pre-empted the defense issue by beefing up military and naval contracts. And as workers streamed into the factories to fill the new orders, unemployment figures dropped as well. In his speeches Roosevelt reminded workers that it was his administration that had provided the defense jobs. When Willkie reversed his approach and accused Roosevelt of being a warmonger, the president promised, "Your boys are not going to be sent into any foreign wars."

Willkie never did come up with an effective campaign issue, and when the votes were tallied on election day, Roosevelt had received 27 million votes to Willkie's 22 million. In the electoral college, Roosevelt buried Willkie 449 to 82. Willkie did manage to win the farm and small-town vote in the Midwest, but as in 1936 Roosevelt triumphed in the cities, primarily among working-class, lower-income, and black voters. Although the New Deal was over, Roosevelt was still riding a wave of public approval.

Any analysis of the New Deal must begin with Franklin Delano Roosevelt. Assessments of his career varied widely during his presidency. In the 1930s a popularity poll among New York schoolchildren produced an easy victory for Roosevelt; God finished a distant second. Other people called Roosevelt a liar, a crook, a madman, a dictator, and a Communist. Most historians have considered him a truly great president, citing his courage, his buoyant self-confidence, his willingness to experiment, and his capacity to inspire the nation during the most somber days of the depression. But those who have criticized him have charged that he was too pragmatic, that he failed to formulate a bold and coherent strategy of economic recovery and political and economic reform.

On this last point, one of Roosevelt's biographers, James MacGregor Burns, has written in Roosevelt's defense: "Everything conspired in 1932 to make Roosevelt a pragmatist, an opportunist, an experimenter." The United States had never faced an economic disaster of the magnitude of the Great Depression. "The country needs," Roosevelt once said, "and, unless I mistake its temper, the country demands bold, persistent experimentation." Burns admits that the New Deal lacked coherence, and that at times the wary president "failed to exercise creative leadership," playing the fox—devious, crafty, and difficult

to pin down—rather than the lion—bold and assertive. Notwithstanding Roosevelt's faults, Burns prefers to see "the lineaments of greatness—courage, joyousness, responsiveness, vitality, faith and, above all, concern for his fellow man."

Though scholars have debated Roosevelt's performance, they all agree that he transformed the presidency. "Only Washington, who made the office,

Strengthening of the Presidency

and Jackson, who remade it," Clinton Rossiter, the political scientist, observed, "did more than Roosevelt to raise it to its present condition of strength, dignity, and independence." Scholars in a later era would charge that Roosevelt laid the foundations of the "imperial presidency" (see page 975). But whether for good or ill, Roosevelt strengthened not only the presidency but the whole federal government. "For the first time for many Americans," the historian William Leuchtenburg has written, "the federal government became an institution that was directly experienced. More than state and local governments, it came to be *the* government." In the past, the federal government had served as a regulator of railroads, corporations, and other businesses; during the New Deal it became a guarantor and stimulater as well.

The New Deal laid the foundation of America's welfare system on which subsequent presidential administrations would build. For the first time the government acknowledged a responsibility to bring relief to the jobless and the needy, and for the first time it resorted to deficit spending in order to stimulate the economy. Millions of Americans benefited from governmental programs that are still operating today. The New Deal not only provided immediate unemployment relief during the worst days of the depression; it also reformed economic institutions for decades to come.

Yet the economy itself remained basically capitalistic under the New Deal. Though the government took on responsibility for public welfare and the vitality of the economy, the profit motive and private property remained fundamental to the system. And though some redistribution of wealth did result from the New Deal, the wealthy survived as a class. In 1929, for example, the most well-to-do 5 percent of the population received 30 percent of the total family income. By 1941, the same group's share of total income had

DISTRIBUTION OF TOTAL FAMILY INCOME[a] AMONG VARIOUS SEGMENTS OF THE POPULATION, 1929–1944 (IN PERCENTAGES)

Year	Poorest Fifth	Second Poorest Fifth	Middle Fifth	Second Wealthiest Fifth	Wealthiest Fifth	Wealthiest 5 Percent
1929	12.5		13.8	19.3	54.4	30.0
1935–1936	4.1	9.2	14.1	20.9	51.7	26.5
1941	4.1	9.5	15.3	22.3	48.8	24.0
1944	4.9	10.9	16.2	22.2	45.8	20.7

[a]Monetary and nonmonetary income.

Source: Adapted from U.S. Bureau of the Census, *Historical Statistics of the United States, Colonial Times to 1970,* Bicentennial Edition (Washington: U.S. Government Printing Office, 1975), p. 301.

shrunk, but was still a healthy 24 percent. Most of the income lost by the wealthy ended up in the pockets of the middle and upper-middle classes, not of the poor (see table).

The New Deal brought about limited change in the nation's power structure. Beginning in the 1930s, business interests had to share their political clout with others. Finally the labor movement gained influence in Washington, and farmers got more of what they wanted from Congress and the White House. But there was no real increase in the power of Afro-Americans and other minorities. And if people wanted their voices to be heard, they had to organize in labor unions, trade associations, or other special-interest lobbies.

The New Deal was a liberal, evolutionary reform program and did not represent a radical, or revolutionary, break with the past. Most New Deal ideas had been around for decades, and prominent New Dealers had been involved in various reform movements since the Progressive era. Some left-wing historians have criticized the New Deal for its conservative commitment to the status quo; a handful of right-wing scholars have argued that the New Deal was a revolution that produced socialism and political cor-

ruption and lowered national morale. But most historians view the New Deal as a reform movement that benefited middle-class Americans. William Leuchtenburg has concluded that the New Deal "swelled the ranks of the bourgeoisie but left many Americans —sharecroppers, slum dwellers, most Negroes—outside of the new equilibrium."

The New Deal failed in its fundamental purpose: to put people back to work. As late as 1938, over 10 million men and women were still jobless. That

New Deal Failure to Solve Unemployment

year unemployment was 19.1 percent; over the next two years it fell no lower than 14.6 percent. What plagued the nation throughout the 1930s was underconsumption: people and businesses either could not or would not purchase enough goods to sustain high levels of employment. In 1929, for example, sales of new cars totaled almost $6.5 billion; by 1933 that figure had dropped to $2.1 billion. Though New Deal pump priming helped to raise auto sales to $5.1 billion in 1936, Roosevelt's attempt to balance the budget reduced the figure to $3.9 billion in 1938. The same thing was true of capital investment in new industrial construction. In 1929 companies had invested $546 million in new buildings, but by 1933 the total had fallen to $128 million. It climbed again to $314 million in 1937, only to plummet in 1938 to $121 million.

In the end it was not the New Deal but massive government spending during the Second World War that put people back to work. In 1941, as a result of mobilization for war, unemployment would drop to 9.9 percent, and in 1944, at the height of the war, only 1.2 percent of the labor force would be jobless.

SUGGESTIONS FOR FURTHER READING

The New Deal

Barton J. Bernstein, "The New Deal: The Conservative Achievements of Liberal Reform," in Barton J. Bernstein, ed., *Towards a New Past* (1968), 263–288; Paul K. Conkin, *The New Deal*, 2nd ed. (1975); Otis L. Graham, Jr., *Encore for Reform: The Old Progressives and the New Deal* (1967); Ellis W. Hawley, *The New Deal and the Problem of Monopoly* (1966); Peter H. Irons, *New Deal Lawyers* (1982); William E. Leuchtenburg, *Franklin D. Roosevelt and the New Deal* (1963); Katie Loucheim, ed., *The Making of the New Deal* (1983); Robert S. McElvaine, *The Great Depression* (1984); Albert U. Romasco, *The Politics of Recovery: Roosevelt's New Deal* (1983); Harvard Sitkoff, ed., *Fifty Years Later: The New Deal Evaluated* (1985).

Franklin D. Roosevelt

James MacGregor Burns, *Roosevelt: The Lion and the Fox* (1956); Frank Freidel, *Franklin D. Roosevelt*, 4 vols. (1952–1973); Joseph P. Lash, *Eleanor and Franklin* (1971); William E. Leuchtenburg, *In the Shadow of FDR* (1983); Arthur M. Schlesinger, Jr., *The Age of Roosevelt*, 3 vols. (1957–1960); Rexford G. Tugwell, *The Democratic Roosevelt* (1957).

Voices from the Depression

James Agee, *Let Us Now Praise Famous Men* (1941); Ann Banks, ed., *First-Person America* (1980); Federal Writers' Project, *These Are Our Lives* (1939); Robert S. McElvaine, ed., *Down and Out in the Great Depression: Letters from the Forgotten Man* (1983); Studs Terkel, *Hard Times: An Oral History of the Great Depression* (1970); Tom E. Terrill and Jerrold Hirsch, eds., *Such as Us: Southern Voices of the Thirties* (1978).

Alternatives to the New Deal

David H. Bennett, *Demagogues in the Depression* (1969); Alan Brinkley, *Voices of Protest: Huey Long, Father Coughlin & the Great Depression* (1982); Harvey Klehr, *The Heyday of American Communism: The Depression Decade* (1984); R. Alan Lawson, *The Failure of Independent Liberalism, 1930–1941* (1971); Mark Naison, *Communists in Harlem During the Depression* (1983); James T. Patterson, *Congressional Conservatism and the New Deal* (1967); Leo Ribuffo, *The Old Christian Right: The Protestant Far Right from the Great Depression to the Cold War* (1983); Frank A. Warren, *An Alternative Vision: The Socialist Party in the 1930s* (1976); T. Harry Williams, *Huey Long* (1969); George Wolkskill, *The Revolt of the Conservatives: A History of the American Liberty League, 1934–1940* (1962).

Labor

Jerold S. Auerbach, *Labor and Liberty: The La Follette Committee and the New Deal* (1966); John Barnard, *Walter Reuther and the Rise of the Auto Workers* (1983); Irving Bernstein, *Turbulent Years: A History of the American Worker, 1933–1941* (1969); Cletus E. Daniel, *Bitter Harvest: A History of California Farmworkers, 1870–1941* (1981); Melvin Dubofsky and Warren Van Tine, *John L. Lewis: A Biography* (1977); Sidney Fine, *Sit-Down: The General Motors Strike of 1936–1937* (1969); August Meier and Elliott Rudwick, *Black Detroit and the Rise of the UAW* (1979); David Milton, *The Politics of U.S. Labor: From the Great Depression to the New Deal* (1980); Ronald W. Schatz, *The Electrical Workers* (1983).

Agriculture

David E. Conrad, *The Forgotten Farmers: The Story of Sharecroppers in the New Deal* (1965); R. Douglas Hurt, *The Dust Bowl: An Agricultural and Social History* (1981); Richard S. Kirkendall, *Social Scientists and Farm Policies in the Age of Roosevelt* (1966); Theodore M. Saloutos, *The American Farmer and the New Deal* (1982); Walter J. Stein, *California and the Dust Bowl Migration* (1973); Donald Worster, *Dust Bowl: The Southern Plains in the 1930s* (1979).

Nonwhites

Abraham Hoffman, *Unwanted Mexican Americans in the Great Depression: Repatriation Pressures, 1929–1939* (1974); Laurence C. Kelly, *The Assault on Assimilation: John Collier and the Origins of Indian Policy Reform* (1983); John B.

Kirby, *Black Americans in the Roosevelt Era: Liberalism and Race* (1980); Carey McWilliams, *North from Mexico* (1949); Donald L. Parman, *The Navajos and the New Deal* (1975); Kenneth Philp, *John Collier's Crusade for Indian Reform, 1920–1954* (1977); Mark Reisler, *By the Sweat of Their Brow: Mexican Immigrant Labor in the United States, 1900–1940* (1976); Harvard Sitkoff, *A New Deal for Blacks* (1978); Nancy J. Weiss, *Farewell to the Party of Lincoln: Black Politics in the Age of FDR* (1983); Raymond Wolters, *Negroes and the Great Depression: The Problem of Economic Recovery* (1970); Robert L. Zangrando, *The NAACP Crusade Against Lynching* (1980).

Women

Julia Kirk Blackwelder, *Women of the Depression: Caste and Culture in San Antonio, 1929–1939* (1984); Glen H. Elder, Jr., *Children of the Great Depression: Social Change in Life Experience* (1974); Joan Hoff-Wilson and Marjorie Lightman, eds., *Without Precedent: The Life and Career of Eleanor Roosevelt* (1984); Alice Kessler-Harris, *Out to Work* (1982); Lois Scharf, *To Work and To Wed: Female Employment, Feminism, and the Great Depression* (1980); Winifred Wandersee, *Women's Work and Family Values, 1920–1940* (1981); Susan Ware, *Holding Their Own: American Women in the 1930s* (1982); Susan Ware, *Beyond Suffrage: Women in the New Deal* (1981); Jeane Westin, *Making Do: How Women Survived the '30s* (1976).

Cultural and Intellectual History

Daniel Aaron, *Writers on the Left: Episodes in American Literary Communism* (1961); Andrew Bergman, *We're in the Money: Depression America and Its Films* (1971); Jerre Mangione, *The Dream and the Deal: The Federal Writers' Project, 1935–1943* (1972); Richard H. Pells, *Radical Visions and American Dreams: Culture and Social Thought in the Depression Years* (1973); Warren I. Sussman, "The Thirties," in Stanley Coben and Lorman Ratner, eds., *The Development of an American Culture*, 2nd ed. (1983), 215–260.

DIPLOMACY
IN A BROKEN WORLD
1920–1941

CHAPTER 27

On *December 24, 1921*, prisoner #9653 strode out of Atlanta's federal penitentiary. After a train ride to Washington, D.C., he entered the White House to meet the man who had just pardoned him. "Well," said the good-natured President Warren G. Harding, "I have heard so damned much about you, Mr. Debs, that I am now very glad to meet you personally." They had a good talk, and Eugene V. Debs told reporters that Harding was a "gentleman" who "possesses human impulses. We understand each other perfectly." The First World War now over for him, Debs went home to Terre Haute, Indiana.

It seemed out of character for a conservative, pro-business Republican who had supported the American effort in the First World War to pardon Eugene V. Debs—Debs the anticapitalist leader of the Socialist party, Debs the antiwar critic, Debs the convict serving a ten-year sentence for violating the wartime Sedition Act, Debs the Socialist presidential candidate in 1920 who ran against Harding from jail and won nearly a million votes. President Woodrow Wilson had snarled a firm "no" to pardoning this "traitor." But Harding was more compassionate, and he believed that Debs's continued imprisonment simply reminded Americans of a troubled past they were trying to forget.

Debs's release was one of Harding's ways of saying that the United States was liquidating the war and returning to what he called "normalcy." "I thought the spirit of clemency was quite in harmony with the things we were trying to do here in Washington." What "things?" A return to peacetime, free from missionary zeal, overseas crusades, huge military expenditures, and domestic divisiveness. Interpreting his 1920 victory as a repudiation of Wilson's League of Nations, Harding also wished to shelve that issue. Henceforth, he said, the United States would not become "entangled" in "Old World affairs."

The president took several other steps in November 1921 that further demonstrated his resolve to put the war behind him. He buried the Unknown Soldier in Arlington Cemetery to initiate, he said, "a new and lasting era of peace." He signed peace treaties with the defeated Central Powers, until then tech-nically still at war with the United States because the Senate had rejected the Treaty of Paris with its offending League provisions. Harding urged acceptance of these treaties "so that we may put aside the last remnant" of the war. That month too he opened an international conference in Washington, where the United States insisted on a major reduction in naval armaments to ensure a stable world order. Harding's pardon of Debs was thus but one element in a self-conscious attempt to chart a new American foreign policy for a warless future.

Harding's desire to shove the war into the past and his emphasis on avoiding entanglements with Europe should not be interpreted to mean that Americans cut themselves off from international affairs after the First World War. To be sure, Americans were disillusioned with their war experience. But they remained quite active in the world in the 1920s—from gunboats on Chinese rivers to negotiations in the financial centers of Europe to interventions in Latin America. The most useful description of interwar foreign policy is *independent internationalism*. That is, the United States was active on a global scale but retained its independence of action, its traditional unilateralism. Even if they had wanted to, Americans could not have escaped the tumult of international relations; their interests were too far-flung and too vast—colonies, client states, overseas naval bases, investments, trade, missionaries.

At the same time, many Americans called themselves *isolationists*. By that label they meant that they wanted to isolate themselves from Europe's political squabbles, from military alliances and interventions, and from commitments like the League of Nations that might restrict their freedom of choice. Americans, then, were isolationists in their desire to avoid war, but independent internationalists in their behavior in foreign affairs.

The desire to avoid war led American leaders to search for nonmilitary means to exercise power. In the aftermath of the First World War, Americans had grown disenchanted with military methods of achieving order and protecting American prosperity and security. "We can never herd the world into the paths of righteousness with the dogs of war," Herbert Hoover said. American diplomats thus put increasing emphasis on conferences, moral lectures and calls for peace, nonrecognition of disapproved regimes, arms control, and economic and financial ties in accord with the principle of the Open Door. They pulled American troops out of Caribbean states, fashioning a Good Neighbor policy that would reduce hostility to United States influence in the region.

American policies and power, however, failed to create a stable world order. The debts and reparations tangle left over from the First World War bedeviled world finance and trade. More than any other event, the Great Depression of the 1930s undercut stability. The global economic cataclysm threatened America's prominence in the international marketplace. It also spawned revolutions in Latin America and political extremism, militarism, and war in Europe and Asia. The peace and disarmament agreements of the 1920s were smashed. In answer especially to the turmoil in Europe sparked by Germany's drive to restore its power, the United States passed the Neutrality Acts.

Yet in the late 1930s, Americans, along with President Franklin D. Roosevelt, changed their minds. Perceiving Germany and Japan as terrible menaces to the national interest, Roosevelt first appealed for preparedness and then begged the nation to abandon its neutrality in order to aid Britain and France. German victory in Europe, he reasoned, would imperil Western political principles, destroy traditional American economic links, threaten America's influence in the Western Hemisphere, and place at the pinnacle of European power a fanatical man—Adolf Hitler—whose ambitions and barbarities knew no limits.

At the same time Japan seemed determined to dismember America's friend China, to squelch the principle of the Open Door, and to surround and isolate the American colony of the Philippines. To deter Japanese expansion in the Pacific, Roosevelt cut off supplies of vital American products like oil. But economic warfare intensified antagonisms. Japan's surprise attack on Pearl Harbor finally brought the United States into the Second World War. Americans had wanted peace. But the relentless march of the militarists boded ill for the kind of world Americans thought necessary to their well-being. By 1941 they were convinced that remaining at peace would be more costly than going to war.

This recruiting poster reflected the postwar American mood of independent internationalism by offering exciting overseas duty to prospective marines. Library of Congress.

THE SEARCH FOR PEACE AND ORDER IN THE 1920s

In the early 1920s Secretary of State Charles Evans Hughes predicted that "there will be no permanent peace unless economic satisfactions are enjoyed." Like the nation's business leaders, Hughes expected American economic expansion to bring about world stability: out of economic prosperity would spring a world free from political extremes, revolution, aggression, and war. The government thus facilitated business activities abroad through the Webb-Pomerene Act (which excluded from antitrust prosecution those combinations set up for export trade); the Edge Act (which permitted foreign branch banks); and the overseas offices of the Department of Commerce. It also stimulated and monitored foreign loans made by American investors, discouraging those that might be used for military purposes.

United States economic influence became conspicuous after the First World War. By the late 1920s the United States produced about half the world's

Economic Expansion

industrial goods, ranked first among exporters ($5.4 billion worth of shipments in 1929), and also acted as the financial capital of the world (see map). During the period from 1914 to 1930 private investments abroad grew fivefold, to over $17 billion. To cite some examples, General Electric joined international cartels and invested heavily in Germany; American companies began to exploit Venezuela's rich petroleum resources; the Radio Corporation of America built Poland's radio system; in the Middle East, American companies began to challenge the British for control of oil resources. Britain and Germany lost ground to American businesses in Latin America, where Standard Oil was active in eight nations, the United Fruit Company was a huge landowner, and International Telephone and Telegraph dominated Cuba's communication network. An American diplomat denied that this impressive economic expansionism meant that selfish private interests were running the State Department. "Any student of modern diplomacy knows," he claimed, "that in these days of competition, capital, trade, agriculture, labor and statecraft all go hand in hand if a country is to profit."

Many foreigners saw United States expansionism as imperialism. A famous Argentine critic, the writer Manuel Ugarte, asserted that the United States was a new Rome: it annexed wealth rather than territory, enjoying the "essentials of domination" without the "dead-weight of areas to administrate and multitudes to govern." To such criticisms the American ambassador to Chile replied that "American capital will be the controlling factor in public and private finance in these countries. . . . American civilization, material and cultural, is bound to impress itself upon, and I believe, benefit these peoples. If anti-American critics wish to describe this as our 'imperialism' let them make the most of it."

Other foreigners were grateful to Americans for a helping hand. Europe lay in shambles at the end of the war. From 1914 to 1921 there were 60 million casualties in Europe from world war, civil war, massacre, epidemic, and famine. Germany and France each lost 10 percent of its workers. Crops, livestock, factories, trains, forests, bridges—little had been spared. The plight of Europeans drew American sympathies and aid. The American Relief Administration delivered food to needy Europeans, including Russians who were wracked by famine in 1921 and 1922. All told, private charities and official relief programs delivered foodstuffs that were valued at over half a billion dollars.

But if Americans won praise from Europeans for their humanitarianism, they earned the nickname Uncle Shylock for their handling of war debts and

First World War Debts and Reparations

reparations, an issue that dogged international relations for a decade. Twenty-eight nations were tangled in the web of inter-Allied debts which totaled $26.5 billion, about half of it owed to the United States. Europeans urged Americans to forgive the debts as a magnanimous contribution to the war. During the war, they charged, Europe had bled while America profited. But American leaders insisted on repayment. "They hired the money, didn't they?" Coolidge reportedly said. Other Americans argued that the victorious European nations had gained vast lands and resources through the war; to cancel their debts would be to increase their spoils even more. Senator George Norris, emphasizing domestic priorities, declared that the United States could build highways in "every county seat" if the Europeans would only pay their debts.

The debts question was linked to Germany's $33 billion reparations bill. Hobbled by inflation and economic disorder, Germany had begun to default on its payments. Americans grew worried that German economic troubles would spawn radicalism. To keep Germany afloat, American bankers poured millions of dollars in loans into the floundering nation. A triangular relationship developed: American investors' money flowed to Germany; German reparations payments went to the Allies; the Allies then paid some of their debts to the United States. The American-crafted Dawes Plan of 1924 greased the financial tracks by reducing Germany's annual payments, extending the repayment period, and providing still more loans. And the United States gradually scaled

Chapter 27: DIPLOMACY IN A BROKEN WORLD, 1920–1941

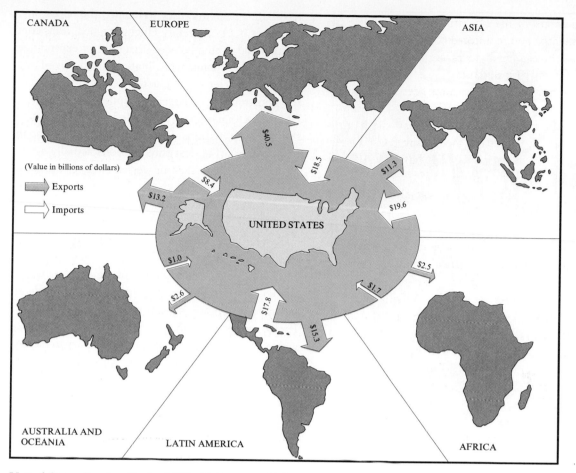

CANADA   EUROPE   ASIA

(Value in billions of dollars)

➡ Exports

⇨ Imports

$40.5

$18.5

$11.3

$8.4

$13.2

$19.6

UNITED STATES

$1.0

$2.5

$2.6

$1.7

$17.8

$15.3

AUSTRALIA AND
OCEANIA   LATIN AMERICA   AFRICA

United States Foreign Trade, 1920–1941

down Allied obligations, cutting the debt by half during the 1920s.

But the triangular arrangement was dependent on continued German borrowing in the United States, and in 1928 and 1929 American lending abroad declined sharply in the face of more lucrative opportunities in the stock market. The American-negotiated Young Plan of 1929, which reduced the total of Germany's reparations, salvaged little as the international economy sputtered and collapsed. That year the British rejected an ingenious offer from Hoover to trade their debt altogether for British Honduras, Bermuda, and Trinidad. By 1931, when Hoover declared a moratorium on payments, the Allies had paid back only $2.6 billion. Wracked by depression, they defaulted on the rest.

In the end, American economic power had proved unable to sustain a healthy world economy. But many nations shared responsibility for the failure. The selfish and vengeful Europeans might have trimmed Germany's huge indemnity. The Germans might have borrowed less from abroad and taxed themselves more. The Bolsheviks might have agreed to pay rather than repudiate Russia's $4 billion indebtedness. And Americans might have tried for a comprehensive, multinational settlement and lowered their tariffs, giving Europeans a market in which to earn the money to pay off their debt.

American influence also failed to curb militarism. During the 1920s and 1930s peace societies advocated numerous strategies to preserve world order: cooperation with the League of Nations; membership in the World Court; disarmament, arms reduction; curbs on exploitative business ventures; arbitration of international disputes; the outlawing of war; and strict neutrality in times of belligerency. The Fellowship

"Come on in. I'll treat you right. I used to know your daddy." Clarence D. Batchelor's haunting antiwar cartoon recalling the human tragedy of the First World War. The artist won a Pulitzer Prize for his statement. *Library of Congress.*

of Reconciliation, the Women's International League for Peace and Freedom, and the National Council for Prevention of War, among others, struggled to remind Americans of the carnage of the First World War and the futility of war as a solution to international problems. Antiwar films like *What Price Glory* (1926) and *Submarine* (1928) emphasized the cruelties of military combat.

At the time, the Washington Conference (November 1921–February 1922) seemed a substantial step toward arms control. There the United States discussed with eight other nations limits on naval

Washington Conference

armaments. Britain, the United States, and Japan, the three top naval powers, were facing a costly

naval arms race, and they welcomed the opportunity to deflect it. As Secretary Hughes argued, arms competition had to stop because large military expenditures endangered economic rehabilitation. In the Five-Power Treaty the delegates set a ten-year moratorium on the construction of large, or capital, ships, and established a total tonnage ratio of 5:5:3:1.75:1.75 among the five top nations (Britain:United States:Japan:France:Italy). The first three nations actually agreed to dismantle some existing vessels to meet the ratio. They also pledged not to build new fortifications in their Pacific possessions (such as the Philippines for the United States).

Several other agreements were reached at the conference. The Nine-Power Treaty reaffirmed the Open Door in China, recognizing Chinese sovereignty. In the Four-Power Treaty, the United States, England, Japan, and France agreed to respect each other's Pacific possessions and to consult in the event of aggression in Asia. In another agreement Japan pledged to pull back from Shandong and Russian Siberia. But although the treaties signed at Washington provided a rare example of mutual disarmament, they did not, critics pointed out, limit submarines, destroyers, or cruisers, and there were no provisions for enforcement of the Open Door declaration. Subsequent conferences in the 1930s produced meager results, and rearmament rather than disarmament became the thrust of the times.

Peace advocates also placed their hopes in the Kellogg-Briand Pact of 1928, eventually signed by sixty-two nations. The signatories agreed simply to

Kellogg-Briand Pact

"condemn recourse to war for the solution of international controversies, and renounce it as an instrument of national policy." The treaty's backers billed it as a first step in a long journey toward international cooperation and the outlawry of war. Though it passed the Senate 85 to 1, many senators thought the document no more than a moral statement, because it lacked provisions for enforcement. The agreement did in fact prove impotent in the 1930s. But however weak it was, the pact reflected a sincere popular belief that war was barbaric, inhumane, and wasteful; and it served a useful educational purpose in getting people to think about peace and war.

The League of Nations, also looked to as a peacemaker, exhibited a conspicuous feebleness, not only because the United States refused to join, but because members themselves usually chose not to use it to settle disputes. Starting in the mid-1920s, however, American officials did participate discreetly in League meetings on public health, prostitution, drug trafficking, and other such questions. By 1930 American "observers" had sat in on over forty League conferences. And individual jurists like Charles Evans Hughes served on the World Court in Geneva, although the United States also refused to join that institution. Neither the World Court, League of Nations, nor the Kellogg-Briand Pact proved capable of keeping the peace once the Great Depression upended an already wobbly world order.

SPHERE OF INFLUENCE IN LATIN AMERICA

In Latin America the interwar themes of independent internationalism, isolationism, nonmilitary means, and the destabilizing impact of the Great Depression were prominent. Before the First World War the United States had thrown an imperial net over much of the region by means of the Platt Amendment, the Roosevelt Corollary, construction of the Panama Canal, military intervention, and economic domination. By the 1920s the supposed benefits of American expansionism—hospitals, schools, roads, telephones, and irrigation systems—were evident in much of Latin America. As one observer put it, America's "imperialistic temper" was "manifested in works of benevolence."

A patronizing attitude permeated United States activities in the region. A leading State Department officer told the Foreign Service School that Latins were incapable of political progress because of their temperament, the tropical climate, and their "low racial quality." They were, however, "very easy people to deal with if properly managed." And indeed managed they were. United States financial advisers supervised government budgets in the Caribbean, and in 1920 American soldiers were occupying Cuba, the Dominican Republic, Haiti, Panama, and Nicaragua.

Yet these military expeditions to Latin America were becoming unpopular and counterproductive. Critics like Senator William Borah insisted that South Americans should be granted the right of self-determination. The president was usurping constitutional power, others protested, by ordering troops to Latin America without a congressional declaration of war. Businesspeople feared that nationalists would direct their anti-Yanqui emotion against American *gringos* and their property. And there was the embarrassment of the double standard. Secretary of State Henry L. Stimson outlined the problem in 1932 when he was protesting Japanese incursions in China: "If we landed a single soldier among those South Americans now . . . it would put me absolutely in the wrong in China, where Japan has done all this monstrous work under the guise of protecting her nationals with a landing force."

Turning away pragmatically from military intervention, then, the United States sought less controversial methods of maintaining its influence in Latin America: Pan-Americanism; support for strong native leaders; the training of national guards; economic penetration; Export-Import Bank loans; and when necessary, political subversion. Although the process began before his presidency, Roosevelt gave it a name in 1933: the Good Neighbor policy. It meant that the United States would be less blatant in its domination—less willing to defend exploitative business practices, less eager to send in military expeditions, and less wary of consultation with Latin Americans. "Give them a share," FDR recommended. In 1936 he approved a treaty that restored some sovereignty to Panama and increased that nation's income from the canal. Roosevelt's popularity in Latin America grew enormously for this and other such acts.

Good Neighbor Policy

So did American interests. From 1914 to 1929, direct American investments in Latin America (excluding bonds and securities) jumped from almost $1.3 billion to $3.5 billion. In the same period American exports to the area tripled in value. In country after country Latin Americans felt the repercussions of American economic and political decisions. The price Americans set for Chilean copper

Often at loggerheads, William E. Borah (1865–1940), chairman of the Senate Foreign Relations Committee (left), and Henry L. Stimson (1867–1950), secretary of state (right), here confer in 1929 on Cuba. The Idaho senator became a passionate anti-imperialist and isolationist who protested United States interventions in Latin America. Because of critics like Borah, Secretary Stimson was eager to find nonmilitary means to maintain United States hegemony in the Western Hemisphere. Library of Congress.

determined whether Chile was up or down in the business cycle. American oil executives bribed Venezuelan politicians for tax breaks. In Honduras, where United Fruit and Standard Fruit accounted for most of the nation's revenue, American interests so manipulated and disrupted politics that American troops were sent there in 1924 to restore calm and protect property. What was more, American businesses drew substantially greater sums out of Latin America in profits than they put in as investments. Latin American nationalists complained that their resources were being drained away, and that many of their own businesspeople put their profits not into investments at home but into New Orleans and New York banks.

The training of national guards went hand in hand with support of dictators: many Latin American dictators rose to power through the ranks of a national guard trained by the United States.

Training of National Guards For example, before the United States withdrew its troops from the Dominican Republic in 1924, American personnel created a constabulary. One of its first officers was Rafael Leonidas Trujillo, who became head of the National Army in 1928. Trujillo became president in 1930 through fraud and intimidation and ruled the Dominican Republic with an iron fist until his assassination in 1961. "He may be an S.O.B.," Roosevelt remarked candidly, "but he is our S.O.B."

In Nicaragua the experience was similar. The United

States occupied Nicaragua from 1912 to 1925 and returned in late 1926 during a civil war. The justification for United States involvement was the need to clean up and stabilize Nicaragua's politics. Anti-Yanqui resistance, led by the rebel Augusto Sandino, and noisy opposition at home and abroad finally prompted Washington to end the occupation, and in 1933 the U.S. Marines departed. But they left behind a powerful national guard headed by General Anastasio Somoza, who "always played the game fairly with us," according to the top-ranked American military officer there. With American backing, the Somoza family ruled Nicaragua from 1936 to 1979 through corruption, political suppression, and torture.

The long Marine Corps occupation of black, French-speaking Haiti from 1915 to 1934 had similarly negative results. Even the most charitable historian must

Occupation of Haiti

point out that American intervention did not establish democracy or improve Haitian life. American officials censored the Haitian press; manipulated elections; wrote the constitution; jailed or killed thousands of protesters; managed government finances; and created a national guard. Under American supervision, the National City Bank of New York became the owner of the Haitian Banque Nationale and the United States became Haiti's largest trading partner. The American High Commissioner, General John H. Russell of Georgia, boasted that the Haitian president "has never taken a step without first consulting me."

American black leaders were particularly alert to Haitian issues. Just before his death, Booker T. Washington spoke of the "benevolence" of American intentions and relished the prospect of establishing another Tuskegee Institute in the island nation. But W. E. B. Du Bois angrily criticized the "rape" of Haiti. And James Weldon Johnson of the National Association for the Advancement of Colored People reported after an investigative trip that Haitians forced to work without pay (the *corvée* system) to build roads "were in the same category with the convicts in the Negro chain gangs" of the American South. Indeed, Jim Crow had cut deeply into Haiti.

When Haitians resorted to violent protest against American rule in 1929, President Hoover vetoed a further military build-up and began plans to withdraw American soldiers. His investigative commission

From the leftist magazine New Masses *came this critique of United States intervention in Nicaragua, a nation occupied by American troops, 1912–1925 and 1926–1933. Library of Congress.*

concluded: "The failure of the Occupation to understand the social problems of Haiti, its brusque attempt to implant democracy by drill and harrow, its determination to set up a middle class—however wise and necessary it may seem to Americans—all these explain why, in part, the high hopes of our good works in this land have not been realized." Indeed, the American occupation brought very few benefits to the Haitian people, who continued to suffer Latin America's highest illiteracy rate, lowest per capita income, and poorest health. Speaking for many of his compatriots, one Haitian called Americans "exploiters" and asked, "How can they teach us when they have so much to learn themselves?"

The Cubans too grew restless under American domination. By 1929 American investments in the

Domination of Cuba

Caribbean nation totaled $1.5 billion, up from $220 million in 1913. Most of this money was bound up in the profitable Cuban sugar industry, about two-thirds of which was in American

Early in the long United States occupation of the black island nation of Haiti (1915–1934), marines stand guard over captured Haitians they called "bandits." National Archives.

hands. And the American military uniform was conspicuous at the naval base at Guantánamo Bay. But during the Cuban revolution of 1933, in open defiance of the American warships cruising offshore, rebels made Professor Ramon Grau San Martín president. Grau declared the Platt Amendment, which accorded the United States the right to intervene in Cuban affairs, null and void, seized some American-owned mills, failed to repay American bank loans, and talked of land reform. A startled United States refused to recognize the new government and encouraged a coup by army sergeant Fulgencio Batista in 1934. During the dictatorial Batista era that lasted until 1959, Cuba protected American investments and granted the United States military sites. In return it received military aid, Export-Import Bank loans, abrogation of the Platt Amendment, and a favorable sugar tariff.

The pattern was different in Mexico. Woodrow Wilson had sent troops to Mexico in 1914 and 1916 in an attempt to rearrange politics in that border state bloodied by revolution and civil war. But the military expeditions only united the Mexican people against the United States. In 1917 the Mexicans adopted a new constitution specifying that all "land and waters" and all subsoil raw materials (like oil) belonged to the Mexican nation—a clear threat to American landholdings and petroleum interests. Here was a unique case: a weak, undeveloped Latin American nation issuing a direct challenge to the powerful United States.

Confrontation with Mexico

Washington and Mexico City wrangled for years over the rights of American economic interests. Then, in 1938, Mexico boldly expropriated the property of all foreign-owned petroleum companies. The United

States countered by reducing purchases of Mexican silver and encouraging a business boycott of the upstart nation. But President Roosevelt decided to compromise, because he feared the Mexicans would sell their oil to the aggressors Germany and Japan. In 1941 the United States conceded that Mexico owned its raw materials and could treat them as it saw fit; and Mexico compensated American companies for their lost property. Although American investments and trade continued to claim an important share of Mexican business, American power had been diminished, setting a precedent to which Latin American nationalists would refer in the future.

Roosevelt's movement toward nonmilitary methods—the Good Neighbor policy—can be seen also in Pan-Americanism. Throughout the 1920s the United States had refused to abandon its right of intervention in Latin America. But in 1936, at the Pan American Conference in Buenos Aires, Americans endorsed nonintervention. Though American interventionism of a nonmilitary sort was still conspicuous in Latin America, the new policy marked a distinct change from the days of the Roosevelt Corollary and sending in the marines. One payoff was the Declaration of Panama (1939), wherein the Latin American governments drew a security line around the hemisphere and warned aggressors away. In exchange for more trade and foreign aid, Latin American governments also reduced their sales of raw materials to Germany, Japan, and Italy and increased shipments to the United States. On the eve of the war, then, the United States' sphere of influence was virtually intact, ready to back American military and diplomatic policies.

THE GREAT DEPRESSION AND GROWING ISOLATIONISM

Cordell Hull, secretary of state from 1933 to 1944, liked to say that the character of international relations derived from economic conditions. In the 1930s the effect of economics was particularly apparent as the Great Depression swept through both hemispheres, shattering international order. Hull pointed in 1935 to political extremism, border squabbles, resurgent militarism, increased military expenditures, and new weapons development as products of maimed economies. "We cannot have a peaceful world, we cannot have a prosperous world," he advised, "until we rebuild the international economic structure." Hull was right; the depression so disoriented the international community that it ranks as one of the main causes of the Second World War.

The depression wrecked international finance and trade. In the late 1920s, when First World War debts and reparations proved too much for the shattered European economies to bear, international finance collapsed. Banks failed as wary investors drained gold and foreign currency reserves. World trade, heavily dependent on an easy and safe exchange of currencies, also faltered: from 1929 to mid-1933, it declined in value by 40 percent. American exports alone slumped from $5.4 billion to $2.2 billion over roughly the same period.

The United States actually added to the burdens of the world economy with the Hawley-Smoot Tariff (1930), a selfish move that shut off the American market to European nations struggling to earn cash to pay off their war debts. President Hoover's moratorium on debts payments in 1931 came too late. By 1932 about twenty-five nations had retaliated against the American tariff by imposing similar restrictions on American imports. In short, economic nationalism gained momentum.

Referring to the world economic emergency in his first inaugural address in 1933, President Franklin D. Roosevelt said that he favored a "practical policy of putting first things first." In other words, he would work to restore world trade, but he would attend first to the emergency at home. Roosevelt thereupon barred American cooperation in international monetary stabilization at the London Conference (1933).

Cordell Hull was beside himself over the world's conspicuous nose-dive into economic nationalism. A start-up of world trade, he insisted, would not only help the United States to pull itself **Cordell Hull's** out of the economic doldrums, but **Economic** would boost the chances for global **Foreign Policy** peace. Calling the protective tariff the "king of evils," Hull successfully pressed Congress to pass the Reciprocal Trade Agreements Act in 1934. This important piece of legislation, which would guide American economic foreign policy thereafter, empowered the president to reduce American tariffs by as much as 50 percent through special agreements with foreign countries. The central feature of the act was the *most-favored-nation principle,* whereby the United States was entitled to the lowest tariff rate set by a nation with which it had an agreement. For example, if Belgium and the United States granted each other most-favored-nation status, and if Belgium negotiated an agreement with Germany that reduced the Belgian tariff on German typewriters, American typewriters would receive the same low rate.

In 1934 Hull also sponsored the creation of the Export-Import Bank, a government agency that provided loans to foreigners for the purchase of American goods. The bank not only stimulated trade but became a formidable diplomatic weapon, allowing the United States to exact concessions through the approval or denial of loans. Though Hull's ambitious programs brought only mixed results in the short term, they stood as rare examples of internationalism in an era of rampant nationalism.

As depression-induced authoritarianism, racial hatred, and military expansion descended upon Europe and Asia, Americans reasserted their isolationist beliefs. And they remembered the First World War largely in negative terms: the shelving of reform; civil liberties abuses; unusual federal and presidential power; race riots; inflation; windfalls for business; government propaganda; and postwar labor strikes (see Chapter 23). A 1937 Gallup poll found that nearly two-thirds of the people asked about the war thought American participation had been a mistake. Conservative isolationists feared higher taxes and increased federal power if the nation went to war again. Liberal isolationists spoke of the need to give domestic problems priority. Senator Gerald P. Nye, for example, complained that the federal government appropriated more for the care of National Guard horses than for the Children's Bureau. And critics of many persuasions predicted that in attempting to spread democracy abroad, Americans would lose it at home.

Isolationist Thought

Although isolationist thought was strongest in the Midwest and among anti-British ethnic groups, especially German- and Irish-Americans, it was a truly national phenomenon that cut across socioeconomic, ethnic, party, and sectional lines and attracted a majority of the American people. Isolationist leadership in the 1930s included Republicans like Congressman Hamilton Fish of New York, Senator William Borah of Idaho, Senator George Norris of Nebraska, and former president Herbert Hoover; Democrats like Congressman Maury Maverick of Texas; Socialists like Norman Thomas; Communists and Nazi sympathizers; and pacifists like Congresswoman Jeannette Rankin. It also included the publisher Robert R. McCormick of the *Chicago Tribune*; the historian Charles Beard; the scientist Albert Einstein; and anti-Semite Father Charles E. Coughlin. What united these people was the opinion that there were alternatives to American involvement in another futile Old World war. Only when events grew uglier and more menacing toward the end of the depression decade did many, like President Roosevelt, change their minds.

Some liberal isolationists, critical of business practices at home, charged that corporate "merchants of death" were undermining the national interest by assisting the aggressors. From 1934 to 1936 a congressional committee chaired by Senator Nye held hearings on the role of business interests in the American decision to enter the First World War. The hearings did not prove that businesspeople and financiers had dragged reluctant Americans into the war, but they did uncover evidence that corporations had bribed foreign politicians to improve arms sales in the 1920s and 1930s, and had lobbied against arms control. And records show that isolationists were correct to suspect American business ties with Nazi Germany and fascist Italy. Twenty-six of the top one hundred American corporations in 1937 had contractual agreements with Germany. And after Italy attacked Ethiopia in 1935, American petroleum, copper, and iron and steel scrap exports to Italy increased substantially, despite Roosevelt's call for a moral embargo on those items. Du Pont, Standard Oil, General Motors, and Union Carbide executives apparently agreed with a Dow Chemical Company officer, who stated, "We do not inquire into the uses of the products. We are interested in selling them." (One exception was the Wall Street firm of Sullivan and Cromwell, which severed lucrative ties with Germany to protest the persecution of Jews.)

Business Ties with the Aggressors

EUROPEAN UPHEAVAL AND AMERICAN NEUTRALITY

I n depression-wracked Germany, where 6 million workers were unemployed in the early 1930s, Adolf Hitler came to power. Like Benito Mussolini, who had gained control of Italy in 1922, Hitler was a fascist. Fascism (called Nazism, or National Socialism, in Germany) was a collection of ideas and prejudices that included supremacy of the state over the individual; of dictatorship over democracy; of authoritarianism over freedom of speech; and of militarism and war over peace. The Nazis vowed not only to revive German economic and military strength, but to "purify" the German "race" of Jewish influence, for which they blamed Germany's problems.

Hitler's Germany

In 1933, resentful of the punitive terms of the 1919 Treaty of Paris, Hitler pulled Germany out of the League of Nations, ended reparations payments, and began to rearm. Secretly laying plans for the conquest of neighboring states, he watched admiringly as Mussolini's troops invaded the African nation of Ethiopia in 1935. The next year Hitler ordered his goose-stepping troopers into the Rhineland, an area the Treaty of Paris had declared demilitarized. Germany's timid neighbor France did not resist this aggressive action. "The world belongs to the man with guts!" crowed Hitler.

Soon the aggressors began to join hands. In fall 1936 Italy and Germany formed an alliance called the Rome-Berlin Axis. Shortly thereafter Germany and Japan united against Russia in the Anti-Comintern Pact. To these events Britain and France responded with a policy of appeasement, hoping to curb Hitler's expansionist appetite by permitting him a few nibbles. But the policy eventually proved disastrous; taking advantage of European caution, the German leader continually raised his demands.

In those hair-trigger times, a civil war in Spain turned into an international struggle. From 1936 to 1939 the Loyalist Republicans battled the fascist-backed insurgents under Francisco Franco. Hitler and

The Nazi leader Adolf Hitler (1889–1945) in a propagandistic German painting. Hitler is surrounded by the images that came to symbolize hate, genocide, and war: Nazi flags with emblems of the swastika; iron cross on the dictator's pocket; saluting Nazi troops. Hitler denounced the United States as a "Jewish rubbish heap" of "inferiority and decadence" that was "incapable of conducting war." This soon proved to be a gross misperception that ultimately caused the downfall of Hitler and forced defeat upon the Germans. U.S. Army.

Mussolini sent military aid to Franco; Russia assisted the Loyalists. France and Britain held to the fiction of a nonintervention pledge that even Italy and Germany had signed. And about three thousand American volunteers known as the Lincoln Battalion joined the fight on the side of the Republicans. When Franco won in 1939, his victory tightened the grip of fascism on the European continent.

Early in 1938 Hitler once again tested the limits of European patience when he sent his soldiers into Austria to annex that nation. In September of the same year he seized the Sudeten region of Czechoslovakia. Appeasement reached its peak that month at the Munich Conference when France and Britain, without consulting the helpless Czechs, agreed to allow Hitler this one last territorial bite. British Prime Minister Neville Chamberlain returned home to proclaim "peace in our time," confident he had satiated the dictator. But in March 1939 Hitler swallowed the rest of Czechoslovakia. Poland was next on his list. Scuttling appeasement, London and Paris announced they would stand by their ally. Undaunted, Germany neutralized Russia by signing the Nazi-Soviet Pact and with Russia struck Poland on September 1. Britain and France declared war on Germany two days later. The Second World War had begun.

President Franklin D. Roosevelt witnessed these events with sadness and anxiety. Like his famous older cousin Theodore, Franklin as a young man

Franklin D. Roosevelt

believed that the United States should exert leadership in the world community and flex its military muscle to ensure American security and prosperity. He was an expansionist and interventionist who had imbibed the belief that Americans knew what was best for other societies. "Sooner or later . . . the United States must go down there and clean up the Mexican political mess," he had remarked in 1914. Later, as assistant secretary of the navy under Wilson, Roosevelt helped write the constitution the United States imposed on Haiti. FDR's later statements, however, would not have pleased his cousin (who died in 1919). Like most Americans during the interwar period, Roosevelt talked less about preparedness and more about disarmament and the horrors of war. Alert to public criticism of American military intervention in Latin America, he moved toward a Good Neighbor policy and stressed economic rather than military ties. When Europe and Asia were torn by economic and political crisis and war in the 1930s, Roosevelt at first declared that the United States should avoid foreign squabbles and he signed the Neutrality Acts.

However much they opposed fascism and disapproved aggression, Roosevelt and his fellow Americans tried to stay clear of the recurrent crises of the 1930s. Americans resented the fact that some Europeans looked to the United States to do what they themselves refused to do: block Hitler. With each crisis isolationist sentiment rose. In a series of acts Congress sought to protect the nation by stopping contacts that had compromised American neutrality

Neutrality Acts

two decades earlier. The Neutrality Act of 1935 prohibited arms shipments to either side in a war once the president had declared the existence of belligerency. Roosevelt had wanted the authority to name the aggressor and apply an arms embargo against it alone, but Congress was reluctant to leave such matters to the president's discretion. The Neutrality Act of 1936 forbade loans to belligerents. A joint resolution in 1937 declared the United States neutral in the Spanish Civil War; Roosevelt then embargoed arms shipments to both sides. And finally, the Neutrality Act of 1937 introduced the cash-and-carry principle: warring nations wishing to trade with the United States would have to pay cash for their purchases and carry the goods away in their own ships. The act also forbade Americans from traveling on vessels of belligerent nations—something Woodrow Wilson had been unwilling to do in the First World War.

Sharing the isolationist sentiment of the times and making a pitch for the pacifist vote in the upcoming election, Roosevelt gave a stirring speech in August 1936 at Chautauqua, New York: "I have seen war. . . . I have seen blood running from the wounded. I have seen men coughing out their gassed lungs. . . . I have seen the agony of mothers and wives. I hate war." He promised that the United States would remain distant from European conflict. During the Czech crisis of 1938 Roosevelt actually endorsed appeasement. The United States, he wrote to Hitler, had "no political involvements in Europe." The results of the Munich Conference, he commented on another occasion, elicited a "universal sense of relief."

But Roosevelt was deeply troubled by the arrogant behavior of the "three bandit nations," Germany, Italy, and Japan. He was disgusted by Nazi persecution of the Jews and by Japanese slaughter of Chinese civilians. Privately he snarled against the refusal of the British and French to collar Hitler in their own backyards. And he worried that the United States was militarily ill-prepared to confront the aggressors.

The United States had not been neglecting its military. Roosevelt's New Deal public works programs included millions for the construction of new ships. In 1935 the president requested the largest peacetime defense budget in American history; three years later, in the wake of Munich, he asked Congress for funds to build up the air force. "Had we had this summer 5,000 planes and the capacity immediately to produce 10,000 per year," he told his chief civilian and military advisers, "Hitler would not have dared to take the stand he did." (Whether Hitler would have been deterred by a militarily superior United States is questionable, given the Führer's view of Americans as a mongrel race incapable of playing an important role in foreign affairs.) The president also began to cast about for ways to encourage the British and French to show more backbone. One result was his agreement in January 1939 to sell bombers to France.

In his annual message early in 1939, the president lashed out at the international lawbreakers. Soon afterward he urged Congress to repeal the arms embargo and permit the sale of mu-

Roosevelt Proposes Repeal of Arms Embargo nitions to belligerents on a cash-and-carry basis. Roosevelt saw repeal as an aid to Britain, which dominated the seas. When the Senate Foreign Relations Committee balked, voting down repeal by a 12-to-11 vote, Roosevelt exploded: "I think we ought to introduce a bill for statues of [Senators] Austin, Vandenberg, Lodge and Taft . . . to be erected in Berlin and put the swastika on them." Although he did not yet have the votes to win repeal, he stepped up his public condemnation of the aggressors, warning them that "we, too, have a stake in world affairs." Hitler shot back that the president was a "contemptible . . . creature."

When Europe fell into the abyss of war in September 1939, Roosevelt declared neutrality. But unlike Woodrow Wilson, he did not ask Americans to be neutral in thought, and he pressed again for repeal of the arms embargo. Senator Arthur Vandenberg, an isolationist from Michigan, roared back that the United States could not be "an arsenal for one belligerent without becoming a target for the other." After much lobbying, debate, and bipartisan consultation, however, Congress revised the neutrality legislation. In November 1939 it lifted the embargo on contraband and approved cash-and-carry exports of arms. Now Roosevelt was ready to aid the Allies— short of war—and to challenge the isolationists more boldly and openly than before.

Soviet Russia was a special problem in American foreign relations. Following Wilsonian precedent, the Republican administrations of the 1920s had not recognized the Soviet government,

Relations with Russia arguing that the Bolsheviks had refused to pay over $600 million for the confiscation of American-owned property and the repudiation of Russian debts. To Americans the Communists were also godless, radical malcontents bent on destroying the American way of life through world revolution. Yet American businesses began to enter the Soviet marketplace, offering technology and machinery. International Harvester and General Electric, among others, struck deals with the Soviets. Henry Ford himself signed a contract in 1929 to build a huge automobile plant using mass-production methods (*Fordizatsia*). By 1930 Russia was the largest buyer of American agricultural and industrial equipment.

In the early 1930s, however, trade began to slump. To stimulate business and help the United States pull out of the depression, some businesspeople began to lobby for diplomatic recognition of Russia. "We would recognize the Devil with a false face if he would contract for some pitchforks," quipped Will Rogers. President Roosevelt agreed that a change in policy was necessary, not only to improve trade. He believed it foolish not to recognize a major country like Russia; nonrecognition had failed to alter the Soviet system; and closer Russian-American relations might deter the Japanese and stabilize Asia.

Roosevelt began negotiations in 1933 with the Soviet Commissar for Foreign Affairs, Maxim Litvinov. In a classic example of personal, one-on-one diplomacy, Roosevelt hammered out a number of agreements, some of them vague in language: United States recognition of Soviet Russia; future discussion of the debts question; a Soviet promise to forgo propagandistic or subversive activities in the United States; and religious freedom and legal rights for Americans in Russia. Although the first American embassy in Moscow opened in 1934, within a few years Soviet-American relations had once again become embittered. Especially upsetting to Americans was Russia's pact with Nazi Germany, its grabbing half of Poland in 1939, and its attack against Finland in 1940, marking Russia as yet another aggressor.

TIME

The Weekly Newsmagazine

Volume XXXI   **MAN & WIFE OF THE YEAR.**   Number 1
"Any year[s] should you be regarded as too early."
(See FOREIGN NEWS)

Jiang Jieshi (1887–1976) and his wife Song Meiling were Time *magazine's Man and Wife of the Year in 1937. Their anticommunism and resistance to Japanese aggression earned Jiang's regime favor in the United States. Reprinted by permission from* Time, *the Weekly Newsmagazine; Copyright Time Inc. 1938.*

A NEW ORDER IN ASIA

If United States power was massive in Latin America and limited in Europe, it was minuscule in Asia. Still, there were American interests in that region that official Washington believed it needed to defend: the Philippines and Pacific islands; religious missions; trade and investments; and the Open Door in China. Americans increasingly saw the Japanese as a threat to these interests, and specifically as strong-willed expansionists bent on subjugating China and unhinging the Open Door doctrine of equal trade and investment opportunity. Pearl Buck's best-selling novel *The Good Earth* (1931), made into a widely distributed film six years later, confirmed their opinion with its image of the noble, persevering Chinese peasant. In traditional missionary fashion, Americans came to believe they were China's special friend, its protector and uplifter. "With God's help," Senator Kenneth Wherry proclaimed, "we will lift Shanghai up and up, ever up, until it is just like Kansas City."

But the Chinese were always uneasy about the American presence in Asia, and the Japanese were forthrightly hostile. Both wished to exclude white foreigners from Asia. The highly nationalistic Chinese Revolution of 1911 still rumbled in the 1920s; anti-foreign riots increased, visiting damage on American property and harassment and violence on American missionaries, business representatives, and sailors. And Chinese nationalists demanded an end to the imperialistic practice of extraterritoriality (the exemption of foreigners accused of crimes from Chinese legal jurisdiction). When nationalist leader Sun Zhongshan (Sun Yat-sen) invited Soviet agent Michael Borodin to help him reorganize the governing Guomindong party, some Americans concluded that the Chinese were going Bolshevik.

In the late 1920s Jiang Jieshi (Chiang Kai-shek) emerged as the pre-eminent leader of this convulsed nation. Jiang ousted Communists from the Guomindong, forcing Mao Zedong and **Rise of Jiang** his followers to flee to the hills, and **Jieshi in China** sent Borodin back to Russia. Americans applauded his anti-Bolshevik measures and his conversion in 1930 to Christianity. Jiang's new wife, Song Meiling, also won their hearts. The American-educated daughter of a Chinese businessman, Madame Jiang spoke flawless English, dressed in western fashion, and cultivated close social and political ties with prominent Americans. Warming to Jiang, United States officials signed a treaty in 1928 restoring control of tariffs to the Chinese. American gunboats and marines remained, however.

The Japanese were suspicious of United States–Chinese ties. In the early twentieth century Japanese-American relations were seldom cordial. Japan intruded more and more into China, driving economic and political stakes into Manchuria, Shandong, and

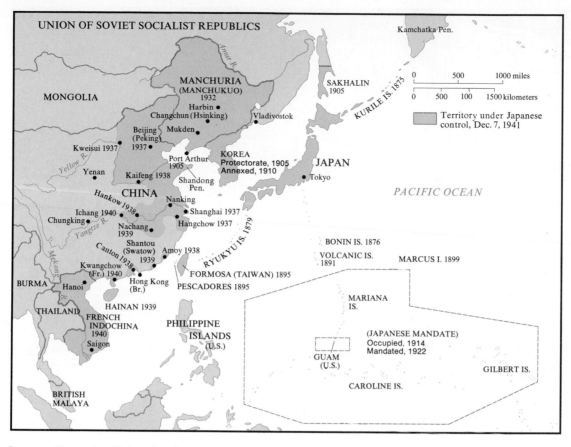

Japanese Expansion Before Pearl Harbor

neighboring Korea. Anti-imperialist only in the sense that they wished to oust Western imperialists from Asia, the Japanese were determined to claim Asian territories that produced the raw materials their island nation depended on. When Americans protested blatant Japanese expansionism, Tokyo reminded Washington of its own sphere of influence in Latin America. The proud Japanese also resented the immigration statute of 1924, which excluded Japanese from entry into the United States. And despite the Washington Conference treaty of 1922, naval competition continued; in fact, American naval officers, betting on a future war with Japan, used that country as the imaginary enemy on the war-game board at the Naval War College. Finally, although the volume of Japanese-American trade was twice that of Chinese-American trade, commercial rivalry strained relations between the two nations. American producers and workers whose profits and jobs were threatened by the im-

portation of inexpensive Japanese goods, especially textiles, organized Buy America campaigns and boycotts.

Relations deteriorated further after the Japanese military seized Manchuria in September 1931 (see map). Only nominally a Chinese region, Manchuria

Japanese Seizure of Manchuria

was important to the Japanese both as a buffer against the Russians and as a vital source of coal, iron, timber, and food. More than half of Japan's foreign investments were in Manchuria; the South Manchurian Railway, which the Chinese had threatened to take over, linked the extensive Japanese holdings. "We are seeking room that will let us breathe," said a Japanese politician, arguing that his tiny, heavily populated nation (65 million people in an area smaller than Texas) needed to expand in order to survive. Though the seizure of Manchuria violated the Nine-Power Treaty and

Victorious soldiers celebrate in the port of Hankow, China, which fell to the Japanese in October 1938. Paul Dorsey, Life Magazine © 1938 Time Inc.

the Kellogg-Briand Pact, the United States did not have the power to compel Japanese withdrawal. The American response therefore went no further than a moral lecture called the Stimson Doctrine (1932): the United States would not recognize any impairment of China's sovereignty or of the Open Door policy, Secretary of State Henry L. Stimson declared.

Hardly cowed by protests from Western capitals, Japan continued to harry China. In mid-1937 full-scale Sino-Japanese war erupted, although Tokyo preferred to call it the "China incident" to maintain the fiction that it had not violated Kellogg-Briand. The Japanese seized cities and bombed innocent civilians. Senator Norris, an isolationist who moved further away from his isolationism with each new Japanese thrust, condemned the Japanese as "disgraceful, ignoble, barbarous, and cruel, even beyond the power of language to describe." In an effort to help China, Roosevelt refused to declare the existence of war, thus not invoking the Neutrality Acts and thereby allowing the Chinese to buy weapons in the United States. In a stirring speech denouncing the aggressors in October 1937, he called for a "quarantine" to curb the "epidemic of world lawlessness." People who thought Washington had been too gentle with Japan cheered; confirmed isolationists warned that the president was edging toward war. Actually, Roosevelt had formulated no program to halt the Japanese. When Japanese aircraft sank the American gunboat *Panay*, an escort for Standard Oil Company tankers on the Chang Jiang Zangbo (Yangtze River), in late 1937, Roosevelt demanded an apology but stopped short of retaliation. He was much relieved when Tokyo apologized and offered to pay for damages.

Japan's declaration of a "New Order" in Asia "banged, barred, and bolted" the Open Door, as one

American official observed. Alarmed, the Roosevelt administration found small ways to assist China and thwart Japan in 1938 and 1939. Military equipment flowed to the Chinese, as did a $25 million loan. Secretary of State Hull declared a moral embargo against the shipment of airplanes to Japan. The navy continued to grow, helped by a billion-dollar congressional appropriation in 1938. And in mid-1939 the United States abrogated the 1911 Japanese-American trade treaty. Yet America continued to ship oil, cotton, and machinery to Japan. The administration hesitated to initiate economic sanctions for fear they would spark an Asian war at a time when the more serious threat was emanating from Berlin. When war broke out in Europe in 1939, Japanese-American relations were stalemated.

ON THE BRINK, 1939 TO 1941

"What worries me, especially," President Roosevelt told interventionist William Allen White in late 1939, "is that public opinion over here is patting itself on the back every morning and thanking God for the Atlantic Ocean [and the Pacific]." The European war, he went on, seriously jeopardized American security, and the American people had better recognize their precarious place in world affairs. Polls showed that Americans strongly favored the Allies, and that most supported aid to Britain and France; but the great majority emphatically wanted the United States to remain at peace. Troubled by this conflicting advice—defeat Hitler, aid the Allies, but stay out of war—the president between 1939 and 1941 gradually moved the United States from neutrality to undeclared war and then to war itself.

During those tense months of inching toward belligerency, isolationist sentiment declined. Alarmed by the swift defeat of one European nation after another, some liberals left the isolationist fold, which became more and more the province of conservatives. Die-hard isolationists organized the America First Committee in fall 1940; interventionists, meanwhile, joined the Committee

Decline of Isolationism

to Defend America by Aiding the Allies (formed in mid-1940). Roosevelt, who now called the isolationists "ostriches," even hinted they were pro-Nazi subversives—"conscious disorganizers or unwitting dupes." The White House began to turn over to the Federal Bureau of Investigation letters criticizing Roosevelt's foreign policy.

In September 1939 Poland succumbed to German stormtroopers in two weeks (see map, page 782). In November Soviet Russia marched into Finland, prompting Roosevelt to denounce "this dreadful rape"; by March 1940 Finland had been defeated. The following month Germany invaded Denmark and Norway, a month later the Netherlands and Belgium. "The small countries are smashed up, one by one, like matchwood," sighed the new British Prime Minister Winston Churchill. In July 1940 France collapsed, frightening Americans even more. Would England be next? After the failure of a peace mission led by his close associate Sumner Welles, Roosevelt told his advisers that though he was "not willing to fire the first shot," he was waiting for some incident to push the United States into war.

In the meantime, assuring people that New Deal reforms would not have to be sacrificed to achieve military preparedness, Roosevelt began to aid the faltering Allies. In May 1940 he ordered the sale of surplus First World War equipment to Britain and France. In July he cultivated bipartisan support for the war by naming Republicans Henry L. Stimson and Frank Knox, ardent backers of aid to the Allies, secretaries of war and navy respectively. In September he announced that by executive agreement he was trading fifty old American destroyers for leases to eight British bases, including Newfoundland, Bermuda, and Jamaica. Two weeks later he signed into law the Selective Training and Service Act, the first peacetime military draft in American history. The act called for the registration of all men between the ages of twenty-one and thirty-five. Soon over 16 million men had been signed up and draft notices were beginning to be delivered. Ironically, Roosevelt won re-election that fall with promises of peace: "Your boys are not going to be sent into foreign wars." Republican candidate Wendell Willkie, who in the emerging spirit of bipartisanship had not made an issue of foreign policy, snapped: "That hypocritical son of a bitch! This is going to beat me!"

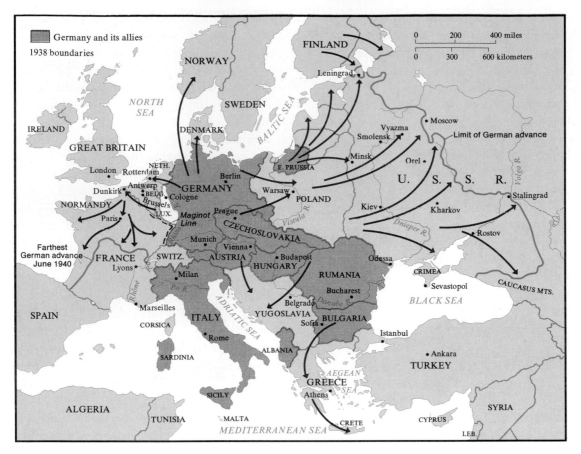

The German Advance, 1939–1942

Through the fall Roosevelt spoke of the need for a huge foreign aid program to save England from the Nazis. The United States, he implored, must become the "great arsenal of democracy."

Lend-Lease Act He justified his pro-Allied stance as a way to keep the United States out of war (by enabling the British to win). In January 1941 the controversial Lend-Lease bill was introduced in Congress. Britain was broke, the president reported. The United States should thus lend military weapons, much as a neighbor lends a garden hose to fight a fire. Roosevelt's analogy did not convince strict isolationist Senator Burton K. Wheeler, who shouted out another comparison: Lend-Lease was "the New Deal's triple A foreign policy; it will plow under every fourth American boy." But in March 1941, with pro-British sentiment running high, the House passed the Lend-Lease Act 317 to 71; the Senate followed suit 60 to 31. The initial appropriation was $7 billion,

but by the end of the war the amount had reached $50 billion, over $31 billion of it for England.

To ensure the safe delivery of Lend-Lease goods, Roosevelt ordered the navy to patrol halfway across the Atlantic and sent American troops to Greenland. Then a stunning turn of events in Europe spurred a new decision. In June 1941 Hitler struck his erstwhile ally Russia, and news from the quiet western front was soon eclipsed by the vicious warfare in the east. Fearing a German attack on Iceland and arguing that the North Atlantic nation was essential to the defense of the Western Hemisphere, Roosevelt sent American troops one step closer to the continent. He talked up the importance of aid to Russia; if the Soviets could hold off the more than two hundred German divisions engaged in the east, Britain would gain some breathing time. By November Lend-Lease aid was flowing to appreciative Russians. Churchill, who had thundered loudly against the Communists for

President Franklin D. Roosevelt reviews the fleet with Admiral Claude Bloch aboard the U.S.S. Houston on July 14, 1938, a time when the United States was expanding its military power.   Library of Congress.

years, now applauded the aid: "If Hitler invaded Hell I would make at least a favorable reference to the Devil in the House of Commons," he said.

In August 1941 Churchill and Roosevelt met for four days off Newfoundland. They got along well, trading naval stories, paying deference to one another, and taking pleasure in the fact that Churchill was half American. "It is fun to be in the same decade with you," Roosevelt later wrote to his new friend. At this conference the two leaders wrote the Atlantic Charter, a set of war aims reminiscent of Wilsonianism: collective security, disarmament, self-determination, economic cooperation, and freedom of the seas. Later, on January 1, 1942, twenty-six nations signed the Declaration of the United

Atlantic Charter

Nations, pledging themselves to fulfill the charter. According to Churchill, the president told him in Newfoundland that although he could not ask Congress for a declaration of war against Germany, "he would wage war, but not declare it, and that he would become more and more provocative."

In September 1941, there occurred the incident Roosevelt had been waiting for: the American destroyer *Greer* was fired on (but not hit) by a German submarine. In a special national radio broadcast the president protested the "piracy" and announced a policy he had privately promised to Churchill. American naval vessels would convoy British merchant ships all the way to Iceland and shoot German submarines, the "rattlesnakes of the Atlantic," on sight. Roosevelt practiced deliberate deception in the *Greer*

IMPORTANT EVENTS

1921	Washington Conference opens		Outbreak of Spanish Civil War
1922	Mussolini comes to power in Italy		Neutrality Act
1924	Dawes Plan for German reparations	1937	Neutrality Act
	U.S. departs Dominican Republic		"China incident"
1926	American troops occupy Nicaragua		Roosevelt's quarantine speech
1927	Jiang Jieshi attacks Communists in	1938	Mexico nationalizes American-
	China		owned oil companies
1928	Kellogg-Briand Pact		Munich Conference
1929	Onset of the Great Depression	1939	Nazi-Soviet pact
	Young Plan for German reparations		Germany invades Poland
1930	Hawley-Smoot Tariff		Second World War begins
1931	Japan seizes Manchuria		U.S. repeals arms embargo
1932	Stimson Doctrine	1940	Soviets invade Finland
1933	Hitler comes to power in Germany		Committee to Defend America by
	U.S. recognition of Soviet Russia		Aiding the Allies formed
	Good Neighbor policy announced		Tripartite Pact
	U.S. subverts Cuban revolution		Destroyer-bases deal
1934	Reciprocal Trade Agreements Act		America First Committee formed
	Export-Import Bank founded		Selective Service Act
1935	Italy invades Ethiopia	1941	Lend-Lease Act
	Neutrality Act		Germany attacks Russia
1936	U.S. votes for nonintervention at		U.S. freezes Japanese assets
	Pan American Conference		Atlantic Charter
			Greer incident
			Japan attacks Pearl Harbor

case, for he did not mention that the *Greer* had been tailing the German U-boat for hours, radioing the submarine's location to British airplanes hunting the ship with depth charges. He and his advisers thought it necessary to manipulate public opinion in order to scare Americans into defending Britain.

The United States had in essence entered into an undeclared war with Germany. When in early October a German submarine torpedoed the American destroyer *Kearny* off the coast of Iceland, the president announced that "the shooting has started. And history

has recorded who fired the first shot." When later that month the destroyer *Reuben James* went down with the loss of over one hundred American lives, Congress scrapped the cash-and-carry policy and further revised the Neutrality Acts to permit the transport of munitions to England on armed American merchant ships. When would war be declared? tense observers asked themselves.

In retrospect it seems ironic that the Second World War came to the United States via Asia, where Roosevelt so wanted to avoid it in order to concentrate

This Japanese photograph of December 7, 1941, was taken soon after an air assault force bombed American ships in Pearl Harbor, Hawaii, making several direct hits. "The wretched enemy's capital ships," read the Japanese caption, "were converted into a sea hell." National Archives.

American resources on the defeat of Germany. In September 1940 Americans read the unwelcomed news of the Tripartite Pact, an alliance between Germany, Italy, and Japan. Roosevelt slapped an embargo on shipments of aviation fuel and scrap metal to Japan. Because the president believed the petroleum-thirsty Japanese would consider a cutoff of oil a life-or-death matter, he did not stop that vital commodity. But after Japanese troops occupied French Indochina in July 1941, Washington froze Japanese assets in the United States, virtually ending trade (including oil) with Japan.

Cutoff of Trade with Japan

Tokyo recommended a high-level meeting between President Roosevelt and Prime Minister Prince Konoye, but the United States rejected the idea. American officials insisted that the Japanese first agree to respect China's sovereignty and territorial integrity, and to honor the Open Door policy—in short, to get out of China. Roosevelt also told the Japanese ambassador that his nation would have to withdraw from the Tripartite Pact. Although the American public, according to polls in fall 1941, seemed willing to risk war with Japan to thwart further aggression, Roosevelt was not ready for an Asian war; Europe still claimed first priority. Yet he would not back down in Asia either. Nor would Japan, now eyeing the oil-rich East Indies, abandon its plans for hegemony in Asia—the Greater East Asia Co-Prosperity Sphere.

Roosevelt told his advisers to string out Japanese-American talks to gain time—time to fortify the Philippines, and time to check the fascists in Europe. "Let us do nothing to precipitate a crisis," he told the cabinet in November 1941. But by breaking the Japanese code through "Operation Magic," Americans learned that Tokyo had committed itself to war with the United States if the oil embargo was not lifted. In late November the Japanese rejected American proposals that they withdraw from Indochina. On December 1 decoding experts informed the president that Japanese task forces were being ordered into battle. Why not attack first? asked aide Harry Hopkins. No, said Roosevelt, "we would have to wait until it came." Secretary Stimson explained later that the United States let Japan fire the first shot so as "to have the full support of the American people" and "so that there should remain no doubt in anyone's mind as to who were the aggressors."

Fearing that they could not win a prolonged war, the Japanese plotted a daring raid on Pearl Harbor in Hawaii. A flotilla of Japanese aircraft carriers crossed 3,000 miles of ocean undetected.

Attack on Pearl Harbor On the morning of December 7, 350 planes stamped with the Rising Sun swept down on the unsuspecting American naval base and nearby airfields, killing more than 2,400 people, sinking or damaging eight battleships, and smashing aircraft. Three American Pacific aircraft carriers, at sea, escaped the disaster.

Though Roosevelt was distressed that his proud navy had been caught by surprise, like many Americans he felt relief after the weeks of tension. But how could Pearl Harbor have happened? Americans asked. Roosevelt did not, as his critics later charged, conspire to leave the fleet vulnerable to attack, so the United States could enter the Second World War through the "back door" of Asia. The base was not ready— not on red alert—because a message of warning from Washington had been sent by Western Union telegraph rather than by navy cable and arrived too late. Base commanders were relaxed, thinking Hawaii, so far from Japan, an unlikely target for all-out attack. They expected the assault to come at British Malaya, Thailand, or the Philippines. Mistakes there were, but not conspiracy.

On December 8, referring to the previous day as a "date which will live in infamy," Roosevelt asked Congress for a declaration of war against Japan. A unanimous vote in the Senate and a 388 to 1 vote in the House thrust America into war. (Representative Jeannette Rankin of Montana alone voted no, matching her vote against entry into the First World War.) Three days later Germany and Italy declared war against the United States. Winston Churchill was pleased that America was now fully at war. "Hitler's fate was sealed," he wrote in his memoirs. "Mussolini's fate was sealed. As for the Japanese, they would be ground to powder. . . . I went to bed and slept the sleep of the saved and thankful."

The war was now a global conflict. The old emphasis on independent internationalism, on economic and nonmilitary means to peace, seemed archaic at that stirring moment. And the Great Depression, which had brought on so much of the international havoc— it too faded in memory as the economy geared up for war. The Neutrality Acts that had been designed to insulate the United States from European troubles had been gradually revised and retired. President Roosevelt had wanted to avoid American entry into a second world war, yet he sought also to aid the Allies and thwart Japanese aggression. What he tried to avoid he could not, because he ultimately believed that the United States, deeply involved in international affairs and with economic and strategic interests to protect, had to defend itself overseas. Moreover, he warned, the Axis nations loomed as threats to Western civilization itself. And there was the perennial American desire to set things right. As the publisher Henry Luce put it in his best-selling book *American Century* (1941), the United States must "exert upon the world the full impact of our influence, for such purposes as we see fit and by such means as we see fit."

As they had so many times before, Americans flocked to the colors. Isolationists now joined the president in spirited calls for victory. "We are going to win the war, and we are going to win the peace that follows," Roosevelt predicted.

SUGGESTIONS FOR FURTHER READING

General and 1920s Foreign Policy

Thomas H. Buckley, *The United States and the Washington Conference, 1921–1922* (1970); Frank Costigliola, *Awkward Dominion: American Political, Economic, and Cultural Relations with Europe, 1919–1933* (1984); L. Ethan Ellis, *Republican Foreign Policy, 1921–1933* (1968); Robert H. Ferrell, *American Diplomacy in the Great Depression* (1957); Peter G. Filene, *Americans and the Soviet Experiment, 1917–1933* (1967); Melvyn P. Leffler, *The Elusive Quest* (1979); Elting E. Morison, *Turmoil and Tradition* (1964) (on Stimson); Arnold A. Offner, *The Origins of the Second World War* (1975); Emily S. Rosenberg, *Spreading the American Dream*

(1982); Raymond Sontag, *A Broken World, 1919–1939* (1971); Joan Hoff Wilson, *Herbert Hoover* (1975).

The Peace Movement and Kellogg-Briand Pact

Charles Chatfield, *For Peace and Justice: Pacifism in America, 1914–1941* (1971); Charles DeBenedetti, *The Peace Reform in American History* (1980); Charles DeBenedetti, *Origins of the Modern American Peace Movement, 1915–1929* (1978); Robert H. Ferrell, *Peace in Their Time* (1952); Harold Josephson, *James T. Shotwell and the Rise of Internationalism in America* (1976).

The United States in the World Economy

Frederick Adams, *Economic Diplomacy* (1976); Derek H. Aldcroft, *From Versailles to Wall Street, 1919–1929* (1977); Herbert Feis, *The Diplomacy of the Dollar, 1919–1932* (1950); Lloyd C. Gardner, *Economic Aspects of New Deal Diplomacy* (1964); Michael J. Hogan, *Informal Entente: The Private Structure of Cooperation in Anglo-American Economic Diplomacy, 1918–1928* (1977); Charles Kindleberger, *The World in Depression* (1973); Carl Parrini, *Heir to Empire* (1969); Mira Wilkins, *The Maturing of Multinational Enterprise* (1974); Joan Hoff Wilson, *American Business and Foreign Policy, 1920–1933* (1971).

Latin America

Jules R. Benjamin, *The United States and Cuba* (1978); Bruce J. Calder, *The Impact of Intervention* (1984) (on Dominican Republic); Alton Frye, *Nazi Germany and the American Hemisphere, 1933–1941* (1967); Irwin F. Gellman, *Good Neighbor Diplomacy* (1979); David Green, *The Containment of Latin America* (1971); Walter LaFeber, *Inevitable Revolutions: The United States in Central America* (1983); Lester D. Langley, *The United States and the Caribbean, 1900–1970* (1980); Neil Macaulay, *The Sandino Affair* (1967); Lorenzo Meyer, *Mexico and the United States in the Oil Controversy, 1917–1942* (1977); Richard Millett, *Guardians of the Dynasty* (1977) (on Nicaragua); Stephen G. Rabe, *The Road to OPEC* (1982) (on Venezuela); Robert I. Rotberg, *Haiti* (1971); Ramon Ruiz, *Cuba* (1968); Karl M. Schmitt, *Mexico and the United States, 1821–1973* (1974); Robert F. Smith, *The United States and Revolutionary Nationalism in Mexico, 1916–1932* (1972); Bryce Wood, *The Making of the Good Neighbor Policy* (1961).

Isolationism and Isolationists

Warren I. Cohen, *The American Revisionists* (1967); Wayne S. Cole, *Roosevelt and the Isolationists, 1932–1945* (1983); Wayne S. Cole, *America First* (1953); Manfred Jonas, *Isolationism in America, 1935–1941* (1966); Thomas C. Kennedy, *Charles A. Beard and American Foreign Policy* (1975); Richard Lowitt, *George W. Norris*, 3 vols. (1963–1978); John Wiltz, *In Search of Peace: The Senate Munitions Inquiry, 1934–1936* (1963).

Franklin D. Roosevelt and Europe

Thomas A. Bailey and Paul B. Ryan, *Hitler vs. Roosevelt* (1979); Edward Bennett, *Recognition of Russia* (1970); James MacGregor Burns, *Roosevelt: The Lion and the Fox* (1956); Mark Chadwin, *The Hawks of World War II* (1968); James V. Compton, *The Swastika and the Eagle* (1967); David H. Culbert, *News for Everyman: Radio and Foreign Affairs in Thirties America* (1976); Robert Dallek, *Franklin D. Roosevelt and American Foreign Policy, 1932–1945* (1979); Robert A. Divine, *The Reluctant Belligerent*, 2nd ed. (1979); Robert A. Divine, *Roosevelt and World War II* (1969); Manfred Jonas, *The United States and Germany* (1984); Warren F. Kimball, *The Most Unsordid Act: Lend-Lease, 1939–1941* (1969); William L. Langer and S. Everett Gleason, *The Undeclared War, 1940–1941* (1953); William L. Langer and S. Everett Gleason, *The Challenge to Isolation, 1937–1940* (1952); Thomas R. Maddux, *Years of Estrangement: American Relations with the Soviet Union, 1933–1941* (1980); Arnold A. Offner, *American Appeasement* (1969); Julius W. Pratt, *Cordell Hull*, 2 vols. (1964); David Reynolds, *The Creation of the Anglo-American Alliance, 1937–1941* (1982); Bruce Russett, *No Clear and Present Danger* (1972).

China, Japan, and the Coming of War in Asia

Charles A. Beard, *President Roosevelt and the Coming of the War, 1941* (1948); Dorothy Borg and Shumpei Okomoto, eds., *Pearl Harbor as History* (1973); R. J. C. Butow, *Tojo and the Coming of the War* (1961); Warren I. Cohen, *America's Response to China*, 2nd ed. (1980); Roger Dingman, *Power in the Pacific* (1976); Herbert Feis, *The Road to Pearl Harbor* (1950); Waldo H. Heinrichs, Jr., *American Ambassador* (1966) (on Joseph Grew); Akira Iriye, *Across the Pacific* (1967); Akira Iriye, *After Imperialism: The Search for a New Order in the Far East, 1921–1931* (1965); Charles Neu, *The Troubled Encounter: The United States and Japan* (1975); Paul W. Schroeder, *The Axis Alliance and Japanese-American Relations, 1941* (1958).

Pearl Harbor

Martin V. Melosi, *The Shadow of Pearl Harbor* (1977); Gordon W. Prange, *At Dawn We Slept* (1981); John Toland, *Infamy* (1982); Roberta Wohlstetter, *Pearl Harbor* (1962).

THE SECOND WORLD WAR AT HOME AND ABROAD

1941–1945

CHAPTER 28

"*We are going* on a mission to drop a bomb different from any you have ever seen or heard about," Colonel Paul Tibbets informed his crew on the small Pacific island of Tinian. Silent and incredulous, they listened to "Old Bull" describe the strange new weapon, which packed the destructive power of twenty thousand tons of TNT. Resting in the bay of a converted B-29 named the *Enola Gay*, after Tibbets's mother, was "Little Boy"—a ten-thousand-pound uranium bomb on which the airmen had scribbled anti-Japanese graffiti.

On August 6, 1945, the *Enola Gay* lumbered down the runway at Tinian. Once airborne, crew members assembled the firing mechanism. "Knock wood," muttered one of them. Several hours later they received a radio message that the weather over Hiroshima was clear. Cruising at over 30,000 feet, they put on welder's goggles and made their run on the unsuspecting city of a quarter-million people.

At 8:15 A.M. the atomic bomb dropped from the aircraft. It exploded in less than a minute over the target. A flash of dazzling light shot across the sky. "Everything just turned white in front of me," Tibbets recalled. Then two violent slaps rocked the ship. "My God!" gasped co-pilot Captain Robert Lewis as he watched a huge purplish mushroom cloud boil 40,000 feet into the atmosphere. Dense smoke, swirling fires, and suffocating dust soon engulfed the ground for miles. Much of the city was leveled almost instantly. "Even though we had expected something terrific," Lewis remembered, "what we saw made us feel that we were Buck Rogers twenty-fifth century warriors."

Approximately 130,000 people were killed at Hiroshima; tens of thousands more suffered painful burns and nuclear poisoning. As Hiroshima suffered its unique nightmare, Washington, D.C., celebrated its military and scientific triumph. "This is the greatest thing in history," exclaimed President Harry S Truman on hearing of the successful mission.

For forty-five months Americans had fought abroad to subdue the Nazi and Japanese aggressors. After military engagements against the fascists in North Africa and Italy, in June 1944 American troops had joined the dramatic crossing of the English Channel on D-Day. The massive invasion forced the Germans to retreat through France to Germany. Battered by merciless bombing raids, leaderless after Adolf Hitler's suicide, and pressed by a Russian advance from the east, the Nazis capitulated in May 1945. In the Pacific, Americans drove the Japanese from one island after another before turning to the just-tested atomic bombs that demolished Hiroshima and Nagasaki and helped spur a Japanese surrender in August.

Throughout the war the Allies—Britain, Russia, and the United States—were held together by their common goal of defeating Germany. But they squabbled over many issues: when the second, or western, front would be opened; how a new international organization would be structured; how Eastern Europe, liberated from the Germans, would be reconstructed; how Germany itself would be governed after defeat. At the end of the war Allied leaders seemed more intent on keeping and expanding their own nations' spheres of influence than on building a community of mutual interest. The United States and the Soviet Union emerged from the war as major competitors in a world facing the task of reconstruction. The prospects for postwar international cooperation seemed bleak, and the advent of an atomic age with nuclear weapons frightened people everywhere.

The atomic bomb was a milestone in world affairs, but events on the home front transformed American life in different ways. The nation united behind the war effort, collecting scrap iron, rubber, and old newspapers and planting victory gardens. But more than national unity and enthusiasm were required to win the war. Essential to victory was the successful mobilization of all sectors of the economy—industry, finance, agriculture, and labor. The federal government had the monumental task of coordinating these several elements, as well as a couple of new ones: higher education and science. For this was a scientific and technological war, supported by the development of new weapons like radar and the atomic bomb.

For millions of Americans the war was a time to relocate in other parts of the country. Between 1941 and 1945, over 16 million men and women served in the armed forces. They traveled to new duty stations in the United States and abroad, acquired new skills, and broadened their horizons. But at war's end they were older, both physically and emotionally, and many felt they had sacrificed the best years of their lives. Also on the move during the Second World War were blacks, Mexican-Americans, and whites who migrated to war-production centers in the North and the West. For numerous Afro-Americans, the war offered new economic and political opportunities, encouraging them to demand their full rights as citizens. But it also provided the ingredients of racial violence; in 1943 race riots erupted across the country.

Employers' negative attitudes toward women workers eased during the Second World War, and millions of married middle-class women, many of them over thirty-five, took jobs in war industries. For some, work was an economic necessity; for others it was a patriotic obligation. Whatever the motivation, paying jobs brought women benefits—financial independence and enhanced self-esteem—that many were unwilling to give up at war's end.

The United States underwent profound change during the course of the war. Its big businesses got even bigger, while hundreds of thousands of neighborhood enterprises and family farms ceased to function. Membership in the nation's labor unions increased dramatically, and the federal government experienced tremendous growth in both its budget and its bureaucracy. Furthermore, the experiences of the First World War and the New Deal proved an inadequate guide in this longer, more demanding conflict. For all of these reasons the Second World War was a turning point in American history.

WINNING THE SECOND WORLD WAR

"We are now in the midst of a war, not for conquest, not for vengeance, but for a world in which this Nation, and all that this Nation represents, will be safe for our children." President Roosevelt was speaking just two days after the surprise attack on Pearl Harbor. Americans believed with

Roosevelt that they were defending their homes and families against aggressive and satanic Nazis and Japanese. Few of them, however, knew much about the principles of the Atlantic Charter (see page 783) or about United States war aims. To most Americans the Second World War was simply a grimy job. Like cartoonist Bill Mauldin's popular GI characters Willy and Joe, who were more interested in tasty food and dry socks than in abstractions, they were eager to get it over with. Americans also seemed wary of lofty rhetoric about the future, remembering how Woodrow Wilson had promised so much and delivered too little during the era of the First World War. The army's Morale Branch, worried that the average American was ignorant or cynical about the reasons for war, hired prominent Hollywood director Frank Capra to produce a series of propaganda films called *Why We Fight.*

In these widely distributed films and in the popular mind, the Allies were heroic partners in a common effort against evil. Actually, wartime relations among the United States, Great Britain, and the Soviet Union ran hot and cold. Although winning the war claimed top priority, Allied leaders knew that military decisions had political consequences. Should one ally become desperate, for instance, it might sue for a separate peace. And the position of troops at the end of the war might determine the politics of the region they occupied. Thus an undercurrent of suspicion ran beneath the surface of Allied cooperation.

Roosevelt, British Prime Minister Winston Churchill, and Soviet Premier Josef Stalin differed vigorously over the opening of a second, or western,

Second Front Controversy front. After Germany conquered France in 1940 and invaded Russia in 1941, the Russians bore the brunt of the war until mid-1944, suffering heavy casualties. By late 1941, before the fierce Russian winter stalled their onslaught, German troops had reached the edge of Moscow and Leningrad and had slashed deeply into the Ukraine, taking Kiev. Stalin pressed for a British-American landing on the northern coast of Europe to draw German troops away from the eastern front, but Churchill would not agree. The Russians therefore did most of the fighting and dying on land, while the British and Americans concentrated on getting Lend-Lease supplies across the Atlantic and harassing the Germans from the air

In January 1944 General Dwight D. Eisenhower arrived in England to assume his duties as Supreme Commander, Allied Expeditionary Forces. His mission was to organize the D-Day invasion of Europe by Allied forces. Here Eisenhower talks with members of the spearhead assault forces. U.S. Army.

with attacks on factories and civilians alike. When Secretary of State Cordell Hull bemoaned the 200,000 American casualties suffered from 1941 to 1943, a Russian official replied, "We lose that many each day before lunch. You haven't got your teeth in the war yet."

Roosevelt was particularly sensitive to the suggestion that Americans were shirking their responsibility by avoiding an invasion of Europe. He feared that Russia might be knocked out of the war, leaving Hitler free to send his goose-stepping soldiers into England. In 1942 Roosevelt told the Russians they could expect the Allies to open a second front later that year. The move across the English Channel, later tagged Operation OVERLORD, was exactly what Stalin sought to take pressure off his wracked country. But Churchill balked. "To postpone that evil day, all his arts, all his eloquence, all his great experience was spent," the prime minister's chief military adviser

later wrote. Churchill feared heavy losses in a premature cross-channel invasion. Though American Generals George C. Marshall and Dwight D. Eisenhower argued for a direct attack on the heart of German power, Churchill held out for a series of small jabs at the enemy's Mediterranean forces. American officials suspected that Churchill's strategy derived from his desire to recover British imperial power in the Mediterranean.

Churchill won the debate. Instead of attacking France, the western Allies invaded North Africa in November 1942. To reduce resistance to the invasion, the Americans agreed to recognize the pro-Nazi Vichy French regime in North Africa—a "deal" many critics denounced as unsavory. Roosevelt deemed it justified in order to get Americans into combat. "We are striking back," the cheered president declared. News from Russia also buoyed Roosevelt. In the battle for Stalingrad (September 1942 to January 1943), probably the turning point of the war, the Red Army defeated the Germans in bloody block-by-block fighting, forcing Hitler's divisions to retreat. But shortly after Stalingrad, the president once again angered the Russians by declaring another delay in launching the second front. Marshal Stalin was not mollified in the summer of 1943 by the Allied invasion of Italy. When Italy surrendered in September, it capitulated to American and British officers; Russian officials were not invited to participate. Stalin grumbled that the arrangement smacked of a separate peace and wondered if Roosevelt and Churchill's policy of unconditional surrender for the Axis, announced that January at the Anglo-American conference at Casablanca, had been violated.

With the Grand Alliance badly strained, Roosevelt sought reconciliation through personal diplomacy. The three Allied leaders met in Teheran, Iran, in December 1943. Stalin dismissed Churchill's repetitious justifications for further delaying the second front. Roosevelt had had enough too; with Stalin he rejected Churchill's proposal for another peripheral attack, this time through the Balkans to Vienna. The three finally agreed to launch OVERLORD in early 1944. An appreciative Russia promised to aid the Allies against Japan once Germany was defeated.

Like a coiled spring bursting free, the second front opened in the dark morning hours of June 6, 1944: D-Day. Two hundred thousand Allied troops under the command of General Eisenhower scrambled ashore in Normandy, France, in the largest amphibious landing in history. Thousands of ships ferried the men within a hundred yards of the sandy beaches. Craft and soldiers became entangled in sharp obstacles and triggered mines, and were pinned down by fire from cliffside pillboxes. Meanwhile, airborne troops dropped behind German lines. Although heavy aerial and naval bombardment and the clandestine work of underground saboteurs had softened up German defenses, the fighting was still ferocious. One soldier felt like a "pigeon at a trap shoot."

After digging in at now-famous places like Utah and Omaha beaches and gaining reinforcements, Allied forces broke through disorderly German lines and gradually ground inland, reaching Paris in August. That same month another force invaded southern France and threw the stunned Germans back. Allied

D-Day

As the Second World War drew to a close in Europe, American and Russian troops linked up in Germany. These Americans from the 82nd Airborne Division met up with Russian soldiers at Grabow, Germany, on May 3, 1945. Five days later, Germany surrendered.   U.S. Army.

troops soon spread across the countryside, liberating France and Belgium and entering Germany itself in September. In December German panzer divisions counterattacked in Belgium's Ardennes Forest, hoping to push on to Antwerp to halt the flow of Allied supplies through that major Belgian port. After weeks of heavy fighting in what has come to be called the Battle of the Bulge—because of the noticeable dent in the Allied line—the Allies pushed the enemy back once again. Meanwhile, battle-hardened Russian troops streamed through Poland and cut a path to the German capital, Berlin. American forces crossed the Rhine in March 1945 and captured the heavily industrial Ruhr valley. Some units peeled off to enter Austria and Czechoslovakia, where they met up with Russian soldiers. In bomb-ravaged Berlin, defended largely by teenage boys and old men, Adolf Hitler killed himself in his bunker. On May 8 Germany surrendered.

Allied strategists had devised a "Europe first" for-

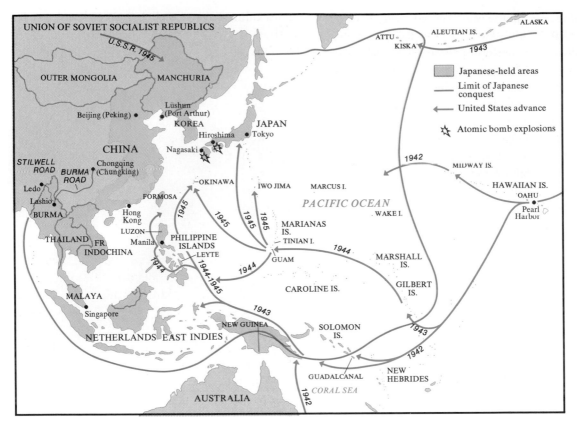

The Pacific War *Source: By permission of the publisher, from American Foreign Policy: A History by Paterson et al., p. 474. (Lexington, Mass.: D.C. Heath and Company, 1977).*

mula: knock out Germany first and then concentrate on an isolated Japan. Nevertheless, the Pacific theater claimed headlines throughout the war, for the American people regarded Japan as the United States' chief enemy. The treacherous Japanese—"monkeys" and "bastards," boomed Admiral William Halsey—had to be repaid for Pearl Harbor. By mid-1942 Japan had seized the Philippines, Guam, Wake, Hong Kong, Singapore, Malaya, and the Dutch East Indies. In the Philippines in 1942 Japanese soldiers forced American prisoners, weak from insufficient rations, to walk sixty-five miles, clubbing, shooting, or starving to death about ten thousand of them. The Bataan Death March intensified the American hatred of the Japanese.

In April 1942 Americans began to hit back. They bombed Tokyo, and in May, in the momentous Battle of the Coral Sea, carrier-based U.S. planes halted a Japanese advance toward Australia (see map). The

next month American forces defeated the Japanese at Midway, sinking four of the enemy's valuable aircraft carriers. Thanks to the success of Operation Magic— the work of American experts who deciphered the secret code used by the Japanese to transmit messages— American naval officers knew ahead of time the approximate date and direction of the Japanese assault. The Battle of Midway broke the Japanese momentum and relieved the threat to Hawaii. Thereafter, Japan was never able to match American manpower, sea power, air power, or economic power. Still, the war in Asia was contested until the very end. "There are no breathers in this schedule," exclaimed General H. H. Arnold in the football jargon of the time. "You take on Notre Dame every time you play!"

American strategy was to "island-hop" toward Japan itself, skipping the most strongly fortified points whenever possible and taking weaker ones. Americans also set out to sink the Japanese merchant marine,

American Offensive in the Pacific

in an effort to strand the Japanese armies in their island outposts and to cut off raw materials from the factories of the home islands. The first American offensive—at Guadalcanal in the Solomon Islands in summer and fall 1942—gave troops their first taste of jungle warfare: thick vegetation, mosquitos, scorpions, tropical heat, and rotting gear. From the Solomons the U.S. military pushed relentlessly on, colliding with the entrenched enemy in the Gilberts, Marshalls, and Marianas in 1943 and 1944. In June 1944 the navy smashed Japanese forces in the Battle of the Philippine Sea. In October General Douglas MacArthur landed at Leyte to reclaim the Philippines for the United States. Then in early 1945 both sides took heavy losses at Iwo Jima and Okinawa. In desperation, Japanese pilots began suicide (*kamikaze*) attacks, flying their planes directly into American ships.

Hoping to avoid a humiliating unconditional surrender (and to preserve the emperor's sovereignty), Japanese leaders refused to admit defeat. They hung on while American bombers leveled their cities. In one staggering attack on Tokyo on May 23, 1945, American planes dropped napalm-filled bombs that engulfed the city in a firestorm. Eighty-three thousand people died; observers described the ghastly scene as a mass burning.

Impatient for victory, American leaders began to plan a fall invasion of the Japanese islands, an expedition that was sure to bring high casualties. But the successful development of an atomic bomb by American scientists provided another route to victory. The secret atomic program, known as the Manhattan Project, began in August 1942 and cost $2 billion. The first atomic bomb was exploded in the desert near Alamogordo, New Mexico, on July 16, 1945. On August 6 the Japanese city of Hiroshima was destroyed by an atomic blast, killing half of the city's inhabitants at a stroke.

American planes continued their devastating conventional bombing and scattered leaflets over other Japanese cities warning that they too would face atomic terror unless the Japanese empire surrendered. On August 9 another atomic attack flattened Nagasaki, killing at least sixty thousand people. The next day a sobered President Truman suspended the further atomic bombing of Japan. He had belated qualms about killing "all those kids." Four days later the Japanese, who had sent out peace feelers since June, surrendered. The victors promised that the Japanese emperor could remain as the nation's titular head. Formal ceremonies were held September 2 aboard the battleship *Missouri*. The Second World War was over.

Most Americans agreed with President Truman that the atomic bombing of two Japanese cities had been necessary, to end the war as quickly as possible and to save American lives. Use of

Why the Atomic Bomb Was Used

the bomb to achieve victory had, in fact, been the primary assumption of the Manhattan Project. At the highest governmental levels and among atomic scientists, alternatives had been discussed: detonate the bomb on an unpopulated Pacific island, with international observers as witnesses; blockade and bomb Japan conventionally; follow up Tokyo's peace feelers; encourage a Russian declaration of war. But Truman's aides had rejected these options on the grounds that they would take too long and would not convince the tenacious Japanese they had been beaten. Then, too, memories of Pearl Harbor played a part. "When you have to deal with a beast you have to treat him as a beast," Truman said.

Diplomatic considerations also sped the decision to use the bomb. Leaders envisioned the real and psychological power the bomb would bestow on the United States. It might serve as a deterrent against aggression; it might intimidate Russia into making concessions in Eastern Europe; it might end the war in the Pacific before Russia could claim a role in the management of Asia. "If it explodes, as I think it will," Truman remarked, "I'll certainly have a hammer on those boys" (the Russians).

ECONOMIC EFFECTS OF THE WAR AT HOME

T he Second World War had been won at great cost not only abroad, but also on the American home front. While the guns boomed in Europe and

ARE *YOU*
PLAYING SQUARE?

GAS

The federal government used a variety of methods to exhort home-front Americans to obey wartime regulations. This Office of War Information poster suggested that the gas cheat was betraying his patriotic duty to support American troops.   National Archives.

Asia, the war changed American lives and institutions. One month after Pearl Harbor, President Roosevelt had established the War Production Board (WPB). First on the WPB's list of tasks was the conversion from civilian to military production. Factories that had manufactured silk ribbons began to turn out silk parachutes; automobile companies switched to the production of tanks and airplanes; adding-machine companies converted to make automatic pistols. Factories had to be expanded and new ones built. The WPB was so successful that the production of durable goods more than tripled. For example, manufacture of military aircraft, which had totaled 6,000 in 1940, jumped to over 47,000 in 1942 and 85,000 in 1943.

The wartime emergency spurred the establishment of totally new industries, the best known of which was synthetic rubber. The Japanese, in their conquest of the South Pacific in the weeks following Pearl Harbor, had captured 90 percent of the world's supply of crude rubber. Though the government resorted to conservation measures, including a national speed limit and gasoline rationing to save wear and tear on tires, neither conservation nor recycling could meet wartime needs. So with an investment of $700 million, the government underwrote the creation of a synthetic-rubber industry based on petroleum. By war's end the nation that had been the world's largest importer of rubber had become the world's largest exporter of rubber—all of it synthetic. New industries, of course, introduced new pollutants: smog (first detected in Los Angeles in 1943); artificially made radioactive elements; and petrochemical wastes from such new products as plastics, detergents, and DDT.

To gain the cooperation of business, the WPB and other government agencies met it more than halfway. The government guaranteed profits in the form of cost-plus-fixed-fee contracts, generous tax writeoffs, and exemption from antitrust prosecution. And it allowed prime contractors to distribute subcontracts as they saw fit, including those involving scarce war-related materials. These rewards made sense for a government—and a nation—that wanted the most possible war goods manufactured in the shortest possible time.

Government Incentives to Business

From mid-1940 through September 1944 the government awarded contracts totaling $175 billion, no less than two-thirds of which went to the top one hundred corporations. General Motors received 8 percent of the total; big awards also went to other automobile companies, as well as to aircraft, steel, electrical, and chemical companies. Almost all these industries had been dominated by big corporations at the beginning of the war; the billions of dollars they received in government contracts only accentuated their dominance. Though no one had yet thought to call it the "military-industrial complex," as President Dwight Eisenhower would in 1961 (see page 875), the web of government-business interdependence had begun to be woven.

The big also got bigger in science and higher education. To develop radar and do other research, the Massachusetts Institute of Technology received contracts valued at $117 million. The California Institute of Technology came next with contracts totaling $83 million, followed by Harvard, Columbia, the University of California, Johns Hopkins, and the University of Chicago. The most spectacular result of a government contract with a university was, of course, the atomic bomb; its testing was run by the University of California at Berkeley.

Big labor also grew bigger during the war. Union membership ballooned from 8.5 million in 1940 to 14.75 million in 1945. Less than a week after Pearl Harbor, a White House labor-management conference produced a no-strike–no-lockout pledge to guarantee uninterrupted war production. "When the nation is attacked," declared John L. Lewis, the gruff president of the United Mine Workers union, "every American must rally to its defense. All other considerations become insignificant." In 1942, to minimize labor-management conflict, President Roosevelt created the National War Labor Board (NWLB), sometimes referred to as the Supreme Court for labor disputes. Unions were permitted to enroll as many new members as possible, but workers were not required to join a union. Thus the NWLB forged a compromise between the unions' demand for a closed shop, in which only union members could be hired, and management's interest in open shops.

When the NWLB attempted to limit wage increases to increases in the cost of living, there were wildcat strikes and other work stoppages that tripled the production time lost in 1943. "Strikes are spreading at an alarming rate," bemoaned a member of the NWLB, "and unless they are checked immediately, the 'no strike–no lockout' agreement will become meaningless." But the worst labor disruptions of 1943 came in the coal fields, where 450,000 soft-coal miners and 80,000 anthracite miners struck. "When the mine workers' children cry for bread, they cannot be satisfied [with words];" declared John L. Lewis, who seemed to forget his earlier patriotic commitment to sacrifice.

Public hostility grew toward organized labor in general and John L. Lewis in particular. To discourage further work stoppages, Congress passed the War Labor Disputes, or Smith-Connally, Act of June 1943. The act conferred on the president the authority to seize and operate any strike-bound plant deemed necessary to the national security, and established a mandatory thirty-day cooling-off period before any new strike

could be called. The Smith-Connally Act also gave the NWLB the legal authority to settle labor disputes for the duration of the war. Over the course of the war the NWLB handled close to eighteen thousand disputes, reducing time lost due to strikes to one-third the peacetime level.

Although the war demanded sacrifices from Americans, it also brought new highs in personal income. Savings deposits jumped from $32.4 billion in 1942 to $51.4 billion in 1945. It was an even more bountiful time both for corporations, which doubled their net profits between 1939 and 1943, and for employees, whose wages and salaries rose more than 135 percent from 1940 to 1945. The government did not tax this extra income as heavily as it might have. Instead it resorted to deficit financing and borrowed approximately 60 percent of the cost of the war, about half of it in the form of war bonds sold to patriotic citizens; the national debt skyrocketed from $49 billion in 1941 to $259 billion in 1945.

Agriculture also made an impressive contribution to the war effort, not only through hard work but through the introduction of labor-saving machinery to replace the men and women who **Increased** had gone to the front or migrated **Mechanization** to war-production centers. Farming **of Agriculture** was in the midst of a transition from the family-owned and operated farm to the large-scale, mechanized agribusiness dominated by banks, insurance companies, and farm co-ops. The Second World War accelerated the trend, for wealthy financial institutions were better able than family farmers to pay for expensive new machinery. From 1940 to 1945 the value of American agricultural machinery rose from $3.1 billion to $6.5 billion, and the average acreage per farm jumped from 175 to 195. The use of the new machines and fertilizers boosted farm output per man-hour by 25 percent. At the same time the farm population fell from 30.5 million to 24.4 million. Like business and labor, agriculture was becoming more consolidated as it contributed to the war effort.

At the head of the burgeoning national economy stood the federal government, whose size and importance, like that of business and labor, was mushrooming: from 1940 to 1945 the federal bureaucracy expanded from 1.1 million workers to 3.4 million. The executive branch, which included the Office of the Commander-in-Chief and bore the responsibility for directing the war effort, grew the most. Besides raising the armed forces, mobilizing industrial production, pacifying labor and management, and controlling inflation, the executive also had to manage the labor supply. Through the War Manpower Commission (WMC), composed of representatives of various agencies, the government determined where labor was most needed, allocated labor between industry and the armed forces, and recruited new workers.

Although the WMC was far from successful in accomplishing its goals, another government agency, the Office of Price Administration (OPA), did succeed in combating inflation by fixing price ceilings on commodities and introducing rationing programs. Consumers became skilled in handling ration stamps, each worth ten points—red for meats and cheese, blue for canned goods—and car windows displayed "A" stamp decals for gasoline. In addition, the OPA issued a series of proclamations and rules that governed the behavior of landlords, employers, rationing boards, wholesalers, retailers, and consumers. In May 1943, as economic mobilization became increasingly bogged down in red tape, President Roosevelt created the Office of War Mobilization which became, in effect, a court of appeal in disputes between conflicting civilian and military claims.

Although government-business-labor relations were sometimes bitter and slowed production, Americans were generally ready to make personal sacrifices. They knew the war would be costly and long. In previous conflicts Americans had flocked to the colors with flags, wild rallies, and militaristic songs, but in the Second World War they fought with a grim, realistic determination. To elicit the people's enthusiasm, the Office of War Administration took charge of domestic propaganda and hired Hollywood filmmakers and New York advertising copywriters to sell the war. But as historian Allan Nevins observed, "In this war there was . . . no such straw fire of frothy enthusiasm." Most Americans wanted to leave behind their concerns about the war, so the motion pictures produced and books published during this war were typically light, fluffy, sentimental escapes from the harsh realities of life. In 1861, 1898, and 1917, Nevins wrote, Americans had thought that "the war would be easy. They knew full well in 1941 that it wouldn't."

THE MILITARY LIFE

In America's forty-five months at war, a total of 16.4 million of its citizens responded to the colors. Some served for the war's duration, others for shorter periods. At the war's conclusion in 1945, over 12 million men and women were serving in the U.S. armed forces. The army topped the list with 8.3 million, including 100,000 WACS (Women's Army Corps). Though women were prohibited from engaging in combat duty, they worked at a variety of noncombat jobs, not only in the WACS but as WAVES (Women Accepted for Volunteer Emergency Service) in the navy, as pilots in the WASPS (Women Air Service Pilots), and as members of the Coast Guard and the Marine Corps Women's Reserve. The WASPS taught basic flying, towed aerial targets for gunnery practice, and flight-tested military aircraft.

American troops served overseas for an average of about sixteen months. Some, of course, never returned: total deaths exceeded 405,000; total wounded, 670,000. In terms of human life, the cost of the war was second only to that of the Civil War. Still, compared with losses suffered by other nations, U.S. figures were low. Less than 1 percent of the population was killed or wounded in the war; the Soviet Union lost 8 percent of its population—about 20 million people.

Many soldiers and sailors, who had never been more than a few miles from home, became homesick. GIs joked, somewhat bitterly, about having found a home in the army. But this loneliness was minor compared with the intense fear that soldiers admitted to feeling in battle. Combat veterans told a group of psychologists that a man who burst out weeping was "not regarded as a coward unless he made no apparent effort to stick to his job." Some Americans became looters. One veteran explained that when soldiers took a town, they "wanted something to drink. Then they wanted a woman. And then they wanted to go out and see what they could loot. And brother, when I say loot, I mean some of them looted."

But if combat's cruelties robbed many GIs of their innocence, military service itself broadened the ho-

B-17 pilots return from a training flight in their Flying Fortress *Pistol Packin' Mama. WAF pilots ferried the planes for the Air Corps. U.S. Air Force Photo.*

rizons of millions of men and women. "Take these kids from the hills," noted one GI,

Broadening of GIs' Horizons

"the service opened their eyes some. . . . And some of these guys from Chicago, why they'd never been outside of Chicago. They talked about fellows 'from the sticks' and they'd never been out in the 'sticks'—they'd never even known what the 'sticks' were."

Wartime service not only broadened horizons but stimulated soldiers' ambitions. A soldier from the Midwest, who reported that he found himself "living among fellows from all over the country," said, "I picked up a lot of ideas from them, not only [about] what the United States was really like—I mean the whole country—but about how to live my own life and to get more out of it. . . . I came out a lot more ambitious than I was before I went in." Finally, many GIs returned to civilian life with new skills they had learned in the military's technical schools. Some became fluent in foreign languages; others became medical technicians, electronics experts, and aircraft mechanics. Still others took advantage of the educational benefits offered in the GI Bill of Rights (1944) to study for a college degree (see page 895).

Still, after two or three years abroad, men and women in the service returned to the United States not knowing what to expect from civilian life. Earlier in the war, troops had been given orientation lectures and booklets introducing them to the historical backgrounds and social customs of the foreign nations where they would serve. Now they were coming home, and yet, as one observer wrote, they were "to a surprising degree, foreigners in their own land." Returning soldiers also feared a postwar economic depression. A B-17 crew chief complained that people were "spending too much money and . . . not saving up for what's coming—you know, unemployment after the war."

But what might have been most disturbing to GIs was the feeling that life at home had passed them by. For one thing, returning GIs were much older in experience and in exposure to brutality; they had lost their innocence. Many came back to the United States convinced that they had sacrificed their youth.

"Just gimme a coupla aspirin. I already got a Purple Heart." The cartoonist Bill Mauldin became famous through his GI characters Willie and Joe, two battle-hardened veterans who hated officers almost as much as they hated the army. By permission of Bill Mauldin and Wil-Jo Associates, Inc.

Still worse, they found that home had changed as well. "Our friends are gone," one GI lamented. "The family and the town naturally had to go on even if we weren't there, and somehow it seems things have sort of closed in and filled that space we used to occupy."

CIVIL LIBERTIES AND THE INTERNMENT OF JAPANESE-AMERICANS

Once the United States entered the war, its leaders had to consider whether enemy agents were operating within its borders and threatening the war effort. It was clear that not all Americans were en-

thusiastic supporters of the nation's involvement in the war. Following Pearl Harbor, several thousand "enemy aliens" were arrested and taken into custody, some of them Nazi agents who had accumulated firearms, shortwave radios, and codes in the course of their work. Other people had conscientious objections to the war, particularly Quakers, Mennonites, and members of the Church of the Brethren. During the Second World War conscientious objectors (COs) had to have a religious (as opposed to moral or ethical) reason for refusing military service. About 25,000 qualified COs accepted noncombat service, most of them as medical corpsmen. An additional 12,000 were placed in civilian public-service camps, where they worked at forestry or conservation or as orderlies in public health hospitals. Some—5,500 in all, three-fourths of whom were Jehovah's Witnesses—refused to participate in any way; they were imprisoned.

The one enormous exception to the nation's generally creditable wartime civil liberties record was the internment in "relocation centers" of more than 110,000 Japanese-Americans. Of these people, 70,000 were Nisei, or native-born citizens of the United States. Their imprisonment was based not on suspicion or evidence of treason; their crime was their ethnic origin—the fact that they were of Japanese descent. As General John L. DeWitt, chief of the Western Defense Command, expressed it:

Internment in "Relocation Centers"

> The Japanese race is an enemy race and while many second and third generation Japanese born on United States soil, possessed of United States citizenship, have become "Americanized," the racial strains are undiluted. . . . It, therefore, follows that along the vital Pacific Coast over 112,000 potential enemies, of Japanese extraction, are at large today.

With strained illogic he declared: "The very fact that no sabotage [by Japanese-Americans] has taken place to date is a disturbing and confirming indication that such action will be taken." DeWitt was not alone in his paranoia.

Charges of criminal behavior were never brought against Japanese-Americans; none were ever indicted or tried for espionage, treason, or sedition. Even their alleged crime, disloyalty to the United States, was

Branded members of an enemy race by the government, more than 110,000 Japanese-Americans were rounded up and shipped to internment camps. Included among the evacuees were children and the elderly.   National Archives.

not against the law. Nevertheless in 1942 more than 110,000 people were rounded up and imprisoned. "It was really cruel and harsh," recalled Joseph Y. Kurihara, a citizen and a veteran of the First World War. "To pack and evacuate in forty-eight hours was an impossibility. Seeing mothers completely bewildered with children crying from want and peddlers taking advantage and offering prices next to robbery made me feel like murdering those responsible." After the war, Kurihara, along with 8,000 other Japanese-Americans, did the next best thing: he emigrated to Japan, a country he had never seen.

The internees were sent to flood-damaged lands at Relocation, Arkansas; to the intermountain terrain of Wyoming and the desert of western Arizona; and to other arid and desolate spots in the West. Although the names were evocative—Topaz, Utah; Rivers, Arizona; Heart Mountain, Wyoming; Manzanar, California—the camps themselves were bleak and demoralizing. Behind barbed wire stood tarpapered

wooden barracks where entire families lived in a single room furnished only with cots, blankets, and a bare light bulb. Toilets and dining and bathing facilities were communal; privacy was almost non-existent. Besides their freedom, the Japanese-Americans lost property valued at $500 million, along with their positions in the truck-garden, floral, and fishing industries. Indeed, their economic competitors were among the most vocal proponents of their relocation.

The Supreme Court upheld the government's policy of internment. In wartime, the Court said in the *Hirabayashi* ruling (1943), "residents having ethnic affiliations with an invading enemy may be a greater source of danger than those of different ancestry." And in the *Korematsu* case (1944), the Court, with three justices dissenting, approved the removal of the Nisei from the West Coast. One dissenter, Justice Frank Murphy, denounced the decision as the "legalization of racism," and Justice Robert Jackson warned that the precedent established by the cases "lies about like a loaded weapon ready for the hand of any authority that can bring forward a plausible claim of an urgent need." But the most damning appraisal of all came from Circuit Court Judge William Denman, who in an earlier ruling wrote that "the identity of this doctrine with that of the Hitler generals . . . justifying the gas chambers of Dachau is unmistakable."

In 1983, forty-one years after he had been placed in a government camp, Fred Korematsu had the satisfaction of hearing a federal judge rule that he—and by implication all the detainees—had been the victim of "unsubstantiated facts, distortions and misrepresentations of at least one military commander whose views were affected by racism." In 1982 the government's special Commission on Wartime Relocation and Internment of Civilians had recommended compensating the victims of this policy. Because of "race prejudice, war hysteria and a failure of political leadership," the commission concluded, the U.S. government had committed "a grave injustice" to more than 110,000 people.

JOBS AND RACISM ON THE
HOME FRONT

For other nonwhite groups in America, the Second World War would prove to be a mixed blessing, providing both the benefits of employment and the insults of racism. For many black Americans, the war was a watershed, the point at which they determined to make a stand against racial discrimination. Several factors highlighted Afro-American involvement in the war: the presence of nearly 1 million black men and women in the armed services; the mass migration of blacks, particularly from the rural South to the urban North and West, to work in war industries; and the participation of black people in all kinds of wartime activities—buying war bonds, serving as air-raid wardens, and volunteering for the Red Cross.

At peak enrollment the army had over 700,000

black troops. An additional 187,000 had enlisted in the navy, the Coast Guard, and the once all-white Marine Corps. In response to the March on Washington Movement of 1941 (see page 753), the Selective Service System and the War Department agreed to draft black Americans in proportion to their presence in the population: about 10 percent.

Though blacks in the service were still segregated, they made some real advances in the direction of racial equality during these years. For the first time

**Black
Troops**

the War Department sanctioned the training of blacks as pilots. After instruction at Tuskegee Institute in Alabama, pilots saw heroic service in such all-black units as the Ninety-ninth Pursuit Squadron, winner of eighty Distinguished Flying Crosses. And some blacks reached positions of leadership. In 1940 Colonel Benjamin O. Davis became the first black brigadier general. Wherever black people were offered opportunities to distinguish themselves, they proved they were just as capable as whites. The performance of black marines in the Pacific theater was such that the Corps Commandant proclaimed: "Negro Marines are no longer on trial. They are Marines, period."

Set against these accomplishments, however, were serious failures in race relations. Race riots instigated by whites occurred on military bases, and white civilians assaulted black soldiers and sailors throughout the South. In North Carolina a white bus driver murdered a black soldier in full view of the passengers, but was found not guilty. When the War Department issued an order in mid-1944 forbidding racial segregation in military recreation and transportation, the *Montgomery Advertiser* replied, "Army orders, even armies, even bayonets, cannot force impossible and unnatural social relations upon us."

Of course, experiences such as these caused black soldiers and sailors to wonder what, in fact, they were fighting for. They recalled the remark of the governor of Tennessee, when blacks urged him to appoint Afro-Americans to local draft boards: "This is a white man's country. . . . The Negro had nothing to do with the settling of America." They noted that the Red Cross separated blood taken from whites and blacks, as if there were some difference. And many considered black participation in the First World War a mistake, for it had resulted not in social advances but in race riots and lynchings. Some even argued that the Second World War was a white man's war. But most telling was the charge that American racism was little different from German racism.

At the same time, there were positive reasons for blacks to participate in the war effort. Perhaps this was an opportunity, as the NAACP believed, "to persuade, embarrass, compel and shame our government and our nation . . . into a more enlightened attitude toward a tenth of its people." Proclaiming that in the Second World War they were waging a "Double V" campaign (for victory at home and abroad), blacks were more militant than before, and readier than ever to protest. Membership in civil rights organizations soared. The NAACP, whose membership had stood at 50,000 in 1940, had 450,000 members by 1946. And in 1942 civil rights activists founded the Congress of Racial Equality (CORE).

Because of the war, blacks found new opportunities in industry. Roosevelt's Executive Order 8802, issued in 1941, required employers in defense industries to make jobs available "without dis-

Black War Workers

crimination because of race, creed, color or national origin." To secure defense jobs, 1.2 million blacks migrated from the South to the industrial cities of the North and West in the 1940s. Almost three-fourths settled in the urban-industrial states of California, Illinois, Michigan, New York, Ohio, and Pennsylvania. More than half a million became active members of CIO unions such as the United Auto Workers, the United Steel Workers, and the United Rubber Workers. Finally, black voters in northern cities were beginning to constitute a vital swing vote not only in presidential contests, but in local and state elections.

But along with the benefits of urban life came liabilities. The migrants had to make enormous emotional and cultural adjustments, and white hostility and ignorance made their task particularly difficult. Southern whites who had migrated north brought with them the racial prejudices of the Deep South. Blacks competed with these whites for housing, jobs, and seats on buses; they rubbed elbows with them in city schools and parks and at the beaches. But just as significant was the ignorance of northern whites, more than half of whom believed in 1942 that blacks should be segregated in separate schools and neighborhoods; that black people were receiving all the

opportunities they deserved; and that if blacks suffered economically, politically, or socially, it was their own fault. These attitudes encouraged racial violence.

Many people, black and white, feared that the summer of 1943 would be like 1919, another Red Summer. And indeed, almost 250 racial conflicts exploded in forty-seven cities that

Race Riots of 1943

year. The worst of the 1943 race riots bloodied the streets of Detroit in June. At the end of thirty hours of rioting, twenty-five blacks and nine whites lay dead. White mobs, undeterred by police, had roamed the city attacking blacks. Blacks had hurled rocks at police and hauled white passengers off streetcars. This was outright racial warfare. In response to the riot a city councilman suggested that the city build a bigger ghetto and pen blacks up in it. Surveying the damage, an elderly black woman said, "There ain't no North any more. Everything now is South."

The federal government did practically nothing to prevent further racial violence. From Roosevelt on down, most federal officials put the war first, domestic reform second. Unquestionably many government leaders were racists themselves; Secretary of War Henry L. Stimson claimed that the riots were "the deliberate effort . . . on the part of certain radical leaders of the colored race to use the war for obtaining . . . racial equality and interracial marriages." But this time governmental neglect could not discourage Afro-Americans and their century-old civil rights movement. By war's end they were ready—politically, economically, and emotionally—to wage the struggle for voting rights and for equal access to public accommodations and institutions.

Not all racial violence was directed against blacks. In the 1943 Los Angeles zoot suit riot, the victims were Mexican-Americans. In the eyes of the rioters, most of whom were sailors and soldiers, people of Mexican origin were as despicable as those whose roots were African. In 1942, American farms and war industries needed workers, and the United States and Mexico had agreed to the *bracero* program, whereby Mexicans were admitted to the United States on short-term work contracts. Although the newcomers suffered racial discrimination and segregation, they seized the economic opportunities that had become available. In Los Angeles, 17,000 people of Mexican descent found shipyard jobs where before

The bloodiest race riot of 1943 struck Detroit, where 34 people, 25 black and 9 white, were killed. At the peak of the rioting a white mob overturned a black person's car, showering trolley passengers with burning gasoline. UPI/ Bettmann Newsphotos.

the war there had been none available. Mexican-American teenagers in that city joined street gangs (*pachucos*), adopted ducktail haircuts, and donned "zoot suits": long coats (called "drapes") with wide, padded shoulders, pegged pants, wide-brimmed hats, and long watch chains. Whites' racial hatred boiled over in June, and for four days mobs invaded Mexican-American neighborhoods. According to one report: "Procedure was standard: grab a zooter. Take off his pants and frock coat and tear them up or burn them. Trim the '. . . ducktail' haircut that goes with the screwy costume." Not only did white policemen look the other way during these assaults, but the city of Los Angeles even passed an ordinance that made it a crime to wear a zoot suit within city limits.

Such experiences made life difficult for people of Mexican descent within the United States. Although the war opened up brief economic opportunities for Mexican-Americans, these years were not the watershed experience that they were for Afro-Americans.

A MILESTONE FOR WOMEN

If the Second World War was a turning point for Afro-Americans, it was equally or even more so for the women of America. During the Great Depression, when millions of men were unemployed, public opinion had been hostile to the hiring of women, but the war brought about a rapid increase in employment. Just when men were going off to war, industry had to recruit millions of new workers to supply the rapidly expanding need for military equipment. Afro-Americans, southern whites, teenage boys and girls, Mexicans and Mexican-Americans, and, above all, women filled these new jobs.

Well over 6 million women entered the labor force during the war years, increasing the number of working women 57 percent in less than five years. Two million

Over six million women entered the labor force during the war, many of them taking skilled jobs that had once been reserved for men. These women on the assembly line at a Douglas Aircraft plant are making bombardier noses for bombers.   National Archives.

took clerical jobs; another 2.5 million worked in manufacturing. The significance of the trend lay not only in the numbers, but in the kinds of women who were entering the work force. Seventy-five percent of the new women workers were married, and 3.7 million were not only married but mothers. Before the war the average woman wage earner had been young, single, and largely self-supporting; by 1945 more working women were married than single, and more were over thirty-five than under.

But statistics, no matter how impressive, tell only part of the story. There was a change in attitude toward heavy labor for women. Up to the early months of the war employers had insisted **Women in War** that women were not suited for in-**Production** dustrial jobs. If women were allowed to work in factories they would begin to wear overalls instead of dresses; their muscles would bulge; they might even drink whiskey and swear like men. As labor shortages began to threaten the war

effort, employers did an about-face. "Almost overnight," said Mary Anderson, head of the Women's Bureau of the Department of Labor, "women were reclassified by industrialists from a marginal to a basic labor supply for munitions making." Women became riveters, lumberjacks ("lumberjills"), welders, crane operators, keel benders, tool makers, shell loaders, cowgirls, blast-furnace cleaners, locomotive greasers, police officers, taxi drivers, and football coaches.

The new employment opportunities increased women's geographic and occupational mobility. Especially noteworthy were the gains made by black women; over 400,000 quit work as domestic servants to enjoy the better working conditions, higher pay, and union benefits of industrial employment. Hundreds of thousands of others, black and white, abandoned menial jobs in dime stores, restaurants, laundries, and hospitals for higher-status, higher-paying jobs. To take these jobs, women uprooted themselves. Over 7 million women moved from their original counties of residence to new locations during the war. Many sought jobs in the rapidly expanding aircraft industry, which increased its employment of women from 4,000 in December 1941 to 310,000 two years later.

Public opinion quickly changed from hostility to support of women's war work. Posters and billboards urging women to "Do the Job HE Left Behind" soon began to appear. Newspapers and magazines, radio and movies proclaimed Rosie the Riveter a war hero. But very few people asserted that women's war work should bring about a permanent shift in sex roles. This was merely a response to a national emergency. Once the victory was won, women should go back to nurturing their husbands and children, leaving their jobs to returning GIs. From "a humanitarian point of view," stated the president of the National Association of Manufacturers, "too many women should not stay in the labor force. The home is the basic American institution." Wartime surveys showed, however, that many of the women wanted to remain in their jobs. Eighty percent of New York's women workers felt that way, as did 75 percent of Detroit's female laborers. "War jobs have uncovered unsuspected abilities in American women," explained one woman. "Why lose all these abilities because of a belief that 'a woman's place is in the home.' For some it is," she added, "for others not."

Though women increased their wages when they acquired better jobs, they still received lower pay than men, even for the same work. In 1945 women in manufacturing earned only 65 **"Women's** percent of what men were paid. An **Work"** important reason for this inequality was the sex-segregated labor market. Although the wartime emergency caused some traditionally male jobs to be reclassified for women, most jobs were defined as either "women's work" or "men's work." Even in factories, most women worked in all-female shops. And working women, particularly working mothers, suffered in other ways as well. Perhaps the most persistent problem was the near-absence of supportive services such as childcare centers and communal kitchens. Some of the most serious wartime social problems were a direct result of the lack of such services. During the war there were increases in juvenile delinquency, venereal disease, teenage pregnancy, and the incidence of "eight-hour orphans,"

Latchkey Children or "latchkey children," left alone while their mothers worked eight-hour shifts in war plants. In 1940 Congress passed the Lanham Act to provide federal aid to communities that had to absorb large war-related populations. Benefits included funds for daycare centers, hospitals, sewer systems, police and fire-fighting facilities, and recreation centers. But provision was made for the care of only 107,000 children. Many of the remaining children roamed the streets or were locked in cars or sent to all-day or even all-night movies. In an area of concentrated war industry in Los Angeles, one social worker counted forty-five infants locked in cars in a single lot.

Crime was another problem: juvenile arrests jumped 20 percent nationwide in 1943. The increase was greater for girls than for boys; in San Diego, arrests increased 55 percent for boys and 355 percent for girls. Many girls became prostitutes: in 1943, arrests for that crime climbed 68 percent. Among boys the most common crime was theft, but vandalism and violence were also problems.

Perhaps because of such statistics, the massive contributions children made to the war effort were often overlooked. Children contributed their own nickels and dimes to buy war stamps and bonds, and they pulled their wagons from house to house collecting old newspapers and tin cans. The Boy Scouts collected 109 million pounds of rubber and 370 million pounds of scrap metal. Even more significant was that thousands of young people went to work during the war. In 1940, for example, 900,000 boys and girls between the ages of fourteen and eighteen were employed. By spring 1944 their number had climbed to 3 million—one-third of their age group. Indeed, some observers felt that the most pressing social problem afflicting teenagers was not juvenile delinquency but failure to finish school. High school enrollments hit new lows during the war, prompting a back-to-school drive in 1944.

At the same time that millions of women and youths were entering the work force, hundreds of thousands of women were getting married. From 1939 to 1942 the marriage rate rose from **Increase in** 73 marriages per 1,000 unmarried **Marriage,** women to 93 per 1,000. Some cou-**Divorce, and** ples scrambled to get married so they **Birth Rates** could spend time together before

In June 1942 Boy Scouts in Stevens Point, Wisconsin, led a parade of trucks carrying more than 80 tons of old automobile and bicycle tires collected in scrap drives. Throughout the nation children aided the war effort by selling bonds and gathering materials for recycling.   Wide World Photos.

the man was sent overseas. Some doubtless married and had children to qualify for military deferments. But the rush to get married was also fueled by prosperity. A justice of the peace in Yuma, Arizona, explained that the marriage rate "began going up as soon as those boys were given employment in those plants at San Diego and Los Angeles and were taken off WPA." He was not exaggerating; 90 percent of the marriage licenses in Yuma went to aircraft workers.

These hasty marriages often did not survive long military separations. As a result, divorces soared too, from 25,000 in 1939 to 359,000 in 1943 and 485,000 in 1945. And as might be expected, the birthrate also climbed: total births rose from over 2.4 million in 1939 to 3.1 million in 1943. Many of these births were "good-bye babies," conceived as a hedge against

the future before the father left for the war, a guarantee that the family would be perpetuated should he die in battle overseas.

Ironically, women's efforts to hold their families together during the war posed problems for returning fathers. Women war workers had brought home the wages; they had taken over the budgeting of expenses and the writing of checks. In countless ways they had proved they could hold the reins in their husbands' absence. When the husbands began returning home in the waning months of the war, many found that the pattern of life for their wives and children seemed to be complete without them. For some men, it was not just a case of appearances; they knew their families could survive and even prosper without them.

And what of the women who wanted to remain in the labor market? Many were forced by employers, or by their husbands, to quit. Others chose to leave their jobs for a year or two, but then returned to work. And throughout the rest of the 1940s and 1950s, millions more who had never worked took jobs.

THE DECLINE OF LIBERALISM AND THE ELECTION OF 1944

Another wartime trend was the decline of political liberalism. Even before Pearl Harbor, liberals had suffered major defeats. Some Democrats hoped to revive the reform movement during the war, but Republicans and conservative Democrats were on guard against such a move. New Dealers, warned Republican Senator Robert Taft early in 1942, "are determined to make the country over under the cover of war if they can." Taft and his fellow conservatives successfully blocked reform.

Aided by a small turnout in November 1942, the Republicans scored impressive gains, winning forty-four new seats in the House and nine in the Senate and defeating Democratic governors in New York, California, and Michigan. Part of the Democrats' problem was that, unlike the 1930s, the war years were a time of full employment. Once people had acquired jobs and gained some economic security, they began to be more critical of New Deal policies. The New Deal coalition had always had the potential for fragmentation. Southern white farmers had little in common with northern blacks or white factory workers. And in northern cities, blacks and whites who had voted for Roosevelt in 1940 were competing for jobs and housing and would soon collide in race riots.

With Republican victories in 1942, the alliance of conservative southern Democrats and Republicans became a formidable threat to New Deal programs. In 1942 and 1943 the conservative coalition actually abolished several New Deal relief and social-welfare agencies, among them the Civilian Conservation Corps and the Work Projects Administration.

But though liberalism was enfeebled, it was far from dead. The liberal agenda began with a pledge to secure full employment. Roosevelt emphasized the concept in his Economic Bill of Rights, delivered as part of his 1944 State of the Union address. Every American had a right, the president declared, to a decent job; sufficient food, shelter, and clothing; and financial security in unemployment, illness, and old age. If to accomplish those goals the government had to operate at a deficit, Roosevelt was willing to do so. But first he had to be re-elected.

In 1944 Franklin D. Roosevelt looked like an exhausted old man. His eyes were tired and puffy; he was almost bald; and the loose flesh that hung on his large frame made him appear emaciated. Though the president's personal physician pronounced "nothing organically wrong with him at all—he's perfectly O.K.," rumors of his ill health persisted. Because Roosevelt expected to survive his fourth term, he believed he could select a running mate who was inexperienced in international affairs. His choice was Senator Harry S Truman of Missouri. During the war Truman had gained favorable publicity for chairing a senatorial watchdog committee on favoritism and waste in the awarding of defense contracts. A representative of both a border state and a big-city machine (the Pendergast machine in Kansas City), Truman was satisfactory both to southerners and to the bosses. As an ardent and loyal New Dealer, the senator was also approved by liberals. But there was little evidence that he possessed the qualities of national and world leadership that he would need as president. And Roosevelt did not take Truman into his confidence; he even failed to inform his running mate about the atomic bomb project.

The Republicans were optimistic about their prospects for regaining the presidency. New York Governor Thomas E. Dewey, who won the nomination on the first ballot, was a moderate who did not advocate repeal of the essentials of the New Deal—social security, unemployment relief, collective bargaining, and price supports for farmers. And he was cautious in his criticism of Roosevelt's foreign policy. But Dewey had one great liability, his public image. Short of stature and dull of personality, Dewey looked, as Alice Longworth, Theodore Roosevelt's daughter, described him, "like the bridegroom on a wedding cake."

Although Roosevelt won a fourth term, the margin

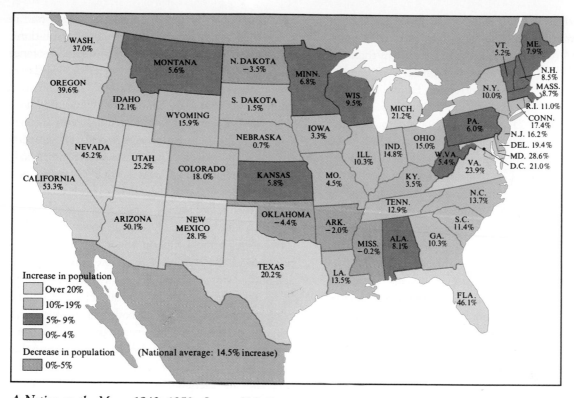

A Nation on the Move, 1940–1950 *Source: U.S. Bureau of the Census,* Portfolio of United States Census Maps, *1950 (Washington: U.S. Government Printing Office, 1953), p. 4.*

of victory in the popular vote was his narrowest ever; it was the closest presidential election since 1916. Nevertheless, he won 53.4 percent of the popular vote and 432 electoral votes to Dewey's 99. It was the urban vote that returned Roosevelt to the White House. Wartime population shifts had much to do with the cities' new political clout. New workers—notably southern whites who had been lifelong Democrats and southern blacks who had never before voted—had migrated to the urban industrial centers (see map). Added to the urban vote was a less obvious factor. Many voters seemed to be exhibiting what has been called "depression psychosis." Fearful that hard times would return once war contracts were terminated, they remembered New Deal relief programs and voted for Roosevelt. Finally, as Senator Taft conceded, the Republicans had "underestimated the difficulty of changing a President at the very height of a victorious war." With victory within grasp, many Americans wanted Roosevelt's experienced hand to guide the nation, and the world, to a lasting peace.

WARTIME DIPLOMACY

The lessons of the post–First World War period weighed heavily on the minds of American diplomats throughout the war. Americans vowed to make a peace that would ensure a postwar world free from depression, totalitarianism, and war. The Atlantic Charter, so reminiscent of Woodrow Wilson's vision of an open world, was their general guide, tempered and compromised by the interests of the great powers. Thus American goals included the Open Door and lower tariffs; self-determination for liberated peoples; avoidance of the debts-reparations tangle that had plagued Europe after the First World War; expansion of the United States sphere of influence; and management of world affairs by what Roosevelt once called the Four Policemen: Russia, China, Great Britain, and the United States.

Although the major Allies concentrated on defeating the aggressors, their suspicions of one another undermined cooperation. More dogged them than the timing of the second front and the Italian surrender. Eastern European questions proved the most difficult. The Russians sought to fix their boundaries where they had stood before Hitler attacked in 1941. In the case of Poland, this meant that the part of the country the Soviets had invaded and captured in 1939 would become Russian territory. The British and Americans hesitated, preferring to deal with Eastern Europe at the end of the war. But the sustained drive of the Russian armies through the region on the heels of the retreating Germans persuaded Churchill to act. In an October 1944 agreement, he and Stalin struck a bargain: Russia would gain Rumania and Bulgaria as a sphere of influence; Britain would have the upper hand in Greece; and the two would share authority in Yugoslavia and Hungary. The two leaders did not, however, agree on Poland.

Allied Disagreement over Eastern Europe

Poland was a special case. In 1943 Moscow had broken off diplomatic relations with the conservative Polish government-in-exile in London. The Poles had angered Moscow when they asked the International Red Cross to investigate German charges that the Russians had massacred thousands of Polish army officers in the Katyn Forest in 1940. Then an uprising in Warsaw in July 1944 complicated matters still further. Taking advantage of the nearness of Soviet troops, the Warsaw underground rose against the occupying Germans. To the dismay of the world community, Soviet armies stood aside as German troops slaughtered 166,000 people and devastated the city. Finally, in late 1944 and early 1945 the Soviets spawned a pro-Communist government in Lublin. Thus near the end of the war Poland had two competing governments, one in London, recognized by America and Britain, and another in Lublin.

Early in the war the Allies had begun talking about a new international organization. At Teheran in 1943 Roosevelt called for an institution controlled by the Four Policemen. The next year, in a Washington, D.C., mansion called Dumbarton Oaks, American, British, Russian, and Chinese representatives conferred on the details.

Creation of the United Nations Organization

Since American participation had been endorsed in public opinion polls and congressional resolutions, United States diplomats proceeded with some assurance that their handiwork would not meet the legislative fate of Wilson's League of Nations. The conferees approved a preliminary charter for a United Nations Organization, providing for a supreme Security Council dominated by the great powers and a weak General Assembly (Roosevelt called it "an investigatory body only"). The Security Council would have five permanent members, each with veto power.

Disagreement surfaced when the United States pushed China forward as a great power entitled to permanent membership on the council: Churchill complained that China was a captive vote on the side of the United States. To mollify him, the United States reluctantly agreed to elevate France to a permanent seat. Russia accepted both France and China, believing that its veto power would protect its national interest against unfriendly decisions. But noting that the United States would have a group of sympathetic votes in the General Assembly among the Latin American states, and that Britain could muster support from members of its Commonwealth, the Soviets asked for a balancing of power. They wanted separate membership in the General Assembly for the sixteen Soviet republics. This issue was not resolved at Dumbarton Oaks, but the meeting proved a success nevertheless. The conferees had achieved 90 percent of their goals, Roosevelt pointed out. "Well, that is what we used to call in the old days a darn good batting average."

The diplomatic batting average on another problem, Nazi treatment of the Jews, was considerably lower. Even before the war Nazi officials had targeted Jews throughout Europe for extermination. By war's end, about 6 million Jews had been forced into concentration camps and systematically killed by firing squads, unspeakable tortures, and gas chambers. Many others who survived the Holocaust could never forget the terror. During the depression the United States and other nations had refused to relax their immigration restrictions to save Jews fleeing persecution. The American Federation of Labor and Senator William Borah, among others, argued that new immigrants would compete with American workers for scarce jobs, and public

Jewish Refugees from the Holocaust

opinion polls supported their position. The fear of economic competition was, of course, fed by anti-Semitism. Bureaucrats applied the rules so strictly—requiring legal documents fleeing Jews could not possibly provide—that otherwise qualified refugees were kept out of the country. From 1933 to 1945 less than 40 percent of the German-Austrian quota was filled.

Even the tragic voyage of the *St. Louis* did not change government policy. The vessel left Hamburg in mid-1939 with 930 desperate Jewish refugees who lacked proper immigration documents. Denied entry to Havana, the *St. Louis* headed for Miami, where Coast Guard cutters prevented it from docking. Aroused American citizens appealed to Washington, but the ship was forced to return to Europe. Some of those refugees took shelter in countries that were later overrun by Hitler's legions. "The cruise of the *St. Louis*," wrote the *New York Times*, "cries to high heaven of man's inhumanity to man."

As news of the Nazi atrocities filled government files during the war years, American officials futilely attempted to persuade Latin American countries to accept refugees. They also approached the British, who proved unhelpful as well: they would not open Palestine. Some American leaders were themselves lax in their attention to the problem. The State Department officer in charge was Breckinridge Long, a Democratic politician who actually hindered private citizens' efforts to save victims.

When evidence mounted that Hitler intended to exterminate the Jews, British and American representatives met in Bermuda (1943) but came up with no plans. Secretary Hull made a discouraging report to the president, emphasizing "the unknown cost of moving an undetermined number of persons from an undisclosed place to an unknown destination." Appalled, Secretary of the Treasury Henry Morgenthau, Jr., charged that the State Department's foot-dragging made the United States an accessory to murder. "It takes months and months to grant the visa and then it usually applies to a corpse," he wrote bitterly. Early in 1944, stirred by Morgenthau's well-documented plea, Roosevelt created the War Refugee Board, which set up refugee camps in Europe and saved thousands from death.

But American officials waited too long to act, and they missed a chance to destroy the gas chambers and ovens at the extermination camp at Auschwitz

in occupied Poland. They had aerial photographs and diagrams of the camp, but they argued that bombing it would detract from the war effort or prompt the Germans to step up the anti-Jewish terror. In 1944 American planes bombed synthetic oil and rubber plants in the industrial sector of Auschwitz, only five miles from the gas chambers and crematoria. "How could it be," historian David S. Wyman has asked, "that Government officials knew that a place existed where 2,000 helpless human beings could be killed in less than an hour, knew that this occurred over and over again, and yet did not feel driven to search for some way to wipe such a scourge from the earth?"

THE YALTA CONFERENCE AND A FLAWED PEACE

With the war in Europe nearing an end, and a host of political questions—including what to do with Germany—yet to be settled, President Roosevelt urged another summit meeting. The three Allied leaders met at Yalta, on the Russian Crimea, in early February 1945. Controversy has surrounded the conference ever since. Roosevelt was obviously ill. "His appearance could change in a couple of hours from looking like a ghost to looking okay," remarked the new Secretary of State Edward Stettinius, Jr. The sixty-two-year-old president suffered from hypertension, heart disease, and hardening of the arteries. His doctors prescribed rest, a reduction in cigarette smoking, and medication, but the president maintained a busy schedule. Critics of the Yalta agreements later charged that Roosevelt was too weak to resist the demands of a guileful Stalin, that he struck a poor bargain. The evidence suggests, however, that Roosevelt was mentally alert and that he managed to sustain his strength during negotiations.

The Yalta meeting has also been criticized because some of its agreements were secret (suggesting the Allies had something to hide) and because it decided the fate of weak nations like Poland and China without their consent. The truth is that some agreements were secret because they contained military information

The three Allied leaders—Winston Churchill, Franklin D. Roosevelt, and Josef Stalin—met at Yalta in February 1945. Having been president for twelve years, Roosevelt showed signs of age and fatigue. Franklin D. Roosevelt Library.

that had to be kept from the still undefeated Japanese and Germans. But the criticism that the Allies paid scant attention to small nations was well deserved. It exposed a general pattern of wartime diplomacy, which assumed that the most powerful of the Allies would dominate international relations after the war.

Each of the Allies entered into the conference with definite goals. Britain sought a place for France in occupied Germany; a curb on Soviet influence in Poland; and protection for the vulnerable British Empire. Russia **Allied Goals at Yalta** wanted reparations from Germany, to assist in the massive task of rebuilding at home; possessions in Asia; continued influence in Poland; and a permanently weakened Germany, so that Russia would never again suffer a German attack. The United States lobbied for the United Nations Organization, where it believed it could exercise influence; for a Soviet declaration of war against Japan; for recognition of China as a major power; and for compromise between rival factions in Poland.

Military positions at the time of the conference helped to shape the final agreements. Soviet troops had occupied much of Eastern Europe, including Poland, while the Western Allies were emerging from the Battle of the Bulge. In Asia the Japanese were still resisting the American advance. Millions of Japanese troops in China, Manchuria, Korea, and the home islands seemed ready to die to the last man for the empire. As near as victory was, Britain and the United States still needed the Soviets to win the war.

The unsettled issue of Poland preoccupied the conferees. Stalin repeatedly pointed out that twice in the century German armies had marched through Poland into Russian territory, killing millions. He insisted on a government friendly to Moscow—the Lublin regime—in order to prevent another German onslaught. And he demanded boundaries that would give Poland part of Germany in the west and Russia part of Poland in the east. Churchill boiled over in protest; he wanted the London regime to return to Poland. A compromise was reached under Roosevelt's leadership: a boundary favorable to Russia in the east; postponement of the western boundary issue; and the creation of a "more broadly based" coalition government that would include members of the London government-in-exile. Free elections would be held sometime in the future. The agreement was vague, but given Soviet occupation of Poland, Roosevelt considered it "the best I can do."

As for Germany, the Big Three agreed that it would be divided into four zones, the fourth to go to France. On the question of reparations, Russia wanted a precise figure, but Churchill and Roosevelt said they would first have to determine Germany's ability to pay. Without the British, the Americans and Russians agreed that an Allied committee would consider the sum of $20 billion as a basis for discussion in the future, with half the amount to go to the Soviet Union.

Other issues found trade-offs. Stalin promised to declare war on Japan two or three months after Hitler's defeat. Since the atomic bomb was still on the drawing boards, American military leaders applauded the commitment. The Soviet premier also consented to sign a treaty of friendship and alliance with Jiang Jieshi (Chiang Kai-shek), America's ally in China, rather than with the Communist Mao Zedong. In return the United States agreed to Russia's taking the southern part of Sakhalin Island and Lüshun (Port Arthur). To the Russians these concessions amounted to a recovery of holdings lost after the Russo-Japanese War in 1905. Regarding the new world organization, Roosevelt and Churchill granted the Soviets three votes in the General Assembly. (Fifty nations officially launched the United Nations Organization in May.) Finally, the conferees accepted the Declaration of Liberated Europe, pledging to establish order and to rebuild economies by democratic methods.

Yalta marked the high point of the Grand Alliance; each of the Allies came away with something, in the tradition of diplomatic give-and-take. But as the great powers jockeyed for influence at the close of the war, neither the spirit nor the letter of Yalta held firm.

Potsdam Conference

The crumbling of the alliance became evident at the Potsdam Conference, which took place between July 17 and August 2, 1945. Roosevelt had died in April, and Harry S Truman had replaced him. Truman was a novice at international diplomacy and less patient with the Russians. Stalin "seems to like it when I hit him with a hammer," he bragged in a letter to his beloved wife Bess. "We had a tough meeting," he also wrote. "I reared up on my hind legs and told 'em where to get off and they got off." Truman seemed especially emboldened after he learned during the conference that the atomic test in New Mexico was successful. "Now I know what happened to Truman," said Churchill. "When he got to the meeting after having read this report he was a changed man. He told the Russians just where they got off and generally bossed the whole meeting."

Despite the "brawl" at Potsdam, as Truman called it, the Big Three did agree on general policies toward Germany: complete disarmament; elimination of industry used for military production; and dissolution of Nazi institutions and laws. In a compromise over reparations, they decided that each occupying nation should take reparations from its own zone; but they could not agree on a total figure. To resolve other issues, such as peace treaties with Italy, Finland, and Hungary, the Big Three created the Council of Foreign Ministers.

Potsdam left much undone. As the war drew to a close, there was little that bound the Allies together. Roosevelt's cooperative style was gone; the spirit of Yalta was evaporating; the common enemy, Hitler, was defeated. And America, with the awesome atomic bomb in the offing to force defeat upon Japan, no longer needed, or even wanted, Russia in the Pacific war. Moreover, the victors were seeking to preserve and enlarge their spheres of influence. The British claimed authority in Greece and parts of the Middle East; the Russians already dominated much of Eastern Europe; and Americans continued their hegemony in Latin America. The United States also seized several Pacific islands as strategic outposts and laid

IMPORTANT EVENTS

1941	Japan attacks Pearl Harbor; U.S. enters Second World War
1942	National War Labor Board established
	War Production Board established
	Internment of 110,000 Japanese-Americans in "relocation camps"
	War Manpower Commission established
	Bataan Death March
	Battles of Coral Sea and Midway
	Office of War Information established
	Manhattan Project established
	Allied invasion of North Africa
	Republican gains in Congress
	Synthetic-rubber program begins
1943	Russian victory at Stalingrad
	Strikes by soft-coal and anthracite miners
	Office of War Mobilization established
	War Labor Disputes (Smith-Connally) Act
	Race riots in Detroit, Harlem, and 45 other cities

Allied invasion of Italy
Teheran Conference

1944	Roosevelt requests Economic Bill of Rights
	War Refugee Board established
	Supreme Court upholds Japanese-American internment
	GI Bill of Rights
	Normandy landings (D-Day)
	Dumbarton Oaks Conference
	Roosevelt re-elected
	U.S. retakes Philippines
1945	Yalta Conference
	Battles of Iwo Jima and Okinawa
	Roosevelt dies; Truman assumes presidency
	United Nations founded
	Germany surrenders
	Potsdam Conference
	First atomic bomb exploded in test at Alamogordo, New Mexico
	Atomic bombs devastate Hiroshima and Nagasaki
	Japan surrenders

plans to dominate a defeated Japan. Let the Americans have their Pacific bases, responded Churchill, "but 'Hands off the British Empire' is our maxim." Furthermore, American interests increased their stake in Middle Eastern oil during the war. By 1944 American petroleum companies controlled 42 percent of the proved oil reserves of the Middle East—a nineteenfold increase since 1936. Both the British and Russians complained about this new evidence of American expansionism.

Hitler once said, "We may be destroyed, but if we are, we shall drag a world with us—a world in flames." Indeed, *rubble* became the word most commonly invoked to describe the global landscape at the end of the war. Hamburg, Stuttgart, and Dresden had been laid waste; three-quarters of Berlin was in ruins. In England, Coventry and parts of London were bombed out. Across the continent transportation systems had been disrupted and water supplies contaminated. Everywhere ghostlike people wandered about searching desperately for food, and mourning those who would never come home. Russia had lost 20 million people; Poland 5.8 million; Germany 4.5 million. In all, about 35 million Europeans died as a result of the war. In Asia untold millions of Chinese and 2 million Japanese died.

Only one major combatant escaped these grisly statistics: the United States. Its cities were not burned and its fields were not trampled. American deaths

Postwar Supremacy of the United States

from the war—about 400,000—were few compared with the losses of other nations. In fact, Americans came out of the Second World War more powerful than they had gone in. They alone had the atomic bomb. The American air force and navy were the largest anywhere. And though the United States demobilized the major part of its regular army after the war, it still had 2 million men in arms in 1946, 1.6 million in 1949. What is more, only the United States had the capital and economic resources to spur international recovery. America was, gloated Truman, a "giant." In the coming struggle to fashion a new world out of the ashes of the old, soon called the Cold War (see Chapter 29), the United States held a commanding position.

Events at home and abroad during the Second World War had transformed the United States. For many Americans in 1945, life was fundamentally different from what it had been before Pearl Harbor. The Academy Award–winning film for 1946 was *The Best Years of Our Lives,* the painful story of the postwar readjustments of three veterans and their families and friends. Not only veterans' lives had been changed by the experiences of war; with the advent of the Cold War, millions of younger men would be inducted into the armed forces over the next thirty years. War and the expectation of war would become part of American life.

Though the gains made during the war by blacks and women were overdue, other changes were less welcome. The war had stimulated the trend toward bigness in business, labor, and government. In the next few years, government agencies that had been conceived as temporary would become permanent and would grow in size and influence. The results are well known—a Department of Defense (consolidating the War and Navy Departments), the Central Intelligence Agency (succeeding the Office of Strategic Services), the Atomic Energy Commission. The seeds of the military-industrial complex were sown in these years. For better or worse—and clearly there were elements of both—the Second World War was a turning point in the nation's history.

SUGGESTIONS FOR FURTHER READING

Fighting the War

Stephen A. Ambrose, *Eisenhower,* vol. 1 (1983); Stephen A. Ambrose, *The Supreme Commander* (1970); Hanson Baldwin, *Battles Lost and Won* (1966); A. Russell Buchanan, *The United States in World War II,* 2 vols. (1964); Peter Calvocoressi and Guy Wint, *Total War* (1972); R. Ernest Dupuy, *World War II* (1969); Dwight D. Eisenhower, *Crusade in Europe* (1948); Kent R. Greenfield, *American Strategy in World War II* (1963); B. H. Liddell Hart, *History of the Second World War* (1970); Max Hastings, *OVERLORD: D-Day and the Battle of Normandy* (1984); Clayton D. James, *The Years of MacArthur, 1941–1945* (1975); David Kahn, *The Codebreakers* (1967); Richard M. Leighton and Robert W. Coakley, *Global Logistics and Strategy, 1940–1945,* 2 vols. (1955–1968); Douglas MacArthur, *Reminiscences* (1964); Samuel Eliot Morison, *The Two-Ocean War* (1963); Samuel Eliot Morison, *Strategy and Compromise* (1958); Forrest C. Pogue, *George C. Marshall,* 3 vols. (1963–1973); Bradley F. Smith, *The Shadow Warriors: O.S.S. and the Origins of the C.I.A.* (1983); R. Harris Smith, *OSS* (1972); Ronald H. Spector, *Fighting Against the Sun: The American War with Japan* (1984); Russell F. Weigley, *The American Way of War* (1973); Gordon Wright, *The Ordeal of Total War, 1939–1945* (1968).

Diplomatic Issues

Robert Beitzell, *The Uneasy Alliance* (1972); James MacGregor Burns, *Roosevelt: The Soldier of Freedom* (1970); Thomas Campbell, *Masquerade Peace: America's UN Policy, 1944–1945* (1973); Winston S. Churchill, *The Second World War,* 6 vols. (1948–1953); Diane Clemens, *Yalta* (1970); Robert Dallek, *Franklin D. Roosevelt and American Foreign Policy, 1932–1945* (1979); Robert A. Divine, *Roosevelt and World War II* (1969); Robert A. Divine, *Second Chance: The Triumph of Internationalism in America During World War II* (1967); Henry L. Feingold, *Politics of Rescue* (1970); Herbert Feis, *Churchill, Roosevelt, and Stalin* (1957); George C. Herring, *Aid to Russia, 1941–1946* (1973); Akira Iriye, *Power and Culture: The Japanese-American War, 1941–1945* (1981); Gabriel Kolko, *The Politics of War* (1968); William R. Louis, *Imperialism at Bay: The United States and the Decolonization of the British Empire* (1978); William H. McNeill, *America, Britain, and Russia* (1953); Vojtech

Mastny, *Russia's Road to the Cold War* (1979); Arthur D. Morse, *While Six Million Died* (1968); Gaddis Smith, *Diplomacy During the Second World War, 1941–1945*, 2nd ed. (1985); Michael Stoff, *Oil, War, and American Security* (1980); Mark Stoler, *The Politics of the Second Front* (1977); Christopher Thorne, *Allies of a Kind* (1977); David S. Wyman, *The Abandonment of the Jews: America and the Holocaust, 1941–1945* (1984).

The Home Front

John Morton Blum, *V Was for Victory: Politics and American Culture During World War II* (1976); Alan Clive, *State of War: Michigan in World War II* (1979); Philip J. Funigiello, *The Challenge to Urban Liberalism: Federal-City Relations During World War II* (1978); Jack Goodman, ed., *While You Were Gone: A Report on Wartime Life in the United States* (1946); Mark Jonathan Harris et al., *The Homefront* (1984); John W. Jeffries, *Testing the Roosevelt Coalition: Connecticut Society and Politics in the Era of World War II* (1979); Richard R. Lingeman, *Don't You Know There's a War On? The American Home Front, 1941–1945* (1970); Francis E. Merrill, *Social Problems on the Home Front: A Study of War-time Influences* (1948); Geoffrey Perrett, *Days of Sadness, Years of Triumph: The American People 1939–1945* (1973); Richard Polenberg, *War and Society: The United States, 1941–1945* (1972); Studs Terkel, ed., *"The Good War": An Oral History of World War Two* (1984).

Mobilizing for War

John Morton Blum, ed., *From the Morgenthau Diaries: Years of War* (1967); Bureau of the Budget, *The United States at War* (1946); Bruce Catton, *The War Lords of Washington* (1948); George Q. Flynn, *The Mess in Washington: Manpower Mobilization in World War II* (1979); Eliot Janeway, *The Struggle for Survival* (1951); Paul A. C. Koistinen, *The Hammer and the Sword: Labor, the Military, and Industrial Mobilization, 1920–1945* (1979); Donald Nelson, *Arsenal of Democracy* (1946); Smaller War Plants Corporation, *Economic Concentration and World War II* (1946); William M. Tuttle, Jr., "The Birth of an Industry: The Synthetic Rubber 'Mess' in World War II," *Technology and Culture*, 22 (1981), 35–67; Gerald T. White, *Billions for Defense: Government Finance by the Defense Plant Corporation During World War II* (1980); Allen M. Winkler, *The Politics of Propaganda: The Office of War Information, 1942–1945* (1978).

Farmers and Workers, Soldiers and Sailors

John L. Blackman, Jr., *Presidential Seizure in Labor Disputes* (1967); Melvyn Dubofsky and Warren H. Van Tine, *John*

L. Lewis: A Biography (1977); Nelson Lichtenstein, *Labor's War at Home: The CIO in World War II* (1983); Bill Mauldin, *Up Front* (1968 ed.); Davis R. B. Ross, *Preparing for Ulysses: Politics and Veterans During World War II* (1969); Joel Seidman, *American Labor from Defense to Reconversion* (1953); Samuel A. Stouffer et al., *The American Soldier*, 2 vols. (1949); Walter W. Wilcox, *The Farmer in the Second World War* (1947).

Japanese-American Internment

Commission on Wartime Relocation and Internment of Civilians, *Personal Justice Denied* (1982); Roger Daniels, *Concentration Camps U.S.A.* (1971); Morton Grodzins, *Americans Betrayed: Politics and the Japanese Evacuation* (1949); Bill Hosokawa, *Nisei: The Quiet Americans* (1969); Peter Irons, *Justice at War: The Story of the Japanese American Internment Cases* (1983); Jacobus tenBroek et al., *Prejudice, War and the Constitution: Causes and Consequences of the Evacuation of the Japanese Americans in World War II* (1954); Michi Weglyn, *Years of Infamy: The Untold Story of America's Concentration Camps* (1976).

Science and Education

James Phinney Baxter, *Scientists Against Time* (1946); Isaac Kandel, *The Impact of War upon American Education* (1948); Daniel J. Kevles, *The Physicists* (1977).

Politics

James C. Foster, *The Union Politic: The CIO Political Action Committee* (1975); Alonzo J. Hamby, "Sixty Million Jobs and the People's Revolution: The Liberals, the New Deal, and World War II," *The Historian*, 30 (1968), 578–598; Maurice Isserman, *Which Side Were You On? The American Communist Party During the Second World War* (1982); Donald R. McCoy, "Republican Opposition in Wartime, 1941–1945," *Mid-America*, 49 (1967), 174–189; Roland Young, *Congressional Politics in the Second World War* (1956).

Afro-Americans and Wartime Violence

A. Russell Buchanan, *Black Americans in World War II* (1977); Dominic J. Capeci, Jr., *Race Relations in Wartime Detroit* (1984); Dominic J. Capeci, Jr., *The Harlem Riot of 1943* (1977); Richard M. Dalfiume, *Desegregation of the U.S. Armed Forces: Fighting on Two Fronts, 1939–1953* (1969); Lee Finkle, *Forum for Protest: The Black Press During World War II* (1975); Phillip McGuire, ed., *Taps for a Jim Crow Army: Letters from Black Soldiers in World War II* (1982); Mauricio Mazon, *The Zoot-Suit Riots* (1984); Harvard Sitkoff, "Racial Militancy and Interracial Violence in the

Second World War," *Journal of American History*, 58 (1971), 661–681; Neil A. Wynn, *The Afro-American and the Second World War* (1976).

Women

Karen T. Anderson, "Last Hired, First Fired: Black Women Workers During World War II," *Journal of American History*, 69 (1982), 82–97; Karen T. Anderson, *Wartime Women: Sex Roles, Family Relations, and the Status of Women During World War II* (1981); M. Joyce Baker, *Images of Women in Film: The War Years, 1941–1945* (1981); William H. Chafe, *The American Woman: Her Changing Social, Economic, and Political Roles, 1920–1970* (1972); Sherna Berger Gluck, "Interlude or Change: Women and the World War II Work Experience," *International Journal of Oral History*, 3 (1982), 92–113; Chester W. Gregory, *Women in Defense Work During World War II: An Analysis of the Labor Problem and Women's Rights* (1974); Susan M. Hartmann, *The Home Front and Beyond: American Women in the 1940s* (1982);

Sally Van Wagenen Keil, *Those Wonderful Women in Their Flying Machines: The Unknown Heroes of World War II* (1979); Ruth Milkman, "Redefining 'Women's Work': The Sexual Division of Labor in the Auto Industry During World War II," *Feminist Studies*, 8 (1982), 337–372; Leila J. Rupp, *Mobilizing Women for War: German and American Propaganda, 1939–1945* (1978).

The Atomic Bomb

Gar Alperovitz, *Atomic Diplomacy* (1965); Barton J. Bernstein, ed., *The Atomic Bomb* (1976); Robert J. C. Butow, *Japan's Decision to Surrender* (1954); Committee for the Compilation of Materials on Damage Caused by the Atomic Bombs in Hiroshima and Nagasaki, *Hiroshima and Nagasaki* (1981); Herbert Feis, *The Atomic Bomb and the End of World War II* (1966); Gregg Herken, *The Winning Weapon* (1981); Richard G. Hewlett and Oscar E. Anderson, *The New World* (1962); Chalmers M. Roberts, *The Nuclear Years* (1970); Martin J. Sherwin, *A World Destroyed* (1975).

THE COLD WAR
AND AMERICAN POLITICS
1945–1953

CHAPTER 29

President Harry S Truman was exhausted on March 13, 1947, as his official plane flew him from Washington to his Florida vacation spot in Key West. "This terrible decision I had to make," he wrote his daughter Margaret that day, "had been over my head for about six weeks." He had known since the Potsdam Conference of 1945 "that there is no difference in totalitarian or police states, call them what you will, Nazi, Fascist, Communist. . . . The attempt of Lenin, Trotsky, Stalin, et al., to fool the world and the American Crackpots Association . . . is just like Hitler's and Mussolini's so-called socialist states. Your Pop had to tell the world just that in polite language."

The day before, in a controversial speech to a joint session of Congress, the president had announced the Truman Doctrine. Without mentioning the Soviet Union by name, he equated its policies with the former "totalitarian regimes" of Germany and Japan. "I believe," he said, "that it must be the policy of the United States to support free peoples who are resisting attempted subjugation by armed minorities or by outside pressures." These words became the backbone of containment, a doctrine that in the coming years would not only lead the United States into armed conflict in Asia, the Middle East, and Latin America but also heighten fears at home that a Communist conspiracy had gained control of the federal government.

The central theme of Truman's presidency was anti-Communism at home and abroad. A week later, on March 21, Truman made another momentous decision. Through an executive order, he announced the Employee Loyalty Program for the executive branch of the government. Henceforth, all agency heads had to ensure that each employee under their jurisdictions was a loyal American. In doubtful cases, the boss had to appoint a loyalty board to hear the evidence and make recommendations. For the first time, government officials had the authority to pass judgment on a job applicant's personal beliefs and past associations. People already on the job who were accused of disloyalty were presumed to be guilty, not innocent. Although some critics argued that Truman's anti-Communist actions were bellicose and a threat to civil liberties and that he shot from the hip, his decisiveness initially won him many followers across the country.

When Franklin D. Roosevelt died in office in April 1945, Truman had acceded to the presidency. Contrary to his later "Give 'em hell, Harry" image, Truman's initial response to this challenge was a deep feeling of inadequacy. "I'm not big enough for this job," he confided to a friend. Even an experienced, well-respected president would have faced an enormous task in guiding the nation's transition from war to peace. But the new president was little more than an obscure politician. "Who is Harry Truman?" Americans asked themselves when they heard the news of Roosevelt's death. As a senator from Missouri, Truman had been a New Deal liberal. He was intelligent, warm, hard-working, and honest, a loving husband and father. But he was also short-tempered, impulsive, headstrong, and quick to call people names ("son of a bitch" was one of his favorites). Neither his virtues nor his defects, however, were well known at the time. People knew Truman mainly from his wartime chairmanship of a special Senate committee on awarding defense contracts. And of course he had received some publicity as his party's vice-presidential nominee in 1944.

Although Roosevelt had chosen Truman as his running mate in 1944, he had left the vice president in the dark about crucial foreign and military policies, even including the development of the atomic bomb. "They didn't tell me anything about what was going on," Truman fretted after a month in the presidency. With the deterioration of Soviet-American relations, however, the new president got a quick education.

In foreign affairs the theme of anti-Communism revealed itself in Cold War policies that protected and expanded American overseas interests, challenged the Soviet Union, created alliance systems, rebuilt Western Europe and Japan, drew the United States into civil wars, and favored a military build-up over diplomacy. The United States emerged from the Second World War the most powerful nation on earth, but the world it faced seemed uninviting to the exercise of that power. Much of Asia and Europe lay in ruins, requiring a huge reconstruction task, and civil wars and colonial rebellions rocked political stability. The United States and the Soviet Union scrambled to win friends and to drive in economic and strategic stakes. The two nations clashed constantly, "like two big dogs chewing on a bone," remarked Senator J. William Fulbright. Truman saw the Soviet threat as global and decided to project American power on a worldwide scale. This new globalism, with the containment doctrine as its guide, brought the United States into crisis after crisis. As Secretary of State Dean Acheson said, the United States was "playing for keeps" in a global contest with the Soviet Union and would go around the world creating "situations of strength."

Just five years after the Second World War, the Cold War turned hot on the peninsula of Korea. Although the threat of world war did not materialize, the Korean conflict significantly accelerated the process toward globalism. The United States began to enlarge its military power and to develop new nuclear weapons.

As in foreign policy, the new president got a crash course in the intricacies of governing the United States. At home in 1945, the nation's reconversion from war to peace was not smooth, and Truman managed to anger liberals, conservatives, farmers, consumers, and union members during his first year as president. In 1946 voters responded to inflation and a wave of strikes by electing a Republican Eightieth Congress. But just two years later, partly because of public approval of his decisive foreign policy, Truman confounded political experts by winning the presidency in his own right. Truman had continued to be loyal to the welfare state fashioned in the 1930s. And his upset victory in 1948 was proof that the New Deal coalition was alive and well.

As Truman's victory indicated, however, Cold War politics were volatile. And the key domestic issues of the period—black civil rights and the anti-Communist witch hunt called McCarthyism—were the most highly charged of all. The outbreak of the Korean War in June 1950 intensified domestic discontent. The military stalemate frustrated war-weary citizens; inflation began another upward climb; and evidence of corruption surfaced in the White House. Truman's popularity plummeted. In 1952 Americans cast their presidential votes for a legitimate hero, General Dwight D. Eisenhower.

THE SOURCES OF THE COLD WAR

After overseeing the defeat of Germany and Japan, President Truman participated in the rapid deterioration of Soviet-American relations—the Cold War. In this new conflict, competitive ideologies, propaganda, reconstruction programs, military alliances, atomic arms development, and spheres of influence condemned the world once again to instability and fear. Some conflict was inevitable after the Second World War, because the international environment was so unsettled. First, the world was in serious economic trouble. Across Europe and Asia, factories, bridges, transportation and communications systems, and houses had been reduced to rubble. Agricultural production was low, and displaced persons wandered around in search of food and family members. How would this devastated world be pieced back together? America and Russia each offered a different model. Second, the collapse of Germany and Japan created power vacuums that drew the two major powers into collision as they sought to claim influence in countries where the Axis had once held sway. Third, political turmoil within nations spurred Soviet-American competition. In Greece and China, for example, where civil wars were waged between leftists and conservative regimes, the two powers favored different sides. Fourth, empires were disintegrating. In this process of decolonization, the European imperial nations were forced to withdraw by nationalist rebels and by their own financial constraints. New nations were born in the Middle East and Asia, and America and Russia competed to win them as friends who might provide military bases, resources, and markets. Finally, conflict seemed inevitable because of the shrinkage of the globe. That is, because of the triumph of the airplane and the advent of the "air age," the world became more compact. Nations were brought closer together by faster travel; at the same time, they became more vulnerable to surprise attack from the air. The Americans and Soviets once again collided

Unsettled International Environment

People and governments in the postwar period faced the awesome job of rebuilding. Berlin, which had been reduced to rubble, was an example.   National Archives.

as they strove to establish defensive positions, sometimes far from home.

Conflict may have been inevitable because of these international conditions, but the Cold War may not have been. That is, the national policies of the United States and the Soviet Union and their leaders' conduct of diplomacy exacerbated rather than resolved postwar issues. Both nations marched into this new Cold War with a sense of righteousness that gave the contest an almost religious character. Each country saw the other as the world's bully. If Americans feared "communist aggression," Russians feared "capitalist encirclement." In mirror image, each side saw the other as the obstacle to peace.

"We are in this thing all over the world to the extent few people realize," Secretary of State James F. Byrnes (1945–1947) told Truman's cabinet. Why were Americans "all over the world"? For one reason, they had determined never to repeat the experience of the 1930s. They vowed no more depressions that would spawn political extremism and in turn produce war; no more Munichs, no more appeasement. It seemed to Americans in the 1940s that Nazi Germany had merely been replaced by Soviet Russia, that communism was simply the flip side of the totalitarian

coin. The popular term "Red fascism" captured this sentiment.

American officials also knew that the nation's economic well-being depended on an activist foreign policy. In the postwar years the United States was the largest supplier of goods to world markets: in 1947 its exports amounted to $14 billion. That trade was jeopardized by the postwar economic paralysis of Europe, traditionally America's major customer, and by discriminatory trade practices that violated the Open Door doctrine. "Any serious failure to maintain this flow," declared an assistant secretary of state, "would put millions of American businessmen, farmers, and workers out of business." Indeed, exports constituted about 10 percent of the gross national product; the automobile, steel, and machine-tool industries, among others, relied heavily on foreign trade. About half of America's wheat was shipped abroad, and surpluses of cotton and tobacco also required foreign outlets. Finally, the United States needed to export in order to pay for imports such as zinc, tin, and manganese. Economic expansionism, so much a part of pre–Cold War history, thus remained a central feature of postwar foreign relations.

New strategic theory also propelled the United

States toward an activist, expansionist, globalist diplomacy. "As top dog, America becomes target

American Strategic Thinking

No. 1," warned Air Force General Carl Spaatz. To be ready for a military challenge in the postwar air age, American strategists believed that the nation's defenses had to begin far beyond its own borders. Thus the United States felt compelled to acquire overseas bases to guard the approaches to the Western Hemisphere. Overseas bases would also permit the United States to launch offensive attacks with might and speed. When asked where the American navy would float, Navy Secretary James Forrestal declared: "Wherever there is a sea."

President Truman, who shared these assumptions, had a personality that tended to increase international tensions. Whereas Franklin D. Roosevelt had been ingratiating, patient, and evasive, Truman was brash, impatient, and direct. He seldom displayed the appreciation of subtleties so essential to successful diplomacy; for him issues were sketched in black and white, not shades of gray. As a friendly Winston Churchill said of him, Truman "takes no notice of delicate ground, he just plants his foot firmly on it."

Shortly after Roosevelt's death, Truman met Soviet Commissar of Foreign Affairs V. M. Molotov at the White House. The president sharply berated Russia for violating the Yalta accords, a charge Molotov denied. When Truman shot back that the Soviets should honor their agreements, Molotov stormed out of the room. The president was pleased with his "tough method": "I gave it to him straight 'one-two to the jaw.' " But the Yalta agreements were vague; although Soviet actions in Poland had been heavy-handed, whether they were in violation of the agreements was a matter of interpretation. Nonetheless, Truman's simplistic display of toughness would become a trademark of American Cold War diplomacy.

As for the Soviets, they were not easy to get along with either. Dean Acheson, a high-ranking diplomat from 1945 to 1947 and secretary of state from 1949 to 1953, found them rude and abu-

American Anti-Soviet Views

sive. This conservative graduate of Yale and Harvard Law School could, he said, talk with "everybody who was housebroken." The Russians, he asserted, were not: "I think it is a mistake to believe that you can, at any time, sit down with the Russians and solve problems." Indeed, Premier Josef Stalin's blunt *nyets* stung American ears. But more than Soviet style bothered Americans. Soviet territorial ambitions—and successes—included a portion of eastern Poland, the Baltic states of Lithuania, Latvia, and Estonia, and parts of Finland and Rumania. In Eastern Europe Russian officials began to suppress non-Communists.

For their part, the Russians remembered how the hostile West had attempted to ostracize them before: "We were always outsiders," complained one Soviet diplomat. Driven by memories of the past, by fear of a revived Germany, by the huge task of reconstruction, and by Marxist-Leninist doctrine, the Soviets suspected capitalist nations of plotting once again to extinguish the Communist flame. They protested that the Americans were surrounding them with hostile bases and practicing atomic and dollar diplomacy.

"After World War II," Senator J. William Fulbright remembered, "we were sold on the idea that Stalin was out to dominate the world." This view pitted a generous United States ready to rebuild a peaceful world against a selfish, uncooperative Soviet Union; Americans were forced to react defensively against expansionist Russians. But Fulbright came to believe that the Soviets probably never intended to dominate the world and they certainly lacked the capability to do so. Russia emerged from the war with a weak military establishment, a hobbled economy, and obsolete technology. Knowing this, American leaders did not expect the Soviets to attack Western Europe or to start a war they obviously could not sustain. The Soviet Union was a regional power in Eastern Europe, but not a global menace.

American officials nonetheless exaggerated the Soviet threat. There are several reasons why, and they sum up the American global perspective in the early

Question of the Soviet Threat

Cold War. First, President Truman liked things in black and white, as his aide Clark Clifford remarked. Nuances, ambiguities, and counterevidence were often glossed over to satisfy Truman's penchant for the simple answer. Second, military officers often overplayed the Soviet threat to persuade Congress to pass larger defense budgets. Third, some Americans fixed their attention, as they had since the Bolshevik Revolution of 1917, on the utopian communist goal of world revolution rather than on actual Soviet behavior, which was limited largely to regions along the Russian border and to bombastic rhetoric. Fourth, American leaders feared that the terrible postwar conditions of poverty and social unrest abroad would leave United States strategic and economic interests vulnerable to political disorders which the Soviets might exploit. In other words, Americans feared less a direct Soviet attack and more the Soviets' potential seizing of opportunities to challenge American interests, perhaps through subversion. Last and overall, the United States, flushed with its own strength, took advantage of the postwar power vacuum to expand its overseas interests and shape a peace on American terms. The American pursuit of nuclear superiority, outlying bases, raw materials and markets, supremacy in Latin America, control of the Atlantic and Pacific Oceans, and air transit rights across other nations aroused a growing number of opponents, in particular the Soviet Union. Americans overreacted to the criticism, unable to understand it except as further evidence of wicked Soviet obstructionism on a worldwide scale. George F. Kennan, one of the chief architects of Cold War policy, later regretted that Americans had created the image of the Soviet Union as "the totally inhuman and malevolent adversary," because this distorted view contributed to the American abandonment of diplomacy during the rash of crises that bedeviled the global community.

COLD WAR CRISES AND THE CONTAINMENT DOCTRINE

One of the first Soviet-American clashes came in Poland in 1945, when the Russians refused to admit conservative Poles from London to the Communist government in Lublin, as agreed at Yalta.

Soviet Domination of Eastern Europe

A visit to Stalin by former Roosevelt aide Harry Hopkins in May of that year brought about some broadening of the Lublin regime, but did not change Poland's status as a subser-vient, Soviet-directed state where the Communists could not claim majority support. The Russians also snuffed out civil liberties in the former Nazi satellite of Rumania. Though they allowed free elections to be held in Hungary and Czechoslovakia, as the Cold War progressed and they came to fear American power more and more, they encouraged Communist coups. First Hungary (1947) and then Czechoslovakia (1948) succumbed to Soviet subversion. Yugoslavia was a unique case: its independent Communist government, led by Josip Broz Tito, successfully broke with Stalin in 1948.

To justify their actions the Soviets complained that the United States was reviving Russia's traditional enemy, Germany. Citing radio broadcasts that encouraged resistance, clandestine meetings with anti-Soviet groups, repeated calls for elections, and the extension or withholding of loans to gain political influence ("dollar diplomacy"), the Soviets protested that the United States was meddling in Eastern Europe. Russia also charged that the United States was pursuing a double standard in intervening in the affairs of Eastern Europe but expecting Russia to stay out of Latin America and Asia. They pointed to the lack of free elections in United States–backed Latin American dictatorships. Americans insisted that their spheres of influence were far more open, their methods far less repressive than the Russians'. But protest as Washington did, it was unable to roll back Soviet influence in Eastern Europe.

Atomic Diplomacy

Another issue that divided America and Russia was the atomic bomb. The Soviets believed that the Americans were practicing "atomic diplomacy"— maintaining a frightening nuclear monopoly and bragging about it to scare the Soviets into diplomatic concessions. At a stormy foreign ministers' conference in London in fall 1945, Soviet Commissar of Foreign Affairs V. M. Molotov asked Secretary of State James F. Byrnes if he had an atomic bomb in his side pocket. Byrnes replied that southerners "carry our artillery in our hip pocket. If you don't cut out all this stalling and let us get down to work, I am going to pull an atomic bomb out of my hip pocket and let you have it." Retiring Secretary of War Henry L. Stimson was one among the few who opposed the use of the bomb as a diplomatic lever. As he told the president in September 1945,

A Soviet tank in Gdansk, Poland, April 1945. After driving the Germans from Poland, the Red Army stayed on to ensure the power of the Communist regime in that war-weary nation. Sovfoto.

if Americans continued to have "this weapon rather ostentatiously on our hip, their [the Russians'] suspicions and their distrust of our purposes and motives will increase."

In this atmosphere of suspicion and distrust, the United States and the Soviet Union could not agree on the international control of atomic energy. The American proposal, called the Baruch Plan, provided for America's abandoning its monopoly after the world's fissionable materials had been brought under the authority of an international agency. The Soviets retorted that this plan denied them the right to develop their own bomb while the United States continued its supremacy. Secretary of Commerce Henry A. Wallace understood why Moscow rejected the Baruch Plan: "We are telling the Russians that if they are 'good boys' we may eventually turn over our knowledge of atomic energy. . . ."

The two adversaries also collided in Iran. By wartime agreement, British, American, and Russian troops occupied Iran. The Russians had some influence in

the north, near the Russian-Iranian border, and the British dominated the country's rich **Crisis in Iran** oil industry. When American petroleum companies asked the Iranian government for an oil concession, Moscow sniffed a capitalist plot on its border. In March 1946, the date agreed on for troop withdrawal, the Russians stayed on in violation of the wartime treaty. Americans angrily accused the U.S.S.R. of intending to take over Iran. The Russians countered that American military advisers remained in Iran, and that British oil interests ensured Anglo-American political influence in the Teheran government. When the American-dominated United Nations investigated only Soviet actions in Iran, Moscow ordered its delegation to boycott the international body.

Still, Iranian and Soviet diplomats managed to negotiate a settlement in April: Soviet soldiers would leave Iran in exchange for an oil concession. Americans claimed a Cold War victory, believing their tough words had forced the Soviets to withdraw. (In

1947 they turned the tables by persuading the Iranians to go back on their promise of a Russian oil concession. Moscow cried that it had been double-crossed.)

Soviets and Americans clashed on every front in 1946. They could not agree on the unification of Germany, so they built up their zones independently. The new World Bank and International Monetary Fund, created at the 1944 Bretton Woods Conference to stabilize trade and finance, also became tangled in the Cold War struggle. The Soviets refused to join because the United States so dominated both institutions. In early 1946 Washington extended a $3.5 billion loan to Great Britain but turned down a similar Soviet request. Already smarting from an abrupt cutoff of Lend-Lease aid in mid-1945, the Soviets denounced the United States for using its reconstruction dollars in order to manipulate foreign governments.

When in early February 1946 Stalin gave a pre-election speech depicting a world threatened by capitalist acquisitiveness, the American chargé d'affaires in Moscow, George F. Kennan, concluded that Russian fanaticism made even a temporary understanding impossible. Kennan's pessimistic "long telegram" to Washington fed the growing belief that only toughness would work with the Russians. On March 5, Winston Churchill made his stirring Iron Curtain speech, warning that Eastern European countries were being cut off from the West by Russia. With the approving Truman sitting on the stage, the former prime minister called for an Anglo-American partnership to resist the Russian menace. Stalin protested that "Russia was not attacking, she was being attacked."

Secretary of Commerce Henry A. Wallace, a critic of Truman's get-tough policy, feared the United States was substituting atomic and economic coercion for diplomacy. " 'Getting tough,' " he told a Madison Square Garden audience in September 1946, "never brought anything real and lasting—whether for schoolyard bullies or businessmen or world powers. The tougher we get, the tougher the Russians will get." Truman fired Wallace from the cabinet, blasting him privately as "a real Commy and a dangerous man." The president crowed that he had now "run the crackpots out of the Democratic Party."

The Cold War escalated further on March 12, 1947, when in response to a request from the British, who could no longer afford to fund their Greek client government, the president asked Congress for $400 million in aid to Greece and Turkey, both of which were threatened by economic dislocation and Communist political pressure. To repeat Truman's famous words: "It must be the policy of the United States to support free peoples who are resisting attempted subjugation by armed minorities or by outside pressures." It was time to draw the line, to contain the Communist menace. The president's statement quickly became known as the Truman Doctrine. Critics correctly pointed out that there was no evidence that the Soviet Union was involved in the civil war in Greece; that the rebel National Liberation Front had good reason to resent the repressive and corrupt regime supported by the British; and that the resistance movement included non-Communists as well as Communists. Others suggested that aid should be channeled through the United Nations. But after much debate the Senate approved Truman's request 67 to 23. Using American dollars and military advisers, the Greek government defeated the insurgents in 1949.

Truman Doctrine

In July 1947 George F. Kennan, now director of the State Department's policy planning staff, offered another statement of what became known as the containment doctrine. Writing under the name "Mr. X" in the magazine *Foreign Affairs*, this expert on Soviet affairs advocated a "policy of firm containment, designed to confront the Russians with unalterable counterforce at every point where they show signs of encroaching upon the interests of a peaceful and stable world." Such a counterforce, Kennan argued, would check Soviet expansion and eventually foster a "mellowing" of Soviet behavior. Together with the Truman Doctrine, Kennan's article became the chief manifesto of Cold War foreign policy.

The highly regarded journalist Walter Lippmann was critical of the containment doctrine. In *The Cold War* (1947), Lippmann called containment a "strategic monstrosity" that did not distinguish between areas vital and peripheral to American security. If American leaders thought every place on earth was of strategic importance, he reasoned, the nation's patience and resources would soon be drained. Nor did Lippmann share Truman's view that Russia was

Debate over Containment

plotting to take over the world. Truman, he asserted, put too little emphasis on diplomacy.

Lippmann was happier with the Marshall Plan for the reconstruction of Western Europe. In 1946 and 1947 an unusually harsh winter swept over Europe. Coal supplies dwindled; meager food stores were exhausted. European nations, still reeling from the war, lacked the dollars to buy American goods. Especially in France and Italy, leftists and Communists gained in political influence. Americans, who had already spent billions of dollars on European relief and recovery by 1947, recalled the troubles of the 1930s: global depression; political extremism; war born of economic discontent. It could not be allowed to happen again. Western Europe, Dean Acheson emphasized, was the "keystone in the arch which supports the kind of a world which we have to have in order to conduct our lives."

On June 5, 1947, Secretary of State George C. Marshall (1947–1949) announced that the United States would finance a massive European recovery program. Though Marshall did not exclude Eastern Europe or the Soviet Union, few American leaders believed that Russia and its allies would want to join an American-dominated project. And indeed, they did not join. Launched in 1948, the Marshall Plan sent $12.4 billion (or 1.2 percent of the United States gross national product) to Western Europe before the program ended in late 1951 (see map, page 828). To stimulate business at home, the legislation provided that the foreign aid dollars must be spent in the United States. The Marshall Plan was a mixed success. In Europe, it caused inflation, failed to solve a serious balance-of-payments problem, and took only tentative steps toward economic integration. But it also sparked impressive Western European industrial production and investment and started the region toward self-sustaining economic growth. By 1952 the recovery program had given way to military assistance. From the beginning the Soviets blasted the Marshall Plan as the enslavement of Europe. They created a special propaganda agency—the Cominform—to harangue against it and the feeble Molotov Plan for Eastern Europe to imitate it.

To strengthen the nation's defenses, Truman worked with Congress to streamline the government's administrative structure under the National Security

Marshall Plan

At Edgewater, New Jersey, in 1949, Ford trucks are being loaded for a shipment to Israel. As America's trade with its allies boomed, so too did business profits at home. Some of the United States's foreign-aid packages required the receiving countries to buy only American goods with the money. National Archives.

Act (July 1947). The act created the Department of Defense, the National Security Council (NSC) to advise the president, and the Central Intelligence Agency (CIA) to conduct spying and information gathering. By the early 1950s the CIA had expanded its functions to include covert (secret) operations aimed at overthrowing unfriendly foreign leaders and, as a high-ranking American official put it, stirring up economic trouble in "the camp of the enemy" through a "Department of Dirty Tricks." In 1953 the United States Information Agency was created to counter Soviet propaganda.

American officials also reached out to find new foreign friends and build new bases. In 1946, when the United States granted the Philippines independence, it maintained its old military, economic, and political ties. And in 1947 American diplomats created

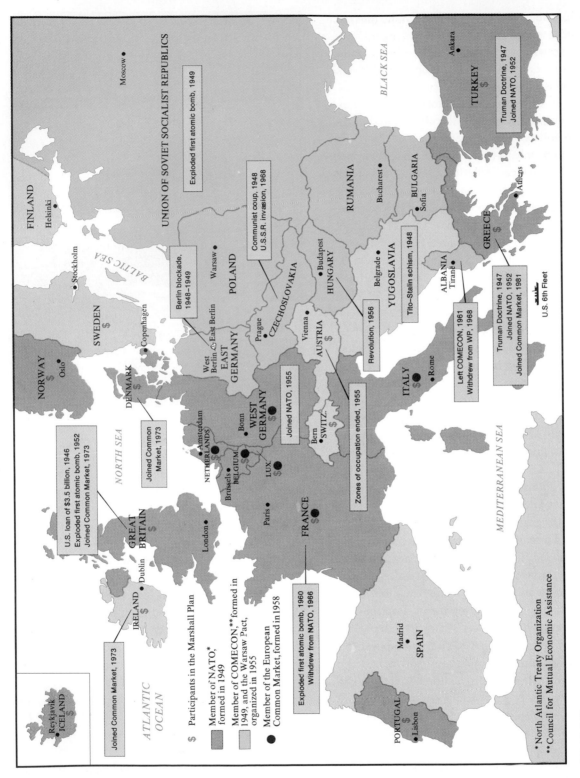

Divided Europe

ATLANTIC OCEAN

Reykjavik •
ICELAND
$
Joined Common Market, 1973

Joined Common Market, 1973

IRELAND
$
Dublin •

GREAT BRITAIN
$
London •

U.S. loan of $3.5 billion, 1946
Exploded first atomic bomb, 1952
Joined Common Market, 1973

NORTH SEA

NORWAY
$
Oslo •

SWEDEN
$
Stockholm •

BALTIC SEA

FINLAND
Helsinki •

DENMARK
$
Copenhagen •

Joined Common Market, 1973

NETHERLANDS
Amsterdam •

Brussels •
BELGIUM
$
LUX.
$

Bonn •
WEST GERMANY
$

Joined NATO, 1955

Paris •
FRANCE
$

Exploded first atomic bomb, 1960
Withdrew from NATO, 1966

SPAIN
Madrid •

PORTUGAL
$
Lisbon •

West Berlin / East Berlin
EAST GERMANY

Berlin blockade, 1948–1949

Prague •
CZECHOSLOVAKIA

POLAND
Warsaw •

Communist coup, 1948
U.S.S.R. invasion, 1968

UNION OF SOVIET SOCIALIST REPUBLICS

Moscow •

Exploded first atomic bomb, 1949

Vienna •
AUSTRIA
$

Budapest •
HUNGARY

Revolution, 1956

Zones of occupation ended, 1955

Bern •
SWITZ.
$

ITALY
$
Rome •

Belgrade •
YUGOSLAVIA

Tito–Stalin schism, 1948

RUMANIA
Bucharest •

BULGARIA
Sofia •

ALBANIA
Tiranë •

Left COMECON, 1961
Withdrew from WP, 1968

GREECE
$

BLACK SEA

TURKEY
Ankara •

Truman Doctrine, 1947
Joined NATO, 1952

Athens •

Truman Doctrine, 1947
Joined NATO, 1952
Joined Common Market, 1981

MEDITERRANEAN SEA

U.S. 6th Fleet

$ Participants in the Marshall Plan

Member of NATO,* formed in 1949

Member of COMECON,** formed in 1949, and the Warsaw Pact, organized in 1955

● Member of the European Common Market, formed in 1958

*North Atlantic Treaty Organization
**Council for Mutual Economic Assistance

the Rio Pact—a military alliance with Latin American countries. To enforce the Rio Pact, the United States helped found the Organization of American States (OAS) the following year. Under this and other agreements the Truman administration sent several military advisory missions to Latin America, and others to Greece, Turkey, Iran, China, and Saudi Arabia. In 1948 Americans activated an air base in Libya. And in May of that year Truman quickly recognized the new state of Israel, which had been carved out of the British-held territory of Palestine after years of Arab-Jewish dispute. America's perceived need for international allies joined the president's desire for Jewish-American votes in the upcoming election to hurry the decision.

One of the most electric moments in the Cold War came a month later. In June 1948 the Russians cut off Western access to the jointly occupied city

Berlin Blockade and Airlift

of Berlin, located well inside the Soviet zone of Germany. Before the Soviets' bold move, the Americans, French, and British had agreed to fuse their zones into what became known as West Germany. The three allies planned to integrate West Germany, including the three Western sectors of Berlin, into the Western European economy, complete with a reformed German currency. The Soviets, fearing a resurgent Germany tied to the American Cold War camp, may have sparked the Berlin crisis to stimulate negotiations. But if they thought Truman would compromise, they guessed wrong. Instead the president ordered a massive airlift of food, fuel, and other supplies to the isolated city— a plane almost every minute. Finally, in May 1949, their image badly damaged, the Soviets lifted the blockade. They had spurred the very result they feared: the creation of the Federal Republic of Germany (West Germany) that month. In retaliation they founded the People's Republic of Germany (East Germany).

On April 4, 1949, believing that a military shield should be added to the economic shield of the Marshall Plan, the United States, Canada, and much of Western

Creation of NATO

Europe founded the North Atlantic Treaty Organization (NATO). The treaty aroused considerable debate at home, for not since 1778 had the United States entered a formal European military

alliance. Senator Robert A. Taft protested that NATO would provoke an arms race with Russia or cause American soldiers to be stationed in Europe. Others complained that the scheme gave the president power to send troops into combat without a congressional declaration of war, and that it would cost too much, ultimately weakening the nation. Truman responded that NATO would give Europeans the will to resist, the confidence to thwart Communism in their midst. And it would function as a "tripwire," bringing the full force of the United States to bear on the Soviet Union if it dared to cross the East-West line with troops—which it was not expected to do, with or without a NATO. Quietly, administration spokesmen also indicated that NATO was designed to knit Western Europe together, to discourage some nations' tendency toward neutrality. The Senate ratified the treaty in July, 82 to 13. Truman then asked for a $1.5 billion Mutual Defense Assistance Act, to which Congress also consented, as it did to all Truman's major foreign policy requests.

Just before passage of the military aid bill (September 1949), an American aircraft carrying sensitive equipment detected unusually high radioactivity in the atmosphere: the Soviets had exploded an atomic bomb. "This is now a different world," commented Senator Arthur Vandenberg. The American nuclear monopoly was no more, and Western Europe now seemed more vulnerable. The Communists were also winning the civil war in China (see pages 830–831) and Moscow was scoring propaganda points by advocating "peaceful coexistence" with the West. American leaders could have responded to this changed state of affairs with diplomatic negotiations. But Secretary of State Dean Acheson announced that there would be no "appeasement." The United States would instead build "situations of strength" around the world. In early 1950 Truman ordered production of the hydrogen bomb. And in May Congress finally endorsed funds for technical assistance to developing nations, to draw them into the American sphere of influence (a plan called the Point Four Program, after point 4 of Truman's 1949 inaugural address).

A month earlier, the National Security Council had delivered to the president a top-secret document numbered NSC-68. Predicting continued tension with the Communists and describing a "shrinking world of polarized power," the report appealed for an enlarged

NSC-68 military budget to counter the Soviet global design American strategists perceived. The authors advised that public opinion would have to be mobilized behind huge defense expenditures. Administration officials worried about how to sell this strong prescription to the voters and budget-conscious congressional representatives. "We were sweating over it, and then—with regard to NSC-68—thank God Korea came along," recalled one of Dean Acheson's aides.

THE COLD WAR IN ASIA

When the Korean War erupted in mid-1950, it came in the wake of vast changes in Asia. The Second World War had accelerated the process of decolonization begun during the First World War. Occupied with defending themselves and then with rebuilding after the war, imperial countries were no longer able to resist their colonies' demands for independence. Britain gave up India and what are now Pakistan and Bangladesh in 1947, Burma and Ceylon in 1948. The Dutch reluctantly let go of Indonesia in 1949. Only the French fought on in Indochina, finally retiring from that outpost in 1954.

The defeat of Japan brought about the division of its empire among the victors. Korea was divided between the United States and the Soviet Union. The Pacific islands (the Marshalls, Marianas, and Carolines) came under American control. Half of Sakhalin went to Russia as agreed at Yalta, and Formosa (Taiwan) was returned to the Chinese. As for Japan itself, the United States monopolized its reconstruction. Though the British and Russians asserted that they too had fought in the Asian theater and de-**Reconstruction** served a say in the occupation, **of Japan** Ambassador W. Averell Harriman answered that Washington was "very firm on the matter of keeping the power in American hands." Stalin wondered what the difference was between American domination of Japan and Russian domination of Rumania. But General Douglas MacArthur, who envisioned turning the Pacific Ocean into "an Anglo-Saxon lake," had the last word in Japan. As director of the American occupation, MacArthur wrote a democratic constitution for Japan, revitalized its economy, and destroyed the weapons of the Japanese military.

Though United States supremacy in Japan was an established fact, the Russians would not recognize it. Thus, after squabbling with Russia for years over a peace treaty with Japan, the United States finally signed a separate peace in 1951. The treaty restored Japan's sovereignty, ended the occupation, granted the United States a military base at Okinawa, and permitted American troops to be stationed in Japan. Tokyo and Washington also initialed a defense pact. The people who had been called beasts after their surprise attack on Pearl Harbor were now American allies in the Cold War. Along with Germany, Japan was, as Kennan noted, one of "our most important pawns on the chessboard of world politics."

Meanwhile, America's Chinese ally was faltering. The United States was feeding and fueling Jiang Jieshi's (Chiang Kai-shek's) Nationalist army in its battle against Mao Zedong and Zhou Enlai's Communists. Immediately **Chinese** after the Second World War Amer-**Civil War** ican troops had occupied northern China, flown Nationalist soldiers to Manchuria, and stayed on to advise Generalissimo Jiang. From 1945 to 1949 the United States sent China $3 billion in aid. But it soon became evident that Jiang was an unreliable friend. His government was corrupt and inefficient; he was out of touch with the rebellious peasants, whom the Communists enlisted with promises of land redistribution; and he tolerated a grossly unfair tax system. Journalist Theodore White thought the Nationalists combined "some of the worst features of Tammany Hall and the Spanish Inquisition," and Truman privately denounced them as "grafters and crooks." Jiang ignored American advice to root out corruption, halt inflation, and begin land reform. He also worked to disrupt the efforts of the Marshall mission (1945–1947) to negotiate a cease-fire and a coalition government. And he rejected American military advice. "We picked a bad horse," Truman admitted. Still, seeing Jiang as the only viable alternative to Mao, Truman backed him to the end.

American officials were divided on the question of whether Mao was a puppet of the Soviet Union. Some diplomats considered him an Asian Tito—

In this 1945 photograph taken at the Chinese Communists' head-quarters at Yenan, Mao Zedong (1893–1976) stands with Lin Biao (at right), a war hero whom Mao had designated his "closest comrade in arms and successor." Four years later, the Communists were victorious over Jiang Jieshi's National-ists and proclaimed the People's Republic of China. In 1971, Biao betrayed Mao and was shot down in a jet airplane while trying to escape from China. Wide World Photos.

Communist but independent—but most believed he was part of an international Communist movement and would thus give the Soviets a springboard into Asia. In the *White Paper* of 1949—a government report written to explain America's efforts to contain Communism through aid to Jiang—Secretary Acheson overstated his case in saying that the "Communist leaders have foresworn their Chinese heritage and have publicly announced their subservience to a foreign power." Thus when the Chinese Communists made secret overtures to begin diplomatic talks in 1945 and again in 1949, American officials rebuffed them. Mao soon decided that he was "leaning to one side" in the Cold War—the Soviet side.

Actually, Americans had overestimated Mao's dependence on the Soviet Union. The Russians gave Mao little support, rejecting his interpretation of

Marxism-Leninism and resenting his determination to resist their influence. For its own purposes Russia preferred a weak China under Jiang to a strong China under Mao, an attitude that derived from a long history of Sino-Russian rivalry.

In fall 1949, after numerous military setbacks, Jiang fled to the island of Formosa, and Mao proclaimed the People's Republic of China. Would the United States extend diplomatic recognition to Mao's new government? Truman hesitated; he tried unsuccessfully to persuade the British to wait. "Are we to refuse to recognize facts, however unpleasant they may be?" asked the British prime minister. "Are we to cut ourselves off from all contact with one-sixth of the inhabitants of the world?" But

Nonrecognition of the People's Republic of China

for several reasons Washington did just that. First, American officials were alarmed by a Sino-Soviet treaty of friendship signed in February 1950. Second, Mao's followers had harassed Americans and seized American-owned property in China. Third, Mao was now openly hostile to the United States, blaming it for prolonging the bloody civil war. Fourth, Secretary Dean Acheson simply wanted to "wait until the dust settles." He predicted that Mao would conquer Formosa, thus eliminating Jiang, and that frictions between Beijing and Moscow would ultimately convince Mao to sever his ties with the Soviets.

Still another reason lay behind the policy of nonrecognition. A noisy group of Republican critics called the China lobby, shattering the postwar spirit of bipartisanship, was seeking to blame Jiang's defeat on Truman. Publisher Henry Luce, Senator William Knowland of California, and Congressman Walter Judd of Minnesota won headlines by charging that the United States had "lost" China. Senator Joseph McCarthy of Wisconsin snorted that "egg-sucking liberals" and "queers" had sold China into "atheistic slavery."

Truman and Acheson answered that the United States had never had China to lose, that Jiang was not willing to help himself, and that large-scale military intervention in the Chinese civil war would have been costly and probably interminable. Moreover, major involvement in China would have drained valuable resources from Europe, the primary front in the Cold War. "The United States cannot furnish determination, it cannot furnish the will, and it cannot furnish the loyalty of a people to its government," Acheson insisted—adding, "China lost itself." For reasons of both domestic politics and international relations, the United States did not open formal diplomatic relations with the People's Republic of China until 1979—thirty years after Mao's government came to power.

Reaching for some way to offset Jiang's collapse, the National Security Council urged the president to fortify "friendly and independent" states in Asia as a bulwark against Communist expansion. In February 1950 the United States recognized the French puppet regime of Bao Dai in Vietnam, and a few months later decided to extend aid to the beleaguered French there. In April the National Security Council sent the president its alarming report NSC-68. And in May more funds went to Jiang Jieshi in Formosa. It is in this context of globalist thought and action that America's response to war in Korea must be seen (see pages 843–845).

A ROUGH TRANSITION AT HOME

Truman's crises abroad were matched by several challenges at home. The atomic bombs that fell on Hiroshima and Nagasaki brought about victory much sooner than the economic planners had anticipated. Mid-1946 was the target date for victory, and administrators had planned a gradual conversion from a wartime to a peacetime economy. But in 1945 the war was over, and important questions remained unanswered. What would be the effect of reconversion—the cancellation of war contracts, the termination of wage and price controls, and the end of wartime labor agreements? Would depression recur once the artificial stimulus of the war was withdrawn, throwing people out of work and sending prices downward? Or would Americans go on a buying spree, driving prices up to record highs? After all, during the Great Depression penny-pinched Americans could not afford to buy autos, houses, appliances, and other consumer durables. During the prosperity of the Second World War civilian items such as these were not manufactured. Therefore, by 1945 Americans had bulging bank accounts, and they wanted to treat themselves.

Most Americans were pessimistic about the future. Even before the war's end, cutbacks in production had caused layoffs. Workers at the Ford Motor Company's massive Willow Run plant **Postwar Job** outside Detroit, where nine thou-**Layoffs** sand Liberator bombers had been produced, were let go in spring 1945. Ten days after the victory over Japan, 1.8 million people received pink slips and 640,000 filed for unemployment compensation. The peak of postwar unemployment came in March 1946, when 2.7 million people were seeking work.

In 1946 ex-servicemen picketed coal mines in Panther Valley, Pennsylvania, complaining that mine owners had hired outside help during the war and then had refused to lay these workers off in favor of the returning veterans, former coalminers themselves.   Wide World Photos.

Swelling the ranks of those seeking jobs were the millions of soldiers and sailors who received their discharges from the armed services in 1945 and 1946. As with the cancellations of government contracts, the demobilization of the armed forces was rapid. The army had expected to muster out 1.1 million people in the eighteen months between V-E and V-J days, but the atomic bombings of Hiroshima and Nagasaki had cut that period to four months. The army's demobilization rate was increased fivefold, with a target of 5.5 million by July 1946. The navy hurriedly converted landing and cargo ships to troop carriers and returned 4 million GIs from abroad in the first year of peace. In mid-1945 the nation's armed forces stood at over 12 million. A year later, the figure had fallen to just over 3 million; in 1947 it hit 1.5 million. "The program we were following," Truman recalled, "was no longer demobilization—it was disintegration of our armed forces."

Truman declared his determination not only to combat unemployment, but also to expand on New Deal programs begun in the 1930s. On September 6, 1945, he delivered to Congress a twenty-one-point message urging extension of unemployment compensation, an increase in the minimum wage, adoption of permanent farm-price supports, and new public works projects. Truman revived Roosevelt's Economic Bill of Rights: every able-bodied American had a right to a job. Should the economy fail to provide one, the government should create it. Congress responded to Truman's message with the Employment Act of 1946, which announced that the government would use its resources, including deficit spending if necessary, to achieve "maximum employment, production, and purchasing power." The act established the Council of Economic Advisers to assist the president. But it fell short of Truman's hopes: Congress had deleted a commitment to absolute full employment.

Truman's Reconversion Plan

Despite high unemployment in the immediate post-war period, the United States was not teetering on the brink of depression; in fact, after a brief period of readjustment, the economy would blast off into a quarter-century of unprecedented boom. People had plenty of savings to spend in 1945 and 1946, and suddenly there were new houses and cars for them to buy. Easy credit and new war-inspired industries like synthetic rubber and electronics promoted the buying spree. As a result, though war production began to wind down in 1944, the gross national product (GNP) continued to rise in 1945. And though there was a slight dip in economic activity in 1946, the GNP jumped from $209 billion to $231 billion the next year. In 1948 it rose to $258 billion (see Chapter 31).

So the nation's postwar economic problem was not depression; it was inflation, fueled by maddening shortages of consumer goods like meat and housing. Throughout 1945 and 1946 prices skyrocketed; the inflation rate for 1946 was 18.2 percent.

Meanwhile, though prices were spiraling upward, many people were earning less than they had during the war. Industrial workers complained that the National War Labor Board had limited them to cost-of-living pay increases, thus preventing them from improving their status. To complicate matters, workers who had put in long hours of overtime during the war were returning to the forty-hour paycheck. Although employers claimed they could not afford to guarantee workers the same take-home pay for fewer hours, most workers believed it was possible. The result was an impasse between management and labor and a spate of strikes. During fall and early winter 1945, daily absences due to strikes ballooned to 28.4 million, more than double the 1943 figure. But although such strikes were massive and frequent, they were peaceful compared with the fiery confrontations that had followed the First World War.

Throughout the period of reconversion the government hesitated to act in the face of competing special-interest groups. Big business and small business, management and labor, farmers and consumers, liberals and conservatives offered conflicting prescriptions, and to serve one interest was to risk offending others. For all these groups, Truman was the perfect scapegoat. "Sherman was *wrong*," Truman told a Gridiron Dinner

audience in December 1945. "I'm telling you I find peace is hell."

As severe as was the discontent of farmers, factory workers, and consumers in 1945, in 1946 it became worse. As volatile as labor-management relations were in 1945, the next year they exploded. And as unpopular as President Truman was in 1945, in 1946 his rating hit new lows.

Over 4.5 million men and women left their jobs to strike in 1946, more even than in 1919. Daily absences due to strikes totaled 113 million—four times as many as in 1945. One reason for workers' discontent was that while wages and salaries had declined slightly in 1946, net profits had reached all-time highs, jumping more than 50 percent from 1945 to 1946. Indignant that they were not sharing in the increased prosperity, workers forced nationwide shutdowns in the coal, automobile, steel, and electric industries and halted railroad and maritime transportation.

Upsurge in Labor Strikes

John L. Lewis's United Mine Workers was among the most powerful unions to walk off the job. Coal was the nation's primary source of energy in 1946; when soft-coal production stopped on April 1, steel and automobile output plummeted, railroad service was canceled, thousands of people were laid off, and twenty-two states reinstituted wartime "dim-outs" to conserve coal. Though the miners' demands were legitimate—higher wages, a federal safety code, and a royalty of ten cents per ton to finance health services and welfare and pension funds—a two-week truce in May failed to produce a solution. On May 21, with time running out and the country still desperate for coal, Truman ordered the seizure of the mines. Lewis and the government reached an accord a week later and the miners returned to work. But within six months the agreement had collapsed, and once again the government seized the mines.

There was no doubt in 1946 about the growing unpopularity of labor unions and their leadership. Many Americans believed that the unions were responsible for strikes that not only restricted the output of consumer goods and inflated prices, but also threatened the national security. In May, when a nationwide railroad

Truman's Attack on the Unions

　　　　Chapter 29: THE COLD WAR AND AMERICAN POLITICS, 1945–1953

strike was threatened, Truman hopped aboard the antiunion bandwagon. A special board appointed to mediate the dispute had managed to satisfy eighteen of the disgruntled unions, but two held out for a better settlement. In exasperation, Truman made a dramatic appearance before a joint session of Congress. If the government seized a strike-bound industry, he said, and the workers in that industry refused to honor a presidential order to return to work, "I [would] request the Congress immediately to authorize the President to draft into the Armed Forces of the United States all workers who are on strike against their government." He also requested authority to strip strikers of seniority benefits, to take legal action against union leaders, and to fine and even imprison them for contempt. Truman's speech alienated not only railroad workers but union members in general. Many dedicated themselves to defeating him in the upcoming presidential election.

Truman fared little better in his direction of the Office of Price Administration. Now that the war was over, powerful interests wanted OPA controls lifted. Consumers were impatient **Consumer** with shortages and black-market **Discontent** prices, and manufacturers and farmers wanted to jack up prices legally. Yet when most controls expired in mid-1946 and inflation rose higher, people became angry. When the OPA price ceilings on beef expired in June, for example, the cost of beef soared, cattle ranchers beamed, and consumers grumbled. When the OPA reimposed ceilings in August, however, producers retaliated by withholding beef from the market. Soon consumers were standing in long lines at the butcher shop and buying beef through the black market. In an election year, they blamed the Democrats. "This is going to be a damn *beefsteak* election," groused Speaker of the House Sam Rayburn.

Truman's popularity rating plunged from 87 percent in late 1945 to 32 percent in 1946. Even liberals were unhappy with the president's performance. Truman had prompted the resignation of Harold Ickes, one of the two New Dealers left in the cabinet, by appointing a California oil and real estate baron (who also happened to be a Democratic fundraiser) as undersecretary of the navy. Fearing another Teapot Dome scandal, Ickes angrily denounced Truman's policy of "government by crony." Seven months later Truman fired Henry A. Wallace, the only remaining New Dealer, for making a speech critical of his containment policy (see page 826). By election time the president was out of favor with labor, consumers, farmers, liberals, and—because of his advocacy of welfare programs—conservative Democrats as well.

Republicans made the most of public discontent. "Got enough meat?" asked Republican Congressman John M. Vorys of Ohio. "Got enough houses? Got enough OPA? . . . Got enough inflation? . . . Got enough debt? . . . Got enough strikes?" When the votes were tabulated, the Republicans had won a majority in both houses of the Eightieth Congress and captured twenty-five of thirty-two nonsouthern governorships. The White House in 1948 seemed within their grasp.

THE EIGHTIETH CONGRESS AND THE ELECTION OF 1948

The politicians who ruled the Eightieth Congress, both Republicans and southern Democrats, were committed conservatives. Although they supported Truman's foreign policy, they perceived the Republican landslide as a mandate to reverse the New Deal, to curb the power of government and of labor. Truman had had little success with the Seventy-ninth Congress; he would have even less success with this one. Ironically, however, it would be the Eightieth Congress that would help him to win the presidency in 1948. For if Truman had alienated labor, farmers, and liberals, the Eightieth Congress made them livid.

One extremely unpopular measure was the Taft-Hartley Act, which Congress adopted over Truman's veto in 1947. A revision of the Wagner Act of 1935, the bill prohibited the closed shop, **Taft-Hartley** in which only union members could **Act** be hired. The framework of the Wagner Act still governed labor-management relations, and workers could still organize, elect a union to represent them, enroll new union members, bargain collectively, and strike. But the Taft-Hartley Act forbade union contributions to political funds in federal elections; required union leaders to sign non-Communist affidavits; and mandated an eighty-day cooling-off period in strikes that imperiled the national security. Although it was not the slave-labor act labor spokespersons said it was, responses to the act quickly distinguished supporters of labor from opponents. Truman's veto therefore vindicated him in the eyes of labor. Just a year earlier, labor leaders had pledged all-out war against the president; now they threw their resources behind him.

Throughout 1947 and into 1948 the Eightieth Congress offended numerous interest groups, which in turn swung back to Truman. For example, the president asked Congress for continued price supports for farmers; the Eightieth Congress responded with weakened price supports. The president requested nationwide health insurance; the Eightieth Congress refused. It was the same with federal funding of public housing and aid to public education; with broadened and increased unemployment compensation, old-age and survivors' benefits, and the minimum wage; with funds for land reclamation, irrigation, and public power; and with antilynching, anti-poll tax, and fair-employment legislation. Truman proposed; Congress rejected or ignored his requests.

But Republicans seemed oblivious to public opinion. Not since 1928 had they been so confident of capturing the presidency, and most political experts agreed. "Only a political miracle," stated

Campaign of 1948

Time, "or extraordinary stupidity on the part of the Republicans can save the Democratic party." At their national convention, Republicans strengthened their position by nominating for president and vice president the governors of the nation's two most populous states: Thomas E. Dewey of New York and Earl Warren of California.

Democrats revealed how fragmented they were when they convened to nominate a candidate and adopt a platform. A curious alliance of big-city bosses and liberals, reasoning that Truman was a loser, tried to dump him in favor of General Dwight D. Eisenhower. But Eisenhower declined the overtures of both Democrats and Republicans, declaring that "life-long professional soldiers should abstain from seeking high

political office." In the end, Truman received the nomination.

Democrats were fighting against more than Republicans in 1948. After his dismissal from the cabinet, Henry Wallace decided to run for president on a third-party ticket. Wallace's Progressive party advocated friendship and negotiation with the Soviet Union and condemned the Truman Doctrine as a "global Monroe Doctrine." Wallace also argued for desegregation and for the nationalization of oil companies, railroads, and other basic industries. Experts predicted that the Progressives would poll at least 5 million and perhaps as many as 8 million votes, thus dashing the Democratic party's hopes for victory. To complicate matters, a fourth party, the Dixiecrats (States Rights Democratic party), nominated Governor Strom Thurmond of South Carolina. The Dixiecrats had bolted the Democratic party when the 1948 national convention adopted a pro–civil rights plank; waving Confederate flags, they had won control of the Democratic party in four southern states. If Wallace's candidacy did not destroy Truman's chances, experts said, the Dixiecrats certainly would.

But Truman had ideas of his own. He called the Eightieth Congress into special session and demanded that it enact all the planks in the Republican platform. If Republicans really wanted to transform their ideals into law, said Truman, this was the time to do it. After Congress had met for two weeks and accomplished nothing of significance, Truman took to the road. Traveling more than 30,000 miles by train, he delivered scores of whistle-stop speeches denouncing the "do-nothing" Eightieth Congress. Still, no amount of furious campaigning on Truman's part seemed likely to change the predicted outcome. Hours before the returns were in, the *Chicago Tribune* had printed a headline announcing "DEWEY DEFEATS TRUMAN."

Yet as the votes were counted early into the morning, it became clear that Truman had confounded the experts. The final tally was 24.1 million popular votes, 304 electoral votes, for Truman; 21.9 million popular votes, 189 electoral votes, for Dewey (see map, page 838). Not only had Truman won four more years in the White House, but the Democrats had regained control of Congress—in the House by a majority of ninety-three, in the Senate by twelve.

So few pollsters predicted that President Harry S Truman (1884–1972) would win in 1948 that the Chicago Tribune announced his defeat before all the returns were in. Here a victorious Truman pokes fun at the newspaper for its premature headline. *UPI.*

How and why had the upset occurred? First, no matter how troubled Truman's presidency had been, the United States was prosperous, at peace, and essentially united on foreign policy. Moreover, the Roosevelt legacy—the New Deal coalition—had endured; the big cities, Afro-Americans, and labor unions had rallied to Truman's support. Many Jewish and Catholic voters also supported Truman, as did voters of Eastern European ancestry who approved of his hard line toward the Soviet Union. Ironically, the Progressive and Dixiecrat parties helped him, for their extremist images made the Democratic party look moderate by comparison. The Democrats, for their part, did not hesitate to distort the facts by denouncing

the Progressives as a pack of Communists. Truman himself was adept at redbaiting; he once declared, "I do not want . . . the political support of Henry Wallace and his Communists." Rather than the predicted 5 million votes apiece, Wallace and Thurmond polled just a little over 1 million each.

There were still other reasons for Truman's victory. Some formidable Democrats also ran for offices that year—Adlai E. Stevenson, Hubert H. Humphrey—and their presence on the ticket helped Truman. Without doubt, too, Dewey's smug campaign did not stand up well to Truman's aggressive effort. But in the end it was the farmers whose votes made the difference. Truman advocated continued high price

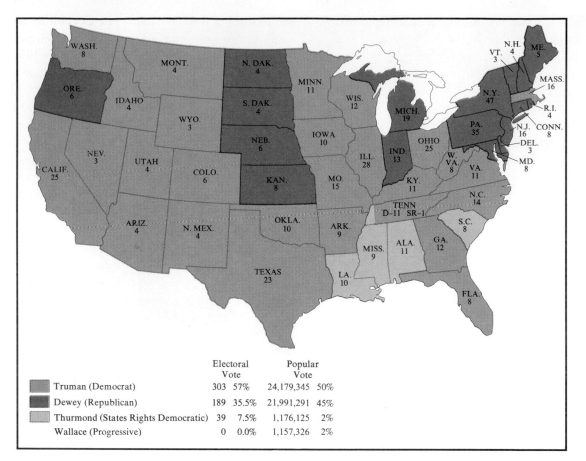

		Electoral Vote		Popular Vote	
	Truman (Democrat)	303	57%	24,179,345	50%
	Dewey (Republican)	189	35.5%	21,991,291	45%
	Thurmond (States Rights Democratic)	39	7.5%	1,176,125	2%
	Wallace (Progressive)	0	0.0%	1,157,326	2%

Presidential Election, 1948

supports for farmers; Republicans wanted to decrease supports. In the bumper-crop year of 1948, Republicans actually wanted to cut back on grain storage. As the harvest mounted, prices began to fall; corn dropped from $1.78 a bushel in September to $1.38 in mid-October. Ever ready, Truman told farmers that the Eightieth Congress had "stuck a pitchfork in the farmer's back." Practically all the midwestern and border states went for Truman.

Truman entered his new term brimming with confidence. He believed that it was time for government to fulfill its responsibility to provide economic security for the poor and the elderly. As he worked on his 1949 State of the Union message, he penciled in an expression of his intentions: "I expect to give every segment of our population a fair deal." Little did Truman know that he had selected the label that historians would hereafter associate with his presidency: Fair Deal.

TRUMAN ON CIVIL RIGHTS

The postwar years were a period of gathering strength for Afro-Americans. Truman and other politicians knew they would have to compete for the growing black vote in urban-industrial states like California, Illinois, Michigan, Ohio, Pennsylvania, and New York. Many Republicans now cultivated the black vote. Thomas Dewey, who as governor of New York had pushed successfully for the establishment of a fair employment practices commission, was particularly popular with blacks. In Harlem, which had gone Democratic by a 4-to-1 margin in 1938, Dewey won by large margins in 1942 and 1946.

Certainly, then, Truman had political reasons for supporting black civil rights. But he also felt a moral obligation to blacks. For one thing, he believed that it was only fair that each American, regardless of race, should enjoy the full rights of citizenship. More than that, Truman was disturbed by the resurgence of racial terrorism. The Ku Klux Klan had taken to the road again, burning crosses and murdering blacks who had had the audacity to vote. Senator Theodore G. Bilbo of Mississippi had exhorted every "red-blooded Anglo-Saxon man in Mississippi to resort to any means to keep . . . Negroes from the polls," and Eugene Talmadge had won the governorship of Georgia with the promise that "no Negro will vote in Georgia for the next four years." But what really horrified Truman was the report that police in Aiken, South Carolina, had gouged out the eyes of a black sergeant just three hours after he had been discharged from the army. Several weeks later, on December 5, 1946, Truman signed an executive order establishing the President's Committee on Civil Rights.

A year later the committee delivered its report, *To Secure These Rights*. Among the committee's recommendations, which would become the agenda for the civil rights movement for the next twenty years, were the enactment of federal antilynching, antisegregation, antibrutality, and anti-poll-tax laws. *To Secure These Rights* also called for laws guaranteeing voting rights and equal employment opportunity, and for the establishment of a permanent commission on civil rights and a civil rights division within the Department of Justice. In February 1948 Truman sent a special message to Congress. The protection of citizens' rights, Truman said, was "the duty of every government which derives its powers from the consent of the governed." Congress made no formal response. Some southerners told Truman that with such a civil rights program, "You won't be elected dogcatcher in 1948." There is evidence that the president did not expect congressional action, and that his real goal was the black vote in 1948. But whatever his motive, this was the first time since Reconstruction that a president had acknowledged the federal government's responsibility to protect Afro-Americans.

President's Committee on Civil Rights

Truman also used the power of the executive to proclaim a policy of "fair employment throughout the federal establishment," and he created the Employment Board of the Civil Service Commission to hear charges of discrimination. His Committee on Equality of Treatment and Opportunity in the Armed Services issued a report, *Freedom to Serve,* in 1950 stating that racial desegregation would "make for a better Army, Navy, and Air Force." Though strong, at times even fierce, opposition to desegregation existed within the military, by the outbreak of the Korean War segregated units were being phased out.

Blacks also benefited from a series of Supreme Court decisions. The trend toward judicial support of civil rights had begun in the late 1930s, when the NAACP established its Legal Defense Fund led by Thurgood Marshall, who in 1967 became the first black Supreme Court justice. Marshall and his staff were trying to destroy the separate-but-equal doctrine established in *Plessy* v. *Ferguson* (1896) by insisting on its literal interpretation. In higher education, the NAACP figured, the cost of racially separate schools was prohibitive. "You can't build a cyclotron for one [black] student," the president of the University of Oklahoma acknowledged. As a result, in the 1940s black students won admission to professional and graduate schools at a number of state universities. The NAACP also scored notable victories in two other cases. In 1944, in *Smith* v. *Allwright*, the Supreme Court outlawed the whites-only primaries held by the Democratic party in some southern states, branding them a violation of the Fifteenth Amendment. Two years later the Court declared segregation in interstate bus transportation unconstitutional (*Morgan* v. *Virginia*).

Supreme Court Decisions on Civil Rights

In 1947 the Department of Justice began to submit friend-of-the-court briefs on behalf of the civil rights movement, most notably in cases involving higher education and restrictive covenants, which were private agreements among white homeowners not to sell to blacks. In the *Thompson Restaurant* case, a Justice Department brief helped to bring about the desegregation of restaurants and eventually hotels in the District of Columbia. But most important was the attorney general's brief supporting the NAACP's effort to desegregate the nation's public schools. Although the Supreme Court did not decide the landmark *Brown* v. *Board of Education of Topeka* until 1954, the Truman administration's legal efforts helped overturn the separate-but-equal doctrine that had been the law of the land since *Plessy* v. *Ferguson* (see page 475).

Jackie Robinson cracked the color line in major league baseball when he joined the Brooklyn Dodgers for the 1947 season. Robinson won rookie-of-the-year honors and was later elected to the Baseball Hall of Fame. In this game against the Philadelphia Phillies, Robinson stole home. Wide World Photos.

A change in social attitudes accompanied these gains in black political and legal power. Books such as Gunnar Myrdal's *An American Dilemma* (1944) and Richard Wright's *Native Son* (1940) and *Black Boy* (1945) had increased white awareness of the social injustice that plagued blacks. A new black middle class had emerged, composed of college-educated activists, veterans, and union workers. Blacks and whites were working together in CIO unions and with service organizations such as the National Council of Churches, the Anti-Defamation League, the National Urban League, and the American Friends Service Committee. And in 1947 a black baseball player, Jackie Robinson, cracked the major-league color barrier and electrified crowds with his spectacular hitting and base running.

Cold War pressures also benefited blacks. As the Soviet Union was quick to point out, the United States could not pose as the leader of the free world, or condemn the denial of human rights behind the Iron Curtain, so long as it condoned racism at home. Nor could it convince new African and Asian nations of its dedication to human rights if Afro-Americans were subjected to segregation, disfranchisement, and racial violence. To win the support of nonaligned nations, the United States would have to live up to its own ideals. That the nation was not doing so was evident. Segregation was still an accepted practice in the 1950s, even if it was no longer the law of the land. Blacks continued to suffer job discrimination and disfranchisement. Nevertheless, in the ten years following the Second World War, Afro-Americans had made considerable progress, more than in any period since Reconstruction.

MCCARTHYISM

A common misconception about the postwar era is that anti-Communist hysteria began in 1950 with the furious speeches of Senator Joseph R. McCarthy. Actually, anti-Communism had been part of the American political temper ever since the First

World War and the Red Scare of 1919 and 1920. The Cold War heightened anti-Communist fears at home, and by 1950 they reached hysterical proportions. McCarthy did not create this hysteria; he manipulated it to his own advantage. He was, though, undeniably the most successful and frightening redbaiter the country had ever seen.

What reason was there to fear Communist influence in the 1940s and 1950s? The party had never been strong, even during the hard times of the depression.

Communist Party Membership When news of the trial and execution of large numbers of anti-Stalinists in the Soviet Union reached America in 1937 and 1938, followed shortly by the signing of the Nazi-Soviet Pact in August 1939, the party had quickly lost much of its following. With the German invasion of Russia in summer 1941, however, American attitudes toward the Soviet Union became more favorable. Suddenly the United States and Russia were allies in the war against Hitler.

At the same time anti-Communism persisted in the United States. In 1940 Congress enacted the Alien Registration, or Smith, Act, which made it unlawful to advocate the overthrow of the U.S. government by force or violence or to join any organization that did so. And politicians began playing on anti-Communist paranoia again. In the 1944 presidential campaign Dewey warned that the Democratic party was about to be captured by the Communists.

Then in March 1945 an incident occurred that tended to confirm anti-Communists' worst fears. In a raid on the offices of *Amerasia,* a little-known magazine whose editors sympathized with the Chinese Communists, the Office of Strategic Services confiscated classified government documents. Who had supplied the documents to the magazine, and why? people asked. Concern was also mounting north of the Canadian border, where in 1946 a royal commission issued a report claiming that Soviet spies were operating in Canada. Among them, the report said, were a member of Parliament and a scientist who had transmitted atomic secrets to a Soviet agent.

Spurred by these revelations, Truman in March 1947 ordered investigations into the loyalty of the more than 3 million employees of the U.S. government. In 1950 the government began discharging people deemed "security risks," among them alcoholics,

Truman's Loyalty Probe homosexuals, and debtors thought to be susceptible to blackmail. In most cases there was no question of these people's loyalty. Without the right to confront their accusers and demand evidence, however, many were ruined for life. Still others became victims of guilt by association—they knew people considered to be subversive, disloyal, or dangerous.

The wellspring of this fear of Communism was, of course, the Cold War. Fear of internal subversion was intertwined with fear of external attack. It was no coincidence that Truman ordered the loyalty probe the same week he appeared before a joint session of Congress to announce his containment policy (see pages 820, 826–827). His alarmist rhetoric only heightened public anxiety.

Truman was not alone in peddling fear; conservatives and liberal Democrats joined him. Republicans used the same technique to attack the Democratic candidates for president in 1948 and 1952; liberal Democrats used it to discredit the far-left, pro-Wallace wing of their party. In many ways, then, the anti-Communist hysteria of the late 1940s was a phenomenon created by professional politicians and promoted by labor union officials, religious leaders, Hollywood moguls, and other influential figures.

People began to point accusing fingers at each other. "Reds, phonies, and 'parlor pinks,' " in Truman's words, seemed to lurk everywhere. Hollywood film personalities who had been ardent left-wingers were blacklisted; some writers and directors were sentenced to prison for contempt of Congress when they refused to answer questions and name names. Schoolteachers and college professors were fired for expressing dissenting viewpoints, and in some communities "pro-Communist" books were removed from school libraries. In labor-union elections and in struggles to dominate local parent-teacher associations, redbaiting became a convenient tactic for discrediting the opposition. The hysteria was particularly damaging to the labor movement, which forsook its class-conscious militancy in favor of patriotism and anti-Communism. In the United Auto Workers, Walter Reuther used redbaiting to destroy his opposition and win the union's presidency. Union bulletin boards that had once bristled with strike notices and photographs of police clubbing strikers were now adorned with such slogans as "UAW Americanism for Us." At its 1949 convention, the

CIO expelled eleven unions with a combined membership of over 1 million for alleged Communist domination. And all this occurred at a time when membership in the Communist party was rapidly declining, from a high of about 83,000 in 1947 to 55,000 in 1950 and 25,000 in 1954.

Despite the false accusations, there was cause for alarm—especially in 1949, which dramatist Arthur Miller called "the year it came apart." Throughout that year a former State Department official, Alger Hiss, was on trial for perjury for denying in congressional testimony that he had passed to the Russians "numerous secret, confidential and restricted documents." When Truman and Secretary of State Dean Acheson came to his defense, charging that the Republicans were publicizing the case to divert attention from their own failures, some people began to suspect the worst. The Democrats, they decided, had something to hide. Republican Congressman Richard M. Nixon of California, a member of the House Committee on Un-American Activities, which had led the investigation of the Hiss case, harped constantly on that theme. Then in September two events shoved the Hiss trial off the front page. The Russians exploded their first atomic bomb, and the Chinese Communists, finally victorious in the civil war, proclaimed the People's Republic of China (see page 831). A howl of indignation arose from the China lobby; Truman and Acheson were now on the defensive.

Hiss Trial

The dawn of a new decade brought no end to the hysteria; indeed, 1950 saw more disquieting news. Hiss was convicted. Scotland Yard arrested Klaus Fuchs, a nuclear scientist, for turning over to Soviet agents secrets from the atomic-bomb project at Los Alamos, New Mexico. And President Truman announced that in response to the Russian atomic bomb, the United States would embark on a crash project to develop a hydrogen bomb. "How much more are we going to have to take?" wailed one right-wing Republican. "Fuchs and Acheson and Hiss and hydrogen bombs threatening outside and New Dealism eating away at the vitals of the nation. In the name of Heaven, is this the best America can do?" The ingredients of the situation were ripe for a demagogue: an irrational blurring of enemies; simplistic conspiracy theories; awareness that the Second World War had not ended the threat of war, but brought a new threat of nuclear holocaust. It was in this atmosphere that on February 9, 1950, Senator Joseph McCarthy mounted a rostrum in Wheeling, West Virginia, and gave a name to the hysteria: McCarthyism.

That day in Wheeling, McCarthy proclaimed, "The reason we find ourselves in a position of impotency is . . . because of the traitorous actions of those who have been treated so well by this nation." The State Department, he asserted, was "thoroughly infested with Communists," and the most dangerous person in the State Department was Dean Acheson. Reporters wrote that the senator claimed to have a list of 205 Communists working in the State Department; later McCarthy lowered the figure to "57 card-carrying members," then raised it to 81. No matter the number. What McCarthy needed was a winning campaign issue, and he had found it. Republicans, distraught over losing what had appeared to be a sure victory in 1948, were eager to support his attack. Here was a chance to discredit both Roosevelt's New Deal and Truman's Fair Deal. "A generation was on trial," wrote journalist Alistair Cooke.

McCarthy's Attack on the State Department

McCarthy and McCarthyism gained momentum throughout 1950. Nothing seemed to slow the senator down, not even attacks by other Republicans. Seven Republican senators broke with their colleagues and publicly condemned McCarthy for his "selfish political exploitation of fear, bigotry, ignorance, and intolerance." A Senate committee reported that his charges against the State Department were "a fraud and a hoax." But McCarthy had much to sustain him, including Julius and Ethel Rosenberg's 1950 arrest for espionage; they allegedly had recruited and supervised a spy at the Los Alamos atomic laboratory.

The widespread support for anti-Communist measures was also apparent in the adoption, over Truman's veto, of the Internal Security, or McCarran, Act of 1950. The act made it unlawful for anyone to "contribute to the establishment . . . of a totalitarian dictatorship," required members of "Communist-front" organizations to register with the government, and prohibited such people from holding defense jobs or traveling abroad. And in a telling decision in 1951 (*Dennis et al. v. U.S.*), the Supreme Court upheld the Smith Act, under which eleven Communist leaders had been convicted and imprisoned.

Senator Joseph R. McCarthy gave his name to the anti-Communist hysteria that infected many people. Testifying in March 1950, he waved a copy of the Daily Worker *published by the Communist Party. National Archives.*

Meanwhile, McCarthy continued to display his unparalleled talent for demagoguery, making unsubstantiated charges, implying guilt by association, interpreting writings out of context, and telling outright lies. "It would seem easy to pin down the preposterous utterances," a reporter covering the Senate observed. "But no; McCarthy is as hard to catch as a mist—a mist that carries lethal contagion." And there is no doubt that the outbreak of the Korean War in June 1950 made McCarthyism even more virulent than before.

THE KOREAN WAR AND ITS GLOBAL CONSEQUENCES

In the early morning hours of June 25, 1950, thousands of troops under the banner of the Democratic People's Republic of Korea (North Korea) moved across the 38th parallel into the Republic of Korea (South Korea). They "struck like a cobra," recalled General Douglas MacArthur. For years the two Koreas had skirmished along the border the great powers had drawn for them in 1945. Both regimes sought reunification of the divided country, but each on its own terms. Now it appeared that the North Koreans, heavily armed by the Russians, would realize their goal by force, for the South Koreans, armed by the Americans, soon disintegrated. When the news reached Washington, D.C., people recalled Pearl Harbor and braced themselves for a third world war.

For the thirty-third president, it was the 1930s all over again. "Communism was acting in Korea just as Hitler, Mussolini, and the Japanese had acted," Truman recalled. After huddling with his advisers, the president decided to intervene; he ordered MacArthur to send arms to South Korea and to attack North Korean forces from the air. Thinking beyond Korea, he directed the Seventh Fleet to patrol the waters between the Chinese mainland and Jiang's sanctuary, Formosa, thus inserting the United States once again into Chinese politics. Finally, on June 30, Truman ordered American troops into battle. "If Washington only will not hobble me," boasted

In 1950, after only five years of peace, the United States intervened in a war in Korea. In San Diego this officer and his wife stare at a waiting aircraft carrier before he departs for Korea. National Archives.

MacArthur, "I can handle it with one arm tied behind my back." After the Security Council, in the Soviet delegate's absence, voted to assist South Korea, MacArthur became United Nations Commander.

Truman acted decisively for war because he believed, in the Cold War mentality of the time, that the Soviets had masterminded the North Korean attack. As an assistant secretary of state put it, the relationship between the Soviet Union and North Korea was "the same as that between Walt Disney and Donald Duck." Though there is little evidence that the Soviets began the Korean War, at the time there was reason to believe that the Soviets were exploiting an opportunity to expand their influence. When most American troops withdrew from Korea in mid-1949, the Joint Chiefs of Staff had secretly declared South Korea nonvital to American

Origins of the Korean War

security. And in a public speech in January 1950, Secretary Acheson had drawn the American defense line in Asia through the Aleutians, Japan, and Okinawa to the Philippines. Although Formosa and Korea were clearly beyond that line, Acheson did say that those areas could expect United Nations (and hence American) assistance in the event of attack. Still, Stalin might have read Acheson's speech as an abandonment of South Korea. Russia may also have been willing to risk war to challenge China for leadership of the Communist world or to disrupt American peace negotiations with its long-time rival Japan.

But unanswered questions dog the thesis that Russia started the Korean War. The Soviet delegate was absent from the Security Council when it voted to aid South Korea because he was protesting the United Nations' refusal to seat the People's Republic of China. If the Soviets had fomented the war in Korea, it is surprising that their delegate was not present to veto aid to South Korea. Were they caught off-guard? And other questions are puzzling. Why did the Soviets give so little aid to the North Koreans once the war broke out? And why, when they were scoring important propaganda points by advocating peaceful coexistence, would they destroy their gains by igniting a war? Some scholars believe that the North Koreans began the war, for their own nationalistic reasons. To suggest this is to emphasize the *Korean* rather than international origins of the conflict—to focus on the civil war between the North Korean Communists led by Kim Il-sung and the South Korean government ruled by Syngman Rhee.

In June 1950 such questions were not being asked. Truman and his aides never doubted that Russia or international Communism was testing their policy of containment; that American prestige was at stake; and that failure to act in Korea would prompt Russian aggression in Iran or Berlin. And having bragged about toughness against Communism before, Truman could not now refrain from acting against North Korea.

At first the war (Truman called it a "police action") went badly. The North Koreans, utilizing tanks and superior firepower, sent the South Korean army into chaotic retreat. The first American troops sent into battle tried to buy time for General MacArthur's effort to amass larger forces. Taking heavy casualties, American soldiers slowed but could not stop the North Korean advance. Within weeks the South Koreans and Americans found themselves pushed into the tiny Pusan perimeter at the base of South Korea. There they dug in.

MacArthur began to plan a daring operation: an amphibious landing at Inchon, several hundred miles behind North Korean lines (see map). Inchon seemed an inhospitable place for such an **Inchon** attack, with high tides, narrow approach channels, mud flats, and heavy enemy fortifications. The Joint Chiefs of Staff balked, but MacArthur insisted. After American naval guns and bombs pounded Inchon, U.S. Marines sprinted ashore on September 15, 1950. By nightfall, 18,000 American troops were inland, ready with tanks and vehicles to move against the South Korean capital of Seoul. Soon they had liberated Seoul and pushed the North Koreans back to the 38th parallel. Even

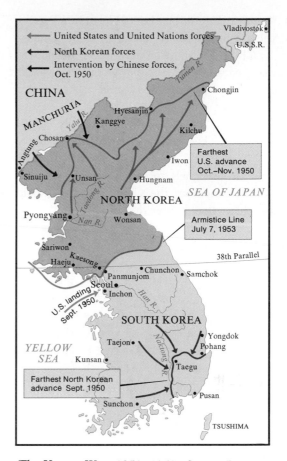

The Korean War, 1950–1953 Source: *By permission of the publisher, from* American Foreign Policy: A History *by Paterson et al., p. 378. (Lexington, Mass.: D.C. Heath and Company, 1977).*

before Inchon, Truman had decided to redefine the American war goal from the containment of North Korea to the reunification of Korea by force. Communism would not only be stopped; it would be rolled back. On September 27 Truman authorized United Nations forces (90 percent of them American) to cross the 38th parallel.

Within several weeks American troops had driven deeply into North Korea. In early November American aircraft began strikes against bridges on the Yalu River, the border between North Korea and the People's Republic of China. The Chinese watched warily, wondering if the Americans who had supported Jiang Jieshi would soon stab at the People's Republic. Mao issued public warnings that China could not permit the continued bombing of its transportation links with Korea or the annihilation of North Korea itself. MacArthur shrugged off the warnings, telling Truman that the Chinese would face the "greatest slaughter" if they entered the war. Officials in Washington agreed.

Chinese Entry into the Korean War

But they were dead wrong. In late October Americans had tangled with some Chinese soldiers, who pulled back quickly after the encounter. This may have been one of many signals to the United States that American advances to the Chinese border should halt, or China would enter the war. A month later an unmoved MacArthur sent his Eighth Army northward in a new offensive. On November 26, tens of thousands of Chinese troops counterattacked, surprising the general's forces and driving them pell-mell southward. Embarrassed, MacArthur demanded that Washington order a massive air attack on China. Truman hesitated, reflecting on the costs and consequences of a wider war. He hinted that he might use the atomic bomb, but he seemed chastened, uneager for a war that might drag on for years.

By March 1951 the military lines had stabilized around the 38th parallel. Truman contemplated negotiations, and the Soviets stated publicly that they favored a political settlement. But MacArthur had other ideas. The theatrical general was making reckless public statements, calling for an attack on China or for Jiang's return to the mainland. Now was the time, he insisted, to smash Communism by destroying its Asian flank. MacArthur also hinted that the president was practicing appeasement. Denouncing the concept of limited war (war without nuclear weapons, confined to one place), he told one member of Congress: "There is no substitute for victory."

Truman Fires MacArthur

On April 10 Truman fired the general for insubordination. MacArthur, who had not set foot in the United States for over a decade, returned home to a ticker-tape parade, and made a televised address to Congress that moved many in the audience to tears. One congressman was so spellbound that he murmured, "We saw a great hunk of God in the flesh."

Although Truman's popularity sagged, he withstood calls for his impeachment. The chairman of the Joint Chiefs of Staff, General Omar Bradley, spoke against MacArthur's provocative ideas. Escalation could bring Russia into battle, Bradley pointed out—American

bombs had already fallen close to the Siberian port of Vladivostok. And it was unwise to exhaust America's resources in an Asian war that promised no victory when there were allies in Europe to be protected. Indeed, a showdown with Asian Communists, Bradley told a Senate committee, would be "the wrong war, at the wrong place, at the wrong time, and with the wrong enemy." MacArthur had overestimated his popularity and soon faded from the public eye.

Armistice talks began in July 1951, but the fighting and dying went on for two more years. Though the new president, Dwight D. Eisenhower, went to Korea personally in December 1952 to fulfill a campaign pledge, his post-election visit brought no settlement.

The POW Question

Once he became president, Eisenhower let it be known privately that he was considering using atomic weapons in Korea. He hoped the Chinese would be frightened into an agreement. The sticking point in the negotiations was the fate of the prisoners of war (POWs): thousands of North Korean and Chinese captives did not want to return home. In violation of international custom, American officials honored their wishes and refused to ship them back against their will. The price for this position proved high: an extended war and 32,000 more American casualties. On July 23, 1953, an armistice was finally signed. The combatants agreed to hand the POW question over to a special panel of neutral nations (which later gave prisoners their choice of staying or leaving). The North Korean–South Korean line was set close to the 38th parallel, the prewar boundary. Thus ended a frustrating war—a limited war that Americans, accustomed to victory, had not won. No celebrations greeted news of the end of the war. The experience was indeed sobering, as was the casualty list of 34,000 Americans dead and 103,000 wounded. Total killed and wounded for all combatants in the Korean War was 1.9 million.

The Korean War had major political consequences. The failure to achieve victory and the public's impatience with a limited war undoubtedly helped to elect Eisenhower (see pages 847–849). Bipartisanship in foreign policy eroded further, and the powers of the presidency grew as Congress deferred to Truman time and again. Truman had never gone to Congress for a declaration of war, for he believed that as commander-in-chief he had the authority to send troops to Korea. A few dissenters like Senator Robert Taft disagreed, but Truman saw no need to debate the matter. Had he asked for a declaration, he would have had majorities in both houses. But as Dean Acheson later explained, Truman did not wish to invite hearings and "ponderous questions" that might have "muddled up" presidential decisions.

The Korean War also set off a great national debate. Conservative critics of globalism, like Taft, former ambassador to England Joseph P. Kennedy, and ex-president Herbert Hoover, suggested

Debate over Globalist Policy that America should reduce its overseas commitments and draw its defense line in the Western Hemisphere. If foreign nations were not willing to commit their own resources to defending themselves, the United States had no obligation to help them, they reasoned. But Republican John Foster Dulles countered that "a defense that accepts encirclement quickly decomposes." Truman himself joined the debate with bloated rhetoric exaggerating the Communist threat: "We are fighting in Korea so we won't have to fight in Wichita, or in Chicago, or in New Orleans, or on San Francisco Bay."

The advocates of global defense won the debate. Increased aid flowed to the French for their die-hard stand in Indochina; by 1954, when the French effort finally collapsed, the United States was paying three-quarters of the war's cost (see Chapter 32). South Korea and Formosa also became major recipients of American foreign aid. And Australia and New Zealand joined the United States in a mutual defense agreement, the ANZUS Treaty (1951), which provided that an attack on any of the three countries would be considered an attack on all.

The Korean War, Acheson noted happily, removed "the recommendations of NSC-68 from the realm of theory and made them immediate budget issues." Indeed, the military budget shot up to $44 billion in 1953 (it had been $14 billion in 1949) and remained at $35 to $44 billion a year throughout the 1950s. The American military acquired new bases in Morocco (1951) and Spain (1953), among other places; developed the hydrogen bomb; and introduced a new long-range bomber, the B-52. The army sent six divisions to Europe, and the administration initiated plans to rearm West Germany. Proponents claimed that the logic of the containment doctrine required

this global military watch, for if the threat was worldwide, the response had to be worldwide as well. "If you don't pay attention to the periphery," diplomat Dean Rusk warned, "the periphery changes. And the first thing you know the periphery is the center."

But the periphery did not in fact always become the center. Some areas were vital and others were not. Nor did a global watch ensure security. One member of Congress compared containment to "sending three policemen to surround a building that has 25 exits." And as Walter Lippmann had warned, blind allegiance to the containment doctrine did lead to repeated overseas ventures and alliances with questionable clients and dictators. Officials also assumed wrongly that threats to world peace always sprang from international Communist intrigue. They overlooked the local, non-Communist roots of many rebellions against the status quo, and they underestimated the independence of non-Russian Communists. In the future, Americans would struggle in a revolutionary world where nationalism rather than Communism was the driving force in international affairs—a force that would be subordinated neither to the United States nor to the Soviet Union.

WARTIME DISCONTENT AND THE ELECTION OF 1952

As Senator Joseph McCarthy raged on and Americans mobilized for the war in Korea, they remembered shortages in the last war and flocked

Korean War on the Home Front to their grocery stores for sugar, shortening, razor blades, and canned goods. And fearing that Detroit would have to convert to the manufacture of military vehicles, Americans bought cars in a hurry. Orders for military supplies flooded factories. Ford built engines for B-36 bombers; the American Locomotive Company contracted for medium-size tanks; other companies filled requests for boots, sandbags, bandages, and jackets. By the end of 1950 U.S. Steel was enjoying its greatest profits since 1917.

Fueled by panic buying and these huge federal expenditures, inflation, which had not been a problem since 1948, began to eat away at the economy again: prices rose 8 percent in the first eight months of the war. In January 1951, after six months of inflation, the government froze wages and prices. Although administering the controls proved to be a nightmare—especially after Truman's unconstitutional seizure of the steel industry in 1952, when it rejected a government-recommended wage increase—inflation had been brought under control by mid-1951. Meanwhile, factories hummed, the gross national product grew, disposable personal income increased, and unemployment fell. Reform-minded Democrats were not altogether pleased, however, for defense mobilization was taking precedence over Fair Deal programs. "Every liberal movement has been stopped cold at the time of national emergency," groaned Senator Hubert Humphrey.

Draft boards registered men between the ages of eighteen and twenty-five and began to call them up. National Guardsmen and reservists were elevated to active duty. There was no rush to join. "Everybody wants out; no one wants in," complained the director of the draft. Husbands and fathers thought single men should go first; parents wrote protest letters when in 1951 the military began to draft eighteen-and-a-half-year-olds. When the government announced that college students would be granted deferments, young people enrolled in universities. Other students hoped that the war would end before their graduation. But the war did not end quickly, and by mid-1952 American military personnel numbered 3.6 million, up from 1.5 million two years earlier.

As the 1952 presidential election approached, the Democrats foundered. Added to frustration with the war and hysteria over Communism was the revelation of influence-peddling by some of Truman's cronies. Known as "five-percenters," these presidential appointees had offered government contracts in return for 5-percent kickbacks. In exchange for help in expediting the importation of perfume ingredients, Truman's military aide and friend Major General Harry Vaughn had accepted a freezer. An employee of the executive branch admitted under oath, "I have only one thing to sell and that is influence." In 1951 Truman's public-approval rating slumped to an all-time low of 23 percent and hovered at that level for

the next year. Once again the Democratic party seemed doomed along with its leader—only this time the prediction was correct. Voters agreed with the 1952 Republican campaign slogan, "It's Time for a Change."

What sealed the fate of the Democratic party was the Republican candidate, General Dwight D. Eisenhower, who had changed his mind about the appropriateness of a military man running for office. "Ike" was a bona fide war hero with a winning smile, a man who seemed to embody the virtues Americans most admired: integrity, decency, lack of pretense, and the ability to rise from humble beginnings. His running mate, Senator Richard M. Nixon, was less likable. Accused during the campaign of having been the beneficiary of a secret slush fund raised by wealthy Californians, Nixon went on television to deny the charge. The only gift his family had received, he explained, was a puppy named Checkers. His daughters loved the little dog, and "we're gonna keep it."

The Republican Ticket

Eisenhower's unlucky Democratic opponent was Adlai Stevenson, the thoughtful, literate, and witty governor of Illinois. From the outset it was never much of a contest. Eisenhower promised to end the Korean War, and though he remained cautiously silent on the subject of McCarthyism, his running mate did not. Nixon scored political points by referring to Stevenson as "Adlai the appeaser . . . who got a Ph.D. from Dean Acheson's College of Cowardly Communist Containment." The result was a landslide: Eisenhower won almost 34 million popular votes and 442 electoral votes, compared with the Democrats' 27 million popular and 89 electoral votes.

Dwight D. Eisenhower's 1952 presidential election victory was a great personal triumph. Several issues, including the Korean War, stirred the voters. By election day, armistice negotiations in Korea had been dragging on for almost one and a half years. There was still sporadic and heavy fighting, and Eisenhower had promised to visit Korea and end the war. Americans were also upset by White House corruption and alleged Communism in the State Department. All these factors coalesced to produce a record turnout of 61.5 million voters, 13 million more than in 1948. Many wanted to express their enthusiasm for Eisenhower, war hero and trusted statesman, who won the votes of Americans from a

IMPORTANT EVENTS

1945	Yalta Conference
	Roosevelt dies; Truman assumes presidency
	United Nations founded
	Germany surrenders
	Potsdam Conference
	Atomic bombs devastate Hiroshima and Nagasaki
	Japan surrenders
	Truman's 21-point economic message to Congress
1946	Crisis over Iran
	Employment Act of 1946
	Churchill's Iron Curtain speech
	Strikes by coal miners
	Paris Peace Conference
	Baruch Plan
	Truman fires Secretary of Commerce Wallace
	Inflation reaches 18.2 percent
	Republicans win both houses of Congress
1947	Truman Doctrine
	Truman's Employee Loyalty Program
	Communist takeover in Hungary
	Taft-Hartley Act
	Kennan's "Mr. X" article
	Marshall Plan announced
	To Secure These Rights
	National Security Act
	Rio Pact
1948	Communist coup in Czechoslovakia
	State of Israel founded
	Berlin blockade and airlift
	Truman elected president
1949	North Atlantic Treaty Organization founded
	Russia explodes atomic bomb
	Communist victory in China
1950	Klaus Fuchs arrested as atomic spy
	Alger Hiss convicted of perjury
	Hydrogen bomb project announced
	McCarthy alleges Communists in government
	Freedom to Serve
	NSC-68
	Point Four Program launched
	Korean War begins
	Julius and Ethel Rosenberg arrested
	Inchon
	Internal Security (McCarran) Act
	U.S. troops cross the 38th parallel
	China enters the Korean War
1951	Armistice talks begin in Korea
	Dennis et al. v. U.S.
1952	Hydrogen bomb exploded
	Eisenhower elected president
	Republicans win both houses of Congress
1953	Korean War ends

diversity of socioeconomic groups, educational levels, and religious faiths. He even captured four states in the once-solid Democratic South. Moreover, Eisenhower's coattails were long enough to carry other Republicans to victory; the party gained control of both houses of Congress, though with only a one-seat margin in the Senate (forty-eight Republicans, forty-seven Democrats, one Independent).

Although Truman was highly unpopular when he left office in 1953, historians now rate him among the nation's ten best presidents. He came to office

Truman's Presidential Legacy

suddenly and with little experience, but in eight years he greatly strengthened the powers of the presidency. At the onset of the Cold War he had announced policies to contain any presumed threat of Soviet expansion. During his presidency the Central Intelligence Agency,

National Security Council, Council of Economic Advisers, and a unified Department of Defense were all created. Truman's main problems stemmed from his overreaction to the alleged threat of Communist subversion in government. His loyalty program ruined innocent people's lives and careers. In drumming up support for his foreign and military policies, Truman presented a frightening picture to the American people of the Communists' aims and with his rhetoric he helped prepare the way for McCarthyism. Finally, he sent American troops to fight in Korea without a declaration of war from Congress.

At the same time, Truman was still a New Dealer who fought for social welfare programs and legislation for farmers and workers. His Fair Deal, most of which was enacted during subsequent presidential administrations, included first-class citizenship for Afro-Americans. He showed his spunk and courage in 1948, when he pulled the biggest upset in American political history. When he left office in 1953, he had set the United States on a course from which it would not veer in the future and had cast a long shadow across the country's twentieth-century history.

SUGGESTIONS FOR FURTHER READING

Origins of the Cold War and Policy Toward Europe

Stephen Ambrose, *Rise to Globalism*, 3rd ed. (1983); Richard J. Barnet, *The Alliance* (1983); Seyom Brown, *The Faces of Power* (1983); Leonard Dinnerstein, *America and the Survivors of the Holocaust* (1982); John L. Gaddis, *The United States and the Origins of the Cold War, 1941–1947* (1972); Louis Halle, *The Cold War as History* (1967); Laurence S. Kaplan, *The United States and NATO* (1984); Gabriel Kolko and Joyce Kolko, *The Limits of Power* (1972); Bruce Kuklick, *American Policy and the Division of Germany* (1972); Walter LaFeber, *America, Russia, and the Cold War, 1945–1980*, 4th ed. (1980); Melvyn Leffler, "The American Concept of National Security and the Beginnings of the Cold War, 1945–1948," *American Historical Review*, 89 (1984), 346–381; David McLellan, *Dean Acheson* (1976); Thomas G. Paterson, *On Every Front: The Making of the Cold War* (1979); Thomas G. Paterson, *Soviet-American Confrontation* (1973); Thomas G. Paterson, ed., *Cold War Critics* (1971); Gaddis Smith, *Dean Acheson* (1972); William Taubman, *Stalin's American Policy* (1982); Adam Ulam, *The Rivals* (1971); Bernard A. Weisberger, *Cold War, Cold Peace* (1984); Imanuel Wexler, *The Marshall Plan Revisited* (1983); Daniel Yergin, *Shattered Peace* (1977). (Also see works cited in Chapter 28 on the diplomacy of the Second World War and the atomic bomb.)

Truman Doctrine, Containment, and the Middle East

Thomas H. Etzold and John L. Gaddis, eds., *Containment* (1978); Richard M. Freeland, *The Truman Doctrine and the Origins of McCarthyism* (1972); John L. Gaddis, *Strategies of Containment* (1982); Charles Gati, ed., *Caging the Bear* (1974); John D. Iatrides, *Revolt in Athens* (1972); George F. Kennan, *Memoirs, 1925–1950* (1967); Bruce R. Kuniholm, *The Origins of the Cold War in the Near East* (1980); Walter Lippmann, *The Cold War* (1947); William R. Louis, *The British Empire in the Middle East, 1945–1951* (1984); Aaron D. Miller, *Search for Security* (1980); Thomas G. Paterson, ed., *Containment and the Cold War* (1973); Michael B. Stoff, *Oil, War, and American Security* (1980); Samuel F. Wells, Jr., "Sounding the Tocsin: NSC-68 and the Soviet Threat," *International Security*, 4 (1979), 116–158; Lawrence S. Wittner, *American Intervention in Greece, 1943–1949* (1982); C. Ben Wright, "Mr. 'X' and Containment," *Slavic Review*, 35 (1976), 1–31.

China and Asia

Robert M. Blum, *Drawing the Line* (1982); Dorothy Borg and Waldo Heinrichs, eds., *Uncertain Years* (1980); Russell Buhite, *Soviet-American Relations in Asia, 1945–1954* (1982); Warren I. Cohen, *America's Response to China*, 2nd ed. (1980); Herbert Feis, *Contest over Japan* (1967); Herbert Feis, *The China Tangle* (1953); Akira Iriye, *The Cold War in Asia* (1974); E. J. Kahn, Jr., *The China Hands* (1975); William R. Louis, *Imperialism at Bay: The United States and the Decolonization of the British Empire* (1978); Gary May, *China Scapegoat: The Diplomatic Ordeal of John Carter Vincent* (1979); Charles E. Neu, *The Troubled Encounter: The United States and Japan* (1975); Michael Schaller, *The United States and China in the Twentieth Century* (1979); Michael Schaller, *The U.S. Crusade in China, 1938–1945* (1978); William W. Stueck, Jr., *The Road to Confrontation: American Policy Toward China and Korea, 1947–1950* (1981); Christopher Thorne, *Allies of a Kind* (1978); Tang Tsou, *America's Failure in China, 1941–1950* (1963); Nancy B. Tucker, *Patterns in the Dust: Chinese-American Relations and the Recognition Controversy, 1949–1950* (1983).

Politics of the Truman Administration

Barton J. Bernstein, ed., *Politics and Policies of the Truman Administration* (1970); Bert Cochran, *Harry Truman and the Crisis Presidency* (1973); Robert J. Donovan, *Tumultuous Years: The Presidency of Harry S Truman, 1949–1953* (1982); Robert J. Donovan, *Conflict and Crisis: The Presidency of Harry S Truman, 1945–1948* (1977); Andrew J. Dunar, *The Truman Scandals and the Politics of Morality* (1984); Robert H. Ferrell, *Harry S Truman and the Modern American Presidency* (1983); Alonzo L. Hamby, *Beyond the New Deal: Harry S Truman and American Liberalism* (1973); Susan Hartmann, *Truman and the 80th Congress* (1971); Donald R. McCoy, *The Presidency of Harry S Truman* (1984).

Truman and the Economy

Stephen K. Bailey, *Congress Makes a Law: The Story Behind the Employment Act of 1946* (1950); Jack Stokes Ballard, *The Shock of Peace: Military and Economic Demobilization After World War II* (1983); Richard O. Davies, *Housing Reform During the Truman Administration* (1966); R. Alton Lee, *Truman and Taft-Hartley* (1966); Maeva Marcus, *Truman and the Steel Seizure Case* (1977); Allen J. Matusow, *Farm Policies and Politics in the Truman Years* (1967); Arthur F. McClure, *The Truman Administration and the Problems of Postwar Labor* (1969).

The Election of 1948

V. O. Key, *Southern Politics in State and Nation* (1949); Norman D. Markowitz, *The Rise and Fall of the People's Century: Henry A. Wallace and American Liberalism, 1941–1948* (1973); Richard Norton-Smith, *Thomas E. Dewey and His Times* (1982); Irwin Ross, *The Loneliest Campaign: The Truman Victory of 1948* (1968), Allen Yarnell, *Democrats and Progressives: The 1948 Presidential Election as a Test of Postwar Liberalism* (1974).

Civil Rights

William C. Berman, *The Politics of Civil Rights in the Truman Administration* (1970); Richard M. Dalfiume, *Desegregation of the U.S. Armed Forces* (1969); Richard Kluger, *Simple Justice: The History of* Brown v. Board of Education *and Black America's Struggle for Equality* (1975); Donald R. McCoy and Richard T. Ruetten, *Quest and Response: Minority Rights and the Truman Administration* (1973); Harvard Sitkoff, "Harry Truman and the Election of 1948: The Coming of Age of Civil Rights in American Politics," *Journal of Southern History*, 37 (1971), 597–616; Jules Tygiel, *Baseball's Great Experiment: Jackie Robinson and His Legacy* (1983).

McCarthyism

Michael R. Belknap, *Cold War Political Justice: The Smith Act, the Communist Party, and American Civil Liberties* (1977); David Caute, *The Great Fear* (1978); Larry Ceplair and Steven Englund, *The Inquisition in Hollywood* (1983); Robert Griffith, *The Politics of Fear: Joseph R. McCarthy and the Senate* (1970); Stanley I. Kutler, *The American Inquisition: Justice and Injustice in the Cold War* (1982); Harvey Levenstein, *Communism, Anticommunism, and the CIO* (1981); Mary Sperling McAuliffe, *Crisis on the Left: Cold War Politics and American Liberals, 1947–1954* (1978); Victor Navasky, *Naming Names* (1980); William L. O'Neill, *A Better World: Stalinism and the American Intellectuals* (1983); David M. Oshinsky, *A Conspiracy So Immense: The World of Joe McCarthy* (1983); Ronald Radosh and Joyce Milton, *The Rosenberg File* (1983); Thomas C. Reeves, *The Life and Times of Joe McCarthy* (1982); Michael Paul Rogin, *The Intellectuals and McCarthy* (1967); Walter and Miriam Schneir, *Invitation to an Inquest* (1983 ed.); Athan Theoharis, *Seeds of Repression: Harry S Truman and the Origins of McCarthyism* (1971); Allen Weinstein, *Perjury: The Hiss-Chambers Case* (1978).

The Korean War and Korean-American Relations

Ronald J. Caridi, *The Korean War and American Politics* (1969), Bruce Cumings, ed., *Child of Conflict* (1983); Bruce Cumings, *The Origins of the Korean War* (1980); Charles Dobbs, *The Unwanted Symbol* (1981); Joseph C. Goulden, *Korea* (1982); Glenn D. Paige, *The Korean Decision* (1968); David Rees, *Korea: The Limited War* (1964); Robert R. Simmons, *The Strained Alliance* (1975); John W. Spanier, *The Truman-MacArthur Controversy and the Korean War* (1959); I. F. Stone, *The Hidden History of the Korean War* (1952); Allen Whiting, *China Crosses the Yalu* (1960).

An Age of
Fragile Consensus
1953–1961

Chapter 30

The signs of patriotism were everywhere. Whether beating Russian athletes at the Olympics, bragging about new records in automobile ownership, or marveling at the nation's powerful military machine, Americans celebrated their country as the best place on earth. Certainly it was better than the Soviet Union. And to trumpet that difference, sermonized the Presbyterian minister George M. Docherty on February 7, 1954, religion should be enlisted. "One nation, indivisible, with liberty and justice for all"— American schoolchildren recited those famous words every morning in pledges of allegiance to the flag. With President Dwight D. Eisenhower sitting in his congregation that day, the Reverend Docherty implored political leaders to insert "under God" after "one nation" in the flag pledge. Nobody could utter *those* words in the Soviet Union, where atheistic Communists ruled. The president agreed, and Congress hastened to make the change.

This small episode conjoining religion, patriotism, and politics befitted the 1950s, an age of consensus. In that decade Americans generally shared a belief in anti-Communism and economic progress. Republican President Eisenhower, hardly the passive, ill-informed chief executive the Democrats tried to depict, was active in articulating the two beliefs and devising programs to satisfy them. But he moved cautiously and preferred a hidden-hand style to conspicuous displays of political arm-twisting.

Believing that Communists posed a mortal danger to the American system, the Eisenhower administration expanded Truman's loyalty program, endorsed restrictive legislation, and purged the State Department. The president was reluctant to confront directly Senator Joseph McCarthy, whose anti-Communist tactics proved reckless. McCarthy eventually destroyed himself with his excesses, but not before he had damaged many people and the nation itself. To maintain economic growth, Eisenhower pursued staunchly Republican goals: a balanced budget, reduced government spending, lower taxes, low inflation, private enterprise, a return of power to the states, and modest federal efforts to stimulate economic development. The Eisenhower officials did not attempt to roll back the New Deal and Fair Deal. In fact, however reluctantly, they expanded the welfare state.

Holding to their consensus thinking, white Americans celebrated their economic system for providing a high standard of living. But recurrent recessions and continued poverty in the midst of plenty raised doubts that economic progress had bestowed its benefits on all. An infant civil rights movement especially challenged the consensus view. Not only were most blacks at the bottom of the economic ladder; they were being denied their constitutional rights. How would blacks be brought into the consensus? The president, Congress, southern whites, black civil rights activists—all gave different answers as they debated the Supreme Court's 1954 *Brown* decision.

In foreign affairs, too, Eisenhower's low-key style and the two features of the consensus were evident. Eisenhower essentially continued Truman's Cold War policies, applying the containment doctrine worldwide. To wage the Cold War, the administration relied on nuclear weapons and interventions, some of them by a major new instrument of foreign policy, the Central Intelligence Agency (CIA). Many of the CIA's covert operations were directed against governments in the Third World, where new states were emerging from colonialism to nationhood. Americans feared that revolutionary nationalism and unrest in Third World countries was or would be exploited by Communists linked to a Soviet-led international conspiracy. Serious obstacles impeded the projection of United States influence into the Third World. And in Latin America the United States faced several revolutionary challenges to its hegemony. Those challenges often took the form of an economic nationalism that threatened American companies. The United States, then, intervened abroad not just to stop communism, but also to protect American economic overseas interests, which traditionally had contributed to economic growth at home.

President Eisenhower left office a disappointed man. The nuclear arms race had accelerated, race relations had deteriorated, and his vice president, Richard M. Nixon, had lost the 1960 presidential election to Senator John F. Kennedy. The young Kennedy had criticized Eisenhower's domestic policies as inadequate to sustain economic progress for all Americans. And he had faulted Eisenhower's foreign policy for not winning the Cold War and for not aligning the Third World with the United States. Yet the consensus, however fragile, remained basically intact, for Kennedy too shared its premises. Scholars largely agree that for all the political rhetoric of the 1960 campaign the Eisenhower presidency was the kind most Americans desired in the 1950s age of consensus. Americans liked "Ike's" traditionalism, caution, and moderation. He reassured them, and they trusted him.

CONSENSUS AND THE POLITICS OF EISENHOWER'S FIRST TERM

Smiling Ike, with his folksy style, displays of confusion, garbled syntax, and frequent escapes from the Oval Office to the golf course, fueled Democratic charges that he failed to lead—"the bland leading the bland." But it was not that simple. Dwight D. Eisenhower was no stranger to hard work. His low-key, hidden-hand style was his way of playing down his political role and highlighting his role as chief of state. He was also timid about tangling directly with the vocal right wing of the Republican party. Eisenhower relied considerably upon staff work, delegated authority to departments, and shied away from close involvement in the legislative process. Sometimes this meant that he was not well informed on details, giving the impression that he was out of touch with his own government. He was not, and he remained a very popular president.

During Eisenhower's presidency, with few exceptions, Americans clung to the status quo. It was a time of both national self-congratulation and worry.

The Consensus Mood

The British journalist Godfrey Hodgson, describing the "consensus mood," wrote that Americans were "confident to the verge of complacency about the perfectibility of American society, anxious to the point of paranoia about the threat of communism." Much as they might bicker about how the Cold War should be waged or about how the economy should be managed, they were one when it came to anti-Communism and a faith in economic progress. Most white Americans believed not only that the United States was the greatest nation in the world, but that its potential was boundless. For middle-class Americans who surrounded themselves with the symbols of economic success—automobiles, televisions, and houses in suburbia—the American dream seemed a reality (see Chapter 31).

Demand for reform at such a time was deemed not only unnecessary but downright unpatriotic. The country was engaged in a moral struggle with Communism, people believed, and during such a crusade one should support, not criticize, the government. Almost everywhere he looked, the historian Henry Steele Commager saw conformity: "the uncritical and unquestioning acceptance of America as it is." College students shunned passionate political convictions, liking instead to be "cool." A weak minority on the left advocated checks on the political power of corporations and a noisy minority on the right vilified the government for a supposed wishy-washy campaign against Communism, but both liberal Democrats and moderate Republicans avoided extremism of any variety, satisfied to be occupying "the vital center."

Along with this attitude of conformity went trust in and respect for established authority. In government, business, labor, the military, religion, and education, Americans let those at the top bargain on their behalf. And they chose to pursue economic goals more than moral ones, believing that the latter were not merely unimportant but also unattainable. Like their leaders, Americans feared mass movements, even those with democratic goals like the civil rights movement, as threats to stability. It seemed preferable for people to spend their time earning a living, raising a family of togetherness, and contributing their tax dollars toward a stronger America than to become involved in an idealistic crusade. "The fifties under Ike," Richard Lingeman of the *New York Times* observed, "represented a sort of national prefrontal lobotomy: tail-finned, we Sunday-drove down the superhighways of life while tensions that later bubbled up in the sixties seethed beneath the placid surface."

Scholars of the 1950s who subscribed to the consensus proclaimed the "end of ideology" in America.

On July 4, 1961, patriotic residents of a Chicago neighborhood posed in front of their flag-draped homes. Patriotism was a prominent characteristic of the age of consensus. National Archives.

Since the early twentieth century, historians had told the American story as one of conflict—rich against poor, North against South, farmer against industrialist and banker. They focused on rebellions, strikes, moral crusades, and wars. But the historians of the 1950s wrote about stability, continuity, and cultural wholeness; they spoke of *the* American experience and *the* national character.

Consensus Historiography

Important books were published on these themes, among them Daniel Boorstin's *The Americans: The Colonial Experience* (1958); Louis Hartz's *The Liberal Tradition in America* (1955); Richard Hofstadter's *The Age of Reform* (1955); and David Potter's *People of Plenty* (1954). Historians did not deny the existence of conflict in the American past, but they ascribed it less to flaws in society than to psychologically disturbed personalities. Among the people historians identified as maladjusted were abolitionists, feminists,

Populists, and progressive reformers. The consensus interpretation thus shifted the focus away from society's faults—slavery, sexism, or political corruption—and placed it on the critics who demanded reform. As the historian John Higham has noted, "A psychological approach to conflict enables historians to substitute a schism in the soul for a schism in society."

In this age of consensus, President Eisenhower approached his duties with a philosophy of "dynamic conservatism," explaining that he would be "conservative when it comes to money and liberal when it comes to human beings." Eisenhower's was "an Administration representing business and industry," admitted Interior Secretary Douglas McKay. One journalist referred to the cabinet as "eight millionaires and a plumber"—an accurate description until the plumber resigned within a year. Eisenhower and his appointees thus gave priority to

"Dynamic Conservatism"

Chapter 30: AN AGE OF FRAGILE CONSENSUS, 1953–1961

reducing the federal budget. Eisenhower officials recognized that they could not dismantle New Deal and Fair Deal programs, because this would have been politically impossible. They knew as well that most government expenditures consisted of fixed, built-in costs such as veterans' pensions, social security benefits, and interest payments on the national debt. Soon the Republican right wing complained that Ike was a "fifth-column Democrat" for not moving more forthrightly against the welfare state and slashing the budget more. In turn, Eisenhower grew impatient with those he privately scorned as "hidebound reactionaries." For the president, "progressive moderates" were more sensible.

True to the principles of the free marketplace and a balanced budget, Eisenhower tried in his first term to get the federal government out of agriculture. Since the 1930s the government had **Farm Program** made payments to farmers based upon the difference between the market price and the higher parity price for farm goods. (The parity price was equivalent in value to the price farmers enjoyed in the good years of 1909–1910.) After paying farmers this price support, the government took and stored their surplus products. Farmers received huge support payments, and government bins bulged with surplus wheat and other commodities. And farm production increased through the accelerated use of chemical fertilizers and machinery. Prices still fell, and farmers' purchasing power declined. Millions of farmers—most of them small landowners—abandoned farming altogether. Eisenhower officials concluded that lower, flexible price supports would discourage production. But the Agricultural Act of 1954 only lowered them to 75 to 90 percent of parity. Two years later the Soil Bank Act provided for federal payments to farmers who agreed to take cropland out of production. Another farm bill in 1958 reduced the price support for some crops to 65 percent of parity. None of this worked; the government spent more and the surpluses grew. All of this was very distasteful to President Eisenhower. He remarked later that the federal farm program was a "national disgrace."

Eisenhower made better headway with other issues. In 1954 Congress approved the St. Lawrence Seaway project to construct a canal between Montreal and Lake Erie. This inland waterway was intended to spur the economic development of the Midwest by linking the Great Lakes to the Atlantic Ocean. The president also made a Cold War case for the joint Canadian-American project: it would strengthen the security of both nations. That year, too, Eisenhower signed into law amendments to the Social Security Act that raised benefits and added 7.5 million workers, largely self-employed farmers, to the program's coverage. In the first of many such measures during the decade, the Housing Act of 1954 provided federal funds for the construction of houses for low-income families displaced by urban renewal's destruction of their neighborhoods. Congress also obliged the president in 1954 with tax reform that increased deductions and raised business depreciation allowances and the Atomic Energy Act, which granted private companies the right to own reactors and nuclear materials for the production of electric power. But there was a legislative setback for the president: his inability to persuade Congress to promote private rather than public development of hydroelectric power (the Dixon-Yates controversy).

The Eisenhower administration also presided over a dramatic change in the lives of Native Americans. In 1953, Congress adopted *termination*, whose purpose it was to liquidate Indian reservations **Termination** tions and end federal services. **Policy for** Eisenhower officials seemed disposed **Native** toward the new policy because it **Americans** would reduce federal costs and serve states rights by eliminating federal trusteeship, making Indians subject to state laws. Critics—including most Indians—denounced termination as another white attempt to grab Indian lands. Between 1954 and 1960, the federal government withdrew its benefits from sixty-one tribes, and about one in eight Indians abandoned their reservations in return for small relocation payments. Under the new policies many Indians joined the urban poor. A Senate committee reported in 1969 that members of the terminated tribe of the Klamath in Oregon suffered "extreme social disorganization" and "many of them can be found in state mental and penal institutions." By the time termination was halted in the 1960s, so much human tragedy had visited Native Americans that observers compared their modern plight to their distress in the late nineteenth century.

In the 1954 congressional elections, voters revealed

Recovering from a heart attack in 1955, President Dwight D. Eisenhower (1890–1969) registers his famous smile from a hospital wheelchair. He went on to win re-election decisively in 1956. Wide World Photos.

the already ailing railroads, and spurred the growth of the suburbs, which were built farther and farther from the central cities (see pages 890–893).

Although Eisenhower suffered a heart attack in September 1955, he regained his strength in months and soon declared his intention to run again. With

Election of 1956

much relief the Republicans nominated the popular president for a second term. The Democrats ran Adlai E. Stevenson once more (see page 848). The campaigns lacked spirit, and the party platforms differed little. With recent crises over Hungary and Suez much on their minds, Americans decided to stick with an experienced military man and statesman at a time of world unrest. Eisenhower won a landslide victory in 1956: 35.6 million votes and 457 electoral votes to Stevenson's 26 million and 73. Still, his personal victory did not aid the Republicans in Congress, where the Democrats continued to dominate.

that while they still liked Ike, at heart they remained loyal to the Democratic party. With a recession just winding down and the controversy over Joseph McCarthy as a backdrop, the voters gave the Democrats control of both houses of Congress. Lyndon B. Johnson became the new Senate majority leader. An energetic, pragmatic politician from Texas, he tried to work with the Republican White House to achieve legislation. A notable ac-

Interstate Highway System

complishment was the Highway Act of 1956. This law authorized the spending of $31 billion over the next thirteen years to build a 41,000-mile interstate highway system, intended to permit the military to move around the nation more easily and to assist commerce. The Highway Trust Fund, fed by new taxes on gasoline, would finance much of the construction. As the largest public works program in American history, the interstate highways invigorated the tourist industry, further weakened

THE DECLINE OF MCCARTHYISM

D uring Eisenhower's first term, one of the most vexing problems for the administration was the conduct of Senator Joseph R. McCarthy (see

Eisenhower on McCarthy

pages 842–843). His no-holds-barred search for subversives in government turned up none, but it did affront political fair play, decency, and civil liberties. The president privately labeled the senator a "pimple on the path of progress," but he avoided directly confronting him, saying he would not "get into the gutter with that guy." Eisenhower also feared that a showdown would splinter the Republican party. Instead the president spoke against unnamed "demagogues thirsty for personal power," and hoped the media and Congress would bring McCarthy down. "You know," Eisenhower told his press secretary, "what we ought to do is get a word to put ahead of Republican. Something like 'new' or 'modern' " so that McCarthy and his ilk would bolt and form a third party. But the president made no such move, even when the senator began to accuse the administration of permitting "treason" to persist in the government.

While Eisenhower tried his quiet strategy to undermine the senator, his administration practiced its own brand of anti-Communism. A new executive order in 1953 broadened Truman's loyalty program (see pages 840–841). The administration periodically announced the number of "security risks" it had dismissed from their government jobs, including State Department officials (see page 863). One of Eisenhower's most controversial decisions came in June 1953 when he denied clemency to Julius and Ethel Rosenberg, who had been convicted of treason (see page 842). They were executed. Late that year, at the urging of the chairman of the Atomic Energy

Oppenheimer Case

Commission, the president suspended the security clearance of J. Robert Oppenheimer, the celebrated physicist who had directed the atomic bomb project at Los Alamos during the Second World War. Oppenheimer's "crimes" were not that he was either disloyal to his nation or a risk to its security, but rather that he had apparently later misrepresented a 1943 conversation with a friend on Soviet interest in atomic secrets and that he had opposed the government's crash program to develop the hydrogen bomb.

In 1954 the Communist Control Act demonstrated that both liberals and conservatives shared the consensus of anti-Communism. In effect making membership in the Communist party illegal, the measure passed the Senate unanimously and the House 265 to 2. The chief sponsor of the bill, liberal Democratic Senator Hubert H. Humphrey of Minnesota, told his colleagues just before he cast his vote: "We have closed all of the doors. These rats [Communists] will not get out of the trap." Years later Humphrey said of his role in the legislation that "it's not one of the things I'm proudest of."

As for Senator McCarthy, he finally undercut himself. He transgressed the limits of what the Senate and the public would tolerate. His crucial mistake was not merely taking on the U.S. Army, but doing so in front of millions of television viewers. At issue was the senator's wild accusation that the army was shielding and promoting Communists; he cited the case of one army dentist. The Army-McCarthy hearings, held by a Senate subcommittee in 1954, became

A falling Senator Joseph McCarthy hands the mud-slinging brush of McCarthyism to fellow McCarthyites Vice President Richard M. Nixon and Indiana Senator William Jenner. "Carry on, lads" says the Wisconsin senator in this cartoon by Herblock. From Herblock's Here and Now (Simon & Schuster, 1955).

a showcase for his abusive treatment of witnesses. At one general, whose loyalty was never in doubt, McCarthy shouted, "You are a disgrace to the uniform. You're shielding Communist conspirators. . . . You're not fit to be an officer. You're ignorant." McCarthy alternately ranted and, appearing drunk, slurred his words. Finally, after he had attacked a young lawyer who was not even involved in the hearings, Joseph Welch, counsel for the army, asked, "Have you no sense of decency, sir?" The gallery erupted in applause, and McCarthy's career as a witch-hunter rapidly came

Senate Condemnation of McCarthy

to a close. In December 1954, in a 67 to 22 vote, the Senate condemned McCarthy, not for defiling the Bill of Rights but for sullying the dignity of the Senate with his contemptuous behavior. He remained a senator, but exhaustion and alcohol took their toll. He died in 1957 at the age of forty-eight.

President Eisenhower's reluctance publicly to discredit McCarthy gave the senator, other right-wing members of Congress, and some private and public institutions enough rein to damage the nation and destroy the careers of many innocent people. The City University of New York, for example, fired eighteen professors—and did not apologize to them until 1980. Eisenhower's own government-sponsored McCarthyism demoralized and frightened federal workers, some of whom were driven from public service. The anti-Communist campaigns of the 1950s also discouraged people from freely expressing themselves and hence from debating critical issues of the time. Fear and a contempt for the Bill of Rights, then, helped sustain the consensus.

AN AWAKENED CIVIL RIGHTS MOVEMENT

If Eisenhower was pleased to be rid of McCarthy, he did not welcome the invigorated civil rights movement. Although the president completed the desegregation of the armed forces started under Truman, he did not seem to want to go further. But black leaders, more and more outspoken against their people's second-class citizenship and poverty in white America, insisted on more. The NAACP challenged segregation in the courts, and young blacks turned to more direct action such as boycotts, sit-ins, and demonstrations.

In 1954 the NAACP won a historic victory against segregation. The Supreme Court's decision in *Brown v. Board of Education of Topeka* involved cases from Kansas, Delaware, South Carolina,

Brown v. Board of Education of Topeka
Virginia, and the District of Columbia, which were grouped under one unanimous ruling. Written by Chief Justice Earl Warren, the Court's ruling concluded that "in the field of public education the doctrine of 'separate but equal' has no place. Separate educational facilities are inherently unequal." Such facilities, Warren wrote, generated in black children "a feeling of inferiority . . . that may affect their hearts and minds in a way unlikely ever to be undone." A year later the Court

demanded the desegregation of schools "with all deliberate speed."

Though some border states quietly implemented the order, a majority of southern communities defied the Court, at times violently. Business and professional people formed White Citizens' Councils for the express purpose of resisting the order. Known familiarly as "uptown Ku Klux Klans," the councils used their economic power against black civil rights activists, foreclosing on their mortgages and seeing to it that they were fired from their jobs or denied credit at local stores. The Klan itself experienced a resurgence, and new groups, such as the National Association for the Advancement of White People, surfaced. But the most effective resistance tactic was the enactment of state laws that paid tuition for white children attending private schools. In some cases, desegregated public schools were ordered closed.

Eisenhower, who had named Earl Warren chief justice in 1953, now pronounced that appointment "the biggest damn fool mistake I ever made." The president had hoped to avoid a confrontation over desegregation, for he tended to side with white southerners and he hoped to continue making Republican inroads in the South. Eisenhower had even approached the chief justice at a White House dinner while the Court was considering the *Brown* case. Referring to the white South, Eisenhower had said, "These are not bad people. All they are concerned about is to see that their sweet little girls are not required to sit in school alongside some big overgrown Negroes."

The president's desire to sidestep the issue was thwarted in September 1957 when the governor of Arkansas, Orval E. Faubus, intervened to halt a local

Little Rock, Arkansas, Crisis
plan for the gradual desegregation of Little Rock's Central High School. Faubus mobilized troops of the Arkansas National Guard to block the entry of black students. Eisenhower made no effort to stop Faubus's actions, and he seemed to agree with the sentiment behind them when he told a press conference that week, "You cannot change people's hearts merely by laws." In late September, after bowing to a federal judge's order, Faubus withdrew the guardsmen. Eight black children slipped inside Central High, as hundreds of jeering whites threatened to storm the school. The next day, fearing violence, Eisenhower federalized

Escorted to school by federal marshals in Little Rock, Arkansas, in 1957, this black student and others had to endure shouted racial slurs, spittings, and thrown objects—this three years after the Supreme Court's Brown decision ordering the desegregation of public schools. By the noted illustrator Norman Rockwell. The Norman Rockwell Museum at the Old Corner House, Stockbridge, MA.

the Arkansas National Guard and ordered 1,100 paratroopers flown in to ensure the children's safety. Troops patrolled the school for the rest of the year, but Little Rock officials closed all public high schools in 1958 and 1959 rather than desegregate them.

Meanwhile, the civil rights movement was gaining momentum elsewhere. In December 1955 Rosa Parks refused to give up her seat to a white passenger on a public bus in Montgomery, Alabama. Jim Crow practices required that blacks sit at the back of the bus and, when asked, surrender their seats to whites. Mrs. Parks's arrest ignited a year-long black boycott of the city's bus system. Blacks walked or carpooled. "My feets is tired," remarked an elderly black woman, "but my soul is rested." With the bus company near bankruptcy and downtown merchants hurt by declining sales, city officials began harassing tactics to frighten blacks into abandoning the boycott. But the black community's leader, Martin Luther King, Jr., urged them to persevere. "This is not a war between the white and the Negro," he said, "but a conflict between justice and injustice."

King was an Atlanta-born, twenty-seven-year-old Baptist minister who had recently earned a Ph.D. at Boston University. He insisted on nonviolent peaceful protest in the spirit of India's leader **Martin Luther King, Jr.** Gandhi. Although he was jailed and a bomb blew the front from his house, King persisted. What King gave to blacks was the "absence of fear," remembered black leader Bayard Rustin. "So Dr. King had this tremendous facility for giving people the feeling that they could be bigger and stronger and more courageous and more loving than they thought they could be." With the aid of a 1956 Supreme Court decision that declared Alabama's Jim Crow laws unconstitutional,

Martin Luther King, Jr. (1929–1968) helped organize the Montgomery, Alabama, bus boycott which led to the desegregation of public transportation. Here, in 1956, he is surrounded by reporters on the first integrated bus run.   Ebony Magazine.

the face of angry white mobs, SNCC members challenged the status quo, all the while singing the anthem of the civil rights movement, "We Shall Overcome." One line goes: "We are not afraid."

EISENHOWER-DULLES FOREIGN POLICY AND THE COLD WAR

Dwight D. Eisenhower had had more experience in foreign affairs than domestic affairs before he became president. He had lived and traveled in Europe, Asia, and Latin America. During the Second World War General Eisenhower came to know Europe well, negotiated with world leaders, and made tough decisions of international consequence. After the war he served as Army Chief of Staff and NATO Supreme Commander and learned the essentials of nuclear weapons development and secret intelligence operations. Like most Americans, Eisenhower accepted the Cold War consensus assumptions about the threat of Communism and the need for a global watch by the United States. As president he controlled the making of foreign policy and enjoyed comfortable vote margins in Congress on key resolutions and programs.

The image of the bumbling, aging hero that partisan Democrats helped create was in part shaped by Eisenhower himself, because he deliberately counted

John Foster Dulles

heavily upon his secretary of state, the strong-willed John Foster Dulles. Polished and articulate, Dulles seemed to have lived his whole life in preparation for the nation's chief diplomatic post. He had studied at Princeton and trained in law at George Washington University before, at age thirty, assisting Woodrow Wilson at Versailles. As a senior partner in a prestigious Wall Street law firm Dulles had handled international cases, and as an officer of the Federal Council of Churches he had participated in programs on behalf of world peace. He had also helped the Truman administration negotiate a peace treaty with Japan. Although experienced, Dulles impressed people as arrogant, stubborn, and preachy—

Montgomery blacks triumphed. They won again in 1957 when Congress passed the Civil Rights Act, which created the U.S. Commission on Civil Rights. Three years later Congress strengthened voting rights.

Martin Luther King, Jr., became president of the Southern Christian Leadership Conference, organized in 1957 to coordinate civil rights activities. He criticized the White House for being "too silent and apathetic" on the issue of race relations. But Eisenhower remained reluctant to move desegregation forward. Blacks tried new tactics. In early 1960 four black students from North Carolina Agricultural and Technical College in Greensboro

The Sit-ins

sat down at a segregated lunch counter and ordered coffee. Though they were refused service and were physically and verbally abused, they would not budge. Thus began the sit-in movement, which spread from the South to the North, rolling back segregation in many public accommodations (see map). Inspired by the sit-ins, some participants organized the Student Nonviolent Coordinating Committee (SNCC) in fall 1960. In

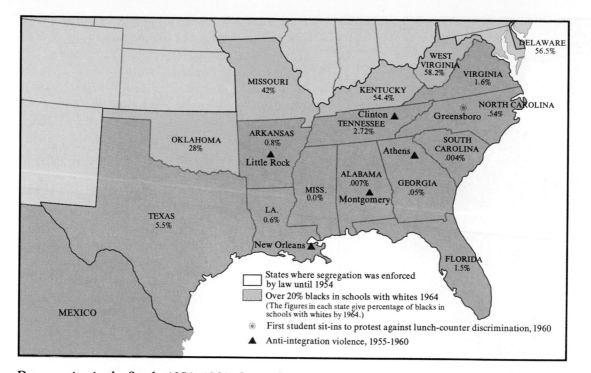

Desegregation in the South, 1954–1964 Source: Re-
drawn by permission of Macmillan Publishing Company,
Inc. by Peter Kingsland. Copyright © 1968 by Martin
Gilbert.

the "conscience and straightjacket of the free world,"
complained one European newspaper. The Eisenhower-
Dulles relationship was mutually cooperative, for they
agreed on basic policies, and the president delegated
authority to Dulles with confidence.

Like his president, Dulles conceded much to the
McCarthyites. He appointed one of Senator
McCarthy's henchmen, Scott McLeod, as chief security
officer of the State Department. McLeod went about
trying to prove McCarthy's charge that the department
was infested with Communists. Making few distinctions
between New Dealers and Communists, he and Dulles
forced many innocent, talented officers out of the
foreign service. They included Asian specialists whose
expertise was later denied to American decision-makers
when they sent the United States to war in Indochina
(see pages 913–915).

For the most part, Eisenhower and Dulles continued
Truman's containment policy, but introduced some
memorable phrases to distinguish their administration
from Truman's. Thinking containment too defensive
a concept, Dulles invented *liberation*. (He did not,

however, explain precisely how the countries of Eastern
Europe could be freed from Soviet
control.) *Massive retaliation* was the
administration's phrase for the nuclear obliteration of the Soviet state
or its assumed client, the People's
Republic of China, if they took aggressive actions.
Eisenhower said it "simply means the ability to blow
hell out of them in a hurry if they start anything."
The ability of the United States to make such a
threat was thought to provide *deterrence,* or the prevention of hostile Soviet behavior.

Related to both massive retaliation and deterrence
was the *New Look* of the American military. Eisenhower and Dulles emphasized air power and nuclear
weaponry and de-emphasized conventional forces. The
president's preference for heavy weapons stemmed in
part from his desire to trim the federal budget ("more
bang for the buck" in the words of the time). With
this huge military arsenal, the United States in the
1950s practiced *brinkmanship:* not backing down in
a crisis, even if it meant taking the nation to the

**Eisenhower-
Dulles
Policies**

Secretary of State John Foster Dulles (1888–1959) became a formidable debater in diplomatic negotiations. Foreigners often complained that he was too rigid, passing up chances for compromise. Although President Eisenhower admired him, he questioned Dulles's "practice of becoming a sort of international prosecuting attorney." Dulles seemed more eager to denounce the Soviets than to negotiate with them. The Reporter, 1956. Copyright 1956 by The Reporter Magazine Company, Inc.

brink of war. Eisenhower also popularized the *domino theory,* according to which small, weak nations would fall to Communism like a row of dominoes if they were not propped up by the United States. Adopting a globalist perspective on wrenching changes in the Third World, the Eisenhower administration conducted a diplomacy of holding the line—against Soviet Russia, Communist China, neutralism, Communism, socialism, nationalism, and revolution everywhere.

After the death of Stalin in 1953, Eisenhower hoped for a relaxation of Soviet-American relations,

but instead witnessed alternating thaws and freezes. The nuclear arms race accelerated as the two superpowers developed new military technology and nuclear delivery systems. In November 1952 the United States detonated the first hydrogen bomb. In March 1954 the biggest bomb the United States has ever tested destroyed the Pacific island of Bikini. This fifteen-megaton H-Bomb packing the power of 15 million tons of TNT, or 750 times as powerful as the atomic bomb that leveled Hiroshima, produced a fallout of radioactive dust that showered a Japanese fishing boat in the area. The crew of the *Lucky Dragon* suffered nausea, fever, and blisters. One of them died, becoming the world's first victim of a hydrogen bomb and setting off international protest in response to the incident.

The Soviets, who had tested their first H-bomb in 1953, shocked Americans in October 1957 by propelling the first man-made satellite, *Sputnik,* into outer space. Just two months earlier, Soviet technicians had fired the first intercontinental ballistic missile (ICBM). Americans now felt vulnerable to air attack and inferior to the Russians in rocket technology. But the United States soon tested its own ICBMs. It also enlarged its fleet of long-range bombers (the B-52s) and deployed intermediate-range missiles in Europe targeted against the Soviet Union. By the end of 1960 Americans had as well produced Polaris-missile-bearing submarines. To ensure future technological advancement, the National Aeronautics and Space Agency (NASA) was created in 1958.

Sputnik and the Missile Race

Through flights by the CIA's U-2 spy planes, American officials knew that the Soviets had deployed very few ICBMs. Yet critics charged that Eisenhower had allowed the United States to fall behind in the missile race. The much-publicized "missile gap" was actually a false notion inspired in part by political partisanship. "Everyone knows," Air Force General Nathan Twining privately told the president, "we already have a [nuclear] stockpile large enough to obliterate the Soviet Union." As the 1950s closed, then, the United States enjoyed overwhelming strategic dominance because of its "triad" of long-range bombers, submarine-launched ballistic missiles (SLBMs), and ICBMs.

Still, President Eisenhower was uneasy about the

arms race. He feared nuclear war, and the cost of the new weapons made it difficult to balance the budget. In his 1953 Chance for Peace speech, the president had noted that "every gun that is made, every warship launched, every rocket fired signifies, in the final sense, a theft from those who hunger and are not fed. . . . The cost of one modern heavy bomber is this: a modern brick school in more than 30 cities." He also doubted the need for more and bigger nuclear weapons. How many times, he once asked, "could [you] kill the same man?" Spurred by such thoughts, by citizens' groups like the Committee for a Sane Nuclear Policy (founded in 1957 and popularly known as SANE), and by neutralist and Soviet appeals, the president cautiously initiated arms control proposals. But because he did not trust the Soviets, arms control talks never became a top priority. Indeed, he intended to preserve the American advantage and, in the propaganda duel with the Soviets, to put them on the defensive.

Eisenhower's 1953 "atoms for peace" initiative called upon the nuclear nations to contribute fissionable materials for use in industrial projects under the auspices of the United Nations. Two years later he issued his "open skies" proposal: aerial surveillance of both Soviet and American military sites to reduce the chances of surprise attacks. Despite numerous attempts at Geneva disarmament talks, neither side could agree on suitable inspection systems to ensure compliance with arms control treaties or bans on nuclear testing. To satisfy world opinion about radioactive fallout, however, the two powers unilaterally suspended atmospheric testing from late 1958 to fall 1961, when the Soviets resumed it. The United States began testing again at the same time, but underground.

While the nuclear arms race gained momentum, Russia and the United States waged the Cold War. The year 1955 provided a brief respite from the intensity of the competition. First, the superpowers agreed to end their ten-year joint occupation of Austria, making it an independent neutral state. And, second, Eisenhower and Soviet leader Nikita Khrushchev journeyed to Geneva for high-level talks. This first summit meeting in ten years produced no important resolutions, but the conferees "disagreed so nicely," as one reporter put it.

Events in Eastern Europe soon returned the Cold War to the more familiar fierce acrimony. In 1956

"So Russia Launched a Satellite, but Has It Made Cars With Fins Yet?"

While American genius was being applied to fancy consumer goods like the tail-finned automobiles of the 1950s, the Soviets were demonstrating their technological abilities by launching the satellite Sputnik—or so Uncle Sam seems to be thinking in this Ross Lewis cartoon. Democratic Senator Lyndon B. Johnson complained that "the Soviets have beaten us at our own game—daring scientific advances in the atomic age." Milwaukee Public Library.

Khrushchev called for "peaceful coexistence" between capitalists and Communists, denounced Stalin, and suggested that Moscow would tolerate different brands of Communism. Soon revolts against Soviet power erupted in Poland and Hungary, testing this new permissiveness. Moscow saw its new military alliance, the Warsaw Pact (1955), endangered and quickly crushed the rebellions. The Eisenhower administration, on record as favoring the liberation of Eastern Europe, found itself unable to aid the rebels without igniting a third world war. All the United States could do was to welcome Hungarian immigrants in greater numbers than American quota laws allowed.

Eastern Europe

Hardly had the turmoil in Eastern Europe subsided when the divided city of Berlin, in East Germany, once again became a Cold War flash point. The Soviets were angry about the placement in West Germany of American bombers capable of carrying nuclear warheads. And they were upset that West Berlin had become an escape route for disaffected

East Germans. In 1958 Khrushchev boldly announced that the Soviet Union would recognize East German control of all of Berlin unless East and West began talks on German reunification and rearmament. The Americans, unwilling to give up their hold on West Berlin, sought to strengthen West German ties with NATO. The two sides talked of war; finally Khrushchev backed away from his ultimatum, resolving to take up the issue at future conferences.

Berlin and Germany were on the agenda of a summit meeting planned for Paris in May 1960. But two weeks before the conference, an American U-2 spy plane carrying high-powered cameras crashed 1,200 miles inside the Soviet Union. Moscow announced that it had been shot down. At first Washington denied that its planes flew over Soviet territory, but Russian officials blasted that story by displaying the captured CIA pilot, Francis Gary Powers, his aircraft, and the pictures he had been snapping of Soviet military installations. Moscow demanded an apology, Washington refused, and the Russians walked out of the Paris summit.

U-2 Incident

While West and East sparred over Europe, both kept a wary eye on the People's Republic of China (PRC). Despite growing evidence of a Sino-Soviet split, most American officials continued to think of Communism as a unified world movement. The United States refused to open diplomatic relations with the Chinese government and continued to give aid to Jiang Jieshi (Chiang Kai-shek) on Formosa, which the Chinese claimed as part of the PRC. Washington worried about PRC calls for colonial rebellion and its support for the revolutionaries in Indochina (see pages 913–915). In 1954 China and the United States negotiated face to face in Geneva to settle the Indochinese crisis, but their relations were marked more by hostility than conciliation.

In 1954 and 1955 a crisis brought the two nations to the brink of war. Just a few miles off the Chinese coast sat the tiny islands of Quemoy and Matsu. Jiang's forces used them as bases for commando raids against the PRC. In fall 1954 China bombarded the islands. Eisenhower decided to defend the outposts, and he let it be known he was considering the use of nuclear weapons. Massive re-

Quemoy and Matsu

taliation over such an insignificant issue? "Let's keep the Reds guessing," advised John Foster Dulles. But what if they guessed wrong? asked critics. Congress passed the Formosa Resolution (1955), which authorized the president to send troops to Formosa and adjoining islands. Two years later the United States installed on Formosa missiles capable of carrying nuclear warheads. Chinese and American diplomats talked in secret meetings in Geneva and Warsaw, but again in 1958 war loomed over Quemoy and Matsu. The crisis passed, but defense of the islands became an issue in the election of 1960 at home.

INTERVENTIONS IN THE THIRD WORLD

If Eisenhower believed that he had contained the Sino-Soviet threat, he was very much less confident about challenges from the Third World. In the 1940s, as a result of changes wrought by the Second World War, a cavalcade of new nations began to alter the international community. In the period from 1943 to 1983 no fewer than ninety countries cast off their colonial bonds. The march to independence was unrelenting: Lebanon (1943), Syria (1944), the Philippines (1946), India (1947), Indonesia (1949), Libya (1951), Morocco (1956), Ghana (1957). In 1960 alone, eighteen colonies became nations (see map, page 868).

These profound stirrings arose in what is now known as the Third World, a general term applied to those parts of the global community belonging to neither of the other two "worlds": the United States and its allies in the capitalist "West" and the Soviet Union and its allies in the Communist "East." Sometimes called developing countries, Third World nations on the whole are nonwhite, nonindustrialized, and located in the southern half of the globe—Asia, Africa, the Middle East, and Latin America. With Cold War lines drawn fairly tightly in Europe by the early 1950s, Soviet-American rivalry shifted increasingly to the Third World. Much was at stake. Third World nations possessed strategic raw materials such as manganese, oil, and tin. They also attracted foreign investment—in 1959 over a third of America's private foreign investments were in Third World countries. Third World nations provided markets, especially for American products and technology. Finally, the great powers looked to these new states for support in the United Nations and for sites to be used as military and intelligence bases.

But many Third World states, like India, Ghana, Egypt, and Indonesia, did not wish to take sides in the contest between the great powers. To the dismay of both Washington and Moscow, they proudly declared themselves neutral, or nonaligned, in the Cold War. Eisenhower and Dulles considered neutralism an immoral stance, a first step along the road to Communism. Nations, they insisted, should take sides in the life-and-death Cold War struggle.

Neutralism

If this negative view of neutralism inhibited United States efforts to strengthen relations with the Third World, so did America's domestic race relations. In August 1955, the ambassador from India, G.L. Mehta, walked into a restaurant at the Houston International Airport, sat down, and waited to order. But Texas law required that whites and blacks be served in separate dining facilities. The dark-skinned diplomat, who had seated himself in a white-only area, was told to move. The insult stung deeply and was not soon forgotten. From Washington, Secretary Dulles telegraphed his apologies for this blatant display of racism, fearing that the incident would injure relations with a nation whose allegiance the United States was seeking in the Cold War.

American Racism as Handicap

Such embarrassments were not uncommon in the 1950s. Burma's minister of education was denied a meal in a Columbus, Ohio, restaurant; and the finance minister of Ghana was turned away from a Howard Johnson's just outside the nation's capital. Secretary Dulles complained that segregationist practices were becoming a "major international hazard," a threat to United States efforts to gain the friendship of Third World countries. Americans stood publicly condemned as a people who did not honor the ideal of equality.

Thus when the attorney general appealed to the Supreme Court to strike down segregation in public schools, his introductory remarks took note of the international implications. "It is in the context of the present world struggle between freedom and tyranny that the problem of racial discrimination must be viewed," he warned. The humiliation of dark-skinned diplomats in Washington, D.C., "the window through which the world looks into our house," was damaging to American interests. Racism "furnished grist for the Communist propaganda mills."

United States hostility toward revolution also obstructed the American quest for influence in the Third World. Despite its own history, the United States has been uncomfortable with significant twentieth-century revolutions—Mexican, Chinese, Russian, Cuban, Vietnamese, and Iranian. Although Americans paid lip service to the Spirit of '76, they were intolerant of revolutionary disorder—in part because Third World revolutions were directed against their Cold War allies, but also because such upheavals threatened American investments, markets, and military bases. Indeed, by mid-century the United States had become an established power in world affairs, eager for the stability and order that seemed to ensure its own prosperity and security. During revolutionary crises, therefore, the United States usually threw its support to its European allies or to the conservative propertied classes in the Third World. When forty-three African and Asian states sponsored a United Nations resolution appealing for decolonization in 1960, the United States abstained from the vote, signaling that it stood with the white imperialists.

American Intolerance of Revolution

Still another obstacle in America's relations with the rising Third World was the country's great wealth. Foreigners both envied and resented the "people of plenty," who had so much and wasted so much while poorer peoples went without. American movies offered enticing glimpses of middle-class materialism; American products drew attention at international trade fairs and were coveted items at native marketplaces. And Americans stationed overseas often flaunted their superior standard of living. The popular novel

America's Wealth as a Problem

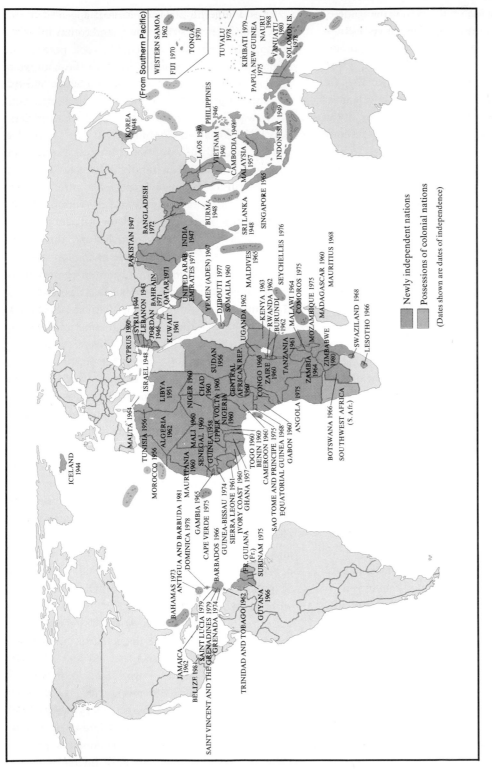

The Rise of the Third World: Decolonization Since 1943

The Ugly American (1958) drew attention to the problem by describing the "golden ghettoes" of American diplomats, separated from their poorer surroundings by high compound walls. Finally, many foreign peoples resented the ample profits that American corporations extracted from them. For all these reasons, the United States found itself often not the model of revolution but the target. Americans were blamed for the persistent poverty of the Third World, although the leaders of those nations made decisions that sometimes hindered their progress. Underfed India, for example, poured millions of dollars into the production of a nuclear bomb when it might have spent those funds improving agricultural production.

The Soviet Union enjoyed only a slight edge, if any, in the race to win friends in the Third World. It was true that Communist ideology encouraged anticolonialism, and that the Soviet
Obstacles to Soviet Influence Union was free of association with the long years of Western European imperialism. But though Moscow kept up a heavy drumbeat of propaganda, it could not easily explain away its subjugation of Eastern European countries. The Soviet invasion of Hungary in 1956 earned Russia international condemnation. Though Khrushchev toured India and Burma in the mid-1950s, those nations refused to become Soviet clients. They were not about to replace one imperial master with another, and Russian aid was minuscule compared with American offers. Even Communist China drifted away from Soviet influence, much as Yugoslavia had in 1948. Ultimately the Soviets, like the Americans, concluded that Third World nations were playing the two superpowers against each other in order to garner larger amounts of aid and arms, and that neutralism was anathema.

Nonetheless, the United States often interpreted Third World anti-imperialism, political instability, and attacks on foreign-owned property as Soviet-inspired, rather than as expressions of nationalism or internal racial, religious, and ethnic divisiveness. Americans too simply labeled radicals, nationalists, reformers, and neutralists as Communists. To thwart these presumed enemies, the United States resorted to alignments with unrepresentative but friendly re-

gimes and large programs of economic assistance (by 1961 over 90 percent of American foreign aid went to the Third World).

The United States also utilized the CIA to meet Third World challenges. President Eisenhower believed that secret operations were as necessary as espionage and the gathering of information,
CIA Covert Operations which had been defined as the CIA's primary functions at its birth in 1947. In the 1950s and later, the CIA bribed foreign politicians, subsidized foreign newspapers, hired mercenaries, conducted sabotage, sponsored labor unions, dispensed "disinformation" (circulation of false information), plotted the assassination of foreign leaders like Cuba's Fidel Castro, and staged coups. These and other spoiling operations were designed to influence foreign governments toward pro-American positions. The CIA helped overthrow the governments of Iran (1953) and Guatemala (1954), but failed in attempts to topple regimes in Indonesia (1958) and Cuba (1961). The CIA and other parts of the American intelligence community followed the principle of "plausible deniability." That is, covert operations should be conducted and the decisions that launched them concealed so that the president could deny any knowledge of them. Thus President Eisenhower denied the United States role in Guatemala, even though he ordered the operation; he also denied that he had ordered the CIA to assassinate Castro, whose government after 1959 became noisily anti-American (see pages 908–912).

In Latin America, long a United States sphere of influence, where poverty, overpopulation, illiteracy, economic sluggishness, and foreign exploitation fed
CIA in Guatemala discontent, anti-American feelings grew. In 1951 the leftist Jacobo Arbenz Guzmán was elected president of Guatemala, a poor country whose largest landowner was the American-owned United Fruit Company. United Fruit was a major force throughout Latin America. Its total assets in 1954 equaled $580 million; it owned three million acres of land and operated railroads, ports, ships, and extensive telecommunications facilities. To fulfill his promise of land reform, Arbenz expropriated United Fruit's uncultivated land and offered compensation. United Fruit dismissed the offer and began an

"It seems the C.I.A. has not been inactive in this area."

Although the Central Intelligence Agency (CIA) became active in far-away, exotic places and enjoyed considerable influence through both conspicuous and covert operations, its effect on foreign peoples probably did not go as far as depicted in this New Yorker *cartoon. Drawing by Dana Fradon; © 1970 The New Yorker Magazine, Inc.*

advertising campaign in the United States to rally official Washington against what the company called a Communist threat to Guatemala. Lacking evidence of actual Communist control of Arbenz's government, United States officials nevertheless cut off aid to Guatemala, and the CIA began a secret plot to subvert its government. When Arbenz learned that the CIA was working against him, he turned to Russia, thus reinforcing American suspicions. The CIA airlifted arms into Guatemala, dropping them at United Fruit facilities, and in June 1954 CIA-supported Guatemalans struck from Honduras. American planes bombed the capital, the invaders drove Arbenz from power, and the new pro-American regime returned United Fruit's land. But Latin Americans wondered

what had happened to the Good Neighbor policy (see page 769). Their growing hostility toward the United States surfaced in 1958, when rioters interrupted Vice President Richard M. Nixon's goodwill trip to South America.

In the boiling Middle East the Eisenhower administration also confronted challenges to United States influence. American stakes there included the survival of the Jewish state of Israel, carved out of the British mandate of Palestine in 1948, and extensive oil holdings (in the 1950s American companies produced about half the region's petroleum). Oil-rich Iran was a special friend, for the ruling shah had granted American oil companies a 40 percent interest in a new petroleum consortium in return for CIA

Chapter 30: AN AGE OF FRAGILE CONSENSUS, 1953–1961

On a "goodwill tour" of Latin America in spring 1958, Vice President Richard M. Nixon met an angry crowd in Caracas, Venezuela. Shouting anti-American slogans, protestors threatened Nixon in his automobile. This mob's expression of bitterness represented increasing Third World discontent with the United States. UPI/Bettmann Newsphotos.

help in the overthrow of his rival, Mohammed Mossadegh (1953). Mossadegh had attempted the unpardonable sin, nationalization of foreign oil interests.

The major threat to American interests in the Middle East came from Egypt, where the fervent Arab nationalist Gamal Abdel Nasser rose to power determined to push the British out of the Suez Canal Zone and the Israelis out of Palestine. The United States was caught in a double bind. It did not wish to anger the Arabs, for fear of losing its oil holdings. Nor did it wish to lose its staunch ally Israel, which was supported by a vocal Jewish-American lobby in American politics. But when Nasser declared neutrality in the Cold War, Dulles lost patience with him. "Do nations which play both sides get better treatment than nations which are stalwart and work with us?" he asked angrily. Eisenhower was not convinced of Nasser's neutrality. "If he was not a Communist," the president wrote later, "he certainly succeeded in making us suspicious of him." In July 1956 American officials withdrew their offer to help finance the Aswan Dam, a project to provide inexpensive electricity and water for thirsty Egyptian farmlands. Nasser quickly nationalized the British-owned Suez Canal, intending to use its profits to build the dam.

Suez Crisis

Western Europe received 75 percent of its oil from the Middle East, much of it transported through the Suez Canal. Fearing an interruption in this vital trade, the British and French conspired with Israel "to knock Nasser off his perch." On October 29, 1956, the Israelis invaded the Suez, joined two days later by Britain and France. Eisenhower fumed that his allies had not consulted him, and that the attack had shifted attention from the Soviet invasion of Hungary. He feared the move might cause Nasser to seek help from the Soviets, inviting the dread enemy into the Middle East. In early November Eisenhower bluntly told London, Paris, and Tel Aviv to pull out. The troops withdrew, Egypt paid $81 million for the canal, and the Russians built the Aswan Dam.

In early 1957, in an effort to improve the Western position in the Middle East and protect American interests there, the president proclaimed what became known as the Eisenhower Doctrine.

Eisenhower Doctrine The United States would intervene in the Middle East, he said, if any government threatened by a Communist takeover asked for help. Fourteen thousand American troops scrambled ashore in Lebanon the next year to quell an internal political dispute that Washington feared might be exploited by pro-Nasser groups or Communists. American critics protested that the United States was wrongfully acting as the world's policeman. But others complained that such a drastic resort to military intervention demonstrated that Eisenhower had failed miserably to thwart challenges to American power in the Third World and to convert the emerging nations to American friends in the Cold War.

As his presidency neared its end Eisenhower was beleaguered by accumulating foreign crises. In 1959 he had had a friendly meeting with Khrushchev at the presidential retreat at Camp David, Maryland; but it was soon followed by renewed Soviet-American tensions, especially over the U-2 incident. In Laos and Vietnam inconclusive yet escalating American intervention threatened a wider war; and Cuba's Castro moved closer to the Soviets (see Chapter 32). And the president suffered the humiliating cancellation of his trip to Japan because of anti-American riots against the United States military presence there. He became short-tempered with critics who charged that America had to regain world leadership, and he blamed everything on the Soviets. When in September 1960 Khrushchev ranted at United Nations sessions— even taking off a shoe to pound it on the table—

Eisenhower angrily commented that were he a dictator he would "launch an attack on Russia while Khrushchev is in New York." Eisenhower was no dictator, and he always tamed such impulses. Americans admired his caution, but they began to wonder if it was time for a younger, more energetic man to carry the anti-Communist torch.

THE SECOND TERM AND THE ELECTION OF 1960

In part because of the demands of overseas activism, Eisenhower faced rising federal expenditures in his second term. In the first three years of his presidency he had managed to trim the budget,

Deficit Spending largely by controlling defense spending. But he discovered that he had to tolerate deficit spending to achieve his goals. In 1959 federal expenditures climbed to $92.1 billion, about half of the amount going to the military. This budget produced the largest peacetime deficit to that point in American history. In all, Eisenhower balanced only three of his eight budgets. One reason for the administration's resort to deficit spending was the need to cushion the impact of three recessions—in the years 1953-1954, 1957-1958, and 1960-1961. A sluggish economy and unemployment (it peaked in 1958 at 7.6 percent) also reduced the tax dollars the federal government collected. But most Americans remained prosperous, and the administration succeeded in keeping inflation down to about 1 percent through the 1950s.

In 1958, a year after *Sputnik*, Eisenhower signed the National Defense Education Act. It created a multimillion-dollar loan fund for college students and granted money to the states for upgrading teaching in the sciences and foreign languages. After this legislative success, the administration was rocked by the resignation of the president's chief aide, Sherman Adams, for influence-peddling and by large Republican losses in the 1958 congressional elections. The Democrats, helped by the public outcry against Adams, the economic slump, and discontent among farmers, took the Senate 64 to 34 and the House 282 to 154. Some Republicans grumbled that Eisenhower had not given his party enough leadership, while others realized that the Democrats were just too great in number to be beaten in the best of times. For the last two years of his presidency, then, Eisenhower had to confront congressional "spenders" who proposed "every sort of foolish proposal" in the name of "national security and the 'poor' fellow." Often at odds with Congress, Eisenhower cast vetoes against bills he thought would plunge the nation into even greater debt, which stood at $286 billion at the end of 1960.

The election of 1960 was one of the closest and most spirited in the twentieth century. Although Democratic candidate John F. Kennedy shared the tenets of the consensus, he asserted

John F. Kennedy

that he could expand the benefits of economic progress and win foreign disputes through more vigorous leadership. People often contrasted his youth (forty-three years old) with Eisenhower's age (seventy years old). Handsome and intelligent, Kennedy was born to wealth, graduated from Harvard, and served as a congressman before joining the Senate in 1953. His running mate in 1960 was Senator Lyndon B. Johnson of Texas, who was added to the ticket to hold white southerners in the Democratic party as the civil rights issue heated up. Republican candidate Richard M. Nixon, the forty-seven-year-old vice president from California, and his running mate, Ambassador Henry Cabot Lodge of Massachusetts, expected a rugged campaign.

Kennedy, exploiting the media to great advantage, ran a risky, yet ultimately brilliant, race. Knowing his major liability was his Roman Catholicism, he addressed that issue head-on. He traveled to the Bible Belt to tell a group of Houston ministers that he respected the separation of church and state and would take his orders from the American people, not the Pope. Seeing a major opportunity in the black vote, and calculating that Johnson could keep the white South loyal to the Democrats, Kennedy appealed to black voters. He responded to an appeal to help Martin Luther King, Jr., gain release from a Georgia county jail; he promised to sign an executive order forbidding segregation in federally subsidized housing.

Foreign policy became a major issue. Nixon claimed that he knew how to deal with Communists; and he charged that because Kennedy lacked experience in foreign affairs he could not stand up to Khrushchev. Kennedy shot back, "I was not the Vice President of the United States who presided over the Communization of Cuba." Kennedy hit hard on Cuba, while Nixon played on the senator's statement that Quemoy and Matsu were not worth defending. Kennedy's most effective theme was that Eisenhower and Nixon had let American prestige and power slip. The Democratic candidate offered Cold War victory instead of stalemate; and he vowed to secure Third World countries as allies.

As Kennedy gained momentum by stressing the anti-Communist theme, Nixon continued to suffer handicaps from the recession of 1960 and the U-2 incident. Nixon also presented an

Nixon's Handicaps

unsavory TV image, because he came across as surly and heavy-jowled in the televised debates with Kennedy. Perhaps worse, Eisenhower gave him only a tepid endorsement. Asked to list Nixon's significant decisions as vice president, the president replied: "If you give me a week, I might think of one."

In an election that saw the highest voter participation (62.8 percent) in half a century, Kennedy defeated Nixon by the razor-slim margin of 118,000 votes. The electoral college margin, 303 to 219, was much closer than the numbers suggest (see map, page 874). Slight shifts in the popular vote in Illinois and Texas would have made Nixon the victor. Kennedy carried most of the large industrial states and most of the South. Black votes were important in providing him with triumphs in North Carolina, South Carolina, and Texas, and blacks in the inner cities turned out in large numbers for him. Electoral fraud in Illinois and Texas may also have figured in Kennedy's narrow victory. Although his Catholicism lost him votes, especially in the Midwest, it also gained him about 80 percent of Catholic voters. Religious bigotry, then, did not decide this election, and Kennedy became the first Roman Catholic president.

Assessments of the Eisenhower administration used to emphasize its conservatism, passive style, limited achievements, and hesitancy to confront difficult issues. And they pointed to Eisenhower's reluctance

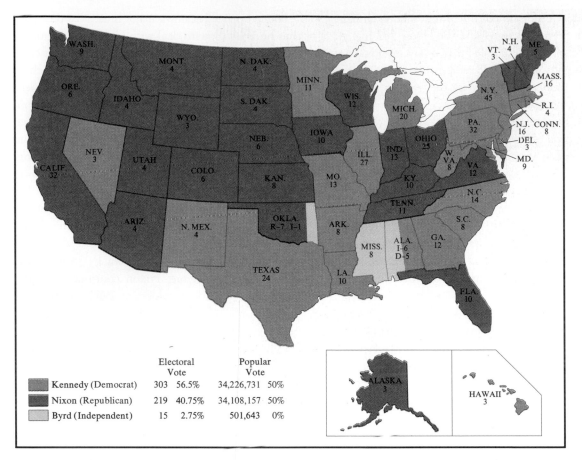

Presidential Election, 1960

to take strong stands, keep abreast of events, or inspire needed reforms. In recent years scholars have

Eisenhower Assessed

been researching in the now declassified documents of the consensus era, and interpretations are changing. Many have begun to stress Eisenhower's influential style, command of policymaking, sensibly moderate approach to most problems, political savvy, and great popularity. He was, in short, not an aging bystander in the 1950s, but a competent, pragmatic, compassionate leader who gave the American people what they wanted—economic growth and unrelenting anti-Communism. Most historians would agree that the record of the Eisenhower presidency is mixed. At home he failed to deal with the problems that would wrack the country in the next decade: racism, poverty, urban decay. He exacerbated the damage done by McCarthyism by refusing to come down hard on the reckless senator, and

the president's own loyalty program was excessive. Eisenhower never solved the farm problem, and he never reorganized his party to reflect the "modern Republicanism" that he championed. In foreign policy, he found no way to relax Cold War tensions, and in the end he accelerated the nuclear arms race that he so disliked. He unleashed the CIA upon the Third World and failed to adjust American diplomacy to the immense changes there.

On the other hand, when compared with his successors, Eisenhower was cautious. He kept military budgets under control and managed crises so that the United States avoided major military ventures abroad. At home he curbed inflation, kept the nation prosperous (GNP rose from $365 billion in 1953 to $504 billion in 1961), and strengthened the infrastructure by building an interstate highway system and expanding social security coverage. He brought dignity to the presidency, and the American people

Secretary of Defense Charles E. Wilson (1890–1961) left the presidency of General Motors to join Eisenhower's cabinet. A symbol of the military-industrial complex that the president came to criticize, Wilson gained a reputation for ill-considered utterances. He once remarked that "what was good for our country was good for General Motors, and vice versa." Eisenhower frequently had to press Wilson to reduce his large defense budget requests—which Wilson's apparent fascination with the weapons of America's military might helped stimulate. Wilson resigned in 1956, much to the president's relief. Hank Walker, © Time, Inc.

respected him. Historians now rank Eisenhower among the top third of American presidents—ahead of his successor John F. Kennedy.

In Eisenhower's final radio and television address before leaving office in early 1961, he issued a warning. Because of the Cold War, he observed, the United States had been "compelled to create a permanent industry of vast proportions," as well as a standing army of 3.5 million. "Now this conjunction of an immense military establishment and a large arms industry is new in the American experience." In it, he went on, resides the "potential for the disastrous rise of misplaced power." The demands of national security, then, had created a powerful interest group that threatened the very existence of liberty. No doubt he was thinking about the 1960 congressional report, which showed that there were 1,400 retired military officers above the rank of major, including 261 generals and admirals, employed by the one hundred leading defense contractors. Eisenhower urged Americans to guard against the "military-industrial complex." They did not.

Eisenhower's Warning Against "Military-Industrial Complex"

1952	Eisenhower elected president First U.S. H-bomb exploded	1957	Eisenhower Doctrine Little Rock desegregation crisis Civil Rights Act *Sputnik*
1953	Stalin dies Korean War ends Oppenheimer case Termination policy for Native Americans	1958	U.S. intervention in Lebanon National Defense Education Act Berlin crisis
1954	*Brown* decision CIA intervention in Guatemala Quemoy-Matsu crisis Senate condemns Senator McCarthy	1959	Castro takes power in Cuba
		1960	Eighteen colonies became independent nations Greensboro, North Carolina, sit-in U-2 incident Kennedy elected president
1955	Montgomery bus boycott begins		
1956	Highway Act Soviets invade Hungary Suez crisis Eisenhower re-elected	1961	Eisenhower warns against "military- industrial complex"

SUGGESTIONS FOR FURTHER READING

An Age of Consensus

Daniel Bell, *The End of Ideology* (1960); Paul A. Carter, *Another Part of the Fifties* (1983); Job L. Dittberner, *The End of Ideology and American Social Thought: 1930–1960* (1979); Marty Jezer, *The Dark Ages: Life in the U.S. 1945–1960* (1982); George Lipsitz, *Class & Culture in Cold War America* (1981); Ronald Lora, *Conservative Minds in America* (1971); Douglas T. Miller and Marion Novak, *The Fifties* (1977); George H. Nash, *The Conservative Intellectual Movement in America: Since 1945* (1976); David M. Potter, *People of Plenty* (1954); David Riesman with Nathan Glazer and Reuel Denney, *The Lonely Crowd* (1950); William H. Whyte, *The Organization Man* (1956).

Dwight D. Eisenhower

Stephen E. Ambrose, *Eisenhower*, 2 vols. (1983–1984); Robert H. Ferrell, ed., *The Eisenhower Diaries* (1981); Peter Lyon, *Eisenhower* (1974); Herbert Parmet, *Eisenhower and the American Crusades* (1972).

Eisenhower and the Politics of the 1950s

Charles C. Alexander, *Holding the Line* (1975); Larry W. Burt, *Tribalism in Crisis: Federal Indian Policy, 1953–1961* (1982); Barbara B. Clowse, *Brainpower for the Cold War: The Sputnik Crisis and the National Defense Education Act of 1958* (1981); David A. Frier, *Conflict of Interest in the Eisenhower Administration* (1969); Fred I. Greenstein, *The Hidden-Hand Presidency* (1982); Emmet John Hughes, *The Ordeal of Power* (1963); Gary W. Reichard, *The Reaffirmation of Republicanism: Eisenhower and the Eighty-third Congress* (1975); David W. Reinhard, *The Republican Right since 1945* (1983); Elmo Richardson, *The Presidency of Dwight D. Eisenhower* (1979); Mark H. Rose, *Interstate: Express Highway Politics, 1941–1956* (1979); Bernard Schwartz,

Super Chief: Earl Warren and His Supreme Court (1983). (See also works cited in Chapter 29 on McCarthyism and in Chapter 31 on social and economic questions.)

Civil Rights

John W. Anderson, *Eisenhower, Brownell, and the Congress: The Tangled Origins of the Civil Rights Bill of 1956–1957* (1964); Numan V. Bartley, *The Rise of Massive Resistance: Race and Politics in the South During the 1950s* (1969); Robert F. Burk, *The Eisenhower Administration and Black Civil Rights* (1984); William H. Chafe, *Civilities and Civil Rights* (1980) (on Greensboro sit-in); Elizabeth Huckaby, *Crisis at Central High, Little Rock, 1957–1958* (1980); Martin Luther King, Jr., *Stride Toward Freedom: The Montgomery Boycott* (1958); Richard Kluger, *Simple Justice: The History of* Brown v. Board of Education *and Black America's Struggle for Equality* (1975); Paul Murphy, *The Constitution in Crisis Times, 1918–1969* (1972); Stephen B. Oates, *Let the Trumpet Sound: The Life of Martin Luther King, Jr.* (1982); Howell Raines, *My Soul Is Rested* (1977); Harvard Sitkoff, *The Struggle for Black Equality, 1954–1980* (1981).

Eisenhower-Dulles Foreign Policy

Blanche W. Cook, *The Declassified Eisenhower* (1981); Robert A. Divine, *Eisenhower and the Cold War* (1981); Louis Gerson, *John Foster Dulles* (1968); Michael Guhin, *John Foster Dulles* (1972); Townsend Hoopes, *The Devil and John Foster Dulles* (1973); Burton I. Kaufman, *Trade and Aid: Eisenhower's Foreign Economic Policy* (1982); Douglas Kinnard, *President Eisenhower and Strategic Management* (1977); Jack M. Schick, *The Berlin Crisis* (1971). (Also see works cited in Chapter 29.)

Nuclear Arms Race

Robert A. Divine, *Blowing in the Wind: The Nuclear Test Ban Debate, 1954–1960* (1978); Lawrence Freedman, *The Evolution of Nuclear Strategy* (1981); Gregg Herken, *Counsels of War* (1985); Jerome Kahan, *Security in the Nuclear Age* (1975); Herman Kahn, *On Thermonuclear War* (1960); Henry A. Kissinger, *Nuclear Weapons and Foreign Policy* (1957); Walter A. McDougall, . . . *The Heavens and the Earth: A Political History of the Space Age* (1985); Michael Mandelbaum, *The Nuclear Question* (1979); George Quester, *Nuclear Diplomacy* (1970); Chalmers M. Roberts, *The Nuclear Years: The Arms Race and Arms Control, 1945–1970* (1970); Herbert York, *The Advisors* (1976).

The United States and the Third World

Stephen E. Ambrose, *Ike's Spies: Eisenhower and the Espionage Establishment* (1981); Richard J. Barnet, *Intervention and Revolution*, rev. ed. (1972); Chester L. Cooper, *The Lion's Last Roar: Suez, 1956* (1978); Richard Immerman, *The CIA in Guatemala* (1982); Donald Neff, *Warriors at Suez* (1981); Robert W. Stookey, *America and the Arab States* (1975). (Also see the works on Vietnam and Southeast Asia cited in Chapter 32.)

AMERICAN SOCIETY DURING THE POSTWAR BOOM

1945–1960s

CHAPTER 31

Five mornings a week through the 1950s and 1960s, the same scene was played out at the bus stop at Pennsylvania Avenue and 12th Street in the District of Columbia. This was the final destination for the Red Line buses traveling from Virginia's northern suburbs to the nation's capital. Eight or nine of every ten people who debarked at that intersection were men dressed in business suits and carrying briefcases. Most were government civil servants. All were white. From shortly after seven in the morning until about ten, the buses unloaded passengers from Alexandria, Falls Church, and other rapidly growing bedroom communities across the Potomac River from Washington. The incoming passengers barely noticed the line of people waiting behind a railing to catch the return trip to the suburbs.

The difference between the busloads could hardly have been more extreme. Practically without exception, every rider on the outbound journey was a black woman from Washington's inner-city neighborhoods. Tidily dressed, many carrying shopping bags with work clothes folded inside, these women were domestic servants in the affluent homes of Washington's lawyers, bankers, politicians, lobbyists, and high-ranking bureaucrats and military officers. Next to the poverty or near-poverty to which these maids, cooks, and laundresses returned at night, the opulent white world stood in sharp contrast and raised gnawing questions. Why should these white people live in such comfort while their black servants lived precariously, wondering not what to have for dinner at night, but knowing there might not be much to eat at all?

The contrast was heightened by the fact that in 1945 the United States had entered a twenty-five-year economic boom, whose cornerstones were the automobile, housing, and defense industries. As the gross national product grew, income levels rose and property ownership spread. Automobiles rolled from assembly lines; houses and schools sprang up throughout the country. More and more Americans, including many unionized blue-collar workers, bought homes in the suburbs and consumed a seemingly endless supply of goods and services.

But while three of every four Americans were enjoying the economy of abundance, the fourth American was poor. Although poverty levels varied regionally, as well as among the cities, suburbs, small towns, and farms, it became clear by the 1960s that the American poor comprised a much larger group than people in the complacent 1950s had imagined (see pages 888–890). As calculated in 1960 by the Bureau of Labor Statistics, a "minimum comfort" budget for an urban family of four varied from $5,370 a year in Houston to $6,567 in Chicago. A widely accepted national average for the poverty line was $3,000, but the five least generous states defined subsistence as $1,600.

With the publication of Michael Harrington's *The Other America*, in 1962, people became aware of this contradiction in their midst. America's poor, wrote Harrington, were "the strangest poor in the history of mankind": they "exist within the most powerful and rich society the world has ever known. Their misery has continued while the majority of the nation talked of itself as being 'affluent.'" Crowded into the cities or living in rural isolation, the poor had "dropped out of sight and out of mind," particularly to comfortable residents in the suburbs.

Just as deprivation and pessimism defined the poor, so material comfort and optimism were the hallmarks of the middle class. Whether considered in terms of income levels or lifestyles, more Americans were better off than ever before. The most obvious expression of postwar optimism was the baby boom. From 1946 to 1961 births hit record highs. And as parents were rearing these millions of children, "family togetherness" took on almost religious significance. Landon Y. Jones, the author of a book on the baby boom, makes the analogy that this generation was like "the pig in the python." As this age group has grown older, it has had a successive impact on housing, elementary and secondary education, fads and popular music, higher education, and now the adult job market.

Postwar Americans benefited from the increase in leisure time that resulted from a return to the forty-hour week. People wanted to be entertained, and entertained they were. Sales of televisions, long-playing records, paperbacks, and comic books ballooned.

Families took to the road on expensive vacations. And, of course, there were the fads. From hula hoops to 3-D movies, the American rush to consume took new and sometimes peculiar forms.

To many people, it seemed that the American dream had come true. Whatever the nation's faults, it was the world's foremost land of opportunity. Americans boasted that they enjoyed political self-determination through the vote and social mobility through the melting pot. And public education, "the engine of democracy," guaranteed a better life to all who were willing to study and work hard. The exceptions to the dream went unnoticed by most Americans. And the lack of equal opportunities for women was concealed by an emphasis on femininity, piety, and family togetherness.

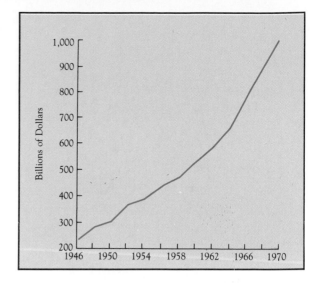

Gross National Product, 1946–1970 *Source: Adapted from U.S. Bureau of the Census,* Historical Statistics of the United States, Colonial Times to 1970, *Bicentennial Edition (Washington: U.S. Government Printing Office, 1975), p. 224.*

THE POSTWAR ECONOMIC BOOM

As Americans entered the postwar era, many wondered whether it would resemble another postwar epoch, the 1920s. In spring 1946 a *New York Times* writer predicted a return of the Roaring Twenties. Not everyone agreed. Reminding readers that the 1920s had culminated in economic depression and world war, another writer responded, "There are too many people who, knowing the results which flowed from the attitudes of 1920, are going to see to it that history does not repeat itself." Indeed, most Americans expected a replay of the 1930s. After all, it was the war that had created jobs and prosperity; surely the end of war would bring a slump.

As it turned out, neither prediction was correct. The United States in 1945 entered one of its longest, steadiest periods of growth and prosperity. The keys to this success were increasing output and increasing demand. In the twenty-five years after 1945 the American economy grew at an average rate of 3.5 percent per year. Even with occasional recessions the gross national product seldom faltered, rising from just over $200 billion in 1946 to close to $1 trillion in 1970 (see figure).

The United States was not alone in establishing new standards for economic growth and stability. Japan and the nations of Western Europe were also booming during the postwar years. "In the 'Golden Age' of the 1950's and 1960's," stated Angus Maddison, a British economist, "economic growth in the advanced capitalist countries surpassed virtually all historical records."

When the economy produced more, Americans generally brought home bigger paychecks and had more money to spend. Between 1946 and 1960 real purchasing power rose 22 percent—but that was only the beginning. In the next decade it jumped another 38 percent. Suddenly many Americans could afford goods and services that had been beyond their means in earlier decades. The result was a noticeable increase in the standard of living. To the vast majority of Americans, this nearly continuous prosperity was a vindication of the American system of free enterprise. Sociologist Seymour Martin Lipset went so far as to announce, "The fundamental problems of the industrial revolution have been solved."

Increased Purchasing Power

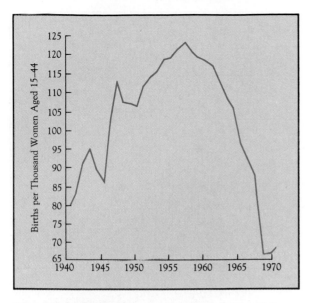

Birth Rate, 1940–1970 *Source: Adapted from U.S. Bureau of the Census, Historical Statistics of the United States, Colonial Times to 1970, Bicentennial Edition (Washington: U.S. Government Printing Office, 1975), p. 49.*

Crucial to the postwar economic boom was the baby boom, which was both a cause and an effect of prosperity. In 1950, 3.5 million babies were born, a sizable jump from the 2.5 million born in 1940. It was natural for the birthrate to soar immediately following the Second World War. What was confounding was that it continued to do so throughout the late 1940s and 1950s. During the 1950s the annual total exceeded 4 million (see figure), reversing the downward trend in birthrates that had prevailed for one hundred fifty years. Between 1946 and 1961, more than 63.5 million babies were born in the United States (compared with 41.5 million born in the fifteen-year period from 1930 to 1945), making the baby-boom generation the largest by far in the nation's history.

Baby Boom

What the baby boom meant was that many women who gave birth to a first child in 1946 or 1947 had second, third, fourth, and even fifth children in the years ahead. According to the Census Bureau, 83 percent of the increase in births from 1940 to 1950 were first children. Of the increased births between 1950 and 1954, however, 84 percent occurred in families that already had at least one child. The

popular belief that an only child was likely to grow up poorly adjusted had something to do with the continued increase. But *Business Week* was closer to the mark in crediting the boom to confidence in America's economic future. Professionals, white-collar workers, and college graduates contributed disproportionately to the baby boom. These were people who knew how to practice birth control and had done so in the past. (During the depression and the war the birthrate had declined most sharply among the urban middle class.) And these were people who were now having children by choice.

The baby boom spelled business for builders, manufacturers, and school systems. "Take the 3,548,000 babies born in 1950," wrote Sylvia F. Porter in her syndicated newspaper column. "Bundle them into a batch, bounce them all over the bountiful land that is America. What do you get?" Porter's answer: "Boom. The biggest, boomiest boom ever known in history. Just imagine how much these extra people, these new markets, will absorb—in food, in clothing, in gadgets, in housing, in services. Our factories must expand just to keep pace."

Of the three cornerstones of the postwar economic boom, two were related to the upsurge in births. The first was a construction boom to provide houses and schools for all these children. Office buildings, shopping centers, factories, airports, and stadiums also sprang up across the country. Much of this construction took place in the suburbs (see pages 890–893). But the postwar suburbanization of America would have been impossible without the second cornerstone, automobile manufacturing, for in the sprawling new communities a car was a necessity. Auto sales had plummeted during the Second World War, when manufacturers shifted to produce tanks and bombers, but from 1946 on sales began to climb. In 1950 they hit 6.7 million, as Americans seized the chance to get back on the road again. The number of registered automobiles climbed from 25.8 million in 1945 to 89.3 million in 1970, and total miles traveled jumped from 250 billion in 1945 to 1.1 trillion in 1970.

Auto Sales

The third cornerstone of the postwar economic boom was military spending. When the Defense Department was finally established in 1949, the nation was spending just over $13 billion a year on defense.

Military Spending

Babies meant big business for companies that produced baby foods, clothing, toys, and diapers. "In its first year as a consumer," read the caption for this 1958 Life photo, "baby is a potential market for $800 worth of products." Yale Joel, Life Magazine © 1958 Time Inc.

But beginning with the Korean War in the early 1950s, defense spending began to eclipse private domestic investment. By 1951, the Defense Department's budget was over $22 billion. Two years later it was over $50 billion. Except for a short dip from 1954 to 1958 (see page 863), it has been going up ever since. Much of the money spent on defense went into weapons research. And from 1949 to 1960 funds spent on space research alone jumped from $49 million to $401 million; by 1966 the expenditures had zoomed to almost $6 billion.

The invention of the transistor in 1948 inaugurated the computer revolution and stunning advances in electronics. Businesses and governments were so eager to buy electronic data-processing machines that sales zoomed from $25 million in 1953 to $1 billion in 1960. By the early 1960s thousands of computers had been produced and sold, marking what economist Herbert A. Simon called "an advance in man's thinking processes as radical as the invention of writing."

The evolution of electronics was a tradeoff for the American people. Computers brought about a rapid rise in productivity through the automation of numerous industries. But in doing so they stimulated technological unemployment: fewer workers were needed to accomplish the same amount of work. Computerized technology caused a decline in the demand for machinists; from 1950 to 1970 their numbers dropped from 535,000 to 390,000.

The spread of electronic technology also promoted the concentration of ownership in industry. Sophis-

Rising automobile sales not only fueled America's postwar economic boom, but also made possible the growth of the suburbs. These Cadillacs rolled off the assembly line in 1949. National Archives.

ticated technology was expensive to develop or purchase. Often only large corporations could afford it; small corporations were shut out of the market. People who believed that competition was the lifeblood of the American economy saw this tendency toward bigness as a dangerous development.

As the need for large amounts of capital increased, companies that were already established in high-technology fields expanded into related industries. General Electric was one example of a large corporation that diversified following the war. Although GE had manufactured a variety of electrical products prior to the 1940s, during the Second World War and the Cold War it expanded further, undertaking the manufacture of jet engines, nuclear-powered generators, computers, and industrial automation systems.

But not all expansion was a matter of diversification into related fields. Beginning in the early 1950s a third great merger wave swept American business. But unlike the first two waves in the 1890s and 1920s, which tended toward vertical and horizontal integration respectively (see pages 487–489, 681),

Conglomerate Mergers

this new wave was distinguished by conglomerate mergers. A *conglomerate* merged companies in totally unrelated fields as a hedge against instability in a particular market or industry. International Telephone and Telegraph, for instance, bought up companies in the fields of car rental (Avis), baking (Continental Baking), suburban development and home construction (Levitt and Sons), food sales (Canteen Corporation), hotels and motels (Sheraton Corporation), and insurance (Hartford Fire Insurance).

This new wave of mergers resulted in unprecedented concentration of industry. The Federal Trade Commission observed that in 1968 the two hundred largest manufacturing corporations held the same proportion of total manufacturing assets as had the one thousand largest in 1941. Reflecting the directions of America's postwar boom, the country's ten largest corporations at this time were in automobiles (GM, Ford, Chrysler), oil (Exxon, Mobil, Texaco), and electronics and communications (GE, IBM, ITT, Western Electric).

Even the labor movement experienced a merger. In 1955 the American Federation of Labor and the Congress of Industrial Organizations put aside their differences and established the AFL-CIO. Union membership remained fairly constant, however, increasing from just under 18 million at the time of the merger to only 20.7 million fifteen years later. Most new jobs were opening up not in the heavy industries that hired blue-collar workers, but in the union-resistant white-collar service trades. And some observers complained that union leaders had become comfortable and lost the organizing zeal that had won over so many workers in the 1930s and 1940s. Revelations of corrupt union practices also tainted the labor movement. The nation's biggest union, the International Brotherhood of Teamsters, had ties to organized crime. When the Teamsters failed to clean their house, the AFL-CIO officially expelled the union in 1957. Two Teamsters' presidents, Dave Beck and James R. Hoffa, served federal prison sentences for offenses ranging from tax evasion to jury tampering.

The postwar economic boom was a good time for unionized blue-collar workers, many of whom not only benefited from real increases in wages, but also enjoyed a middle-class lifestyle that heretofore had been the exclusive province of white-collar workers, businesspeople, and professionals. Because most union jobs paid well, these workers could obtain mortgages for suburban homes, especially if their spouses were also working. Many enjoyed job security, including a paid two-week vacation. With Social Security and union and company pension plans, they could look forward to retirement. They aspired to college educations for their children. And they were more secure against inflation. In 1948 General Motors and the United Auto Workers Union agreed on automatic cost-of-living adjustments (COLAS) in workers' wages, a practice that spread to other industries.

The trend toward economic consolidation brought changes in agriculture as well as business and labor. While new machines such as mechanical cotton-, tobacco-, and grape-pickers and **Agricultural** crop-dusting planes revolutionized **Consolidation** farming methods, increased use of fertilizers and pesticides raised the cash value of farm output by 120 percent (in constant dollars) between 1945 and 1970. Meanwhile labor productivity tripled. The resulting improvement in profitability drew large investors into agriculture. Average acreage per farm almost doubled, from 195 in 1945 to 374 in 1970. Simultaneously the value of farmland skyrocketed from $69 billion in 1945 to $266 billion in 1970. By the 1960s it took money—big money—to become a farmer. In many cases only banks, insurance companies, and other large businesses could afford the necessary land, machinery, and fertilizer.

By no means did all the effects of economic growth benefit the average American. In agriculture the movement toward consolidation threatened survival of the family farm. From 1945 to 1970 the nation's farm population declined from 24.4 million to just under 10 million, or from 17.5 percent of the population to 4.8 percent. When the harvesting of cotton in the South was mechanized in the 1940s and 1950s, more than 4 million people were displaced. One result was a shift of this poverty to the North and the cities. As one farmer lamented, "We lost country life when we moved to tractors." What was more, many of the people who stayed on did so, not because they could still make a good living, but because they were too old to leave their lifelong homes and follow their children and grandchildren to the cities. Living in relative isolation on limited incomes, the rural aged were among the hidden victims of mechanization.

The significant changes that postwar growth produced in industry and agriculture were matched by changes in Americans' buying habits and lifestyles. For many Americans the postwar economic boom brought what the economist John Kenneth Galbraith called the affluent society.

THE AFFLUENT SOCIETY

As America's productivity grew by leaps and bounds in the postwar years, so did its appetite for goods and services. During the depression and the Second World War, many Americans had dreamed about buying a home or a car. In the affluent postwar years they could satisfy their deferred desires. Families purchased not one but sometimes two cars and equipped their new homes with the latest appliances and amusements—dishwashers, television, and stereophonic sound systems. When they lacked cash to buy what they wanted, they borrowed money. Credit

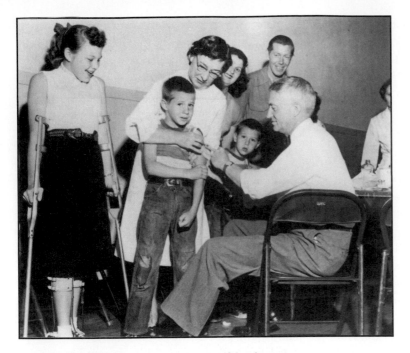

In 1955 the Salk polio vaccine was approved by the government for general use, and millions of children like this one received the vaccine. By 1962 the incidence of reported polio cases had dropped 97 percent.   UPI/Bettmann Newsphotos.

to support the nation's shopping spree grew from over $8 billion worth of short- and intermediate-term loans in 1946 to $127 billion in 1970. Here was the economic basis of the consumer culture.

As Americans consumed goods and services, they were using up the world's resources. Consumption of crude petroleum soared 118 percent from 1946 to 1970, but domestic production increased only 97 percent. The extra oil had to be imported. Electricity use jumped too, from 270 billion kilowatt-hours to 1.6 trillion. By the mid-1960s the United States, with only 5 percent of the world's population, produced and consumed over one-third of the world's goods and services.

Advances in public health were a particularly happy effect of postwar prosperity. The average life span increased from 65.9 years in 1945 to 70.9 in 1970, due especially to a dramatic decline **Improvements** in the death rate among the young. **in Public** Affluent Americans could afford **Health** regular prenatal and pediatric care, and they benefited from increased federal funding for medical research. As a result the

infant mortality rate dropped from over 38 deaths per 1,000 live births in 1945 to 20 per 1,000 in 1970. At the same time the discovery of wonder drugs such as streptomycin (1945) and aureomycin (1948) reduced deaths from influenza and postsurgical infection. And the Salk polio vaccine, approved for public use in 1955, reduced the number of reported cases of polio 97 percent by 1962. Other diseases, like tuberculosis, whooping cough, and diphtheria, became little more than bad memories.

Millions of Americans began their search for the affluent society by migrating to the Sunbelt. This mass migration had started during the Second World War, when GIs and their families **Growth of** were ordered to new duty stations **the Sunbelt** and war workers moved to the shipyards and aircraft factories of San Diego and other cities of the West and South. Soon the Sunbelt encompassed most of America's southern rim, the area running from southern California across the Southwest and South all the way to the Atlantic Coast. Between 1940 and 1950 Houston's population jumped from 385,000 to 596,000. Other Sunbelt

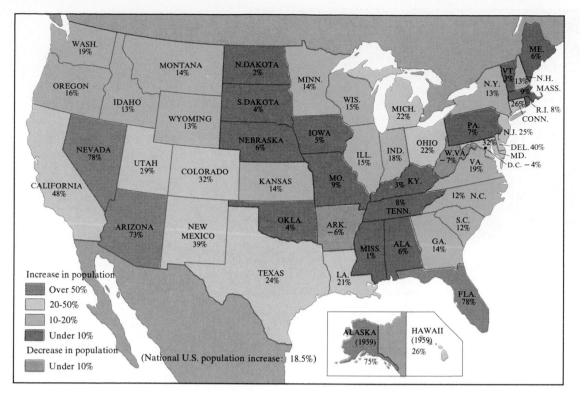

Rise of the Sunbelt, 1950–1960

cities that boomed in the 1940s were Baton Rouge, Long Beach, Miami, Mobile, and Phoenix.

The southward and westward migration continued to swell in the 1950s and 1960s (see map). Houston became a center not only of the aerospace industry but of oil and petrochemical production. Tucson, which had been scarcely more than a watering hole in the desert in 1950, grew to a city of 213,000 ten years later. California absorbed no less than one-fifth of the nation's entire population increase in the 1950s—enough, by 1963, to make the Golden State the most populous state in the union.

The economic bases of the Sunbelt's spectacular growth were easy to identify: agribusiness, the aerospace industry, the oil industry, real estate development, recreation, and, of course, defense spending. Government policies—such as large tax breaks given to oil companies and decisions about where to build military bases and award defense and aerospace contracts—were crucial to the Sunbelt's development. Industry was also drawn to the southern rim by right-to-work laws, which outlawed the closed union shop, and by low taxes and heating bills.

The millions of people who left the chilly industrial cities of the North and East for sunnier climes strengthened the political clout of the Sunbelt. In a book published in 1969, Kevin Phillips, a conservative Republican, predicted an emerging Republican majority based on the votes of the South and West. Richard Nixon's triumph in the presidential election of 1968 seemed to support Phillips's thesis. So did the tendency of political parties to nominate Sunbelt candidates for national office. (The nation's four most recently elected presidents have hailed from the Sunbelt—one from Texas, two from California, and one from Georgia. And in 1980 the Census Bureau made it official: for the first time in the nation's history, voters in the South and West accounted for a majority of those eligible to cast ballots.)

The economic boom that made for the political pre-eminence of the Sunbelt also brought increased security for whole classes of Americans. And the expanding economy combined with federal welfare legislation to reduce poverty (see Chapter 33). But even with the reduction in poverty, there was little redistribution of income. The portions of total national

Year	Poorest Fifth	Second Poorest Fifth	Middle Fifth	Second Wealthiest Fifth	Wealthiest Fifth	Wealthiest 5 Percent
1947	3.5	10.6	16.7	23.6	45.6	18.7
1950	3.1	10.5	17.3	24.1	45.0	18.2
1960	3.2	10.6	17.6	24.7	44.0	17.0
1970	3.6	10.3	17.2	24.7	44.1	16.9

[a]Monetary income only.

Source: Adapted from U.S. Bureau of the Census, *Historical Statistics of the United States, Colonial Times to 1970,* Bicentennial Edition (Washington: U.S. Government Printing Office, 1975), p. 292.

income taken home by the rich, the middle classes, and the poor remained about the same from 1947 to 1970 (see table).

THE OTHER AMERICA

In the postwar age of abundance, most Americans found it especially hard to acknowledge the presence of poverty in their midst. But according to the Bureau of Labor Statistics, in 1962 about 42.5 million Americans (nearly one out of every four people) were poor. These Americans earned less than $4,000 per year for a family of four, or $2,000 per year for a single person living alone. Age, race, sex, education, and marital status were all factors in their poverty. One-fourth of the poor were over sixty-five; many lived alone on fixed incomes, their meager purchasing power continually reduced by inflation. More than a third of the poor were under eighteen. One-fifth were nonwhite, including almost half the nation's black population and more than half the Native

American population. Two-thirds lived in households headed by a person with an eighth-grade education or less, and one-fourth lived in households headed by a single woman. For all these people, there was little reason for hope. The bureau constructed a budget to show what a poor family of four could afford: one book a year; a new car every twelve to eighteen years; no telephone; a movie once every three weeks; a wool suit every two or three years for the husband. It is clear from this meager budget that no matter how much the economy might boom, there was a limit to the money that would trickle down to the poor.

In the years after 1945, while millions of Americans, most of them white, were settling in the suburbs, the poor were congregating in the inner cities. Starting with the wartime industrial boom of the early 1940s and continuing through the 1960s, almost 4.5 million blacks, many of whom were unskilled and illiterate, trekked to the cities from the rural South. By 1970 the black population, which had been 48.6 percent urban in 1940, had become 81.4 percent urban. Joining Afro-Americans in the exodus to the cities were poor whites from the southern Appalachians, who moved to Cincinnati, Baltimore, St. Louis, Columbus, Detroit, and Chicago. Latin Americans were arriving

Despite America's postwar economic boom, many people still lived in poverty. In 1945, these black farm workers in Belleglade, Florida, had little hope for the future. Fifteen years later their plight was unchanged, as the historic television documentary "A Harvest of Shame" made clear in 1960. National Archives/Photo Researchers.

in growing numbers from Mexico, Puerto Rico, the Dominican Republic, Colombia, Ecuador, and Cuba. New York City's Puerto Rican population spurted from 70,000 to over 600,000 in just twenty years.

Next to Afro-Americans, the largest group of urban newcomers were the Mexican-Americans, or Chicanos. Millions came during and after the war as farm workers, and increasingly they remained to make their lives in the United States. Despite the initiation in 1953 of Operation Wetback, a program to find and deport illegal aliens, Mexicans continued to enter the country in large numbers, many of them illegally. Many settled in cities. According to the 1960 census, over 500,000 Mexican-Americans had migrated to the *barrios* of the Los Angeles–Long Beach area since 1940. If estimates of uncounted illegal aliens were added to the census figure, the total was far higher. The same was true of the *barrios* of El Paso, Phoenix, and other southwestern cities, as well as Chicano

communities in Denver, Kansas City, Chicago, Detroit, and other northern cities.

Native Americans made up the country's poorest group with an average annual income that was half the amount of the poverty level. Indians moved to the cities in the 1950s and 1960s, particularly after Congress in 1953 adopted the policy of termination that ended the status of certain tribes as wards of the United States (see page 857). Accustomed to the rural, semicommunal life of the reservation, many had difficulty adjusting to the city. Indeed, the tragedy of many groups who migrated to cities was that, instead of finding a place to prosper, they found only a dumping ground for the poor.

Not all the poor, however, lived in cities. By 1960, 30 percent lived in small towns and 15 percent on farms. Tenant farmers and sharecroppers, both black and white, suffered economic hardship. Migratory farm workers lived in abject poverty. And elderly people tended to be poor regardless of where they lived.

These Americans were poor partially because they had been shortchanged by New Deal and Fair Deal legislation. Postwar housing laws primarily helped the middle class (see page 893). The Wagner Act and federal farm programs established during the New Deal chiefly helped unionized workers and big farmers (see pages 741 and 746). Neither Social Security nor the minimum wage covered hospital janitors and orderlies, bus boys, dishwashers, and other restaurant employees, or migratory farm workers. The programs available to the poor were generally designed to give them direct relief, not to better their chances of maintaining an independent income.

Naturally, the number of people living in poverty fluctuated with the economy. During the postwar years, poverty was most widespread during the 1950 recession, when 36 percent of Americans were classified as poor. By 1962 poverty had fallen to about 25 percent; economic growth was clearly reducing the ranks of the poor. President Lyndon B. Johnson's war on poverty cut the figure further, and it fell to 13 percent by 1969. Still, it was evident that many people slipped into poverty for a variety of reasons.

A large share of the poor were women. Well-paying employment opportunities were limited and there was extensive occupational segregation, with low-paying positions being labelled women's work and better-paying positions being reserved for men. Although in 1945 many women had wanted to remain in the factories and shipyards, they were pushed out to make way for returning veterans. And those who tried later to return to industrial work were discouraged. "Rosie [the Riveter] feels something like Typhoid Mary when she applies for a factory job," stated the *Detroit Free Press*. In 1960 the median annual earnings for full-time women workers stood at 60 percent of men's earnings. Moreover, many women's jobs were not covered by either the minimum wage or Social Security. Finally, if divorce, desertion, or death did rend a family, it was usually the woman who was left to bear responsibility for the health and welfare of children. Many ex-husbands did not make their child-support payments. And on welfare, or a salary that paid women sixty cents for each dollar a man got, many single mothers and their children slipped into poverty.

One of the least-known effects of economic hardship on the poor has been physical and emotional illness. A study done in the late 1950s in New Haven, Connecticut, found that the rate of treated psychiatric illness was three times as high for the lowest fifth of income earners as it was for the upper-middle and upper classes. Psychiatrists at Cornell University's Medical School described the "low social economic status individual" as "rigid, suspicious," and having "a fatalistic outlook on life. . . . They are prone to depression, have feelings of futility, lack of belongingness . . . and a lack of trust in others."

Graphic evidence of the emotional costs of poverty came during the economic recession of 1960, when the National Federation of Settlements and Neighborhood Centers assembled reports from around the country on the effects of the downturn. A social worker from Rochester, New York, bemoaned a sharp rise in "marital discord and desertions of families by the father, increased welfare dependency, increased crime, especially robberies, burglaries and muggings, and alcoholism." Ironically, all of this suffering was occurring in a nation that was being heralded as the affluent society.

THE GROWTH OF SUBURBS

Suburban growth was closely associated with the affluent society. During the first six decades of the twentieth century, cityward migration steadily increased. But in the 1940s another migration—from the city to the suburbs—began to swell. By 1970 more Americans resided in suburbs than in central cities (see table).

A combination of motives drew people to the suburbs. Many wanted to leave behind the sounds and smells of the city and be closer to nature. They also wanted homes with yards so that, as one suburbanite put it, "every kid [would have] an opportunity to grow up with grass stains on his pants." Or they wanted the privacy and quiet that detached homes provided, as well as family rooms, extra closets, and utility rooms. Many were also looking for a community of like-minded people, a place where they could have

GEOGRAPHIC DISTRIBUTION OF U.S. POPULATION, 1930–1970 (IN PERCENTAGES)

Year	Central Cities	Suburbs	Rural Areas and Small Towns
1930	31.8	18.0	50.2
1940	31.6	19.5	48.9
1950	32.3	23.8	43.9
1960	32.6	30.7	36.7
1970	31.4	37.6	31.0

Source: Adapted from U.S. Bureau of the Census, *Decennial Censuses, 1930–1970* (Washington, U.S. Government Printing Office).

a measure of political influence. Big-city government was dense and impenetrable. In the suburbs citizens could become involved in government and have an impact, particularly on the education their children received. "The American suburb," mused a Pittsburgh building executive in 1960, "is the last outpost of democracy, the only level on which the individual citizen can make his wishes felt, directly and immediately."

Judging from the massive numbers of three- and four-bedroom houses built in the suburbs, there was no question that suburbanites' major concern was their children. "This is a paradise for children," observed a newspaper writer in 1950, referring to the new suburb where he lived. "There are so many babies here," commented one of his neighbors, "you would think everybody would be blasé about them. Still, when a new one is coming, all the neighbors make a fuss over you."

Another allure of the suburbs was closeness in age and shared experience. In many suburbs most adults were young parents between the ages of twenty-five and thirty-five, and almost all the children were toddlers. In one suburb of nine thousand homes there were eight thousand children, only about one hundred of whom were old enough for high school; most of the rest were still in playpens. "People could not outdo each other," one resident of this community reported, "because they almost all have the same income. . . . Nobody talks about the [Second World] war much, because they've all been in it. And most of the men have the same . . . commuting problem— which many have solved by car pools. All this helps to cement neighbors into friends."

Government funding and policies helped these new families to settle in the suburbs. Low-interest GI mortgages and Federal Housing Administration mortgage insurance made the difference

Housing Boom for people who would otherwise have been unable to afford a home. Such easy credit combined with postwar prosperity to produce a construction boom. In 1944 there had been only 142,000 housing starts, many of which represented temporary housing for soldiers and war workers. From 1945 to 1946 housing starts climbed from 326,000 to over 1 million, and in 1950 they approached 2 million. Never before had new starts exceeded 1 million; not until the early 1980s would they dip below that level.

To produce so much new housing so fast, contractors had to operate on a massive scale. Arthur Levitt and Sons, a firm that built planned communities (Levittowns) in New York, New Jersey, and Pennsylvania, developed the pattern adopted by other companies: using interchangeable materials and designs, Levitt erected rows of nearly identical houses on uniform

The suburbs promised a haven for the families of the baby boom. In this housing project in Lakewood Park, California, new families moved in at a rate of 25 per day during the last three months of 1950.   National Archives.

treeless lots. As suburbia spread, pasture lands yielded to whole neighborhoods with astounding rapidity. To supply the new communities, supermarkets, gas stations, shopping centers, and malls—all of them surrounded by vast parking lots—soon dotted the countryside.

At the same time highway construction opened up rural lands for the development of suburban communities. In 1947 Congress authorized the construction of a 37,000-mile chain of highways, and in 1956 President Eisenhower signed the Highway Act, which launched a 41,000-mile nationwide network. Federal funds spent on highways swelled from $79 million in 1946 to $429 million in 1950, $2.9 billion in 1960, and a huge $4.6 billion in 1970. State and local highway expenditures also mushroomed.

Highway Construction

By the 1970s most of the interstate system had been completed, and some towns along the way had prospered. Route I-70, for example, gave Junction City, Kansas, six new motels, several restaurants, and an economic boost. But the new road also siphoned traffic away from older roads. Small towns along two-lane highways withered as residents left to seek a better living in the city. "They [the towns] didn't dry up and blow away," observed the editor of Junction City's daily newspaper, "but they are much like the towns left off the railroad [lines] 100 years ago."

The spurt in highway construction combined with the mushrooming of suburbia to produce the *megalopolis*, a term first used by urban experts in the early 1960s to refer to the almost uninterrupted metropolitan complex stretching along the northeastern seaboard of the United States. Beginning in Boston and extending 600 miles south through New York, Philadelphia, Baltimore, and Washington, "Boswash" encompassed parts of eleven states and a population of 49 million people, all tied together by interstate highways. Although the suburbs within the megalopolis were politically independent, they were economically dependent on the cities and connecting highways. Other megalopolises that took shape following the Second World War were "Chipitts," a band of heavy industry and dense population stretching from Chicago to Pittsburgh, and "San-San"—San Francisco to San Diego.

Middle-class whites benefited more than other Americans from the government-supported housing and highway boom. In 1948 the government cut mortgage subsidies for rental-unit construction and increased subsidies for privately owned single-family houses, a policy that worked against the poorest Americans. Moreover, the FHA refused to guarantee suburban home loans to the poor, nonwhites, Jews, and other "inharmonious racial and ethnic groups." Some federal programs actually worsened conditions for the poor. The National Housing Act of 1949, passed to make available "a decent home and a suitable living environment for every American family," failed in several respects. The primary features of the act were "urban redevelopment," or slum clearance; the construction of public housing for low-income people (810,000 units in four years); and FHA mortgages for home buyers. But the program was poorly coordinated, and slums were replaced not with low-income housing but with parking lots, shopping centers, luxury high-rise buildings, highways, and factories. The planned 810,000 housing units for the poor were constructed not in four years but in twenty.

Socially, the suburban emphasis on family togetherness tended to isolate families. Writing in 1957, sociologist David Riesman criticized "the decentralization of leisure in the suburbs . . .

Critics of Suburban Life

as the home itself, rather than the neighborhood, becomes the chief gathering place for the family—either in the 'family room' with its games, its TV, its informality, or outdoors around the barbecue." The floor plan of the ranch-style home, at whose center was the TV set enthroned on a swivel, was suited to the stay-at-home lifestyle. Even when families traveled, they were isolated in the family car.

Riesman was only one of many critics of suburban living. Other observers denounced the suburbs for breeding conformity. Some writers criticized suburbanites for trying to keep up with the Joneses by buying new cars and appliances. The word *suburbia*,

These commuters from their jobs in Chicago departed the train at their suburban destination in Park Forest, Illinois. The novel The Man in the Gray Flannel Suit (1955) was the best-selling account of one such commuter. *Dan Weiner photo, courtesy Sandra Weiner.*

Scott Donaldson wrote in *The Suburban Myth* (1969), had "unpleasant overtones, suggesting nothing so much as some kind of scruffy disease." The titles of magazine articles and books echoed his diagnosis: "Trouble in the Suburbs," "The Crabgrass Roots of Suburbia," *The Split Level Trap*. In Sloan Wilson's novel *The Man in the Gray Flannel Suit* (1955), the main character led a treadmill existence commuting to his white-collar job in the city. And C. Wright Mills, a sociologist, castigated white-collar suburbanites, who "sell not only their time and energy but their personalities as well. They sell . . . their smiles and their kindly gestures."

When all the pluses and minuses were tallied, however, most residents of suburbia seemed to prefer family togetherness to any other lifestyle of which they were aware. Of the college students interviewed by Riesman in the 1950s, the vast majority looked forward to living in the suburbs.

IDEALS OF MOTHERHOOD AND THE FAMILY

In the early twentieth century, Sunday dinner had been an exasperating occasion for the youngest child in a large family, for the youngest was traditionally served last. If the dinner was chicken, the little one often got the back or the neck. "I was the youngest of five children" recalled one young father shortly after the Second World War, "and by the time I was served, all the white meat was gone. . . . I swore to myself that when I grew up I would eat all the white meat I could. So I'm grown up and a father—and my children get first choice!" Times had changed, and so had the ways of the American family.

A good deal of the change was due to the publication in 1946 of Dr. Benjamin Spock's *Baby and Child Care*. The book, which quickly became a bible for new parents, answered many common questions about childrearing.

Dr. Spock on Childrearing

But unlike earlier manuals, *Baby and Child Care* urged mothers (but not fathers, because Spock assigned them little formal role in childrearing) to think of their children first, even at the expense of their own mental and physical health. Dr. Spock's predecessors during the previous thirty years had advised mothers to consider their own needs as well as their children's. They had recommended early and strict toilet training; "putting away your children at six o'clock" in order to enjoy "the quiet comfort of a still household in the evening"; and ignoring a baby's crying except at feeding time. Now Dr. Spock urged the mother to be constantly available to feed and communicate with her baby, and to remember that "feeding is learning." Spock encouraged the baby's "self-realization," self-discovery," and "self-motivated behavior."

Though no mother could be all things to her baby, women who embraced Dr. Spock's teachings tended to believe they had failed if they were not. Guilt was the inevitable result of the effort to be not only mother but teacher, psychologist, and buddy. The mother of an epileptic son wrote to Dr. Spock: "I

try to give him a great deal of affection, although I am a working woman. . . . Sometimes it is so difficult to maintain my control that my hands shake. . . . Does he need the help or do I?" Another mother wrote, "We like to read and listen to music. Maybe we have neglected some aspects of A's development in our own selfishness."

At the same time Philip Wylie, author of the book *Generation of Vipers*, denounced such selfless behavior as Momism. In the guise of sacrificing for her children,

Momism

Wylie wrote, Mom was pursuing "love of herself." She smothered her children with affection so they would become emotionally dependent on her and would not want to leave home. Other experts agreed. Army psychiatrists blamed recruits' nervous disorders on mothers who, as a psychiatric adviser to the Secretary of War wrote, had "failed in the elementary mother function of weaning [their] offspring emotionally as well as physically."

But women were caught in a double bind, for if they pursued a life outside the home they were accused of being "imitation men" or "neurotic" feminists. Echoing the psychoanalyst Sigmund Freud, critics of working mothers contended that a woman could be happy and fulfilled only through domesticity. "Anatomy is destiny" was their catch phrase; a woman's gender determined her role in life. Reflecting on the contradictory expectations of women, anthropologist Margaret Mead wrote in 1946, "Choose any set of criteria you like, and the answer is the same: women—and men—are confused, uncertain, and discontented with the present definition of women's place in America."

A reason for woman's dilemma was the conflicting roles she was expected to fulfill. On the one hand, the home was premised on a full-time housewife who, with little regard for her own needs, provided her husband and children a haven from the outside world. In 1963 Betty Friedan gave this situation a name—*The Feminine Mystique*. On the other hand, women continued the wartime trend toward work outside the home. The female labor force rose from 16.8 million in 1946 to 23.3 million in 1960 and 31.6 million in 1970. These women entered the labor force lacking the support of an organized women's movement and refraining from challenging sex-role stereotypes. But because of the rough division of the labor market into "men's jobs" and "women's jobs," many women found themselves segregated in low-paying work as clerks, secretaries, and nurses, while men commanded comfortable incomes as tradesmen, business managers, and doctors.

Many women, of course, were their families' sole source of income; they had to work. Still others took jobs not to challenge male dominance but to earn additional family income, enjoy adult company, or bolster their self-esteem. Despite the cult of motherhood, most new entrants to the job market were married, a trend that had begun during the Second World War (see figure), and most were mothers.

Immediately after the Second World War, many American families moved into Quonset huts on college campuses. Accompanied by wives and babies, former GIs were getting an education. The **GI Bill** legislation making it possible was the Servicemen's Readjustment Act of 1944, or GI Bill of Rights, which provided living allowances and tuition payments to college-bound veterans. Over 1 million enrolled in 1946—almost one out of every two students. Despite dire predictions to the contrary, the veterans succeeded as students. Benjamin Fine, education editor of the *New York Times*, called it "the most astonishing fact in the history of American higher education. . . . The G.I.'s are hogging the honor rolls and the Dean's lists. . . . Far from being an educational problem, the veteran has become an asset to higher education." But there was nothing astonishing about it. Veterans saw higher education as the key to upward mobility.

These veterans were determined to succeed so they and their families could prosper, so their children could grow up in grassy suburban yards and attend good public schools. Men and **Family Togetherness** women of their generation had been children and adolescents during the economic deprivation of the 1930s. They had experienced young adulthood during the Second World War, when many had been physically separated from their families and friends. Glen H. Elder, the sociologist, has written that men and women who had grown up in the 1930s "in Depression-marked homes were most likely to anchor their lives around family and children, perhaps reflecting the

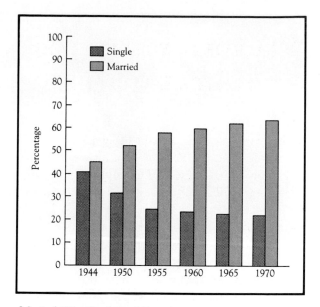

Marital Distribution of Female Labor Force, 1944–1970 *Source: Adapted from U.S. Bureau of the Census, Historical Statistics of the United States, Colonial Times to 1970, Bicentennial Edition (Washington: U.S. Government Printing Office, 1975), p. 133.*

notion of home as a refuge in an unpredictable world." These men and women became parents of the baby boom and exponents of "family togetherness." Such togetherness included family TV-watching, outings to parks and beaches, and Little League games. The destination of many family vacations was Disneyland, which opened in Anaheim, California, in 1955.

Popular periodicals echoed the importance that these parents attached to togetherness. "Ed and His Family Live Together and Love It" was the title of a typical article in a 1954 *McCall's*. "Caring for three lively children makes tremendous demands on Carol. . . . But Ed is a cheerful working partner to her, helps with the children and housework whenever he can, gives everything he has to make his family happy." In return, Ed's wife and children "give him all the love and affection a husband and father could hope for." Carol even took over some household tasks traditionally performed by men: "Paneling that extra room in the cellar used to be the man's job. But Ed and Carol do it together." Despite *McCall's* advocacy of shared tasks, the magazine stopped short of advocating complete equality. "For the sake of every

Complete with their addition to the baby boom generation, these smiling parents stand proudly in front of their suburban home and new automobile. After a dozen years of economic depression and world war, many young couples enjoyed the togetherness afforded by life in the suburbs. UPI/Bettmann Newsphotos.

member of the family, the family needs a head. This means Father, not Mother."

Most American families were preoccupied with education. As the baby boom became a grade-school boom, parents rushed to join the parent-teacher association so they would have a voice in the educational process. They expressed concern that schools were overcrowded, understaffed, and aimless, or that teachers were using obsolete methods. Educators encouraged their participation. "Just as war is 'too serious a matter to be

Education of the Baby Boom Generation

left to the generals,' so, I think, the teaching of reading is too important to be left to the educators," wrote Dr. Rudolf Flesch in 1955, in his best-selling book *Why Johnny Can't Read.*

Two years later when the Russians launched *Sputnik,* the first earth-orbiting satellite, education became a matter of national security. The Russian success challenged American military and technological superiority, based ultimately on the nation's school system. James B. Conant, Hyman G. Rickover, and other critics argued that what the United States needed to regain its technological leadership was new emphasis on mathematics, foreign languages, and the sciences. In 1958 Congress responded with the National Defense Education Act (NDEA), which funded elementary and high school programs in those disciplines and offered fellowships and loans to college students. Parents were quick to endorse the new programs. After all, public education was the engine of democracy, a guarantee of both upward social mobility and military superiority.

Just as education became intertwined with national security, religion became synonymous with patriotism. As President Eisenhower put it, "recognition of the Supreme Being is the first, the most basic expression of Americanism." After all, the United States was locked in mortal combat with an atheistic enemy. In America's Cold War with the godless Soviet Union, ministers, priests, and rabbis became foot soldiers in the battle for souls. Religious leaders emphasized family togetherness in their appeals for new converts. "The family that prays together stays together" was a famous slogan used during the 1950s and 1960s. The Bible topped the best-seller lists, and books with religious themes, such as the Reverend Norman Vincent Peale's *The Power of Positive Thinking* (1952), sold in the millions. Meanwhile evangelist Billy Graham exhorted television viewers and stadium audiences throughout the country. From 1945 to 1970 church membership nearly doubled.

Although Americans were eager to improve their minds and souls, they were not ready until the 1960s to liberate themselves sexually. When Dr. Alfred Kinsey, director of the Institute for Sex Research at Indiana University, published his pioneering book *Sexual Behavior in the Human Male* (1948), the American public was shocked. On the basis of interviews with numerous men, Kinsey estimated that 95 percent of American men had engaged in masturbation, premarital or extramarital intercourse, or homosexual behavior. Princeton's President Harold Dodds denounced the volume as "the work of small boys writing dirty words on fences." Five years later Kinsey caused even more of a disturbance with *Sexual Behavior in the Human Female*, which revealed that 62 percent of women masturbated and 50 percent had intercourse before marriage. Some angry Americans condemned the report as a slanderous attack not only on women, but on motherhood and the family as well. A

congressional representative from New York, who tried to bar the report from the mails, charged Kinsey with "hurling the insult of the century against our mothers, wives, daughters and sisters." Sex was nothing new, of course, but its existence was seldom acknowledged in polite conversation or respectable publications—and most Americans preferred that situation.

AMERICA AT PLAY

The prosperity that marked the postwar era was reflected in the materialistic values and pleasures of the period. Having satisfied their basic needs for food, clothing, and shelter, growing numbers of Americans turned their attention to luxury items. "More appliances make mom's work easier," read a typical advertisement. As families strove to acquire the latest conveniences, shopping became a form of recreation.

Of the new luxuries, television was the most revolutionary in its effects. One man who grew up in the postwar era recalled the purchase of the first family TV set in 1950. "And so the

TV Enters the American Home

monumental change began in our lives and those of millions of other Americans. More than a year passed before we again visited a movie theater. Money which previously would have been spent for books was saved for the TV payments. Social evenings with friends became fewer and fewer still because we discovered we did not share the same TV program interests." By 1950 television had broken radio's grip on the American public. The number of households with TVs climbed from 8,000 in 1946 to 3.9 million in 1950 and 60.6 million in 1970.

Entertainment was TV's number one product. Situation comedies and action series were among the most popular shows. Topping these categories in the 1950s were *I Love Lucy*, starring Lucille Ball, and *Dragnet*, a detective series. Family togetherness was a theme of *Father Knows Best* and *Leave It to Beaver*. There were programs for all age groups, ranging from

The Howdy Doody Show was one of the most popular children's television shows. The show's stars were Clarabelle the clown, Howdy Doody (sitting on the back of Flubadub), and Bob Smith.   National Archives.

Ding Dong School, quiz shows, and westerns to the roller derby. As daily average TV viewing in the United States reached five hours in 1956 and six hours in 1971, the danger presented itself that television would become more than just entertainment. Some critics worried that with this much viewing, TV's distorted presentation of the world would significantly define people's sense of reality.

Advertising was the foundation of the television industry, as it had also been for radio. The first TV commerical, made by the Bulova Watch Company in 1941, was a one-minute effort that cost nine dollars. By the end of the decade, American families were spending several hours a day before the television set, and bargain rates had vanished; annual expenditures for TV advertising totaled $50 million. By 1970 the figure had soared to $3.6 billion.

Critics of the television industry have often wondered why American viewers put up with advertising. The answer is that, far from being an unwanted interruption, television advertising was a valuable service to consumers. Because keeping up with the Joneses was a goal of some suburbanites, television advertising provided visual evidence of just what the Joneses were buying. In the comfort of their living rooms Americans could study how to elevate their status through the purchase of a particular automobile, cigarette, or electric appliance. Indeed, it was not only commercials but programs themselves that tantalized viewers with glimpses of the sumptuous life. Situation comedies and dramas were nearly always set in well-furnished suburban homes; the characters dressed in the latest styles and drove the newest cars.

As television brought the world into their living

Important Events

1945	Demobilization of 12 million GIs	1955	Salk polio vaccine approved for use AFL-CIO merger *Rebel Without a Cause*
1946	Beginning of the baby boom Spock, *Baby and Child Care* Over 1 million GIs enroll in colleges	1956	Highway Act Ginsberg, *Howl*
1947	Gross national product ($231.3 billion) begins postwar rise Levittown, New York, begun 8,000 families own TVs	1957	Peak of baby boom (4.3 million births) Soviet Union launches *Sputnik I* Kerouac, *On the Road*
1948	Kinsey, *Sexual Behavior in the Human Male*	1958	National Defense Education Act
1949	National Housing Act	1960	Gross national product reaches $503.7 billion
1952	Peale, *The Power of Positive Thinking* Ellison, *Invisible Man*	1962	Harrington, *The Other America*
1953	*The Wild One* Kinsey, *Sexual Behavior in the Human Female*	1963	Friedan, *The Feminine Mystique*
		1970	Gross national product reaches $977.1 billion Suburbs surpass central cities in population

rooms, Americans began to read newspapers and news magazines a little less carefully, and to listen to radio a lot less frequently. But despite the lure of the tube, book readership went up. One reason for the increased consumption of literature was the mass marketing of the inexpensive paperbound book. Pocket Books hit the market in 1939; soon westerns, detective stories, and science fiction filled the newsstands, supermarkets, and drug stores. "The paperback democratized reading in America," Kenneth C. Davis has written in his history of "the paperbacking of America." The comic book, which had become popular in 1939 with the introduction of Superman, became another drug store standard. Reprints of hardcover books and condensed books also did well. All in all, funds spent for books increased by 220 percent between 1946 and 1960 and by another 265 percent between 1960 and 1970.

Paperback Books

One obvious casualty of the stay-at-home suburban culture was the motion picture. While Americans continued to buy paperbacks and comic books in large numbers, many of them stopped visiting movie theaters. Why fight traffic to go to a movie when you could watch TV in the comfort of your living room? Why pay a babysitter? From 1946 to 1948 Americans had attended movies at the rate of nearly 90 million a week. By 1950 the figure had dropped to 60 million a week; by 1960, 40 million. Thus the postwar years saw the steady closing of movie theaters—with the notable exception of the drive-in, which appealed to car-oriented suburban families.

There was one crucial exception to the downturn in moviegoing. By the late 1950s the first children of the postwar baby boom had become adolescents, and though their parents preferred to stay home and watch television, they themselves flocked to the theaters. No less than 72 percent of moviegoers during

The most popular rock-and-roll star of the 1950s was Elvis Presley. Presley's records sold millions of copies, but so freely did he bump and grind that Ed Sullivan, the host of a popular weekly television variety show, pronounced him "unfit for a family audience." Leviton-Atlanta/Black Star.

the 1950s were under age thirty. Hollywood responded to this youthful new audience with films portraying young people as sensitive and intelligent, adults as boorish and hostile: *The Wild One, Rebel Without a Cause, Blackboard Jungle*. The cult of youth had been born.

Rise of the Youth Subculture

Soon the music industry was catering to teens with cheap 45 rpm records. Bored with the era's syrupy music, young Americans welcomed the driving energy and hard beat of rock-and-roll. Bill Haley, the Everly Brothers, and Buddy Holly thrilled teenagers with their music. Elvis Presley horrified their parents with his suggestive gyrations. Before long, Presley's ducktail haircut and leather jacket had become the uniform for rebellious teenage males. Although the roots of the new music lay in black rhythm-and-blues, most white stars did not acknowledge the debt. Presley's hit tune "Hound Dog," for example, had originally been performed by the black singer Big Mama Thornton, but Thornton received little credit for her contribution. Among the black rock-and-roll stars of the 1950s were Chuck Berry and Little Richard.

While white performers copied black rhythm-and-blues, serious black jazz artists like Charlie Parker and Dizzy Gillespie were experimenting with "bebop." In the 1950s jazz became increasingly fused with classical themes, compositions, and instrumentation.

Intellectuals began to study this art form, which had once been looked down on as vulgar.

In the arts Martha Graham was lauded in international dance circles, and Jackson Pollock became the pivotal figure of the abstract expressionist movement, which in the 1950s established New York City as a center of the art world. Rather than work with the traditional painter's easel, Pollock spread his canvas on the floor, where he was free to walk around it, "work from the four sides and literally be *in* the painting." He and other "action painters" worked with sticks, trowels, and knives, and they played with new materials like heavy impasto with "sand, broken glass and other foreign matter added." In the 1960s artists of the Pop Art movement satirized the consumer society, using commercial techniques to depict everyday objects. Andy Warhol painted Campbell soup cans; other artists did blowups of ice-cream sundaes, hamburgers, and comic-strip panels.

Every era has its fads. Slinky, selling for a dollar, began loping down people's stairs in 1947; silly putty was introduced in 1950. The 1950s also had 3-D movies and hula hoops. Within **Fads** months of the hula hoop's introduction in 1958, over 30 million had been sold. And then there were signature items such as Hoppy watches, emblazoned with pictures of cowboy star Hopalong Cassidy. Although most crazes were short-lived, they created multimillion-dollar industries and effectively promoted dozens of movies and TV shows. Other postwar crazes are still with us—Scrabble, paint-by-number sets, and Barbie dolls, to name just a few. Between 1959 and 1980 more than 120 million Barbie and Barbie family dolls were sold. Frisbee-throwing has not only survived but has prevailed over similar outdoor games. Many of these toys and games succeeded because they brought the whole family together.

Some prewar activities flourished in the 1950s and 1960s, notably golf and bowling. But though Americans still hunted and fished, they no longer did so at the farm pond or in the woods down the road; they had to travel to get to the country. And travel they did. With more money and leisure time and a much-improved highway system, middle-class families took vacations that had formerly been restricted to the rich. They visited national monuments and parks, went camping, and even ventured abroad.

Andy Warhol's Campbell's Soup *(1965), a Pop Art satire of the consumer culture. Collection, The Museum of Modern Art, New York, Elizabeth Bliss Parkinson Fund. Oil silkscreened on canvas, 36⅛ × 24⅛".*

Needless to say, the consensus society of the 1950s and early 1960s was not receptive to social criticism. The filmgoing public preferred noncontroversial doses of Doris Day and Rock Hudson, and Dean Martin and Jerry Lewis. Readers bought novels and retreated into the criminal underworld, the wild West, or science-fiction fantasy. Even serious artists tended to ignore the country's social problems.

There were exceptions. Ralph Ellison's *Invisible Man* (1952) gave white Americans a glimpse of the psychic costs to black Americans of exclusion from the white American dream. **Beat** Two films—*Gentleman's Agreement* **Generation** (1947) and *Home of the Brave* (1949)—examined anti-Semitism and white racism. And in the 1950s, one group of writers repudiated the conventional world of the middle class and the suburbs. Rejecting the same social niceties Kinsey had challenged, the writers of the Beat (for "beatific") Generation flaunted their freewheeling sexuality and consumption of drugs. The Beats produced some memorable prose and poetry, including Allen Ginsberg's long poem *Howl* (1956) and Jack Kerouac's *On the Road* (1957), and they offered American youth an alternative to their parents' materialism and righteous self-congratulation. Though the Beats were mostly ignored during the fifties, millions of young Americans discovered their writings and lifestyle in the late 1960s.

One of the most influential books of postwar years was the best-selling *The Affluent Society* (1958), by economist John Kenneth Galbraith. Galbraith's thesis dovetailed with the prevalent belief that economic growth would bring prosperity to everyone. Some would have more than others, of course, but in time everybody would have enough. "Production has eliminated the more acute tensions associated with [economic] inequality," Galbraith wrote. Not until Chapter 23 did the author mention poverty; when he did, he dismissed it as not "a universal or massive affliction," but "more nearly an afterthought."

Only in the 1960s would comfortable Americans of the middle class discover that millions of poor people lived in America (see Chapter 33). Politically and culturally, the later 1960s would be vastly different from the consensus years that preceded them. Ironically, it would be the products of suburbia—the children of the baby boom—who formed the vanguard of the assault not only on poverty, but on the whole value system of the American middle class.

SUGGESTIONS FOR FURTHER READING

The Affluent Society

Carl Abbott, *The New Urban America* (1981); Robert H. Bremner and Gary W. Reichard, eds., *Reshaping America: Society and Institutions* (1982); David P. Calleo, *The Imperious Economy* (1982); John Kenneth Galbraith, *The Affluent Society* (1958); John Kenneth Galbraith, *American Capitalism* (1952); Robert Heilbroner, *The Limits of American Capitalism* (1966).

Farmers and Workers

Willard W. Cochrane and Mary E. Ryan, *American Farm Policy, 1948–1973* (1976); Gilbert C. Fite, *American Farmers* (1981); James R. Green, *The World of the Worker* (1980); Howell John Harris, *The Right to Manage: Industrial Relations in the 1940s* (1982); John L. Shover, *First Majority—Last Minority: The Transforming of Rural Life in America* (1976).

The Baby Boom

Richard A. Easterlin, *Birth and Fortune* (1980); Landon Y. Jones, *Great Expectations: America & The Baby Boom Generation* (1980); Diane Ravitch, *The Troubled Crusade: American Education, 1945–1980* (1983).

The Other America

Joseph H. Cash and Herbert T. Hoover, eds., *To Be an Indian: An Oral History* (1971); Harry M. Caudill, *Night Comes to the Cumberland* (1963); J. Wayne Flynt, *Dixie's Forgotten People: The South's Poor Whites* (1979); Leo Grebler et al., *Mexican-American People* (1970); Michael Harrington, *The Other America* (1981 ed.); August B. Hollingshead and Frederick C. Redlich, *Social Class and Mental Illness* (1958); Oscar Lewis, *La Vida* (1966); Herman P. Miller, *Rich Man, Poor Man* (1971); Dorothy K. Newman et al., *Politics and Prosperity: Black Americans and White Institutions, 1940–75* (1978); James T. Patterson, *America's Struggle Against Poverty, 1900–1980* (1981); David S. Walls and John B. Stephenson, eds., *Appalachia in the Sixties* (1972).

Suburbia

Bennett M. Berger, *Working-Class Suburb* (1960); William B. Dobriner, *Class in Suburbia* (1963); Herbert J. Gans, *The Levittowners* (1967); Mark I. Gelfand, *A Nation of Cities* (1975); Dolores Hayden, *Redesigning the American Dream* (1984); Kenneth T. Jackson, "The Crabgrass Frontier: 150 Years of Suburban Growth in the United States," in R.A. Mohl and J.F. Richardson, eds., *The Urban Experience* (1973), 196–221; Zane L. Miller, *Suburb* (1982); John B. Rae, *The American Automobile* (1965); Robert C. Wood, *Suburbia* (1959); Gwendolyn Wright, *Building the Dream: A Social History of Housing in America* (1981).

Women, Motherhood, and the Family

William H. Chafe, *The American Woman: Her Changing Social, Economic, and Political Role, 1920–1970* (1972); Ruth Schwartz Cowan, *More Work for Mother* (1983); Carl Degler, *At Odds: Woman and the Family in America from the Revolution to the Present* (1980); Betty Friedan, *The Feminine Mystique* (1963); Susan M. Hartmann, *The Homefront and Beyond: American Women in the 1940s* (1982); Susan Estabrook Kennedy, *If All We Did Was to Weep at Home: A History of White Working-Class Women in America* (1979); Alice Kessler-Harris, *Out to Work: A History of Wage-Earning Women in the United States* (1982); Mirra Komarovsky, *Blue-Collar Marriage* (1962); Susan Strasser, *Never Done: A History of American Housework* (1982); Nancy Pottisham Weiss, "Mother, the Invention of Necessity: Dr. Spock's *Baby and Child Care*," *American Quarterly*, 29 (1977), 519–546.

Popular Culture

John W. Aldridge, *In Search of Heresy: American Literature in an Age of Conformity* (1956); Peter Biskind, *Seeing Is Believing: How Hollywood Taught Us to Stop Worrying and Love the Fifties* (1983); Paul A. Carter, *Another Part of the Fifties* (1983); Ann Charters, *Kerouac* (1973); Kenneth C. Davis, *Two-Bit Culture: The Paperbacking of America* (1984); Andrew Dowdy, *The Films of the Fifties* (1973); Maxwell Geismar, *American Moderns* (1958); Charlie Gillett, *The Sound of the City: The Rise of Rock 'N' Roll*, rev. ed. (1983); Serge Guilbaut, *How New York Stole the Idea of Modern Art* (1983); Jeffrey Hart, *When the Going Was Good: American Life in the Fifties* (1982); Douglas T. Miller and Marion Novak, *The Fifties* (1977); Gerald Nicosia, *Memory Babe: A Critical Biography of Jack Kerouac* (1983); Nora Sayre, *Running Time: Films of the Cold War* (1982).

Television

Erik Barnouw, *Tube of Plenty*, rev. ed. (1982); Leo Bogart, *Age of Television* (1958); George Comstock et al., *Television and Human Behavior* (1978); Jerry Mander, *Four Arguments for the Elimination of Television* (1978); Frank Mankiewicz and Joel Swerdlow, *Remote Control: Television and the Manipulation of American Life* (1978).

VIETNAM
AND THE COLD WAR:
AMERICAN FOREIGN POLICY
1961–1981

CHAPTER 32

The *Joint Chiefs* of Staff (JCS) memorandum lay on the table. Its recommendation: add another 100,000 to the 80,000 American troops already in Vietnam, because the war was not going well. "Is there anyone here of the opinion we should not do what the memorandum says?" asked President Lyndon B. Johnson of his advisers, assembled for a tense meeting on the morning of July 21, 1965. Only Undersecretary of State George W. Ball spoke up: "Mr. President, I can foresee a perilous voyage, very dangerous." Johnson asked, "What other road can I go?" Ball answered directly, "Take our losses, let their government fall apart, negotiate, discuss, knowing full well there will be a probable take-over by the Communists." The president, who had actually already made up his mind to escalate the American intervention in Vietnam but was willing to listen to Ball's oft-stated objections again so that he could always say he had carefully weighed all alternatives, did not like that answer. The hard-driving Texan recoiled from thoughts of losing. He simply could not accept that a small, primitive country like Vietnam could deny the United States victory.

At an afternoon session, Ball again forthrightly argued a case he knew few of his colleagues endorsed. "The war will be long and protracted. The most we can hope for is a messy conclusion." Not only did dangers arise from possible Chinese intervention, negative world opinion, and domestic politics, but "the enemy cannot be seen in Vietnam. He is indigenous to the country." Ball seriously doubted that "an army of Westerners can successfully fight Orientals in an Asian jungle." He pressed on, "It is like giving cobalt treatment to a terminal cancer case." In the long run, then, the war "will disclose our weakness, not our strength." Johnson jumped in: "But George, wouldn't all these countries say that Uncle Sam was a paper tiger," with America losing its credibility? "No sir," Ball retorted. "The worse blow would be that the mightiest power on earth is unable to defeat a handful of guerrillas."

The next day Johnson huddled with the military brass. The generals told him that more men, more bombings, and more money were needed to keep America's South Vietnamese ally in power against the North Vietnamese and Vietcong. "But if we put in 100,000 men won't they put in an equal number, and then where will we be?" Johnson asked. He became excited, asking tough questions. When an admiral claimed that if the United States did not back the faltering South Vietnamese regime, allies around the world would lose faith in America's word, Johnson knew better: "We have few allies really helping us now." And have the bombing raids hurt the enemy? Not really, the generals answered, but if more sites were added to the target list, they would. Johnson grew worried: "Isn't this going off the diving board?" The secretary of defense argued that the United States had a "commitment" to South Vietnam. Johnson shot back, "But, if you make a commitment to jump off a building and you find out how high it is, you may want to withdraw that commitment."

In late July a troubled President Johnson nonetheless decided to keep that "commitment" by giving the JCS what it wanted. A major decision of the Vietnam War, it meant that the United States was assuming, for the first time, primary responsibility for fighting the war. Fearing a national debate, Johnson muted his decision's importance when he announced it. By the end of 1965 nearly 200,000 American combat troops were at war in Vietnam. Yet Congress had not passed a declaration of war, and the American people remained largely ignorant of the government's massive venture in Southeast Asia. Ball later concluded that Johnson's July decision was "the greatest single error that America had made in its national history." Measured by the wrenching impact of the war on the United States, he was probably correct.

Vietnam, either because of the searing war experience itself or because of the lessons Americans later drew from that experience, bedeviled the Kennedy, Johnson, Nixon, and Carter presidencies. Other themes crowded the international agenda in the 1960s and 1970s: continued Soviet-American competition for global influence with dramatic swings from conciliation to confrontation in the Cold War, an accelerating nuclear arms race, turmoil in the Third World, much of it anti-American, eruptions in the Middle East, mean-spirited Cuban-American hostilities, and disorder in the world economy. But Vietnam, where Cold War and Third World issues seemed to merge, at least in American thinking, dominated American foreign policy. Kennedy enlarged a United States presence in Southeast Asia, Johnson Americanized the war, Nixon spent considerable energy trying to end the war without losing it, and Carter struggled with the postwar consequences of defeat. As he wound down the American combat role in Vietnam, Nixon also inched toward détente with the Soviet Union and China and intervened in Third World disputes to protect American interests he thought threatened. Carter sought to reverse the deterioration of American influence in the Third World and to continue détente, but the Iranian hostage crisis and a flare-up in Soviet-American relations dashed most of his hopes and returned the world to frigid Cold War.

Throughout the 1960s and 1970s Americans became uneasy not only about the troubled position of the United States in world affairs, but also about the disorder wrought at home by foreign entanglements. Foreign policy and domestic developments had been traditionally interconnected, and foreign policy had always sprung from the domestic setting of the nation — its needs, wants, moods, and ideals. Yet the experience of the Vietnam War called into question those needs, wants, moods, and ideals, because a majority of Americans came to see the effects of the war as a threat to their economic well-being, social stability, and political system (see Chapters 33 and 34). By 1981 Americans had not reached a consensus about the lessons of Vietnam; but, fearing America's slippage from its high world rank, they were eager to restore its pre-eminence and repair their own frayed society.

KENNEDY AND THE QUEST FOR COLD WAR VICTORY

John F. Kennedy's diplomacy owed much to the past. He remembered the tragedy of appeasement in the 1930s as well as the triumph of containment

Kennedy as Cold War Activist

in the 1940s. Just as Nazism had been turned back and Communism contained, now in the 1960s Communism would be routed. Kennedy's dynamic personal style suggested a new departure in foreign policy; actually it meant a bolder, more vigorous prosecution of the Cold War. An eloquent speaker, energetic worker, and fierce competitor, Kennedy was an "incandescent man. He was on fire, and he set people around him on fire," recalled Secretary of State Dean Rusk. As a diplomat, Kennedy was eager to prove his toughness. His administration kept box scores on the missile race, the arms race, the space race, and the race for influence in the Third World. When the young president prepared for his first meeting with Russian Premier Nikita Khrushchev, he seemed poised for a contest rather than a talk: "I have to show him that we can be as tough as he is," remarked Kennedy. "I'll have to sit down with him and let him see who he's dealing with."

Kennedy appointed a staff of bright, often arrogant, people who were determined to score Cold War victories. Journalist Theodore White called them "action intellectuals." A disenchanted Undersecretary of State Chester Bowles complained later that the Kennedy team was "full of belligerence." And Adlai Stevenson told a friend privately that "they've got the damnedest bunch of boy commandos running around down there [in Washington] you ever saw." That there would be no halfway measures was apparent in Kennedy's inaugural address: "Let every nation know that we shall pay any price, bear any burden, meet any hardship, support any friend, oppose any foe to assure the survival and the success of liberty."

Khrushchev matched Kennedy's rhetoric with an endorsement of "wars of national liberation" in the Third World. And in fall 1961 the Soviet Union ended a moratorium on above-ground nuclear testing by exploding a giant 50-megaton bomb. Khrushchev also bragged about Russian ICBMs, raising American anxiety over Soviet capabilities. Intelligence data soon proved the premier's claim false. Kennedy nonetheless sought to fulfill his campaign commitment to a military buildup based on the principle of *flexible response*. Junking Eisenhower's concept of massive retaliation, which emphasized nuclear weapons, Kennedy sought ways to meet any kind of warfare, from guerrilla combat in the jungles to a nuclear

When the ugly Berlin wall first went up in 1961 along the border between East and West Berlin, it was hastily constructed of barbed wire. Later East German troops added heavy concrete slabs to the barricade, as they are doing here. President John F. Kennedy drew criticism from West Germans for not stopping construction of the wall; some students even sent him an umbrella—symbol of appeasement in the 1930s. Two years later, however, West Berliners gave the president a warm reception. UPI/Bettmann Newsphotos.

showdown. In this way, he reasoned, he could contain both the Soviet Union and Third World revolutionary movements. In 1961 the military budget shot up 15 percent, ICBM arsenals swelled further, and plans were laid to increase NATO's nuclear firing power. The government even encouraged citizens to build fallout shelters in their backyards. By mid-1964 strategists measured a 150 percent increase in the number of American nuclear weapons. Though Kennedy could claim credit for the Arms Control and Disarmament Agency and a test-ban treaty with Russia (1963), which banned nuclear testing in the atmosphere, in outer space, and under water, his real legacy was an accelerated arms race.

During this time Berlin continued to claim headlines. The Russians again demanded negotiations to end the Western occupation of Berlin. But Kennedy saw the historic city as "the great testing place of Western courage and will." Instead of negotiating, he asked Congress in 1961 for an additional $3.2 billion for defense and the authority to call up reservists. Events took an ugly turn in August 1961 when the Soviets erected the Berlin Wall, a concrete-and-barbed-wire barricade designed to halt the exodus of East Germans into the more prosperous and politically free West Berlin. Yet another example of Soviet repression, the wall inspired protests all over the non-Communist world. When Kennedy visited the wall in 1963 he stirred a mass rally of West Berliners with the words "Ich bin ein Berliner" ("I am a Berliner").

Berlin Wall

But it was over Cuba, a nation whose allegiance the United States had taken for granted since the turn of the century, that Kennedy had his most serious confrontation with the Soviet Union (see map). Cuba became an obsession of American policymakers in

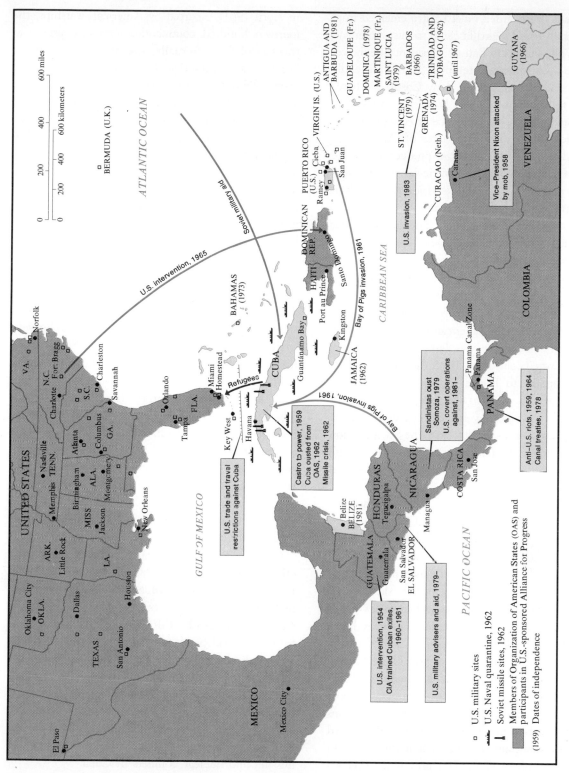

The following labels and annotations appear on the map:

Scale:
600 miles
600 kilometers
0 200 400 600

Oceans and seas:
ATLANTIC OCEAN
GULF OF MEXICO
CARIBBEAN SEA
PACIFIC OCEAN

United States cities and states:
UNITED STATES
Norfolk — VA.
Fort Bragg — N.C.
Charlotte — S.C.
Charleston
Savannah — GA.
Atlanta
Columbus
Orlando
Tampa — FLA.
Miami
Homestead
Key West
Havana
Nashville — TENN.
Memphis
Birmingham — ALA.
Montgomery — MISS.
Jackson
New Orleans — LA.
Little Rock — ARK.
Oklahoma City — OKLA.
Dallas — TEXAS
Houston
San Antonio
El Paso
MEXICO
Mexico City

Caribbean / Central America:
BERMUDA (U.K.)
BAHAMAS (1973)
CUBA
Guantánamo Bay
HAITI
Port au Prince
DOMINICAN REP.
Santo Domingo
PUERTO RICO (U.S.)
Ramey — Ceiba
San Juan
VIRGIN IS. (U.S.)
GUADELOUPE (Fr.)
DOMINICA (1978)
MARTINIQUE (Fr.)
SAINT LUCIA (1979)
ANTIGUA AND BARBUDA (1981)
BARBADOS (1966)
ST. VINCENT (1979)
GRENADA (1974)
TRINIDAD AND TOBAGO (1962)
CURACAO (Neth.)
GUYANA (1966)
VENEZUELA
COLOMBIA
Caracas
JAMAICA (1962)
Kingston
BELIZE (1981)
Belize
GUATEMALA
Guatemala
EL SALVADOR
San Salvador
HONDURAS
Tegucigalpa
NICARAGUA
Managua
COSTA RICA
San José
PANAMA
Panama
Panama Canal Zone

Annotation boxes:
Soviet military aid
U.S. intervention, 1965
Bay of Pigs invasion, 1961
Refugees
Bay of Pigs invasion, 1961

Vice-President Nixon attacked by mob, 1958

U.S. invasion, 1983

Sandinistas oust Somoza, 1979
U.S. covert operations against, 1981–

Anti-U.S. riots, 1959, 1964
Canal treaties, 1978

U.S. trade and travel restrictions against Cuba

Castro to power, 1959
Cuba ousted from OAS, 1962
Missile crisis, 1962

U.S. intervention, 1954
CIA trained Cuban exiles, 1960–1961

U.S. military advisers and aid, 1979–

Legend:
□ U.S. military sites
⚓ U.S. Naval quarantine, 1962
⚓ Soviet missile sites, 1962
█ Members of Organization of American States (OAS) and participants in U.S.-sponsored Alliance for Progress
(1959) Dates of independence

The United States in the Caribbean and Central America

909

1959, when the bearded Fidel Castro emerged from his mountain-based guerrilla camp to oust America's long-time ally Fulgencio Batista. President Eisenhower had made a last-minute attempt to install a friendly military regime there and to deny Castro his hard-fought revolutionary triumph. From the start Castro determined to break the influence of American business, which owned 3 million acres of Cuban land, controlled 40 percent of its sugar production and 90 percent of its telephone and electric service, and sold Cuba 70 percent of its imports. Indeed, American investments in the island at the time of Castro's victory totaled about $1 billion. The Cuban leader nationalized some American-owned property, suspended promised elections, indulged in a barrage of anti-American rhetoric, and in early 1960 signed a trade treaty with Russia.

In mid-1960 President Eisenhower grew impatient with Castro and reduced American purchases of Cuban sugar. Castro's response was large-scale seizures of American-owned companies. Soon the Cuban premier began to appeal to Russia for support. Historians disagree on whether Castro was always a Communist, or whether Washington's vehement opposition pushed him into Russia's arms. In any case, the Soviet Union gradually came to Cuba's assistance with loans and trade. The Monroe Doctrine, Moscow declared, was dead.

In March 1960, Eisenhower had ordered the CIA to train Cuban exiles for an invasion of their homeland. Just before he left office Eisenhower broke diplomatic relations with Castro and advised Kennedy to advance plans for the invasion. The picture sketched by the CIA appealed to Kennedy: Cuban exiles would land at the Bay of Pigs and secure a beachhead; the Cuban people would rise up against Castro; a Revolutionary Council organized in the United States would enter Havana in triumph. Kennedy was nonetheless uneasy over such a blatant attempt to topple a sovereign government; he ordered that no Americans be directly involved in the invasion so that the United States could maintain the fiction that the operation was solely a Cuban affair. The president never attempted to negotiate with Castro over Cuban-American troubles; Kennedy preferred victory over compromise.

The CIA-directed expedition departed Nicaragua

Bay of Pigs

in April 1961. Escorted by American warships, the fourteen hundred commandos scrambled ashore at the Bay of Pigs. Actually, the first man to hit the beaches was an American CIA operative. The Cuban people did not rise up against Castro and within two days most of the commandos had been captured. Many of them later blamed Kennedy for the disaster, citing his refusal to permit a second air strike. But the operation, with or without more air support, had little chance of success. Boats went aground on coral reefs that the CIA had dismissed as seaweed; equipment malfunctioned; the Bay of Pigs was Castro's favorite fishing spot and he knew the details of its landscape; had the exiles of Brigade 2506 managed to move inland they would have encountered swamps; and the mountains that might have served as a sanctuary were eighty miles away. Before it was over, four Americans had died. "How could I have been so stupid to let them go ahead?" Kennedy asked himself.

Kennedy did not suffer defeat easily. Soon he and his advisers set about finding other means to unseat Castro. "My idea," Attorney General Robert Kennedy said, "is to stir things up on the island with espionage, sabotage, [and] general disorder." The president's brother instructed the CIA to let "no time, money, effort—or manpower—be spared" in a project that came to be known as Operation Mongoose. Government agents worked to disrupt the island's trade; they continued to aid anti-Castro groups in Miami; and they plotted with organized crime leaders to assassinate Castro.

Cuba soon became the site of one of the scariest crises of the Cold War. Had there been no Bay of Pigs and no Operation Mongoose, Fidel Castro has said, there would have been no missile crisis. For Castro, American hostility represented a real threat to Cuba's independence. And for the Russians, American actions were a challenge to the only pro-Communist regime in Latin America. "We had to think up some way of confronting America with more than words," recalled the Soviet premier. So Castro and Khrushchev devised a daring plan to deter any new American intervention: installation of Soviet missiles and nuclear bombers in Cuba.

Although the Kennedy administration was aware of a Soviet military buildup on the island, it was not until October 14, 1962, that a U-2 plane photographed medium-range missile sites. Whether the Soviets had

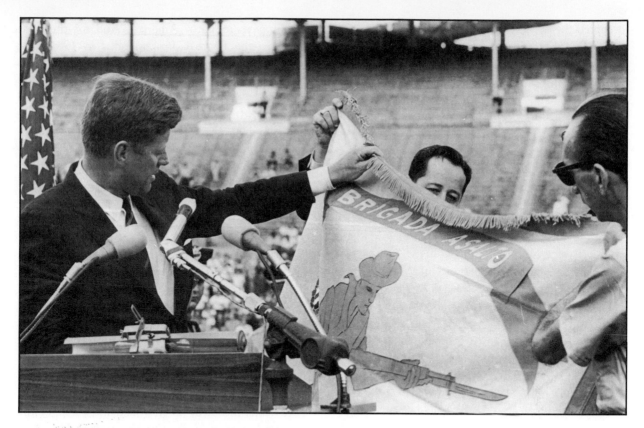

In December 1962, in Miami's Orange Bowl, President John F. Kennedy (1917–1963) welcomed home the newly released members of the CIA-sponsored landing force captured by the Cuban militia at the Bay of Pigs. Still determined to unseat Castro, Kennedy received the troops' combat banner, promising, "This flag will be returned to this Brigade in a free Havana." Wide World Photos.

acted to protect Cuba, to improve their own nuclear capability, to trigger negotiations over Berlin, or to force the United States to pull its missiles out of Turkey was not clear. In any case, the president organized an executive committee and ordered it to find a way to remove the missiles from Cuba. Some members advised a surprise air strike, likely to kill both Russian technicians and Cubans. But Robert Kennedy scotched that idea; he wanted no Pearl Harbors on his brother's record. The JCS recommended a full-scale military invasion—a Bay of Pigs with American soldiers. But that approach risked a prolonged war with Cuba, a Soviet attack against Berlin, or even nuclear holocaust. Soviet expert Charles Bohlen unsuccessfully urged quiet, direct ne-

Cuban Missile Crisis

gotiations with Soviet officials. It was Secretary of Defense Robert S. McNamara who proposed the most acceptable formula: a naval quarantine of Cuba, to prevent further military shipments. Halfway between armed warfare and doing nothing, it left the administration free to attack or negotiate, depending on the Russian response.

Over national television on October 22, Kennedy informed the Soviets of American policy and demanded their retreat. American warships headed for the Caribbean, B-52s loaded with nuclear bombs took to the skies, and American military forces around the globe went on alert. Khrushchev first replied that the missiles would be withdrawn if Washington pledged never to attack Cuba again. Then he demanded the removal of American missiles from Turkey. Kennedy accepted the first condition but rejected the second. (Privately the administration made an informal promise to the Russians to withdraw the missiles from Turkey in the future.) On October 28 Khrushchev accepted the American pledge to respect Cuban sovereignty and promised to ship the missiles back to the Soviet Union. Americans breathed a collective sigh of relief; this was, said many, Kennedy's finest hour.

But critics then and now have asked whether the crisis was really necessary. Why, they have asked, did the president attempt to solve the crisis with public brinkmanship instead of private negotiations? Television addresses and public confrontations are not the stuff of statesmanship, but of politics—and the congressional elections were just weeks away. They have noted too that Kennedy passed up a chance to protest the presence of the missiles when he met privately with Foreign Minister Andrei Gromyko in the White House on October 18. Finally, critics have claimed that the strategic balance of power was not seriously altered by the placement of Soviet missiles in Cuba. The United States had about four hundred missiles capable of reaching Russia, the Soviets only less than one hundred capable of hitting North America. Kennedy went to the nuclear brink when he did not need to, his critics have said.

The Cuban missile crisis humiliated the Soviets. (In the world of diplomacy, it is wise to give the enemy a chance to save face.) Exposed as nuclear inferiors, the Soviets vowed to catch up—and they managed to do so by the late 1960s. The crisis did produce some relaxation in Soviet-American relations. The superpower leaders installed a teletype "hot line" between Washington and Moscow staffed round the clock by translators and technicians, signed a test-ban treaty, and refrained from further confrontation in Berlin.

Elsewhere in the Third World, Kennedy called for "peaceful revolution" based on the concept of *nation building.* Drawing on the ideas of the economist Walt W. Rostow, who joined the Kennedy administration, the president determined to build goodwill in Third World countries by helping them through the infant stages of nationhood. One method would be programs aimed at improving agriculture, transportation, and communications. Kennedy thus created the multibillion-dollar Alliance

Nation Building

for Progress in Latin America. And for the same purpose, the Peace Corps, founded in 1961, sent teachers, agricultural specialists, and health workers into developing nations throughout the world. Within three years ten thousand idealistic young men and women had volunteered for service. But the Peace Corps' humanitarian purpose competed with the administration's political needs. Periodic conflicts arose between corps members in the field, who identified with Third World peoples and their desire for neutralism, and headquarters in Washington, where the goal was aligning those peoples with American foreign policy.

Besides such special development programs, Kennedy relied on *counterinsurgency:* the training of native police forces by American military and technical advisers. The assumption was that American soldiers—especially the Special Forces units, or Green Berets—would provide a protective shield against insurgents while American civilian personnel worked on economic projects.

Nation building and its methods did not work. Americans assumed, as they had for much of the twentieth century in the Caribbean, that they could simply transfer their own model of capitalism and democracy to foreign cultures. But many foreigners resented American meddling in their affairs. And because monetary aid was usually funneled through a self-interested elite, it often did not reach the very poor. And to people who preferred the relatively quick solutions of a managed economy, the American emphasis on private enterprise seemed inappropriate. "In the end," the presidential adviser Arthur M. Schlesinger, Jr., later wrote, counterinsurgency proved "a ghastly illusion. Its primary consequence was to keep alive the American belief in their capacity and right to intervene in foreign lands."

The CIA became one of the primary instruments of counterinsurgency (see pages 869–870). In the Congo (now Zaire) in 1960–1961 the CIA plotted to poison Premier Patrice Lumumba through the lethal injection of a virus; before that could be done, a CIA-backed Congolese political faction murdered Lumumba, who had turned to Russia for help after the Belgians and United Nations sent troops to protect white Europeans during a civil war. In Brazil, the CIA spent $20 million to influence

CIA Interventions

the 1962 elections against President Joao Goulart, who had earned American disapproval by expropriating the property of the American firm International Telephone and Telegraph and refusing to vote to oust Cuba from the Organization of American States. When Goulart's followers nonetheless won, the CIA then helped organize opposition groups. In 1964, with United States complicity, the Brazilian military overthrew Goulart. After failure at the Bay of Pigs, the CIA could claim the outcomes in the Congo and Brazil as Cold War successes.

DESCENT INTO THE LONGEST WAR: VIETNAM

The belief in the right to influence the internal affairs of other countries led to disaster in Southeast Asia. How Vietnam became the site of America's longest war (it lasted a quarter-century, from 1950 to 1975); how the world's most powerful nation spent itself in a futile attempt to subdue a peasant people; how those people suffered enormous losses of life and property and yet persisted, is one of the tragic stories of modern history.

The story begins with the French takeover of Vietnam during the late nineteenth century (see Vietnam Chronology). For decades the French exploited the colony for its rice, rubber, tin, and tungsten, beating back peasant rebellions. Not until the Second World War, when the Japanese moved into Indochina, did French authority collapse.

History of Imperialism in Vietnam

Seizing their chance, the Vietminh, an anti-imperialist coalition led by Communists, began guerrilla warfare against the Japanese. Led by the nationalist Ho Chi Minh, they collaborated with American Office of Strategic Services (OSS) agents to harass the Japanese. OSS officers who worked with Ho in Vietnam were impressed by his determination to free his country of outsiders, and by his frequent references to the United States as a revolutionary model. When Ho declared Vietnam's independence in September 1945, his words sounded familiar: "We hold these truths to be self-evident. That all men are created equal." But though Ho wrote to the Truman administration requesting support for his new government, his letters were never answered. When the Second World War ended, the French returned, and Ho and the Vietminh took up arms to defend their independence.

The United States did not recognize Vietnamese independence (and in fact attempted to undermine it) for several reasons. First, France was a valued ally in the emerging Cold War. Second, Southeast Asia was important as the world's largest producer of natural rubber and a rich source of other commodities. Third, the area seemed strategically vital to the defense of Japan and the Philippines. Finally, Ho Chi Minh was a Communist who had lived for a time in Russia. Thus Vietnam became another test in the containment of Communism—the Berlin of Asia. Overlooking the native roots of the revolution and the tenacity of a people fighting on and for their own land, American leaders from Truman through Nixon took a globalist view, interpreting events through a Cold War lens.

In the 1940s Vietnam was a French problem that few Americans watched with keen interest. More dramatic crises in Europe commanded their attention. But when Jiang Jieshi went down to defeat in China, the United States was aroused to action. The Truman administration made two crucial decisions in early 1950. First, it recognized the French puppet government of Bao Dai. Thus in Vietnamese eyes the United States became in essence a colonial power, an ally of the hated French. Second, the administration agreed to send weapons, and ultimately military advisers, to the French. By 1954 the United States had invested over $2 billion in the war and was bearing 78 percent of its cost.

Despite American aid, the French lost steadily to the Vietminh. Finally, in 1954 Ho's forces surrounded the French fortress at Dienbienphu. What would the United States do? Could the French be saved? President Eisenhower huddled with his advisers. The Chairman of the Joint Chiefs of Staff urged the president to unleash a massive air strike, using nuclear weapons if necessary. Secretary Dulles recommended that he seek help from Great Britain. Other advisers suggested sending American troops. But Eisenhower was cautious. If American forces became directly involved in the war—as distinct from merely advising

1861–87	French consolidate colonial rule in Indochina
1890	Ho Chi Minh born
1920	Ho Chi Minh joins Communist party
1940	Japan occupies Indochina
1941	Vietminh organized
	OSS cooperates with Vietminh
1945	Ho declares independence
1946	Anticolonial war against France begins
1950	U.S. recognizes government of Bao Dai
	U.S. sends military aid to French for war in Vietnam
1954	Dienbienphu crisis
	Geneva conference and accords
	Temporary partition of Vietnam
	U.S. backs government of Diem
1955	Diem, with U.S. support, rejects Geneva accords
1956	Diem begins crackdown on opponents
1957	Anti-Diem insurgents begin terrorist attacks
1959	North Vietnam begins sending aid to Communists in the South
1960	National Liberation Front (Vietcong) organized in the South
1961	President Kennedy decides to increase U.S. military role in Vietnam

Note: For Vietnam events after 1961, see Important Events, page 934.

the French—he might not be able to limit the nation's involvement. As one high-level doubter remarked, "One cannot go over Niagara Falls in a barrel only slightly." Army Chief of Staff Matthew Ridgway was also wary. He warned the president that American troops would be fighting in hostile terrain, that air power could not guarantee victory. And American soldiers would have to be moved from elsewhere in Asia and Europe, a shift that might leave other regions vulnerable.

Nevertheless, Eisenhower worried aloud at the prospect of a Communist victory, comparing the weak nations of the world to a row of dominoes, all of which would topple if just one fell. He asked the British to help, but they would make no commitment.

At home, members of Congress refused to support military action unless the British went along.

To add to the administration's problems, the French wanted out. They agreed to peace talks at Geneva, where France, the United States, Russia, Britain, China, Laos, and Cambodia joined the two competing Vietnamese regimes of Bao Dai and Ho Chi Minh.

Geneva Conference

It was an unpleasant job for Dulles, who conducted himself, according to one biographer, like a "puritan in a house of ill repute." The 1954 Geneva accords, signed by France and Ho's Democratic Republic of Vietnam, temporarily divided Vietnam at the 17th parallel, with Ho's government confined to the North. National elections would be held in

1956, and the country would thereupon be unified. Neither North nor South was to join a military alliance or permit foreign military bases on its soil.

Certain that the Geneva agreements would ultimately mean Communist victory, the United States and Bao Dai refused to accept them and set about their sabotage. Soon after the conference a CIA team entered Vietnam and began secret operations against the North, including commando raids across the parallel. In the South, the United States cultivated the friendship of Ngo Dinh Diem. A Catholic in a Buddhist nation, Diem had no mass support and many enemies. But with American aid he outmaneuvered his opponents, including Bao Dai, and staged a fraudulent election that gave him a remarkable 98 percent of the vote. When Ho called for national elections in keeping with the Geneva agreements, Diem and Eisenhower refused, fearing the charismatic Vietminh leader would win. In September 1954 the United States joined Britain, France, Australia, New Zealand, the Philippines, Thailand, and Pakistan in an anti-Communist pact called the Southeast Asia Treaty Organization (SEATO). In a special protocol SEATO extended protection to South Vietnam.

From 1955 to 1961 Diem received more than $1 billion worth of American aid, most of it military. American advisers organized and trained the South Vietnamese army. Michigan State University police experts helped to create a national guard. And American agriculturalists worked to improve crops. As American consumer products flowed into a land of peasant villages, Diem's Saigon regime became dependent on the United States for its very existence.

Meanwhile, Diem became bent on dictatorial leadership. He abolished village elections and appointed people beholden to him to public office. He threw dissenters into jail and shut down **Civil War in** newspapers that criticized his regime. **South Vietnam** In the South non-Communists and Communists alike began to strike back at Diem's corrupt and repressive government. The Vietminh embarked on a program of terror, assassinating hundreds of Diem's village officials. In late 1960 the Vietminh organized the National Liberation Front. Called the Vietcong (Vietnamese Communists) by Diem and Americans to discredit them as tools of Moscow and Beijing, they attracted Communists and other anti-Diem groups in the South.

It became clear that the war against imperialism had become a civil war.

In the United States, the newly elected President Kennedy decided to stand firm against the Vietcong. He had suffered the humiliations of the Bay of Pigs and the Berlin Wall; he feared further criticism should the United States back down in Asia. But more important, he sought a Cold War victory. "How do we get moving?" he asked his advisers in his first meeting on Vietnam. Soon he ordered more military advisers and Special Forces units to South Vietnam, and millions of dollars worth of additional aid. Yet Diem showed no signs of using the assistance effectively, and his enemies grew in number. Fearing Diem would drag the United States down to defeat, Kennedy pressed him to reform. Meanwhile, Project Beefup was sending more Americans to South Vietnam; by late 1963 16,700 American "advisers" were stationed there. That year 489 Americans were killed, and an American project called the strategic hamlet program actually strengthened resistance to Diem. That program, which aimed to isolate peasants from the Vietcong by uprooting them into barbed-wire compounds, simply alienated villagers. When Diem's troops attacked Buddhists who opposed his religious repression, the country sank further into civil war. Protesting monks poured gasoline over their robes and ignited themselves in the streets of Saigon.

American officials began to think that if Diem could not be reformed, he should be removed. "We could not sit still and be puppets of Diem's anti-**Removal** Buddhist policies," recalled a high-**of Diem** ranking State Department officer. Moreover, Diem, who knew that American officials were preparing to dump him, was apparently trying to make peace with the North—"a possible basic incompatibility with U.S. objectives," worried General Maxwell Taylor. Through the CIA, the United States quietly encouraged disaffected South Vietnamese generals to stage a coup. With the ill-concealed backing of Ambassador Henry Cabot Lodge, the generals struck in early November 1963. Diem was captured and murdered—only a few weeks before Kennedy himself met death by an assassin's bullet.

With new governments in Saigon and Washington, some analysts thought it an appropriate time for reassessment. The Vietcong, United Nations General

Secretary U Thant, France, and others called for a coalition government in South Vietnam. But the new American president, Lyndon B. Johnson, would have none of it. He declared that America's purpose was victory, for anything less "would only be another name for a Communist take-over."

JOHNSON AND THE WAR
WITHOUT VICTORY

Lyndon B. Johnson was a Texan who liked to say that he lived by the lessons of the Alamo—fight to the end. An old New Dealer, he talked about building Tennessee Valley Authorities around the world. "I want to leave the footprints of America there [in Vietnam]. I want them to say, 'This is what Americans left—schools and hospitals and dams.'" But Johnson's drive to become a global social worker—some commentators called it welfare imperialism—proved a tragic mistake, especially in Vietnam, where America's footprints were those of over 500,000 soldiers, and where bombs and chemical defoliants destroyed instead of built.

Johnson saw the world in simple terms—them against us—and privately disparaged both his allies and his enemies. Vietnam was a "raggedy-ass fourth-rate country," his critics at home "rattlebrains" or "nervous nellies." Johnson sometimes lied or exaggerated, creating what reporters referred to as a credibility gap. His public speeches, larded with trite metaphors and delivered in a belabored drawl, led some to suggest that he was unintelligent. They were wrong, for Johnson had a quick mind; his limitation was that he held firmly to fixed ideas about American superiority, the menace of Communism, and the necessity of global intervention. The problem, said Senator J. William Fulbright, chairman of the Foreign Relations Committee, was that both Johnson and the American people suffered from an "arrogance of power."

By early 1964 the Vietcong controlled nearly half of South Vietnam. Because the new Saigon government was shaky and seemed to be leaning toward neutralism, United States officials cooperated in a second coup. In neighboring Laos, American bombers hit supply routes connecting the Vietcong with the North Vietnamese. Laos, where the CIA had manipulated politics for years and where in 1962 non-Communists and Communists agreed to a neutralist government, was increasingly drawn into a wider Southeast Asian war. The bombings were kept secret from the American Congress and people; yet, as Ambassador William H. Sullivan admitted, "we ran Laos."

In August 1964 an incident in the Gulf of Tonkin, off the coast of North Vietnam, led to accelerated American warmaking (see map). On August 2, 1964, the U.S.S. *Maddox*, while monitoring South Vietnamese commando raids against North Vietnam, came under attack from northern patrol boats, which suffered heavy damage.

Tonkin Gulf Incident

The unharmed *Maddox* sailed away. "If they do it again," said Secretary of State Dean Rusk, "they'll get another sting." On August 4, now joined by another destroyer, the *Maddox* moved again toward the North Vietnamese shore as if to bait the Communists. During bad weather, sonar technicians reported what they thought were enemy torpedoes; the two destroyers began firing ferociously. Yet when the captain of the *Maddox* asked his crew members what had happened, not one had seen or heard hostile gunfire.

President Johnson, although knowing that the evidence was very questionable, and unwilling to acknowledge that American ships were participating in covert raids against North Vietnam, went on television to announce that the United States was retaliating against an "unprovoked" attack: American planes would bomb North Vietnam. On August 7 Congress gave him the Tonkin Gulf resolution, passed 466 to 0 in the House and 88 to 2 in the Senate after brief debate. Only Wayne Morse of Oregon and Ernest Gruening of Alaska dissented from the resolution's sweeping language that authorized the president to "take all necessary measures to repel any armed attack against the forces of the United States and to prevent further aggression." Over time the Tonkin Gulf resolution would come to serve as the declaration of war Congress never voted on. Only in 1970 would senators repeal it, realizing too late

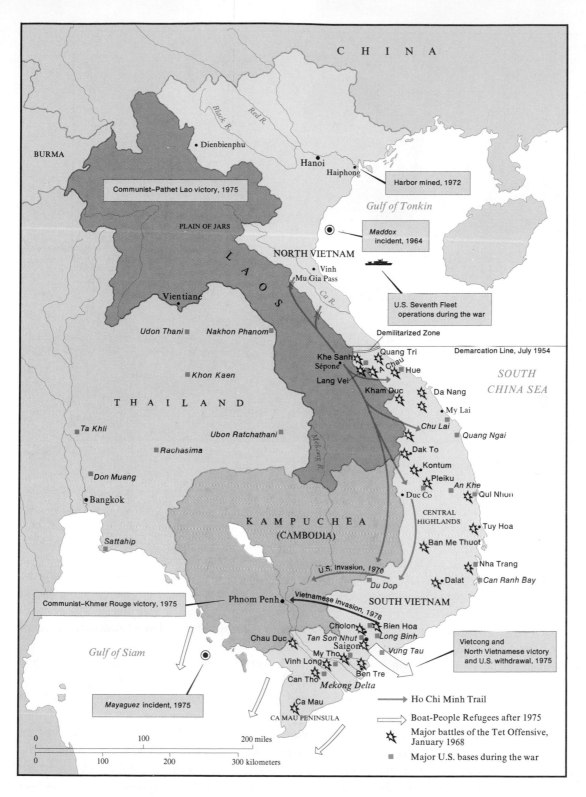

CHINA

Dienbienphu

BURMA

Hanoi

Haiphong

Harbor mined, 1972

Gulf of Tonkin

Maddox incident, 1964

Communist–Pathet Lao victory, 1975

PLAIN OF JARS

NORTH VIETNAM

Vinh
Mu Gia Pass

U.S. Seventh Fleet operations during the war

Vientiane

L A O S

Ca R.

Demilitarized Zone

Demarcation Line, July 1954

Udon Thani   Nakhon Phanom

Khe Sanh   Quang Tri

Sépone   A Chau   Hue

Lang Vei

SOUTH CHINA SEA

Khon Kaen

Kham Duc   Da Nang

My Lai

T H A I L A N D

Chu Lai

Quang Ngai

Ta Khli

Dak To

Ubon Ratchathani

Kontum

Rachasima

Pleiku

An Khe

Duc Co   Qui Nhon

Don Muang

CENTRAL HIGHLANDS

Tuy Hoa

Bangkok

K A M P U C H E A
(CAMBODIA)

Ban Me Thuot

Nha Trang

Sattahip

Can Ranh Bay

U.S. invasion, 1970

Du Dop   Dalat

Communist–Khmer Rouge victory, 1975

Vietnamese invasion, 1978   **SOUTH VIETNAM**

Phnom Penh

Mekong R.

Cholon   Bien Hoa

Gulf of Siam

Chau Duc   *Tan Son Nhut*   Long Binh

Saigon

Vietcong and North Vietnamese victory and U.S. withdrawal, 1975

My Tho   *Vung Tau*

Vinh Long

Ben Tre

Can Tho

Mekong Delta

Mayaguez incident, 1975

Ca Mau

CA MAU PENINSULA

→ Ho Chi Minh Trail

⇨ Boat-People Refugees after 1975

✪ Major battles of the Tet Offensive, January 1968

■ Major U.S. bases during the war

| 0 | 100 | 200 miles |

| 0 | 100 | 200 | 300 kilometers |

Southeast Asia and the Vietnam War

An American marine tries to revive a wounded GI in the inhospitable terrain of Khe Sanh Valley, near the Demilitarized Zone in South Vietnam in 1967. The fallen marine soon died, as did over 57,000 other Americans in their nation's longest war. Wide World Photos.

that they had surrendered their powers in the foreign policy process by giving the president wide latitude to conduct the war as he saw fit.

His popularity buoyed by his forceful response to the Tonkin Gulf incident, Johnson won the presidency in his own right in the fall of 1964. At his direction the military mapped plans for stepped-up bombing of North Vietnam and Laos. Undersecretary of State George Ball urged caution: "Once on the tiger's back we cannot be sure of picking the place to dismount." Nonetheless, when a Vietcong attack on an American airfield at Pleiku took nine American lives in February 1965, Johnson ordered carrier jets to ravage the North. Soon Operation Rolling Thunder—a sustained bombing program above the 17th parallel—was under way. Before the longest war was over, more bombs would fall on Vietnam than American aircraft had

dropped in all of the Second World War. But the North Vietnamese would not give up. They hid in shelters and rebuilt roads and bridges with a perseverance that frustrated and awed American decision-makers.

The president, in his momentous decision of July 1965, also sent more troops to the South. By the end of 1965 184,000 Americans were assigned to

Americanization of the War

Vietnam; in 1966 the figure reached 385,000; in 1969 it peaked at 543,400. But Ho only increased the flow of arms and men to the rebels in the South; in this seemingly endless war of attrition, each American escalation begot a new Vietnamese escalation. "I feel like a hitchhiker caught in a hailstorm on a Texas highway," groaned Johnson. "I can't run, I can't hide, and I can't make

American troops in the field faced thick jungle growth—and well-hidden Vietcong and North Vietnamese opponents more familiar than Americans with an environment suited to guerrilla warfare. This photograph was taken in 1969. U.S. Army.

it stop." He and his aides just could not believe that the Vietnamese could tangle successfully with the greatest power on the face of the earth—at least not for very long.

The "Americanization" of the war in Vietnam under Johnson bothered growing numbers of Americans, especially as increased television coverage brought the ugliness of combat into their homes every night. The pictures and stories were not pretty. Innocent civilians were caught in the line of fire; refugees flooded "pacification" camps; villages considered friendly to the enemy were burned to the ground. To destroy Vietcong hiding places, pilots whose motto was "Only You Can Prevent Forests" sprayed chemical defoliants like Agent Orange over the landscape. The Vietcong and North Vietnamese added to the carnage, but American guns, bombs, and chemicals

took by far the greatest toll, and the Vietnamese people knew it. Indeed, America's search-and-destroy missions were counterproductive; rather than winning the war, they were molding an ever-growing population of anti-American peasants who gave secret aid to the Vietcong. An American official later admitted, "It was as if we were trying to build a house with a bulldozer and wrecking crane."

Stories of atrocities made their way home. Most gruesome was the My Lai massacre in March 1968 (not made public until twenty months later because of a military cover-up). An American unit, frustrated by its inability to pin down an elusive enemy and eager to revenge the loss of some buddies, shot to death scores of unarmed women and children. Private Paul Meadlo, the father of two children himself, was there. "We huddled them up. We made them squat down. . . . I poured about four clips into the group. . . . The mothers was hugging their children. . . . Well, we kept right on firing. They was waving their arms and begging. . . . I still dream about it. About the women and children in my sleep. Some days . . . some nights, I can't even sleep."

Although many incidents of the deliberate shooting of civilians, torturing and killing of prisoners, taking of Vietnamese ears as trophies, and burning of villages have been recorded, most American soldiers were not committing atrocities. They were trying instead

American Troops in Vietnam

to save their young lives (their average age was only nineteen) and serve the United States mission by killing enemy troops, whom they usually called "gooks." Many of these Americans made up the rear-echelon forces that supported the "grunts" or "boonierats" in the field. Wherever they were, soldiers met an inhospitable environment, for no place in Vietnam was secure. Well-hidden booby traps blasted away parts of the body. The enemy was everywhere yet nowhere, often burrowed into elaborate underground bunkers or melded into the population, where every Vietnamese might be a Vietcong terrorist.

Infantrymen on maneuvers humped heavy rucksacks into thick jungle growth, their every step precarious. "In places the bamboo was over fifteen feet high," wrote the veteran John M. DelVecchio in his novel *The 13th Valley* (1982). "The point man felt as if he were breaking trail through knife blades of spring steel. His arms were soon slashed and bloody and his face had multiple tiny lacerations." Leeches sucked at weary bodies. Boots and human skin rotted from the rains, which alternated with withering suns. "It was as if the sun and the land itself were in league with the Vietcong," recalled the marine officer Philip Caputo in his book *A Rumor of War* (1977), "wearing us down, driving us mad, killing us." Wounded GIs shouted for a medic, who in turn might call in a "medevac" (medical evacuation helicopter), praying that it would not be shot down, knowing that a successful departure could carry the wounded to operating tables within minutes. "What I saw were young men coming in, eighteen or nineteen years old . . . and they would be without a leg," remembered Gayle Smith, a nurse at the 3rd Surgical Hospital.

As the war ground on to no discernible conclusion, the army grew troubled, and morale sagged. Racial tensions intensified as "black power" militants tangled with whites muttering racial slurs. Drug abuse became serious. Many soldiers smoked plentiful, cheap marijuana; about one-third of the troops were addicts to opium and heroin, according to a 1971 official report. "Fragging," the murder of an officer by soldiers using hand grenades or other weapons, also increased. "Grenades leave no fingerprints. Nobody's going to jail," recalled a helicopter pilot. The military elite in Washington grew alarmed as well by numerous reports of disobedience—and peace symbols scratched on helmets.

Such antiwar sentiment drew strength from dissent in the United States. In early 1966 Senator J. William Fulbright began to hold public hearings on whether the national interest was being served by pursuing the war in Asia. What exactly was the threat? senators asked. To the surprise of some, the father of the containment doctrine, George F. Kennan, testified before television cameras that his theory was meant for Europe, not the volatile environment of Southeast Asia. Within the administration, too, disenchantment rose. Secretary of Defense Robert McNamara and Undersecretary Ball resigned, unable to justify further escalation of the war. And in a direct challenge to Johnson's policies, antiwar Senator Eugene McCarthy of Minnesota announced his candidacy for the Democratic presidential nomination.

Johnson dug in, snapping at his critics and vowing to continue the battle, cheered by opinion polls that showed Americans actually favoring escalation over withdrawal. "We are not going to shimmy," he insisted. At times he halted the bombing to encourage Ho Chi Minh to negotiate. Such pauses, however, were often accompanied by increases in American troop strength. And in some cases the United States resumed or accelerated the bombing just when a diplomatic breakthrough seemed imminent—such as in late 1966, when a Polish diplomat's efforts were inexplicably cut short by a resumption of the bombing. Unpersuaded, the North demanded a stop to the bombing raids before sitting down at the conference table. And American terms were unacceptable to the Communists: nonrecognition of the Vietcong; withdrawal of northern soldiers from the South; and an end to North Vietnamese military aid to the Vietcong.

In July 1968, a war-weary President Johnson. Just months before, stunned by the Tet offensive, Johnson had decided to drop out of politics and initiate peace talks.   Lyndon Baines Johnson Library.

THE PAINFUL WITHDRAWAL

FROM VIETNAM

In January 1968 a shocking event forced Johnson to reappraise his position. During Tet, the Vietnamese lunar new year, Vietcong and North Vietnamese forces struck all across **Tet Offensive** South Vietnam, hitting and capturing provincial capitals. In Saigon raiders actually occupied the American embassy for several hours. American and South Vietnamese units eventually regained much lost ground, inflicting heavy casualties on the enemy. But the destruction of the village of Ben Tre revealed the cost of driving the Vietcong out. "It became necessary to destroy the town to save it," reported a sober-faced American officer.

The Tet offensive jolted Americans. Hadn't the Vietcong and North Vietnamese demonstrated that they could strike when and where they wished? Didn't they have the advantage of fighting on home territory? Why did "their Vietnamese" fight harder than "our Vietnamese"? If all of America's firepower and dollars and half a million troops couldn't defeat the Vietcong, could anything? Had the American public been lied to? One television reporter asked, "Isn't there something Orwellian about it, that the more we kill, the stronger they get?"

The Tet offensive and its impact on public opinion hit the White House like a thunderclap. The new secretary of defense, Clark Clifford, told Johnson the war could not be won, even if the 206,000 more soldiers requested by the army were sent to Vietnam. The Cold Warrior of Cold Warriors, Dean Acheson, bluntly told a surprised president that the military brass did not know what they were talking about. Strained by exhausting sessions with advisers, realizing that further escalation would not bring victory, and faced with serious opposition within his own party, Johnson changed course. In an appearance on television (March 31) he announced that he had stopped the bombing of most of North Vietnam and asked Hanoi to begin negotiations. Then he surprised the nation by dropping out of the presidential race.

The United States, knowing it could not win, would at least try not to lose. As the diplomats talked in Paris, the war ground on. Late in 1968 president-elect Richard M. Nixon met with Johnson and his key advisers to discuss the war. "The travail of the long war was etched on the faces around me," Nixon recalled. "They had no new approaches to recommend to me. I sensed that, despite the disappointment of defeat, they were relieved to be able to turn this morass over to someone else."

Nixon initiated a policy of "Vietnamization"—building up South Vietnamese forces to replace American troops. And he announced the Nixon Doctrine: that the United States would help those Asian nations that helped themselves. Slowly he began to withdraw American troops from Vietnam, decreasing their number to 139,000 by the end of 1971. But he also increased the bombing in the North, hoping to pound Hanoi into making concessions. Nixon's national security adviser, Henry A. Kissinger, called it jugular diplomacy.

In April 1970 American and South Vietnamese troops invaded Cambodia in search of arms depots and enemy forces that used it as a sanctuary. The escalation sparked renewed protest at home. Demonstrations swept college campuses; the Senate forbade the expenditure of funds on the new war. But Nixon and Kissinger were unmoved. They continued to escalate the war, ordering "protective reaction strikes" against the North; acceleration of the CIA's Operation Phoenix (the assassination of thousands of enemy civilians in the South); the secret bombing of Cambodia; the mining of Haiphong harbor, near the northern capital, Hanoi; and in December 1972, a massive air strike called the Christmas bombing, or as one of Kissinger's aides put it, "calculated barbarism."

Invasion of Cambodia

Meanwhile the peace talks seemed to be going nowhere. The South Vietnamese delegate saw defeat coming and purposely stalled the negotiations. But Kissinger was meeting privately with Le Duc Tho, the chief delegate from North Vietnam. Finally the administration, impatient to improve relations with Russia and China, win back the allegiance of its allies, and restore stability at home, made concessions. On January 27, 1973, Kissinger and Le signed a cease-fire agreement. The United States promised to withdraw its remaining troops within sixty days. Other troops would stay in place, and a coalition government that included the Vietcong would eventually be formed in the South. Pleased that a peace had been made, critics nonetheless noted that the terms of the agreement could have been accepted in 1969, and over twenty thousand American lives could have been spared.

Cease-fire Agreement

Leaving behind some advisers, the United States pulled its troops out of Vietnam and reduced its aid program. Both North and South soon violated the cease-fire, and full-scale war erupted once more. As many had predicted, the feeble South Vietnamese government, for so long an American puppet, could not hold out. Just before its surrender, hundreds of Americans and Vietnamese who had worked for them were hastily evacuated by helicopter from the roof of the American embassy in Saigon. In those desperate last moments, crying South Vietnamese surged toward the embassy and the departing aircraft, only to be shoved violently back. On April 29, 1975, South Vietnam collapsed, and shortly after Saigon was renamed Ho Chi Minh City.

The next month a bizarre episode compounded the tragic American failure in Southeast Asia. The Communist Khmer Rouge had triumphed in Cambodia. That May Cambodian patrol boats seized the American cargo ship *Mayaguez* along with its crew. President Gerald Ford, who had taken over the presidency following Nixon's resignation (see page 975), ordered the marines to attack. Patience would have brought the news that the crew members had been released unharmed. Instead, forty Americans died in the needless venture, many of them in a helicopter accident. Nonetheless, Americans applauded the show of force at a time when the United States appeared to be on the retreat.

After twenty-five years, American intervention in Southeast Asia had come to this panicky end. The overall costs of the war were immense. Over 57,000 Americans and hundreds of thousands of Asians died in the struggle. In monetary terms the war cost the United States more than $150 billion, and as was inevitable, billions more would be paid in future veterans' benefits. At home the war brought inflation, political schism, attacks on civil liberties, and retrenchment from reform programs (see Chapter 33). The war also had negative consequences internationally: delay in moving toward better relations with the Soviet Union and the People's Republic of China, friction with allies, and the alienation of Third World nations.

Meanwhile, in South Vietnam, Cambodia, and Laos, Communists assumed power and instituted repressive governments. Acute hunger afflicted the people of those devastated lands. Soon refugees were crowding aboard unsafe vessels in an attempt to escape their battered homelands. Many of these "boat people" immigrated to the United States, where Americans, reluctant to be reminded of their defeat in Asia, received them with mixed feelings. But thoughtful Americans realized that the United States, which had relentlessly bombed, burned, and defoliated once-rich agricultural lands, bore more than a slight responsibility for the plight of the Southeast Asian peoples.

This sad conclusion prompted an American ambassador to ask the central question about the American defeat: "how so many with so much could achieve so little for so long against so few"? Rather than seek the answer to that question, most Americans preferred to put the disaster out of mind. But the Vietnam veterans were unable to forget. In the words of one veteran,

The longest war is over
Or so they say
Again
But I can still hear the gunfire
Every night
From
My bed.

The longest nightmare
Never seems to
Ever
Quite come
To
An end. [1]

---

[1] Jan Barry, "The Longest War," from *Winning Hearts & Minds: War Poems by Vietnam Veterans.* Copyright © 1972 by 1st Casualty Press. Reprinted by permission of the author.

NIXON, KISSINGER, AND DÉTENTE

For President Nixon, Vietnam was a "short-term problem"; for Kissinger it was a mere historical "footnote." Both considered the central question of international affairs to be the relationship between the United States and the Soviet Union. As a congressman, senator, and vice president, Nixon had been an ardent cold warrior. As one Soviet official commented, "We very well know with whom we have to deal." Kissinger was a German-born political scientist teaching at Harvard and a noted writer on diplomatic topics. Nixon appointed him national security adviser, a post he held until 1973, when he became secretary of state. Ambitious, witty, knowledgeable, and deliberate, Kissinger was a formidable negotiator. Critics, however, thought he adhered too callously to the principle that the end justifies the means. They cited his willingness to unseat foreign governments through secret operations, as in Chile (see page 927), and to sell massive amounts of arms to dictators like the shah of Iran. Kissinger also had his own staff wiretapped.

Together Nixon and Kissinger pursued a grand strategy designed to promote a global balance of power, or "equilibrium." The first part of the strategy was

Détente

détente, meaning limited cooperation with the Soviets through negotiations within a general environment of rivalry. Its purpose, like the containment doctrine it resembled, was to check Soviet expansion and limit a Soviet arms buildup. The second part of the strategy was the curbing of revolution and radicalism in the Third World so as to resist threats to American interests. The grand design seemed attractive to its architects, for the Cold War and limited wars like Vietnam were costing too much. And increased trade with a friendlier Russia might reduce the huge balance-of-payments deficit. Critics, even those who endorsed détente, faulted the Nixon-Kissinger posture for its arrogant assumption that the United States had the ability and the right to manipulate a disorderly world.

The architects of détente, Soviet party boss Leonid Brezhnev (1906–1982) and President Richard M. Nixon (1913–   ), enjoy a light moment during the 1972 Moscow summit meeting that produced the Strategic Arms Limitation Treaty (SALT-I).   Photo J. P. Laffont/Sygma.

SALT Talks   prices. To slow the costly arms race, the Nixon administration initiated Strategic Arms Limitations Talks (SALT) with the Soviets. In 1972 the talks produced a SALT treaty that limited antiballistic missile (ABM) systems. ABM systems were defensive systems that made offensive missiles less vulnerable to attack—and hence encouraged the other side to build more missiles to overcome ABM protection. Limiting ABMs was thus a step toward halting a spiraling arms race. A second agreement placed a five-year freeze on the number of offensive nuclear missiles each side could have. At the time of the agreement the Soviets held an advantage in total missiles, but the United States had more warheads per missile (see table, p. 931) because of its MIRVs (multiple independently targeted re-entry vehicles). One missile loaded with MIRVs could send several nuclear warheads to different targets. In short, the United States had a 2-to-1 advantage in deliverable warheads. Because SALT did not restrict MIRVs, the nuclear arms buildup continued.

Nixon and Kissinger also cultivated détente with the People's Republic of China, ending almost three decades of Sino-American hostility. In February 1972 the president made an historic trip to what he used to call "Red" China. The Chinese Communists welcomed him because they sought to improve trade and they hoped friendlier Chinese-American relations would make the Soviets—the new Chinese enemy—more cautious. Nixon reasoned the same way. In China the president visited the Great Wall and exchanged 150-proof rice-liquor toasts with Mao Zedong and Zhou Enlai. In the end, the conferees agreed to disagree on a number of issues, except one: Russia should not be permitted to make gains in Asia. The opening of this Chinese-American dialogue ended one of the Cold War's most troublesome contests. Official diplomatic recognition and exchange of ambassadors was effected in 1979.

Opening to China

Tortuous events in the Middle East, however, revealed how fragile the Nixon-Kissinger grand strategy was. When Nixon took office in 1969 the Middle East was, in the president's words, a "powder keg."

In the Six-Day War (1967) Israel had used American weapons to score victories against Egypt and Syria.

Arab-Israeli Hostilities

They complained that the administration paid too much attention to archaic Cold War thinking and too little to the force of nationalism, which in the Third World generated instability deriving not from Soviet intrigue but from local conditions. Rather than decreasing the need for intervention, said critics, the new design actually increased it.

Nixon and Kissinger nonetheless pursued détente with extraordinary energy and fanfare. They expanded trade relations with Russia; a 1972 deal sent $1 billion worth of American grain to the Soviets at bargain

Zhou Enlai (1898–1976) and Henry A. Kissinger (1923–) toast better Sino-American relations during President Richard M. Nixon's celebrated trip to China in 1972. As Nixon's assistant for national security affairs, Kissinger had secretly negotiated with the Chinese to arrange the visit—symbol of the new détente between Washington and Beijing. Foreign Minister Zhou had long sought the normalization of diplomatic relations, broken since 1949 when the Communists assumed power and the Truman administration refused to recognize the new People's Republic of China. National Archives, Nixon Project.

The Israelis had seized the West Bank and the ancient city of Jerusalem from Jordan, the Golan Heights from Syria, and the Sinai Peninsula from Egypt (see map, page 926). Soviet arms had backed the Arab nations that Israel fought. To further complicate matters, Palestinian Arabs, many of them expelled from their homeland in 1948 when the nation of Israel was created, had organized the Palestine Liberation Organization (PLO) and pledged to destroy Israel. PLO sympathizers made hit-and-run raids on

Jewish settlements, hijacked jetliners, and murdered Israeli athletes at the 1972 Olympic Games in Munich, West Germany.

On October 6, 1973, Egypt and Syria attacked Israel. In spite of détente, Moscow, backing Egypt, and Washington headed for a confrontation; both superpowers put their armed forces—including nuclear—on alert. At the same time, in an attempt to pressure Americans into taking a pro-Arab stance, the Organization of Petroleum Exporting Countries

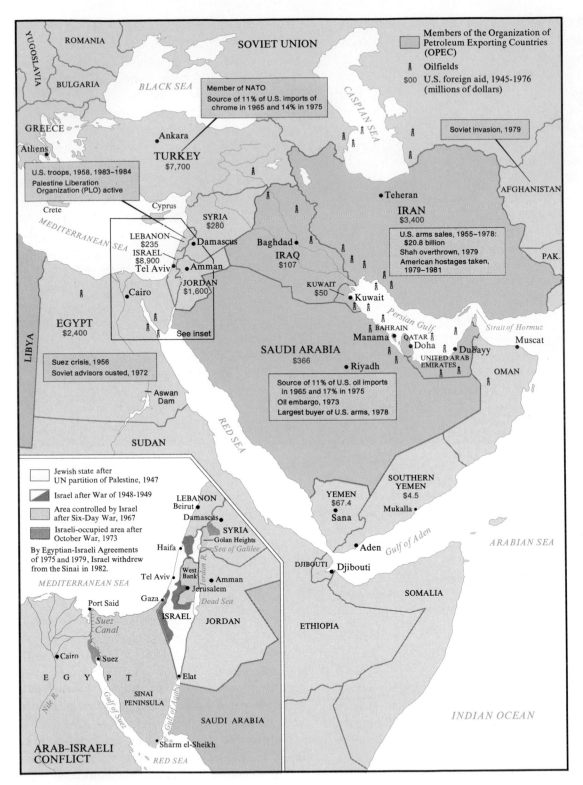

The Middle East

(OPEC) imposed an embargo on shipments of oil to the United States and a dramatic increase in oil prices occurred.

Faced with an energy crisis at home, the Nixon administration had to find a way to end Middle Eastern hostilities. Kissinger arranged a cease-fire and undertook "shuttle diplomacy," flying back and forth repeatedly between Middle Eastern capitals in an exhausting search for a settlement. In March 1974 OPEC lifted the oil embargo. The next year Kissinger persuaded Egypt and Israel to accept a United Nations peace-keeping force in the Sinai. But other problems remained: the homeless Palestinian Arabs; Israeli occupation of Jerusalem and the West Bank; Israel's insistence on building settlements in occupied lands; and Arab threats to destroy the Jewish state. Furthermore, Soviet-American rivalry was still very much alive in the Middle East, especially after the exclusion of the Soviets from the peace negotiations and after Egypt moved closer to the United States, snubbing the Soviet Union.

In Latin America, Nixon continued President Johnson's interventionist policies. Johnson had dispatched twenty thousand American troops to the **Intervention in Latin America** Dominican Republic in 1965 to prevent a leftist government from coming to power. And in the Johnson Doctrine—the United States would prevent Communists from coming to office in the Western Hemisphere—the president had reiterated the Roosevelt Corollary's insistence on United States policing powers in the region. Thus in 1970, when the people of Chile elected a Marxist president, Salvador Allende, it was all too easy for Nixon to see him as a Communist threat who had to be removed. The CIA began secret operations to disrupt the Chilean economy; funneled money to newspapers critical of Allende; and apparently encouraged military officers to stage a coup. In 1973 a military junta ousted and killed Allende and installed an authoritarian regime in his place. Nixon and Kissinger privately pronounced their policy of "destabilization" successful, while publicly denying their role in the affair.

In Africa, Nixon-Kissinger maneuvers proved less successful. During the 1960s and early 1970s the CIA **Angola** channeled funds to some of the groups fighting for the liberation of Angola from Portuguese colonial rule—at the same time that Washington publicly supported Portugal. After Angola won its independence in 1975, civil war erupted. The United States, which stepped up covert aid, and South Africa, which sent troops, backed one faction while the Soviets helped another. When Congress learned about the secret aid, it voted to cut all funds. Kissinger complained that the Soviets would gain a foothold in Africa. But many members of Congress argued that Americans could not decide the outcome of an African civil war; that the United States should not be aligned with the white racist regime of South Africa; that it was very unlikely that Angola would become a Soviet puppet; and that diplomacy should have been tried. After a leftist government came to power in Angola, Washington took a keener interest in the rest of Africa, building economic ties, sending arms to friendly black nations, and putting more distance between the United States and the white minority governments in Rhodesia (now Zimbabwe) and South Africa. It was important, Kissinger said, to "prevent the radicalization of Africa."

Like other Americans before him, Kissinger clung to the belief that the United States had the answers to most international problems. In his view the Third World was a mere sideshow to the Soviet-American confrontation; and the United States had to defend its interests there against nationalist challenges. Thus in the mid-1970s about 686,000 American military personnel were stationed abroad; the United States had military links with ninety-two nations; and American arms sales overseas climbed to about $10 billion. These so-called commitments were maintained not only to impress Moscow with American might and will, but to serve as a counterrevolutionary force against nationalist stirrings that threatened American economic and strategic interests. Nixon and Kissinger stood, then, in a long line of leaders who counterpoised American power against foreign peoples determined to decide their own fate. Even American allies thought the United States too meddlesome. "Living next to you is in some ways like sleeping with an elephant," said Canadian Prime Minister Pierre Trudeau. "No matter how friendly and even-tempered is the beast, if I can call it that, one is affected by every twitch and grunt."

RICH NATIONS, POOR NATIONS: THE NORTH-SOUTH DIALOGUE

If disputes in the Middle East, Latin America, and Africa bedeviled the Nixon-Kissinger grand design for world order, global economic issues also heightened political disorder. Kissinger explained that "international political stability requires international economic stability." But in the 1970s there was little economic stability; troubles could be seen everywhere. The worldwide recession in the early part of the decade was the worst since the 1930s. Inflation and high oil prices pinched rich and poor nations alike. Protectionist tendencies raised tariffs and impeded world trade. Very poor Third World countries suffered massive famines and built up huge international debts to meet internal needs. The North-South dialogue became acrimonious when Third World countries (the "South") insisted that the wealthier, industrial "North" share economic resources and the power to exploit them. The gulf between rich and poor nations threatened world peace.

The United States could not escape these problems because it was a major participant in the world economy. Although America's economic standing had declined since the olympian days of the 1940s and 1950s as other nations, such as Japan and West Germany, had recovered from the devastation of the Second World War and as Third World countries had gained more control over their raw materials, Americans remained the richest people in the world. The United States produced about one-third of the world's goods and services. Many American companies, like Coca-Cola and Exxon, earned over half their profits abroad. One-fourth of agricultural sales came from exports; one out of every nine manufacturing jobs depended upon exports. The American economy also depended upon imports of strategic raw materials: three-quarters of the tin, over 95 percent of the manganese, and over half of the zinc consumed in the United States came from abroad. Such ties, as well as American investments abroad totaling over

$133 billion in the mid-1970s, explain in part why the United States was an interventionist power; threats to markets, investments, and raw materials were read as deadly stabs at the high American standard of living. American economic holdings did in fact become targets. Venezuela nationalized American oil properties in 1976, and terrorists around the world destroyed American facilities and kidnapped and sometimes murdered American business executives.

Multinational corporations became a symbol and a target of the conspicuous American economic position overseas. American-based multinationals like

Multinational Corporations Exxon and General Motors actually enjoyed budgets and incomes larger than most countries. These giant firms brought home profits and exported American culture. But they aroused criticism. American workers protested that these global oligopolies stole their jobs by moving their plants abroad in search of cheaper labor. People of the "South" also complained that multinationals exploited poor countries, robbing them of their natural resources; that they corrupted politics, as when International Telephone and Telegraph tried to undermine President Allende in Chile and Lockheed Aircraft bribed foreign leaders to promote sales; that they sometimes provided "cover" for CIA agents; and that they evaded taxes by clever manipulations of their books.

Multinational officers and government officials defended these enterprises, pointing out that they invested in risky ventures that brought economic progress, including the transfer of technology. Multinationals, they insisted, helped rationalize a chaotic world economy, and privately owned multinationals made more rational economic choices—hence benefiting the consumer—than government-owned companies. Nonetheless, many countries passed laws requiring a certain percentage of native ownership; India, for example, legislated that its nationals own a majority of voting shares in industrial firms. Other states simply nationalized multinational properties.

Besides placing restraints on multinationals, the Third World of the South pressed for lower prices on technology and manufactured goods, low-interest loans, and higher prices for raw materials. In 1974 the United Nations issued the "New International Economic Order" encompassing many of these points, but the North made few concessions. Food was another divisive issue in the North-South dialogue. Droughts, meager harvests, high birthrates, and swelling populations condemned millions to hunger. In Africa in the early 1970s famine killed 10,000 people a day. The United States sent food aid, especially to those nations considered political friends, but it preferred to sell its surplus food for profit, as evidenced by the large grain sales to the dollar-paying Russians. Although total American foreign aid rose from $6.6 billion in 1970 to $7.8 billion in 1977, the aid dollars actually bought less because of rampant inflation.

Another question that pitted North against South was the Law of the Sea treaty, patiently composed in the 1970s through extended negotiations. Developing nations argued that the rich seabed resources of petroleum and minerals should be shared among all nations as a "common heritage of mankind." The industrial states, alone having the capital and equipment to conduct the excavating and drilling, tended to prefer private enterprise or national exploitation, reaping the profits and raw materials for themselves. In the early 1980s the global community hammered out a compromise between international and national controls and rights, but the United States rejected the treaty in 1983. Angry Third World nations railed against what they perceived as selfish economic imperialism, whereas many American allies who supported the compromise predicted a chaotic future of competing claims of ownership, territorial disputes, and threats to freedom of navigation similar to the colonial powers' scramble for advantage in Africa and Asia in the late nineteenth century. Like other international economic issues, this one promised a future of political instability—and perhaps war.

Law of the Sea

CARTER AND A REINVIGORATED COLD WAR

President Jimmy Carter was "deeply troubled by the lies our people had been told" during the Vietnam War, and he asked Americans to put their "inordinate fear of Communism" behind them. His secretary of state, Cyrus R. Vance, said that he had learned from the Vietnam War that the United States could not "prop up a series of regimes that lacked popular support" and that "there can be no going back to a time when we thought there could be American solutions to every problem." If Carter, the first post-Vietnam president, and Vance, once an architect of the war, drew lessons from the Vietnam experience, many tried to forget the nightmare. "Coming back to America," recalled a Vietnam veteran, "I was shocked . . . that no one even talked about it." But debate about the causes and consequences of the war did develop, making the Carter administration forge its foreign policy in an unsteady setting: the old Cold War consensus seemed fractured, and Americans were both angry and confused. The historian William Appleman Williams observed that for the first time in their history Americans were suffering from a serious case of "empire shock."

Hawkish leaders who debated the meaning of the war claimed that America's ignoble failure in Vietnam undermined the nation's credibility and tempted enemies to exploit opportunities at the expense of United States interests. They pointed to a Vietnam syndrome—a mood suspicious of foreign entanglements—which would inhibit the United States from exercising its power. They advised that next time the military should be permitted to do its job, free from the constraints of whimsical public opinion and timid politicians. America lost in Vietnam, they asserted, because the American people lost their guts and will at home. They urged Carter to stop at no expense to expand the military and face down America's many adversaries.

Lessons of Vietnam

Others drew different lessons. Some people blamed the war on strong-willed presidents like Johnson and pusillanimous Congresses that had conceded too much power to the executive branch, as evident in the Tonkin Gulf resolution. Trim the powers of the imperial presidency, they counseled, and America would become less interventionist. Others took a more hardheaded, even fatalistic, view: as long as the United States remained an industrial giant, with strong ideological, strategic, economic, and political needs that could only be satisfied through activism abroad, then the nation would continue to be expansionist and interventionist. Still others found fault with the containment doctrine: it failed to make distinctions between areas peripheral and areas vital to the national security and relied too heavily upon military means. The widely read journalist Walter Lippmann endorsed "neo-isolationism." "Compared to people who thought they could run the universe," he remarked, "I *am* a neo-isolationist and proud of it." Many of these critics thus advised Carter: not more, but less, bluster; not more, but less, military; not more, but less, interventionism.

During Carter's presidency public discussion of the Vietnam War intensified. Some of the war's 2.8 million veterans called for better benefits, especially asking for help to deal with "post-traumatic stress disorder." This illness of nightmares and extreme nervousness was different from the shell shock of the First World War or the battle fatigue of the Second. Doctors reported that the disorder stemmed largely from the fact that soldiers saw so many women, children, and elderly killed in Vietnam. Many returning veterans were also stung by the unsympathetic glances of Americans who did not want to be reminded of the unpleasant war or who blamed them for losing a war that could not be won. Films like *Coming Home* (1978), *The Deer Hunter* (1978), and *Apocalypse Now* (1979), personal accounts like Philip Caputo's *A Rumor of War* (1977), and novels like James Webb's *Fields of Fire* (1978) focused attention on the soldier's Vietnam, stimulating questions about whether defeat was inevitable given the jungle conditions and elusive enemy.

In this environment of conflicting answers and lessons Carter vowed to chart a new course. When he took office in 1977 he pledged to give as much attention to North-South as to East-West

Carter's Goals   issues, to reduce the American military presence overseas, to cut back arms sales, which had reached unprecedented heights under Nixon, and to slow the nuclear arms race. "The soul of our foreign policy," he intoned, would be the championing of individual human rights abroad—the freedom to vote, worship, travel, speak out, and get a fair trial. A deeply religious man, Carter intended to infuse international relations with moral force.

From the start Carter's statements were inconsistent, and administration officials squabbled among themselves. One source of the problem was Zbigniew Brzezinski, a Polish-born political scientist who became Carter's national security adviser. The stern-faced Brzezinski was an old-fashioned Cold Warrior, a critic of détente who tended to view foreign crises in globalist terms—that is, he blamed them on the Soviet Union. One State Department official likened him to a rat terrier constantly nipping at Secretary Vance's ankles. More and more Carter listened to Brzezinski; Vance resigned in April 1980, deploring the American drift toward military power as a substitute for diplomacy.

Despite Carter's goals, détente deteriorated and the Cold War revived. The president first angered the Soviets by calling on them to respect their citizens' human rights and tolerate dissent. Moscow told him to mind his own business. Then American officials denounced Russia for sponsoring Cuban troops in Africa. And as Sino-American relations improved following the Nixon visit, Soviet leaders worried that the United States was playing its "China card"— building up their rival in order to threaten them.

A thaw came in 1979 when negotiations produced a new treaty, SALT-II, that acknowledged Soviet-American nuclear parity (see table). The agreement placed a ceiling of 2,250 deliv-

SALT-II   ery vehicles (long-range bombers, ICBMs, and submarine-based missiles) on each side and imposed limits on the number of warheads and the development of new kinds of nuclear weapons. Critics from the right charged that the treaty favored the Soviets; critics from the left protested that it did not go far enough toward quelling the arms race. As if to prove both sides correct, Carter soon announced that the United States would construct an expensive new MX missile system that would shuttle ICBMs back and forth along a vast maze of underground tunnels designed to confuse attackers. The president was gambling that the MX system would win votes for the SALT-II treaty from skeptical senators without alarming Moscow. He did not get the votes, but he did alarm the Soviets.

As doubts about Senate ratification of SALT-II mounted and Moscow fumed over the MX, events in Afghanistan led to a Soviet-American confrontation. In December 1979 the Red Army bludgeoned its way into the Soviets' southern neighbor to shore up the faltering Communist government, under siege

STRATEGIC NUCLEAR FORCES AT THE TIME OF SALT-I, 1972

	U.S.	U.S.S.R.
Intercontinental ballistic missiles (ICBMs)	1054	1607
Submarine-launched ballistic missiles (SLBMs)	656	740
Strategic bombers	450	200
Nuclear warheads	5700	2500

STRATEGIC NUCLEAR FORCES AT THE TIME OF SALT-II, 1979

	U.S.	U.S.S.R.
Intercontinental ballistic missiles (ICBMs)	1054	1400
Submarine-launched ballistic missiles (SLBMs)	656	950
Strategic bombers	350	150
Nuclear warheads	9200	5000

Sources: U.S. Department of Defense; U.S. Department of State

by Moslem rebels. But the rebels persisted, with some aid from the CIA, and analysts predicted that the Soviet Union had sunk into its own Vietnam. Determined to make the U.S.S.R. "pay a concrete price for their aggression," an embittered Carter shelved SALT-II, suspended shipments of grain and high-technology equipment to Russia, and launched an international boycott of the 1980 Summer Olympics in Moscow. In the United Nations the United States pressed for a resolution condemning the Soviet Union and was heartened by the positive response of many Third World nations. But all these efforts proved fruitless: the Soviets refused to withdraw their forces from Afghanistan.

The president also announced what was quickly dubbed the Carter Doctrine: the United States would intervene, unilaterally and militarily if necessary, against further Soviet aggression in the petroleum-rich Persian Gulf. Prominent critics spoke out against the declaration. Senator Edward M. Kennedy declared that Americans would rather ration gas than spill the blood of their children for Middle Eastern oil. And George F. Kennan, the father of containment, who like Kennedy was critical of Soviet opportunism, called Carter's reaction exaggerated. It was wrong to assume that the Soviets would attack elsewhere in the Middle East, said Kennan. He faulted Carter for not trying diplomacy first, and for playing all his nonmilitary cards prematurely. "Was this really mature statesmanship on our part?" Kennan asked.

On November 4, 1979, an Iranian mob encouraged by government officials seized the American embassy in Teheran and took American personnel prisoner. For more than a year, shouting Iranians taunted the United States to do something about it. The crisis, which had its roots in close American ties to the unpopular government of the fallen shah, frustrated President Jimmy Carter, who remarked that he felt "the same kind of impotence that a powerful person feels when his child is kidnapped." Wide World Photos.

Carter met his toughest test in Iran, where in early 1979 the shah was toppled from his throne by revolutionaries under the leadership of Ayatollah Ruhollah Khomeini, a wrathfully anti-American Moslem cleric. Khomeini remembered that the United States had restored the shah to power in 1953 through a CIA-staged coup and that the CIA had trained and supplied the shah's ruthless secret police. Iranian rebels also resented the huge infusion of American arms into their country—$19 billion worth in 1973 through 1978 alone. In November, after the exiled shah was admitted to the United States for medical treatment, mobs stormed the American embassy in Teheran and

Hostage Crisis in Iran

took American personnel as hostages, demanding the return of the shah for trial, along with his wealth.

Although the Iranians eventually released a few of the prisoners, fifty-two others languished over a year under Iranian guard. Frequently blindfolded or bound, they were subjected to solitary confinement, beatings, and terrifying mock executions. All the while the theocratic Khomeini regime hurled insults at Washington.

Carter would not return the shah to Iran or apologize for past American involvement there. Unable to gain the hostages' freedom through public appeals, foreign emissaries, or United Nations delegations, the president took steps to isolate Iran economically. He froze Iranian assets in the United States and appealed to American allies, largely unsuccessfully, to reduce trade with the Moslem state. In April 1980, frustrated and at low ebb in the public opinion polls, Carter broke diplomatic relations with Iran and ordered a daring rescue mission. Colonel Charles A. Beckwith eagerly led the operation, saying "America needs a win. We need one real, real bad." But the rescue effort miscarried after an equipment failure in the sandy Iranian desert. During the hasty withdrawal two aircraft collided, killing eight American soldiers. The hostages were not freed until January 1981, 444 days after their capture. In the agreement that led to their release, the United States unfroze Iranian assets and promised not to intervene again in Iran's internal affairs.

Elsewhere in the Middle East, Carter enjoyed some success. Through his tenacious personal diplomacy at a Camp David meeting in 1979, the president persuaded Egypt and Israel to agree to Israel's phased withdrawal from the Sinai, which had been occupied since 1967. Other Arab states denounced the agreement for not requiring Israel to relinquish other occupied territories. But the treaty at least ended warfare along one boundary in this troubled area of the world.

Carter also had some success elsewhere in the Third World. His appointment of Andrew Young, a black

Egypt's President Anwar al-Sadat (1918–1981), President Jimmy Carter (1924–   ), and Israeli Prime Minister Menachem Begin (1913–   ), left to right, clasp hands to celebrate the historic signing, on March 26, 1979, of the Egyptian-Israeli Peace Treaty. A triumph of American diplomacy by the president in intense negotiations with the two Mideast leaders at Camp David, Maryland, the document provided only a brief respite from the violent politics of the region.   National Archives, Carter Project.

civil rights activist and member of Congress, as ambassador to the United Nations earned goodwill among developing nations. Young believed that the United States should stay out of local disputes, even if Communists were involved. Thus when warfare broke out in 1979 between Zaire and Angola, where Cuban troops and Soviet advisers were stationed, Young persuaded the president to stand back until the fighting

subsided, and no American interests were sacrificed. Third World leaders were shocked, however, when Young was forced to resign in 1979 after meeting privately with representatives of the Palestine Liberation Organization, which the United States had refused to recognize as a legitimate group.

In Latin America, Carter concluded two treaties with Panama that provided for gradual return of the

IMPORTANT EVENTS

1960	Kennedy elected president		1971	*Pentagon Papers* released
1961	Peace Corps founded Alliance for Progress Bay of Pigs invasion Berlin crisis U.S. military buildup		1972	Nixon visits China SALT-I treaty Nixon re-elected
1962	Cuban missile crisis		1973	Vietnam cease-fire agreement Allende ousted in Chile Arab-Israeli War Arab oil embargo

1963	Test-ban treaty
	Diem assassinated in Vietnam
	Kennedy assassinated; Johnson
	    assumes presidency
			1974	Nixon resigns; Ford becomes
				    president
				New International Economic Order

1964	Tonkin Gulf incident and resolution Johnson elected president		1975	Egyptian-Israeli peace agreement Communists take power in South Vietnam Civil war in Angola
1965	U.S. invasion of Dominican Republic Johnson Americanizes Vietnam War		1976	Carter elected president
1965–66	Antiwar teach-ins		1977	Human rights policy launched
1967	Peace rallies across the nation Six-Day War in the Middle East		1978	Panama Canal treaties

1968	Tet offensive in Vietnam
	My Lai massacre
	Vietnam peace talks open in Paris
	Nixon elected president
			1979	Egyptian-Israeli peace accord (Camp
				    David)
				Hostages taken in Iran
				SALT-II treaty
				Soviets invade Afghanistan
				Grain embargo and boycott of
				    Olympic Games against Soviets

1969	543,400 U.S. troops in Vietnam Nixon begins withdrawal Détente policy announced		1980	Secretary Vance resigns Reagan elected president
1970	Invasion of Cambodia		1981	American hostages in Iran released

Canal Zone to that Central American country. The treaties, endorsed by the Senate in 1978, aroused heated debate. Former governor of California Ronald

**Panama
Canal
Treaties**

Reagan, running hard for the presidency, went so far as to claim that the Canal Zone was sovereign American territory. But others saw

that without the treaty the United States might have to fight the Panamanians, who longed for the restoration of territory they believed had been wrongfully severed from their nation in 1903 (see pages 638–639).

In Nicaragua in 1979 leftist revolutionaries overthrew Anastasio Somoza, a graduate of West Point, long-time ally of the United States, and member of the dictatorial Somoza family that had ruled the Central American nation since 1936. The revolutionaries called themselves Sandinistas after the Nicaraguan who had fought American marines in the early 1930s (see page 771). President Carter at first tried to tame their radicalism, but, failing, he recognized the new government. In early 1981 he shut off aid to Nicaragua to demonstrate disapproval of the Sandinistas' curbing of civil liberties, growing ties with Castro's Cuba, and alleged assistance to rebels in El Salvador, where another regime friendly to the United States was threatened by internal upheaval (see Chapter 35).

Debate on Carter's Record

Carter's diplomatic record never met his aspirations. More American military personnel were stationed overseas in 1980 (489,000) than in 1976 (460,000); the defense budget climbed; foreign arms sales grew from $8.3 billion in 1977 to $15.3 billion in 1980; and the United States and NATO agreed to install cruise and Pershing-II missiles in Western Europe. Carter's human rights policy also proved inconsistent. In four years the president did gain the release of hundreds of political prisoners, but he left himself vulnerable to the charge that he followed a double standard. That is, he applied the human rights test to some nations (the Soviet Union, Argentina, and Chile), but not to American allies (South Korea, the shah's Iran, and the Philippines). Carter's successes in the Middle East, Latin America, and Africa became overshadowed by the shrillness of an invigorated Cold War.

Carter's performance did not satisfy Americans who wanted superiority in foreign affairs—a reinstatement of the considerable military edge the United States had had in the early days of the Cold War. As one Tennessee woman mused: "Growing up we learned in history that America was the best in everything. We had the respect of the whole world. But where can you go today and be respected for being American?" Her bluntly chauvinistic attitude reflected a broad segment of American public opinion. An Oklahoma couple urged Carter to take up once again Teddy Roosevelt's big stick. "And club the hell out of them if you need to," grumbled the husband.

This nostalgia for old-fashioned American militancy found a ringing voice in President Ronald Reagan,

elected in 1980 after a campaign in which he charged that the United States was falling behind the Soviets in the arms race and retreating under fire from the Third World. Reagan promised to abandon détente and SALT-II, dramatically increase the military budget, and support right-wing governments that stood by American foreign policy. About the Vietnam War, Reagan said, "It is time we recognized that ours was, in truth, a noble cause." The United States, it appeared, had come full circle—back to 1961 when John F. Kennedy had decided to win the Vietnam War.

SUGGESTIONS FOR FURTHER READING

General and Soviet-American Relations

Stephen Ambrose, *Rise to Globalism*, 3rd ed. (1983); Richard J. Barnet, *The Alliance* (1983); John L. Gaddis, *Strategies of Containment* (1982); John L. Gaddis, *Russia, the Soviet Union, and the United States* (1978); Alexander L. George and Richard Smoke, *Deterrence in American Foreign Policy* (1974); Raymond L. Garthoff, *Détente and Confrontation: American-Soviet Relations from Nixon to Reagan* (1985); Robert C. Johansen, *The National Interest and the Human Interest* (1980); Walter LaFeber, *America, Russia, and the Cold War, 1945–1985*, 5th ed. (1985); James A. Nathan and James K. Oliver, *United States Foreign Policy and World Order*, 2nd ed. (1981); Alvin Z. Rubenstein and Donald E. Smith, eds., *Anti-Americanism in the Third World* (1985); Adam B. Ulam, *Dangerous Relations* (1983).

Kennedy and Johnson Diplomacy

George W. Ball, *The Past Has Another Pattern* (1982); Warren I. Cohen, *Dean Rusk* (1980); Philip Geyelin, *Lyndon B. Johnson and the World* (1966); David Halberstam, *The Best and the Brightest* (1972); Jim Heath, *Decade of Disillusionment* (1975); Lyndon B. Johnson, *The Vantage Point* (1971); Madeleine G. Kalb, *The Congo Cables* (1982); Doris Kearns, *Lyndon Johnson and the American Dream* (1976); Montague Kern et al., *The Kennedy Crises* (1984); Richard D. Mahoney, *JFK: Ordeal in Africa* (1983); Herbert S.

Parmet, JFK (1983); Walt W. Rostow, *Diffusion of Power* (1972); Arthur M. Schlesinger, Jr., *Robert Kennedy and His Times* (1978); Arthur M. Schlesinger, Jr., *A Thousand Days* (1965); Richard Walton, *Cold War and Counterrevolution* (1972).

Latin America and Cuba

Graham Allison, *Essence of Decision: Explaining the Cuban Missile Crisis* (1971); Samuel Baily, *The United States and the Development of South America, 1945–1975* (1977); Cole Blasier, *Hovering Giant* (1974); Herbert Dinerstein, *The Making of a Missile Crisis* (1976); Walter LaFeber, *Inevitable Revolutions: The United States in Central America* (1983); Walter LaFeber, *The Panama Canal* (1979); Stephen G. Rabe, *The Road to OPEC: United States Relations with Venezuela* (1982); Peter Wyden, *Bay of Pigs* (1979).

Middle East

George Lenczowski, *The Middle East in World Affairs*, 4th ed. (1980); William B. Quandt, *Decade of Decision: American Policy Toward the Arab-Israeli Conflict, 1967–1976* (1977); Bernard Reich, *Quest for Peace: United States–Israel Relations and the Arab-Israeli Conflict* (1977); Barry Rubin, *Paved with Good Intentions: The American Experience and Iran* (1980); Robert W. Stookey, *America and the Arab States* (1975).

The Vietnam War and Southeast Asia

Larry Berman, *Planning a Tragedy* (1982); Frances FitzGerald, *Fire in the Lake* (1972); Leslie H. Gelb and Richard K. Betts, *The Irony of Vietnam* (1979); George C. Herring, *America's Longest War* (1979); Arnold R. Isaacs, *Without Honor: Defeat in Vietnam and Cambodia* (1983); Stanley Karnow, *Vietnam* (1983); Guenter Lewy, *America in Vietnam* (1978); Archimedes L.A. Patti, *Why Viet Nam?* (1980); John C. Pratt, ed., *Vietnam Voices* (1984); Al Santoli, *Everything We Had* (1981); Herbert Y. Schandler, *The Unmaking of a President: Lyndon Johnson and Vietnam* (1977); William Shawcross, *Sideshow: Kissinger, Nixon, and the Destruction of Cambodia* (1979); Ronald H. Spector, *United States Army in Vietnam* (1983); Wallace Terry, *Bloods: An Oral History of the Vietnam War by Black Veterans* (1984); Nancy Zaroulis and Gerald Sullivan, *Who Spoke Up? American Protest Against the War in Vietnam, 1963–1975* (1984).

The Lessons of Vietnam

Walter H. Capps, *The Unfinished War* (1982); Michael Charlton and Anthony Moncrieff, eds., *Many Reasons Why* (1978); Herbert Hendin and Ann P. Haas, *Wounds of War: The Psychological Aftermath of Combat in Vietnam* (1984); Myra MacPherson, *Long Time Passing: Vietnam and the Haunted Generation* (1984); Robert E. Osgood, *Limited War Revisited* (1979); Norman Podhoretz, *Why We Were in Vietnam* (1982); Earl C. Ravenal, *Never Again* (1978); Harrison E. Salisbury, ed., *Vietnam Reconsidered* (1984); Harry G. Summers, Jr., *On Strategy: A Critical Analysis of the Vietnam War* (1982); W. Scott Thompson and Donaldson D. Frizzill, eds., *The Lessons of Vietnam* (1977).

Nixon, Kissinger, and Détente

Richard J. Barnet, *The Giants: Russia and America* (1977); Seymour M. Hersh, *The Price of Power: Kissinger in the Nixon White House* (1983); Stanley Hoffmann, *Primacy or World Order* (1978); Stanley Hoffmann, "The Case of Dr. Kissinger," *New York Review of Books*, 26 (December 6, 1979), 14ff.; Bernard Kalb and Marvin Kalb, *Kissinger* (1974); Henry Kissinger, *Years of Upheaval* (1982); Henry Kissinger, *White House Years* (1979); Roger Morris, *Uncertain Greatness: Henry Kissinger and American Foreign Policy* (1977); Richard Nixon, *RN* (1978); Andrew J. Pierre, *The Global Politics of Arms Sales* (1982); Tad Szulc, *The Illusion of Peace* (1978).

Carter's Foreign Policy

Zbigniew Brzezinski, *Power and Principle* (1983); Jimmy Carter, *Keeping Faith* (1982); Warren Christopher et al., *American Hostages in Iran* (1985); James Fallows, *National Defense* (1981); Kenneth A. Oye et al., *Eagle Entangled* (1979); Gaddis Smith, *Morality, Reason, and Power* (1986); Cyrus Vance, *Hard Choices* (1983); Sandy Vogelgesang, *American Dream, Global Nightmare* (1980).

The CIA and Counterinsurgency

Philip Agee, *Inside the Company* (1975); Douglas S. Blaufarb, *The Counterinsurgency Era* (1977); Ray Cline, *Secrets, Spies and Scholars* (1976); Victor Marchetti and John D. Marks, *The CIA and the Cult of Intelligence* (1974); Thomas Powers, *The Man Who Kept the Secrets* (1979); John Stockwell, *In Search of Enemies* (1978); David Wise, *The American Police State* (1976); David Wise, *The Invisible Government* (1964); David Wise and Thomas B. Ross, *The Espionage Establishment* (1967).

Nuclear Arms Race and SALT

Desmond Ball, *Politics and Force Levels: The Strategic Missile Program of the Kennedy Administration* (1980); John Newhouse, *Cold Dawn: The Story of SALT* (1973); Samuel B. Payne, Jr., *The Soviet Union and SALT* (1980); Glenn T.

Seaborg, *Kennedy, Khrushchev, and the Test Ban* (1981); David N. Schwartz, *NATO's Nuclear Dilemmas* (1983); Stanford Arms Control Group, *International Arms Control*, 2nd ed. (1984). (See also works listed in Chapter 30 under "Nuclear arms race.")

The World Economy and North-South Issues

Richard J. Barnet, *The Lean Years* (1980); Richard J. Barnet and Ronald Müller, *The Global Reach: The Power of the Multinational Corporations* (1974); David P. Calleo, *The Imperious Economy* (1982); Alfred E. Eckes, *The U.S. and the Global Struggle for Minerals* (1979); Charles A. Jones, *The North-South Dialogue* (1983); Stephen D. Krasner, *Defending the National Interest* (1978); Robert K. Olson, *U.S. Foreign Policy and the New International Economic Order* (1981); William Paddock and Paul Paddock, *Time of Famines* (1976); Joan E. Spero, *The Politics of International Economic Relations*, 2nd ed. (1981).

Reform, Radicalism, and Disappointed Expectations

1961–1973

Chapter 33

The first dreadful flash from Dallas clattered over newsroom teletype machines across the country at 1:34 P.M., Eastern Standard Time. Carried immediately over radio and television, the news was soon on the streets. People still remember precisely where they were and what they were doing when they heard that President John F. Kennedy had been shot and killed. For them, time stopped at that moment in what psychologists call flashbulb memory, the freeze-framing of an exceptionally emotional event down to the most incidental detail. For an earlier American generation, the indelible memory was of December 7, 1941, when radio reports of the Japanese attack at Pearl Harbor had stunned the nation into silence. But now, it was November 22, 1963, the day John Kennedy's promise was snuffed out.

In New York City that afternoon, a man braked his car to a halt in the middle of a busy intersection and ran over to a sidewalk luncheonette. "Is it true?" he asked. Without looking up, the counterman replied, "Yes, he's dead." The man returned to his car and slumped behind the wheel, oblivious to the impatient honking around him. In Detroit, Sister Kate Seidenwand was the co-principal of a parochial grade school. Upon hearing that the president had been shot, she took the children into chapel and "started the Rosary, praying that it wasn't serious. And when we were in the midst of the Rosary, the secretary came in and said that he had died. And I was personally so overwhelmed . . . I had to wait a few minutes to compose myself in order to tell the students. When I finally could announce it, you could hear the children's sighs and groans, and some of them were crying." Ken Kesey's play *One Flew Over the Cuckoo's Nest* had just opened on Broadway, and he and a couple of friends were driving triumphantly back to the West Coast. They were in Pennsylvania when "the news came in over that car radio, and [as] we stopped in at service stations and Howard Johnson's and little fast-food places across the United States, a really profound thing happened to us. We felt like we were seeing the real soul of America with its shirt torn open in grief."

For four days in late November 1963, Americans wept, prayed, and stared at their television sets, numbed by the unbelievable. Throughout the afternoon and night before the funeral, 250,000 people trod silently past the coffin in the Capitol Rotunda. Jacqueline Kennedy and her daughter Caroline paid a last visit to kneel and kiss the coffin. On the fourth day, a million people lined the streets of Washington and millions more watched on television as the president's body was borne by horse-drawn caisson from the Capitol to St. Matthew's Cathedral to Arlington Cemetery. Throughout the country, people mourned. "He was our man," sobbed an elderly black man in Harlem, "and now he's gone."

Some of America's postwar confidence was riding on the caisson that carried Kennedy's body to the grave. "In retrospect," the British journalist Godfrey Hodgson has written, "people looked back to Friday, November 22, 1963, as the end of a time of hope, the beginning of a time of troubles." What was ironic about America's outpouring of grief was that the Kennedy administration had failed in many of its goals. In the final months of his presidency Kennedy had been criticized for being ineffectual in domestic affairs and reckless in foreign affairs. Few successes distinguished his legislative record, and there was already opposition to America's deepening involvement in Vietnam. But John Kennedy's assassination was a national tragedy. In their grief Americans remembered how handsome and eloquent he had been and how he had inspired their hopes for peace, prosperity, and social justice.

In the early 1960s, hope had run high among millions of Americans, including the nation's poor. Kennedy's call for a New Frontier had inspired liberal Democrats and young idealists to work to eliminate poverty, segregation, and voting rights abuses. Americans also supported Kennedy's desire to court the Third World and prevail in the Cold War. Lyndon B. Johnson, Kennedy's successor in the White House, presided over the Great Society, and Congress responded to his urgings with a flood of legislation. The 1960s saw more economic, political, and social reform than any period since the New Deal. But even during these years of liberal triumphs, anger occasionally flared into violence. Beginning with the assassination in 1963, ten years of events ensued—including bloody race riots, the murders of other political and civil rights leaders, and the war in Vietnam—that shattered the Kennedy and Johnson optimism.

In the cities, many Afro-Americans were angry that they still lived in poverty and segregation despite the civil rights movement and the passage of landmark civil rights laws. Their discontent exploded during the 1960s' "long hot summers." In July 1967, for example, twenty-six people were killed in Newark, New Jersey, in warfare between blacks, the police, and army troops. This event was followed a week later by the Detroit race riot, which led to the deaths of forty-three persons. The next year the National Advisory Commission on Civil Disorders, chaired by Governor Otto Kerner of Illinois, released its report on the causes of the race riots. "The nation is rapidly moving toward two increasingly separate Americas . . . a white society principally located in suburbs, in smaller central cities, and in peripheral parts of large central cities; and a Negro society largely concentrated within large central cities."

This social turbulence along with the growing movement opposing the Vietnam War brought down the presidency of Lyndon Johnson and gave rise to Black Power, the radical politics of the New Left, and a revived women's movement. But Johnson's departure from office did not produce calm. Richard Nixon, who was elected president in 1968, polarized the nation still further. Nixon's two immediate predecessors had been destroyed in office: both Dallas and Vietnam evoked those tragedies. A third place, Watergate, was to signify Richard Nixon's downfall. Battered by these events, by 1973 many Americans had ceased to believe in the American dream.

Caroline Kennedy kisses her father as her mother watches. President John F. Kennedy (1917–1963) and his wife, Jacqueline, seemed to symbolize youthful energy and idealism. Kennedy's New Frontier gave hope to nonwhites and the poor. National Archives.

KENNEDY AND THE NEW FRONTIER

He was, as Norman Mailer wrote of President John F. Kennedy, "our leading man." The handsome, vigorous new chief executive was young, the first president born in the twentieth century. Perceived by the public as an intellectual, he had a genuinely inquiring mind, and as a patron of the arts, he brought wit and sophistication to the White House.

Kennedy had been born to wealth and politics. His Irish-American grandfather had been mayor of Boston; his millionaire father, Joseph P. Kennedy, served as ambassador to Great Britain. In 1946 the young Kennedy, home from the Second World War a hero, continued the family tradition by campaigning in Boston for a seat in the House of Representatives. He won easily.

As a Democratic politician, Kennedy inherited the New Deal commitment to the welfare state. He generally cast liberal votes in line with the prolabor sentiments of his low-income, blue-collar constituents. But on issues of no direct concern to his district—flood control, farm price supports, the Tennessee Valley Authority—he cast his votes with some of the most conservative members of Congress. Kennedy avoided controversial issues such as civil rights and the censure of Joseph McCarthy. Though he won a Pulitzer Prize for a book *Profiles in Courage* (1956), a study of politicians who had acted on principle, some critics complained that he himself showed too much profile and not enough courage. And he shaded the truth when he claimed sole authorship of this book, which had been largely written by others. Kennedy nevertheless enjoyed an enthusiastic following, especially after his landslide re-election to the Senate in 1958.

Although he was elected president in 1960 by a razor-slim margin (see page 873), Kennedy's vitality and style captured the imagination of many Americans.

"The Best and the Brightest" In a departure from the Eisenhower administration's staid, conservative image, the new president surrounded himself with young men of intellectual verve who proclaimed that they had fresh ideas for invigorating the nation. (On the other hand, Kennedy appointed no women to significant posts.) The writer David Halberstam called these men "the best and the brightest." Secretary of Defense Robert McNamara, forty-four, had been an assistant professor at Harvard at age twenty-four and later the whiz-kid president of the Ford Motor Company. Kennedy's special assistant for national security affairs, McGeorge Bundy, forty-one, had become a dean at Harvard at age thirty-four with only a bachelor's degree. Kennedy himself was only forty-three, and his brother Robert, the attorney general, was thirty-five.

Kennedy's program, the New Frontier, was immensely ambitious, and he promised more than he could deliver: an end to racial discrimination, federal aid to farmers and to education, medical care for the elderly, and government action to halt the recession the country was suffering. But long-time members of Congress saw him and his administration as publicity hungry. Some also feared the president would seek federal aid to parochial schools. The result was the defeat of federal aid to education and of a Kennedy-sponsored boost in the minimum wage. By August 1961, eight months into his first year, it was evident that Kennedy lacked the ability to move Congress, which was largely ruled by a conservative coalition of Republicans and southern Democrats.

Still struggling to work with these conservatives, the new president pursued civil rights with a lack of vigor. On the one hand, Kennedy established the President's Committee on Equal Employment Opportunity to eliminate racial discrimination in government hiring. But on the other hand, he waited until November 1962 before finally honoring a 1960 campaign pledge to issue an executive order forbidding segregation in federally subsidized housing. Meanwhile he appointed five diehard segregationists to the federal bench in the Deep South, one of whom in open courtroom referred to blacks as "chimpanzees." Kennedy's performance disheartened civil rights advocates.

Despite the White House's lack of interest, black civil rights activists continued their struggle through the tactic of nonviolent civil disobedience. Volunteers organized by the Southern Christian Leadership Conference (SCLC), headed by Martin Luther King, Jr., deliberately violated segregation laws by sitting in at whites-only lunch counters, libraries, and bus stations throughout the South. When arrested they went to jail as an act of conscience. In May 1961 "Freedom Riders" with the racially integrated Congress of Racial Equality (CORE) boarded buses and braved attacks by southern white mobs for daring to desegregate interstate transportation. Meanwhile black students in the South were joining the Student Non-Violent Coordinating Committee (SNCC). More than any other volunteers, it was these field workers who walked the dusty back roads of Mississippi and Georgia, encouraging blacks to resist segregation and register to vote. Some SNCC volunteers were white, but most were black and many were from low-income families. These volunteers understood from experience how racism, powerlessness, and poverty intersected in the lives of Afro-Americans.

Civil Rights Movement

As the civil rights movement gained momentum in the early 1960s, President Kennedy gradually made a commitment to first-class citizenship for blacks. In September 1962 he ordered U.S. marshals to protect and assist James Meredith, the first black student to attend the University of Mississippi. Under court order the following spring, federal officials ignored the defiant governor of Alabama, George C. Wallace, and forced desegregation of the University of Alabama. In June 1963 Kennedy finally requested legislation to outlaw segregation in public accommodations.

In 1963 the center of white resistance to the civil rights movement was Birmingham, Alabama. And every evening on the television news millions of Americans watched the violence. From many sides pressure mounted on the Congress to pass civil rights legislation. Charles Moore/Black Star.

When more than 250,000 people, black and white, gathered at the Lincoln Memorial for a March on Washington that August, they did so with the knowledge that President Kennedy was at last on their side. Those congregated also heard Martin Luther King, Jr., speak. "I have a dream," he told the crowd, "that my four little children will one day live in a nation where they will not be judged by the color of their skin but by the content of their character."

Meanwhile, television news programs brought civil rights struggles into Americans' homes. The story was sometimes grisly. In 1963 Medgar Evers, director of the NAACP in Mississippi, was murdered in his own driveway. That same year police under the command of Sheriff "Bull" Connor of Birmingham, Alabama, attacked civil rights demonstrators with snarling dogs, firehoses, and cattle prods. And William Moore, a white postman who attempted his own freedom march from Baltimore to Mississippi carrying a sandwich board that read "Eat at Joe's, Both Black and White" and "Equal Rights for All," was shot and killed just after entering Alabama.

Then, while Kennedy's public accommodations bill was being held up by a Senate filibuster, two horrifying events helped to convince reluctant politicians that action on civil rights was long overdue. In September white terrorists exploded a bomb during Sunday-morning services at Birmingham's Sixteenth Street Baptist Church. Sunday school was in session, and four black girls were killed. A little more that two months later, on November 22, 1963, John Kennedy was assassinated in Dallas.

Kennedy's murder still baffles many Americans. Was the accused assassin, Lee Harvey Oswald, acting alone or as part of a conspiracy, possibly involving organized crime, pro-Castro or anti-Castro groups, or even the Central Intelligence Agency? Was he the only gunman, or were there more? What was Oswald's motive? Whatever the answers, Kennedy's death traumatized the entire nation. Then two days later, in full view of millions of TV viewers, Oswald himself was shot dead by Jack Ruby, a nightclub owner and small-time Mafia figure. The same question was asked: what was Ruby's motive?

Assassination of President Kennedy

Historians have wondered what John Kennedy would have accomplished had he lived. Although his legislative achievements were meager, he inspired idealism in Americans. When Kennedy said in his inaugural address, "Ask not what your country can do for you. Ask what you can do for your country," tens of thousands of Americans volunteered to spend two years of their lives in the Peace Corps. "We had such faith in what Kennedy was doing," recalled one volunteer, "and we all wanted to be a part of it." And the new president created a sense of national purpose through his vigorous support of the space program. Americans beamed when on February 20, 1962, Marine Lieutenant Colonel John Glenn orbited the globe in a space capsule, and they embraced Kennedy's challenge to put a man on the moon by the end of the decade.

In recent years, however, some writers have described not Kennedy's idealism, but his recklessness in world events, such as authorizing CIA assassination attempts on the life of Cuba's Premier Fidel Castro. To counteract that assessment, it is clear that

Kennedy in Retrospect

Kennedy had begun to grow as president during his last few months in office. He made a moving appeal for racial equality, and he called for reductions in Cold War tensions. Then there was the Kennedy aura. James Reston of the *New York Times* called Kennedy "a story-book President," handsome, graceful, "with poetry on his tongue and a radiant young woman at his side." Jacqueline Kennedy said that for her the Kennedy era evoked the image of Camelot. Partly because of this aura, John Kennedy came to have a higher reputation in death than he enjoyed in life. Although he had been elected in 1960 with only 49.7 percent of the popular vote, by June 1963, even before his assassination, 59 percent of those polled claimed to have voted for him. Immediately after the assassination, his retrospective landslide swelled to 65 percent. And in a bizarre way he accomplished more in death than in life. In the post-assassination atmosphere of grief and remorse, Lyndon Johnson pushed through Congress practically the entire New Frontier agenda. Johnson had done, Walter Lippmann wrote, "what President Kennedy could not have done had he lived."

JOHNSON AND THE GREAT SOCIETY

The new president, Lyndon Johnson, was a big man and a passionate one. The Senate majority leader from 1954 to 1960, he knew how to manipulate people and power to achieve his ends. "This ponderous . . . Texan knows more about the sources of power in the political world of Washington than any President in this century," wrote columnists Rowland Evans and Robert Novak. "He can be gentle and solicitous as a nurse, but as ruthless and deceptive as a riverboat gambler." In the aftermath of the assassination, Johnson determined to unite the country behind the unfulfilled legislative program of the martyred president. But more than that, he wanted to realize Roosevelt's and Truman's unmet goals. He called his new program the Great Society.

Shortly after the assassination of President Kennedy, Vice President Lyndon B. Johnson (1908–1973) was sworn in as the thirty-sixth president of the United States. The ceremony took place on the presidential plane as it returned to Washington from Dallas. Standing on Johnson's right is his wife, Lady Bird; on his left, a stunned Jacqueline Kennedy. AP/ Wide World Photos.

Johnson made civil rights his top legislative priority. "No memorial oration or eulogy," he told a joint session of Congress five days after the assassination, "could more eloquently honor President Kennedy's memory than the earliest passage of the civil rights bill." It was a happy coincidence for the civil rights movement that Johnson, a southerner, had become president. According to Clarence Mitchell, chief lobbyist for the NAACP, Johnson "made a greater contribution to giving a dignified and hopeful status to Negroes in the United States than any other President, including Lincoln, Roosevelt and Kennedy." Within months Johnson had signed into law the Civil Rights Act of 1964, which outlawed

Civil Rights Act of 1964

discrimination not only in public accommodations but also in employment on the basis of race, color, religion, sex, or national origin. An Equal Employment Opportunity Commission was established the same year to investigate and judge complaints of job discrimination. The act also authorized the government to withhold funds from public agencies that discriminated on the basis of race, and it gave the attorney general powers to guarantee voting rights and end school segregation.

Johnson enunciated another priority in January 1964, in his first State of the Union address: "The administration today, here and now, declares unconditional war on poverty." Eight months later, he signed into law the Economic Opportunity Act of

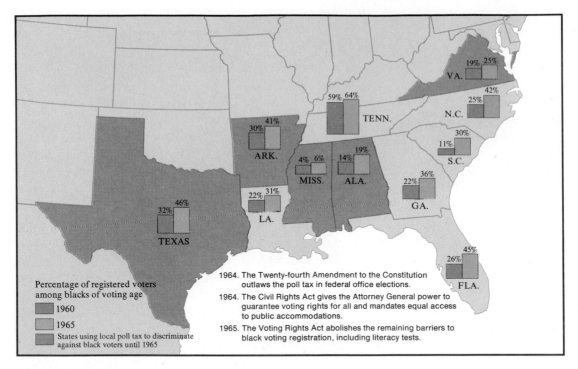

Black Voting Rights, 1960–1965

Within the map:

VA. 19% 25%
TENN. 59% 64%
N.C. 25% 42%
ARK. 30% 41%
S.C. 11% 30%
MISS. 4% 6%
ALA. 14% 19%
GA. 22% 36%
TEXAS 32% 46%
LA. 22% 31%
FLA. 26% 45%

Percentage of registered voters among blacks of voting age
- 1960
- 1965
- States using local poll tax to discriminate against black voters until 1965

1964. The Twenty-fourth Amendment to the Constitution outlaws the poll tax in federal office elections.

1964. The Civil Rights Act gives the Attorney General power to guarantee voting rights for all and mandates equal access to public accommodations.

1965. The Voting Rights Act abolishes the remaining barriers to black voting registration, including literacy tests.

1964, which allocated almost $1 billion to fight poverty. The act, which became the opening salvo in Johnson's War on Poverty, promised "to eliminate the paradox of poverty in the nation by opening to everyone the opportunity to live in decency and dignity." Finally, Johnson secured the $13.5 billion tax cut for which Kennedy had labored unsuccessfully.

In the year following Kennedy's death, Johnson sought to govern by consensus, appealing to the shared values and aspirations of the majority of the nation.

Election of 1964

Judging by his lopsided victory over his Republican opponent in 1964, Senator Barry Goldwater of Arizona, he succeeded. Johnson garnered 61 percent of the popular vote and the electoral votes of all but six states. Goldwater's narrowness certainly enhanced Johnson's appeal. The Republican candidate alienated voters by suggesting that Social Security be voluntary and the Tennessee Valley Authority be abolished, and he appeared reckless and provocative when he advocated using nuclear weapons in Vietnam. Republican leaders from the liberal eastern wing of the party either refused to support Goldwater or gave him half-hearted endorsements. He seemed to have solid support in only a few states in the Southwest and South.

Riding on Johnson's coattails, the Democrats won staggering majorities in both the House (295 to 140) and the Senate (68 to 32). Johnson knew that the moment for further reform had arrived. "Hurry, boys, hurry," Johnson told his staff just after the election. "Get that legislation up to the Hill and out. Eighteen months from now ol' Landslide Lyndon will be Lame-Duck Lyndon." Congress responded in 1965 and 1966 with the most sweeping reform legislation since 1935. Skillfully guided by Johnson, the liberal Democratic majorities passed a remarkable 69 percent of the president's legislative proposals. The powerful conservative coalition of Republicans and southern Democrats, which had had its way on 74 percent of House roll-call votes in 1961 and 63 percent in 1963, was victorious on only 25 percent of the votes in 1965.

Three bills enacted in 1965 were legislative milestones. The Medicare program insured the elderly against medical and hospital bills. The Elementary and Secondary Education Act became the first general program of federal aid to education. And the Voting Rights Act of 1965 empowered the attorney general to supervise voter registration in areas where fewer than half the minority residents of voting age were registered (see map). When Johnson became president, only one-fourth of the South's black population was registered to vote; when he left office in 1969 the proportion was approaching two-thirds. Even in the most resistant states, that trend has continued. Only 6.7 percent of Mississippi's black citizens were registered to vote in 1964; in 1981 the figure was 70 percent.

Other accomplishments during Johnson's presidency included establishment of the Department of Housing and Urban Development and the National Foundation on the Arts and Humanities; water and air quality improvement acts; the Teacher Corps to work in impoverished school districts; college scholarships and loans; liberalization of immigration laws; and appropriations for the most ambitious federal housing program since 1949, including rent supplements to low-income families. And in 1968 Johnson signed his third civil rights act, banning racial and religious discrimination in the sale and rental of housing. Another provision of this legislation, known as the Indian Bill of Rights, extended those constitutional protections to reservation Indians living under tribal self-government.

Even more ambitious was Johnson's War on Poverty. Because the gross national product had increased, Johnson and his advisers reasoned that the government **War on Poverty** could expect a "fiscal dividend" of several billion dollars in additional tax revenues. They decided to spend the extra money to wipe out poverty through education and job training programs. As the War on Poverty evolved in 1965 and 1966, it included the Job Corps and Neighborhood Youth Corps, to provide marketable skills, work experience, remedial education, and counseling for young people; the Work-Experience Program for unemployed fathers and mothers; Project Head Start, to prepare low-income preschoolers for grade school; and Upward Bound, for high school students from low-income families who aspired to a college education. In an innovation that was to arouse the ire of mayors and city councils, these programs encouraged "maximum feasible participation" by the poor in the administration of community action programs. Other antipoverty programs were Legal Services for the Poor; Volunteers in Service to America (VISTA); and the Model Cities program,

which directed federal funds toward upgrading employment, housing, education, and health in targeted neighborhoods.

Confusion abounded in this ambitious program. Not even R. Sargent Shriver, who as head of the Office of Economic Opportunity (OEO) administered the War on Poverty, could deny this. "It's like we went down to Cape Kennedy and launched a half dozen rockets at once," he later conceded. Another serious criticism was that the War on Poverty did little to reduce suffering in the countryside or to check the South-to-North migration that exacerbated the already overwhelming northern urban problems. In a Brookings Institution study, James Sundquist noted that "when it comes to the solution of the poverty problem, a good many of the urban poverty thinkers have written off the rural areas and have concluded that the only way to deal with rural poverty is to let the people move and then handle them in the cities." Another group that remained poor despite the government's antipoverty efforts included those—mostly children—living in female-headed families, who comprised 40 percent of the poor in the United States. While the booming economy from 1963 to 1969 lifted 12 million people in male-headed families out of poverty, it stranded there 11 million in families headed by women, the same number as in 1963.

Still, the War on Poverty, in tandem with a rising gross national product, substantially alleviated hunger and suffering in the United States. The tax cut and fresh infusions of federal funds for **Successes in Reducing Poverty** defense ended the recession of 1960 and 1961, and beginning in the mid-1960s, the social welfare budget soared. Between 1965 and 1970 federal spending for Social Security, health, welfare, and education more than doubled. During the same years, the GNP leapt from $685 billion to $977 billion. Some of this prosperity trickled down to the poor, but of more direct importance in eradicating poverty was the government's funding of specific welfare programs. The result was a startling reduction in the number of poor people, from 25 percent of the population in 1962 to 11 percent in 1973. Particularly fortunate were the elderly, who benefited from large increases in Social Security benefits; poverty among the elderly dropped from about 40 percent in 1960 to 16 percent in 1974.

The War on Poverty lifted many people out of suffering. But this Harlem woman, photographed with her children in 1966, had a bleak future. Being black, a woman, and a single mother all contributed to her poverty.   John Launois/ Black Star.

liberalism. Its liberal majority included Justices Hugo Black, William Brennan, and William O. Douglas in addition to Chief Justice Earl Warren. After the 1954 and 1955 school desegregation cases (see page 860), the Warren Court did not roil the political waters for the remainder of the 1950s. But the next decade was to be markedly different. According to one constitutional historian, in the 1960s the United States "changed irrevocably," and the Warren Court was "midwife to that change—if not its sire."

In 1962 the Court began handing down a series of liberal decisions. In *Baker v. Carr* (1962) and subsequent rulings, it declared that the principle of "one person, one vote" must prevail at both state and national levels. This decision required the reapportionment of state legislatures so that each representative would serve the same number of constituents. Prior to this decision, some legislators from sparsely settled rural areas represented only half as many people as their counterparts from populous urban areas. The Court also outlawed required prayers in public schools, explaining that such practices placed an "indirect coercive pressure upon religious minorities" (1962). In 1963 it struck down a Pennsylvania law requiring daily Bible readings in all public schools. Some religious groups denounced these decisions, and a few communities, feeling they were losing their freedoms, announced their refusal to comply.

The Court also attacked the constitutional basis of McCarthyism, ruling in 1965 that a person need not register with the government as a member of a subversive organization, for to do so would violate constitutional safeguards against self-incrimination. It also ruled on birth control, holding in *Griswold v. Connecticut* (1965) that a state law prohibiting the use of contraceptives by married persons violated "a marital right of privacy" and was unconstitutional. The Court upheld the Civil Rights Act of 1964 and the Voting Rights Act of 1965, and it broadened the interpretation of the Fourteenth Amendment by outlawing segregation in private businesses. In *Jones v. Mayer* (1968) it decided that private discrimination in the rental or sale of housing was prohibited by the Civil Rights Act of 1866. In ruling the 1866 act constitutional under the Thirteenth Amendment, the Court opened new avenues for the pursuit of legal battles for equal rights. With its de-

Civil Rights Rulings

Despite the War on Poverty's successes, the period of liberal ascendancy it represented was short lived, with its legislative achievements occurring from 1964 to 1966. Disillusioned with America's deepening involvement in Vietnam (see Chapter 32), many of Johnson's allies began to reject both him and his liberal consensus. But one branch of government continued the liberal tradition—the Supreme Court.

THE WARREN COURT

In the volatile 1960s, the Supreme Court was disposed by political sentiment and a belief in judicial activism to play a major role in the resurgence of

cisions on prayer and contraception, the Court had deeply affected people's personal lives. And in other rulings that particularly upset conservatives, the Court decreed that books, magazines, and films could not be banned as obscene unless they were "found to be utterly without redeeming social value."

Perhaps most controversial was the Court's transformation of the criminal justice system. Beginning with *Gideon* v. *Wainwright* (1963), the Court ruled that a poor person charged with a felony had the right to a state-appointed lawyer. In *Escobedo* v. *Illinois* (1964), it decreed that the accused had the right to counsel during interrogation and could remain silent. And in *Miranda* v. *Arizona* (1966), it added that police had to inform criminal suspects that they could see a lawyer and remain silent and that any statements they made could be used against them. Critics denounced the decisions as victories for criminals, and the John Birch Society, a right-wing organization, began a campaign to impeach Earl Warren.

Despite demands for Warren's removal, most constitutional historians judge him to have been perhaps the most influential chief justice in the nation's history. Whether or not one approved of the Warren Court, which ended with his retirement in 1969, there was no denying its impact on the American people. In 1983 Bernard Schwartz, constitutional law professor at New York University, made this appraisal: "In expanding civil liberties, broadening political freedom, extending the franchise, reinforcing freedoms of speech, assembly, and religion, limiting the power of the politicians in smoke-filled rooms, [and] defining the limits of police power, the Warren Court had no equal in American history."

RACE RIOTS AND THE MOVEMENT TOWARD BLACK POWER

Even as the civil rights movement registered legal and constitutional victories, some activists began to grumble that the federal government was not to be trusted. During the Mississippi Summer Project of 1964, hundreds of college-age volunteers from the North had joined SNCC and CORE field workers to establish "freedom schools" for black children. Many of these volunteers believed that the Federal Bureau of Investigation was hostile to the civil rights movement. They alleged that FBI Director J. Edgar Hoover was a racist, and they were disturbed by rumors, later confirmed, that Hoover had wiretapped and bugged Martin Luther King, Jr.'s rooms and planted stories in the newspapers about his sexual improprieties. Why, activists asked themselves, had Johnson allowed Hoover to remain in office?

Indeed, some FBI informants had not only joined the Ku Klux Klan; they had reportedly become leaders of the terrorist group. One of them had organized several atrocities, including the bombing of Birmingham's Sixteenth Street Baptist Church in 1963. Small wonder that during summer 1964 there was an upsurge in racist violence in the South, particularly in Mississippi. White vigilantes bombed and burned two dozen black churches there between June and October, and three civil rights workers were murdered in Philadelphia, Mississippi, by a group including sheriff's deputies. Instead of protecting the civil rights workers, southern police had assaulted and arrested them.

Violent Attacks on Civil Rights Workers

Amid the terror, SNCC volunteers joined with black Mississippians to establish the Mississippi Freedom Democratic party (MFDP) and sent an opposition delegation to the Democratic national convention. Arguing that the MFDP supported civil rights, while the state's regular Democratic organization was vehemently segregationist, the MFDP demanded that the convention honor its credentials. But Johnson, fearful of alienating southern whites and more committed to consensus than to civil rights, offered the MFDP only two token at-large seats. Johnson's offer was inconsistent with his earlier civil rights actions, and Democratic commitment to racial equality was thrown into question.

The year 1964 also brought the first of the "long hot summers" of race riots in northern cities. In Harlem and Rochester, New York, and in several New Jersey cities, black anger exploded. A cleaning woman in Harlem expressed her rage. When the riot

Explosion of Black Anger began, "something happened to me. I felt like something was crawling in me, like the whole damn world was no good, and the little kids and the big ones and all of us was going to get killed. . . . And I see the cops are white and I was crying. . . . And I took this pop bottle . . . and I threw it down on the cops and I was crying and laughing."

Whites wondered why blacks were venting their frustration in violence at at time when real progress was being made in the civil rights struggle. Part of the reason was that the movement had been largely southern in focus, geared to abolishing Jim Crow and black disfranchisement. In the North public accommodations and the vote had been available to Afro-Americans for decades, but blacks were still living in deep poverty. The black median income was little more than half that of whites: for every dollar the white worker took home in 1964, the black worker earned 54 cents. Black unemployment in the mid-1960s was twice that of whites, and for black males between eighteen and twenty-five it was five times as high. Many black families, particularly those headed solely by women, lived in perpetual poverty, and their numbers were increasing rapidly. One reason was that Aid to Families with Dependent Children (AFDC), part of the 1935 Social Security Act that had been expanded in 1950 to include payments to the mothers as well as their dependent children, would provide these payments only if there were no able-bodied man in the household. As a result, some unemployed men left home rather than make their families ineligible for AFDC. But more important, the payments themselves were inadequate to cover a family's rent, utility bills, and household expenses, let alone its food. On the basis of food budgets in 1970, it was estimated that over 60 percent of America's black children were being raised in poverty.

As northern blacks learned of the economic and civil rights gains of the 1960s, they wondered when they would benefit from the Great Society. Unlike southern blacks, northern blacks made up a small percentage of the population and tended to be concentrated in the inner cities. When blacks looked around the ghettos in which they lived, they knew their circumstances were deteriorating. Their neighborhoods were more segregated than ever, for whites had responded to the black migration from the South by fleeing to the suburbs. And as inner-city neighborhoods became all black, so did the neighborhood schools. As one writer commented, "It doesn't cost anything to move a few feet along a hamburger counter to make room for a Negro. But the cost—economic, social, psychological—of abolishing forever a Negro ghetto of half a million souls is only now becoming apparent."

If 1964 was fiery and violent, 1965 was even more so. In August blacks gutted the Los Angeles neighborhood of Watts; thirty-four people were killed (see map). Unlike the race riots of 1919

Watts Race Riot and 1943, white mobs did not provoke the violence; instead, blacks exploded in anger over their joblessness and lack of opportunity, looting white-owned stores, setting fires, and throwing rocks. "Get Whitey!" they screamed. "Burn, Baby, Burn!" "What white Americans have never fully understood," stated the Kerner Commission in its report several years later, "but what the Negro can never forget—is that white society is deeply implicated in the ghetto. White institutions created it, white institutions maintain it, and white society condones it."

Other cities exploded in riots between 1966 and 1968. Besides expressing their rage, rioters increasingly sought the material wealth on display in store windows. "On Twelfth Street," a black resident of Detroit explained during the 1967 riot, "everybody was out, Mama, Papa, the kids, it was like an outing. . . . The rebellion—it was all caused by the [TV] commercials. I mean you saw all those things you'd never be able to get. . . . Men's clothing, furniture, appliances, color TV,"

It was obvious that many blacks, especially in the North, had begun to question whether the nonviolent civil rights movement had ever addressed their needs. In 1963 Martin Luther King, Jr., had appealed to whites' humanitarian instincts in his "I have a dream" speech. But another voice was beginning to be heard, one that urged blacks to seize their freedom "by any means necessary." It was the voice of Malcolm X, a one-time pimp and street hustler who, while in prison, had converted to the Nation of Islam religion, commonly known as the Black Muslims.

The Black Muslims, a small sect that espoused

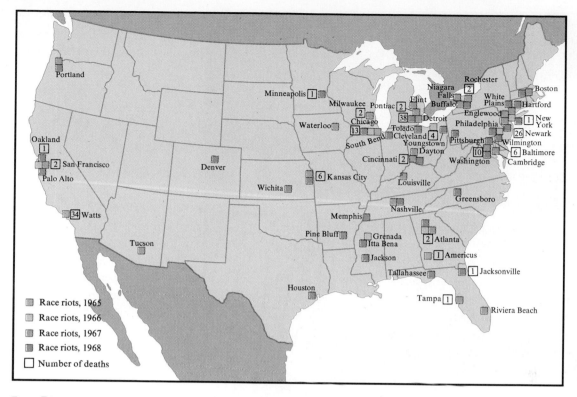

Race Riots, 1965–1968

Map legend:
- Race riots, 1965
- Race riots, 1966
- Race riots, 1967
- Race riots, 1968
- Number of deaths

Cities labeled on map: Portland, Minneapolis 1, Rochester 2, Boston, Milwaukee, Pontiac 2, Niagara Falls, Flint, Buffalo, White Plains, Hartford, Chicago 2, Detroit 38, Englewood, New York 1, Waterloo, Toledo, Cleveland 4, Philadelphia, Newark 26, Oakland 1, South Bend 13, Youngstown, Pittsburgh, Wilmington, San Francisco 2, Cincinnati 2, Dayton, Washington 10, Baltimore 6, Palo Alto, Cambridge, Denver, Kansas City 6, Louisville, Wichita, Greensboro, Watts 34, Nashville, Memphis, Tucson, Pine Bluff, Grenada, Itta Bena, Atlanta 2, Jackson, Americus 1, Tallahassee, Jacksonville 1, Houston, Tampa 1, Riviera Beach

separatism from white society, condemned the "white devil" as the chief source of evil in the world. They

Malcolm X attempted to dissociate themselves from white society and exhorted blacks to lead sober lives and practice thrift. Unlike Martin Luther King, Jr., they advocated violence in self-defense. By the early 1960s Malcolm X had become their chief spokesperson, and his advice was straightforward: "If someone puts a hand on you, send him to the cemetery."

Malcolm X was murdered in a hail of bullets in February 1965; his assassins were Black Muslims who believed he had betrayed their cause. It was true that he had modified some of his ideas just before his death. He had met whites who were not devils, he said, and he had expressed cautious support for the nonviolent civil rights movement. Still, for both blacks and whites, Malcolm X symbolized black defiance and self-respect. A powerful figure in life, in death he would become even more of a hero to increasing numbers of black nationalists and proponents of Black Power.

Although Martin Luther King, Jr., continued to be the most admired leader of the civil rights movement, many younger blacks began to question not only his tactic of nonviolence but

Black Power his dream of racial integration. In 1966 Stokely Carmichael, chairman of SNCC, called on blacks to assert Black Power. Carmichael believed that in order to be truly free from white oppression, blacks had to control their own institutions—businesses, politics, schools. They had to elect black candidates and teach black students in black schools. Soon organizations that had been committed to racial integration and nonviolence began to embrace Black Power. SNCC and CORE purged white members and repudiated integration, arguing that black people needed power, not white friendship.

The wellspring of this new militance was black nationalism, the concept that black peoples everywhere in the world shared a unique history and cultural heritage that set them apart from whites. College students pressed for black studies programs, and blacks began to call themselves black or Afro-American

Malcolm X (1925–1965), a one-time pimp and street hustler, became the leading spokesman not only for the Black Muslims but also for many black nationalists and separatists. His autobiography, published after his death, became a classic statement of black pride.   Eve Arnold/Magnum Photos.

rather than Negro. More than at any time since the 1920s, Afro-Americans saw themselves as a nation within a nation.

To white America, one of the most fearsome of the new black groups was the Black Panther Party. Armed and wearing leather jackets, Panther leaders Bobby Seale and Huey Newton dedicated themselves to destroying capitalism. What worried white parents was that some of their own children agreed with the Panthers. Denouncing the major political parties, big business and big labor, middle-class affluence and the suburban lifestyle, even the American dream itself, this vocal minority of the baby-boom generation set out to "change the system."

THE NEW LEFT AND THE COUNTERCULTURE

"I'm tired of reading history," a philosophy student at the University of California complained in a letter to a friend in early 1964. "I want to make it." By autumn of that year, Mario Savio would realize his ambition as the leader of the Free Speech Movement (FSM), and Berkeley would become a synonym for the campus unrest of the 1960s.

In many ways the University of California in 1964 was a model university, with a worldwide reputation for excellence. Its chancellor, the economist Clark

Free Speech Movement

Kerr, had written *The Uses of the University*, in which he likened the university to a big business. But that was what bothered some students. Berkeley, a "multiversity" with tens of thousands of students, had become hopelessly impersonal. "I am a student," rang one lament of the FSM. "Do not fold, spindle, or mutilate."

After teaching in SNCC's Mississippi Summer Project, Savio and other students had returned to Berkeley suspecting that the same power structure that dominated blacks' lives also controlled the bureaucratic machinery of the university. "Last summer I went to Mississippi to join the struggle there for civil rights. This fall I am engaged in another phase of the same struggle, this time in Berkeley. . . . The same rights are at stake in both places," Savio wrote. The struggle began in September 1964, when the university administration banned political recruitment in Sproul Plaza, the students' traditional gathering place. Savio and other students defied Kerr's ban; the administration suspended them or had them arrested. On October 1 several thousand students surrounded a police car in which a militant was being held, immobilizing it for thirty-two hours. Then in December the FSM seized and occupied the main administration building. Governor Pat Brown dispatched state police to Berkeley, and over eight hundred people were arrested. Angry students shut down classes for several days in protest. By the end of the decade, the activism born at Berkeley would spread to hundreds of other campuses.

Over two years before the confrontation in Berkeley, another group of students had met in Port Huron, Michigan, to form Students for a Democratic Society

Students for a Democratic Society (SDS)

(SDS). Like their leaders, Tom Hayden and Al Haber, most SDS members were white college students, the children of middle-class Americans. In their platform, the Port Huron Statement, they condemned racism, poverty amidst plenty, the antidemocratic tendencies of powerful corporations, and "the enclosing fact of the Cold War," symbolized by the hydrogen bomb. Above all, SDS called upon America to practice its democratic

ideals, not just pay them lip service. SDS sought nothing less than the revitalization of democracy through the return of power to the people.

Inspired by the Free Speech Movement and SDS, a minority of students joined the New Left. Although the people in the New Left were united in their

New Left

hatred of racism and the Vietnam War, they were divided in other ways. Indeed, the New Left was not a single organization or even a single movement. Some people were Marxists, others black nationalists, anarchists, or pacifists. Some believed in pursuing social change through negotiation; others were revolutionaries who regarded compromise as impossible.

In the wake of the New Left appeared a phenomenon that observers called the counterculture. Revolu-

Counter-cultural Revolution

tionary figures like Mao Zedong and Fidel Castro became campus idols, "Mao caps" a cult uniform, and "right on" an all-purpose greeting. Led by Timothy Leary, the LSD prophet, millions of students experimented with marijuana, amphetamines, and hallucinogenic drugs.

But it was music more than anything else that reflected the new attitudes. In 1962, the year the founders of SDS gathered at Port Huron, four young musicians from Liverpool, England, recorded "Love Me Do." Long before the Beatles sang "you say you want a revolution," it was evident that their music had inspired one. Soon music was the chief vehicle for the countercultural assault on the status quo. Barry McGuire warned of nuclear holocaust in "Eve of Destruction," and Bob Dylan promised revolutionary answers "blowing in the wind." Young people cheered Jimi Hendrix, who sang of life in a drug-induced "purple haze"; Janis Joplin, who brought black blues to white Americans; and the Buffalo Springfield, who urged youth to stop and "look what's goin' down." Unlike the 1950s counterparts, the rock superstars of the 1960s acknowledged their roots in black rhythm-and-blues. Joplin, who moved crowds with her version of "Ball and Chain," was quick to credit its composer, Big Mama Thornton.

Rock festivals became cultural happenings, the most famous of which was Woodstock (1969), an upstate New York festival that attracted 400,000 people. The huge crowd endured several days of rain and mud together, without shelter and without violence. Some

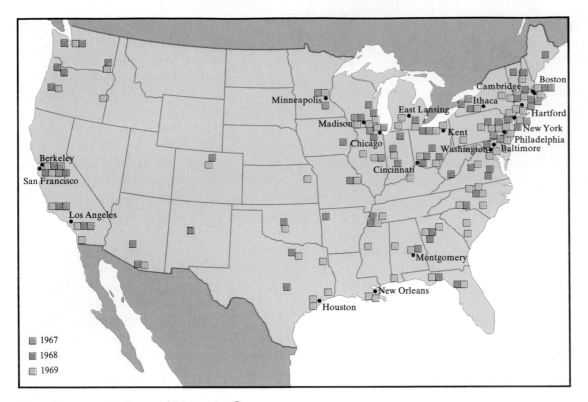

Disturbances on College and University Campuses, 1967–1969

among them began to dream of a peaceful "Woodstock nation" based on love, drugs, and rock music. Beatle John Lennon expressed it best: "All we are saying is give peace a chance."

While some youths sought alternative experiences through drugs and music, others tried to construct alternative ways of life. Among the most conspicuous were the hippies. In the Haight-Ashbury section of San Francisco, "flower children" created an urban subculture as distinctive as that of any Chinatown or Little Italy. "Hashbury" inspired numerous other communal living experiments. Throughout the country, hitchhikers hit the road in search of communes, America, and themselves.

Just as the New Left attracted a minority of students, so the counterculture represented only a small proportion of American youth. But to disconcerted middle-class parents, hippies seemed to be everywhere. Parents carped about long hair, love beads, and patched jeans. They complained that "acid rock" was loud, discordant, even savage. And they feared their chil-

Drugs and Sex

dren would suffer lifelong damage from drugs. Perhaps most disturbing were the casual sexual mores their children adopted, partly as a result of the availability of birth-control pills. For many young people, living together no longer equaled living in sin. And as attitudes toward premarital sex changed, so did notions about pornography, homosexuality, sex roles, and familial relationships.

For both cultural and political reasons, the slogan "Make Love, Not War" became popular at mid-decade. As the war in Vietnam escalated, the New Left and the counterculture discovered a common cause. Students held teach-ins on the war—open forums for discussion among students, professors, and guest speakers.

Thousands of young men also expressed their opposition to the war by fleeing the draft. By the end of 1972 more than 30,000 draft resisters were living in Canada, an additional 10,000 had fled to Sweden, Mexico, and other countries, and 10,000 more were living under false identities in the United States. During the war half a million men committed draft violations, including an estimated quarter-million who

During the March on Washington in 1967, this demonstrator attempted to disarm the troops by placing flowers in their rifle barrels. Bernie Boston.

never registered and another 110,000 who burned their draft cards in protest.

Marches and demonstrations against the war became a popular protest tactic (see map). In April 1965, 25,000 people marched on the White House, and in October the National Committee to End the War in Vietnam mobilized over 80,000 in demonstrations across the country. During the next two years SDS-led groups organized antiwar marches of several hundred thousand people in New York and San Francisco. And in October 1967, the March on the Pentagon of 100,000 people confirmed government officials' fears that the convergence of student activists, the New Left, and the counterculture threatened the nation's warmaking powers.

Antiwar Protests

By this time growing numbers of Americans, young and old, had quit believing their elected leaders. Though President Johnson claimed the United States was fighting for honorable reasons, people wondered what goal could justify the murder of Vietnamese women and children. As troop levels increased, many recalled ruefully that they had voted for Johnson as the more cautious of the two candidates in 1964. By 1968 almost half a million American soldiers were stationed in Vietnam, and Johnson's credibility had vanished.

1968: A YEAR OF PROTEST, VIOLENCE, AND LOSS

As stormy and violent as the years from 1963 through 1967 had been, many Americans were still trying to downplay the nation's distress in hopes it would go away. "We were in a kind of national sleepwalk," the novelist John Hersey wrote, "aware, on a dream level, of black rage; of the undertow of

Vietnam . . . of the way Lyndon Johnson's credibility gap was beginning to show." But in 1968 the sleepers awoke to a series of violent quakes.

The first shock hit in late January 1968, when the U.S.S. *Pueblo*, a navy intelligence ship, was captured by the North Koreans near the port of Wonsan; not until Christmas of that year would the crew of eighty-two be released. On January 30 came the Tet offensive in Vietnam (see page 921). For the first time many Americans believed they might lose the war. Meanwhile, American casualties had been climbing. In a two-week period in May more than eleven hundred U.S. soldiers died, more by far than in any previous two weeks. In fact, more Americans died in the first six months of 1968 than in all of 1967; on July 4, 1968, total American fatalities surpassed thirty thousand.

Controversy over the war deepened. Within the Democratic party, two men rose to challenge Johnson for the 1968 presidential nomination. One of them, the war hawk Governor George C. Wallace of Alabama, exhorted Americans to "stand up for America." The other, Senator Eugene McCarthy of Minnesota, entered the New Hampshire primary solely to contest Johnson's war policies. On March 12 McCarthy won 42 percent of the popular vote and 20 of 24 convention delegates. Yet another Democrat, Senator Robert F. Kennedy of New York, would soon enter the fray.

On March 31, President Johnson went on national television and announced a scaling-down of the bombing in North Vietnam. Then he hurled a political thunderbolt—he would not be a candidate for reelection.

Less than a week later a white assassin named James Earl Ray shot and killed Martin Luther King, Jr., in Memphis. People still wonder whether Ray was a deranged racist acting alone or a pawn in an organized conspiracy. Whatever his motive, his crime aroused instant rage in the nation's ghettos. Blacks rioted in 168 cities and towns, looting and burning white businesses and properties. Thirty-four blacks and five whites died in the violence. Tough talk flared from Maryland Governor Spiro Agnew, who denounced Baltimore's black leaders for not controlling "your people," and from Chicago's Mayor Richard

Assassination of Martin Luther King, Jr.

Daley, who ordered police to shoot to kill arsonists. The terror provoked a white backlash against blacks, and hatred mounted on both sides. "When white America killed Dr. King last night, she declared war on us," charged Stokely Carmichael.

Student protests multiplied that spring not only in the United States but in Paris, Mexico City, and elsewhere in the world. Between January and June 1968 over two hundred demonstrations rocked colleges and universities across the country. Students protested university involvement in the military-industrial complex. In New York students at Columbia University occupied the president's office and other buildings for ten days. On April 30, at the request of Columbia's president, one thousand club-swinging city policemen stormed the occupied buildings, injuring 150 protesters and onlookers.

Most Americans, of course, were not personally threatened by the violence. But nearly all owned TV sets and watched the evening news. As two scholars wrote in the *Columbia Journalism Review*, it was the nightly news that "made social disorganization a realistic threat to the comfortably-off middle-class urbanites, to suburbanites, to rural residents—to all those, in short, who have seldom faced robbery, mugging, protest marching . . . black power salutes, or perhaps even hostile questions about their values."

In April and May Gallup polls reported Robert Kennedy the front-running presidential candidate among Democrats. Kennedy had lost to McCarthy in the Oregon primary but won in California that June. While celebrating his victory in Los Angeles's Ambassador Hotel, he decided to take a short cut through the kitchen to a press conference. Suddenly a young man named Sirhan Sirhan stepped forward with a .22-caliber revolver and fired repeatedly at Kennedy. The assassin, it turned out, was an Arab nationalist who despised Kennedy for his unwavering support of Israel. But the cumulative effect of so many assassinations made some Americans wonder and worry. Whenever a charismatic, progressive leader rose to prominence, it seemed, he was mowed down.

Assassination of Robert Kennedy

The poor were especially grief-stricken by the assassination, because Kennedy had befriended blacks and Mexican Americans. When Cesar Chavez led

Americans mourned when Robert F. Kennedy was assassinated. Earlier in 1968, Kennedy had joined Cesar Chavez as the Mexican-American leader of the United Farm Workers ended a fast.   UPI/Bettmann Newsphotos.

the United Farm Workers' strike against growers in 1965, Kennedy had traveled to California to stand with them. Antiwar liberals also felt they had lost a friend in Kennedy.

Violence erupted again in August at the Democratic national convention in Chicago. The Democrats were divided among supporters of Vice President Hubert Humphrey (Lyndon Johnson's candidate), peace candidate Eugene McCarthy, and Senator George McGovern of South Dakota, who had inherited some of Kennedy's support. Adding to the dissension were several mule-drawn wagons driven by blacks from the Poor People's Campaign; thousands of antiwar protesters; and the Youth International Party, or Yippies, who had traveled to Chicago for a Festival of Life, which they contrasted pointedly to "Lyndon and Hubert's celebration of death."

The Chicago police force was still in the psychological grip of Mayor Daley's shoot-to-kill directive. Twelve thousand police were assigned to twelve-hour shifts and another twelve thousand army troops and National Guardsmen were on call with rifles, bazookas, and flamethrowers. On Michigan Avenue, in front of the Conrad Hilton Hotel, they attacked, wading into ranks of demonstrators, reporters, and TV camera operators. Throughout the nation viewers watched as club-swinging police beat protesters to the ground. When onlookers rushed to shield the injured, they too were clubbed. Inside the convention hall, Senator Abraham Ribicoff of Connecticut put aside his prepared speech to denounce "those Gestapo tactics in the streets of Chicago."

**Violence
at the
Democratic
Convention**

The Democratic convention nominated Humphrey for president and Senator Edmund Muskie of Maine for vice president. Like Johnson and Kennedy before him, Humphrey was a political descendant of the New Deal, committed to the welfare state and supported by a coalition of northern liberals, big-city bosses, blacks, and union members. First elected to the Senate from Minnesota in 1948, Humphrey was known not just as a champion of civil rights, but as a supporter of the Cold War doctrine of containment that had led to Vietnam. Humphrey's unstinting public support of the war angered some and saddened others, who repudiated him as the candidate of Johnson, Daley, and the war.

The Republicans selected Richard M. Nixon as their presidential nominee. After his defeat by Kennedy in 1960 and his loss in the California gubernatorial race in 1962, Nixon's political career had seemed to be over. But he spent much of the decade campaigning for fellow Republicans and had built up credits with party regulars and officeholders around the country. In 1968 Nixon cashed in his credits and defeated Governors Nelson Rockefeller of New York and Ronald Reagan of California for the nomination. For his running mate, Nixon chose Governor Spiro Agnew of Maryland.

There was little voter enthusiasm for either Humphrey or Nixon. A Gallup poll taken at the time of the convention showed that 66 percent of Americans believed the United States should turn over more of the fighting to the South Vietnamese and begin withdrawing its troops. Not only independents and McCarthy followers favored an end to hostilities: large majorities of Humphrey and Nixon supporters agreed. Yet both major candidates endorsed the continuation of the war while negotiations stalled in Paris. In 1968, the nation was deeply divided between the "doves" and the "hawks" (who favored escalation of the war). The Gallup Poll reported that 41 percent of the people described themselves as doves and 41 percent as hawks, with 18 percent holding no opinion.

Election of 1968

The candidate with the most appeal for conservatives was George Wallace, the nominee of the American Independent party, who argued that the United States should bomb North Vietnam to rubble with nuclear weapons. Wallace also appealed to people concerned about law and order, code words for the suppression of protest. If a civil rights protester ever lay down in front of his car, Wallace declared, he would drive over the person.

When the votes were tabulated, Nixon emerged the winner. Just four years after the Goldwater debacle, the Republicans had captured the White House, though by the slimmest of margins. Wallace collected almost 10 million votes, or 13.5 percent of the total, the best performance by a third party since 1924. His strong showing made Nixon a minority president, elected with only 43 percent of the popular vote (see map). Moreover, the Democrats maintained control of the House (243 to 192) and the Senate (58 to 42). Soon there would be a new president and a new decade, but Americans doubted whether they could heal the wounds of war, poverty, racism, sexism, black rage, youthful disaffection, and the shattered promise of the American dream.

THE REBIRTH OF FEMINISM

During the turbulence of the 1960s, another liberation movement gained momentum, at first quietly and then on the picket line. Following the adoption of the Nineteenth Amendment in 1920, the women's rights movement had languished. But in the 1960s feminism was reborn. In *The Feminine Mystique* (1963), Betty Friedan wrote that the American home had become a "comfortable concentration camp." TV advertisers, magazine writers, beauticians, and psychiatrists had conspired to create the image of a woman "gaily content in a world of bedroom, kitchen, sex, babies and home." Any woman who was dissatisfied with such surroundings was considered neurotic. But as Friedan pointed out, the woman who spent her life in a world of children sacrificed her adult frame of reference and sometimes her very identity. Friedan quoted a young mother: "I've tried everything women are supposed to do—hobbies, gardening, pickling, canning, and

The Feminine Mystique

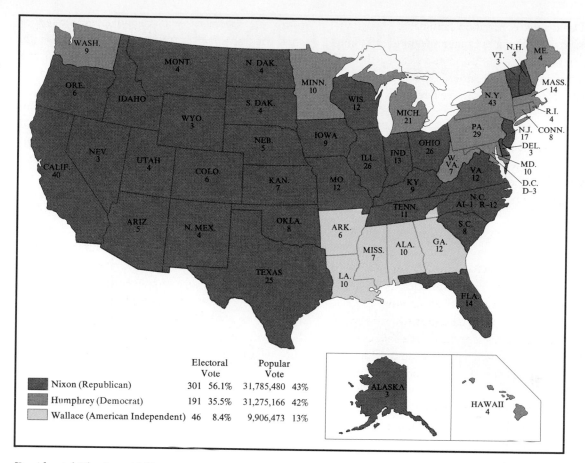

Presidential Election, 1968

<table>
<tr><th></th><th>Electoral
Vote</th><th></th><th>Popular
Vote</th><th></th></tr>
<tr><td>Nixon (Republican)</td><td>301</td><td>56.1%</td><td>31,785,480</td><td>43%</td></tr>
<tr><td>Humphrey (Democrat)</td><td>191</td><td>35.5%</td><td>31,275,166</td><td>42%</td></tr>
<tr><td>Wallace (American Independent)</td><td>46</td><td>8.4%</td><td>9,906,473</td><td>13%</td></tr>
</table>

being very social with my neighbors. . . . I love the kids and Bob and my home. . . . But I'm desperate. I begin to feel that I have no personality. . . . Who am I?" Friedan's book inspired the founding in 1966 of the National Organization for Women (NOW). A reform organization, NOW battled for "equal rights in partnership with men" by lobbying for legislation and testing laws in the courts.

Not long after NOW's formation, a new generation of radical feminists emerged—once again, the baby boom was making an impact on American life. Most

Radical Feminism

were white and well educated; many were the daughters of working mothers. Most had been raised in the era of sexual liberation, in which birth-control pills and other contraceptives were taken for granted. The intellectual ferment of their movement produced a new feminist literature: Shulamith

Firestone's *The Dialectic of Sex*; Kate Millett's *Sexual Politics*; Robin Morgan's *Sisterhood Is Powerful*. Feminists challenged everything from women's economic, political, and legal inequality to sexual double standards and sex-role stereotypes. And unlike the members of NOW, the radical feminists practiced direct action, as when they picketed the 1968 Miss America contest in Atlantic City. One woman auctioned off an effigy of Miss America: "Gentlemen, I offer you the 1969 model. . . . She walks. She talks. She smiles on cue. *And* she does the housework." Into the "freedom trash can" the pickets dumped false eyelashes, curlers, girdles, and *Playboy*. These feminists were protesting the view of women as servants and sex objects who were pressured to conform to male-imposed "beauty standards." They were also practicing "personal politics." "There is no private domain of a person's life that is not political," explained Charlotte Bunch, a

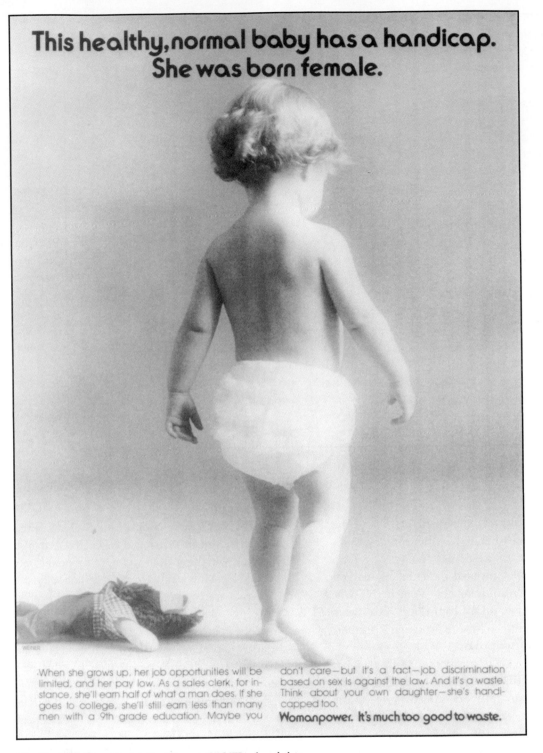

This healthy, normal baby has a handicap.
She was born female.

When she grows up, her job opportunities will be limited, and her pay low. As a sales clerk, for instance, she'll earn half of what a man does. If she goes to college, she'll still earn less than many men with a 9th grade education. Maybe you don't care—but it's a fact—job discrimination based on sex is against the law. And it's a waste. Think about your own daughter—she's handicapped too.

Womanpower. It's much too good to waste.

The National Organization for Women (NOW), founded in 1966, went from 1,000 members in 1967 to 40,000 members in 1974. NOW's advertisements about sexual inequality were simple and to the point.   NOW Legal Defense and Education Fund, Inc.

feminist, "and there is no political issue that is not ultimately personal."

Many radical feminists had struggled earlier for black civil rights, but they had discovered they were second-class citizens even in movements dedicated to equality. Instead of making policy, they were expected to make coffee, take minutes, and even provide sexual favors. During a staff retreat in 1964 Stokely Carmichael was challenged by women who asked for a discussion of the SNCC position paper on "women in the movement." To male laughter he replied: "The only position for women in SNCC is prone."

Radical feminists joined in consciousness-raising groups where they discussed sensitive issues such as homosexuality. In 1969 and 1970 NOW had forced

Gay Rights Movement

lesbians to resign from membership and offices in the organization. This rift was healed in 1971, largely because homosexuals had begun to fight back. Examples of militancy—by blacks, radical feminists, and antiwar protesters—helped inspire the gay rights movement. Throughout the 1950s and most of the 1960s, many homosexuals had feared that disclosing their sexual preference would cause them to lose not only their jobs, but even their friends and families. But in June 1969 that began to change. In New York City's Greenwich Village, a riot erupted between police and the patrons of the Stonewall Inn, a gay bar on Christopher Street. Police who raided the bar were not prepared for the volley of beer bottles that greeted them. Rioting continued well into the night, and graffiti calling for "Gay Power" appeared along Christopher Street. As John D'Emilio has written in *Sexual Politics, Sexual Communities: The Making of a Homosexual Minority in the United States, 1940–1970* (1983), "Stonewall thus marked a critical divide in the politics and consciousness of homosexuals and lesbians. A small, thinly spread reform effort suddenly grew into a large, grass-roots movement for liberation. The quality of gay life in America was permanently altered as a furtive subculture moved aggressively into the open."

For working women in the 1960s, the problems were sex discrimination in employment, lack of professional opportunities, unequal pay for equal work, lack of adequate day care for children, and prohibitions against abortion. In 1963 the average woman earned

63 cents for every dollar a man earned. Ten years later the figure had fallen to 57 cents. What this gender-based discrimination meant for many women was less food on the table and no new shoes for the kids.

Another harsh reality women encountered was "occupational segregation," which became even more pronounced as women flooded entry-level jobs in

Occupational Segregation

female-dominated fields like secretarial and clerical work. Women complained of occupational ghettos in which work was broken down into men's jobs and women's jobs and where women were concentrated in the lower-paying positions. The number of women workers jumped from 23.2 million in 1960 to 31.5 million in 1970 and 34.1 million in 1972, but "men's jobs" still paid higher wages. Many women with college educations earned less than men with eighth-grade educations. It was natural that two feminist goals of the 1960s were equal job opportunity and equal pay for equal work.

Opposition to feminist goals was widespread and intense. In December 1971 President Nixon vetoed a bill that would have set up a national system of day-care facilities for the children of working mothers. The bill, Nixon asserted, would have committed government to "communal approaches to child-rearing over against the family-centered approach," thus imperiling "the keystone of our civilization," the American family.

Despite such opposition, women made impressive gains. They entered professional schools in record numbers: from 1969 to 1973, the numbers of women

Educational and Legal Advances for Women

law students almost quadrupled and of women medical students more than doubled. Under Title IX of the Educational Amendments of 1972, female college athletes gained the right to the same financial support as male athletes. In the same year Congress approved the Equal Rights Amendment (ERA) and sent it to the states for ratification. (The Equal Rights Amendment states, "Equality of rights under the law shall not be denied or abridged by the United States or by any State on account of sex.") In two 1973 cases (*Roe* v. *Wade* and *Doe* v. *Bolton*), the Supreme Court struck down state laws that made abortion a crime. Ruling that such laws violated a woman's right of privacy, it held that the Constitution protected a woman's decision as to whether or not to end her pregnancy. Only in the last three months of pregnancy could a state absolutely bar abortion; otherwise, the state's power to regulate abortion was either nonexistent or subordinate to the issue of maternal health. As a result of these victories the women's movement gained new confidence. "If the 1960s belonged to the blacks, the next ten years are ours," remarked one feminist.

NIXON AND THE PERSISTENCE OF CHAOS

Richard Nixon's presidency was born in chaos. In 1969 a hundred black students armed with rifles and shotguns seized the student union at Cornell University and occupied the building for thirty-six hours. Harvard students took over the president's office before being evicted by police. Bloody confrontations occurred at Berkeley, San Francisco State, Wisconsin, and scores of other colleges and universities. And in October 1969, three hundred Weathermen, members of an SDS splinter group, raced through Chicago's downtown district, smashing windows and attacking police officers in an attempt to incite armed class struggle. A month later half a million people assembled peacefully at the Washington Monument on Moratorium Day to call for an end to the Vietnam War. While they appealed to the nation's leaders, President Nixon watched football on TV.

One bright spot for Nixon in 1969 was the flight of *Apollo 11*, a manned spaceship, to the moon. After separating in space from the *Apollo* craft, the lunar module reached its destination in **Moon Landing** mid-July, and on July 21 astronaut Neil Armstrong made history by taking the first step onto the moon's surface. After taking rock and soil samples, Armstrong and his flightmate Edwin Aldrin successfully rendezvoused with the *Apollo* command ship, docked, and returned to earth, splashing down 950 miles southwest of Hawaii on July 24. Led by the president, the nation cheered this accomplishment.

But this was a momentary respite. Back on earth, 1970 would prove to be even bloodier and more turbulent than 1969 had been. On April 30, 1970, President Nixon appeared on television to announce that the United **Kent State** States had launched an "incursion" **and Jackson** into Cambodia (see page 922), a **State** neutral country. The war at home escalated in response. On May 4, Ohio National Guardsmen fired into a group of protesting students at Kent State University, killing four and wounding eleven. Enraged students elsewhere went on strike, shutting down 250 campuses and pouring into the nation's capital to lobby against the war. Nixon referred to the protesters contemptuously as "these bums, you know, blowing up the campuses." Ten days after the Kent State killings, police and state highway patrolmen armed with automatic weapons blasted a women's dormitory at Jackson State, an all-black university in Mississippi, killing two students and wounding nine others. No evidence of student sniping could be found; the police fired no tear gas or warning shots.

While police and soldiers waged official violence in 1970, revolutionaries conducted an unofficial campaign of terror. They bombed the New York offices of Mobil Oil, IBM, General Telephone and Electronics, and various banks. In March a bomb factory exploded in Greenwich Village, blowing up at least three young revolutionaries. And there were scores of politically motivated skyjackings.

Worst of all, as far as many Americans were concerned, was street crime. "Fortress America: A nation behind locked doors," proclaimed the heading of a *Newsweek* article on crime. Sales of **Fear of Crime** pistols, burglar alarms, and bulletproof vests soared, as did the demand for private guards and special police. Conservatives accused liberals of causing the crime wave by coddling criminals. "You know what a conservative is?" asked Frank Rizzo, the hard-line police-chief-turned-mayor of Philadelphia. "That's a liberal who got mugged the night before."

Campus protests and confrontations between students and police escalated. In 1969, these Berkeley protesters picked up tear gas cannisters and hurled them back at the police. Copeland/Black Star.

In the tense atmosphere, government officials sometimes overreacted. Governor Nelson Rockefeller of New York did so in September 1971, when more than a thousand inmates of the Attica State Correctional Facility seized thirty-eight guards and took over a cellblock. Rather than give in to the prisoners' demand that he visit Attica to negotiate, Rockefeller ordered state troopers, sheriff's deputies, and guards to storm the prison. Under a pall of tear gas Rockefeller's army regained control, but at a horrifying cost: twenty-nine inmates and ten hostages dead.

In the wake of this new wave of riots and violent crime, Nixon became convinced that the nation was plunging into anarchy. And he worried, as had Lyndon Johnson before him, that the antiwar movement was Communist-inspired. In June 1970 he ordered the FBI, the CIA, the National Security Agency, and the Defense Intelligence Agency to formulate a co-ordinated attack on "internal threats." "Everything is valid," a Nixon aide told the group, "everything is possible." Had it not been for FBI Director J. Edgar Hoover's refusal to cooperate in the illegal plot, the group would have had free rein to open mail, tap telephones, and break into citizens' homes and offices.

The administration also worked to put the Democratic party on the defensive. Vice President Agnew took to the road in September to warn the country of threats to its internal security and exhort people to vote Republican in the upcoming congressional

Politics of Divisiveness

elections. "Will America be led by a President elected by . . . the American people," he asked, "or will we be intimidated and blackmailed into following the path dictated by a disruptive, radical, and militant minority?" The same month Jeb Stuart Magruder, an assistant to White House Chief of Staff H.R. Haldeman, defined the theme of the upcoming congressional elections in a memorandum. "The Democrats should be portrayed as being on the fringes: radical liberals who . . . excuse disorder, tolerate crime, apologize for our wealth, and undercut the President's foreign policy," Magruder wrote. But Republican attempts to discredit the Democrats failed. In the election the Democrats gained nine seats in the House and dropped only two in the Senate. The Republicans lost eleven state governorships.

Nixon's fortunes declined further in 1971. On June 13 the *New York Times* began to publish the Pentagon Papers, a top-secret study of the Vietnam War ordered in 1967 by then Secretary of Defense McNamara. The *Times* had obtained the papers from Daniel Ellsberg, a disillusioned defense analyst with the RAND Corporation, a think tank for analyzing national defense policies. The study revealed that the government had consistently lied to the American people about the war. For instance, in August 1964, when President Johnson announced that North Vietnamese patrol boats had attacked the U.S.S. *Maddox* and *C. Turner Joy* (see page 916), he did not reveal that the destroyers had been supporting a South Vietnamese raiding party. And the emergency resolution Johnson introduced in Congress as a result of the attack turned out to have been drafted several months before. Some analysts concluded that the attacks themselves might have been a lie, invented to rally public opinion in favor of the war.

Pentagon Papers

In 1971 Nixon also had to contend with inflation, a problem not entirely of his making. Rather, it was Lyndon Johnson's policy of guns and butter—massive deficit financing to support both the Vietnam War and the Great Society—that had fueled inflation. Not until 1967 had Johnson proposed tax increases to reduce the government deficit and dampen inflation, and not until June 1968 had Congress responded with a 10-percent tax surcharge. Johnson had also trimmed federal spending by

Skyrocketing Inflation

$6 billion, but the cut was too little too late. Nixon's policies, including a $2.5-billion tax cut in late 1969, only boosted rising prices. By January 1971 the United States was suffering from a 5.3-percent inflation rate and a 6-percent unemployment rate. Soon the word *stagflation* would be coined to describe this coexistence of economic recession (stagnation) and inflation.

That January Nixon shocked both critics and allies by declaring, "I am now a Keynesian." Like his Democratic predecessors, he would try to stimulate the economy through government spending. The budget for fiscal 1971 would have a built-in deficit of $23 billion, just slightly under the all-time high of $25 billion (1968 to 1969). Then in August, in an effort to correct the nation's balance-of-payments deficit, Nixon announced he would devalue the dollar by allowing it to "float" in international money markets. He also requested a tax on imports, the repeal of certain excise taxes, and tax concessions to industry for new capital investments. Finally, to curb inflation, the president froze prices, wages, and rents for ninety days, then set limits on their increase. Nixon's commitment to the controversial wage and price controls buckled the next year under pressure from businesses and unions. Though some economists, businesspeople, and politicians argued that the controls were bound to fail, others contended that they would have been successful had they been allowed more time to work.

The wage and price controls were just one sign of what surprised observers called Nixon's "great turnabout." Another was his announcement in July 1971 that he would travel to the People's Republic of China, an enemy Nixon had denounced for years. It was clear that the president was preparing for the 1972 presidential election.

THE SOUTHERN STRATEGY AND THE ELECTION OF 1972

Political observers believed that Nixon would have a hard time running for re-election on his first-term record. Having urged Americans to use "cool" words and "lower our voices," he had ordered

Vice President Agnew to denounce the press and student protesters. Having espoused unity, he had practiced the politics of polarization. Having campaigned as a fiscal conservative, he had authorized near-record budget deficits. And having promised peace, he had widened the war in Southeast Asia.

Moreover, congressional accomplishments had been made more in spite of Nixon than because of him. The Democrats dominated both houses of Congress during his first term, and they continued to follow a liberal agenda. Eighteen-year-olds gained the vote, Social Security payments and food-stamp funding were increased, and the Occupational Safety and Health Administration was established. Congress responded to the growing environmental movement by passing the Clean Air Act, the Water Quality Improvement Act, and the Resource Recovery Act. (Nixon opposed most of these social welfare, environmental, and voting rights bills.)

Democratic Legislative Victories

One Nixon innovation that bore fruit in 1972 was revenue sharing, a program that returned federal funds to the states to use as they saw fit. Nixon's effort to shift responsibility to state and local governments was known as the New Federalism. A less popular program was the Family Assistance Plan (FAP), under which a family of four would receive a guaranteed income of $1,600 per year plus $860 in food stamps. (Welfare payments fell below that level in twenty states.) Michael Harrington, the author of *The Other America*, called the plan "the most radical idea since the New Deal"; most conservatives denounced it. But a handful of conservatives, among them the economist Milton Friedman, supported the FAP, arguing that simple cash payments to the poor would do away with the mammoth welfare bureaucracy. The program did not pass Congress, in part because Democrats considered the benefit payments too low.

In his campaign for re-election, Nixon was less interested in running on his record than in employing a "southern strategy" of political conservatism. A product of the Sunbelt himself, Nixon was attuned to the growing political power of that conservative region. Thus he appealed to "the silent majority," the white suburbanites, blue-collar workers, Catholics, and ethnic

Nixon's Southern Strategy

groups of "middle America." As in the 1970 congressional elections, Nixon equated the Republican party with law and order and the Democratic party with permissiveness, crime, drugs, pornography, the hippie lifestyle, student radicalism, black militancy, feminism, homosexuality, and the dissolution of the family.

Actually, Nixon had been pursuing a southern strategy all along. A furor had arisen in February 1970 when the press published a memorandum written by Daniel Moynihan, Nixon's adviser on urban affairs and social welfare. While insisting that blacks should continue to make progress, Moynihan had recommended that "the issue of race could benefit from a period of benign neglect." Moreover, Attorney General John Mitchell had courted southern white votes by trying to delay school desegregation in Mississippi and to prevent extension of the 1965 Voting Rights Act. Mitchell sought vigorous prosecution of antiwar activists as well.

The southern strategy had also guided Nixon's nomination of Supreme Court justices. After appointing Warren Burger, a conservative federal judge, to succeed Earl Warren as chief justice, Nixon had selected two southerners to serve as associate justices. One of them, Judge G. Harrold Carswell of Florida, was a segregationist. When the Senate declined to confirm either nominee, Nixon protested angrily, "I understand the bitter feelings of millions of Americans who live in the South." By 1972, however, the president had managed to appoint three more conservatives to the Supreme Court: Justices Harry Blackmun, Lewis F. Powell, and William Rehnquist. Ironically, the new appointees did not always vote as Nixon would have wished. The Court's decisions on abortion, publication of the Pentagon Papers, the death sentence, wiretapping, and busing for school desegregation all ran counter to Nixon's politics.

The Court was at the center of one of the most emotional issues of the 1972 election: busing. In 1971, in *Swann* v. *Charlotte-Mecklenburg*, the justices had upheld a desegregation plan that required a school system in North Carolina to work toward racial integration through massive crosstown busing. The decision generated widespread protest. In March 1972 Governor George Wallace of Alabama won the Democratic primary in Florida after taking a strong antibusing stand. Three days later Nixon proposed that Congress pass a busing moratorium, and he appeared

President Nixon and Vice President Spiro T. Agnew (1918–) celebrate their re-election in 1972. Both resigned in disgrace before completing the second term. National Archives, Nixon Project.

on television to denounce busing as a reckless and extreme remedy for segregation. Though Nixon's response to busing was a well-planned part of his southern strategy, his stand clearly appealed to northern whites as well.

Besides Wallace, Democratic candidates for the 1972 presidential nomination included Senators Hubert Humphrey, Edward Kennedy, George McGovern, and Edmund Muskie. After his defeat by Nixon in 1968, Humphrey inspired little enthusiasm. And for many Americans, Kennedy had ceased to be a contender in 1969, when he left the scene of an accident at Chappaquiddick, on Martha's Vineyard, in which a woman passenger in his car drowned. Senator Muskie fell victim to a dirty trick, a forged letter published during the New Hampshire primary that accused the senator of laughing at disparaging remarks about Canadian-Americans. When the letter and other slurs brought Muskie to the point

Election of 1972

of tears in public, he too ceased to be a serious candidate. Governor Wallace was shot by a disturbed young man named Arthur H. Bremer and began a long convalescence. After his shooting the right-wing law-and-order vote had no place to turn but to Nixon. Meanwhile, Senator McGovern won several primaries and arrived at the Democratic convention with enough votes for the nomination.

Nixon campaigned by assuming the elevated role of world statesman: in February 1972 he traveled to China and in May to the Soviet Union. Both trips were elaborately staged and televised for maximum political effect. But it was the campaign waged by George McGovern that handed victory to the Republicans. When McGovern committed himself to a $30-billion cut in the defense budget, people began to fear he was a neo-isolationist who would reduce the United States to a second-rate power. McGovern's proposals split the Democrats between his supporters—blacks, feminists, antiwar activists, young militants—

IMPORTANT EVENTS

1960	Kennedy elected president	1968	U.S.S. *Pueblo* captured by North Korea
1961	Freedom Ride		Tet offensive
1962	John Glenn orbits globe		Martin Luther King, Jr., assassinated
	SDS's Port Huron Statement		Race riots in 168 cities and towns
			Civil Rights Act of 1968
1963	Friedan, *The Feminine Mystique*		Antiwar protests escalate
	March on Washington		Robert F. Kennedy assassinated
	Birmingham, Alabama, Baptist church bombed		Violence at Democratic convention
	Kennedy assassinated; Johnson assumes the presidency		Nixon elected president
1964	Beatles perform in the United States	1969	Stonewall riot
	Economic Opportunity Act		*Apollo II* moon landing
	Civil Rights Act of 1964		Woodstock festival
	First of the "long hot summers"		Moratorium Day
	Free Speech Movement	1970	U.S. invades Cambodia
	Johnson elected president		Students killed at Kent State University and Jackson State University
1965	Malcolm X assassinated		
	March from Selma to Montgomery	1971	Pentagon Papers
	Antiwar demonstrations		Nixon's New Economic Policy
	Voting Rights Act of 1965		Attica prison revolt
	Watts race riot	1972	Nixon visits China and Russia
1966	National Organization for Women (NOW) established		Equal Rights Amendment (ERA) approved by Congress
			George Wallace shot
1967	Race riots in Newark, Detroit, and other cities		Break-in at Watergate
	March on the Pentagon		Revenue-sharing adopted
			Nixon re-elected

and old-guard urban bosses, labor and ethnic leaders, and southerners.

Much to Nixon's advantage was the rumor that the Vietnam War was near its end. Troops were being pulled out; by September 1972 the death rate was almost zero. Then in late October, less than two weeks before the election, Henry Kissinger announced a breakthrough in the peace negotiations. "Peace is at hand," he proclaimed. The announcement proved inaccurate, but it helped persuade some people to vote for Nixon.

Nixon's victory in November was overwhelming. He polled 47 million votes, 60.7 percent of the votes cast. McGovern received only 29 million and won in just one state, Massachusetts, and the District of Columbia. Nixon's southern strategy was supremely successful: he carried all of the Deep South, which had once been solidly Democratic. He also gained a majority of the urban vote, wining over such long-time Democrats as blue-collar workers, Catholics, and ethnics. Only blacks,

Nixon's Landslide Victory

Jews, and low-income voters stuck by the Democrats. Remarkably, the Democrats retained control of both houses of Congress and won two additional seats in the Senate. Democratic voters were becoming independent, resorting to ticket-splitting when they perceived a Democratic candidate to be unacceptable.

When John F. Kennedy delivered his inaugural address in 1961, he had challenged Americans to "pay any price, bear any burden, meet any hardship" to defend freedom and inspire the world. Twelve years later, Richard M. Nixon echoed that rhetoric: "Let us pledge to make these four years the best four years in America's history, so that on its 200th birthday America will be as young and vital as when it began, and as bright a beacon of hope for all the world." Largely because of the president's own actions, however, the next four years would be among the most dismal in the nation's history. As for Nixon, he would resign well before the nation celebrated its bicentennial in 1976.

SUGGESTIONS FOR FURTHER READING

General

Godfrey Hodgson, *America in Our Time* (1976); Peter Joseph, *Good Times: An Oral History of America in the Nineteen Sixties* (1973); Allen J. Matusow, *The Unraveling of America: A History of Liberalism in the 1960's* (1984); Charles R. Morris, *A Time of Passion: America 1960–1980* (1984); William O'Neill, *Coming Apart: An Informal History of America in the 1960s* (1971); Milton Viorst, *Fire in the Streets: America in the 1960s* (1979).

The Kennedy Administration

Henry Fairlie, *The Kennedy Promise* (1973); David Halberstam, *The Best and the Brightest* (1972); Jim F. Heath, *Decade of Disillusionment: The Kennedy-Johnson Years* (1975); Ralph G. Martin, *A Hero for Our Time* (1983); Bruce Miroff, *Pragmatic Illusions: The Presidential Politics of John F. Kennedy* (1976); Herbert S. Parmet, *J.F.K.—The Presidency of John F. Kennedy* (1983); Herbert S. Parmet, *Jack* (1980); Arthur M. Schlesinger, Jr., *A Thousand Days: John F. Kennedy in the White House* (1965); Theodore C. Sor-

enson, *Kennedy* (1965); Theodore H. White, *The Making of the President* (1961); Garry Wills, *The Kennedy Imprisonment* (1982).

The Kennedy Assassination

Edward Jay Epstein, *Legend: The Secret World of Lee Harvey Oswald* (1978); Edward Jay Epstein, *Inquest* (1966); Michael L. Kurtz, *Crime of the Century* (1982); William Manchester, *The Death of a President* (1967); President's Commission on the Assassination of President John F. Kennedy, *The Warren Report* (1964); Anthony Summers, *Conspiracy* (1980).

The Johnson Administration

Carl M. Brauer, "Kennedy, Johnson, and the War on Poverty," *Journal of American History*, 69 (1982), 98–119; Robert A. Divine, ed., *Exploring the Johnson Years* (1981); Ronnie Dugger, *The Politician* (1982); Hugh Davis Graham, *The Uncertain Triumph: Federal Education Policy in the Kennedy and Johnson Years* (1984); Lyndon B. Johnson, *The Vantage Point* (1971); Doris Kearns, *Lyndon Johnson and the American Dream* (1976); Sar A. Levitan, *The Great Society's Poor Law* (1969); Sar A. Levitan and Robert Taggart, *The Promise of Greatness* (1976); Charles Murray, *Losing Ground: American Social Policy 1950–1980* (1983); James T. Patterson, *America's Struggle Against Poverty 1900–1980* (1981); Frances Fox Piven and Richard A. Cloward, *Regulating the Poor* (1971); Hugh Sidey, *A Very Personal Presidency* (1968); Carl Solberg, *Hubert Humphrey* (1984); Theodore H. White, *The Making of the President 1964* (1965).

Civil Rights and Black Power

Carl M. Brauer, *John F. Kennedy and the Second Reconstruction* (1977); Clayborne Carson, *In Struggle: SNCC and the Black Awakening of the 1960s* (1981); William H. Chafe, *Civilities and Civil Rights: Greensboro, North Carolina, and the Black Struggle for Freedom* (1980); David J. Garrow, *The FBI and Martin Luther King, Jr.* (1981); David J. Garrow, *Protest at Selma* (1978); David L. Lewis, *King* (1970); August Meier and Elliott Rudwick, *CORE* (1973); Malcolm X and Alex Haley, *The Autobiography of Malcolm X* (1965); Stephen B. Oates, *Let the Trumpet Sound: The Life of Martin Luther King, Jr.* (1982); Frances Fox Piven and Richard A. Cloward, *Poor People's Movements* (1977).

Warren Court

William O. Douglas, *The Court Years 1939–1975* (1980); Gerald Dunne, *Hugo Black and the Judicial Revolution* (1977); Anthony Lewis, *Gideon's Trumpet* (1964); Charles Morgan, Jr., *One Man, One Voice* (1979); Bernard Schwartz, *Super*

Chief: Earl Warren and His Supreme Court (1983); Earl Warren, *The Memoirs of Earl Warren* (1977).

The New Left and the Antiwar Movement

Wini Breines, *Community and Organization in the New Left* (1983); Todd Gitlin, *The Whole World Is Watching: Mass Media in the Making and Unmaking of the New Left* (1980); Kenneth Keniston, *Young Radicals* (1968); Thomas Powers, *Vietnam, the War at Home* (1984); Stanley Rothman and S. Robert Lichter, *Roots of Radicalism: Jews, Christians, and the New Left* (1982); Kirkpatrick Sale, *SDS* (1973); Sohnya Sayres *et al.*, eds., *The 60s, Without Apology* (1984); Jon Wiener, *Come Together: John Lennon in His Time* (1984); Nancy Zaroulis and Gerald Sullivan, *Who Spoke Up? American Protest Against the War in Vietnam 1963–1975* (1984).

The Counterculture

Stanley Booth, *Dance with the Devil: The Rolling Stones and Their Times* (1984); Morris Dickstein, *Gates of Eden: American Culture in the Sixties* (1977); Michael Medved and David Wallechinsky, *What Really Happened to the Class of '65* (1976); Philip Norman, *Shout! The Beatles in Their Generation* (1981); Charles Reich, *The Greening of America* (1970); Theodore Roszak, *The Making of a Counter Culture* (1968); Philip Slater, *The Pursuit of Loneliness*, rev. ed. (1976); Tom Wolfe, *The Electric Kool-Aid Acid Test* (1968).

The Nixon Administration

John Ehrlichman, *Witness to Power* (1982); Daniel P. Moynihan, *The Politics of a Guaranteed Income* (1973); Richard M. Nixon, *RN: The Memoirs of Richard Nixon* (1978); Leon E. Panetta and Peter Gall, *Bring Us Together: The Nixon Team and the Civil Rights Retreat* (1971); Kevin Phillips, *The Emerging Republican Majority* (1969); Raymond Price, *With Nixon* (1977); Jonathan Schell, *The Time of Illusion* (1975); Leonard Silk, *Nixonomics* (1972); Theodore H. White, *The Making of the President 1972* (1973); Theodore H. White, *The Making of the President 1968* (1969); Garry Wills, *Nixon Agonistes* (1970).

The Rebirth of Feminism

William H. Chafe, *The American Woman: Her Changing Social, Economic, and Political Role, 1920–1970* (1972); Sara Evans, *Personal Politics* (1978); Jo Freeman, *The Politics of Women's Liberation* (1975); Betty Friedan, *The Feminine Mystique* (1963); Judith Hole and Ellen Levine, *Rebirth of Feminism* (1971); Alice Kessler-Harris, *Out to Work: A History of Wage-Earning Women in the United States* (1982); Kate Millett, *Sexual Politics* (1970); Robin Morgan, ed., *Sisterhood Is Powerful* (1970); Sheila M. Rothman, *Women's Proper Place* (1978); Gayle Graham Yates, *What Women Want: The Ideas of the Movement* (1975).

DISILLUSIONMENT AND ECONOMIC UNCERTAINTY

1973–1981

CHAPTER 34

*N*ight watchman Frank Wills was making his rounds at the Watergate apartment-office complex in Washington, D.C., on June 17, 1972, when he noticed that two doors connecting the building to an underground garage had been taped to keep them from locking. Wills removed the tape, but when he returned thirty minutes later he found it had been replaced. He promptly telephoned the police to report the illegal entry. At 2:30 A.M., police arrested five men who were attaching listening devices to telephones in the sixth-floor offices of the Democratic National Committee. The men had cameras, and they had been rifling through files.

One of the men arrested was James W. McCord, a former CIA employee who had become security coordinator of the Committee to Re-elect the President (CREEP). The other four were anti-Castro Cubans from Miami. Unknown to the police, two other men had been in the Watergate building illegally at the time of the break-in. One was E. Howard Hunt, a one-time CIA agent who had become CREEP's security chief. The other was G. Gordon Liddy, a former FBI agent serving on the staff of the White House Domestic Council. What were these men trying to find in the Democrats' offices? What did they hope to overhear on the telephones? Most important, who had ordered the break-in?

In the next twenty-two months the American people would learn the answers to some but not all of these questions. What had at first appeared to be a third-rate burglary would turn out to be part of an official plot to destroy a free presidential election. As the shoddy story of Watergate unfolded, Americans' disillusion would grow. Most had grown up believing their country was the most powerful, the most righteous, the most democratic, and the most bountiful in the history of humankind. By the early 1980s, far fewer Americans clung to such beliefs, and many wondered why they had not shed their innocence earlier.

The Watergate scandal came to light at a time when Americans were still recovering from their country's defeat in the Vietnam War. Perhaps for that reason it was more traumatic than earlier national scandals; in 1974 it caused the first presidential resignation in American history.

While Americans worried about morality in government, economic events touched their lives even more deeply. The years between 1973 and 1981 were filled with uncertainty as the American people reeled under the assault of stagflation (see page 964). The first blow was dealt by the 1973 Arab oil embargo, which led to the realization that the United States was not a fortress that could stand alone; it was dependent for its survival on imported oil. Long gasoline lines, the declining value of the dollar, and persistent stagflation dogged Americans; the postwar economic boom was over.

Politicians seemed unable to cope with the floundering economy. President Gerald Ford's weak WIN program to Whip Inflation Now did not impress voters, who turned him out of office in 1976. Jimmy Carter, who defeated Ford by arguing that the nation needed an outsider to bring integrity, efficiency, and fiscal responsibility to Washington, fared just as badly. Under Carter inflation reached new heights and unemployment remained high.

Women and nonwhites were particularly hard hit by inflation and unemployment, for they were usually the last hired and the first to be laid off. Even when they had jobs, women and Afro-Americans were paid less than white men, and experts pointed to the growing "feminization" and "blackening" of poverty. Minorities did achieve some victories in the 1970s, though. Women made educational gains and won legislative seats in Washington and in various state houses. Many Afro-Americans attended college and joined the middle class or were elected to political office. But opposition to the aspirations of both groups mounted steadily. The feminist movement was confronted by an increasingly vocal and effective antifeminist, or "profamily," movement. And blacks had to contend with antibusing agitation and a resurgent Ku Klux Klan.

Some Americans decided that if they could not reform society, they could at least develop their own individual potential. For them, the 1970s were the Me Decade. Millions of people took to jogging; others meditated, ate health food, or developed their assertiveness skills. But some observers thought they detected an undercurrent of desperation. By 1980 public opinion polls disclosed that most Americans found the present worse than the past and believed the future would be worse yet. "We've gone almost overnight from a nation of optimists to a nation of pessimists," reported pollster Daniel Yankelovich.

As the 1980 presidential election approached, Americans looked back on a decade of economic difficulties. With the purchasing power of their paychecks eroded by inflation, many people had raided their savings, sacrificing future security to present needs. They had seen once-proud automobile and steel plants age and close. "It's an open question," one steel company president lamented in 1980, "whether this industry will survive." As a result of "deindustrialization," many jobs were jeopardized and some disappeared forever. Increases in foreign imports on store shelves became constant reminders that the competition was gaining.

It was in this grim context that Ronald Reagan rode a wave of conservatism into office. Reagan promised a return to old-fashioned morality and a balanced budget. He blamed government for fettering American economic creativity. America could again be what it once was, he declared, and Americans believed him.

NIXON AND THE WATERGATE SCANDAL

Watergate actually began in 1971, when the White House established not only CREEP but the overlapping Special Investigations Unit, known familiarly as the Plumbers, to stop the leaking of confidential information to the press. Following publication of the Pentagon Papers (see page 964), the Plumbers burglarized the office of Daniel Ellsberg's psychiatrist in an attempt to find information to discredit Ellsberg. It was the Plumbers who broke into the Democratic National Committee's headquarters to photograph documents and install wiretaps. And it was CREEP that raised money to pay the Plumbers' expenses both before and after the break-in. CREEP's official duty was to solicit campaign contributions. The committee had managed to collect $60 million, much of it donated illegally by corporations.

The arrest of the Watergate burglars generated furious activity in the White House. Incriminating documents were shredded, E. Howard Hunt's name was expunged from the White House telephone directory, and Nixon ordered his chief of staff, H. R. Halderman, to discourage the FBI's investigation into the burglary on the pretext that it might compromise national security.

White House Cover-up

Soon after the break-in, the Democrats filed a damage suit against CREEP and the five burglars for invasion of privacy. John Mitchell, who had resigned as attorney general to chair Nixon's re-election campaign, called the suit "another example of sheer demagoguery." CREEP "did not authorize and does not condone the alleged actions of the five men apprehended there," Mitchell said. Later, Nixon announced to the press that his White House counsel, John W. Dean III, had conducted a "complete investigation," and that no one in the administration "was involved in this very bizarre incident." At the same time, Nixon privately authorized CREEP payments in excess of $460,000 to keep Hunt and others from implicating the White House in the crime.

Thanks to White House efforts to cover up the scandal, the break-in went practically unnoticed by the electorate. Had it not been for the diligent efforts of reporters, government special prosecutors, federal judges, and congressional representatives, Nixon might have succeeded in disguising his involvement in Watergate. Slowly, however, the ball of lies and distortions began to unravel. In early 1973, U.S. District Court Judge John Sirica tried the burglars, one of whom, James McCord, implicated his superiors in CREEP and at the White House. From May until November, the Senate Select Committee on Campaign Practices, chaired by Senator Sam Ervin, heard testimony from White House aides. John Dean acknowledged not only that there had been a cover-up, but that the president had directed it. Another aide, Alexander Butterfield, shocked the committee and the nation

Watergate Hearings and Investigations

During testimony before a Senate committee investigating Watergate, a White House aide revealed that President Nixon had had tape recorders installed in the White House. This cartoon, which needs no caption, suggests the public's reaction to the electronic surveillance.   Reprinted by permission of the Chicago Tribune–New York News Syndicate, Inc.

by disclosing that Nixon had had a taping system installed in the White House, and that conversations about Watergate had been recorded.

Nixon feigned innocence, but on April 30, 1973, he announced the resignations of his two chief White House aides, John Ehrlichman and H. R. Haldeman. Speaking to a national television audience, the president pledged that he would find the facts and act on them. "There can be no whitewash at the White House," he intoned.

As if to give meaning to his words, the president appointed Elliot Richardson, the secretary of defense, to the post of attorney general. Richardson in turn selected Archibald Cox, a Harvard law professor, for the new position of special Watergate prosecutor. But when Cox, supported by Richardson, sought to

Saturday Night Massacre

obtain the White House tapes by means of a court order, Nixon forced Richardson and Deputy Attorney General William Ruckelshaus to resign and ordered the next-ranking official in the Department of Justice to send Cox back to Harvard. The public outcry provoked by the so-called Saturday Night Massacre (October 20, 1973) compelled the president to agree to the appointment of a new special prosecutor, Leon Jaworski. When Nixon still refused to surrender the tapes, Jaworski took him to court.

In the same month as the Saturday Night Massacre, the Nixon administration was stung by another scandal. Vice President Spiro Agnew resigned after pleading no contest to charges of income-tax evasion and

Agnew's Resignation acceptance of bribes. Under the provisions of the Twenty-fifth Amendment, ratified in 1964 after President Kennedy's assassination, Nixon nominated Gerald R. Ford, congressman from Michigan and the House minority leader, to replace Agnew. Ford's voting record showed him to be a conservative; he had opposed most of the 1960s reform legislation. But Ford was congenial and popular on Capitol Hill, and his nomination was confirmed promptly by both houses of Congress. Once he had taken the oath of office, the new vice president staunchly maintained that Nixon was innocent of involvement in the Watergate cover-up.

Throughout 1973 and 1974, enterprising reporters uncovered details of the break-in, the hush money, and the various people from Nixon on down who had taken part in the cover-up. White House aides and CREEP subordinates began to go on trial, with Nixon cited as their "unindicted co-conspirator." *Washington Post* reporters Carl Bernstein and Bob Woodward found an informant in the White House known as Deep Throat, who provided damning evidence against Nixon and his aides. As Nixon's story became less credible, his hold on the tapes became more tenuous. In late April 1974 the president finally released an edited version of the tapes, which, he explained, would "at last, once and for all, show that what I knew and what I did with regard to the Watergate cover-up were just as I described them to you from the very beginning."

The tapes, however, were replete with gaps. They swayed neither the public nor the House Judiciary Committee, which had begun to draft articles of impeachment against the president. Nixon was still trying to hang onto the tapes when on July 24 the Supreme Court, in *U.S.* v. *Nixon*, unanimously ordered him to surrender the recordings to Judge Sirica. At about the same time, the Judiciary Committee began to conduct nationally televised hearings. After several days of testimony the committee voted for impeachment on three of five counts: obstruction of justice through the payment of hush money to witnesses, lying, and withholding of evidence; defiance of a congressional subpoena of the tapes; and the use of the CIA, the FBI, and the Internal Revenue Service to deprive Americans of their constitutional rights of privacy and free speech.

On August 5 the president finally handed over the complete tapes, which he knew would condemn him. Four days later he resigned.

Nixon's successor was Gerald R. Ford. His congressional colleagues hailed the new president as a "decent" and "good" man, respected by both Republicans and Democrats, who would bind up the wounds of Watergate. But Ford's first substantive act was to pardon Nixon, though he had said he would not do so. When the pardon was announced, some people concluded that Ford and Nixon had struck a deal.

The Watergate scandal prompted the reform of abuses that had existed before the Nixon administration. The development of what the historian Arthur M. Schlesinger, Jr., called "the imperial presidency" dated from Franklin D. Roosevelt's administration. Roosevelt had signed executive agreements with foreign nations that were in effect treaties, but had never sent them to the Senate for its advice and consent. President Johnson had led the nation into the Vietnam War without securing a congressional declaration of war as required by the Constitution, and Nixon had authorized secret bombing of Cambodia. Finally, Nixon also had impounded (refused to spend) $15 billion in funds appropriated by Congress for social programs.

Post-Watergate Restrictions on Executive Power

To remedy many of these abuses, Congress in 1973 passed the War Powers Act, which mandated that "in every possible instance" the president must consult with Congress before sending American troops into foreign wars. The law required the president to withdraw troops after sixty days unless Congress specifically directed otherwise. But the act did not specify what Congress could do if the president refused to comply. In 1974 Congress produced the Congressional Budget and Impoundment Control Act, which prohibited impounding federal money. In actions directly related to Watergate, Congress attacked campaign fund-raising abuses and the misuse of government agencies. The Federal Election Campaign Act of 1972 had restricted campaign spending to no more than ten cents per constituent, and required candidates to report individual contributions of more than $100. In 1974 Congress enacted additional legislation that set ceilings on campaign contributions and expenditures for House, Senate, and presidential elections. Finally, to aid citizens who were victims of dirty-tricks campaigns, Congress strengthened the Freedom of Information

Act, originally passed in 1966. The new legislation permitted access to "reasonably" described government documents and provided penalties if the government "arbitrarily or capriciously" withheld such information.

THE ENERGY CRISIS AND THE END OF THE POSTWAR ECONOMIC BOOM

The fallout from Watergate was not the only problem confronting the nation in the early 1970s. More disruptive in the long run was the Arab oil embargo of 1973 (see page 925), which Americans denounced as an "energy Pearl Harbor." Even before the embargo the United States had suffered occasional shortages of natural gas, heating oil, and gasoline. But the American people, who had grown up on cheap, abundant energy, made no effort to conserve; they drove big cars and lived in poorly insulated homes. By fall 1973 the country had to import one-third of its oil supplies.

Price increases ordered by the Organization of Petroleum Exporting Countries (OPEC) struck the United States another blow. From January 1973 to January 1974 oil prices rose 350

OPEC Price Increases and Rising Inflation

percent. In March 1974 the majority of OPEC members lifted the five-month-old oil embargo, but prices remained high. Government officials began to fear that the price of home air conditioning and heating would soar beyond the reach of even middle-class Americans. As people grappled with the social and political costs of the price hikes, multinational oil companies prospered. Profits jumped 70 percent in 1973 and another 40 percent in 1974. Public resentment of oil companies mounted; many citizens suspected company officers were in league with the Arabs.

The boost in the price of imported oil reverberated through the entire economy. High-cost oil drove up both inflation and unemployment and considerably slowed overall economic growth. Inflation jumped from 3.3 percent in 1972 to 6.2 percent in 1973 and a frightening 11 percent in 1974. At the same time recession hit the auto industry. In Detroit General Motors laid off thirty-eight thousand workers—6 percent of its domestic work force—indefinitely and put another forty-eight thousand on leave for up to ten days at a time. The reason was obvious: sales of gas-guzzling American autos had plummeted as consumers rushed to purchase energy-efficient foreign subcompacts. Like Ford and Chrysler, GM was stuck with mostly large-car assembly plants. First-quarter 1974 profits fell 85 percent at GM, 66 percent at Ford, and 98 percent at Chrysler.

For years the American automobile industry had based production on the presumption that large autos were more profitable to manufacture than small ones.

Recession in the Auto Industry

They had ignored the steady shift to smaller cars, which accelerated suddenly in late 1973. In December compact-car sales exceeded standard-size sales, a turnaround that auto makers, with the exception of American Motors, had not expected to occur before 1977. Buyers rushed to showrooms displaying Japanese, German, and other foreign cars. Moreover, the ailing American auto companies that were not selling cars were not buying steel, glass, rubber, or tool-and-die products either. Soon the recession in the auto industry spread to other manufacturers, who not only quit hiring new workers, but also began laying off experienced employees with seniority.

Unlike earlier postwar recessions, this one did not fade away in a year or two. Part of the reason was the coexistence of inflation. In the earlier recessions, Democrats, as well as many Republicans, had held to a policy of neo-Keynesianism. That is, they had manipulated federal policies to minimize the swings in the business cycle—both fiscal policies, covering taxes and government spending, and monetary policies, including interest rates and the money supply. Thus they hoped to keep employment up and inflation down. The federal government could heat up, or stimulate, the economy by increasing spending, cutting taxes, increasing the money supply, and decreasing the interest rates charged to banks that borrowed from the Federal Reserve System. And it could lower the flame by reversing these policies. Beginning in the 1970s, however, joblessness and prices both began to rise sharply. Policies to correct one problem seemed only to exacerbate the other. In 1974, as unemployment mounted, so too did inflation, but government officials hesitated to fuel it further through massive federal spending.

Even in the best of times, the economy would have been hard pressed to produce jobs for the millions of baby boomers who would join the labor market in the 1970s. As it was, economic

The Shifting Occupational Structure

activity created 26.5 million additional jobs during the decade, a remarkable increase of 32.3 percent. (By contrast, during the 1960s, total jobs increased by 12.2 million, or 17.4 percent.) But because of deindustrialization, there was a shift in the occupational structure. In Youngstown and Pittsburgh, steel mills sat idle, and in Detroit weeds grew in the empty parking lots next to abandoned automobile factories. As these heavy industries collapsed, laid-off workers took jobs in fast-food restaurants, all-night gas stations, and convenience stores, but at half their former wages. Workers who had held high-paying blue-collar jobs saw their middle-class standard of living slipping away.

There were other problems too. One was a slowing of growth in productivity, or the average output of goods per hour of labor. Between 1947 and 1965 American industrial productivity had

Decreased Productivity

increased an average of 3.3 percent a year, raising manufacturers' profits and decreasing the cost of products to consumers. But from 1966 to 1970 the annual productivity increase averaged only 1.5 percent; it fell further to 1.4 percent between 1971 and 1975 and to a mere 0.2 percent between 1976 and 1980. Economists blamed the lack of business investment in state-of-the-art technology, the shift from an industrial to a service economy, and an alleged erosion of the work ethic. Whatever the causes, American goods cost more than those of foreign competitors. During the 1970s, Japanese productivity, stimulated by heavy automation, grew at four times the American rate. In 1979, for example, Toyota produced fifty cars per production worker, five times the American average. The savings to Japanese manufacturers made

A homemade gas-station sign graphically illustrates the discomfort Americans felt when Arab oil-producing nations cut back fuel shipments in 1973. Dennis Brack/Black Star.

their products more competitive in the American market, and cut into American manufacturers' sales.

The lag in productivity was not matched by a decrease in workers' expectations. Wage increases regularly exceeded production increases, and some economists blamed the raises for inflation. Indeed, wages and prices that went up seldom came down again, regardless of market conditions. Managers of the nation's basic industries—steel, autos, rubber— complained that the automatic cost-of-living adjustments in their labor contracts left them little margin to restrain price hikes. Congress's Joint Economic Committee warned, "The average American is likely to see his standard of living drastically decline in the 1980s unless the United States accelerates its rate of productivity growth."

Another spur to inflation was easy credit, particularly

between 1975 and 1979. Fearing an era of scarcity, many people went on a buying spree. Household and

Easy Credit and Inflation

business borrowing more than tripled (from $94 billion to $328 billion). More people had credit cards; Master Charge cardholders jumped from 32 million in 1974 to 57 million five years later. This credit explosion helped bid up the price of everything, from houses to gold. What also encouraged borrowing was that interest expenses were tax deductible and that interest-rate increases lagged behind the soaring inflation rate. But some people borrowed more than they could afford. Farmers bought new farm land and expensive machinery and irrigation equipment. The nation's farm debt in 1971 was $54.5 billion; by 1977 it was $122.7 billion, and by 1980 it had reached $165.8 billion. Overburdened with debts, many farmers would face bankruptcy in the 1980s.

Every expert had a scapegoat to blame for the nation's economic doldrums. Labor leaders cited foreign competition and called for tariffs to protect American goods. Some businesspeople and economists said the cost of obeying federal health and safety laws and pollution controls added to the price of goods. Critics estimated that regulations not only discouraged business investments, but also cost industry tens of billions of dollars annually, much of this borne by industries already hurt by recession. They urged officials to abolish the Environmental Protection Agency and the Occupational Safety and Health Administration, and pressed for deregulation of the oil, airline, and trucking industries on the theory that competition would bring prices down.

Above all, critics attacked the federal government's massive spending programs; the mounting national debt, they said, was the sad result. Since the New Deal, both Republican and Democratic administrations had resorted to pump priming to cure recessions. But the Johnson administration's attempt to finance both the War on Poverty and the Vietnam War evidently had backfired. To pay for these costly programs and to service interest on the national debt, the government needed to compete with private businesses for investment funds. This competition forced up interest rates, further fueling inflation and making it more difficult for businesses to expand. Critics of neo-Keynesian pump priming pointed to the resulting stagflation as evidence of the failure of New Deal and Great Society economics.

Inflation was certainly getting out of hand. It had begun to climb in 1966 and 1967; when it reached 5.9 percent in 1970, President Nixon had reacted

Government Response to the Economic Crisis

by trying to restrain federal spending, and the Federal Reserve Board had tightened credit (see page 964). The results had been a stock market collapse, the bankruptcy of the Penn Central Railroad, and a national recession. By the time Gerald Ford became president in 1974, OPEC price increases had pushed the rate to 11 percent. Appalled, Ford created WIN, a voluntary program that encouraged businesses, consumers, and workers to save energy and form grassroots anti-inflation organizations. In the 1974 congressional elections, voters responded to WIN, Watergate, and the Nixon pardon by giving the Democrats forty-three additional seats in the House and four in the Senate.

Ford's ultimate response to inflation, like Nixon's, was to curb federal spending and encourage the Federal Reserve Board to tighten credit. As before, these actions prompted a recession—only this time it was the worst in forty years. Unemployment jumped to 8.5 percent in 1975, and because the economy had stagnated, the federal deficit for the fiscal year 1976 and 1977 hit a record $60 billion.

Neither Nixon nor Ford devised lasting solutions to the energy crisis. In 1973, in response to the oil embargo, Congress did consider gasoline rationing, higher fuel taxes to encourage conservation, and a windfall-profits tax on oil companies. Encouraged by rising prices, coal companies began to increase production. President Nixon outlined an energy program that called for lowering thermostats in government buildings, cancelling 10 percent of airline flights, and expediting the construction of nuclear power plants. For a few months the government even banned Sunday gasoline sales. But when OPEC ended the embargo, the crisis seemed to pass, and with it the incentive to prevent future shortages.

The energy crisis intensified public debate over nuclear power. For the sake of energy independence, advocates asserted, the United States had to rely more on nuclear energy. Environmental activists

Three Mile Island, the site of a major nuclear accident in March 1979. When the fail-safe system of one of the reactors failed, 800,000 gallons of radioactive water spurted from a defective valve. UPI/Bettmann Newsphotos.

countered that the risk of nuclear accident was too great and there was no safe way to store nuclear waste. In March 1975 an accident **Nuclear Power** in one of the world's largest nuclear reactors at Brown's Ferry, Alabama, gave credence to the activists' cause. And in March 1979, in a plant at Three Mile Island, Pennsylvania, a stuck valve overheated the reactor core and raised fears of meltdown and radiation poisoning; it forced the evacuation of a hundred thousand nearby residents. By that time ninety-six reactors were under construction throughout the nation, and thirty more were on order.

Meanwhile, the combined effects of the energy crisis, stagflation, and the flight of industry and the middle class to the suburbs and the South were producing fiscal disaster in the nation's cities. Not since 1933, when Detroit defaulted on its debts, had an American city gone bankrupt. But in November 1975 New York City was near financial collapse, unable to meet its payroll and make payments on bonds.

Ford vowed "to veto any bill that has as its purpose a federal bail-out of New York City," but after the Senate and House Banking Committees approved loan guarantees, he relented, and the city was saved. New York was not alone in its financial problems; other Frostbelt cities in the North and East were in trouble, saddled with growing welfare rolls, deindustrialization, and a declining tax base. In December 1978 Cleveland became the first American city to default since the Great Depression.

Throughout Ford's term Congress enjoyed new power. Though Ford almost routinely vetoed its bills, Congress in most cases overrode his vetoes. Watergate and the new criticism of the imperial presidency accounted for Congress's new self-confidence. There was also the fact that, for the first time in the nation's history, both the president and the vice president lacked the popular mandate of having been elected to office. One of Ford's first acts as president was to select former Governor Nelson Rockefeller of New York to be his vice president.

THE FAILED PROMISE OF THE CARTER PRESIDENCY

While Ford struggled with a Democratic Congress, the Democratic party prepared for the presidential election of 1976. Frontrunners included

Election of 1976

Senators Birch Bayh of Indiana, Lloyd Bentsen of Texas, and Henry Jackson of Washington. But against the background of Watergate secrecy and corruption, one candidate in particular promised honesty and openness. "I will never lie to you," pledged Jimmy Carter, an obscure former one-term governor of Georgia. A graduate of the U.S. Naval Academy, Carter had served aboard nuclear submarines before returning to Georgia to follow his father as a peanut farmer and politician. When this born-again Christian promised voters efficiency and decency in government, they believed him.

Carter was as ambitious as he was sincere. For two years he and his advisers plotted his campaign strategy. When the 1976 Democratic primaries began, they were ready to canvass the country state by state, primary by primary. Carter worked harder and longer than the other candidates, and he arrived at the national convention with more than enough delegates to win the nomination. His selection of Senator Walter Mondale of Minnesota as his running mate strengthened his candidacy by cementing relations with northern liberals, blacks, union members, and political bosses.

Carter presented himself as a fiscal conservative who would restrain government spending and a social liberal who would fight for the poor, the aged, non-whites, workers, urban dwellers, and farmers. He stressed that in foreign affairs the United States should work for human rights, arms control, and nonintervention (see page 930). But most of all he emphasized his character: a simple, down-home farmer and family man; a white southerner who had won the support of blacks and northern liberals; an honest politician.

President Ford won his party's nomination after a bitter struggle with Ronald Reagan, former governor of California and champion of the party's right wing.

Ford had grown in the public's estimation since his pardon of Nixon, and the economy had improved while he was in office: inflation had dropped to 5.8 percent. But neither Ford nor Carter inspired much interest, and on election day only 53.5 percent of the electorate stirred itself to vote. Nevertheless, an analysis of the turnout was instructive. One political commentator concluded that the vote was "fractured to a marked degree along the fault line separating the haves and have-nots." Carter gained nearly 90 percent of the black and Mexican-American vote and squeaked to victory by a slim 1.7 million votes out of 80 million. Ford's appeal was strongest among middle- and upper-middle-class voters.

Carter's major domestic accomplishments were in energy, transportation, and conservation policy. To encourage domestic production of oil he instituted

Carter Administration

phased decontrol of oil prices. To moderate the social effects of the energy crisis he called for a windfall-profits tax on excessive profits resulting from decontrol, and grants to the poor and elderly for the purchase of heating fuel. Carter also reformed the civil service and created separate Departments of Energy and Education. He deregulated the airline, trucking, and railroad industries and persuaded Congress to ease federal control of banks. His administration established a $1.6 billion "superfund" to clean up abandoned chemical-waste sites. And finally, in what Carter called "the most important decision on conservation matters that the Congress will face in this century," he placed over 100 million acres of Alaskan land under the federal government's protection as national parks, national forests, and wildlife refuges.

Despite these accomplishments, Jimmy Carter's popularity flagged early. He seemed cold and uncommanding, and he lacked leadership qualities. He

Carter's Flagging Popularity

never established a close working relationship with congressional leaders, nor did he forge friendly relations with other power bases, such as the AFL-CIO. Elected as an outsider, he remained one throughout his presidency.

Carter's conservative policies alienated Democrats who had grown up in the party's New Deal liberal tradition. His support of deregulation and his opposition to wage and price controls and gasoline rationing ran counter to the liberal Democratic position. Seeing inflation as more of a threat to the nation's health than either recession or unemployment, Carter announced that his top priority would be to cut federal spending, even though doing so would add to the jobless rolls. But inflation continued to rise. Liberals grumbled that Carter was a closet Republican, the most conservative Democratic president since Grover Cleveland. In November 1979 Senator Edward Kennedy announced that he would contest the president's renomination.

Carter's problems were not entirely of his own making. In 1979, the shah of Iran's government fell to revolutionary forces; the new government then cut off oil supplies to the United States. And in November Iranian militants stormed the United States embassy in Teheran, taking sixty-six Americans hostage (see page 932). OPEC also raised its prices in 1979, and the cost of crude oil nearly doubled. During the summer, as Americans waited in long lines at gasoline pumps, public approval of the president reached new lows. The Carter administration did respond to the economic woes of the Chrysler Corporation, which had reported losses of $466 million in the first six months of 1979. In the Chrysler "bailout" of January 1980, Congress authorized loan guarantees of $1.5 billion on condition that Chrysler obtain wage reductions from employees, concessions from banks, and state and local aid.

Carter also inherited certain political problems. Not since Eisenhower's eight-year presidency had a president served two full terms; some observers worried

Decline of Presidential Authority

that America had invented the "disposable president," to be discarded every four years. And in the wake of Vietnam and Watergate, Congress had put the president in what Nixon's secretary of state, William Rogers, called "a straitjacket of legislation": campaign laws, the impoundment act, and the War Powers Act. Power had clearly shifted from the White House to Capitol Hill. At the same time Congress was filling up with political newcomers, men and women unused to blind obedience to established leadership. Party discipline seemed a thing of the past.

To complicate matters, Capitol Hill was crawling with lobbyists from a multitude of special-interest

On inauguration day, President Jimmy Carter (1924–) and his wife, Rosalynn, caught the public's fancy by walking from the Capitol to the White House. Despite this symbolic beginning, Carter became increasingly isolated both from the American people and from Congress. National Archives, Carter Project.

groups: trade associations, corporations, labor unions, and single-issue groups like the National Rifle Association. Carter complained that the nation had become "fragmented, Balkanized." In 1980, there were 2,765 political action committees (PACs), more than four times as many as in 1974. Partly responsible for this proliferation was the Campaign Finance Law of 1974, which put a lid of $5,000 on PAC contributions to each candidate, but weakened this provision's impact by placing no limit on the number of PACs from which politicians could accept money.

With party discipline in tatters and each group

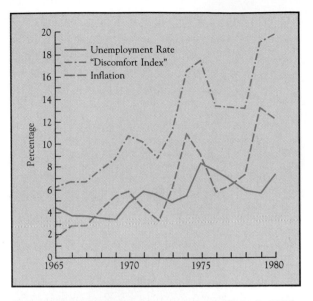

Discomfort Index (Unemployment plus Inflation), 1965–1980 Source: *Economic Report of the President: 1980* *(Washington: U.S. Government Printing Office, 1981),* *pp. 238, 263.*

clamoring for its own program, the president was forced to form what one White House aide called a "roll-your-own majority" for each proposal. The task called for skills Carter did not possess—trading pork-barrel projects for votes, mobilizing public opinion, and massaging politicians' egos.

By 1980 the economy was a shambles. Inflation had jumped in 1979 to 13.4 percent, and buyers around the world had lost confidence in the dollar, causing unprecedented increases in the price of gold. To steady the dollar and curb inflation, the Federal Reserve Board had taken drastic measures in late 1979: it had raised the rates at which it loaned money to banks. As a result auto loans became more difficult to obtain, mortgage interest rates leaped beyond 15 percent, and the prime lending rate (the rate charged to businesses) hit an all-time high of 20 percent.

Worse still, by 1980 the nation was in a full-fledged recession, with an unemployment rate of 7.5 percent. For two consecutive quarters it had experienced no growth in the gross national product. The combined high inflation and high unemployment rates had produced a staggeringly high discomfort index of just under 20 percent (see figure). Moreover, the Iranian hostage

Economic Discomfort in 1980

crisis made Carter and the United States appear ineffectual. In 1976 Carter had gibed at the incumbent, President Ford, by saying, "Anything you don't like about Washington, I suggest you blame on him." In 1980 Carter was the incumbent, and many Americans blamed him for the problems that beset the country.

NONWHITES AND NEW IMMIGRANTS

Carter and his predecessors in the 1970s, Nixon and Ford, presided over a nation in which many nonwhites saw their economic fortunes decline. Joblessness plagued blacks, Native Americans, and Hispanics, as well as the new immigrants who arrived during the decade. As a result of the sluggish economy, poverty was still a national problem in 1980, and blacks made up a disproportionate share of the poor. In the 1970s inner-city blacks experienced a 21 percent increase in poverty. By 1978, though the overall poverty rate had decreased to 11.4 percent, the rate for black families was 27.5, compared with 6.9 percent for white families.

The weight of poverty fell heavily on black children. A 1981 Children's Defense Fund survey reported that black children in the United States were four times more likely than whites to be born in poverty, twice as likely to drop out of school before twelfth grade, five times as likely as white teenagers to be murdered, and three times as likely to be unemployed. "Millions of black children lack self-confidence, feel discouragement, despair, numbness or rage as they try to grow up on islands of poverty, ill health, inadequate education . . . crime and rampant unemployment in a nation of boastful affluence," the report concluded. Indeed, in 1980 the unemployment rate for black male teenagers in the inner cities hovered around 50 percent. For each single percentage-point increase in the nation's overall unemployment rate, the increase for young black men was 6.3 percent.

Tied to the high unemployment rate was the increase in the number of young black families headed by single women. Between 1960 and 1975 the number of fatherless black families rose 130 percent. Many of these families were headed by unmarried teenagers who were forced to rely on welfare to support their children. Other mothers earned meager incomes as domestic servants, laundresses, or kitchen helpers. Like young black males, welfare mothers suffered from a sense of futility. Many were children of the welfare system; it was the only life they knew.

Some whites and even other blacks grumbled that poor blacks were responsible for their own poverty. Their own forebears had seized the opportunities at

Declining Job Opportunities for Blacks

hand and raised themselves up by their bootstraps, whites insisted; why couldn't today's blacks do the same? But the job market was far different in the 1980s from what it had been

twenty-five, fifty, or seventy-five years before. In the past, unskilled European immigrants and black migrants from the South had been able to obtain blue-collar jobs during periods of rapid industrialization. But in the 1970s few such jobs were available; the auto, steel, rubber, and coal industries were contracting, not expanding. Blue-collar jobs in the inner cities were disappearing or moving to the suburbs. New York City alone had 234,000 fewer blue-collar workers in 1980 than it had at the beginning of the decade. This loss of jobs added to inner-city poverty. In 1970, the median household income in the cities was 80 percent of that in the suburbs. By 1980, it had fallen to 74 percent.

In the 1970s, the labor demand was for skilled workers such as computer operators, bank tellers, secretaries, and bookkeepers. Most jobless blacks could not qualify. During these years, too, the labor movement was no longer committed to unionizing the unskilled and the semiskilled. Instead, unions were devoting much of their energy to organizing white-collar workers. As a result the portion of the nonfarm labor force belonging to unions dropped from 33 percent in 1958 to 24 percent in 1978. The situation was tragic for young black men and women who lacked marketable skills. As the black psychiatrist Alvin Poussaint has observed, "A lot of black kids simply feel they don't count. . . . In terms of what makes this society run, they're expendable."

But even as the plight of the black poor worsened, the black middle class expanded. Black college students increased from 282,000 in 1966 to over 1 million in

Black Middle Class

1976. During this period an estimated 30 percent of the urban black population joined the middle class, and many moved to the suburbs or to better housing in the cities. By 1980 about one-third of all black high school graduates were going on to college, the same proportion as among white youths. At least at the upper levels of black society, the dream of equality was being realized.

In his provocative book *The Declining Significance of Race* (1978), William Julius Wilson, the University of Chicago sociologist, spoke of the emergence of two black Americas, one very poor, the other affluent. Blacks living in inner cities and possessed of few job skills found themselves "locked in the low-wage sector . . . where there is little opportunity for advancement and rates of job turnover are high." Meanwhile middle-class blacks, better educated than poor blacks, were able to obtain jobs in government and business, in part because of the pressures of affirmative action. Wilson concluded that "the life chances of blacks" were "based far more on their present economic class position than on their status as black Americans."

Some scholars criticized Wilson's thesis, but other observers supported it. As early as 1970 Andrew F. Brimmer, a black governor of the Federal Reserve System, had warned about "the deepening schism" between poor and middle-class blacks. "There is growing estrangement," Alfred Smith, a black social worker in Boston, admitted in 1978. "The empathy is there, but there's less contact between the middle class and poor blacks."

As middle-class blacks were making gains, resentful whites complained that they were being victimized by "reverse discrimination." To meet federal affirmative-action requirements, some

White Backlash

schools and companies had established quotas for minorities and women. In some cases the requirements for quota groups were lower than those for whites. In a 5-to-4 ruling in 1978 the Supreme Court outlawed quotas but upheld the principle of affirmative action (*Bakke* v. *University of California*).

Anger over a special standard for blacks combined with the effects of stagflation and opposition to busing to produce an upsurge in racism in the 1970s. In Louisville in 1975, bumper stickers urged people to "Honk if you oppose busing." The Ku Klux Klan

In Boston in 1976, antibusing protesters tried to impale a black man with a flagstaff. This photograph of the ugly incident won a Pulitzer Prize. Stanley Forman/Boston Herald-American.

stepped up its recruiting in Louisville, and violence soon erupted: over two days, one hundred people were injured and two hundred arrested. In Boston, where busing caused numerous riots, a group of white students protesting busing attacked a black passer-by outside City Hall. "Get the nigger; kill him," one shouted, and they ran at him with the sharp end of a flagstaff flying an American flag. Tension rose not only in Boston and Louisville, but all across the nation. Membership in the Ku Klux Klan grew from about five thousand in 1978 to ten thousand just two years later.

Blacks were tense, too, and they showed it more openly than in the past. "After 350 years of fearing whites," Charles Silberman wrote in *Criminal Violence, Criminal Justice* (1978), "black **Black Anger** Americans have discovered that fear runs the other way, that whites are intimidated by their very presence. . . . The taboo

against expression of anti-white anger is breaking down, and 350 years of festering hatred has come spilling out." That hatred erupted several times in summer 1980, most notably in Miami and Chattanooga, after all-white juries acquitted whites of the murder of blacks. (In Miami the defendants were white policemen; in Chattanooga, Ku Klux Klansmen.) Miami's three days of rioting left eighteen dead, four hundred injured, and $100 million worth of property damage. Surveying the wreckage, Vernon Jordan of the National Urban League remarked, "The ingredients that caused the explosion in Miami are present in every city in this country." Just a few days later, Jordan was seriously wounded in Fort Wayne, Indiana, by an unidentified gunman.

Every bit as angry as blacks were American Indians. Their new militancy had burst into the headlines in November 1969, when a small group of Indians seized Alcatraz Island in San Francisco Bay. Arguing that

In February 1973, angered by federal government policies and by the actions of conservative Indian leaders, militant members of the American Indian Movement seized hostages at Wounded Knee, South Dakota. The militants exchanged gunfire with federal marshals and their Indian allies, whom the militants disdained as "Uncle Tomahawks."   Michael Abramson/Black Star.

an 1868 Sioux treaty entitled them to possession of unused federal lands, the Indians occupied the island until summer 1971. But more was at stake than an abandoned federal penitentiary. "Not just on Alcatraz," explained Richard Oakes, a spokesperson for the Indians, "but every place else, the Indian is in his last stand for cultural survival." Two years later, members of the American Indian Movement (AIM) seized eleven hostages and a trading post on the Pine Ridge Reservation at Wounded Knee, South Dakota, the place where troops of the 7th Cavalry had massacred the Sioux in 1890 (see page 465). Their seventy-one-day confrontation with federal marshals ended with a government agreement to examine the treaty rights of the Oglala Sioux.

Indian Militancy

White society posed more than a cultural threat to Indians, however. The unemployment rate among Indians was 40 percent in the late 1970s. The average per capita income on large reservations was $974, well below the poverty line. Nine out of ten Indians lived in substandard housing, and the high school dropout rate averaged 53 percent. Being an Indian was also unhealthy: Native Americans suffered the highest incidence of alcoholism, tuberculosis, and suicide of any ethnic group in the United States. Though their population had risen since the Second World War to about 1 million (650,000 on or near reservations and 350,000 in the "red ghettos" of the cities), that was only a fraction of their number when the first Europeans arrived in North America.

Since 1924 Indians have had dual legal status as United States citizens and as members of tribal nations subject to special treaty agreements with the United States. But their dual status has proved a curse, in large part because the government has not honored its treaty commitments—especially

Indian Suits for Lost Lands

when Indian lands contained valuable minerals. In 1946 Congress established the Indian Claims Commission to compensate Indians for lands stolen from them. Under the legislation lawyers for the Native American Rights Fund and other groups scored notable victories in the 1970s. The Chippewa in the upper Midwest, Indians in the Puget Sound area of Washington, and the Cheyenne-Arapaho tribes in Oklahoma won protection of their hunting and fishing rights and restitution of their land and water. In 1971 President Nixon signed a bill returning to the Taos Pueblo their sacred forest of Blue Lake in New Mexico. And in 1980 the Supreme Court ordered the government to pay $117 million plus interest to the Sioux Indian Nation for the Black Hills of South Dakota, stolen from them when gold was discovered there in the 1870s.

Compared with earlier treatment, the court decisions, land settlements, and legislation of the 1960s and 1970s were heartening. At the same time, though, corporations and government agencies still coveted Indian lands and disregarded Indian religious beliefs. In the 1960s a coal company strip-mined a portion of the Hopi Sacred Circle, which according to tribal religion is the source of all life. And once again the Black Hills of South Dakota were being mined, this time for uranium.

As Indians fought to regain old rights, Hispanics struggled to make a place for themselves in the United States. An influx of immigrants unequaled since the

Hispanic-Americans

turn of the century coupled with a high birthrate had made Hispanic peoples America's fastest-growing minority by the 1970s. Of the more than 20 million Hispanics living in the United States in the 1970s, 8 million were Mexican-Americans concentrated in Arizona, California, Colorado, New Mexico, and Texas. Several million Puerto Ricans and perhaps 1 million Cubans clustered principally on the East Coast. In 1980 New York City's Planning Commission estimated that the city had almost 2 million Hispanic residents, over half of Puerto Rican descent and the rest Dominicans, Colombians, Ecuadorans, and Cubans.

Besides these officially acknowledged Hispanics, between 8 million and 12 million more undocumented workers, or illegal aliens, lived in the United States. Beginning in the mid-1960s, large numbers of poverty-stricken Mexicans began to cross the poorly guarded 2,000-mile border between Mexico and the United States. The movement north continued in the 1970s; in the last eight years of that decade the Chicano population increased 60 percent. Pressure mounted on Congress to curtail this flow and perhaps to provide amnesty for those aliens already living illegally in the United States. In 1979 a congressional commission undertook a two-year re-examination of America's immigration policies. By 1980, one out of every four Texans and one out of every five Californians was Mexican-American. Many newcomers settled in East Los Angeles, the nation's largest barrio. As David Lizarraga, director of the East Los Angeles Community Union, explained: "If I were in Mexico now, I'd be running across that wire as fast as I could. This is the land of opportunity."

But poverty awaited these new immigrants, as it had previous groups of newcomers. The median family income for Mexican-Americans in 1979 was $11,421, as compared with $16,284 for non-Hispanic families. Nineteen percent of Mexican-Americans lived below the poverty line. Puerto Ricans were worse off, with a median family income of about $8,300, and 30 percent of their number living in poverty. Though the problems with which Hispanics contended were similar to those confronting other nonwhites, they also faced a language barrier. Most inner-city schools were ill equipped to serve the needs of bilingual students. As a result, only 30 percent of Hispanic high school students graduated, and fewer than 7 percent finished college. Finally, the larger the Hispanic population has become, the more widespread has been the discrimination against them. "Anglos are afraid," said California Assemblyman Richard Alatorre. "They think they will get to be the minorities and we'll be opposing them."

Most Hispanics preferred their family-centered culture to Anglo culture, and for that reason they resisted assimilation. "What we are saying," explained Daniel

Hispanic Cultural Pride

Villanueva, a TV executive, "is that we want to be here, but without losing our language and our culture. They are a richness, a treasure that we don't care to lose." A Puerto Rican woman in New York added, "We have been trying to become American for too long, and we are forgetting our roots, culture and the values of our nationality."

The 1970s were a decade of massive immigration to the United States. These Vietnam refugees were among twenty-eight "boat people" who were rescued in the South China Sea by American sailors. U.S. Navy.

Instead, like other minorities, Hispanics wanted power—"brown power." Cesar Chavez's United Farm Workers had been the first Hispanic interest group to gain national attention. Another group, the militant Brown Berets, attracted notice for their efforts to provide meals to preschoolers and courses in Chicano studies and consciousness-raising to older students. And throughout the 1970s the Mexican-American political party La Raza Unida was a potent force in the Southwest and East Los Angeles. Still, for a group soon to become the nation's largest minority, Hispanics exercised a disproportionately small share of political power. One reason was that Hispanic America was a tremendously diverse community. Although they shared a language and a religion, Mexican-Americans, Puerto Ricans, Cubans, and other groups differed in countless ways. "We need a Spanish Bobby Kennedy or Martin Luther King," observed Daniel Villanueva. "Right now he's just not there."

During the late 1970s and early 1980s, still other new immigrants joined America's nonwhite population. Between 1970 and 1980 the United States absorbed more than 4 million immigrants and refugees and perhaps twice that number of illegal aliens—more new residents than in any one decade in American history. Refugees of the Vietnam War arrived from Indochina, and other immigrants came from the Philippines, Korea, Taiwan, India, the Dominican Republic, and Jamaica. In 1980, 160,000 boat people poured in from the islands of Cuba and Haiti. Although well-wishers were on hand to greet these people, the history of the nation's treatment of nonwhites, along with the severe recession that began in 1979, did not augur well for them. "Clearly, some people derive great benefit from the present situation," explained Leon Castillo, former commissioner of immigration, in referring to the low wages paid to aliens. The new residents faced a long struggle.

New Influx of Immigrants

WOMEN'S STRUGGLES

In the 1970s, while civil rights struggles were engaging the energies of various racial and ethnic groups, increasing numbers of women were committing themselves to the struggle for equality with men. Feminists had scored some impressive legislative victories. In 1974 Congress passed the Equal Credit Opportunity Act, which enabled women to get bank loans and obtain credit cards on the same terms as men. Many states revised their statutes on rape, prohibiting lawyers from stressing the previous sexual experience of rape victims.

Women also made gains in education: between 1970 and 1975 the number of women enrolled in college rose 45 percent. And they campaigned for and were elected to various political offices. In 1976 Ella Grasso was elected governor of Connecticut, and two years later Nancy Kassebaum of Kansas was elected to the Senate. Perhaps most significant were women's gains, along with blacks and other minorities, from affirmative action in hiring. As mandated by the Civil Rights Act of 1964 and the establishment of the Equal Employment Opportunity Commission, women and minorities had to receive the same consideration as white males when applying for a job. To take advantage of new opportunities, many women delayed having children until they were in their thirties and had established themselves in their careers.

Still, women continued to encounter barriers in their quest for equality. One of the most formidable was the antifeminist, or "profamily," movement, which contended that men should lead and women should follow, particularly within the family. The backlash against feminism became an increasingly powerful political force in the 1970s. In defense of the family—especially the patriarchal, or father-led, family—antifeminists campaigned against the Equal Rights Amendment (ERA), the gay rights movement, and abortion on demand. Anita Bryant and Phyllis Schlafly gained fame by arguing that all these issues were interrelated and that they endangered traditional American values.

Antifeminist Movement

For one thing, antifeminists blamed the women's movement for the country's spiraling divorce rate; they charged that feminists would jettison their husbands and even their children in their quests for job fulfillment and sexual equality. Although the number of divorces almost tripled from 1960 to 1976, the decision to terminate marriages and dissolve families was often made, not by the wives, but by their husbands. According to Barbara Ehrenreich, a feminist scholar, men first started walking out on their families in large numbers in the 1950s, well before the rebirth of feminism. Tired of fulfilling their male role as financial provider and final arbiter of family disputes, many men also responded to the image of bachelorhood presented in the pages of *Playboy*. Some felt trapped emotionally, as well as financially and sexually. Beginning in the 1950s, *Playboy* and other magazines attacked wives as parasites who gobbled up their husbands' salaries but were too sexually repressed to give much in return. Increasingly, many men came to see their wives as the source of their entrapment and in their "flight from commitment," they chose divorce.

In the political arena antifeminists successfully stalled ratification of the Equal Rights Amendment, which after quickly passing through thirty-five state legislatures fell three states short of success in the late 1970s. Schlafly's STOP ERA campaign falsely claimed that the ERA would abolish alimony and legalize homosexual marriage. The ERA debate was vicious at times. Refusing to acknowledge the gender-based discrimination that was so injurious to women's welfare, morale, and aspirations, Schlafly derided ERA advocates as "a bunch of bitter women seeking a constitutional cure for their personal problems."

Equal Rights Amendment

Many antifeminists also participated in the antiabortion, or "prolife," movement, which sprang up almost overnight in the wake of the Supreme Court's 1973 decisions in *Roe* v. *Wade* and *Doe* v. *Bolton* (see page 961). People whose opposition to abortion was heartfelt and uncompromising denounced those rulings and called for an amendment to the Constitution that would define human life as beginning at conception. The battle between the prolife and prochoice forces had been joined. Along with Catholics, Mormons, and other religious opponents of abortion, the prolife movement also supported the

The struggle over the Equal Rights Amendment was heated on both sides. It pitted these ERA supporters against the antifeminist campaign led by, among others, Phyllis Schlafly's STOP ERA organization.   Diana Walker/Gamma Liason.

successful legislative efforts of Representative Henry Hyde of Illinois in 1976 to cut off most Medicaid funds for abortions. In summer 1980 the Supreme Court upheld the Hyde amendment, deciding that the government had no obligation to make even medically necessary abortions available to the poor (*Harris v. McRae*).

As activists in the women's struggle looked to the future, they had to acknowledge certain harsh realities. One was the impact of the economic recessions of the 1970s and early 1980s. In a tight job market, it was difficult for most outsiders—women and non-whites—to become insiders. Though affirmative action had certainly helped women to gain employment and receive promotions, jobs had to be available in the first place for women to benefit. "The economic environment," predicted one analyst, "may prove to be the major determinant of women's role in 1980. . . . Scarcity of jobs in the next decade [will] produce a greater

Effects of a Glutted Job Market

competition in the labor market and a tremendous backlash against women." Added to job scarcity was the continuing problem of occupational segregation in which women were concentrated in lower-paying positions while most men enjoyed much higher incomes (see page 961). By the end of the 1970s, female workers still took home only 59 cents to every male worker's dollar.

Perhaps the most disturbing trend was what *Newsweek* called "the Superwoman Squeeze." According to a report by the Worldwatch Institute in 1980, most working wives and mothers, even those with full-time jobs, "retained an unwilling monopoly on unpaid labor at home." Husbands were generally less than eager to do household tasks, and there were few readily available marketplace substitutes for loving, caring, and responsiveness to emergencies. Predictions were that by 1990 only one in four wives would be a full-time housewife and mother. The rest would be trying to

Increased Burdens on Women

balance the more-than-full-time demands of work and homemaking.

It appeared, too, that the feminist ferment of the 1970s had dwindled by the early 1980s. Some women seemed to take for granted the gains of that decade, believing that equality of opportunity had been secured for all time. Others were concentrating on planning their lives so they could have both a career and a family without shortchanging either—or themselves—in the process.

THE ME DECADE

At the beginning of 1980, the editors of *Time* magazine observed that the 1970s had been "erected upon the smoldering wreckage of the '60s. Now and then, someone's shovel blade would strike an unexploded bomb; mostly the air in the '70s was thick with a sense of aftermath, of public passions spent and consciences bewildered."

The nation had turned apathetic, and perhaps nowhere was this new attitude more evident than among youth. In the 1960s American youths had worked for change in the nation's social, political, and cultural life. But by the mid-1970s the aspirations of young Americans had been transformed. A student at Vassar commented: "We saw it all. We were freshmen in high school when our older brothers and sisters were going off to war or to exile or to revolution. . . . We saw the waste of lives and I think that determined that we would not ruin our own for lost causes." Older Americans took refuge, too, from a lost war, political scandal, and economic distress. As a theologian put it, Americans "have a beleaguered sense in their bones that the old order is dying. Very few want a radical alternative, but few also are working to develop a rationale for the system we've got."

Instead, in the 1970s Americans turned inward and concentrated on self-expression and personal improvement. As a popular beer commercial proclaimed, "You only go 'round once in life and you've got to grab for all the gusto you can get." That gusto ranged from recreational vehicles to roller skates, disco to punk rock, *The Godfather* to *Star Wars*. Social commentator Tom Wolfe branded the 1970s the Me Decade, a time of diversion and material consumption designed to make Americans' private worlds, in the midst of public confusion, at least tolerable.

In the self-centered new decade, suggestions for realizing one's full potential were consumed as readily as jogging shoes and health foods. Transactional Analysis (TA), a form of psychotherapy emphasizing interpersonal relationships, was popularized in Eric Berne's *Games People Play* (1969) and Thomas Harris's *I'm OK—You're OK* (1969). Transcendental Meditation (TM), a yogic discipline, drew 350,000 adherents and spawned over two hundred teaching centers. Est (Erhard Seminars Training), a system of encounters meant to enable people to "get in touch with themselves," was grossing $10 million a year in 1975. In addition to these fads, other new therapies and exotic religions flourished, as did such eastern religions and practices of long-standing as Zen and yoga.

Human Potential Movement

As millions of Americans sought to fill spiritual and emotional voids through esoteric movements, millions more were drawn to traditional Christian beliefs. According to a 1977 survey, about 70 million Americans defined themselves as born-again Christians, and 10 million claimed to have had the experience since 1975. President Jimmy Carter, singers Pat Boone and Johnny Cash, professional football player Roger Staubach, former Black Panther Eldridge Cleaver, and Watergate felons Jeb Stuart Magruder and Charles Colson all counted themselves among the saved. Religious revivals and evangelical sects were not new, of course, but by the mid-1970s they were a growth industry. In the latter years of the decade evangelicals were grossing $200 million annually in sales of religious books, and the Virginia-based Christian Broadcast Network was earning nearly $60 million from its four stations and 130 affiliates.

Spiritual Revival

Besides the relatively harmless human potential movements and the traditional religious enthusiasms, a dark undercurrent of cult-like adherence to charismatic leaders ran through the 1970s. In 1973 and 1974, the Reverend Sun Myung Moon, Korean

Messianic Cults

founder of the Unification Church, converted young Americans to his religion, a curious blend of Christianity, anti-Communism, and worship of Moon as a messiah. "Moonies" disposed of their possessions, moved into communes, and raised funds for the church by selling ginseng tea, candles, flowers, and peanuts. Critics charged that Moon and his disciples had brainwashed their converts. Soon worried parents were attempting to kidnap their children from the Unification Church and its influence.

For most of those who followed the Reverend Jim Jones to Guyana, attempts at rescue came too late. Jones's California cult, the People's Temple, had begun as a church committed to social reform and civil rights. But in 1977 stories began to surface alleging that Jones had made death threats and had committed extortion. Jones moved the cult to Guyana, in South America, where he established a colony named Jonestown. In November 1978, convinced that the United States was about to destroy the colony and embark on an apocalyptic race war, the crazed leader ordered his followers to poison their children and then kill themselves with a mixture of Kool-Aid and cyanide. The mass murder and suicide of 911 people at Jonestown added a satanic headline to the history of cults in the United States.

Many Americans in the 1970s were in quest not only of the "ideal self," but also of their personal identity. For this reason, another facet of "me-ness" was the phenomenon called "Roots." The 1977 television series, based on a best-selling book by Alex Haley, dramatized the author's family history beginning with his ancestor, Kunta Kinte, a Gambian boy sold into slavery. "Roots" spawned an interest in family trees that touched all races and ethnic groups. More important, the sheer numbers of Americans exposed to the book and television series (130 million watched the eight-part series) helped to sensitize the public to the agonies of slavery and racism.

When Americans went running to libraries to research their family trees during the 1970s, they usually did so in an expensive pair of Nikes, Pumas, or Adidas, for this was the decade of the jogger. James Fixx's *Complete Book of Running* (1977) enjoyed tremendous popularity, and literature on running, physical fitness, diet, and health jammed

Physical Fitness Craze

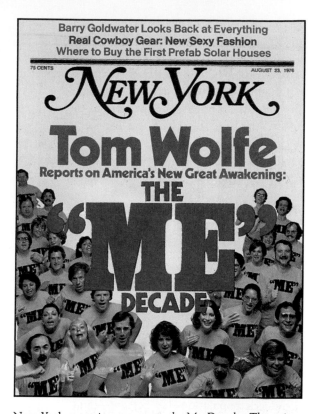

New York *magazine announces the Me Decade. The writer Tom Wolfe, who gave the label to the seventies, sensed that Americans had become self-indulgent and apolitical.* © 1976 *by News Group Publications, Inc. Reprinted with the permission of* New York Magazine.

bookshelves and magazine racks. Perhaps America was no longer the best nation it could be, but Americans were determined to make themselves the healthiest individuals they could be. Saunas, hot tubs, and Jacuzzis became popular, and membership in tennis and racquetball clubs, health centers, and diet clinics boomed. At the supermarket, consumers kept a careful eye out for products marked "no preservatives" or "all natural."

The dominant sound of the later 1970s was disco. One writer called disco "the affirmation of the 'unreal' seventies, the fantasies, fashions, gossip, frivolity and fun. . . . Disco emphasizes surfaces over substance, mood over meaning." Millions of Americans of various ages and backgrounds flocked to clubs to dance, display their latest fashions, and watch each other.

As the decade drew to a close, Christopher Lasch, a history professor at the University of Rochester, condemned the nation's behavior as self-indulgent and apolitical. In *The Culture of Narcissism* (1979), Lasch branded Americans an emotionally shallow, anxiety-ridden people desperately trying to ignore the waning of their nation's power. He cited advertising and the human potential movement as causes of the nation's malaise. But there was little evidence that the trend was changing. In a decade of exhausted public passions, private passions reigned supreme.

RONALD REAGAN AND THE ELECTION OF 1980

The year President Carter ran for re-election the federal government published its decennial census of the population. The figures released by the Bureau of the Census revealed significant growth in the elderly population—24 percent— and a two-year rise in the median age. By 1980 there were as many people over thirty as under, and the number of retired persons had increased by more than 50 percent since 1972. Translated into political terms, the census figures meant that the American population was becoming more conservative.

The census also documented the continuing movement of large numbers of people from the politically liberal Frostbelt states of the Northeast and Midwest to the more conservative Sunbelt states of the South and West (see map). The census findings meant that seventeen seats in the House of Representatives would shift from the Frostbelt to the Sunbelt by the 1982 elections. Florida would gain four seats and New York would lose five; Texas would gain three, California two.

Besides gaining political power, the Sunbelt enjoyed abundant energy resources and a wider tax base than the North. In 1980 Louisiana produced over four times its energy needs, New Mexico over three, and Texas over two. By contrast, Michigan and New York had to import most of their energy, at a price jacked up by export taxes imposed by producing states. Taxes were lower in the Sunbelt, too; Texas families paid less than half as much of their incomes for state and local taxes as New York families did.

The census only confirmed what had already become obvious to politicians: conservatism was the dominant mood of the nation in the late 1970s. Americans doubted government's capacity to serve the people. In 1977 Senator Gary Hart, a Colorado Democrat, characterized this mood as "a non-ideological skepticism about the old, Rooseveltian solutions to social problems." But there were hard-working conservatives whose goal was to repeal the welfare state. In 1978 California voters approved a tax-cutting referendum called Proposition 13, which reduced property taxes and put stringent limits on state spending for social programs. On the national level conservatives lobbied for a constitutional amendment to prohibit federal budget deficits and organized for the 1980 elections. One conservative campaign group, the National Conservative Political Action Committee (NCPAC), targeted a number of liberal senators for defeat.

Resurgence of Conservatism

Conservative politicians were joined by evangelical Christians, who believed they had a moral obligation to enter politics on the side of righteousness, which they defined as "a pro-life, pro-traditional family, pro-moral position." In summer 1979 the Reverend Jerry Falwell, a radio-TV minister from Lynchburg, Virginia, helped to found the Moral Majority, which in the next fourteen months registered beween 2 and 3 million new voters, raised $1.5 million, started a newspaper, and bought daily time on 140 radio stations. Together with conservative think tanks like the Hoover Institution and conservative magazines like the *National Review*, these church groups formed a flourishing network of potential supporters for conservative candidates.

In 1980 several conservative Republican politicians ran for the White House, but the champion of them all was Ronald Reagan, former Hollywood movie star and two-term governor of California. A small-town boy from Dixon, Illinois, Reagan had been a radio sportscaster before moving to Hollywood in the mid-1930s. As president of the Screen Actors Guild, his politics had been those of a New Deal Democrat. But in the

Ronald Reagan's Early Career

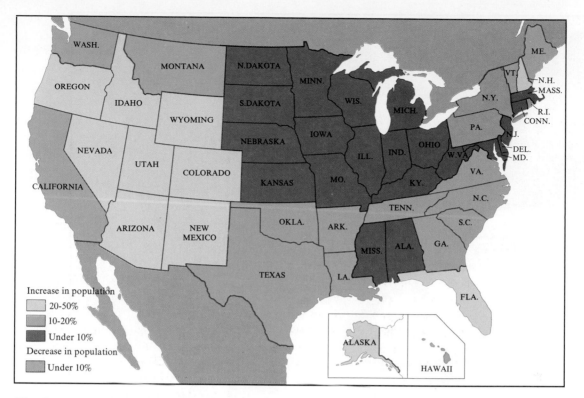

The Continued Shift to the Sunbelt.

Increase in population
- 20-50%
- 10-20%
- Under 10%

Decrease in population
- Under 10%

1950s, as he toured the country as host of the television program "General Electric Theatre," Reagan became increasingly conservative. In 1964 he made a televised appeal for Senator Barry Goldwater, the conservative Republican presidential candidate. His persuasive speech not only catapulted him to the forefront of conservative politics; it became his personal platform for the presidency. America, Reagan said, had come to "a time for choosing" between free enterprise and big government, between individual liberty and "the ant heap of totalitarianism." Two years later he was elected governor of California.

During his two four-year terms as governor Reagan maintained his conservatism, but also displayed a pragmatic approach to governing. While denouncing welfare, he presided over reform of the state's welfare bureaucracy. While demanding that student radicals at the University of California either obey the rules or face the prospect of a "bloodbath," he worked to fund most of the university's budget requests. And he signed one of the nation's most liberal abortion laws.

In 1980 Reagan triumphed easily over moderate Republicans Representative John Anderson of Illinois and former CIA director George Bush of Texas. And

Election of 1980

his appeal to the voters in the presidential campaign was much more widespread than observers had predicted. He promised economy in government and a balanced budget, and he committed himself to "supply-side" economics, or tax reductions to businesses to encourage capital investment. But while he planned to slash federal spending, Reagan also pledged to cut income taxes and boost the defense budget—a prescription that George Bush dismissed as "voodoo economics." Reagan declared that he now opposed legalized abortion, and his stand against the ERA recommended him to the profamily movement. Indeed, his candidacy united the old right wing with the new. The old right, explained one fundraiser, had never been very interested in social issues. "But when political conservative leaders began to reach out and strike an alliance with social conservatives—the pro-life people, the anti-ERA people,

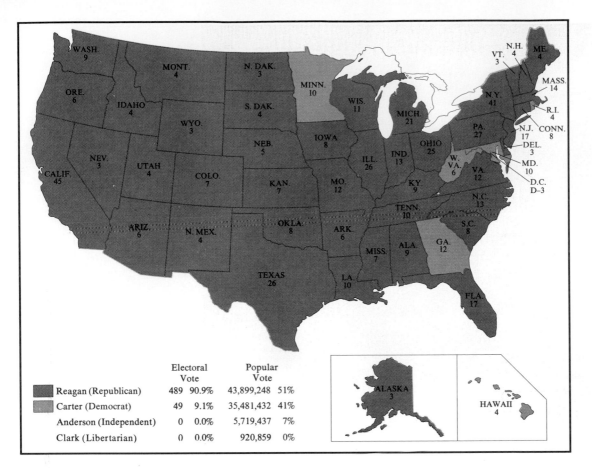

		Electoral Vote		Popular Vote	
■	Reagan (Republican)	489	90.9%	43,899,248	51%
▨	Carter (Democrat)	49	9.1%	35,481,432	41%
	Anderson (Independent)	0	0.0%	5,719,437	7%
	Clark (Libertarian)	0	0.0%	920,859	0%

Presidential Election, 1980

the evangelical and born-again Christians, the people concerned about gay rights, prayer in the schools, sex in the movies or whatever—that's when this whole movement began to come alive. It's happened in a big way just in the last two years, and its just exploding."

For his part, President Carter had little difficulty beating back Senator Edward Kennedy's challenge. Kennedy's New Deal liberalism seemed out of place in the 1980s, and memories of Chappaquiddick lingered in voters' minds. The president had more formidable problems. American hostages were still held captive in Iran, and stagflation beset the economy. Carter retreated into the White House, contending that the nation's problems were too serious to allow him time to campaign. His supporters worried about the independent candidate, John Anderson, who had bolted the Republican party in the primaries.

As election day approached, some political analysts thought they detected a resurgence of support for Carter. Polls predicted a Reagan victory by 3 to 5 percent, a small margin given the country's problems. But on election day voters gave Reagan and his running mate, George Bush, 51 percent of the vote to 41 percent for Carter and 6.6 percent for Anderson (see map). Reagan's sweep was nationwide; Carter carried only six states and the District of Columbia. Although the vote was partially an affirmation of Reagan's conservatism, it also signified deep dissatisfaction with Carter. In addition, the Republicans were better organized and had more campaign money to spend. And Reagan espoused ideas that most Americans found relevant and sensible.

More startling than Reagan's sweep was the capture of eleven Senate seats by Republican candidates, a victory that gave the party a majority in that house.

February 2, 1981 / $1.25

Newsweek

A Day to Remember

SPECIAL
★ISSUE★

Ronald Reagan began his presidency auspiciously. On his inauguration day, the American hostages were released from Iran. Borrel/SIPA–Special Features and Susan T. McElhenney, Newsweek Magazine.

Conservative advertising campaigns had succeeded in defeating most of the targeted liberals, including Senators George McGovern and Frank Church. Republicans also gained thirty-three seats in the House and four state governorships. It seemed clear that Democrats would be running scared in the 1980s.

On January 20, 1981, Ronald Reagan was inaugurated as president. He pledged to work for "an era of national renewal," for "a healthy, vigorous, growing economy that provides equal opportunities for all Americans." On the same day, after 444 days in captivity, the American hostages boarded an airplane that flew them from Teheran to freedom. Yellow ribbons welcomed the freed Americans, and the nation rejoiced. Seldom had a new administration had a more auspicious beginning.

IMPORTANT EVENTS

1973	Trials of Watergate burglars	1976	Hyde amendment on abortions
	Ervin Watergate hearings		Carter elected president
	White House aides Ehrlichman and Haldeman resign	1977	"Roots" serialized on television
	Wounded Knee confrontation		
	War Powers Act	1978	*Bakke v. University of California*
	Arab oil embargo		California voters approve Proposition 13
	Agnew resigns; Ford appointed as vice president		Mass suicides in Guyana
	Saturday Night Massacre	1979	Three Mile Island nuclear accident
1974	OPEC oil price increases		Moral Majority established
	Supreme Court orders Nixon to release White House tapes		Federal Reserve Board tightens money supply
	House Judiciary Committee votes to impeach Nixon		American hostages seized in Iran
	Nixon resigns the presidency; Ford becomes president	1980	Economic recession
	Rockefeller appointed as vice president		Phased decontrol of oil prices and deregulation of transportation industries
	Ford pardons Nixon		Race riots
	Ford's WIN program		Reagan elected president
1975	Brown's Ferry nuclear accident	1981	American hostages in Iran released after 444 days
	Antibusing agitation		

SUGGESTIONS FOR FURTHER READING

Watergate

Richard Ben-Veniste and George Frampton, *Stonewall* (1978); John W. Dean, *Blind Ambition* (1976); Seymour M. Hersh, "The Pardon: Nixon, Ford, Haig, and the Transfer of Power," *Atlantic Monthly*, 252 (1983), 55–78; Jim Hougan, *Secret Agenda* (1984); Leon Jaworski, *The Right and the Power* (1976); J. Anthony Lukas, *Nightmare: The Underside of the Nixon Years* (1976); Arthur M. Schlesinger, Jr., *The Imperial Presidency* (1973); John J. Sirica, *To Set the Record Straight* (1979); Theodore White, *Breach of Faith* (1975); Bob Woodward and Carl Bernstein, *The Final Days* (1976);

Bob Woodward and Carl Bernstein, *All the President's Men* (1974). (For works on the Nixon administration, see Chapter 33.)

Energy Shortages, Economic Woes

Richard J. Barnet, *The Lean Years: Politics in the Age of Scarcity* (1980); Daniel Bell, *The Coming of the Post-Industrial Society* (1973); John M. Blair, *The Control of Oil* (1976); Barry Bluestone and Bennett Harrison, *The Deindustrialization of America* (1982); David P. Calleo, *The Imperious Economy* (1982); Barry Commoner, *The Politics of Energy* (1979); Robert L. Heilbroner, *An Inquiry into the Human Prospect* (1974); Harry Mauer, *Not Working: An Oral History of the Unemployed* (1979); Emma Rothschild, *Paradise Lost: The Decline of the Auto-Industrial Age* (1973); John E. Schwarz, *America's Hidden Success* (1983); Robert Sherrill, *The Oil Follies of 1970–1980* (1983); Robert Stobaugh and Daniel

Yergin, eds., *Energy Future* (1979); Lester C. Thurow, *The Zero-Sum Society* (1980).

The Ford Administration

Gerald R. Ford, *A Time to Heal* (1979); Robert T. Hartmann, *Palace Politics* (1980); Ron Nessen, *It Sure Looks Different from the Inside* (1978); A. James Reichley, *Conservatives in an Age of Change: The Nixon and Ford Administrations* (1981); James L. Sundquist, *The Decline and Resurgence of Congress* (1981).

The Carter Administration

Griffin Bell, *Taking Care of the Law* (1982); Joseph A. Califano, *Governing America* (1981); Jimmy Carter, *Keeping Faith* (1982); Rosalynn Carter, *First Lady from Plains* (1984); Betty Glad, *Jimmy Carter: From Plains to the White House* (1980); Haynes Johnson, *In the Absence of Power* (1980); Hamilton Jordan, *Crisis* (1982); Jody Powell, *The Other Side of the Story* (1984); Laurence H. Shoup, *The Carter Presidency & Beyond* (1980).

Women and the Family

Susan Brownmiller, *Against Our Will: Men, Women and Rape* (1975); Andrea Dworkin, *Right-Wing Women* (1983); Barbara Ehrenreich, *The Hearts of Men: American Dreams and the Flight from Commitment* (1983); Kenneth Keniston, *All Our Children: The American Family Under Pressure* (1977); Christopher Lasch, *Haven in a Heartless World: The Family Besieged* (1977); Kristin Luker, *Abortion and the Politics of Motherhood* (1984); Maggie Scarf, *Unfinished Business: Pressure Points in the Lives of Women* (1980).

Nonwhites and New Immigrants

Thomas J. Archdeacon, *Becoming American* (1983); John Crewden, *The Tarnished Door: The New Immigrants and the Transformation of America* (1983); Vine Deloria, *Behind the Trail of Broken Treaties* (1974); Dorothy K. Newman *et al.*, *Protest, Politics, and Prosperity: Black Americans and White Institutions, 1940–1974* (1978); Carol B. Stack, *All Our Kin: Strategies for Survival in a Black Community* (1975); Arnulfo D. Trejo, ed., *The Chicanos: As We See Ourselves* (1979); J. Harris Wilkinson III, *Fron Brown to Bakke: The Supreme Court and School Integration, 1954–1978* (1979); William Julius Wilson, *The Declining Significance of Race: Blacks and Changing American Institutions*, 2nd ed. (1980).

The Me Decade

Peter Clecak, *America's Quest for the Ideal Self: Dissent and Fulfillment in the Sixties and Seventies* (1983); Jim Hougan, *Decadence: Radical Nostalgia, Narcissism, and Decline in the Seventies* (1975); Christopher Lasch, *The Culture of Narcissism* (1978); Edwin Schur, *The Awareness Trap: Self-Absorption Instead of Social Change* (1976); Gail Sheehy, *Passages: Predictable Crises in Adult Life* (1976); Tom Wolfe, "The 'Me' Decade and the Third Great Awakening," *New York*, 9 (1976), 26–40; Daniel Yankelovich, *New Rules: Searching for Self-Fulfillment in a World Turned Upside Down* (1981).

The New Conservatism and the Election of Ronald Reagan

Peter N. Carroll, *It Seemed Like Nothing Happened: The Tragedy and Promise of America in the 1970s* (1982); Alan Crawford, *Thunder on the Right* (1980); Elizabeth Drew, *Portrait of an Election* (1981); Jack W. Germond and Jules Witcover, *Blue Smoke and Mirrors: How Reagan Won and Why Carter Lost the Election of 1980* (1981); Jeff Greenfield, *The Real Campaign* (1982); David W. Reinhard, *The Republican Right Since 1945* (1983); Kirkpatrick Sale, *Power Shift: The Rise of the Southern Rim and Its Challenge to the Eastern Establishment* (1975); Peter Steinfels, *The Neo-conservatives* (1979); F. Clifton White, *Why Reagan Won* (1981).

A SHARP TURN TO THE RIGHT
AMERICA SINCE 1981

CHAPTER 35

*I*t *was a* political first. The vice-presidential candidate for the Democratic party was a woman. And that woman, Geraldine Ferraro, had decided to confront union members. Campaigning in October 1984, Ferraro toured a Chrysler assembly plant in Rockford, Illinois, and told a group of workers, "When I read the polls that one third of the United Auto Workers are going to vote for Ronald Reagan, I'm absolutely floored. I want to know why." Her listeners stared back in uncomfortable silence. Finally a man spoke up, "They blame Jimmy Carter for a lot of our problems. Record high interest rates. Iran. A weak foreign policy."

"I don't know how in the hell to explain it," moaned a UAW official. "We've got Chrysler workers saying they're going to vote for Reagan when he opposed the Chrysler recovery program [see page 981]. . . . Do these people know their roots?"

Ferraro knew that the Democratic percentage of the union vote had dropped from 64 percent in the 1976 presidential election to 47 percent in 1980, but she believed that the 1980 vote had signified a rejection of President Jimmy Carter, not an endorsement of Reagan's conservatism. However, in 1984 the economy was on the upswing, and Reagan's policies appeared to have conquered inflation and high interest rates, and dealt a blow to unemployment as well. Many Americans also applauded Reagan's foreign policy; they said they were proud that their country would stand up to the Russians again. Patriotism was back in style.

Yet there was a further explanation for the president's popularity. A proponent of prayer in the public schools and an opponent of abortion, Reagan argued for a return to the morality that had dominated American culture prior to the 1960s. Many Americans, including Catholics and born-again Christians, agreed. A soft-spoken woman standing near Geraldine Ferraro touched on the campaign's most volatile moral and cultural issue when she told the candidate, "My Christian friends don't like the ticket because of how you feel about abortion." "I can't change my views on abortion," Ferraro replied. "I would never have an abortion. But if I were raped I'm not sure I would

be that self-righteous. And that decision would be mine. I wouldn't leave it to you to make," she told the woman, "or you to make," pointing to a man who had just praised President Reagan's morality. There was no bridging the gulf between their position and Ferraro's.

Voters in 1984 had a clear choice, and in forty-nine states they chose the Republican ticket. Only Minnesota—the home state of Walter Mondale, the Democratic candidate—kept it from being unanimous. The election returns were the most convincing evidence yet that by 1984 the nation had taken a sharp turn to the right.

Reagan had, nonetheless, suffered severe criticism during his first term. Opponents lambasted his economic policies ("Reaganomics"), particularly the massive cuts in income taxes accompanied by large social welfare cuts, as favoring the rich and penalizing the poor. From 1981 to 1983, Reaganomics became synonymous with human suffering. In October 1982, unemployment reached 10.1 percent, the highest rate since 1940. So depressed had the economy become by January 1983 that the *New York Times* declared: "The stench of failure hangs over Ronald Reagan's White House;" the president's "loss of authority only halfway through his term should alarm all Americans." Although Reagan's policies failed for three years to produce the promised results, he urged Americans to "stay the course" and stick with his conservative agenda.

Reagan's conservatism also shaped his foreign policy. He surrounded himself with people who believed that previous administrations had shown weakness toward the Soviet Union, Cuba, Third World countries, and terrorists. The Reagan administration set out to swell the American military arsenal, denounce and intimidate the Soviets, unseat leftist governments through military intervention or covert operations, and settle civil wars in the Middle East and Latin America. Reagan was hesitant to engage in arms control talks or in negotiations to quiet regional conflict in Central America. His administration virtually ended the North-South dialogue, lecturing Third World nations that they should practice free-enterprise economics. Although many Americans and foreigners grew alarmed at the rapid acceleration of the nuclear arms race and at the application of military power to political problems, most Americans approved Reagan's harsh anti-Sovietism and emphasis on military strength. Indeed, a vibrant patriotism swept through the American people, buoyed in part by the successful invasion of the Caribbean island of Grenada.

As Reagan geared up for the 1984 election, he was alert to the mounting criticism not only of his policies, but also of his appointees for their insensitivity to ethical standards for officeholders. Despite several scandals, however, Reagan's re-election prospects seemed to improve, not deteriorate, in 1983 and 1984. For one thing, the president was a master at distancing himself not only from controversies within his administration, but even from problems in foreign and domestic policy. Representative Patricia Schroeder, a Colorado Democrat, gave this phenomenon a memorable label, saying that Reagan was "perfecting the Teflon-coated presidency. . . . He sees to it that nothing sticks to him."

Even more helpful to Reagan's campaign was that the economy showed unmistakable signs of recovery; during the first quarter of 1984, it grew at an annual rate of 8.8 percent. People were spending their tax cuts on video recorders, new cars, and other goods. Lower interest rates boosted housing sales, and renewed activity meant more jobs. Reagan's re-election bid was spurred also by the Democrats' lack of a winning candidate. Walter Mondale did not inspire Americans; most people identified him with the ineffectuality of the Carter administration. And he lost votes early when he announced in his acceptance speech that if elected he would raise taxes.

Reagan's victory was never in doubt, but his immense margin made political observers speculate that he had fashioned a new right coalition that could dominate national politics for years to come. By 1984 the New Deal coalition was in shambles. The only groups still voting for the Democratic ticket were blacks, Hispanics, Jews, the poor, and the unemployed. Reagan scored solid victories with all other voting groups, including young people, white men and women, high school and college graduates, Protestants and Catholics, and families with incomes exceeding $12,500. Whether or not Reagan had forged a lasting

coalition, there was no doubt that he had secured his place in history. After reviewing Reagan's first-term successes, a Columbia University history professor proclaimed, "He has a chance to make somebody move over on Mt. Rushmore." Still, the president confronted unsolved problems that would bedevil his second term. Heading the list were the federal budget deficit and the need to halt the nuclear arms race. Sober analysts revealed too that the United States was facing a depressing agenda of international problems—including economic instability, famine, terrorism, weakening alliances, and religious and racial tensions—that were not susceptible to military solutions and that promised a future of global disorder and threats to American tranquility.

"REAGANOMICS"

Upon taking office, President Reagan wasted little time in announcing his plans for what he called "a new beginning." In February 1981 he launched a double-barreled attack on problems in the economy. First, he asked Congress for $43.5 billion in spending cuts from domestic programs, including urban aid, Medicare and Medicaid, food stamps, welfare subsidies for the working poor, and school meals. In July Congress met most of Reagan's demands by paring $35.2 billion from social and cultural programs. Veteran agencies of the War on Poverty, such as the Community Services Administration, were gutted or dismantled. Some 300,000 public service jobs under the Comprehensive Employment and Training Act were eliminated. Reagan initiated a second round of budget cuts totaling $13 billion in September, resulting, among other things, in the trimming of 1 million food-stamp recipients from government rolls.

Massive tax cuts constituted the second part of Reagan's economic plan. Reagan was a fervent believer in supply-side economics, which called for reductions

Tax Cuts   in the income taxes of the affluent and of corporations in order to stimulate savings and investments.

New capital would be invested, the argument went, and would produce new plants, new jobs, and new products, and as prosperity returned, the profits at

Ronald Reagan assumed the presidency confident that his policies and leadership would restore both prosperity and national pride. In the manner of Franklin D. Roosevelt fifty years earlier, Reagan's confidence was infectious.   Bill Pierce/Time Magazine.

the top would trickle down to the middle classes and even to the poor at the bottom. Economic growth and expanding opportunities would again be the hallmarks of American society. Reagan thus proposed slashing income taxes by 30 percent over three years. And with cross-over votes given to the Republicans by conservative southern Democrats, Congress responded in August with a five-year, $750-billion tax cut, the largest ever in American history. The act's major feature was a 25-percent reduction in personal income taxes over the next three years. Other provisions increased business investment tax credits and depreciation allowances and lowered the maximum tax on all income from 70 to 50 percent. Wealthy people gained the most from these tax cuts. In an unguarded moment, budget director David Stockman acknowledged that Reagan's supply-side doctrines were a "Trojan horse" for tax relief to the rich. "It's kind of hard to sell 'trickle down,'" Stockman explained, "so the supply-side formula was the only way to get a tax policy that was really 'trickle down.'"

A third item occupied Reagan's agenda: a vigorous assault on federal environmental, health, and safety regulations that, Reagan believed, unnecessarily and excessively reduced business profits and discouraged economic growth. A lightning rod for this effort was Secretary of the Interior James Watt, who said that

his objective was to "mine more, drill more, cut more timber, to use our resources rather than simply keep them locked up." Watt began by opening up federal lands and coastal waters to rapid exploitation of oil, gas, and coal. He also proposed that 80 million acres of wilderness be turned over to developers by the year 2000. And Watt had Reagan's support. Even the business-oriented *Wall Street Journal* observed that the president was "naming regulators who by virtue of attitude or inexperience are more likely to be nonregulators."

Some critics said this approach to presidential appointments resulted in the proverbial foxes guarding the chicken coops. An example was Anne Gorsuch Burford, administrator of the Environmental Protection Agency, who delayed implementing a groundwater protection program, weakened enforcement of the Clean Air Act, and resigned in March 1983 because of her controversial handling of the $1.6-billion "Superfund" for cleaning up toxic waste. Reagan's appointee to head the Occupational Safety and Health Administration was Thomas Auchter, president of a Florida construction company that had amassed forty-eight OSHA violations since 1972. ("Nobody is perfect," Auchter explained.) In Reagan's first six months, OSHA inspections were down 16 percent and penalties were down 40 percent. Reagan officials announced that slackened enforcement was necessary to reduce business costs and make American goods competitive in world markets, but environmentalists countered that such policies invited human disaster, such as toxic-waste poisoning or nuclear reactor accidents.

Reagan scored two notable economic successes during his first two years in office: the inflation rate plummeted, as did the cost of borrowing money. With the Federal Reserve Board leading the way by lowering its discount rate (see page 982), the prime rate for bank loans, which had stood at a record high of 21.5 percent in early 1981, dropped to 10.5 percent by early 1983. Inflation fell from 12.4 percent in 1980 to less than 7 percent in 1982. Oil led the way in price declines. In 1981 the United States was awash with oil, as world production exceeded demand by 2 million barrels a day; after eight years the Organization of Petroleum Exporting Countries (OPEC) at last had to put a lid on its oil prices. Americans

Weakened Environmental Enforcement

The "smokestack industries" were hard hit economically in the 1980s. At Christmastime 1982, workers left Bethlehem Steel's plant in Lackawana, New York, forever. Once the largest steel plant in the world, the Lackawana facility had closed. © 1983 Jamey Stillings/Black Star.

had also become conservation-minded. Homeowners by the millions turned down their thermostats and installed insulation. Partly because of declining energy costs, in 1981 food prices rose only 4.3 percent, less than half the 10.1 percent increase of 1980.

But there was also a sobering explanation for the decline in inflation. "It wasn't just luck on food and oil," said an economist with Data Resources, a leading economic-forecasting firm. "It was very much the result of the stagnant economy that brought the prices down." By mid-1981 the nation was mired in a recession that not only persisted, but deepened. During the last three months of the year, the gross national product fell 5.3 percent, and there was a sharp drop in sales of cars and houses; housing starts were down more than half from 1978. With declining economic activity, unemployment went up, soaring in October to 8 percent, the highest level in almost six years. But the worst economic news was still to come.

A year later, in October 1982, unemployment had reached 10.1 percent. On top of the 11.3 million people who were out of work, a record 6.6 million Americans were forced to work part-time because they could not find full-time jobs. Most of the jobless were adult men, particularly black men who suffered an unemployment rate of 19.8 percent. Many of the unemployed were blue-collar workers in such ailing "smokestack industries" as autos, steel, and rubber. Unemployment was 15.6 percent for industrial workers and over 20 percent for construction workers, compared with white-collar unemployment, which stood at just 4.8 percent.

Rising Unemployment

Reagan and his advisers had hoped that his supply-side economics would produce demand-side results and that consumers would lift the economy out of the recession by spending their tax cuts. But as late as April 1983, unemployment stood at 10.2 percent, and people were angry. Jobless steelworkers paraded through McKeesport, Pennsylvania, carrying a coffin that bore the epitaph "American Dream." "I used to have big plans for myself," said one laid-off steelworker. "But not anymore. It's like I've fallen into hell and there isn't anyone who's going to pull me out." Unemployment in some West Virginia coal-mining towns hovered at 90 percent, while the state's overall rate was 20.4 percent. Michigan ranked second with 17 percent. Facing a bleak future, people took to the road; most headed to the South and Southwest.

Just as heavy industry was in shambles, so too agriculture was faltering and near collapse. Farmers suffered not only from floods and droughts, but also from burdensome debts they had incurred at high interest rates. Many lost their property through mortgage foreclosures and farm auctions. Others filed for bankruptcy. "Only in the last couple years," observed Judge Richard Stageman, a veteran of twenty-two years on the federal bankruptcy bench in Des Moines, Iowa, "have I seen grown men cry on the witness stand, and always it's the farmers. Some want reorganization when there's nothing left to reorganize. They're on the ragged edge of nowhere."

As the recession deepened in 1982, poverty rose to its highest level since 1965. (An urban family of four was classified as poor if its annual cash income was under $10,178.) The Bureau of the Census reported that the number of Americans living in poverty increased from 26.1 million (11.7 percent) in 1979 to 34.4 million (15 percent) in 1982. Poverty increased most among blacks (35.6 percent of whom were poor) and Hispanics (29.9 percent). Predictably, the largest single category of poor families consisted of households headed by women (36.3 percent). In 1983 poverty continued its rise, to 35.3 million Americans (15.2 percent). With one exception, poverty had returned to the levels that existed before the enactment of President Lyndon B. Johnson's Great Society. That exception was the elderly. For the first time in the history of federally defined need, the poverty rate among Americans over sixty-five (14.6 percent) was lower than that for the population at large, revealing that politicians had been paying attention to the needs of this rapidly growing group.

Poverty was literally painful. Federal officials announced in October 1982 that more than 16 million Americans had lost health insurance coverage as a

In 1982 and 1983, unemployment rose to the highest levels in forty years. At the same time, Reagan cut welfare benefits for the poor. Paul Conrad, cartoonist of the Los Angeles Times, suggested that Herbert Hoover's dour face lived behind the smiling Ronald Reagan mask. Paul Conrad, Los Angeles Times Syndicate.

result of unemployment, and many appeared to be deferring necessary medical care just when they most needed it. A sociologist who studied unemployed aircraft workers near Hartford, Connecticut, found evidence of "serious physical or emotional strain," including alcoholism, increased smoking, high blood pressure, insomnia, and nervous exhaustion. A few said they suffered from "recession depression" or had a bad case of the "pink slip blues." In 1982 M. Harvey Brenner, a sociologist at Johns Hopkins University, reported that for each 1 percent rise in unemployment, suicides increased 4.1 percent, homicides 5.7 percent, and mental hospital admissions 2.3 percent for women and 4.3 percent for men.

Poverty's Effects

President Reagan had announced that while his administration would reduce the rate of expansion of social and health programs, it would retain a "safety net" that would catch the "truly needy" before they hit bottom. But he reneged on his promise. Facing a budget deficit in excess of $200 billion in mid-1982, Reagan had three choices, and in each case he made a conservative decision. First, he could cut back on his rearmament plans to spend $1.7 trillion over five years, but this he refused to do. In fact, the budget signed by Reagan raised defense spending another 13 percent. Second, he could suspend or reduce the second installment of his tax cut, but this too he found unacceptable. Third, he could—and did—cut welfare and social programs. Reagan chose to push through Congress further cuts of $27.2 billion over three years in Medicare and Medicaid, food stamps, federal pensions, and government-guaranteed home mortgages. Still, in the absence of other budget cuts, the deficit continued to grow.

A *Los Angeles Times* poll in August 1982 showed that despite Reagan's personal popularity, more than a third of the people who had voted for him in 1980 said they would not support him again, largely because they lacked confidence in his economic policies. "People see little or no reason for optimism," explained a Los Angeles businessman. "I think we're headed for the bread lines," said a retired domestic worker in Miami. With the 1982 elections nearing, Democrats predicted big victories for their party.

Just a week before the 1982 elections, however, a *New York Times*/CBS News poll reported that the American public was being tugged sharply in different directions: toward the Democrats by unemployment, but toward the Republicans by declining inflation and the president's popularity. There was no denying Reagan's winning style. Nothing revealed this better than his courageous response to the attempt made on his life in March 1981. Although John W. Hinckley, Jr., failed to kill his target, he shot the president in the left side and wounded Reagan's press secretary, a Secret Service agent, and a police officer. Reagan's grace on that day caused his popularity ratings to soar. He walked into the George Washington University Hospital on his own with his blood oozing away, an undetonated explosive bullet in his chest, and his fighting spirit and sense of humor very much intact. "Honey, I forgot to duck," he told his wife.

In the 1982 elections, twenty-six House seats swung to the Democrats, giving them a lead of 267 to 166. Even with massive campaign funding, the Republicans

1982 Elections

came close to losing their majority in the Senate; four incumbents survived only narrowly. But with a continued Republican majority of 54 to 46, the Senate remained pro-Reagan. In another two years, there would be a presidential election. By then, the president had to prove that he could restore prosperity. Additionally, in order to be re-elected, Reagan had to demonstrate that his Cold War crusade would not lead to American participation in war in Central America, the Middle East, or, worst of all, against the Soviet Union.

REAGAN'S FOREIGN POLICY: THE SOVIETS AND THE NUCLEAR ARMS RACE

Ronald Reagan's foreign policy was driven by four beliefs rooted in America's past. "His is a kind of 1952 world," remarked one of Reagan's former aides. First, Reagan and the

Reagan's Foreign Policy Views

conservatives he selected to advise him believed that a malevolent Soviet Union was the source of the world's troubles. They saw almost everything through an East-West lens. If détente was already dead when Reagan became president, he buried it in an avalanche of strident anti-Soviet rhetoric. Barely settled into the White House, Reagan charged that the Soviets were prepared "to commit any crime, to lie, to cheat" to achieve a Communist world. He attributed Third World disorders to Soviet intrigue, rejecting analyses that argued, for example, that the civil wars in Central America derived not from Soviet meddling, but from deep-seated local sources of economic instability, poverty, and class oppression.

Second, the Reagan administration believed that a major American military build-up would thwart the Soviet threat and intimidate the Soviets into negotiating on terms favorable to the United States. Reagan launched an eight-year, $2.3-trillion defense budget, most of which Congress approved. He pushed plans for the B-1 bomber, a much enlarged navy, production of poison gas, beefed-up special forces units for counterinsurgency, the MX missile, and an antimissile defense system in space (titled the Strategic Defense Initiative but quickly dubbed "Star Wars"). "They're screaming like they're sitting on a sharp nail," crowed Reagan when the Soviets protested the largest peacetime arms build-up in American history. In 1985 the Pentagon was spending an average of $28 million an hour, twenty-four hours a day, seven days a week. A warmongering image soon settled around the Reagan administration, especially when it became clear that the new president assigned low priority to arms control talks. Veteran diplomat George W. Ball lamented that once again "we shiver in the icy winds of the Cold War. Diplomacy is for sissies."

Third, Reagan and his advisers believed that nations must embrace private capitalism and reject managed economies. They frequently lectured Third World countries on the virtues of private enterprise. The United States even voted against—it was the only "no" vote—a United Nations resolution to restrict the marketing of baby formula in developing nations. Medical authorities had complained that the baby formula companies were marketing their product so aggressively that many mothers were foregoing healthy breast-feeding in favor of the artificial liquid, which they mixed with polluted water (all that was available to them), thus spreading disease. Regardless, Reagan officials would tolerate no interference with private business. The United States also refused to sign the Law of the Sea Treaty, protesting that it did not adequately protect private American deep-sea mining companies. Overall, the Reagan administration silenced the North-South dialogue (see pages 928–929).

Fourth, Ronald Reagan believed Americans must abandon their post-Vietnam "self-doubt" and renew their mission of converting foreign peoples to the American model. Most Americans shared Reagan's feeling that the United States had been ignobly retreating from global power and leadership—witness the treaty to return the canal to Panama, the Iranian hostage crisis, and Soviet achievement of nuclear parity. Besides talking tough and enlarging the military to reverse this trend, Reagan revitalized the Central Intelligence Agency and expanded its covert operations abroad. "America is back, standing tall," bragged the president in 1984 during a revival of passionate American patriotism.

In this atmosphere, Soviet-American relations became "white hot, thoroughly white hot," noted a Soviet leader. Actually, Reagan's first decision affecting the Soviets was to lift the grain embargo that President

Carter had imposed after the Soviet invasion of Afghanistan. A grain deal worth about $3 billion was soon negotiated. Reagan thereby fulfilled a campaign promise to American farmers eager to sell wheat and corn in foreign markets. But this decision was followed in late 1981 by hostility when the Soviets cracked down on the Solidarity labor movement in Poland. In response, Washington restricted some Russian-American trade and hurled angry words at Moscow. As Soviet troops struggled to subdue Afghanistan, the CIA channeled aid to the Afghan rebels.

Reagan's expansion of the military, his coolness toward arms control, his utterances about winning a limited nuclear war, his quest for nuclear supremacy, and his insistence on placing new **Nuclear** cruise and Pershing-II missiles in **Arms Race** Western Europe stimulated a lively international debate. In fall 1981 hundreds of thousands of marchers in London, Rome, Bonn, and other European cities demanded Soviet-American negotiations to prevent a nuclear holocaust. Talks on limiting intermediate-range nuclear forces (INF) based in Europe—such as the Soviet SS-20 missiles targeted against Western Europe and the American cruise and Pershings aimed at Russia—did get under way in late November 1981. The American proposal was called the zero option: the United States would not deploy its missiles in Western Europe if the Soviet Union would dismantle all of its SS-20s. Moscow replied that the plan did not take into account that, already, American long-range bombers and submarine-based missiles could reach the Soviet Union. Moreover, the Soviets said, Reagan's scheme did not count British and French nuclear forces aimed at the Soviet Union. Critics believed that Reagan's plan was more a propaganda ploy to quiet a worried public than a serious step toward arms control. The INF talks collapsed in November 1983 after the first American cruise and Pershing-II missiles were installed in Western Europe.

Reagan's substitute for the SALT talks, the Strategic Arms Reduction Talks (START), began in June 1982. But in December of the next year they too faltered. These difficult negotiations attracted intense American public interest. Evangelist Billy Graham and the National Council of Churches joined peace groups and prominent politicians such as Senator Edward Kennedy in appeals for a freeze in the nuclear arms race. In

In this 1983 test, the United States Army launched a Pershing-II missile on a long-range flight from Cape Canaveral, Florida. The plan to install these missiles in Western Europe provoked antinuclear weapons demonstrations in the United States and other parts of the world. Official U.S. Navy photo.

the largest peaceful protest in American history in June 1982, 1 million people marched through New York City to support a freeze. The Roman Catholic bishops of the United States issued a long pastoral letter that said, "We are the first generation since Genesis with the power to virtually destroy God's creation." They condemned nuclear weapons as "immoral" and urged an end to the arms race, "which robs the poor and the vulnerable."

Doctors in Boston pointed out that if their city were hit by nuclear warheads, half a million people would die, thousands would suffer serious burns and fatal radiation poisoning, and hospitals would be so wrecked that they could not treat the wounded. Scientists predicted a "nuclear winter" after a nuclear war: the earth, cut off from the sun's rays, would turn cold, and food sources would disappear. An ABC television dramatization titled "The Day After" stunned Americans in fall 1983 with its vivid depiction of the human costs of nuclear war. Even before this movie, towns across the nation had passed resolutions to freeze either the development, production, or deployment of new weapons. Despite opposition from the Reagan administration, the House of Representatives in 1983 also passed a freeze resolution. Because of such public opinion, pressure from NATO allies, worry that a more expensive and more dangerous nuclear arms race loomed, and the belief that reinvigorated American military power gave the United States a strong bargaining position, Reagan officials resumed discussions on arms control with the Soviets in early 1985.

While concern over nuclear war escalated, so did American-Soviet tensions. In early September 1983

Shooting Down of South Korean Airliner a Soviet fighter pilot tailed a South Korean commercial jet that had strayed over Soviet territory. When the airliner did not change course after having been warned, it was blasted out of the sky, killing 269 people. The world was shocked. Reagan went on television to denounce this "act of barbarism." Russian leaders claimed that the passenger plane was mistaken for an American spy aircraft. Although American spy planes did regularly travel a route close to that flown by Korean Air Lines Flight 007, few Americans accepted the Soviet explanation. Reagan halted commercial flights between the United States and the Soviet Union, but did little more. He seemed content to let the tragedy confirm in the American mind his dark view of the Soviets.

INTERVENTIONS IN THE THIRD WORLD AND FOREBODING FORECASTS

Reagan's dark view included the belief that the Soviets and their clients the Cubans were fomenting disorder in the Third World, especially in Central America. The region of Guatemala, Honduras, El Salvador, Nicaragua, and Costa Rica was a traditional sphere of influence for the United States, characterized by large economic holdings, political influence, and repeated interventions. Americans had long called Central America their backyard. For Reagan officials, El Salvador appeared to be a textbook case of Communist aggression. In that very poor country, revolutionaries challenged the government, which was dominated by the military and a small, landed elite. The regime used (or could not control) right-wing "death squads" that killed thousands of dissidents and other citizens, as well as some American missionaries who worked with landless peasants. Believing that the war against the rebels could be successfully concluded in a short time, Reagan eschewed negotiations and instead increased military assistance to the Salvadoran regime.

The controversial intervention in the Salvadoran civil war sparked a debate that sounded much like that which had erupted over Vietnam years before. Those who urged negotiations thought Reagan wrong to interpret the conflict as an East-West contest. Oppression and poverty, not Communist plots, caused people to pick up guns to fight the regime, they argued. "The region will continue to seethe with revolution—with or without the Soviets," said Connecticut Senator Christopher Dodd. Resurrecting the discredited domino theory, Reagan warned that if the "Communists" were not stopped in El Salvador they would soon be at the Mexican-American border. When that exaggerated argument convinced few, Reagan turned to a strategic case. Central America, he said, hugs the Caribbean Sea—"our lifeline to the outside world." In time of war, the Soviets could cripple American shipping from Caribbean bases. All of this assumed, of course, that the Soviets were in fact trying to take over El Salvador; critics rejected that assumption.

Although Congress voted funds for the American involvement in El Salvador, it stipulated that the United States government would have to certify every six months that the Salvadoran government was making improvements in human rights or the funds would be cut off. To keep the aid flowing, American officials made strained yet positive statements every six months that left many human rights observers incredulous. The Reagan administration's case was helped somewhat in May 1984 when a United States–influenced election produced a government under the popular José Napoleon Duarte. Still, civilian deaths mounted and land reform languished. And the guerrillas fought on and grew in numbers, showing no signs of being deterred by the continued infusion of substantial American arms, economic assistance, and CIA operatives.

Elsewhere in Central America the Reagan administration intervened, threatening a regional war. Nicaragua was ruled by a leftist government, the Sandinistas (see page 935). To succeed with their plans for improvements in health and education, they had invited several thousand Cubans into their hospitals and schools. Cuban military advisers helped them reorganize their army, and Soviet arms were ordered. Reagan early denounced the government, charging that it was becoming a Soviet puppet and was sending

The Russians (bear) and Americans (Uncle Sam) often explained their meddling in the affairs of other nations by claiming that they had to intervene in order to halt the expansion of the other. To the unhappy people whose sovereignty was violated, however, such an explanation was not convincing because it ignored the conspicuous, self-interested drive of the two great powers for control of small countries. By Auth for the Philadelphia Inquirer.

arms to the rebels in El Salvador. The Reagan administration soon strove to topple the Nicaraguan government. The United States conducted military maneuvers off the coast and staged war games in neighboring Honduras, where major American bases were built. The CIA also began, in 1982, to train, arm, and direct over ten thousand counterrevolutionaries, called *contras*. Many of these anti-Sandinista rebels were former supporters of the Somoza dictatorship, which the Sandinistas had overthrown in 1979. From Honduras the *contras* killed Nicaraguan officials and innocent civilians and destroyed oil refineries, transportation facilities, medical clinics, and day-care centers.

Actions Against Nicaragua

In the spring of 1984 it became known that the CIA had mined the harbors of Nicaragua with explosives, causing merchant ships to be blown up. Negative international and American opinion cascaded down on Washington. The French helped clear the harbors; the World Court ruled that Nicaragua had the right to sue the United States for damages. Conservative Republican Senator Barry Goldwater of Arizona boomed, "This is an act violating international law. It is an act of war. For the life of me, I don't know how we are going to explain it." Both houses of Congress passed a nonbinding resolution to halt the mining operations. In mid-1984 Congress voted to stop American aid to the *contras*. Then, in the fall, American journalists revealed that a CIA manual prepared for the *contras* told them not only how to conduct sabotage and incite mob violence, but also how to "neutralize" (that is, assassinate) Nicaraguan leaders. But the undeclared war against well-armed Nicaragua continued, prompting critics to assert that the United States was forcing Nicaragua into the

Americans mourned their war dead in Lebanon. These marines carried the body of a navy pilot from a helicopter after its arrival aboard the USS John F. Kennedy, an aircraft carrier. The pilot's aircraft had been shot down during a bombing raid over Lebanon. Official U.S. Air Force photo.

Communist camp. Moreover, they protested, the United States was bypassing opportunities to negotiate. The Nicaraguans, for example, accepted the objectives of the Contadora group (Mexico, Venezuela, Colombia, and Panama), which included the reduction of foreign military bases and advisers in Central America. But by 1985 the Reagan administration had refused to endorse the Contadora peace plan. As in El Salvador, the Reaganites preferred a military solution. His goal, the president declared in early 1985, was to remove the Sandinista government—to force it to say "uncle." And he soon imposed an economic blockade against Nicaragua.

In the Middle East too Reagan tried to use military power. Sophisticated airplanes worth $8.5 billion were sold to Saudi Arabia. United States relations with Israel cooled because of this deal, but also because the Israelis repeatedly bombed suspected Palestine Liberation Organization (PLO) camps inside Lebanon,

killing hundreds of civilians. In December 1981, without warning, Israel annexed the Syrian territory of the Golan Heights. Secretary of Defense Caspar Weinberger, like many Americans impatient with Israel's provocative acts toward its neighbors, stormed: "How long do we have to go on bribing Israel [with American aid]? If there is no real cost to the Israelis, we'll never be able to stop any of their actions." When, after the annexation, Reagan suspended an American-Israeli agreement on strategic cooperation in an attempt to punish Israel, Israeli Prime Minister Menachem Begin castigated Washington for treating his nation like a "banana republic."

Then, in June 1982, Israeli troops invaded civil war–torn Lebanon, cutting their way to the capital Beirut and inflicting massive damage. The beleaguered PLO and various Lebanese factions called upon Syria to contain the Israelis. Civilian deaths rose to at

Crisis in Lebanon

least ten thousand, and a million people became refugees. In August, as part of a peace-keeping force, U.S. Marines entered Lebanon and eventually dug in around Beirut. "Too few to fight and too many to die," protested one member of Congress. Their mission ill-defined, the American troops soon became allied with the faction that controlled the Lebanese government and exchanged fire with other factions and with Syrians. In October 1983, terrorist bombs demolished a marine barracks, killing 240 American servicemen. In February of the next year, with Lebanon reeling from civil war and Syrian and Israeli occupation, Reagan recognized failure and pulled the marines out. In the wake of the Lebanese tragedy, American leaders grew wary of Mideast ventures. Secretary of State George P. Schultz, upset that moderate Arab states like Jordan and Saudi Arabia were doing little to stabilize the region, muttered that "somehow or other we have to get over the notion that every time things don't go just to everybody's satisfaction in the Middle East, it's the U.S. fault or it's up to the U.S. to do something about it." Still, the United States had commitments (defense of Israel), political friends (Saudi Arabia), enemies (Iran and Libya), and oil supplies that would continue to draw it into the area.

Just before the terrorist bombing of the barracks in Lebanon, a Reagan aide remarked that "we need a major victory somewhere to show we can manage

Invasion of Grenada

foreign policy." On October 25, 1983, just after the terrorist attack, the president ordered marines to invade Grenada. This tiny Caribbean island was troubled by political strife and ruled by a leftist government friendly with Cuba. Announcing that the invasion was necessary in order to protect several hundred Americans studying medicine there and once again trumpeting the Soviet threat, the United States implanted a new government and deported Cubans. The casualty list included about a hundred dead; the expedition cost the United States $75 million. The United Nations passed a resolution condemning this revival of gunboat diplomacy, but most Americans cheered Reagan's action. It was, said one senator, America's "Grenada high."

The euphoria was short-lived, for Americans faced bewildering international problems that seemed immune to military solutions. First, global economic issues were threatening world order and American prosperity. Third World nations were sinking more and more deeply into debt, less able to repay loans or to purchase goods. Between 1980 and 1983, American exports to developing nations declined by over $18 billion; that meant the loss of over 1 million jobs in the United States. In 1984 alone, America's trade deficit (more imports than exports) stood at a staggering $102 billion. Second, hunger and famine were not only taking a ghastly human toll, but also contributing to political instability. In the early 1980s population experts estimated that annual hunger-related deaths numbered between 13 and 18 million people—twenty-four people per minute. Drought-ravaged Africa was hardest hit; Ethiopia, wracked as well by civil war, counted over 6 million people on the verge of starvation in 1984.

A third major, long-term international problem was the deterioration of the global environment. Soil erosion hurt food production at a time when the world's population was growing rapidly. Toxic wastes, acid rain, shortages of clean water, and the overcutting of forests escalated environmental decline, which, in turn, burdened governments that seemed unable to respond. Fourth, international drug traffic was causing health problems for millions, enriching criminals who sometimes gained political influence (as in Bolivia and Colombia), and financing the activities of terrorists (as in Peru). American programs to eradicate crops of opium poppies (used to make heroin) in Asia and Mexico and coca (used to make cocaine) in Latin America cost a great deal, but were failing. Fifth, terrorism was increasing at an alarming rate. Terrorists struck at will without warning. Forty percent of terrorist attacks in 1983 were directed against the United States; 271 Americans were killed. In June 1985, Shiite Moslem terrorists from Lebanon hijacked an American jetliner, killed one passenger, beat others, and held 39 Americans hostage for seventeen days. Sixth, America was facing a future of uneasy relations with allies. NATO was splintering, and once-valuable allies like the Philippines were rocked by political unrest. At stake were military bases and intelligence-gathering stations. Seventh, religious and racial tensions undermined stability and spawned war. Sikhs and Hindus fought one another in India, where in 1984 Prime Minister Indira Gandhi was assassinated; Christians and Moslems battled in Lebanon; the Shiite

Moslems governing Iran were at war with the Sunni Moslems of Iraq; Roman Catholics and Protestants bloodied each other in Northern Ireland.

Finally, South Africa represented a special problem. There a blatantly racist white minority ruled a predominantly nonwhite people (85 percent) through the segregationist policy of *apartheid* **South Africa** and political repression. The Reagan administration refrained from criticizing South Africa, preferring instead what it called "constructive engagement." To many Americans it seemed necessary to pressure South Africa by cutting imports or by urging the 350 American companies operating there—led by Texaco, General Motors, Ford, and Goodyear—to stop doing business with the racist government. By early 1985 eleven cities and five states had passed divestment laws; that is, they were withdrawing dollars (such as pension funds used to buy stocks) from American companies active in South Africa. Many analysts were predicting that revolution was inevitable in South Africa. Wherever Americans turned, then, they faced unattractive questions and seemingly intractable problems that spelled global disorder and threats to American well-being both at home and abroad far into the future.

REAGAN'S OPPOSITION: WOMEN, NONWHITES, ORGANIZED LABOR

As the American people entered 1984, it was evident that several important groups desperately opposed Ronald Reagan's re-election. His most vocal critics were women, nonwhites, and labor leaders. In late 1983 the *New York Times* reported a "gender gap" between men's and women's opinions of Reagan's performance: far fewer women (38 percent) than men (53 percent) believed Reagan deserved re-election. The poll also found that 49 percent of women, but only 33 percent of men, feared that he would get the United States into a war. Reagan's opposition to the Equal Rights Amendment and

abortion on demand had already won him the enmity of many feminists. But what really caused the gender gap to yawn widely were Reagan's social welfare, health, and education cuts. Eleanor Holmes Norton, speaking for the Coalition on Women and the Budget, said in early 1984: "For three years we have seen unwarranted cuts in domestic survival programs that have weakened, not strengthened, families; that have made children hungrier, not healthier." Kathy Wilson, a Republican and president of the National Women's Political Caucus, was more direct: "Ronald Reagan is quite simply the most anti-woman president in history."

In May 1983, the Labor Department announced that for the first time in United States history, more than half (50.5 percent) of all women aged twenty and older held jobs. Some were blue-**Working** collar workers, including 9,000 new **Women** female carpenters and 29,000 new female truck drivers who had joined the work force since 1970. Nevertheless, in 1985 half of all working women still occupied only 20 of the 441 job categories of the United States census, mostly at the low end of the pay scale. Eighty percent worked in such "female" occupations as clerking, selling, teaching, nursing, and waitressing.

Many working women were also mothers shocked by the Reagan administration's insensitivity to child welfare. Edwin Meese, counselor to the president, lacked the facts when he said that people went to soup kitchens "because the food is free," and added that he had seen no "authoritative evidence" that children in America went hungry. That evidence appeared in 1984 when the House Select Committee on Children, Youth and Families reported: "The number of poor children increased by two million between 1980 and 1982. Today, one out of five children and one out of two black children live in poverty."

Women still earned only 60 percent as much as men, and partly for this reason an additional 2 million women fell into poverty between 1981 and 1983. Reagan's critics assailed him not only for failing to stop this "feminization of poverty," but also for approving policies, such as cuts in food stamps and school meals, that added to the woes of poor women and their children. The Reagan administration was also hostile to the feminist goal of "equal pay for jobs of comparable worth." Why, women asked, should a grade-school teacher earn less than an electrician, if the two jobs required comparable skills and involved comparable responsibilities? But "comparable worth" was only one of many feminist goals opposed by Reagan. In response, for the first time in its history, the National Organization for Women (NOW) endorsed a presidential candidate before the primaries. NOW's choice was Walter Mondale, former Minnesota senator, vice president under Jimmy Carter, and the frontrunner for the Democratic nomination.

Black civil rights leaders also opposed Reagan's re-election; they joined feminists in assailing the president's appointments. Whereas 12 percent of President Carter's high-level jobholders were black and 12.1 percent women, Reagan's comparable totals were 4.1 percent black and 8 percent women. Reagan had appointed three women to his cabinet, and he had made history by appointing Sandra Day O'Connor the first woman associate justice of the Supreme Court, but blacks could find little to applaud in Reagan's performance. After the U.S. Commission on Civil Rights issued a report expressing its concern that Reagan had not appointed more blacks, women, and Hispanic Americans to full-time, high-level positions, the president fired the commission's outspoken liberals and replaced them with opponents of affirmative action in hiring and in education.

Reagan announced in early 1982 that his administration favored tax exemptions for fundamentalist Christian schools that cited the Bible to justify racial segregation and whites-only admissions policies. (In mid-1983, the **Retreat in** Supreme Court ruled against Reagan **Civil Rights** 8 to 1 and ordered the Internal Revenue Service to deny tax exemptions to Bob Jones University in South Carolina and the Goldsboro Christian Institute in North Carolina.) Although Reagan denounced as "plain baloney" the allegation that "we are taking a less active approach to protecting the civil rights of all Americans," his record proved otherwise. William Bradford Reynolds, Reagan's civil rights chief in the Justice Department, fought against renewing intact the Voting Rights Act of 1965, expressed opposition to busing and affirmative action, and was criticized for lax enforcement of fair-housing laws and laws banning sexual and racial discrimination in federally funded education programs.

Hispanic and Native Americans joined Afro-Americans in blasting the Reagan administration. The League of United Latin American Citizens censured Reagan for his "very, very dismal record" in dealing with their problems, and the National Tribal Chairman's Association charged that within two years of Reagan's election, "the delivery of services by federal agencies to Indians was in a shambles."

Joining women and nonwhites in the anti-Reagan camp was the AFL-CIO. Even without Reagan in the White House, hard times would have hit the labor unions. Faced with the reces-**Hard Times** sion and unemployment, union ne-**for Labor** gotiators had to settle for less than **Unions** they were accustomed to receiving. American workers who ratified contracts during the first three months of Reagan's term settled for pay increases averaging only 2.2 percent in the first year, a stunning decline from the 9.8-percent hikes that had prevailed the year before. The drop in wage settlements was the biggest since the government began collecting such data in 1954. Unions had suffered large membership losses as unemployment hit the "smokestack industries," and their efforts to unionize the high-growth electronics and service sectors of the economy were failing. In February 1984 the Supreme Court ruled that companies declaring bankruptcy could unilaterally cancel union contracts to which they had agreed earlier, without even having a hearing.

Reagan made the unions' hard times worse. He presided over the government's busting of the Professional Air Traffic Controllers Organization (PATCO) during the union's 1981 strike. His appointees to the National Labor Relations Board consistently voted against labor and for management. Although it seemed that Reagan was clearly labor's enemy, union leaders could not rally their members to oppose his re-election. An estimated 44 percent of union families had voted for Reagan in 1980; many still responded positively to his genial personality, his espousal of old-fashioned values, and his anti-Communism. Wanting to use its political muscle against Reagan as soon as possible, the AFL-CIO followed NOW's lead and endorsed Mondale for president.

Reagan's opponents decried the "country club ethics" of his appointees, several of whom resigned after accusations that they had behaved illegally or

During the high unemployment of 1982 and 1983, jobless Americans came to Washington, D.C., to protest their situation. In October 1982, these demonstrators stood in a row in Lafayette Park, opposite the White House, and called attention to the loss of jobs in basic industries. AP/Wide World Photos.

down on her former employer, Aerojet-General Corporation. And in 1984 when Reagan nominated his close friend Edwin Meese to be attorney general of the United States, allegations arose that Meese had accepted "sweetheart loans" from individuals who were later appointed to positions in the Reagan administration.

In ordinary political times, the Democrats would have profited from the Republicans' misfortunes. Added to the nation's economic woes, the issue of corruption in government ("the sleaze factor") should have bolstered the Democrats in 1984. But 1984 produced a stunning victory for the Republican incumbent, Ronald Reagan, whose Teflon coating protected him from personal responsibility for his administration's failings.

REAGAN'S 1984 RE-ELECTION LANDSLIDE

As the political parties mounted their 1984 presidential campaigns, it became evident early that Reagan could defeat any Democratic nominee.

Reagan's Re-election Assets

Topping the list of Reagan's re-election credentials was the rebound in the economy. The gross national product rose 6.8 percent in 1984, the sharpest increase since 1951, and mid-year unemployment fell to a four-year low of 7.1 percent. And while the economy was heating up, it did so without causing inflation to boil. Indeed, inflation (4 percent in 1984) fell to its lowest level since 1967. A second factor in Reagan's favor was people's perception of him as a strong leader in foreign as well as national affairs. In contrast, Walter Mondale had to struggle to prove that he was not a "wimp" and that he too would stand up to the Soviet Union and to terrorists. Third, Reagan was the enthusiastic choice of the political right as well as of social, cultural, and religious conservatives across the country. And he won the approval of millions of other Americans who agreed with his television ads that "America is back" after two decades of turmoil and self-doubt.

improperly. The number-two administrators in both the CIA and the Department of Defense left office after newspaper reports that they had taken part in questionable stock transactions. The deputy secretary of defense, W. Paul Thayer, pleaded guilty to criminal charges of obstruction of justice and giving false information to the Securities and Exchange Commission and was sentenced to four years in a federal prison. Another resignation was that of Richard Allen, the national security adviser, after the disclosure that he had accepted gifts, including money and watches, from Japanese journalists for arranging interviews with Nancy Reagan, the president's wife. Rita Lavelle, an assistant administrator of the Environmental Protection Agency, was convicted of perjury and obstructing a congressional investigation for covering up her role in halting an EPA crack-

Finally, the Democrats did not pose a convincing alternative. The party was in disarray, its policies seemed timeworn, and its presidential candidate aroused little excitement, even within his own party.

Nor did the Democratic party have an appealing platform to present to the American voters in 1984. The party was fragmented into numerous caucuses for union members, blacks, women, Jews, homosexuals, Hispanics, and **Democratic Divisions** other groups. Each group had its own agenda, and at the 1984 Democratic national convention, each threatened to walk out if its demands were not met. One divisive issue was the Simpson-Mazzoli bill to change immigration laws. Organized labor supported the bill because it promised to curtail the illegal flow of undocumented Mexican-born workers to the United States. But the bill was denounced by Hispanics, an increasingly important voice in the Democratic party, who argued that punishing employers who hired undocumented workers would increase job discrimination against all Hispanics. Many Americans gained the impression that the Democratic party was not concerned with the national welfare, but rather with dividing up the spoils among its special-interest groups.

Still worse for the party's prospects, the leading contenders for the Democratic presidential nomination fought a bitter contest throughout the primaries. Walter Mondale spoke for the New Deal tradition of the welfare state and received preconvention endorsements from NOW, the AFL-CIO, and various civil rights organizations. Senator Gary Hart of Colorado evoked the image of John F. Kennedy: the tousled hair, the appearance of youthful vigor, the talk about "new ideas" and a "new generation." Hart denounced Mondale as the tool of the unions and other special interests and aimed his campaign at "Yuppies" (young urban professionals) and members of the baby boom, those 63.5 million Americans born between 1946 and 1961. When polled, Yuppies generally said they would vote for Reagan if Hart did not win the Democratic nomination. The third Democratic contender was Jesse Jackson, a former co-worker of Martin Luther King, Jr., in the southern civil rights struggle. Jackson had moved to Chicago to organize economic and educational programs for the poor, and in 1984 inspired a massive voter-registration drive among blacks. An eloquent preacher,

The Democratic party nominated Congresswoman Geraldine Ferraro to be its vice-presidential candidate in 1984. Her choice was a historic first.   Photograph for Time by P. F. Bentley/Time Magazine.

Jackson campaigned on his dream of forming a "Rainbow Coalition" of the "rejected"—blacks, women, Hispanics, the physically handicapped. Jackson was the first black candidate in history to win mass support in a bid for the presidential nomination of a major party.

What enthusiasm there was for the Democratic ticket arose from Mondale's historic selection of Congresswoman Geraldine Ferraro as his vice-presidential running mate. Feminists hailed this **Geraldine Ferraro** choice, as did numerous women and men throughout the country. Ferraro showed herself to be an intelligent, indefatigable campaigner who won the respect of even her opponents.

But the Democratic party was out of step with the nation's social and cultural conservatism. During the 1930s the New Deal coalition had gained the allegiance of economic liberals who subscribed to the welfare state. In 1984, however, many Democrats held conservative views on such issues as abortion and homosexuality, and they switched their votes to Ronald Reagan. The Democratic party was badly split, its confidence shaken, and it would need to redefine what it had to offer the American voter.

Reagan's personality, on the other hand, seemed to fit the public mood. In the summer of 1984, Americans carrying the Olympic torch ran from one coast of the United States to the other, through hundreds of cities, by night and day. This public relations pageantry was in harmony with a new optimism. In 1980 the pollster Daniel Yankelovich had reported that the United States had gone "almost overnight from a nation of optimists to a nation of pessimists." Four years later Yankelovich's polls told him that "the defeatism is gone. There is a reassertion of the familiar kinds of American optimism and can-do spirit—in many ways more realistic than in the 1960s." The invasion of Grenada brought not demonstrations, but a surge of new enrollments in ROTC programs. As shown in the moral and cultural conservatism of the antiabortion and profamily movements, a deep reaction also was occurring against the sexual liberalization that had begun in the 1960s. The cycle had turned sharply to the right once again, as it had in the 1920s and 1950s.

During the campaign Mondale attempted to debate what he defined as the issues, but Reagan preferred to invoke the theme of leadership and communicate traditional values to his audience. Rather than discuss the federal deficit, tax policy, and the nuclear arms race, Reagan relied on slogans and on his unofficial campaign song, "I'm Proud to Be an American." Mondale chastised Reagan for the federal deficit, which had run at $175 billion in fiscal year 1984 and was projected to jump to $210 billion in fiscal year 1985. But when Mondale announced that he would raise taxes to cut the deficit, he lost votes.

Religion became an unexpectedly hot issue. Mondale predicted that if Reagan were re-elected, he would nominate only conservative, prolife justices to the Supreme Court and thus **Religious** overturn the Warren Court's liberal **Issues** legacy (see page 949). Mondale even hinted that Reagan's Supreme Court appointments would be approved in advance by Jerry Falwell, the radio-TV minister and founder of the Moral Majority. Falwell's benediction delivered at the 1984 Republican national convention described Reagan and Vice President George Bush as "God's instruments in rebuilding America." Reagan responded that "religion and politics are necessarily related" and called opponents of school prayer "intolerant of religion." Mondale then denounced the Moral Majority's role in Reagan's campaign and declared, "Most Americans would be surprised to learn that God is a Republican." Still, millions of religious conservatives saw a vote for Reagan as an extension of their moral commitments; an expression of their "personal politics," just as walking an antiabortion picket line would be.

Mondale also attacked Reagan's foreign policy, but to little avail. "Mr. Reagan's approach could be summarized this way," Mondale asserted. "If there's an arms agreement, oppose it. If there's a dangerous weapon, buy it. . . . If there's a diplomatic problem, militarize it. If there's a regional conflict, Americanize it. If your policies fail, blame someone else." The Democratic candidate favored a mutual freeze in nuclear testing, arms control talks, an end to the covert war against Nicaragua, and negotiations over Central America. Reagan dismissed Mondale's suggestions as "policies of weakness." But Mondale agreed with the president that military aid should go to El Salvador and that missiles should be deployed in Western Europe. Despite Reagan's minimal success in world affairs, Mondale was unable to make political gains on foreign policy issues largely because Reagan had generated a flag-waving patriotism that supported the president's military build-up and sharp anti-Soviet utterances.

Reagan's victory in 1984 was never in doubt, but his forty-nine-state total led observers to conclude that he had transformed American politics. Columnists and scholars wrote that he had **Reagan's** forged a new right coalition that **Victory** could dominate national politics for years to come. Some compared this election to Franklin D. Roosevelt's comparable sweep in 1936 (he took forty-six of forty-eight states) that had put the final stamp on the New Deal coalition (see page 747). But Reagan's triumph had reduced Roosevelt's coalition to rubble.

Reagan and Roosevelt were alike in several ways. Both were skillful performers; both projected warm

In 1985, these farmers protested the foreclosure auction of a 300-acre farm in Toledo, Iowa, by standing silent and refusing to bid. Burdened by debts and low prices, few family farmers looked forward to the future. Max Winter/Picture Group.

images that inspired confidence. Reagan had never hidden his admiration of Roosevelt's style. The writer David McCullough, after interviewing Reagan in the White House, concluded that he "sees Roosevelt as his 'kind of guy'—confident, cheerful, theatrical, larger than life." The irony, of course, was that Reagan's goal was to repeal Roosevelt's New Deal, not to champion it. Indeed, in his second inaugural address in 1985, Reagan announced that his "new American Emancipation" would "tear down economic barriers and liberate the spirit of enterprise" by eradicating the excesses of fifty years of Democratic liberalism.

Whether Reagan had put together a lasting new right coalition was debatable. What was not debatable was that he had succeeded in his principal aims during his first term and had restored the presidency to its central role in politics and the government. Columnist David Broder wrote in 1985 that "with the nation prosperous and at peace and his personal popularity high," Reagan could already lay claim to being "a historically significant president." Still, as Broder also noted, Reagan had "given many hostages to fortune." Although personally popular, Reagan presided over a polarized people. In the second half of the 1980s, the gap was growing between affluent whites and poor nonwhites, between Frostbelt and Sunbelt states, between the country's social and defense needs, and between liberal lifestyles and religious conservatism. Uncertainties in the economy threatened its continuing rebound. While many businesspeople made money in the mid-1980s, farmers were burdened by debts they could not possibly repay. Around them, banks collapsed and small towns died. The budget deficit during Reagan's second term was projected to add more than $700 billion to the national debt. At stake too were Reagan's commitment and ability to achieve arms control and peace in the Middle East, Africa, and Central America. By taking the oath for a second term, President Ronald Reagan had put his place in history on the line.

SUGGESTIONS FOR FURTHER READING

The Conservative Politics of Ronald Reagan

Ronald Brownstein and Nina Easton, *Reagan's Ruling Class* (1983); Lou Cannon, *Reagan* (1982); Joan Claybrook, *Retreat from Safety: Reagan's Attack on America's Health* (1984); Robert Dallek, *Ronald Reagan: The Politics of Symbolism* (1984); Ronnie Dugger, *On Reagan* (1983); Fred Greenstein, ed., *The Reagan Presidency* (1983); Jonathan Lash, *A Season of Spoils: The Story of the Reagan Administration's Attack on the Environment* (1984); John L. Palmer and Isabel V. Sawhill, eds., *The Reagan Experiment* (1982); Gillian Peele, *Revival and Reaction: The Right in Contemporary America* (1984); Kevin Phillips, *Post-Conservative America* (1982).

Reaganomics

Frank Ackerman, *Reaganomics* (1982); Michael Harrington, *The New American Poverty* (1984); Robert Lekachman, *Greed Is Not Enough* (1983); Frances Fox Piven and Richard Cloward, *The New Class War* (1982); Sidney Weintraub and Marvin Goodstein, eds., *Reaganomics in the Stagflation Economy* (1983).

Reagan's Foreign Policy and the Nuclear Arms Race

Ruth Adams and Susan Cullen, eds., *The Final Epidemic: Physicians and Scientists on Nuclear War* (1981); William M. Arkin and Richard Fieldhouse, *Nuclear Battlefields* (1985); Richard J. Barnet, *The Alliance: America, Europe, Japan* (1983); Alexander Haig, *Caveat: Realism, Reagan, and Foreign Policy* (1984); Harvard Nuclear Study Group, *Living with Nuclear Weapons* (1983); Ole R. Holsti and James R. Rosenau, *American Leadership in World Affairs: Vietnam and the Breakdown of Consensus* (1984); George F. Kennan, *The Nuclear Delusion* (1982); National Academy of Sciences, *Nuclear Arms Control* (1985); Kenneth A. Oye *et al.*, eds., *Eagle Defiant* (1983); Strobe Talbott, *Deadly Gambits: The Reagan Administration and the Stalemate in Nuclear Arms Control* (1984); Strobe Talbott, *The Russians and Reagan* (1984). (Also see the *America and the World* series published by *Foreign Affairs* magazine and the *Great Decisions* series published by the Foreign Policy Association.)

Central America

Raymond Bonner, *Weakness and Deceit: U.S. Policy and El Salvador* (1984); Tom Buckley, *Violent Neighbors* (1984); Charles Clements, *Witness to War* (1984); Kenneth M. Coleman and George C. Herring, eds., *The Central America Crisis* (1985); Martin Diskin, ed., *Trouble in Our Backyard* (1984); Walter LaFeber, *Inevitable Revolutions*, rev. ed. (1984); Robert S. Leiken, ed., *Central America* (1984); Richard A. White, *The Morass* (1984).

APPENDIX

HISTORICAL REFERENCE

BOOKS BY SUBJECT

Encyclopedias, Dictionaries, Atlases,
Chronologies, and Statistics

General

Geoffrey Barraclough, ed., *The Times Atlas of World History* (1979); *Concise Dictionary of American Biography* (1980); *Concise Dictionary of American History* (1983); *Dictionary of American Biography* (1928–); *Dictionary of American History* (1976–1978); Robert H. Ferrell and John S. Bowman, eds., *The Twentieth Century: An Almanac* (1984); Edward W. Fox, *Atlas of American History* (1964); George H. Gallup, *The Gallup Poll: Public Opinion, 1935–1971* (1972) and *1972–1977* (1978); John A. Garraty, ed., *Encyclopedia of American Biography* (1974); Bernard Grun, *The Timetables of History* (1975); Stanley Hochman, *Yesterday and Today* (1979); *International Encyclopedia of the Social Sciences* (1968–); Kenneth T. Jackson and James T. Adams, *Atlas of American History* (1978); R. Alton Lee, ed., *Encyclopedia USA* (1983–); Michael Martin and Leonard Gelber, *Dictionary of American History* (1981); Richard B. Morris, *Encyclopedia of American History* (1982); *National Cyclopedia of American Biography* (1898–); Arthur M. Schlesinger, Jr., ed., *The Almanac of American History* (1983); *Scribner Desk Dictionary of American History* (1984); U.S. Bureau of the Census, *Historical Statistics of the United States* (1975); U.S. Department of the Interior, *National Atlas of the United States* (1970).

The American Revolution

Mark M. Boatner, III, *Encyclopedia of the American Revolution* (1974); Lester J. Cappon, ed., *Atlas of Early American History: The Revolutionary Era, 1760–1790* (1976); Douglas W. Marshall and Howard H. Peckham, *Campaigns of the American Revolution* (1976); Gregory Palmer, ed., *Biographical Sketches of Loyalists of the American Revolution* (1984); *Rand-McNally Atlas of the American Revolution* (1974).

Architecture

William D. Hunt, Jr., ed., *Encyclopedia of American Architecture* (1980).

Blacks

Peter M. Bergman, *The Chronological History of the Negro in America* (1969); Rayford W. Logan and Michael R. Winston, eds., *The Dictionary of American Negro Biography* (1983); W. A. Low and Virgil A. Clift, eds., *Encyclopedia of Black America* (1981); Harry A. Ploski and James Williams, eds., *The Negro Almanac* (1983); Erwin A. Salk, ed., *A Layman's Guide to Negro History* (1967); Mabel M. Smythe, ed., *The Black American Reference Book* (1976); Edgar A. Toppin, *A Biographical History of Blacks in America* (1971).

Cities and Towns

Charles Abrams, *The Language of Cities: A Glossary of Terms* (1971); John L. Androit, ed., *Township Atlas of the United States* (1979); Ory M. Nergal, ed., *The Encyclopedia of American Cities* (1980). *See also* "Politics and Government."

The Civil War

Mark M. Boatner, III, *The Civil War Dictionary* (1959); *The Civil War Almanac* (1983); E. B. Long, *The Civil War Day by Day* (1971); Mark E. Neely, Jr., *The Abraham Lincoln Encyclopedia* (1982); Craig L. Symonds, *A Battlefield Atlas of the Civil War* (1983); U.S. War Department, *The Official Atlas of the Civil War* (1958); Jon L. Wakelyn, ed., *Biographical Dictionary of the Confederacy* (1977); Ezra J. Warner and W. Buck Yearns, *Biographical Register of the Confederate Congress* (1975). *See also* "The South."

Conservation

Forest History Society, *Encyclopedia of American Forest and Conservation History* (1983).

The Constitution and Supreme Court

Congressional Quarterly, *Guide to the Supreme Court* (1979); Leon Friedman and Fred I. Israel, eds., *The Justices of the United States Supreme Court, 1789–1978* (1980); *Judges of the United States* (1980).

Crime

Sanford H. Kadish, ed., *Encyclopedia of Crime and Justice* (1983); Carl Sifakis, *The Encyclopedia of American Crime* (1982).

Culture and Folklore

M. Thomas Inge, ed., *Handbook of American Popular Culture* (1979–1981); Marjorie Tallman, *Dictionary of American Folklore* (1959); Justin Wintle, ed., *Makers of Nineteenth Century Culture, 1800–1914* (1982). *See also* "Entertainment," "Music," and "Sports."

The Economy and Business

Christine Ammer and Dean S. Ammer, *Dictionary of Business and Economics* (1983); Douglas Auld and Graham Bannock, *The American Dictionary of Economics* (1983); Douglas Greenwald, *Encyclopedia of Economics* (1982); John N. Ingham, *Biographical Dictionary of American Business Leaders* (1983); Glenn G. Munn, *Encyclopedia of Banking and Finance* (1973); David W. Pearce, *Dictionary of Modern Economics* (1983); Glenn Porter, *Encyclopedia of American Economic History* (1980).

Education

Lee C. Deighton, ed., *The Encyclopedia of Education* (1971); Joseph C. Kiger, ed., *Research Institutions and Learned Societies* (1982); John F. Ohles, ed., *Biographical Dictionary of American Educators* (1978).

Entertainment

Tim Brooks and Earle Marsh, *The Complete Directory to Prime Time Network TV Shows, 1946–present* (1979); Barbara N. Cohen-Stratyner, *Biographical Dictionary of Dance* (1982); John Dunning, *Tune in Yesterday* [radio] (1967); Stanley Green, *Encyclopedia of the Musical Film* (1981); *Notable Names in the American Theater* (1976); *New York Times Encyclopedia of Television* (1977); Andrew Sarris, *The American Cinema: Directors and Directions, 1929–1968* (1968); Evelyn M. Truitt, *Who Was Who on Screen* (1977). *See also* "Culture and Folklore," "Music," and "Sports."

Foreign Policy

Alexander DeConde, ed., *Encyclopedia of American Foreign Policy* (1978); John E. Findling, *Dictionary of American Diplomatic History* (1980); *International Geographic Encyclopedia and Atlas* (1979); Warren F. Kuehl, ed., *Biographical Dictionary of Internationalists* (1983); George T. Kurian, *Encyclopedia of the Third World* (1981); Richard B. Morris and Graham W. Irwin, eds., *Harper Encyclopedia of the Modern World* (1970); Jack C. Plano, ed., *The International Relations Dictionary* (1982); Jack E. Vincent, *A Handbook of International Relations* (1969).

Immigration and Ethnic Groups

American Jewish Biographies (1982); Stephanie Bernardo, *The Ethnic Almanac* (1981); Matt S. Meier and Feliciano Rivera, *Dictionary of Mexican American History* (1981); Stephan Thernstrom, ed., *Harvard Encyclopedia of American Ethnic Groups* (1980).

Indians

Frederick J. Dockstader, *Great North American Indians* (1977); *Handbook of North American Indians* (1978–   ); Barry Klein, ed., *Reference Encyclopedia of the American Indian* (1978).

Labor

Gary M. Fink, ed., *Biographical Dictionary of American Labor Leaders* (1974); Gary M. Fink, ed., *Labor Unions* (1977); Philip S. Foner, *First Facts of American Labor* (1984).

Literature

James T. Callow and Robert J. Reilly, *Guide to American Literature* (1976–1977); *Dictionary of Literary Biography* (1978–   ); Eugene Ehrlich and Gorton Carruth, *The Oxford Illustrated Literary Guide to the United States* (1982); Jon Tuska and Vicki Piekarski, *Encyclopedia of Frontier and Western Fiction* (1983). *See also* "Culture and Folklore," "The South," and "Women."

Medicine

Martin Kaufman, *et al.*, eds., *Dictionary of American Medical Biography* (1984).

Music

John Chilton, *Who's Who of Jazz* (1972); Edward Jablonski, *The Encyclopedia of American Music* (1981); Roger Lax and

Frederick Smith, *The Great Song Thesaurus* (1984). *See also* "Culture and Folklore" and "Entertainment."

Politics and Government: General and Elections

Congressional Quarterly, *Congress and the Nation, 1945–1976* (1965–1977); Congressional Quarterly, *Guide to U.S. Elections* (1975); Jack P. Greene, ed., *Encyclopedia of American Political History* (1984); Kenneth C. Martis, *The Historical Atlas of United States Congressional Districts, 1789–1983* (1982); Edwin V. Mitchell, *An Encyclopedia of American Politics* (1968); Svend Peterson, *A Statistical History of the American Presidential Elections* (1963); William Safire, *Safire's Political Dictionary* (1978); Richard M. Scammon, ed., *America at the Polls* (1965); Edward L. and Frederick H. Schapsmeier, eds., *Political Parties and Civic Action Groups* (1981); Arthur M. Schlesinger, Jr., and Fred I. Israel, eds., *History of American Presidential Elections, 1789–1968* (1971); Robert Scruton, *A Dictionary of Political Thought* (1982); Hans Sperber and Travis Trittschuh, *American Political Terms* (1962). *See also* "The Constitution and Supreme Court," "States and the West," and the following section.

Politics and Government: Leaders

Roy R. Glashan, comp., *American Governors and Gubernatorial Elections, 1775–1978* (1979); Otis L. Graham, Jr., and Meghan R. Wander, eds., *Franklin D. Roosevelt: His Life and Times* (1985); Melvin G. Holli and Peter d'A. Jones, eds., *Biographical Dictionary of American Mayors, 1820–1980: Big City Mayors* (1981); Joseph E. Kallenbach and Jessamine S. Kallenbach, *American State Governors, 1776–1976* (1977); Thomas A. McMullin and David Walker, *Biographical Directory of American Territorial Governors* (1984); *Political Profiles, Truman Years to . . .* (1978); John W. Raimo, ed., *Biographical Directory of American Colonial and Revolutionary Governors, 1607–1789* (1980); John W. Raimo, ed., *Biographical Directory of the Governors of the United States, 1789–1978* (1978); John W. Raimo, ed., *Biographical Directory of the Governors of the United States, 1978–1983* (1984); Robert Sobel, ed., *Biographical Directory of the United States Executive Branch, 1774–1977* (1977); U.S. Congress, Senate, *Biographical Directory of the American Congress, 1774–1971* (1971); Robert Vexler, *The Vice-Presidents and Cabinet Members* (1975). *See also* the previous section.

Religion

Henry Bowden, *Dictionary of American Religious Biography* (1977); John T. Ellis and Robert Trisco, *A Guide to American Catholic History* (1982); Edwin S. Gaustad, *Historical Atlas of Religion in America* (1976); Samuel S. Hill, Jr., ed., *Encyclopedia of Religion in the South* (1984); J. Gordon Melton, *The Encyclopedia of American Religions* (1978); Mark A. Noll and Nathan O. Hatch, eds., *Eerdmans Handbook to Christianity in America* (1983); Arthur C. Piepkorn, *Profiles in Brief: The Religious Bodies of the United States and Canada* (1977–1979).

Science

Charles C. Gillispie, ed., *Dictionary of Scientific Biography* (1970–   ); National Academy of Sciences, *Biographical Memoirs* (1877–   ).

Social Issues

Louis Filler, *A Dictionary of American Social Reform* (1963); Louis Filler, *Dictionary of American Social Change* (1982); Robert S. Fogarty, *Dictionary of American Communal and Utopian History* (1980); Mark E. Lender, *Dictionary of American Temperance Biography* (1984); Alvin J. Schmidt, *Fraternal Organizations* (1980). *See also* "Crime."

The South

Robert Bain, *et al.*, eds., *Southern Writers: A Biographical Dictionary* (1979); Kenneth Coleman and Charles S. Gurr, eds., *Dictionary of Georgia Biography* (1983); William C. Ferris and Charles R. Wilson, eds., *Encyclopedia of Southern Culture* (1986); David C. Roller and Robert W. Twyman, eds., *The Encyclopedia of Southern History* (1979); Walter P. Webb, *et al.*, eds., *The Handbook of Texas* (1952, 1976). *See also* "Politics and Government" and "States and the West."

Sports

Ralph Hickok, *New Encyclopedia of Sports* (1977); Ralph Hickok, *Who Was Who in American Sports* (1971); Zander Hollander, *The NBA's Official Encyclopedia of Pro Basketball* (1981); Frank G. Menke and Suzanne Treat, *The Encyclopedia of Sports* (1977); *The NFL's Official Encyclopedic History of Professional Football* (1977); Paul Soderberg, *et al.*, *The Big Book of Halls of Fame in the United States and Canada* (1977). *See also* "Culture and Folklore."

States and the West

John Clayton, ed., *The Illinois Fact Book and Historical Almanac, 1673–1968* (1970); Doris O. Dawdy, *Artists of the American West* (1974–1984); Howard R. Lamar, ed., *The Reader's Encyclopedia of the American West* (1977);

Mose Y. Sachs, ed., *The Worldmark Encyclopedia of the States* (1981). *See also* "Politics and Government" and "The South."

Wars and the Military

R. Ernest Dupuy and Trevor N. Dupuy, *The Encyclopedia of Military History* (1977); Holger H. Herwig and Neil M. Heyman, *Biographical Dictionary of World War I* (1982); Michael Kidrow and Dan Smith, *The War Atlas: Armed Conflict, Armed Peace* (1983); Roger J. Spiller and Joseph G. Dawson, III, eds., *Dictionary of American Military Biography* (1984); U.S. Military Academy, *The West Point Atlas of American Wars, 1689–1953* (1959); *Webster's American Military Biographies* (1978). *See also* "The American Revolution," "The Civil War," and "World War II."

Women

Edward T. James, *et al.*, *Notable American Women, 1607–1950* (1971); Lina Mainiero, ed., *American Women Writers* (1979–1982); Barbara Sicherman and Carol H. Green, eds., *Notable American Women, The Modern Period* (1980).

World War II

Marcel Baudot, *et al.*, eds., *The Historical Encyclopedia of World War II* (1980); Simon Goodenough, *War Maps: Great Land Battles of World War II* (1983); Robert Goralski, *World War II Almanac, 1931–1945* (1981); John Keegan, ed., *The Rand-McNally Encyclopedia of World War II* (1977); Thomas Parrish, ed., *The Simon and Schuster Encyclopedia of World War II* (1978); Louis L. Snyder, *Louis L. Snyder's Historical Guide to World War II* (1982); U.S. Military Academy, *Campaign Atlas to the Second World War: Europe and the Mediterranean* (1980); Peter Young, ed., *The World Almanac Book of World War II* (1981). *See also* "Wars and the Military."

Declaration of Independence in Congress, July 4, 1776

The unanimous declaration of the thirteen United States of America

When, in the course of human events, it becomes necessary for one people to dissolve the political bonds which have connected them with another, and to assume, among the powers of the earth, the separate and equal station to which the laws of nature and of nature's God entitle them, a decent respect to the opinions of mankind requires that they should declare the causes which impel them to the separation.

We hold these truths to be self-evident: That all men are created equal; that they are endowed by their Creator with certain unalienable rights; that among these are life, liberty, and the pursuit of happiness; that, to secure these rights, governments are instituted among men, deriving their just powers from the consent of the governed; that whenever any form of government becomes destructive of these ends, it is the right of the people to alter or to abolish it, and to institute new government, laying its foundation on such principles, and organizing its powers in such form, as to them shall seem most likely to effect their safety and happiness. Prudence, indeed, will dictate that governments long established should not be changed for light and transient causes; and accordingly all experience hath shown that mankind are more disposed to suffer, while evils are sufferable, than to right themselves by abolishing the forms to which they are accustomed. But when a long train of abuses and usurpations, pursuing invariably the same object, evinces a design to reduce them under absolute despotism, it is their right, it is their duty, to throw off such government, and to provide new guards for their future security. Such has been the patient sufferance of these colonies; and such is now the necessity which constrains them to alter their former systems of government. The history of the present King of Great Britain is a history of repeated injuries and usurpations, all having in direct object the establishment of an absolute tyranny over these states. To prove this, let facts be submitted to a candid world.

He has refused his assent to laws, the most wholesome and necessary for the public good.

He has forbidden his governors to pass laws of immediate and pressing importance, unless suspended in their operation till his assent should be obtained; and, when so suspended, he has utterly neglected to attend to them.

He has refused to pass other laws for the accommodation of large districts of people, unless those people would relinquish the right of representation in the legislature, a right inestimable to them, and formidable to tyrants only.

He has called together legislative bodies at places unusual, uncomfortable, and distant from the depository of their public records, for the sole purpose of fatiguing them into compliance with his measures.

He has dissolved representative houses repeatedly, for opposing, with manly firmness, his invasions on the rights of the people.

He has refused for a long time, after such dissolutions, to cause others to be elected; whereby the legislative powers, incapable of annihilation, have returned to the people at large for their exercise; the state remaining, in the mean time, exposed to all the dangers of invasions from without and convulsions within.

He has endeavored to prevent the population of these states; for that purpose obstructing the laws for naturalization of foreigners; refusing to pass others to encourage their migration hither, and raising the conditions of new appropriations of lands.

He has obstructed the administration of justice, by refusing his assent to laws for establishing judiciary powers.

He has made judges dependent on his will alone, for the tenure of their offices, and the amount and payment of their salaries.

He has erected a multitude of new offices, and sent hither swarms of officers to harass our people and eat out their substance.

He has kept among us, in times of peace, standing armies, without the consent of our legislatures.

He has affected to render the military independent of, and superior to, the civil power.

He has combined with others to subject us to a jurisdiction foreign to our constitution, and unacknowledged by our laws, giving his assent to their acts of pretended legislation:

For quartering large bodies of armed troops among us;

For protecting them, by a mock trial, from punishment for any murders which they should commit on the inhabitants of these states;

For cutting off our trade with all parts of the world;

For imposing taxes on us without our consent;

For depriving us, in many cases, of the benefits of trial by jury;

For transporting us beyond seas, to be tried for pretended offenses;

For abolishing the free system of English laws in a neighboring province, establishing therein an arbitrary government, and enlarging its boundaries, so as to render it at once an example and fit instrument for introducing the same absolute rule into these colonies;

For taking away our charters, abolishing our most valuable laws, and altering fundamentally the forms of our governments;

For suspending our own legislatures, and declaring themselves invested with power to legislate for us in all cases whatsoever.

He has abdicated government here, by declaring us out of his protection and waging war against us.

He has plundered our seas, ravaged our coasts, burned our towns, and destroyed the lives of our people.

He is at this time transporting large armies of foreign mercenaries to complete the works of death, desolation, and tyranny already begun with circumstances of cruelty and perfidy scarcely paralleled in the most barbarous ages, and totally unworthy the head of a civilized nation.

He has constrained our fellow-citizens, taken captive on the high seas, to bear arms against their country, to become the executioners of their friends and brethren, or to fall themselves by their hands.

He has excited domestic insurrection among us, and has endeavored to bring on the inhabitants of our frontiers the merciless Indian savages, whose known rule of warfare is an undistinguished destruction of all ages, sexes, and conditions.

In every stage of these oppressions we have petitioned for redress in the most humble terms; our repeated petitions have been answered only by repeated injury. A prince, whose character is thus marked by every act which may define a tyrant, is unfit to be the ruler of a free people.

Nor have we been wanting in our attentions to our British brethren. We have warned them, from time to time, of attempts by their legislature to extend an unwarrantable jurisdiction over us. We have reminded them of the circumstances of our emigration and settlement here. We have appealed to their native justice and magnanimity; and we have conjured them, by the ties of our common kindred, to disavow these usurpations, which would inevitably interrupt our connections and correspondence. They, too, have been deaf to the voice of justice and of consanguinity. We must, therefore, acquiesce in the necessity which denounces our separation, and hold them, as we hold the rest of mankind, enemies in war, in peace friends.

We, therefore, the representatives of the United States of America, in General Congress assembled, appealing to the Supreme Judge of the world for the rectitude of our intentions, do, in the name and by the authority of the good people of these colonies, solemnly publish and declare, that these United Colonies are, and of right ought to be, FREE AND INDEPENDENT STATES; that they are absolved from all allegiance to the British crown, and that all political connection between them and the state of Great Britain is, and ought to be, totally dissolved; and that, as free and independent states, they have full power to levy war, conclude peace, contract alliances, establish commerce, and do all other acts and things which independent states may of right do. And for the support of this declaration, with a firm reliance on the protection of Divine Providence, we mutually pledge to each other our lives, our fortunes, and our sacred honor.

JOHN HANCOCK
and fifty-five others

Constitution of the United States of America and Amendments

Preamble

We the people of the United States, in order to form a more perfect union, establish justice, insure domestic tranquillity, provide for the common defense, promote the general welfare, and secure the blessings of liberty to ourselves and our posterity, do ordain and establish this Constitution for the United States of America.

Article I

Section 1 All legislative powers herein granted shall be vested in a Congress of the United States, which shall consist of a Senate and a House of Representatives.

Section 2 The House of Representatives shall be composed of members chosen every second year by the people of the several States, and the electors in each State shall have the qualifications requisite for electors of the most numerous branch of the State Legislature.

No person shall be a Representative who shall not have attained to the age of twenty-five years, and been seven years a citizen of the United States, and who shall not,

when elected, be an inhabitant of that State in which he shall be chosen.

Representatives and direct taxes shall be apportioned among the several States which may be included within this Union, according to their respective numbers, *which shall be determined by adding to the whole number of free persons, including those bound to service for a term of years and excluding Indians not taxed, three-fifths of all other persons.* The actual enumeration shall be made within three years after the first meeting of the Congress of the United States, and within every subsequent term of ten years, in such manner as they shall by law direct. The number of Representatives shall not exceed one for every thirty thousand, but each State shall have at least one Representative; *and until such enumeration shall be made, the State of New Hampshire shall be entitled to choose three, Massachusetts eight, Rhode Island and Providence Plantations one, Connecticut five, New York six, New Jersey four, Pennsylvania eight, Delaware one, Maryland six, Virginia ten, North Carolina five, South Carolina five, and Georgia three.*

When vacancies happen in the representation from any State, the Executive authority thereof shall issue writs of election to fill such vacancies.

The House of Representatives shall choose their Speaker and other officers; and shall have the sole power of impeachment.

Section 3 The Senate of the United States shall be composed of two Senators from each State, *chosen by the legislature thereof,* for six years; and each Senator shall have one vote.

Immediately after they shall be assembled in consequence of the first election, they shall be divided as equally as may be into three classes. The seats of the Senators of the first class shall be vacated at the expiration of the second year, of the second class at the expiration of the fourth year, and of the third class at the expiration of the sixth year, so that one-third may be chosen every second year; and if vacancies happen by resignation or otherwise, during the recess of the legislature of any State, the Executive thereof may make temporary appointments until the next meeting of the legislature, which shall then fill such vacancies.

No person shall be a Senator who shall not have attained to the age of thirty years, and been nine years a citizen of the United States, and who shall not, when elected, be an inhabitant of that State for which he shall be chosen.

The Vice-President of the United States shall be President of the Senate, but shall have no vote, unless they be equally divided.

The Senate shall choose their other officers, and also a President *pro tempore,* in the absence of the Vice-President, or when he shall exercise the office of President of the United States.

Passages no longer in effect are printed in italic type.

The Senate shall have the sole power to try all impeachments. When sitting for that purpose, they shall be on oath or affirmation. When the President of the United States is tried, the Chief Justice shall preside: and no person shall be convicted without the concurrence of two-thirds of the members present.

Judgment in cases of impeachment shall not extend further than to removal from the office, and disqualification to hold and enjoy any office of honor, trust or profit under the United States: but the party convicted shall nevertheless be liable and subject to indictment, trial, judgment and punishment, according to law.

Section 4 The times, places and manner of holding elections for Senators and Representatives shall be prescribed in each State by the legislature thereof; but the Congress may at any time by law make or alter such regulations, except as to the places of choosing Senators.

The Congress shall assemble at least once in every year, and such meeting *shall be on the first Monday in December, unless they shall by law appoint a different day.*

Section 5 Each house shall be the judge of the elections, returns and qualifications of its own members, and a majority of each shall constitute a quorum to do business; but a smaller number may adjourn from day to day, and may be authorized to compel the attendance of absent members, in such manner, and under such penalties, as each house may provide.

Each house may determine the rules of its proceedings, punish its members for disorderly behavior, and with the concurrence of two-thirds, expel a member.

Each house shall keep a journal of its proceedings, and from time to time publish the same, excepting such parts as may in their judgment require secrecy; and the yeas and nays of the members of either house on any question shall, at the desire of one-fifth of those present, be entered on the journal.

Neither house, during the session of Congress, shall, without the consent of the other, adjourn for more than three days, nor to any other place than that in which the two houses shall be sitting.

Section 6 The Senators and Representatives shall receive a compensation for their services, to be ascertained by law and paid out of the treasury of the United States. They shall in all cases except treason, felony and breach of the peace, be privileged from arrest during their attendance at the session of their respective houses, and in going to and returning from the same; and for any speech or debate in either house, they shall not be questioned in any other place.

No Senator or Representative shall, during the time for which he was elected, be appointed to any civil office under the authority of the United States, which shall have been created, or the emoluments whereof shall have been increased, during such time; and no person holding any office under the United States shall be a member of either house during his continuance in office.

Section 7 All bills for raising revenue shall originate in the House of Representatives; but the Senate may propose or concur with amendments as on other bills.

Every bill which shall have passed the House of Representatives and the Senate, shall, before it become a law, be presented to the President of the United States; if he approve he shall sign it, but if not he shall return it with objections to that house in which it originated, who shall enter the objections at large on their journal, and proceed to reconsider it. If after such reconsideration two-thirds of that house shall agree to pass the bill, it shall be sent, together with the objections, to the other house, by which it shall likewise be reconsidered, and, if approved by two-thirds of that house, it shall become a law. But in all such cases the votes of both houses shall be determined by yeas and nays, and the names of the persons voting for and against the bill shall be entered on the journal of each house respectively. If any bill shall not be returned by the President within ten days (Sundays excepted) after it shall have been presented to him, the same shall be a law, in like manner as if he had signed it, unless the Congress by their adjournment prevent its return, in which case it shall not be a law.

Every order, resolution, or vote to which the concurrence of the Senate and House of Representatives may be necessary (except on a question of adjournment) shall be presented to the President of the United States; and before the same shall take effect, shall be approved by him, or being disapproved by him, shall be repassed by two-thirds of the Senate and House of Representatives, according to the rules and limitations prescribed in the case of a bill.

Section 8 The Congress shall have power

To lay and collect taxes, duties, imposts, and excises, to pay the debts and provide for the common defense and general welfare of the United States; but all duties, imposts and excises shall be uniform throughout the United States;

To borrow money on the credit of the United States;

To regulate commerce with foreign nations, and among the several States, and with the Indian tribes;

To establish an uniform rule of naturalization, and uniform laws on the subject of bankruptcies throughout the United States;

To coin money, regulate the value thereof, and of foreign coin, and fix the standard of weights and measures;

To provide for the punishment of counterfeiting the securities and current coin of the United States;

To establish post offices and post roads;

To promote the progress of science and useful arts by securing for limited times to authors and inventors the exclusive right to their respective writings and discoveries;

To constitute tribunals inferior to the Supreme Court;

To define and punish piracies and felonies committed on the high seas and offenses against the law of nations;

To declare war, grant letters of marque and reprisal, and make rules concerning captures on land and water;

To raise and support armies, but no appropriation of money to that use shall be for a longer term than two years;

To provide and maintain a navy;

To make rules for the government and regulation of the land and naval forces;

To provide for calling forth the militia to execute the laws of the Union, suppress insurrections, and repel invasions;

To provide for organizing, arming, and disciplining the militia, and for governing such part of them as may be employed in the service of the United States, reserving to the States respectively the appointment of the officers, and the authority of training the militia according to the discipline prescribed by Congress;

To exercise exclusive legislation in all cases whatsoever, over such district (not exceeding ten miles square) as may, by cession of particular States, and the acceptance of Congress, become the seat of government of the United States, and to exercise like authority over all places purchased by the consent of the legislature of the State, in which the same shall be, for erection of forts, magazines, arsenals, dock-yards, and other needful buildings;—and

To make all laws which shall be necessary and proper for carrying into execution the foregoing powers, and all other powers vested by this Constitution in the government of the United States, or in any department or officer thereof.

Section 9 The migration or importation of such persons as any of the States now existing shall think proper to admit shall not be prohibited by the Congress prior to the year 1808; but a tax or duty may be imposed on such importation, not exceeding $10 for each person.

The privilege of the writ of habeas corpus shall not be suspended, unless when in cases of rebellion or invasion the public safety may require it.

No bill of attainder or ex post facto law shall be passed.

No capitation, or other direct, tax shall be laid, unless in proportion to the census or enumeration herein before directed to be taken.

No tax or duty shall be laid on articles exported from any State.

No preference shall be given by any regulation of commerce or revenue to the ports of one State over those of another; nor shall vessels bound to, or from, one State, be obliged to enter, clear, or pay duties in another.

No money shall be drawn from the treasury, but in consequence of appropriations made by law; and a regular statement and account of the receipts and expenditures of all public money shall be published from time to time.

No title of nobility shall be granted by the United States: and no person holding any office of profit or trust under them, shall, without the consent of the Congress, accept of any present, emolument, office, or title, of any kind whatever, from any king, prince, or foreign state.

Section 10 No State shall enter into any treaty, alliance, or confederation; grant letters of marque and reprisal; coin money; emit bills of credit; make anything but gold and silver coin a tender in payment of debts; pass any bill of attainder, ex post facto law, or law impairing the obligation of contracts, or grant any title of nobility.

No State shall, without the consent of Congress, lay any imposts or duties on imports or exports, except what may be absolutely necessary for executing its inspection laws: and the net produce of all duties and imposts, laid by any State on imports or exports, shall be for the use of the treasury of the United States; and all such laws shall be subject to the revision and control of the Congress.

No State shall, without the consent of Congress, lay any duty of tonnage, keep troops or ships of war in time of peace, enter into any agreement or compact with another State, or with a foreign power, or engage in war, unless actually invaded, or in such imminent danger as will not admit of delay.

Article II

Section 1 The executive power shall be vested in a President of the United States of America. He shall hold his office during the term of four years, and, together with the Vice-President, chosen for the same term, be elected as follows:

Each State shall appoint, in such manner as the legislature thereof may direct, a number of electors, equal to the whole number of Senators and Representatives to which the State may be entitled in the Congress; but no Senator or Representative, or person holding an office of trust or profit under the United States, shall be appointed an elector.

The electors shall meet in their respective States, and vote by ballot for two persons, of whom one at least shall not be an inhabitant of the same State with themselves. And they shall make a list of all the persons voted for, and of the number of votes for each; which list they shall sign and certify, and transmit sealed to the seat of government of the United States, directed to the President of the Senate. *The President of the Senate shall, in the presence of the Senate and House of Representatives, open all the certificates, and the votes shall then be counted. The person having the greatest number of votes shall be the President, if such number be a majority of the whole number of electors appointed; and if there be more than one who have such majority, and have an equal number of votes, then the House of Representatives shall immediately choose by ballot one of them for President; and if no person have a majority, then from the five highest on the list said house shall in like manner choose the President. But in choosing the President the votes shall be taken by States, the representation from each State having one vote; a quorum for this purpose shall consist of a member or members from two-thirds of the States, and a majority of all the States shall be necessary to a choice. In every case, after the choice of the President, the person having the greatest number of votes of the electors shall be the Vice-President. But if there should remain two or more who have equal votes, the Senate shall choose from them by ballot the Vice-President.*

The Congress may determine the time of choosing the electors and the day on which they shall give their votes; which day shall be the same throughout the United States.

No person except a natural-born citizen, *or a citizen of the United States at the time of the adoption of this Constitution,* shall be eligible to the office of President; neither shall any person be eligible to that office who shall not have attained to the age of thirty-five years, and been fourteen years a resident within the United States.

In case of the removal of the President from office or of his death, resignation, or inability to discharge the powers and duties of the said office, the same shall devolve on the Vice-President, and the Congress may by law provide for the case of removal, death, resignation, or inability, both of the President and Vice-President, declaring what officer shall then act as President, and such officer shall act accordingly, until the disability be removed, or a President shall be elected.

The President shall, at stated times, receive for his services a compensation, which shall neither be increased nor diminished during the period for which he shall have been elected, and he shall not receive within that period any other emolument from the United States, or any of them.

Before he enter on the execution of his office, he shall take the following oath or affirmation:—"I do solemnly swear (or affirm) that I will faithfully execute the office of the President of the United States, and will to the best of my ability preserve, protect and defend the Constitution of the United States."

Section 2 The President shall be commander in chief of the army and navy of the United States, and of the militia of the several States, when called into the actual service of the United States; he may require the opinion, in writing, of the principal officer in each of the executive departments, upon any subject relating to the duties of their respective offices, and he shall have power to grant reprieves and pardons for offenses against the United States, except in cases of impeachment.

He shall have power, by and with the advice and consent of the Senate, to make treaties, provided two-thirds of the Senators present concur; and he shall nominate, and by and with the advice and consent of the Senate, shall appoint ambassadors, other public ministers and consuls, judges of the Supreme Court, and all other officers of the United States, whose appointments are not herein otherwise provided for, and which shall be established by law: but Congress may by law vest the appointment of such inferior officers, as they think proper, in the President alone, in the courts of law, or in the heads of departments.

The President shall have power to fill up all vacancies that may happen during the recess of the Senate, by granting commissions which shall expire at the end of their next session.

Section 3 He shall from time to time give to the Congress information of the state of the Union, and recommend to their consideration such measures as he shall judge necessary and expedient; he may, on extraordinary occasions, convene both houses, or either of them, and in case of disagreement between them, with respect to the time of adjournment, he may adjourn them to such time as he shall think proper; he shall receive ambassadors and other public ministers; he shall take care that the laws be faithfully executed, and shall commission all the officers of the United States.

Section 4 The President, Vice-President and all civil officers of the United States shall be removed from office on impeachment for, and on conviction of, treason, bribery, or other high crimes and misdemeanors.

Article III

Section 1 The judicial power of the United States shall be vested in one Supreme Court, and in such inferior courts as the Congress may from time to time ordain and establish. The judges, both of the Supreme and inferior courts, shall hold their offices during good behavior, and shall, at stated times, receive for their services a compensation which shall not be diminished during their continuance in office.

Section 2 The judicial power shall extend to all cases, in law and equity, arising under this Constitution, the laws of the United States, and treaties made, or which shall be made, under their authority;—to all cases affecting ambassadors, other public ministers and consuls;—to all cases of admiralty and maritime jurisdiction;—to controversies to which the United States shall be a party;—to controversies between two or more States;—*between a State and citizens of another State;*—between citizens of different States;—between citizens of the same State claiming lands under grants of different States, and between a State, or the citizens thereof, and foreign states, citizens or subjects.

In all cases affecting ambassadors, other public ministers and consuls, and those in which a State shall be party, the Supreme Court shall have original jurisdiction. In all the other cases before mentioned, the Supreme Court shall have appellate jurisdiction, both as to law and fact, with such exceptions, and under such regulations, as the Congress shall make.

The trial of all crimes, except in cases of impeachment, shall be by jury; and such trial shall be held in the State where said crimes shall have been committed; but when not committed within any State, the trial shall be at such place or places as the Congress may by law have directed.

Section 3 Treason against the United States shall consist only in levying war against them, or in adhering to their enemies, giving them aid and comfort. No person shall be convicted of treason unless on the testimony of two witnesses to the same overt act, or on confession in open court.

The Congress shall have power to declare the punishment of treason, but no attainder of treason shall work corruption of blood, or forfeiture except during the life of the person attainted.

Article IV

Section 1 Full faith and credit shall be given in each State to the public acts, records, and judicial proceedings of every other State. And the Congress may by general laws prescribe the manner in which such acts, records, and proceedings shall be proved, and the effect thereof.

Section 2 The citizens of each State shall be entitled to all privileges and immunities of citizens in the several States.

A person charged in any State with treason, felony, or other crime, who shall flee from justice, and be found in another State, shall on demand of the executive authority of the State from which he fled, be delivered up, to be removed to the State having jurisdiction of the crime.

No person held to service or labor in one State, under the laws thereof, escaping into another, shall, in consequence of any law or regulation therein, be discharged from such service or labor, but shall be delivered up on claim of the party to whom such service or labor may be due.

Section 3 New States may be admitted by the Congress into this Union; but no new State shall be formed or erected within the jurisdiction of any other State; nor any State be formed by the junction of two or more States, or parts of States, without the consent of the legislatures of the States concerned as well as of the Congress.

The Congress shall have power to dispose of and make all needful rules and regulations respecting the territory or other property belonging to the United States; and nothing in this Constitution shall be so construed as to prejudice any claims of the United States, or of any particular State.

Section 4 The United States shall guarantee to every State in this Union a republican form of government, and shall protect each of them against invasion; and on application of the legislature, or of the executive (when the legislature cannot be convened), against domestic violence.

Article V

The Congress, whenever two-thirds of both houses shall deem it necessary, shall propose amendments to this Constitution, or, on the application of the legislatures of two-thirds of the several States, shall call a convention for proposing amendments, which, in either case, shall be valid to all intents and purposes, as part of this Constitution, when ratified by the legislatures of three-fourths of the several States, or by conventions in three-fourths thereof, as the one or the other mode of ratification may be proposed by the Congress; provided *that no amendments which may be made prior to the year one thousand eight hundred and eight shall in any manner affect the first and fourth clauses in the ninth section of the first article;* and that no State, without its consent, shall be deprived of its equal suffrage in the Senate.

Article VI

All debts contracted and engagements entered into, before the adoption of this Constitution, shall be as valid against the United States under this Constitution, as under the Confederation.

This Constitution, and the laws of the United States which shall be made in pursuance thereof; and all treaties made, or which shall be made, under the authority of the United States, shall be the supreme law of the land; and the judges in every State shall be bound thereby, anything in the Constitution or laws of any State to the contrary notwithstanding.

The Senators and Representatives before mentioned, and the members of the several State legislatures, and all executive and judicial officers, both of the United States and of the several States, shall be bound by oath or affirmation to support this Constitution; but no religious test shall ever be required as a qualification to any office or public trust under the United States.

Article VII

The ratification of the conventions of nine States shall be sufficient for the establishment of this Constitution between the States so ratifying the same.

Done in Convention by the unanimous consent of the States present, the seventeenth day of September in the year of our Lord one thousand seven hundred and eighty-seven and of the Independence of the United States of America the twelfth. In witness whereof we have hereunto subscribed our names.

GEORGE WASHINGTON
and thirty-seven others

Amendments to the Constitution*

Amendment I

Congress shall make no law respecting an establishment of religion, or prohibiting the free exercise thereof; or abridging the freedom of speech, or of the press; or the right of the people peaceably to assemble, and to petition the government for a redress of grievances.

Amendment II

A well-regulated militia being necessary to the security of a free State, the right of the people to keep and bear arms shall not be infringed.

Amendment III

No soldier shall, in time of peace, be quartered in any house without the consent of the owner, nor in time of war, but in a manner to be prescribed by law.

Amendment IV

The right of the people to be secure in their persons, houses, papers, and effects, against unreasonable searches and seizures, shall not be violated, and no warrants shall issue but upon probable cause, supported by oath or affirmation, and particularly describing the place to be searched, and the persons or things to be seized.

---

*The first ten Amendments (the Bill of Rights) were adopted in 1791.

Amendment V

No person shall be held to answer for a capital, or otherwise infamous crime, unless on a presentment or indictment of a grand jury, except in cases arising in the land or naval forces, or in the militia, when in actual service in time of war or public danger; nor shall any person be subject for the same offense to be twice put in jeopardy of life or limb; nor shall be compelled in any criminal case to be a witness against himself, nor be deprived of life, liberty, or property, without due process of law; nor shall private property be taken for public use without just compensation.

Amendment VI

In all criminal prosecutions, the accused shall enjoy the right to a speedy and public trial, by an impartial jury of the State and district wherein the crime shall have been committed, which district shall have been previously ascertained by law, and to be informed of the nature and cause of the accusation; to be confronted with the witnesses against him; to have compulsory process for obtaining witnesses in his favor, and to have the assistance of counsel for his defense.

Amendment VII

In suits at common law, where the value in controversy shall exceed twenty dollars, the right of trial by jury shall be preserved, and no fact tried by a jury shall be otherwise reexamined in any court of the United States, than according to the rules of the common law.

Amendment VIII

Excessive bail shall not be required, nor excessive fines imposed, nor cruel and unusual punishments inflicted.

Amendment IX

The enumeration in the Constitution, of certain rights, shall not be construed to deny or disparage others retained by the people.

Amendment X

The powers not delegated to the United States by the Constitution, nor prohibited by it to the States, are reserved to the States respectively, or to the people.

Amendment XI
[Adopted 1798]

The judicial power of the United States shall not be construed to extend to any suit in law or equity, commenced or prosecuted against one of the United States by citizens of another State, or by citizens or subjects of any foreign state.

Amendment XII
[Adopted 1804]

The electors shall meet in their respective States, and vote by ballot for President and Vice-President, one of whom, at least, shall not be an inhabitant of the same State with themselves; they shall name in their ballots the person voted for as President, and in distinct ballots the person voted for as Vice-President, and they shall make distinct lists of all persons voted for as President, and of all persons voted for as Vice-President, and of the number of votes for each, which lists they shall sign and certify, and transmit sealed to the seat of government of the United States, directed to the President of the Senate;—the President of the Senate shall, in the presence of the Senate and House of Representatives, open all the certificates and the votes shall then be counted;—the person having the greatest number of votes for President shall be the President, if such number be a majority of the whole number of electors appointed; and if no person have such majority, then from the persons having the highest numbers not exceeding three on the list of those voted for as President, the House of Representatives shall choose immediately, by ballot, the President. But in choosing the President, the votes shall be taken by States, the representation from each State having one vote; a quorum for this purpose shall consist of a member or members from two-thirds of the States, and a majority of all the States shall be necessary to a choice. And if the House of Representatives shall not choose a President whenever the right of choice shall devolve upon them, before *the fourth day of March* next following, then the Vice-President shall act as President, as in the case of the death or other constitutional disability of the President.

The person having the greatest number of votes as Vice-President shall be the Vice-President, if such number be a majority of the whole number of electors appointed; and if no person have a majority, then from the two highest numbers on the list the Senate shall choose the Vice-President; a quorum for the purpose shall consist of two-thirds of the whole number of Senators, and a majority of the whole number shall be necessary to a choice. But no person constitutionally ineligible to the office of President shall be eligible to that of Vice-President of the United States.

Amendment XIII
[Adopted 1865]

Section 1 Neither slavery nor involuntary servitude, except as a punishment for crime whereof the party shall have been duly convicted, shall exist within the United States, or any place subject to their jurisdiction.

Section 2 Congress shall have power to enforce this article by appropriate legislation.

Amendment XIV
[Adopted 1868]

Section 1 All persons born or naturalized in the United States, and subject to the jurisdiction thereof, are citizens of the United States and of the State wherein they reside. No State shall make or enforce any law which shall abridge the privileges or immunities of citizens of the United States; nor shall any State deprive any person of life, liberty, or property, without due process of law; nor deny to any person within its jurisdiction the equal protection of the laws.

Section 2 Representatives shall be apportioned among the several States according to their respective numbers, counting the whole number of persons in each State, excluding Indians not taxed. But when the right to vote at any election for the choice of Electors for President and Vice-President of the United States, Representatives in Congress, the executive and judicial officers of a State, or the members of the legislature thereof, is denied to any of the male inhabitants of such State, being twenty-one years of age and citizens of the United States, or in any way abridged, except for participation in rebellion, or other crime, the basis of representation therein shall be reduced in the proportion which the number of such male citizens shall bear to the whole number of male citizens twenty-one years of age in such State.

Section 3 No person shall be a Senator or Representative in Congress, or Elector of President and Vice-President, or hold any office, civil or military, under the United States, or under any State, who, having previously taken an oath, as a member of Congress, or as an officer of the United States, or as a member of any State legislature, or as an executive or judicial officer of any State, to support the Constitution of the United States, shall have engaged in insurrection or rebellion against the same, or given aid or comfort to the enemies thereof. Congress may, by a vote of two-thirds of each house, remove such disability.

Section 4 The validity of the public debt of the United States, authorized by law, including debts incurred for payment of pensions and bounties for services in suppressing insurrection or rebellion, shall not be questioned. But neither the United States nor any State shall assume or pay any debt or obligation incurred in aid of insurrection or rebellion against the United States, or any claim for the loss of emancipation of any slave; but all such debts, obligations, and claims shall be held illegal and void.

Section 5 The Congress shall have power to enforce, by appropriate legislation, the provisions of this article.

Amendment XV
[Adopted 1870]

Section 1 The right of citizens of the United States to vote shall not be denied or abridged by the United States or by any State on account of race, color, or previous condition of servitude.

Section 2 The Congress shall have power to enforce this article by appropriate legislation.

Amendment XVI
[Adopted 1913]

The Congress shall have power to lay and collect taxes on incomes, from whatever source derived, without apportionment among the several States, and without regard to any census or enumeration.

Amendment XVII
[Adopted 1913]

Section 1 The Senate of the United States shall be composed of two Senators from each State, elected by the people thereof, for six years; and each Senator shall have one vote. The electors in each State shall have the qualifications requisite for electors of [voters for] the most numerous branch of the State legislatures.

Section 2 When vacancies happen in the representation of any State in the Senate, the executive authority of such State shall issue writs of election to fill such vacancies: Provided, that the Legislature of any State may empower the executive thereof to make temporary appointments until the people fill the vacancies by election as the Legislature may direct.

Section 3 This amendment shall not be so construed as to affect the election or term of any Senator chosen before it becomes valid as part of the Constitution.

Amendment XVIII
[Adopted 1919; Repealed 1933]

Section 1 After one year from the ratification of this article the manufacture, sale, or transportation of intoxicating liquors within, the importation thereof into, or the exportation thereof from the United States and all territory subject to the jurisdiction thereof, for beverage purposes, is hereby prohibited.

Section 2 The Congress and the several States shall have concurrent power to enforce this article by appropriate legislation.

Section 3 This article shall be inoperative unless it shall have been ratified as an amendment to the Constitution by the legislatures of the several States, as provided by the Constitution, within seven years from the date of the submission thereof to the States by the Congress.

Amendment XIX
[Adopted 1920]

Section 1 The right of citizens of the United States to vote shall not be denied or abridged by the United States or by any State on account of sex.

Section 2 The Congress shall have power to enforce this article by appropriate legislation.

Amendment XX
[Adopted 1933]

Section 1 The terms of the President and Vice-President shall end at noon on the 20th day of January, and the terms of Senators and Representatives at noon on the 3d day of January, of the years in which such terms would have ended if this article had not been ratified; and the terms of their successors shall then begin.

Section 2 The Congress shall assemble at least once in every year, and such meeting shall begin at noon on the 3d day of January, unless they shall by law appoint a different day.

Section 3 If, at the time fixed for the beginning of the term of the President, the President-elect shall have died, the Vice-President-elect shall become President. If a President shall not have been chosen before the time fixed for the beginning of his term, or if the President-elect shall have failed to qualify, then the Vice-President-elect shall act as President until a President shall have qualified; and the Congress may by law provide for the case wherein neither a President-elect nor a Vice-President-elect shall have qualified, declaring who shall then act as President, or the manner in which one who is to act shall be selected, and such persons shall act accordingly until a President or Vice-President shall have qualified.

Section 4 The Congress may by law provide for the case of the death of any of the persons from whom the House of Representatives may choose a President whenever the right of choice shall have devolved upon them, and for the case of the death of any of the persons from whom the Senate may choose a Vice-President whenever the right of choice shall have devolved upon them.

Section 5   Sections 1 and 2 shall take effect on the 15th day of October following the ratification of this article.

Section 6   This article shall be inoperative unless it shall have been ratified as an amendment to the Constitution by the Legislatures of three-fourths of the several States within seven years from the date of its submission.

Amendment XXI
[Adopted 1933]

Section 1   The eighteenth article of amendment to the Constitution of the United States is hereby repealed.

Section 2   The transportation or importation into any State, Territory, or Possession of the United States for delivery or use therein of intoxicating liquors, in violation of the laws thereof, is hereby prohibited.

Section 3   This article shall be inoperative unless it shall have been ratified as an amendment to the Constitution by conventions in the several States, as provided in the Constitution, within seven years from the date of submission thereof to the States by the Congress.

Amendment XXII
[Adopted 1951]

Section 1   No person shall be elected to the office of President more than twice, and no person who has held the office of President, or acted as President, for more than two years of a term to which some other person was elected President shall be elected to the office of President more than once. But this article shall not apply to any person holding the office of President when this article was proposed by the Congress, and shall not prevent any person who may be holding the office of President, or acting as President, during the term within which this article becomes operative from holding the office of President or acting as President during the remainder of such term.

Section 2   This article shall be inoperative unless it shall have been ratified as an amendment to the Constitution by the legislatures of three-fourths of the several States within seven years from the date of its submission to the States by the Congress.

Amendment XXIII
[Adopted 1961]

Section 1   The District constituting the seat of Government of the United States shall appoint in such manner as the Congress may direct:

A number of electors of President and Vice-President equal to the whole number of Senators and Representatives in Congress to which the District would be entitled if it were a State, but in no event more than the least populous State; they shall be in addition to those appointed by the States, but they shall be considered for the purposes of the election of President and Vice-President, to be electors appointed by a State; and they shall meet in the District and perform such duties as provided by the twelfth article of amendment.

Section 2   The Congress shall have the power to enforce this article by appropriate legislation.

Amendment XXIV
[Adopted 1964]

Section 1   The right of citizens of the United States to vote in any primary or other election for President or Vice-President, for electors for President or Vice-President, or for Senator or Representative in Congress, shall not be denied or abridged by the United States or any State by reason of failure to pay any poll tax or other tax.

Section 2   The Congress shall have the power to enforce this article by appropriate legislation.

Amendment XXV
[Adopted 1967]

Section 1   In case of the removal of the President from office or of his death or resignation, the Vice President shall become President.

Section 2   Whenever there is a vacancy in the office of the Vice President, the President shall nominate a Vice President who shall take office upon confirmation by a majority vote of both Houses of Congress.

Section 3   Whenever the President transmits to the President pro tempore of the Senate and the Speaker of the House of Representatives his written declaration that he is unable to discharge the powers and duties of his office, and until he transmits to them a written declaration to the contrary, such powers and duties shall be discharged by the Vice President as Acting President.

Section 4   Whenever the Vice President and a majority of either the principal officers of the executive departments or of such other body as Congress may by law provide, transmit to the President pro tempore of the Senate and the Speaker of the House of Representatives their written declaration that the President is unable to discharge the powers and duties of his office, the Vice President shall immediately assume the powers and duties of the office as Acting President.

Thereafter, when the President transmits to the President pro tempore of the Senate and the Speaker of the House of Representatives his written declaration that no inability exists, he shall resume the powers and duties of his office unless the Vice President and a majority of either the principal officers of the executive department[s] or of such other body as Congress may by law provide, transmit within four days to the President pro tempore of the Senate and the Speaker of the House of Representatives their written declaration that the President is unable to discharge the powers and duties of his office. Thereupon Congress shall decide the issue, assembling within forty-eight hours for that purpose if not in session. If the Congress, within twenty-one days after receipt of the latter written declaration, or, if Congress is not in session, within twenty-one days after Congress is required to assemble, determines by two-thirds vote of both Houses that the President is unable to discharge the powers and duties of his office, the Vice President shall continue to discharge the same as Acting President; otherwise, the President shall resume the powers and duties of his office.

Amendment XXVI
[Adopted 1971]

Section 1 The right of citizens of the United States, who are eighteen years of age or older, to vote shall not be denied or abridged by the United States or by any State on account of age.

Section 2 The Congress shall have power to enforce this article by appropriate legislation.

THE AMERICAN PEOPLE AND NATION: A STATISTICAL PROFILE

Population of the United States

Year	Number of States	Population	Percent Increase	Population Per Square Mile	Percent Urban/ Rural	Percent Male/ Female	Percent White/ Nonwhite	Persons Per Household	Median Age
1790	13	3,929,214		4.5	5.1/94.9	NA/NA	80.7/19.3	5.79	NA
1800	16	5,308,483	35.1	6.1	6.1/93.9	NA/NA	81.1/18.9	NA	NA
1810	17	7,239,881	36.4	4.3	7.3/92.7	NA/NA	81.0/19.0	NA	NA
1820	23	9,638,453	33.1	5.5	7.2/92.8	50.8/49.2	81.6/18.4	NA	16.7
1830	24	12,866,020	33.5	7.4	8.8/91.2	50.8/49.2	81.9/18.1	NA	17.2
1840	26	17,069,453	32.7	9.8	10.8/89.2	50.9/49.1	83.2/16.8	NA	17.8
1850	31	23,191,876	35.9	7.9	15.3/84.7	51.0/49.0	84.3/15.7	5.55	18.9
1860	33	31,443,321	35.6	10.6	19.8/80.2	51.2/48.8	85.6/14.4	5.28	19.4
1870	37	39,818,449	26.6	13.4	25.7/74.3	50.6/49.4	86.2/13.8	5.09	20.2
1880	38	50,155,783	26.0	16.9	28.2/71.8	50.9/49.1	86.5/13.5	5.04	20.9
1890	44	62,947,714	25.5	21.2	35.1/64.9	51.2/48.8	87.5/12.5	4.93	22.0
1900	45	75,994,575	20.7	25.6	39.6/60.4	51.1/48.9	87.9/12.1	4.76	22.9
1910	46	91,972,266	21.0	31.0	45.6/54.4	51.5/48.5	88.9/11.1	4.54	24.1
1920	48	105,710,620	14.9	35.6	51.2/48.8	51.0/49.0	89.7/10.3	4.34	25.3
1930	48	122,775,046	16.1	41.2	56.1/43.9	50.6/49.4	89.8/10.2	4.11	26.4
1940	48	131,669,275	7.2	44.2	56.5/43.5	50.2/49.8	89.8/10.2	3.67	29.0
1950	48	150,697,361	14.5	50.7	64.0/36.0	49.7/50.3	89.5/10.5	3.37	30.2
1960	50	179,323,175	18.5	50.6	69.9/30.1	49.3/50.7	88.6/11.4	3.33	29.5
1970	50	203,302,031	13.4	57.4	73.5/26.5	48.7/51.3	87.6/12.4	3.14	28.0
1980	50	226,545,805	11.4	64.0	73.7/26.3	48.6/51.4	86.0/14.0	2.76	30.0
1983	50	236,600,000*	4.4	64.0	NA/NA	48.7/51.3	85.3/14.7	2.73	30.9

*1984 figure.
NA = Not available.

Vital Statistics

Year	Birth Rate*	Death Rate*	Life Expectancy in Years					Marriage Rate	Divorce Rate
			Total Population	White Females	Nonwhite Females	White Males	Nonwhite Males		
1790	NA	NA	NA	NA	NA	NA	NA	NA	NA
1800	55.0	NA	NA	NA	NA	NA	NA	NA	NA
1810	54.3	NA	NA	NA	NA	NA	NA	NA	NA
1820	55.2	NA	NA	NA	NA	NA	NA	NA	NA
1830	51.4	NA	NA	NA	NA	NA	NA	NA	NA
1840	51.8	NA	NA	NA	NA	NA	NA	NA	NA
1850	43.3	NA	NA	NA	NA	NA	NA	NA	NA
1860	44.3	NA	NA	NA	NA	NA	NA	NA	NA
1870	38.3	NA	NA	NA	NA	NA	NA	NA	NA
1880	39.8	NA	NA	NA	NA	NA	NA	NA	NA
1890	31.5	NA	NA	NA	NA	NA	NA	NA	NA
1900	32.3	17.2	47.3	48.7	33.5	46.6	32.5	NA	NA
1910	30.1	14.7	50.0	52.0	37.5	48.6	33.8	NA	NA
1920	27.7	13.0	54.1	55.6	45.2	54.4	45.5	12.0	1.6
1930	21.3	11.3	59.7	63.5	49.2	59.7	47.3	9.2	1.6
1940	19.4	10.8	62.9	66.6	54.9	62.1	51.5	12.1	2.0
1950	24.1	9.6	68.2	72.2	62.9	66.5	59.1	11.1	2.6
1960	23.7	9.5	69.7	74.1	66.3	67.4	61.1	8.5	2.2
1970	18.4	9.5	70.9	75.6	69.4	68.0	61.3	10.6	3.5
1980	15.9	8.8	73.7	78.1	73.6	70.7	65.3	10.6	5.2
1983	15.5	8.6	74.7	78.8	75.3	71.6	67.1	10.5	5.0

Data per one thousand for Birth, Death, Marriage, and Divorce rates.

NA = Not available.

*Data for 1800, 1810, 1830, 1850, 1870, and 1890 for whites only.

Immigration Totals by Decade

Years	Number	Years	Number
1820–1830	151,824	1911–1920	5,735,811
1831–1840	599,125	1921–1930	4,107,209
1841–1850	1,713,251	1931–1940	528,431
1851–1860	2,598,214	1941–1950	1,035,039
1861–1870	2,314,824	1951–1960	2,515,479
1871–1880	2,812,191	1961–1970	3,321,677
1881–1890	5,246,613	1971–1980	4,493,000
1891–1900	3,687,546	Total	49,655,620
1901–1910	8,795,386		

Source: U.S. Bureau of the Census, *Historical Statistics of the United States, Colonial Times to 1970* (1975), Part I, pp. 105–106; U.S. Bureau of the Census, *Statistical Abstract of the United States, 1984* (1983), p. 88.

Regional Origins of Immigrants (in percentages)

Period	Total Europe	Europe North and West[a]	Europe East and Central[b]	Europe South and Other[c]	Western Hemisphere	Asia	All Other
1821–1830	69.2	67.1	—	2.1	8.4	—	22.4
1831–1840	82.8	81.8	—	1.0	5.5	—	11.7
1841–1850	93.3	92.9	0.1	0.3	3.6	—	3.1
1851–1860	94.4	93.6	0.1	0.8	2.9	1.6	1.1
1861–1870	89.2	87.8	0.5	0.9	7.2	2.8	0.8
1871–1880	80.8	73.6	4.5	2.7	14.4	4.4	0.4
1881–1890	90.3	72.0	11.9	6.3	8.1	1.3	0.3
1891–1900	96.5	44.5	32.8	19.1	1.1	1.9	0.5
1901–1910	92.5	21.7	44.5	26.3	4.1	2.8	0.6
1911–1920	76.3	17.4	33.4	25.5	19.9	3.4	0.4
1921–1930	60.3	31.7	14.4	14.3	36.9	2.4	0.4
1931–1940	65.9	38.8	11.0	16.1	30.3	2.8	0.9
1941–1950	60.1	47.5	4.6	7.9	34.3	3.1	2.5
1951–1960	52.8	17.7	24.3	10.8	39.6	6.0	1.6
1961–1970	33.8	11.7	9.4	12.9	51.7	12.9	1.7
1971–1979	18.4	4.8	4.4	9.2	44.9	34.1	2.6

Note: dash indicates less than 0.1 percent.

[a] Great Britain, Ireland, Norway, Sweden, Denmark, Iceland, Netherlands, Belgium, Luxembourg, Switzerland, France.

[b] Germany (Austria included, 1938–1945), Poland, Czechoslovakia (since 1920), Yugoslavia (since 1920), Hungary (since 1861), Austria (since 1861, except 1938–1945), U.S.S.R. (excludes Asian U.S.S.R. between 1931 and 1963), Latvia, Estonia, Lithuania, Finland, Romania, Bulgaria, Turkey (in Europe).

[c] Italy, Spain, Portugal, Greece, and other European countries not classified elsewhere.

Source: Stephan Thernstrom, ed., *Harvard Encyclopedia of American Ethnic Groups* (1980), p. 480; and U.S. Bureau of the Census, *Statistical Abstract of the United States, 1984* (1983), p. 9. Reprinted by permission of Harvard University Press.

Major Sources of Immigrants by Country (in thousands)

Period	Germany	Italy	Britain	Ireland	Austria-Hungary	Russia[a]	Canada	Denmark, Norway, Sweden[b]	Mexico	West Indies
1820–1830	8	—	27	54	—	—	2	—	5	4
1831–1840	152	2	76	207	—	—	14	2	7	12
1841–1850	435	2	267	781	—	—	42	14	3	14
1851–1860	952	9	424	914	—	—	59	25	3	11
1861–1870	787	12	607	436	8	3	154	126	2	9
1871–1880	718	56	548	437	73	39	384	243	5	14
1881–1890	1,453	307	807	655	354	213	393	656	2[c]	29
1891–1900	505	652	272	388	593	505	3	372	—	—[d]
1901–1910	341	2,046	526	339	2,145	1,597	179	505	50	108
1911–1920	144	1,110	341	146	896	922	742	203	219	123
1921–1930	412	455	330	221	64	89	925	198	459	75
1931–1940	114	68	29	13	11	7	109	11	22	16
1941–1950	227	58	132	28	28	4	172	27	61	50
1951–1960	478	185	192	57	104	6	378	57	300	123
1961–1970	191	214	206	40	26	7	413	43	454	470
1971–1979	68	124	122	11	15	31	156	13	584	668
Total	6,985	5,300	4,906	4,727	4,317	3,423	4,125	2,495	2,176	1,726

Notes: Numbers are rounded. Dash indicates less than one thousand.

[a]Includes Finland, Latvia, Estonia, and Lithuania.

[b]Includes Iceland.

[c]Figure for 1881–1885 only.

[d]Figure for 1894–1900 only.

Source: U.S. Bureau of the Census, *Historical Statistics of the United States: Colonial Times to 1970* (1975), Part I, pp. 105–108; U.S. Bureau of the Census, *Statistical Abstract of the United States, 1984* (1983), p. 91.

The American Farm

Year	Farm Population (in thousands)	Percent of Total Population	Number of Farms (in thousands)	Total Acres (in thousands)	Average Acreage Per Farm	Corn Production (millions of bushels)	Wheat Production (millions of bushels)
1850	NA	NA	1,449	293,561	203	592[a]	100[a]
1860	NA	NA	2,044	407,213	199	839[b]	173[b]
1870	NA	NA	2,660	407,735	153	1,125	254
1880	21,973	43.8	4,009	536,082	134	1,707	502
1890	24,771	42.3	4,565	623,219	137	1,650	449
1900	29,875	41.9	5,740	841,202	147	2,662	599
1910	32,077	34.9	6,366	881,431	139	2,853	625
1920	31,974	30.1	6,454	958,677	149	3,071	843
1930	30,529	24.9	6,295	990,112	157	2,080	887
1940	30,547	23.2	6,102	1,065,114	175	2,457	815
1950	23,048	15.3	5,388	1,161,420	216	3,075	1,019
1960	15,635	8.7	3,962	1,176,946	297	4,314	1,355
1970	9,712	4.8	2,949	1,102,769	374	4,200	1,370
1980	6,051	2.7	2,428	1,042,000	427	6,600	2,400
1983	5,787	2.5	2,370	1,024,000	432	4,200	2,400

[a]Figure for 1849.
[b]Figure for 1859.
NA = Not available.

The American Worker

Year	Total Number of Workers	Males as Percent of Total Workers	Females as Percent of Total Workers	Married Women as Percent of Female Workers	Female Workers as Percent of Female Population	Percent of Labor Force Unemployed	Percent of Workers in Labor Unions
1870	12,506,000	85	15	NA	NA	NA	NA
1880	17,392,000	85	15	NA	NA	NA	NA
1890	23,318,000	83	17	13.9	18.9	4 (1894 = 18%)	NA
1900	29,073,000	82	18	15.4	20.6	5	3
1910	38,167,000	79	21	24.7	25.4	6	6
1920	41,614,000	79	21	23.0	23.7	5 (1921 = 12%)	12
1930	48,830,000	78	22	28.9	24.8	9 (1933 = 25%)	7
1940	53,011,000	76	24	36.4	27.4	15 (1944 = 1%)	27
1950	59,643,000	72	28	52.1	31.4	5	25
1960	69,877,000	68	32	59.9	37.7	5.4	26
1970	82,049,000	63	37	63.4	43.3	4.8	25
1980	108,544,000	58	42	59.7	51.5	7.0	23
1983	113,226,000	57	43	58.9	52.9	9.5	19[a]

[a]1984 figure.
NA = Not available.

Year	Gross National Product (GNP) (in $ billions)	Steel Production (in short tons)	Automobiles Registered	New Housing Starts	Foreign Trade Exports (in millions of dollars)	Imports
1790	NA	NA	NA	NA	20	23
1800	NA	NA	NA	NA	71	91
1810	NA	NA	NA	NA	67	85
1820	NA	NA	NA	NA	70	74
1830	NA	NA	NA	NA	74	71
1840	NA	NA	NA	NA	132	107
1850	NA	NA	NA	NA	152	178
1860	NA	13,000	NA	NA	400	362
1870	7.4[a]	77,000	NA	NA	451	462
1880	11.2[b]	1,397,000	NA	NA	853	761
1890	13.1	4,779,000	NA	328,000	910	823
1900	18.7	11,227,000	8,000	189,000	1,499	930
1910	35.3	28,330,000	458,300	387,000 (1918 = 118,000)	1,919	1,646
1920	91.5	46,183,000	8,131,500	247,000 (1925 = 937,000)	8,664	5,784
1930	90.7	44,591,000	23,034,700	330,000 (1933 = 93,000)	4,013	3,500
1940	100.0	66,983,000	27,465,800	603,000 (1944 = 142,000)	4,030	7,433
1950	286.5	96,836,000	40,339,000	1,952,000	10,816	9,125
1960	506.5	99,282,000	61,682,300	1,365,000	19,600	15,046
1970	992.7	131,514,000	89,279,800	1,469,000	42,700	40,189
1980	2,631.7	111,800,000	121,600,000	1,313,000	220,783	244,871
1983	3,304.8	84,600,000	125,382,000	1,712,000	200,538	258,048

[a]Figure is average for 1869–1878.
[b]Figure is average for 1879–1888.
NA = Not available.

Federal Spending and Debt

Year	Defense[a]	Interest on Public Debt[a]	Veterans Benefits and Services[a]	Income Security[ad]	Health[a]	Education and Manpower[a]	Federal Debt (dollars)
1790	14.9	55.0	4.1[b]	NA	NA	NA	75,463,000[c]
1800	55.7	31.3	.6	NA	NA	NA	82,976,000
1810	48.4 (1814 = 79.7)	34.9	1.0	NA	NA	NA	53,173,000
1820	38.4	28.1	17.6	NA	NA	NA	91,016,000
1830	52.9	12.6	9.0	NA	NA	NA	48,565,000
1840	54.3 (1847 = 80.7)	.7	10.7	NA	NA	NA	3,573,000
1850	43.8	1.0	4.7	NA	NA	NA	63,453,000
1860	44.2 (1865 = 88.9)	5.0	1.7	NA	NA	NA	64,844,000
1870	25.7	41.7	9.2	NA	NA	NA	2,436,453,000
1880	19.3	35.8	21.2	NA	NA	NA	2,090,909,000
1890	20.9 (1899 = 48.6)	11.4	33.6	NA	NA	NA	1,222,397,000
1900	36.6	7.7	27.0	NA	NA	NA	1,263,417,000
1910	45.1 (1919 = 59.5)	3.1	23.2	NA	NA	NA	1,146,940,000
1920	37.1	16.0	3.4	NA	NA	NA	24,299,321,000
1930	25.3	19.9	6.6	NA	NA	NA	16,185,310,000
1940	15.7 (1945 = 85.7)	10.9	6.5	15.2	.5	.8	42,967,531,000
1950	30.4 (1953 = 59.4)	13.3	20.5	10.9	.6	.5	257,357,352,000
1960	49.0	7.5	5.9	20.6	.9	1.1	286,330,761,000
1970	40.1	7.3	4.4	26.6	3.0	4.4	370,918,707,000
1980	23.6	9.1	3.7	41.1	4.0	5.3	914,300,000,000
1983	26.4	11.3	3.1	43.4	3.6	3.3	1,381,900,000,000

[a]Figures represent percentage of total federal spending for each category.
[b]1789–1791 figure.
[c]1791 figure.
[d]Includes Social Security and Medicare.
NA = Not available.

TERRITORIAL EXPANSION OF THE UNITED STATES

Territory	Date Acquired	Square Miles	How Acquired
Original states and territories	1783	888,685	Treaty with Great Britain
Louisiana Purchase	1803	827,192	Purchase from France
Florida	1819	72,003	Treaty with Spain
Texas	1845	390,143	Annexation of independent nation
Oregon	1846	285,580	Treaty with Great Britain
Mexican Cession	1848	529,017	Conquest from Mexico
Gadsden Purchase	1853	29,640	Purchase from Mexico
Alaska	1867	589,757	Purchase from Russia
Hawaii	1898	6,450	Annexation of independent nation
The Philippines	1899	115,600	Conquest from Spain (granted independence in 1946)
Puerto Rico	1899	3,435	Conquest from Spain
Guam	1899	212	Conquest from Spain
American Samoa	1900	76	Treaty with Germany and Great Britain
Panama Canal Zone	1904	553	Treaty with Panama (returned to Panama by treaty in 1978)
Corn Islands	1914	4	Treaty with Nicaragua (returned to Nicaragua by treaty in 1971)
Virgin Islands	1917	133	Purchase from Denmark
Pacific Islands Trust (Micronesia)	1947	8,489	Trusteeship under United Nations (some granted independence)
All others (Midway, Wake, and other islands)		42	

ADMISSION OF STATES INTO THE UNION

State	Date of Admission	State	Date of Admission
1. Delaware	December 7, 1787	26. Michigan	January 26, 1837
2. Pennsylvania	December 12, 1787	27. Florida	March 3, 1845
3. New Jersey	December 18, 1787	28. Texas	December 29, 1845
4. Georgia	January 2, 1788	29. Iowa	December 28, 1846
5. Connecticut	January 9, 1788	30. Wisconsin	May 29, 1848
6. Massachusetts	February 6, 1788	31. California	September 9, 1850
7. Maryland	April 28, 1788	32. Minnesota	May 11, 1858
8. South Carolina	May 23, 1788	33. Oregon	February 14, 1859
9. New Hampshire	June 21, 1788	34. Kansas	January 29, 1861
10. Virginia	June 25, 1788	35. West Virginia	June 20, 1863
11. New York	July 26, 1788	36. Nevada	October 31, 1864
12. North Carolina	November 21, 1789	37. Nebraska	March 1, 1867
13. Rhode Island	May 29, 1790	38. Colorado	August 1, 1876
14. Vermont	March 4, 1791	39. North Dakota	November 2, 1889
15. Kentucky	June 1, 1792	40. South Dakota	November 2, 1889
16. Tennessee	June 1, 1796	41. Montana	November 8, 1889
17. Ohio	March 1, 1803	42. Washington	November 11, 1889
18. Louisiana	April 30, 1812	43. Idaho	July 3, 1890
19. Indiana	December 11, 1816	44. Wyoming	July 10, 1890
20. Mississippi	December 10, 1817	45. Utah	January 4, 1896
21. Illinois	December 3, 1818	46. Oklahoma	November 16, 1907
22. Alabama	December 14, 1819	47. New Mexico	January 6, 1912
23. Maine	March 15, 1820	48. Arizona	February 14, 1912
24. Missouri	August 10, 1821	49. Alaska	January 3, 1959
25. Arkansas	June 15, 1836	50. Hawaii	August 21, 1959

PRESIDENTIAL ELECTIONS

Year	Number of States	Candidates	Parties	Popular Vote	% of Popular Vote	Electoral Vote	% Voter Participation[b]
1789	11	**George Washington**	No party			69	
		John Adams	designations			34	
		Other candidates				35	
1792	15	**George Washington**	No party			132	
		John Adams	designations			77	
		George Clinton				50	
		Other candidates				5	
1796	16	**John Adams**	Federalist			71	
		Thomas Jefferson	Democratic-Republican			68	
		Thomas Pinckney	Federalist			59	
		Aaron Burr	Democratic-Republican			30	
		Other candidates				48	
1800	16	**Thomas Jefferson**	Democratic-Republican			73	
		Aaron Burr	Democratic-Republican			73	
		John Adams	Federalist			65	
		Charles C. Pinckney	Federalist			64	
		John Jay	Federalist			1	
1804	17	**Thomas Jefferson**	Democratic-Republican			162	
		Charles C. Pinckney	Federalist			14	
1808	17	**James Madison**	Democratic-Republican			122	
		Charles C. Pinckney	Federalist			47	
		George Clinton	Democratic-Republican			6	
1812	18	**James Madison**	Democratic-Republican			128	
		DeWitt Clinton	Federalist			89	
1816	19	**James Monroe**	Democratic-Republican			183	
		Rufus King	Federalist			34	
1820	24	**James Monroe**	Democratic-Republican			231	
		John Quincy Adams	Independent Republican			1	

Year	Number of States	Candidates	Parties	Popular Vote	% of Popular Vote	Electoral Vote	% Voter Participation[b]
1824	24	John Quincy Adams	Democratic-Republican	108,740	30.5	84	26.9
		Andrew Jackson	Democratic-Republican	153,544	43.1	99	
		Henry Clay	Democratic-Republican	47,136	13.2	37	
		William H. Crawford	Democratic-Republican	46,618	13.1	41	
1828	24	Andrew Jackson	Democratic	647,286	56.0	178	57.6
		John Quincy Adams	National Republican	508,064	44.0	83	
1832	24	Andrew Jackson	Democratic	688,242	54.5	219	55.4
		Henry Clay	National Republican	473,462	37.5	49	
		William Wirt	Anti-Masonic	101,051	8.0	7	
		John Floyd	Democratic			11	
1836	26	Martin Van Buren	Democratic	765,483	50.9	170	57.8
		William H. Harrison	Whig			73	
		Hugh L. White	Whig	739,795	49.1	26	
		Daniel Webster	Whig			14	
		W. P. Mangum	Whig			11	
1840	26	William H. Harrison	Whig	1,274,624	53.1	234	80.2
		Martin Van Buren	Democratic	1,127,781	46.9	60	
1844	26	James K. Polk	Democratic	1,338,464	49.6	170	78.9
		Henry Clay	Whig	1,300,097	48.1	105	
		James G. Birney	Liberty	62,300	2.3		
1848	30	Zachary Taylor	Whig	1,360,967	47.4	163	72.7
		Lewis Cass	Democratic	1,222,342	42.5	127	
		Martin Van Buren	Free Soil	291,263	10.1		
1852	31	Franklin Pierce	Democratic	1,601,117	50.9	254	69.6
		Winfield Scott	Whig	1,385,453	44.1	42	
		John P. Hale	Free Soil	155,825	5.0		
1856	31	James Buchanan	Democratic	1,832,955	45.3	174	78.9
		John C. Frémont	Republican	1,339,932	33.1	114	
		Millard Fillmore	American	871,731	21.6	8	
1860	33	Abraham Lincoln	Republican	1,865,593	39.8	180	81.2
		Stephen A. Douglas	Democratic	1,382,713	29.5	12	
		John C. Breckinridge	Democratic	848,356	18.1	72	
		John Bell	Constitutional Union	592,906	12.6	39	
1864	36	Abraham Lincoln	Republican	2,206,938	55.0	212	73.8
		George B. McClellan	Democratic	1,803,787	45.0	21	
1868	37	Ulysses S. Grant	Republican	3,013,421	52.7	214	78.1
		Horatio Seymour	Democratic	2,706,829	47.3	80	
1872	37	Ulysses S. Grant	Republican	3,596,745	55.6	286	71.3
		Horace Greeley	Democratic	2,843,446	43.9	[a]	
1876	38	Rutherford B. Hayes	Republican	4,036,572	48.0	185	81.8
		Samuel J. Tilden	Democratic	4,284,020	51.0	184	

Year	Number of States	Candidates	Parties	Popular Vote	% of Popular Vote	Electoral Vote	% Voter Participation[b]
1880	38	**James A. Garfield**	Republican	4,453,295	48.5	214	79.4
		Winfield S. Hancock	Democratic	4,414,082	48.1	155	
		James B. Weaver	Greenback-Labor	308,578	3.4		
1884	38	**Grover Cleveland**	Democratic	4,879,507	48.5	219	77.5
		James G. Blaine	Republican	4,850,293	48.2	182	
		Benjamin F. Butler	Greenback-Labor	175,370	1.8		
		John P. St. John	Prohibition	150,369	1.5		
1888	38	**Benjamin Harrison**	Republican	5,477,129	47.9	233	79.3
		Grover Cleveland	Democratic	5,537,857	48.6	168	
		Clinton B. Fisk	Prohibition	249,506	2.2		
		Anson J. Streeter	Union Labor	146,935	1.3		
1892	44	**Grover Cleveland**	Democratic	5,555,426	46.1	277	74.7
		Benjamin Harrison	Republican	5,182,690	43.0	145	
		James B. Weaver	People's	1,029,846	8.5	22	
		John Bidwell	Prohibition	264,133	2.2		
1896	45	**William McKinley**	Republican	7,102,246	51.1	271	79.3
		William J. Bryan	Democratic	6,492,559	47.7	176	
1900	45	**William McKinley**	Republican	7,218,491	51.7	292	73.2
		William J. Bryan	Democratic; Populist	6,356,734	45.5	155	
		John C. Wooley	Prohibition	208,914	1.5		
1904	45	**Theodore Roosevelt**	Republican	7,628,461	57.4	336	65.2
		Alton B. Parker	Democratic	5,084,223	37.6	140	
		Eugene V. Debs	Socialist	402,283	3.0		
		Silas C. Swallow	Prohibition	258,536	1.9		
1908	46	**William H. Taft**	Republican	7,675,320	51.6	321	65.4
		William J. Bryan	Democratic	6,412,294	43.1	162	
		Eugene V. Debs	Socialist	420,793	2.8		
		Eugene W. Chafin	Prohibition	253,840	1.7		
1912	48	**Woodrow Wilson**	Democratic	6,296,547	41.9	435	58.8
		Theodore Roosevelt	Progressive	4,118,571	27.4	88	
		William H. Taft	Republican	3,486,720	23.2	8	
		Eugene V. Debs	Socialist	900,672	6.0		
		Eugene W. Chafin	Prohibition	206,275	1.4		
1916	48	**Woodrow Wilson**	Democratic	9,127,695	49.4	277	61.6
		Charles E. Hughes	Republican	8,533,507	46.2	254	
		A. L. Benson	Socialist	585,113	3.2		
		J. Frank Hanly	Prohibition	220,506	1.2		
1920	48	**Warren G. Harding**	Republican	16,143,407	60.4	404	49.2
		James M. Cox	Democratic	9,130,328	34.2	127	
		Eugene V. Debs	Socialist	919,799	3.4		
		P. P. Christensen	Farmer-Labor	265,411	1.0		
1924	48	**Calvin Coolidge**	Republican	15,718,211	54.0	382	48.9
		John W. Davis	Democratic	8,385,283	28.8	136	
		Robert M. La Follette	Progressive	4,831,289	16.6	13	

Year	Number of States	Candidates	Parties	Popular Vote	% of Popular Vote	Electoral Vote	% Voter Participation[b]
1928	48	**Herbert C. Hoover**	Republican	21,391,993	58.2	444	56.9
		Alfred E. Smith	Democratic	15,016,169	40.9	87	
1932	48	**Franklin D. Roosevelt**	Democratic	22,809,638	57.4	472	56.9
		Herbert C. Hoover	Republican	15,758,901	39.7	59	
		Norman Thomas	Socialist	881,951	2.2		
1936	48	**Franklin D. Roosevelt**	Democratic	27,752,869	60.8	523	61.0
		Alfred M. Landon	Republican	16,674,665	36.5	8	
		William Lemke	Union	882,479	1.9		
1940	48	**Franklin D. Roosevelt**	Democratic	27,307,819	54.8	449	62.5
		Wendell L. Wilkie	Republican	22,321,018	44.8	82	
1944	48	**Franklin D. Roosevelt**	Democratic	25,606,585	53.5	432	55.9
		Thomas E. Dewey	Republican	22,014,745	46.0	99	
1948	48	**Harry S Truman**	Democratic	24,179,345	49.6	303	53.0
		Thomas E. Dewey	Republican	21,991,291	45.1	189	
		J. Strom Thurmond	States' Rights	1,176,125	2.4	39	
		Henry A. Wallace	Progressive	1,157,326	2.4		
1952	48	**Dwight D. Eisenhower**	Republican	33,936,234	55.1	442	63.3
		Adlai E. Stevenson	Democratic	27,314,992	44.4	89	
1956	48	**Dwight D. Eisenhower**	Republican	35,590,472	57.6	457	60.6
		Adlai E. Stevenson	Democratic	26,022,752	42.1	73	
1960	50	**John F. Kennedy**	Democratic	34,226,731	49.7	303	62.8
		Richard M. Nixon	Republican	34,108,157	49.5	219	
1964	50	**Lyndon B. Johnson**	Democratic	43,129,566	61.1	486	61.7
		Barry M. Goldwater	Republican	27,178,188	38.5	52	
1968	50	**Richard M. Nixon**	Republican	31,785,480	43.4	301	60.6
		Hubert H. Humphrey	Democratic	31,275,166	42.7	191	
		George C. Wallace	American Independent	9,906,473	13.5	46	
1972	50	**Richard M. Nixon**	Republican	47,169,911	60.7	520	55.2
		George S. McGovern	Democratic	29,170,383	37.5	17	
		John G. Schmitz	American	1,099,482	1.4		
1976	50	**Jimmy Carter**	Democratic	40,830,763	50.1	297	53.5
		Gerald R. Ford	Republican	39,147,793	48.0	240	
1980	50	**Ronald Reagan**	Republican	43,899,248	50.8	489	52.6
		Jimmy Carter	Democratic	35,481,432	41.0	49	
		John B. Anderson	Independent	5,719,437	6.6	0	
		Ed Clark	Libertarian	920,859	1.1	0	
1984	50	**Ronald Reagan**	Republican	54,451,521	58.8	525	53.3
		Walter Mondale	Democratic	37,565,334	40.5	13	

Candidates receiving less than 1 percent of the popular vote have been omitted. Thus the percentage of popular vote given for any election year may not total 100 percent.

Before the passage of the Twelfth Amendment in 1804, the Electoral College voted for two presidential candidates; the runner-up became vice president.

Before 1824, most presidential electors were chosen by state legislatures, not by popular vote.

[a]Greeley died shortly after the election; the electors supporting him then divided their votes among minor candidates.

[b]Percent of voting-age population casting ballots.

PRESIDENTS, VICE PRESIDENTS, AND CABINET MEMBERS

The Washington Administration

President	George Washington	1789–1797
Vice President	John Adams	1789–1797
Secretary of State	Thomas Jefferson	1789–1793
	Edmund Randolph	1794–1795
	Timothy Pickering	1795–1797
Secretary of Treasury	Alexander Hamilton	1789–1795
	Oliver Wolcott	1795–1797
Secretary of War	Henry Knox	1789–1794
	Timothy Pickering	1795–1796
	James McHenry	1796–1797
Attorney General	Edmund Randolph	1789–1793
	William Bradford	1794–1795
	Charles Lee	1795–1797
Postmaster General	Samuel Osgood	1789–1791
	Timothy Pickering	1791–1794
	Joseph Habersham	1795–1797

The John Adams Administration

President	John Adams	1797–1801
Vice President	Thomas Jefferson	1797–1801
Secretary of State	Timothy Pickering	1797–1800
	John Marshall	1800–1801
Secretary of Treasury	Oliver Wolcott	1797–1800
	Samuel Dexter	1800–1801
Secretary of War	James McHenry	1797–1800
	Samuel Dexter	1800–1801
Attorney General	Charles Lee	1797–1801
Postmaster General	Joseph Habersham	1797–1801
Secretary of Navy	Benjamin Stoddert	1798–1801

The Jefferson Administration

President	Thomas Jefferson	1801–1809
Vice President	Aaron Burr	1801–1805
	George Clinton	1805–1809
Secretary of State	James Madison	1801–1809
Secretary of Treasury	Samuel Dexter	1801
	Albert Gallatin	1801–1809
Secretary of War	Henry Dearborn	1801–1809
Attorney General	Levi Lincoln	1801–1805
	Robert Smith	1805
	John Breckinridge	1805–1806
	Caesar Rodney	1807–1809

Postmaster General	Joseph Habersham	1801
	Gideon Granger	1801–1809
Secretary of Navy	Robert Smith	1801–1809

The Madison Administration

President	James Madison	1809–1817
Vice President	George Clinton	1809–1813
	Elbridge Gerry	1813–1817
Secretary of State	Robert Smith	1809–1811
	James Monroe	1811–1817
Secretary of Treasury	Albert Gallatin	1809–1813
	George Campbell	1814
	Alexander Dallas	1814–1816
	William Crawford	1816–1817
Secretary of War	William Eustis	1809–1812
	John Armstrong	1813–1814
	James Monroe	1814–1815
	William Crawford	1815–1817
Attorney General	Caesar Rodney	1809–1811
	William Pinkney	1811–1814
	Richard Rush	1814–1817
Postmaster General	Gideon Granger	1809–1814
	Return Meigs	1814–1817
Secretary of Navy	Paul Hamilton	1809–1813
	William Jones	1813–1814
	Benjamin Crowninshield	1814–1817

The Monroe Administration

President	James Monroe	1817–1825
Vice President	Daniel Tompkins	1817–1825
Secretary of State	John Quincy Adams	1817–1825
Secretary of Treasury	William Crawford	1817–1825
Secretary of War	George Graham	1817
	John C. Calhoun	1817–1825
Attorney General	Richard Rush	1817
	William Wirt	1817–1825
Postmaster General	Return Meigs	1817–1823
	John McLean	1823–1825
Secretary of Navy	Benjamin Crowninshield	1817–1818
	Smith Thompson	1818–1823
	Samuel Southard	1823–1825

The John Quincy Adams Administration

President	John Quincy Adams	1825–1829
Vice President	John C. Calhoun	1825–1829
Secretary of State	Henry Clay	1825–1829
Secretary of Treasury	Richard Rush	1825–1829
Secretary of War	James Barbour	1825–1828
	Peter Porter	1828–1829
Attorney General	William Wirt	1825–1829
Postmaster General	John McLean	1825–1829
Secretary of Navy	Samuel Southard	1825–1829

The Jackson Administration

President	Andrew Jackson	1829–1837
Vice President	John C. Calhoun	1829–1833
	Martin Van Buren	1833–1837
Secretary of State	Martin Van Buren	1829–1831
	Edward Livingston	1831–1833
	Louis McLane	1833–1834
	John Forsyth	1834–1837
Secretary of Treasury	Samuel Ingham	1829–1831
	Louis McLane	1831–1833
	William Duane	1833
	Roger B. Taney	1833–1834
	Levi Woodbury	1834–1837
Secretary of War	John H. Eaton	1829–1831
	Lewis Cass	1831–1837
	Benjamin Butler	1837
Attorney General	John M. Berrien	1829–1831
	Roger B. Taney	1831–1833
	Benjamin Butler	1833–1837
Postmaster General	William Barry	1829–1835
	Amos Kendall	1835–1837
Secretary of Navy	John Branch	1829–1831
	Levi Woodbury	1831–1834
	Mahlon Dickerson	1834–1837

The Van Buren Administration

President	Martin Van Buren	1837–1841
Vice President	Richard M. Johnson	1837–1841
Secretary of State	John Forsyth	1837–1841
Secretary of Treasury	Levi Woodbury	1837–1841
Secretary of War	Joel Poinsett	1837–1841
Attorney General	Benjamin Butler	1837–1838
	Felix Grundy	1838–1840
	Henry D. Gilpin	1840–1841
Postmaster General	Amos Kendall	1837–1840
	John M. Niles	1840–1841
Secretary of Navy	Mahlon Dickerson	1837–1838
	James Paulding	1838–1841

The William Harrison Administration

President	William H. Harrison	1841
Vice President	John Tyler	1841
Secretary of State	Daniel Webster	1841
Secretary of Treasury	Thomas Ewing	1841
Secretary of War	John Bell	1841
Attorney General	John J. Crittenden	1841
Postmaster General	Francis Granger	1841
Secretary of Navy	George Badger	1841

The Tyler Administration

President	John Tyler	1841–1845
Vice President	None	
Secretary of State	Daniel Webster	1841–1843
	Hugh S. Legaré	1843
	Abel P. Upshur	1843–1844
	John C. Calhoun	1844–1845
Secretary of Treasury	Thomas Ewing	1841
	Walter Forward	1841–1843
	John C. Spencer	1843–1844
	George Bibb	1844–1845
Secretary of War	John Bell	1841
	John C. Spencer	1841–1843
	James M. Porter	1843–1844
	William Wilkins	1844–1845
Attorney General	John J. Crittenden	1841
	Hugh S. Legaré	1841–1843
	John Nelson	1843–1845
Postmaster General	Francis Granger	1841
	Charles Wickliffe	1841
Secretary of Navy	George Badger	1841
	Abel P. Upshur	1841
	David Henshaw	1843–1844
	Thomas Gilmer	1844
	John Y. Mason	1844–1845

The Polk Administration

President	James K. Polk	1845–1849
Vice President	George M. Dallas	1845–1849
Secretary of State	James Buchanan	1845–1849
Secretary of Treasury	Robert J. Walker	1845–1849
Secretary of War	William L. Marcy	1845–1849
Attorney General	John Y. Mason	1845–1846
	Nathan Clifford	1846–1848
	Isaac Toucey	1848–1849
Postmaster General	Cave Johnson	1845–1849
Secretary of Navy	George Bancroft	1845–1846
	John Y. Mason	1846–1849

The Taylor Administration

President	Zachary Taylor	1849–1850
Vice President	Millard Fillmore	1849–1850
Secretary of State	John M. Clayton	1849–1850
Secretary of Treasury	William Meredith	1849–1850
Secretary of War	George Crawford	1849–1850
Attorney General	Reverdy Johnson	1849–1850
Postmaster General	Jacob Collamer	1849–1850
Secretary of Navy	William Preston	1849–1850
Secretary of Interior	Thomas Ewing	1849–1850

The Fillmore Administration

President	Millard Fillmore	1850–1853
Vice President	None	
Secretary of State	Daniel Webster	1850–1852
	Edward Everett	1852–1853
Secretary of Treasury	Thomas Corwin	1850–1853
Secretary of War	Charles Conrad	1850–1853
Attorney General	John J. Crittenden	1850–1853
Postmaster General	Nathan Hall	1850–1852
	Sam D. Hubbard	1852–1853
Secretary of Navy	William A. Graham	1850–1852
	John P. Kennedy	1852–1853
Secretary of Interior	Thomas McKennan	1850
	Alexander Stuart	1850–1853

The Pierce Administration

President	Franklin Pierce	1853–1857
Vice President	William R. King	1853–1857
Secretary of State	William L. Marcy	1853–1857
Secretary of Treasury	James Guthrie	1853–1857
Secretary of War	Jefferson Davis	1853–1857
Attorney General	Caleb Cushing	1853–1857
Postmaster General	James Campbell	1853–1857
Secretary of Navy	James C. Dobbin	1853–1857
Secretary of Interior	Robert McClelland	1853–1857

The Buchanan Administration

President	James Buchanan	1857–1861
Vice President	John C. Breckinridge	1857–1861
Secretary of State	Lewis Cass	1857–1860
	Jeremiah S. Black	1860–1861
Secretary of Treasury	Howell Cobb	1857–1860
	Philip Thomas	1860–1861
	John A. Dix	1861
Secretary of War	John B. Floyd	1857–1861
	Joseph Holt	1861
Attorney General	Jeremiah S. Black	1857–1860
	Edwin M. Stanton	1860–1861
Postmaster General	Aaron V. Brown	1857–1859
	Joseph Holt	1859–1861
	Horatio King	1861
Secretary of Navy	Isaac Toucey	1857–1861
Secretary of Interior	Jacob Thompson	1857–1861

The Lincoln Administration

President	Abraham Lincoln	1861–1865
Vice President	Hannibal Hamlin	1861–1865
	Andrew Johnson	1865
Secretary of State	William H. Seward	1861–1865
Secretary of Treasury	Samuel P. Chase	1861–1864
	William P. Fessenden	1864–1865
	Hugh McCulloch	1865
Secretary of War	Simon Cameron	1861–1862
	Edwin M. Stanton	1862–1865
Attorney General	Edward Bates	1861–1864
	James Speed	1864–1865

Postmaster General	Horatio King	1861
	Montgomery Blair	1861–1864
	William Dennison	1864–1865
Secretary of Navy	Gideon Welles	1861–1865
Secretary of Interior	Caleb B. Smith	1861–1863
	John P. Usher	1863–1865

The Andrew Johnson Administration

President	Andrew Johnson	1865–1869
Vice President	None	
Secretary of State	William H. Seward	1865–1869
Secretary of Treasury	Hugh McCulloch	1865–1869
Secretary of War	Edwin M. Stanton	1865–1867
	Ulysses S. Grant	1867–1868
	Lorenzo Thomas	1868
	John M. Schofield	1868–1869
Attorney General	James Speed	1865–1866
	Henry Stanbery	1866–1868
	William M. Evarts	1868–1869
Postmaster General	William Dennison	1865–1866
	Alexander Randall	1866–1869
Secretary of Navy	Gideon Welles	1865–1869
Secretary of Interior	John P. Usher	1865
	James Harlan	1865–1866
	Orville H. Browning	1866–1869

The Grant Administration

President	Ulysses S. Grant	1869–1877
Vice President	Schuyler Colfax	1869–1873
	Henry Wilson	1873–1877
Secretary of State	Elihu B. Washburne	1869
	Hamilton Fish	1869–1877
Secretary of Treasury	George S. Boutwell	1869–1873
	William Richardson	1873–1874
	Benjamin Bristow	1874–1876
	Lot M. Morrill	1876–1877
Secretary of War	John A. Rawlins	1869
	William T. Sherman	1869
	William W. Belknap	1869–1876
	Alphonso Taft	1876
	James D. Cameron	1876–1877
Attorney General	Ebenezer Hoar	1869–1870
	Amos T. Ackerman	1870–1871
	G. H. Williams	1871–1875
	Edwards Pierrepont	1875–1876
	Alphonso Taft	1876–1877

Postmaster General	John A. J. Creswell	1869–1874
	James W. Marshall	1874
	Marshall Jewell	1874–1876
	James N. Tyner	1876–1877
Secretary of Navy	Adolph E. Borie	1869
	George M. Robeson	1869–1877
Secretary of Interior	Jacob D. Cox	1869–1870
	Columbus Delano	1870–1875
	Zachariah Chandler	1875–1877

The Hayes Administration

President	Rutherford B. Hayes	1877–1881
Vice President	William A. Wheeler	1877–1881
Secretary of State	William B. Evarts	1877–1881
Secretary of Treasury	John Sherman	1877–1881
Secretary of War	George W. McCrary	1877–1879
	Alex Ramsey	1879–1881
Attorney General	Charles Devens	1877–1881
Postmaster General	David M. Key	1877–1880
	Horace Maynard	1880–1881
Secretary of Navy	Richard W. Thompson	1877–1880
	Nathan Goff, Jr.	1881
Secretary of Interior	Carl Schurz	1877–1881

The Garfield Administration

President	James A. Garfield	1881
Vice President	Chester A. Arthur	1881
Secretary of State	James G. Blaine	1881
Secretary of Treasury	William Windom	1881
Secretary of War	Robert T. Lincoln	1881
Attorney General	Wayne MacVeagh	1881
Postmaster General	Thomas L. James	1881
Secretary of Navy	William H. Hunt	1881
Secretary of Interior	Samuel J. Kirkwood	1881

The Arthur Administration

President	Chester A. Arthur	1881–1885
Vice President	None	
Secretary of State	F. T. Frelinghuysen	1881–1885

Secretary of Treasury	Charles J. Folger	1881–1884
	Walter Q. Gresham	1884
	Hugh McCulloch	1884–1885
Secretary of War	Robert T. Lincoln	1881–1885
Attorney General	Benjamin H. Brewster	1881–1885
Postmaster General	Timothy O. Howe	1881–1883
	Walter Q. Gresham	1883–1884
	Frank Hatton	1884–1885
Secretary of Navy	William H. Hunt	1881–1882
	William E. Chandler	1882–1885
Secretary of Interior	Samuel J. Kirkwood	1881–1882
	Henry M. Teller	1882–1885

The Cleveland Administration

President	Grover Cleveland	1885–1889
Vice President	Thomas A. Hendricks	1885–1889
Secretary of State	Thomas F. Bayard	1885–1889
Secretary of Treasury	Daniel Manning	1885–1887
	Charles S. Fairchild	1887–1889
Secretary of War	William C. Endicott	1885–1889
Attorney General	Augustus H. Garland	1885–1889
Postmaster General	William F. Vilas	1885–1888
	Don M. Dickinson	1888–1889
Secretary of Navy	William C. Whitney	1885–1889
Secretary of Interior	Lucius Q. C. Lamar	1885–1888
	William F. Vilas	1888–1889
Secretary of Agriculture	Norman J. Colman	1889

The Benjamin Harrison Administration

President	Benjamin Harrison	1889–1893
Vice President	Levi P. Morton	1889–1893
Secretary of State	James G. Blaine	1889–1892
	John W. Foster	1892–1893
Secretary of Treasury	William Windom	1889–1891
	Charles Foster	1891–1893
Secretary of War	Redfield Proctor	1889–1891
	Stephen B. Elkins	1891–1893
Attorney General	William H. H. Miller	1889–1891
Postmaster General	John Wanamaker	1889–1893
Secretary of Navy	Benjamin F. Tracy	1889–1893
Secretary of Interior	John W. Noble	1889–1893
Secretary of Agriculture	Jeremiah M. Rusk	1889–1893

The Cleveland Administration

President	Grover Cleveland	1893–1897
Vice President	Adlai E. Stevenson	1893–1897
Secretary of State	Walter Q. Gresham	1893–1895
	Richard Olney	1895–1897
Secretary of Treasury	John G. Carlisle	1893–1897
Secretary of War	Daniel S. Lamont	1893–1897
Attorney General	Richard Olney	1893–1895
	James Harmon	1895–1897
Postmaster General	Wilson S. Bissell	1893–1895
	William L. Wilson	1895–1897
Secretary of Navy	Hilary A. Herbert	1893–1897
Secretary of Interior	Hoke Smith	1893–1896
	David R. Francis	1896–1897
Secretary of Agriculture	Julius S. Morton	1893–1897

The McKinley Administration

President	William McKinley	1897–1901
Vice President	Garret A. Hobart	1897–1901
	Theodore Roosevelt	1901
Secretary of State	John Sherman	1897–1898
	William R. Day	1898
	John Hay	1898–1901
Secretary of Treasury	Lyman J. Gage	1897–1901
Secretary of War	Russell A. Alger	1897–1899
	Elihu Root	1899–1901
Attorney General	Joseph McKenna	1897–1898
	John W. Griggs	1898–1901
	Philander C. Knox	1901
Postmaster General	James A. Gary	1897–1898
	Charles E. Smith	1898–1901
Secretary of Navy	John D. Long	1897–1901
Secretary of Interior	Cornelius N. Bliss	1897–1899
	Ethan A. Hitchcock	1899–1901
Secretary of Agriculture	James Wilson	1897–1901

The Theodore Roosevelt Administration

President	Theodore Roosevelt	1901–1909
Vice President	Charles Fairbanks	1905–1909
Secretary of State	John Hay	1901–1905
	Elihu Root	1905–1909
	Robert Bacon	1909

Secretary of Treasury	Lyman J. Gage	1901–1902
	Leslie M. Shaw	1902–1907
	George B. Cortelyou	1907–1909
Secretary of War	Elihu Root	1901–1904
	William H. Taft	1904–1908
	Luke E. Wright	1908–1909
Attorney General	Philander C. Knox	1901–1904
	William H. Moody	1904–1906
	Charles J. Bonaparte	1906–1909
Postmaster General	Charles E. Smith	1901–1902
	Henry C. Payne	1902–1904
	Robert J. Wynne	1904–1905
	George B. Cortelyou	1905–1907
	George von L. Meyer	1907–1909
Secretary of Navy	John D. Long	1901–1902
	William H. Moody	1902–1904
	Paul Morton	1904–1905
	Charles J. Bonaparte	1905–1906
	Victor H. Metcalf	1906–1908
	Truman H. Newberry	1908–1909
Secretary of Interior	Ethan A. Hitchcock	1901–1907
	James R. Garfield	1907–1909
Secretary of Agriculture	James Wilson	1901–1909
Secretary of Labor and Commerce	George B. Cortelyou	1903–1904
	Victor H. Metcalf	1904–1906
	Oscar S. Straus	1906–1909
	Charles Nagel	1909

The Taft Administration

President	William H. Taft	1909–1913
Vice President	James S. Sherman	1909–1913
Secretary of State	Philander C. Knox	1909–1913
Secretary of Treasury	Franklin MacVeagh	1909–1913
Secretary of War	Jacob M. Dickinson	1909–1911
	Henry L. Stimson	1911–1913
Attorney General	George W. Wickersham	1909–1913
Postmaster General	Frank H. Hitchcock	1909–1913
Secretary of Navy	George von L. Meyer	1909–1913
Secretary of Interior	Richard A. Ballinger	1909–1911
	Walter L. Fisher	1911–1913
Secretary of Agriculture	James Wilson	1909–1913
Secretary of Labor and Commerce	Charles Nagel	1909–1913

The Wilson Administration

President	Woodrow Wilson	1913–1921
Vice President	Thomas R. Marshall	1913–1921
Secretary of State	William J. Bryan	1913–1915
	Robert Lansing	1915–1920
	Bainbridge Colby	1920–1921
Secretary of Treasury	William G. McAdoo	1913–1918
	Carter Glass	1918–1920
	David F. Houston	1920–1921
Secretary of War	Lindley M. Garrison	1913–1916
	Newton D. Baker	1916–1921
Attorney General	James C. McReynolds	1913–1914
	Thomas W. Gregory	1914–1919
	A. Mitchell Palmer	1919–1921
Postmaster General	Albert S. Burleson	1913–1921
Secretary of Navy	Josephus Daniels	1913–1921
Secretary of Interior	Franklin K. Lane	1913–1920
	John B. Payne	1920–1921
Secretary of Agriculture	David F. Houston	1913–1920
	Edwin T. Meredith	1920–1921
Secretary of Commerce	William C. Redfield	1913–1919
	Joshua W. Alexander	1919–1921
Secretary of Labor	William B. Wilson	1913–1921

The Harding Administration

President	Warren G. Harding	1921–1923
Vice President	Calvin Coolidge	1921–1923
Secretary of State	Charles E. Hughes	1921–1923
Secretary of Treasury	Andrew Mellon	1921–1923
Secretary of War	John W. Weeks	1921–1923
Attorney General	Harry M. Daugherty	1921–1923
Postmaster General	Will H. Hays	1921–1922
	Hubert Work	1922–1923
	Harry S. New	1923
Secretary of Navy	Edwin Denby	1921–1923
Secretary of Interior	Albert B. Fall	1921–1923
	Hubert Work	1923
Secretary of Agriculture	Henry C. Wallace	1921–1923
Secretary of Commerce	Herbert C. Hoover	1921–1923
Secretary of Labor	James J. Davis	1921–1923

The Coolidge Administration

President	Calvin Coolidge	1923–1929
Vice President	Charles G. Dawes	1925–1929
Secretary of State	Charles E. Hughes	1923–1925
	Frank B. Kellogg	1925–1929
Secretary of Treasury	Andrew Mellon	1923–1929
Secretary of War	John W. Weeks	1923–1925
	Dwight F. Davis	1925–1929
Attorney General	Henry M. Daugherty	1923–1924
	Harlan F. Stone	1924–1925
	John G. Sargent	1925–1929
Postmaster General	Harry S. New	1923–1929
Secretary of Navy	Edwin Derby	1923–1924
	Curtis D. Wilbur	1924–1929
Secretary of Interior	Hubert Work	1923–1928
	Roy O. West	1928–1929
Secretary of Agriculture	Henry C. Wallace	1923–1924
	Howard M. Gore	1924–1925
	William M. Jardine	1925–1929
Secretary of Commerce	Herbert C. Hoover	1923–1928
	William F. Whiting	1928–1929
Secretary of Labor	James J. Davis	1923–1929

The Hoover Administration

President	Herbert C. Hoover	1929–1933
Vice President	Charles Curtis	1929–1933
Secretary of State	Henry L. Stimson	1929–1933
Secretary of Treasury	Andrew Mellon	1929–1932
	Ogden L. Mills	1932–1933
Secretary of War	James W. Good	1929
	Patrick J. Hurley	1929–1933
Attorney General	William D. Mitchell	1929–1933
Postmaster General	Walter F. Brown	1929–1933
Secretary of Navy	Charles F. Adams	1929–1933
Secretary of Interior	Ray L. Wilbur	1929–1933
Secretary of Agriculture	Arthur M. Hyde	1929–1933
Secretary of Commerce	Robert P. Lamont	1929–1932
	Roy D. Chapin	1932–1933
Secretary of Labor	James J. Davis	1929–1930
	William N. Doak	1930–1933

The Franklin D. Roosevelt Administration

President	Franklin D. Roosevelt	1933–1945
Vice President	John Nance Garner	1933–1941
	Henry A. Wallace	1941–1945
	Harry S Truman	1945
Secretary of State	Cordell Hull	1933–1944
	Edward R. Stettinius, Jr.	1944–1945
Secretary of Treasury	William H. Woodin	1933–1934
	Henry Morgenthau, Jr.	1934–1945
Secretary of War	George H. Dern	1933–1936
	Henry A. Woodring	1936–1940
	Henry L. Stimson	1940–1945
Attorney General	Homer S. Cummings	1933–1939
	Frank Murphy	1939–1940
	Robert H. Jackson	1940–1941
	Francis Biddle	1941–1945
Postmaster General	James A. Farley	1933–1940
	Frank C. Walker	1940–1945
Secretary of Navy	Claude A. Swanson	1933–1940
	Charles Edison	1940
	Frank Knox	1940–1944
	James V. Forrestal	1944–1945
Secretary of Interior	Harold L. Ickes	1933–1945
Secretary of Agriculture	Henry A. Wallace	1933–1940
	Claude R. Wickard	1940–1945
Secretary of Commerce	Daniel C. Roper	1933–1939
	Harry L. Hopkins	1939–1940
	Jesse Jones	1940–1945
	Henry A. Wallace	1945
Secretary of Labor	Frances Perkins	1933–1945

The Truman Administration

President	Harry S Truman	1945–1953
Vice President	Alben W. Barkley	1949–1953
Secretary of State	Edward R. Stettinius, Jr.	1945
	James F. Byrnes	1945–1947
	George C. Marshall	1947–1949
	Dean G. Acheson	1949–1953
Secretary of Treasury	Fred M. Vinson	1945–1946
	John W. Snyder	1946–1953
Secretary of War	Robert P. Patterson	1945–1947
	Kenneth C. Royall	1947
Attorney General	Tom C. Clark	1945–1949
	J. Howard McGrath	1949–1952
	James P. McGranery	1952–1953

Postmaster General	Frank C. Walker	1945
	Robert E. Hannegan	1945–1947
	Jesse M. Donaldson	1947–1953
Secretary of Navy	James V. Forrestal	1945–1947
Secretary of Interior	Harold L. Ickes	1945–1946
	Julius A. Krug	1946–1949
	Oscar L. Chapman	1949–1953
Secretary of Agriculture	Clinton P. Anderson	1945–1948
	Charles F. Brannan	1948–1953
Secretary of Commerce	Henry A. Wallace	1945–1946
	W. Averell Harriman	1946–1948
	Charles W. Sawyer	1948–1953
Secretary of Labor	Lewis B. Schwellenbach	1945–1948
	Maurice J. Tobin	1948–1953
Secretary of Defense	James V. Forrestal	1947–1949
	Louis A. Johnson	1949–1950
	George C. Marshall	1950–1951
	Robert A. Lovett	1951–1953

The Eisenhower Administration

President	Dwight D. Eisenhower	1953–1961
Vice President	Richard M. Nixon	1953–1961
Secretary of State	John Foster Dulles	1953–1959
	Christian A. Herter	1959–1961
Secretary of Treasury	George M. Humphrey	1953–1957
	Robert B. Anderson	1957–1961
Attorney General	Herbert Brownell, Jr.	1953–1958
	William P. Rogers	1958–1961
Postmaster General	Arthur E. Summerfield	1953–1961
Secretary of Interior	Douglas McKay	1953–1956
	Fred A. Seaton	1956–1961
Secretary of Agriculture	Ezra T. Benson	1953–1961
Secretary of Commerce	Sinclair Weeks	1953–1958
	Lewis L. Strauss	1958–1959
	Frederick H. Mueller	1959–1961
Secretary of Labor	Martin P. Durkin	1953
	James P. Mitchell	1953–1961
Secretary of Defense	Charles E. Wilson	1953–1957
	Neil H. McElroy	1957–1959
	Thomas S. Gates, Jr.	1959–1961
Secretary of Health, Education, and Welfare	Oveta Culp Hobby	1953–1955
	Marion B. Folsom	1955–1958
	Arthur S. Flemming	1958–1961

The Kennedy Administration

President	John F. Kennedy	1961–1963
Vice President	Lyndon B. Johnson	1961–1963
Secretary of State	Dean Rusk	1961–1963
Secretary of Treasury	C. Douglas Dillon	1961–1963
Attorney General	Robert F. Kennedy	1961–1963
Postmaster General	J. Edward Day	1961–1963
	John A. Gronouski	1963
Secretary of Interior	Stewart L. Udall	1961–1963
Secretary of Agriculture	Orville L. Freeman	1961–1963
Secretary of Commerce	Luther H. Hodges	1961–1963
Secretary of Labor	Arthur J. Goldberg	1961–1962
	W. Willard Wirtz	1962–1963
Secretary of Defense	Robert S. McNamara	1961–1963
Secretary of Health, Education, and Welfare	Abraham A. Ribicoff	1961–1962
	Anthony J. Celebrezze	1962–1963

The Lyndon Johnson Administration

President	Lyndon B. Johnson	1963–1969
Vice President	Hubert H. Humphrey	1965–1969
Secretary of State	Dean Rusk	1963–1969
Secretary of Treasury	C. Douglas Dillon	1963–1965
	Henry H. Fowler	1965–1969
Attorney General	Robert F. Kennedy	1963–1964
	Nicholas Katzenbach	1965–1966
	Ramsey Clark	1967–1969
Postmaster General	John A. Gronouski	1963–1965
	Lawrence F. O'Brien	1965–1968
	Marvin Watson	1968–1969
Secretary of Interior	Stewart L. Udall	1963–1969
Secretary of Agriculture	Orville L. Freeman	1963–1969
Secretary of Commerce	Luther H. Hodges	1963–1964
	John T. Connor	1964–1967
	Alexander B. Trowbridge	1967–1968
	Cyrus R. Smith	1968–1969
Secretary of Labor	W. Willard Wirtz	1963–1969
Secretary of Defense	Robert F. McNamara	1963–1968
	Clark Clifford	1968–1969

Secretary of Health, Education, and Welfare	Anthony J. Celebrezze	1963–1965
	John W. Gardner	1965–1968
	Wilbur J. Cohen	1968–1969
Secretary of Housing and Urban Development	Robert C. Weaver	1966–1969
	Robert C. Wood	1969
Secretary of Transportation	Alan S. Boyd	1967–1969

The Nixon Administration

President	Richard M. Nixon	1969–1974
Vice President	Spiro T. Agnew	1969–1973
	Gerald R. Ford	1973–1974
Secretary of State	William P. Rogers	1969–1973
	Henry A. Kissinger	1973–1974
Secretary of Treasury	David M. Kennedy	1969–1970
	John B. Connally	1971–1972
	George P. Shultz	1972–1974
	William E. Simon	1974
Attorney General	John N. Mitchell	1969–1972
	Richard G. Kleindienst	1972–1973
	Elliot L. Richardson	1973
	William B. Saxbe	1973–1974
Postmaster General	Winton M. Blount	1969–1971
Secretary of Interior	Walter J. Hickel	1969–1970
	Rogers Morton	1971–1974
Secretary of Agriculture	Clifford M. Hardin	1969–1971
	Earl L. Butz	1971–1974
Secretary of Commerce	Maurice H. Stans	1969–1972
	Peter G. Peterson	1972–1973
	Frederick B. Dent	1973–1974
Secretary of Labor	George P. Shultz	1969–1970
	James D. Hodgson	1970–1973
	Peter J. Brennan	1973–1974
Secretary of Defense	Melvin R. Laird	1969–1973
	Elliot L. Richardson	1973
	James R. Schlesinger	1973–1974
Secretary of Health, Education, and Welfare	Robert H. Finch	1969–1970
	Elliot L. Richardson	1970–1973
	Casper W. Weinberger	1973–1974
Secretary of Housing and Urban Development	George Romney	1969–1973
	James T. Lynn	1973–1974

Secretary of Transportation	John A. Volpe	1969–1973
	Claude S. Brinegar	1973–1974

The Ford Administration

President	Gerald R. Ford	1974–1977
Vice President	Nelson A. Rockefeller	1974–1977
Secretary of State	Henry A. Kissinger	1974–1977
Secretary of Treasury	William E. Simon	1974–1977
Attorney General	William Saxbe	1974–1975
	Edward Levi	1975–1977
Secretary of Interior	Rogers Morton	1974–1975
	Stanley K. Hathaway	1975
	Thomas Kleppe	1975–1977
Secretary of Agriculture	Earl L. Butz	1974–1976
	John A. Knebel	1976–1977
Secretary of Commerce	Frederick B. Dent	1974–1975
	Rogers Morton	1975–1976
	Elliot L. Richardson	1976–1977
Secretary of Labor	Peter J. Brennan	1974–1975
	John T. Dunlop	1975–1976
	W. J. Usery	1976–1977
Secretary of Defense	James R. Schlesinger	1974–1975
	Donald Rumsfeld	1975–1977
Secretary of Health, Education, and Welfare	Casper Weinberger	1974–1975
	Forrest D. Mathews	1975–1977
Secretary of Housing and Urban Development	James T. Lynn	1974–1975
	Carla A. Hills	1975–1977
Secretary of Transportation	Claude Brinegar	1974–1975
	William T. Coleman	1975–1977

The Carter Administration

President	Jimmy Carter	1977–1981
Vice President	Walter F. Mondale	1977–1981
Secretary of State	Cyrus R. Vance	1977–1980
	Edmund Muskie	1980–1981
Secretary of Treasury	W. Michael Blumenthal	1977–1979
	G. William Miller	1979–1981
Attorney General	Griffin Bell	1977–1979
	Benjamin R. Civiletti	1979–1981
Secretary of Interior	Cecil D. Andrus	1977–1981

Secretary of Agriculture	Robert Bergland	1977–1981	Secretary of Treasury	Donald Regan	1981–1985
				James A. Baker, III	1985–
Secretary of Commerce	Juanita M. Kreps	1977–1979	Attorney General	William F. Smith	1981–1985
	Philip M. Klutznick	1979–1981		Edwin A. Meese, III	1985–
Secretary of Labor	F. Ray Marshall	1977–1981	Secretary of Interior	James Watt	1981–1983
Secretary of Defense	Harold Brown	1977–1981		William P. Clark, Jr.	1983–1985
				Donald P. Hodel	1985–
Secretary of Health, Education, and Welfare	Joseph A. Califano	1977–1979	Secretary of Agriculture	John Block	1981–
	Patricia R. Harris	1979			
			Secretary of Commerce	Malcolm Baldridge	1981–
Secretary of Health and Human Services	Patricia R. Harris	1979–1981	Secretary of Labor	Raymond Donovan	1981–1985
				William E. Brock	1985–
			Secretary of Defense	Casper Weinberger	1981–
Secretary of Education	Shirley M. Hufstedler	1979–1981			
			Secretary of Health and Human Services	Richard Schweiker	1981–1983
Secretary of Housing and Urban Development	Patricia R. Harris	1977–1979		Margaret Heckler	1983–1985
	Moon Landrieu	1979–1981			
			Secretary of Education	Terrel H. Bell	1981–1985
				William J. Bennett	1985–
Secretary of Transportation	Brock Adams	1977–1979	Secretary of Housing and Urban Development	Samuel Pierce	1981–
	Neil E. Goldschmidt	1979–1981			
Secretary of Energy	James R. Schlesinger	1977–1979			
	Charles W. Duncan	1979–1981	Secretary of Transportation	Drew Lewis	1981–1983
				Elizabeth Dole	1983–
The Reagan Administration			Secretary of Energy	James Edwards	1981–1982
				Donald P. Hodel	1982–1985
President	Ronald Reagan	1981–		John S. Herrington	1985–
Vice President	George Bush	1981–			
Secretary of State	Alexander M. Haig	1981–1982			
	George P. Shultz	1982–			

PARTY STRENGTH IN CONGRESS

Period	Congress	House					Senate					Party of President
		Majority Party		Minority Party		Others	Majority Party		Minority Party		Others	
1789–91	1st	Ad	38	Op	26		Ad	17	Op	9		F	Washington
1791–93	2nd	F	37	DR	33		F	16	DR	13		F	Washington
1793–95	3rd	DR	57	F	48		F	17	DR	13		F	Washington
1795–97	4th	F	54	DR	52		F	19	DR	13		F	Washington
1797–99	5th	F	58	DR	48		F	20	DR	12		F	J. Adams
1799–1801	6th	F	64	DR	42		F	19	DR	13		F	J. Adams
1801–03	7th	DR	69	F	36		DR	18	F	13		DR	Jefferson

Period	Congress	House					Senate						Party of President
		Majority Party		Minority Party		Others	Majority Party		Minority Party		Others		
1803–05	8th	DR	102	F	39		DR	25	F	9		DR	Jefferson
1805–07	9th	DR	116	F	25		DR	27	F	7		DR	Jefferson
1807–09	10th	DR	118	F	24		DR	28	F	6		DR	Jefferson
1809–11	11th	DR	94	F	48		DR	28	F	6		DR	Madison
1811–13	12th	DR	108	F	36		DR	30	F	6		DR	Madison
1813–15	13th	DR	112	F	68		DR	27	F	9		DR	Madison
1815–17	14th	DR	117	F	65		DR	25	F	11		DR	Madison
1817–19	15th	DR	141	F	42		DR	34	F	10		DR	Monroe
1819–21	16th	DR	156	F	27		DR	35	F	7		DR	Monroe
1821–23	17th	DR	158	F	25		DR	44	F	4		DR	Monroe
1823–25	18th	DR	187	F	26		DR	44	F	4		DR	Monroe
1825–27	19th	Ad	105	J	97		Ad	26	J	20		C	J. Q. Adams
1827–29	20th	J	119	Ad	94		J	28	Ad	20		C	J. Q. Adams
1829–31	21st	D	139	NR	74		D	26	NR	22		D	Jackson
1831–33	22nd	D	141	NR	58	14	D	25	NR	21	2	D	Jackson
1833–35	23rd	D	147	AM	53	60	D	20	NR	20	8	D	Jackson
1835–37	24th	D	145	W	98		D	27	W	25		D	Jackson
1837–39	25th	D	108	W	107	24	D	30	W	18	4	D	Van Buren
1839–41	26th	D	124	W	118		D	28	W	22		D	Van Buren
1841–43	27th	W	133	D	102	6	W	28	D	22	2	W	W. Harrison
												W	Tyler
1843–45	28th	D	142	W	79	1	W	28	D	25	1	W	Tyler
1845–47	29th	D	143	W	77	6	D	31	W	25		D	Polk
1847–49	30th	W	115	D	108	4	D	36	W	21	1	D	Polk
1849–51	31st	D	112	W	109	9	D	35	W	25	2	W	Taylor
												W	Fillmore
1851–53	32nd	D	140	W	88	5	D	35	W	24	3	W	Fillmore
1853–55	33rd	D	159	W	71	4	D	38	W	22	2	D	Pierce
1855–57	34th	R	108	D	83	43	D	40	R	15	5	D	Pierce
1857–59	35th	D	118	R	92	26	D	36	R	20	8	D	Buchanan
1859–61	36th	R	114	D	92	31	D	36	R	26	4	D	Buchanan
1861–63	37th	R	105	D	43	30	R	31	D	10	8	R	Lincoln
1863–65	38th	R	102	D	75	9	R	36	D	9	5	R	Lincoln
1865–67	39th	U	149	D	42		U	42	D	10		R	Lincoln
												R	Johnson
1867–69	40th	R	143	D	49		R	42	D	11		R	Johnson
1869–71	41st	R	149	D	63		R	56	D	11		R	Grant
1871–73	42nd	R	134	D	104	5	R	52	D	17	5	R	Grant
1873–75	43rd	R	194	D	92	14	R	49	D	19	5	R	Grant
1875–77	44th	D	169	R	109	14	R	45	D	29	2	R	Grant
1877–79	45th	D	153	R	140		R	39	D	36	1	R	Hayes
1879–81	46th	D	149	R	130	14	D	42	R	33	1	R	Hayes

Period	Congress	House Majority Party		House Minority Party		Others	Senate Majority Party		Senate Minority Party		Others	Party of President	
1881–83	47th	D	147	R	135	11	R	37	D	37	1	R	Garfield
												R	Arthur
1883–85	48th	D	197	R	118	10	R	38	D	36	2	R	Arthur
1885–87	49th	D	183	R	140	2	R	43	D	34		D	Cleveland
1887–89	50th	D	169	R	152	4	R	39	D	37		D	Cleveland
1889–91	51st	R	166	D	159		R	39	D	37		R	B. Harrison
1891–93	52nd	D	235	R	88	9	R	47	D	39	2	R	B. Harrison
1893–95	53rd	D	218	R	127	11	D	44	R	38	3	D	Cleveland
1895–97	54th	R	244	D	105	7	R	43	D	39	6	D	Cleveland
1897–99	55th	R	204	D	113	40	R	47	D	34	7	R	McKinley
1899–1901	56th	R	185	D	163	9	R	53	D	26	8	R	McKinley
1901–03	57th	R	197	D	151	9	R	55	D	31	4	R	McKinley
												R	T. Roosevelt
1903–05	58th	R	208	D	178		R	57	D	33		R	T. Roosevelt
1905–07	59th	R	250	D	136		R	57	D	33		R	T. Roosevelt
1907–09	60th	R	222	D	164		R	61	D	31		R	T. Roosevelt
1909–11	61st	R	219	D	172		R	61	D	32		R	Taft
1911–13	62nd	D	228	R	161	1	R	51	D	41		R	Taft
1913–15	63rd	D	291	R	127	17	D	51	R	44	1	D	Wilson
1915–17	64th	D	230	R	196	9	D	56	R	40		D	Wilson
1917–19	65th	D	216	R	210	6	D	53	R	42		D	Wilson
1919–21	66th	R	240	D	190	3	R	49	D	47		D	Wilson
1921–23	67th	R	301	D	131	1	R	59	D	37		R	Harding
1923–25	68th	R	225	D	205	5	R	51	D	43	2	R	Coolidge
1925–27	69th	R	247	D	183	4	R	56	D	39	1	R	Coolidge
1927–29	70th	R	237	D	195	3	R	49	D	46	1	R	Coolidge
1929–31	71st	R	267	D	167	1	R	56	D	39	1	R	Hoover
1931–33	72nd	D	220	R	214	1	R	48	D	47	1	R	Hoover
1933–35	73rd	D	310	R	117	5	D	60	R	35	1	D	F. Roosevelt
1935–37	74th	D	319	R	103	10	D	69	R	25	2	D	F. Roosevelt
1937–39	75th	D	331	R	89	13	D	76	R	16	4	D	F. Roosevelt
1939–41	76th	D	261	R	164	4	D	69	R	23	4	D	F. Roosevelt
1941–43	77th	D	268	R	162	5	D	66	R	28	2	D	F. Roosevelt
1943–45	78th	D	218	R	208	4	D	58	R	37	1	D	F. Roosevelt
1945–47	79th	D	242	R	190	2	D	56	R	38	1	D	Truman
1947–49	80th	R	245	D	188	1	R	51	D	45		D	Truman
1949–51	81st	D	263	R	171	1	D	54	R	42		D	Truman
1951–53	82nd	D	234	R	199	1	D	49	R	47		D	Truman
1953–55	83rd	R	221	D	211	1	R	48	D	47	1	R	Eisenhower
1955–57	84th	D	232	R	203		D	48	R	47	1	R	Eisenhower
1957–59	85th	D	233	R	200		D	49	R	47		R	Eisenhower

Period	Congress	House Majority Party		House Minority Party		Others	Senate Majority Party		Senate Minority Party		Others		Party of President
1959–61	86th	D	284	R	153		D	65	R	35			R	Eisenhower
1961–63	87th	D	263	R	174		D	65	R	35			D	Kennedy
1963–65	88th	D	258	R	177		D	67	R	33			D	Kennedy
													D	Johnson
1965–67	89th	D	295	R	140		D	68	R	32			D	Johnson
1967–69	90th	D	246	R	187		D	64	R	36			D	Johnson
1969–71	91st	D	245	R	189		D	57	R	43			R	Nixon
1971–73	92nd	D	254	R	180		D	54	R	44	2		R	Nixon
1973–75	93rd	D	239	R	192	1	D	56	R	42	2		R	Nixon
1975–77	94th	D	291	R	144		D	60	R	37	3		R	Ford
1977–79	95th	D	292	R	143		D	61	R	38	1		D	Carter
1979–81	96th	D	276	R	157		D	58	R	41	1		D	Carter
1981–83	97th	D	243	R	192		R	53	D	46	1		R	Reagan
1983–85	98th	D	267	R	168		R	55	D	45			R	Reagan
1985–87	99th	D	253	R	182		R	53	D	47			R	Reagan

AD = Administration; AM = Anti-Masonic; C = Coalition; D = Democratic; DR = Democratic-Republican; F = Federalist; J = Jacksonian; NR = National Republican; Op = Opposition; R = Republican; U = Unionist; W = Whig. Figures are for the beginning of first session of each Congress, except the 93rd, which are for the beginning of the second session.

JUSTICES OF THE SUPREME COURT

	Term of Service	Years of Service	Life Span		Term of Service	Years of Service	Life Span
John Jay	1789–1795	5	1745–1829	Henry B. Brown	1890–1906	16	1836–1913
John Rutledge	1789–1791	1	1739–1800	George Shiras, Jr.	1892–1903	10	1832–1924
William Cushing	1789–1810	20	1732–1810	Howell E. Jackson	1893–1895	2	1832–1895
James Wilson	1789–1798	8	1742–1798	Edward D. White	1894–1910	16	1845–1921
John Blair	1789–1796	6	1732–1800	Rufus W. Peckham	1895–1909	14	1838–1909
Robert H. Harrison	1789–1790	—	1745–1790	Joseph McKenna	1898–1925	26	1843–1926
James Iredell	1790–1799	9	1751–1799	Oliver W. Holmes	1902–1932	30	1841–1935
Thomas Johnson	1791–1793	1	1732–1819	William R. Day	1903–1922	19	1849–1923
William Paterson	1793–1806	13	1745–1806	William H. Moody	1906–1910	3	1853–1917
John Rutledge*	1795	—	1739–1800	Horace H. Lurton	1910–1914	4	1844–1914
Samuel Chase	1796–1811	15	1741–1811	Charles E. Hughes	1910–1916	5	1862–1948
Oliver Ellsworth	1796–1800	4	1745–1807	Willis Van Devanter	1911–1937	26	1859–1941
Bushrod Washington	1798–1829	31	1762–1829	Joseph R. Lamar	1911–1916	5	1857–1916

	Term of Service	Years of Service	Life Span		Term of Service	Years of Service	Life Span
Alfred Moore	1799–1804	4	1755–1810	Edward D. White	1910–1921	11	1845–1921
John Marshall	1801–1835	34	1755–1835	Mahlon Pitney	1912–1922	10	1858–1924
William Johnson	1804–1834	30	1771–1834	James C. McReynolds	1914–1941	26	1862–1946
H. Brockholst				Louis D. Brandeis	1916–1939	22	1856–1941
Livingston	1806–1823	16	1757–1823	John H. Clarke	1916–1922	6	1857–1945
Thomas Todd	1807–1826	18	1765–1826	William H. Taft	1921–1930	8	1857–1930
Joseph Story	1811–1845	33	1779–1845	George Sutherland	1922–1938	15	1862–1942
Gabriel Duval	1811–1835	24	1752–1844	Pierce Butler	1922–1939	16	1866–1939
Smith Thompson	1823–1843	20	1768–1843	Edward T. Sanford	1923–1930	7	1865–1930
Robert Trimble	1826–1828	2	1777–1828	Harlan F. Stone	1925–1941	16	1872–1946
John McLean	1829–1861	32	1785–1861	Charles E. Hughes	1930–1941	11	1862–1948
Henry Baldwin	1830–1844	14	1780–1844	Owen J. Roberts	1930–1945	15	1875–1955
James M. Wayne	1835–1867	32	1790–1867	Benjamin N. Cardozo	1932–1938	6	1870–1938
Roger B. Taney	1836–1864	28	1777–1864	Hugo L. Black	1937–1971	34	1886–1971
Philip P. Barbour	1836–1841	4	1783–1841	Stanley F. Reed	1938–1957	19	1884–1980
John Catron	1837–1865	28	1786–1865	Felix Frankfurter	1939–1962	23	1882–1965
John McKinley	1837–1852	15	1780–1852	William O. Douglas	1939–1975	36	1898–1980
Peter V. Daniel	1841–1860	19	1784–1860	Frank Murphy	1940–1949	9	1890–1949
Samuel Nelson	1845–1872	27	1792–1873	Harlan F. Stone	1941–1946	5	1872–1946
Levi Woodbury	1845–1851	5	1789–1851	James F. Byrnes	1941–1942	1	1879–1972
Robert C. Grier	1846–1870	23	1794–1870	Robert H. Jackson	1941–1954	13	1892–1954
Benjamin R. Curtis	1851–1857	6	1809–1874	Wiley B. Rutledge	1943–1949	6	1894–1949
John A. Campbell	1853–1861	8	1811–1889	Harold H. Burton	1945–1958	13	1888–1964
Nathan Clifford	1858–1881	23	1803–1881	Fred M. Vinson	1946–1953	7	1890–1953
Noah H. Swayne	1862–1881	18	1804–1884	Tom C. Clark	1949–1967	18	1899–1977
Samuel F. Miller	1862–1890	28	1816–1890	Sherman Minton	1949–1956	7	1890–1965
David Davis	1862–1877	14	1815–1886	Earl Warren	1953–1969	16	1891–1974
Stephen J. Field	1863–1897	34	1816–1899	John Marshall Harlan	1955–1971	16	1899–1971
Salmon P. Chase	1864–1873	8	1808–1873	William J. Brennan, Jr.	1956–	—	1906–
William Strong	1870–1880	10	1808–1895	Charles E. Whittaker	1957–1962	5	1901–1973
Joseph P. Bradley	1870–1892	22	1813–1892	Potter Stewart	1958–1981	23	1915–
Ward Hunt	1873–1882	9	1810–1886	Byron R. White	1962–	—	1917–
Morrison R. Waite	1874–1888	14	1816–1888	Arthur J. Goldberg	1962–1965	3	1908–
John M. Harlan	1877–1911	34	1833–1911	Abe Fortas	1965–1969	4	1910–
William B. Woods	1880–1887	7	1824–1887	Thurgood Marshall	1967–	—	1908–
Stanley Matthews	1881–1889	7	1824–1889	Warren C. Burger	1969–	—	1907–
Horace Gray	1882–1902	20	1828–1902	Harry A. Blackmun	1970–	—	1908–
Samuel Blatchford	1882–1893	11	1820–1893	Lewis F. Powell, Jr.	1971–	—	1907–
Lucius Q. C. Lamar	1888–1893	5	1825–1893	William H. Rehnquist	1971–	—	1924–
Melville W. Fuller	1888–1910	21	1833–1910	John P. Stevens, III	1975–	—	1920–
David J. Brewer	1890–1910	20	1837–1910	Sandra Day O'Connor	1981–	—	1930–

*Appointed and served one term, but not confirmed by the Senate.

Note: Chief justices are in italics.

CHAPTER OPENER CREDITS

Chapter 1
Columbus on the island of Hispaniola. Etching. Spanish. The Granger Collection.

Chapter 2
Mrs. Elizabeth Freake and Baby Mary. Unknown artist, ca. 1674. Oil on canvas, 42 ½″ × 36 ¾″. Worcester Art Museum, Massachusetts/The Granger Collection.

Chapter 3
Wedding needlepoint, 1756. American Antiquarian Society, Worcester, Massachusetts.

Chapter 4
Tory Stamp agents being tarred and feathered. J. Trumbull. The Granger Collection.

Chapter 5
The Battle of Bunker's Hill (detail). John Trumbull. Oil on canvas, 1786. Copyright Yale University Art Gallery.

Chapter 6
Mr. and Mrs. Thomas Mifflin (Sarah Morris). J. Singleton Copley, 1773. Oil on canvas, 60 ½″ × 48″. Historical Society of Pennsylvania, Philadelphia/The Granger Collection.

Chapter 7
Arrival of George Washington at the Battery, New York City, for his inauguration. The Granger Collection.

Chapter 8
Andrew Jackson at the Battle of New Orleans. The Granger Collection.

Chapter 9
Powerloom weaving at textile mill. The Granger Collection.

Chapter 10
American Farm Scene by Currier & Ives. J. Martin/Scala/Art Resource.

Chapter 11
Slave coffle passing unfinished Capitol Building, Washington, D.C., ca. 1820. The Granger Collection.

Chapter 12
Stump Speaking. George Caleb Bingham. Oil, 1854. From the Collection of the Boatman's National Bank of St. Louis.

Chapter 13
American troops storming the palace of Chapultepec, 1847. The Granger Collection.

Chapter 14
General Stonewall Jackson at the Battle of First Bull Run, 21 July 1861. The Granger Collection.

Chapter 15
The First Vote. Colored engraving, 1867. The Granger Collection.

Chapter 16
Emigrant waiting room of the Union Pacific railroad depot, Omaha, Nebraska. Colored engraving, 1877. The Granger Collection.

Chapter 17
Bessemer steel manufacturing at Carnegie's Pittsburgh Steelworks, 1886. Contemporary colored engraving. The Granger Collection.

Chapter 18
Intersection of Orchard and Hester Streets on Lower East Side, New York City. Oil over photograph, 1905. The Granger Collection.

Chapter 19
Columbia Bicycles and Tricycles. Poster, ca. 1900. The New-York Historical Society.

Chapter 20
The Lost Bet. Library of Congress.

Chapter 21
Teddy Roosevelt campaigning for president, summer of 1912. Oil over photograph. The Granger Collection.

Chapter 22
Battle before Caloocan, Philippines. Free Public Library of Philadelphia/Joseph Martin/Scala/Art Resource.

Chapter 23
Rock of the Marne: 30th and 38th U.S. Infantry Regiments in action near Mézy, France, July 1918. Painting by Mal Thompson. The Granger Collection.

Chapter 24
Fisk Tire Advertisement. Free Library of Philadelphia/Joseph Martin/Scala/Art Resource.

INDEX

American Railway Union, 502, 577
American Relief Administration, 766
American Renaissance, 329
American Revolution, *see* Revolutionary War
American Society for the Promotion of Temperance, 330
"American System," 227, 337, 339; of manufacturing, 247–248
American Tobacco Company, 489
American Union Against Militarism, 655
American Woman Suffrage Association, 567
Ames, "Doc," 527
Amnesty Act (1872), 443
Anarchism, 500, 502, 577, 689, 953
Anderson, John, 993, 994
Anderson, Marian, 752, 753
Anderson, Mary (Labor Department), 805
Anderson, Mary (WTUL leader), 503
Anderson, Sherwood, 630, 723
Andros, Sir Edmund, 63
Anglican Church (Church of England), 20; in America, 20–21, 25, 43, 88, 101, 133, 203. *See also* Religion
Anglicans: vs. New England Puritans, 60; in Boston, 64; in Irish law, 74
Angola, 51, 927, 933
Annapolis Convention, 172
Anne, queen of England, 63, 74
Anthony, Susan B., 429, 567
Anti-Catholicism, 256, 283, 326, 330
Anti-Comintern Pact, 775
Anti-Defamation League, 840
Antietam: battle of, 387, 399
Antifederalists, 176–177, 178, 184
Antifeminist movement, 988, 989
Anti-Imperialist League, 633
Antimasonry, 334–335, 341
Anti-Saloon League, 595
Antislavery movement, *see* Abolitionism
Antitrust laws, 493, 607, 661, 674; Supreme Court decisions on, 493, 607, 682; Sherman Act, 493–494; Clayton Act, 611; Webb-Pomerene Act, 661, 765; World War II, 796. *See also* Monopoly
Anzus Treaty, 847
Apaches, 19, 462, 464. *See also* Indians
Apartheid, 1012
Apocalypse Now, 930
Apollo 11, 962
Appomattox, Lee surrenders at, 413
Arabic, sinking of, 652
Arbenz Guzman, Jacobo, 869
Arbuckle, Fatty, 699
Archbold, John D., 453
Architecture, 157–158, 704
Argentine-U.S. relations, 230, 935. *See also* Latin America
Arikara Indians, 7
Arizona, 259, 357, 453, 457
Arkansas, 319, 377
"Arkies," 743, 755
Arms Control and Disarmament Agency, 908
Arms race, *see* Nuclear weapons

Armstrong, Louis, 704
Armstrong, Neil, 962
Army, *see* Military, U.S.
Army Industrial College, 675
Arnold, Benedict, 148–149
Arnold, Gen. H. H., 794
"Arrogance of Power," 916
Arthur, Chester A., 565, 569, 570
Arthur, Timothy Shay, 330
Articles of Confederation, 155, 165, 167–171, 172–173, 176, 178, 210
Arts, the, and republican virtue, 157–158; and women, 158; and New Deal, 734, 745; and Kennedy, 941; of alienation, 703
MUSIC AND DANCE: blacks and, 314, 703–704, 953; musical comedy, 549–550; jazz, 703–704, 900–901; rock-and-roll and rock, 900, 953–954; Martha Graham, 901; disco, 991
PAINTING: of republican period, 157; 1920s (O'Keeffe, Marin), 704; WPA artists and, 745; 1950s–60s (Pollock, Warhol), 901
See also Entertainment
Asante, 51
Ashley, William Henry, 260
Assassinations, of 1960s, 956
Astor, John Jacob, 260, 274, 276
Aswan Dam, 871, 872
Atkins, Josiah, 161
Atlanta, Georgia, 403, 460, 520, 522, 688, 717; battle at, 410
Atlanta Compromise, 601, 602
Atlanta University, 438, 723
Atlantic Charter, 783, 791, 809
Atlantic and Pacific Tea Company (A&P), 542–543
Atomic bomb, 790, 795, 797, 813, 815, 820, 824, 832, 833, 846
Atomic energy, international control of, 825
Atomic Energy Act, 857
Atomic Energy Commission (AEC), 815, 859
Attica prison, riot at, 963
Auchter, Thomas, 1002
Augusta, Treaty of, 135
Auschwitz, 811
Austin, Moses and Stephen, 348
Austin, Warren T., 777
Australia, 513, 794, 847, 915
Austria, 671, 775, 865
Austria-Hungary: immigrants from, 514; in World War I, 649, 659, 671
Automation, 883
Automobile, *see* Transportation
Automobile industry, 685, 686, 882, 884, 976
Avery, William Waightstill, 318
Awful Disclosures of Maria Monk, The, 283
Axson, Ellen, 611
Ayer, N. W. & Son, 553
Azores, New England trade with, 5
Aztecs, 4, 8–9, 16, 17, 18. *See also* Indians

Babcock, Orville, 625
Baby boom, postwar, 880, 882, 977, 1015
Baby formula ban, 1006
Backus, Isaac, 203
Bacon, Nathaniel, and Bacon's Rebellion, 56–57, 65
Bahamas, Columbus lands in, 15
Bailey v. Drexel Furniture Company, 682
Baker, Newton D., 656, 659
Baker v. Carr, 948
Bakke v. University of California, 983
Balboa, Vasco Núñez de, 16
Baldwin, Roger, 667
Ball, George, 906, 918, 920, 1006
Ball, Lucille, 897
Ballinger, Richard A., 609
Baltimore, Lord (Cecilius Calvert), 25, 45
Baltimore, Maryland, 80, 224, 240, 271, 292, 888, 892
Baltimore and Ohio Railroad, 245
Bangladesh, 830
Bankhead, Tallulah, 720
Banking Act: of 1933, 741; of 1935, 747
Banking and finance: failures and closings, 231, 253, 575, 576, 608, 714, 716, 737; industry and railroads, 251, 253; national bank, 188–189, 227, 229, 231, 253; state banks, 227, 253, 341; free banking, 253; independent treasury system, 344, 345; Civil War and after, 392, 394, 414, 440; savings and investment, 489; home mortgages, 523, 752, 891, 893, 982, 1005; Federal Reserve system, 612; foreign investment, 622, 638, 639, 766, 769, 771–772, 867, 910, 928; Emergency Banking Relief Bill (1933), 737; city defaults, 979. *See also* Banking Act; Bank of the United States
CREDIT SYSTEM, 231, 251, 253, 262–263, 341; in triangular trade, 59; in tobacco trade, 79; specie circular, 342; collapse of, 344; National Banking Acts, 396; and stock market, 489; from chain stores, 543; installment buying, 681; and Great Depression, 716; postwar, 886, 978; and women, 968; interest rates, 982, 1000, 1001, 1002, 1018
CURRENCY, 167, 188, 341, 344, 396, 566–567, 575–576; distrust of, 227; greenbacks, 444; and crop-lien system, 472; free silver, 574, 581–582, 583; gold standard and gold reserves, 566, 738, 741
INTERNATIONAL: and Great Crash, 715–716; U.S. leadership in, 766; Export-Import Bank, 772, 774; World Bank, 826; International Monetary Fund, 826; devaluation of dollar, 964; Third World debt, 1011

Economic conditions (cont.)
through 1960s, 881, 887–888; guaranteed (FAP), 965; in cities vs. suburbs, 983; 1970s (nonwhites), 985, 986

INFLATION, 16, 21; 1779–80, 167; Civil War, 383, 390, 394; from 1889 to 1913, 538; in Coxey's plan, 578; World War I, 662, 670; 1930s, 738, 749; World War II, 798; postwar, 827, 834; Korean War, 848; in 1950s, 872, 874; COLA clauses and, 885, 977; 1960s–70s (stagflation), 928, 964, 972, 976–978, 979, 980, 981, 982, 994; in 1980s, 1000, 1002–1003, 1014

MARKET ECONOMY, 239; agriculture in, 239–240, 257–258, 262, 366; development of, 239–240, 298; boom-or-bust in, 240–241; and wage workers, 256; consumerism, 248, 536–537, 540, 542–543, 552–553, 614, 680–681, 685–688, 694, 835, 886, 898, 901, 950, 990; and yeomen, 303, 319; Populists against, 562; and Eisenhower era, 857

POVERTY: in colonies, 76–77; and social conflict, 268, 274–275; urban, 274, 283, 327, 519, 857; Civil War and, 389; crop-lien system and, 472–473; of blacks, 474, 721, 854, 880, 888, 889, 948, 950, 972, 982–983, 1004; of elderly, 692, 743; in 1928, 705; in 1950s, 854, 880, 885, 887–890, 902; and illness, 890; legislation against and war on, 890, 946, 947; of women, 890, 947, 972, 1004, 1012; in 1960s, 947, 950; of Indians, 985; of Hispanics, 986; in 1980s, 1004; definition of, 1004; of children, 1012

WEALTH, DISTRIBUTION OF: 1830s–50s, 273–274, 275–276; in the South, 302, 319; in Gilded Age, 562; income tax and, 614 (see also Taxation); 1920s, 715; and Share Our Wealth Society, 743–744; and New Deal, 758; and U.S. world image, 867, 869. See also Social class
See also Banking and finance; Labor; Lifestyle; Trade

Economic Opportunity Act (1964), 945–946
Economic Recovery Tax Act, 1018
Economies of scale, 486
Economy Act, 737, 743
Ecuador, 889, 986
Edenton Ladies Tea Party, 117, 118
Ederle, Gertrude, 680, 700
Edge Act, 765
Edison, Thomas A., 481–484, 504, 550, 551, 556, 588, 613, 621
Edmondston, Catherine Devereux, 308
Education: religion in, 331; for clerical work, 496; moral, 596; progressive, 596–597, 598; quantity stressed in, 598–599; and World War II, 806;

post-Sputnik, 872, 896–897; federal aid to, 942, 946, 947

AND BLACKS: after Revolution, 162; during Reconstruction, 434, 438; "separate but equal" in, 475, 598; and southern high schools, 601; at universities, 721, 723, 942, 983; and busing, 965–966

COLLEGE AND UNIVERSITY: colonial, 89, 90; and football, 548–549; in Progressive Era, 597; for women, 598, 988; increase in, 599; and civil liberties, 666; military training in, 675; increased enrollment, 692; football in, 699; for blacks, 721, 723, 942, 983; GI Bill, 895; black nationalism in, 951–952; "multiversity," 953; student unrest in, 953, 954, 956, 962, 963; female athletes in, 961; public segregation in, 475, 601, 860, 950; and immigrants, 517; and upward mobility, 540; increase in, 596, 598; and busing, 965–966; for Hispanics, 986

AND WOMEN: and republicanism, 154; Murray on, 158–159; as teachers, 277–278; among upper-class southerners, 308; sports in, 549; college, 598, 988

Education, U.S. Department of, 980
Educational Amendments Act (1972), 961
Edwards, Jonathan, 94–95
Eggleston, Edward, 557
Egypt, 409, 440, 867, 927; Suez Canal, 638, 871; Aswan Dam, 871, 872; Israel and, 924–925, 932
Ehrenreich, Barbara, 988
Ehrlichman, John, 974
Eighteenth Amendment, 595, 728
Einstein, Albert, 774
Eisenhower, Dwight D., 647, 724, 848–849, 862; as general, 792, 793, 821, 836; presidency of, 796, 846, 854–855, 856–860, 862–865, 866, 867, 869, 871, 872–875, 892, 897, 910, 915; and Eisenhower Doctrine, 872; and Vietnam, 913–914
Elder, Glen H., 895
Elderly, see Demographic factors, AGE
Elections, congressional: of 1788, 184; of 1834–40s, 343; of 1854, 364–365; of 1862, 1863, 406, 407; of 1865, 426, 427; of 1866, 427, 429; of 1874, 443; of 1878, 569; of 1918, 670; of 1932, 730; of 1934, 742, 745; of 1938, 749; of 1942, 808; of 1946, 821, 835; of 1948, 836; of 1950s, 849, 857–858, 872–873; of 1962, 912; of 1970s, 964, 968, 978; of 1980, 994–995; of 1982, 1005
Elections, presidential, 563; of 1789, 185–186; of 1792, 190; of 1796, 194–195; of 1800, 198–199, 218; peaceful transition of power in, 233; of 1804, 216; of 1808, 221; of 1812, 226; of 1816, 228; of 1820, 231, 263, 336; of 1824, 233, 336–

337, 336 (map), 343; caucus system ends, 336–337; of 1828, 335, 337; of 1832, 341; of 1836, 344; voting participation increase, 343; of 1840, 343, 344–345; of 1844, 348–349, 354; foreign policy issue arises, 348; of 1848, 357–358; of 1852, 363; of 1856, 370; of 1860, 354–355, 374, 375; of 1864, 410; of 1868, 442; of 1872, 442; of 1876, 445 (map), 445–446; of 1880, 569; of 1884, 570; of 1888, 570; of 1892, 571; of 1896, 562, 581–584; of 1900, 584, 635; voting participation decrease, 589; of 1904, 607; of 1908, 608; of 1912, 609, 610 (map), 684; of 1916, 809; of 1920, 683; of 1924, 684; of 1928, 705, 711; of 1932, 710–711, 728–731, 736; of 1936, 735, 747; of 1940, 756–758; of 1944, 808–809; of 1948, 836–837, 838, 850; of 1952, 821, 846, 848–849; blacks and, 803; of 1956, 858; of 1960, 855, 873, 874, 942, 944; of 1964, 918, 946; of 1968, 887, 921, 956, 958, 959; of 1972, 964–968, 972; Election Campaign Act, 975; of 1976, 980, 1000; of 1980, 935, 993–994, 1000; of 1984, 1000, 1014–1016

Electrical industry, 481–484
Electricity, see Technology, ELECTRICITY
Electronics, 883
Elementary and Secondary Education Act (1965), 946
Eleventh Amendment, 185
Eliot, Charles W., 597
Eliot, John, 32
Eliot, T. S., 703
Elizabeth I, queen of England, 13, 19, 20
Elizabethton textile strike, 713
Ellison, Ralph: Invisible Man, 901
Ellsberg, Daniel, 964, 973
Ellsworth, Oliver, 173, 185
El Salvador, 935, 1008–1009, 1010, 1016
Ely, Richard, 492, 599
Emancipation, see Slavery, EMANCIPATION FROM
Emancipation Proclamation, 399–400
Embargo Act, 219, 221
Emergency Banking Relief Bill, 737
Emergency Quota Act, 697
Emergency Relief Appropriation Act, 745
Emerson, Ralph Waldo, 329, 373
Empire State Building, 712
Employee Loyalty Program, 820
Employment Act of 1946, 833
Employment Board of the Civil Service Commission, 839
"End of ideology," 855–856
Energy, see Natural resources; Technology
Energy, U.S. Department of, 980
England: pre-1400 unimportance of, 13; Reformation in, 20–21; social disruption in, 21, 26; ethnocentrism

England (*cont.*)

of, 47; slave trade by, 51–52; and French Revolution, 191; and American manufacturing system, 247–248; immigrants from, 514; and Samoa, 625; and Venezuela, 627, 629; and China, 635; in World War I, 649, 650, 651; and Ireland, 652; at Paris Peace Conference, 671; and Middle Eastern oil, 766; in inter-war treaties, 768; and Munich, 775–776; in World War II, 782, 790, 791–792; in postwar world, 809, 810, 812; and Iranian oil, 825; and Greece, 826; decolonization of, 830; and Suez, 871–872; and Vietnam, 913, 914, 915. *See also* Revolutionary War

AND COLONIES, 16, 19–25; as trading with Indians, 53, 54; and French and Indian War, 100–101; American virtue contrasted with, 156. *See also* Colonies, English

U.S. RELATIONS WITH: Jay Treaty, 192–193; impressment by, 219; events leading to War of 1812, 219–222; continued conflict with, 226; and Monroe Doctrine, 230–231; and cotton trade, 299, 440; *1830s* tensions, 345; and Republic of Texas, 348, 349; and Oregon, 355; and Civil War, 409–410; and *Alabama* dispute, 410, 445, 625; rapprochement with, 625; loan to, 826

English Civil War, 41, 43

Enlightenment, the, 71, 87, 89–90, 91, 94, 203, 334

Enola Gay, 790

Entertainment: and republican virtue, 157; circuses, 549; as homogenizing influence, 551–552; in *1920s*, 698–699; in *1950s–1960s*, 880–881; television, 897

MOVIES: 551, 693, 699; and sexual freedom, 694; stars of, 700–701; in Great Depression, 720; black roles in, 721; in World War II, 798; anti-Communist blacklists in, 841; and TV, 897, 899; and adolescent audience, 899–900

SPORTS: baseball, 547, 699, 840; croquet and cycling, 547–548; golf, 548; tennis, 548, 699; football, 548–549, 699; and sports news, 554–555; in *1920s*, 699–700; heroes in, 700; in *1950s* and *1960s,* 901

THEATER: 268; popular drama, 549; musical comedy, 549–550; vaudeville, 550–551

See also Arts; Lifestyle, SOCIAL LIFE AND RECREATION

Environment: destruction and pollution of, 796, 1002; legislation protecting, 965. *See also* Natural resources

Environmental Protection Agency, 978, 1014

Epstein, Abraham, 693

Equal Credit Opportunity Act, 988

Equal Employment Opportunity Commission, 988

Equality: and republicanism, 156; of opportunity, 156, 278, 588; and women, 160, 988 (*see also* Feminism; Women); and racism, 163, 164 (*see also* Civil rights; Racism); and Second Awakening, 204; Tocqueville on, 273; among whites, 369; and bigotry, 520; and white male culture, 601; automobile as symbol of, 686; U.S. hypocrisy on, 867; and family life, 895–896; and Kennedy, 944; as feminist goal, 961; for middle-class blacks, 983. *See also* Economic conditions, WEALTH, DISTRIBUTION OF

Equal Opportunity Commission, 954

Equal Rights Amendment (ERA), 694, 961, 988, 1012

Equiano, Olaudah, 40–41, 47, 51, 53

Era of Good Feelings, 229

Erie Canal, 238, 245, 251, 258, 262, 269, 326

Ervin, Sam, 973

Escobedo v. *Illinois,* 949

Espionage Act (1917), 666, 667

Est (Erhard Seminars Training), 990

Estonia, 671, 823

Ethiopia: Italy invades, 774, 775; famine in, 1011

Ethnicity: in politics, 194, 532; and Whigs vs. Democrats, 343; chipping away of, 516; and neighborhoods, 524; and lifestyle, 532; and social relations, 540; and show business, 551; and law, 599; and World War I, 649; and isolationism, 774; of Hispanic immigrants, 986; and "Roots," 991. *See also* Immigrants; Racism

Europe: social organization of, 13; political and technological change in, 14; American virtue contrasted with, 156; Napoleonic Wars in, 218; American disengagement from, 226; *1890s* slump in, 576; World War I effect on, 766; World War II devastation in, 820, 821; division of, 828 (map); U.S. troops in, 847

European exploration and expansion, 4, 14–17, 22 (map); cultural contact through, 5; motives for, 15; disease spread by, 17–18; plant/animal exchange through, 18–19; impact of, 36

European Recovery Plan (Marshall Plan), 827

Evangelism, *see* Religion, EVANGELICAL

Evans, Rowland, 944

Evans, Hiram Wesley, 695

Everly Brothers, 900

Evers, Medgar, 943

Exceptionalism, American, 650

Executive branch: and separation of powers, 175, 430; and executive privilege, 193; and Jackson, 339;

and veto, 342; and Civil War, 383, 392, 396; and World War II, 797–798; and Vietnam War, 929; impoundment by, 975. *See also* Government, federal; Presidency

Exodusters, 446

Exogamy, and European social organization, 13

Expansion and expansionism, 199–201, 206, 210–211, 214, 354, 618, 623, 628, 638; and War of 1812, 222; and Adams, 229; and slavery, 232, 234, 363; commercial and industrial, 238–239, 487; Indian resistance to, 285; economic, 343, 508, 622–623, 674–675, 765–766, 822; overseas revival of, 618–621, 623–626, 640; as "manifest destiny," 619; and foreign commerce, 621–623; annexation of Hawaii, 626–627; imperialist–anti-imperialist debate, 631–635; Roosevelt Corollary, 639–640; and Middle East oil, 814; and Cold War, 822–823 (*see* Cold War); in post-Vietnam debate, 929–930. *See also* Foreign affairs; Westward expansion

Ex parte Milligan, 441

Export-Import Bank, 772, 774

Extended family, 86, 542, 545

Extraterritoriality, 778

Exxon Oil, 884, 928

Factors, Scots, 79–80

Factory Girl, 255

Factory Girl's Garland, 255

Fairbanks, Douglas, 700–701

Fairbanks House, Dedham, Massachusetts, 33

Fair Deal, 838, 842, 848, 850, 854, 857, 890

Fair Employment Practices Committee (FEPC), 753

Fair Labor Standards Act (1938), 749, 752, 755, 756

Fall, Albert, 684

Fallen Timbers, battle of, 170, 171

Fall River, Massachusetts, 241

Falwell, Rev. Jerry, 992, 1016

Family Assistance Plan (FAP), 965

Family life: slavery and, 86, 201, 315, 439; extended family, 86, 544, 555; of yeomen, 303, 305; and boarding, 538, 545; industrialization and, 543–546; and other institutions, 546; and working women, 664, 694, 894–895, 989; and Great Depression, 719; "profamily" views, 972, 988

CHANGE IN, 277, 279; and automobile, 686; in *1920s,* 691; in World War II, 806; and counterculture, 954; and feminism, 958–959

CHILDREN: slum, 274–275; juvenile delinquency, 806; child-care facilities, 806, 961; in World War II, 806; postwar baby boom, 880, 882, 894–896, 897; in suburbs, 891, 893; in poverty, 982–983, 1012

Family life (cont.)
IN COLONIES, 27–28, 34, 81–83; patriarchal system, 13
See also Demographic factors; Women
Famine, in Africa, 929, 1011
Farm Credit Act, 738
Farmers' Alliances, 573–574, 579
Farmers' Holiday Association, 723–724, 736–737, 743
Farming, see Agriculture; Lifestyle, RURAL
Farm Security Administration (FSA), 755
Farragut, Adm. David, 383–384
Fascism, 745, 775; "Red," 822
Father Knows Best, 897
Faubus, Orval, 860
Faulkner, William, 703
Federal Bureau of Investigation (FBI), 781, 949, 963, 973
Federal Council of Churches, 862
Federal Deposit Insurance Corporation (FDIC), 735, 741
Federal Election Campaign Act of 1972, 975
Federal Emergency Relief Act, 738, 756
Federal Farm Board, 726
Federal Farm Loan Act of 1916, 612
Federal government, see Government, federal
Federal Highway Act, 686
Federal Housing Administration (FHA), 752, 891, 893
Federalist, The (political essays), 178, 187
Federalist party, 190, 193–195, 210, 211, 221, 226–227, 229, 336, 337; and Supreme Court, 212, 213; and Younger Federalists, 216–217, 218, 221, 226
Federal Republic of Germany (West Germany), see Germany
Federal Reserve Act (1913), 612
Federal Reserve Board/System, 716, 749, 976, 978, 982
Federal Securities Act, 741
Federal Trade Commission (FTC), 611–612, 682, 715, 884
Federal Writers', Theatre, and Music Projects (1930s), 745
Fellowship of Reconciliation, 767–768
Female Moral Reform Society, 327
Feminism: of Abigail Adams, 154; of Murray, 158–159; and mother's role, 160; Seneca Falls meeting, 280; and antiprostitution movement, 327; and Shakers, 328; rise of, 331; of the Grimkes, 331–332; and abolitionism, 331–332, 429, 604–605; female suffrage, 433, 646; suffrage movement, 567, 568, 604–605; and female identity, 603, 604; and Ederle, 680; economic, 694; social, 756; in consensus history, 856; as maladjusted or neurotic, 856, 894, 988; radical, 959, 961; and gay rights, 961; and civil rights movement, 961; vs. "profamily" movement, 988; of 1970s, 988–

990; and comparable worth, 1012–1013; and Ferraro, 1015. See also Civil rights; Women
Fenian Brotherhood, 623
Ferdinand, king of Spain, 14
Ferraro, Geraldine, 1000, 1015
Fifteenth Amendment, 421, 431, 442, 447, 579, 839
"Fifty-four Forty or Fight," 348
Filene, E. A., 591
Fillmore, Millard, 357, 370
Films, see Entertainment, MOVIES
Finance, see Banking and finance
Fine, Benjamin, 895
Finland, 671, 777, 781, 823
Finlay, Carlos, 637–638
Finney, Charles G., 326–327
Firestone, Shulamith: The Dialectic of Sex, 959
First World War, see World War I
Fish, Hamilton, 445, 625, 774
Fisher, Sidney George, 240
Fisk University, 438
Fitch, George: The City, 513
Fitzgerald, F. Scott, 703
Fitzhugh, George, 362–363
Five Nations, see Iroquois/Iroquois Confederacy
"Five-percenters," 848
Five Points, N.Y., 274, 275, 281
Five-Power Treaty, 768
Fixx, James: Complete Book of Running, 991
Flappers, 694
Fleming, Samuel, 318
Flesch, Dr. Rudolf: Why Johnny Can't Read, 896
Fletcher, Benjamin, 94
Fletcher v. Peck, 229
Flexible response, 907
Flint, C. R., 477
Flintoff, John F., 303–305
Florida: Spanish, 53, 54, 105, 150, 224, 229–230, 289, 319; Indians in, 54; negotiations for and purchase of, 259, 346; secedes, 376
"Flower children," 954
Floyd, John, 341
Flynn, Elizabeth Gurley, 592
Food Administration, 661
Food riots, 403, 508
Food stamps, 965, 1001, 1005
Football, 548–549
Forbes, Charles, 683
Forbes, John M., 396
Force Act(s), 340, 442
"Force bill," 571
Ford, Gerald, 922, 972, 975, 978, 979, 980, 982
Ford, Henry, 484, 522, 550, 588, 685, 688; and Ford Motor Company, 484; "peace ship" of, 655; in Soviet Union, 777
Ford Hunger March, 710
Ford Motor Company, 484, 495, 832, 884, 942, 976, 1012
Fordney-McCumber Tariff, 682
Foreign affairs: president given charge of, 175; and Washington's Farewell

Address, 194; "Quasi-War" with France, 195–196, 198; in Civil War, 409–410; and Gilded Age presidents, 569; and McKinley, 584; and expansionism, 618, 619–620, 822 (see also Expansion and expansionism); domestic roots of, 619; and foreign policy elite, 620; and U.S. racism, 620, 840, 867; and Seward's expansionism, 623, 625; disputes with England, 625; and Hawaii, 626–627; and Spanish-American War, 628–631; debates on, 649; and Wilson vs. Congress, 652; and war debts, 671, 726, 766–767, 773; and New Deal demise, 748, 749; and Latin America, 769–773 (see also Latin America); and Great Depression, 773; and Soviet Russia, 777 (see also Soviet Russia,–U.S. RELATIONS); and China, 778; and Japanese aggression, 778, 780–781, 785–786; in World War II, 809–815; Cold War, 820, 821–832, 854 (see also Cold War); and foreign aid, 827, 929; and Korean War, 846–847; Asian specialists lost, 863; and Third World, 866–872 (see also Third World); and revolutionary disorder, 867, 927; in 1960 election, 873; and Vietnam War, 907, 929 (see also Vietnam War); chauvinism in, 935; current problems in, 1011–1012
POLICIES: neutrality between British and French, 191; Open Door policy, 635–636; dollar diplomacy, 637, 640; and Panama Canal, 638–639; Roosevelt Corollary, 639–640; collective security vs. unilateralism, 673, 764; independent internationalism, 764; Hull's internationalism in, 773–774; isolationism in, 774, 776, 781; Neutrality Acts, 776; support of Allies, 781–784; anti-Communism, 820–821; globalism, 821, 847, 864, 913; Eisenhower-Dulles policies, 863–865, 867; Eisenhower Doctrine, 872; human rights campaign, 930; under Reagan, 1000–1001, 1005–1012, 1014, 1016
See also specific nations, presidents, treaties, and wars
Foreign investments, 622, 638, 639, 766, 769, 771–772, 867, 910, 928
Formosa, 635
Formosa Resolution, 866. See also Taiwan (Formosa)
Forrest, Edwin, 268
Forrest, Gen. Nathan Bedford, 389
Forrestal, James, 823
Fort Christina, 16
Fort Dearborn, 223
Fort Donelson, 384
Fort Duquesne, 104, 106
Forten, James, 293
Fort Henry, 384
Fort Necessity, 104

Ginsberg, Allen: *Howl*, 902
Gish, Lillian, 551
Gitlow, Benjamin, 669
Gladden, Washington, 529, 629
Glenn, Lt. Col. John, 944
Globalism, 821, 847, 864, 913
"Glorious Revolution" (England), 63–64, 92, 110
Gnadenhuetten; massacre at, 149
Godkin, E. L., 565, 623
Golan Heights, 925, 1010
Gold Coast, 11, 49
Goldman, Emma, 669
Gold Rush, 261–262
Goldsboro Christian Institute, 1013
Gold standard, 566, 738, 741
Gold Standard Act (1900), 584
Goldwater, Barry, 946, 958, 993, 1009
Golf, 548
Gompers, Samuel, 501, 583, 632, 633, 662
Good Neighbor Policy, 765, 769–773, 776, 870
Goodyear, 1012
Gordon, Thomas, 109
Gore-McLemore resolution, 652, 654
Gorgas, Josiah, 388, 389, 405
Goulart, Joas, 912–913
Gould, Jay, 396
Government, colonial: representative, 25, 28, 31, 44, 45, 62–63, 92; legal system, 61; rebellion against, 56–57, 63–64, 94; and "virtual representation," 108, 110; British vs. American view of, 109; and Parliamentary power over colonies, 110, 111, 115, 120, 121; and Townshend Acts, 115; revolutionary, 129–132
Government, federal: checks and balances in, 165, 174; first revenues of, 170, 189 (*see also* Tariff; Taxation); representation in, 174–175; cabinet in, 185; executive privilege in, 193; and public lands, 456; and New Deal, 758; bureaucratic growth in, 797–798; loyalty program in, 820, 841–842, 850, 854, 859, 874; revenue sharing by, 965
CENTRALIZATION AND DECENTRALIZATION OF, 182, 187–188, 324, 338–339; Confederacy and, 388; war and, 659, 661, 674
DESIGN OF, 173–176; Virginia and New Jersey plans, 174, 175
INTERVENTION: trade regulation, 461–462; trademark law, 553; and change, 605; in economy, 606–607, 610–611, 612–613, 712, 736, 739, 758, 978, 1002. *See also* Economic conditions, GOVERNMENT INVOLVEMENT WITH
SUBSIDIES AND AID: highway, 227, 686, 745, 858, 892; technology, 242, 481; railroad, 460; business, 490–491, 681–684; housing, 519, 857, 893, 947; hydroelectric power, 857. *See also* Business, AND GOVERNMENT

See also Congress; Executive branch; Foreign affairs; Presidency
Government, state: and federal assumption of debt, 187–188; and economic growth, 243–244; agriculture promoted by, 258; and Civil War, 427; railroad regulation by, 461
Grady, Henry, 476
Graham, Rev. Billy, 897, 1006
Graham, Martha, 901
Grain Coast, 11
Grand Army of the Republic, 564
Grand Coulee Dam, 726
Grange, Harold ("Red"), 700
Grange movement, 572–573
Grant, Madison: *The Passing of the Great Race*, 696
Grant, Ulysses S.: as general, 384, 386, 404–405, 408, 410, 412–413, 430; presidency of, 442–443, 444, 445, 565, 618, 625
Grasse, Comte de, 149
Grasso, Ella, 988
Grau San Martín, Ramon, 772
"Great Awakening," 70, 71, 94–96, 201; Second, 201–205, 232, 287, 324, 326–327, 331
Great Britain, *see* England
Great Depression, *see* Depression, Great
Greater East Asia Co-Prosperity Sphere, 785
Great Lakes, 224, 245, 247, 857
Great Lakes Naval Training Station, 500
Great Society, 940, 944–948, 950, 964, 1004
"Great White Fleet," 637
Greece: postwar, 810, 813, 821, 826, 829; U.S. aid to, 826
Greeley, Horace, 368, 399, 442
Green, William, 749, 750
Green Berets, 912
Green Corn Rebellion, 665
Greene, Gen. Nathanael, 148
Greenland, 782
Greensboro, North Carolina, 862
Greenville, Treaty of, 171, 183, 193, 201, 286
Greenwood, John, 60
Greer incident, 783–784
Grenada invasion, 1001, 1011, 1016
Grenville, George, 108–110, 114
Gresham, Walter Q., 620
Grey, Edward, 650
Grey, Zane, 555
Griffith, D. W., 551, 664
Grimké, Angelina, 317, 331–332
Grimké, Sarah, 158, 317, 331–332
Griswold v. *Connecticut*, 948
Gromyko, Andrei, 912
Grossman, Meyer, 522
Gross national product, 685, 716, 827, 834, 848, 874, 881, 947, 1014
Gruening, Ernest, 916
Guadalcanal, 795
Guadelupe-Hidalgo, Treaty of, 357
Guam, 631, 794
Guantánamo Bay, Cuba, 631, 637, 772
Guatemala, 869–870, 1008

Guerrilla warfare, 148, 149, 204, 919
Guilford Court House, battle at, 148
Guinea, *see* West Africa
Guiteau, Charles, 565, 569
Gulflight (tanker), 652
Gullah dialect, 48
Guyana, 991

Habeas corpus, writ of, 176–177; suspended, 396, 407
Haber, Al, 953
Hague peace conferences, 640
Haight-Ashbury, 954
Haiti, 987; slave revolt in, 204, 291; U.S. intervention in, 639, 640, 769, 771, 772, 776
Halberstam, David, 942
Haldeman, H. R., 964, 973, 974
Hale, Eugene, 635
Hale, John P., 363
Haley, Alex, 991
Haley, Bill, 900
"Halfway Covenant," 58
Hall, G. Stanley, 596
Halsey, Adm. William, 794
Hamilton, Alexander, 156, 168, 178, 186–187, 188, 189, 190, 191, 192, 193, 194, 195, 212, 218, 227, 229, 593, 606; "Report on Manufactures," 189, 250
Hamilton, Dr. Alexander, 70–71, 90
Hammond County, Indiana, 292
Hampton Institute, 602
Hampton Roads Conference, 400–401, 425
Hampton's magazine, 590
Hancock, John, 100, 118
Hancock, Thomas, 78
Hancock, Winfield Scott, 569
Handsome Lake, Chief, 205–206
Hanna, Marcus Alonzo, 581, 583, 605
Harding, Warren Gamaliel, 682, 683–684, 703, 705, 736, 764
Hard Labor, Treaty of, 135
Hardy, Irene, 269–270
Harlan County, Kentucky, 724
Harlem Renaissance, 703
Harlem Tenants' League, 723
Harmer, Gen. Josiah, 171
Harper's Ferry, Virginia, 248, 373
Harper's Monthly, 467
Harriman, E. H., 593
Harriman, W. Averell, 830
Harrington, Michael: 965; *The Other America*, 880
Harris, Abram L., 752
Harris, Joel Chandler, 557
Harris, Thomas: *I'm OK—You're OK*, 990
Harris, William T., 529
Harrison, Benjamin, 569, 570–571, 627
Harrison, William Henry, 224, 286, 344, 570; presidency of, 344–345
Harris v. *McRae*, 989
Hart, Albert Bushnell, 673
Hart, Gary, 992, 1015
Harte, Bret, 457, 557
Hartford, Connecticut, witchcraft panic, 65

Ideology (cont.)
  "end of," 855–856. See also
  Communism
Illinois, 232, 244, 269, 361, 407, 719;
  blacks in, 291
Illinois Central railroad, 263
I Love Lucy, 897
Immigrants: and Great Awakening, 94;
  in textile mills, 250, 255, 256; and
  social tensions, 273; women, 280;
  numbers of, 280, 646; and cities,
  281–282; in rural areas, 282; disenchantment of, 282–283; personal
  conflicts of, 284; and western settlement, 467; and South, 476; in
  factories, 494; and labor unions,
  500, 504; institutions of, 516; and
  crime, 520; and police, 520; and
  occupational mobility, 522; and
  family pattern, 544; as boarders,
  545; fertility among, 545; in show
  business, 550, 551; diplomatic
  problems from, 620; in Seward's
  plans, 623; and World War I, 655,
  666, 673; blacks contrasted with,
  983; economic prospects for, 986,
  987; statistics, A-18–A-19
  MAJOR WAVES OF: 1848–1860, 365;
  1870–1920, 514–517; newest influx, 987
  NATIONALITIES: Jews, 74, 284, 516,
  517; Irish, 268, 280, 281, 283,
  284, 305, 330, 344, 407, 458, 514,
  649; Germans, 280, 281, 282,
  283–284, 330, 407, 514, 647, 648;
  Puerto Rican, 689–690; 986; Mexican, 689–690, 889 (see also Mexico, MEXICAN-AMERICANS); Japanese,
  779; Jews refused as, 810–811; of
  Indochinese, 923; Hispanic, 986–
  987. See also other countries of
  emigration
  AND POLITICS, 194, 532; and Federal-
  ist-Republican split, 194; and Hartford Convention proposals, 227;
  freethinkers, 284; and machine politics, 528; and populism, 575; and
  political reformers, 590
Immigration: and social diversity, 268–
  269; hardships of, 280; stimulus to,
  280, 282; and labor demand, 394;
  after Civil War, 444; and industrialization, 481, 508; and city
  growth, 513; and 1890s depression,
  576; opposition to, 695–696, 696–
  697, 698; and Simpson-Mazzoli
  bill, 1015
Impeachment, 175–176, 212–213, 420,
  430–431, 975
Imperialism, 618, 620–621, 623, 627;
  vs. anti-imperialism, 631–635; in
  China, 635; toward South America, 640; economic expansionism
  as, 766, 929; and Japan, 779; in
  Vietnam, 913, 915; welfare, 916.
  See also Expansion and
  expansionism
"Imperial" presidency, 758
Impressment, 219, 220, 226

Incas, 16, 17. See also Indians
Inchon landing, 845
Income, see Economic conditions,
  INCOME
Income tax, 612, 614, 662
Indentured servitude, 26, 47, 48, 73–
  74, 79
Independent internationalism, 764
India, 409, 440, 672, 830, 866, 867,
  869, 928, 987, 1011
Indiana, 232, 407, 570, 719
Indian Affairs, Bureau of, 464
Indian Bill of Rights, 947
Indian Claims Commission, 986
Indian Reorganization Act, 753–754
Indian Rights Association, 448
Indians, American, 5–9, 6 (map), 22
  (map), 102 (map); colonists aided
  by, 4; and European diseases, 4,
  17–18, 47; and Paleo-Indians, 5;
  social organization of, 5, 7–8, 9;
  population of, 9, 985; Columbus
  names, 15; and Spanish, 16, 53–
  54; trade with, 17, 23, 54; and
  horses, 19; European attitudes toward, 23, 24, 47, 55; and Virginia
  settlement, 23–25; and property
  rights, 24; and New England settlers, 29–30, 31–32; and slavery,
  47, 54; and blacks, 75; and French-
  English rivalry, 100–101, 101–103,
  106; in Revolutionary War, 135–
  136, 146, 148, 149–150; and Jay
  Treaty, 192–193; and War of 1812,
  222, 224, 226, 285, 286; as frontier guides, 259; assimilation of,
  287, 290, 464; and buffalo, 452,
  464; on western frontier, 455; and
  Philippine Insurrection, 636; in
  Great Depression, 719; in cities,
  889; militancy of, 984–985; illnesses among, 985. See also other
  specific tribes or groups
  GOVERNMENT POLICY TOWARD: Penn's
  policies, 46; lands ceded by, 169,
  169 (map), 171; and westward expansion, 206, 287, 290, 462–465;
  and Louisiana Purchase, 214; removal, 242, 269, 284, 285, 287–
  290, 299, 346; as sovereign nations, 284–285; agency system,
  287; reservations, 464–465; and
  New Deal, 734, 753–754; allotment policy, 754; termination policy, 857, 889; dual legal status,
  985–986; and Reagan administration, 1013
  MASSACRES OF: at Conestoga, 107; at
  Gnadenhuetten, 149–150; at
  Wounded Knee, 465
  TREATIES WITH, 24, 285, 287, 463–
  464; of Augusta (1773), 135; of
  Lochaber (1770), 135; at Hard Labor Creek (1768), 135; at Fort
  Stanwix (1768), 135; at Fort Stanwix (1784), 169; at Hopewell
  (1785–86), 169; of Greenville,
  171, 183, 193, 201, 286; coercion
  in, 285; of Fort Wayne, 286; with

Cherokees (1835), 289; Payne's
  Landing, 290; and Alcatraz take-
  over, 985; and dual legal status,
  985–986
Indian wars: against Powhatan Confederacy, 25; Pequot War, 32; Pueblo
  rebellion, 53; Tuscarora War, 54,
  65; Yamasee War, 54, 65; against
  Susquehannock, 56–57; King Philip's War, 57; and King William's
  War, 64; on Carolina and Virginia
  frontiers, 106; Pontiac's uprising,
  106–107; Lord Dunmore's War,
  136; against Creeks (1780s), 169;
  against Miami confederacy, 171; in
  War of 1812, 222, 224; Creek
  War, 224; Seminole Wars, 285,
  290; against Plains Indians, 464
Indigo, 49, 58, 61
Individualism: of yeomen, 303, 318; of
  Romanticists, 329; and Jackson,
  339; and frontier, 452; economic,
  528, 588; vs. consumerism, 540;
  FDR on, 606; prior to Great
  Depression, 712, 713; of Hoover,
  712, 721
Indochina, 785, 830, 847, 863, 866,
  913, 987. See also Vietnam
Indonesia, 830, 866, 867, 869
Industrialization and industrialism, 480–
  481; and women's role, 268; ambivalence toward, 324, 325; in
  Confederate states, 388; in North
  during Civil War, 392; during Reconstruction, 434; and Civil War
  debt, 444; in South, 453, 472,
  475–476; and labor conditions,
  480; and invention, 481–485; and
  efficiency study, 486; social imbal-
  ance from, 494; mechanization of
  labor in, 494; and unions, 500,
  501; results of, 504; and cities,
  511; and violence, 520; problems
  seen solved for, 881; and employment opportunities, 983; Industrial
  Workers of the World (IWW),
  502, 504, 592, 662, 666–667, 669
Industrial Workers of the World
  (IWW), 502, 504, 592, 662, 665,
  666–667, 669
Industry: Hamilton's report on, 189,
  250; government investment in
  support of, 227; and market economy, 239–241, 256; and patent
  system, 242; American system in,
  247–248; and industrial revolution,
  248; and War of 1812, 211, 226,
  233–234, 240, 251; and tariffs, 231
  (see also Tariffs); water power in,
  250; "putting-out" vs. Waltham
  system, 250; and credit systems,
  251, 253; in frontier cities, 264;
  specialization in, 277, 481; southern, 302; in Confederacy, 388; in
  North during Civil War, 392; and
  railroad expansion, 459–460; 1919
  production from, 483; mass production, 483, 681; mechanization of,
  494–495, 497–498; in World War

Jones v. Mayer, 948
Joplin, Janis, 953
Jordan, Vernon, 984
Jordan, Israel vs., 925, 1011
Jordan Marsh department store, 542
Journalism, see News media
Juan de Fuca Strait, 229
Judd, Walter, 832
Judicial branch, 184, 185; and judicial veto, separation of powers, 175–176; impeachment of, 212–213. See also Courts; Supreme Court, U.S.; and individual court cases
Judicial review, 214
Judiciary Acts, 185, 212, 214, 216
Judiciary Reorganization Bill, 748
Julian, George, 427
Justice Act, 123

Kamikaze attacks, 795
Kansas, 286, 468; settlement of, 290, 467; slavery controversy over, 369–370, 372–373; black migration to (Exodusters), 446, 601; cattle population of, 465; farmers' alliances in, 573, 574
Kansas City, as model, 778
Kansas City machine politics, 526, 527, 808
Kansas-Nebraska Act, 363–364
Kansas Pacific Railroad, 452
Kassebaum, Nancy, 988
Katyn Forest massacre, 810
KDKA, Pittsburgh, 688
Kearney, Col. Stephen, 357
Kearney incident, 784
Keaton, Buster, 699
Kelley, Florence, 529–530, 592–593, 600
Kelley, Oliver H., 572
Kellogg, Paul, 655
Kellogg-Briand Pact, 768, 769, 779–780
Kelly, "Honest John," 527
Kemble, Fanny, 298
Kennan, George F., 824, 826, 920, 931
Kennedy, Edward M., 931, 966, 981, 994, 1006
Kennedy, Jacqueline, 940, 941, 944, 945
Kennedy, John F.: presidency of, 854–855, 873, 875, 907–912, 915, 940–944, 945, 958, 968, 1015; and Vietnam, 906, 907, 935; assassinated, 915, 940, 944, 945; Profiles in Courage, 942
Kennedy, Joseph P., 847, 941
Kennedy, Robert, 910, 911, 942, 956–957
Kent State University, 962
Kentucky, 201, 238, 319, 339, 386–387; rejects secession, 377, 383
Kentucky Resolutions, 197–198
Kern, Jerome, 549–550
Kerner, Otto, and Kerner Commission, 941, 950
Kerouac, Jack: On the Road, 902
Kesey, Ken, 940
Keynes, John Maynard, 739
Khmer Rouge, 922

Khomeini, Ayatollah Ruhollah, 932
Khrushchev, Nikita, 865–866, 869, 872, 873, 907, 911–912
Kim Il-sung, 845
King, Martin Luther, Jr., 861–862, 873, 943, 949, 950, 951, 956, 1015
King, Rufus, 173, 216, 221, 228
King George's War, King William's War, 64, 77–78, 80, 93, 103
King Kong (film), 720
"King Philip," see Metacomet, Chief
King Philip's War, 57
King's College, 70. See also Columbia University
King's Mountain, battle at, 148
Kingston, New York, 270, 271
Kinsey, Dr. Alfred, 897, 902
Kiowas, 446. See also Indians
Kipling, Rudyard, 509, 632–633
Kissinger, Henry A., 922, 923–928, 967
Kitchen, Claude, 655
Klamath tribe, 857
Knights of the Golden Circle, 407
Knights of Labor, 500, 501, 502, 504, 573
Knowland, William, 832
Knowlton, Dr. Charles: Fruits of Philosophy . . . , 279
Know-Nothing party, 365–366, 370
Knox, Frank, 781
Knox, Henry, 186
Knox College (Illinois), 416
Koale-xoa, 260
Komarovsky, Mirra, 755
Konoye, Prince Fumimaro, 785
Korea: Japan and, 635, 636–637, 778–779, 830, 847; immigrants from, 637, 987; and Pueblo, 956
Korean Air Lines incident, 1008
Korean War, 821, 830, 832, 843–847; and Eisenhower, 848; and military spending, 882–883
Korematsu, Fred, 802
Korematsu case, 801
Krock, Arthur, 742
Krutch, Joseph Wood, 681
Ku Klux Klan: during Reconstruction, 421, 436–437, 442, 580; revivals of, 551, 664, 680, 684, 695, 698, 839, 860, 972, 983–984; and FBI, 949
Kurihara, Joseph Y., 801

Labor: indentured, 26, 47, 48, 73–74, 79; workplace for, 254–256; farm, 258; of landless whites, 305; free, 367, 369, 423, 440; industrialization and, 480–481, 494–495, 497–498, 538–539, 547; and scientific management, 486; of women, 495–496, 498, 503 (see also Women, WORKING); legislation on, 498; foreign competition for, 632; migrant, 754–755; in World War II, 806; 1960s–1970s labor market, 977; statistics, A-20
BLACK, 318, 409, 518; wartime, 662–663, 803; in Great Depression, 716–717, 721

CHILD, 496–497, 538; regulations on, 497, 595, 612, 614, 682–683, 693
UNEMPLOYMENT: industrialization and automation and, 504; and urban economy, 519; post-World War I, 681; 1930s, 710, 716–717, 717–718, 720, 721, 724, 717–718, 720, 721, 724; among blacks, 721, 735, 742, 749, 759, 1003; World War II and postwar, 760, 832, 833–834, 872; technological, 883; 1960s–80s, 964, 976–977, 978, 982, 1000, 1003–1004, 1014, 1018; among Indians, 985; effects of, 1004
Labor strikes: by women, 254–255; Civil War, 394; of 1877, 498–499, 569, 577; and Knights of Labor, 500; Haymarket riot, 500, 577; employers' associations against, 500–501; Pullman, 502, 571–572; Homestead, 502, 577; mineworkers', 502, 577, 607–608, 646, 724, 797, 834; garment workers', 503; New Orleans general strike, 577; World War I, 662; of 1919, 668; Seattle general strike, 668; police, 668, 684; steelworkers', 668–669; textile workers', 713; farmers', 723–724; sit-down, 750–751; Mexican-American, 754–755; World War II, 797; postwar, 834
Labor unions, 256–257, 499–504; Civil War and, 394; antitrust provisions and, 494; membership in, 500, 502–503, 682, 885, 983; women in, 500, 502–504; blacks in, 500, 504; and non-union workers, 504; World War I and, 662, 674; in 1920s, 682, 712–713; and yellow-dog contracts, 721; and New Deal, 739, 746, 749–752; craft vs. industrial, 749; struggle within, 749–750; Mexican-American, 754–755; and World War II, 791, 797; and politics, 834–835; and Taft-Hartley Act, 835–836; and right-to-work laws, 887; white collar, 983; and Reagan, 1000, 1013; and immigration, 1015
ORGANIZATIONS: National Trade Union, 256; National Labor Union, 499; Knights of Labor, 500, 501, 502, 504, 573; American Federation of Labor (AFL), 501–502, 504, 662, 721, 749–750, 810, (AFL-CIO), 884–885, 980, 1013, 1015; United Mine Workers (UMW), 502, 607, 749, 834; Industrial Workers of the World (IWW), 502, 504, 662; Women's Trade Union League (WTUL), 503–504, 734; American Railway Union, 577; Congress of Industrial Organizations (CIO), 734, 747, 750, 752, 803, 840, (AFL-CIO), 884–885; International Ladies' Garment Workers Union (ILGWU), 749; United Brewery Workers, 749; Teamsters, 749, 885; United Auto

Military (cont.)
hearings, 859. See also Conscription and recruitment; specific wars
COLONIAL MILITIA, 103–104, 105–106; recruitment of, 105; in Revolutionary War, 137, 138–139, 141, 143 (see also NATIONAL MILITIA, below; state militia, above)
MARINE CORPS: in Tripoli, 219; in Latin America, 637, 771; blacks in, 802; at Inchon, 845; and Mayaguez, 922
NATIONAL GUARD, 723, 848; and violence, 724, 860–861, 957
NATIONAL MILITIA: callup authorized (1803), 214; blacks barred from (1792), 290
NAVY: in War of 1812, 222, 223–224; enlargement of, 619, 626, 629, 655, 776; as "Great White Fleet," 637
TROOPS ABROAD: Cuba, 630; Philippines, 630, 636; Siberia, 667; Vietnam, 906, 918–922, 923; 1970s, 927. See also Korean War; World War I; World War II
See also Defense, U.S. Department of; Foreign affairs; War(s); War veterans
Military-industrial complex, 647, 796, 815, 875, 956
Military Reconstruction Act (1867), 430
Military spending, 882–883, 1004–1005, 1005–1006
Miller, Arthur, 842
Miller, David, 334
Miller, Thomas W., 683
Millett, Kate: Sexual Politics, 959
Milligan, Lambdin P., 441
Mills, C. Wright, 893
Milwaukee, Wisconsin, 264, 284, 511, 516
Miniature golf, 691, 699
Mining, 453–454, 456, 608
Minnesota, 423, 453
Minor, Frances and Virginia, and women suffrage case, 567
Minority groups: on western frontier, 455; and police, 520; and machine politics, 528; in Great Depression, 710. See also Blacks; Hispanics; Women
Minstrel shows, 551
Miranda v. Arizona, 949
MIRVs (missiles), 924
Miss America Pageant, 680, 959
Missiles, 864, 907, 908, 924, 930, 931
Mississippi, 299, 302, 319, 579; admitted to Union, 232; slavery in, 291; secedes, 376; black voters in, 947; and civil rights movement, 943, 949, 953, 965; Jackson State killings, 962
Mississippi Freedom Democratic Party (MFDP), 949
Mississippi River: navigation rights on, 168, 193; as transportation route, 214, 244, 246, 247

Mississippi Summer Project (1964), 949, 953
Missouri: admission of, to Union (Missouri Compromise), 232 (map), 233, 234, 290, 334, 359, 364, 371; rejects secession, 377, 383
Mitchell, Clarence, 945
Mitchell, John (labor leader), 607
Mitchell, John, 965, 973
Mobil Oil, 884, 962
Mobile, Alabama, 292, 306, 388, 403, 887; population, 302
Mobility: Tocqueville on, 273; promise of, 521–522, 525; through property acquisition, 522, 523; occupational, 522–523; residential, 523–524; and education, 540, 895; and nuclear household, 544; for women, 805
Moctezuma (Aztec ruler), 16
Model cities program, 947
Mohawk and Hudson Railroad, 238
Mohawk River Valley, 73, 74, 144, 145
Mohawks, 55, 145. See also Indians
Moley, Raymond, 736
Molotov, V. M., 823, 824
Molotov Plan, 827
Momism, 894
Mondale, Walter, 980, 1000, 1001, 1013, 1014–1015, 1016
Monetary policy, 566, 976
Monetary system, during Revolutionary War, 167–168
Money, see Banking and finance
Monongahela Valley, 106
Monopoly, 490, 611; fears of, 493, 500, 562, 588; Sugar Trust, 493; and trust-busting, 607, 614, 682, 736. See also Antitrust laws
Monroe, James, 214, 219, 221; presidency of, 228–231, 287, 288, 336
Monroe Doctrine, 211, 230–231, 625, 627, 671, 673, 910; Roosevelt Corollary to, 639, 769, 773, 927
Montana, 355, 453, 456, 465
Montcalm, Louis Joseph, 104
Montgomery, Alabama, 861
Montgomery, Lucy M.: Anne of Green Gables, 557
Montgomery Ward, 470
Monticello, 141
Montreal, 16, 64, 105, 223
Moon, Rev. Sun Myung, 990–991
Moon landing, 639, 962
Moore, W. H., 489
Moore, William, 943
Moral education, 256, 331
Moral Majority, 992, 1016
Moravian sect, 73, 149
Morgan, Brig. Gen. Daniel, 148
Morgan, J. P., 484, 489, 490, 576, 593, 607, 608, 625, 727; and Company, 713
Morgan, Robin: Sisterhood Is Powerful, 959
Morgan, William, and Morgan Affair, 334–335
Morgan v. Virginia, 839
Morgenthau, Henry, Jr., 811

Mormons, the, 259, 274, 329, 344, 444, 456, 599, 988
Morocco, 640, 847, 866
Morrill Land Grant Act, 395, 471, 598
Morris, Gouverneur, 173, 175
Morris, Robert, 168
Morse, Samuel F. B., 242, 247
Morse, Wayne, 916
Mortality rate, see Demographic factors, MORTALITY RATE
Moscow Olympics, 931
Mossadegh, Mohammed, 871
Most-favored-nation principle, 774
Motherhood, cult of, 895
Mott, Lucretia, 332
Moving pictures, see Entertainment, MOVIES
Moynihan, Daniel, 965
Muckrakers, 555, 590, 591, 595, 607
Mugwumps, 570
Muir, John, 456
Mulberry Plantation, South Carolina, 49
Muller v. Oregon, 498, 599
Mullett, Mary B., 701–702
Multinational corporations, 928, 976
Multiversity, 953
Munich Conference, 775–776, 777, 822
Munich Olympic Games, 925
Municipal Voters League, 591
Munn v. Illinois, 461
Murfee, Mary Noailles, 557
Murphy, Frank, 801
Murray, Judith Sargent, 158, 159
Murray, William Vans, 198
Muscle Shoals dam, 682, 741
Music and dance, see Arts, the, MUSIC AND DANCE
Musical comedy, 549–550
Muskie, Edmund, 958, 966
Muskogean peoples, 8
Muslims, 9; West Africans as, 11; Spain expels, 14; as Portuguese or Spanish slaves, 15, 47
Mussolini, Benito, 775
Mutual Defense Assistance Act, 829
MX missiles, 930, 1005
My Lai massacre, 919–920
Myrdal, Gunnar: An American Dilemma, 840

Nagasaki, 790, 795, 832
Napoleon Bonaparte, 222, 226
Napoleonic Wars, 218–219, 222, 224, 280
Napoleon III, 625
Narragansetts, 29–30, 32, 57. See also Indians
Nasser, Gamal Abdel, 871, 872
Nast, Thomas, 432
National Advisory (Kerner) Commission on Civil Disorders, 941
National Aeronautics and Space Administration (NASA), 864
National American Woman Suffrage Association, 567, 589, 605, 694
National Association for the Advancement of Colored People (NAACP), 603, 657, 721, 723, 753, 803;

Phillips, David Graham: *Treason of the Senate*, 590
Phillips, Kevin, 887
Physical fitness, 991
Pickering, John, 212
Pickering, Timothy, 217
Pickford, Mary, 551
Pierce, Franklin, 363, 364
Pike, Zebulon, 215
Pilgrims, *see* Plymouth Colony
Pinchback, P. B. S., 438
Pinchot, Gifford, 608, 609
Pinckney, Charles, 173
Pinckney, Charles Cotesworth, 195, 199, 216, 221
Pinckney, Thomas, 193, 195
Pinckney, William, 219
Pinckney Treaty, 193, 214
Pingree, Hazen S., 528
Pitt, William, 105, 115
Pittsburgh, Pennsylvania, 104, 264, 271, 511, 526, 666, 893
Pizarro, Francisco, 16, 17
Plains Indians, 8, 9, 19, 452, 462–464
Plan of Union, 103
Plantations, *see* South
Platt Amendment, 637, 639, 769, 772
Plattsburg, New York, 655
Playboy, 988
Pledge of Allegiance, "under God" in, 854
Pleiku, 918
Plessy v. Ferguson, 475, 839
"Plumbers," 973
Plunkett, George Washington, 526
Pluralism: cultural, 530–532, 552, 599; and politics, 584; and Klan, 695
Plymouth Colony, 29–30
Plymouth Company, *see* Virginia Company
Pocahontas, 23, 24
Pocket Books, 899
Pocket veto, 342
Point Four Program, 829
Pokanoket (Wampanoag) Indians, 29–30, 57
Poland, 671, 766, 814; immigrants from, 516; Germany and, 776, 781; Soviet Union and, 777, 793, 810, 811, 812–813, 823, 824, 865, 1006
Polio, Salk vaccine for, 886
Political action committees (PACs), 981, 992
Politics: in colonies, 70, 74–75, 88, 91–92, 113 (*see also* Government, colonial); and public rituals, 88, 116; factionalism in, 182, 189–190, 191–192, 193, 195, 210, 427, 442; and spoils system (patronage), 339, 530, 562, 564–565, 569, 618, 626; economic conditions and, 274–275; immigrants enter, 284, 532 (*see also* Immigrants); radicalism, 500, 666–667, 696–697 (*see also* Radicals and radicalism); "boss" and "machine," 525–528, 591, 595; of divisiveness, 963–964, 965; Hispanics in, 987

BRIBERY AND CORRUPTION IN, 436, 443, 570, 873, 1001, 1013–1014; overseas, 764, 915
CAUCUS SYSTEM, 336–337
EDUCATION IN: from colonial rituals, 88; through prerevolutionary protests, 116; from Constitution-ratification processions, 183–184
PARTISAN: rise of, 192, 193–194, 210; ethnicity and religion and, 194, 344; and Constitution, 195; popular campaigns in, 216–217; first party system, 218; and Era of Good Feelings, 228–229; and second party system, 324, 343, 364; and convention system, 335; and party platform, 341; and North-South differences, 366–367, 369; and pluralism, 531–532, 584; and Gilded Age, 563, 569, 571; and party differences, 563–564; reform of, 590; in *1970s* Congress, 981–982

See also Government, federal; Reform
Polk, James K., 348, 349, 354, 355, 357, 363
Polk, Leonidas, 575
Pollock, Jackson, 901
Poll tax, 474, 752
Pollution, *see* Environment
Polo, Marco: *Travels*, 14
Polo Grounds, 548
Ponce de Leon, Juan, 16
Pontiac, Chief, 106
Pools (economic), 488, 493
Poor People's Campaign (1968), 957
Poor Richard's Almanack, 90, 557, 680–681
Pop Art, 901
Popé (Pueblo medicine man), 53
Popular sovereignty, 357–358, 359–360, 361, 364, 371, 372, 373
Population: Indian, 9, 985; world increase in, 19; doubling of in world, 21; New England increase in, 57; 18th-century growth of, 71; of colonies, 76, 83; slave, 79; black post-Revolution, 161; United States *1820*, 252 (map); 19th-century growth of, 270; of New York City, 271; black *1800–1860*, 292; in North vs. South, 301; of southern cities, 302; and westward expansion, 452; *1870–1910* rise in, 467; and industrialization, 480; urban vs. rural, 508, 688; and city growth, 512, 515; of blacks in cities, 518; Sunbelt increase in, 886–887; geographic distribution of, 891; increase of elderly in, 992; statistics, A-16
Populist movement and party, 562, 574–575, 579, 581, 583–584, 589; and yeomen, 473; and Knights of Labor, 500; and Cleveland, 572; and free silver, 574, 580–581, 583; and Debs, 577; and Bryan campaign, 582; and Progressives, 588;

war as unifier against, 629; in consensus history, 856
Porter, Sylvia F., 882
Port Huron Statement, 953
Portsmouth Conference (1905), 637
Portugal, 15, 47, 51, 927
Post, Louis, 670
Post Office, U.S., 242, 262, 555; and censorship and seizure of the mails, 333, 334, 666; RFD, 470
Potawatomis, 106, 169, 222, 223, 226, 286. *See also* Indians
Potsdam Conference (1945), 813, 820
Potter, David, 375; *People of Plenty*, 856
Pound, Ezra, 703
Pound, Roscoe, 599
Poussaint, Alvin, 983
Poverty, *see* Economic conditions, POVERTY
Powderly, Terence V., 500
Powell, Lewis F., 965
Powers, Francis Gary, 866
Powhatan, Chief, and Powhatan Confederacy, 23, 24–25, 57. *See also* Indians
Preemption Act, 263
Pregnancy, *see* Demographic factors, BIRTHS AND BIRTH RATE
Presbyterians, 163, 201, 326, 344. *See also* Religion
Prescott, Dr. Samuel, 136
Presidency: checks and balances on, 174; and cabinet, 185; and Washington, 186, 195; in Gilded Age, 562, 569–572; revival of, 605; Roosevelt's transformation of, 758; "imperial," 758, 975; and Eisenhower, 874; resignation from, 922, 975; "disposable," 981; decline of, 981; Teflon-coated, 1001, 1014; Reagan's restoration of, 1017
AND PRESIDENTIAL POWERS: under Constitution, 175; to dismiss appointed officials, 185; to withhold information (executive privilege), 193, to call up and send abroad troops, 846–847, 850; and Truman, 849

See also Executive branch
President's Committee on Civil Rights, 839
President's Committee on Equal Employment Opportunity, 942
President's Organization on Unemployment Relief (POUR), 726
Presley, Elvis, 900
Press, *see* News media
Preston, Col. John S., 318
Price, Victoria, 722
Princeton, battle of, 142
Princeton University, 89, 173, 611
Prisoners of War (POWs), in Korean War, 846
Prison uprising at Attica, 963
Proclamation of 1763, 107
"Profamily" movement, 988, 1016
Professional Air Traffic Controllers Organization (PATCO), 1013

Stageman, Richard, 1004
Stagflation, 964, 972, 976–978, 979, 994
Stalin, Josef, 791, 792, 793, 810, 811, 812, 813, 820, 823, 826, 830, 844, 864
Stalingrad, battle of, 792–793
Stamp Act (England, 1765), 109–114, 117, 130; sites of demonstrations against, 113 (map)
Stamp Act Congress, 114
Standard Fruit, 770
Standard Oil Corporation, 488; expansion and influence of, 489, 490–491, 493, 686; abroad, 766, 774, 780
Stanford, Leland, 396, 457
Stanton, Edwin M., 392, 425, 430
Stanton, Elizabeth Cady, 332, 429
Stanwix, Fort, treaties of, 135, 169
State, U.S. Department of, McCarthy's charges against, 842, 863; and Eisenhower, 854, 859
State government, see Government, state
States' rights: federal powers vs., 185; federal payment of state debts and, 187–188; Jefferson and Madison and, 197–198; and Hartford Convention, 226–227; political party views on, 369; Jackson and, 336, 339, 340; and nullification, 339; and slavery, 363, 369; in the South, 388; and Civil War, 388, 402, 414–415; Democrats on, 407; and Johnson, 425
Staubach, Roger, 990
Steamboats, 246–247
Stearns, Harold, 704
Stearns, Sarah Ripley, 279–280
Steel, Ferdinand L., 305
Steel industry, see Industry, IRON AND STEEL
Steel Workers Organizing Committee (SWOC), 751. See also Labor unions
Steffens, Lincoln, 590, 724, 725; The Shame of the Cities, 590
Steinbeck, John, 745
Stephens, Alexander H., 378, 406, 426
Stephenson, David, 695
Stettinius, Edward, Jr., 811
Stevens, John L., 627
Stevens, Thaddeus, 427, 430
Stevenson, Adlai E., 576, 848
Stevenson, Adlai E. (II), 837, 858, 907
Stimson, Henry L., 769, 770, 780, 781, 785, 803, 824; and Stimson Doctrine, 780
Stockman, David, 1002
Stock market, 489; Great Crash in, 710, 713–714; speculation in, 713, 714, 715
Stockton, Richard, 142
Stono Rebellion, 93
Stowe, Harriet Beecher: Uncle Tom's Cabin, 361
Strasser, Adolph, 501

Strategic Arms Limitation Talks (SALT), 924, 930, 931, 935
Strategic Arms Reduction Talks (START), 1006
Strategic Defense Initiative ("Star Wars"), 1005
Stratification, see Social class
Stratton-Porter, Gene, 557, 558
Strauss, Levi, 262
Strikes, see Labor strikes
Strong, George Templeton, 271
Strong, Josiah, 528, 619, 622
Stuart, Gilbert, 157
Stuart, Gen. J. E. B., 387
Stuart, John, 135
Stuart Restoration, 43, 60
Stuarts (rulers of England), 20, 63; and Puritans, 21, 29; and representative government, 44; and colonial rebellion, 64, 71. See also Charles I; Charles II; James I; James II
Student Non-Violent Coordinating Committee (SNCC), 862, 942, 949, 951, 953, 961
Student protest, 922, 952–953, 954–955
Students for a Democratic Society (SDS), 953, 955, 962
Submarine (film), 768
Subtreasury plan, 573, 584, 612
Suburbs, 509, 510, 512, 690–691, 882, 890–893, 896, 950, 983
Suez Canal, 638, 639, 858, 871–872
Suffragists, see Vote, the, FOR WOMEN
Sugar, 40, 61, 299, 910
Sugar Act (1764), 109, 115, 130
Sugar Trust, 493
Sullivan, Ed, 900
Sullivan, "Big Tim," 527, 591
Sullivan, General John, 146
Sullivan, William H., 916
Sullivan and Cromwell law firm, 774
Summit conference(s): Geneva (1953), 865; Paris (1960), 866; Kennedy-Khrushchev, 907
Sumner, Charles, 370, 427, 445, 625
Sumner, William Graham, 490, 631
Sumter, Fort, attack on, 377
Sunbelt, migration to, 886–887, 965, 992, 993
Sundquist, James, 947
Sun Zhongshan (Sun Yatsen), 778
"Superfund" for environmental cleanup, 1002
"Supply-side" economics, 1002, 1003
Supreme Court, U.S.: establishment and first cases, 184, 185; members impeached, 212–213; Federalism of (under Marshall), 213–214, 229; and national unity, 233; and slavery, 361, 370–371, 372; and Reconstruction, 441; and Sherman Act, 493; and court-packing plan, 748; Warren Court, 948–949, 1016; first woman on, 1013
DECISIONS: on constitutionality, 185, 723; on rights of contract, 242, 599, 683; on Indians, 288–289, 986; Dred Scott, 371–372, 373;

Slaughter-House cases, 441–442; and retreat from Reconstruction, 441–442; on interstate commerce, 461–462, 493; on civil rights, 474–475; on working hours and conditions, 498, 595, 599, 682–683; on Debs' sentence, 502; on suffrage, 567; on 15th Amendment, 579; on states' power, 599; antitrust, 607, 674; and progressivism, 614; on freedom of speech, 667; Scottsboro case, 721, 722; on New Deal, 745, 746, 748; on Japanese internment, 801; on civil rights and desegregation, 839, 854, 860, 948–949; on alien registration, 842; on voting rights, 948; on church and state, 948; on criminal justice, 949; on school busing, 965–966; on Watergate tapes, 975; on abortion, 988–989; on labor practices, 1013; on tax-exempt fundamentalist schools, 1013
Surinam, 60
Susquehanna River Valley, 106
Susquehannocks, 56. See also Indians
Sussex (French vessel), 652
Swann v. Charlotte-Mecklenburg, 965
Swanson, Gloria, 694, 701
Sweden, 16, 43, 954
Swift, Gustavus, 486, 489
Swift, Tom, 555–556, 558
Sylvis, William H., 394
Syphilis, 18
Syria, 866, 924–925, 1010–1011

Taft, Robert A., 777, 808, 809, 829, 847
Taft, William Howard, 595, 608–609, 640, 682, 684
Taft-Hartley Act, 835–836
Taft-Katsura Agreement, 637
Taiwan (Formosa), 830, 832, 843, 987; as Jiang's headquarters, 831; U.S. aid to, treaty with, 847, 866
Talleyrand, Charles Maurice de, 195
Tallmadge, James, Jr., 232, 233
Talmadge, Eugene, 839
Tammany Hall, 527, 591, 705
Taney, Roger, 243, 371
Tanguay, Eva, 550–551
Tappan, Lewis, 253
Tarbell, Ida, 664
Tariff: by Britain on colonies, 61, 109, 115, 121; by First Congress, 184; 1816, 228, 231, 251; 1828 (of Abominations), 251, 339; 1832, and nullification controversy, 340; 1833, 340; 1864, 395; reciprocity in, 566; 1890 (McKinley), 566, 584, 628; 1894 (Wilson-Gorman), 566, 627–628; 1897 (Dingley), 566, 584; Mills bill (1888), 570; 1909 (Payne-Aldrich), 608; 1913 (Underwood), 612; 1922 (Fordney-McCumber), 682; 1930 (Hawley-Smoot), 727, 773; most-favored-nation principle for, 774

GREENLAND
(DEN.)

ALASKA
(U.S.)

CANADA

Aleutian Is.

UNITED STATES

Azores

Bermuda

Midway Is.

ATLANTIC OCEAN

BAHAMAS
DOMINICAN
REP.
MEXICO   CUBA   SAINT CHRISTOPHER AND NEVIS
Hawaiian Is.   Virgin Is.   ANTIGUA AND BARBUDA
Wake I.   JAMAICA HAITI   DOMINICA   CAPE
BELIZE   Puerto Rico   BARBADOS   VERDE
Marshall Is.   HONDURAS   SAINT LUCIA
GUATEMALA   GRENADA SAINT VINCENT AND
PACIFIC OCEAN   EL SALVADOR NICARAGUA   THE GRENADINES
COSTA RICA   TRINIDAD AND TOBAGO
KIRIBATI   PANAMA   VENEZUELA GUYANA
Equator   SURINAME
NAURU   Galapagos Is. ECUADOR COLOMBIA   FR. GUIANA
TUVALU
SOLOMON IS.
PERU   BRAZIL
VANUATU   W. SAMOA
FIJI   BOLIVIA
New   TONGA   PARAGUAY
Caledonia
Easter I.
URUGUAY
CHILE
NEW   ARGENTINA
ZEALAND

Falkland Is.